FOUR YEARS OF WAR-TIME WIT AND HUMOUR IN THE ROYAL SIGNALS/ATS/INTELLIGENCE CORPS

- 🟩 Original house/outbuildings
- 🟥 Wooden huts
- ⬛ Brick construction
- ▨ Pre-fabricated (Portal Hut)

Not to scale!!

H HUT (MORSE) COTTAGE (Civilian manned)

...METER TRACK

L HUT (late 1944)

(...tion and ...s Room)

M BLOCK (GREENHOUSE) (CANTEEN/RECREATION ROOMS)

I HUT (MORSE) COTTAGE (Civilian/ATS manned)

BRICK ICE HOUSES NEAR LANE →

J HUT (HIGH-SPEED MORSE) COTTAGE (Civilian/ATS Manned)

(...Section)

K HUT (MORSE) FARM SHED (ATS Manned)

Does not show aerials, feeder routes etc.

X Position of ship's figurehead mounted on ornamental horse trough/fountain

↑ approx N

THE BEAUMANOR STAFF MAGAZINE
1941–1945

THE WOYGIAN
1945–1949

First published in Great Britain 1993
By Hugh Skillen, 56 St. Thomas Drive,
Pinner, Middlesex HA5 4SS
to whom all enquiries should be addressed.

By the same author:

> Spies of the Airwaves (1989) ISBN 0 9515190 X
> The Y Compendium (1990)
> Knowledge Strengthens the Arm (1991) ISBN 0 9515190 1
> Enigma and its Achilles Heel (1992) ISBN 0 9515190 2 6
> The Enigma Symposium 1992 (1992) ISBN 0 9515190 3 4

All rights reserved. No part of this publication may be reproduced, stored in a retrieval system, or transmitted, in any form or by any means, electronic, mechanical, photocopying, recording or otherwise, without prior permission of the author/publisher. Such permission, if granted, is subject to a fee depending on the nature of the use.

Printed by Hobbs the Printers of Southampton.

© Copyright by Hugh Skillen
ISBN 0 9515190 4 2

British Library Cataloguing-in-Publications Data

A catalogue record for this book is available from the British Library.

WAR OFFICE Y GROUP (WOYG)

1939–1940

Fort Bridgewoods, Chatham

1940–1941

Chicksands Priory

1941–1951

Beaumanor Hall

Acknowledgements

I am very grateful to Major John Ellingworth and Dr. Philip Blenkinsop not only for their encouragement but also for the substantial help they have given me in providing documents and photographs, as well as actual copies of the BSM to photocopy, including the vital first issue.

I am also grateful to Mrs. D. E. Fisher of Ipswich who made it possible to contemplate the re-issue of the BSM by lending me the majority of the issues two years ago.

Mrs. Dorothy Coggan has supplied photographs of groups at Forest Moor and material concerning the running of both Kedleston Hall and Forest Moor, which fulfilled the same functions as WOYG. These valuable contributions are at the end of the book.

I am also happy to acknowledge both photographs of the personnel at WOYG and her own story of the bombing of Fort Bridgewoods, Chatham, from Mrs. Gladys Earle and individual copies of the BSM from Mrs. Leadbeater and others whose names are enshrined on the covers by the distributor.

I am grateful to William Grayson, author of *Chicksands—A Millenium of History*, for permission to quote from his book.

Hugh Skillen

Dedicated to all Service men and women and civilians who served at

Beaumanor
Bishops Waltham
Bletchley Park
Brora
Canterbury
Cheadle
Chicksands
Denmark Hill
Flowerdown
Forest Moor
Kedleston Hall
Knock Holt
Sandridge
Scarborough
Shenley
Whitchurch
Wincome Etousa (for Santa Fe)

Beaumanor - The Secret Years

Background

Many visitors to the Beaumanor of today will be aware that the house and its grounds were occupied by 'the Army' during the war years. Some may also be vaguely aware that the role of Beaumanor had something to do with wireless. Until the publication of three books during the last fifteen years, the secrecy that surrounded the activities of the war-time occupants, a secrecy which persisted into the post-war period, meant that few could be aware of the true story of Beaumanor and the 'Y' Service.

That the facts have remained hidden is a great pity since Beaumanor played a vital role in one of the most interesting and exciting developments in the struggle to achieve victory.

The notes which follow draw heavily from two of the three books. The first of these is 'The Ultra Secret' by F W Winterbotham who first revealed the secret to the public in 1974. The other is 'The Hut Six Story' by Gordon Welchman who was the first to mention Beaumanor by name. I am also fortunate in possessing a several editions of the Beaumanor Staff Magazine (BSM) which was published monthly between 1941 and 1945. This house magazine provides much anecdotal information and atmosphere about the period. Lastly, I have combined a little speculation with snippets of information gleaned from my father who was stationed at Beaumanor from 1941 until its closure in 1969/70. I do not claim, therefore, that this is an accurate account but I hope that it fills in some of the gaps in the long history of Beaumanor and its parklands.

In this account I shall persist in using the term 'wireless' rather than the modern term 'radio' since that is how it was referred to at the time.

The Secret

In the years leading up to Munich, the British Intelligence organisations were anxious to gain as much information about the intentions of the German government as possible. Anticipating the outbreak of war, they foresaw that this information would become increasingly important. Apart from conventional intelligence gathering methods, the monitoring of German diplomatic and military wireless traffic was recognised as being a direct and immediate means of reading the enemy's mind. The problem was that, for some time, the

Germans had been enciphering their messages on a machine known as Enigma which - in theory at least - provided over 200 quintillion (two hundred million million million!) combinations of possible keys to a message. It was generally thought to be unbreakable. Fortunately for Britain, the Foreign Office had established between the wars the Government Code and Cipher School, initially based in Broadway Buildings in London, but by 1938 housed in the Victorian Gothic mansion of Bletchley Park in the centre of Bletchley (now regrettably Milton Keynes). Here a collection of mathematicians, classics scholars, and intelligence experts worked upon the difficult task of breaking the German ciphers.

At this time, the main listening post for Bletchley Park was the naval wireless station, Fort Bridgewoods, based in the Victorian fort on a hill just south of Chatham. Intercepted messages would be sent daily from Chatham to Bletchley where work would begin on deciphering the codes.

Bletchley Park had discovered that (or more strictly, had extended the ground-breaking work carried out by Polish Intelligence) because of poor German encryption practice, the number of possible cipher keys could be reduced from 200 quintillion to around a million and that by using fairly simple hand methods - and given a fair degree of good fortune - the key to the messages could be broken. By December of 1939, Bletchley Park were regularly reading German Air Force and Army messages.

Throughout 1940 the ciphers continued to be broken but gradually decryption became more and more difficult and the volume of wireless traffic needing to be examined increased dramatically. Heavy bombing raids on Chatham during 1940 and the close proximity of German forces just across the channel stimulated a move from Fort Bridgewoods to Beaumanor which had been requisitioned from Mr William Curzon-Herrick so displacing his tenant Mrs Frances Abel Smith. The move was interrupted by a short stay at Chicksands Priory, another naval signals base a few miles east of Bletchley. The huts which still stand today were rapidly built in the grounds and teleprinter circuits installed linking Beaumanor to Bletchley Park.

From this point, Beaumanor became the main Army 'ear' listening to the Germans and providing raw intelligence to Bletchley.

Once decoded by Bletchley, the messages would be passed selectively to British commanders in the field as well as to the War Cabinet. Only a small number of people were allowed to know the origin of the intelligence such was the importance of the source. Since much of the material gave a strong indication of the strategic plans of the German High Command, it is not unfair to argue that many of the key military decisions taken by the British during the middle years of the war began their life in the huts scattered round Beaumanor's grounds.

The Job

To understand what went on in those huts it is necessary to know a little about the way in which the German military units communicated with each other. This is complicated but I will try to keep it simple.

A group of German military units needing to exchange orders and messages would operate what was known as a 'net'. To do this, one control unit would transmit on a particular frequency at a pre-arranged time and the other units would then tune in to that frequency. Once all the units were tuned in or 'netted', the controller would permit units to transmit to each other. The nature of the 'net' could vary from a Luftwaffe unit in France to a higher level command unit deep in Germany itself.

To ensure that eavesdroppers could not read the messages, the details would be entered into the typewriter-like Enigma machine and the enciphered message then transcribed by hand on to signal pads. The message would then be sent using Morse Code as groups of five letters - QZXYP ENDLF GRKTY and so on. Without the key the transmission appeared to be gibberish.

To add to the security, the Germans would change the setting of their Enigma machine each midnight so that a key was only valid for a day. The consequence of this was that Bletchley had, on average, only 24 hours to obtain the raw signals from Beaumanor and elsewhere and then decode them. This put considerable pressure on the Beaumanor staff to work quickly and accurately.

Short-wave signals travel for long distances which is why it was relatively easy to pick up messages from, say, the Eastern Front by a wireless set located in the middle of rural Leicestershire. Nevertheless, fading and interference would have made the wireless operator's life very difficult. Their task was to tune in to a specific net and write down the signals on message pads. Reception of every letter was important and so, if the signal faded, an intelligent guess as to how many characters had been lost would have to be made.

The handwritten message sheets would be sent via pneumatic tube from the intercept huts to the control hut (my guess is that this was one of huts A, B, or C). Here they would be logged and collated and then sent on to Bletchley Park. In the early days nearly everything was sent down the A6 by motorcycle despatch rider but later sufficient teleprinter lines were installed to allow direct transmission of much of the material.

The German transmissions would have been made at regular times on known frequencies but, to ensure that no material was lost, the huts needed to be manned continuously. The 'listeners' were thus organised into four shifts or watches - A, B, C, and D.

No attempt at deciphering the signals was made at Beaumanor since there were no facilities for doing this. However, much useful information could be gleaned from the basic facts and figures to do with frequencies, call-signs, and times of transmission. To handle this, a group of people known as the log-readers, part of the Military Intelligence organisation MI8, moved into the mansion when the wireless operators moved into the huts. This group ultimately moved down to Bletchley in 1942. I imagine that to aid the log-readers, some of the wireless operators would be engaged upon Direction Finding work (in K Hut ?) - trying to obtain accurate bearings on the location of specific transmitters.

Although removed from the immediate dangers of the battlefield, life at Beaumanor must have been difficult at times. Having travelled from cramped billets some distance away, usually in the middle of the night, the operational staff would be confined to their huts for eight hours at a time with only limited periods for breaks. The huts would be cold in winter (blankets were issued to the occupants of H hut in 1944) and stuffy in summer.

For most of the time their task would be routine and humdrum and no-one can have been absolutely certain that their work was contributing to the war effort rather than simply adding to a pile of worthless 'bumf'.

The Technology

By today's standards, the equipment used then was primitive. The front end of the 'Ear' was the aerial farm. This consisted of some two dozen or so masts located in the fields to the North-West of the huts. Strung between the masts were the aerial wires themselves, connected in various configurations with names like Rhombic and Beveridge. Co-axial cables fed the received signals to the set-rooms.

I am not sure which of the huts were set-rooms but logic suggests that they were H, I, and J. Each set-room was filled with a number of wireless sets. Initially, these were HROs, (still remembered with affection by present-day radio enthusiasts), but these were later replaced by more modern sets such as the Hallicrafters. Using these sets, operators would search and listen for signals using headphones. Having worn a pair of war-time 'cans' I can vouch that they bore no relationship to modern designs and must have been extremely uncomfortable to have worn for long periods.

The pneumatic message tubes which linked set-room to control have already been mentioned. To my knowledge, these tubes, laid underground and of pure copper, are still *in situ* so the present occupants of the house should beware nocturnal scrap-merchants. Apparently, during wet weather, condensation would form on the inside of the tubes and the receiving hut would often be greeted by the arrival of a slug of cold water.

The teleprinters clattering away at 10 characters per second must have been a limitation to communications with Bletchley and, in addition, gave scope for introducing errors. The despatch riders used to augment the teleprinter links avoided this problem and were probably the unsung heroes of this period of Beaumanor's history. Clambering aboard their BSA M20 side-valve machines and rattling through the stable block in the small hours of the night to face a long journey down the A6 in the blackout, their life cannot have been easy.

Despite the crudeness of much of the equipment, and the haste with which it had been assembled, the system worked and worked smoothly for close on four years.

The People

Reading through the pages of BSM one gains the impression of a very strong sense of community surrounding Beaumanor during the war. Much of this must have stemmed from the isolation brought about by the inability to talk about their work, even to spouses or close relatives. It is also apparent that the mixture of social backgrounds contributed to the atmosphere of the place. Equally clear is that the quality of intellect was considerably above that of a conventional military unit largely because of the need for administrative an technical skills.

Beaumanor was at this time part of the War Office 'Y' Service and was thus known as War Office Y Group or WOYG. To the staff, the station became known as 'Woygland' and the inhabitants 'Woygites'. Other terms in common use at the time included 'Beaumaniacs' and 'Manor Beaus' for some of the more dashing male members. In overall charge of the Woygites was Commander Ellingworth, an ex-naval man who had been in charge at Chatham and had moved to Beaumanor via Chicksands. Known behind his back as 'Trunky' he was apparently well liked by all of his subordinates.

There would appear to have been three groupings of Woygites.

The Hard Cores, as they were referred to, presumably because they had been on site since its reception, were the civilian staff. These were known as Experimental Wireless Assistants or EWAs. This slightly misleading title was an attempt to disguise the nature of their work. Many of the EWAs had transferred from Chatham in 1941. Others had joined from the Merchant Navy or the Post Office as well as the Royal Signals. It would seem that those EWAs recruited from the services dressed in 'civvies' but remained part of the forces. All the EWAs were skilled wireless operators and were paid about £5 a week.

The EWAs were mostly billeted with private families or landladies either in Loughborough or the bigger villages around Woodhouse. I believe that some of the single EWAs may have had rooms in the old part of the mansion at one time.

The second group of Woygites were the ATS (Auxiliary Territorial Service) girls whose numbers increased rapidly during 1942. The ATS were trained to carry out a number of duties including acting as intercept and teleprinter operators, operating the typing pool, as well as the more humble tasks such as the 'runners' who carried messages and supplies of stationery. The ATS were billeted in Garats Hey, in several large houses in Quorn, Barrow, and Swithland, as well as a special camp at Brand Hill in Woodhouse Eaves. The curious can still find traces of this camp in the field directly opposite the old Zachary Merton convalescent home.

JUNE, 1944
VOL. I - No. 4 (NEW SERIES)

The third group were the Army personnel themselves. I know little about their duties but assume that they were Royal Signals personnel who supplemented the numbers of wireless operators as well as supplying the despatch riders, guards, technical maintenance, and other miscellaneous staff. It should be pointed out that a significant activity of the station was the training of the ATS girls and I believe that both Army and civilian staff took on this teaching role. Other groups were on the site at various times. At one time a number of Post Office Technical Staff were recruited only to be moved elsewhere after a short time. Towards the end of the war I believe that US Intelligence Corps staff were based in Hut C.

Despite the rigours of shift work life at Beaumanor seems to have been very active. Scanning the pages of BSM reveals that there were:

- *fortnightly dances in the mansion*
- *active football, rugger, and hockey teams*
- *400 hours of booked time on the tennis courts in 1944!*
- *an active Beaumanor Music Society which organised the Beaumanor Proms*
- *various rambling, shooting, and other social clubs*

When I described this view of the social life to an ex-ATS who was there she took me to task for making it sound very staid. Life, it seems, was rather more Radio 1 than the Radio 3 picture I've presented! More informal entertainment seems to have centered around The Pear Tree, The Curzon Arms, and other local hostelries. The arrival of American troops in the area in 1944 made an immediate impact upon the life of the ATS.

A major product of Beaumanor in those days was gossip and the pages of BSM are full of examples. This was inevitable given that large numbers of single and married EWAs (age range 25 to 35 ?) were working closely alongside equal numbers of ATS (age range 18 to 30 ?). Liaisons, both innocent and otherwise, undoubtedly took place and the wives of married EWAs, often living far way and not knowing the nature of their husband's work, must have felt grounds for concern. This is neatly summarised in one cartoon from the pages of BSM in 1943.

MY JOB - AS SEEN BY MY WIFE

BSM itself had grown by 1944 to a sizeable publication - impressive considering that it relied totally upon voluntary contributions. Started as a rather thin Roneo'd newssheet at Chicksands in 1941, it grew to a professionally produced magazine of some 25 pages by early 1944. The unusual mixture of backgrounds shows in the curiously democratic style of the magazine. The presence of the civilians shows in the irreverent and sometimes radical nature of the articles (topics included feminism and the role of socialism in post-war Britain!) whilst the ATS presence prevented it from becoming the self-indulgent joke sheet normally associated with all-male communities.

All-in-all, my impression is that Beaumanor was a happy place to work in during the war years and that it made a lasting impression on those who served there.

The Ear continues to listen

Like most close-knit wartime units, Beaumanor staff must have experienced a strong feeling of anti-climax once the war had ended. The ATS departed, the mansion continued to provide administration, but the German signals - the entire reason for the station's existence - had ceased. Soon, however, new work was found for the site. The Ear continued to listen but this time its focus was further to the east than the old enemy. The recipients were no longer Bletchley Park but the newly formed Government Communications Headquarters (GCHQ) based in Cheltenham.

In this role the park continued as a Composite Signals Organisation Station. Gradually, as more modern equipment became available and the nature of the interception business changed, the need for Beaumanor once again diminished. It was decided to close the station and transfer its activities to other sites such as Irton Moor near Scarborough, Taunton, and Cheadle. In 1970 the last of the EWAs and their post-war successors left and over the following eighteen months the site was dismantled. The sentiments of those who had worked at Beaumanor during those years are captured in the verses written by one of their number and reproduced below.

Today

Today, apart from the huts, there are few signs of the wartime role of Beaumanor. The aerial farm has gone as has the sentry box that once stood at the top of the drive. More mysteriously, the figurehead of Admiral Cornwallis that once stood on the plinth in the stable yard has disappeared and is believed to be in the USA.

A Farewell from the House of Beaumanor

I stand by the Forest of Charnwood,
Not far from the River Soar,
I've stood here for hundreds of years, Sirs,
And expect to remain many more.

The Herricks have now left my staterooms,
Their Arms show their heritage,
But the Lebanons will grow here for ever,
To the end of my Beaumanor days.

You came in the crisis of War, Sirs,
From Chicksands and places unknown,
A.T.S. girls worked alongside you,
And together the Station was born.

Officers in Charge I remember,
Ellingworth, Duvivier and Wort,
Jack Kelsall, Eddy Goddard, and Basted,
They came, went, and left their mark.

I remember the year '65, Sirs,
Upheavals and suchlike bestirred,
Army Department deleted for ever,
Cheltenham's name now first heard.

Personalities came and departed,
The canteen fell by the wayside,
Let's hope you remember dear Emma,
The cook who filled your inside.

There was Peddie and Hutch and of course Andy,
Olly, Slap, Phillips, and more,
They were all here at Beaumanor,
Not forgetting, of course, the 'hard core'.

The year is now nineteen seventy,
Your voices are now getting dim,
Not many left in the chairs now,
Personnel now getting very thin.

July is now upon us,
I bid you a fond farewell,
To new stations and in your retirement,
I bid you adieu — keep well.

You've gone and deserted my rooms, Sirs,
Haunting echos fill my inside,
Who knows, you may come back to see me,
Till then leave the ghosts by my side.

REDMAN

During a visit to Beaumanor some time ago, I was pleased to feel, as I walked round the perimeter path by the huts, that many of the ghosts of that time were still present and that if one listened hard enough, it was still possible to decern the crackle of static as well as the faint sounds of the occasional weak Morse signal.

[This monograph is based upon notes written in 1985 in response to a request by the current staff of Beaumanor Hall for more information about the history of the park during the war years]

Philip Blenkinsop

War Office Y Group (WOYG)

The main provider of raw material for Bletchley Park from 1939 until after the end of the war was WOYG. It was in operation when the war began at Fort Bridgewoods in Chatham until it was bombed out in October 1940.

The personnel were male civilians, radio operators recruited from the Royal Signals, the Royal Navy, the Merchant Navy and the Post Office. A signalman of the Royal Signals who wrote to the Eastern Command Signal Company for information was informed in a letter dated 27 July 1939 that it would be convenient if he attended at that station, Fort Bridgewoods, for interview on 16 August 1939 at his own expense.

If he possessed the necessary skills he would be rewarded at the rate of 80/- per week rising to 84/- p.w. after one month and then by annual increments to 96/- p.w. as an Experimental Wireless Assistant (EWA) and would be eligible for pensionable establishment after three years of unestablished service. Leave would be granted for 18 days a year plus public holidays. It was pointed out that candidates for appointment must possess a high standard of proficiency in reception of wireless signals under all conditions. Tests would include reception of weak signals with interference. "Candidates will also require a good standard of general intelligence. Their handwriting must be good and they must be able to write block letters legibly at speed. In your interest you should consider whether you are suitable before incurring travelling expenses for this test".

He was asked to attend at Eastern Command Signal Company for a test at his own expense on 16 August, 1939. And so at a time when most of the young men and women were donning uniforms to serve their country these men were taken out of uniform. Their commanding officer was Commander M J N Ellingworth, Royal Navy, a veteran of WW1. There were 200 male civilians and these were later joined by an equal number of ATS wireless operators trained at the Special Operators Training Battalion (SOTB) at Trowbridge and later at Douglas, Isle of Man.

Royal Signals personnel provided supervisors for the setrooms and despatch riders to carry the Enigma intercepts to BP, while Cdr Ellingworth sent the preambles of messages by teleprinter to give the code-breakers advance material to begin their researches.

From Chatham the formation went to Chicksands Priory in Bedfordshire (SYG) Special Y Group, working alongside the RAF and WAAF intercept operators until a permanent home was ready at Beaumanor Hall in Leicestershire. This was not an easy time for the "lost tribe" as they were called in their house magazine, the Beaumanor Staff Magazine (BSM) and their tribulations were recorded even before they left Chicksands in "The Gospel According to St. Upid", (translated from the English by Disciple Millhouse). The first issue of this fascinating history was printed in October 1941 and continued in forty monthly chapters. In chapter IV *The Prophet and the Exodus* translated from the English by disciple Millhouse) it runs:—

Now it came to pass, when the year drew nigh unto the Feast of the Pullover, and the Ewas were shaking forth the mothballs from their Roltops and Veenecks, that the Prophet Osee communed with his peoples again, and spake unto them in this wise, saying:

Verily my heart is full, for I bring thee tidings of great joy. Full many a moon have I believed I have done my task and delivered my peoples into the Promised Land. But behold, a parchment has come into mine hand from the mighty Red Tabs in Wyt Awl and thus sayeth the parchment, in the tongue of Red Tabs, which is called Verbossitee!

WE REGRET TO INFORM YOU THAT, OWING TO AN ERROR, YOU HAVE BEEN WRONGLY DELIVERED.

Yes verily, by the beer of the Prophet, inasmuch as ye think not, this is a promised land, but the land was given by Red Tabs unto another tribe called Glamma Boiz. But Red Tabs saith my peoples shall have a new and greater land, a land flowing with beer and skittles and the land shall be called Lesta or Leiks.

Therefore I say unto you before another moon hath ascended the heavens ye must take up thy beds, and mount the chariots again, and depart for ever out of the land of Beds, taking with thee thy ox, and thy ass, and thy pencil, but not everything that is thy neighbour's—lest thy neighbour looketh and splitteth unto Koppa.

And the multitude went up into the Hill of Klop, and sundry other places where they were assured of solitude, and meditated, and Behold, they were glad in their hearts and rejoiced, yea, even without the persuasion of mead.

And the onions and leeks which the tribe had planted at Setrum flourished not from their weepings.

And be it known that the Glamma Boiz found the back view of the tribe better to the eye than the front view.

ORDER YOUR GOSPEL IN ADVANCE AND THUS BE SURE OF THE NEXT THRILLING INSTALMENT. SPECIAL FREE GIFT WITH EVERY COPY; THE TEN COMMANDMENTS.

In the Gossip column are other clues:

"The event of the season was the "Farewell to SYG" dance held at Silsoe and a great time was drunk by all.

Various members of the seearar appeared, but we were dismayed to learn that Mr. Fillyparnold's pig was unable to be with us, owing to a mislaid waistcoat button.

Lady ATT looked as charming as ever, in her gown of khaki serge, and spent her entire evening persuading her RAF partner that "SYG" did not stand for "silly young girls" and that she'd seen the moon before.

Seabreeze was supplied by Admiral Goldcuff. Sqd. Ldr. Morgan made the most of having two arms in commission at long last.

(Editor's note: seearar to the initiated is CRR (Compilation and Registration Room). The C.O. at Chicksands was Rear-Admiral Miller).

According to the MI8 Diary No VI Intelligence School was formed on 25 March 1941 and opened by Lieut Colonel Thompson on 1 August. Red Tabs in Whitehall boobed when they sent me to Loughborough on 28 June to be met by Col Thompson and spend an idle five days in the empty Beaumanor Hall until I returned to London and was despatched to SYG at Chicksands on 5 July to begin my duties as Night Duty Officer at WOYG, which as we have seen from the BSM was still at Chicksands in October.

At this point it should be said that my training in MI8 and the Y Service was long as my initiation into the army was short and brutish. For example, I went straight from Teachers Training College after six a half years at universities in Scotland and France preparing to be a teacher of Modern Languages to Mytchett Barracks, Ash Vale Aldershot. A graduate and a volunteer I was paid 14/- per week until I had completed the two weeks' course in Field Security, when half of us were promoted to L/Cpl at 27/6 p.w. In WW1 uniforms, breeches and puttees long, we were sent on Christmas Leave and told to cadge some practice from friends on motor-cycling as the roads in S. England were frozen and rutted for some months in the winter of 1939–40. When we returned we were told it was our embarkation leave and we were issued with the new battle dress and spent hours unravelling the pieces of webbing and fastening them together. We had no rifle drill and were denied pistol practice because there was no ammunition for our .38 Smith & Wessons. We drew these on the eve of departure for Southampton and thereby several lives were no doubt saved. The CSM refused us ammunition which was very wise and we faced the German panzers with empty pistols. Some were poorly after inoculations and the Section set off on frozen rutted roads mostly inexpert in controlling their BSAs and several times five or more were entangled with and under our heavy motorcycles when someone skidded. Four weeks earlier I had been a civilian.

At Cherbourg conditions were identical and we travelled in convoy with the HQ 50 (Northumbrian) Division to Lille in January in a fearsome journey which lasted a week. Little more need be said except that a month after Dunkirk I was in liaison with the 51 Division during the Battle of the Somme and brought back to England the only motor-cycle possessed by the 50th Div then on coastal defence in Dorset.

By contrast after being commissioned as an infantry officer at Sandhurst in April 1941 I spent months visiting intercept stations, Harpenden (HPN) RAF Cheadle, Shenley and its jamming stations, Chicksands and Beaumanor as well as Field Y Sections at varous Corps HQs on exercises before assuming command of my first W I Section with 9. Armoured Division.

At Chicksands I saw the aerial farm with long low aerials stretching for hundreds of yards side by side in the direction of various sectors of the Mediterranean and I now have photographs of the aerial farm in Beaumanor Park and of the installations ready for a published version of the BSM. As there is no war diary for WOYG the BSM is an invaluable record of a large intercept station.

There were four main groups of Woygites. Dr Philip Blenkinsop has already described three of these in the Foreword.

The fourth group was No. VI Intelligence School. Until it was in operation at Beaumanor, Major Jolowicz, the second in command, in charge of the CRR (Compilation and Registration Room) at Chicksands, supervised the first sorting of Enigma messages by call-sign and discriminant to give the correct priorities to messages to be decrypted. Intelligence Corps Officers were on duty by day and night to direct the setroom supervisors.

By the time I returned from Tunisia in July 1943 No. VI IS had moved to 57 Netherhall Gardens, Hampstead, into the private residence of Major Jolowicz. Commanded by Lieut Colonel Lithgow it had become the Training and Research Wing of the Army Y Service, leaving an Intelligence control group with WOYG. At Hampstead recruits were trained in decryption procedures and the vocabulary of military German. The British and Canadian officers and NCOs destined for D-Day landings in Normandy were trained in the latest techniques.

GC and CS moved when the war ended to Eastcote, Pinner, where the WRENS had been operating the "Bombes" to decrypt German Enigma, before the last move to Oakley in Cheltenham. Beaumanor is now the Admin Library HQ of Loughborough and the giant statue of Admiral Cornwallis has disappeared. In the cellars are still traces of the old station and the letters WOYG clearly painted in white.

The Woygian replaced the BSM in the next four years after the war ended and many pages kept readers informed of their comrades' postings, marriages, etc. It also contained two more chapters of the Epistle of St. Upid to the Woygians, no longer the Gospel According to St. Upid, which was published in book form by the Woygian Association in 1946, with the title *The Chronicles of St. Upid*.

Beaumanor Staff Magazine

There had been an attempt to produce a magazine either at Chatham or Chicksands because, when the first number of the BSM appeared in October 1941, it contained Chapter 4 of the Gospel According to St. Upid.

We can reproduce the first three chapters of the Gospel from the published book and it will be useful to introduce these with the Author's Prefatory Note and the Foreword by Cdr Ellingworth and the cartoon of him by Wilk.

AUTHOR'S PREFATORY NOTE

THIS seems to be the place to answer the various people who from time to time have been curious to know how I came to write this nonsense.

The simple fact is that it just "happened"—and then grew up. After the Department moved to Bedfordshire the analogy of the Children of Israel was too palpable to escape notice, and after a little reflection that which now appears as Chapter I of this book was scribbled out on an odd piece of paper and passed, rather diffidently, to a colleague.

Some days later a friend produced a neatly typewritten copy of it, with an enquiry as to when the next instalment would be forthcoming. It was, soon afterwards; and thus the variously-titled epistles were scrawled out and passed on, to eventually find their mysterious way to the obliging typist. By the time the third screed had acquired legibility Messrs. Jones and Staddon had conceived the idea of a monthly staff journal, and asked me to contribute something in the same vein. So, with the emergence of the *Beaumanor Staff Magazine,* which grew from extremely modest beginnings to achieve a circulation approaching a thousand, it became necessary to give the series a proper title. Thus was born the new "saint," whose name even now fails to "register" in some quarters.

Thenceforth it devolved upon me to produce each month some topical record of the activities of the Tribe. Times were when a theme was very difficult to find, although on several occasions events seemed to cry out to be recorded in this style. The chapter concerning the "Yanks" (Chapter XXIX of this book) acquired a fame all of its own. Following a visit to the *B.S.M.'s* printers by an American officer seeking to buy copies of the issue concerned (which request, incidentally, was refused by the printers on the grounds of "security!") I learned that an enterprising Yank at the Quorn Camp, albeit unacquainted with the law of copyright, had reeled off a thousand copies of the epistle on a duplicator and distributed them among his comrades. Many of these sheets must have migrated across the Atlantic.

But it seemed obvious that this stuff could not go on indefinitely; that it must grow stale and boring, as undoubtedly it did to some people; yet on the whole the series maintained its popularity until the end. Even though there were times when the perpetrator wanted to call a halt, editorial persuasion, plus the seemingly magical manifestation of suitable topics, prolonged the output until the end of the War. Then the *B.S.M.* ceased publication, and, although the first number of its successor, *The Woygian,* contained an epistle, the whole *raison d'etre* of the series seemed to have vanished. At least, the potentialities for its regular appearance no longer existed.

So now let me tender my best thanks to those who sometimes furnished me with details of an episode which they felt ought to be chronicled, and to those who made helpful suggestions when I was hard pressed for a theme; to those who delved among their belongings to find the earlier chapters of which I had no copy, (not forgetting those who convinced me that there never had been a Chapter XXVIII!); to "Wilk," whose splendid illustrations so greatly enhance this book; to Ron Hyder for his delightful rendering of Beaumanor House; and to all those who have assisted, in various ways, with its production; and finally, I suppose, to Itla the Hunnite, who, after all, was primarily responsible for the whole thing!

If I may lapse for a last time into "Stupidese," let me recount a true little episode which came to my ears quite early in our days of exile:

Now a certain young man went unto his Lady of the Land and shewed her a parchment. And on the parchment was writ: Gospel according to St. Upid. And when she had read the writings he saith unto her: What thinkest thou? And she answered him, saying: Yea, I am well pleased, but verily I say unto ye, it is indeed a blasphemy.

After that I felt glad for Samuel's sake that the Bible didn't happen to be written in the phraseology of Pepys' Diary. E. C. M.

Beaumanor Park,
    Near Loughborough,
        Leicestershire.
11th March, 1946.

FOREWORD

BY THE PROPHET OSEE

THIS little book records the wanderings and doings of a small body of men—afterwards reinforced by a large number of women—during the war years 1941-45.

Written in Mr. Millhouse's delightful and inimitable style, the monthly instalments in the *Beaumanor Staff Magazine* were eagerly sought after. Always topical, never controversial, they gave just the right amount of light relief required in strenuous times.

Although probably unintelligible to some extent to those outside the fold, "*The Chronicles of St. Upid*" will, I am sure, bring back happy memories of their war service to *Woygians* now dispersed to the four corners of the earth.

I am proud to have had the honour and privilege of leading the Tribe through the war years, and may they all ultimately reach their promised land.

[signature: Illingworth]

"—the Prophet Osee appeared before them and spake" (*Chap. I.*)

Contents

CHAPTER		PAGE
I	Exodus	13
II	Quest for Bilits	14
III	The Temple at Chiksanz	15
IV	Second Exodus	17
V	The Promised Land	18
VI	The Box	19
VII	A Great Do	21
VIII	Winter in Woyg	23
IX	Weeds	24
X	Raiment and Ohmgard	26
XI	A Bright Idea	27
XII	The Temple Floor	28
XIII	Holy Days at Home	30
XIV	The Atsites	31
XV	Six Weeks Shalt Thou Labour	33
XVI	Glad Tidings from Egg-wiped	34
XVII	Eksmas	36
XVIII	A New Prophet	38
XIX	Concerning the Hop	40
XX	A Man called Klark	41
XXI	A Scribe on a Grid (I)	44
XXII	A Scribe on a Grid (II)	45
XXIII	Musso the Wop	47
XXIV	A Man in Baro	49
XXV	Plague of Flag Staffs	50
XXVI	Bil and the Koppas	52
XXVII	Purification of the Temples	54
XXVIII	Plague of Apathy	55
XXIX	The Iankis	57
XXX	Banishment to Bedublyu	59
XXXI	The House of Pawtle	61
XXXII	Kantin	63
XXXIII	The Two Flocks	65
XXXIV	Darken Thy Lightness	66
XXXV	No Ell and Bebe	68
XXXVI	Ohmgard	71
XXXVII	Hot Air	73
XXXVIII	Atsites called Beetoo	74
XXXIX	Juke Boxes	76
XL	The Battle Ceaseth	78

CHAPTER I

The great Tribe and their Prophet. The King commandeth. Guides and Bilits in the land of plenty. They journey forth. Weeping and wailing. The man Green. The Damij. The Tribe's new name.

Now THERE WAS IN BRIJWUDS which is nigh unto the city of Rochista in the land of Qent, a great tribe which was named Chm.

And it came to pass that the Prophet Osee appeared before them and spake, saying: Behold, the King that is in Smowk hath commanded me to bring my peoples forth from the land of Qent unto the promised land which is called Chiksanz. And verily, verily I say unto ye, ye shall each one be met with guides who shall bear ye unto Bilits where ye shall dwell in the land of plenty.

And they journeyed forth through the wilderness and came over the ford of Shef into the promised land.

And there was weeping and wailing and gnashing of teeth, for no guides came forth and there were no Bilits.

Now as the sun was going down the Prophet Osee appeared again, and taking the Tribe with him he went up into the hill of Klop. And when they were nigh unto the inn of the man Green he saith unto them: Come hither, and buy thee each some mead, and I will give shekels unto the man Green.

And the multitude rejoiced and entered therein, calling: Ginis, and: Wervington, and all manner of strange names. And when they were refreshed the Prophet spake unto the man Green, saying: Wotsa damij? And behold, the damij was great; and the man Green took many shekels from Osee, and Osee smiled a smile which was verily sickly.

And the Tribe knew not why they had been brought forth. And because they knew not why, they were henceforth called SYG, which is: Special Why Group.

Until the missing issues are found it will be appropriate to fill in the missing spaces with background information on WOYG.

Mrs Gladys Earle and her sister Hazel Webb completed their initial training at the ATS Intake Centre at Butlins Ocean Hotel, Saltdean, in Sussex in March 1940. As they both had clerical jobs before the war they expected to be posted to the Pay Corps. They were somewhat surprised when answering "yes" to the question "Have you ever seen a typewriter?" they were told they were "born" teleprinter operators. They had never seen a teleprinter until they arrived at the Central Telegraph Office in Kensington where they were given three days training and posted to the Signal Corps at Chatham to join fourteen other "born" teleprinter operators. As they were not expected accommodation seemed to be a problem. This was solved by taking them to the village of Borstal where they knocked on doors asking villagers if they would take them in temporarily. Gladys and Hazel were very fortunate to be welcomed by a couple who had three sons all away in the Forces and treated them like long lost daughters.

They were divided into four groups of four to cover the twenty-four hour duties, eight hours each shift and one group off duty. They made their own way across the fields and back to Fort Bridgewoods. The wireless operators were all civilians and worked underground as they did. At that time they had no ATS Officer and rarely saw Commander Ellingworth or his deputy Mr Wort.

After six months in private billets they were transferred to Brompton Barracks living four to a house in married quarters. This was some way from the Fort so they had to be transported to and fro by lorry driven by a member of the F.A.N.Y. "The bombing raids became pretty regular every night about September 1940 and I can remember completing more than one sixteen-hour shift when it became impossible for the transport to get through Chatham, owing to craters or being turned back by the Military Police. Just after midnight on 16 October the off-coming shift, including myself were already seated in the back of the Ford Transit, and the sergeant of the R.E. guard was fixing the tail-board as he always did when there was a terrific explosion and the lorry caught fire. There had been no "alert" and we had not heard any aircraft overhead. It seems to have been a stray bomb dropped from an enemy plane on its way back from London. All I can remember is someone shouting to me to "Jump!" which I did. It was a civilian wireless "op" coming on duty who realised there was still someone alive in the inferno. My hair was burnt and I had shrapnel wounds in my arm. A naval doctor was soon on the scene and I was taken to hospital for treatment and allowed to return to my billet. It was not until the next day that I learned that three ATS operators on the lorry had been killed, also the F.A.N.Y. driver, the sergeant of the guard and one civilian WTO. We used to say in those days, "if your name is on it you will get it". I guess my name was not on it. We were not sorry when in early 1941 we moved to Chicksands for a little peace and quiet".

At Chicksands WOYG joined the RAF Y Group for some months until a permanent home was ready at Beaumanor. They were billetted at Barrow-on-Soar and were joined there by their young sister Betty who is shown manning the machine in the TP hut which received messages transmitted through copper tubes underground from the intercept huts. Her last posting was to Bishops Waltham a subsidiary of Beaumanor to the northwest of Southampton where she was sergeant in charge of a small TP group transmitting from Upham. It was not until 1943 that the GOC Southern Command presented to her the Certificate for Devotion to Duty which she earned in 1940.

The group photograph shows A and C Watches with some HQ staff, the civilians left to right being Mr Wort, later Major Wort, commanding at Forest Moor, Lt Cdr Ellingworth and the Rev A. Barrow. Gladys Earle is holding the scroll presented to her in the front row with the TP operators. All are named in the same photograph in the Y Compendium.

Photo of TP Room

The three Webb sisters

CHAPTER II

The Prophet and Koppa. The Tribe go forth and Koppa haileth the peoples. The flock is shepherded in. The comparing of notes. Fish-payst. There is no health in them.

Now THE PROPHET CAME before the multitude again with a great man who was the chief of the tribe of Konstabuls in the land of Bedz. And the Prophet saith unto them: Woe is me that my peoples are without Bilits. But behold, the great Koppa hath come from afar to seek them out for thee.

And he commanded them to their chariots, and they journeyed forth. And they travelled from Klop unto the Hurst called Graven, and into the city which is named Sil because it is so. And everywhere the Prophet and Koppa hailed the peoples, crying: Behold, here is the wandering tribe of Syg; open up thy stables, we beseech thee, and let them enter therein.

And it came to pass that when the moon was high and the innkeepers were saying their evening prayer, which is: Time, brethren, we beseech thee, the last of the flock was shepherded into his Bilit. And they were even as the corn; for some fell among thorns, and some fell upon stony ground, and some dropped into the Star and Garter.

And upon the day following, the Tribe met and spake amongst themselves, which is called the comparing of notes. And behold, all were sad, and the laughter had departed from them. For some had seen swine come and go even as they brake bread. And some had gone to stool and found the stool passing strange.

And as the days passed many among them fed upon strange foods, for the Ladies of the Land gave them not gold, frankincense nor myrrh, but Fish-payst, Fish-payst, and verily I say unto ye, Fish-payst. And many dwelled only until the first sunrise, and rising from their beds, gave unto their Ladies that which is called Notis. And the Ladies were glad to see their backs, and they were verily pleased to shew them unto them.

And some were sick of the palsy, and some were sick of the Priory, and there was no health in them.

Major John Ellingworth has done some research on the bombing of Rochester Airport which lay across the Rochester—Maidstone Road, Bridgewoods being on the Western side. Any one of these raids could have involved the odd stray bombs falling on or in the vicinity of the fort.

Friday 9 August 1940. Rochester Airport was the target of a heavy raid. 6 Short Stirling bombers. N3645, N3647–N3651 were destroyed as they came off the production line.

Thursday 15 August 1940. 30 Dornier Do 17s of Stabskette, I and II. KG3 attacked Rochester Airport. Bombs fell across the runways, hangars and amongst parked aircraft. Showers of 100 lb fragmentation bombs (SC 50 kg bombs) crashed into aircraft factories on the northern boundary. Incendiaries and delayed action bombs were also released. The "store of finished products" (components store) was burnt out and production of the Stirling was delayed. Luftwaffe aerial photographs taken during an air raid show bombs falling across the A229 road near Fort Horsted, a sister fort to Bridgewoods. These may well have included some falling on or near Bridgewoods.

Saturday 24 August 1940. Luftwaffe aircraft attacked aircraft factories at Rochester (Shorts) and Kingston (Hawkers). ("Defence of the United Kingdom" Basil Collier, HMSO 1957).

Monday 2 September 1940 Day attacks on airfields in the East Kent/Thames areas including Rochester.

Wednesday 4 September 1940. Attack on the Pobjoy aero-engine works at Chatham (located at Rochester Airport). Pobjoys was a subsidiary of Shorts.

Wednesday 16 October 1940. Additional to the report by Mrs Earle—The main attacks in the evening were on London and the suburbs. 3 Luftwaffe aircraft were destroyed, 1 badly damaged. The Home Office gave the following casualties:

<u>LONDON</u>   40 killed, 209 injured.
<u>Elsewhere</u>   24 killed. 44 badly injured, 46 slightly injured.

Fort Bridgewoods had its own L D V (Home Guard) designated Fort Bridgewoods Company, 2nd Battalion, Kent Home Guard. The incident involved two members of the WOYG staff at the Fort:—

In his report the Zone Commander expressed his high appreciation of the conduct of Section Commander T S G Worster, Rochester Battalion, Home Guard.

On 16 October 1940 at 21.35 hours a high explosive bomb fell setting fire to a stationary Army lorry in which there were FANY drivers and six members of the ATS.

Section Commander Worster, who was about twenty feet away, though partially stunned by the explosion, dashed to the blazing lorry and at great personal risk rescued one of the FANY drivers who was badly injured and whose clothing was on fire. He dragged her from the driver's seat, beat out the flames with his bare hands, and took her to a place of safety. He then, with the assistance of Mr R. Hilder, of the A R P service, rescued three of the A.T.S. personnel, who were still alive, from the blazing lorry.

Though suffering from his injuries and shock, Section Commander Worster refused to give up his rescue work till forced to do so. But for his gallantry and presence of mind the death roll of five would have been considerably higher.

I direct that the above be entered on Section Commander Worster's A.F.W. 3056 and be republished in the Battalion Orders of all Battalions in the Kent Home Guard.

Even far removed from the battlefield many suffered from stress because of the exacting and precise nature of their duties. While an Intelligence Officer in the field might have a recurring nightmare that he had missed an enemy tank strength—a routine report of prime value to the Allied commander—missed in the sense that the duty corporal had forgotten to telephone the information to HQ—the wireless operator suffered from nightmares that he had slept in, been late in reporting for duty, or had missed his rendezvous with his opposite number on the Morse key on the enemy side, etc. It was a great strain on the operators working in shifts week after week, sometimes two hours on and four hours off. In the field off duty there was no recreation, no amusements, no pub, just a muddy field or a scorching desert and the fear of scorpions in your bedroll or in your boots, and the incessant distant thunder of guns and the danger of enemy bombers. With no respite, not even weekend leave in eight months it is no wonder that there was even suicide among the young nineteen and twenty year old Oxbridge graduates. We were a happy band of brothers but it may be significant that like the disciples there were always twelve NCOs in a Field Security and a Wireless Intelligence Section.

A nervous consequence of concentration on weak signals through "mush" (interference) resulted in operators suffering from deafness and I remember visiting several in hospital in Tunisia when the campaign ended and many of them became temporarily completely deaf.

When the Woygian Association was wound up all members were presented with a copy of one of Wilk's cartoons as a souvenir. The personal nightmare of Wilkinson, himself an operator, is shown as the unwilling victim. On his left is Noel Royle with pipe, author of the poem "Night Bomber" on p.9 of the May 1944 B S M and on his right Mr Walton one of the supervisors. Major John Ellingworth who supplied this cartoon says: "My late father wears his three hats, as a civilian, as Lt Cdr RN retd at Fort Bridgewoods, and dressed as a Lt Col Royal Signals when he was reluctantly put into khaki from I think 1943–1945. On being demobilised he promptly reverted to his retired naval status and remained a civilian until he retired from Beaumanor in 1953. One slightly ironic fact was that although required to wear uniform he was still paid as a civil servant and was given a gratuity from the Army which he was promptly asked to repay.

The simulated receiver shows the watch changeover times on the main tuning dial and the Germanic Vulture is of course self-explanatory."

MY NIGHTMARE
BY WILK

A souvenir of the Woygian Association reproduced by kind permission of Wilk—May 1951

CHAPTER III

The temple and its many boxes. The Chief Rabbi. The boxes speak. Rabbi playeth tunes. A maiden called Eighty-ess. Kisses for the Rabbi. A Twerp. Wine and bread. Alms for the blessed one.

Now BE IT KNOWN among all men that the great Tribe of Syg built them a temple in the Promised Land. And they call it: Setrum. And men journeyed from afar by day and by night, and hearkened therein. Yea, even from the green field did they come and from their bed in the ford.

And in the temples were many boxes, which were Aycharos, and Amalunds, and Diestys; and the Scribes sat before the boxes and put a crown upon their heads, and a great peace fell upon them. Yea, for some were even as in a trance. And among their number was one, the Chief Rabbi, who moved back and forth many times bearing fresh parchments unto their flocks, and comforting them in sundry ways.

Now the Scribes put many strange scriptures upon the parchments. For many writ in this wise: Verily verily, have I hearkened, and none hath spoken, or inasmuch as they have spoken their voices became too faint in mine ears. Which in the tongue of Syg sounded like unto: Naktivnordibul, and: Nillerd. Yea, it was a strange temple. And some among the Scribes were assuredly sick in their heads, for even as their boxes spake unto them, which speakings were buzzings, and scrapings, and clickings and roarings; yea, and sounds like even unto the very tempest, they writ upon their parchments in this wise: Quiet.

And some cried aloud in the temple, saying: Begone, I beseech thee, even as music like unto the song of the nightingale came forth from their boxes. And some spake of logs, but of timber there was none; and of traffick, but the chariots came not. And some spake often of dropping something, but be it known that these were ofttimes bricks.

And some were without music whatsoever, and cried aloud in their agony. Wherefore the Chief Rabbi came unto them bearing another box which is called Meat Waver and played tunes thereon until they were happy again. Verily this Rabbi was a good and kindly man.

THE CHRONICLES OF ST. UPID

Now in the temple also was one, a maiden, called Eighty-ess, who had much parchment. And inasmuch as she loved the parchment she went among the Scribes pleading for gifts of it. And in the goodness of their hearts they gave it unto her, and of the fruits of the earth; yea, and even of the fowls of the air, and the hues of the rainbow. And she bore the gifts from thence into the tabernacle which is called Tepee.

And it came to pass that the Chief Rabbi often sought kisses, for he came before each Scribe in turn and they gave unto him one, or two, or three, or even four, as was their regard for him; and he marked them upon his parchment. And verily, some there were who gave no kisses and the Chief Rabbi was in a great measure dismayed. But he came not in this wise before the maiden.

Now a certain Scribe who is nameless writ much one day, and great was the sweat of his brow, for his parchments rose high unto the roof. And the Chief Rabbi came before him and saw that the parchments were full of E's. And behold, he was of great wrath and seized the Scribe, and smote him hip and thigh, cursing him mightily, saying: Verily, thou art a Twerp of boundless magnitude, for thou has hearkened unto the great Orto which revveth.

Now at certain times one of the Scribes called Kee would go forth from the temple and return bearing a chalice of rare wine called Naficha, and other names. And each of the Scribes took unto himself a goblet of the wine and brake bread with it. And when the ceremony was come to a finish the Chief Rabbi moved among the peoples, calling upon them for alms for the blessed one of the Kantin tribe. And behold, the multitude showered their shekels upon him. And be it known: In this manner was a great prophet made.

For the unitiated the boxes in the set-room were wireless receivers Aycharos HROs, Hammerlunds etc. When there was no wireless traffic on the required frequencies the operator wrote, Inactive, or Inaudible or Nil Heard. The unhappy operator who tried to take automatic morse "the great OTTO which revveth" was scolded. Naficha is NAAFI tea. And Meat Wavere is Wave-meter.

WOYG AT CHICKSANDS PRIORY

The Priory was built by the Gilbertine order in the XII Century on the north bank of the R. Flit as a pair of adjacent cloisters one for men and one for women with an east/west dividing wall following the established rule for combined Gilbertine Houses. It was a place of refuge for Thomas a Becket in 1164 when he fled from Canterbury to escape the king's wrath on his way to exile in France. With the Act of Suppression in 1536 all religious houses with incomes under £200 were dissolved. Chicksands came just above the threshold at £220 and the Priory escaped destruction. The Prior was given the alternative of surrendering the property voluntarily and receiving a pension of £30 or being gibbetted from a nearby tree. Gibbeting was most cruel. The victim was suspended in iron fetters in a man-sized cage till he died of dehydration and hunger. There were six canons and sixteen nuns. The canons receivd a pension of £2 and the nuns two silver marks or two-thirds of a Pound. Chicksands' religious era came to an end after 388 years in October 1538.

In 1598 the title of Chicksands with its 2,500 acres passed to the Osborne family who retained it till 1936 when it passed to the Crown and the Air Ministry. King James 1 (VI of Scotland) used to visit the Priory as a form of pilgrimage and knighted John Osborne in 1618. There is an octagonal tower incorporating the King James Bedroom and for centuries it was furnished with King James bed.

In August 1936 the Air Ministry allowed the Royal Navy to become sole tenants in 1939 and the RAF began to develop the site as a secret signals station. Although the RN remained at Chicksands throughout the 1939–45 War and even posted an admiral in the Priory as its senior officer it was an RAF base and the Navy were always tenants. The RN and the Army maintained a small intercept presence throughout the war.

The sprawling estate afforded ground for the large antenna arrays necessary for High Frequency (HF) radio intercepts. In the summer of 1940 with the Battle of Britain raging Air Ministry surveyors were tramping across the meadows planning sites for the radio intercept antennae and the new camp buildings, and soon the first of the RAF Y Service personnel arrived to join their RN counterparts. At first the aerials were slung between the Priory windows and nearby trees pending the erection of the proper 240 ft HF antenna masts.

There were two air raids which caused the authorities to think the Germans had discovered the nature of the work at Chicksands, the first on 20 Sep 1940 when seven bombers of LG 1 based on Orleans joined 135 other bombers of LG 2 and LG 3 for a raid on England. They dropped sixteen bombs of which six fell on RAF Henlow 5 miles southeast of Chicksands and ten others at Chicksands Farm destroying the outside lavatory.

Nearby Bedford was bombed on 22 Sep and eight were killed. Luton was struck on 14 Oct with 13 killed. On 16 Nov KG 55 sent 42 HE 111s from Dreux, Chartres and Villacoublay to attack London and targets as far to the north as Birmingham and Coventry. Eleven Heinkels were reported over their target from 0520 to 0600 (German time). Using Knickebein to bomb through cloud they dropped eleven 1,000 pound bombs and many smaller ones and some came down only 100 yards south of the Priory using Knickebein as there was a great deal of cloud. Damage was done to trusses in the roof of the ancient building and WAAF and RAF operators in the second-floor Music Room were thrown to the ground amid shattered glass.

All the Heinkels returned safely to base.

In 1941 the first WAAF arrived, many only seventeen years of age and away from home and working for the first time in their lives. At first they had to share billetting, ablution and latrine arrangements with the men until two self-contained and separate living camps were constructed: one for the RAF south of the River Flit and one for the WAAF on the other side of the river. Not all Y personnel were in camps, many were billetted at Campton and Shefford and other nearby villages.

The upper rooms in the Priory served as intercept rooms until the Technical Site "A" was completed. Their targets were Luftwaffe ground radio nets in German-occupied Europe, North Africa and the Russian Front. The networks of Italian Air Force formations were intercepted in an attic of the Priory by seven Special Operators. There were three Squadrons of operators numbered 1, 2 and 3 working eight-hour shifts over twenty-four hours so that each squadron had its share of evening and night shifts. No. 4 Squadron was allocated daytime admin duties.

The drill was to have a squadron roll-call in the cobble-stoned yard outside the octagon-shaped tower of The King James Bedroom and then 30 operators marched up the main staircase to Watch Rooms in the magnificent rooms with vaulted ceilings and Gothic windows. The walls were

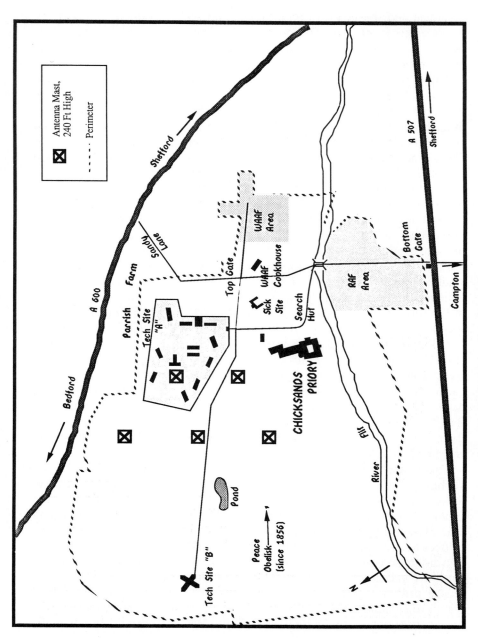

RAF Chicksands in the 1940s

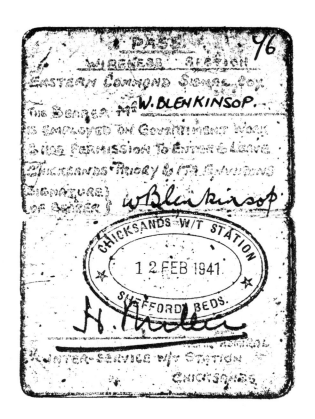

Chicksands Priory with two of the five 240ft antenna masts in the background
Courtesy of W. Grayson: Chicksands—A Milennium of History

lined with wooden shelves for the radio intercept receivers. The teletype message centre was the King James Bedroom and its inception in 1941 obviated the necessity of despatch riders rushing "E" messages 20 miles to Bletchley Park.

It was at Chicksands that the fate of the German battleship Bismarck was sealed. On 18 May 1941 the 42,500 ton ship left Bergen with the cruiser Prinz Eugen to break into the North Atlantic to wreak havoc among Allied merchant ship convoys and fast enough to catch the pride of the British fleet the Queen Mary and Queen Elizabeth each of which could transport an American division to Europe. They were spotted by RAF reconnaissance Spitfires from Wick and shadowed by HMS Norfolk and HMS Suffolk northwest of Iceland. Churchill, desperately worried by the loss of Crete knew that eleven convoys including a precious troop convoy were at sea or about to sail. In fact during the chase the battleships left the troop convoy south of Ireland and joined the hunt for the Bismarck. He was wakened at 7 a.m. on the 24th to hear that the Hood had been lost with its complement of 1500 men and that the Prince of Wales was damaged under water aft and out of action with four direct hits from the Bismarck's 15 inch guns, one of which wrecked the bridge killing or wounding nearly everyone on it. The Prince of Wales had inflicted damage on Bismarck with two heavy shells one of which had holed an oil tank below water level and the loss of oil was to have important consequences. Meanwhile Admiral Somerville had left Gibraltar with Force H, (Renown, Ark Royal and the cruiser Sheffield) at high speed to protect the troop convoy or join in the battle.

Bismarck should have headed home victorious but was going southwards and the British had lost contact. During this period of uncertainty Bismarck had sent 22 signals some announcing her change of plans. Naval Enigma was not being read at BP until 28 May by which time Bismarck had been sunk but during thirty minutes on the air she had been repeatedly plotted by D/F bearings. According to Hinsley (British Intelligence in the Second World War Vol 1) "British intercept stations had submitted the signals to analysis by RPF, whch filmed the type and the peculiarities of a transmitter and by TINA, the process which studied the morse characteristics of individual wireless operators. These precautions proved valuable when the Bismarck, slow to grasp that she had shaken off her shadowers and possibly by false intelligence which included a reconnaissance report to the effect that part of the Home Fleet was still at Scapa Flow transmitted three further signals during the forenoon of 25 May. It was the DF bearings and the RPF and TINA characteristics of these signals that in the end enabled the British authorities to decide correctly which option of the three available to her the Bismarck had adopted. But it was only after considerable delay that this decision was reached."

At 0832 hours on 25 May Admiral Luetjens broke radio silence. He began a long Enigma-enciphered message requesting support from German air and sea units. The Navy Y Service at Chicksands intercepted Bismarck's long transmission and the RDF bearings taken by Y Service in Gibraltar provided repeated "cuts" from the south that located the Bismarck at 0948 and 1054 at 55°15′N 30 to 31′W and 55°N 31′W slightly south and east of that of 0854. "The Admiralty ordered HMS Rodney at 1158 to act on the assumption that the enemy was proceeding to a Bay of Biscay port. At 1244 Flag Officer Submarines disposed his force on the same assumption . . . As it happened the Naval Section's close watch on the German naval W/T system yielded only one piece of evidence in the course of 24 May. It informed the OIC by telephone that whereas the normal W/T control station for the Bismarck frequency was Wilhemshaven, the control had been transferred to Paris, a good sign that the Bismarck was moving south. German naval records establish that the Bismarck was ordered to shift to the Paris control at midday on 24 May."

"Admiral Tovey in the King George V" wrote Churchill," was still a long way off but signalled that he hoped to engage by 9 a.m. on the 25th. The Admiralty summoned all forces. The Rodney, five hundred miles to the SE, was ordered to steer a closing course. The Ramillies was ordered to quit her homeward bound convoy and place herself to the westward of the enemy and the Revenge, from Halifax, was also directed to the scene. Cruisers were posted to guard against a break-back by the enemy to the north and east, while all the time Admiral Somerville's force was pressing northwards from Gibraltar.

That evening about 6 p.m. the Bismarck suddenly turned to engage her pursuers and there was a brief encounter. We now know that this movement was made to cover the escape of the Prinz Eugen which then made off at high speed to the south, and after refuelling at sea reached Brest quite unchallenged ten days later. Admiral Tovey had sent the Victorious ahead to make an air attack in the hope of reducing the enemy's speed. At 10 p.m. covered by four cruisers she released her nine Swordfish torpedo-aircraft on a 120-mile flight against a strong head wind with rain and low cloud. Two hours later they found the Bismarck and scored a torpedo hit under the bridge.

Once more everything seemed set for a morning climax and once more the Admiralty's hopes were dashed. Soon after 3 a.m. on the 25th the Suffolk suddenly and unexpectedly lost contact with the Bismarck. She had been shadowing by Radar with skill from a position on the enemy's port quarter. All ships were now zigzagging as they moved south into waters infested by U-boats. The Bismarck had managed to slip through the cordon and gain a commanding lead in her race for safety, but short of oil through leakage. The Rodney with her 16-inch guns still lay between her and home, but she too was moving to the north-eastward and crossed ahead of the Bismarck during the afternoon. The day which had begun so full of promise ended in disappointment and frustration. Happily from the south, breasting the heavy Atlantic seas, the Renown, the Ark Royal, and the cruiser Sheffield were steadily approaching on an intercepting course.

By the morning of 26 May the problem of fuel for all our widely scattered ships, which had now been steaming hard for four days, began to clamour for attention. Already several of the pursuers had had to reduce speed. It was clear that in these wide expanses all our efforts might yet be in vain. However at 10 30 a.m. just as hopes were beginning to fade a Catalina working from Lough Erne in Ireland located the fugitive steering towards Brest and still about 700 miles from home. The Bismarck damaged the aircraft and contact was lost. But within an hour two Swordfish from the Ark Royal spotted her once more. She was still to the westward of the Renown and not yet within the German air cover radiating powerfully from Brest. The Renown could not face her single-handed and had to await the arrival of King George V and Rodney both still far behind the chase.

Admiral Somerville hastening northwards sent on the Sheffield to close and shadow the enemy and she held her for sure . . . Fifteen Swordfish left the Ark Royal a little after 7 pm. The enemy was now less than forty miles away and this time there was no mistake. By 9.30 their work was done. Two torpedoes had certainly hit and possibly a third. A shadowing aircraft reported that the Bismarck had been seen to make two complete circles and it seemed she was out of control. Captain Vian's destroyers were now approaching and throughout the night surrounded the stricken ship attacking with torpedoes whenever the chance came.

The German commander had no illusions. Shortly before midnight he reported: "Ship unmanoeuvrable. We shall fight to the last shell. Long live the Fuehrer!" Her main armament was uninjured and Admiral Tovey decided to bring her to battle in the morning. The Rodney opened fire at 8.47 am followed a minute later by the King George V. The British ships quickly began to hit and after a pause the Bismarck too opened fire. For a short time her shooting was good and with her third salvo she straddled the Rodney but thereafter the weight of the British attack was overwhelming. Within half an hour most of her guns were silent. A fire was blazing amidships and she had a heavy list to port. The Rodney now turned across her bow, pouring in a heavy fire from a range of no more than 4,000 yards. By 10.15 all the Bismarck's guns were silent and her mast was shot away. The ship lay wallowing in the heavy seas, a flaming and smoking ruin: yet even then she did not sink.

It was the cruiser Dorsetshire that delivered the final blow with torpedoes, and at 10.40 the great ship turned over and foundered. With her perished nearly 2,000 Germans and their Fleet Commander, Admiral Luetjens. One hundred and ten survivors, exhausted but sullen, were rescued by us. The work of mercy was interrupted by the appearance of a U-boat and the British ships were compelled to withdraw. Five other Germans were picked up by a U-boat and a ship engaged in weather reporting."

In 1941 the first of the Tech Site "A" buildings called blocks were completed. Italian traffic was copied in D Block at the northeast corner of Tech Site "A" and very near to Sandy Lane, which runs through the Parish Farm to the A600 road. The blocks were flat-roofed, one storey buildings dispersed through the site to minimise their vulnerability to air attack. Each had a brick blast wall protecting the doors at either end and an underground shelter immediately outside. At its peak Chicksands was operating approximately 100 intercept positions against the Germans and another ten against the Italians.

According to Grayson, Chicksands served as a major RAF communications control centre, functioning as the hub of RAF high-frequency radio nets in the UK and abroad on the continent. After D-Day 6 June 1944 the Allies pushed the Germans steadily out of France and the Low Countries. Airfields liberated by the Allies were brought into service for units redeployed from the UK. Their communications overseas were handled by lorry-mounted radio units at the forward airfields by Heavy Mobile Units such as No 15 HMU of the 2nd Tactical Air Force. It was formed and trained in the UK as part of Operation Overlord and shipped to France in July 1944. RAF communications were handled at Chicksands by Technical Site "B" located to the west of the Priory. It formerly occupied a single building in the shape of a Christian cross, housing receivers, transmitters and maintenance facilities. Much of the traffic was sent as Automatic Morse. The specialists in the Priory and Technical Site "A" were never told what was going on in Technical Site "B".

Long before the despatch of mobile HMUs to France, RAF Chicksands had begun to transmit messages to Allied agents in Occupied France. These had been sent by BBC Bristol but the blitz had forced important offices to evacuate London and the South Coast generally. Studios were set up in Bedford for this purpose and the messages were routed by GPO cable to the aerials of RAF Chicksands seven miles away. It was a two-way traffic as agents abroad were able to send back vital information from all over Europe. The messages were made up probably at BP in stanzas of poetry or innocent greetings. The messages were read in different languages by announcers who had no idea of the concealed meanings.

Readers of *Enigma and its Achilles Heel* will remember that Bertrand and his wife learned that the message "Les lilas blancs sont fleuris" had been passed at 12.30 and would be repeated twice more at 19.30 and 21.30. The first time it meant "The Lysander intends to come", the second "It's on" and the third "We are coming as planned". Usually only the agent for whom the message was intended could understand it. As D-Day drew near there were thousands of these messages and they made the Germans feel very uncomfortable indeed. The immortal poem of Verlaine was chosen to signal the start of D-Day. It was sent from Chicksands in two parts, the first repeated over several days:

Les sanglots longs des violons de l'automne

was capped on the eve of 6 June 1944 with the following verse:

Blessent mon coeur d'une langueur monotone

It was necessary to give this warning as on a previous occasion the Maquis had risen and attacked the Germans when the Allies landed in North Africa in November 1942 especially on the plateau of Vercors in the Drome where they had an impregnable position. This premature offensive was put down with the utmost severity by the Germans who launched gliders with paratroops and armoured cars on the plateau and even slaughtered the patients and nurses in the hospital among the rocks.

Grayson makes an interesting point about Glenn Miller who was a major in the USAAF. As Bedford was a hub for the many U.S. formations stationed in the area the Corn Exchange in the Market Square and the old Granada Theatre (pulled down in 1991) were visited by Bob Hope, Bing Crosby, Bea Lillie, Gracie Fields and many others to entertain the troops.

"Glenn Miller brought his band to Bedford in 1944 and gave live performances for the troops at the Granada Theatre and dances at the Corn Exchange. Miller had a flat in Waterloo Road while the rest of the band was billetted in the Red Cross Officers' Club in town. At one performance at the Corn Exchange on 10 July, Humphrey Bogart and David Niven were in the audience. David Niven was Miller's senior and in his chain of command. It seemed a natural progression that the live performances should be sent by radio to troops on their bases and this was soon being routinely done via the American Forces Network. Next came an idea attributed (but with virtually no evidence) to General Eisenhower himself. Glenn Miller's music could be broadcast to the Continent where it would be accepted as neutral, innocent entertainment by listening Germans and the populations of occupied countries. In some cases the stations' announcers attempted to give the deceptive impression that the transmissions originated in Germany, although many went through Chicksands Technical Site "B". At these times propaganda and disinformation produced by the Political Warfare Executive, lodged at the Duke of Bedford's estate, Woburn Abbey, was included in the broadcasts.

With a studio set up in Milton Earnest Hall, just north of Bedford, Glenn Miller and his band recorded for subsequent transmission. What Miller had not even been told from the start was that Milton Earnest Hall another country house that had joined the war effort, also housed special service elements engaged in the various tricks and ploys of unconventional warfare. One of these was a newly developed technique of hiding messages under other recorded material, such as music, so that an unsuspecting listener would hear only the music. This, it was planned, would permit a greater number of subliminal messages to be sent with less danger of German jamming and less of a risk to non-Germans caught listening.

The doctored Glenn Miller recordings with the hidden agent traffic was sent by telephone cable from Milton Earnest Hall to RAF Chicksands and also to the studios of the American Forces Radio for radio broadcasting.

A Continuing Mystery: The Disappearance of Glenn Miller

Several post-war writers have documented various scenarios purportedly explaining Miller's mysterious disappearance. The facts as they are known are that on 15 December 1944 the bandleader and Colonel Norman Baesell, the Executive Officer at the super-secret Milton Earnest Hall, boarded an Army Air Force UC-64 "Norseman" utility transport at RAF Twinwoods three miles north of Bedford. The Canadian-built aircraft took off at 1255 GMT. Miller was en route to Bordeaux, France with stops at RAF Bovingdon and Air Base A-42 at Villacoublay, ironically one of the re-taken Luftwaffe fields in France which may have supported the 6 November attack on Chicksands Priory, four years earlier. The Norseman, with Flight Officer John "Nipper" Morgan at the controls disappeared without trace after departing Bovington. No other Allied aircraft went missing over the Channel on 15 December 1944. Nothing more is positively known.

The most bizarre theory attributes Miller's disappearance to his being eliminated (murdered) as a security risk by the U.S. Office of Strategic Services. In this unfounded account, an agitated Miller was about to blow the whistle on the propaganda and secret broadcasting activities at Milton Earnest Hall and Chicksands . . .

On the other hand if it is claimed that a Miller visit to Chicksands was connected with the technical aspects of the base's transmitter operations, we must await confirming evidence, since none is openly available. It requires, however, a great leap of faith to believe that the band leader would have had any interest at all in the broadcast system's transmission interfaces . . .

Admittedly it is curious that, if Miller was on his way to France to perform, (and the other band members did arrive in Bordeaux the day of the disappearance) what was Colonel Norman Baessel doing on the same plane, going to France? Just a strange coincidence? One explanation suggests that it was Baessel who provided the "hop" to Miller.

The currently favoured explanation for the disappearance has it that "Nipper" Morgan, the luckless Norseman pilot, unknowingly flew into falling bombs jettisoned by aborting RAF Lancaster bombers over the English Channel, also unaware of the UC-64's presence below. In this version the explosions disintegrated the fabric-covered transport, which is supposed to have sunk in the Channel without trace.

This plausible account is bolstered by the published recollections (1988) of a Number 149 Squadron Lancaster crew in question, which was returning to England with unused bombs to jettison. The entire squadron, each carrying a single 4000 pound "blockbuster" bomb set to explode above the surface, was recalled halfway to their target at Siegen because of a scheduling problem with their planned fighter escort. Fred Shaw, a Lancaster navigator, was watching the squadron's ditched bombs exploding above the Channel when the bomb aimer shouted there was a plane below. Shaw spotted what he is certain was a high-winged monoplane, heading south at about 1300 feet and remembers seeing the plane go down in the water. According to Shaw two other crew members, deceased before 1988, also claimed to have seen the incident. Shaw, an experienced airman who had seen UC-64s previously identified the crashed plane as a UC-64. With a speed of only 135 knots, a surprised Flight Officer Morgan would have had no chance of evasive action.

Because the Siegen mission had been aborted the usual post-mission debriefings were not conducted and the accident was not reported by the crew, everyone reasoning that someone else would report it. The crucial Battle of the Bulge began the next day and Number 149 Squadron's attention was fully occupied, the "Norseman" incident rapidly decreasing in relative importance. This version of the disappearance of Glenn Miller is the one officially accepted by historians at the Ministry of Defence.

Just as at Beaumanor and Bletchley the main entertainment was the cinema, and the pubs. At Beaumanor they had the Odeon Cinema and the Empire Theatre at Loughborough for films and the Theatre Royal for dramatic performances. At Chicksands the camp cinema was also used for live performances and near the base favourite pubs were the White Hart in Campton, and the White Hart, the Black Swan and White Swan in Shefford. As at Beaumanor and BP bicycles were the usual means of transport but there was a rail connection by LMS between Shefford and Bedford Midland Road station and it was only a short walk from the camp by a footpath from the camp to Shefford station.

There was a great deal of sporting activity as at other Y stations and the camp fielded teams for Rugby, soccer cricket etc against other Services as RAF Cardigan, Dunstable and Henlow and the Royal Navy made its contibution by raising teams from Letchworth versus Vauxhall Motors and Luton Corporation. There was fishing in the River Flit and the editor remembers boating on the river at Bedford with his wife and visits to the pub at Shefford with Captain Burgess. He also joined the fencing club at BP which had a professional coach.

Now let the BSM tell its own story!

FOREWORD.

I am very glad to write a word or two for the first number of the B.S.M. and to wish the Editorial Staff all good luck in their venture.

Apart from the stimulation of interest in current affairs, a journal of this nature has a very distinct historical value.

I still treasure my first copy of the "Tenedos Times", a double sheet produced in the Dardenelles in 1914 on an ordinary hectograph jelly.

At that time the Captain of our Destroyer parent ship hated tobacco in any shape or form, therefore the "Tenedos Times" in its first issue had a cartoon shewing this officer chasing a trail of cigarette ashes laid by a certain Lieut-Commander A.B. Cunningham, Captain of one of the destroyers of the Flotilla. Lieut-Commander Cunningham is now Admiral Sir A.B. Cunningham, KCB., DSO., etc., Commander-in-Chief, Mediterranean Fleet. So keep your copies of the B.S.M. to show your children - you never know!

The issue of the first number of the B.S.M. is coincident with our departure from our temporary home. I doubt whether, even in this war, such a mixture of all sorts and conditions of men - and women - , service and civilian, could have been made bearable without the greatest consideration and forbearance on the part of the Commanding Officer of the Station, and of the C.O, Officers and other ranks of the R.A.F. We thank them all and wish them all good fortune in the future.

And now we go ahead in our new location. There will be many changes and many new faces, but I have no doubt that if we all pull together as in the past, we shall still be able to play our small part in the War Effort, and one day rejoice in the "Victory" that must be ours.

Oct. 1941.   M.E.

Editorial

WELL HERE IT IS: WE HOPE YOU LIKE IT:

OUR THREE POINT AIM:-

To be HELPFUL; INTERESTING and AMUSING
Constructive criticisms-Facetious criticisms WELCOMED
and VENTILATED. In this column we will endeavour to
interpret the feelings and wishes of the staff.
With this issue we say farewell CHICKSANDS and
H O L D T I G H T LEICESTER. Pigs, Billets, Free buses,
wonderful canteen, plenty of Smokes? here, have all
helped to liven up a not uneventful 8 months. We may,
we hope, look forward to Happier, Freer and Smokier days.
We understand our Club committee are a body of GENTLEMEN;
to whom miracles are matter of small moment. Gentlemen,
we await the first miracle.

Re our title "B.S.M." The Editor is fully aware of the
almost irresistible temptation to "gag" on these
initials and, wishing to be first with the news, in the
traditional "Press" manner, we say to our readers, "It
is our intention to make each months' issue of the
"B" Staff Magazine, a better one than its predecessor."

THE EDITOR DOES NOT NECESSARILY ASSOCIATE HIMSELF WITH
VIEWS EXPRESSED BY CONTRIBUTORS.

Staff Club News.

The members of the Section are thanked for the manner in which they responded to the appeal by the Committee for a loan of a minimum of 2/6d. per member to meet the initial expenditure in connection with the canteen.

Times of opening of the Canteen at our new station have been provisionally arranged as follows:-
```
                    0000-0430
                    0800-1400
                    1600-2200
```

During the first few weeks, the Committee crave the indulgence of ALL members, as only a limited type of goods will be on sale, and, owing to the difficulty of obtaining labour, only a small staff operating in the Canteen. As time goes on however, it is hoped that with more staff, it will be possible to provide a larger variety of food, drinks and other commodities.

The following drinks will be on sale from the commencement: Tea, Coffee, Cocoa, Oxo and Bovril.

An ample supply of Daily and other papers will be available.

The Committee ask ALL members to assist in keeping the Canteen Hut as clean & tidy as possible by using the receptacles which are being provided for waste paper and other rubbish.

It is hoped to provide Railway and Omnibus Timetables and other books of information for the use of the members. These, nor the daily papers or other magazines, should not be taken away from the Canteen Hut.

The Editor regrets that production is not up to his expectations, owing to technical difficulties. Profiting by experience the next issue will show improvements.

("J" is Major Jolowicz my colleague in No. VI IS at Chicksands and Hampstead. He was Professor of Roman Law at University College, London and I sat at his feet 1946–47 in my first year in Law School.—Ed)

"HINTS ON EVACUATION TO NEW BILLETS"   "Freelance"

Prior to moving, listen attentively to details regarding bus transport, then humming "You don't have to tell me - I know" take your cycle.

Do not arrive in a "browned off" mood as in this event you will notice no change.

Do not be mislead by the size of landladies. Remember that invariably the "bomber" type are easier to handle than the "spitfire" specie.

If asked, "would you mind sleeping with the children", ask for names, ages and photos, then well "what would you do chums"?.

When asked if you like certain items of food, which happen to be your particular fancy, give a very definite no. This will ensure you receiving a fairly regular supply.

If billeted in a place with all modern conveniences, do not display a too childish delight in the wondrous workings of a cistern. This will assist you in maintaining your "pull" with your hosts.

It is recommended that some kind of reserve ration be taken and for convenience a FISHPASTE sandwich is advisable. If not required, this could be framed as a keepsake and in years to come, would be found to "speak for itself". It is hoped this is not carried too far, as in the case of Reg.Hilder, who, the writer understands, has ensured his own rations and in the process has left the village of Silsoe to face a winter of famine.

PACKING:- It will first be found necessary to endeavour to obtain your suitcase from the person who last borrowed same. Finding it to be severely mauled, throw away and purchase a new one. Next, consider how you will pack your working suit, your evening suit and your best or Sunday suit and then decide to wear it. As the case will no longer be required, offer to loan it to one of your borrowing circle. In the event of being let down by people refusing to borrow this it will be found by those working a 7 day week plus overtime, or those engaged on the eight to "plus four" watch, to be a useful receptacle for transporting the "kitty".

The Anglers File   A H Appleton

Fish, nature, streams, discourse, the line, the hook shall form the motley subject of my book.

The idea behind the Anglers page is firstly to help my fellow-anglers to make progress by interchange of ideas, in our fascinating sport.

Secondly to try to convert those unbelievers and scoffers who only think of fishermen as "a fool at one end and a worm at the other".

Fishing has a lure of its own which is very difficult to describe to the uninitiated. I sometimes wonder if fishermen are born and not made, because one is either very keen or has no interest in it at all. I have often heard people exclaim "Fancy watching a float all day".

Of course, no angler likes a blank day but the bait must be in the water whether the fish are feeding or not.

The true angler is, however a student of nature. By observation many interesting things may be learned about the birds, the animals, the insects, the flowers etc. that haunt the riverside.

The habits of fish can be studied to advantage, also other animals are easily watched in their own element but not so with our finny friends. Even the scientists are puzzled still, by many oddities in the fish world. For instance the astounding life story of the eel has only just been unfolded and proved. This I hope to tell you about later on.

In future articles I wish to deal in detail with the various forms of fishing whether sea or river. I shall welcome criticisms and compliments (if any)!

In my next article I shall discuss the tackle to be used for river fishing.

A.H.A.

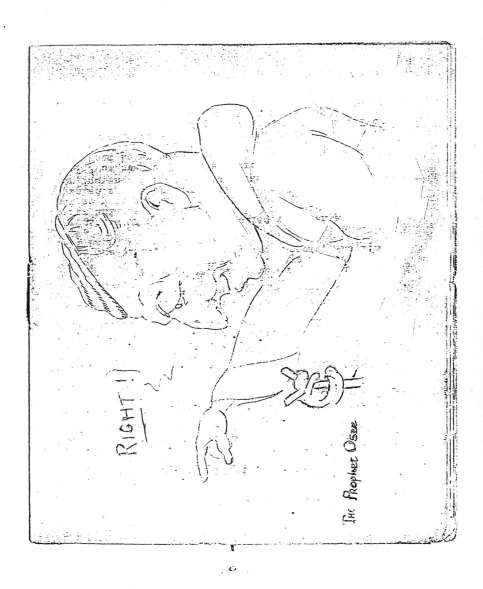

THE GOSPEL ACCORDING TO ST.UPID. CHAPTER IV.

THE PROPHET AND THE EXODUS (translated from the English by disciple Millhouse).

Now it came to pass, when the year drew nigh unto the Feast of the Pullover, and the Ewes were shaking forth the mothballs from their Roltopz and Veenekz, that the Prophet Osee communed with his peoples again, and spake unto them in this wise, saying:

Verily my heart is full, for I bring thee tidings of great joy. Full many a moon have I believed I have done my task and delivered my peoples into the Promised Land. But Behold, a parchment hath come into mine hand from the mighty Red Tabz in Wyt Awl and thus sayeth the parchment, in the tongue of Red Tabz, which is called Verbossitee!

WE REGRET TO INFORM YOU THAT, OWING TO AN ERROR YOU HAVE BEEN WRONGLY DELIVERED

Yea, verily, by the Beer of the Prophet, inasmuch as ye think not, this is a promised land, but the land was given by Red Tabz unto another tribe called Glamma Boiz. But Red Tabz saith my peoples shall have a new and greater land, a land flowing with beer and skittles and the land shall be called Lesta or Leiks.

Therefore I say unto ye, before another moon hath ascended the heavens ye must take up thy beds, and mount the chariots again, and depart for ever out of the land of Bedz, taking with thee thy ox, and thy ass, and thy pencil, but not everything that is thy neighbour's-lest thy neighbour looketh and splitteth unto Koppa.

And the multitude went up into the Hill of Klop, and sundry other places where they were assured of solitude, and meditated, and Behold, they were glad in their hearts and rejoiced, yea, even without the persuasion of mead.

And the onions and leeks which the tribe had planted at Setrum flourished not from their weepings.

And be it known that the Glamma Boiz found the back view of the tribe better to the eye than the front view.

ORDER YOUR GOSPEL IN ADVANCE AND THUS BE SURE OF OUR NEXT THRILLING INSTALMENT. SPECIAL FREE GIFT WITH EVERY COPY! THE TEN COMMANDMENTS.

```
............................................
............................................
```

TRAVELOGUE by R.G.D.

Beautiful Bedfordshire

Biggleswade This industrious town set in a countryside which could not be described as hilly, boasts a spacious market square. (One side practically invisible from the other). Many people come and languish in this town at no cost whatever to themselves, His Majesty bears all expenses. **Bedford Mile** Quite distinct from all others. Found almost anywhere in the Shire. Actually measures 2.125 miles. **Beaver** It appears that for many years strangers (always welcome) to this part, have been under a misapprehension regarding Beaver and dealing with it. Instead of shaving, the working man of Bedford eats his beaver, which is a nourishing apertif, round about 10.0 oclock or 4.0 oclock time. **Industry** For those who wisely contemplate permanent residence within the Shire, a healthful and progressive future is offered in Brusselin' and Muck Spreddin!
Conclusion The hospitality of this "Garden of Eden" is renowned, and to anyone passing who is in need of sanctuary, we say, "You can do nothing better than keep passing.

BITS and PIECES

Related by "Win"

An ARP Warden spotting a light showing through a crack in a door, knocked and said to the woman, "I have just seen a chink coming through your door". The woman exclaimed, "The .... he told me he was a Polish airman.

From R.G.D. (for which, many thanks)

We have our co-editors Staddon & Jones: one bounces, the other appears of no bones. They hope that by publishing topical themes to bring about what has been in all our dreams; a chance for the staff to express its own tones.

All healthy young men in Silsoe
can tell how to coo and bill, so
not going too far but just far enough
they pick out some grass, a nice bit of fluff
and murmur "Don't mind if I do though".

Flowers in CRR. This is not to be taken as a precedent. The O.C's hand basin must not be used for Goldfish.
....

Dances will no longer be attended by kind permission of the R.A., but by kind permission of your Lumbago.

We hear that two publicans in a village not far from the Old Homestead are entering the Workhouse on Oct. 11th. By "George" !!! Slap me on the "Star & Garter"

Looking back over the past months, we have many things to remember (I'll say we have).

The Priory,—its quiet and peacefulness??? the formidable figures that parade its corridors, rings round their arms and under their eyes, guarding its sacred walls as did those in days gone by.

Its history is famous. Mentioned in literature, it is by no means unknown. Legend has it that a Nun, who did what none should have done, wanders through the grounds in the not so still of the night, I understand she did'nt live long enough to become a Mother-Superior.

I doubt whether our presence within its walls will go down in history, yet, surely history has been made for I cannot recall having heard where the two womens services have worked in such close co-operation. Many thought it impossible, but the age of miracles is not past, and women do not have their claws out all the time.

Now that the A.T.S. seek fresh fields to conquer, we look forward to the day when once again we can meet in happier circumstances.

We wish everyone the very best of luck.

Farewell .... Priory. Time and the A.T.S. marches on.......

G.B.

C.S.R.O.A.

B.R.Kelly
Hon. Sec.

I am going to summarize my estimate of the CSROA, as formed through a study of association business at general meeting in Carlisle.

There was a considerable amount of business which entailed much discussion, but very few of the proposals affected us closely. Regarding that side, details of the proceedings will appear in the Association Mag's next issue.

The most interesting part of the agenda to me, as your representative, was the annual reports of the various secretarys. These were very enlightening and left me with a very favourable impression of the strength and efforts the Association was prepared to expend in pushing through any claim which affected it.

I went to the meeting with an absolutely open mind and returned satisfied we have backed the right horse. Finally, I can wholeheartedly recommend the Carlisle brew. It's O.K. B.R.K.

GOSSIP

BRILLIANT SOCIAL EVENT AT SILSOE.

The event of the season was the "Farewell to SYG" dance held at Silsoe, and a great time was drunk by all.

Various members of the seearar appeared, but we were dismayed to learn that Mr.Fillyparnold's pig was unable to be with us, owing to a mislaid waistcoat button.

Lady Att looked as charming as ever, in her gown of khaki serge, and spent her entire evening persuading her RAF partner that "SYG" did not stand for "silly young girls" and that she'd seen the moon before.

Sea breeze was supplied by Admiral Goldsuff. Sqd.Ldr.Morgan made the most of having two arms in commission at long last.   M.P.

How To Keep Your Man - Joan Clark

Don't see him too often (every night is enough).

Don't keep him waiting too long (One hour is enough on a chilly night, any longer is apt to kill all his ardour)

<u>Do</u> be bright but not too bright or you may make him get the idea that he is dumb.

Be a little motherly but not a little mother, or he might think you are older than you look.

Don't order pints when he takes you for a drink or he will think you are a regular drinker, which will spoil his romantic mood.

Don't mention any other fellows you may know or may have known. Let him claim he is the shining light that has come into your life and that you have always been looking for him.

Don't grab his hand in the flicks, wait till a crucial moment (murders-love scenes etc)

Don't kiss him every night - every other night will do (even if you are dying to). He may start thinking you have always made a habit of kissing.

Don't take an instant dislike to his mother when you go to his home to meet her. You can always put aresenic in her tea when she comes to visit you after the wedding bells have rung <u>and</u> they will if only you will follow my few simple hints.

I THANK YOU
or, perhaps
you should thank me

The aims of the magazine have been outlined on another page, but some elaboration is felt necessary. We want if possible, to fill our pages with the spontaneous efforts of our readers, but in order to maintain some kind of continuity we are going to have a series of regular features: details later.

Amongst other items we want to cover, are Sports and Entertainments. So, let us have your ideas on any subject coming under these headings and we will endeavour to bring interested parties together.

Do not be sceptical of your own abilities: who knows we may have a new "Edgar Wallace" or "Ethel M. Dell" in our midst.

Our help, such as it is, on make-up etc. is available to all.

ROLL OUT YOUR JOKES, STORIES, SCANDAL, HINTS, EXPERIENCES and WHAT HAVE YOU?!

Closing date for next issue:- 7th. NOVEMBER.

Publishing date - Mid-November.

STOP PRESS.

CHAPTER V

The issues for November, December 1941, January, February and March 1942 are still unobtainable but the Chapters of the Gospel in them are extant:

CHAPTER V

November
The Tribe is delivered.

The ATS were accommodated all round Beaumanor.
HQ Y Signals ATS: The Towers, Chaveney Road, Quorn.
C.O. Commander Rabaglichi, ATS.
Teleprinter personnel: The Lodge, Barrow-on-Soar (now a hotel) and a property (name unknown) at Newton-Linford.

Operators: Garats Hay. Hutted accommodation now all demolished.
"The Old Bull's Head" Quorn (now a private residence)
"The Hurst" Quorn (now a hotel)
Brand Hill Camp, Woodhouse Eaves (purpose-built. Demolished at end of war and reverted to agriculture).

C.R.S. Private residence. Gardens regularly open to the public. (Camp Reception Station)

ATS Sick Bay "Long Close" Main Street, Woodhouse Eaves.
Some ATS lived in Beaumanor itself.

Training Fearon Hall, Loughborough (now in civic/communal use).

Facility
All out-station ATS personnel moved from various areas to Beaumanor by Bedford 3-ton QLT TCVs (Troop Carrying Vehicles). They were all driven by ATS MT Personnel.

Civilian Grades at WOYG
TEWA   Trainee Experimental Wireless Assistant
EWA   Experimental Wireless Assistant
SEWA   Senior/Supervisory Experimental Wireless Assistant
ADEWO   Assistant Deputy Experimental Wireless Officer
DEWO   Deputy Experimental Wireless Officer

CHAPTER V

The Tribe is delivered. Wyt and the Bilits. A strange people. The Tribe see Bilits. A new temple. Barkus and the Grids. The three shekels. Prophet crieth: Bukshee.

EVEN AS THE PROPHET had spake, so by the bounteous mercy of Red Tabz, were the Tribe delivered out of the land of Bedz, and, by the peoples this was verily Oki Doke.

Now Red Tabz sent his disciple Wyt ahead of the Tribe and charged him with a great task, saying: Go thou forth and find Bilits, and let the Bilits be good and of great comfort, yea, even having Dublusee and all Modkon.

And when the chariots of the Tribe halted, they found a strange land, and a strange people, for it did seem that many of the Lestrites had brethren who wehked in the sheht-wehks in Behmingham. And behold, there were Bilits. And as the Tribe did look upon some of the Bilits they saith, one unto another: Dekko; and: Bly Me; and of a truth thou couldst have knocked them down with a steam roller.

Now there was built in the land a new temple for the Tribe and when the multitude came and saw it, they cried out saying; O Temple thy name is Mudd, and it was so.

And it came to pass that some of the Wehkmen who built the temple liked it not, and, seizing hammers and chisels struck at it and knocked Ell out of it, even though the Tribe were within. But it became not strange to the Tribe, for verily, in the words of St. Oli, they had had some.

Now there was in the land one Barkus, of the caravans, of whom it was said: Barkus delivereth the carcase. But many of the Tribe delivered their own carcases, for had they not 'Grids, yea, and even Flivvas and Lizzies? But they who possessed only Shanks', and they who needed new flints, and they who suffered with Punk, journeyed with Barkus and were poorer by three shekels. But they heard the voice of the Prophet crying; Verily must it be Bukshee; and they murmured among themselves, saying; Red Tabz is a mean beggar, or words sounding like unto these.

CHAPTER VI

The Wehkmen leave a certain box. The Great Noises rejoice. The Scribes breathe out. Confusion rageth and air is blue. Scribes compassion for sardines. Prophet maketh cheeses.

Now IT CAME TO PASS that when the Wehkmen which built the temple were finished their labours, and departed from thence, there was left lying close unto the walls thereof, a small box.

And when the Great Noises came and beheld the box they rejoiced and were exceeding glad, crying: Verily this box cometh from heaven itself. And forthwith they gave a name unto the box saying: Henceforth shall the box be called Klowkrum.

Yet when the Scribes beheld the box there was no gladness in their hearts. Thrice daily did they come unto the temple, which prayers were called Sikstertoo, Tootaten, and Nytz; and

"And when all were come into the box—" (*Chap. VI.*)

did enter thereinto through the box. And when all were come into the box, except a few odd dozen, who, standing without, exhorted their brethren to breathe out, the Chief Rabbi appeared before them, and sang unto them a psalm.

Then with a shoe-horn did he ease the Scribes one by one into the temple. And likewise those which were already within the temple, and had Done Theirs, sought to come out into the box. Yea, verily, this was the General Idea. And it is written: a Great Time was had by All. For within the box a great confusion did rage, and they which wished to depart from hence were sorely tried to put upon themselves their outer raiment. Yea, a great vexation was visited upon them, and many spake not without divers oaths, and the air was become blue. For coat-sleeves did contain more than one arm, and two arms went not into the same coat. Likewise did hats come upon wrong heads, and scarves were found to contain sundry extra necks. And the Scribes did cry aloud, not in the tongue of Drawingrum, saying: Bly Me, verily wouldst I journey unto Calcutta and relax within the Black Hole thereof.

And when they had departed from hence a certain man called Laybra did come into the box to Clear Up. And behold, he findeth ribs, and sundry other pieces of Sivilservant, which is good for Salvage.

And henceforth when the Scribes beheld a Tin of Sardines, they uncovered and bowed their heads, saying: These are our brethren, for they also cry for Lebensraum.

Now in these days were certain among the Scribes chosen to be Cheeses of greater or lesser degree. For it was written that henceforth there should be Ewers, Tewers, yea, and even Sewers; and of these three the greatest were Sewers. But ere the Prophet Osee brought forth his parchment which is called Short List and spake unto the multitude, there was put upon the road where all did tread an Notis, for all to behold. And the Notis saith:

CAUTION: *HEADROOM* 8ft. 6ins.

Which was exceeding wise.

THE EXILES

New Year's Party

LOUGHBOROUGH TOWN HALL

FRIDAY, JANUARY 2nd
1942

AUTOGRAPHS

PROGRAMME
Commencing 6-45 p.m.

MUSIC WHILE YOU GRIP

WHIST AND TOMBOLA
Duggie

REFRESHMENTS
Hazel and her Nippies

FRED STADDON'S FLAW SHOW

DANCING
No Clinching

THE W O Y G CHORUS
Q R M by Charles (No Cap)

ALL IN—NOTHING BARRED

GOD SAVE THE KING

Organisers: Dix, Fox and Gilliard

The best of luck to you all in 1942.
May this year bring you all the happiness you desire, and, above all may it bring "Victory" to our Arms.

M.J.W.E.

January, 1942.

52

CHAPTER VII

Glad tidings. The house of Mare and crashing of gates. There is no Fish-payst. The Holy of Holies. Musick and minstrels. Multitude answereth the call.

Now WHEN THE YEAR of the Tribe's banishment drew to an end, certain disciples of the Prophet did publish a Griffin, and inasmuch as the Tribe had had many Griffins since their banishment, this was a welcome Griffin bringing glad tidings of a Do.

Now in Luff, the city nigh unto Woyg, is a house called Townorl, a mighty house of many cubits length and breadth, wherein dwelleth one Mare and the men of Alder. And in Mare's house are many mansions; and the greatest of these is Corn Exchange. Howbeit if thou art afflicted with thy feet and bringeth them unto the Corn Exchange, thou shalt receive no succour. And it came to pass that it was in Corn Exchange that the great assembly, called Do, was held.

And upon the day appointed came many of the Tribe with their handmaidens into Luff. And there came also Luffites, and Kwarnites, and Raffites, and Swaddites, and Atsites, and it is written in the chronicles that many who were not Woygites crashed gates, though the Woygites heard not the crashing thereof.

And behold, the six-forty-five commencement began promptly at a half after eight, when the multitude went forth on a Drive. Yea, verily, and with much vigour did victorious maids Move Up, and defeated brethren Moved Down. Then saith Emsee: Whist ye not. And they Whisted not.

And because the moon was already high, a certain Tom the Bowler, which was to entertain them, came not. But instead came Asel and her Nipis, bearing Char and Korfi, and Fickuns, and Kike. And be it known that the Fickuns were good because they were not Fish-payst.

Now at one side of Corn Exchange was the Holy of Holies, called Barr. There, were gathered together Aridiks, Misisdiks, and Fredifoks, and a mighty host of Womp. And unto whosoever came thither they spake, saying: Art thou registered with us? For verily there was the Pints Rationing Scheme, and the Law of Mare is written: No Kewpongs; No Wallop.

THE CHRONICLES OF ST. UPID

And so great was the thirst of the multitude, that a great tumult of noise arose.

And about this time, there began a Flawsho. Here was one Fredi conjuring musick from his push-pull amplifier. Also were there Joaks, and this was Frederick Staddon cracking them. And the maid Ilda brought forth the fatted Metcalfe, and these two made pretty tinklings upon Joanna, whereat the multitude cried out: Oh Kay; which was in no wise a rebuke, for the tinkles fell softly upon the ears, which is written: Oh Kay for Sound.

But the clamouring at Barr was in great measure; and many heard naught of the Musick and Joaks and Tinkles, causing the Prophet to rise up; and he exhorteth them in a loud voice to insert socks in it. And then the Musick was good, as it is written: QSA5.

Then did one Dugi bring forth Musick from a Pan of Tripe, causing the multitude to trip the light fantastic called Hop. And when Dugi was become weary, St. Anthony gathered certain of his brethren which could blow, and suck, and thump, and the multitude stepped and trotted in the manner of the fox.

Then came forth Aridod, brother of John the road widener, with Mr. Brown of Woygite Town, and their minstrels. And great was their lament for one Clementine who was lost and gorn forever, inasmuch as she lay over the ocean down among the dead men.

And when the minstrels were athirst and dried up, there was more Dugi and Pan of Tripe, and Hop, but Womp diminished; and one by one the multitude hearkened and answered the call of the great Kip.

CHAPTER VIII

A Great Voice. The Tribe knoweth something. The snow is red. Agony of the Scribes. Swaddling clothes and the palsy. Certain Scribes cry out for Birdman. They earn another name.

AND IT CAME TO PASS in these days that a great voice called Bebesee came over the wilderness, and spake unto the peoples of the Tribe of Osee, saying: Now let it be known among all men that two weeks past ye suffered snow, and ice, and blizzards, and this is Alvar Lidell revealing it.

This was the Low Down, and the Tribe rose up, and cried as with one voice: Thou telleth us!

But Alvar heard them not, for their voice was as a whisper beside his own, for Alvar was possessed of a mess of Wattage.

Yea, verily, the Tribe had knowledge of the snow, and the ice; for they had inherited a Basin Full. And the roads from the cities were paved with glass, and many amongst the Scribes forsook their Grids, and did beseech Barkus to deliver the Carcase, being thus poorer by three shekels, unless they were from the Tribe of Peo. And whomsoever was Tough and scorned Barkus did find the Deck rise up and smite him hip and thigh, and divers other places, and was sorely cheesed.

And it is written that the snow was white as the lilies of the field, yet did the Scribes, beholding it, call it red, which was passing strange. Thus saith many: This is Oke—upon Krismuz Kards.

And the tempest in all its fury was visited upon them; yea, even upon the Scribes which sat in the Temples of Aych and Eye, for the walls thereof were only blastproof, and withstood it not. And the roofs of the temples opened up, and spat upon them, and they were become baptised in snow and ice. and the Laybras ran hither and thither setting down buckets, excepting Tom, who walked hither and thither. And when there were many buckets, musick filled the air, for it was here a Ping, there a Ping, everywhere a Ping.

And in their agony the Scribes cried out: Give us a Break. And whomsoever was given a Break, which was Draft Leave, waded forth on to dry land to thaw himself in Kantin. And they which remained, sat wrapped in swaddling clothes; yet were many sick of the palsy.

THE CHRONICLES OF ST. UPID

Now it was said that the temples had been builded by one Jeri. And certain of the Scribes which were vexed with their anointment, cried in great wrath, saying: That which Jeri hath built, let Jeri also destroy. And they spake thus not of Jeri the Electricks man, who is a Sarge of Ohmgard; neither spake they of Jeri who dwelleth with Alik; but of the Birdman who layeth eggs in sundry places, for they prayed that he might transport the temples unto Halifax, for it is written: there is great warmth.

And it came to pass in these days, that the Tribe of Woyg were known throughout the land as God's Frozen People.

CHAPTER IX

The Tribe multiplieth. They seek fragrant weeds. A merchant called Gil. Publicans shut their doors and Scribes sup Korfi. In the Band. A certain Hunnite. Levying of taxes.

Now WITH THE PASSING of time the Tribe continued to sojourn in the Promised Land, and their numbers grew and multiplied, and they waxed exceeding strong. And new temples were builded for them, for the Woygites were a pious and devout people.

But the new land was not a Land of Plenty. Verily, oftimes it was not even a Land of Twenty, notwithstanding that the brethren tarried in long files in the cities, seeking fragrant weeds. And upon many days did they seek in vain and were without succour. And curiously it seemeth at these times they encountereth ever one maiden, albeit this maiden was in divers places. For behold, they spake one to another of Sweet Fanny Adams.

And ofttimes when there were weeds, these had gone bad and lost their fragrance, being called Tenerz, and certain other names. And for whomsoever receiveth these there was weeping and wailing and coughing of blood.

But a certain merchant called Gil and his brethren of Kantin was blest at certain times with lashings of weeds. And when this was come about he giveth unto all a token. And the multitude, descending upon Kantin, cried unto the serving maid therein: Gimme.

WEEDS

And the maid saith: Inasmuch as ye give unto me one token, so shall this be a land of Twenty.

And it was so.

Now there was also in these times a famine in Womp. And the publicans shut their doors upon the sinners. Peradventure certain publicans did leave unfast their back doors, and some of the sinners did enter thereby. And of these it was said they were In the Band. Yet behold, they bore with them neither push-pulls, nor cymbals, nor tinkling brass, nor yet their musick parchments.

And those who knew not the back doors were constrained to visit Empiah and other like places and sup Korfi and break bread and rare welshbits. And be it known that rare Welshbits were in no wise strange unto the Scribes.

Now all these things were come about because of one Schicklegruber, a Hunnite, also named Itla the Misbegotten. Thus was it said by all men; yea, and by their womenkind also. But the womenkind spake thus among themselves in dark places and in whispers, for it is neither meet nor seemly for maidens so to speak.

And because Schicklegruber desired vast deliveries of heavy equipment in sundry places, the King in Smowk levied a mighty tax upon the peoples, and commanded the Prophet to collect it. And the Prophet delivered the monies unto a man in a far off and distant place whom the King called Inlan Revnew. And because of Schicklegruber this man came to be known as Shekelgrabber. And certain of the Scribes spake in this wise: Verily it were better that Shekelgrabber taketh all mine pay, and payeth unto me the tax. Thus would I possess more shekels.

BSM

3D VOL 1 NO. 7

APRIL · 1942

FIRST HALFHOUR

B.S.M. APRIL 1942
Vol. 1 No. 7

General Editor:- L.P.Jones
Editor:- F.C.Staddon

Editorial Board
R.Wilkinson.
P.Wade.
E.Millhouse.
A.Carr.
R.G.Denny.
T.Brister.

-oooOOOooo-

With this issue we introduce our first competition. It has been designed to give full scope to your creative minds, and the only stipulation is "nothing barred". We have decided that if the worst comes to the worst we will have a private view of the best effort. The prize was decided on before the Budget, but we will add the extra cost to our already large overdraft.

Having read the "MY PEACE TIME JOB" article we can understand why there is very often a smell of cooking in Hut C. It does prove, however, that even those jobs which seem mundane can have an interesting story weve round them, so get on with your own story and let us have it.

The Disciple has picked on a topical theme for his sermon this month, but if he is thinking of obtaining some buckshee Kewpongs by this underhand method he had better think again.

The "Travellers Log" will carry us a stage further in our tour round the countryside, we hope that you are following your guide faithfully, as we have more than a germ of an idea for a competition, based on these rambles, later on.

The two illustrations are by E.Millhouse and L.C.Moore respectively. The cover design is by "WILK".

At the time of preparing this Editorial, it was obvious to us that this issue was going to be unavoidably late, so we will apologise in advance.

NEXT PUBLICATION:- 29th. May.   CONTRIBUTIONS by the 15th. May.

GOSSIP.

CONGRATULATIONS to "Hilda" (Watson) on her engagement, 18th April, to Sgm. Jack Kellow, late of this section.
To Mr. Geo. Coles on his marriage to Miss Edith Hill at St. Paul's Church, Woodhouse Eaves, on 11th April. The happy couple were blessed with fine weather, and we hope this continues during their future life together.
To Pte. "Connie" (Praegar) (our Dumb Blonde) who attained her 22nd birthday on the 2nd. April. When a Ewa remarked, if he had known he would have taken her out on the "razzle" she was reputed to have replied "I didn't know you had a "razzle".
To A/C.S.M. "Bunny" (Bunyard) who celebrated her 25th. birthday on 14th. of this month. This probably accounts for the cute bonnet now being worn.
THAT STORK AGAIN. To Mr. & Mrs. A.J.Fielding,(S.V.) the gift of a girl on 8th April. Father doing as well as can be expected.
Very pleased to report that Sgt. "Molly" (Ling) and Pte. "Olive" (Millward) are now out of hospital, regret, however, that Pte. "Dot" (Dingle) is still confined to sick bay.
We regret that "Joan" (Clarke) is indisposed and having an enforced rest in Leicester Infirmary. We hope she will soon be with us again.
PROMOTIONS. Congratulations to "Angela" (Wiffen) and "Dora" (**Blackett**) on their promotion to the rank of A/L/Cpl.
THE ATS GO GARDENING.
Vegetable marrow, tomatoes, celery
We dig for victory in slacks.
When some of us bend down too far
Oh! boy you should hear the "cracks".

THE ATS GO HORSE RIDING.
Some Ats now go horse riding,
They've done it now for weeks.
It keeps them young and healthy,
You should see their rosy cheeks.
(they always could "stand up" for themselves.)

BOATING. Now available at the Boat House, Barrow-on-Soar. There is a Cafe adjoining which can invariably provide a reasonable meal. Skiffs, Punts, Canoes available from 8.0 a.m. to 8.0 p.m. on the following terms:-
Persons
1... 2/- per hour)
2... 2/6 "   "   )
3... 3/6 "   "   ) Then 6d. per person per hour
4... 4/- "   "   ) after first hour.
5... 5/- "   "   )
6... 6/- "   "   )

? One of our runners reported having been chased by a small man, whilst on night duty. We have long felt there was still too much wishful thinking in the country.
Presumed returned "Not Known"! Envelope found addressed "The Director of Organisation" War Office.
WITHOUT COMMENT. One chorister to another: "Harry (Dodd) has been picking up some new stuff in London during a long week-end". Whilst on the subject of the choir, we feel that it was a little inconsiderate of them to include "England Arise" in their last public performance. A good deal of England embodied in those present was <u>arising</u> at 4.30 the following morning.(or should have done.)

THE GOSPEL ACCORDING TO ST.UPID. Chapter X
(Translated from the English by Disciple Millhouse).

Now when the Feast of the Pullover was drawing to an end and the red snow departed from out the land, the Tribe knew there was a Sun in the heavens, even as there had been upon several days in the land of Bedz. And their hearts were glad for themselves and for all brass monkeys. And they put away their warm raiment and made ready for the Feast of the Casting of the Clout.

And most diligently did they count their Kewpongs, for it was proclaimed throughout the land that those who were possessed of a score and six, could purchase a Futility Suit, but they who had wasted their substance and possessed only one Kewpong could inherit one new neck rope or two nose cloths until the Sabbath of Trinity, when the Kind had promised unto them three score more.

And some which were poor in Kewpongs and whose raiment became ragged in the rear, went unto the centurion Dik and saith:
O Dik, I am without raiment. Therefore I say unto you, lest I suffer to go forth in the cities and in the land clad only in fig leaves, give unto me the garments of a soldier, for I would be a warrior in thy command.
And Dik was glad, and straightway putteth another pip upon his shoulder.

And the Prophet Osee, who dwelleth in an High Place, looking forth from his window, beheld the centurion and his soldiers. And Dik saith in a might voice: Slope thy pikes.

And the Prophet was well pleased and lefteth up his eyes to the heavens saying: My Squad and my Staff they comfort me.

Now at this time a great wind arose, yea, a greater wind even than bloweth when Red Tabz cometh unto Woyg. And a certain man who possessed a Grid, journeyed daily upon it from Luff unto the Temple. And the wind pleased him not. For when he turneth into the lane of the House of Wood it meeteth him with all its fury, so that he knew not whether he cometh or goeth. Therefore did he labour diligently upon his Grid and was become mightily hot and bothered. And when he was come toward the Iron Road, where is the house of Lner set upon a hill, he standeth upon his pedals to ascend the hill in the teeth of the great wind. And when he reacheth the summit and was nigh unto being flaked out, he see-eth a parchment upon the house of Lner. And it is written upon the parchment: Is the journey really necessary?.

And the man waxeth exceeding wrath, and teareth out his hair, saying in a loud voice, even though there is none other which hearkeneth unto him,: What thinkest thou?
-x-x-x-x-x-x-x-x-x-x-x-

The Gospel's Special Correspondent regretteth that he couldst not send his usual eye-witness parchment from Townorl on the Dance of the Day of All Fools. For that day he was commanded to labour upon the Dance of the Seven Teils.

"MORE LIGHT PLEASE".

The war has altered the lives of all in diverse ways. Some are more affected than others, but everyone has to suffer one thing - the BLACK OUT.

This has brought home to us, in no uncertain fashion, the blessings of our lighting systems in city, town and village, before the present conflict.

The controversial question is, however, whether the dangers and discomforts are outweighed by the reasons for the black-out. We are told that the enemy will drop bombs wherever a light can be seen. That may, or may not be; the average person has not the necessary data to argue about this.

In spite of the black-out, however, did the enemy have any difficulty in finding and setting fire to the City of London?. Again, did the black-out save Coventry, Portsmouth, Liverpool, Plymouth, Hull, etc. from the prolonged and savage attacks made on them?. The answer is, of course, most emphatically NO! I purposely leave out the rest of London because it is obviously easy to drop bombs at random on the sprawling mass of Greater London.

I do not suggest, of course, for one moment, a return to pre-war lighting. The authorities have made certain modifications, such as Star-lighting and increase in light on vehicles.

The worst feature of the black-out is the high number of accidents, many of them fatal, on the roads. I know from my own experience what a nerve-racking ordeal it is driving a car at night. We are all cyclists or pedestrians and we know by experience the dangers and difficulties incurred as we go about our lawful occasions.

For these reasons I vote for "MORE LIGHT PLEASE".

A.H.A.

The Editors will publish any comments on this controversial subject.
XXXXXXXXXXXXXXXXXXXXXXXXXXXXXXXXXXXXXXXXXXXXXXXXXXXXXXXXXXXXXXXX

"ABOU BEN EWA!" by "Snikmot".

Abou Ben Ewa (may his pay increase)
Awoke one night from a deep dream of peace
And saw within the arclight of the room
(Tho' filled with smoke, he could still pierce the gloom)
A Super writing in a book of brown.
Some loud guffaws had made Abou feel cold
And turning to the Super standing near; he said
"What writest thou?". The Super raised his head
And with an accent sounding all grade two, replied
"The names of those that want to sleep - and do".
"And is mine one" cried Abou?.
"No not much!" replied the Super.
The Super wrote and vanished.
Next night he came again, and showed
The names of those on whom Grade 1 was pressed;
And Lo! that Super's name led all the rest.

AN END TO THE GOSSIP FOR THIS MONTH.

MRS.CAVE DESCRIBES ONE OF US   "He has nice dark spaniel eyes and doesn't take sugar."

We have witnessed Mr.Walton and his "Commandos" making lightening raids on the canteen from time to time, and have no doubt he would have welcomed their support when a difference of opinion occurred with the Police at a Halt Sign. We understand the following proceedings finished on quite a good note - a ten-shilling one to be precise.

Dickie Akhurst was the cynosure of all eyes in his impromptu role as star performer in "Hanky Panky" at the Theatre Royal the other week. Co-starring was Miss La Rue, better known as the Dumb Blonde of the Sunday Pictorial. Picking Dicky, she couldn't have been quite so dumb, neither was Dicky, as a kiss and a bouquet proved. Miss La Rue evoked a mild storm of derision from other members of the "Theatre Going Club" when she asked the "gentleman" on the end of the fifth row to accompany her - the said gentleman was Dicky, hence the derision.

Outside Loughborough Town Hall. Placard on one side advertising Loughborough Warship Week Aim, on the other side a placard advertising a performance of the "Messiah". One Ewa reading one placard, another Ewa reading the other. 1st. Ewa: "I see it's the Messiah this week", 2nd. Ewa: "Yes! what is it, a Cruiser?".

xxxxxxxxxxxxxxxxxxxxxxxxxxxxxxxxxxxxxxxxxxxxxxxxxxxxxxxxxx

SPORTS.

We are now passing from one season into another. Both hockey and football teams have had many enjoyable games, also a number of practise games. Messrs. Hartill & Worster are to be congratulated on obtaining fixtures in these difficult times.

Sport is now a luxury and in the future it will be difficult, if not impossible, to obtain any kind of Sports goods. Therefore, it is of great importance for all of us to preserve what we have, very carefully. Your committee intend to have the tennis-court in readiness in the immediate future.

In regard to cricket, the home ground will be the Quorn Cricket Cricket Ground at Spinney Drive. A fixture list is now being prepared. Further details will be posted on the notice-board.

A.H.Appleton.
(Hon.Sec. Sports Committee).

xxxxxxxxxxxxxxxxxxxxxxxxxxxxxxxxxxxxxxxxxxxxxxxxxxxxxxxxxx

OMISSIONS FROM TEXT.

Owing to unforeseen circumstances the Drawing by L.C.Moore will not appear in this issue but in the next.

The Crossword Puzzle solution in this issue refers to the puzzle set last month.

All entries for the Limerick Competition to be addressed to the Editor, B.S.M., C.R.R.

"DE PROFUNDIS"   by Ollie Pearce.

When as a lad my fond relations,
Asked what would be my occupation,
With all the wisdom of short pants,
I chose adventure and romance,
And thought that when grown up I'd be
A film star of celebrity.

The years of my alleged discretion,
Brought me conviction that the station,
To which I had received my call,
Was not adventurous at all,
It will not take me very long
To show how sadly I was wrong.

Most of my waking hours are spent,
Cramped in a chair with shoulders bent,
Intent on all the feeble sounds,
Which, underneath the din abound,
Straining each nerve as signals fade,
Neath interference - British made.

On all sides men incinerate,
Tobacco of a doubtful date,
To which is cunningly allied,
A virulent insecticide,
Half choked with dust by Doll & Ena,
Why don't they use a Vacuum Cleaner?.

I glance up as some strangers enter,
and hear a voice proclaim "Nerve Centre",
With vacant stares they gaze about,
In wonderment, without a doubt,
Regarding me as people do,
Uncommon species at the Zoo.

The slamming door as they depart,
Contributes just a minor part,
To all the usual din and clamour,
From tinkling phone to builder's hammer,
Which, at great cost, the powers upkeep,
For fear that I might fall asleep.

These noises I have long since found,
Essential to the daily round,
Without them there would only be,
an increase in efficiency,
In which event, what would they do,
With all those pencils, red and blue?.

I stagger off to have my break,
And seek solace in tea and cake,
But Gladys, whilst the news I see,
Collects my cup, half full of tea,
And mumbles as she fills it up,
No sugar in the second cup.

(Cont...)

"ONCE UPON A TIME"

I had twelve bottles of whisky in my cellar, and my wife made me empty the contents of each and every bottle down the sink. I promised to do this, and proceeded as follows.

I withdrew the cork from the first bottle, and poured the contents down the sink, with the exception of one glass which I drank.

I extracted the cork from the second bottle and did likewise, with the exception of one glass which I drank. I then withdrew the cork from the third bottle, and emptied the good old booze down the sink, with the exception of a glass, which I devoured. I pulled the cork from the fourth sink, and poured the bottle down the glass which I drank.

I pulled the bottle from the cork of the next and drank one sink out of it, and then threw the rest down the cork. I pulled the sink out of the next cork, and poured the bottle down my neck. I pulled the next cork from my throat, and poured the sink down the bottle. Then I corked the sink with the glass, bottled the drink, and drank the pour.

When I had them all emptied, I steadied the house with one hand, and counted the bottles, which were 24, so I counted them again when they came round, and I had 74. Finally I had them all counted except one house, and one bottle which I drunk.

"BY.JMY"

-XXXXXXXXXXXXXXXXXXXXXXXXXXXXXXXXXXXXXXXXXXXXXXXXXXXXXXXXXXXXXXXXXXXX

"De Profundis" Cont....

The break is brief, and I return,
My bread and margarine to earn,
Unwittingly park in the chair,
For weeks past threatened with repair,
And while the other fellows roar,
I pick myself up..off the floor.

At long, long last it's time to leave,
I gently extricate my sleeve,
Caught in the tacks which line the bench,
More darning for my faithful wench,
Then hurry out into the rain,
To find my tyre is flat again !!!

"My Peace Time Job" – N° 2
THE AUDITORS ARE HERE
ENTER A. H. APPLETON.

My job took me all over London and sometimes into the country. The work of an audit clerk may seem dull but this is not so. Once the necessary spade work is overcome it is quite interesting.

The main objects of an audit are as follows: 1. The detection of fraud. 2. The checking of clerical errors. 3. Checking or or preparation of Balance Sheet & Profit & Loss Account for clients and Inland Revenue. The auditor is bound by Company Law when conducting an audit of Limited Liability Companies whether Public or Private. He is also bound by certain acts when auditing Partnerships. Owing to the high rate of Income Tax this has become very important. The great thing is to get as many legitimate set-offs against profits as the Inspector will allow. An audit clerk must have a thorough knowledge of book-keeping and Company Law and a certain knowledge of Liquidation & Bankruptcy Law. In this connection I have been astonished at the small number of really efficient book-keepers there are. This particularly applies to women. It seems to me as if women are more ready to take a chance and say they know, when actually they haven't the faintest idea what it is all about. Of course eventually they get completely sunk and then the audit clerk is sent for to pull them out of a hole. I remember one case where the firm were in the habit of dealing in Bills Payable. That was quite simple but one day they had a couple of Bills Receivable and these were discounted. I was sent for and I soon realised that the woman book-keeper was quite lost and floundering. I mention this to show that while the job remained mechanical everything was all right, but as soon as something new appeared she was lost.

My regular audits, whether monthly, quarterly or yearly, were of a varied nature, covering the following professions and businesses:- Solicitor, Leather Merchant, Commercial College, Furrier, Estate Agent, Cinema, Tailor, Farmer etc. etc. Among the people I met were some well known characters. One was Horatio Bottomley, then a tired old man at the end of his career. I also met Leslie Burgin, the eminent international lawyer recently Minister of Supply. He is a brisk, clever, little man who speaks several languages fluently. Mr Clark of Clark's College, who, as you would expect, is genial and imposing. Several years ago I met Inspector Collins, who afterwards became famous in a murder case, and latterly I met Inspector Burt.

Of course, the work is usually routine and humdrum. Some of it is done in one's own office. These are usually the smaller businesses and one-man concerns. Amongst these were a Fishmonger, a Nurseryman, a Fried Fish & Chip Shop, a Boarding House and many others. In fact, I suppose we had clients representing nearly every trade or profession.

68

One client, for instance, was a carnation grower. He did for a time give this up and grow other plants but the buyers in Covent Garden requested him to return to his carnation growing. The reason for this was that he could grow them better than anyone else.

Investigations are generally the most exciting and also the most lucrative. Investigations cover a wide scope, such as the purchase or sale of businesses, or where there is a suspicion of fraud or embezzlement. There is a certain amount of drama when the accountants are called in to try to save a tottering business. On the result of my work the livlihoods of many people were at stake. On these occasions sometimes we have been successful in pulling a firm round, sometimes not. In recent years one of our biggest failures to keep the business going was Glaves of New Oxford Street, London, and Croydon. Owing to circumstances it was impossible to make it pay. I am glad to say that everyone of the employees, except those who retired, were soon given jobs by the other big stores.

The most important investigations are when fraud and embezzlement are suspected. Then one is truly a human bloodhound and the quarry is hunted through books and papers until run to earth. I remember one case of suspected fraud at a well-known London Departmental Store. My colleagues and I spent many weeks on this until it was finally cleared up. We discovered several departments were affected, collusion between them was proved, with the result that cash and goods were misappropriated. One employee actually stole a lawn mower!

Bankruptcy and Liquidations also provide both comedies and tragedies. The tragedies are generally that the chief actors in them go to prison. Only rarely do they end as one I remember. A bankrupt wrote to my principal saying he would not stand his trial at the Old Bailey on the following Monday but his body would be found in the river at Richmond on Saturday. The Police were informed but it was too late to save him and his body was found in the river.

Looking back over sixteen years experience I now realise it was rather exacting but interesting because I met so many people of all grades of society.

The above Account is a true statement of my peacetime job and in accordance with what I can remember of my experiences.

ENTERTAINMENTS.

J.H. Appleton
Late Audit Clerk.

The Dance/Cabaret held on April 1st. produced a profit of £14.14.1d.
By previous agreement the Sports Section will receive the balance, to help them with the Summer programme.
The show provided a pleasant social evening for most of the Staff, and the committee wish to thank the choir for an excellent performance.
Our efforts during the Winter months here have realised a total of £63.5.0. With the exception of our first Charity Show, it was not the primary aim to make maximum profit, but the surplus has served a very useful purpose. Over £45 to charity and the rest to our Sports Section.

F.Fox (Sec. Ents.Committee

TRAVELLER'S LOG.   W. Dalton.

Since my last notes I regret that my travels have been somewhat curtailed through a slight incapacitation, so on this occasion have no new points of interest to bring to your notice. But, with the advent of summer-like weather in Spring such as we have experienced recently, it seems that the time has come for those who are so minded to explore the possibilities of the places described in my previous articles.

While living at Gravenhurst I had for a neighbour an elderly lady who, whenever she saw me setting forth on my lawful occasions used to transfix me with a penetrating glance and exclaim "I know where you are going - 'gelling'!" (the present participle of a verb which so far has not appeared in the grammatical structure of the English language). My plea of "not guilty" was so much waste of breath, being received always with a snort of scornful unbelief. The point I wish to make is that those of you who do indulge in the pastime referred to could not do better than conduct the victim to any of the spots previously mentioned and of which herewith a brief resumé.

Woodhouse Eaves offers much that is attractive. There is its own Windmill Hill which is a most pleasant spot; Beacon Hill which affords one of the finest panoramic views I have yet seen; and the "Rockies" and their surrounds which go to make up the local golf links from which visitors are not excluded. I should particularly like to mention that part of Charnwood Forest lying between the golf links and Beacon Hill. Nearly all the trees in this immediate vicinity are Silver Birches, forming a most charming picture, while in a few days now there will be interspersed among them a profusion of rhododendron bloom which alone will be worth a visit.

Somewhat further afield, but within easy reach by cycle or bus, are the picturesque reservoirs of Swithland and Cropston. Last but by no means least is the vastness of Bradgate Park with its historical ruins, and the "Old John" prospect tower from which another splendid view is to be enjoyed.

The foregoing notes provide the basis for many delightful excursions, which I venture to suggest will offer a relaxation from official duties, and a welcome contrast to the indoor amusements of the winter months.

-----oOo-----

(H)ATS OFF TO CUPID.

Barrow towns' near Woodhouse
Near famous Leicester city
And that old river known as Soar
Rushes past with a mighty roar
A pleasanter spot you never saw
But when begins my ditty
In nineteen hundred and forty two
You never saw such a how d'you do
with ladies - from the city.

ATS, they brought their coats
They brought their hats
They brought their kit bags in a lorry
Blonde ATS, Black ATS, Short ATS
                              Tall ATS,
ATS from flats and ATS from houses
ATS in skirts and ATS in trousers
ATS for "C" and ATS for "J"
They overran the Garrets Hey.

At last the scribes in one big army
To the Prophet went alooking
Do you think we can keep our minds
                              on working
Now they've been and brought this
                              skirt in?
At this his corporation quaked with
               a mighty consternation
Up by phone to Whitehall City
He sang his short but doleful ditty
"Why must they make the ATS so pretty
Perhaps if we had Wrens on duty
Or even Waafs all proud and snooty"
Just as he said that, what should
                              hap
At the office door but a gentle tap
"Bless me" cried he "what's that?
Only a scraping of feet on the mat?
Anything like the sound of an AT
Makes my heart go pit a pat".
"Come in" said he looking bigger
And in did come the strangest figure
Straight from his stand -
                         Piccadilly
Where he'd gazed on the world so
                              silly.
But gazing now with courteous smile
That held for him a world of guile
His only garment was a quiver
Enough to make the small chap
                              shiver
And in his left hand held a bow

With which it was his wont to sow
The seeds of love; the one desire
That set all young mens' hearts
                            afire.

He advanced to the council table
And "Please" said he "I'm able
To set your mind at rest from
                           vexing
O'er this problem so perplexing
To me the whole thing's really
                           stupid
For I'm the son of Venus - Cupid!
And if you'll let me do my worst
I'll twang my bow string till I
                           burst
For all the scribes who now are
                           single
I'll set the wedding bells a
                           jingle
And when at last they're man and
                           wife
Twill rid your land of all this
                           strife!"

Barrow Towns' near Woodhouse
Near famous Leicester City
But if you go down there be sure
To keep away from River Soar
For here the arrows fly the
                           thickest
They catch the cutist and the
                           quickest
But if you're single at 95
Feel more dead than you do alive
If you should feel an arrow
                           sticking
Its probably your conscience
                           pricking.

                    SNIKMOT.

P	A	C	I	F	I	C	I	S	L	A	N	D
R		A		A		P				E		A
I		S	A	T	U	R	N		N	E		N
N		P		E		I		T		S		G
C	U	E	S		F	L	Y		S	P	E	E
I		A		A		E		A		E		R
P	A	R	A	D	I	S	E	B	I	R	D	S
A		M		O		S		C		A		I
L	A	R		E	Y	E		S	N	A	G	G
R		N		I		O		S		T		N
O		T	I	M	B	U	C	T	O	O		A
Y			P		T		U					L
S	P	A	N	I	S	H	O	N	I	O	N	S

LIMERICK COMPETITION.

Having been compelled to listen to many Limericks, clean and otherwise, we have decided that for our first Competition we will ask you to complete any of the following lines. There are no restrictions, no entrance fee, and no limit to the number of entries submitted. We are offering a prize of 100 CIGARETTES for the best entry. It does not, however, necessarily follow that the judges choice will be the winner, as to a certain extent this must be controlled by the question: "Dare we publish it". CLOSING DATE FOR ENTRIES, 5th May.
The judges panel consists of:- O.C., Messrs. Millhouse, Wade and Carr. In the event of equal voting, the Editor will lodge the casting vote.

LINES FOR COMPLETION.
(1) A wheezy young lady of Rye
....
....
....
(2) The curious habits of men
(3) A weary young lady of Chatham
(4) A frivolous filly of Bicester
(pronounced Bister)

xxxxxxxxxxxxxxxxxxxxxxxxxxxxxxxxxxxxxxxxxxxxxxxxxxxxxxxxxxxxxxxx

POSTCRIPT TO "DE PROFUNDIS"   by Ollie Pearce.

Due to the recent innovation
Of female scribes now at our station,
Life's taken on a different hue
And interest has been born anew.
Some fellows, anxious to impress,
Now take more interest in their dress.
Vocabularies have grown quite small
Some words are never heard at all!
And when the fairer sex have gone
The Supt. asks how they're getting on,
In answer to "How does she shape?"
Some fellow, grinning like an ape
Will wave his two hands in the air
Describing curves beyond compare,
Or, if the chap's a different type,
In answer to "What is she like?"
He turns with rapture in his eye
And gives a long, heart-rendering sigh,
In tones of awe comes his reply- "<u>She's wonderful</u>".

ROYAL NAVAL OLD COMRADES ASSOCIATION.

Landlubbers are now quite familiar with the "bunker plate" which shines resplendently from the lapels of the ex matelots in this Section. By the time you are reading this, I hope the Loughborough Branch of the R.N.O.C.A. will be an established fact. This will be another feather in the W.O.Y.G's already well plumed halo.

Among the earliest members was the O.C. whose "date of joining the service" sank most of us. A little known fact came to light on his enrolment. How many of you knew he was decorated for Distinguished Service in the last war?.

One word about the Badge. It consists of a plaque with the letters R.N.O.C.A. inscribed surmounted by the Naval Crown. The Naval Crown itself is very old and is made up from the sterns of old ships with square sails alternating.

As to its origin. I quote from a book dated 1764, "Signals for R.N. Convoys and Sailing & Fighting Instructions" in which is an interesting picture of one with the inscription: "Naval or Rostral Crown anciently given to the officers etc. who were the first to grapple on board an enemy's ship". Whether this means that an actual crown was given to adorn the brows of the said officers, etc. or whether it was awarded as an honorary distinction, is not quite clear.

As far back as the first century of the Christian Era the Roman Emperor Claudius invented a Golden Crown consisting of galley prows arranged in a circle to form the rim, which was given as a reward for sea service. This seems likely to be the original.

The Association is open to all ranks and ratings who have served not less than 12 months in any branch of the naval services. The objects of the Association are to perpetuate the comradeship which began in the service, to foster good fellowship, render service to one another and to encourage and promote social gatherings among the members.

The motto of the Association is: "UNITY, LOYALTY, PATRIOTISM AND COMRADESHIP". The only obligation is that every member undertakes to act up to the motto of the Association and to do everything in his power to assist members to obtain civil employment.

The inclusive membership fee is 4/6d.

```
          Entrance Fee         1.0.
          Badge                1.0.
          Annual Subscription  2.6.
                               4.6
```

We are on the lookout for new members, particularly among the P.O. men. Anyone who has the necessary qualification and wishes to join can obtain an enrolment form from myself or any other member.

E.F.TOMKINS.

"B.S.M." MAY 1942.
Vol. 1 No. 8

General Editor:- L.P. Jones.
Editor:- F.C. Staddon.

Editorial Board
R. Wilkinson.
P. Wade.
E. Millhouse.
A. Carr.
R.G. Denny.
T. Brister.

....

First we must ask your indulgence for a rather lengthly Editorial, and this having been granted, will proceed to ruminate over the contents of the present issue.

The "PEACE TIME JOB" article is one more proof of the mixed crowd that goes to make up the Woygite Tribe, and we have no doubt that future articles will show an even more varied selection, especially if some of the female element will only take the plunge.

An interesting new series is introduced under the title "REFLECTIONS"; the idea for which, we are indebted to the first contributor. All of you have experienced or witnessed some incident or other, on which you look back with varied feelings; let us have it, as it will undoubtedly prove of interest to your fellow readers. Number of words is not important, keep it short and snappy if you can, but if of real interest, make it as long as you like.

Our thanks to the Proprietors of "Men Only" for permission to reproduce "EMPTY ACRES" from the May, 1936 issue of that excellent magazine. Having the fortune to read this article some 6 years after publication, we felt it was well worth reproducing.

We feel that "AH REMEMBER" is really descriptive. We have often thought that the Tower of Babel had nothing on our Canteen, particularly at night.

The Club accounts which make interesting reading and reflect good stewardship, are presented for your perusal.

Now we come to something a little more personal. As you all know, the cost of producing the "B.S.M." is very high and is likely to go higher still. This high cost coupled with the sum outstanding on Capital outlay, prevents us from putting into effect some ideas we have for improving the methods of production.

Our numbers are growing, we want more drawing materials, we would like to improve the quality of the paper as well as the number of pages, although this will probably prove to be "wishful thinking". Therefore we have decided to accept Annual Subscriptions, and ask if you, or as many of you as possible, will pay to us 1 Years' sub. for the "B.S.M." It is only a matter of 3/0d. and we have no doubt in our own minds that you think the magazine, which is one of the few, if not only, material record of the Tribe, worthy of your support.

It is understood of course, that any subscriber who leaves, will have the balance of his subscription returned, unless any other specific arrangement is arrived at. We invite your confidence and trust, and assure you they will not be misplaced. Please address subscriptions to:- THE EDITOR-"B.S.M."-HUT "C".

COVER DESIGN BY:- E. Millhouse. INNER DRAWING BY:- L.C. Moore
Illustrations by:-Messrs. Carr & Denny.
NEXT PUBLICATION:- 26th. June.   CONTRIBUTIONS by the 13th. June.
(The Limerick Competition is dealt with on another page).

TO THE EDITOR OF THE "B.S.M."

Sir,
The following quotation from "A History of Mediaeval Political Theory in the West", By R.W. and A.J. Carlyle, Vol. V, Page 118, though not exactly stop-press news, may be considered to have a certain topical interest. History, it is said, repeats itself.

"In the proceedings related to the deposition of Adolf of Germany in 1298, we find that the princes concerned assumed that they were acting by due process of law, and it is worth while to observe the procedure in a little detail. The Archbishop of Maintz called a Council to consider the troubled condition of Germany, and to this he summoned both the princes who had the right of election and Adolf himself.....They enumerated various charges against him, the violation of Churches and ecclesiastics, the toleration of violence against women, the interference with ecclesiastical liberties, especially by demanding gifts before he would grant the "Regalia" to the bishops, and various acts of aggression upon the rights of the German princes, counts, barons etc. They found Adolf guilty of these crimes, and declared that he had proved himself to be incompetent and useless for so great an authority, and therefore, after careful deliberation and by the common council and will of all the electoral princes, the bishops, dukes, counts, barons and wise men present, the electoral princes declared Adolf deposed, and also absolved all men from their oath of allegiance to him."

I enclose my name (written of course on the back of a secret document) in proof of good faith, but prefer to subscribe myself,

Your constant reader,

Hushton-on-Silence
May 5th. 1942.

Crystal Gazer.

Ah Remember

Ah remember dowlfully t'hoil weer ah wor born
afore yon blighter started t'war, and ah from ooam wor torn
ah ewsed ter sit in slippered ease wi book an pipe complete
an nowt were sed if mantel-ward ah raised me weary feet
aye ah remember, ah remember, sitting ere in pain
wi things clamped on me lug hoils an a buzzin in me brain.

"Ee gow"! them appy days is gone
in exile ah sojourn
we lahtl bacca in me pouch
but lots er time ter burn.

A stroll around t'graveyard
a tour er Deead Man Lane
a coffee at t'Empire
an "ooam" ter bed again.

Some day when t'war is ower
an thers justice ter be done
some fooils ull say, "Let's string im up"
an others, "Fotch a gun".

Eres punishment fer Itler
more suited to me taste
just billet im in Loughboro
an feed im on fishpaste.

N.B. The above lesson in Kings English was inspired by the conflicting Babel of Tongues heard in the canteen. Translation can be obtained from the erstwhile savages of "i" hut, into whom, Professors Allison, Bacon, and myself, have finally succeeded in inculcating some elementary rudiments of purer English diction.

G.B.Mason.

REFLECTION N°1

It was a beautiful Spring day in Palestine, blood-red anemones made a rich carpet for one's feet and the sun shone in a blue, cloudless sky. We were travelling from Sarafand to Jerusalem and thence to the Dead Sea.

Palestine - so dusty, hot and breathless during the Summer months, seemed fresh and invigorating on this May morning. The plains with their undulating rows of orange groves were now behind us and we gradually ascended the rugged Judean Hills.

Tiny mud villages were passed and little dark-eyed children in long gowns came out to wave and stare. Here and there was a shepherd tending his flock and whistling a mournful tune on a pipe made of reeds. Seemingly unending lines of tawny-coloured camels made slow progress along the narrow, winding roads, lead by a small donkey on who's back sat a fat, nodding Arab.

Jerusalem is a strange place, where East and West rub shoulders. Large, opulent Western hotels stand cheek by jowl with pale, rounded mosques. The Arabs shoo their dirty sheep and goats from the path of a sleek, high-powered car.

The Mount of Temptation was on our left as we descended from the hills to the flat plain where the Dead Sea lies. It lay still and very blue beneath the now hot sun, with just a faint ripple stirring its surface.

Swimming in the Dead Sea is one of the queerest experiences I have ever had. When I say swimming I am wrong - one cannot swim in the Dead Sea. It is so full of salt that your legs suddenly bob to the surface of the water. One cannot, either, stay in for any length of time - the saltiness of the water makes one tingle and burn.

After an excellent meal eaten in one of the comfortable hotels that stand on the edge of this famous stretch of water, we commenced our journey back. There is no twilight in Palestine but the sun was slowly making way for the moon and long shadows reflected in the sea as we left it behind us.

I was very conscious of the fact that I had seen and visited a place that many people are not fortunate enough to jot down in their "memory books" - and I realised their loss.

Irene Smith

P.S. Many people imagine that my swimming in the Dead Sea is the reason why I am only half-alive.

ED. We would have said you had swum in Niagara Falls!

EMPTY ACRES.

By Lieut.-Colonel T.A.Lowe, D.S.O.

(Reprinted from "MEN ONLY" (May,1936) by permission of the Proprietors)

During a tour of some of the Dominions' offices in London, I saw bottles of prize plums, cases of luscious apples, pictures of fat sheep and woolly lambs, delightful panoramas of acres and acres of golden corn; but, when making enquiries inside, I rather gathered that those bottles of fat plums were just a joke on the window gazers. Canada doesn't want you, and neither does Australia. The plums are there, but the reaping requires no assistance.

Canada, of course, has been completely closed for the last six or seven years because of severe economic troubles-and rightly so, for immigration would only have aggravated the matter. Nor will Canada open up again until schemes have been arranged with the British Government ensuring stability. There will be none of those unorganised, mad rushes like there were in the old days. The new idea will be the establishment of whole communities-if people will allow themselves to be transferred like that!

The cinema and the radio have made our potential Empire builders "soft". That was the information I got from a man in one of the offices with a window exhibiting golden corn. He said our young men would sooner watch the covered wagons bobbing over the vasty prairies from comfortable seats in the nine-pennies than drive the old buggy carts themselves. I said I didn't believe that; the radio was having the other effect. But the chap in the London office wouldn't listen to any argument. He said a concert on the radio was just about as near to the Rockies as most Englishmen ever wanted to get. I said: "Naturally, when you don't give him any encouragement. Do you want us to go to your country, or don't you?"

Well, we had a long talk. He said: "Listen-British Columbia, in common with the rest of the world, has been passing through a period of acute depression, and there is no possibility of employment being obtained by a new-comer unless he creates his own sphere of activity with his own capital. On the other hand, to people of limited means with an assured income, British Columbia is a grand country. It is possible, for example, at a comparatively small cost, to acquire what would be in England the equivalent of an estate, superbly situated-and immune from that particular brand of taxation known as Schedule A."

I gathered that they weren't getting a large number of that semi-prosperous type of Englishman, which was why he had made up his mind we were all going a bit "soft".

Continued.

half the gold in the world. I had a long chat with a chap who seemed to know the country inside out, and he seemed quite hurt when I asked him if his Dominion was another of the "lock-out" ones. "On the contrary", he said, "we have helped over 7,000 people from Great Britain to go to South Africa since 1925, and some of these had no private means at all". Some were nursery governesses, some were mining engineers, some (about half of the total) were farmers, but he said mere land hunger wouldn't see you very far in South Africa, unless you knew how to farm beforehand. Small farming is different though. A man with a pension is welcomed and can live a marvellous life on a small-holding or garden (the produce of which will reduce his expenses), because he can fish and enjoy surf-bathing as well.

We came back, of course, to the old argument about Englishmen having got "soft". Boys are encouraged to go to South Africa and learn farming at special colleges which do everything for them until they get settled on the land. But our boys won't go, apparently...the cinema and the radio again?

Puzzled about it all, I went to the window with the fat woolly lambs, and asked to see the boss. He wasn't in, but a nice lad gave me a pile of literature about New Zealand. He knew a lot about the All-Blacks too, and we forgot all about the Empire and talked Rugby football instead. That's the worst of it! A German or an Italian or a Greek would have pumped that young man dry about his country. He would have found out what they grow in it, what the wages are, how much it costs to get there, how many families to the acre, and everything, but here were we talking animatedly about Gilbert's place-kicking...

Thoroughly ashamed of myself, I studied the pamphlets at home afterwards. I gathered that if you have a job or a spot of cash, they don't mind you going to New Zealand. They prefer you to go as a child or as a very young man (you might get into the All-Black side of 1946), but whatever age you are they don't actually forbid you to go. The new Premier says that New Zealand's one claim to territory is that it shall not remain empty and unused. He says the best way to defend New Zealand is to fill it up with prosperous people...

That word "prosperous" again!

I'm still puzzled about this heritage we are not allowed to touch unless we pay our own passages, bring our own sheets and blankets, and buy farms when we get there. Is it any wonder that every country in Europe seems so mightily interested in the "empty spaces" of the British Empire? We go on ignoring the persistent way Germany has of demanding back her Colonies. We laugh at Italy for going to all the trouble to fight a big war for possession of a country no self-respecting white man would ever think of living in. We are bored when Japan gets fussy about a place in the sun. But the fact remains that every "empty" acre in Canada, Australia, New Zealand, and South Africa is capable of supporting about three Germans, or five Italians, or, say, a hundred Japanese. In moments of depression, I see myself sitting in a dug-out de-lousing my shirt the way one used to do, and all because of a lot of darned <u>empty acres</u>.

7
THE B———— PRIVATE ROAD.

(FROM THE "WHEELER'S" POINT OF VIEW.)

(FROM THE PEDESTRIAN'S POINT OF VIEW.)

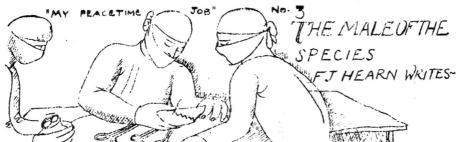

"MY PEACETIME JOB" No. 3
THE MALE OF THE SPECIES
F J HEARN WRITES-

Most people dislike hospitals, but I often get nostalgia when I smell iodine. A hospital, colony of healing, where the strong smell of antiseptics and pungent odour of chloroform and ether pervade every nook and cranny is really a wonderful place. I worked in various hospitals for many years.

In a hospital, tragedy is often apparent, but so also, is hope. Hope that someone desperately sick or injured, will recover. Hope that is realised scores of times, due in no small measure to the skill of the surgeon and tender care of the nurses.

For a period I was on duty in a casualty ward, and saw nothing else but broken and torn limbs and maimed bodies. How some of them were ever made well again is a miracle of modern medicine and surgery. The casualty ward is a common leveller of what we call society. I have assisted the doctor attend a company director in one cubicle, and gone straightway to a tramp in the next. They were both just cases to us.

My most embarrassing experience in the casualty ward occurred very late one night. A noted walker of the local streets, a lady we all knew well, was brought in extremely intoxicated and suffering from some slight mishap. My female counterpart on the womens' side was away for a few minutes, so I had to keep my eye on the new arrival. Hearing her call I entered the ward, and was horrified when a nude figure leapt forward, threw two skinny arms round my neck and called me "Ducky". I immediately decided that a blanket draped around her figure, would look much better than lying idle on a stretcher.

The worst experience I had was when I had to tell a woman with a brood of children clustered round her skirt, that her husband had died ten minutes after the ambulance had brought him in. I dare not meet her eyes, and I was only just quick enough to catch her as she fell.

Work in the main wards of a hospital is not so varied but quite as interesting. I got to know the patients much more intimately, and all their likes and dislikes. Their families also, I got to know, and made some very good friends.

A hospital, as far as is practical, works to a schedule. I expect many of you have been in hospital and grumbled at being called early in the morning to be washed. Believe me, it has to be, for the sake of the nurses as well as the patients. You are usually one in a ward of thirty patients, and twenty-nine others need the same individual care and attention as you.

If there is a very special case in a hospital, everybody is interested. I remember one particular case of a man who had his heart scraped, a very ticklish operation. All the hospital staff were most disappointed when the man died after two days.

I was always pleased when I bid, "Goodbye and good luck" to patients I had tended. Many of them added to that pleasure by coming to see me at the hospital on visiting days, and also inviting me to their homes. One patient of mine, who afterwards went to Australia, still corresponds with me.

I have watched many operations and have always been thrilled by the skill of the surgeon. I have assisted at post-mortems and given evidence at several inquests. I had a gruelling time at one inquest on a patient of mine, whom I had cut down after he had successfully hanged himself. I actually saw another patient commit suicide. He threw himself from the second flight of a fire-escape on to the concrete at my feet. The dull thud his body made was the most horrible sound I have ever heard, and I must confess, it made me miss a meal.

A hospital often has tragedy and pathos intermingled with comedy and laughter.

A hard job, sometimes a thankless one. An interesting job, but always a worthwhile one.
XXXXXXXXXXXXXXXXXXXXXXXXXXXXXXXXXXXXXXXXXXXXXXXXXXXXXXXXXXXXXXXXXX

A LAMENT.

A Bus driver whose route had been changed so many times that he eventually became insane was heard to say the following prayer:-

    Our Father who art in Hendon, Harrow be thy name,

    Thy Kingston come, thy Wimbledon, in Erith as it is in Hendon,

    Give us this day our Leatherhead, and forgive us our bye-passes,

    As we forgive them that bye-pass against us,

    And lead us not into Thames Ditton, but deliver us from Ewell,

    For thine is the Kingston, the Purley and the Crawley,
                                          For Esher and Esher,
                                                Crouch End.

BEAUMANOR STAFF CLUB.

BALANCE SHEET.   31st March 1942.

Loans from Members. 18. 5. 6		Cash at Bank and in hand.	
Less Repaid. 17.13. 0	12. 6	Float. 1. 0. 0	
		In hand. 80. 1.10	
		At Bank. 300. 6. 6	381. 8. 4
Sundry Creditors.	352.14. 7	Stock 31st March 1942.	173.14. 4
New Canteen Reserve Fund	150. 0. 0	Sundry Debtors.	6.13. 6
Profit and Loss.	58. 9. 1		
	£561.16. 2		£561.16. 2

TRADING and PROFIT & LOSS ACCOUNT for three months to 31.3.42.

To Stock 31.12.41.	52.13. 6	By Sales	814.18.10
" Purchases.	749. 0. 1	" Stock 31.3.42.	173.14. 4
" Gross Profit c/d.	186.19. 7		
	£988.13. 2		£988.13. 2
To Wages.	6. 0. 0	By Gross Profit b/d.	186.19. 7
" Crockery.	4. 0.10		
" Newspapers.	4. 3. 0		
" Cleaning Materials.	1. 4. 9		
" Cigarettes for Dance.	1. 7. 1		
" First Aid Kit.	1. 0. 8		
" Darts and Flights.	4. 5		
" Tobacco Licence.	2. 7		
" Stamps, Stationery, Fares and General Expenses.	1. 2. 0		
	19. 5. 4		
" Net Profit c/d.	167.14. 3		
	£186.19. 7		£186.19. 7

APPROPRIATION ACCOUNT.

To Grants		By Net Profit for period 9.10.41 to 31.12.41 b/f	75.14.10
Sports Section	20. 0. 0		
Christmas Party.	10. 0. 0		
Choir Section.	5. 0. 0	" Net Profit for the three months to 31.3.42 b/d.	167.14. 3
" New Canteen Reserve Fund.	150. 0. 0		
" Balance carried to Balance Sheet.	58. 9. 1		
	£243. 9. 1		£243. 9. 1

TRAVELLER'S LOG.   by W. Dalton.

Before going further afield it may be of interest to consider a few points of interest concerning the history of the estate, within the precints of which, we perform our daily task. On delving into records I found some confliction of opinion regarding the origination of the demesne, but it seems fairly certain that the first Lord of the Manor, early in the 12th. century, was Geoffrey Le Depenser. He was succeeded in occupation by Henry de Beaumont, of French royal extraction, and from whom the estate apparently derived its name. It was actually known for a long period as Beaumond Park, and at that time was said to have a boundary 20 miles in circumference, while the mansion itself was surrounded by a moat. Other famous persons to occupy the Manor included the Earl of Essex, and the Duchess of Suffolk, mother of Lady Jane Grey. Following the tragic fate which overtook members of her own family, the Duchess married her Keeper of Horse. By this act it was surmised that in thus lowering her social status she would escape the dangers attached to a more exalted position.

The name of Herrick has a long and inseparable association with Beaumanor, dating from 1596 when Sir William Herrick came into occupation. The present building (which is actually the third manor in the estate's history) was erected to the order of William Perry Herrick, nearly a hundred years ago. Mr. Railton was the designer and the mansion has been described as a perfect example of the late Tudor or Jacobean style. Among the old customs recorded in connection with the Manor under the Feudal System were the tribute of "a pound of pepper from Barrow" and "four flights of arrows from Frisby". On St. Valentine's Day all the children of the district presented themselves at the Manor and received a gratuity in return for their Valentines.

Antiques which have been preserved, include the old family stage coach which can be seen in the building at the back of the Court Yard; and the famous oak chair, of which a contemporary writer gave this description:- "A liveing chair which did grow in the park at Beaumanor in the yeare 1695, is cut down and being beautified is now placed in the Hall there as a real wonder of the world, to the admiration of all that see it". The Chair remains on view in the Hall, and judging from its bulk would take a bit of shifting.

LOUGHBOROUGH.   As so many members of the staff reside in Loughborough, a few high lights which stand out during its evolution from a small scattered village to its present dimension may be worthy of attention. The town is of Saxon origin, and was first officially recorded in the Domesday Book as LUCTEBURNE. In those early days it became noted for its wool industry, the very rich pastures of the district being ideal for raising sheep of a very high quality. The textile trade became the staple industry as the town expanded, and when the first serious signs of industrial unrest arose through the introduction of lace making machinery at Nottingham, the trouble naturally spread to Loughborough. On one occasion a large body of people entered the town bent on destruction, but while gathered in the market square, they were addressed by Dr. Hardy, rector of the Parish Church, and prevailed upon to disperse peaceably. (Continued)

-- The market square has been the centre of much activity, and has undergone considerable change. There was formerly a row of cottages in the square, opposite the Lord Nelson Hotel, while at the other end was a building known as the "Shambles" which comprised trading premises with a public room overhead. The square also contained a butter market, stocks and whipping post, all in regular use. During a parliamentary contest in 1857, when the prospective candidates harangued the electors from hustings, tumultuous scenes were witnessed, resulting in the reading of the Riot Act, while the keepers of law and order belaboured the crowd with their batons. Religious meetings in the square were frequent, and John Wesley is known to have conducted part of his campaign here. During the time of the Civil War, King Charles visited the town, but being not in great favour was honoured by only "5/8d worth of bell-ringing". Prince Rupert, who followed in his wake, was even less fortunate, being saluted with but a shillingsworth. At one time cock-fighting was very prevalent and popular. It began in the yard of one of the taverns, and culminated in the erection of a special pit in Ashby Square. One of the regular patrons was a certain Dan Lambert of Leicester, who was reputed to weigh 50 stone. Among notable visitors to Loughborough, was Dr.Johnson, who stayed at the "Bull's Head", and who subsequently described the ladies of the town as being "more faithful and virtuous than in former days". I regret I am not in a position to state how far the rate of improvement has been maintained.

TO WHOM IT MAY CONCERN.   "The Slaughter of the Innocents".

During the cold months of February and March, those who had eyes to note it, were gladdened by the sight of what promised to be a truly magnificent sight, namely, thousands of daffodil leaves growing, not in serried ranks but as nature intended amid carpets of grass. Alas, when April came, they were to many, an unfulfilled promise, a Barmicidean feast. For no sooner dare a daffodil show a bud than selfish people, not content with what they would have taken from a florists (where money has to be paid for them) exterminated in a few days, what would have been a vision to many of us city dwellers. In the coming weeks, no doubt we will have roses, rhododendrons etc. in bloom and I would make a plea that if these are permitted to flower unscathed, they will be a daily pleasure to appreciate on our way to and from our task.   H.Landless.

ANNOUNCEMENT:- GARDEN FETE - "THE BRAND" - WOODHOUSE EAVES. 13th. June - 3.0 to 7.0 p.m. then Dance in Village hall. Entrance fee 6d. Children 3d. Light teas available at 1/0d. Fancy dress parade from "Bull's Head" at 2.0 p.m. Function in aid of British Red Cross and Order of St.John's Funds. SIDESHOWS-ENTS.- MAY-POLE - COMPETITIONS-RAFFLES-ANKLE COMPETITION-BAND. ROLL UP!

G O S S I P.

MARRIAGES From-"The Times"-of the 11th. May:-

CATON:ELLINGWORTH.-On May 9, 1942, at St. Augustine's, Highgate, by the Rev. Martin Caton, brother of the bridegroom, FLYING OFFICER MICHAEL FRANCIS CATON, younger son of Mr. and Mrs. H. Caton, 79, Torrington Park, Finchley, to JOYCE ELEANOR, elder daughter of LIEUT.-COMMANDER and Mrs. ELLINGWORTH, formerly of Rochester.

On behalf of the Staff, we tender "all best wishes" to the happy couple.

CONGRATULATIONS:- To Geo. Billingsley on his recent marriage to a charming young lady, "Dorothy". We need no longer ask, "Where's George?".

To "Micky" Griffiths on her promotion to the rank of A/Cpl.
To "Marie" Newman on her promotion to the rank of A/L/Cpl.

Reported by the Apostles - Advert. seen in Leicester:-
"Women wanted for boiling". We always did like boiled "sweets".

WOODHOUSE EAVES GARDEN FETE Details will be seen on another page, but we would emphasise that this will be well worth a visit, even if only to see the lovely grounds, The Brand, which are being lent for the occasion, by Sir Robert & Lady Martin. Rumour has it that the O/C is judging the "Ankle" competition. Apparently the O/C also has "it".
LEFT WITH NOTHING AT WHICH TO GRUMBLE. 14 days leave. The expected petition from "7 day weekers" asking for this to be reduced to 12 days, has not yet materialised.

We understand that our Home Guard recently attacked "Charley Knoll". This gentleman however, has not even bothered to visit his panel doctor.

A recent Ministry order dealing with second-hand furniture, has ruled that an antique is to be regarded as something made prior to this century. On this basis, it appears that Woyg has quite a collection of these rare pieces. If you persist in thinking only in terms of furniture, it is felt that elucidation will gladly be supplied by that most accommodating gentleman, Mr. "Smart".

TENNIS COURT. During the early days of the opening of the court, it was suggested by many people, that the idea of playing tennis on it should be abandoned, and that it be handed over to the Home Guard, for training in desert warfare. However, defects have now been remedied, and Mr. Cairncross is no longer heard singing, "Sand in my shoes".

There have been a number of complaints recently regarding the obnoxious smell pervading Hut "C". We have applied all our talents to the solving of this mystery and are now in a position to report on our findings. It is a kind of fifth column intrusion into the Woygite atmosphere, and is generally known as fresh air.

We notice a reference in "Traveller's Log", to a tribute of pepper from Barrow. We have long maintained that Barrow was a pretty hot spot, and in these days, is certainly no place to be sneezed at.
ANTICIPATED ADVERT. "Wanted to sell, Pitch & Toss outfit, or would exchange for acute insomnia. Apply through official channels."
SO LONG FOLKS! WE CONTINUE SNOOPING. "The eyes and ears of Woyg".

(translated from the English by Disciple Matthede).

Now in the days when the Tribe began their sojourn in the Promised Land, it came to pass that a certain man had a Bright Idea. And the Wehkmen who built the Temples were summoned before their superior, the man Fore, who saith unto them :-

Go ye and build on to each Temple another room. And the layers of bricks, and the hewers of wood, and the swingers of lead went forth into the builderness and cleaned the rust from their tools, and began to build right diligently. Yea, even though the frost was ofttimes visited upon the land, for it was the season when layers of bricks do hibernate, which is called the Feast of the Dotted Line, for it is a right Doleful time.

And the man Fore, spake again, saying :-

Get ye bouncing, for verily I say unto you this task is King Robert.

And the Wehkmen, hearing this, toiled mightily until the rooms were raised up. Yea verily, such was their haste that they tarried not even to ensure that the roof leaked satisfactorily. And when they were finished and done they went for their shekels, and putting the rust back on their tools, departed out of the land.

And when the Scribes beheld the Wehkmen they ruminated greatly and saith, one to another :-

Peradventure this is to be a room of rest. While others scornfully did say :- Nay, of a certainty this shall be a padded cell, for is it not become most necessary ?. Do not the bats dwell in our belfry ?.

And they saith unto the Wehkmen :- Oi mate, For what build ye this room. And the Wehkmen put their fingers unto the lips and whispered :- Whist ye not that this is Ush-Ush ?. None knoweth except a certain man.

And the rooms stood many moons and none came nigh nor entered thereinto. And the Scribes marvelled at this, saying :- Is it not strange ?. For a certain man commandeth :- Let there be rooms, and there were rooms. Yet none cometh to toil therein. Neither are there beds, nor tea-urns, nor yet daily parchments.

And one among their number, who saith he possesseth the Low Down, spake in this wise, saying :-

Verily, verily, I say unto you, the certain man hath died. And they rose up crying :- How know ye he kicketh the bucket, if ye know not who is this man ?. And the man with the Griffin answered them, saying :- Is it not plain for all to see ?. Is not Woygland blessed with new rooms upon each temple yet none knoweth for what to use them ?. Therefore I say unto you, the certain man hath snuffed it, and borne unto the grave with him his Bright Idea.

CHAPTER XI

A Bright Idea. Much building occurreth. The Scribes ruminate. None entereth the rooms. One saith he hath the Low Down. He passeth it on.

Now IN THE DAYS when the Tribe began their sojourn in the Promised Land, it came to pass that a certain man had a Bright Idea. And the Wehkmen who built the temples were summoned before their superior, the man Fore, who saith unto them:

Go ye and build on to each temple another room. And the layers of bricks, and the hewers of wood, and the swingers of lead went forth into the builderness and cleaned the rust from their tools, and began to build right diligently. Yea, even though the frost was ofttimes visited upon the land, for it was the season when layers of bricks do hibernate, which is called the Feast of the Dotted Line, for it is a right Doleful time.

And the man Fore, spake again, saying:

Get ye bouncing, for verily I say unto ye this task is King Robert.

And the Wehkmen, hearing this, toiled mightily until the rooms were raised up. Yea verily, such was their haste that they tarried not even to ensure that the roof leaked satisfactorily. And when they were finished and done they went for their shekels, and putting the rust back on their tools, departed out of the land.

And when the Scribes beheld the Wehkmen they ruminated greatly and saith, one to another: Peradventure this is to be a room of rest. While others scornfully did say: Nay, of a certainty this shall be a padded cell, for is it not become most necessary? Do not the bats dwell in our belfry?

And they saith unto the Wehkmen: Oi mate. For what build ye this room? And the Wehkmen put their fingers unto their lips and whispered: Whist ye not that this is Ush-Ush? None knoweth except a certain man.

And the rooms stood many moons and none came nigh nor entered thereinto. And the Scribes marvelled at this, saying: Is it not strange? For a certain man commandeth: Let there be rooms, and there were rooms. Yet none cometh to toil therein. Neither are there beds, nor tea-urns, nor yet daily parchments.

And one among their number, who saith he possesseth the Low Down, spake in this wise, saying:

Verily, verily, I say unto you, the certain man hath died. And they rose up crying: How know ye he kicketh the bucket, if ye know not who is this man?

And the man with the Griffin answered them, saying: Is it not plain for all to see? Is not Woygland blessed with new rooms upon each temple yet none knoweth for what to use them? Therefore I say unto you, the certain man hath snuffed it, and borne unto the grave with him his Bright Idea.

CHAPTER XII

A costly carpet. The Elders are dismayed. The Scribes are banished unto the stables. Powder maketh Scribes exceeding red. Many Huddles. The mat and Meat Waver.

Now IN THE DAYS when the Tribe were newly come into the Promised Land, there was laid upon the floor of the temple of Aych, a rare and costly carpet called Li-No.

And it came to pass, because the Scribes of the temple did shift-work, that the shifting of their chairs and their sandals did wear grievous holes into the carpet.

And when the Elders and the Powers that Be beheld this, they were sore dismayed, and forthwith went into an Huddle.

And coming forth from the Huddle they saith: Behold, Li-No cannot take it. And it was so. And they straightway

THE TEMPLE FLOOR

sendeth word unto Red Tabz in Wyt Awl, saying: Li-No hath become too holy for this humble temple. Therefore we beseech thee, ere we put it away privily, send thou us Kom-Po to put upon the floor, lest thy servants wear out thy concrete with their sandals.

And so it came to pass that the Scribes were banished unto the Stables of Kay, and the Wehkmen came yet again, and got bouncing.

And when the Scribes returned from thence, they beheld a fine red powder sprinkled upon the floor in the temple, and they marvelled at it, saying: If yonder is Kom-Po, I will in very truth devour my Titfa.

And a certain wise man spake unto them, saying: Whist ye not that this is Red E broken up?

And the floor was like unto the Desert. Yea, verily, the Devil's Cauldron and El Alamein in a dust-storm were as naught beside this. For the air was becoming exceeding red, insomuch as it had been blue. And it is written: the raiment of the Scribes and their sandals, and everything that was the Scribes, would have found favour in the eyes of one Jo who dwelleth in Kremlin.

And when the Elders and the Powers beheld this, they were cast down and becometh sick with an headache, and taking each unto himself an aspirin, they goeth into another Huddle. And they bringeth forth a long mat called Koka-Nut, and spreadeth it in the middle of the temple, lest the Recording Angels, and those others which prowleth up and down, should wear a deep trench where they walketh, for it is written: in those days the cost of periscopes was exceeding great.

And the Mat was a boon and blessing, so that the Scribes murmured, each unto his neighbour: Not so dusty.

Yet because of this, the Scribes toiled and sweated greatly, picking Meat-Waver up from the floor, for in this wise it Waveth a right poorly Meat.

No.1   Beaumanor Hall from the H Stable blocks on left.

No.2 (below)   'Garage in 1944 on left MORRIS COMMERCIAL 15 cwt truck on right Standard Utility Humber of Major RS Clifton R.Sigs. 2 I/C who is tall figure in Battledress leaning over the bonnet.

No.3   GIANT EFFIGY OF ADMIRAL CORNWALLIS—ship's figurehead.

No.4   'M' Block with Clock Tower in background.

The warship's figurehead was discovered in the Beaumanor woodyard and erected by Cdr Ellingworth in the courtyard after the paintwork had been restored by an EWA. It represented Admiral Cornwallis (Admiral of the Blue). The effigy was erected as a fountain/horse trough. Embossed on the stonework was a monogram WPH- William Percy Herrick. His frockcoat was blue and he wore the Garter Star. Breeches etc were white. At the end of the war he was removed from his location and given to the Sea Cadet Corps in Loughborough. He may subsequently have emigrated to the United States.

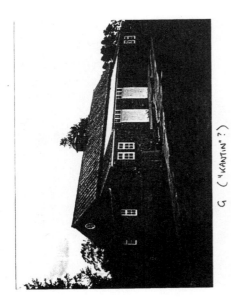

G ("KANTIN"?)

J (SET-ROOM?)

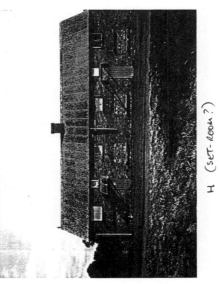

H (SET-ROOM?)

K (D.F.?)

No.5   L to R 'J' Hut 'H' Hut 'I' Hut. In left background row of wooden huts 'A' to 'O'.

No.6   'K' Hut with two occupants (unidentified).

No.7   J Hut right K Hut both taken from 'H' Hut Cloakroom.

No.8   House from SW. Pole carries feeder route for aerials for AR-13 located top right of house on uppermost floor.

No.6 Intelligence School, Hampstead, August 1945. Back: L. Cahill, R. Frawley, H. Knox, N. Forsyth, A. Richardson, A. Jauraude, J. Milligan, R. Remington. Front: Pip Cadman, Jane Barnett, Maj. Jolowicz, Col. Lithgow, K. Slaney (Adj), Anne Edwards, Joan Partridge

Inset: left: H. Skillen, centre: Mrs. M. Bennett, right: The Hon J. Acland Hood who were members of the School in 1943–44.

In this issue is a two-page article on Admiral Cornwallis whose effigy by Wilk appears on the cover.

"B.S.M." AUGUST 1942.
Vol. 1   No. 11

General Editor :- L.P. Jones.

Editorial Board
R. Wilkinson.
P. Wade.
E. Millhouse.

A. Carr.
R.G. Denny.
T. Brister.

Editor :-   F.C. Staddon.

Next publication 26th. Sept.   Contributions by 12th. Sept.

    We regret the slight delay in publishing this number, but the supply question has been a little difficult; we have however, now made arrangements which will cover our production requirements for the next few months. We will be on time next month (we hope).
    The article by "M.E." on Earl Cornwallis, will be of particular interest to members of the R.N.O.C.A., and will no doubt, be of enlightenment to landlubbers. At the same time it will serve as an explanation of the trojan efforts with paint brush, by Dick Whitford. "M.E." writes :- "so much for the man. Next month I hope to tell you something about H.M.S. "Cornwallis".
    The Disciple is very much to the point, in what we consider is his best effort to date.
    The Home Guard article is a reasoned commentary on that organisation, and is published purely as such.
    "Traveller's Log", contains some excellent suggestions for spending a pleasant day, and the prevailing weather will, no doubt, send many of you following in the footsteps of the Dalton.
    "My Peacetime Job", this month, extolls the virtues of our forgetful friend, the plumber. You may have heard the story of the gentleman, (probably Charlie), who, whilst engaged on a bathroom job, opened the door to discover the bath filled with a lady. With great tact he withdrew, exclaiming, "I beg your pardon, sir!".
    You will, no doubt, detect the touch of the Disciple behind "Moulin Maison", and his attempts at "Christening" the Wops, is admirable. In spite of being unable to invent a final appropriate name, "Moulin Maison" can reconcile himself with the knowledge that there is no lack of Godfathers for the Wops.
    Call it "Zoosh", is an excellent account of an apparently true episode, written in the Damon Runyon style.
    "Said the Bishop", in the July No. has resulted in one letter to the Editor, which is published in this issue. We would like other readers to air their views on this important subject, which is fundamental to the improved era we would all like, at least, after the successful conclusion of the present conflict.

        "Do not neglect to rectify an
        evil because it may seem small,
        for, though small at first, it may
        continue to grow until it overwhelms you" - CONFUCIUS.

    With regard to National Savings, we would like to record thanks to "Duggie" and all the helpers involved on this great piece of work, performed on behalf of their colleagues. We would like to see more of this type of thing.
    With the next issue, we intend celebrating our first birthday with a BUMPER number, and ask you all to rally round with articles, cartoons, ideas etc., whether old contributors or new talent.

EARL CORNWALLIS - ADMIRAL OF THE WHITE.

You have all seen his figure-head in the court-yard and some notes about him may not be amiss.

Cornwallis was born in 1744, and entered the Royal Navy in 1755. He served in various junior ranks until 1776, when as a Post Captain in H.M.S. "Pallas" he was in charge of a convoy of 104 Merchantmen sailing from Jamaica to England. Owing to the carelessness and obstinacy of the Masters the ships separated and "Pallas" arrived in the Channel with only 10 left. In July 1779 he took part in the Battle of Grenada as Captain of the "Lion", 64 guns.

His next appearance was on June 20th 1780, where according to a contemporary account, whilst detached with 4 ships, two 64's, one 50 and a 32 frigate, he sighted a fleet of transports carrying M. de Rochambeau and French troops to N. America with an escort of 9 ships of the line, three 80's, two 74's and four 64's. Cornwallis reconnoitred the force, but "Ruby" 64, was so far to the lee, that if the enemy kept the wind, they would pass between him and her. Cornwallis formed line of battle, and edged toward the "Ruby". Should the French keep their wind, "Ruby" would be cut off, and Cornwallis would have to fight tremendous odds, to prevent her being taken prize. The French, however, bore off and Cornwallis pushed them so far to the lee, that the "Ruby" on our lee bow was able to rejoin. The French squadron tacked, and forming parallel lines with our force, exchanged shots. No serious effort was made to crush our force. Cornwallis very properly declined to further engage so superior a force. He had already done much in saving a ship so far greatly exposed.

The French account differs not in essentials from our own. The French Captains were much incensed by their Admiral's cautious action. De Ternay, however, had to consider that an equal or superior force might be encountered at Narragansett Bay, and he could not risk crippling his squadron. The charge of 6,000 troops, under the prevailing conditions, was no light responsibility. Comment on his action, does not belong to British Naval history, to which the firmness and seamanship of Capt. Hon. William Cornwallis added a lasting glory.

At the end of the year he returned to England in the "Lion" 64, with him as a passenger was Capt. H. Nelson, invalided from the "Janus". His friendship contracted with Nelson, lasted throughout their whole lives.

After a long spell of shore service he was appointed to H.M.S. "Crown" as Commodore and Commander-in-Chief East Indies. Quoting from a contemporary account...In November, 1791, "Crown" lying at Tellicherry, learned that the French frigate "Resolue" was leaving Mahe with two merchantmen, Cornwallis sent the frigates "Phoenix" Captain Sir Richard Strachen, and "Perseverance", each more powerful than the "Resolue", to intercept and search for contraband. On being told to heave to, "Resolue" replied with a broadside at the "Phoenix" and a sharp action followed. "Resolue" struck her colours. "Perseverance" meanwhile had examined the merchant ships and finding them clear of contraband, directed them to pursue their voyage. "Resolue", however, refused to sail, and insisted on considering

Contnd.

103

herself a prize. She was taken to Tellicherry, whence Cornwallis sent her to Mahe. The French Commodore protested at his action, but no further objection was made in the searching of French ships.

War being declared with France, Cornwallis seized all French ships within reach, made himself master of Chandernagore, and with Colonel Braithewaite, reduced Pondicherry.

Promotion came fairly rapidly, and on June 16th 1795, we find him in Command of a Squadron of the Channel Fleet as Vice Admiral of the Red. While cruising in the Channel on June 16th, 1795, in H.M.S. "Royal Sovereign" 100 guns, with five ships of the line and 3 frigates he fell in with the French Fleet of twelve ships of the line and other large vessels totalling 30 sail in all under M. Villaret Joyeuse. Cornwallis retreated but "Bellerophon" and "Brunswick" being heavy sailers, lagged behind, and the French Fleet were able to draw up two divisions on each quarter. By Monday 17th the English Squadron was within range. The French Fleet opened fire, and action was joined. "Mars", who was in the rear, suffered considerable damage, and Cornwallis, fearing she might be cut off, wore round to her support. This bold front, in face of such heavy odds, together with deceptive signals from the frigate "Kingfisher" and the fortunate appearance of sails on the horizon, deceived the French, who bore up, fearing the approach of the English Fleet. Cornwallis was able to proceed to Plymouth with the intelligence of the French Fleet at sea. This escape from a force so enormously superior, especially the bold manoeuvre of the "Royal Sovereign", raised the reputation of the Vice Admiral to a very high pitch. It is clear that if the French had attacked, the English would have been crushed. In Parliament, the thanks of both Houses was conveyed to the Vice Admiral, his officers and men.

In February 1796, Cornwallis was appointed Commander-in-Chief, West Indies, and was ordered to proceed with ships of the line and transports to Barbadoes. Down Channel "Royal Sovereign" fouled one of the convoy, sustaining such damage, that after seeing the convoy safely to sea, Cornwallis returned to port. This action was met with disapproval by the Admiralty, who ordered him to hoist his flag in the frigate "Astraea" and proceed with all dispatch to Barbadoes. This order was conveyed by formal letter from the Board on the 15th February and Cornwallis replied on the 16th assuring Their Lordships he was ready to proceed in the "Royal Sovereign", as soon as the defects were made good, but that his precarious state of health obliged him to decline going in a frigate, a stranger to all on board, without accomodation or comfort. This refusal was considered an act of disobedience, and he was ordered to be court martialled.

The Court Martial pronounced censure for not pursuing the voyage in one of the other ships, but acquitted him on disobedience of orders, accepting his defence, that he had not remonstrated against the order,--"that his health would not permit him to go out under such circumstances, and that he would have resigned his command, if the order had been made positive; but as to disobeying it, he had no thought of it." (Minutes of the Court Martial). Notwithstanding his acquittal, Cornwallis considered himself ill treated, and requested permission to strike his flag. **(Contnd.)**

SPORTS PAGE

TENNIS

The news of the month, is of course, our success in the Tennis Tournament held during the Holidays at Home Week in Loughborough. Messrs. Thompson & Waldron and their respective partners, are to be congratulated on reaching the final.

Members taking part were Messrs. Thompson, Waldron, Dalton, and Hobden.

CRICKET

Owing to bad weather and other reasons, four matches were scratched during this month. This was much regretted by the committee. Results:-

15/8 v R.A.F. Won. R.A.F. 32 (Smart 5 for 15)
Exiles 47 (Ridgeway 6 for 14, Cornthwaite 4 for 16)
(Reedman 15, Last, not out, 12).

NOTE:- A General Meeting for all interested in Sport, will be held Wednesday, Sept. 2nd. in Town Hall, Loughborough, at 1800 Hrs.

A.H. Appleton.
Hon. Sec. Sports Sectn.

xxxxxxxxxxxxxxxxxxxxxxxxxxxxxxxxxxxxxxxxxxxxxxxxxxxxxxxxxxxxxx

EARL CORNWALLIS - ADMIRAL OF THE WHITE. (Contnd.)

This was readily granted, and he had no further employment under that administration.

He was appointed Admiral of the Blue in 1799, and succeeded Lord St. Vincent as Commander-in-Chief Channel Fleet. In 1804 Cornwallis was appointed Admiral of the White, and in 1806 he was himself succeeded by Lord St. Vincent and had no further service. He was nominated Grand Cross of the Bath in 1815, and died in 1819.

Cornwallis was described as being of middle size, stout and portly, though strictly temperate. He had a jovially red face, which procured for him among the seamen of his day, the nickname "Billy go tight". He had however a wealth of names, such as "Blue Billy", "Coachee", "Mr. Whip". These not ill-natured jokes point to his being a favourite.

The following story, probably incorrect in detail, but possibly founded on fact, gives an insight to the type of man he was. While in Canada the men mutinied, and signed a round robin declaring they would not fire a gun until they had been paid. Cornwallis turned the hands up and addressed them. "Lads, the money cannot be paid until we return to port, and as to your not fighting, I'll clap you alongside the first ship of the enemy that I see, then the devil himself couldn't stop you."

He never won a victory, and never had a chance of winning one, but in command of both fleets and single ships he distinguished himself repeatedly when circumstances seemed dead against him. M.E.

TRAVELLER'S LOG. by W. Dalton.

Within the last few days I have visited a number of villages in the neighbourhood of Loughborough, which I had been advised were worthy of attention, so herewith particulars of small circular tour.

It is very easily accomplished by cycle, or on foot, aided by a 'bus ride over the longer distances.

The starting point is from Meadow Lane, Loughborough, and after passing over the railway, the only rule of direction to remember is to keep left all the time. The first village reached is Stanford, which is made up of a picturesque church, a few cottages, and an old rustic bridge over the River Soar. Places of special interest in the immediate neighbourhood are Stanford Hall, the residence of Sir Julien Cahn, and Stanford Park and Fish pond. The latter place provides facilities for other than a passing visit, according to the time at one's disposal.

From Stanford it is but a short stretch to Normanton-on-Soar, and when the distance is about half accomplished, one reaches the summit of a hill from which a striking view of the winding river, with the sleepy village spread along its right bank, is obtained. One of Normanton's show pieces is a half-timbered cottage of considerable age, but in good preservation. One of those places which might be described as " a bit of old England ". There are pleasant walks by the river-side, and boating is available from the gardens of the "Plough" tavern. Near the beautiful church one can cross the river by a ferry service which has survived from very olden times. As a matter of fact, the river here divides the counties of Leicestershire and Nottinghamshire.

Next we come to Zouch, and here the river temporarily divides so that the village is mainly built on an island. This is one of the prettiest spots I have yet visited, and, I am informed, is a favourite haunt of fishermen. Certainly there were quite a number following their patient hobby the other day when I was there, but I did not wait sufficiently long to witness a landing. Or, it may be, that I was more interested in a gratifying glimpse of some stream-lined feminine figures - "qui sait". The fact that there are a number of Summer bungalows and caravans round about here is proof of the deserved popularity of the district. I strongly advise you all to make this trip before the Summer season comes to an end.

From Zouch it is not much more than a stone's throw to the main Derby road at the foot of Hathern hill, and thence back to Loughborough.

XXXXXXXXXXXXXXXXXXXXXXXXXXXXXXXXXXXXXXXXXXXXXXXXXXXXXXXXXXXXXXX

OUR DUMB BLONDE

Overhearing a remark about "Jamming" by a British Station, exclaims, "I can't understand where they get all the sugar from".

CHRISTENING.

by:- Moulin Maison.

Now females thin, and fat, and old,
and females young and vital
are toiling in our midst, 'tis time
someone gave them a title.
Whate'er she's been - a debutante
or humble "char" or waitress,
She wouldn't care for anyone
to call her OPERATRESS.

So sitting down, we gave this thing
most earnest contemplation,
and silently, with fever'd brow,
we waited inspiration.
The greatest minds when thus engaged
are often wont to play tricks,
and rather shyly, and ashamed,
we thought of OPERATRIX.

With guilty blush we cast it back
from whence it sprang, and pondered
until a gleam of hope shone as
through fancy's realm we wandered
-but then again, on second thoughts
we doubted if Marina,
or Ag. or Mag. or Ermyntrude
would fall for OPERINA.

Continuing our efforts to
discover fitting names,
another monicker was born,
for pencil-pushing dames.
'Twas stillborn, this, for we suspect
that Gladys, Grace, or Gwen,
would gaze at us in sympathy
if hailed as OPIENNE.

But after that we thought we had
produced a proper "snorter",
quite good enough for anyone's
"discriminating" daughter,
until we realised, 'way back,
someone had gone one better,
and put our word to other use,
-so much for OPERETTA!

In any case we would not stoop
to copyright purloining,
while, scratching heads, and
               gnawing pens
we're capable of coining
an epic name like-but we fear
the Janes and Joans and Jessies
would give a "language" lesson
we styled them OPERESSES. (if

We thought it rather apt, to
                          give
our effort Service flavour,
The only brainwave we contrived
was viewed with great disfavour,
'cause of the danger that some
                           guy
would start enlisting cats
to kill the plague of rodents,
                           if
we dubbed them OPERATS.

So after all we havn't thought
of any graceful title
for females thin, and fat, and
                           old,
and females young and vital.
And so despite its usage for
Il Duce's little flops,
we'll carry on as heretofore,
and simply call 'em WOPS.

7

THE GOSPEL ACCORDING TO ST. UPID. Chapter XIII
(Translated from the English by Disciple Millhouse).

Now at the time of the year when the Brittites were sometimes blest with a day of sunshine, called Summer, it was the custom of the peoples to journey forth along the Iron Road to the Sea, with buckets and spades. And these were the Holy Days.

But because the patience of Itla the Hunnite, also called Misbegotten, was still exhausted, he continued to send his Birdmen, who lay their eggs upon the seashore. Wherefore did the King in Smowk command his peoples not to come hence with their buckets. And the order went forth throughout the land: Holy Days at Home.

And accordingly the Mare and the Elders of the city called Luff did forgather in Townorl, and consulted one with the other, saying; Ee, what a mook-oop. Which, being translated, meaneth they knew not what to do. For, saith the Elders, the Broosh ceaseth to labour seven days and seven nights, likewise also Empress, and many other houses of craft. Therefore, if the peoples are to obey the King, we must bring them musick and whoopee into the city. Likewise also must we find them sand for their buckets.

And a certain man called Jaybee, a right priestly man, who dwelleth in Smowk with Alvar, came down through the wilderness into Luff, bringing a host of fellowers. There was one Malcolm of the three chevrons and his philanthropic musick players, and the man Muddlecombe, and a certain Sanger with his beasts, and many others. Yea, it was a mighty host, and this was Bruce Belfrage leading it. And such Woygites as journeyed not unto the Temples joined with the multitudes in Luff, and were filled with rejoicing.

But because the Holy Day of Bank fell about this time, the skies opened up as was customary, and a plague of cats and dogs descended upon the city. Yea verily, the situation was become extremely fluid. But Jaybee heeded this not, and spake with the Great Voice called Bebesee unto all the Brittites, saying: Here found I happy sunny days, for was it not a hundred and ten in the shade?. And the echo answered unto him saying: Was it?.

And at the close of the week, there came to pass the ceremony of Putting back the Sundial, for henceforth noon was to be at 11 o'clock instead of 10 o'clock. And certain scribes of the Temples of Woyg conceived that this was a Great Idea, but deserving of improvement, and straightway putteth back their sundials two hours, which enabled them to come later unto the Temples.

And this is the parable of the Hungry Man. Now a certain Scribe returning from his labours in Woyg, was possessed of a great hunger. And coming unto his Bilit, he saith unto the Lady of the Land: Verily I say unto you, I am starving.

And she answered him saying: Be of good cheer, and I will light the fire for thee.

GOSSIP.

CONGRATULATIONS:- To Miss Joyce Kempin (canteen) on her marriage to a Sergeant of the R.E. at St. Paul's Church, Woodhouse Eaves 22/8/42. All best wishes are extended to the happy couple.

We are delighted to be able to announce the engagement of our smiling runner, Sally Hullet, to British Constable Fred Raymond, now serving with the Palestine Police.

"ROMANCE IS IN THE AIR"

HER name is Norrie Smart,	HIS name is Ron:
And I think there must be an art,	You'll find him in Hut "E"
In stealing a WOYGITE's heart,	Or chatting to little Norrie
It must have been the Spring.	over a cup of tea!
So do not raise a questioning brow,	MY name must remain Anon,
And wonder "Why and Where and How",	But I'm sure that everyone
I feel that I must tell you now	Will join me in wishing the
She wears an engagement ring.	best of luck
	To little Norrie and Ron:
	"Ever Hopeful".

Congratulations to Mr. & Mrs. Chisman (P.O.), on the arrival of a son and heir, (Robert), on Saturday August. 1st.

Also to Mr. & Mrs. A.M.Hilder, on the arrival of a son, Edward John, on the 15th.July. To prove that he was not claiming undue fame, "Mac" produced the birth certificate for the Editor's inspection. It is regretted that space will not allow us to reproduce this historic document.

Both scribes and ATS were present at the 20th. birthday party of "Don" Barber, which was held at the "Bull's Head", Woodhouse Eaves. A good time was had by most, a bad time was had by some, and a lousy time was had by the "puncture repairing party" on Woodhouse Lane at 2330. However, there were no repercussions, save the one which preceded the puncture; "more things are wrought by prayer than this world dreams of".

FAGGOTS IN THE CANTEEN. We can now look forward to saveloys and pease pudding, not to mention the possibility of onions to go with the tripe we hear about in the canteen. The fact that the O/C was heard plaintively calling, "Laddie", during the faggot selling era, was purely coincidental.

MIRRORS. We are pleased to note that the much discussed mirrors, have at last materialised after the repeated promises that they would be "looked into". The occupants of Hut "C", have however, undergone a good deal of embarrassment, due to the location of the mirror, by apologising to their own reflections and postponing matters of often, extreme urgency.

APPEAL. We have been asked by the "Riff-Raffs" Concert Party, to appeal for the names of any members of the staff, who are able and willing to entertain in any capacity. They are particularly anxious to contact a pianist (male or female), who can tackle typical Concert Party music, with particular accent on rhythm. The "Riff-Raffs" intend to devote their energies in support of local charities. All communications to F.C.Staddon, c/o Hut "C", please.

MUSICAL CHAIRS We understand there have been one or two impromptu games of musical chairs in the canteen recently. In future, any persons wishing to indulge in these hilarities, are requested to approach the Entertainments Committee. So long folks'.

MY PEACETIME JOB No. 6.

"THE GILBERTIAN PERIOD"

A butcher, a baker and a candlestick maker-so goes the old song:- but what about a Plumber?. Rarely, if ever, do you hear of a Plumber mentioned in song or story. You do not see his name blazoned on the Great White Way of Broadway, or hear some crooner with a "come kiss me" voice telling the unseen millions of the Glamorous Plumber. No sir.

Still if you want your sink repaired, or your old joints soldered, or your pipes renewed, or your lavatory seen into, you send for a Plumber, and there he is-bowler hat, walrus moustache, bag of oily tools-not to mention his smiling mate-at your service.

In peace time I was a Plumber, spelt P-L-U-M-B-E-R. The B is silent as in Church. Let me tell you right now that a modern Plumber is a qualified engineer who has to serve a long apprenticeship and pass several difficult trade examinations. Thermostatics, Bio-chemistry, Constructional engineering, and Manipulative handwork, are only some of the things you must know. Add to that the delicate touch of a Plastic surgeon with the practised eye of a Gunsmith and the studied art of soldering a Midges thyroid gland without a tremor. You need the patience of Job coupled with the tenacity of a bulldog.

Of course, we have our thrills and our disappointments, but who hasn't?. We are known in the trade as Housemaids Delight. We get into all sorts of odd corners and dirty holes. We are at home in the Duke's mansion or the Peasant's hovel. The frost and the snow are our friends, at all times and in all climes you will find us-seeking out your discomforts-adding to your pleasures,and as Gracie Fields says, "watching all your troubles go swinging down the drain".

Just now I'm on a War-time job, but when I've given old 'Itler a sock on the jaw, I'll go back to Plumbing and the sooner the better. I'll go back to Sunny Sussex by-the-sea, where you don't see "Trespassers will be prosecuted" at every woodland pathway, or nailed to every tree.

My hobby is gardening. I think my longevity is due to hard work and old ale. I think the Loughborough policemen are wonderful. I like to read Medieval History. Give me Gibbon's "Decline and Fall", or Finlay's "History of the Byzantine Empire", or even a history of Loughborough 200 years ago, and I am content. I don't like Spearheads, or Pincer movements, or Cauldron battles, they give me a nasty feeling in me innards.

Peace and quietness is my motto. When this ruddy war is over, and you go south young man with your charming wife and your squalling kids, for a holiday at Brighton, you may perchance see a big sign in letters of gold, saying-Plumbers & Joiners. Expert work at reasonable rates-well that's me mates. Your old friend,

C. Gilbert.

CALL IT "ZOOSH" YONC

With the acuteness of mind common to all Woygites, you lot will wonder - why?.

Well, it's this way..........
You see, my pal's landlady has a bungalow for a fortnight out by ZOOSH. Well, my pal and old Freddy, get on well enough by themselves for about a week, except for a pile of washing up to do at the end of it, and all the cigarette ash to clear up, and all the cushions and things as well, where we'd been doing a spot of P.T. one morning. However, with a little help from me and the carpet-beater, we get the place cleaned up.

Well - that's O.K., but Freddy goes on leave on Saturday, so my pal says, "Oh no!", "Oh no!" he says, "I'm not staying by myself". So he goes over to ZOOSH to stay with MR. and MRS. for three days.

Well - on the last day, we both are on the morning watch, so my pal says to come over this afternoon, and I say it's O.K., and I doll up in glad rags at 4.30 a.m. because I am going straight there after work.

Well, at work, my pal says he wants to get into best bib and tucker, and will I meet his girl-friend, because he can't make it by 2.30. I, being a self-sacrificing sort of chap, agree, and I arrive at rendez-vous at 2.15, Barkus being a bit earlier that day.

I find that my pal's girl-friend is not in evidence, so I walk up and down, wearing grooves in the pavement. I see Buzz across the road, so I trickle over and cadge a light. Then I wander back and re-commence work of making grooves.

My pal's girl-friend arrives ten-minutes late in a big hurry and a new uniform. She says the peak is too big, and I say "yes it is."

I explain my presence, and she, knowing my pal, understands. So then we wander away to the 'bus stop and my pal, he rolls up just after, having done himself proud.

We wait in the crowd for the ten-to-three 'bus which is leaving just on ten-past. We are inside, by the help of a judicious and adroit method of infiltration, which makes us all laugh, but not the other people, because they are left behind.

We get to the bungalow and have a belated lunch on the verandah. Then the fun begins - for me.

My pal goes for a walk with the girl-friend and the puppy, so I take MRS. up the river in a punt. I find punting very awkward, and we are going up the river in a series of v's as it were. We go round in circles once or twice, but on the whole, except for the attentions of a few wet willow trees, we are getting on O.K.

So we go up as far as the "Plough", which is the name of a pub. Because it is afternoon, we do not get out, but turn round and start to go back. It is now MRS's turn for a paddle, so she paddles and makes a better fist of it, so that I am jealous of her prowess and drag the other paddle in the water to make her go funny like I did. But she isn't having any, and tells me to shut up. So I shut up, because she is bigger than I am, and she has a bigger paddle too, and we continue in a nearly straight line.

Contnd.

LIMERICK COMPETITION

We were a little disappointed at the small number of entries, and hope that the published limericks will spur others on to "have a go" when we decide to run a similar competition.

We are constantly hearing that the chief fault in Government departments is the complete lack of competition as compared with private enterprise, but in spite of this, believe that the Staff are still sufficiently immune from this beaurocratic disease, to justify the entry of an occasional competition in the pages of your magazine.

The panel of judges:- O/C, Messrs. Millhouse, Wade and Carr, were each given a copy of all entries with names omitted, and a reference number inserted. The Editor then took a census of opinion from their rulings, and from the final result it will be clearly seen that MR. SPOONER is a very worthy winner, and thoroughly deserves the prize of 100 CIGARETTES, which have already been received by him. (It's a pity he isn't a non-smoker).

WINNER :- J.M. Spooner.
The curious habits of men
do not seem very odd, except when
the women have course
to adopt them in force
they are certainly curious then.

2nd. :- J.R. Pearce.
A frivolous filly of Bicester
attended a dance as a Mister
but regretted the hoax
when she went to the "cloaks"
where the standing room didn't assist her.

3rd. :- Capt. Burgess.
The curious habits of men
seem even more curious when
indulged in by those
who wear female clothes
such as A.T.S., F.A.N.Y, & W.R.E.N.

4th. :- F.C. Staddon.
A wheezy young lady of Rye
was staring away at the sky
she exclaimed with a squint
when a bird dropped a "hint"
carrier pigeon, be blowed-mind my eye.

5th. :- J.M. Spooner.
The curious habits of men
defy the most eloquent pen
each woman in turn
for herself has to learn
what they are-or might be now and then.

6th. :- P. Carrington.
The curious habits of men
like the lecture, on loading the Bren
caused many a snigger
so Dick pulled the trigger
and thus ends my story-Amen!

SPORTS

The Tennis Court is proving very popular, especially with the A.T.S. In this connection, I have noticed cups of tea being swallowed rather hastily, in order to spend part of the "break" watching the tennis (Ats?). This proves we are providing recreation for everyone.

As you will observe from the Sports Notice Board, I have arranged a number of Cricket fixtures. These of course, will be added to in the future. It is now up to you to show interest and back up your committee. In response to enquiries, I should like to mention we have now bought sufficient kit.

I take this opportunity to thank the O/C for the interest and help he has given us, particularly in regard to the Tennis.

I should also like to record my appreciation of the efforts of the Entertainments Committee, in raising the sum of £14.14.1 at the last Dance, on our behalf.

A.H. Appleton. (Hon. Sec)
Sports Section.

He grabbed me round my slender waist
I could not yell or scream
he dragged me to a dingy room
where we should not be seen
he tore away my flimsy wrap
and gazed upon my form
I was so very cold and damp
while he was hot and warm
his fevered lips he pressed to mine
I gave him every drop
he drained me of my very self
I could not make him stop
he made me what I am today
that's why you find me here
a broken bottle thrown away
that once was full of beer!!

A corrupted mind like yours would
think this poem very hot
but when you read the last few lines
you'll soon find out it's not.

"Kohdist".

First Name(s)	Surname
Gloria	Adams
Terrie	Aiken
Roy	Aldridge
Fred	Alldred
Ina	Anderson
P.K.	Antrum
A.H.	Appleton
Harry	Appleton
Philip	Arnold
Joyce	Askew
Don	Barber
Rose	Barlow
J.C.M.	Barnes
Myrtle	Barnes
Marjorie	Bartram
Ted	Beckwith
G	Billingsley
Doreen	Blake
Anne	Boughey
Jo	Brind
T	Brister
Charles	Brown
Helen	Brown
Hilda	Brownlow
Freddie	Burgess
Bobbie	Burr
?	Burton
Mabel	Cage
Ann	Campbell
Wally	Cecil
Peggy	Chaffin
Ralph	Champion
Audrey	Chope
Joan	Clarke
Isobel	Clay
J	Colville
Joan	Cook
Alice	Cooke
Betty	Coombs
Lynda	Courtnage
Molly	Cronin
Gerry	Dalton
'Midge'	Dawson
?	Denne
Ron	Denny
Harry	Dix
Charley	Dobson
Eric	Dobson
Harry	Dodd
John	Dodd
Peggy	Doherty
Jean	Donlon
Marie	Down
R	Downer
Margaret	Dunn
Jimmy	Edge
Peggy	Evans
Muriel	Fidoe
'Spike'	Forster
Janet	Fourdrinier
Freddie	Fox
Hilary	Fry
Muriel	Furniss
Hilda	Gamble
Peter	Gardner
'Tubby'	Garnham
Bill	Ghent
Mary	Gill
W.J.	Gilliard
Sybil	Gregory
Cecile	Groves
Priscilla	Hall
Jean	Hammond
Roy	Hardy
Victor	Hartill
Bill	Hayward
Fred	Hearn
Jimmy	Hewson
Max	Hilder
Reg	Hilder
Johnny	Hodge
Audrey	Holland
E.A.	Hooper
Jimmy	Hunter
Laurie	Isaacs
Muriel	Jellings
Leonard P	Jones
Margaret	Jones
Alex	Keenlyside
Paddy	Kelly
George	Kenneally
Peter	Kingsland
D.A.	Kirby
N	Leadbetter
F.W.	Leedham
Netta	Lees
Henry	Lewis
Doris	Light
'Bobby'	Lord
Dorothy	Louch
Fred	Mayne
Irene	Mayor
Hilary	McCauslan
Paddy	McGrath
V.	Merritt
Kay	Metcalfe
Hazel	Miller
Eric C	Millhouse
Molly	Morgan
Peggy	Morgan
Joan	Morley
Sam	Murgatroyd
Jean	Murray
F.	Mutton
Geoff	Nicol
Joan	Nixon
Kay	Norman
Mary	Norris
Bernard	Norwood
Joan	Oakey
Lew	Owen
Mary	Parker
Ollie	Pearce
Connie	Praeger
Kay	Price
Pat	Price
Joan	Price
M	Reed
E	Reedman
Norman	Rees
Margaret	Rhodes
Bob	Roberts
Audrey	Robinson
Jimmy	Rogers
Ida	Romer
Noel	Royle
'Trixie'	Scillitoe
Dorothy	Sharman
Eddie	Sims
Ellen	Smith
E.D.	Smith
R.M.	Smith
?	Snell
G.M.	Spooner
Fred	Staddon
Kay	Statham
Kathleen	Sutcliffe
Harold	Sweeten
Ken	Talbot
Ginger	Talbot
Muriel	Taylor
Gordon	Terry
Dudley	Truin
P.M.	Tuke
P.E.	Turner
Edith	Turner
F	Vickers
?	Vickers
Ivy	Walton
Freda	Ward
Mavis	Warren
Hazel	Webb
Rex	Welch
Fred	Wells
May	Wesson
George	White
R.W.	Whitford
R	Wildblood
Peggy	Wilding
Dick	Wilkinson
Mary	Willcock
Margaret	Willet
Joan	Williams
Bungy	Williamson
Elma	Wood
Evelyn	Woodhouse
Daphne	Workman
Ron	Worster
R.G.	Yaxley

A list of some of the first operators at WOYG

"B.S.M." SEPTEMBER 1942.
Vol. 2   No. 1.

General Editor:- L.P. Jones.   Editorial Board:-
                                    R. Wilkinson.   A. Carr.
Editor:-   F.C. Staddon.   P. Wade.   R.G. Denny.
                                    E. Millhouse.   T. Brister.

Next publication 30th.Oct. .... Contributions by 17th.Oct.

A personal note from the General Editor. With this issue, the "B.S.M.", the child of an idea born on a quiet 2 - 10 watch last September, reaches its first birthday.

I would like to take this opportunity to extend my thanks to all those who have so loyally stood by us during the difficult stages. To the O.C. for his unflagging personal interest, to the members of the Editorial Board who have given so freely of their time whenever called upon, and above all to my colleague, Mr. Staddon, who has so cheerfully shouldered the by no means small financial burden, necessary to put the "B.S.M." on its feet.   L.P.J.

xxxxxxxxxxxxxxxx

The growth of the "B.S.M." has been rapid, from a small paper, limited in size and production, to the familiar publication which is now so well known. Our first production figure was 50 (small size), this month we have had to produce 350 (double the size) in order to satisfy our reader's requirements. We are naturally, proud of this figure but it must be remembered that the "B.S.M." is not produced without a few headaches. We had not intended to stress the many difficulties of supplies these days, but the following inside information, may help you to understand why we are so insistent that readers should take up their specially printed copies, in spite of the fact that they may already have read someone elses copy.

On July 21st, we commenced negotiations to cover us for this production and over the next 4/5 months. No reply was received for some time, but after numerous communications, culminating in a telegram, we received confirmation on the 24th.Aug. An official order was immediately despatched, with the accompanying numerous certificates, but in spite of still further reminders, nothing had come to hand by Thursday the 24th. Sept. We then decided to buy a further stock to cover this issue, locally, and made a dash into Leicester, buying at advanced prices. That same afternoon the whole of our 10Gn. order arrived from London. Such are the joys of publishing!

We have been magnificently supported by our contributors during the past year and hope they will continue the good work. At the same time we should like to see this small circle widening. There are signs of this already. A special tribute should, we think, be paid to the Disciple, who preaches to us in such a polished style month after month. Thank you, "Mouse".

THIS IS YOUR MAGAZINE. WHY NOT TAKE UP THE PEN?   or what "Peacetime Job", "Reflection" have you?

A BIRTHDAY TRIBUTE (OR IS IT?).
Collected by F.Hearn.

The first anniversary of the "B.S.M."! The Editors deserve a bouquet at least, but I am not a fit person to hand them one.

I wonder what a few well-known writers would say about the magazine, if they were allowed to read the copies of the past year?. I have let my imagination roam, and this is what I think they would say. :-

BERNARD SHAW. "A magnificent example of the innate wit of the contemporary plebeian mass. I myself, wrote similar stuff at the age of thirteen, but then, am I not the G.B.S"

GODFREY WINN "The drawings are well executed, the articles superbly written, with a humour that is unmistakeably British. In fact, everything is blended judicially together, to make a fit magazine for a section of the community, who are really doing their bit for their country. It reminds me of the time when I was on the bridge of a destroyer which was on convoy duty. I said to the skipper, "You know, it is you and these tramp steamer fellows who are really winning this war. You chappies are an inspiration to the country", and he replied, "If those damned Jerries hit the Magazine we'll all be inspired..... in heaven."

SYDNEY HORLER "The whole thing is dynamic. Crisp action, suspense and racy dialogue, are all contained in this dramatic periodical".

H.G. WELLS. "An outpouring of a section of the community, which gives a true idea of the mentality of the people who are now trying to shape the things to come."

EDWARD LYND. "Reviewing periodicals is rather out of my sphere, but when I started to read the "B.S.M." I could not put it down, until I had finished. I was at once arrested by the beautiful simplicity of the writing. In these days of adjectives and more adjectives, it is a sublime pleasure to read a work that dispenses with a few of them. It is a periodical worthy of note, and should set an example to others in a similar vein. I have no hesitation in recommending this as something to read. If you cannot buy it, borrow it from your local library."

AN E.W.A. " (CENSORED) "

"**N E S S I E**".   from Montrose.

The Balmacaan Estate in Inverness, which comprises a large portion of Loch Ness and the whole of Glen Urquhart, has recently been sold. The Vale of Urquhart abounds in tradition from as far back as the Roman times. Ptolemy has it, that in his day, about A.D.120, the country of Urquhart was peopled by the Caledonii, who a century later, formed one of the tribes of the Pictii, a name dreaded during the later years of the Roman Occupation.

Beyond these records, we must rely on legend, such as the tradition that where the waters of Loch Ness are seen today, there was once a great Glen sheltered from every blast by high mountains clothed with trees and herbs of richest hues.

This vale was covered with verdant pasture over which roamed the flocks of the people, and through it flowed a majestic river in which was found every fish, good for the food of man.

There was a spring in this happy vale which was blessed by Daly the Druid, who enjoined that whenever the stone which protected its waters from pollution, was removed, it should be immediately replaced, or desolation would overtake the land.

The words of the Druid were remembered until one day, when drawing water, a woman who had left her child by the fireside was distracted by its cry and forgot, in her anxiety, to replace the stone. Immediately the waters rose and overflowed the Vale, and the people escaped to the mountains and filled the air with lamentation so that the rocks echoed back the cry - "Tha loch 'nis ann" ("There is a Loch now" - for the benefit of those not blessed with the Gaelic).

After the Romans, the records of Scottish history pass into an era of impenetrable mist, and then we find the Pictish King, Brude MacMailcon in sway. His Seat was on the banks of Loch Ness. To this Court came Saint Columba in 563 A.D.

The Saint's deeds at this Court made a great impression on the inhabitants of Urquhart, and on one occasion, according to Adaman in his Vita Sancti Columbae, the Holy Man, being obliged to cross the Ness, found a number of people burying a man who had just been killed by a Water Monster.

Nothing dismayed, he directed his companion, Lugne, to swim the stream. Lugne obeyed, but when half-way across, the Monster gave an "Awful Roar" and darted after him. Columba, observing this, raised his hand, while all the rest were stupified with terror, and forming the "Saving Sign", commanded the ferocious Monster not to touch the man or go further, but to return with all speed.

At the voice of the Saint, the Monster was terrified and, as the records have it, "fled more quickly than if he had been pulled by ropes".

Now, don't dismiss the Monster as a lot of pifflo. It is an actual fact that a "large sea monster, of irregular proportions, humped, with a long neck, a heavy mane and the head of a cow", was seen in the South Atlantic, by the Captain and members of the crew of the "Mauretania" and the fact was actually entered in the Ship's Log!

"Cabar Feidh".

COGS and COGITATIONS   by "Jone".

Well, we've never heard of this place Loughborough until old Larry tells us we are going there, and that is one year ago.
We came here in October and it's October again, and there are no Octobers in between, so that's a year isn't it? - If you can see what I mean.
So we are all coming down here from London, and I am sitting with my pal and old Freddy and Bill, too. There are some other oddments, but they are not sitting with us. We are debating the possibilities of Loughborough most of the way, and since Larry says to be ready to meet someone, we are wondering what we will get in the way of Civil Servants and their Regulations.
Well, we get out of the train at Loughborough, and at once we are caught in the dreadful cogs of Civil Service machinations. The chief cog is wearing a black hat, so I think at first that he is the chief cog of Woygland, who is down there to meet us and do us proud. Well, he says he isn't _that_ chief cog but that he is going to take us to see him, or at least to see the next biggest one. He has a couple of lesser cogs with him and he says he is going to take us straight to Woygland in this. So we all look for "this" and we see it is a lorry, that looks as if it might do anything but move. But he climbs into the back O.K., along with a smaller cog, and he says to us to climb in behind him. So we pile our whats and nots in, and ourselves as well, and my pal bangs the cog with his trousers-press, which he has done all up in brown paper, but it still hurts him a lot and nearly knocks his teeth out which cannot make him happy because I know it wouldn't me.
But we don't mind because we are feeling like a Sunday School treat grown up, except that we don't sing when we are driving through Loughborough, and we cannot even speak, because we are mighty surprised at what we see. Someone says that the "Oughborough" should be left out of the name, which expresses our feelings and nearly makes us laugh only we can't.
We are a bit cheered when we see a cinema, but someone sits on it by pointing out that "King Kong" is still running. But anyway we are at least close to civilisation and we are nearly happy again, and someone hums. So then we stop outside the place where all the big cogs live, although I am still trying to find out why we stopped, and after five-minutes of the view we are going on again, for miles and miles, until we arrive at Woygland. Well we see some of the mud and toil and tears, and we see some sweat too although it is wintertime; but they haven't got the fan yet, so that's why, I think.
(Contnd.)

"COGS and COGITATIONS" (Contnd.)

Well, then the big cog in a black hat says it's his job to take us all round to our digs, and we try not to look surprised and some sap says "Is it?", or he would have done only a stamp on his feet, which I couldn't miss anyway. Well first he shows us where to find Barkus, and then we get into "this" again and go back to "L" without "Oughborough".

Well we dump some chaps and then we stop at another house, and the big cog says "you" to me, and I say "me" to him and we settle that O.K. So then I get down and my whats and nots, with me underneath talk up a path, accompanied by a pink form and a small cog.

Well, this little cog bangs the door, and I think he makes a lot of noise for a little one, but it brings results, so it's alright with me. Well, then the door opens and I paste on my smile of welcome, but the door is not so pleased and she tells the cog that she can't feed me which is a bit thick, though when her mouth opens I see that she has no teeth, and I think maybe she doesnt feed and so she isn't expecting to feed anyone else. She says she can give me a bed, but the little cog says I cannot eat a bed and I agree, and they are arguing the merits of beds and watercress as staple diets, for about five minutes.

Well, finally, the little cog brings her round, by brute force and he goes down the path happily enough. Well the door says to come in then, so I say "Goodbye" to my pals because that's what it feels like, and I go in. Then the door says to come up stairs to the bedroom, so we go up and when we get there she opens a thing like a box and says that this is it. I say "what?", and she says "the bedroom". I say "Oh", and then the door says she can't get any food for me, but she's got some watercress and where on earth am I going to put my clothes?, and that's the bathroom and nearly blushes only wood can't and I'm on radio-location, aren't I?, and as for food................

So she has introduced me to herself, and shall I come down for tea because she has already mashed it but she's only got watercress. I look at her and I think she could mash things a lot stronger than weak tea, but I go down and the door's husband comes in. I think the door has probably mashed the husband a bit as well as the tea, because he hasn't got any teeth either, and I wonder what they would do if they had to go abroad and chew biltong or something; But the point does not arise because we are eating watercress anyway.

Well, I look out into the garden, and I ask the door if she keeps chickens. She says "No, why?", and I tell her because something has obviously been scratching there lately, and the husband unmashes for a bit and says "Heh!", which means that he thinks it's funny although the joke's on him because he did the scratching. But the door creaks, which shows that she is not amused, although the joke's not on her and I think she is jealous because she did not think of it first.

So then I finish my watercress and mosey down to the "town", where I meet my pals and we discover the "Empire" and Michael that's gone away gets excited about some girls, which is silly, because he cannot afford to take them out. My pal is playing chess which is a dopey thing to do anywhere, and hopelessly insane in Loughborough, and the "Empire" in particular. (Concluded at foot of page 9).

A LAMENT by "Freelance".

Oh! where, Oh! where can our runner be
Oh! where, Oh! where has she gone
I sent her over to visit hut "C"
So expect she'll be gone for long.

I miss her form, I miss her face
I miss her glances admiring
As she sits and watches me at my desk
When to be a 'Big Shot' I'm aspiring.

How can she treat me in this way
My work's all going to pot
What have they over there in hut "C"
That us poor fellows have not.

Dear little runner be good to me
Else in anguish I'll ask for a shift
Although we've run right out of clips
Please don't let us come adrift.

I tried to find her by telephone
But then I became quite enraged
For a gloating voice floated over the line
I'm sorry old man, she's "engaged".

Oh! how I miss my runner dear
I miss her pattering feet
My chances are spoilt by those in hut "C"
At Chatham, the snag was the FLEET.

HELP US HARVEST! from "Anon".

Here's a tale I will unfold
About some Woygites very bold,
Who ventured out in wind and rain
To help the farmers harvest grain.

A plucky spirit you'll admit
Possessed these lads to do their bit,
Who after working six to two
Went searching for more work to do.

SO ALL YOU CHAPS WITH TIME TO SPARE
COME OUT INTO THE OPEN AIR,

Into the fields they were sent
And to the task their bodies bent,
From 4 to 8, they would "stook"
At first, success was just a "fluke"

But soon these lads became expert
To get more work was now a "cert"
From far and wide, voices call
"Help us harvest, before fall".

TO THE FIELDS OF GODS CREATION
TO HELP UPKEEP THE BRITISH
                    NATION.

G O S S I P.

CONGRATULATIONS:- To the undermentioned, whose engagements have been announced since our last issue.
   Cpl. Gladys Webb...to Armament Qtr.Mstr.Sgt. E.J. Earle of R.A.O.C.
   Pte. Mary Pearce...to Cpl. H.W. Jackson.
Other engagements are, Pte. Lily Minto - Pte. Doreen Sills - Pte. Audrey Warren and Pte. "Vicky" Hunt. We have been unable to ascertain any information regarding the fortunate gentlemen concerned with this attractive bunch, but extend congrats. to the lucky unknowns.
   Congratulations to Mr. & Mrs. D.A. Kirkby on the arrival of a son and heir, (Christopher John), on Tuesday, August 25th.
WORTHY OF MENTION, is the celebration held on Sept.10th., at The Bell Hotel, Leicester (dinner), of the 4 Sergeants, C.S.M. Bunyard, Sgts. Thorp, Browne and Jones, the 4 Maidstone girls who worked together, joined-up together, and descended on Chatham together, 3 years ago. Some record! and still going strong.
   A DISCOVERY. We noted with pleasure, the inclusion of a charming vocalist, A.T.S. Margaret Lindbury, with the Exiles band on Sept.8th. We hope to hear more of this tuneful lady, whom, we understand, has appeared at the Coconut Grove, (London) and with Jack Jackson. The footlights temporary loss, should be the Exiles gain.
SPORTS GENERAL MEETING. It is not true that Mr. Appleton had to co-opt the Town Hall doorkeeper, in order to have his proposals seconded. FOOTBALL BOOTS. We understand that a number of people have stolen, or refused to pay for pairs of "non-coupon, subsidised", (did you ever hear of such a thing), football boots. Our sentiments are, that we hope these "gentlemen" manage to secure plenty of games this season, and that in the process, these ill-gotten boots will cripple them.
   BATHS. Certain high personages are restricting their number of baths, and adhering to the 5" plimsoll line,in accordance with the National Fuel Campaign. Whilst searching for the soap in our hip-bath, we feel neither joy nor gratitude at this information, but, on the contrary, would have been highly indignant had this not been the case. Surely there is hardly a more social leveller than the bath!
NOTICE SEEN IN A WAR OFFICE ESTABLISHMENT "Is your conversation really necessary?" Things to come?, "Must you breathe?". Thank God, for a sense of humour.
   NORTHERN COMMAND A.T.S. ORDER to the affect that A.T.S. must not walk arm in arm with male escorts.
   O discipline! what sort of vagaries are touched with thy name, that thou should arm in arm with true hypocrisy, while martyrdom awaits the Providential hour - (Eternity).
FOR SALE   COMPLETE SET SUPERVISORS' AUTOGRAPHS (ALL GENUINE)
            OR WOULD EXCHANGE FOR BOX OF THROAT PASTILLES
            OR RELIABLE PENCIL-SHARPENER.   APPLY BOX 56.
   OUR DUMB BLONDE (just makes it)   Signalling to Sup. "Look, I've got the whole of Monday Night at Eight".
                         ooooooooooo
                         ooooooooooo (Doodler!)
Keep your Gossip writer advised of your (or your friend's) escapades. No births or engagements recognised, unless reported to your favourite columnist..   YOU MAKE IT, I'LL WRITE IT.

CHOIR

The Choir commences its second season with a SOCIAL on FRIDAY, OCTOBER 9th, at 7.0 pm, in the CHURCH ROOM, QUORN, to which everybody interested is invited, whether a present or prospective member of the Choir or not.

The Social will be an informal affair and we hope that it will provide the opportunity for many new members to enlist. We shall be particularly glad to number A.T.S. Wops among our ranks, as well as newcomers drawn from the A.T.S. staff and from the male element.

We had many enjoyable practices last season and we discovered that there is surprisingly good fun to be had by more or less inexperienced singers practising carefully a simple part-song, or singing, perhaps rather less carefully but with considerable gusto, such songs as "John Brown's Body" and "Clementine". We also proved that the possession of a good solo voice is by no means necessary for enjoyable participation, while we have always borne in mind the fact that not all of us can read music with facility.

Our attempts to obtain new members have frequently been met with such replies as "Oh, I sing only in my bath", or "I sing only for my own amusement; nobody else could possibly be amused". These excuses are really not valid; indeed, they even serve to prove that you should in fact join us, since you admit that you can and do sing, albeit perhaps imperfectly! Practice, after all, makes perfect.

We haven't the slightest intention of confronting new members with the terror of an audition, and we therefore submit that you have every possible encouragement to join. So come along on October 9th for an evening's entertainment and prove our claims for yourself.

The first practice of the new season will be held on Monday, October 12th, at 6.0 pm, in the Church Room, Quorn, and we propose to commence proceedings then with a "General Meeting", for the purpose of electing a new committee and for approving the general plans for the coming season.

Don't forget, then, to book this date:

FRIDAY, OCTOBER 9th, 7-11 pm.

QUORN CHURCH ROOM
(opposite the new Bull's Head Hotel)

Dancing,   Games,   Community Singing,   Entertainments.

No charge for admission.   Light refreshments at usual charges.

MY PEACETIME JOB NR 7 — SELLING TRANSPORT
BY W GORDON

A whistle is heard in the distance and there is sudden activity by staff and passengers alike, as in a few minutes the important Night Express, "The Aberdonian", draws into a Main Line station of the L.N.E.Rlwy., on the commencement of its journey to London.

In my capacity of Chief Passenger Traffic Clerk, at this particular station, I was connected with this, and other famous trains, for many years. My duties were many. I was responsible for the correct and efficient collection, despatch and delivery of all classes of traffic handled by the passenger dept, for arranging supplies of passenger rolling stock to the various stations in our Control area, such as Sleeping Cars, Diners, Luggage Vans, Horse Boxes etc. Other duties comprised the supervision of the Telegraph Dept., Cloak Room, Lost Property, these being a few of the many indispensable units.

During our peak seasons we have passed through our hands, in one day, anything from 15 to 20 thousand Baskets of Fruit, 6 to 10 tons Salmon, Horses, Corpses, tons of luggage, parcels, mail bags, and other small consignments, and you can see that myself and staff were kept with our noses to the grindstone.

We will take the "Aberdonian" as an example. This train was one of our heaviest and carried traffic consigned to all over South of England and France. At 6.p.m. traffic would commence to be marshalled for this train, and up to time of departure, 7.30 p.m., the office would be a hive of activity, with arranging Sleeper and Seat accomodation, waybilling of traffic, registration of baggage for the Continent, and despatch of telegrams to the various stations, arranging for a quick delivery of the perishable traffic, to be in time for the first early morning markets.

Another side was the accounting work, balances to be struck, dozens of books to be entered up, claims and letters to be attended to, public complaints to be settled, wages paybills to be made up and other little duties that go to the efficient and smooth working of the passenger department.

The work is varied and interesting requiring a knowledge of British Geography, Mileage Distances, Engine and Vehicle capacities, Market Times and Tact when dealing with the public. I have been with the industry for 24 years, passing through all the stages and departments, until now I specialise in the Traffic and Control side of the Passenger Dept., in which I take a great pride and pleasure.

So friends, if ever you wish to travel in my area after the war, look me up, you can rest assured my services will be at your disposal for your comfort in travelling by L.N.E.R.

"IS YOUR JOURNEY REALLY NECESSARY?"

AN APPRECIATION
by Ollie Pearce.

Time slips away, it's just a year
Since first we ventured to appear,
Recording for posterity
Events at W-O-Y-G,
And striving month by month to fill
Each page with samples of our skill
Which should, I'm sure, convince all men,
The sword is mightier than the pen.

Scanning these efforts, it would seem
That articles upon the theme
Of our pet grievances and such,
Though gilded with a humorous touch,
Remain predominating features,
Revealing us as selfish creatures,
Whilst if we only look around,
Our blessings virtually abound.

Remember, when you're feeling hateful
These reasons why you should be grateful:-
The canteen spoon, though hitherto
Exclusive to the chosen few,
Is not impossible to lure,
Even by members most obscure,
From its enshrouding cotton wool,
For Barbara is most bountiful.

And when you feel inclined to swear
Because at break you had no chair,
A chair-less break you must agree
Is just ideal for you and me,
A very thoughtful innovation,
Affording well earned relaxation
To the part which does most work,
Whilst behind our box we lurk.

And though your watch could but attend
One dance in five, you may depend
Those dates were given contemplation,
And fixed with due consideration
For your health, and to allay
Your fears of being late next day.

These instances are but a few,
Intended merely as a cue,
I could write on for evermore
Of things we should be thankful for,
This proves a point which needs no stressing,
The paper shortage is a blessing.

TEN LITTLE WOPSIES.

by "Tim".

Ten little Wopsies, noses all ashine
The C.O. sent for one of them
And then there were NINE.

Nine little Wopsies, got up rather late
One went and missed the 'bus
And then there were EIGHT.

Eight little Wopsies, one seated at "eleven"
Got caught playing battleships
And then there were SEVEN.

Seven little Wopsies, one was full of tricks
Doodled on her writing pad
And then there were SIX.

Six little Wopsies, only half alive
One overstayed her break
And then there were FIVE.

Five little Wopsies, their food is very poor
One ate her breakfast
And then there were FOUR.

Four little Wopsies, hoping to be free
One stayed out all night
And then there were THREE.

Three little Wopsies, feeling rather blue
One got psycho analysed
And then there were TWO.

Two little Wopsies, pretty nearly done
One completely lost her grip
And then there was ONE.

One little Wopsy, having all the fun
Vows she'll never leave us
TILL VICTORY IS WON.

---

from A.E.J.C.

The valley is quiet now:
Blue smoke curls towards the sky;
Only the blackened rafters,
And the child sleeping in the sun –
Dead before his course had run –
Show the invader halted there,
And passed by.

HEARD COLOGNE'S FIRST SIREN
SAYS RALPH CHAMPION

"Thousand RAF bombers blitz Cologne". That was the inspiring news flash we read in 1942.

Yet it was as long ago as six years that I heard the first air raid warnings wailing in Cologne. Their deafening clamour greeted me as my train, punctual to the minute, steamed into the City's magnificent, Cathedral-like station, on a dark September night in 1936.

My mouth felt unaccountably dry as with the eerie clamour continuing, I wandered through strangely deserted and blacked-out streets to the small hotel where I was to stay. I could not understand. It flashed across my mind that possibly a giant organ in the Cathedral had gone wrong and that all the pipes were blaring in a frightful cacophony. It was some time later before I realised the truth.

Yet what I had seen earlier in my stay in other parts of Germany, should have prepared me. On all sides, there had been frantic activity of a directly military character, or on civil works which could be adapted readily for war.

Even in the gay, friendly vineyard villages where they were celebrating the harvest with wine festivals, the preparations went on unobtrusively. English visitors who had linked arms with their German hosts and danced through the village streets, returned some nights to find the houses where they stayed, darkened by black curtains. Men in sinister grey uniforms entered brusquely to see that buckets of water and sand bags were ready. When war began we treated A.R.P. rather derisively in England. In 1936 Germany, it would have been foolhardy to joke.

At my hotel, I found the lift not working. I asked why. The hall porter looked embarrassed. "Not till it's over", he replied enigmatically, and walked off to avoid further questions. Waiters were distinctly sheepish as they served my roast chicken, salad and sauerkraut, and poured my Hock. For, though the sirens were at long-last silent, outside the blacked-out windows I could hear the marching of jack-booted soldiers, and guttural shouts of command.

Next night I returned to the hotel from the Kaiserhof music hall where bright lights, dancing and generous supplies of beer, had put war preparations far from mind. Climbing into the deep feather bed, I pulled the eiderdown, like a domestic barrage balloon, on top of me.

Then, again - the sirens! Lights were extinguished, I heard waiters running and chamber-maids whispering excitedly outside, the deserted streets echoed again to the marching of soldiers.

As I paid my bill next day, I asked the cashier to explain. He peered cautiously over his shoulder. Then he whispered: "The hooters are to warn us when the French bombers come over. England will always be our friend".

"GIVE WAY TOGETHER!"

"Snikmot"

Simultaneously with the report of the starting gun, the racing whaler's crew stand to their oars, and give six strong, swift, strokes the impetus of which, almost throws me backwards over the stern. I cling to the tiller, and as the six strokes finish, the crew resume their seats, and I take up the count. One! Two! - One! Two! Somewhat fast at first, as I am anxious to maintain the lead we have acquired by our flying start.

Some distance astern on the starboard quarter, I can hear the deep throated voice of the coxswain of the Impregnable's racing whaler, exhorting his crew to more powerful, if slower strokes. They are the favourite for this race, having by far the fastest whaler in the Fleet, and at the same time, having the crew that won the race in last years regatta. We, on the other hand have never rowed as a crew in a race before. Though for some months past, we have been out every evening going over the course with a stop watch, until now, we are certain, that, barring accidents, we shall beat the Impregnables crew by four seconds, on their last years time. If, however, they have decreased this time, then the battle is to the strongest, and I for one, will see my boats crew dead, before we yield a foot of our present lead.

Such are the thoughts that course through my mind, as my body sways in harmony with the rhythmic motion of the oarsmen. The whaler is riding through the water as though towed by some gigantic Gulliver. The sea is calm, and save for the swirling whirlpools that synchronously appear, as the oars dip simultaneously into its blue smooth surface, the white wake flows swiftly from the clean cut bows, and goes eddying round the stern in one continuous, and swift flowing line.

All this I notice as we approach the half way buoy. The stroke is lying well back on his oar, and the remainder of the crew, copy his movement in such detail, that it would appear that they move up and down, controlled by some connecting rod, rather than by their own volition.

I take a swift glance at the Impregnable. She is still astern, though I fancy from the intonation, that the coxswain has increased the number of strokes, and, what is more alarming they seem to be moving faster than we are. I bend nearer the stroke, lowering my voice, and quickening the count. "One! Two! One! Two!"

My voice is urgent. We must go faster. The stroke responds. The veins on his neck stand out like whipcord. The skin is drawn tight over the rapidly responding and relaxing muscles of his arms. His breath comes in sharp bursts, that seem to explode from within him, and the sweat runs down his face and neck, in a never ending stream. One! Two! One! Two!

(Contnd.)

"GIVE WAY TOGETHER!" (Contnd.)

I take another backward glance. The Impregnable's whaler is almost on us. I can hear the grunts from its labouring crew, while the voice of the coxswain, rings like a death knell in my ears. I raise my voice almost to a frenzy. "Faster faster, One! Two! One! Two!.., and for a few minutes, we seem to hold them. Neck and neck, the two whalers seem to fill the entire ocean. The screeching of the rowlocks, the grunts of the crews, and the cries of the coxswains, fill the air. The pace is terrific.

Then in a split second it happens. Our whaler gives a jar, that shakes her from stem to stern, as number 2's oar drops from his nerveless fingers, and disappears under the stern. His hands clutch frantically at his stomach. His face is white. His body convulses, and blood shoots from his mouth in torrents.

"Away enough!" I cry, and as the stroke comes back on his oar, number 2 collapses. All is confusion. As I drop the tiller the crew turn in wonderment and horror, to see what has befallen. Number 2 lies in the bottom of the whaler, groaning in agony, his white face bathed in sweat, his head lolling on one side, and his vacant eyes, staring into nothing. Meanwhile the other whalers sail past, their coxswains turning to stare at the tragedy. While from the Flagship, some hundred yards distant, I can hear the hubbub of speculation, from the spectators lining the upper deck.

Sadly I resume the tiller, and as I give the order, "Give way together!", I set course for the Flagship's gangway. As I approach, the Quartermaster hails me, and I reply, asking for the Doctor. Already the sideboy is running, and as I come alongside, he returns, carrying a small medical bag, and preceded by a Surgeon Cdr., hatless, and with a stethoscope dangling from his fingers. With swift step the Doctor descends the gangway, and into the whaler. Number 2 is still doubled up in the bottom, but he seems conscious, while from the guard rail of the Flagship tense faces peer down at the drama enacted below.

The Surgeon Cdr. crosses over to Number 2. Number 2 looks rather sheepish, though still very white, the Doctor lifts his eyelid, and gazes into it, then siezing Number 2's singlet, he examines it intently. For the first time I notice the blood on it, seems peculiar.

Straightening his back, the Surgeon Cdr. looks down at Number 2, "What was your last meal, before the race?", he enquires. Number 2 lowers his eyes, and upon my astounded ears falls the answer. "TOMATOES, sir!"

"COGS and COGITATIONS" (Concluded).

I am fed up to the few back tooth I have left, already, and I decide that I dislike cogs and doors and watercress, and "L" without "Oughborough", and I can't stick this 'till the end of the war. But a year of it has gone during which, the door practises mashing on me and the coffee nearly poisons me and I am nearly driven mad in the temples of Woyg, and I have to do "Rotate" too. But I am still here alive, and, once in a while I manage a feeble kick.

REFLECTION No 3

MY TAKING WAYS!

by F C STADDON

I own an 18 footer, and around my little auxiliary ketch, "Cygnet II", Naval Control permit No.3CB (now withdrawn), occurred one of my most expensively amusing episodes, on which I often reflect.

My moorings are on the Middlesex side of Eel Pie Island (a place with an unjustifiably naughty reputation) at Twickenham, which is a delightful spot at the extreme tidal end of the Thames, just before the river comes under the authority of the Thames Conservancy Board, at Teddington.

I was on 7 days leave, and naturally, availed myself of the opportunity to spend a few days cruising up and down the very restricted war-time area, in company with my youngest brother, (you heard), Dennis, aged 14.

Whilst pottering around one day, I chanced to investigate a wreck of a cabin cruiser, which to my certain knowledge had been derelict, submerged with each tide and generally wastefully breaking up over a period of 2 years. I was at this time on the look out for a petrol tank, and indeed to goodness, look you, there it was, a petrol tank, mildewy, full of the famous Thames mud and slime, but nevertheless, a petrol tank.

I endeavour to be logical in my outlook, and basing my action on the fact that the wreck had been there for 2 years, the petrol tank was simply wasting away, I unscrewed the tank without one word of reproach being uttered by my young brother. Then without any shadow of furtiveness, I rowed back to my boat and left the very dirty tank in the open cockpit, for all to see.

By this time the inner man was calling, and I crawled into the small cabin in order to attend to the important business of tea, not a care in the world and my portable wireless playing (I think it must have been, "You started something"). Suddenly I felt a bump on the starboard bow, and dashed into the cockpit with a "mind my paint" look on my face, and behold the arm of the law sitting in a leaky dinghy, with what appeared to be one of the dead end kids. At this stage, the following conversation ensued:-

    A.O.L. "Does that tank belong to you?".
    Me. "No, but I've just taken it off that old wreck".
    A.O.L. "Well, it belongs to this gentleman".
    Me. "(turning to apparent D.E.K.) I'm awfully sorry old man, I'll put it back at once".
    A.O.L. "I'm afraid you can't do that, he insists on charging you".
    Me. "Oh! Well look, you go back to the embankment, I'll lock my boat up safely, and then I'll come across. (Contnd:)

"REFLECTION" (Contnd.)

A.O.L. "I'm sorry, you can't do that, you're under arrest".
Me. "Okeydoke. Come on Dennis".
    I must say the law was awfully nice to me, agreed that it was a stupid mistake, but as the apparent D.E.K. insisted on going through with it, he had no option. He would however, not suffer me to undergo the indignity of being marched through the streets, but would ring for the Black Maria. This duly arrived, and as Dennis and I entered, I remarked to the law, "It's foolish, but it's fun", then we started on the 5 minute ride to the station.
    On arrival, the charge was read over to me with the rider, that "anything I said, would be taken down in evidence against me". I endeavoured to explain the difference between a motor launch and a wreck, but did not seem to make any headway. I was then asked to empty my pockets, and naturally, being in a police station, kept a very careful eye on the cash part of the collection. My young brother also did likewise, and was told "allright Dennis, you can put your 3d back".
    After a little confusion, caused by the fact that my young brother had left his identity card at home, and that I was arrested aboard my boat at Twickenham, gave my home address as London, showed them a Chatham pass, and said I was billeted at Shefford, I was informed that whilst they would not insist on it, they could ask to take my finger prints. I replied that as far as I was concerned, they could add my prints to their collection, (I wanted to see how they did this). This willingness to co-operate however, appeared to upset their system, and the subject was dropped. During this station interlude, various people kept dashing in and out, and invariably siezed on the apparent D.E.K. as the guilty party, which, I found most gratifying. One plain clothes man however, sidled up to me and said, "I'm a C.I.D. man". I felt like replying, "I'm an E.W.A", but merely shrugged my shoulders and said, "As far as I'm concerned, the whole thing is a stupid mistake and damned funny". I must have convinced him, because he said, "I won't bother you any more", and went off stage. The sergeant then told me that they had the power to detain me overnight, but consented to my departure on the following terms:-
"Frederick Cyril Staddon. You are hereby bound over in the sum of £5.0.0. to appear at the......Police Court.......at 10.30 a.m., Wednesday, 6th.August,1941, to answer the charge of larceny".
                                                                Inspr.

A similar billet-doux was issued in respect of Dennis.
    Why do they put these Police Courts in the most outlandish places?. Allowing as I thought ample time, the seat of "justice" was not reached until 11.0 a.m. I have on occasions had small boys waiting for my autograph at stage doors, but this was something bigger, a whole Court room literally on their toes, waiting for me. Yes, I was pleased with my entrance, it had been rehearsed well, with just the right touch of nonchalance, but somehow the magistrate did not appear to be entering into the spirit of the occasion.
                                                                          (Contnd).

"REFLECTION" (Contnd). I was escorted into the box, and the following repartee ensued, enlivened by the fact that the magistrate used the age old dodge of most slow thinking people, in asking you to repeat what you have just said, in order to give them time to think. I replied in kind, and am convinced that we had a mutual feeling of keen dislike.

I was then formally charged with removing a petrol tank, valued 30/-d. from a Motor Launch etc. and was given the option of pleading guilty, or not guilty. This vision of a Sopwith yacht was too much for me, and I replied, that I was prepared to plead guilty to taking an abandoned tank, value nil whilst on the wreck, and now of very doubtful value, from a wreck laying alongside the Island. I had never played this game before, but apparently this was cheating, and I was requested to plead guilty, or not guilty. Realising that on purely technical grounds, I had committed theft, I replied, I must confess in a very offhand manner, "O.K. guilty!" I was then asked if I had anything to say about it. I said, "yes, the charge was wrongly worded, that the tank was valueless whilst on the wreck, and had been rotting for two years, and even now I questioned the value of 30/-d. placed on it. Also, as I understood it, a Motor Launch was a vessel that could be propelled along by a motor, but this wreck could not have been shifted by anything (short of a crane). These finer points did not interest the Bench, who had quite definitely written me off as a complete scoundrel, from whose clutches, no petrol tank was safe.

My brother was next charged as an accessary, and in accordance with rehearsals, pleaded not guilty. As he had admitted to the police that he was with me at the time, the Bench decided that he was nevertheless an accessary. I protested, and endeavoured to explain that he was most decidedly not guilty, he merely happened to be with me at the time, and if he had objected to my taking the tank, would probably have felt my brotherly hand on his pants. The Bench, however, confirmed the saying, "The law is an ass", by ignoring this logic and saying that he was nevertheless an accessary.

The D.E.K. next appeared, and proceeded to say his party piece, "It was like this ere, I was working on my boat sort a peaceful like when I eres scraping on the shingle. I looks over the side, and spots a couple of luvvers in a canoe, but I don't take any notice like, I pops back and minds me own business. The Bench; "That's quite enough of that". The D.E.K. then proceeded to tell the Bench that he heard voices later on, and saw "Al Capone" and "Lefty" removing the tank from the "Daisy". He watched this intrepid piece of smash and grab, saw the gangsters row off in a dinghy marked, "Tender to Cygnet II", then went for the police.

The Bench then addressed me with words of wisdom. I had done a very foolish thing. I agreed. But, not only had I stolen this magnificent petrol tank, I had also taught my young brother to take things. I felt an utter cad. My young brother would have the charge against him dismissed. AND YOU SIR! YOU WILL BE FINED 40/-d.

I heard later from the local police, with whom, by now, I was on very good terms, that the D.E.K. had served a 6 months sentence fairly recently, for stealing from boats. I do however, still consider the 40/-d. well spent. That court room scene beat anything that Mr. Muddlecombe, J.P., has yet produced.

N.B. I have a receipt for 40/-d. as a memento. (YOU HAVE BEEN WARNED!)

CHAPTER XIV

The tribe of Atsites and their divers families. A dearth of handmaidens. The Manorites and the Fearonites. Scribes put on fine raiment and remove their beards. Scribes and Atsites go places.

Now IN THE DAYS of their exile the Woygites perceived that a new tribe were come among them. And these were the Atsites, a warlike people, with long hair, and war-paint, and enamel mugs.

And there were divers families among the Atsites. For in the beginning there was the Tepee. And when the Quarter Blokess conceived that she was possessed of sundry pairs of Slacks, and because there was an abundance of war-paint in the land, she summoned more Atsites, and called them Runners. And they set up a tabernacle and called it Butiparlor.

Now there was a great dearth of handmaidens in the land of Woyg, and accordingly the Trowites, who dwelled in a far off and distant land, journeyed up through the wilderness, and came nigh unto the fair city of Luff and tarried awhile, and were henceforth called Fearonites. And when they had learned that Woyg was a land flowing with beer and skittles they came

THE CHRONICLES OF ST. UPID

hence and entered into the temples, and their name was Manorites. And they found no beer, yet was there an abundance of Ops, and the skittles were gone forth for salvage.

Now the Manorites pitched their tents by the House of Wood, and journeyed into Woyg upon Shanks', and the Fearonites dwelled in Kwarn which is beside the caravan trail into Luff. But when the sisters and wives of Red Tabz, which ruleth over all the Atsites from afar, heard of these things they were gravely displeased, and cried out, saying: Woe is us. For as a metter of fect, we ectually don't use enough Juice. And they forthwith commanded the Manorites and the Fearonites to change places. And it was so. And because the Manorites now took unto themselves a caravan, and the journey of the Fearonites caravan was become greater, an abundance of Juice was consumed. And the sisters and wives of Red Tabz were exceeding glad in their hearts, and straightway bought another roll of Red Tape.

And the Atsites grew and multiplied, and waxed exceeding strong in their numbers. And it came to pass that many of the Scribes took unto themselves handmaidens, which were called Nice Bits of Homework. And those Scribes which sought favour in the eyes of the Atsites attired themselves in fine raiment, and put a crease upon their slacks, and removed their beards daily. And henceforth when they were provoked to anger within the temples they forsook their familiar curses, saying instead: Verily is this a nuisance, and: Bless my soul; and: Tut; and: Flick; and: Blow. And the air which was blue became sanctified.

And the Scribes went forth in the land with their handmaidens, and knocked Ell out of a tennis ball. And others took their handmaidens into the Palaces of Dark, to behold Greta, and Robert the Tailor. Yea, this was the General Idea; but they beheld them not, for they gazed only upon one another and were become exceeding Goofy. And because oftimes the war-paint upon the handmaidens was become curiously transferred unto the countenance of the Scribes, the rulers of the Palaces of Dark commanded that the light of the candles therein be lessened, lest the Luffites and others beheld the war-paint upon the Scribes and mocked them.

CHAPTER XV

The Prophet commandeth: Six weeks shalt thou labour. Punishment of the seventh day. The pilgrimage. Adewo hath a grievous cramp. Scribes look in the Book of Words.

Now IN THE BEGINNING the Prophet Osee appeared before the multitude and spake unto them in this wise, saying: Six weeks shalt thou labour, and do all thou hast to do, and upon the seventh thou shalt rotate. And when thou rotateth thou shalt be blessed with a week-end of exceeding great length, and verily, verily I say unto thee, thou wilt sorely need it. Five days shalt thou labour, but in them thou shalt do six days' toil, so that thou knoweth not whether thou cometh or goeth, nor whether thou art boiled, scrambled or poached.

And it was so for many moons, even after the Tribe were sent into exile in Bedz, and were wrongly delivered, and came up into the Promised Land.

And upon the seventh week called Rotate, the Scribes dwelt in the temples, except when their fish-payst tins were become empty, when they hastened to their Bilits, and crying unto the Lady of the Land: Refill, were revictualled, and returned from whence they came, and put their snouts again upon the grindstone.

And the rest of the Scribes laboured six days, for the seventh day was called Dayorf, and they were not permitted to enter the temples.

Now it came to pass when the Tribe came up into the Promised Land that the Prophet suffered many of the Scribes to visit the temples daily, and the punishment of Dayorf was lifted from upon them. And those which desired to preserve their souls continued to labour six days, and those who wished to give more alms to Inlan Revnew laboured seven days, and rotated not. And the Scribes who were blessed with a week-end went forth along the Iron Road upon a pilgrimage to Saint Pank and divers other places where there are no Skeds, and where Light Blue still meaneth a colour which is fair to look upon.

And in the course of time the Rotatites conceived that they could increase their Week-end, and this was the Swap. And Adewo who sitteth upon the right hand of Osee wore out

C

sundry fountain pens putting his name upon a multitude of Chitties. And accordingly the Prophet made another ordinance and coming before the brethren said unto them: Get a load of this: Hitherto all ye who rotateth hath done six labours in five days. Now, inasmuch as Adewo is afflicted with a grievous cramp, ye shall do them in four days, and whatsoever remaineth of ye on the morning of the fifth day shall go forth upon a pilgrimage.

And it was so. And when the Scribes had heeded this they went and looked in the Book of Words, and beheld there writ: Rotate meaneth: To spin, and to whirl, and to gyrate. And they lifted up their voices, crying: Verily dost thou know something, O Nuttall, for thou has truly slobbered a bib-full.

CHAPTER XVI

The sun vanisheth. The Great Voice bringeth glad tidings. Rom speaketh and biddeth soldier's farewell to Itis. Tinkles throughout the land. Iankis cast out the devil. Jo is almost pleased. The peoples reason and rejoice.

Now IT WAS THE TIME when there was no sun in the heavens. And there was no room within the cycle racks. And there was November. Yet, despite these things the hearts of all Brittites were lifted up in rejoicing, for the Great Voice called Bebesee had brought them glad tidings. And here was the Tidings for today, and this was Stuart Hibberd tiding it. For behold, the King's soldiers which were in a far off and distant land called Egg-wiped had triumphed. And Bebesee spake thus:

The King's soldiers with all their chariots and horses, under the centurions Alex and Mont, have reaped the fields of mines, and are retreating unto Lib. And the mighty and victorious hosts of Itla advanceth away from them. Now did not Rom, head over all the Hunnites and Itis speak in this wise: I come not to Alamein to beat it from hence. Thus reasoneth he: When I am prepared I shall wipe up Egg-wiped. But it is written: he hath another think which cometh. For the Brittites are armed with 25-pounder slings and a mighty array of weighty weapons, and their birdmen layeth

GLAD TIDINGS FROM EGG-WIPED

an abundance of eggs; and Rom and his hosts are afflicted with grievous headaches. And behold, Rom speaketh a soldier's farewell unto his comrades the Itis, and grabbeth all their chariots, and hasteneth away.

Now whereas the mighty Hunnites did in days past take Tobruk and Matruh, they now showeth signs of having taken Cascara. Likewise have they taken Fright, and To Their Heels.

And Jurjil commanded: Let there be tinkles throughout the land. And it was so. And be it known that the tinkles were exceeding soothing unto the Scribes which had done Nytz and were afflicted with a Quick Changeover.

And it came to pass that the winter pilgrimage to Benghazi began. For every year the Brittites come unto Benghazi as pilgrims, but this time they cometh betimes, and intendeth to tarry long days in the land.

And about this time the Iankis, who were comrades of the Brittites since they cast out the devil called Splendid Isolation at the Harbour of Pearls, came in the Back Door of Afrik in countless legions. And Itla was dismayed, and forthwith commanded that Pet and Lav who licketh his sandals, be also dismayed. And it was so. For Pet and Lav were Frogs, and the lands of Afrik, wherein came the Iankis, belongeth unto the Ruler of the Frogs. And Itla sendeth his birdmen to Afrik, and likewise disposeth of many superfluous Itis. But the Iankis marched towards them, and made ready to give unto them De Woiks.

And Jo, who dwelleth in Kremlin, was almost pleased, and knocking back a vodka, he saith: Inasmuch as we desireth a Second Front in Urop, thy effort in Afrik is exceeding good. And he commandeth: Up Reds, and at 'em. And it was so.

And in all the lands where the peoples were yet suffered to think for themselves there was great rejoicing. And they reasoneth among themselves in this wise: For whereas we have had Dunkirks, and Cretes, and a Harbour of Pearls, it did seem that the fight must endure for ever. But yet now that we getteth cracking, we perceiveth the wisdom of Chamb. For notwithstanding we groweth not younger day by day, even yet there may be Peace in our Time.

"B.S.M." JANUARY, 1943.
Vol.2   No.4.

General Editor:- L.P.Jones.   Editorial Board:-
                                R.Wilkinson.   R.G.Denny.
Editor:-   F.C.Staddon.   E.Millhouse.   T.Prister.

Next publication 26th.Feb.   Contributions by 10th.Feb.

FRONT COVER DESIGN by R.Wilkinson.

    This month we say "Au Revoir" to two of our colleagues on the Editorial Board. We thank Messrs. Carr & Wade for their past co-operation and assistance, and wish them well in their new sphere.
    Congratulations are also due to E.Millhouse, better known to you all as "St.Upid". His worth has been recognised by "London Opinion", who have merely confirmed "Beaumanor Opinion". More power to your pen, Mouse.
    Also in line for good wishes, is F.C.Staddon (our Financial Pillar), on his engagement to Kay (L/Cpl.Metcalfe). We feel that following on her article of last month, she thought, "well here goes, I will put my ideas into practice". No offence pals.
    This Editorial seems to consist of nothing else but boquets for members of our Editorial Board, but such is fame.
    What is the matter with you all, have you gone coy and bashful, or is it that all those people with respectable "Peace Time Jobs", have contributed to the series, and the remainder dare not let daylight in on their past.
    25 people failed to take up their copies last month. Perhaps they think it is not worth reading, but they might have the decency to cancel their order in a straightforward manner. They have had their last chance, in future they will not have the pleasure of leaving their copies on the canteen counter, unpaid for. In this instance, the 25 copies represented an actual outlay of 6/3d, and leaves a debit of this amount to the "B.S.M." accounts. This could have been avoided by straight dealing.
    The Canteen General Meeting is due next Thursday,(4th.Feb.), step right up critics and justify yourselves. Otherwise, henceforth temper your criticism with caution. To the present Committee, we say thank you for your past efforts, and to their successors, remember one thing, "actions speak louder than words".
    Your General Editor, having in common with most, seen his Income Tax assessment form, happened on a visit to a Loughborough office, to note on the Income Tax Officer's door, "PLEASE WALK IN". This was an occasion when the slogan, "Is your journey really necessary", seemed to have something.

oooooooooooooooooooooo

MAY I PRESUME?

There appeared in last months' magazine, an article written by a most luscious member of the opposite sex who called herself Auntie Kay.

Equal rights for women, bah! that's what comes about by giving them too much rope, the plague of every mans life. Who is it that is at the root of all trouble?. Why, women.

Man has been cursed by this creature ever since the days of the Garden of Eden. Had it not been for Eve tempting Adam and encouraging him to take a bite from that rosey apple, man would not be in the state that he is today.

Just think of it fellows, we might have been able to live in peace and contentment, in a world full of the wonderful riches, and never having to worry. Look at us now, down trodden, dejected, browbeaten, ill-used, the thing that takes the money home, that's how they look on us, just an ornament that can be displayed when and where they think fit. "This is my husband my dear, oh he is so sweet, why,he comes home early every night, pays up sharp on the dot on Friday, never says a word out of place, never drinks or smokes, see's to the washing up before he has his dinner, puts the children to bed, attends to the washing on Sunday morning while I go over to mothers, and spends all his spare time in the garden".

Have we ever done anything right since that fateful day, when we said "I will". Why, they are always moaning about something or other. "Why don't you throw the bed clothes back, and fold up your pyjamas when you get up, put this away behind you, put that back where you found it, don't do this, don't do that". Why, we are sinking lower and lower into the depths of despair.

MEN, lets put our foot down before it is too late, let's take the bull by the horns and turn the tables once and for all. We must put these Auntie Kays in their place. This is what I suggest. Insist on your morning cup of tea in bed, and your shaving water boiling hot, a clean shirt every day, make them clean your boots every night before retiring. If they start to cut up rough, don't weaken, just stop the money for a week or two, they will soon come round again. They will no doubt put up the old argument, no money, no food, but that's not much to worry about, because we shall still have the money in our pockets, which will enable us to eat outside.

If we have a good stiff whiskey and soda before going home at night, that should put us in good fighting trim to meet the tempest that is bound to be waiting on our arrival. Don't put up with any frying pan dish, we want a real good hot meal, carpet slippers, and a big fire. Another clean shirt, and off to the club for a couple of hours. On returning home, another hot meal then off to bed, which has been warmed with a half dozen hot-water bottles, but make sure she attends to all the washing up, and has the breakfast laid ready for morning. I think this will do for a start, the rest can come later, but if needs be we must become brutal. Go to it lads! "Uncle Jimmie".

GENUINE EXTRACTS FROM LETTERS TO THE MINISTRY OF PENSIONS etc.

I cannot get sick pay. I have six children. Can you tell me why this is?

Mrs.B. has no clothes; has not had any for a year. The clergy have been visiting her.

The reply to your letter, I have already co-habited with your officers, so far without result.

I am glad to say that my husband that was missing is now dead.

Sirs, I am forwarding my marriage certificate, had two children one of which is a mistake.

Unless I get my husband's money I shall be forced to lead an immortal life.

I am writing these lines for Mrs.J. who cannot write herself. She expects to be confined next week and can do with it.

I am sending my marriage certificate and six children. I had seven and one died which was baptised on a half sheet of paper by the Rev.T.

Please find out if my husband is dead as the man I am now living with wont eat or do anything until he is sure.

You have changed my boy to a little girl. Will this make any difference?

I have no children as my husband is a bus driver and works all day and night.

According to your instructions I have given birth to twins in the enclosed envelope.

Milk is wanted for my baby, and father is unable to supply it.

Re your dental enquiry the teeth on the top are all right, but the ones in my bottom are hurting terribly.

Please send money as I have fallen into errors with my landlord.

I want money as quick as you can send it. I have been in bed with doctor for a week and he does not seem to be doing me any good. If things do not improve I shall have to take in another doctor.
"YAHUDI".

"CABAR FEIDH"

"Jewels and Women are the Devil's two best pawns on Life's Chessboard". Somebody knew both his jewels AND his Women. Jewels have always fascinated me. Even from earliest times, jewels have been granted SEX, the darker stone the male and the lighter stone the female, but to me, all jewels are Female, more so, because they are mysterious, and what could be more mysterious than Woman.

According to Theophrastus, one of the earliest Greek Writers, certain jewels, especially Diamonds, were capable of reproducing their kind. Re Kunz's "Curious Lore of Precious Stones", a member of the house of Luxembourg backed up Theophrastus' theory by stating that she owned two diamonds which "engendered progeny", but don't take my word for it. Even our own Sir John Mandeville states that jewels "grow together, male and female and are nourished by the Dews of Heaven".

With little imagination, one can see the WIT of woman in the DIAMOND, her LOVE in the RUBY, her CHASTITY in the SAPPHIRE, and her INTUITION in the EMERALD - PEARLS for Sorrow, her TEARS, those keys to our male susceptibility, and the lesser gems, Jasper, Agate, Topaz, Sunstone or Alexandrite, the rags and tags of her temperament which get us men tied into such impossible knots at times.

A famous Author once said - "To me, a woman should represent the Seasons' four great jewels. SPRING the EMERALD, her Youth, Beauty and Chastity, standing on the threshold of life. SUMMER the RUBY, her womanhood and early motherhood. AUTUMN the SAPPHIRE, her Constancy and Fidelity, her steadfastness come to her through overcoming. Then WINTER the DIAMOND, Peace, the peace of deep knowledge and understanding".

To me, the World's most famous jewels are possibly unknown to any of my readers. I refer to the Breastplate of Aaron (See Exodus Ch.28 v20). The Breastplate was a bag or receptacle holding four rows of three stones, each set in an Ouche or knot of gold, not a Claw as that setting is comparatively more modern. The claw setting, by the way, is one of the reasons for the ill-luck attributable to the Opal. The Opal contracts under certain temperatures, and if in a claw setting, quickly loosens and falls out. To return to the Breastplate, each stone was named after one of Jacob's twelve sons, and inscribed on each was the name of one of the Twelve Tribes.

No-one really knows what became of the Plate after the Trek through the Wilderness. We know that the Tabernacle Plate was placed in the Temple in Jerusalem, but the Breastplate is not directly mentioned as being part of it. Titus the Roman sacked Jerusalem about 60-70 A.D., the Plate being carried to Rome. Rome in its turn was sacked by the Visigoths. At that period the Plate was last heard of as being placed in the vaults of St.Sophia in Constantinople for safe keeping. Thenceforth - silence. Any of the great Jewel collectors would, I'm sure, give up their entire collection to possess one of those stones from the Breastplate, even though they were worthless from a material point of view, being possibly only Spinel, Chysophrite or Feldspar. They were "Occult or Glowing" stones, and it is said that through these stones, Jehovah communicated with Aaron.

contnd."
Page 7.

A. H. Appleton reflects on sport.

REFLECTION No 6

During and after my school-days, I have always been interested in any sporting activities. To my great sorrow, I have never been any good at games, but have always tried to help those who are.

After leaving school, I obtained a position in London. This was a great advantage as it enabled me to see some great sporting events. *Cricket.* I have seen a number of Test Matches including the Australians, South Africans, West Indians, and Indians. The Australians are of course easily the most formidable, next the S.A's, followed by W.Indians and lastly Indians. The personalities of our visitors that struck me most, were Warwick Armstrong, McCartney, Ponsford and Bradman. Bradman, "the record-breaker", is a scoring machine and can be rather boring to the spectator. The Australians attitude of mind is different from ours. Having made 100, they then try to make it 200 and so on. Living in Kent, I visited some of the many Kentish grounds, Canterbury, Maidstone, Tonbridge etc. Frank Woolley was the idol of the crowds and deservedly so. When he was on top of the bowling and in form,he was the most graceful batsman I have ever seen. The most effective match winning county for many years was Yorkshire. There is no doubt however, the backbone of English Cricket is the Club and Village--the Saturday afternoon cricketer. Without Club Cricket, there would be no County Cricket or Test Matches. I used to umpire for my brothers club, and very enjoyable it was.
Soccer Football. I have seen two Cup Finals. The first when Everton beat Manchester and the second when Arsenal won against Sheffield United, then a 2nd. Division team. I followed Arsenal and Gillingham regularly. C.Bastin was the complete footballer. The late Herbert Chapman said he was the only player, even at the age of 17, that did not require teaching. Dean (Everton), was the best centre-forward I have seen and Blenkinsop (ED.Sit down Blenk.) (Sheffield Wednesday), the best back. Again the Village and small clubs are the foundation of the professional clubs. I suppose it is correct to say Soccer is the most popular of all games. In Scotland they seem to play nearly all the year round and migrate to England, where there is one or more Scotsman in every league team. I think Cup Matches are the most exciting. There is no doubt each player does go all out. I know that professionals treasure a Cup Final medal more than anything else.
Rugby Football. I know nothing of Rugby League, but have seen a lot of Rugby Union. On balance I think Rugby is the best game to play and Soccer, the best game to watch. For some years I went to Twickenham to every International. Given a dry day with plenty of handling and it is a very fine spectacle. During one season I had a personal interest in the Internationals, as a near relative had the honour of playing for England. I have not seen Rugby League, but I believe it is a faster game than the Union.
Tennis The growth of Tennis during the last 20 years is amazing, and probably due to the fact that women were able to partake in this. I could write pages on why I think Sport is necessary for the wellbeing of the country. I do believe however, that the inbred love of Sport and the split second decisions engendered by it, was a deciding factor in the Battle of Britain.

A H Appleton

HUMPING THE BLUEY

F.W. LEDHAM

There is a small curiosity shop on the quayside in Freemantle, Western Australia. Over the shop front is written "The First and Last Shop in Australia". Here you can buy curios, knick-knacks, picture postcards and bright novelties for the delight of your friends.

Outside on the quay, on the beaches, in the streets, in the bush, you will find other curios, human curiosities----the swagmen, the beachcombers, and the bushmen.

Who are these men?. Where are they from?. They are an oddly assorted band of men; mostly British with perhaps a sprinkling of Norwegians, Swedes and Italians. They are men desparately looking for work or desparately trying to avoid it. Some of them are seamen who have missed their ship; a few may be emigrants tired of life in the open spaces so they come to Freemantle, hoping to find a ship that will take them home. One or two are twopenny-halfpenny adventurers.

A few are unwashed, unshaven, with tattered clothes and down at heel shoes. An odd one or two are there from choice, but most of them are victims of misfortune, cast up by a relentless sea of bad luck.

Some few years ago I found myself in Australia. For one year I lived, or perhaps it would be better to say I existed in Western Australia. From Freemantle I made frequent trips into the bush. A swagman myself, I met many other swagmen and beachcombers.

The swagman's wardrobe consists of the clothes he stands up in, a change of underclothes and a few personal items. All the spare articles of clothing are carried in either a small bag, or more usually rolled up in a cloth. According to tradition the cloth should be blue and the bundle is known as a bluey.

I addition, every swagman worthy of the name, carries a billy-can, a small quantity of dry tea and sugar. If he is lucky, a tin of milk is also included in the ration bag. When travelling in the bush a canvas water bag holding about four pints of water is always carried.

Usually we travelled about in pairs for company. It is not a particularly happy state to be alone in the Australian bush. One of the greatest imperfections of a swagman's life, apart from securing enough food to keep him alive, is the inability to obtain a good nights sleep. We used to talk and dream about luxurious beds with clean white sheets and cool soft pillows. With me, beds almost became an obsession.

It seemed beyond the bounds of human possibility to enjoy a sound nights sleep in the Australian bush without blanket or overcoat. Most of us had no blankets, but we found that by taking our jackets off and covering our heads and shoulders with them, we did manage to keep out some of the chilly night air. At times the winter nights in West Australia could be decidedly cold.

In the bush, a swagman can always light a fire to make a billy-can of tea and cook some supper. The fire is kept going all night, partly for warmth and partly to keep snakes away. Of course, food is the real problem, but it speaks volumes for the open "handedness" and hospitality of the Australian farmers and bush dwellers, when I say that during my stay in Australia, I never once heard of a starving swagman.

Contnd.

If a swagman wanted to travel from one town to another, he could choose one of two alternatives. He could either try and jump a train or set out to hike along the bush roads. Jumping the train was perhaps the quickest way, although when travelling by road the swagman invariably managed to obtain a lift in some travellers car.

It is worth mentioning here that hitch-hiking has become a popular means of travel in this country, especially with members of the forces.

The swagmen are nearly always able to find a job of some kind in the bush. It may be stooking, haycarting, felling trees, clearing land, lumping wheat, loading trucks and chopping sticks. Unfortunately, when a swagman had earned a few pounds, his thoughts would turn to city life; the gay life. Perhaps he would be filled with a desire to clear out of Australia altogether. Back he would come to Freemantle; back ultimately to the beach.

If the bush life was hard, life in Freemantle was infinitely harder for the beachcomber. Jobs were like angels visits, few and far between. It was more difficult to obtain food in Freemantle than in the bush. It was certainly harder to find a place to sleep. It was impossible to light a fire, so a billy-can was useless. We managed to have a few meals on the ships that were tied up in port. We slept in woodyards and railway carriages.

In Freemantle lived a priest. Gossip had it that he was not quite right in the head, but he had a heart as big as his head. Every day he gave meal tickets to the swagmen. With these tickets a swagman could get a decent meal in one of the local restaurants. This cleric was very generous and even gave a large part of his salary away. His exceeding generosity was widely known among beachcombers and he never had a moments peace. The poor man was never free of them. If they were not knocking at his door, they were button-holing him in the streets.

Sunday in Freemantle was the swagmens red letter day. In the early evening the "Stiffs Banquet" was held. A philanthropical gentleman had died and left some of his money to be put aside for the express purpose of feeding the "down and outs". Hence every Sunday evening in an upstairs room, the philanthropist's wishes were religiously obeyed. The last supper of the week! A veritable feast for the hungry hobo.

But perhaps the high spot of the evening was the cinema. Every Sunday evening in Freemantle, when the church services were finished and altar candles had been snuffed out, the lights of a cinema, reds, greens and blues would brightly proclaim to the public that a film was about to be shown. The price of admission was----a silver collection taken at the door.

I think I can say without exaggeration that practically every swagman in town would be in the cinema enjoying the show.

For a brief space the swagman had ceased to be a curiosity. He was just another fellow being taking his pleasure at the pictures.

LETTERS TO THE EDITOR :-

Sir, For some considerable time, "Vox Plebis", our distinguished politician and writer of the article "Apres la Guerre" has tried in vain to arouse criticism and argument over his ideas of a model post-war British Government. Up to now however, his brainwaves have caused to stir among the readers, a fact which, in itself, tends to show just how little interest has been caused.

Apparently he has forgotten that the whole constitution of the British Government depends upon the popular opinion of the electors, who, if they were dissatisfied would not continue to support the existing regime. Nationalisation of transport, factories and similar institutions may be a good thing for the country, but this could, and would, apparently, if "Vox Plebis" had his way, be taken too far.

England has, since first becoming civilised, had its rich and poor, and its class distinction. It does not seem to have suffered in any way by this. Indeed it has, for years, been a prosperous, contented, and well governed country. It has, certainly, had its slumps and unemployment, but then, other countries have had the same, and in most cases have had these stigmas on a larger scale.

Now, as a contrast, take a "nationalised" country, Russia, China, or any other. Their people have lived on the verge of poverty for years, most of their cities are on a par with the East of London, dirty, overcrowded to the extreme. Who, do you suppose, is the better off?. The Englishman or the Russian?. Or to put the question another way; how many people would give up life in England and voluntarily go to live in Russia?. There are not many.

Why, if "Vox Plebis" is right, was De Montfort given so much support in his quest to establish the first Parliament?. This was, you may say, a long time ago, but the spirit of the NORMAL Briton has not changed. But enough of this. I commenced with the intention of saying, in a roundabout way, that the majority do not want politics in a Staff Magazine, then in my enthusiasm, unwittingly sidetracked into the very thing I sought to eliminate. Let us, minors as we are, in the hazards of British politics, ignore for the moment what will happen "Apres la Guerre", and try to amuse each other "pendant que nous assistons a achevoir la victoire finale".

"VOX MULTITUDINUM"

"VOX PLEBIS" replies :- The present regime is maintained in this country because the masses are either deceived by the propoganda of the ruling class, or are apathetic towards political matters, and are quite prepared to allow someone else to do their political thinking for them, regarding these affairs which are perhaps the most significant influences on their lives, as something outside their sphere.

Until my correspondent and thousands of others like him, cease to regard themselves as "minors in the hazards of British politics", the present state of affairs will continue. Every man if he would improve the conditions of his existence in the community must regard politics as part of his own personal affairs. Contnd.

LETTERS TO THE EDITOR (Contnd.) ("Vox Plebis" replies to
"Vox Multitudinum" Cntd.
Not yet having discussed the Nationalisation of the major industries,
it seems strange that my correspondent should suggest that "if Vox
Plebis had his way, Nationalisation would be taken too far."
   It would be interesting to have evidence to prove the statement
that "most of the cities of Russia are dirty and overcrowded".
Photographs and descriptions which can be obtained, indicate no
grounds for believing that living conditions in these towns are worse
or even, as bad in many English towns. In modern Russian centres,
systematic town-planning has been carried out on a scale which rivals
the best that the rest of the world can produce.
   The Russians by making great sacrifices in peacetime, have made
great strides forward in their social services and community life.
Their system though as yet, immature, crude and still behind the
times, is in advance in many respects of the rest of the world, and
as such will have a significant influence on the future.
   "Not many people", says my correspondent, "would leave England to
live in Russia". That is not a particularly sound argument, but
replying in similar vein; However small the number may be, it would
hardly be exceeded by the number of Russians who would leave their
newly evolved civilization to live in this country!

....

TO THE EDITOR :-

Sir, In effect, "Vox Plebis" states tradition is a snare and
delusion. We must banish our flags and banners commemorating past
deeds of our regiments and exchange Empire and tradition for a
spineless Internationalism. Also he trails the good old red herring
of an alleged decadent and opulent British aristocracy. How utterly
wrong and false is this conception, I will prove. In fact there is
nothing basically true in his lucid and comprehensive survey.
  As a matter of fact, the anti-traditionists held full sway in
current affairs from 1918 onwards, they will go down to posterity
as the worst collection of nitwits who dominated the British political
arena. Under their direction, Empire prestige declined to the lowest
level in the annals of history, as events proved.
Three times the traditional Empire has saved the world, incidentally
Homo Sapiens, from opression and worse, namely, 1588, 1815 and again
in 1940. On these are based tradition which is really service to
country, self effacing and maybe unrewarded.
  Sea power is the basis of Empire and tradition, the clothes we
wear, our food, in fact the very air we breathe depend on the fact
that the Empire commands the seas, otherwise we cease to exist.
Realising this the first objective of the anti-traditionists was to
take advantage of current public opinion, organised conferences,
innumerable committees, with the object of whittling down Britain's
sea power and other forces necessary for our well being. To a great
extent they succeeded, treaties were signed by which Britain and
the Commonwealth practically relinquished their heritage.
A battleship squadron of the Grand Fleet was scrapped with the
exception of one unit, many other destroyers and cruisers laid up,
and the personnel was discharged, or as they politely termed it
retired, tonnage was cut by agreement, the stage seemed set for a
                                                                      Contnd.

Shssh! G O S S I P Shssh!

CONGRATULATIONS:- We take pleasure in congratulating the following on their recent engagements:-

Pte. Nora Gledstone to Cfm. Fred Lucas, R.E.M.E.
" Anne Slee to Trooper W. Park, Green Howards.
" "Dicky" Bird ("Hello" girl) to Mr. Tony Bone, G.P.O.
" Mary Watson to Mr. Bert Norris, E.W.A., W.O.Y.G.
L/Cpl. Kay Metcalfe to Mr. F.C. Staddon, E.W.A., W.O.Y.G.

We have two weddings to report this month:-
Pte. Muriel Corden to Cpl. J. Archer, R.A.O.C. The ceremony took place at St. Matthew's Church, Skegness, on Nov. 21st.
Sgt. Gladys Webb to Q.M.S. Earle, R.E.M.E. (Loughboro!). The ceremony took place at St. John's Church, Moordown, Bournemouth, on Dec. 23rd.

Our very best wishes for their future happiness are extended to the happy couples.

One of our snoops reports that Ben Hurley (at present at Aldershot), has recently been presented with a little daughter. We understand that mother and daughter are well, and father is bearing up under the strain. Congrats. Ben.

Met our old friend "Chick" Henbest (now L/Cpl), the other day. He was looking as ruddy faced as ever, and very pleased with life. May he continue to prove the value of Woygite training by obtaining still more rapid promotion.

CHRISTMAS PARTY   The Entertainments Committee deserve our congratulations and thanks on the promotion of this herculean task. We could well have done without the unruly element which gatecrashed in the later hours, but suspect this was aggravated to some extent by our own people. Why do the Forces, who receive such good treatment with regard to entertainment, invariably spoil themselves by bursting in on private functions of this nature?. It was observed that people wearing the uniform of "an officer and a gentleman", were indulging in the general scrimmage. Perhaps the answer is to engage a policeman or professional thrower-out on the door in future. In any case the Committee were not to blame, as they had presumably based their programme on the fact that they were dealing with decent people.

You have probably heard the story of the stranger walking down Whitehall, enquiring of a passer by, "which side is the War Office on", the answer being, "ours I hope". Recent events confirm this, but we often think on how we could shorten the struggle if we had a 100% War Effort at home. Is it right to shower praise on workers who are being paid fantastic wages for turning out jobs, often of a repetitive and mechanical nature. We do not think so. We hear of long hours and 7 day weeks, when in many cases, better production figures could be attained by a 48 Hr. week of good labour.

NEW CANTEEN. We seem to be settling down in our new abode and the option of purchasing a 1½d, 2d, or 3d. tea is proving quite an attraction. A night watch is often enlivened by a feeling of going on the binge when one indulges in a large moog/3d. tea.

We understand that some of the Ats have been barred from wearing slacks whilst on duty. Well, for ever more!

LETTERS TO THE EDITOR:-

Sir, Whilst agreeing with most of the things that Vox Plebis has to say regarding tradition and the failings of the British Colonial administration, I hope Vox Plebis is not confusing the handing over to Gandhi of India, who does not represent India any more than the House of Lords represents Gt.Britain, or its people.

The whole of the Empire, including the coloured peoples, must be given the right of self government. It must be the job of the British peoples to see that we, along with all the people that go to make up the British Empire, reach a broader and better understanding; that we on our side, prove to the coloured races that we are at one with them and that we sincerely wish to see them travelling along the road that will lead to happiness for us all, remembering that he who oppresses another, can never himself be free.

One of the first tasks of the people after this war, should be to remove the bodies who by reason of birth, reject or alter as to make useless, bills passed by the peoples duly appointed representatives.

One of our biggest tasks will be to introduce some form of proportional representation. Let us rid ourselves of the farce of the last General Election, when one party obtained something like 50% of the total votes polled, and got nearly three-quarters of the seats in the lower house, whilst the other 50% were represented by a mere handfull. A serious study of this will show that a large body of opinion has no voice in an election. Whilst I am on the subject of peoples and their representatives, and the so called tradition that surrounds them, might I as a Britisher, put in a word for the so called foreigner. We, as men and women, are no better than they. Let us not forget that most of the people of occupied Europe, were defeated not by sheer force of arms, as much as by the enemies in their midst, who posed as their friends, of which, we in this country have our quota who, if they thought their ancient privileges were going to be taken from them, would just as soon go over openly to the enemy.

It has been my privilege and honour, to soldier and fight in this war alongside the French, Poles and Norwegians, and I never desire any better, or braver Allies. Willingly would I serve alongside them again to enable them to free their own countries, for by helping them will we help ourselves.   "GREYHOUND"

"VOX PLEBIS" replies:-
Fully endorsing "Greyhound's" tribute to our allies, I certainly agree that we are no better than they; let us hope that fact is remembered in the years to come.

There was no implication in "Fine Traditions", that the fate of India, should be left in the hands of Mr.Gandhi, who seems from many of his activities to be more concerned with his own welfare than the welfare of the Indian peoples as a whole!

The ultimate fate of India would seem to be a matter for an International Commission, in co-operation with Indian political leaders, to decide as the Indian people are so divided in their racial and caste systems, that for the present at least, they are incapable of democratic self-government.

LETTERS TO THE EDITOR:-

Sir, While I admire both articles by Vox Plebis, there are certain points which can be challenged. The sneer at the House of Lords is only a half-truth. The Lords is admittedly composed partly of traditional peers, but it is being constantly reinforced by men who have been rewarded for the business, social, artistic or political work they have performed. Do such men because of this, suddenly lose those qualities which have brought them to their high position? In other words it is absurd to suggest that society is in sharply defined classes and it is not possible to pass from one to the other. In fact, society is in a constant state of flux, and individuals and families are constantly rising or falling.

Whether the Lords should be allowed to function in a democratic state is arguable. If titles were abolished altogether, we should have the same situation as obtains in other democratic countries; namely much political graft, and where money and only money counts.

It is easy for us to talk about the colour-bar, because we have not got that problem. In America it is acute and will become more acute. In S.Africa, the Government have always steered a middle course between on the one hand complete domination of the natives, and on the other of complete political and social freedom. If Vox Plebis wishes for the latter, two things will happen.

(1) The native will gain complete control by reason of their overwhelming majority.

(2) On the social side, marriage between black and white will no longer be considered anti-social.

My answer to the first is obvious, and to the second, ask yourself this question, " would I like my sister to marry a black man!"

Returning to the political. In this country there is one point on which I feel rather strongly. The only religious body officially represented in Parliament, is the Established Church. This seems very wrong to me. All denominations and creeds should have a representative.

I shall look forward with interest to further articles by "Vox Plebis"

A.H.Appleton.

"VOX PLEBIS" replies:-

In reply to Mr.Appleton's remarks about the House of Lords, I can only repeat that "Democracy" is "government for the people by the people"-If this is to be truly applied, no-one, whatever his qualifications or however "blue-blooded" he may be, has any right to a seat in the government of the land unless elected by the popular vote.

Our colour-bar system is a very serious obstacle to real inter-national understanding, and as long as it survives, so long will discord exist between the different races on earth, and discord between nations has usually the result we know too well.

The answer to the question my correspondent asks, is simply that if my sister wished to marry a negro and saw a way to happiness by doing so, it would be purely her concern, and my own attitude would be one of complete impartiality.

A NEW YEAR'S OLIVE BRANCH

To Paddy McGrath. From Ollie Pearce

Last June, a short biography
Produced by your exalted pen,
Extolled the aristocracy
And glorified the "upper ten",
Disparaging the common men,

Who've never had the chance to know
The pleasures of the idle rich,
Whose literary tastes are low,
A fault in your opinion, which,
In our relations caused a hitch.

Because I do not much peruse
The words that Schopenhauer penned,
Locke's, Kant's and Hegel's lofty views
I don't aspire to comprehend,
Because, in short, my worthy friend,

I'm, like yourself, a man of prose,
A man of commonplace belief,
Who doubts, and disbelieves, and knows,
And aims at joy, and flies from grief,
And has a taste for beer and beef.

The ruddy warmth of arduous toil,
The spasm of triumphant strife,
A friend to serve, a foe to foil,
A cause with noble purpose rife,
The common bond 'twixt man and wife.

Men, women, children, speech and song,
The thrill a hard-solved problem brings,
The pulses of a busy throng,
I'm grateful for these common things
Unknown to those who "walk with kings".

But, even though we have disputes,
Can't we agree to disagree?
It's foolish to remain like mutes,
So why not sink a pint with me
Some evening in the Apple Tree?

THE GOSPEL ACCORDING TO ST.UFID.   Chapter XVII
(Translated from the English by Disciple Millhouse).

    Now it came to pass in the second year of their banishment, that the great tribe of Woyg were afflicted with another Xmas. And there was, in Townorl, in the fair city of Luff, where dwelleth Mare and the Elders of the city, a Great Do, even as there had been in the year preceding.
    And a mighty host of Scribes and their handmaidens the Atsites came hither. And whereas at other Do's the Scribes and Atsites came in one's and fives, this day they came forth in two's and tens. Yea! For it was written upon the tablets of Woyg : The Do shall be Buckshee.
    And Aridiks and his brethren of Amity gave unto each of the Tribe a parchment, saying : Let this be a token that the blood of Woyg runneth in thy veins. Bring it forth with thee to Townorl, for without it ye shall not enter into the portals thereof. And they came unto Townorl, and saith unto Aridiks : What cooketh? And behold, there was exceeding much which was cooking. For it was written upon the parchments in this wise:-
    For the peoples which are like unto Gigolo's, and worshippeth at the shrine of the Twerpsichorean god, shall trot in the manner of the fox, and divers other wondrous ways, and shall exhort one another in this wise, saying: Thou putteth thy right arm forth, and thou turnest it round about.
    And for the peoples which are flowers of the wall, or leaners upon the bar, or are afflicted with corns and bunions, or stampeth exceeding much upon the corns and bunions of their partners, or are flat in the foot, for such as these to behold there shall be the maiden Dorna, who tappeth a right nifty sandal. (Likewise she tappeth a left nifty sandal) And for these also the minstrels of Broosh shall make musick and song, and shall crack jokes of exceeding great wit.
    And for the peoples which hunger there shall be an abundance of Char and Wads and pieces of unleavened bread containing succulent morsels of Dog.
    And for the Sinners there shall be Womp.
    And the peoples went amongst the crowd with their parchments, and exhorted one another to scratch thereon, saying: Saign heah, or Sign ere, according to their salary. And some spake only one word, saying: Hic! For it is written: If a sinner suppeth one over the eight, he shall be possessed of a full skin, and like unto a cricket, and shall henceforth say: Hic!
    Now when the multitude were all assembled the Atsites were numbered as the sands of the desert, and the oases thereof were the Scribes. And the doors were opened unto the Raffites, and the Swaddites, and the Luffites, and there was much crashing of gates. And they all descended upon Townorl until the Woygites were verily hidden by their numbers.
    And upon the Eve of Xmas there was set up in Kantin in Woygland a mighty gambling den called Owsi-Owsi. And the prophet Osce and Dewo came hence, and the shekels and womp flowed exceeding free. And when the multitude were wearied of gaining shekels, and were engaged in other wise, which is an old Xmas custom, one Ej spake unto them, saying: Owsi hath ceased, in case ye have not noticed it.
                                                                Contnd.

"B.S.M." FEBRUARY, 1943.
Vol.2 No.5.

General Editor:- L.P.Jones.
Editor:- F.C.Staddon.

Editorial Board:-
R.Wilkinson.   R.G.Denny.
E.Millhouse.   T.Brister.

Next publication 26th.March.   Contributions by 15th.March.

FRONT COVER DESIGN:- R.Wilkinson.   ILLUSTRATIONS:- R.G.Denny.

What a storm in a teacup our last issue caused. Never since the inception of the "B.S.M." has there been so much talk about an issue. Feeling on both sides ran high, but our Editorial head remains unbowed. Surely the kernel of the whole matter is this. We invited criticism and comment and got it, then published it. We published it all, because we must at all costs avoid any charge of favouritism and to have picked out one, or perhaps two letters, would have given rise to this complaint. At the same time, we must point out that the publication of such a weight of matter, was achieved by adding 6 pages to our normal size production.

Although we require no justification of our action, it is of interest to note that the issue was disposed of far more quickly than any of the last six numbers. Would be readers who had not taken up their copies for some months past, were indignant that their copy had been disposed of. In fact, some people were so eager to read the "B.S.M.", that in their eagerness they forgot to pay for their copy.

We would reiterate that the contents of a Staff Magazine, depend upon the contributions received from the aforesaid Staff. We hope our many critics will be constructive, and assist us in producing an interesting number each month, by sending in their Mss.

In conclusion, may we once more state the Editorial policy of the "B.S.M." The pages of the "B.S.M." are open to any who have the urge to write or draw and can interest our readers in so doing. (subject to passing the censorship of the O.C.). That is the only proviso, and whatever else we think or say about him, "Vox Plebis" has certainly aroused reader interest.

xxxxxxxxxxxxxxxxxxxxxxxxxxxxxxxxxxxxxxxxxxxxxxxxxxxxxxxx

THE GOSPEL. Chap. XVIII. Contnd.

And there were many which sniffed, and likened his writings unto the entrails of a sheep, saying: Verily, this man causes a sore affliction in my neck. And yet others saith: Truly there is a place for everything, and the place which they counselled for Politicks was afar off from Beer Sugar Monkey.

And Fred and Jonah, which were Big Cheeses of Beer Sugar Monkey were chastised by the multitude, and they knew not how to answer. Yet if they questioned all and sundry they could know the wishes of the peoples, and therefore could there be a VOX PLEBISCITE.

THINGS TO COME

What did you do in the War Daddy?
Oh! will you to me please relate
An adventure or two or a battle or so
That settled old Hitler's fate.

Oh! I was a Ewa my laddie
My part I most nobly did play
And although I aint got any medals
I sure took my part in the fray.

And were you a soldier my Daddy
Or a sailor in navy so smart?
Or perhaps a bold airman way up in the sky
Your bombs dropping true as the dart.

No, I didn't wear any posh clobber
And I didn't go up in no plane
And I didn't take part in no battles or fights
So I can't be a claimant to fame.

But Daddy, I don't understand you
If you didn't go out to the front
And you didn't help making munitions
(You'll excuse me for seeming so blunt)
But what _did_ you do in the war dad?
I'm anxious to hear of your fame
But you don't seem to have any answers
(Forgive me for speaking so plain).

Why go durn your hide, you young blighter
My words aren't believed I can see
But the proof of the puddings in eating
And the proof is forthcoming you'll see
Just go to the chest in my bedroom
And ten pairs of trousers you'll find
A record of service unstintingly given
I completely wore out each "behind".   "Shiner"

THE GOSPEL ACCORDING TO ST. UPID. Chapter XVIII
(translated from the English by Disciple Millhouse).

Now the Great Tribe of Woyg continued to flourish, and their days were long in the land. Yea, verily, their days were exceeding long, and their nights were even longer. But now the Clerk of the Weather blessed them with a good and mild winter, and so little snow fell from the heavens that it was even as if the price was controlled by His Majesty's Government.

And in these days there rose up among them a great new prophet, and he was named Vox Plebis. And he journeyed amongst the peoples preaching the gospel of Politicks. Now it is written that when Father Plebis begat his son Vox, he took the suckling babe and oped his mouth, and looked therein. And he was sore dismayed, and cried: Behold mine son hath no silver spoon within his mouth. And Vox Plebis heard the words of his father, and the words lived with him all the days of his life. So it came to pass when Vox Plebis was become almost old enough to call himself a man, that he went forth teaching. And he read the writings of Wells and divers other wise men. And when he had perceived the Shape of Things to Come, he was sore dismayed, because he saw that it was a bad shape. And he cried unto the multitude : Verily I say unto ye, ye are become afflicted with an apathy which is exceeding dangerous. Rise up therefore and learn the gospel of Politicks, before ye are consumed by the Upper Ten. And there were some who doubted if the Upper Ten were that much hungry, even though their swine and other victuals were portioned out among all the peoples.

And because there were many who hearkened not unto Vox Plebis, and because he could not find himself a Soap-box, he writ his gospel upon the tablets of Beer Sugar Monkey for all peoples to behold. And when they had read what he had writ, (excepting those sinners who left their Beer Sugar Monkey's upon the counter in Kantin) they marvelled at it, and said: Truly how doth this man mind so well the words which wise men have writ?

And there rose up among them some Latin men and divers others, and even one who knew the spelling of his name, and they disputed with Vox Plebis.

And Vox Multitudinum taxed him thus, saying: How many of thy brethren would journey forth to dwell in Russland? and the Wise One answered him, saying: Nay, rather shouldst thou ask thyself: How many Russites would cast away their hammers and sickles and come hither to abide in Brit? And they neither knew the answers, for peradventure their brethren and the Russites were the only ones which did.

And one Aplton saith unto Vox Plebis: Wouldst thou have a nigger take thine own sister to wife? And the Wise One answered saying: Verily, if mine own sister had a crush on a nigger, I would say unto her :Get cracking sister, for truly it is thy wedding. But they knew not if the Wise One was possessed of a sister, nor, if he were, whether she was fair to look upon in the eyes of a nigger.

And the peoples of Woyg were divided among themselves, for some saith: This man knoweth his stuff. And others, considering he knew no stuff at all, yet loving an argument, were wishful to see his writings continue, that they might argue themselves blue in their faces.

(Contd. at foot of Editorial).

SOME STANZAS FROM THE RUBAIYAT OF OMAR EWA.

(with apologies to the Astronomer-Poet of Persia.)

Wake! The Alarum on the washstand white
Has hurled its Summons in the dead of night
And, from my bed I scramble up in haste,
To find Renascent Dawn is barely light.

Dreaming with half-cooked breakfast in my hand
I ease away my coat from the hall stand
And gliding slowly through the creaking gate
I stumble off, to join the drowsy Band.

And, as the clock strikes Six, those who sit
Within the Temple, cry out, "What's to do?
We've only been here eight hours yet,
And once departed, mayn't return e'er two".

Christmas indeed is gone with all it's cheer,
Its Skylarks, Dances, Parties, and free beer
But still the Scribes, their daily toil pursue
And still a Rotate to be done I fear.

I sometimes think that never lasts so long,
A Forenoon, when there's very little done
And, far from wanting, "Penny and the Cake"
E'en hungry, I would sooner wait my break.

With me along the Path now lined with mould
That just divides the huts from Canteen cold.
Past little signs "en route", so oft' ignored,
Whose warnings cry aloud, "Keep to the Road".

Here with a Canteen Wad of half-cooked cow,
A Mug of Tea, a Daily Rag,-and Thou
Beside a screaming untuned Radio,
And Paradise, is Hell on Earth enow.

Ah, make the most of thirty minutes brief
Before, we too, return to give relief,
And when our toil is done, we leave at last,
Sans Voice, sans Thought, sans Feeling, and - Sans Grief!

(Contnd.)

Indeed the hours I have toiled so long
Have done my concentrative powers much wrong
Have drowned my spirit in antipathy's cup
And sold my gay good humour for a song.

Oh Thou, who didst with Night Watch and Rotate,
Beset the Course that was to be my Fate
Thou wilt not after two long years like these,
Impute my Sanity's decrepit state?.

Ah Time of my Delight, who knows't no wain,
The ticking clock is nigh to two again,
How quickly after that sweet hour you'll seek,
In this same corner, after me in Vain.

    Ackar Vikkak.

(Done into English by "Snikmot")

It is our aim to crush the Hun
To kill or maim, yes - everyone
Of those who sought to conquer all the earth
Lands of the FREE, land of our birth.

Remember Rotterdam and Warsaw too,
Galki, Skoby, Lidice, - where they slew
For killings sake - all and everyone
Yes - We'll remember, - Adolf Hitler, - Mighty HUN.

For now it is OUR turn to strike a blow,
With all the strength and MIGHT that we can give
To crush for once and all this common foe
So that FREEDOM once again shall rightly live.
          R.G.Stevens.

NOTE:- GALKI and SKOBY were two villages that were annihilated by the Germans during the occupation of Poland. In GALKI all the women were driven into a school and burnt to death.

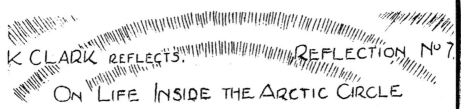

K CLARK REFLECTS. REFLECTION No 7.
ON LIFE INSIDE THE ARCTIC CIRCLE

After an exciting trip across the North Sea on a once luxury liner lasting eight days, during which we were supposed to have been sunk half a dozen times, we awoke one morning to find ourselves in what appeared to be a large lake, with several big brothers of the Royal Navy to keep us company, and everywhere a mantle of white.

We had several unwelcome visitors during the day, but in the evening as the weather turned foul we made a dash for it on a destroyer. I spent about three hours on the deck of that ship in a blinding snowstorm and do not think I have ever felt so miserable before or since. We eventually landed at a place called Karstad, in the Lofoten Islands, and what a sight met our eyes, snow everywhere, anything up to thirty feet deep, with quaint wooden houses built on loose stones about six feet above the ground. Unfortunately, some were in ruins.

The snow continued until about the middle of May, during which time it was fatal to touch metal with the bare hands, or go far away without snow glasses. Towards the end of May, a wonderful transformation took place. The sun shone for twenty-four hours a day and the snow seemed to vanish before our eyes, mountain streams, green valleys, and pine woods taking the place of what had appeared to be just rocks and bushes poking out of the snow.

In the valleys, an amazing variety of multi-coloured flowers appeared as if by magic, and wild strawberries were to be seen growing on the mountain sides, whilst the Norwegian gardens were a galaxy of colour, where they had been lucky enough to escape damage.

Wild life of such variety, I have yet to see elsewhere. Things looked good and the Farmers began to plant out their hardy crops, for the sun shines for twenty-four hours a day until the end of August and winter returns in September.

Unfortunately, we were not to stay much longer with our Norwegian friends, and the last I remember of that unhappy country as I stood on the deck of a destroyer, was a densely wooded countryside bathed in sunshine, with a British soldier running towards the ship, yelling out, "oh feet do your stuff".

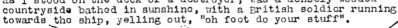

ED. Let us have your "Reflection". This will be of interest to your colleagues and at the same time provide you with a written record, the value of which, will increase as the years pass.

APRÈS LA GUERRE.

A provocative series by "Vox Plebis".

No.3 "PEACE IN OUR TIME".

The sober-minded student of history investigating war and its causes in past centuries, may well despair that the fervent wish for "peace in our time", will ever be fullfilled. History seems to be little more than a record of homicide on varying scales - but with an alarming tendency to increase the rate in recent years, as the devices for mass-annihilation become more efficient.

"There'll always be wars", is a popular if disturbing clique, and the person who makes the remark has a very convincing argument to prove his words.

Are we not part of Nature, and although Mother Nature may be bounteous, she is unquestionably a callous mistress, to whom the lives of millions of her subjects are of no consequence. Who arranges in animal and insect life the destruction of countless thousands of species, in order (in the words of Dickens) "to reduce the surplus population!"

It would seem then that the wars which disrupt our national and private lives every twenty or thirty years, are the inevitable part of Natures grand scheme of things, and, whatever our desires may be, we have no alternative but to grin (if possible!) and bear it.

But even assuming this argument to be true (although there is no conclusive reason why we should) there is even so, a definite ray of hope.

In many fields where Nature has held sway since time began, the hand of Man has taken a part, and by use of his scientific knowledge has utilized Nature's resources for his own betterment. The force of a mountain stream is harnessed to provide power and heat for Man's industries. Irrigation has turned barren desert into fertile fields; and scientifically controlled inter-breeding has produced finer varieties of plants and animals than Nature alone could originate. In these spheres and in numerous others, the intelligence of Man is utilizing Nature for his own purposes when at one time Nature employed Man for hers.

If Man is capable of changing the laws of Nature (so to speak) in this way it seems fairly reasonable to suppose he can, in time, change the laws of Nature in other fields as well.

It is probably quite safe to say that 99% of the people engaged in the present conflict had no desire for war in the first instance. War to the common man means misery, suppression, hunger and often death. Before the war thousands of people signed peace-ballots, attended peace-meetings, shouted for peace and wrote for peace. The result of their effort was that on 3rd.September,1939 they ran into their air-raid shelters, and have been doing the same pretty regularly ever since, whilst most of their younger and many of their older relations and friends are exposed to much greater perils.

This indeed is true not only of the English but of the vast majority of people engaged in the present malestrom. (Contnd.)

APRÈS LA GUERRE. No.3 "PEACE IN OUR TIME" (Contnd.)

It would seem obvious therefore to the dullest intellect that something is wrong - and if we are to have our long-hoped-for lasting peace, that wrong must be rectified.

The chief reason for the present world chaos is simply that Mankind's international outlook has not kept pace with his scientific knowledge. "The abolition of distance" which airplane, the fast liner and wireless communication have affected, have given warfare a potency which is truly amazing - indeed there is no part of the world, however remote, which is beyond the range of the nearest bombing-plane.

With such a state of affairs existing, we are compelled if we wish to survive, to become international in our outlook and to regard ourselves as part of a World Community, not to regard events in China as something outside our sphere, as they are very much our concern. If the first Japanese agression in China had been met by concerted action on the part of the rest of the world's governments, we might still have been at peace. The Chinese, Abyssinian and Spanish campaigns were little more then trial manoeuvres for World War II.

Every Englishman imagines in his heart that the English as a whole are the finest race on earth - this belief would not be dangerous if the German, the Russian and American did not hold similar views about his own people. These views and the traditions, national ideaologies, tariffs, currencies and monopolies which they bring in their train, clash every twenty or thirty years, and several hundred thousand more mothers and sweethearts are once again mourning their dear ones. Methods of governments still in use throughout the greater part of the world are little more than survivals from a time when China was remote from Europe and when local warfare had no international significance. Times have changed but governments remain the same. Traditional methods however old, are for the most part obsolete and drastic reorganisation of the world as a whole, is the only solution to our present plight.

There are in existence many barriers towards any such reorganisation, and these forces of reaction to the old order of things, are both powerful and subtle. Big Business organisations which exist on a world-wide basis, stand to profit by the recurrence of wars.

The bombs used in the attack on Pearl Harbour were made from metal sent from America. In 1938, American Big Business supplied 91% of Japanese scrap metal imports and as late as March, 1941, was supplying Japan with huge quantities of petrol, the trade being stopped only five months before America entered the war. It is also quite feasible that big banking groups in Britain, America, and even France, still hope one day to collect their "blood money" in enemy countries.

If we are to obtain a lasting peace, such forces must obviously be brought under control, and if necessary liquidated - for whilst they are at large, peace will be in jeopardy.

The B.B.C. is largely influenced by these forces of reaction and much of propoganda, though subtle, is for reversion to the old order of things.   (Contnd.)

APRÈS LA GUERRE. NO.3 "PEACE IN OUR TIME" (Contnd.)

A large section of Press, High Society, and the old Universities in this country and other countries are subjected to similar influences, and if the common man is not on his guard, they will succeed.

The future of the world and mankind is in the balance and Nazism is not the only peril. When the German barbarians have been finally vanquished the main task will begin.

That task is of re-adjusting our social standards and governments to meet the world situation. For the cost of one day's warfare and with a reasonable amount of clear-thinking throughout the world, Man's future destiny could be assured. A World Congress which made all international decisions, which controlled an International Police Force and Air Force, and which was proportionally representative of all the nations and tribes on Earth, is the only practical solution.

This Congress would control the bulk of the armed forces (enough to maintain law and order throughout the world) and the amount allowed to independant states would be strictly limited. Every country would be compelled to membership and any agressive acts would be met by prompt action by the World Congress.

The argument may be made that all this has been tried before and has failed. The League of Nations, whilst the precursor of the scheme, was a weak, ineffective organisation without the membership of some of the major powers of the world. Its acts were too much influenced by the demands of international finance and by the ultra conservatism of the major European powers.

The scheme may be condemned as a Utopian dream, Utopian it is, but unless it is converted from a dream into a powerful reality, we have no alternative but a continual repetition of the social and economic collapses which have been the lot of Mankind since civilization began.

An A.T.S. girl on a cold northern hill
Wrote to her mother concerning the chill
She said that the stores bloke had made so bold
As to issue mens pants to keep out the cold.

Now I'm all for the girls keeping cosy and warm
Whilst away from the fireside flickers
But I hope that the summer won't bring a reverse
So that menfolk get issued with knickers.

"Shiner".

Somniloquistic Soliloquies

My landlady warned me not to eat tinned lobster before retiring to bed, but ignoring the warning I enjoyed a good supper.

Some hours later I was awakened by Gabriel, who informed me he had brought a group of Angels to be made wise to the mode of living of my colleagues and I.

I became fully conscious to find the sunlight streaming through the skylight into Jay and beheld the Angels seated at the tables awaiting my words of wisdom.

In order to aid identification of the Angels, it was decided to number them, so they became Angel Number One, Angel Number Two, etc. This was later abbreviated to A1, A2, A3, etc.

In due course these Angels multiplied. I mean that further groups were posted here. Some came by slow and steady routes and were very sedate, but others apparently came by swifter but circuitous routes and were very Dizzy. They seemed to be of that ilk known to our American cousins as Dizzy Dames.

The Sedate Angels were very industrious, but the Dizzy Ones wanted to make Whoopee. They were, however, frowned upon and lectured by the Wet Blanket who spoke of pains in the neck.

Angels have on occasion been shown in association with Father Time, but to these particular Angels, time means nothing, except Break Time and Knocking-off Time. The first movement in each case being carried out at great speed.

Strangely enough, they worship at the shrine of Time and contort their bodies and shuffle their feet in sympathy with sundry shrieks and wails emitted by divers instruments of torture. This is known as Jazz Time. In some cases this cult dominates their thoughts, conversation, dreams and existence.

Harps have not been issued to the Angels so they decided to adopt the subject of Leave and they now Harp on it at every opportunity.

Some of the Angels are very sweet and like unto Rosebuds, so they are billeted in Rose Cottage. Others feel sore at being posted here so they live in Soar House, while yet another group dwells in huts. These are known as Crackers (arn't we all).

The Angels are not normally equipped with wings and halos, but wear war-time utility clothing which is very becoming and gives the impression of extreme youthfulness. The Ministering Angels wear their halos and crowns, but not their hearts, on their sleeves.

All dark clouds, they say, have a silver lining and we regard these Angels as the silver lining to our particular portion of the cloud. (Contnd.)

Shush! GOSSIP Shush!

CONGRATULATIONS:- On the gift of a son, David Robert, to Mr.&Mrs. R.G.Stevens, at 33, Chapel Row,. Bucklebury, Reading, on 13th.February

HEARD OVER THE INTER-COM! "Just a minute, there's 72 girls changing "shift!" Sudden increase of people on search

WOULD YOU MIND PASSING THE SALT! Understand it has been possible to obtain chips in the canteen recently. We hope one day to be able to boast having eaten a canteen chip, but so far have had to satisfy ourselves with the tantalizing aroma left by these delicious morsels, plus very longing glances at the condiment containers, whose appearance we welcome.

We are amused by the system of handing over your pass/identity card, in order to justify your right to receive the loan of a knife and fork. We are also puzzled as to how the act of returning a knife and fork can establish your identity, for the return of your correct pass/identity card. However, we are prepared not to be amused, if there is any possibility of this causing us to be unable to receive the necessary utensils for the consumption of canteen chips. In the words of Douglas Young, "I likes em, very tasty, very sweet".

DANCING CLASSES! Pleased to note this further branch of our social activities, and also to observe that one of our more youthful members, namely, "Victor Silvester" Carrington, is proving extremely useful in the training of wayward logs. To the organisers we say, "Thanks for supplying a definite need".

WITHOUT COMMENT! Extract from Administrative Instruction No.34. "Breaks-Day Staff" "no member of the Day Staff will take their morning break before 1045 hours".

LEICESTER METHODS! To Ewa who had ordered 2 buns & tea (8d), at a "help yourself establishment". "I havn't any coppers, would you like butter with your buns". Gormless Ewa. "Yes please". "Okay that will be a 1/0d". Incidentally, this establishment was asking (but not getting from this source), 6d. for a cheese roll. They must buy from somebody who buys retail!

?????????? Noticing the variety of social activities now running in the section, we pondered on the possibilities of the "Drama" and "Debating Society". Is there a desire for both or either of these, and have we the people with the necessary capabilities and willingness to undertake their organisation?

Reverting to the apparent theme of this Gossip column, namely, "Canteen Chips", we understand from one of our snoops, that contrary to orders, these tasty titbits have been consumed in the Canteen Lounge by people who appear to hold "privilege" tickets. On the particular occasion observed, the chips could very appropriately be referred to, as "Smith's Crisps".

CRITICISM! There have been numerous criticisms of the "B.S.M", which we welcome. Some of these criticisms have, however, been added to by the threat that certain people are seriously considering dropping their subscriptions. For other reasons, and particularly in view of paper supply difficulties, we say to these people, "If you feel you are overdoing the philanthropic cum Lord Nuffield act over the payment of 3d. for the "B.S.M.", please drop your subscription. We have no desire that anyone should become impoverished over this."

LETTERS TO THE EDITOR:-

Sir,
    Although spring seems rather premature this year, there is every evidence of its approach in the grounds surrounding this establishment. Already snowdrops are in bloom, whilst the daffodils are showing their first green shoots.
    May I appeal to the nobler ideals of the many people whose duties fetch them here, to leave these flowers alone this year so that everyone may enjoy their beauty in natural surroundings.
                                                    "GREYHOUND".

ED. We agree whole-heartedly with the above sentiment.

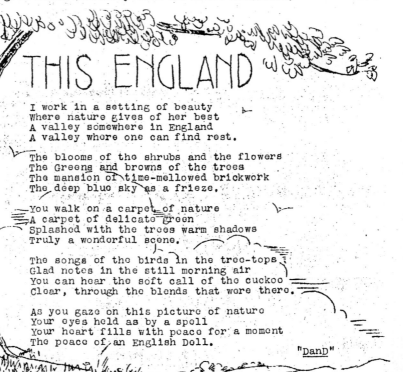

THIS ENGLAND

I work in a setting of beauty
Where nature gives of her best
A valley somewhere in England
A valley where one can find rest.

The blooms of the shrubs and the flowers
The Greens and browns of the trees
The mansion of time-mellowed brickwork
The deep blue sky as a frieze.

You walk on a carpet of nature
A carpet of delicate green
Splashed with the trees warm shadows
Truly a wonderful scene.

The songs of the birds in the tree-tops
Glad notes in the still morning air
You can hear the soft call of the cuckoo
Clear, through the blends that were there.

As you gaze on this picture of nature
Your eyes held as by a spell
Your heart fills with peace for a moment
The peace of an English Dell.
                                        "DanD"

"Somniloquistic Soliloquies" (Contnd.)
                        We shall miss all their smiling faces and trim figures when we return to normal routine at the end of the end. Good luck and a happy sojourn here to them all. E.Catchpole.

SPORTS PAGE

FOOTBALL — We lost badly to Hathern at home. Two visits were made to Shepshed, the results being one win and one loss. The best match this season, was a friendly, on Saturday, 20th. February, versus the R.A.F. The few W.O.Y.G. spectators who turned up, saw a fast and lively game. Our defence was very strong and the R.A.F., although pressing hard, only beat Hobden once. Both our goals came from free-kicks just outside the penalty area, taken by Gerry Dalton.

Several players have, unfortunately, been injured. Bob Roberts has now recovered. Bill Smart has also recovered, but will be unable to play this season, at least.

During the R.A.F. match, Gilliard (Gilly to us), was badly injured, which means the end of his playing career. He has had a very long playing career, and is well past the age when the average player hangs up his boots for the last time. We understand Gilly has performed this ceremony on many occasions previous to this, but has been unable to restrain the urge to lace them on again. He is emphatic in his protestation that this is "really the last time", but time will tell. We take this opportunity to say, "Well done, Grandpa!".

A.H.Appleton.
Hon.Sports Sec.

Oi! hang on. I've mixed my wiskers with my laces

RESULTS:—

ALLIANCE LEAGUE

1943
- Jan.23rd. — Hathern.   Home.   Lost 8-2
- 30th. — Shepshed Rangers. Away. Won. 2-1
- Feb.13th. — Shepshed H.G.   Away. Lost 1-0

FRIENDLIES

- Feb.20th. R.A.F. Loughborough.   Away. Won 2-1
- 21st.   Brush Students   Away. Won 7-2

ED. We shall be pleased to receive matter relating to any Sports activities in connection with the Section. INDOOR or OUTDOOR.

"B.S.M." MARCH, 1943.
Vol.2 No.6.

General Editor:- L.P.Jones.
Editorial Board:-
R. Wilkinson.   R.G. Denny.
Editor:-   F.C. Staddon.   E. Hillhouse.   T. Brister.

Next publication 30th.April.   Contributions by 15th.April.
FRONT COVER DESIGN:- Miss Muriel Fidoe (A.T.S.)   ILLUS. (various)

     Some time after the last issue had been prepared for press, the Editor received a letter signed "Cabar Feidh", purporting to be a criticism of "Vox Plebis" articles. In fact it was no more than a scurrilous attack on a personality, who, to say the least, is honest in his purpose and takes very great pains to confirm all facts and figures where he can.

     Apart from the above paragraph, the Editor has no desire to enter into a personal discussion as to the merits, or otherwise, of "Vox Plebis", but in order to avoid the accusation of bias, and as we cannot afford to devote 2 pages to the letter, excluding our Editorial reply, we have adopted the following procedure. The letter will be placed on our portion of the Notice Board, for scrutiny by those interested.

     We are pleased to note that our requests for more MSS. are meeting with some success, but there is still room for improvement. We hope you will keep us supplied with more articles, particularly of a humourous nature.

     This month's cover is drawn by a member of the A.T.S. (Miss Muriel Fidoe), whom we welcome as a member of our team of artists. May we now look forward to more contributions from her colleagues in the female element?

     Ralph Champion has offered to act as reporter in cases where members of the Section would prefer a verbal interview in preference to the more laborious business of preparing a Mss. We feel this will be of particular value to our "Peace Time Job" & "Reflection" series, but anyone wishing to make use of this service is asked to contact Mr. Champion. Thanks Ralph!

REMEMBER . THIS IS YOUR MAGAZINE.   KEEP US SUPPLIED WITH:-

                      MSS.
                      CARTOONS
                      IDEAS.

NOTES ON MUSICAL TOPICS (1) The Orchestra.

by Harry Dodd

Several of the leading British symphony orchestras pay frequent visits to Leicester and a number of Voygites often take the opportunity of hearing a fine orchestra "in the flesh", an experience which the broadcast concert or the gramophone recital, however enjoyable, can never replace. Here are a few points about the orchestra which will, I hope, interest you, whether you are a confirmed concert-goer or not.

It has taken about 300 years for the orchestra as we know it to develop. The art of writing unaccompanied choral music had reached perfection (never attained since) in the closing years of the 16th. Century, perhaps the greatest composer of that time being William Byrd, an Englishman, who died in 1623. The first that is known of an orchestra is of an odd collection of instruments, consisting of a viola-da-gamba (the forerunner of the 'cello), a harpsichord (the piano's ancestor), a guitar and two flutes, which was employed in a choral work written in 1600 by an Italian composer. The development of the orchestra was, however, quite rapid once it had started, and when Purcell wrote for it in the latter half of the 17th. Century it had established itself in a form which was clearly the precursor of the modern orchestra.

At first, the orchestra was used solely to accompany singers and merely "doubled" the voice parts, but enterprising composers soon realised that instrumental music had possibilities quite different from those of choral music with its restrictions imposed by the limitations of the human voice. Bach, Haydn and Mozart in the 18th. Century, Beethoven, Berlioz, Wagner, Rimski-Korsakov and several other composers in the 19th. Century, all played important parts in developing the orchestra, the tendency being to write music requiring an increasingly large and complex orchestra. The full modern orchestra has over 100 players, but those visiting Leicester are usually about 70 strong.

Here is a diagram of the orchestra as we see it at the De Montfort Hall. (the arrangement varies slightly with different orchestras)

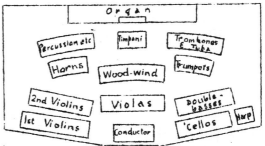

The orchestra comprises four distinct "families" of instruments:

(1) <u>Strings</u> (1st. and 2nd. Violins, Violas, 'Cellos and Double-basses)
(2) <u>Wood-wind</u> (Flutes, Oboes, Clarinets and Bassoons)
(3) <u>Brass</u> (Trumpets, Horns, Trombones and Tuba)
(4) <u>Percussion</u> (various kinds of drums and "effects" - familiarly termed "the kitchen department".) (<u>Contnd.</u>)

3

Relieved, I sally gaily forth, for thirty minutes free
to reinforce my jaded self with grub and cups of tea,
but as the long road I traverse, towards the canteen door,
those minutes tick, relentless, by, one, two, and three, or more.
Within the door a queue I find, a surging, motley crew
of Ops, and Wops, and "gentlemen", "G" Girls, and Day Staff too.
I tack myself on to their tail, resigned and woebegone,
"They also serve, who stand and wait"--but Time goes marching on.
At length my wilting form arrives against the serving bar
in time to see the pot exude its final drip of Char.
Maud goes to fill it up with stalks, and, from the time she's gone
I judge she must be putting through a call to far Ceylon.
At last she does return, and dumps the pot, and sadly shrugs,
That tea's so near, and yet so far, -- she's out of cups and mugs!
The ruthless hand upon the clock moves on a stage or two
before a mug is found and filled with fragrant, frothy stew.
I grab the mug with grateful hand, and join the crush for "Eats",
my empty paunch athrob with joy at sight of cheese and meats.
The unforgiving minutes pass -- Time for no man will wait --
and minutes spent in queues fly at a most alarming rate.
At length a plate's toward me pushed : "Sixpence ha'penny please"
I quickly pay, and seize with greed the bun, and roll and cheese.
I raise the tempting morsel, and prepare to take a bite --
a Hand upon my shoulder falls, I shudder, turning white.
My Super., stern, confronts me, and he indicates the clock:
"You've had your thirty minutes, so, get moving back, Old Cock!"

MOULINMAISON.

<u>NOTES ON MUSICAL TOPICS (1) The Orchestra (Contnd.)</u>   In addition,
harp, piano and organ are sometimes used.
    A book which I think you would find both entertaining and
instructive (and sometimes very amusing) is "The Orchestra Speaks", by
Bernard Shore (until recently the leader of the violas in the B.B.C.
Symphony Orchestra). Loughborough Public Library has a copy in the
Lending Department.
    In a few further articles I propose to discuss, in as much
detail as space will allow, the various orchestral instruments and
their characteristics.

4

"WHY IS A BEE WHEN IT SPINS?"   By: "Yone".

The war had been over for some years now, and the world was passing through a stage of Halcyon Happiness. Birds sang and made merry, and the Voice of the People was heard in the land. The modern Beau Brummel now wore spectacles and spoke with a Yorkshire accent. Parents would read H.G.Wells to the children as a bedtime story, and Ollie Pearce was Poet Laureate. Paddy roamed the world, drinking Vodkas at Vassilieu's and Sidecars at Sam's. Ginger had retired on a pension of four pints per night and Charlie was back at Brighton. Bill bounced his grandchildren on his bony knee, and told them what Percy did at Garats Hey.

In fact, everything in the garden of England was, as you might say, lovely. Millenium as it were. A bit of Utopia. Health, Happiness, and all the rest, what? No grumbles in fact.

But look deeper. Examine more closely. Probe as it were. There is something wrong. Not quite right perhaps. An air of "je ne sais quoi" as the French used to say before Esperanto became all the rage. People were worried.-Irritated you know. The Poet Laureate has fits of moodiness. Paddy forgets himself and runs ashore at Wigan Pier. Bill muddles up Percy's tricks and makes them appear really naughty. Things are chaotic. Not running smoothly in fact. There is a spot of grit in the works. Utopia, is as you might say, a bit limited.

You see everyone was pondering a question. Deep thought was the thing then. "Ruminate" said the wind.-"Think, oh think!" sang the birds. Racking the old grey matter was the order of the day.

The reason of course was a question sent to a still-existent Brains Trust, consisting of some of the most Sapient Homoes in the land, from one, Mr. Oldewa. An enigmatic sort of question you might think. Puzzling, almost. "Why is a Bee when it spins?"

Cmdr.Ellingwoyg didn't know, though he said that when he was somewhere in England, spinning was the usual thing. Quite common in fact. A weekly occurence as it were. They were all puzzled. They might have submitted to the bitter pill and said that they didn't know. But the world had changed. People knew the answers to everything. I mean, every child knew all about democracy, and Nietszche and that sort of thing. A wise crowd as you will admit. A brainy lot, forsooth. Not used to puzzles. Ambiguity was not the thing. No Enigmas.

Hence the somewhat irritated air of worry. Peevishness almost. Overshadowing things like a grey cloud. Rumours flew hither and thither with some abandon. "Outer darkness returned" said some. That sort of thing. Then Cmdr.Ellingwoyg had the idea. "Find Mr.Oldewa" he said, "Search him out. Leave no stone unturned, nor corner undiscovered. Roust, as it were, and dig deeply."

He was discovered roaming the fields near Colney Hatch, crying mysterious nonsense to the winds. He seemed prematurely old, did Mr.Oldewa. A wrinkled face, rheumy eyes, and big dark circles under his ears. He looked tired. Trouble seemed to rest on his shoulders. He was, you might say, careworn.

So they asked him if he knew the answer to his own question:- "Why is a Bee when it spins?", they asked. All he replied was "Yes it is". So they said "What is it?" and he said "A Bee" and they said "When?", and he said "When it spins, of course".~   Contnd.

"Shiner" who is quite a poet
knew, and thought that we should know it,
That, the north winds being chilly rousers
The A.T,S. were wearing trousers.

But he didn't know and couldn't guess,
What a rank, outstanding mess,
On which the Brasshats would decide,
For other jesters to deride.

So now young Joan and Pat and Doris
Must wear the breeches of Cornwallis
And venture over dale and lea
With trousers ending at the knee.
                    "NOSWEH"

For ever more

"WHY IS A BEE WHEN IT SPINS?" (Contnd.)
-Which was just as bad. The same position as before. No headway made, if you see what I mean. So they asked him to explain. "Elucidate" they said "And set out your facts in an orderly way. Be more explicit you know".
   Mr.Oldewa began:-
            "Many years ago, in the war, I was Somewhere in England. I worked at a place called Y. We were ornithologists, mostly; although there were some low people there calling themselves florists and market gardeners". He sniffed disparagingly, perhaps "We used to go home every seven weeks, and in order to get home we had to Rotate-spin, as it were" Cmdr.Ellingwoyg jumped. Bounded, you might say. The startled hare, perhaps. "This spinning was a bit thick" Mr.Oldewa went on. "We had to do six days work in four and a bit. We were, you might say, all over the place. It was a bit of a Bind. A-well-a B- in fact".
   Cmdr.Ellingwoyg's hand rested on his drooping shoulder. "I understand. Y must have been a B-" he said, "when it spun". Mr.Oldewa smiled. Wanly you know. "It was" he said. And so the great mystery was explained and generally elucidated, and the world went back to Halcyon Happiness. The sun shone again, and everything was up and coming. The Voice and Paddy, and people generally got cracking again and Bill wandered far afield telling stories of the Great Lover of Gerats Hey.
   A Fund was formed for Mr.Oldewa's benefit, but he said that all he wanted was one of the new "Skyrider" inter-planetary cars. When it was presented to him he whispered a delighted confidence in Cmdr.Ellingwoyg's ear. "I'm going to turn it into a mobile W-S st-n" he said, "and go on a general hunt about".
   The other smiled. Paternally, almost, and pointed to the number plate "I chose that myself" he said proudly. "DST 100".
   Mr.Oldewa smiled through his tears.

MENTAL ABERRATION.

By "Ollie" Pearce.

Dear Mr. Editor; I wish to say,
If you have no objection to my writing it,
But I've been used, since childhood's happy day,
If I should think of something, to inditing it,
To do this often, one must be courageous,
I seldom think; which is most advantageous!

I overheard at break the other day,
A protest from a fellow civil servant,
"We need more big mugs here" I heard him say,
I couldn't help but think - How unobservant!
But stay, I have no time for idle chatter,
My purpose deals with much more pressing matter.

Oh!, by the way, I have no doubt you've seen,
(Tea queues afford much time for observation)
The growth of a brick wall in the canteen,
It's function has provoked much speculation,
"Not ornamental", "Much too solid looking",
Perhaps it's so that we won't know what's cooking!

I still appear to wander from my theme,
This badinage is really out of place,
And that reminds me; lately, it would seem,
"Vox Plebis" has encroached on too much space,
These pages should be for our recreation,
Not filled by the wrong-righters of the nation!

At proper times and places I have room,
For politics, and rather like his brand,
But I don't have to use a nom-de-plume,
The consequences I'm prepared to stand!
I'm straying from my purpose. To the point;
The time, as Hamlet said, is out of joint.

Now, I had something pressing to impart;
If you recall the way this rhyme begins,
That was my implication at the start,
Before I trailed off on to other things,
And why I mentioned them, I do not know,
Nor what I "wished to say" a while ago!

7

R U G G E R   R E V I E W.

"A Man must serve his time to ev'ry trade
Save censure - critics all are ready made."
                                  English Reviewers.

Once again the section has seen more enthusiasm over a friendly game of Rugger, than it has ever seen over the most keenly contested football match. This enthusiasm was equally divided between players and spectators. The number of the latter having greatly increased since the last game, in spite of the fact that we lost. May this dual enthusiasm continue to grow as I think it will. Once you are imbued with the "spirit" of Rugby Union" it never leaves you. It is the finest of all games, and one of the few remaining "big games", untainted with the "Greed for Gold", (it is open ONLY to bona fide amateurs). Thanks being due to the stern measures adopted by the R.U. Association.
How a man can be a "paid sportsman" surpasses my comprehension, but of course that is just my personal opinion.
Last Wednesday's game showed a great all round improvement, which spoke volumes for the good work in training undertaken by the Capt., "Freddie" Hirstwood. The match opened with a fast bout of exchanges in which we pinned the Navy well down in their own 25 from which they could only emerge occasionally. This pressure was kept up throughout the first half, and in spite of many near goes we could not score. The ground conditions were against us in the second half, and the Navy seizing every opportunity pressed home a scrambled attack which led to their touching down very near the posts. The Navy failed to convert, their kick going some 10 foot wide of the post. Maintaining their pressure, the Navy scored twice more each time failing to convert. Final score; Navy 9 pts. Exiles nil.
The match as a whole was good considering it was only our second attempt, and we did very well to hold them to 9 points. Of the players; Reedman proved a very pleasant surprise at Full Back. "Slap" played a very safe game, his positioning was good, and even under pressure his kicks seldom failed to find touch and some over a considerable distance. It was a shame we had no opportunity to see his "place kicking". He played a good game, and as far as I remember was never once "caught in possession". The scrum results being as they were, we had no good opportunity of seeing our "threequarters" in action. Defensively they played very well. "Alec" Keenlyside and "Bob" Broom (both seasoned veterans) in the centre ruthlessly stopping any attempt at breaking through, while Anderson and Owen on the wings both did their share of stopping. Andy also putting in some good kicks to touch. Pollard at "Stand-off" had little chance to shine in attack, but his tackling was very safe, and few could elude "Snubby's" clutches. In the loose he showed no hesitation in flinging himself down on the ball under the feet of the opposing forwards. Which is the usual privilege of a good scrum or stand off. "Freddie" Hirstwood at "scrum-half" did not see much of the ball owing to slow heeling. I thought he was too much inclined to "blind side tactics", which invariably failed due to the quick way the opposing forwards broke up, and the fact that their scrum was almost permanently "oof-side".
The Forwards, like the P.B.I. do all the work, and got none of the credit. Our forwards really were too slow in "heeling", and far too slow in "breaking up".   (Contnd.)

REFLECTION No. 8 — My Ship by Gilly

On Aug. 8th. 1912, the first keel plate of H.M.S. Lowestoft was laid at No. 8 Slipway in Chatham Dockyard. On the same day another event of lesser National, but greater personal, interest occurred. I commenced my Apprenticeship as a Shipwright. The instructor-shipwright who was to have the thankless task of teaching me the rudiments of the trade, belonged to the party working on the keel-laying. (I might add that the poor man also had to see that I didn't go on train-riding excursions all over the yard, play football and cricket with the other lads, pelt seagulls with nuts and bolts etc. etc. -for which a most unappreciative Admiralty paid him an additional 2/- per week!)

The slipway is uncovered and points obliquely up the river: it can be seen from the Sun Pier at Chatham. The work of laying the outer and inner keels did not interest me a lot, I'm afraid, as it took me some time to get accustomed to the infernal din of hundreds of machines, worked by compressed air, rivetting, cutting, caulking and drilling. The long hours, 7 a.m. to 5 p.m. were also a source of worry to me after the school hours. I had just left. I was just 14, and still wearing shorts, an Eton collar and scull-cap. Gradually, however, I fitted in to the routine and as the frames were erected, giving the mass of iron a ship-like appearance, my interest was stimulated; within me was born a "pride of craftmanship"- an emotion which, I fear, has been slowly strangled in recent years by "mass production" methods.

We worked all through the winter on the plate-wharf alongside the slipway, selecting and preparing the plating for bulkheads, decks, partitions, engine and boiler room flooring and so on; from there the iron and steel plates went to the machine shops for cutting, drilling, etc. and when they returned we went aboard to fix them in position. Higher and higher went the ships sides and higher the scaffolding. Compartments were tested for water-tightness, A-brackets fitted for propellor shafting, stem and stern posts erected and built in. Eventually we were working on the upper-deck. It was not long before preparations were commenced for the great event-the launching. An army of painters appeared, and after a few coats of oxide and anti-rust, dressed the vessel in her best suit of Naval grey - "crab-fat" to all seafaring men. Scaffolding was dismantled and in June 1913, she was ready for her christening. On the morning of launching we were all in to work early to catch the low tide and "set her up". All shoring and supports were removed, except the dog-shore. Launching was timed for 12.30 and an hour or so before this the ceremonies commenced.

Contnd.

"MY Ship" Contnd.

The Royal Marine Band, the Chaplain and choir from the Dockyard Church and a host of Naval and Admiralty officials, resplendent in gold braid and trimmings took part in the Service. A bunting-bedecked platform had been built against the bow and the ceremony of naming and launching was carried out by the Mayoress of Lowestoft. I, together with the other apprentices, was in a "grand-stand" seat, perched, precariously, high up in a derrick. I saw the champagne bottle break against the bow, and watched, with eyes rivetted, for movement in the huge hulk. She moves! Immediately hundreds of sirens broke into a chorus of "Cock-a-doodle-do's"; she slid gracefully and with increasing speed into the river. I was thrilled. She took the water beautifully and as the tide swung her upstream her clean, graceful lines gave an impression of immense power and great speed. No Captain or Admiral has ever been prouder of his vessel than I was at that moment. I, an insignificant little lad of 4'6", had helped build that grand ship-and there she now lay, safe in the arms of Father Neptune and an inspiring sight indeed. I assisted in the building and launching of many vessels in later years, but never did I get quite the same "kick", as I did from the launching of **MY** Ship, the light cruiser "Lowestoft" in June 1913.

RUGGER REVIEW (Contnd.)

As soon as the ball is out, you must break up, otherwise there are 8 good men out of the game, and 9 if the scrum throws himself flat when passing. In the loose there was good individual play, "Theo" Smith, Mitchell, Hobden, James, etc. But what was lacking, was a "leader of the pack", to impress on them the spirit of working as a pack, running as a pack, and hunting as a pack. There should be little difference between hounds after a fox, and forwards after the ball. Where the ball is, there should the forwards be also. After all, 8 men in a bunch with the ball at their feet want a lot of stopping. Instead we saw "Theo" Smith half way up the field with the ball at his feet, and not another man within 30 yards of him, finally having to kick into touch as his breath gave out. Whereas with another 7 forwards, they might have gone the length of the field and touched down for a try. It must always be remembered that the game is "football", and passing movements are actually subsidiary to kicking the ball over the line and touching down.

From the spectators point of view it was a good game and we all enjoyed it. If we enjoy it when you lose, how much more shall we enjoy it when you win?. But win or lose, the "game" is the thing, and let us make a name for ourselves as sportsmen who "count not how we win or lose, but how we played the game".

"Snikmot".

Aegrescit Medendo

I'll tell you all a simple tale,
Which, when you've read it, if you fail
To sympathise with this poor youth,
Your heart must be of stone forsooth.
Down in a hunting town hard by
There lived a youth who well might cry
That ne'er a vice he did possess
Except in smoking, more or less.
However one day as he smoked,
His active mind this scheme evoked,
If cigarrettes he ceased to crave,
Look at the money he would save.
His mind made up, he loathed to tarry,
And ran to an apothecary,
Demanding something to inure him,
Pills, guaranteed to kill or cure him.
Thereafter in the hut of "K"
He strove his best to win the day
And every time he longed to smoke,
Into his mouth Pink Pills he'd poke.
These pills both noxious and bad,
Did almost kill our gallant lad.
Their taste was bitter, almost rancid
And yet in time it seemed he fancied
Their taste upon his palate growing,
Was as a river gently flowing.
And in his hours of idle leisure
To him it soon became a pleasure
To take a pill and suck it slowly
Producing happy melancholy.
Until his yearning for them rated
That he could not be satiated.

Now months elapsed before our hero
Reached what we call financial zero
For though by now he didn't smoke
He yet was nearly always broke
And running through his file of bills
He found they all were for Pink Pills.
This situation that he saw
Staggered and shook him to the core
That, part in earnest, part in joking
He soon resolved to restart smoking
And so this tale of simple annals
Returns right through its previous channels
But the mental anguish that he passed through
None but our hero ever knew
Now, through his folly clearly sees
The cure was worse than the disease.

"Shikmot".

THE GOSPEL ACCORDING TO ST. UPID. Chapter XIX
(Translated from the English by Disciple Millhouse).

Now, at certain times, and in certain places, men took maids in their arms and staggered about on a slippery floor in divers strange and wondrous ways. And it was called a Hop. Now in Voyg there were some Scribes who hopped exceeding well. And there were some who hopped in a manner fair. And there were some who had simply No Idea.

Now the Tribe of Atsites in the land of Voyg had multiplied and waxed exceeding strong, until their numbers were become greater than the numbers of the Scribes. And when the Atsites descended upon Townorl and sundry other places where hoppers assembled, they did find they were without Partners. And those Scribes with No Idea which ventured into Townorl, propped up the Bar, and consumed an abundance of Womp and Firewaters, and went not upon the floor save when they were possessed of a Full Skin and an abundance of Dutch Courage. And at these times they had even less Idea.

And the publicans, and the brewsters who made the Womp, were sore dismayed and filled with disquiet, saying: Woe is us! For these sinners do consume all our Womp. Verily, the land shall be stricken with a Womp famine unless all these which have No Idea learn the art of Twerpsichore.

And the Atsites, hearkening unto them, lifted up their voices with the publicans and brewsters, crying: Yea! Ere the fountains of Mild and Bitter are dried up, let these sinners learn the magic of the Hop, that we may be blest with a multitude of Partners. For in these days a maid must Hop with a maid, which is like unto Bread and Bread. Let there therefore be Bread and Butter.

And it came to pass that Hari, the Fruit Man, and Karinton called Peter, and the maid Ilari, hearing these things, were cast down, and forthwith went into a huddle. And they saith unto the peoples: Come hither into Lownj of Kantin, all ye which have No Idea, and we will teach the Gospel according to Victor Sylvestor.

And they came forth, and entered Lownj, and the Apostles gave them the Dope. And one or two Atsites which were exceeding brave, being blest with stout sandals, and knowing not the suffering of corns and bunions, came hither also. And the Scribes with No Idea experimented upon the Atsites, and shewed them all manner of Unnatural Turns and Flat Spins, until they were afflicted with a Crossed Chassis. And the Apostles saith unto them: Do This. And they straightway did That. And this was called Contrary Body Movement.

And certain of these men with No Idea were also men of Ohmgard. And when they returned to the centurion, and he commanded them: Left, Left, Left, Right, Left, they saith unto him: Nay! Henceforth say unto us: ONE, two, three, ONE, two, three, or we know not what to do.

And the publicans and the brewsters, who were fearful of a Womp famine, and the Atsites, who had no partners, prayed daily, saying: Let it come to pass that these Awkward Crabs may soon acquire Some Idea.

Shssh!   G O S S I P   Shssh!

CONGRATULATIONS:- To L/Cpl. Jessie Adams on her marriage to Mr. G.F. Reeves, of Woodhouse Eaves, at Quorn Parish Church, on Saturday 20th March.
To Mr. & Mrs. R. Wilkinson on their happy event. A baby daughter. No further information is available, but you know what these artists are!

SABOTAGE! Our snoop reports that his "holiness" has been guilty of daffodil bulb extraction, in complete disregard of the appeal in our last month's issue. May his daffodils turn out to be "pansies" and not survive the rigours of the changing elements.

CANTEEN! We can now report having seen members of the staff eating cooked dinners in the canteen, and reporting on watch as usual the following day. We understand that Mr. Appleton, our fishing expert, has secured the contract to supply fish to the canteen, in spite of keen competition from Macfisheries. "Apple" regrets his inability to supply them "wholesale".

NATIONAL SAVINGS! We record our very warmth thanks to the officials and helpers of the Group, for the efficient manner in which this continues to function. We well know the tedious and laborious work involved, but with regard to the writing out of certificates, wish that we personally, could have provided them with much more labour.

THE EWA WHO TRIED TO JOIN UP!   "I go------------I coom buck".

PRESENTATION! An impressive ceremony took place at Barrow recently, when the O/C, accompanied by a large selection of A.T.S. Officers (including the Group Commander, Senior Commander Carter, O.B.E.) presented Sgt. Gladys Earle (née Webb) with a certificate for "bravery and devotion to duty". This was awarded by the War Office for her outstanding conduct during the catastrophic bomb incident at Chatham. A little tardy but none the less deserved.

EXILES TABLE TENNIS CLUB! With reference to the notes on another page, we welcome the wording "in turn, and regardless of ability, represent the "Exiles"." Here is an attempt at real "non-subsidised" sport. Good luck to them.

RUMOURTISM! The atmosphere in the Section has recently been choked with irresponsible rumours as to "where we will go". We have taken the liberty of engaging the services of a very rude old man, who will take great pleasure in telling them "where they can go".

BILLETING! Have recently noted the gradual influx of still more E.W.A's into Woodhouse Eaves. From our own experience, we say it is a good move. Woodhouse has no illusions about you and doesn't give a damn for a "civil servant", but accepts you as you are. We like them.

WE NOTED! A WORD FOR THE DAY   "To live long, one must live slowly". From certain observations we fear there will be an awful drag on the Old Age Pensions later on.   LET'S HAVE THE "DIRT".

DUDLEY TRUIN REVIEWS :-

WHAT'S ON?

LOUGHBOROUGH "FLICKS"

WEEK COMMENCING APRIL 5th.

"A GENTLEMAN AFTER DARK" is Heliotrope Harry (Brian Donlevy). A jewel snatcher "who gave law and order such a kick in the pants that he took the war off the front page". He reforms when his daughter is born, only to be black-mailed into murder by his wife; a real gangster melodrama. On the same programme (EMPIRE, first three days) there is Ralph Byrd in "BROADWAY BIGSHOTS".

"HEART OF THE RIO GRANDE" showing at this cinema at the end of the week is a romantic western with Gene Autry in the lead, singing "Deep In The Heart Of Texas". The supporting film is your old friend Edward Everett Horton in "THE BODY DISAPPEARS".

It's a pretty safe bet that when Bing Crosby, Bob Hope and Dorothy Lamour get together, they are on the road to somewhere or other. This time it is "THE ROAD TO MOROCCO" (ODEON, all the week). It's the mixture as before, with the story a mere incidental, a background to those perfectly timed wisecracks, bevies of lovelies, haunting melodies, romantic moons and the irresistible fooling of the entire population of Dorothy's sheik infested country. More than somewhat of a contrast is "WRECKING CREW" with Richard Arlen & Chester Morris.

Another comedy of a more slapstick nature is "CHARLIE'S AMERICAN AUNT" (VICTORY, first three days) with Jack Benny as "the aunt in pants" and Kay Francis as Dona Lucia. "SUNDOWN JIM" is a supporting western.

"TEN GENTLEMEN FROM WEST POINT" (last three days) deals with that famous military academy at the beginning of the nineteenth century. George Montgomery is tough as the ardent young man from Kentucky who mistakes society lady Maureen O'Hara for a kitchen maid, but Victor Francen as a French instructor of tactics, steals the picture from an excellent cast.

WEEK COMMENCING APRIL 12th.

Lon Chaney Jr. has in my opinion more than lived up to the high standard of acting set by his world famous father. He appears with that polished British actor, Sir Cedric Hardwicke, in another horror film ,"GHOST OF FRANKENSTEIN". EMPIRE this week, first three days; also "ON THE SUNNY SIDE", with Jane Darnell.

In "ALIBI" (last three days), Margaret Lockwood as an ingenuous night club "hostess" takes money from a charlatan to say he spent the night with her when, actually, he was out "bumping off" an enemy. When James Mason turns up "all drunk and loving" only to have the murder pinned on him, things begin to look a trifle awkward you must admit. Also, Kent Taylor, in "HALF WAY TO SHANGHAI".

British films before the war, were a subject for derision and justifiably so; but since 1939, in spite of immense difficulties, they have gone from strength to strength, and now, in Noel Coward's "IN WHICH WE SERVE" they have given the world one of the finest films of the war. It is the story of a destroyer and her crew, from the time she is commissioned until she is finally sunk in the battle of
Crete.

"WHAT'S ON " (Contnd.)
Noel Coward, who plays the part of the captain, has written and produced a film for which he deserves the highest praise. ODEON, all the week. Don't miss it.

Will Hay, with his pince nez always on the point of dropping off his nose, is surely one of the best loved of British comedians. Personally I have yet to see a funnier film than ("OH MISTER PORTER"). Wherever he goes he always lands himself in trouble, so it is hardly surprising that he was "THE BLACKSHEEP OF WHITEHALL". (VICTORY, first three days). In an all laughter programme, there is also Laurel & Hardy in "SAPS AT SEA".

In "ONE FOOT IN HEAVEN", (last three days), Fredric March with Martha Scott as his wife, gives a sincere performance as a parson, whose unselfish work is hampered by rich busybodies, and how he eventually triumphs over all obstacles.

WEEK COMMENCING APRIL 19th.

Humphrey Bogart is well cast as an unscrupulous private detective in "THE MALTESE FALCON" (EMPIRE, first three days). Mary Astor's charm and beauty mean nothing to him and when it happens to suit his plans, he betrays her without the slightest compunction, to achieve his ends. The supporting film is Richard Arlen in "RAIDERS IN THE DESERT". At the end of the week Mickey Rooney is a bell hop in "YESTERDAY'S HERO" who gets involved in a scheme to cheat a group of co-operative dairy farmers. How the unfuriated farmers eventually bar the road with logs to stop the milk trucks getting through, is one of the film's high lights. Jimmy Durante in "YOUR IN THE ARMY NOW" is the second feature.

"THE MAJOR AND THE MINOR" (ODEON, all the week) is an amusing story of a girl's masquerade as a twelve year old, in order to travel from New York to her home at half fare. Suspected by the guard the girl, (Ginger Rogers) takes refuge in the compartment of an army major, (Ray Milland) who befriends her and takes her to the military school at which he is an instructor. How the major's fiancee sees through her disguise and how Ginger Rogers then poses as her own mother and wins the major's heart is romantically told. Alan Mowbray in "THE DEVIL WITH HITLER" is the supporting film.

At the VICTORY, first three days, there is a lively musical with Ann Miller "PRIORITIES ON PARADE". The members of a struggling band join an aircraft factory in the hope of winning fame by their entertainment of the workers, only to throw their chance away when it comes, in order to do the more vital job of the two. Supporting, there is Kent Taylor in "FRISCO LIL".

At the end of the week, in "TOMBSTONE", Richard Dix is a frontier marshall who gives you plenty of fighting in the old tale of rounding up the bad men in Arizona. A jungle drama is the other feature. "AFRICA IN THE RAW."

"WHAT'S ON" (Contnd.)

WEEK COMMENCING APRIL 26th.

"THE VALLEY OF THE SUN" (EMPIRE, first three days) is a robust western picture with James Craig & Lucille Ball, set against realistic backgrounds. It tells of a scout's intervention between Indians and their rascally agent. The supporting number is "NINE LIVES ARE NOT ENOUGH" with Ronald Reagan.

Judy Canova is appearing at the end of the week in "SLEEPYTIME GAL" in which she plays the part of a kitchen maid in a pastrycooks shop. But her voice attracts attention and she is entered for a radio contest by her friends. A novel musical comedy. On the same programme there is "THE MAN FROM HEADQUARTERS".

"THE FALCON'S BROTHER" (ODEON, first three days) is the last in that excellent series based on Michael Arlen's famous character. George Sanders as the amateur detective meets his end but the tradition is carried on by his brother (Tom Conway) who incidentally is his brother in real life. Also showing is "GERT & DAISIE CLEAN UP", with Elsie & Doris Walters.

For the last three days there is a gangster comedy "A HAUNTING WE WILL GO" with Laurel & Hardy and Dante the Magician, together with some excellent trick photography, the film's best feature. On the same programme there is Alan Jones in "MOONLIGHT IN HAVANA".

Do you remember ("CITIZEN KANE"), that novel and successful experiment in production by Orson Welles?. Producers, with few exceptions mean little to the public, but here is a name you should not forget. In "THE MAGNIFICENT AMBERSONS" (VICTORY, first three days) Orson Welles has given us another penetrating study of ordinary people, no legs or sex but first class acting from Agnes Moorehead, whose performance won for her the title of "Best Actress Of 1942". (Greer Garson was only second for Mrs. Minivor), given by the New York critics; Tim Holt & Dolores Costello. This is a film I strongly recommend "ESCAPE FROM HONGKONG" (last three days) deals with events there on the EVE of the Japanese declaration of war.

EXILES TABLE TENNIS CLUB

The lately-formed Table Tennis Club is now going strong, and there is a gratifying number of the Staff taking a keen interest.

So far we have played off the long-drawn out Tournament and Two-Club matches. The first of the Club Handicap Tournaments is, at the time of writing, getting into stride. Our first Tournament was won by T.Bancroft, and the Runner up was T.J.R.Smith.

The first club match played against the Mission Hall Club was won, and the second, against the Brush Sports Club, was lost. We are confident, however, that after more practice and more matches, a good representative team from any shift can be turned out.

We have quite a few fixtures against local clubs, including a return match with the Brush, and all club members will, in turn, and regardless of ability, represent the "Exiles". (Contnd. at foot of back page).

SPORTS PAGE

SOCCER. The two matches against R.A.O.C. were lost by narrow margins. The match versus Brush Car Shop was lost by one goal although on this occasion we only had ten men. The Cobbin Trophy Cup match against 320 Coy. Pioneer Corps, was drawn.

RUGBY. A description of the last match will be found on another page.

CRICKET. The Home ground will again be at Quorn and I am now arranging fixtures. Last season was disappointing because of cancellation of fixtures through bad weather etc. I hope for better luck this year.

TENNIS. The court will be opened very shortly. New or second-hand balls are urgently needed. If anyone knows where these can be obtained, please let me know.

A.H. Appleton.
Hon. Sec.

THE CANTEEN.

It was hoped that by now the Canteen would be serving a full programme of cooked meals, throughout the day. The Committee would like it to be known and understood as widely as possible, that they are far from satisfied with the present arrangements. The main obstacles to be overcome are :-   (a) shortage of Canteen Staff.
(b) incomplete cooking equipment.

(a) This is the most serious problem and the co-operation of all Club members is asked for to overcome it. Full and part time workers, of any reasonable age and either sex are urgently needed as Assistants, Cooks and Cleaners. If YOU know of any person who may be interested, please have a word with the Manager, who will gladly give all details and will, if necessary, arrange an interview.

(b) The cooking range is slowly taking shape, after a lengthy period of "no progress". Numerous other kitchen alterations are proceeding. As soon as the workmen are clear of the kitchen AND the necessary Staff is available the complete quota of meals as originally promised will come into operation.

The Committee are aware of the sense of disappointment prevalent amongst some sections of the Staff, and, in fact, share this feeling themselves. They do ask, however, that members will appreciate the real difficulties, and realise that everything possible is being done under the present trying circumstances.

W.J. Gilliard (Secretary)
Staff Club.

There is an acute shortage of Table Tennis balls. The Club is willing to pay 6d. each for them, to anyone with any to dispose of.

RESULTS:- Exiles v Mission Hall Club. Away. WON.
Exiles v Brush Sports Club. Away. LOST.

M.A. Reed.
Recorder.

"B.S.M". APRIL, 1943.
Vol.2.   No.7.

General Editor:- L.P.Jones.   Editorial Board:-
                                R.Wilkinson.   R.G.Denny.
Editor:-   F.C.Staddon.   E.Millhouse.   T.Brister.

Next publication:- 28th.May.   Contributions by:- 15th.May.

FRONT COVER DESIGN BY:- R.G.DENNY.
Inner cartoon executed by Miss Muriel Fidoe (A.T.S.)

Owing to a technical process known in Hut "C" as "scrubbing", a number of people will find themselves without a copy of this august publication. Despite all our warnings and pleadings, we found ourselves left with a considerable number of the March issue of the "B.S.M." Many of these were in the names of people who had previously been spasmodic in the honouring of their commitment, and who seem to think it only right and proper that we should print a copy for them specially. They, apparently retaining the right to purchase or not, as the whim guided them from month to month.

Well, this will not do, and from now on every listed subscriber failing to take up his specially printed copy will have his name deleted from our books. The name will only be reinstated on special application to the Editors and a gentleman's agreement that they will take their copy up each month until such time as they may have cancelled same in a proper manner.

In the event of any members of the Section leaving this locality, would you please inform us if you wish to have the magazine sent on to you. Given full details, we are prepared to offer this service.

Our A.T.S. artist has executed what we feel to be a very apt cartoon. Various people have been tested with this, and whilst expressing amusement, have not been able to give a very clear explanation of what was in the Editorial mind when commissioning the drawing.

As a matter of interest, we offer a small prize for the best description of what was brewing in this noble cranium when Muriel was asked to "get cracking". Mss. are confined to 50 words.

HELP US TO MAKE THE "B.S.M." INTERESTING BY SENDING IN YOUR MSS.,

SKETCHES, IDEAS, GOSSIP ITEMS etc.

EPISODE IN N. ATLANTIC - 1940   A. A. HASTINGS.

We sailed in convoy from a British Colonial port on a beautiful summers day in September, bound for home; with cork and turpentine on deck and wines, brandy and sardines below. A lovely sight, about 50 ships in 5 lines, with their escorts dotted in and around the lines of ships, and signal flags fluttering in the nice fresh breeze.

Next morning, what a change! Big Atlantic rollers crashing over the ships and the destroyers rising halfway out of the water, and almost disappearing in the troughs the next minute. The wind was now a gale, blowing right ahead at about 50 miles an hour, and by nightfall the neat lines of ships were gone. The escorts were trying to keep in touch with all of them but the ships were widely separated. We were with 3 others, about 15 miles astern of the Commodore's ship, just out of sight of him. Luckily, no enemy attacks took place during the 3 days the gale lasted, but when the convoy reassembled, 3 ships had failed to catch up, and we had used so much coal in keeping up, that we were unable to continue with the convoy, and had to start off alone for Limerick, which was the best port we could make with our remaining bunkers.

During the next 7 days we saw nothing except sea and sky. We really had amazing luck, as we had crossed the track of raiding subs and aircraft from France to the Atlantic, and none had seen us, though 2 ships of our convoy had been bombed and I had read 8 subs. reported positions and about 20 aircraft reports during that time, and some were very close to us.

During the 7 days alone on the sea, all of us had been at high tension night and day, with our 4" gun manned all the time, but unfortunately we had no anti-aircraft guns, except 2 service rifles, if they can be called that, and it was F.W's of which we were most concerned. However-10 a.m. on the 8th. day "Land ahead sir" and up loomed the rugged coast of southwest Ireland, and in 2 hours we were in territorial waters of I.F.S. and also in very high spirits. Lunch at 12.30 was a merry meal as we discussed what we would do ashore at Limerick, where we were due at 7.30 p.m. that day. But alas for our hopes, at 1321, when I was on watch and the Captain and 2nd.Officer on the bridge, a F.W. appeared, slowly circled, and finding only rifles as opposition, came in at mast height, opened up with incendiary machine-gun fire, every bullet of which started the cork burning, and dropped one bomb in the engine room and another at the base of the block comprising Captain's cabin, bridge and wireless room.

As soon as the plane was near enough to be identified, the Captain commenced swerving violently at full speed and I commenced the aircraft distress signal "AAAA" 3 times, position, name of ship, and "bombed" AR. The time available was so short, that though I sent as fast as I can move a key, I had only completed the position for the second time when CRASH!!!, up went wireless set, operator and everybody else on the bridge.

When I regained consciousness, my head was out in the open and the rest of me covered in burning debris, and the first thing I saw was the F.W. still hovering nearby, but he was satisfied and had stopped firing.   Contnd.

I got a bit panicky when my hair began to singe and after fierce struggles, during which I put my foot out, I was able to stand up and look around. Only the sky above and the ship a mass of flames below, coupled with the roar of escaping steam from the boilers.

The Captain was near me and just freeing himself and the Bosun appeared suddenly and as suddenly disappeared as he fell off the heap of debris, which had once been a bridge etc., on to the deck below. The Captain and I failing to see any sign of life around us, had just decided to slide off into the sea, when the Steward's welcome voice shouted, "just a minute, I'll come and help you down". It was a nightmare getting down to the deck and thence to the boat, but eventually all were there but 6, who had been located and found dead in various places, but much to my surprise the Bosun was there with nothing worse than a broken bone in one foot.

As the boat pushed off in a hurry to get away before the 4" magazine blew up, the F.W. flew away to the North and then I collected my wits, which had been stunned by the explosion and shock. I then realised I was saturated in blood to the waist and was bleeding from 4 wounds in the face and head; a lump of the stuffing (I forgot the name) of the lifebelt, a nice soft cotton, soon stopped the bleeding, and after the Captain who was severely injured internally and had a broken leg, had been laid flat, the brandy was passed round and we all began to take an interest in where we were going, and set course for Valentia Island.

A few minutes later, a fishing trawler, who had received my message and with amazing courage had steamed towards us while they could see the F.W. still there, in order to save as many as possible, picked us up. Within the hour the 8 wounded were in hospital beds and the 14 unhurt were knocking back Guinness in the hotel.

That night lying in bed, I heard Haw Haw make one of his rare true accounts of a success. He said, "An enemy cargo ship of 2500 tons was attacked off the S.W. coast of Ireland and its cargo destroyed". The F.W. did not stop to see the ship sink and neither did we, but we heard that at 8 p.m. when she sank, the sea was covered with a mass of flames over an area of several square miles.

While we were still in the boat and later in the trawler, we had seen the overheated drums of turpentine shoot high into the air, burst and come down in a cascade of flame. A beautiful sight, once we were out of range of them.

SEQUEL TO THIS STORY:-

While I was still in hospital, our rescue trawler was machine-gunned by a F.W. but escaped without damage. Three weeks later, a F.W. bombed and sank them, 2 only surviving from a crew of about a dozen very brave men. Incidentally, the Skipper was a naturalized Britisher of Russian birth.

My Native Twang

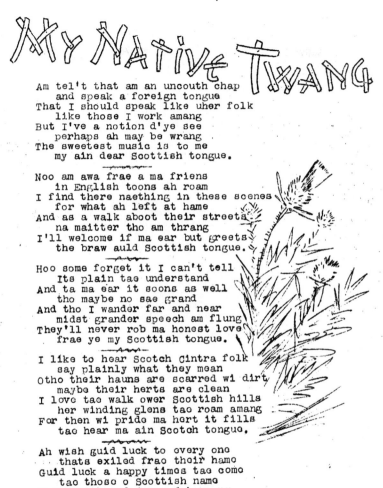

Am tel't that am an uncouth chap
   and speak a foreign tongue
That I should speak like uher folk
   like those I work amang
But I've a notion d'ye see
   perhaps ah may be wrang
The sweetest music is to me
   my ain dear Scottish tongue.

Noo am awa frae a ma friens
   in English toons ah roam
I find there naething in these scenes
   for what ah left at hame
And as a walk aboot their streets
   na maitter tho am thrang
I'll welcome if ma ear but greets
   the braw auld Scottish tongue.

Hoo some forget it I can't tell
   Its plain tae understand
And ta ma ear it soons as well
   tho maybe no sae grand
And tho I wander far and near
   midst grander speech am flung
They'll never rob ma honest love
   frae ye my Scottish tongue.

I like to hear Scotch Cintra folk
   say plainly what they mean
Otho their hauns are scarred wi dirt
   maybe their herts are clean
I love tae walk ower Scottish hills
   her winding glens tao roam amang
For then wi pride ma hert it fills
   tao hear ma ain Scotch tongue.

Ah wish guid luck to every one
   thats exiled frae their hame
Guid luck a happy times tae come
   tao those o Scottish name
May health and joy and harmony
   for ever dwell amang
Frae honest herted Scottish folk
   that speak the Scottish tongue.

                                        W. Gordon.

Bill Baker "Scooped the Pool at Monte Carlo"

Monte Carlo had welcomed me with a perfect sky and glorious sunshine. I found her offering even more than all the picturesque descriptions I had previously read. After London and Paris she came as champagne to a glass of stale beer.

The dome on the Casino glittered under the powerful rays of the sun. My eyes rested on it for the first time from a distance of two hundred yards, and at the same moment my heart seemed to miss the usual beat. So this was the place that had lured me 1,500 miles to risk my all. I strode hastily forward.

On top of the steps leading into the Casino I hesitated, and turning around looked down...... When I return down these steps I shall either be the new edition of the "man who broke the Bank at Monte Carlo" or just another guy whom Monte Carlo broke. And then forward into the Casino. Within a few minutes I was gambling--I was winning! It was too good to be true!

Very soon I was noticed. It was very obvious my luck was right in, and the little group of people that gathered around me grew in size. I could sense their keen interest and excitement. Their eyes followed the numbers as keenly as mine. In their excitement they reacted in the same way as I did--as amazed as I with my good fortune.

Each time it was my number--each time my fortune increased, and the crowd sighed with me in sympathetic excitement. This was life with L in gold. I hung on grimly to my lucky farthing--clutched in my left hand. I had always known this farthing, picked up outside the Post Office at distant Clapham Common, would bring me luck.

In seconds my thoughts raced ahead-- if my luck held that day--who knows--my own yacht--a nice bungalow in the South of France--sunshine and swimming in the Med. forever mine--my thoughts were disturbed by more good fortune....I could do nothing wrong.

And then the blow fell--like a dark cloud passing over the sun--my luck changed. I was losing! it seemed unbelievable--it couldn't happen to me--it wasn't cricket. I was tempted to back out still well on the right side, but no, this moment would pass-- I hung on.

Still hanging on fifteen minutes later, my pile of francs had diminished until there was one left. I jammed it in the infernal, glorified Fruit Machine, and left the results-- if any--from the racing mechanism to the tourists standing by. With a sigh I strode quickly away from the Fruit Machine in the Foyer and passed into the Casino proper.

In a few minutes I was replacing a crestfallen looking soul just leaving a chair next to the Croupier. At last, ready to risk my all.

AS WE SEE THEM

Nr. 2.

SIR GALAHAD SETS FORTH

194

THE SOUTH SEAS

F.W. LEEDHAM.

In the late 1920's I was a member of the crew of the s.s."Antonib". In spite of her Italian sounding name, she was a typical British tramp steamer, flying a tattered red ensign at her stern.

We had been chartered to carry phosphates from the lonely South Sea Islands to Australia and New Zealand.

For nearly a year we cruised about in the warm turquoise Pacific Ocean. Then, one day, we received orders to carry a cargo of coal from Westport, New Zealand to Tahiti. I had been told that Tahiti was an island paradise and a Garden of Eden. I was certainly not disappointed.

Tahiti is the principal member of a group of islands called the Society Islands and is under French administration. It has an area of approximately sixhundred square miles, is of volcanic origin and thoroughly mountainous. We were to take our coal to Papeete - often called "The Pearl of the Pacific". Papeete is the chief port and capital of the island.

We arrived at Tahiti in the early hours of the morning and in the grey light of dawn the island loomed ahead dark and mysterious. Shortly after sunrise we entered the small bay known as Papeete Pass, and I had my first view of the little port.

I was enraptured with the scene that lay in front of me. The tiny white buildings of Papeete shining in the sun, the light green foliage of the banana and bread-fruit trees. The tropical plants with their colourful and sweet-smelling flowers; and, rising up in the background, the dark misty blue mountains of the interior.

Papeete has only one main street of a somewhat sandy character with a number of side streets running off it. The population is slightly less than fourthousand. There are Hotels,Banks,Government offices, an 'American Bar' and numerous fruit shops owned by Chinamen.

There is one small cinema in Papeete. I saw a silent film shown here and during the whole performance an interpreter explained the picture and translated the dialogue to the audience in their native language.

The Tahitians are robust and have well proportioned bodies. They are brown skinned, have black hair and beautiful white teeth. Tahitian girls are lovely and graceful of form. They present a very attractive and fascinating picture in their simple and gayly coloured dresses. Usually their wealth of dark hair is adorned with highly perfumed flowers.

The Tahitians are very friendly, the girls especially so. They treated life as a game, were easily amused and thoroughly enjoyed a joke but their love and affection has a superficial and ephemeral quality. I saw one girl drink a large bottle of wine in less than an hour without any change in her deportment. Nevertheless in such a romantic and amatory atmosphere the pulse of life was quickened and we surrendered gladly to the magical charm of the island.

(Contnd.over)

Beaumanor National Savings Group

I have for some time been intending to write an article, but for one reason or another it has remained unwritten. However, I feel that the time has arrived when the shareholders in this mighty concern should be presented with a balance sheet, this I append. Exact figures for the present cycle are not possible at present as there is a certain fluctuation in membership, but the general trend of saving is ever in an upward direction.

First of all I would like to thank the collectors, past and present, who have helped to make the Group what it is today. We have had to overcome obstacles such as the collection on rota system of shift work, and I think that this has now been brought to almost a fine art, thanks to co-operation. Also, it is sometimes difficult to make the elusive sixpence fit in, especially when money is handed to us in the Canteen, on the roads, and even in the streets of Loughboro'.

Next, the shareholders themselves. I thank you for your words of commendation, they amply repay us for our labours. Also, thanks to those who have uttered words of criticism, when meant kindly it has assisted us in the work, and it does show that you take an interest in the movement beyond the merely personal one of amassing riches. To words not kindly spoken (and I am pleased to say that these are few) we either turn a deaf ear or give a suitable reply.

As many of you are probably aware, our Treasurer, Mr.Manington, has spent some very weary days writing up certificates. I am glad to say that, with the help of the Regional Commissioner, we have devised a scheme whereby the work will be spread over the cycle, and certs. will be issued at intervals. A fuller explanation of this scheme will appear shortly on the Canteen notice board. Also, new members may join, and increases may be made at any time without worrying about paying back to the beginning of the cycle.

Some of our old members will have left us by the time these words appear in print, nevertheless I wish them all the best of luck in their new stations. I also extend a hearty greeting to all new members, and, although many of the fairer sex will not agree, I hope that they will remain members for a long time.

Regarding local "Wings for Victory" weeks, I would like to help both Loughborough and the Barrow areas. The dates are, Barrow, May 1-8, Loughborough, June 29 - July 6. I would therefore ask any members who intend making outright purchases during these weeks, to let us do the business for them, it will help our own Group, and we will see that the money gets to the right place. (Balance sheet at foot of next page)

The decrease in weekly average per member in the 3rd. cycle would appear to be due to the increased A.T.S. membership. It must be realised that the A.T.S. cannot save so much as the more affluent members of the Staff, but it is expected that the average at the end of the cycle will be higher than 4/2d.

It is impossible to give a definite figure showing Group saving per member based on total staff for 1st.&.2nd. cycles owing to increases in personnel on the station, but at the time of going to press it is 1/3½d. This is the way competition averages are reckoned, not just on the number of subscribing members.

F.A.Fairbanks
Hon.Sec.

To all of you I wish Good Luck and - GOOD SAVING.

BEAUMANOR NATIONAL SAVINGS GROUP-Balance Sheet:-

```
1st.Cycle 1.1.42 - 31.7.42   By Group Subscriptions  £592.10.0
                             "  Outright Purchases    191. 5.0
                             "  Sale of Stamps         17.14.0
                                                                801. 9.0
2nd.Cycle 1.8.42 - 27.2.43   By Group Subscriptions  £994.10.0
                             "  Outright Purchases    442.10.0
                             "  Sale of Stamps        147. 1.0
                                                               1584. 1.0
3rd.Cycle to 8.4.43          By Group Subscriptions  £200. 0.0
                             "  Outright Purchases     65.15.0
                             "  Sale of Stamps          7.15.0
                                                                273.10.0
                             Total 1.1.1942 - 8.4.1943     £2659. 0.0

Weekly Averages:-
           1st.Cycle £26.14.3½  - Per member  3/4d. - 160 members
           2nd.Cycle £52.16.0   -     "    "  4/9d. - 240    "
           3rd.Cycle £54.14.0   -     "    "  4/2d. - 263    "
```

££

GOSSIP.

<u>CONGRATULATIONS</u>:- To Mr. & Mrs. Reedman on the gift of a son and heir, John Stuart, 3rd. April, 1943. We anticipate that "Slap" will be severely chastised for giving his son a cricket ball to play with.
<u>MR. APPLETON</u>. We understand that Mr. A.H. Appleton has had an unfortunate occurence of breakage with his spectacles. This occured during a very proper "long week-end". That's his story and he's sticking to it. In view of this we have no hesitation in electing him as auditor to any ventures in which we are interested.
<u>THE REVERSE</u>. We understand that a small unfortunate incident occurred in the Canteen recently. An observor informs us that this was not a case of pouring oil on troubled waters, but pouring water on troubled oils.
<u>WE WERE AMUSED</u> ex "Daily Telegraph"-Situations Vacant:- "A lady secretary to director-West End-£5 and prospects".
<u>CHOIR SOCIAL</u> This proved to be a great success and the Choir Committee wishes to say "Thank You" to those who assisted in various ways.
   Regular choir practices are suspended for the summer months, but it is planned to have in the meantime, occasional rambles, so watch the Canteen Notice Board for details.
   Respectability is overwhelming the Section. The Gossip writer cries out for scandal, titbits etc.

<u>YOU INSTITUTE THE"GOSSIP", I'LL MAKE IT SOUND A DARN SIGHT WORSE</u>.

HERE IS THE NEWS
(REPRINTED FROM "LONDON OPINION", JAN.)
by ERIC C. MILLHOUSE.

Too bad that fool Biddle kept me, jawing about his confounded tomatoes. When there is no Biddle to hinder me I reach home just in time to hear the six o'clock "pips", and settle down to listen to the news in comfort. But to-night, Alvar Lidell is already embarking on "To-night's announcements", as I tear in.

Almost before I have awarded the Missus the daily salutation I burst out:

"Did you listen to the news?"

"Yes, dear", she replies, then, after a few moments, in which she presumably marshals her facts:

"The Japs have sunk something or other of ours-would it be a cruiser? Or perhaps it was we who sunk one of theirs. Some American troops have been landed in Mandalay------"

"Mandalay?" I interject, incredulously. "You don't mean Madagascar, I suppose?"

"Why, of course, that's right," she resumes hurriedly. "These foreign names are so confusing, dear. The R.A.F. raided somewhere or other in Germany, in daylight to-day - sounded like Santa Mare", then after an anxious, almost guilty pause - "but wouldn't that be in Spain, dear?"

"Not Spain or Germany, love," I respond encouragingly, "but probably St.Omer in France. How many did we lose?"

"Seventy-four," she replies brightly, then, hurriedly, "Oh no! That was the number the Russians claimed on the Western Front."

"Eastern front, dear," I say patiently. "Did Jerry come over here last night?"

"Oh yes!" she says, a worried look clouding her face. "He said there was a sharp attack on a North-west town. I do hope Molly and Jack are all right."

Mentally deciding that as Molly and Jack live in Hendon their safety can hardly have been seriously threatened, I callously continue:

"How many did we bag?"

"Four," she replies promptly. Then doubt once more shadows her face. "Or perhaps it wasn't four. Any way, he either said four persons were killed, or else four Jerries were destroyed."

"Anything new from Russia?" I ask, somewhat hopelessly.

"Er-the Soviets have nearly captured a place with a name I couldn't possibly pronounce, much less remember, dear."

"Anything about Libya?" I enquire forlornly.

She meditates.

"I don't think there was anything important, but I believe he said we had captured a few Japs."

My tact forbids an enquiry as to whether the Afrika Korps has reached Port Darwin, and I regretfully abandon the field of foreign news.

Contnd. over.

Matewa Reflections
(Looking Forward To Looking Back)

I remember son, in days of yore,
When youthful, I was but a score,
I dwelt in Woygland, land of wonder,
While a common foe split towns asunder.
We cared not then for tyrants wrath,
With hair askew and lips afroth,
For on our work we'd concentrate,
To bring about the present state
Of peace and friendship o'er the earth
And joy and happiness and mirth.

Our work was arduous, none could know
Our untold misery and woe;
"They also serve who sit and wait",
I served, my trousers shone like plate,
We sat through all the hours God made,
We toiled while watching daylight fade,
And even as the dawn came creeping
And birds and beasts alike were sleeping
Still we sat and laboured on,
Tired and weary every one.

Not all the time was melancholy,
At times, nay frequently, t'was jolly.
We had our football, cricket, dancing,
Beery hops and much romancing,
With women to relieve our sorrow
We worried not about the morrow.
And so, on looking back, my son,
I think that I should like to run
Back to the days I thought were hellish,
But this time every hour I'd cherish.

"NOSWEH".

"HERE IS THE NEWS" (Contnd.)

"What's new on the Home Front, my dear?"
"Darling!" she whoops, eagerly. "Lord Woolton says we're all to have six eggs next month, and there is no immediate prospect of the meat ration being reduced. Oh! and the cheese ration is going to be increased!"

No doubt when I get my newspaper to-morrow morning I shall find she is perfectly right about the eggs, and the meat, and the cheese.

FRED HEARN'S FABLE

A certain E.W.A. returned from his break with a far-away look in his eyes. An observant colleague offered him a penny for his thoughts, but was offered them free, gratis and for nothing, to whit:-

"I have just had a most marvellous meal, the like of which I never thought to see in these difficult times. I walked into the canteen, and was met by a trim waitress dressed in a short black dress covered by a small white pinny — you know, the sort carriers of trays used to wear before we went on the 'Coupon Standard'. She led me to a table spread with a pure white damask table-cloth, held down by a motley collection of silver knives and forks, and the usual condiments necessary to a choice and appetising repast.

On taking my order, she was back in a flash with the necessary provender, and it was then I had my real shock. Instead of the "Spam Rolls" I had asked for, a bowl of hot rich turtle soup was placed before me. Before I could remonstrate with her, she was gone, so I tackled the job in front of me, and was it good? Having wiped the bowl clean with a nice new roll, I sat back with a sigh, when low and behold, the "Angel", (for that is what I had christened her by now) appeared with another tray, and gently put in front of my stomach, that is on the table, a neatly piled up plate of roast chicken and vegetables to match.

Dazedly I reached for the knife and fork and tackled the miracle, conveying it where it would do most good, in the shortest time I could.

More than satisfied, I was wiping my moustache with a napkin (I forgot to mention this) when a dish of cheese and biscuits appeared, together with hot coffee. I managed to polish most of this off, and glancing at the clock, I noticed my half hour was up, so rising, I staggered away, quite forgetting to ask for my bill, and here I am."

"You must have been dreaming", said his colleague.

"That's right", was the answer. "How did you guess?"

"Well", replied his colleague, "THEY DON'T HAVE NAPKINS IN THE CANTEEN".

"Observations in 'K'

THREE ORDERS UNIVERSALLY OBEYED WITH ALACRITY:-

A. "BREAK" (a staccato order rapped out between teeth tightly clenching pipe)

B. "WILL YOU GO FOR YOUR BRAICH Mr...." (savouring slightly of Scotland)

C. "TAKE YOUR BREAK MATE"   R.G.W.

NOTES ON MUSICAL TOPICS (2)   The Orchestra (contd.)
by Harry Dodd.

Last month I enumerated the four "families" of instruments of which the modern orchestra is composed; I am now going to discuss two of them: the Strings and the Wood-wind.

The Strings are the backbone of the orchestra, their number being about two-thirds of the total strength of the orchestra. You will see from last month's diagram that the 1st and 2nd Violins are on the conductor's left. The Violins used by the 2nd Violin players are, of course, exactly the same as those of the 1st Violins, the difference being merely one of function. The Violas are usually in one line facing the conductor. The Viola looks like a Violin and is played in the same manner but is larger and has a range five tones lower. To the right of the conductor are the 'Cellos, and behind them, the Double-basses. The Double-bass looks like a large edition of the 'Cello; it is usually required to play an octave lower than the 'Cello. The player sits on a tall stool so as to bring his unwieldy instrument into a comfortable playing position.

For a good example of string-playing, listen to Elgar's "Serenade in E minor" and, for the use of the "pizzicato" method of playing (i.e. plucking the strings instead of bowing them) listen to the 3rd movement of Tschaikowsky's 4th Symphony.

The Wood-wind players are in one or two lines facing the conductor, behind the Violas. In a normal-sized orchestra there are two of each main Wood-wind instrument. The orchestral Flute is transverse; i.e. it is played in a horizontal position by blowing across a hole at one end of the instrument. Its sleepy, mellow qualities are admirably exploited by Debussy in his "L'Après-Midi d'un Faune". The Piccolo, the Flute's small brother, plays an octave higher; its shrill tone is sparingly employed, usually in colourful and exciting music.

The Oboe is a "double-reed" instrument, the mouthpiece consisting of two long, thin pieces of reed bound together. Its tone is penetrating and reedy. The slow movement of Tschaikowsky's 4th Symphony opens with an Oboe solo. The Cor Anglais, the Oboe's cousin, is larger than the Oboe, having a range five tones lower. The double-reed mouthpiece is bent so as to bring it within easy reach of the player's mouth. Its hollow, nasal tone is quite different from that of the Oboe. Dvorak gives to it the main tune of the slow movement of his "New World" Symphony.

The Clarinet is a single-reed instrument; the reed lies against the tip of the tube, forming the mouthpiece. The Minuet in Mozart's 39th Symphony has a graceful duet for two clarinets. The Bass Clarinet, with a range five tones lower, has the lower end of its tube turned up, like that of a saxophone; it is only an occasional member of the orchestra.

The Bassoon, the largest of the Wood-wind instruments, is an 8-foot tube bent back on itself in the form of a U. The long, thin double-reed forming the mouthpiece is at right-angles to the tube, the end of the latter extending above the level of the player's head. Its tone is dry and reedy and is often used for humorous effect, as, for example, in the amusing dialogue between the Piccolo (the highest in pitch of the Wood-wind) and the Bassoon (the lowest) in Johann Strauss's "Perpetual Motion". There is also a Double Bassoon, but this, like the Bass Clarinet, is not often employed. (Next: Brass/Percussion)

DUDLEY TRUIN
REVIEWS:-

WHAT'S ON
Loughborough "Flicks".

EMPIRE. May 3rd.(3 days) Clifford Evans in SUSPECTED PERSONS.
                          also "PACIFIC RENDEZVOUS"
         May 6th.(3 days) Chester Morris in "NO HANDS ON THE CLOCK"
                          also "LAW OF THE JUNGLE"
ODEON.   May 3rd.(6 days) Brian Donlevy, Robert Preston in "WAKE ISLAND"
                          also "FLYING WITH MUSIC"
VICTORY. May 3rd.(6 days) Jack Benny, Carol Lombard in "TO BE OR NOT
                          TO BE" also "WE SAIL AT MIDNIGHT"
EMPIRE. May 10th.(3 days)Ann Sothern in "SHE GOT HER MAN"
                          also "TODAY I HANG" with Mona Barrie.
         May 13th.(3 days)Ellen Drew in "MY FAVOURITE SPY"
                          also "THE MAN WITH TWO LIVES"
ODEON.   May 10th.(3 days)Kathryn Grayson, Van Heflin in
                          "SEVEN SWEETHEARTS"
                          also "AFFAIRS OF JIMMY VALENTINE"
         May 13th.(3 days)Ann Sothern in "PANAMA HATTIE"
                          also Albert Dekker in "HITTING THE HEADLINES"
VICTORY. May 10th.(6 days)Bette Davis, Ann Sheridan, Monty Woolley in
                          "THE MAN WHO CAME TO DINNER"
EMPIRE. May 17th.(3 days)Leslie Banks, Will Hay in "BIG BLOCKADE"
                          also Richard Arlen in "FORCED LANDING"
         May 20th.(3 days)Basil Rathbone in "FINGERS AT THE WINDOW"
                          also "ALONG THE RIO GRANDE"
ODEON.   May 17th.(3 days)Victor Mature, Lucille Ball in
                          "SEVEN DAYS LEAVE"
                          also Andy Devine in "DANGER IN THE PACIFIC"
         May 20th.(3 days)Brian Donlevy, Diana Barrymore in "NIGHTMARE"
                          also "MRS. WIGGS OF THE CABBAGE PATCH"
VICTORY. May 17th.(6 days)Abbott & Costello in "RIO RITA"
EMPIRE. May 24th.(3 days)Burgess Meredith in "STREET OF CHANCE"
                          also Edgar Bergen in "HERE WE ARE AGAIN"
         May 27th.(3 days)Robert Preston in "PACIFIC BLACKOUT"
                          also Eastside Kids in "MR. WISEGUY"
ODEON.   May 24th.(6 days)Dick Powell, Mary Martin in "HAPPY GO LUCKY"
                          also "LITTLE TOKYO U.S.A"
VICTORY. May 24th.(3 days)Nelson Eddy, Jeanette Macdonald in
                          "BITTER SWEET"
         May 27th.(3 days)Eleanor Powell in "SHIP AHOY"
EMPIRE. May 31st.(3 days)Mickey Rooney in "A YANK AT ETON"
                          also Richard Carlson in "HIGHWAYS BY NIGHT"
         June 3rd.(3 days)Jackie Cooper in "SYNCOPATION"
                          also Ann May Wong in "BOMBS OVER BURMA"
ODEON.   May 31st.(6 days)John Payne, Betty Grable, Victor Mature in
                          "FOOTLIGHT SERENADE" also "NATASHA"
VICTORY. May 31st.(3 days)"THE DOCTOR AND THE DEBUTANTE" with
                          Lew Ayres, Lionel Barrymore.
                          also "DAWN EXPRESS"
※ ※ ※   June 3rd.(3 days)"HER CARDBOARD LOVER" Norma Shearer, Taylor.
          THE PICK OF THE MONTH:- "STREET OF CHANCE" (Empire, May 24th).
"WAKE ISLAND"(Odeon, May 3rd). "THE MAN WHO CAME TO DINNER"(Victory, May 10th).

IT WASN'T HANGOVER (OR WAS IT?) AK.

That confounded alarm broke in on my heavy sleep. Knocking the angels off their perch on the bedrail, 'cos they do watch over you during the dark hours. However, the insistent rattle of my alarm would unsettle anything within a radius of a couple of miles, and even I have to make a move when it commences its ether disturbing din.

I reached out, and knocked this ingenious type of siren off its perch, where it continued its unearthly din, making it imperative for me to get out of bed and switch off. I leaped (did I say, leaped) out of bed, and a pain smote me between the eyes; just seemed as though the floor came up and connected with my head, GOSH, where had I been last night, and what had I been up to?

I fumbled around and eventually turned it off, but there was no relief for my poor head. I stumbled along to the bathroom, and indulged in a few guaranteed pain killers. The pain will go, if you take sufficient, and we always found it cheaper to buy them in bottles of a hundred. Anyway, after being indulgent I commenced with soap and cold water.

After washing and whilst drying, I had occasion to bend down. As I bent down, something seemed to snap right between my eyes and everything went black. I very nearly screamed. I felt my eyes, they were wide open. I must be blind. What should I do?. I felt like screaming, my stomach turned over, and the saying that your heart comes into your mouth is certainly not exaggerated. I was in a cold sweat, and started repeating my prayers. I had gone through everyone I know in the first ten seconds.

I said to myself, I must be brave and walk downstairs, and try and tell my landlord as nonchalantly as possible, that I had been stricken with blindness. If everyone else were filled with panic, I'd have to enact the lone brave hero for a little while. I moved in the darkness and my hand caught the blackout curtain and dragged it to one side, and behold, I saw light. Was I pleased or just pleased. I would willingly have given my clothing coupons to some poor, and needy A.T.S. at that moment. I was really overcome and even my headache vanished like a flash.

After various tests known to us scientists, I found that the meter wanted another bob in, and the lights had gone out simultaneously with my bending down. Tame aint it?.

"THE SOUTH SEAS" (Contnd.)

We stayed in Papeete for three days, They were three glorious days and two delightful nights. Work became an intolerable vexation. We worshipped at the shrine of Venus. We drank deeply from the Bacchanal cup.

The time passed. On the evening of the third day as the sun, a ball of flaming gold, was dipping down to the distant horizon, we said farewell to Tahiti. Our friends on the island came to see us off, throwing coloured paper streamers to members of the crew not on duty. Soon we were moving slowly away - the streamers parted and the last link with the island was broken. The girls dived into the sea in their dresses, shouting and laughing, swimming and splashing. An hour later, Tahiti faded into the dark Pacific night.

SPORTSPAGE

FOOTBALL. Dickenson had the misfortune to break a collar-bone in the match against Brush Apprentices. This was the result of an awkward fall. The committee wish him a speedy recovery.

The re-played Cup match was won by us by the narrow margin of one goal. This was a hard match, played in hot weather. Dalton scored from a penalty given for a handling offence. 320 Coy. had a dangerous forward line, but our defence kept them out. The high-light of the game was when Hobden made a magnificent save from a penalty kick.

RESULTS:-   Alliance League.

Feb.27th.	v R.A.O.C.	Away.	Lost	3-0
Mar. 6th.	v R.A.O.C.	Home.	Lost	2-1
" 13th.	v Brush Car Shop	Away.	Lost	1-0
" 26th.	v Brush Reserves	Away.	Lost	5-1
Apr.16th.	v Brush Apprentices	Home.	Won	2-0
" 26th.	v Hathern	Away.	Lost	2-1

Cup.

" 3rd.	v 320 Coy.		Won	1-0

(Dalton)

TENNIS. I am sorry that it has not been possible to open the Court yet. The chief problem being that the roller has been claimed and taken away.

All the tennis-balls I had, have been sent away to be re-covered and re-inflated. When these will be done, I have not the least idea. Probably three months at least.

CRICKET. The committee have elected M.Musgrave as Captain for this season. The Selection Committee is composed of:-Messrs. M.Musgrave-W.H.Anderson-F.J.Mayne-A.H.Appleton.

A.H.Appleton.
Hon.Sec.

EXILES TABLE TENNIS CLUB. We have now passed successfully through the initial stages of awkward adolescence and the club is going ahead well.

We stand on an exceedingly sound financial footing, mainly because members have kept well up to date with subs: and because we received a very generous grant from the Staff Club, for which we were very grateful. The position now, is such that the weekly subscription has been reduced to 3d., and new members are asked for an entrance fee of 2/6d.

No Club matches have been played to date and as yet the Club Handicap Tournament has not begun.

At the Club, besides Table Tennis, we have the use of a billiards table and darts-board. Space is somewhat limited, but we have managed, so far, to get by.

Table Tennis is still the main occupation, so that any non-member who is interested and willing for a game, should come along on Monday Nights between 6 and 10, and join up with us.

M.A.Reed.
Recorder.

"B.S.M". MAY, 1943.
Vol.2. No.8.

General Editor:- L.P.Jones.   Editorial Board:-
                                 R. Wilkinson.   R.G.Denny.
Editor:-   F.C.Staddon.   E.Hillhouse.   T.Brister.

Next Publication:- 30th.June.   Contributions by:- 15th.June.

FRONT COVER by:R. Wilkinson.
Illustrations by:R.G.Denny.

  Up to the time of going to press, we have only received one contribution on the theme of the cartoon in our last issue. This has come from our old friend, "Poet Laureate" Ollie Pearce. Whilst Ollie has failed to explain the idea that we were trying to convey, his is such a good effort (in spite of exceeding the 50 word limit), that providing no more than a dozen people forget to pay for their magazine, we will award the Editorial biscuit to him.
  Whilst various people had threatened to send in their Mss on this subject, here is a further case of the one solitary person having the necessary real interest or sufficient energy to actually do so.
  We conclude that either our artist disguised the meaning behind the cartoon too cleverly, or that we were the only people who heard all the rumours, and they were many and varied, as to where we were likely to end up. For reasons of secrecy, that is the only pointer we can give you but feel sure that you will all get the point now.

  We would ask you to collect your "B.S.M." as early as possible to avoid this being left in the Canteen for too long a period. When this happens there is a tendency for your copy to become about "fourth-hand" and to contain contributions that were never passed by the Editor, in the form of Jam, Spam etc. etc.

  We are anxious that you should continue to send in your Mss. and ideas during the summer months, in spite of the many counter attractions. The Editorial Board feel this outdoor urge as much as the rest of the staff and often have to take ourselves severely in hand in order to make it possible to produce this publication at all. The forthcoming months give boundless scope for your literary efforts and we hope you will inundate us with MSS. IDEAS. CARTOONS. etc. etc.

  We have only recently received a suggestion that we should run a series called "The Daftest Thing I Ever Did". We think it wise to point out that the obvious theme has already been considered by the Editor, and discarded due to the inability of passing the Mss. through the censor. Well what about it?. We hope next month to publish a Mss. from one of our readers on this theme.

THE GOSPEL ACCORDING TO ST. UPID.   Chapter XX
(Translated from the English by Disciple Millhouse).

    Now in Oliwud, which is in Usa, dwelled a famous man called Klark Gabel. And Klark was good to look upon, even so that he was become a Heart Throb to many maidens in many distant lands. For Klark was the Answer to a Maiden's Prayer.
    And it came to pass that Klark's Uncle Sam fought a war with Hit and Tojo, wherefore Klark pinned back his ears and became a centurion of Uncle Sam's soldiers. And he sailed across the oceans and came unto Brit.
    Now certain ladies of the Atsite tribe in Woyg learned that Klark was indeed in Brit, and they were straightway in a Flutter. And they communed one with another, and saith: Behold, we will hold a Hop privily, and bid Klark and his comrades hither.
    Now in Kwarn, which is nigh unto Woyg, was a habitation called Urst (and sundry other names) wherein dwelled some lesser Atsites. And the ladies came unto Urst and arrayed it with garlands of flowers, and prepared many good things for Klark. And when they beheld certain lesser Atsites who were weary of their toils and slept in the lower bedchambers, they spake unto them saying: Take up thy beds and walk, for Klark cometh.
    And they went into Kantin and took from thence the Musick Box, saying: Peradventure we will hop with Klark to the melodies from the Musick Box. And perchance the students of Twerpsichore shall not miss it, for is it not believed among all men that the Twerps hop better when there is no Musick?
    But it is written that Klark journeyed from afar and was nigh unto Kwarn, when he came upon a maiden of exceeding good countenance. Likewise in divers other places was she also exceeding good. And she gave unto Klark the Glad, and Klark tarried and was lost.
    And in Urst the hour appointed came and passed, and Klark came not, and the ladies were cast down. And they went into a huddle, and saith unto a servant: Go out quickly into the streets and lanes of the city and bring us some men. And the servant said: It is done as thou hast commanded, but behold there are no men, for they have all departed from hence and gone up the road for a Quick One. And the ladies said unto the servant: Go out into the highways and hedges, and bring in hither the sick, and the halt, and the lame. And the servant said: This I have done and now must needs have a chariot to bear these peoples hither.
    Now at this time there were chariots assembled without, to bear pilgrim Atsites to the Temples. But the ladies seized the chariots and sent them forth into Luff, saying unto the Pilgrims: Verily, it is a pleasing night for a walk, so get ye going. And when the pilgrims were set forth the ladies were filled with remorse and summoned a small chariot, and sent it after them. But because the chariot was small it could contain but six pilgrims, wherefore it journeyed back and forth divers times, for the walking pilgrims were numbered three score.
    And the other chariots returned out of Luff bearing the sick, and the halt, and the lame. And they cried unto the ladies: Behold, we cannot Hop, for we are on crutches. And they looked, and it was so.

                                                       (Contnd. over)

YOUR PROBLEM PICTURE AS I SEE IT

By: Ollie Pearce.

How shall I spend them?, - Down by the sea?,
On broad Scottish moors, or in meadow and lea?,
Lounging, perhaps, in the smart haunts of town?,
I weigh every prospect, but turn each one down,
Decision evades me, I'm restless in bed,
Anxiously wondering what lies ahead,
You can't make your plans when you'll probably be
Slicing up spuds in a suit of khaki!

(Refers to the April cartoon).

∧∨

THE GOSPEL (Contd.)

Now a certain maid who had toiled well in the temples and was exceeding weary, returned into Urst seeking her bed. And upon a door she beheld a parchment on which was writ: Klowkrum. And she cried out: Woe is me. For until this night this was the door of my bedchamber, and is no longer. And she was sorely cheesed, and sat without and wept.

And when the day was come to an end and the moon was high in the heavens, the pilgrims returned unto Urst and perceived that all the peoples were Browned Off even unto their very eyebrows. And upon the tables they beheld an abundance of Cream Buns and delicacies. And crying aloud: Nice work, they fell hungrily upon them and devoured them all, saying: Behold. We are not Browned, for Klark hath nobly favoured us by his absence. We pray that next time ye are disappointed it may be by Teddy Brown.

DUDLEY TRUIN —

In the playground of Europe

The train has hardly left Samaden before the rain, which has been threatening all the morning while we have been exploring the Via Mala, starts to fall with a vengeance. A solid curtain, obliterating the entire landscape.

I turn from the window with a grunt of disgust and glance across at Ben, but Ben is already nodding; the hard wooden seats of the third class carriages on the Swiss Federal Railways are no determent to Ben. We've had a pretty tough week and he never could stand getting up early in the morning, anyhow. The Duck is sitting next to me; Nino had christened him the Duck way back; I don't know why; probably because apart from "One Hundred Damn" it was one of the few English words that he knew. But the name had stuck and the Duck he has remained. On the other side of the compartment a peasant woman is listening to the chatter of her little girl; they are speaking in Romansch, the nearest living tongue to the Latin of ancient Rome.

The train is climbing steadily through the storm, and its getting jolly cold for the 15th. July; I'm just putting on my rain coat when we plunge into one of those never ending tunnels which you find everywhere "En Suisse". In five minutes or so we're out on the other side and "Sacré Cochon" its snowing. Snowing steadily as though it were the middle of January not July. "Say Ben does it always snow like this in the Engadine in the middle of Summer?" I yell across the carriage; only in French of course. On our arrival in Switzerland we had agreed to speak only French "Il faut avoir la pratique vous savez" and French it had remained. Ben says he doesn't know and in turn asks the peasant woman; but she only smiles and shakes her head so as none of us speak Romansch or are likely to, the conversation flags and we gaze dismally at the ever whitening countryside.

Its still snowing hard when we pull into St.Moritz. We shoulder our packs, button up our macs at the neck and stagger out to investigate this mecca of society, the home of the idle rich. The station nestling at the bottom of the mountain on the lake side is a garish futuristic affair painted in vivid, contrasting colours of brilliant reds and mauves and greens quite out of tune with nature. But looking upwards at the skyline we find something strangely familiar and reminiscent. The huge luxury hotels towering skywards up there on the mountain, brings to mind that famous view of New York of skyscrapers and colossal buildings brought to every corner of the globe by the men of Hollywood, and now we understand the incongruity of the station below.

We have a look around, visit that renowned tower of some antiquity but are not much impressed by this vaunted little place. Maybe the snow doesn't help matters any. Our trousers are wet through and sticking to our legs so we decide to have a meal. After we've eaten we feel much better; Swiss food is guaranteed to have that effect on you but we come out of the restaurant to find it still snowing, so the Duck says its about time to find somewhere to sleep. We trudge off down the hill again for the luxury hotels are not for us. We are members of the Jugendherberge — no nothing to do with the Hitler youth, for we are in those halcyon days of 1930 — (Contnd.)

Its a Swiss Youth movement which boasts of hostels in most places in Switzerland where for a franc - or I should say a bob - you can get a couple of blankets and a paillasse for the night with maybe cheap eats as well.

Our present objective is a converted barn by the lake - up to now we've been lucky and havn't found any difficulty in getting accomodation but when we arrive at the barn "Quel Horreur!" the place is absolutely swarming with people. Evidently St.Moritz exercises its spell over the humble as well as the rich. Though its quite early, still only about nine o'clock most of the people seem to be settling down for the night and forms are stretched out on either side of the barn as far as we can see. Some one tells us that there is a "Balcon" at the end with straw on it and that's all there is left and its pretty full already. "Tout pis" c'est la vie" we scrounge a blanket each, lucky to get that, and mount the ladder which gives access to our bed of straw. Its rather dark and its as much as we can do to find ourselves a place to stretch out in. We drag off our wet coats and trousers soddened and heavy - beastly prickly stuff this straw - and its only when we are wrapped in our blankets that we begin to feel better.

Ben lights a cigarette and then the form between myself and the wall rolls over and says something in that vile language Swiss German, of course I don't understand a word and reply, "Pardon Qu'est-ce Que Vous Dites?" and to my surprise a girls voice replies "C'est Défendu de Fumer - you are English N'est-ce Pas?" "Oui- Je Suis Anglais" "Oh I am pleased to meet you I am Rosa Muller of Bâle, please tell your friend he must not smoke on account of the straw", but Ben has already put out his cigarette. We endeavour to continue the conversation in French but Rosa Muller isn't having any, crushingly she tells us that our accent is appalling and so we can do nothing else but talk to her in English. So perched up there on our balcony of straw under the roof of the barn she tells us how she is a governess in her native Bâle and is now "en vacances", how she spent 18 months at Manchester High School for girls and how she hated it. I keep intending to ask her what in heavens name prompted her to go to Manchester of all places but somehow I never do and so I've kept wondering ever since. She says she went to learn our language because as everyone knows English is the national language of Switzerland and every Swiss worth his salt speaks "les quatre langues".

Before I realise it, morning is here and the snow is melting fast in the bright sunshine. Snow doesn't stay long in July not even at St.Moritz. We stroll by the lake side clad in pyjamas and raincoats while Rosa irons our bedraggled trousers back into some semblance of respectability with her travelling iron; and after we've shaved before the barn door - all rather primitive - Rosa appears with some hot coffee and crisp rolls and butter apologizing for not having any tea. Well Swiss coffee is good enough for me anywhere anytime. Nice girl Rosa, don't you think? in spite of what she said last night about our rotten French accents. (Contnd.)

212

IN THE PLAYGROUND OF EUROPE (Contnd.)

We're on our way again. We wave goodbye to Rosa, swearing eternal friendship - I've never seen her since - as we set off towards the station along the edge of the lake.

A layer of mist hangs in the valley tinted a warm gold by the rays of the early morning sun. It divorces the lake from the mountains so that with their peaks, freshly whitened by yesterdays snow, they seem to be floating in the sky mingling with those fleecy clouds, which like pieces of cotton wool, are drifting across its face of eggshell blue. The air is like wine, fresh and invigorating. We draw in great draughts and feel good. We think maybe there is after all something in what people say, when they rave about St.Moritz.

Very soon we are in an electric train on a cog railway slowly climbing the Bernina Pass. We are passing through some superb scenery, fairy like in its mantle of white and gold. On our right high on the mountain side lies Pontresina. The real home of the winter sports enthusiasts and from here they go to attack the famous Cresta run, and, strange as it may sound, such are its hazards, it is never covered successfully by more than thirty different people annually.

We are rising steadily, round a bend in the track and there over on the right in all their vastness are the giant peaks of Piz Palü and Piz Bernina, awe inspiring and aloof, towering above the small ranges which lie at their base sparkling in the sunlight and wreathed here and there with wisps of clouds, trailing veils, smoke like and transparent.

We weave our way through a short tunnel and there in front of us is the Lej Alv - the black lake, its inky waters are due to the river which feeds it filtering through beds of peat. Cows are wandering round its edge, puzzling no doubt over this snow in July and we can hear the tinkle of their bells quite clearly above the steady hum of the train. We pass from the black to the white; for the next lake along whose borders we are now travelling, appears to be filled with milk. The Lej Nair or white lake is fed direct by the stream from the white Cambrena glacier.

Still higher and we're glad of the electric heaters which have been switched on in the carriage, for though the sun is shining as brightly as ever, its getting jolly cold. Finally one more tunnel and we are at the Bernina Hospice and the top of the pass. We are about a mile and a half above sea level 7,644 feet to be precise. A post here shows the highest point reached by the snow each year. The highest being 12 feet on the 24th.May, 1879.

Down the other side the first station is Alp Grüm our destination. From here we have one of the finest views in the whole Bernina pass. The railway glued like a piece of tape to the mountain side winds away down the Poschiavo valley towards Tirano and Italy. Directly opposite us rises the Piz Palü that white hell, pitiless and majestic and from it pours that lava like erruption the blue white Palü glacier ending in a thin trickle of water, which by the time it reaches the sea has swollen to a mighty river. Far, far below us the valley through which it runs seems nothing more than a model, with doll like farm houses and miniature cows and trees, with winding paths and roads.

Here on the balcony of Alp Grüm station with this fascinating panorama spread out before us we lunch. (Contnd.)

RADIO MANNERS = CUIMR'HA

```
If she is after a date............METER.
If she calls for you..............RECEIVER.
If she is afraid of the dark......CONDUCTOR.
If she tries to act like an angel..TRANSFORMER.
If she tries to pick your pockets..DETECTOR.
If she eats too much..............REDUCER.
If she is wrong...................RECTIFIER.
If she makes advances.............RESISTOR.
If her hands are cold.............HEATER.
If she wants a vacation...........TRANSMITTER.
If she talks too much.............INTERRUPTER.
If her views are narrow...........AMPLIFIER.
If she feels romantic.............OSCILLATOR.
If she talks to a guy who writes
                odes to Radio.........ELIMINATOR.
```

(ED. We are indebted to our furthest outpost for "Radio Manners").

IN THE PLAYGROUND OF EUROPE (Contnd.)

The Duck takes innumerable photos as usual and as we stand there arguing about exposures and colour filters and the like, we hear a very pucka Englishman say to his lady "you know my deah, ten or even five years ago to see those fellahs standing there; you'd say immediately ah English! flannel bags, sports coat, Englishman's uniform what? But there they are spouting some foreign lingo. Really you don't know where the hell you are these days, "Pon my word you don't". Oh Rosa ma chérie, would that you were here to hear it.

We say goodbye regretfully and humbly to that breath taking scene and soon we're back again in St.Moritz for a fleeting minute. Another train ride and we are at Coire where we await the Rome - Cologne Express. It arrives and we make a dash for the German carriages on the train they're so much cleaner than the Italian. Ben settles himself comfortably, he should get a good sleep we've a four hour journey north before us.

And so with the setting sun turning the capital of the Grisons, to blood, the train takes us on the first stage of our trip to Winterthur and Hanny Laufer

- but that's another story.

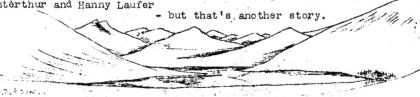

Shssh! G O S S I P Shssh!

CONGRATULATIONS:- To Mr. & Mrs. L.P. Jones on the gift of a son, Michael John, who arrived in the wilds of Diseworth on 6th. May. The Editorial Board anticipate that with this extra help it should be possible to accelerate the publication of the magazine in future.

Congrats. also to A.T.S. Hazel Webb on her promotion to the rank of Sergeant, and Ats Callcut & Please on their elevation to the rank of Corporal.

ALSO RAN! Good old George.

SYMBOLICAL! Canteen serving "trifles".

CAMOUFLAGE! Our observer one recent Sunday morning noticed what appeared to be a mass evacuation. On closer acquaintance however, this proved to be none other than Lt. "Dick" Whitford, mounted on an armoured cycle with various militant oddments a la Sid Walker. Unlike most of us, he was not looking for a new billet, but parachutists, which the writer ventures to suggest is probably a much less difficult job.

R.N.O.C.A. Dance. This was a very convivial event and it was a particular treat to see "Tommo" being taken around the floor by various partners. In spite of many rumours to the contrary, the writer insists that it was possible to distinguish a few of the Woygite personnel amongst the crowd.

SHOULD WE HAVE BEEN AMUSED? During a recent visit to Barrow, met a soldier who had cycled from Leicester, in uniform with sandals as footwear. During a pleasant afternoon canoeing, the sandals had been discarded for comfort and mislaid or stolen. Climax! A cycle ride back to Leicester, in uniform with bare feet plus rat trap pedals.

HOW NOW, BROWN COW? In spite of the appearance of Home Guardsman Jock Smyth on a recent occasion, we understand that no exercises involving the use of mustard gas, have been held here.

IS YOUR JOURNEY REALLY NECESSARY? Apparently from the official viewpoint, "No", unless they can think up some ridiculous place from which to collect your ration book.

THIS LIQUID! Is it not possible to provide a drink not only possessing the quality of warmth, but also a tantalizing suggestive flavouring of tea? We have heard rumours of an increase in price, presumably on a 33-1/3% basis. The writer would support this heavy increase, providing it would then be possible to purchase a cup of TEA in the canteen.

TENNIS:- Emphasising the plea on the Sports Page, we would point out that the court cracks up very quickly and could do with watering and rolling each day.

"Appie" badly needs some hose
The size threequarter inch
He calls upon you tennis fans
Buy, borrow, beg or pinch.
(What a "squirt")

Please send your Gossip titbits to the Editor.   SO LONG FOLKS!

TYPICALLY ENGLISH

The preparation of the Exiles cricket pitch did not seriously disrupt the Military manoeuvres.

With apologies to Rayon Stockings

Ex:
Daily Press.

Twenty seconds' care in putting stockings on can add months to their life. Turn leg inside out — slip foot on, and then smoothly roll leg up. Don't suspender too tightly.

(A PRESS CUTTING DUGGANISED)

We mere males had an idea there was some mystery connected with legs. Little did we guess however that the fair sex could do all these things with them, and what's more wonderful, in exactly twenty seconds.

The last sentence is presumably a necessary precautionary measure which has to be taken to ensure that the legs don't remain rolled up. Be careful girls that after having rolled the legs up as far as possible, you can always return them to their normal position.

It is a pity the advertisement doesn't tell you what to do after the leg has been unrolled - It's important, but of course perfectly obvious - After the leg has been unrolled and turned correct side out again, the stocking should be put on and a chic garter placed around the upper end to indicate just where the stocking ends and the leg proper begins.

As a further refinement, some of you may care to make use of ladders. The really smart girl of course will see that these never lead quite to the garter. Ladders might, if they finish at the garter give quite the wrong impression - care should be used to see they finish abruptly just anywhere. The more obvious you can make the end of the ladder the better, provided the end does not draw attention to any other adornment. The cuteness of this little idea of course being the symbolical use of the ladder to convey an impression. If the ladder finishes just "nowhere in particular", it may give the impression that you will stop at nothing in the same way as the ladder stops at "nowhere in particular". If you grasp this idea correctly, Romance will almost inevitably come your way.

Those of you whose ambitions soar to the more sober aspect of matrimony, might try the same basic idea with this difference. Let the ladder run right to the garter which should be finished off with a large knot, tied for preference in the gordian fashion.

THE R.A.F. BLAST RUHR DAMS!

We hear that Hitler raved and cursed
When the Raf dropped eggs on Hamm
But since they've visited the Ruhr
Can't bear the sound of DAMN!

"Freelance".

TRIBUTE TO THE 8TH ARMY

by Ollie Pearce

From every kind of home, from every
    county in the land,
Men from each trade and calling came
    to form this gallant band,
Though differing in class and creed,
    they had, in every case
One common trait, tenacity, the
    birthright of their race.

What they achieved historians will
    competently tell,
What they endured through those long
    months may not be told so well,
The dangers and the hardships which
    they bore by night and day;
Their anxious thoughts for those they'd
    left so many miles away.

Reversals too they suffered but their
    spirit still remained,
For every inch of ground they lost a
    dozen more were gained,
Against a highly organised, well trained
    and ruthless foe,
This novice army battled and returned
    each stinging blow.

On to Tunisia they went, and with
    their comrades won
The victory of Africa which saved it
    from the hun.
The failures of Norway, of France and
    Greece are past,
The army's prestige is restored,
    Dunkirk avenged at last.

HOMEGUARD

On village street, on field and green
In towns throughout the land,
On guard for Country, King and Queen
Have stood a gallant band.

A band of hundreds-thousands strong
Who in the hour of need
Came forth and joined the mighty throng
That shunned the foe's mad greed.

Three years have passed since that dark hour
When we stood battle scarred,
And now we are a Mighty Power
Our thanks to you - HOME GUARD.

                        R.G.Stevens.

NOTES ON MUSICAL TOPICS: (3) The Orchestra.

by: Harry Dodd.

It now remains for me to consider the Brass and Percussion sections to complete my hurried tour of the Orchestra.

The French Horn is a descendant of the hunting horn (much used in France at one time-hence its name). It is capable of great contrasts in tone; when played softly it sounds not unlike a clarinet, only fuller and rounder, but can also, as one writer has said, "bark like a wild animal". A good example of its solo use is the well-known tune of the slow movement of Tschaikowsky's 5th Symphony. The orchestra usually has four horns; they can be seen at the back of the orchestra, on the conductor's left. It is one of the most difficult instruments to play.

The Trumpet (which has a long pedigree, going back to Biblical times) is, I think, familiar to most of us. Bach and Handel wrote florid parts for it (e.g. the brilliant obligato part in "The Trumpet Shall Sound", from "The Messiah"), but modern composers have tended to restrict its use to fanfares and similar passages. The orchestra has two, sometimes three, trumpets.

Freddie Burgess has familiarised us with the Trombone, so that I need say little about it. There are three in the orchestra: two tenors and a bass (Freddie's is a tenor trombone). Like the French Horn, it has a wide range of tone. Here are two contrasted examples of its use: the "storm" section of "William Tell" Overture (brilliant scale passages) and the slow movement of Brahms' 2nd Symphony, where, in one part, the trombones provide a background of quiet, solemn, chords.

The last representative of the Brass section is that cumbersome instrument the Tuba, which supplies the bass part of the Brass "choir". It is rarely used as a solo instrument. There is usually just one in the orchestra, on the right of the trombones.

The Percussion section has many members, so that I can do little more than mention those most commonly met with. The section consists of two kinds of instruments: those of definite pitch and those of indefinite pitch. Chief of the former are the Timpani (or Kettle Drums) which you will always see in the middle of the back row of the orchestra. The three drums forming the unit have a combined range of one octave, and are tuned by means of screws altering the tension of the parchment. The Celesta, looking like a miniature piano, consists of metal bars suspended over resonating boxes of wood, played from a keyboard. "The Dance of the Sugar Plum Fairy" in Tschaikowsky's "Nut-Cracker" Suite, is an example of its use. The Xylophone, Harp and Piano are included under this heading. Remember, however, that here I refer to the use of the Piano as a member of the orchestra, not as the solo instrument in a concerto.

Instruments of indefinite pitch are: Side and Bass Drums, Cymbals, Gong, Tambourine and Triangle. The Triangle, has, however, the curious property of sounding in tune at all times, no matter in what key the rest of the orchestra is playing. The use of many Percussion instruments in the orchestra is a comparatively recent development: you will realise this when, at a concert, you hear, for example, a Beethoven Symphony (where the Timpani are the only representatives of the Percussion) and "Scheherazade" by Rimski-Korsakov, where many Percussion "effects" are employed.

Compiled by Dudley Irwin

WHAT'S ON

Loughborough 'Flicks'

* **EMPIRE.** June 7th. 3 days. "BLACK DRAGONS" with Bela Lugosi.
* June 10th. 3 days. Vic. Maclaglen in "POWDER TOWN"
  "KLONDYKE FURY" with Edmund Lowe.
  Nat. Pendleton in "TOP SERGEANT MULLIGAN"

** **ODEON.** June 7th. 6 days. "FOR ME AND MY GAL" with Judy Garland, Gene Kelley & George Murphy.
Richard Goulden in "MISTAKEN IDENTITY"

*** **VICTORY.** June 7th. 6 days. "THE BRIDE CAME C.O.D." Bette Davis. James Cagney. "MARCH OF TIME. No.8"

* **EMPIRE.** June 14th. 3 days. "TALK ABOUT JACQUELINE" with Hugh Williams.
Ricardo Cortez "I KILLED THAT MAN"
** June 17th. 3 days. "WOMEN ARN'T ANGELS" Robertson Hare. Drayton.
Rochelle Hudson "RUBBER RACKETEERS"

* **ODEON.** June 14th. 3 days. "MY SON ALONE" with Richard Dix. Preston Foster & Leo Carrillo.
Lucan & McShane "OLD MOTHER RILEY. M.P."
** June 17th. 3 days. "THE NAVY COMES THROUGH" with Pat O'Brien.
George Murphy & Jackie Cooper.

* **VICTORY.** June 14th. 3 days. "ONE THRILLING NIGHT" with John Beal.
Kent Taylor "ARMY SURGEON"
** June 17th. 3 days. "CALLING DOCTOR GILLESPIE" with L. Barrymore.
Grace Hayes "ZIS BOOM BAH"

*** **EMPIRE.** June 21st. 3 days. "ASK A POLICEMAN" with Will Hay.
Guy Kibbee "SCATTERGOOD SURVIVES A MURDER"
** June 24th. 3 days. "THE BIG SHOT" with Humphrey Bogart.
Bill Henry "PARDON MY STRIPES"

*** **ODEON.** June 21st. 6 days. "MOON AND SIXPENCE" with George Sanders.
Herbert Marshall. Doris Dudley.
* Joad. Huxley. Campbell etc. "THE BRAINS TRUST"

**** **VICTORY.** June 21st. 6 days. "PRIDE OF THE YANKEES" with Gary Cooper and Teresa Wright.

*** **EMPIRE.** June 28th. 6 days. "FLYING FORTRESS" with Richard Greene.
* Tim McCoy "CODE OF THE RANGERS"

*** **ODEON.** June 28th. 6 days. "STAR SPANGLED RHYTHM" with Bob Hope. Bing Crosby. Fred McMurray. Ray Milland. Franchot Tone. Alan Ladd. Paulette Goddard. Dorothy Lamour. Veronica Lake. etc. etc.

** **VICTORY.** June 28th. 6 days. "SOMEWHERE I'LL FIND YOU" with Clark Gable.
Lana Turner. also "MARCH OF TIME. No.9"

BEST OF THE MONTH:- Somerset Maugham's "MOON AND SIXPENCE"

SPORTS PAGE

EXIT FOOTBALL

ENTER CRICKET

FOOTBALL:- I am pleased to report that Mr. Dickenson has now recovered from his injury.

It was not possible to complete our League Fixtures, two matches being left unplayed. Our record is:- Played 20. Won 6. Drawn 1. Lost 13. Goals for, 36. Goals against, 47. Points 18.

Several of the matches were lost by the odd goal although it must be admitted the defence was generally better than the attack. The Semi-Final of the Cobbin Trophy was lost by the odd goal of five. This was a match in which our defence played well, Hobden making some grand saves. Our forwards were individually good but lacked combination. The Brush on the other hand showed better understanding and found their men with well-timed passes. The Brush pressed at first, but Mackender scored for us after Keenlyside made a good run on the left wing. We retained this advantage until the interval. Brush soon equalised and went ahead with two more goals. Dalton made no mistake with a penalty kick and up to the end we might have equalised, as we never gave up trying. Some of our players had difficulty in keeping their feet. This was because they neglected the elementary precaution of knocking a few studs in their boots.

CRICKET:- We have lost 3 and drawn one. Rain has interfered with 3 matches.

Some of the enthusiastic younger men, have been practising on the Quorn ground. They are making progress and anyway it is grand fun to say the least.

RESULTS:-

May 1st. Loughborough College continuative dept. 2nd. XI. LOST.

" 12th. Loughborough College continuative dept. evening XI. LOST.

(No details for these two matches)

" 15th. Mountsorrell Castle. LOST. Exiles 51.(Wildblood 21. Stafford 5 for 21) Mountsorrell 136.(Rose 35. Polfrey 35. Smith 28)

" 22nd. Woodhouse Eaves. 21 for 7. (R.P.L.Smith 6 for 7) (rain stopped play).

TENNIS:- A roller has been purchased and we now require a ¾" hose and pipe to fit the tap at the side of the court. If anyone knows where these can be obtained, please pass the information on to me.

THANKS! To all concerned in making such a success of the recent dance in the canteen. Our funds have benefited to the extent of £13.9.6½d.

A.H. APPLETON HON. SEC.

"B.S.M." JUNE, 1943.
Vol.2.   No.9.

General Editor:-   L.F. Jones.   Editorial Board:-
                                       R. Wilkinson.   R.G. Denny.
Editor:-   F.C. Staddon.   E. Millhouse.   T. Brister.

....
....

Next publication:- 30th.July.   Contributions by:- 15th.July.

FRONT COVER by:- R. Wilkinson.
Illustrations and Cartoon by:- Muriel Fidoe (A.T.S)

     Things being what they are, we thought that the efforts of our contributors on the topic of LEAVE, would interest and amuse you. We asked our artist "Wilk" to illustrate the lack of travel vouchers, but after several attempts he gave up, being unable, as he expressed it, "to put enough venom into the drawing". Muriel Fidoe, A.T.S. artist attached to the "B.S.M.", found the thought of an EWA being recalled from his leave, a subject more to her liking. We sincerely hope that this is only wishful thinking on her part.
     St. Upid has gone all H.V. Morton, in search of something or other, and preaches to you this month from the saddle. As usual, he rings the bell.
     We have in addition a contribution from Mr. Catchpole, an old friend of ours, who this month offers "OUT STATION DUTY".
     Our thanks are due to Hwfa Pryse for his personal note on his friend Esmond Knight and to Dudley Truin for the interest he showed in getting same for the "B.S.M." This we feel sure will make interesting reading to all our nautical readers.
     We hope the "Griffin on B.W." will interest you as this subject has been the cause of much speculation.
     We should like to receive more Mss. from the outstations and hope that this reminder will bring a flood of contributions into the Editorial office.

     The General Editor and his wife thank everyone for their good wishes but regret that it will be sometime before the latest addition to their family will be able to lend any real assistance to reach that laudible objective, the publishing of the "B.S.M" on its due date.

     Now gang, see that we are kept well supplied with articles, ideas and drawings, in order that we may continue to provide you with a magazine of real interest.

"How RIGHT he was !!! ..... or WAS he ???"

The didn't even mutter
When they heard their Feuhrer utter
"We want guns not mouldy butter",
      He was right.

And then they didn't natter
As the Feuhrer he grew fatter,
For they knew on every matter
      He was right.

"We shall win without a doubt
"And before the war is out",
They heard their Feuhrer shout.
      He was right.

"We will send our Luftwaffe over"
Said their Feuhrer,"and, moreover
"We will land our ships at Dover".
      He was right.

But why was not this done ?
Began to think the Hun,
Why had not they now won ?
      Was he right ?

Day and night the thunder
Of our aircraft made them wonder,
If they'd made an awful blunder,
      Was he right ?

And now each night they dread
(Not gloat, as he'd once said)
The sound of planes o'erhead
      Was he right ?

I am sure in their great fright
As the raids increase each night,
They know he was not right,
      HE WAS WRONG.

                    Hilary H. Fry.

THE GOSPEL ACCORDING TO ST. UPID. Chapter XXI.
(Translated from the English by Disciple Millhouse.)

Now the Prophet Osee appeared before a certain Ewa and commanded him thus, saying: "Go thou forth on a pilgrimage, and come not nigh unto Woyg fourteen days and fourteen nights." And the Ewa was sore dismayed because he loved the temples and Woyg and all that therein is, but he concealed his grief and brought out his Grid and went forth into the wilderness.

And on the evening of the first day he passed through Cov and came unto Ken. And he hungered greatly and went into the houses of Ken and begged for food. And they all answered him saying: Sold out. Neither have we beds nor breakfasts. And when he was nigh unto being Flaked Out, a kindly Publican smiled upon him and gave him bread and cheese and two pints of Womp, and succoured him. And the Ewa slept in the Inn and woofed Egg and Bacon at sunrise and went on his way.

And he came unto the Spa of Leam, where it was said that many peoples took the Waters. But the Ewa was an honest man and he laid off the waters and they were quite Safe. And he passed on with his Grid and came unto Worik and beheld a fine Castle and a Soldier of Uncle Sam who was sojourning in Brit came with him and gave the Castle the Once Over. And because Uncle Sam was possessed of no Castles the Soldier marvelled at it and cried: Oh Boy, Oh Boy.

And the Ewa bade farewell to the Soldier and sat again upon his Grid until it bore him unto Strat and here was a mighty theatre, and the pilgrim entered in and beheld the work of one Will, who was the Bard of Avon.

And he sojourned the night in Strat and woofed more Egg and Bacon. And on the morn of the third day he went out into the City and beheld the place where Will was begotten, and the cottage of Ann, who was his Missus.

And he sat again upon his Grid and came unto Eves Ham. And when he was passed through, the heavens opened up and a plague of cats and dogs descended. And the Ewa was sorely cheesed, but he put on his outer raiment and proceeded. And when he was nigh drowning he came upon an Inn shewing a parchment on which was writ: Luncheons. And he saith unto the Publican: Pray thee, give me lunch. And the Publican answered him saying: Behold all the lunches are eaten, but thou canst have a sandwich if thou likest.

And after the Ewa had told him what to do with his sandwich, he went on his way in the rain and came presently unto Tewk. And he swam into the Restaurant called Brit and ate a mighty Grubstake and dried his wet sandals upon the hotplate. And when the rains ceased he went on his way upon his Grid and came unto Chelt, where the peoples also took the Waters. But the Ewa had taken sufficient waters to last him all his days in the land and he passed on and rested the night in Gloster.

(To be continued).

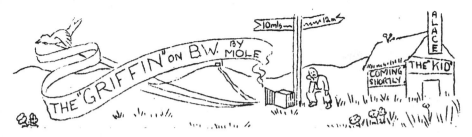

For the benefit of those going down there, and for the interest of those who aren't, I shall now endeavour to describe the "fair and wondrous city of B.W.", a village (or town, if you'd rather call it that) quite near three cities way down South. Two are within a distance of ten miles and B.W. is seventeen miles from the other.

"That's good" says you. BUT - the most accessible place is none of these but a joint which boasts two cinemas and a few shops, which is ten miles away as the crow flies or whichever way you go.

B.W., you know, has got a cinema. It wasn't one originally, but I suppose some brilliant person came to the conclusion (I don't know how) that the three thousand men, women and kids in the town (or village, whichever you prefer) must have a cinema. With the result that the Oddfellows' Hall built in 1898 (or '89; I don't know which) was converted into a "super cinema" known as the "Palace". This marvellous building holds about one hundred and fifty full up. Needless to say, the films are the latest releases, arriving as they do at least six months after leaving Chatham. Of course, they don't always arrive, and also the complete programme isn't always shown (the projector is liable to breakdown at any moment).

Having told you that, you shouldn't be surprised when I tell you that there is a railway station there. But you needn't go thinking that you're going to be all set for a nice run to London, for it's Goods only - and then they only run one train a day in each direction!

As I see you are all waiting for some "gen" on the liquid properties of the place, I'll say that the seven pubs sell mostly Strong's & Brickwood's, but personally speaking, I can recommend neither.

Many Woygites and others seem to be of the opinion that there is a Workingmen's club in the town, but that is wrong. What there is, is a Social club, and anybody can join, providing they "pay up" at the right time. Knowing our people, I'm surprised that even the old Super. of our "home from home" down there was able to be a member.

Now I've brought up the subject of our "home from home" (hum!) and here I'll say that people who love a nice long walk before starting work are going to be lucky - there's a nice steep hill they'll have to go up.

For those few of you who might be interested in ancient buildings, you'll have to be satisfied with the Bishops' Palace, while part of the Parish church is certainly Saxon.

And to finish with I'll "dole out" a bit of fatherly advice: don't, whatever you do, rely on the 'buses - they're terrible. I know, 'cos I've had some!

OUT-STATION DUTY

Red Barracks, Abbassia, Cairo, is no more. Even the millions of bugs which infested the place were unable to prevent the floors collapsing.

Some years ago this ugly edifice was the headquarters of the Wireless Company, Egypt and Palestine and from its guarded gateway departed an NCO and three men for duty in Palestine.

The journey from Cairo to Palestine was marked chiefly by heat, smells, flies and sand. Very little of the countryside was seen as every endeavour was made to exclude from the carriage the above - mentioned discomforts.

Arriving at Haifa, at the foot of Mount Carmel, a change was made to the narrow guage railway; continuing the onward journey after a convivial evening with the personnel of the local sub-wireless station, who although complete strangers were extremely hospitable and unearthed a few bottles of internal lubricant which had been buried in wet sacking to keep cool.

The rail journey terminated at Semakh on the edge of Lake Tiberias (Sea of Gallilea if you know your Bible). The name Semakh means "fish" and probably denotes a fishing village. Not a very attractive place on the whole. A broad flat valley consisting of sand, scrub, cactus and dust - mostly dust, with hills on either side.

The site for the wireless station consisted of two Nissen huts with a double skin or cavity wall and a layer of mud bricks overall to keep out the heat (what a hope). Lighting was by candle and night watches on the set were accompanied by the buzzing of flying beetles, pinging of mosquitoes, fluttering of moths and ravenous onslaughts by a variety of pests.

Eventually a supply of evil-smelling ointment was forthcoming which was smeared on the hands and face to avoid being eaten alive.

In the excitement of successfully arranging that the wireless stores and personnel arrived at the same place at the same time, the authorities had quite forgotten such trifles as rations and beds.

After a night on the floor it was decided that centipedes and scorpions were not good bedfellows. A little judicious scrounging produced a roll of canvas hessian, timber and tools and the question of "kip" was successfully solved.

The ration question also progressed favourably with unlimited supplies of jam, tea, sugar and tinned milk - especially jam. Bread, however, was unobtainable, but this problem was partly solved by exchanging with the Indian regiment (31st Lancers) tins of jam for chupattis. This measure continued for some time until a bread ration was arranged.

Although a military wireless station, communication was not restricted by the cumbersome official procedure; a modified form of post office procedure being used, speed and accuracy being the watchwords. (Contnd.)

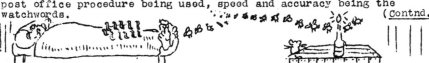

Each member of the staff had a day off during the week which was spent according to the very limited amenities of the place.

Fishing along the banks of the Jordan passed the day very quietly and pleasantly while an occasional swim in the cool running water was most refreshing. Costume and towel being quite unnecessary.

A surprising variety of flowers grow near the water's edge and the writer possesses quite a number of flowers and leaves collected and pressed during these trips.

An occasional meeting with natives, usually of the Bedouin type, invariably gave one the impression that they are very courteous people. This may be accounted for by the murmer of "Ingleezi Magnoon" (Mad Englishman) which one sometimes heard.

Two jolly little native boys acted as general cleaners on the station and their greatest treat was to be presented with a tube of toothpaste, which they consumed with obvious enjoyment.

It was surprising to find how many of their games were so very similar to those played by schoolboys at home.

On viewing Lake Tiberias one wondered, how, in view of the surrounding hills, storms, such as are mentioned in the Bible, could arise. But arise they do, as a most unpleasant buffeting in a small launch soon proved. Bad enough in fact to cause a commissioned Indian rank on board to strip to his loin cloth and pray in readiness for a watery grave. Which made one ponder on the truism of clothes making the man.

While on another out-station near the Syrian border, the writer was unfortunate enough to contract fever and was ordered to hospital. Administrative work being of a high order, the patient had to walk seven miles down the hills to the lake, take a launch, (when available) cross fourteen miles of water and thence seventy miles by train to hospital.

Needless to say that after surviving that journey there was no trace of fever on arriving at the hospital. Nevertheless, it was decided not to lose a good customer and the patient was detained for a month and quite enjoyed the rest.

A bottle of beer or stout was issued daily and cigarettes were a free issue and formed the currency for the Pontoon School. Whist Drives were held frequently and life was pleasant if lazy.

It came as a pleasant surprise on being discharged to duty to find (according to the discharge chit) that the patient was completely recovered from <u>pneumonia</u>.

Shssh!   G O S S I P   Shssh!

Congratulations and sincere good wishes to Pte Mary Watson and Mr. Bert Norris on their recent marriage which, we understand, was solmnized in the Big City on the 1st of June.

Congratulations to Fred Pike on his recent promotion to Grade 1; to "Lofty" Cook on promotion to Grade II and also to "Duggie" who has managed to crawl on to the next rung at last.

As the B.S.M. is only published once a month it is impossible to keep up to date with promotions in the A.T.S. It would of course be absurd to offer congratulations to say "Pte Atkins" on her appointment to L/Cpl, as it is almost a certainty that before the item appeared in print, she would be wearing anything from two stripes to a crown. However, we wish all concerned the best of luck.

Sgt. Doris Mackinley left the fold during the past month and will shortly be listening to shrieks and howls of a different origin. We also said goodbye to our old friend Lily Minto for similar reasons. We wish both of them the best of luck.

To the numerous recent arrivals we say "Welcome to BMR." May you learn to love it as we do!

As our regular gossip writer is on leave, I have been given the extremely difficult task of trying to find out what goes on in the section, and as I have only just returned from civilization myself, I am somewhat out of touch with current affairs at BMR. In our community it is never easy to find out how the other half lives, which reminds me - whilst on leave I attended a dance and the following notice was exhibited at the entrance:- "The Directors have the right to refuse admission to any lady they think proper." I should imagine the local gossip columnist puts in a lot of overtime.

On my first appearance in public for about four weeks I ran into one of the "C" Hut fraternity who was burning with indignation. It appears that he had had a date with a certain "Pte X" who turned up very late and informed him that she had been talking to one of the "K" Hut staff. Questioned as to his identity she said:- "I don't know his name, but he is a fair haired chap with a small fair moustache, and is about as tall as you." On hearing this, our hero drew himself up to his full 61 inches and exclaimed:- "What! that little so-and-so as tall as me, I can give him at least half an inch." No doubt our hero will write in and complain that his correct height is $61\frac{1}{4}$ inches, then we shall all know who it is.

A well known and regular contributor to the B.S.M. is at present spending all his spare time looking for a new billet. If any reader happens to know of a prospective landlady who will not want to know why our friend had to leave his previous address, please forward particulars to the Editor. This is your chance to do something in the cause of humanity. A prompt reply might prevent another death from "exposure."

We understand that Mr. Harry Appleton is a candidate for the post of Canteen Manager. We have no comments to make at this stage.

"GOSSIP" (Contnd.)

TAILPIECE

Where is our Doll? No one has seen her,
She used to knock around with Ena,
The last named of the pair is leaner,
Of course you know her, she's the cleaner.

That's all for now, before I sign off I think it is only fair to point out that my glasshouse is built with Triplex so you will need fairly hefty stones. Well, have your fun.   Cheerio,   Ollie.

MY LOVE *by Chloris*

We are sitting tonight in the fireglow,
Just you and I alone,
And the flickering light falls softly,
On a beauty that's all your own,
It gleams where your round smooth shoulder,
From a graceful neck sweeps down,
And I would not exchange your beauty,
For the best dressed belle in town.

I have drawn the curtains closer,
And from my easy chair,
I stretch my hand towards you,
Just to feel that you are there,
And your breath is laden with perfume,
As my thoughts around you twine,
And I feel my pulses beating,
As your spirit is mingled with mine.

And the woes of the world all vanish,
When I press my lips to yours,
And to feel your life blood flowing,
Is, to me, the best of cures,
You have given me inspiration,
For many a soulful rhyme,
You're the finest old Scotch Whisky,
I've had for a long, long time.

ESMOND KNIGHT (An Appreciation)

In the winter of 1928 some students were selected from the Royal Academy of Dramatic Art, London, to play small parts in a special Sunday evening performance of a new play at the Savoy Theatre. I was one of those students. Three names on the cast of this play who had leading roles were Colin Clive, Lawrence Olivier and Esmond Knight. The two former names were then quite unknown to me and to the general public, but the third, Esmond Knight, was an already established one as a juvenile actor of the West End theatre. His performance at the old Alhambra as Johann Straus in "Waltzes from Vienna" and later as Danny in "Night Must Fall" give some idea of the ability and versatility of this accomplished actor.

It was not until the early summer of 1940 that I came to act in the same play with Mr Knight again. By this time he was a star of the screen as well as the stage, but like most true artistes he could not forsake the footlights altogether in favour of films, so together with a colleague he opened the King's theatre, Hammersmith, as a Repertory Company, and between pictures he played there himself in a different production each week. He was there at the outbreak of war in 1939.

In the months that followed, theatres suffered many ups and downs and in the early part of 1940 showed signs of a possible boom, but as the news from the Continent grew steadily worse our "public" gradually faded away and London itself showed signs of becoming quite desolate. It was then that " Teddy", as his friends knew him, decided that something should be done about it, so he left the studios where he had been working since his King's theatre was closed down, and persuaded a management to put on a new play that had already been "tried out" by his own Repertory Company. It was a small cast with one setting and not a very expensive production. Nevertheless, at that time, it was a brave venture. Although musical shows were still doing quite well, there were only two straight plays left in the West End, "Rebecca" at the Queens and "Jeannie" at Wyndham's. My own season at the Westminster had closed, so I was only too glad when the offer came to play a part in this play. It was entitled "The Peaceful Inn". On the opening night substantial queues formed at the pit and gallery entrances and taxis were drawing up in numbers at the main doors, but on our way to the theatre that memorable evening, newspaper posters everywhere bore the news that Belgium had capitulated. Not very encouraging for a "first night". The play was enthusiastically received by that packed house and by the press the following day, but future bookings were far from hopeful. After struggling along for a month Teddy's gallant effort for his associates and the profession had proved a failure. Throughout the brief run of our play Esmond Knight talked continually of his burning desire to join the Navy. He had volunteered many months before but had been told he must await his turn to be called up. His services were soon sought however for another film, Michael Powel's "49th Parallel". Almost coinciding with this offer came the news that he had been accepted for the Navy, and although he could very easily have obtained time to do the picture first, he turned down the offer and went to sea.

233

The next time Esmond Knight's name was to appear in the press, it was regrettably to announce that he had been wounded while serving as a Lieutenant on board the "Prince of Wales" in the action against the "Bismarck". The entire theatrical profession and his many followers were stunned and horrified when the nature of his injuries became known. Standing on the deck of the "Prince of Wales" a shell bursting near to him had rendered him totally blind. What his own thoughts, or those of his friends were, on receiving that terrible news cannot be described or even imagined. When he was brought back to England all the stars in London organised and appeared in a special performance at the London Palladium in his benefit, and Noel Coward paid a tribute to his work in the theatre and the great sacrifice he had made.

Esmond Knight then went to St. Dunstan's to begin another life all over again. While there, Emlyn Williams visited him and afterwards devoted a Sunday night postscript for him for the B.B.C. Then followed the idea that although Esmond Knight had been robbed of his sight, he still had his memory and capacity of learning. With the help of his actress wife, Frances Clare, who read lines over and over again to him, committing them to his memory, he made a series of talks himself for the B.B.C. It then became evident that if he could learn and speak lines before a microphone he could very easily do the same before a camera, so it was not long before Esmond Knight found himself back in the profession he must have thought was lost to him for good.

In a film production moves are often mapped out by chalk marks beyond which the actor travels at his peril. They are to indicate the limits of the camera's range and focus, and to walk out of that range ruins the "take", several tempers and often reputations as well. Ask the most experienced actor to traverse those chalk marks innumerable times, speak the lines the author has written, not forgetting of course to try to act at the same time, and then ask him to do it again blindfold, he would swoon on the spot. Esmond Knight achieved it and astounded the critics by giving a magnificent performance in one of the best films to come out of British Studios. It was a great personal triumph. In it he plays the part of Von Shiffer, the Gestapo Chief, and although the situation has often been reversed in fictional drama, it is the first time in the history of pictures that a blind man has played the part of a character with sight. This month "The Silver Fleet" which stars Ralph Richardson as well as Esmond Knight will be shown at the Loughborough Odeon for one week.

Besides making this picture he has appeared personally at the Albert Hall and other places in the country for Charity organisations and war effort drives. He spoke at the De Montfort Hall, Leicester, some three of four months ago. Last month he published his Autobiography under the title of "Seeking The Bubble" and it is now having a popular sale.

During the last war the British film industry was ignored and neglected to such an extent that afterwards the market was lost to America. In this war there are already encouraging signs that the position may be reversed, and when seeing this picture of Esmond Knight's I am sure you will feel a sense of pride and admiration in seeing this man triumph over one of the most dreaded and crippling of war's disabilities, knowing that in him we have a strong pillar towards building up a leading industry.

John Hwfa Pryse.

TRUIN'S Flicks GUIDE

EMPIRE. July 5th. 3 days. "FALSE FACES"(✱) with Richard Arlen.
Lyle Talbot in "THEY RAID BY NIGHT"
July 8th. 3 days. "DANGEROUSLY THEY LIVE(✱✱) with John Garfield.
Laurel & Hardy in "PACK UP YOUR TROUBLES(✱).

ODEON. July 5th. 3 days. "LUCKY JORDAN"(✱✱) with Alan Ladd
"THE STORY OF STALINGRAD" (✱✱✱)
July 8th. 3 days. "ONCE UPON A HONEYMOON"(✱✱✱) with
Ginger Rogers and Cary Grant.

VICTORY. July 5th. 3 days. "THE BIG STREET"(✱✱✱) with Henry Fonda.
East Side Kids in "LETS GET TOUGH"(✱)
July 8th. 3 days. "ALWAYS IN MY HEART"(✱✱) with Kay Francis.
Robert Lowery in "LURE OF THE ISLANDS".

EMPIRE. July 12th. 3 days. "LAST OF THE MOHICANS"(✱✱) with Randolph Scott
Robert Pryor in "SO'S YOUR AUNT EMMA".
July 15th. 3 days. "BLUES IN THE NIGHT"(✱) with Lloyd Nolan
J.Anthony Hughes in "MEN OF SAN QUENTTIN"(✱)

ODEON. July 12th. 3 days. "EYES IN THE NIGHT"(✱✱) with Edward Arnold
and Ann Harding.
Leo Carrillo in "TOP SERGEANT"(✱)
July 15th. 3 days. "SOMEWHERE ON LEAVE"(✱) with Harry Korris.
John Hubbard in "YOUTH ON PARADE"(✱)

VICTORY. July 12th. 6 days. "BAMBI"(✱✱✱) Walt.Disney's full length
Cartoon.
George O'Brien in "LEGION OF THE LAWLESS".

EMPIRE. July 19th. 3 days. "BERLIN CORRESPONDENT"(✱✱) with Virginia
Gilmore.
Sid Blackmer in "PANTHERS CLAW"(✱)
July 22nd. 3 days. "QUIET PLEASE! MURDER"(✱✱) with George
Sanders.
Preston Foster in "SECRET AGENT OF JAPAN"(✱)

ODEON. July 19th. 6 days. "THE SILVER FLEET"(✱✱✱) with
Ralph Richardson, Googie Withers, Esmond
Knight
Bing Crosbie & Joan Blondell in
"EAST SIDE OF HEAVEN"(✱✱)

VICTORY. July 19th. 6 days. "SQUADRON LEADER X"(✱✱✱) with ERIC PORTMAN.
East Side Kids in "SMART ALECKS"(✱)

EMPIRE. July 26th. 3 days. "WHISTLING IN DIXIE"(✱) with Red Skelton.
Lyle Talbot in "SHE'S IN THE ARMY"(✱)
July 29th. 3 days. "WILD BILL HICKOK RIDES"(✱) with Bruce
Cabot
George Meeker in "HUMAN SABOTAGE".

A CHALLENGE

A raw recruit in years gone by,
I scorned to dance; and did not try.
A year of army life had passed,
Ere friends persuaded me at last
To seek admittance to a hall -
Half a crown for a Loughborough ball.
I viewed - I sneered with proud disdain -
Then slowly, scorn gave place to pain,
My partners, few, and far between,
Somehow were not awfully keen.
I used to tell my friends I wouldn't;
Now 'twas plain to all, I couldn't.
Anger, fury, indignation
Above all determination,
But every effort seemed in vain,
I wondered, was it worth the strain?
Then came the news upon the board,
A dancing class at last! Good Lord!
So, feverishly, in haste to learn
The Chasse, spin and natural turn
I joined the class, and from the start
My dancing efforts gained new heart,
Now there are more superior folk,
Who think our class is just a joke,
If you look on with scornful eye,
I'm daring you - just come and try.

Avril Wiseman (A.T.S.)

"FLICKS" (Contnd.)

ODEON. July 26th. 3 days.   "JOURNEY FOR MARGARET (✶) with Robert Young, Laraine Day.
             Dick Foran in "HE'S MY GUY" (✶)
        July 29th. 3 days.   "THE MAGNIFICENT DOPE" (✶✶) with Don Ameche, Henry Fonda.
             Marsha Hunt in "ONCE UPON A THURSDAY" (✶)

VICTORY. July 26th. 3 days.   "THE COUNT OF MONTE CRISTO" (✶✶✶) R.Donat.
        July 29th. 3 days.   "THE VANISHING VIRGINIAN" (✶✶) Frank Morgan.
             Roy Rogers in "SOUTH OF SANTA FE"

THE BEST OF THE MONTH:-

                             WALT DISNEY'S   "BAMBI"
                             In Technicolor.

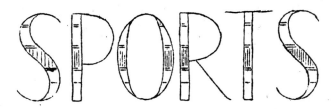

SPORTS

CRICKET.

The weather has again interfered with our matches. I must apologise for two matches being cancelled. The first was owing to a misunderstanding as to which ground the match was to be played on. On June 26th. we journeyed to Shepshed, only to find that the Army unit we were supposed to play had left 6 weeks ago. I regret the inconvenience that was caused to those sportsmen who turned up.

Results:-

29/5	v Mount Sorrel	Lost.	(No details)
8/6	v Loughborough College Army XI	Lost.	Army XI 50. Palmer 20. Dalton 4 for 7. Exiles 44. Cohen 5 for 9.
12/6	v Loughborough College Continuative dept.	Won.	(No details).

TENNIS.

The court is being used by quite a number of people. Owing to good reconnaissance by Mr. Hartill, we have now purchased a hose and pipe for the court. The only rules to be observed are:-

(1) Use the booking sheet provided.

(2) Soft shoes to be worn.

(3) Slacken net after playing, if no-one else is due to play.

ANGLING.

The season has now started. I am a member of two societies, and will be pleased to give details to any one interested. The fishing in the Soar is only moderate, but I have some knowledge of the river and will be pleased to pass on this information.

A.H.Appleton.
Hon.Sec.

BSM

3D.
VOL 2
NO. 10

JULY 1943

"Vies!"

"B.S.M." JULY, 1943.
Vol.2.   No.10.

General Editor:- L.P. Jones.   Editorial Board:-
                                R. Wilkinson.   R.G. Denny.
Editor:-   F.C. Staddon. E. Millhouse.   T. Brister.

Next publication:- 27th. August.   Contributions by:- 15th. August.

FRONT COVER by:- R. Wilkinson.
Illustrations and lettering by:- Muriel Fidoe
                                  R. Wilkinson
                                  H. Dodd.

This month we ask for assistance from any artistic members of the Woygite domain, who are able and willing to carry out free hand drawing and lettering, either from rough sketches or based on their own ideas. We have always been anxious to contact these people, but this direct appeal has been made very necessary due to the fact that Mr. R.G. Denny, who had been chiefly responsible for the illustration and lettering work has been exported down South. We have been very fortunate to obtain the services of Miss Muriel Fidoe, and of course our old friend "Wilk" is always a pillar of strength, but many hands make light work. We would like about six people who we could call on from time to time and ask any interested person to please contact any member of the Editorial Board.

To those of our colleagues who have gone down South we send best wishes and trust they have been treated kindly in the matter of billets. We have made arrangements for the "B.S.M." to reach you in your re-exile, through Mr. R.G. Denny who will be only too pleased to forward any complaints, suggestions and what is more important, contributions to the Editors.

Although publications are not officially allowed to report weather conditions it is nice to note that we have recently been visited with the kind of weather that sends a shiver down the backs of cinema managers. May they continue to shiver for some little time.

STOP PRESS.

We send our belated congratulations to Bet Browne on her recent marriage to a member of H.M. Naval Forces. We used to hear a lot from our A.T.S. friends about glamorous sailors in their lives, but "Bet" appears to be one of the very few, if not the only one, who has remained faithful to the Navy. Happy times "Bet" and best wishes that everything will come safely into port and that you will finally settle down in a nice little anchorage.

NIGHTS SO BOLD

ANON

It was one of those first few warm days in March. The Sun seemed to issue a challenge to everyone: "Here's a nice warm day in Spring - what are you going to do about it?". Accordingly T. and I meet by chance, two of our A.T.S. friends on the Windmill and prepare for a nice long walk. I say prepare, actually what happens runs something like this. T. suggests going on the Beacon, gazing slowly at that distant peak which would have taken him hours to reach, at the speed he normally travels. J. suggests Hanging Stone rocks, vaguely waving an elegant arm in a haphazard arc which embraces everything from the Carillon at L. to the Pumping Station at the Reservoir. The only area of interest excluded being of course Hanging Stone. I, am all for making our way over the Beacon down through the golf course and back to the tea-room. We all look towards M., she appears to be wrapped in meditation so deep, that only the words 'tea-room' seem to penetrate. Even so, the words create a sort of mental riot, you can almost see her mind revolve for a few seconds and come to a jarring stop. We all wait. With a click of her teeth, (which sign from M. always signifies further argument will be useless,) she half turns in the direction of the village, and announces: "I'm hungry - I want my tea!". M. is most emphatic on this point. Clutching at straws, I suggest walking round the back of the Windmill, round the road and on to the tea-room. M. is adamant, the quickest way to the tea-room is down through the village, and that is the way we are going. This, despite T's, plea that if he walks past any house in the street with an At, it will be known throughout the village, and will form the sole topic of mealtime conversation at his digs, for the next three weeks.

We negotiate the village C , and are stepping out along the main road arm-in-arm, suddenly J. dro /my arm in a panic, ejaculating, "Look!" All is confusion. With peremptory "Stand still!" from both of them, we mere males remain rigid. M. and J. dart behind us. There is much handbag activity, badges are whipped out and thrust into hats, which in turn are thrust hastily on heads. Then the object of terror appears - one small, demure A.T.S. officer. I take a quick look at M. and J., yes their appearance is neat and they are all set for the raising of arms. Whether the officer has witnessed this performance I do not know. If she has, she is showing no sign of it in her face, yet I cannot help thinking that had she seen them she would have died laughing. As we draw near, the air grows tense - three paces apart - M. and J's. arms go up as one in a salute that must have taken hours to perfect. The salute is returned, together with, "Good afternoons!" on each side, which sound like the cooing of doves, fatuous smiles are exchanged, and the air is redolent of 'esprit de corps'. As we pass, M. says to J; "Oh isn't she sweet!" - which makes me wonder what they would have called her had she caught them in their previous state.

The tea goes down good. J. tries some time-exposures in the cafe, but as we are all reduced to laughter at the antics she has to resort to to get us in focus, I doubt if they will be an outstanding success.

(Cont'd).

"NIGHTS SO BOLD" (Cont'd).
After, we walk to G.H. with the girls, and at my suggestion we arrange to meet at the Bull in Q. where we hope to have some dinner, after which we shall have a few convivial glasses. On the way over to T's. place, we 'phone the Bull, only to be told that there is no possible hope of getting the semblance of a meal that night. (M. will be furious.) At T's. place, we have a wash and brush up, and courteously refusing an invitation to tea, we make our way down to the bus which will take us to Q. Passing G.H. en route, we offer up a silent prayer that M. and J. have stopped for supper. Arrived at the Bull we partake of a few glasses, and it is not long before the girls arrive. Thank heaven they do not seem at all disappointed at the prospect of no dinner. The evening goes quickly, shortly after nine Y. joins us. He will be leaving shortly, so we must stop and join him in a drink. Now Y. is a particular friend of ours, which makes it rather awkward. We want to stay and talk to him, yet T. and I are on at ten, we have to take the girls home to G.H. and then get back to work. Y. says: "What about the service bus?". I point out that we have no passes, and in any case M. and J. couldn't join us. T. apparently coming out of a trance says: "Easy - leave it to me", and proceeds to unfold his idea, "there are several members of the night shift present", says T., "they will board the bus at the cross roads - right?. If we ask them, they will hang fire on boarding, delaying the operation as long as possible, meanwhile, you S. and myself, together with the girls will attack the bus from the rear, boarding it from the emergency door at the back. Once inside, we can give the tip to the people in the bus, and they can pass word to the people getting on in front, that everything is O.K. Speed is the keynote." The plan looks simple in theory; M. jibs slightly, saying it means she will have to go down to BMR. and then back to G.H. We pacify her by saying that we shall at least be able to get something to eat in the canteen at BMR. This seems to have the desired effect, so we drink up and prepare to leave.

It is almost dark outside, and as we make our way past the Old Bull, an icy voice rings out: "Excuse me! may I speak to the two A.T.S?" We acquiesce moving on a few paces. In the distance we can hear a few, "Yes ma'ams!", and "No ma'ams!" and I wait with almost childish expectation for a "Three bags full! Ma'am". The conversation seems inordinately long, we begin to wonder whether we shall miss the bus completely. Our ruminations are cut short by M. and J. rejoining us. They are both fuming. Apparently it is 'verboten' for us to link our arms with those of our companions who happen to be wearing an A.T.S. uniform. T. says he wonders whether it is from a sense of frustration that some A.T.S. officers compel obedience to this rule, which in itself, he thinks, is ridiculous. What M. and J. think is best forgotten, I am uncertain if it comes under the heading of, 'insubordination', 'conduct to the prejudice of good order etc.', 'mutinous conduct', or, downright 'sedition'. Once again the conversation drops as with a roar the bus approaches. We pick up the double in an effort to reach the cross roads first. After the run, our tempers are once more congenial, in fact, with the prospect of adventure ahead our good spirits are completely renewed.
(Cont'd).

"NIGHTS SO BOLD" (Cont'd). As the bus pulls up, Y. and his party make for the door, T. and I, together with the girls dive for the back. The bus seems pretty full already. Seizing the emergency handle T. gives it a wrench, the door flies open, and out drop two of the night shift, with such speed, that only with the greatest effort T. and I catch them. What they say, is nobody's business, suffice to say they are friends of ours, (or were,) and T., shoving them back, jumps, in himself, with a few rapid words of explanation to the other occupants of the bus, they - good fellows - appreciating the situation, quickly connive, and are soon helping M. and J. into the bus, so much so in fact, that J. practically takes off from the road, and lands inside the bus, which at that moment chooses to start off. The delay in restoring to their seats the people who had fallen out, had cost us valuable seconds. However once along the road, everything is all right. At BMR. the situation is reversed, us four getting out through the rear, there being plenty of time this end, as there are some twenty or so getting out in front, we see that the door is securely locked on leaving.

Now, we are all safe inside the canteen. M. is ensconced behind a spam roll of monstrous proportions. J. is avidly sipping a glass of milk. T. looks at me with a broad grin suffusing his features, "As I always say S, it isn't the money you get in life, it's the fun you have, which counts!"

I smile - mentally, I commune with the Sun - it seems to say: "Went the day well?" - Again I smile.

"EVERY SOLDIER CARRIES A MARSHAL'S BATON IN HIS HAVERSACK".

O/C desirous of congratulating one of the recently promoted A.T.S. quads in Hut "C", inquires:-

O/C. "Where's your stripe?".

A.T.S. Quad. "It's in my saddle-bag, sir".

ED. You are allowed four guesses to name the person concerned.
      (It wasn't Bob Hope!)

"I RECOMMEND IT"

by Mole

The book of the film, 'The Shape of Things to Come', is really a discussion of social and political problems in the future, but as a film is no place for arguments, a new story has been invented to display the conclusions reached in the book.

The story is written round the lives of two people, both played by Raymond Massey, John Cabal, an aviator, and Oswald Cabal his grandson. It is essentially a spectacular film, showing the world devastated by war and then a new plague - the Wandering Sickness, in which the sufferer wanders aimlessly until he dies.

After a short time modern civilization as we know it has vanished and most countries are under the control of warring brigands, but some technicians under John Cabal escape to Basra and build up a new civilization.

The film passes swiftly through the opening stages of the war and broadens out to display a reconstructed world, where the social and economic problems of today have been solved. The cities are half underground, and have artificial lighting and air conditioning.

Because of the incessant exploration many younger people are anxious to travel to the moon. Even Cabal's daughter has volunteered and, with her lover, has been accepted. But the expedition has roused great opposition, and so the film ends on a conflicting note, with the question of Catherine Cabal's reaching the moon in doubt.

The book, 'The Shape of Things to Come', was specially 'treated' by H.G. Wells for film production, and certain points were stressed in a special memorandum circulated by the author to all concerned. The first point is that in the final stages of the film a better civilization than ours is portrayed and that in it, a more organised world, there will be no hurry, the people will not be crowded, there will be more leisure, more dignity.'

The present-day rush and jumble due to mechanisation 'are not to be raised to the nth power. On the contrary they are to be eliminated.'

Another point H.G. Wells makes is that of costume. He anticipates a dress that is broad-shouldered and fine around the legs and feet. A long gauntlet will be worn on one wrist, containing small conveniences corresponding to our fountain pen, etc. 'I would say to our designers: "For God's sake let yourselves go." But remember, fine clothes, please; not nightmare stuff, not jazz. People are not going about in glass jars or aluminium boilers or armour or cellophane. They are not going to dress like super-sandwich men.'

This 'treatment' by H.G. Wells is published in book form by the Cresset Press, is called 'Things to Come,' and can be bought at, Sketchley's (Leicester Road) price 4/-.

"LA BELLE AT SANS STRIPE"

"To those that wouldn't but could,
And to those that haven't but should,
This poem is dedicated."

Oh what can ail thee little AT.
In khaki coat with buttons bright
Demeanour showing service seen,
But why no stripe?

Oh what can ail thee little AT.
With laughing eyes and step so light,
Who've worn this rig some few years now,
And still no stripe.

I see no wrinkles on your brow,
Or jealous glance at favoured few,
And in your eyes ambitions light
Fast withereth too.

One night while dreaming on my bed,
I dreamed a dream - ah pity me
For in that dream, I dreamt that I
Shall stripeless be.

I saw full Corporals, Sergeants too
Drawn from a hat, A topper tall,
Who murmured: "La Belle AT sans Stripe",
It shook them all.

I saw their eyes light with surprise,
At their distinctions cheaply won,
And they all wondered how it was
I hadn't one.

So that is why I sojourn here,
And why promotion I will shun,
Such dreams it seems, have left me now
Sans ambition.

— "Snikmot".

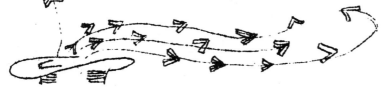

An A.T.S. Soliloquises on a Topical Grievance

When walking out, if the weather is kind,
I can push a pram, if I feel inclined,
And there's nothing mentioned in local orders
To prevent me carrying herbaceous borders,
Or a box of bricks, or a bathing ring,
In fact, I can carry anything,
Except a handbag.

I can hold in my hand, when the moon is high,
An Irish sweep, or the Isle of Skye,
Or a photograph of Sir Stafford Cripps,
Or a fragrant parcel of fish and chips,
And later on, if the night gets colder,
I can sling a Commando over my shoulder,
But not a handbag.

It is most difficult, dispersin'
Necessities about my person,
Oh, why should I be so afflicted!
My chest expansion is restricted
By pockets full of odds and ends.
My outline shows alarming trends,
Without a handbag!

My indiarubber will appear,
Protruding from behind my ear,
My cutlery - this may sound shocking,
I tuck demurely in my stocking,
My lipstick nestles in my shoe,
But, damn it, what's a girl to do
Without a handbag?

I can carry a flea
Or a packet of tea,
Or a peir or a deer,
Or a barrel of beer
Or a rector, a reflector,
Or a sanitary inspector -
Or even a sandbag -
BUT NOT A HANDBAG!

Mary D. Gill.

THE GOSPEL ACCORDING TO ST. UPID.   Chapter XXII.
(Translated from the English by Disciple Millhouse.)

(Cont'd from Chap. XXI.)

And on the morning following, the Ewa rose and broke his fast and all records for leaving Glosta for he was Not Struck. And when strangers accosted him in the highways, saying: Whither goest thou? he answered them truly, saying: Wye. And they straightway replied: All right mate keep thy shirt on. We only wondereth.

And as he came nigh unto Ross, the plague of cats and dogs followed him, and the sun vanished, and he trembled, and brought out his warmer raiment and wrapped himself in swaddling clothes.

And as he journeyed toward Mon he turned aside from the highway and came unto the Yat of Symond. And being Full of Beans he pushed his Grid up a mighty hill to survey the land. And there he chanced upon two maidens from Lon, and he spoke with them and broke bread. And when the maidens were ready to descend to their own Grids which they had wisely left upon the foot of the hill, he might have sped all the way down upon his Grid, but he was a gallant man, and likewise a very Civil Servant, wherefore he pushed his Grid all the way down again.

Now when he had bidden the maidens farewell he rode on and came into Mon and bided the night there. And it was here that a Gremlin crawled into his Gear of Three Speeds and cut the balls thereof into little pieces. And because his Grid did not work so well that way, he gave it into the hands of a craftsman who made it new and likewise nine shekels for his labour. And thus having tarried many hours in Mon in fair weather he set forth again and another plague descended and the situation became extremely fluid. And he passed the Abbey of Tintern tarrying not even to swim around it because he was sorely cheesed. And he sheltered the night with a publican in Chep. And the day following he put his Grid upon a ship and voyaged over the Sev. And here were also two maidens with Grids who were Atsites of Paicor and he rode with them to Weston which is a Super place. And the sun shone brightly and the Ewa's skin became Browned Off and he was loth to leave the seashore. But the next day he journeyed to Chedda and descended the Gorge, and, having gorged a mighty meal and strawberries, he entered into the wondrous Caves of Gof. And here he met a maid who was even as mad as himself for she was on a pilgrimage. Likewise was she on her Todd. And they journeyed together to the Hole of one Wookey, and to Wels, and to the Mallet of Shepton. And the next day they returned to Wels and beheld a mighty temple there where is a wondrous clock which giveth a Variety Performance of knights, and horses, and men with battle-axes, each hour. And because the air in his back tyre was worn out, he put therein a new lot, and bidding the maiden farewell he turned his Grid toward Lon. And he journeyed through Bath and Chip, and tarried the night in Swin. And the woman of the house wherein he slept charged him ten shekels for her bed and her breakfast. And she writ her name upon the parchment which she gave him. And it was truly writ thus: Mrs. Fidler.

(Cont'd).

SOUND PICTURE

Whoops and whistles, splutters, clangs,
buzzing, bawls, explosions, bangs,
grating, grinding, grunts, and thumps,
scratching, scraping, clatter, bumps,
fizzing, frying, liquid splashes,
gurgles, giggles, creaks, and crashes,
chugging, chirping, booming, pinging,
droning, squawking, knocking, ringing,
detonations, echoes, yells,
trumpets, bagpipes, drums, and bells,
barking, braying, whimpers, yapping,
mooing, whinneys, chirrups, clapping,
howling, hooting, piercing shrieks,
rushing, roaring, screeches, squeaks,
humming, hissing, cracks, and squeals,
prattle, titters, chuckles, peals,
whining, wheezing, wailing, groans,
tinkles, thuds, miauing, moans,
 raving, ranting, crying, fizzles,
swishing, screaming, snorting, sizzles,
croaking, quacking, fiendish cackles,
rustling, rattling, clanks, and crackles,
utter discord, utter riot,
--time to write another : QUIET !

"Moulinmaison"

THE GOSPEL (Cont'd).

        And the last day the Ewa journeyed through the Vale of White Horse yet he saw no horse, for it was Blacked Out to deceive the birdmen of Itla. And riding through the Valley of Temz he came on the evening of the eighth day to Lon, where the streets are paved with broken milk bottles. And because he now saw writ upon the ometer of his Grid : Four hundred and fifty, he decided he ought to be tired, and stopped.
    Likewise there was no rear left in his raiment.

LEAVE it alone!

BY F.J. HEARN

The majority of our readers will have had their leave, and are now regretful they did not choose to have it later, but there is an old saying "Two weeks taken is better than three weeks to be so". On the other hand, it is probable that those who have not yet been on any leave have also "had it".

Some, doubtless followed the country's slogan and had their "holiday at home", and thereby became a nuisance to their wives and their neighbours, by the noisy smashing of crockery when doing the chores.

The visit to the hardware shop later to make good the damage, not being fruitful, I hesitate to think what their families are drinking out of now. Still, the local has a few glasses left, and what other drink would a man prefer?.

One or two other members of the staff decided that a cycling tour would doubtless brace them up for the next twelve months, as if they did not sit down enough. I understand that now, back at work, a substantial cushion rests where it will do most good. Incidentally, have you noticed, if you go cycling, the capricious weather clerk decides to damp your ardour, or keep you cool, whichever you prefer, and rain trickles down incessantly; whereas, if you go on a long train journey, the sun shines, it is stifling hot, and sitting in a railway carriage, you wish it was raining, and the carriage roof leaked.

One member of the staff had the courage to try a camping holiday, and pitched his tent within sight of his place of work.(ED.Very "Andy") He had once worked before the mast, he tried a holiday behind. What a thrill? he must have had at 5.45 a.m., when lying in state, or in a state, he looked through the tent flap and espied his colleagues hurrying to get at it. (That is if he was awake at that unearthly hour). I have often wondered what birds see to be so chirpy about at that hour in the morning.

Camping is all very well, especially if you have a good cook to see to your inmost needs, but if you havn't hired a cook, good or otherwise, when the stomach calls, to keep it quiet you adjourn to the local canteen. Now one cheese roll tastes very much like another, and when you have partaken of scores of them, your stomach says "Cheese it", and you do, and have a lettuce roll.

Still it's great fun, as the fisherman's wife said when having a busman's holiday, she used her husband for bait. He was such a worm.

Shssh! G O S S I P. Shssh!

In view of the very good work of the relief Gossip writer last month, I feel that I am faced with two alternatives. One is to slash out right and left, (which is comparatively easy), the other, to steer a nice clean course, bringing to light only those things which insist on comment owing to their interest, humour, or just plain stupidity.

WE WOULD LIKE TO KNOW! Who is the girl with the golden voice who knows all the answers?. As the hut supervisor said, "Aren't men beasts".

We notice that stripes are once again abundant, but considered it very bad taste when we heard one person remark, "I see the July sales are on".

'TWAS A FAMOUS VICTORY! As my Sports Secretary crony Appleton remarked, "There's one thing that we can do at this place, and that is to play Tennis".

TENNIS. EXILES v R.N.A.S on College Grounds 28th.July.

Thompson-Kelly. Lost 4-6,6-5,4-6. Won 6-4,6-1. Won 6-0,6-1
Dalton-Keenlyside. Won 6-5,6-2. Won 6-2,6-0. Won 6-4,6-2
Hobden-Reedman. Won 6-5,6-4. Won 6-4,2-6,6-5. Won 6-3,6-4
Total Result:- EXILES 8 Matches. R.N.A.S 1.
17 Sets to 3.

EDDIE SIMS, THAT CONSCIENTIOUS SUPERVISOR, CONTINUES TO ARRANGE "BREAKS" EVEN AFTER DUTY HOURS!
One of our peeping Toms reports that during a round of golf he was overcome with sympathy for the ball, and made contact with the turf instead. This resulted in his partner's Mashie Niblic collapsing into half a dozen pieces. The spot has now been commercialised, and is pointed out to visitors in Woodhouse Eaves as "Where the big-un dropped".

AN APPEAL FOR CLOTHING COUPONS! Whilst on a visit to Barrow Weir with my piscatorial friend ("Appie") recently, espied Ollie (Body Beautiful) Pearce pulling up stream in a rowing boat. He was blessed with very charming company who was dressed most suitably for the occasion. Ollie was dressed in the body beautiful in a nice shade of pink, finished off with a natty pair of flannel bags. He looked cute. If anybody should think of bribing me for the name of the charming company, please do not waste your time. Since receiving my 'cost of living' bonus, plus an annual increment of net result 6d, I am no longer interested in further monetary gains.

KEEPING UP THE OLD TRADITIONS! Recently met one of the dwarfs referred to in last month's Gossip as "that little so-and-so". He proudly showed me an A.T.S. belt round his waist, this support being very necessary as two buttons had parted from the back of his pants during a "Harry Dodd" ramble. We think that the fact of showing this, was due to a desire to prove that although small, he did not mix with small "Fry". What the result was to the A.T.S. concerned, we are not in a position to report. However, we will not turn a hair if a local order is issued to the effect that A.T.S. must not wear coloured knickerbockers. Cheerio! No Triplex, no name.

"MUTUAL ADMIRATION CO. LTD."
"K" HUT. BMR.

TO: THE GENTLEMEN OF "K".   FROM: "B" WATCH No.7 Wing A.T.S.
                                            19.July,43.

We're sorry that you're going,
We wish that you could stay
It wo'nt seem quite the same somehow
When you are not in 'K'.

You've set us a good standard
Which we'll try to maintain
(But maybe if we're bad enough,
They'll have you back again.)

You've helped us all tremendously
We're really grateful too
And take this opportunity
Of saying 'thanks' to you.

The war will soon be over now,
Just leave that to the troops
Till then, to you from all of us,
Good Luck! and better scoops.

TO: "B" WATCH No.7 Wing A.T.S.   FROM: "K" HUT 19/20th.July,43.

We thank you for your poem,
And the bouquet it contains,
You've made a splendid effort
To assist, we've been at pains.

We've had a grand time with you.
Good things perforce must end;
So now that we're all going,
On yourselves you must depend.

So gird up loins and pencils,
Go forth in great array
Let your credit reach the housetop,
And your praise be sung all day.

Till Hitler in his fury,
At the moment of his fall,
Will curse the "lady" Companies,
And the 'Seventh' most of all.

FOOTNOTE

So bear up as well as you can girls,
For there's always tomorrow to meet
The others as well,
Who'll have the same hell -
Of - a - mess on their first duty sheet.

WHAT'S ON?	WHAT'S ON?	F I L M S. Truin's Guide Assists You.
EMPIRE.	Aug. 2nd. (3 days)	"FEATHER YOUR NEST". George Formby. Sidney Blackmer "GALLANT LADY".
	Aug. 5th. (3 days)	"JUKE GIRL". Ann Sheridan. Guy Kibbee "SCATTERGOOD RIDES HIGH".
ODEON.	Aug. 2nd. (3 days)	"SING YOU SINNERS". Bing Crosby, Fred McMurray. The Ritz Brothers "EVERYTHING HAPPENS TO US"
	Aug. 5th. (3 days)	"WHITE CARGO". Walter Pidgeon Hedy Lamarr. Action Picture of the N.F.S. "FIRES STARTED"
VICTORY.	Aug. 2nd. (3 days)	"QUEEN VICTORIA". Anna Neagle, Anton Walbrook. "WE DEPEND ON IT". "MARCH OF TIME".
	Aug. 5th. (3 days)	"DR. GILLESPIE'S NEW ASSISTANT". Barrymore. Wendy Barrie "PUBLIC ENEMIES".
EMPIRE.	Aug. 9th. (3 days)	"SAN FRANCISCO". Spencer Tracy, Clark Gable. "A LETTER FROM ULSTER".
	Aug.12th. (3 days)	"LARCENY (INC.)" Edward G. Robinson. "STARDUST ON THE SAGE". Gene Autry.
ODEON.	Aug. 9th. (3 days)	"SOCIAL ENEMY No.1". Leon Ames, Luana Walters. "MANILA CALLING". Carole Landis, Lloyd Nolan.
	Aug.12th. (3 days)	"ESCAPE TO HAPPINESS". Leslie Howard, Ingrid Bergman. "THE HOUSE OF MYSTERY". Bela Lugosi.
VICTORY.	Aug. 9th. (3 days)	"YOU CAN'T ESCAPE FOR EVER". George Brent "HI! NEIGHBOUR". Jean Parker.
	Aug.12th. (3 days)	"ORCHESTRA WIVES". George Montgomery. Full Supporting Programme.
EMPIRE.	Aug.16th. (3 days)	"CHINA GIRL". George Montgomery, Gene Tie "THE OLD HOMESTEAD". Weaver Bros.
	Aug.19th. (3 days)	"WINGS FOR THE EAGLE". Dennis Morgan, Ann Sheridan. "JUST OFF BROADWAY". Lloyd Nolan.
ODEON.	Aug.16th. (6 days)	"THE AMAZING MRS. HOLLIDAY". Deanna Durbin "THE BODY VANISHED". Anthony Hulme.
VICTORY.	Aug.16th. (3 days)	"ALL THROUGH THE NIGHT". Humphrey Bogart. Musical, Interest films.
	Aug.19th. (3 days)	"WENT THE DAY WELL". Frank Lawton, Leslie Banks. "SWEETHEART OF THE FLEET". Joan Davis.
EMPIRE.	Aug.23rd. (6 days)	"SPRINGTIME IN THE ROCKIES". Betty Grable, (Technicolor) John Payne. "CAREFUL, SOFT SHOULDER". Virginia Bruce.
ODEON.	Aug.23rd. (6 days)	"SHADOW OF A DOUBT". Jos.Cotton, T.Wright. "OPERATIONAL HEIGHT".
VICTORY.	Aug.23rd. (6 days)	"RANDOM HARVEST". Ron.Colman, Greer Garson.
EMPIRE.	Aug.30th. (3 days)	"QUEEN OF SPIES". Joe E. Brown. "COUNTER ESPIONAGE". Warren William.
	Sept.2nd. (3 days)	"IN OLD CALIFORNIA". John Wayne. "TIME TO KILL". Lloyd Nolan.
ODEON.	Aug.30th. (3 days)	"OLD MOTHER RILEY DETECTIVE". Lucan, McShane. "SUBMARINE ALERT". R.Arlen, Wendy Barrie.
	Sept.2nd. (3 days)	"NO TIME FOR LOVE". Colbert, McMurray. "NIGHT PLANE FROM CHUNGKING". Preston, Drew.
VICTORY.	Aug.30th. (6 days)	"IN THIS OUR LIFE". Bette Davis. Full Supporting Programme.

SPORTS PAGE

CRICKET.

The match with Woodhouse Eaves at Quorn was a close one, as this was won by the small margin of two runs. Castleman, although injured, scored a splendid 43 for Woodhouse Eaves. R.Wildblood, R.P.L.Smith and John Dodd batted well for the Exiles.

We lacked bowlers against R.N.A.S., both their opening bats reaching the half-century.

In the match against Shepshed, G.Spooner, going in No.4, made 35 not out; our total being 82. Although our bowling was weak, the match was lost owing to dropped catches. It was however, an enjoyable game.

We have lost some of our active members who have left us for other scenes. We wish them the best of luck.

We have had difficulty recently in getting a team together. It may be that the new arrivals do not know of the sporting activities here. If anyone is interested, please contact me.

RESULTS:

3/7. Woodhouse Eaves 83. (Castleman 43, Edge 5 for 10)
Exiles 85. (R.Wildblood 27)

7/7. Exiles 63. (R.P.L.Smith 29, Nutman 5 for 22)
R.N.A.S. 122 for 1. (Charter 53, Bloxham 56 (not out)

17/7. Exiles 82. (Spooner 35 (not out), Wilmot 5 for 39)
Shepshed 123 for 3. (Deacon 52, Wilmot 50)

A.H.Appleton.
Hon.Sec.

"WHAT IS IT ?"

From tree to tree through woodland glade,
He moves with accuracy sublime,
To reach his woodland home he made,
With leaf and twig last Autumn time.
His bushy tail and coat of grey,
Will make his life a life of grief,
He doesn't give himself away,
Because he's wanted as a thief.
This woodland gangster cares for none,
Bird's nests by the score he'll rob,
But very soon the keeper's gun,
Will catch him while he's on the job.
Then off will come his tail and coat,
Cured and dressed, it soon will be,
Hung around some Lady's throat,
Or on some Gloves that's made for me.

R.G.Stevens.

"B.S.M." AUGUST, 1943.
Vol.2.   No.11.

General Editor:-   L.P.Jones.   Editorial Board:-
                                    R.Wilkinson.   R.G.Denny.
Editor:-   F.C.Staddon.   E.Millhouse.   T.Brister.

Next publication:- 30th.Sept.   Contributions by:- 15th.Sept.

FRONT COVER by:- R.Wilkinson.
Illustrations etc. by:- Muriel Fidoe.

It is with reluctance that we return to the question of the failure of certain people to take up their "specially printed" copies of this magazine. On the publication of this number we find that we are left still holding 45 copies of the July issue. This absurd and unbusinesslike situation cannot be allowed to continue, and we have therefore decided to adopt the following policy rigidly.

Any person not having taken up their copy by the date the subsequent issue is ready to go to press, will have their name erased from our register of subscribers. In the event of an application for re-instatement, it will only be agreed to, providing all outstanding copies are taken up, and a 3/0d. subscription deposited with us as a sign of good faith.

We make no excuses for this action, but mention that we have an obligation to the Paper Control authorities, and are not really interested in casual subscribers to the magazine. The publication of the "B.S.M." is no mean task, and this "dithering" about by certain people is a further hurdle which we have decided to jump over/on.

We hope you want the magazine and will do our utmost to see that you get it, meanwhile, look out for a competition next month, introduced by "Wilk".

Having mentioned subscriptions already, we would add that we would like more people to make use of this system and give the Editor's word that in the event of any liquidation, all refunds would be made. A reserve fund is kept for this purpose.

DISTRIBUTION:-   This has been a further headache. Our effort to distribute them in the huts did not meet with full approval, and the Canteen system is unsatisfactory as the copies are ill-treated and the container used as a waste-paper receptacle. Well, being democratic, we fully acknowledge the right of opinion.
DECISION:- ALL COPIES WILL, IN FUTURE, BE KEPT IN HUT "C".

"THE GENTLE SEX"

To go to sea an urge they had
so in cute hats and navy clad
they climb the rigging, salvage wrecks
and on occasions - scrub the decks,
The Gentle Sex.

The girls in khaki, just a few
whose ranks so very quickly grew
have tackled almost every trade
and learned the meaning of parade,
The Gentle Sex.

Far from the madding crowd they camp
in winter often cold and damp
wading through mud to reach a winch
determined not to yield an inch,
The Gentle Sex.

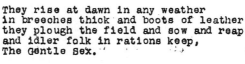

They rise at dawn in any weather
in breeches thick and boots of leather
they plough the field and sow and reap
and idler folk in rations keep,
The Gentle Sex.

In slacks and turbans - any shade
they did not scorn to wield a spade
without the loss of dainty manner
they quickly learned to use a spanner,
The Gentle Sex.

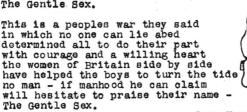

This is a peoples war they said
in which no one can lie abed
determined all to do their part
with courage and a willing heart
the women of Britain side by side
have helped the boys to turn the tide
no man - if manhood he can claim
will hesitate to praise their name -
The Gentle Sex.

Joan Howarth.

THE GOSPEL ACCORDING TO ST. UPID.   Chapter XXIII.
(Translated from the English by Disciple Millhouse.)

  Now in the days when Itla, chief over all the Hunnites began his war against Brit he sought out a number of Stooges. And unto one Musso who was a Dirty Little Wop, he saith: I have decided to conquer the world. Wherefore if thou armest all thy ice-cream merchants and send them to fight for me, and likewise lendest thou me thy big boats, when I am done, thou Musso shalt share in the Mighty Carve-up.
  But Musso being exceeding cautious and anxious to be on the Right Side, answered Itla saying: Ackess. Go thou forth and fight the Brittites and their friends, and when thou pauseth for thy second wind, I will join thee with my mighty and glorious army.
  And it came to pass that Musso perceived that Itla was Doing All Right and winning an abundance of Lebensraum. Wherefore he assembled all his chiefs and elders and told them that the time was come for a Stab in the Back. And he reminded them of the Wops glorious victory over the Ethiopites, and their colossal success in Alban. But he cautioned them, saying: 'Tis indeed a misfortune that the Brittites are armed with weapons, for we are not so accustomed. But fear not, for the Hunnites have made them exceeding weary.
  And there were trumpetings throughout the land of It. and the Wops knew the peoples of Brit must be shuddering in their sandals. For the Wops saith one to another: Did not our forefathers the Romans conquer Brit? But the Brittites were not afflicted with the Jitters, for they happened to remember that all the Romans had died a very long time ago.
  Now in these days the Wops possessed parts of Afrik which no one else wanted, but they coveted Egg-wiped and other places where the Brittites were, and they decided to conquer them. But they Did It All Wrong, and advanced the wrong way, and fell into the sea. And mighty hosts of them Got A Shake On and decided to live in Brit, which was exceeding silly because the King of Brit would not let his peoples eat ice-cream any more.
  And Musso was exceeding sad, and would not let his sailors sail their big boats because the Brittites might make holes in them, which spoiled them.
  And Itla, hearing of this, was sorely vexed and consumed a great length of carpet in his rage.
  And when the Wops possessed no more of Afrik wherein to fly their white flags they came nigh unto their home and did likewise in Sis. And Musso, perceiving that Hit still ate too much carpet, was sorely cheesed, and decided to Save his Skin. And he went to the King and asked him for his cards. And the King gave them unto him and Musso was no longer a Big Noise. And because the King was really only half a king he summoned a bad man called Oglio to fight his war for him.
  And Musso departed from hence, but his name liveth for evermore as a Mighty Windbag. For it is written: Whomsoever buildeth an empire on macaroni shall surely lose it all.

ED. Here endeth the first Lesson. We hope the second is like unto it.

4

The fact that we were going lion-hunting did not imply that we were a band of 'Dead-Eye-Dicks', or 'Buffalo Bills'. Nor must it be taken to indicate we were in any sense a group of 'Bahrams', or any other such great hunters. It merely arose through the fact that our special license allowed us to shoot "ONE LION". That such things as springboks, antelopes etc., were also included, were not taken into consideration. We were going shooting, we had permits, these permits stated we could shoot the maximum of one lion, therefore if we were hunting, it followed suit that it could only be lion-hunting. That we did by sheer bad luck run into a lion was a matter of deep regret to all concerned.

The island on which we had landed was a typically tropical one, after the best M.G.M. tradition, with thick vegetation reaching right down to the coast, and from it arose the scream of paroquets by day, and the roar of beasts by night. Not exactly my idea of a holiday camp. We picked up our boy in the village; we had decided not to hire gun-bearers. I for one was of the opinion that if I went into that jungle, my gun was not going to leave my hands, and the safety catch would be permanently off. Not for me the bubble reputation.

The boy expressed his delight at the gifts we had brought him, and assured us with liberal gesticulations that he was the finest hunter around those parts, in evidence of which he showed us huge scars of ill-healed wounds, which he assured us were obtained in combat with 'Cimba' King of Beasts. Bearing in mind the old adage that a good boxer never carries the marks on his face, this exhibition left me singularly unmoved. I fell to thinking if that's what you get for being a good hunter - what must you get for being a bad one? The horrible truth dawning on me - there are no bad hunters - for long; made me instinctively push forward my safety catch. We moved off into the jungle.

How far we had traversed into it I cannot remember. The heat was oppressive, hot, and moist, it reminded me vaguely of the greenhouse at home - a sort of nostalgic paradox. Suddenly a silent whoop came from our boy, and the magic word; 'Cimba!', escaped his lips. I took a quick glance round the surrounding foliage. I could see no lion, and I fervently hoped he could see no Snikmat. We gathered round the boy, as with eyes rolling and finger raised over his lips he repeats; 'Cimba!' 'Where?', we all whispered in unison. 'Here, Master', said the boy, and pointed to the ground beneath us. Such was the state of my nerves that it was only with an effort I restrained myself from jumping, as for a split-second, I imagined we were stood on the beastly thing. However, the boy dropped to one knee, and there on the ground he pointed to the clear heavy imprint of a lions foot. It took me exactly two seconds to work out that if that was the size of his foot, that lion must stand three feet if it stood an inch, and there must be some good nine feet of it.

(<u>Contnd.</u>)

"HOLD THAT TIGER" (Contnd.)

Well, a lion in a zoo, or a lion in a circus, where in both cases the public are reasonably safe, are quite different propositions to a lion in a jungle, especially a lion the size I estimated this one to be. I realised instantly there was no room in that jungle for both the lion and myself, and, as it was his jungle, I was perfectly willing to withdraw. Unfortunately I was not in a position to do as I pleased, and if the other members of the party wished to go chasing what was now a harmless lion, I knew I would have to go with them.

It was the boy who decided, with a wave of his arm, and a whispered; 'Cimba, go this way, Master', he set off in the direction the lion had taken, and with studied carefree attitude, my compatriots and I followed. I noted with satisfaction an absence of alacrity in taking up the first position behind the boy. Evidently these people did speak my language. As we moved on, I became aware of a thumping noise which seemed to reverberate right down my legs and into the ground. It seemed to come from somewhere in my chest - surely it couldn't be? - I cautiously raised my hand and felt - it was. The reaction was instantaneous, the thought flashed through my mind - If that lion is one half as scared as I am, he'll be half way to Cape Town by now. This reflection was too much for me, and I burst out laughing. Immediately I was hushed into silence, the boy was on his knee once more, (a bad sign that). 'Cimba not far away, Master!' he announced. 'How do you know?', we whisper. 'Look Master!', says the boy, and he pointed to the grass which had been trampled down by the beast. Slowly and surely it was raising itself back into its normal position, the lion must have passed over that spot less than two minutes previously. As I gazed semi-hypnotised at the slowly erecting grass, I was painfully aware of the fact that the hair on my scalp was elevating itself in an identical manner inside my sun helmet. My 'Cape Town hope', was looking pretty sick.

I was now in a quandary. I knew that when a lion suspects he is being hunted, he will frequently describe a huge "P", and endeavour to come back upon his pursuers from the rear. This meant that if I was in the van, I ran the chance of coming upon the lion first, and receiving the initial onslaught. On the otherhand, if I was in the rear, I ran the chance of getting some four cwt. of infuriated lion in the small of my back. Of the two, I preferred neither. The jungle was breaking away rapidly now, giving place to large areas of parkland. As we came up to one, we saw the object of the lions attention, covering an area of some hundreds of square yards was a herd of wild boar. Here was something more worthy of our mettle. In spite of the boys almost tearful pleadings, they, (excluding myself) fired. The results were wonderful. One or two of the beasts jumped as they were hit, but as one unit, the herd wheeled, and with heads and tusks down, foam pouring from their mouths, they roared down on us in a whirl of dust and hooves. Clutching his assegai - his only weapon, save a knife, the boy held his ground. 'Don't shoot yet, Master!', he cried. (The idea being to wait till they were within a hundred yards of you, then open up a rapid fire on the leaders, the devastation caused having the effect of making the remainder withdraw in disorder - if you believe the screen pictures.)

'Right! shoot now, Master' shouts the boy, and turns round. Where there should have been a row of stalwart men lined up with rifles to their shoulders - there was nothing.   (Contnd.)

L is for Loughborough – You all know the route
and it's ten to one you'll end up at the "Boot".

A is for Anstey – a snug little place
after one over the eight there you'll land up in disgrace.

N is for Nottingham – not bad, but oh dear!
what a queer looking liquid they serve you, called Beer.

D is for Diseworth 'way out in the blue
a far cry for billettees, but I know of two.

M for Mountsorrel – Mount Sorry, should be
"open on Thursday" was all I could see.

A is for 'Anchor" – a pub so they say
you may be lucky – it's down Narborough way.

R is for Rothley – on a sort of a plain
you walk miles and miles, then walk home again.

K is for Knighthorpe – there's one at the 'Cross'
but you'll only get beer there, if you're well in with the boss.

S is for 'summing up' – what!stay here?, no fear
I wanna go home folks, where you can get Kentish Beer.

"Thirsty".

"HOLD THAT TIGER" (Contnd.)
                        I seemed to see generations of British mythical courage with which the boy had been instilled, fall from his eyes as though a veil had been taken from them. He surveyed the fleeing figures, they were leaping into trees with an agility which would have made Tarzan look a cripple. With a despairing cry he hurled his assegai at the foremost boar, dropping it dead in its track, then he too took to his heels.
    After a while we climbed down. Having rudely interrupted the boars mealtime, ruined the boy's chances of bagging a lion, and the lion's chances of getting a dinner: – we retired. What the boy must have thought of us, I neither know or care – comparisons at the best are odious , but I do find solace in the fact that had we dropped him on a traffic island at Piccadilly Circus during the rush hour, perhaps even he wouldn't exactly shine.

"Snikmot".

7

Shssh! G O S S I P Shssh!

From "The Times" Aug 17th. 1943
-On Aug. 15 1943, to Joyce (nee Ellingworth), wife of Flight-Lieut. Michael Caton - a son.

We are very sorry to hear that Mr.F.R.Thornton has been seriously ill for some time, and is in Hospital at Leatherhead. We send him our best wishes for a speedy recovery, and hope he will soon be with us again.

'INTO BATTLE.' A small dejected little man creeping up to Canteen counter through a maze of khaki (all ranks-all sorts). "Excuse me, do you serve civilians here?!" Recently arrived for 1400-2200 hrs. duty at 1345 i.w.t.(Ingersoll Wristwatch Time), to find that it was 1405 s.c t.(Signing-on Clock Time), and 1355 c.c.t.(Courtyard Clock Time). However, variety is the spice of life, and the fact that the 0600-1400 watch were still working,(on duty) make it highly probable that 1345 i.w.t. was correct. Although we do not usually drag this publication down to the commercial level, we suggest the wayward clocks contact Dickie (Repairum) Akhurst. That's Okay Dickie, just give me 10%.

CONGRATULATIONS:- to Don Barber on attaining his majority, on a splendid birthday party, and, on not getting thrown out of his billet. Also to 'Mac', on a splendid solo effort which brought him safely home after a hectic night at approx. 3 a.m. Incidentally 'Mac' there never have been any brakes on that byke, but then I doubt if you noticed it.

GARDEN PARTY:- We hear a great success was No.7 Coy's Garden Party and Dance on Bank Holiday Monday, which realised some £60 for the 'comforting' of that very charming Company. We understand the 'buried treasure' was found beneath an Olive tree. A tribute to the 'Ankle-Judge', was the quick spotting of a soldier intruder complete with khaki stockings. We appluad the soldier's gallant attempt-but we know our 'Ankle-Judge', who incidentally, was keeping close to the law later in the evening. An outstanding figure was the EWA, who insisted on telling everyone all the way home, that he was,"Mr. ...of the War Dept." The evening ended with that most enjoyable of games called, "In and Out the Passion Waggon". This game, which has much in common with the feeding of the five thousand,(Mark 6 41) is best played with one 40 seater troop carrier, 350 ATS, and one Officer 1/c, who cannot make her mind up. The game commences with the order:"All girls in the troop-carrier!", which is immediately countermanded by:"All girls not going on duty-out of the troop-carrier!" Having thus set the ball rolling, it is left to the ingenuity of the Officer or NCO i/c, to follow up with orders, in which the variety vies only with the rapidity of their utterance:to the increasing perplexity of the performers, and the intense amusement of the spectators. Such gems as: "All girls who can't get in-Get out!" - "All girls who can't sit down-stand up!", only serve to show the skill in contrivance which can be brought to bear. AFTERMATH:- ATS to EWA:"I saw you having a good time,last night"
                EWA. "Oh yes!-You mean in the 'Bradgate Arms'?"
                ATS. "No, not the 'BRADGATE' arms."
He's still wondering whose arms it could have been-No names,no James.

FLICKS

What's on?

TRUINS GUIDE ASSISTS YOU.   STAR RATING IN BRACKETS

EMPIRE.	Sept. 6th.(3 days)	"MADAMOISELLE FRANCE" (2) Joan Crawford. Bill Elliott "PROMISE FULFILLED".
	Sept. 9th.(3 days)	"FLYING TIGERS" (2) John Carroll. Chester Morris "BLACKIE GOES TO HOLLYWOOD".
ODEON.	Sept. 6th.(3 days)	"I MARRIED A WITCH" (3) Veronica Lake, Fredric March. James Craig "SEVEN MILES FROM ALCATRAZ"
	Sept. 9th.(3 days)	"REBECCA" (4) Laurence Olivier Joan Fontaine, George Sanders.
VICTORY.	Sept. 6th.(3 days)	"THUNDER ROCK" (3) Michael Redgrave. The Fleet Air Arm "FIND FIX AND STRIKE".
	Sept. 9th.(3 days)	"SEVEN SWEETHEARTS" (2) Kathryn Grayson, Van Heflin.
EMPIRE.	Sept.13th.(3 days)	"STAGE COACH" (3) Claire Trevor, J.Wayne. John Hubbard "SECRETS OF THE UNDERGROUND".
	Sept.16th.(3 days)	"ICE CAPADES REVUE" (2) Ellen Drew. Zasu Pitts "TISH".
ODEON.	Sept.13th.(6 days)	"CARGO OF INNOCENTS" (3) Robert Taylor, Chas.Laughton, Brian Donlevy.
VICTORY.	Sept.13th.(6 days)	"TALES OF MANHATTAN" (3) Boyer, Rogers, Fonda,Laughton,Robeson etc. also "JEWEL OF THE PACIFIC".
EMPIRE.	Sept.20th.(3 days)	"SCARLET PIMPERNEL" (3) Leslie Howard. Rin Tin Tin "FANGS OF THE WILD".
	Sept.23rd.(3 days)	"BELLS OF CAPISTRANO" (1) Gene Autry. Dennis O'Keefe "MOONLIGHT MASQUERADE".
ODEON.	Sept.20th.(3 days)	"MAN AND HIS MATE" (1) Victor Mature. Macdonald Carey "SALUTE FOR THREE" (2)
	Sept.23rd.(3 days)	"CHINA" (2) Loretta Young,Alan Ladd. Gale Storm "RHYTHM PARADE".
VICTORY.	Sept.20th.(6 days)	"KEEPER OF THE FLAMES" (3) Spencer Tracy, Katherine Hepburn.
EMPIRE.	Sept.27th.(6 days)	"YANKEE DOODLE DANDY" (3) James Cagney, Walter Huston.
ODEON.	Sept.27th.(6 days)	"THE GENTLE SEX" (3) Leslie Howard's Prod. Frank Albertson "KEEP'EM SLUGGING".
VICTORY.	Sept.27th.(6 days)	"KATINA" (2) Sonja Henie.

THE FILM OF THE MONTH:- The Revival of Daphne Du Maurier's "REBECCA".
(Odeon, Sept. 9th. (3 days).)

THE PERFORMANCE OF THE MONTH:- Jas.Cagney's portrayal of George M.Cohan in "YANKEE DOODLE DANDY".
(Empire, Sept. 27th. (6 days).)

STANDING ORDERS

THEIR'S NOT TO REASON 'Y' GROUP (OR ANY OTHER)

The A.T.S. seems to hold quite a position
as a repository for ancient military tradition
although Jerry has shown us, despite all our swank
it takes more than tradition to stop Bomber and Tank.

Khaki-clad girls so trim and neat
marching to meals through the main street
each carrying cutlery - knife, fork and spoon
a military custom as old as the moon.
    See Standing Orders.

Recreation in 'civvies' to ease the strain
merely serves to cause more mental pain
for military conception of 'organised sport'
would confound the logic of a lawyer in court.
    See Standing Orders.

To carry a few treasures from one's bombed out home
in suitcase or box wherever one may roam
seems hardly a crime when doing one's bit
no hope - it's not issue - 'Dispose of that kit'.
    See Standing Orders.

During spells of hot weather clad in thick khaki skirt
with collar and tie on neatly ironed shirt
no respite while officialdom sits and sighs
and thanks heaven for red tape and old school ties.
    See Standing Orders.

Of the handbag theme you've had your fill
from the pen of charming Mary Gill
with bulging pockets, clutching box and tin
the girls go on duty no longer so trim.
    See Standing Orders.

To travel by warrant the quickest way
seems quite obvious, so one would say
but time is no object - only the miles
so look out for deductions and pay up with smiles.
    See Standing Orders.

Some people read Beachcomber, and others who gaily
publish their foolishness in the newspapers daily
but where sanity reigns - although close to the borders
I heartily commend you to -
    See Standing Orders.

                                    E. Catchpole.

MOSTLY ABOUT JU-JU

By:- T.L.Hobday.

Before leaving England I was warned that Africa was a continent of surprises, and that the West Coast had at least its share of them. The truth of this statement and warning was first made clear to me when, after a quiet swim near Accia, Gold Coast, I found a tree-viper in my trousers: its truth was finally proved to me immediately after embarkation for home, when I found that my native servant, amid tears of regret at my departure, had decided to allot himself generous souvenirs from my kit, mercifully confining himself to W.D. property.

Old Coasters, - as we reverently call those sun-tanned, gin-soaked happy exiles who have passed decades on the Coast and lost the desire to return - say that the springs of human effort are two, varying according to colour: gin for the white massa and ju-ju for the black man.

I don't wish to rekindle old longings by mentioning gin here; it is enough to say that in Africa it has the same effect as here, except that the hallucination-stage provides more exotic shape and colours than it does at home, and that there appears to be a more general public sympathy towards the temporary loss of muscular power at times associated with gin.

Ju-ju however, has a claim to more detailed and careful analysis. Of course, events which might startle a newcomer into shrieking 'ju-ju' are dismissed as childs-play by the hardened coasters: for example, there have been people frightened to insensibility by the spectacle of a white vest and a pair of white underpants stalking along the road at night with apparently nobody inside them. That, of course, is the normal appearance of a scantily-clad black man in the dark.

Real ju-ju is very different, and holds black and white in frequent thrall. By definition and practice, ju-ju is the ability of one man - or, more probably, one woman - to exert, at a distance, influences for good or bad, upon another man: blessing and curse, in other words. Many tribes and communities have well-organised ju-ju administered by a "ju-ju-man", who maintains himself in luxury by the simple process of blackmail. Failure to pay due forfeit might result in the sudden appearance of triplets in the unfortunate man's family, or some other economic disaster. It seems fairly certain that, whether by supernatural means or by some unexplained extension of natural means, apparent miracles are performed.

Personal "ju-ju", however, is the more intriguing study: the ability of a single individual, suddenly provoked, to put a spell, or ju-ju upon the person or object annoying him. Again discussion of its possibility is difficult, but it seems to have the desired effect very frequently.

(Contnd.)

"MOSTLY ABOUT JU-JU" (Contnd.)

I was once the victim of a ju-ju, which had been put upon a bicycle, which the disgruntled black boy thought was to be his, but which was given to me instead. I had had normal cycling experience, but this cycle was definitely possessed. I fell off so frequently, and for such ludicrously slender reasons, that finally I had to give it away. I risked a still greater ju-ju by not giving it to the well-wisher who administered the spell.

When I was at GHQ, West Africa, an African from the Defence Platoon - Kwami Mensa, I believe - slipped away for his months annual leave and came back very dejected and downcast. He said that his brother had caught him looking rather thoughtfully at his, the brother's wife, and had immediately put a ju-ju on him, and that he would inevitably die soon. A few days later, when we were on an early morning P.T. parade, someone noticed a surprising thing - a rifle stuck in the fork of a tree. We went over to see and Kwami Mensa was dead beneath the tree, shot through the chest. He had killed himself in the terror of suspense. That night the tom-toms were beating in the nearby bush villages, from dusk to dawn, to ward off the ju-ju that had accounted for Kwami.

The actual administration of a ju-ju usually takes this form; the aggrieved person withdraws about twenty or thirty feet from the victim, cups his hands, and mumbles into them, looking from time to time at the victim; his mumbling consists of the curse, and the fate he suggests will meet the occasion.

A less tragic example is that told of a bank in West Africa; one day a ragged native turned up and, after palaver and insistence, had an interview with the manager. His point was simple; he demanded a weekly pension, in return for which he would condescend not to burgle the bank. Well, the bank was substantial, and the manager soon cleared him out. The next night fifty pounds was missing, though none of the entrances, either to the bank or to the strong-room, had been interfered with; guards were put on the second night, and the manager himself stayed on the premises. No sound or movement was heard; in the morning another fifty pounds had gone. The native got his pension the following week.

Precautions against ju-ju are common, and usually take the form of objects which have received blessing, and are then capable of exorcision; three of the most common are flails of animal hair looking rather like a torch - which incidentally almost every African M.T. driver carries with him to ward off accidents -, small leather pads, which have a chapter of the Koran woven into them, and are worn round the upper arm, fastened by a cord, and finally small bracelets of elephant hair, worn round the wrist. All three are very commonly seen, and I myself was fully equipped. I have all three with me if anyone wishes to see them.

Fine, gaudy clothes impress Africans greatly; in this respect I had a rather amusing experience which, though not directly connected with Ju-ju, throws a rather instructive light on the African character.

(Contnd.)

"MOSTLY ABOUT JU-JU" (Contnd.)

I didn't know what the conditions for recreation would be in West Africa, so I optimistically took flannels and a blazer with me. My first native servant - he didn't stay long as he didn't "savvy press proper" (couldn't iron) - was highly intrigued by this blazer, and asked my permission to borrow it to wear for Church. I don't suppose he had ever been to Church before. Anyway, I graciously granted him the required permission, adding however, that in England, when one wore a blazer for Church, it was the custom to wear "blazer-trousers" as well. Luckily my pyjamas were nearly as gaudy and stripey as the blazer, so I easily tempted him to wear the "pyjama-trousers" with the blazer. The blazer was black, blue and white, in vertical stripes, and the pyjamas were orange, green and white, also in vertical stripes. I finally equipped him with a navy-blue Army dress hat and an Army belt to go round the blazer, and resisted with difficulty his appeal to sew three stripes on the blazer. Finally he went off to Church in that condition: I soothed my conscience by equipping him with Hymns Ancient and Modern but, as he couldn't read, I don't suppose that helped him very much.

I questioned him about his reception in Church, later. "Massa", he said, with full pride, "when I go for come for inside Church, singing palaver finish one-time, all men, all women go turn look for me. Plenty say I be fine fine boy, clothes shine past all!"

Who wouldn't weep to leave Africa!

There was hardly a soul to be seen in the gloom,
The boys had all gone to the big briefing room,
Out there on the tar-mac, dark shapes in the night
The bombers like great birds, were ready for flight,
How many would lie, before darkness was o'er,
A mass of steel wreckage on some foreign shore,
But the boys who were ready, no dark thoughts were theirs,
I don't suppose one of them uttered his prayers,
They boarded the crates with the usual grin,
Yelled 'contact' and started the trip to BERLIN.
                                    Joan Howarth.

"THE BOMBARD STORY" (Cont'd.)

The rest of t'crew eased their bayonets
Tho' they knew they'd nowt to beware,
But wi' thirty-bob here in t'kitty,
It seemed best to make sure of their share.

As 'Nic' wi' one hand salutes Col.
While t'other held thirty-bob tight,
Col. says: "And as tha's so efficient,
Tha's best stop and clear up t'site."
                              "Snikmot".

THE BOMBARD STORY

"Snikmot".

Now I'll tell you a Home Guard story
Of some lads what won honour and fame,
Under 'Dick', at their last competition,
Blacker-Bombard's crew, that were their name.

They were some of the boys from our section,
Their job when t'action begun
Was to set up their bombard and fire it -
As quick as they could, at the Hun.

And to make competition t'keener
Home Guards for miles had rehearsed,
Tho' some didn't expect to beat Rothley,
They all thought they'd beat 21st.

Now t'Col. thought Rothley would win it,
As t'smartest team out on t'field,
And to honour the best exhibition
He decided to offer a shield.

At blast of t'whistle for starting
All teams rushed to get on their boots,
Then hurried to rig up their bombards
Whilst 2 loads, and No.1 shoots.

At t'height of t'rush were a shambles
And one team was disqualified,
They wanted to fire wi'out legs hammered in,
And t'recoil would have meant suicide.

As our No.1's hand pressed on t'trigger,
Of his teams hopes and threats, he'd a list,
It was: Scotch, if his shot hit t'target,
And a kick where it hurts, if he missed.

At last when their gun were assembled,
And t'shot on t'target did fall,
They gazed at t'opponents around 'em,
And found they'd beaten 'em all.

Now when t'Adjutant announced them t'winners,
Col.'s face grew exceedingly red,
He says: "Well lads, shield's not ready-yet,
Wiltha' take thirty-bob instead?"

Now 'Nick' was Detachment Commander
And wanted that shield really bad,
But thirty-bob split up between 'em
Gave some recompense to t'lad.

SPORTS PAGE

A.H.Appleton.

The Cricket Selection Committee have found it increasingly difficult to raise teams. The match with Quorn on 28th.Aug. had to be cancelled for this reason.

I endeavoured to arrange a Water-Polo match, but only one person was brave enough to put his name down.

I also tried to get names for an Athletic match, but again the few names put forward made it farcical.

Owing to the reasons already stated at the recent general meeting, "Exiles" will not enter the Alliance League this winter.

From the foregoing, it is quite obvious that sport in this Section is dying. After nearly two years, I can only say that I and other committee-men have tried every means to stimulate interest. I, and other people, have spent a lot of our spare time arranging fixtures, leasing grounds, buying kit etc. We do not get the support we should. When I notice young men lounging about the locality with their hands in their pockets, it does seem pitiful that they do not take up some active recreation.

I should like to thank the Cricket Selection Committee, Messrs. Musgrave, Anderson and Mayre, for their invaluable help and advice this season. Also J.Dodd and P.Carrington for mending the cricket practice-nets, and setting up same for the few practices we had. I should also particularly like to thank Mr. Carrington's Landlord, for storing our cricket gear so conveniently close to the ground.

A close game against Woodhouse Eaves resulted in a win by 4 runs. We had the vocal support of a crowd of Woygites, which was most encouraging. Another grand game against R.N.A.S. We only had 9 men on this occasion but the match was thoroughly enjoyed, although we lost. The local Derby v Quorn, we also lost.

The match against Brush Students, proved the old adage of the "glorious uncertainty of cricket". Exiles scored 34, and when the last man came in for Brush, their score was only 19. The score was doubled, the last man scoring 14 not out!! The 10th. wicket fell after the winning score had been made so Brush won by 4 runs. That is Cricket.

RESULTS:-

31/7 Woodhouse Eaves 52. (A.Dobson 18, R.P.Smith 3 for 16, A.Keenlyside 6 for 14).
      Exiles   56. (Musgrave 26, A.Dobson 6 for 24).

4/8   Exiles   83. (W.Anderson 25, Nutman 5 for 43).
      Royal Naval Air Section. 86. (Irvine 54, Grundy 24, R.P.Smith 5 for 41).

14/8 Exiles   35. (A.Dexter 4 for 9, A.Darby 5 for 23).
      Quorn   49. (R.P.Smith 4 for 14, J.Edge 5 for 20).

21/8 (No details of Exiles score) Lost.

28/8 Brush Students   38. (Martin not out 14, R.P.Smith 6 for 14, Edge 3 for 15).
      Exiles   34. (Dobson 17, Anderson 4 for 6, Winkley 6 for 21)

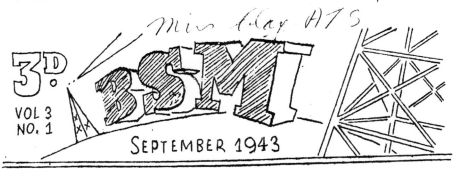

"B.S.M." SEPTEMBER, 1943.
Vol.3.   No.1.

General Editor:-	L.P.Jones.	Editorial Board:-	
		R.Wilkinson.	R.G.Denny.
Editor:-	F.C.Staddon.	E.Millhouse.	T.Brister.

Next publication:- 29th October. Contributions by:- 15th. October.

FRONT COVER by:- R.Wilkinson.
Illustrations etc. By:- E.Hobden, R.Wilkinson.

Time flies! Indeed, this last 12 months have flown so fast, that we were a little surprised ourselves, when we realised that this was our SECOND BIRTHDAY NUMBER.

Although our publication dates are qualified by a certain amount of elasticity, we do feel that the "B.S.M." has so far made the grade, and having gone thus far, see no reason why it should not continue to make its monthly, though often tardy, appearance.

It is regrettable that this number should be unduly late, but as usual we present the perfect alibi. Our printing works are located in the wilds of Diseworth and come under the benevolent management of our General Editor, Mr.L.P.Jones, often referred to somewhat disrespectfully as "Jonah". This gentleman (Hut "C"), has been indisposed recently, and this has aggravated the customary end of the month rush which our contributors, artists, helpers and Editorial staff indulge in with such amazing regularity. We will ignore the fact that the Editor could not resist the lure of a long week-end.

By the time you read this, it is hoped that our General Editor will be his usual boisterous self again.

In retrospect we can observe quite a few changes since we arrived in Toygland. Our feminine element has ceased to be "new", in fact what was an adjunct to the whole, contributes the main part of it. What with the departure of so many of our colleagues to warmer climes (no offence blokes) we are fast becoming a rare specie. Nevertheless, the spirit is still there, and sometimes we think our girl friends like us just a little.

Another change that has taken place, is in the Canteen arrangements. After 2 years of honest endeavour and hard work, it has been found necessary and advisable to hand the management over to an outside organisation. Let us hope that they, with their vast knowledge and resources, will approach the task before them in the same spirit as existed in our own Canteen Committees.

In this issue you will notice a new style in some of the headings and sketches, which serve to introduce you to our latest recruit, Mr.E.Hobden ("Hobby"). Please relax your black-out restrictions and make contact with the Editorial Board. A magazine is always hungry for contributions, sketches, ideas, and the "B.S.M." is no exception. Please help us to see that it keeps 'alive' and not merely 'exist'.

From the General Editor. My very best thanks to all those who have so ably assisted in the production of the "B.S.M."

Three College Cads.

They studied maths from A to Z,
Even when they went to bed.
They bought each other pints of ale
While studying the metric scale.
The Empire was a haunt of theirs,
And there they studied roots and squares;
Until they thought that they would go
And see what more there was to know.
So off they went to Loughborough College
To improve their swelling knowledge.
At first the work was their concern;
They soon learned all there was to learn.
And then they looked around and saw
The style of clothes the others wore.
"Ah", thought they, "this will not do,
We three must look all 'sporty' too!"
They weren't quite sure what they would wear,
But something that would make men stare.-
"And then we'll learn the college lingo,
Drawling out 'By Gad'; 'By Jingo'."
It took some time to change their style,
So let us leave them for awhile.

  x x x x x x x

We'll join our trio 3 months later.
Already 'Dad's' become 'the Pater'.
Everything is, 'nifty, what?'
The other lads are, 'A rum lot'.
"Though the Tutor's rather crusty
College life is not so dusty.
The actual works a frightful bore"
(A thing I didn't know before.)
They call each other by, 'You Cad',
And every sentence starts, 'By Gad',
Their clothes are startling to the eye-
The brightest blazers, socks and tie
Canes and vivid shirts and spats,
And all varieties of hats.
Do you think the life in College
Really has improved the knowledge
Of these three young men, whose names
Are, BRISTER, CARRINGTON and JAMES?

Hilary H. Fry.

THE HAMMER OF THE P.O.T.S. By "YONC"

The Hammer of the P.O.T.S. was worried. As the bodily leader and spiritual guide of all P.O.T.S. in the flourishing fellowship of Woygland he had reason. The ruffled brow was understandable: The lines of worry only to be expected. As head cook and bottle-washer of all the P.O.T.S. such things were not to be wondered at.

The P.O.T.S. (People On Three Shifts) were a recalcitrant race - A motley crew forsooth, and one much given to weeping and wailing and the gnashing of molars and eye teeth. They needed some handling, did the P.O.T.S. Strong will and iron heel were essentials.

But that was beside the point. The Hammer was used to it. He'd done it for so long now, and such things left no mark or stain upon a never very refractory conscience.

No. He had a bigger worry; Something more vital than ordinary P.O.T.S; More nerve-wracking: A thing to make the strongest man dither more than a bit. Yes sir! It sure would!

Now, one of the P.O.T.S. was a very clever sort of chap. Brainy, you know. Surfeit of grey matter and all that. This chap didn't work with the usual run of P.O.T.S. No man! He used to wait for the telephone to ring:

"Ullo! Aychere - sixisdis"

Then this chap, whose name was Priest, (a lissom man and a willowy; graceful in all his ways) this chap would say "O.K." pick up a hammer and a screwdriver, and with easy, swinging strides, proceed to the scene and do the necessary.

That, as I say, was his normal procedure. His way of life as a P.O.T.S. developed through long years of Woygland environment. Being a brave man and a thoughtful, he decided to change all that. This wanderlust was not to his liking. The country ramble was definitely not his strong suit.

So, having a super-abundance of what it takes, he invented something, and called it "Er" - which was what worried the Hammer of the P.O.T.S. He thought "Er" a good thing - nothing better. It was a funny little animal, obtained after some research by the diligence of Mr. Priest. By crossing a hammer and a screwdriver, and feeding the result on bits of wire and bakelite knobs, he'd managed to produce a fine specimen of prototype, Er.

Er was like a screwdriver at the top, and completely bald, and it had hammer-toes, smoked a pipe, and spoke only in phonetics, with a Cockney accent. It was so educated, that when the 'phone rang and someone said in a high-pitched voice (Mr. D- probably) "Aychere Sixisdis", all Mr. Priest had to do was to give Er the tip. At once, Er would get up, and, hopping along on his hammer-toes, would walk round to Aych, say GM, or GN or H.H. O.M. to the man (Mr.D-probably), go up to six, jump around on it a bit with his hammer toes, stand on its screwdriver head and go round and round a few times, jump on to the floor, say OK inkemmerink, and walk out, saying G.B. nicely to the man (still probably Mr.D-).

This, as everyone was prepared to admit with customary P.O.T.S. generosity was a good thing, and a piece of fine business. All the same, it worried the Hammer of the P.O.T.S. Yes Sir! It certainly made him think.   (Contnd.)

"THE HAMMER OF THE P.O.T.S." (Contnd.)

You see he had reason to suspect that the two brilliant secret agents from Pershire Kewessay-fyv and his assistant Kewessay-wun were on the track of the secret invention.

Of course, Er was dreadfully sub human and would easily be lured away with promises of shorter hours, more food, and above all the irresistable temptation of a leather bag like the one Mr. Priest himself carried. It was obvious therefore, that Mr.Priest should take precautions, and the Hammer of the P.O.T.S. was there to see that he did it. Preparing for the worst was his motto in life. Making sure, his guiding star. So he told Mr.Priest:

"Mr.Priest" he said. "I'm sorry Mr.Priest, but just until we've captured Kewessay-fyv and Kewessay-wun, we can't possibly let Er go out by itself. It doesn't even know the rule of the road, so I'm afraid, Mr.Priest, you'll have to go with it, just to keep the old fatherly eye on it y/know."

Mr.Priest exercised, at first, the true British perogative of having a jolly good grumble, but like all Englishmen, he finally buckled to, and girded up his mental loins for fight, because girding up his physical loins would have taken too long.

From then on he accompanied Er wherever it went, teaching it everything he knew, even the elementary principles of geometry, such as lines and rhombics. Er soon got the hang of things, even to the extent of tickling the girls in Jay and arguing with the nobs in Aych. He was popular and the girls thought him just too cute for words. In fact, everything in the land was lovely, and it looked as if the awe-inspiring presence of Mr.Priest had finally put a stop to the dreadful machinations of those two Pershirian rapscallions.

Things were deceptive however, A calm before the storm you might say. All the air a solemn stillness held if I might say so. The storm did not break suddenly; It began like the first gentle breeze heralding a summer storm. Like flickers of summer lightning without the noisy companionship of thunder, the silent wickedness of Kewessay-fyv and his attendant sprite began to make itself felt.

It began when Mr.Priest began to see things. No one else saw them, because when anyone else was there, the cunning thing, the beast, the monster, whatever it was, hid its frightening light under a sinister bushel. Which is why no one else saw it. But when Mr.Priest and Er were walking by themselves, the gremlin-like thing would be there. Over their respective shoulders they would feel its presence, and once in a while, it would be seen, flitting lightly through the lengthening shadows, or disappearing into the man made forests of Woygland. It would float with a kind of sinister ethereal grace, and with half-drawn sword, and eyes lifted piously to heaven, he Cornwallis, Admiral of the White (or is it "Blue" sir?) would haunt the weary footsteps of Mr.Priest and Er. No one could catch him, because no one but they could ever see him; yet all knew that it was in reality, the evil genius of Kewessay-fyv that had caused this thing. Some black magic of a far Eastern clime had found its way in, and somehow, it had to be ejected.

Then, one evening, Mr.Priest and Er were hurrying over to Aych in answer to an urgent call. Suddenly behind them they heard a thunder, as of many broadsides, and a dreadful rattling, like unto grappling irons fastening their iron teeth into the bulwarks of some unfortunate ship. (Contnd.)

Retribution

Two years ago on British homes,
On towns and cities lofty domes,
The hun, in bitter fury hurled
Destruction from another world.
Through nights of slaughter and suspense,
We took it on the chin, too tense
To think or even reason why
Men, women and children had to die.

But with the dawning of respite
Men viewed it in a different light,
They saw, as through an opening door,
That now it was their turn to score,
The factories roared and woke to life,
They toiled and sweated, man and wife
To make the bombs and build the planes,
That we might keep our fields and lanes.

But now the day has really come
When we can crush and smash the hun,
Why should we stop to think it out,
They started this without a doubt,
They shall be battered more and more
Until they've paid in full the score
They totted two long years ago,
For they must reap what they did sow.

The wanton flame roars ever higher,
What will they salvage from the pyre,
These people who for countless ages
Have soiled the glistening history pages,
Now force is being met by force,
Their hymn of hate has run its course,
And they can only hope and wait
To be reprieved, some future date.

Joan Howarth.

xxxxxxxxxxxxxxxxxxxxxxxxxxxxxxxxxxxxxxxxxxxxxxxxxxxxxxxxxxxxxxxxx

"THE HAMMER OF THE P.O.T.S."(Contnd.)

Then with a fearful roar of "Repel Boarders , to me my merry men, English all; with a hey nonny nonny and I don't mean maybe", Admiral Cornwallis fell upon them, eyes flashing fire and brimstone, and silver sword unsheathed. Mr.Priest and Er turned at bay, ready to fight for England home and beauty.

"And I awoke; and behold! It was a dream", only don't tell Alec, because I was on nights at the time.

"Yonc"

Shssh! **G O S S I P** Shssh!

CONGRATULATIONS! To Mr. E.K.Ratcliffe on the occasion of his marriage to Miss Sarah Jane Hurst (A.T.S.). This happy ceremony was held at St.Augustines Church, Darlington, on 14th. September. Here's to happiness.
Also to Bobby/Billy Burr on reaching the almost impossible age of 21 on the 12th.Sept. The writer has distinct memories of Mr.Burrs arrival in our midst, when he seemed to personify the proverbial office boy with his cheekiness, brightness and efficiency. Whilst celebrating this unique event with Bobby/Billy and a few friends, in the customary manner/manor, your Gossip writer felt that he too must be getting really old. Still feeling in this mood I was handed a cutting from a local newspaper, contaning this advert:-
"For sale. unoccupied grave. University-rd., near entrance; best offer"
It's an idea anyway.
FOLLOW UP! Whilst on the subject of adverts., have you noticed what a lot of humour is often contained in the "personals". I liked this one: "Will anonymous person who sent white feather please send rest of bird - 'Amused'."
RESIGNATIONS:- We understand that Messrs. H.Appleton,Sweeten & Truin have resigned from the Staff Club Committee. We await developments, but a word of thanks for their past services would not be amiss.
CANTEEN! We hope that the management of the Canteen by the CO-op will show appreciable dividends, particularly with regard to service. To corrupt the popular advert,"10 minutes to wait-mine's a chance of a cup of tea." However, we have high hopes for the future.
We are a little disappointed to hear that BEER will be available in the Canteen shortly. We feel that the incentive for holding dances in this building, will no longer exist.
MOST SECRET (The Lemon) For the first time in his life, Eddie Sims found that the answer "was a lemon". This gay racketeer plus cloak room tickets and a LEMON,recently raised the magnificent sum of £5.14.0 for the Red Cross. We believe he had a nice rake off in the way of commission from Loughborough hardware stores on lemon squeezers, bought by crowds of optimistic Woygites. Anyway, anybody who can squeeze £5.14.0 out of a lemon, is O.K. by us.
RUMOUR! "Have you heard about the ..". "Well somebody said it was only ...". "Oh no, I understand it's ....".
DARK NIGHTS! Now that we are about to face winter evenings it is appropriate to draw your attention to possible activities. You know the existence of the Music Club and there is also the "Riff-Raff" Concert Party (contact F.C.Staddon. Hut "C"). All interested persons. will be welcomed by these bodies.
REFLECTION! This being our 2nd. birthday edition it is interesting to look back on the career of this page. During our existence we have been threatened with one libel action and been "on the carpet" once. I hesitate to say whether this proves we have fulfilled our function, or not. We have had our scoops as well. On one occasion the "B.S.M." was the first intimation a young A.T.S. had, that she was engaged. We keep our fingers crossed. Bye, bye,and I'll be snooping.

7
Galahad Rides Again.
By "PADDIE"

It was one of those lovely afternoons in mid-June. The sun was shining. A blackbird sang in a neighbouring tree. Myriads of grasshoppers beat out the opening bars of the Fifth Symphony. A cuckoo could be faintly heard, and the bells of the church in Woodhouse Eaves rang out a message of joy and hope. God was in his heaven and all was well with the world.

I strolled slowly over the Bridge of Sighs and ere I crossed the Hellespont leading towards the Canteen, the scene suddenly changed. A cloud came over the sun, a cold bitter wind swept across the grass and the birds stopped singing and the grasshoppers were mute.

A small cyclone was proceeding down the hill from the main gate. As it rounded the bend it gathered momentum and with a screeching noise stopped right in front of me and out of its vortex stepped----Galahad.

You all know him. It is he who rides a buckled contraption called a bicycle. One of his feet points SSE whilst the other bears NNW. He was ably portrayed by that famous artist called Wilk, I think.

He greeted me effusively with all that bonhomie which denotes a well-filled stomach and a bulky purse, and throwing his bike into a clump of nettles, he wiped the copious perspiration from his brow and escorted me to the Canteen.

"Whither goest thou?" I queried, to which he replied "Oh! just amusing myself with a run out here from Loughborough." I gasped.

The Canteen! - Here you may find food for man but not his beast. All the arts are here combined. You have Royle's Reveries coupled with Reed's Reminiscences and there is Harry Dodd in deep discussion with Charles Brown on wood and wind - especially wind, and Pearce's Poetry rivals Omar Khayyam at his best. Add to that, Truin's Truisms or his Yodels from the Tyrols which are indeed, a treat.

We sat at a table and talked of a voyage to the South Seas when the war was over. The calm warm nights. Tropic moons. Hula-hula girls, hibiscus flowers and hula-hula girls.

A half-hour passes quickly in such lovely company. He came out with me as far as the old mill-stream and ere he left, he whispered in my ear these five magic words, "MERCHANT NAVY FOR THE DERBY", and so he left me. Bless him.

The sun came out in all its glory as he disappeared through the gateway. The grasshoppers struck up that enchanting melody - The Pile-drivers Symphony by Sledgehammer.

... ...

As I went South for my annual holiday the train seemed to thunder out "Merchant Navy", "Merchant Navy", Merchant Navy", till my whole being was wrapped up in these exquisite words.

I am well known in my home town. It was generally whispered abroad that what I didn't know about horse-racing wasn't worth knowing. You see, in peace time I had been fortunate enough to guess the winner of the Derby two years in succession. (Contnd.)

Odds And Ends

by: "Ollie" Pearce.

September, and our little Mag,
Is celebrating it's birthtag;
I never thought, when it was born
That we should live to see the dawn,
When those concerned could proudly say,
"The BSM is two today",
And yet it looks as though we'll see
It reach the ripe old age of three.
My contributions hitherto,
Have dealt with things we say and do,
I've always thought our Mag should be,
Confined to Woygiteland, you see.
I don't know whether we've reformed,
Or whether I am ill-informed,
But local matter now is rare,
And so I seek my theme elsewhere,
Which method is most up to date;
Most things are rare, "ersatz" our fate.
Dead horse may be quite good to eat,
But I prefer accustomed meat;
It is enough to make one start,
To see the horse upon the carte.

Talking of "making do" reminds me; I read recently of a debate at a women's Institute in Essex on the subject of husbands.

In Essex some wives had the time of their lives,
Discussing this marital game;
And after debate, I am able to state,
'Twas to this conclusion they came;
Some kind of a mate, though he may not be great,
A regular son-of-a-gun,
A loafer, a sot, and a shocking bad lot,
Is very much better than none.

It occurred to me that we men also have our little cross to bear in these trying times.

A hungry man must make the most of a crust,
If he can't get the crumb - that is clear,
Half a loaf, it is said, is preferred to no bread;
But what, I would ask, about beer?
The bitter and mild wouldn't cheer up a child;
And drinking the stuff is no fun,
So all you can say of the wallop today,
Is - Lousy - But better than none!

Well to tincture my tale with a modicum of brevity, I told them, Oh yes, I told them. Why!, Merchant Navy of course, nothing to touch him. Old ladies, old gentlemen, old-age pensioners, school teachers, bank clerks and even the parson - oh yes, I told them. Of course they said a horse named Straight Deal was rumoured to be the best of the bunch, but I pooh-poohed the idea.

And then the fateful day came. I had put my shirt on Merchant Navy and I waited for the fateful hour with heart beating, feeling all taut and tense.

Why describe the scene of carnage. suffice to say I escaped from that lovely Southern town at the dead o'night, clothed in a barrel and dire vengeance in my heart.

Have any of you seen Galahad? I mean that tall guy who rides a bicycle with one foot pointing SSE and the other NNW. If you have, let me know, as I have polished up my Irish Shillelagh to a glassy hardness. I have threaded it through with horsenails and a few rusty razor blades are inserted with a careless abandon, and I want to pat Galahad and Merchant Navy hard - pretty hard. Oh Boy!

XXXXXXXXXXXXXXXXXXXXXXXXXXXXXXXXXXXXXXXXXXXXXXXXXXXXXXXXXXXXXXX

"ODDS and ENDS" (Contd.)   by:- "Ollie" Pearce.

T A I L P I E C E.
(with reference to a recent North Sea Incident (Press and B.B.C.)

Some German fishing boats were spied,
And soon the Navy got 'em,
And as they sank beneath the tide
Rejoicingly the sailors cried,
"More smacks upon the bottom!"

This is the end - dit-dah-dit-dah-dit.

XXXXXXXXXXXXXXXXXXXXXXXXXXXXXXXXXXXXXXXXXXXXXXXXXXXXXXXXXXXXXXX

HERE COMES THE STORK.
STOP PRESS:-

We hear rumours that "Jock" Miller has recently joined the exalted ranks of father Ewas. We are unable to tell you at this stage whether the baby is an Angus or a Mary, but will issue the full dope next month. In the meantime congratulations are due to "Jock" and Mrs. Miller.

WE MAKE THE POINT.

7 days a week lowers efficiency and makes no appreciable difference to your bank balance.

TO THOSE CONCERNED:- 'Workers Playtime' is usually from 12.30 to 1.0 p.m. only.

Can you write a DERISIVE DITTY?

THIS MONTH'S LIMERICK COMPETITION

Heres the idea boys and girls. We want Limericks about our organisation and its inmates. A chance to win immortal fame, and meet your favourite supervisor on equal terms.
Let's make sure you know how a Limerick goes. Here is an example for you, and you can take it that all Limericks have the same type of construction.

> The fellows looked up and said "Gosh!
> Our Alec has grown a moustache
> There's a sprout here and there
> Hardly worth calling hair"
> But now it's come off in the wash!

Get the idea? Mine may be a rotten effort, but let's see what you can do yourselves. Your editors reserve the right to suppress the too too indiscreet contributions, but anyway send them all in and we will sort them out.
In the meantime, "Pass me the pen and vitriol Emma, and give me a rhyme for McGrath!"

"Wilk".

JUDGES:- Messrs. Wilkinson, Millhouse, Brister.
PRIZE:- For best of published Limericks - 50 CIGARETTES.

THE GOSPEL ACCORDING TO ST. UPID. Chapter XXIV.
(Translated from the English by Disciple Millhouse.)

Now in Baro, which is an exceeding sore place, is an habitation called Loj. And nigh unto Loj are other habitations called Sowfeels, Mownt, and Holil. And there dwelleth here a tribe of Atsites, named Tepee. Now Tepee are a lonely people, for Baro is far off from the cities, and hath no Bright Lights, nor Flicks, nor yet many Heart Throbs. And it is written in the chronicles : Whensoever there are no Bright Lights, nor Flicks, even so a maiden shall survive. But, verily, if there are no Heart Throbs, she shall surely perish.

Now a few brave men, who had conceived mighty Crushes for certain maidens of Tepee, did at divers times venture through the wilderness of Slabz, and come into Baro. And at these times, when they stood without the walls of the habitations, which is called Keeping Him Waiting, other maidens would gaze enraptured from behind the curtains, and one of them, seizing another by her raiment, S.D., A.T.S., for the use of, would proclaim : Behold! there is a real live Man! And get thou this in thy thick head : I saw him first. And her companion would marvel at it, and cry : Lo! By the Beer of the Prophet, so this is the wondrous thing called Man. Verily, I have oft heard tell of these.

But then the maiden for whom the Man had conceived his Crush appeareth, and beareth him off in triumph, and giveth him That For, for giving the Glad unto other maidens, or What Have You. And the maidens for whom no Crushes were conceived were filled with sorrow, and were cast down, and forthwith went into a Huddle.

And it came to pass that these maidens came into their habitations from their labours in the hours of darkness. And when a maiden was alone in the darkness, she uttereth a mighty shriek and flee-eth into the bedchambers of her sisters. And being recovered of her breath, she cryeth : Woe is me, for I have seen The Man. And yea! I have no doubt at all that he is indeed a Man. Yet he scrammeth, and getteth away.

And when two or more Atsites were gathered together, and cometh into the habitations in darkness, and one beholdeth The Man, she straightway becometh mute, and findeth no tongue wherewith to say : Don't look now, but I think we are in luck's way. Wherefore her sister knoweth not the presence of The Man until they are come up into the bedchamber. And here, having searched beneath the bed, and found none other than crockery, the first maiden findeth her tongue, and telleth her sister that which she hath seen. And her sister answereth, saying : Well slap me in the region of Smolensk!. Why tellest thou not me when I couldst have grabbed him? For is not a Man in the Loj worth two in Luff? And the first answereth, saying : Verily I was afflicted with the jitters. And they both straightway seized weapons, and hastened to the place where The Man had been, but there was no Man.

And in the course of time many maidens beheld The Man, and proclaimed unto their sisters that which they had seen. And the fame of The Man spread throughout Loj, and Sowfeels, and Mownt, and Molil, yea, and throughout the length and breadth of Lesta. For it is written : The Man is an air man, likewise also is he a Corp, and a Sarge, and a Civi, and Uncle Tom Cobleigh and all.

P S Y C H O M A N I A

Our khaki friends, the ATS,
Do have hard times I must confess
And though they've got, just what it takes,
Are not averse to "double-breaks".

Now in our case to put it brief,
We only get one meal relief,
On top of that, we are surprised-
We've not been psycho-analysed.

A psychopat's analysis
May bring to light things so amiss,
That War Office to put them right,
Might have to sit up all the night.

Devising schemes whereby the men
Might work for thirty minutes, when,
In spite of their still being 'keen'
They'd then adjourn to the canteen.

There to imbibe with ecstasy,
Ambrosia, on some sweet ATS's knee,
Drinking long and drinking deep,
Then falling gently off to sleep.

Yet psychopathists sometimes err,
And in their keeness to be fair,
Might go so far as to decree
That beer at dances should be free!

And then in wild abandonment,
To every Ewa's wonderment,
To rid him of some "complex" fear,
Ordain a six months leave a year.

But here, at least, I must **digress**,
Six months! - without the ATS?
I'm sorry! - that, at anyrate,
I really couldn't tolerate.

                                              "<u>Snikmot</u>".

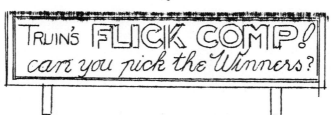

What types of film do you think are popular in Loughborough? What are the pictures that cause the queues and bring the money pouring in at the box office?

Here are the twenty-four films that have taken the most money in Loughborough during the past year:-

THE EMPIRE

(1) UNCENSORED.
(2) YANKEE DOODLE DANDY.
(3) COMMANDOS STRIKE AT DAWN.
(4) DESERT VICTORY.
(5) EAGLE SQUADRON.
(6) DESPERATE JOURNEY.
(7) BROADWAY.
(8) SPRINGTIME IN THE ROCKIES.

THE ODEON

(9) IN WHICH WE SERVE.
(10) MY GIRL SAL.
(11) THIS ABOVE ALL.
(12) THE ROAD TO MOROCCO.
(13) THE GENTLE SEX.
(14) FIVE GRAVES TO CAIRO.
(15) THE MAJOR AND THE MINOR.
(16) THE BLACK SWAN.

THE VICTORY

(17) BAMBI.
(18) THE IMMORTAL SERGEANT.
(19) CASABLANCA.
(20) YOU WERE NEVER LOVELIER.
(21) HOW GREEN WAS MY VALLEY.
(22) RANDOM HARVEST.
(23) THE MAN WHO CAME TO DINNER.
(24) THE ARABIAN NIGHTS.

Now this is the idea. You have to pick the THREE biggest Box Office winners from each cinema, making nine films altogether, and place them in the order in which you consider they were most successful. EXAMPLE:-
EMPIRE. 1-6-7.   ODEON. 9-12-15.   VICTORY. 17-22-23.

THE PRIZES.

1st. TWO FREE BALCONY SEATS FOR EACH CINEMA (six in all, to be used whenever you like.)

2nd. A STEEL FRAMED TRAVELLING MIRROR (7" x 5")

3rd. A WRITING PAD (Rexine Bound)

4th. 50 PLAYERS CIGARETTES.

CONDITIONS. Closing date JAN.10th. One entry per listed reader.
Editors decision final.
Don't forget to put your name, followed by ATS, EWA etc. on the paper.
ENTRIES TO:- "Truin's Flicks Comp." B.S.M. via the letter rack.
Exiled readers please address:- "The Editor, B.S.M., (usual postal address)
DON'T FORGET-NOT THE BEST FILMS-YOU HAVE TO PLACE THE MONEY MAKERS.

HOCKEY

REPORTED BY :— G. A. LOWES.

We have had some very good games this season and on the whole have done rather well. Out of 21 matches, including men, mixed and ladies, we have only lost 3, although several games have resulted in a draw. Still a drawn game generally signifies a tough fight, and that's how we like it.

Spectators at our matches are few and far between, but I am sure the teams would do much better if they had some 'backing up' from the side lines, so if you want to yell and exercise your lungs, come and give the EXILES hockey team your support. They'll appreciate it, A.T.S. included; it is marvellous what effect their sweet voices have on our play.

RESULTS.   A.-Away. H.-Home.

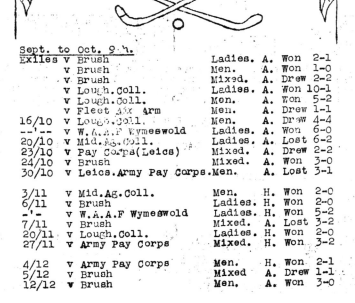

Date		Opponent	Team	A/H	Result	Score
Sept. to Oct. 9.h.						
Exiles	v	Brush	Ladies.	A.	Won	2-1
	v	Brush	Men.	A.	Won	1-0
	v	Brush	Mixed.	A.	Drew	2-2
	v	Lough.Coll.	Ladies.	A.	Won	10-1
	v	Lough.Coll.	Men.	A.	Won	5-2
	v	Fleet Air Arm	Men.	A.	Drew	1-1
16/10	v	Lough.Coll.	Men.	A.	Drew	4-4
--'--	v	W.A.A.F Wymeswold	Ladies.	A.	Won	6-0
20/10	v	Mid.Ag.Coll.	Ladies.	A.	Lost	6-2
23/10	v	Pay Corps(Leics)	Mixed.	A.	Drew	2-2
24/10	v	Brush	Mixed.	A.	Won	3-0
30/10	v	Leics.Army Pay Corps.	Men.	A.	Lost	3-1
3/11	v	Mid.Ag.Coll.	Men.	H.	Won	2-0
6/11	v	Brush	Ladies.	H.	Won	2-0
-'-	v	W.A.A.F Wymeswold	Ladies.	H.	Won	5-2
7/11	v	Brush	Mixed.	A.	Lost	3-2
20/11	v	Lough.Coll.	Ladies.	H.	Won	2-0
27/11	v	Army Pay Corps	Mixed.	H.	Won	3-2
4/12	v	Army Pay Corps	Men.	H.	Won	2-1
5/12	v	Brush	Mixed.	A.	Drew	1-1
12/12	v	Brush	Men.	A.	Won	3-0

Vol. 3.   No. 2.

General Editor:-	L.P. Jones.	Editorial Board:-		
		R. Wilkinson.		R.G. Denny.
Editor:-	F.C. Staddon.	E. Millhouse.		T. Brister.

....

Next publication:- 30th. November.   Contributions by:- 15th. November.

FRONT COVER by:- R.G. Denny.
Illustrations etc. by:- E. Hobden, Muriel Fidoe, W. Stuart.

Our new artist "Hobbie", has started something which we hope he can finish. Since the appearance last month of his glamorous A.T.S. models, everyone has been asking us, "where does he keep them!" The only suggestions we can make are either that working with them all the time makes him biased, or that he is scared. We of course, feel that he only gives them their just dues. We shall have to get "Wilk" and "Hobbie" to give us a full page drawing of their ideal A.T.S., to adorn the walls of our Editorial Sanctum. However, glamour apart, "Hobbie" is a worthy recruit to our ranks.

In this issue, an old contributor, "Snikmot", enlarges upon a theme which has intrigued him for a long time; the magnetism of the Letter Rack. We who only go there to collect Mss. for this magazine, approach it with embarrassment since reading his Mss, "Love in the Midst."

We note with pleasure the increase in A.T.S. contributions. May it continue to grow in volume. This month we have a contribution from Miss Phyllis Borrett (A.T.S.) which deals with that much maligned but very cheerful body of Ats, the RUNNERS. God bless 'em.

We feel sure that "Jackson's Dream" will be enjoyed by all 'Rotaters!

It will be observed that the front cover has been executed by Ron Denny from Beer Willie. We look forward to a regular supply of Mss. from this direction.

We like the Home Guard 'gen' supplied by "Mars" and hope it will prove possible to continue this feature. What about it "Yonc"?. Our old friend St. Upid of course, remains as topical as ever.

Once again we would ask our readers to see that we are kept supplied with all types of contributions. If you have not written before, now is the time to try. If you feel you are able to assist the "B.S.M." in any way at all, please contact the Editorial Board. Remember, this is a STAFF magazine, keep it alive with matter relating to the staff and also see that the 'Gossip' writer is bombarded with the latest titbits of gossip. Thank you!

We feel it our duty to record for posterity, the fact that since our last issue the O/C and Mr. Wort have changed their civilian garments and now appear before us in uniform, with the rank of Lt. Col. and Major, respectively. We wish them well in these unaccustomed roles and find a certain satisfaction in the realisation that most of their best work will almost certainly have been done as civilians.

JACKSON'S DREAM
By "LAMO"

Jackson had made it!. Rotate was over!

For seven weeks this typical Woyger had slogged and now he could go home to "recuperate". That week he had felt as if he had been here, there and everywhere and often somewhere else as well. Come to that, he had. For not only had he rotated; he had also attended a gruelling Home Guard Proficiency Test and had fitted in a Canteen Beer Dance as well.

But Jackson kidded himself that he still felt fit. Other people said that after rotate they had nightmares and told him he must have been mad to go to Home Guard and a Dance as well. He'd feel it, they warned him.

Jackson smiled to himself as he recalled their warnings. He was on the train for Jacksonville and in fine fettle, dragging nervously at a cigarette, his fourth in a row. The train wheels reminded him of Victory as they went "click click click clack", but he tried to ignore them. At times he would find himself looking out the window for places that would afford a good "natural cover", but he got over that by not looking out of the window. When he shut his eyes he could see swirling ATS skirts, but he got over that by not shutting his eyes. In short, Jackson refused to appreciate that his brain was muddled. He was homeward bound, feeling that although Monday night at eight would be on the air at its appointed time, Monday night at ten would never come. He settled down to read the War Office edition of "The Compleat Wangler". He was indoors, having a last smoke before he went to bed. He'd got the best armchair, which dad had sacrificed.

The family was around him, tending to his needs. When he told them what a rotten week rotate was, they all sympathised and said they could never do it. Jackson's chest expanded its full half inch, he took a puff of his cigarette and with a wave of the hand he said "S'nothin', really". He then recounted with his usual modesty, how well he had done at a recent Home Guard exercise. He told in detail how, single handed, he had wiped out a convoy with a Northover. He had never fired one really, but they were'nt to know. They gave him an admiring look that made him unfold his tongue even more and tell them about the dance. He was just going to tell them about the girls who liked him, when they broke in and asked if there was a bar at the dance. He wanted to lick his lips and answer "I'll say", but instead he controlled himself, made out he was trying to remember and then replied "Er-yes, I believe there was", and hurriedly added "I didn't use it, of course". They all nodded approvingly and said "That's right. Don't you".

He announced that he was going to bed and they all jumped up to prepare the way. His mother whispered "Goodnight, son" as she handed him his hot water bottle. Before he went away things weren't like this at all. But now his sister came forward and kissed him tenderly. She never used to do that, but as he was only home once in seven weeks, she took the plunge.

He was in bed. Boy, it was grand to be back home. It was worth rotating. What he wanted now was a good snooze. He yawned contentedly, and was soon in slumberland.

(Contnd.)

JACKSON'S DREAM (Contnd.)

"Jackson! Jackson!"

Jackson turned round to see who could be calling him. He was mad. He'd only just dropped off. "Wotcha want", he asked, angrily. Then he saw who it was and he mellowed his coarse enquiry. He put on his best dark brown voice. "Did you want me, sir?", he asked, purringly. It was Harry. Or was it Alec. He couldn't decide. But he recognised him as the bloke at work who consulted everybody about his four aways on his football coupon almost every hour. Harry (or was it Alec) smiled sweetly at Jackson as he always did and asked him if he'd take number six, please, - as if he'd say he wouldn't!

On arriving at number six he was rather surprised to find a Home Guard officer standing there. Jackson couldn't help noticing what a resemblance he bore to Dick. He sat down, ready to do his best. Dick didn't seem pleased and let him know in no uncertain manner. "Now, now", he bawled. "That's not right. Don't forget what we've taught yer. Remember yer essentials!"

Jackson was looking dumb. He couldn't quite follow the trend of events. He tried to change his expression to one of intelligence by smarming what was intended to be an enlightened smile across his face. It turned out to be nothing better than a snarling glare. He tried to hide his face behind number six and this delighted Dick. "That's better", he bawled. Then to a sergeant standing nearby, "He's passed! Righto, call the roll!"

Jackson looked up again and moaned. He felt like a "drag". He put his hand in his pocket for his cigarette case, but when he brought it out, it looked more like a hand grenade. Uniforms pounced on him and reminded him of the safety precautions.

When things had cleared a bit, he noticed a finger pointing at him. This wasn't Harry or Alec. He couldn't see the face, but somehow it reminded him of Victor. He looked behind him to see for whom it was intended. All he could see was a bunch of Home Guards on the floor with a lighted V in their tin hats, pulling crackers. It must be Christmas, he figured absentmindedly. They were showing each other how to imitate a cat and a monkey crawling. One was even giving the rest the low down on what to do when told to have a funny roll. Bewildered, Jackson looked back at the finger and shrugged his shoulders suggestively. In reply, the finger pointed towards a door. Instinctively, Jackson knew he was meant to take his break. He got up and as he staggered towards the door, he heard familiar voices shouting:-

"I got 'im, Mr. Dix!" "This blokes on nah, Alec!" "All the way!" "You stay here; I'll go downstairs!"

Jackson made his way thoughtfully, out of the mad house. It was dark and a voice, which he recognised as belonging to a Mr. Barkus, shouted: "Anymore for the agony wagon!" Jackson got on the bus, but no sooner had it started than he was bundled off again. Music filled the air. He looked round to see where he was. Ah! the canteen - the place where the tea cups are so clean you can still taste the soap flakes they were washed in!

He entered the den. A trombone was being played by a small man everybody greeted familiarly as "Freddie". "Freddie" was surrounded by other interesting characters all similarly letting off wind, to produce what sounded to Jackson's distorted brain as the Horst Wessel song.

(Contnd.)

JACKSON'S DREAM (Contnd.)

But the dancers, hundreds of them, in two layers, seemed to be quite contented to accept it as either a waltz or a quickstep.

Jackson staggered over to the bar and there met "Ginger", a male character dressed in trousers, with an A.T.S. skirt over them. He was surrounded by a crowd of laughing cronies, who a few minutes previous had been crawling around "No.6" snap-shooting at each other. Jackson enquired what was going on and it was explained to him that they were preparing for a combined operation to storm Garats Hey. The method was to drink beer until you were "ready for it", spilling some to drown those left. Everybody laughed, hi ha hi ha hi - except poor bewildered Jackson, who now felt like a drink himself. He asked for it, but Harry (definitely not Alec) was behind the bar. "Half an' hour is the correct time for your break, Jackson", he said. Jackson apologised, although he didn't know why. In fact, he didn't even know he was at break, why he was, or how he'd got there. His brow was damp with sweat as the terrible truth dawned on him. He was going nuts!

They'd warned him when he started the job. He decided. He must get out of here. He ran forward blindly, right into "her" arms. But now "she" looked different, not at all like the sweet Pte. he raved about. She eyed him up and down - he was nearly on his knees so it didn't take long. "Come on, snake, let's crawl", she leered. As they whirled round to the noise of a trombone plus, everything went black to Jackson. Then, from the distance came voices, gradually getting louder, pounding into his sick brain.

"Get down!". "Nights, afternoons, mornings". "Have yer got 'im?". "Nights, afternoons, mornings". "It's not the flash eliminator!". "Rotate, ROTATE, ROTATE......

"Why, boy, what's the matter? wake up! It's nine o'clock". Jackson opened his eyes. It was still black. He was suffocating, frothing at the mouth. He struggled. Presently the sheets parted and he poked his head out the bottom of the bed. He was muttering -"Rotate, Home Guard, Dances". He looked up and saw his mother. She patted him on the head. "It's the strain of being home", she said. "You will soon be better when you settle down at work again!"

Jackson couldn't tell her the awful truth. But he had to tell someone, so he told me and I thought you might like to know. Don't worry about him, though. He's alright now. He's gone on to seven days a week. No rotate, see?

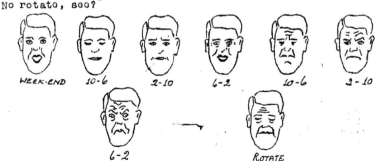

LETTER TO THE EDITOR

20th. October, 1943.

Dear Sir,

The moment seems to be ripe for something to be said on the subject of Entertainment in this Station. May I therefore be allowed a little of your valuable space in order to set the ball rolling?

The New Canteen has now been in action for something like twelve months. Yet who can say the present Entertainments Committee have made any serious attempt to take advantage of the facilities for social activities which it provides? True we have had dances, but these have been, well, just Dances - a Band, a Bar, and dancing. Doesn't anyone on the Committee possess any imagination? Hasn't anyone any original ideas? I submit, and stand ready to be contradicted, that the majority of the Staff on this Station want something novel to entice them out of their billets to this otherwise dreary hole. Whist Drives, Social Evenings, Tombolas, and a dozen other social functions, would, if properly organised and advertised attract a lot of the Staff, of both sexes, to many an enjoyable evening in the Lounge.

Lest anyone raise the matter of the new Canteen Management, let me say that I am assured by the Staff Club Secretary that the new management are anxious, in the matter of social activities, to live up to their name, and co-operate! I do not suggest that the present Entertainments Committee have not worked extremely hard in organising Dances but the arranging of other functions has been left to the various other bodies, acting quite independently of themselves.

Since they seem to have exhibited such a singular lack of initiative and imagination, isn't it time we found ourselves a new Committee before another dull winter is upon us? What do other readers think?

Many will doubtless raise the snag of the inaccessibility of B.M. and the transport question, which has not escaped my notice. In the case of our feminine friends, this difficulty can, I believe, be overcome, if there are sufficient persons. In the instance of the male staff, is the position insurmountable?

Yours faithfully,
Eric C. Millhouse.

HOME — GUARDS

APOLOGIA.~ *For the use of !!*

All this stuff was written way back in September, when Bombards and Beer were all the rage! The Bombard has faded out of the picture a bit just now, and any news contained herein has probably gone a bit cloudy; We therefore make apologies for any sins of ommission or commission or even Non-commission, particularly the latter, all you chaps that have got extra stripes flapping about on your brawny arms.   'Mars!

       I may make digs at officers,
       I may make digs at men,
       I may make digs at N.C.O's,
       But I shall give the gen,
       The dope, the info:, all reports,
       For one I know who sits and snorts,
       And doesn't realise it's a boon,
       To have a 21st. Platoon.

CASUALTY COMMUNIQUÉ No. 1.

In Action - Nil.   On Active Service.

Missing Pte. L.W.S. H.
Injured Pte. BA.B.R. D.
Nature of injury. One bruise, abrasion or confusion in the region of the left temple where the raven black hair sweeps back and away from the broad intelligent forehead. His deep black eyes, soft and compelling etc. etc.
Cause of injury. One left boot, L/Cpl: TA..OT ("Goldylocks") for the use of.
Location. Home Guard camp: 1st. tent on the right as you all fall over the gate when you're half-seas-over.

FROM UNDER THE HAT.

We hear that Pte. Wilk....N. R. sings his cycle to sleep every night, and that his wife is getting jealous. Anyway, he takes it on 'buses with him.

Sgt: E.ge has delicate feet. You ask him and he'll show you if you let him get close enough.

Strange Noises, other than those normally heard in the vicinity, may be attributed to the efforts of Pte. Wil...ms. E.L.

SERGEANT EDGES BOOK OF WORDS (Scotsmen, for the use of)

WORD OR WORDS.	MEANING.
Gra' a ri-ul an' ger'ou'si'.	Take in the hand a .300 P.17 rifle and move on to the parade ground with all possible speed.
Marrrrrrrr.	On receipt of this order the N.C.O or O.R. detailed as marker should fall in.
Squo' quee kmarrrr.	Platoon, squad or body should immediately start marching.
Squo' arrrrr.	On receipt of this order when marching, come to the halt.
Squo' arrrrr.	When at the "stand at ease" position spring smartly to attention.
P'ray (pause) Deesmsssssss.	Parade turn smartly to the right, salute and break off.

A further instalment next month, if I'm still alive.

ADVERTISEMENTS

Private dressing rooms for hire. Apply Pte. F.GG. T.
Squads turned inside out and made as good as new. E.DGE, WIL...MSON, O.EN and Co.
Rifles cleaned free of charge. Apply Pte. W.LLS F, "Old Boot" Hotel.

The Year Grows Old.

We have seen the golden harvest field
Yeilding its precious grain
And watched the plough cut through the earth
Preparing it again.

We have seen the apples on our trees
Blushing a deeper red.
In cottage grates, where flowers bloomed
A wood fire burns instead.

We watched the laden brush of Autumn
Painting each leaf with gold,
But 'neath their coloured canopy
'Tis strangely sad and cold.

The wind that blows across the meadow
Breathes now a hint of frost.
A hawk, high circling overhead
Swoops down - a mouse is lost.

We who watched the months of Autumn
Pass by with queenly grace,
Are waiting with a silent shiver
To see King Winter's face.

Noelene Leadbeater.
(A.T.S.)

xxxxxxxxxxxxxxxxxxxxxxxxxxxxxxxxxxxxxxxxxxxxxxxxxxxxxxxxxxxxxxx

HOME GUARDS - FOR THE USE OF   (Contnd.)

PROFICIENCY TESTS.

So far, 21 platoon has had 100% passes in the proficiency tests held in the Battalion, and has on both occasions, been congratulated by the Battallion Commanding Officer, Lt.Colonel Martin on an effective demonstration of general efficiency.

ELLINGWORTH TROPHY.

It's not in the "London Gazette" you fellows, but we hear that Prayvate Owen (pronounced "Loo") has won the jollay old mug don't y'know.
This we think (in all seriousness) is pretty good. To any A.T.S. coming on watch at 7, we might make it clear that all the tumult and shouting, was Pte.Owen winning it.

Shsssh! G O S S I P Shsssh!

Well, it was an "Angus". Congrats. to Mr.&Mrs. "Jock".Miller on the gift of a son, Ian Campbell, who made this world on the 30th.Sept.'43. We regret to report that Mr.Alec Keenlyside has received a summons to appear at Loughborough Police Court. It appears that although he had "double-banked" his rear lighting, the familiar red glow was conspicuous by its absence when entering a police trap. There is a moral here for all Ewas, but we trust Alec will be dismissed with a caution. Whilst on the subject of 'Alec' it may be reported that he has spent a certain amount of time in Hut "C" recently. It was considered a nice compliment to the occupants of this brain centre, when he appeared garbed in black coat and striped trousers. The writer did not however, observe the proverbial bowler. Incidentally, he did try to emulate Mr.Littlewood.

It is rumoured that when A.T.S. Hammond was questioned by the arm of the law regarding the absence of a front light, she replied," Oh! I've got one, but I only switch it on when I see a policeman". It is not clear whether this was an intended insult to the inquirer, or just sheer frankness.

Reverting to t'other end. A certain policeman recently spent a very puzzling time over a queer looking rear-light which tantalised him at the same time each night. In sheer desparation he attacked, to discover George Curd still trying to get by with the lighted stub of a cigarette held rearwards. The mention of George Curd reminds me that the newly formed "Racketeers" Concert Party are anxious to enlist more male members. We can fully recommend Concert Party work as a very enjoyable and satisfying hobby.

HEARD & DROPPED. Our old friend Charlie Dobson recently pounced on what appeared in the half light, to be a well filled bag. The object however, contained even more surprises than the average young ladies handbag. It was a Hedgehog, who was quite capable of sticking up for itself.

IMPERTINENCE!! Overheard in canteen recently. (not verbatim).
Invariably polite Ewa. May we have a light please.
Person in charge of canteen. No. We have to economise on light.
Invariably polite Ewa. Well, I can't see to read my paper.
Person in charge of canteen. It's people like you who ought to be in uniform.

We would mention to the person concerned that if they were as ready with thier service as with their ignorant insults, we would be a good deal more satisfied.

PSEUDO CELEBRATION. During Sam's (the Murgatroyd) absence (the Bradford lad being unavoidably detained - Blonde, I think!) a small party of friends celebrated his 20th. birthday in the usual "manor". It was discovered later, on Sam's return, that his birthday is not until 27th. November after all. Anyway, the other Saturday was a good rehearsal for the real thing - to be held in the Manor House Hotel on Saturday, December 4th. (ADVT.)

SECURITY! A.T.S. to 'bus conductress:- "Where is this 'bus going to?". Conductress:-"Yes".

FLASHES. Barrow A.T.S. celebrated 2nd. Birthday on October 10th.
THE LIGHT FANTASTIC! A dance is being held at "The Lodge", Barrow-on-Soar, on November 17th. Hungerston Dance Band (R.A.O.C.). All welcome. Plenty of (bottled) wallop!

ADDRESS YOUR GOSSIP TO "GOSSIP", "B.S.M." LET US HAVE THE JUICY BITS.

THE GOSPEL ACCORDING TO ST. UPID. Chapter XXV.
(Translated from the English by Disciple Millhouse.)

Now it is written, since the days when the great Tribe of Woyg began their sojourn in the Promised Land, the Plague of Flag Staffs was ever visited upon them. For there were certain among them who loved to play with Flag Staffs, and these seized upon the slightest excuse to thrust their Staffs into the earth of Woygland, and to decorate them with an abundance of String, which they called by divers strange and wondrous names.

And it came to pass, when they had planted their Staffs and String, the chief among them came forth and beheld their work. And he shaketh his head gravely, and saith unto them: Nay. And they were exceeding sad, and straightway pulled down their Staffs and String, and journeyed back and forth, and planted their Staffs and String, and digged them up again, and went into many Huddles. And the soil of Woygland became truly like unto an honeycomb.

And there were days when they could think of no goodly reason wherefore to pull down the Staffs, nor to alter the Strings. And at these times a mighty wind arose and blew them down, and broke the Strings. And when they saw that the wind had done they were exceeding glad.

And the ceremony of Pulling Them Down and Putting Them Up Again continued throughout the years. And when these peoples were weary of their labours they hired certain of the tribe of Peoh to have fun with the Staffs and Strings. And the men of Peoh had new ideas for the positions of the Staffs. Likewise did they conceive fresh designs for the Strings. And they were very happy.

And it came to pass that the War against the Hunnites ended. Likewise several other Wars happened and finished. And one day a man of Poeh rushed into the temple in a mighty frenzy. Yea, verily, he was All Het Up. And he cried out in a loud voice: Behold. We have builded the Staffs and the Strings in the right manner at last.

And the Ewa which sat in the temple before him, awoke, and hearkened unto his words. And when the Ewa had heard what the man said he sniffed, and shaking a score of pencils out of his beard, he croaked unto the man: Whist ye not that Staffs and String went out of fashion fifty years ago?

DERISIVE DITTIES.

Owing to lack of entries, it has been decided to cancel the competition introduced last month. We have a sneaking suspicion that the Staff were fully capable of "dishing it out", but were a little anxious as to the resultant effect and decided to "avoid the come-back" by thinking instead of writing. Anyway, here are 50% of the entries which we feel are at least worthy of publication. Thanks "Bonus". Having saved 50 cigarettes, the "B.S.M." will probably be able to declare one.

        Paddy McGrath looks nautical - very,
        Done up in his gum boots and beret,
        It's hard to conceive.
        He spends all his leave
        Pinching rides on the Woolwich Free Ferry.   "Bonus".

Skilful is she whose natural charm,
Ne'er causing curious eyes alarm;
And super-skilful are those men
Who dodge Dame Gossip's knowing ken;
Superlative, those with the knack
To use ad. lib. the Letter Rack.

BY "SNIKMOT."

Of the many manifestations of a young man or maid, in the initial stages of that oft' abused passion - Love. None make themselves so patently obvious, in this section, as the disposal of the "billet doux". Unobservant he must be, who has never noticed the self-conscious manoeuvres of both sexes, around the Canteen Letter Rack. Seek to hide it how they will, their every precaution stamps the hall-mark of their uneasiness. If people ignore them, it is not because they have foiled the observer. Rather is it, that they have made him so 'aware' of them, that out of the milk of human kindness, he turns aside.

Consider the female of the species. A smart young At. arrives in the canteen, complete with writing case. She takes a table in the far corner and commences to write. She has a far away look in her eyes. She writes to the man she loves. He, from her very demeanour, must be miles away. Cairo!,- Karachi! Somewhere out in the wilds, (actually, he is out in Woodhouse Eaves, but will be on at 10pm. - which on second thoughts, is wild enough, anyhow.). The letter finished, she gets up to square herself off, and walks nonchalantly out of the canteen. Watch carefully as she passes the rack. With complete aplomb, she whips the letter adroitly into it, with the speed of a "compur-shutter". Her face still wearing that smile of blissful serenity, confident that no one has seen her. I advise her to read the para on 'cynics'.

Now, the "proud man". With wild abandon, bred of the flow of erotic juices. He writes his love-chit during his work - this, in utter contempt of regulations, - "Oh throats of Hell, and Hopes of Paradise!" - it's worth it. Impatiently he waits his 'break'. When it comes, he rushes to the canteen, but - just as his hand touches the cold brass of the door handle, his courage deserts him. Relentlessly however, he hurls back the door, to find the canteen half full of people. This for some reason seems temporarily to suspend his animation. He recovers, and hesitates between walking to the counter and walking to the rack. In doing this, he gives a superb exhibition of the continuous readjustment of the orbit of a planetary electron in an atom of an insulator, when an alternating E.M.F. is applied. (Bristow X.B.) A kind of distorted rotation about his own axis. This latter almost disentegrates him. When he finally decides on the rack, it is not to put in his "billet doux". He adopts an offhand interest in the letters already appearing there. All the time longing to slip in his own missive, which he is fingering tentatively in the security of his left hand coat pocket. Eventually he walks away, only to return again to repeat the performance. This time, as a variation, he takes a casual look at the clock and finds he has been away 35 mins. already. This realisation brings him down to earth with a thud. His cheeks pale, and with a convulsive shudder of despair he rushes from the canteen, running all the way back to his hut. Arrived there - under the furious glances of the charge hand, he gives his precious envelope to his bosom chum, charging him carefully as to its delivery. (Contnd.)

"THIS LETTER RACKET" (Contnd.)

Conscious free, his chum takes it, and drops it into the rack with such a jolt as to shake the fragrant sentences from off the turquoise paper.

We all know the type. The human epitome of the "Prudential" - self-assurance personified. He swaggers up to the rack, proclaiming in a loud voice to all and sundry, that: "No one ever writes to me!" - Incidentally, no one ever does. This of course, is all a pose. The boisterous bonhomie of an inferiority complex. This type is always hoping against hope that: "One day his Princess will come" - if I may coin a phrase.

Then, we have the Don Juans of the section; whose panther like strides setting their undulating forelocks ('permanently theirs') in violent agitation, glide up to the rack with complete savoir-faire. Yes! - she's written. You can almost hear them purr with satisfaction. They extract it from the rack as though they are removing something the cat's brought in, and slide it carelessly into their swagger-coat pocket. Don't they read it? Oh yes! - later, much later. It is a matter of no moment! Casanova was notoriously careless in his "affaires". Verb. sap.

So much for the successful amourettes. What of the not so successful, or even the jilted? Of these, volumes could be written. The course of true love may not run smooth - we don't expect it to. But, from the haggard looks of some of the miserable wretches, as they turn bitter with chagrin, from an empty rack. One would imagine that the course at present, is decidedly rough. Sometimes the looks are bitter, sometimes bewildered. They come all uncomprehendingly away; then go back to make sure their name is not "Catchpole", or to see if the one marked "Dancing Club Committee" couldn't be a distorted version of their name. Disappointed, they stagger back, like Tennyson's "Eagle".

> He grips the chair with grasping hands,
> Close to the place the chit-rack stands,
> And feels not: though he understands.
>
> The milling crowd around him crawls,
> He gazes at the reeling walls,
> And, like a 'sack of spuds' he falls.

As an embittered friend of mine remarked recently, "My God! I know now why they call that thing a rack!"

Lastly we have the cynics. The people who know the price of everything and the value of nothing. Married, and single, they occupy their breaks, drinking tea preferably without sugar. One eye glued on a "News of the World" - the other glued to the rack: its contents, its contributors, and its recipients. Like the Stoic's of Greece and the heretic's of Torquemada, they glory in their own martyrdom. "No woman will ever get me!" they say. Their pity extends to the less fortunate who have a girl already, oblivious of the fact that Pity and Envy, are twins. So the play goes on.

Enough! Why all this deception and sham? Why go on pretending? Let us place this problem in its proper perspective. Let us wear our hearts on our sleeves - together with our proficiency badges H.G. To the diffident male, I would point out - Love, is merely a transitory stage, remember: "One man in his time, plays many parts" - but not too many at once, or they may make him a charge hand - of a type.

"Y – I pass." BY F. HEARN.

According to the neat little pieces of pasteboard we have recently been issued with, the war will last at least another twelve months. Disturbing thought, for when coming on watch at ten, and a stentorian voice challenges me, together with a very noisy rattling of his rifle bolt, I hope I shall always be ready to answer as I am now.

Now I anticipate the voice, and almost before the "there" has left his lips, and certainly before it has died amongst the trees behind me, I reply "Friend".

I wonder what would be the reaction if I answered "Foe", or "Co-belligerent". Maybe I am a "Co-optimist", but I think the sentry would be too amazed to do anything.

I heard a queer answer to a challenge the other evening, when the sentry challenged a colleague of his. The reply was "It's all right, Arthur". I have been puzzling over this ever since. "Arthur" was undoubtedly the sentry's name, for he let his colleague pass without demur, but I could not understand the "It's all right". What was all right? The weather certainly was not, for it was raining and blowing from the west, a direction I abhor as I have to cycle that way, and anyway, what had the weather to do with entering those mystic gates?

"It" could not possibly mean himself, for who would speak of oneself as "it".

Some persons, usually feminine, (they are "all right" with me) have what is commonly called "It", but the person I espied in the dull glow of my cycle lamp, certainly had not that elusive quantity.

Well, I give up, but being a "Y" – I Pass".

"THIS LETTER RACKET."

"IT'S FROM THE HOME GUARD HONEST IT IS!!"

What's on FLICKS

(STAR RATING IN BRACKETS)
Truin's Guide Assists You.

EMPIRE.	Nov. 1st. (6 days)	"WE'LL MEET AGAIN"(2) Vera Lynn, Geraldo. John Beal "ATLANTIC CONVOY"(1).
ODEON.	Nov. 1st. (3 days)	"ASSIGNMENT IN BRITTANY"(2) Pierre Aumont. Robert Paige "HOW'S ABOUT IT".
	Nov. 4th. (3 days)	"FLIGHT FOR FREEDOM"(2) R.Russell,F.McMurray. Tom Brown,Jean Parker "PERSONAL HONOUR"(1).
VICTORY.	Nov. 1st. (3 days)	"MY SISTER EILEEN"(2) Brian Aherne,R.Russell. Bill Elliott "THROUGH THE STORM"(1).
	Nov. 4th. (3 days)	"CONVOY"(2) Clive Brook,John Clements. Charles Starrett "WRONGLY ACCUSED"(1).
EMPIRE.	Nov. 8th. (3 days)	"THUNDER BIRDS"(2) Gene Tierney,Preston Foster. Dick Foran "HI BUDDY".
	Nov.11th. (3 days)	"FLIGHT LIEUTENENT"(1) Pat O'Brien. Penny Singleton "A BUNDLE OF TROUBLE".
ODEON.	Nov. 8th. (6 days)	"FOREVER AND A DAY"(3) Chas.Laughton,R.Milland, Anna Neagle,Merle Oberon etc
VICTORY.	Nov. 8th. (6 days)	"TALK OF THE TOWN"(3) Jean Arthur,Colman,Grant.
EMPIRE.	Nov.15th. (6 days)	"COMMANDOS STRIKE AT DAWN"(3) Paul Muni. Laurel & Hardy "JAIL BIRDS"(1).
ODEON.	Nov.15th. (6days)	"WE DIVE AT DAWN"(3) Eric Portman,John Mills, Men of H.M.Submarines.
VICTORY.	Nov.15th. (3 days)	"THEY ALL KISSED THE BRIDE"(2) Douglas,Crawford. Warren Williams "ONE DANGEROUS NIGHT"(1).
	Nov.18th. (3 days)	"TRADE WINDS"(2) Fred.March,Joan Bennett. Tex Ritter "FALSE CLUES"(1).
EMPIRE.	Nov.22nd. (6 days)	"GET CRACKING"(3) George Formby. Chester Morris "CONFESSIONS"(1).
ODEON.	Nov.22nd. (6 days)	"THE LIFE AND DEATH OF COLONEL BLIMP"(3) Anton Walbrook,Deborah Kerr,Roger Livesey.
VICTORY.	Nov.22nd. (6 days)	"ARABIAN NIGHTS"(2) Sabu,Maria Montez. The Story of Lidice "THE SILENT VILLAGE"(3).
EMPIRE.	Nov.29th. (3 days)	"CLOSE QUARTERS"(3) Men of H.M.S. "TYRANT". Freddie Bartholomew "JUNIOR ARMY"(1).
	Dec. 2nd. (3 days)	"STRANGE CASE OF DR. R.X."(1) Patrick Knowles. Bert Gordon "LAUGH YOUR BLUES AWAY".
ODEON.	Nov.29th. (3 days)	"STRIPTEASE LADY"(2) Barbara Stanwyck. Joan Bennett "MARGIN FOR ERROR"(1).
	Dec. 2nd. (3 days)	"SLIGHTLY DANGEROUS"(2) Lana Turner. Margaret Lindsay "A CLOSE CALL"(1).
VICTORY.	Nov.29th. (6 days)	"A NIGHT TO REMEMBER"(2) Brian Aherne,Lt.Young. Bill Elliott "THE ANCHOR"(1).

The development of the documentary film has been one of the major war time achievements of the British film industry.
Two first class examples by "THE CROWN FILM UNIT" are available this month.
"CLOSE QUARTERS" (Empire,Nov.29th.) deals with the exploits of a British submarine in Norwegian waters.
The other is "THE SILENT VILLAGE" (Victory,Nov.22nd.) a re-enactment of the massacre of Lidice as if it had taken place in a Welsh Valley.

SPORTS PAGE

A.H. Appleton, Hon. Sec.

It is now two years since Sport was started in this station. Looking back over this period, many changes have taken place. Of the old committee, only one or two are left. During the whole of this time, Mr. Hartill, has been, and still is, in charge of the Hockey section. He has always done the Hockey secretarial work, which has relieved my task considerably.

We have had two seasons of Cricket. Those who played have, I think, enjoyed it.

The Tennis court has proved to be most popular. Over 600 hours were booked during the first season. This year there has been a falling-off, due to the lack of tennis balls which are unobtainable. May I mention that the Tennis has always been completely free of charge.

At the beginning of this season I had to make a hard decision. It was obvious we should not be able to run a league Soccer team so we have withdrawn from the league.

It has taken two winters to expose the fallacious argument that the good players kept others out of the team. Those few "good" players are now playing for another team or have retired from the game and we are as far off as ever in raising a side.

Two Rugby and one Soccer match have been cancelled this season. As a result, the offer of the Home Guard to take over the remaining fixtures was accepted. I wish them the best of luck.

To sum up for the last two years, I think the effort has been worth while. If we cast our minds back it will be remembered we came here not knowing anyone, and the Sport section has undoubtedly helped us to settle down and make social contacts otherwise impossible.

As a last word may I thank those who have helped me in this work.

THE FOLLOWING NOTICE HAS BEEN CIRCULATED.

FOR SALE.

GENTS SPORTS CYCLE.
LIGHTWEIGHT MACHINE IN SPLENDID CONDITION.
X 2 NEW TYRES.
X WHEELS JUST RESPOKED.
X FIXED AND FREE WHEEL.
REASON FOR SALE:- OWNER PURCHASING HEAVIER MACHINE WITH LARGER FRAME.
PRICE £4.10.0 CASH.   APPLY:-BILL BAKER.

This will come as a great surprise to many of the Staff, as most of them tend to regard the "mangle" as symbolic of its owner. It is rumoured that Bill was born on this bike. At any rate it has done him good service. Apparently the trouble is that although Mr. Baker has sized tremendously, the cycle was not equal to it and stopped growing at 21 yrs.

The only snag so far as I can see is that the bicycle, once free of the gentle, mastering hand of its lifelong employer will completely and finally give up the ghost. It has been suggested however, that the now almost legendary machine might fetch a good price from any collector of genuine antiques. However, be that as it may, the breaking-up of this age-old association can be viewed with nothing but regret by the many admirers of the wonderful feats of balance performed by the owner.

CHAPTER XXVI

The King's commandment concerning chariots. The Koppas of Luff. Their Chief bids them go forth. Sins of the Woygites. They are Wheeled Up. A certain Bil is displeased and causeth a Flat Spin. A goodly profit is made.

Now IT CAME TO PASS during the War against the Hunnites, that the King, who dwelleth in Smowk delivered many commandments unto his peoples, because of the War Effort. And he bade the multitudes not to drive their chariots, except on National Service. Wherefore there were exceeding few chariots upon the highways.

Now there was in Luff a mighty force of Koppas, as it was in all the cities of Brit. And before the War they busied themselves with chariot drivers who transgressed, charging them with all manner of deadly sins, and collecting many shekels from them. But when the King commanded the drivers not to bring their chariots out the Koppas were cast down, and knew not what to do. And the Chief Koppa, perceiving not that his men might do more good in another kind of uniform, saith unto them: Go ye out into the highways and byways, and pinch as many riders of Grids as ye can. And verily, I say unto ye, the more ye pinch, the greater shall be thy reward.

And a certain Koppa, who dwelled nigh unto Luff, perceived that the peoples of Woyg were a Piece of Cake, and accordingly he stationed himself nightly by the highway where they travelled upon their Grids. And upon a certain day after sundown he procured a Big Bag of Woygites, and charged them, saying unto one: Why haltest thou not at Major Road Ahead?, and unto another, Behold, thy rear lamp showeth a black light. And the Koppa beheld a vision of sergeant's stripes, and was well pleased.

And in due course he Wheeled Them Up before the Beaks. And the Beaks possessed a mighty Court, but someone had forgotten to buy the Blackout. Wherefore they held their Court in a small chamber which was exceeding comfortable with a goodly fire. And the King had commanded that the Publick be admitted to these Courts.

BIL AND THE KOPPAS

But the Court flowed over with Beaks and Koppas, and clerks, and witnesses. And the Publick hearkened from without the doors, for had not someone forgotten to buy the Blackout?

And the Koppa spake long and earnestly of what they had done, and the Beaks were struck with horror, and cried: Verily, these are dastardly crimes. And they caused the transgressors to pay their tributes unto the Court.

But one Bil, a maker of bread, when he came before the Beaks, was gravely displeased, and saith unto them: Get a load of this. And turning unto the Koppa and his stooges, he taxed them thus, saying: How far stood ye from the scene of this ghastly crime? And they told him: Thirty cubits. And he saith: What of the night? And they remembered not whether the night was dark or light, nor whether the moon shone, nor whether Bil halteth, nor yet whether they even saw Bil. And they were become in a mighty Flat Spin. And Bil turned unto the Beaks and saith: Behold, I have a righteous friend Eddi, who accompanied me this night. Wilt thou summon him hither, that he may shew ye that these beans which I have spilled are good beans?

And the Beaks sent Bil, and the Koppas, and the witnesses from the Chamber, and went into an Huddle. And when they were come out of the Huddle, they summoned Bil, and saith: We have counted our shekels, and have made good profit this night. Therefore, go thou forth from hence without a stain on thy Grid. Only don't do it again.

And no one told them there was a War on.

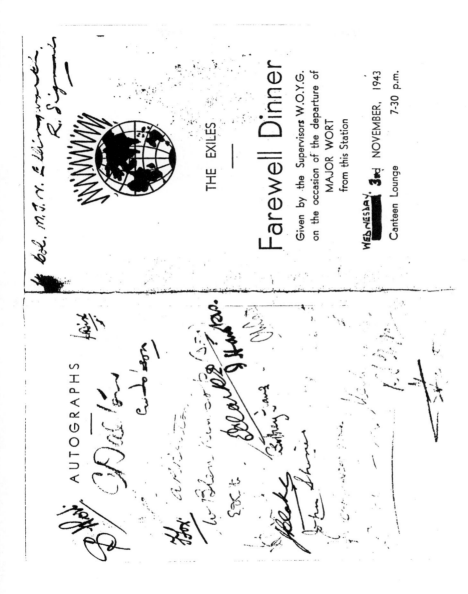

THE EXILES

Farewell Dinner

Given by the Supervisors W.O.Y.G.
on the occasion of the departure of
MAJOR WORT
from this Station

WEDNESDAY, 3rd NOVEMBER, 1943
Canteen Lounge   7-30 p.m.

"B.S.M" DECEMBER, 1943.
Vol.3.   No.4.

General Editor :- L.P.Jones.   Editorial Board :-
                                  R. Wilkinson.   R.G.Denny.
Editor :-   F.C.Staddon.   E. Millhouse.   T. Brister.

Next publication :- by 31st. January. Contributions by :- 15th. January.
FRONT COVER by :- "Wilk". Illustrations by :- "Wilk", E. Hobden, Muriel Fidoe.
NEW FEATURE: "MANORBEAUS" sketched by "Bill" Baker.   (Ron Denny)

Omission :- A.T.S. "Off Duty" (Nov) was by Miss Joan Howarth.
Truin's Flick Competition. We draw your particular attention to this competition, details of which appear on another page, and hope you will help to make it a success by sending in your entry.

MESSAGE from O.C.

A very Happy Christmas and New Year to you all. This is the fifth Christmas of the war and probably the last, but this next year will be a hectic one as far as we are concerned. Nevertheless, I'm sure we shall all do our best to hasten the day of Victory, and those of us who, if all goes well, should be back in civilian life by next Christmas will not entirely regret our wartime experiences.

This fourth year of war has been a period of strain. Some of us are getting a bit tired and wish we could 'shut up shop' for a week or so. Unfortunately this is not possible, and we have no alternative but to carry on with our job. We have, however, the full knowledge that the job is a worthwhile one, and of real use in the war effort. So stick it out during the next few months and perhaps we shall get a spell earlier than we believe.

To all, who have so loyally supported the Group during these wartime years I send my warmest thanks.

The old "hard core" of civilians in all Departments, never daunted, despite changes and difficulties, is as good as ever. I hope their efforts will be recognised in the near future.

The feminine element, still increasing, is doing a splendid job, and we hope the girls will not run away from us too quickly when this bother is over.

Finally, enjoy yourselves as much as you can this Christmastide, and may it not be very long before we listen to the final 'V', the 'V' that means Victory.   M.J.W.E.

We'll fight like demons on the square,
And we will never quit,
How can we end this war affair
'Til someone signs a chit?

You may be wealthy as a king,
You may be fighting fit,
But in the ATS you're not a thing
Unless you've got a chit.

Dash in the mess at ten past eight,
The ATS her brows will knit,
"Yuv 'ad it, yuv got 'ere too late,
Where's your bl---y chit?"

You make a date for Thursday night
With a boy in the park to-er-sit,
The picquet pests your hopes will blight,
"On domestic night? no chit?"

Plead with the AT in the clothing store
With a tunic that won't fit,
"Yes we could change it" (what a bore),
"Oh! but you're not without a chit?"

At last they've got you in a spot,
They're here to see your kit,
To hide things that you haven't got,
For Pete's sake scrounge a chit.

What rights we have, what powers we hold,
How prettily we sit,
We could not change for countless gold
Our grubby, tattered chit.

But when at last we've beat the Hun
And the lamps of peace are lit,
They may release us one by one,
But they'll still want a bl---y chit.

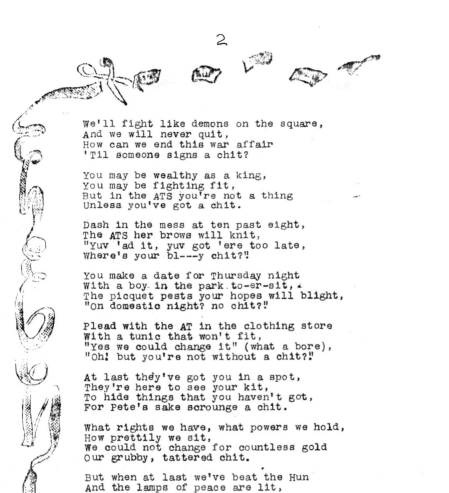

Shssh! G O S S I P Shssh!

CONGRATULATIONS! To Pte. Mickey Hunt who celebrated her majority on the 11th.Dec. We hear it was quite a binge.

ANOTHER PROUD FATHER! Congratulations to Mr.&Mrs.Crick upon the arrival of a daughter at the end of last month.

?????????????? Whose was the party which was mistaken for a collection of honeymooning couples in the Manor Hotel early this month? No boys! You can't do 'that-there' - there.

Is it true that Joyce and Margaret have a stripe between them? It is rumoured that, as a half tape would look rather out of place, they are wearing the whole one for three months each.

Mr.E.Beckwith. On behalf of the Editorial Board and readers of the "B.S.M", we have forwarded £2 to this gentleman at Markfield Sanitarium, with seasonal greetings and best wishes for his early recovery.

PERSONAL. We have received an anonymous letter with regard to the "personal" item in the Nov. gossip. The writer describes our offer of 10½d. for a new battery as miserly and points out that present prices are 11d. or 1/1d. We gather that if we can see our way to bring our offer up to these levels, he is prepared to divulge his name. That may be, but the establishment has already produced its quota of impostors willing to sacrifice themselves at the cut-price of 10½d.

MOVE DOWN THE 'BUS PLEASE! We are informed that a certain highly respected member of the staff recently caused a minor congestion on a Barrow 'bus due to his rather overdone portrayal of a faithful old Airedale. Eventually the idea "Pearce(d)" his mind that he was meant to move down to the back of the 'bus. Why couldn't she have sat on his lap, or doesn't Ollie approve of this kind of thing?

WELFARE! We are very pleased to note the inclusion of this word in the title of the Staff Committee now being formed. Our Woolworth 6d. Dictionary gives the following meaning:"health;happiness;prosperity!" Boy oh Boy'. At last,"they shall not be forgotten".

A PRICKLY SUBJECT! Although many of us frequently enter this establishment without any challenge, it is amusing to record that the 'bus has recently been boarded on its <u>outward</u> journey, and the occupants asked "Has anybody got any holly?" Ah! well, things do get out of control sometimes and these incidents will "Bob" up. We now joyfully anticipate an enterprising AT endeavouring to board with "Has anybody got any mistletoe?"

SO THERE! We didn't even mention it.

YOU'RE LETTING US DOWN. It is quite obvious that we are not being supplied with the amount of "Gossip" which this establishment manufactures so efficiently. Will you please make a resolution for 1944 that you do not hold out on us? Give us the Griffin, supply us with the dope. We are always discreet and in any case invariably twist it so that you know exactly to whom we are referring.

On behalf of the Editorial Board we offer all our readers our sincerest good wishes and trust that your Christmas is/was cheerful, and that 1944 will treat you kindly.

<u>YOU HAVE THE GOSSIP!</u> <u>WE WANT IT!</u> <u>DON'T FORGET PASS IT ON TO US.</u>

4

THE EPIDEMIC CONTINUES

BY ANON.

"You can earn money in your spare time"."Writing short stories can be everyman's source of easy money". "Join our correspondence school and see how surprised you will be!". Sooner or later everybody reads one of these lures to literature and writes a short story; but then, where is it to be published. Naturally, the answer is in the Staff Magazine.

Well, there is a Staff Magazine; and remembering that opportunity knocks at the door but once in a nightgown, I want to rush into print - a complaint very similar to breaking out in spots. But I have a cold- not, I would emphasise, a polite, sneeze once and "Scuse me" sort of cold; but such a cold as makes the usual running cold seem a mere crawling one. I cannot keep a hand on paper long enough to write two consecutive words and anything I write is washed out at once by the portable fountain which is misnamed my nose. I can think only of how many handkerchiefs I have left, I can say nothing but "Oh! DAB" (and that not all in one breath), I have visions of the attractions of death, I bust hab a day off, and I cad'ht write anything for the magazine.

MORAL: PREVENTION IS BETTER THAN CURE!!

311

Mainly about Christmas
By:- 'OLLIE

Now that you have bought your Xmas shopping expeditions to a successful conclusion and posted all your cards and parcels, you will be preparing to consume huge chunks of turkey, Xmas pud, oranges and other nuts, after which you will feel extremely uncomfortable and seek some form of amusement which will not call for too much physical exertion.

In connection with the latter I would like to offer a few suggestions, and as they will make a certain amount of demand on your mental capacity, the first thing to do is to set your mind completely at rest.

Stop worrying about those handkerchiefs you sent to Mary. Supposing they are the ones she sent you in 1940, you've only washed them twice, and she'll never recognise them after all this time, especially now that you have embroidered her initials in the corner. And that tie you sent to George, you couldn't possibly have worn a thing like that yourself, and if it was him that gave it to you, well, at least you've got even with him. I don't suppose you will have any similar worries about cards as it is quite easy to make a note of the original sender when removing the inside.

Owing to the coupon system the more usual type of present is not so conspicuous, and books seem to be most popular. I gave one to a certain lady. It is entitled "When Nights Were Cold" and tells how a small section of the cream of England's youth, recognisable by their cycle clips and dirty macs, set the rapidly declining Empire on it's feet again. I can't tell you who the lady is as a certain bloke whose initials could be mistaken for a bad smell might object.

Whilst doing my Christmas shopping I had a most terrifying ordeal. It was in a big London store and I was wandering aimlessly from one department to another when suddenly I became conscious of an ear-splitting roar and a feeling of being torn to pieces. In a frantic effort to get away I slipped, and after being almost trampled to death I managed to crawl to the door. I have read about the Christians being thrown to the lions and have often wondered how they must have felt. At the door I glanced back and saw a card hanging above the counter, it bore one word which explained everything: It was allright for the Christians, they only had lions to contend with. The word was "COSMETICS" - and they call them the gentle sex!!

That reminds me, some months ago an article appeared in the "B.S.M" bearing that title. It was in verse, one line of which caused a certain amount of controversy, particularly among the ex-sailors of our community- No, not you Paddy, I said sailors. The argument seemed to be whether or not it was true that the gentle sex salvaged wrecks. Well, if any of you are still in doubt, you can take it from me that they most certainly do. I very often see them out with 'em!

To get back to our after dinner pastimes. First of all, each person must have paper and pencil. If any of you are unfamiliar with these articles you can get the low down from any encyclopedia. Each person is then provided with a set of simple problems, you know the sort of thing - if two EWA'S do a certain amount of work in 8 hours etc; etc; the answer to that one of course is, sound A. Should anyone mention anything about any sort of a miracle, his or her answer is obviously absurd - or is it?

The whole point about this is that the "B.S.M" is published so far in advance that you will undoubtedly have mislaid it by the time Christmas comes round so I think I will leave you to your own devices whilst I rush off to "L" to see what can be done about my landlady's pink form.

THE GOSPEL ACCORDING TO ST.UPID.   Chapter XXVII.
(Translated from the English by Disciple Millhouse.)

    Now the days of the great Tribe of Woygites were long in the land, and the third Feast of Eksmas drew nigh.
    And the Prophet Osee had changed his name. For the King, who dwelleth in Smowk, was well pleased with him, and had made him a centurion, and henceforth he was called Seeo.
    Now the temples wherein the scribes worshipped were become exceeding unclean; for it is written, they were a Lousy Lot. And when the Prophet Seeo beheld the temples, and saw that they were unclean, he was cast down, and summoned the Wehkmen before him. And he spake unto them in this wise, saying: Go ye unto the temples, and fumigate them, and make them clean. But first be certain there are no scribes left within the temples, for I still have need of them, yea, and their pencils, and their rubbers.
    Wherefore the Chief over all the Wehkmen went forth to the temple of Atsites which is named Jug and saith unto the Sargess: Beat it. Thou and all thy Wopites, and take from hence all that is thine, but leave thy musick boxes in the temples. And they beated it, taking with them their parchments, and their pencils, and their rubbers.
    And it came to pass that he visited each of the temples in turn, and Turfed Out all the scribes, causing them to tarry awhile in another temple. And in the empty temples the Wehkmen laboured mightily, and fumigated the places, for many plagues had been visited upon the peoples during their sojourn.
    And when the time came for the scribes to return into their own temples, with their parchments, and their pencils, and their rubbers, they perceived divers great and wondreus changes. For the walls of the temples which had been a neutral tint, were now exceeding belligerent. And they were glad in their hearts. And the floors of the temples which had been covered with Kompo which was not there any more, were laid with a costly carpet, called Li-No. And they were glad in their hearts. And the centurion of Woygiteshops promised them he would lighten their darkness before many days were passed. And likewise he spake of giving unto them an extra ration of the rare and priceless perfume called Fresh Air. And they were glad in their hearts.
    Yet when they turned and beheld the tables which were in the temples, they perceived that these were unchanged. For the musick boxes were yet even where they had left them. And they were exceeding sad in their hearts.

Sweet FANNY ADAMS replies

Dear Friends,

You haven't provided me with a very large postbag for this my debut in the pages of the "B.S.M", but I expect you have all been busy with your Christmas mail, so I look forward to being able to help you all in the New Year.

The first letter comes from "PUZZLED" - Woodhouse Eaves, who wants to know something of the etiquette of Proposals. He has grown very fond of a girl and wants to marry her, but is a little uncertain about how to set about it. Well, "Puzzled", in our forefathers time when a young man became very enamoured of a particular lady, it was customary for him to pay a visit to the father of the object of his desire, and acquaint him with the detailed facts of his income, position, and ability to support the stern father's daughter. If it all was found to be satisfactory, he then took the young lady to some convenient blossom-scented bower and sinking on his knees before her, took her lily-white hand in his, and pleaded at great length to be allowed the exquisite joy of seeing her face on the pillow every morning for the rest of his life. If she agreed, a betrothal was in due course formally announced. Nowadays however, a young couple meet and form a friendship and then if it ripens into something deeper, they gradually drift into an understanding, and he buys her a ring. If you feel this is rather a slipshod way of going on, and yet are a little shy about popping the question, I suggest you take your courage in both hands and have a shot at it. There is no need to be particularly verbose. When the moment seems ripe, just say: "I love you. What about it?"

M.-Garats Hey. I am very sorry to hear about your pimples. Yes it is definitely one of the most difficult areas of the body to clear. Send me a S.A.E. for address of firm supplying reliable remedy, and let me know if you find it suitable. Meantime do try to avoid beer for a while.

CONSCIENCE-STRICKEN-Loughborough. I would get the whole matter off your mind if I were you. Forward a 1½d. stamp through the post direct to Manageress Woygite Canteen, or if you are afraid your handwriting may be recognised, send the money to me, and I will personally explain that the girl gave you the cup of tea and then walked away.

Other Replies In Brief:

MYRTLE. Not if he is married, dear.

M.J.W.E. No.

"SUPERVISOR". Write to "The Phsycologist". They may be able to help.

Do write and let me help you, Friends,

Sweet Fanny Adams.

THESE LITTLE THINGS
"ARCHANGEL"

Nights aren't so bad, and I don't mind afternoons, but I hate mornings. I <u>hate</u> and <u>loathe</u> the six to two watch with all my heart and soul. Mornings - a <u>merciless</u> and ruthless 'Thing' which rears its ugly head above my horizon at periodic intervals.

At sometime or another I must have made an enemy; a foul, underhand enemy who gets his revenge by shortening the nights when I'm on six to two. I'm convinced that he does, because I just get into bed and close my eyes when the blarming alarm clock goes. Sleep? Ha! not when I'm on mornings. And that alarm clock. If ever I have to commit murder I shall do it at 4.45 a.m. and use the alarm to wake me. I could kill anything and everybody then. Murder most foul would be a delight; brutal deeds I would adore.

How lovely bed seems at a quarter to five in the morning, what thoughts enter your mind as you have a five-minute-gape at the ceiling. How blarming awful it is when you stagger to the bathroom for a wash-force of habit makes you do this because if you stopped to think for a moment you would'nt do it at 5.0'clock in the morning. Then you totter down the stairs - if <u>you</u> don't, <u>I</u> do-and prepare breakfast, and it's one of those mornings when nothing ever goes right,-I have an average of four days per week like that-and people actually say they like six to two!

Do you cook your own breakfast? You do? So do I. Do you make a lot of smoke? No? I do,-clouds of it! It's a funny thing, one might almost say uncanny, because it frightens me, but I can watch the wife cook bacon, I can see my mother cook bacon; and the landlady too, but-no smoke, not a wisp. Now when <u>I</u> cook bacon(low, medium, or high gas) I get smoke. It billows out of the pan and plays around my head; it gets itself into layers all over the kitchen, and everything looks far away in a distant blue haze;-I'm a haze expert I am. I can conjure up blue smoke from nowhere. It follows me about, and it won't leave me alone. My life is made up of two things-six to two and blue smoke.

By the way, talking of bacon, here's a bit of advice. <u>Never</u> turn your back on it for even a split second. Why? I'll tell you <u>why</u>,-I know. Your bacon is cooked, you put it on a plate-at least, I hope you do-and take it into the dining room. Just as you commence the attack, the blarming kettle boils and you have to leave off to make the tea. It only takes thirty seconds to do it, but that's all your rasher needs.

(Contnd.)

When you come back into the room, just look at it. Study it, notice its' form, its' shape, look at it grinning up at you. There are more waves in that one piece of bacon than there are waves in the Atlantic Ocean. It' gone dry too, drier than a year old bone, and it makes you mad, oh, so mad You feel like throwing the fork at it, but instead you stab it viciously with one. But your bacon wants you to do that, you've played right into its hands; as soon as the fork touches it, it flies everywhere, in about a hundred pieces.

I have one regret when this happens to me. It's so early in the morning that I can never remember what I say. If I could, I should be ruler of the world by my tongue alone. Whilst we're on the subject of these little things which annoy us so much, I might as well have a few seconds about 'The Early Morning Back-swiper'.

You know the fellow. He creeps up behind you, with one of those silly grins on his face, draws back his arm, summons all his energy, then lets you have it slap between the shoulder blades at nine o'clock in the morning. Of all the things which madden me most, I think this is the worst. I must look terrible when this happens to me; my face must change from its' normally vacant look to one of calculated ferocity. I say to him- but no, on second thoughts perhaps I had'nt better tell you, I love the ATS too much. They're such innocent dears!

Yes, there are many incidents which annoy me, but there, they are sent to try us-these little things.

"MOLLY TAKES THE PLUNGE"

(Owing to his recent acquisition, will any callers at the residence of Mr. 'Molly' Morgan, please KNOCK before entering!)

RETROSPECTION À LA "SNIKMOT"

I've Xmased out at Aden
In the torrid tropic heat
I've Xmased up in Scapa
In Orcadian's icy sleet.

I've Xmased in Atlantic
Where the mighty breakers roll
And I've Xmased just off Mudros
On a submarine patrol.

But to me the finest Xmas's
That I so far have seen
Have been the last two efforts
That we've spent in our Canteen.

Where the ATS had fun in plenty,
Was it "B" watch formed a ?
And marched past old Cornwallis
Decorated in the yard?

And if I remember; Charlie
Had a little game of 'nap'
With the girls, who thrashed him soundly
-But his bank-book took the rap.

And several others all agreed
Their frolics took the 'bun'
But after all 'twas Xmas,
"Let's be foolish, let's have fun".

Let's make the most of this one
Though to you it seems a bore
Just bear in mind that maybe
It's the last one of the war.

WRITE UP BY MORGAN

Some of you saw a notice in the Canteen. Across it was written "We've had it - We've enjoyed it - We want more". The "more" was underlined; which is evidence. Evidence of the good time we had at the Social.

Run by 'Showman Smith' and 'Coin-a-phrase Owen', it was remarkable for several things. Firstly, you don't often see a rather large A.T.S. trying to pick up a matchbox from the floor with her nose. Secondly, you rarely see Andy with two pairs of trousers on, both of them sewn together. Thirdly, the spectacle of Jimmy Edge having his trousers patched by an A.T.S. is not often encountered. Besides that, it's not everywhere that you can blow up paper bags and burst them with umpunity. It's not everywhere that you can walk along with a book balanced on the head, and doughnuts are rather uncommon just now.

Yes, we enjoyed it, Shaker and Lew; And we have come to the conclusion with due apologies to an unknown poet that;-

> "After deep consideration
> And profound deliberation
> On the various petty projects that have here been shown,
> Not a scheme in agitation
> For Woygland's amelioration
> Has a grain of common sense in it -
> Except your own".

"MANORBEAUS' 43

WHAT'S ON FLICKS

Star Rating in brackets.

Truin's guide assists you.

EMPIRE.	Jan. 3rd. (3 days)	"JUNGLE SIREN"(1) Buster Crabbe.
		East Side Kids "KID DYNAMITE"(1).
	Jan. 6th. (3 days)	"SIN TOWN"(2) Constance Bennett.
		Penny Singleton "TROUBLES THRU' BILLETS"(1).
ODEON.	Jan. 3rd. (6 days)	"CONEY ISLAND"(3) Betty Grable, Geo. Montgomery.
		"THE GLORY OF SEBASTOPOL"(2).
VICTORY.	Jan. 3rd. (6 days)	"THE MAN IN GREY"(3) M. Lockwood, James Mason.
EMPIRE.	Jan. 10th. (6 days)	"PITTSBURGH"(3) Marlene Dietrich, R. Scott.
		H.B. Warner "A YANK IN LIBYA"(1).
ODEON.	Jan. 10th. (6 days)	"MR. LUCKY"(2) Cary Grant, Laraine Day.
		Stuart Erwin "HE HIRED THE BOSS"(1).
VICTORY.	Jan. 10th. (6 days)	"PRESENTING LILY MARS"(2) J. Garland, Van Heflin.
EMPIRE.	Jan. 17th. (3 days)	"AIR RAID-WARDENS"(1) Laurel & Hardy.
		Buck Jones "FORBIDDEN TRAILS"(1).
	Jan. 20th. (3 days)	"SILVER SKATES"(2) Ken Baker.
		Tim McCoy "GUNMAN FROM BODIE"(1).
ODEON.	Jan. 17th. (6 days)	"WHITE CAPTIVE"(2) Sabu, Maria Montez.
		Chester Morris "ALIAS BOSTON BLACKIE".
VICTORY.	Jan. 17th. (3 days)	"THE SILENT WITNESS"(2) Otto Kruger.
		East Side Kids "'NEATH BROOKLYN BRIDGE"(1).
	Jan. 20th. (3 days)	"THE YOUNGEST PROFESSION"(2) Virginia Weidler.
		Frances Day "THE GIRL IN THE TAXI"(1).
EMPIRE.	Jan. 24th. (3 days)	"ROOKIES"(2) Abbott & Costello.
		Dead End Kids "MUGTOWN"(1).
	Jan. 27th. (3 days)	"JOHNNY COMES MARCHING HOME"(2) G. Jean, A. Jones.
ODEON.	Jan. 24th. (3 days)	"THE RAINS CAME"(3) Tyronne Power, Myrna Loy.
		Annabella "TONIGHT WE RAID CALAIS"(1).
	Jan. 27th. (3 days)	"UNDERCOVER"(2) John Clements.
		Virginia Bruce "BUTCH MINDS THE BABY"(1).
VICTORY.	Jan. 24th. (6 days)	"HELLO, FRISCO HELLO"(3) Alice Faye, Jack Oakie, John Payne.
EMPIRE.	Jan. 31st. (6 days)	"CRASH DIVE"(3) Tyronne Power, Ann Baxter.
ODEON.	Jan. 31st. (6 days)	"DIXIE"(3) Bing Crosby, Dorothy Lamour.
		Richard Arlen "AERIAL GUNNER"(1).
VICTORY.	Jan. 31st. (3 days)	"THE LIGHT OF HEART"(3) Ida Lupino, M. Woolley.
		Richard Travis "THE POSTMAN DIDN'T RING"(1).
	Feb. 3rd. (3 days)	"GIRL TROUBLE"(2) Don Ameche, Joan Bennett.
		Richard Cortez "THE MAN WITHOUT A CONSCIENCE"

"DIXIE" (ODEON, JAN. 31st. (6 days)
This film is in technicolour, a medium which lends itself to the picturesque period settings in which Bing plays the part of DANIEL EMMETT the first of the KENTUCKY MINSTRELS. Look out for BILLIE DE WOLFE, who, though a newcomer to the screen, is outstanding in this delightful show.

Dudley Truin.

WHAT'S ON? Flicks WHAT'S ON?
(STAR RATING IN BRACKETS) Truin's Guide Assists You.

Cinema	Date	Duration	Films
EMPIRE.	Oct. 4th.	(6 days)	"DESPERATE JOURNEY"(2) Errol Flynn. Russell Hayden "LUCKY LEGS".
ODEON.	Oct. 4th.	(3 days)	"THE CRYSTAL BALL"(2) R.Midland,P.Goddard. C.Boyer,Hedy Lamarr "ALGIERS"(3).
	Oct. 7th.	(3 days)	"HAPPIDROME"(1) Harry Korris. Chester Morris "HIGH EXPLOSIVE"(1)
VICTORY.	Oct. 4th.	(3 days)	"THE AMATEUR GENTLEMAN"(2) Doug Fairbanks. Roy Rogers "SOUTH OF SANTA FE".
	Oct. 7th.	(3 days)	"THREE HEARTS FOR JULIA"(2) Melvyn Douglas.
EMPIRE.	Oct.11th.	(3 days)	"SHE'S MY LOVELY"(2) Gloria Jean. Tommy Trinder "SAILORS THREE"(2).
	Oct.14th.	(3 days)	"PETERVILLE DIAMOND"(1) Douglas Wakefield. Gene Autry "HOME IN WYOMIN".
ODEON.	Oct.11th.	(6 days)	"HIT THE ICE"(2) Abbott & Costello. Jimmy Lydon "HENRY ALDRICH, EDITOR".
VICTORY.	Oct.11th.	(6 days)	"THE IMMORTAL SERGEANT"(3) Henry Fonda, Maureen O'Hara,Thomas Mitchell.
EMPIRE.	Oct.18th.	(6 days)	"MUCH TOO SHY"(3) George Formby. John Howard "SUBMARINE RAIDER"(1).
ODEON.	Oct.18th.	(6 days)	"THE BLACK SWAN"(3) George Sanders, Maureen O'Hara,Tyrone Power,Thos.Mitchell.
VICTORY.	Oct.18th.	(6 days)	"CASABLANCA"(4) Ingrid Bergman,H.Bogart, Paul Henreid,Claude Rains,P.Lorre,C.Veidt. Gerry Wilmot "PLAYTIME FOR WORKERS".
EMPIRE.	Oct.25th.	(3 days)	"INVISIBLE AGENT"(2) Peter Lorre. Chas.Starrett "FORESTALLED".
	Oct.28th.	(3 days)	"TWO YANKS IN TRINIDAD"(2) O'Brien,Donlevy. Virginia Gilmore "THAT OTHER WOMAN".
ODEON.	Oct.25th.	(6 days)	"FIVE GRAVES TO CAIRO"(3) E.Von Strohein, Franchot Tone. Frances Langford "COWBOY IN MANHATTAN".
VICTORY.	Oct.25th.	(3 days)	"STAND-IN"(3) Leslie Howard. Dick Purcell "PHANTOM KILLER".
	Oct.28th.	(3 days)	"GEORGE WASHINGTON SLEPT HERE"(2) J.Benny. Marjory Chapman "A MAN'S WORLD".

xxxxxxxxxxxxxxxx

"CASABLANCA" VICTORY. Oct. 18th. 6 days. Here we have, I think, not only the film of the month but, with the exception of "IN WHICH WE SERVE", the film of the year.
    It is a dramatic story of refugees, romance and international intrigue set in the capital of French Morocco while still under the doubtful control of Vichy.
    It is difficult with such a brilliant constellation of stars, all of whom give memorable performances, to choose the brightest, but I hand a bouquet to DOOLEY WILSON, who is perfect as SAM, the negro piano player and singer of "As time goes by".
    Casablanca is a film you will remember if only for that very moving moment in the singing of the Marseillaise. Dudley Truin.

Sports Page

A.H. Appleton.
Hon. Sec.

RUGBY

The first fixture v Brush had to be cancelled. I still have hopes, so stick your name on the board for the remaining matches.

SOCCER

An exciting game v R.N.A.S was lost by the odd goal in seven.
Results:-
    22/9 v R.N.A.S Lost 4-3 Keenlyside 2, Musgrave 1

HOCKEY

This has again started well under V. Hartill's leadership.
Results:-
    19/9 Won. Exiles (A.T.S.) 2. Brush Ladies 1.
    25/9 Won. Exiles (Men) 1. Brush 0.
    25/9 Won. Exiles (A.T.S.) 10. Loughborough College Ladies 1.

WATER POLO

I must apologise for any annoyance caused by my remarks last month. I understand that most of the other 15 who originally put their names down as players, were either on leave or on duty on the day in question.

CRICKET Result:-

    8/9 v Rothley. Won. Rothley 35. Exiles 106.
    (Spooner 35 rtd., E. Smith 20 rtd)

MUSIC. Harry Dodd.

We begin our 3rd. Season with a Social on Friday, October 8th, (7 to 11 p.m.) at Quorn Church Room. As on previous similar occasions, non-members will be welcome, and we hope that YOU will come for an evening of dancing and entertainment. Tickets (price 1/-, including refreshment charge) are limited, so get yours soon. They can be obtained at the Canteen counter, and from the following:- Sgt. Maj. Timon, L/Cpl. Metcalfe, Mr. C.E.W. Brown, Mr. J. Smyth, Mr. H. Dodd, Mr. J. Dodd, and Mr. A. Keenlyside.

The weekly Club meetings will be held on Wednesday evenings, from 6 to 8 p.m., at the Hurst Canteen, Quorn. We are greatly indebted to the Officers of No.1 A.T.S. "Y" Wing for their permission to use the Hurst Canteen again. The first meeting will be on Wednesday, Oct. 13th.

Once more we extend to all W.C.Y.G. personnel interested in music an invitation to join the Club. It does not matter if you consider you know little about music, or if you "can't sing much". Those who were at our Social in April last will, we think, agree that the Choir's performance of "The Blue Danube" showed that a group of quite inexperienced singers can achieve much, given enthusiasm, in spite of the relatively little practice which shift duties inevitably entail, so come along and join in what we believe to be a most pleasurable way of spending a winter's evening.

We intend to incorporate into our weekly programme a short gramophone recital on the lines which proved quite successful last season. We look forward to meeting old, and new, friends.

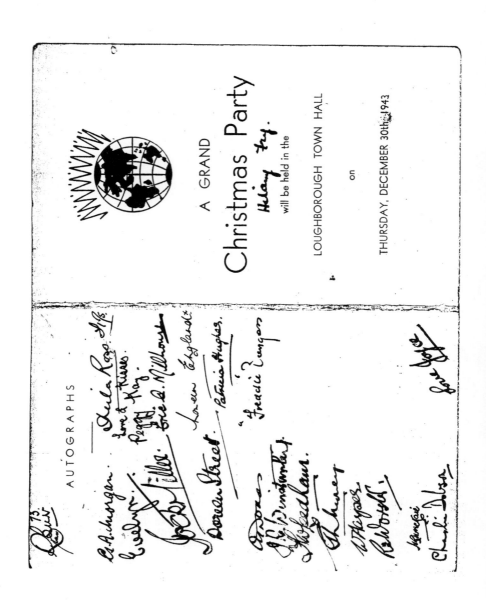

PROGRAMME

4 p.m.
TEA DANCE
in the
CORN EXCHANGE

6 p.m.
CONCERT
in the
VICTORIA ROOM

7-30 p.m.
GRAND TWILIGHT BALL
in the
CORN EXCHANGE

BUFFET   BAR

A Very Happy Christmas to you all. The race is nearly run. Keep Smiling for the last lap, and may your next Christmas be a "Victory Christmas."

M.J.W.E.

Beaumanor,
Christmas, 1943.

MARCH, 1944
VOL. I. No. 1 (NEW SERIES) - **6d.**

YOUR FILM ATTRACTIONS for MARCH

SUNDAY, MARCH 5th. — Melvyn Douglas & Virginia Bruce in
WHAT A WOMAN
also Otto Kruger in **SCANDAL SHEET**

MONDAY, MAR. 6th—3 days
Claudette Colbert, Paulette Goddard & Veronica Lake in
So Proudly We Hail

THURS., MAR. 9th—3 days
Frank Randal, George Doonan and Suzette Tarri in
Somewhere in Civvies

SUNDAY, MARCH 12th. — Walter Connolly & Iris Meredith in
GATES OF ALCATRAZ
also Chester Morris in **MEET BOSTON BLACKIE**

MONDAY, MAR. 12th—6 days: Roddy McDowall & Preston Foster in
MY FRIEND FLICKA
(in Technicolor)
and Tom Conway & Harriet Hilliard in
THE FALCON STRIKES BACK

SUNDAY, MARCH 19th. Boris Karloff in
BEHIND THE DOOR
and Warren William in **SECRETS**

MONDAY, MAR. 20th—3 days
Spencer Tracy, Mickey Rooney, Freddie Bartholomew & Lionel Barrymore in
Captains Courageous

THURS., MAR. 23rd—3 days
Mary Martin, Franchot Tone and Dick Powell in
True to Life
also Walt Disney's Special
Saludos Amigos

SUNDAY, MARCH 26th. — Melvyn Douglas & Rosalind Russell in
MARRIED BUT SINGLE
also Frank Craven in **THE RICHEST MAN IN TOWN**

MONDAY, MAR. 27th—3 days
Robert Taylor, George Murphy and Thomas Mitchell in
BATAAN

THURS., MAR. 30th—3 days
Mary Astor, Herbert Marshall and Susan Peters in
Young Ideas
also Dorothy Lamour & Jack Benny in
THE MAN ABOUT TOWN

Continuous Performance Every Day except Sunday, One Perf. at 6 p.m.

B.S.M.

Vol. I. No. I (New Series)
MARCH, 1944.

Editors: LEONARD P. JONES, ERIC C. MILLHOUSE
A.T.S. Editresses: KAY PRICE, MARY GILL, MURIEL FIDOE.
Editorial Board: DICK WILKINSON, OLLIE PEARCE, DUDLEY TRUIN.

THERE can be no more fitting opening to this new series of the B.S.M. than a tribute to our retiring Editor, Mr. F. C. Staddon. For the past two and a half years he has given up a large proportion of his spare time to the editing and financial care of the magazine. That he has derived a great amount of satisfaction in seeing the tangible results of his labour, Mr. Staddon will be the first to admit, but at the same time it has provided him with many a headache. Now that he has found it necessary to lay aside his task we feel that the occasion should not be allowed to pass without putting on record the gratitude of the Editorial Board, and, we feel sure, that of all the readers and contributors. Our ability to produce the B.S.M. in its new form is due in no small way to the careful handling of our financial side by Mr. Staddon.

As with all new ventures, there must be some concern as to whether our efforts are going to meet with approval. During our preliminary enquiries into the support we might be able to anticipate we frequently ran up against the query: "IS IT GOING TO BE BETTER?"

We feel that the only way in which we can answer that is by reminding you that this is YOUR magazine, and it will be as good (or bad) as YOU make it, and to briefly state our policy thus :—The B.S.M. has never pretended, and could never hope, to compete with the large National magazines. Nor does it presume to be a literary masterpiece. Our principal efforts are directed towards furnishing the Station with a printed record of its activities, and to provide some outlet for your pent-up literary urges. We do not expect, or desire, to go outside the ranks of the Staff for material, and, in view of the extremely varied cross-section of the public that we have here, may we add that we think it would be a shame if we were obliged to. So is it not worth sixpence to have a copy of an intimate, friendly magazine, which you have had a share in shaping? In view of the very greatly increased present-day costs we feel that it is not an excessive amount for something which may, in years to come, provide an interesting and amusing record of your days in Woygland.

For the first time we have a section devoted exclusively to the A.T.S. We hope they will enjoy it, and reward their Editresses' efforts by keeping them well supplied with all News and Gossip of the Group, as well as with suitable contributions.

So, all of you, take up your pens, and let us all see what journalistic giants we have in captivity here. And, if you do not like the new B.S.M., write and tell us why, but make your criticism fair and reasonable, and, above all, constructive.

THE EDITORS.

Next Issue ready: March 31st.   All contributions to reach Editors by March 18th.

APPRECIATION

BY ERIC DOBSON.

INTO a land so fair and rosy,
    Safe from the rigours of the strife,
Into a job so snug and cosy,
    Understood to last for life,
Cajoled thence by promise fair,
    Taught to think themselves secure,
Came a crowd of civil servants
    Leaping at the toothsome lure.

Some were promised, Never doubt,
    Come what may you're safe and sound,
We shall never throw you out,
    We are thus by honour bound.

Promises of quick promotion,
    Promises of increased pay,
Vows all uttered with emotion,
    What's a promise worth to-day?

They who came can go unwanted,
    But not until the war is done,
They're not allowed to go unhindered
    Till the glorious peace is won.

When that day arrives they'll go
    And join the ever-swelling queue,
"Are you soldiers, sailors, airmen?
    Sorry, civvies, you won't do."

Do they want peace soon, these people,
    When they know they'll be thrown out?
Do you wonder that they question:
    "What's this peace we fight about?"

Do you question that they grumble,
    Having hoped for just their due?
Is it strange that they should mumble
    That their interest is through?

You can make Atlantic charters
    You can set all Europe free,
But don't forget your humble servants,
    Branches of the parent tree.

In their job once called essential,
    They have done well for the fight,
What they want is safe employment,
    It's theirs by effort, theirs by right.

TEWA: "What is the date?"
CEWA: "Well, if the day before yesterday had been the day after to-morrow, to-morrow would be 13th."
What is the date in question? Answer next month.

Snoop's Corner

Stop Press! Four Extra Pages This Issue!

CONGRATULATIONS to George and Mrs. Kenneally on the arrival of twins, a boy and a girl, on Jan. 20th last. Some months ago George was suffering with severe pains in the back, which he attributed to the draught in "K" hut. He is now prepared to admit that this might not have been the real cause. It **could** have been due to his golfing activities. Belated congratulations to Mr. and Mrs. Michael Francis on the arrival of a daughter Ann, at Bristol on Dec. 21st.

We understand that L/Cpl. Light is to be a June bride. Doris has been running a long time now; it looks as though she has caught up at last. "Tubby" Fagg tells me that the date for his forthcoming marriage with Miss Joan Dale, of Woodhouse Eaves, is uncertain, but will probably be next quarter-day. The date is significant.

DEPARTURES.—Since our last issue we have said good-bye (in one case *fair*well) to several old friends. Messrs. **Carrington** (Peter), whose place on (and off) the dancing class committee is being so adequately filled by Mr. Brister; **Tomkins** (Snikmot), whose loss will be keenly felt by the B.S.M.; **Akhurst** (Dickie) who, by the way, has just had an addition to his family; **Cole** ((George); **Edge** (Jimmy); and more recently **C.S.M. Timon.** We wish them all the best of luck in their new spheres.

During a conversation with Sgt. Jessie Reeves, *nee* Adams, whose marriage on 20th March last was reported in this column, I learned (1) that she is not now able to ride a bicycle, (2) she doesn't expect to stay at her present job much longer. Since the arrival of American troops in this area an increasing number of our A.T.S. friends are finding it necessary to walk home. This, *they* tell me, is due to the extra strain on the inadequate local bus service.

I met Phillip Johnson the other day outside a jeweller's shop, where he had been trying, unsuccessfully, to buy an engagement ring. Perhaps the "I" Corps could put him on to someone who apparently has no further use for such an article.

Since we were first asked to announce the engagement of Bill Ghent and Pte. Muriel Furniss (Fiery?) we have lost track of the number of times it has been broken off, so that at the time of going to press we are uncertain of whom is engaged to whom, or why. An army, Muriel, breaks off an engagement when it has had enough of battle.

On Feb. 9th a section of Control Staff spent an enjoyable evening at the Theatre Royal, followed by a trip to the Old Boot, finishing up at the Town Hall dance. The outing was organised by "Slap," who, I am told, is almost human when off duty.

We are familiar with the stories about young ladies who hide under their favourite film star's bed, etc., but I don't think even Robert Taylor could compete against the overwhelming popularity enjoyed by one of the "K" hut supervisors who was recently besieged, in the most intimate manner, by two ardent young ladies who, in an effort to avoid competition, arrived some time ahead of the remainder of "D" watch.

We always knew that a certain unmarried Grade II. had a considerable bank balance. He also seems to have influence, judging by the amount of chocolate and fruit (in winter too) which he presents to an A.T.S. sergeant, whose name suggests that she would make a competent wife.

It is rumoured that an empty cigarette packet of **English** origin was found in "J" hut the other day. We can only suggest that it must have been left there by the duty I.M., or some other male member of the staff.

We are pleased to see that "Mouse" has moved up in the literary world. Not satisfied with having a short story published in the "London Opinion," he has now succeeded in gate-crashing the exclusive pages of "Punch."

We are also interested to learn that Wally Cecil has been doing some free-lance recording in connection with the B.B.C.!

According to the wording of his bus pass Mr. Antrum (The Weasel) is authorised to travel to *and* from Loughborough. As he seems to think that this must be taken literally, we should like to point out it is customary to let either 16 or 8 hours elapse between the "to" and the "from."

It wound be interesting to know whether Paddy Kelly enjoyed his weekend in Nottingham, or has he **really** reformed?

We have just been informed of the engagement of Mr. J. Dodd to Miss Mary Carter, of Gillingham. Congratulations!

In case anyone should get confused, and to avoid unnecessary heartache, we hasten to point out that the "J" stands for Jimmy and not John.

Explanation re Sergt. Reeves: (1) She never could anyway, (2) She thinks the war will soon be over—which just goes to show!

We are still uncertain whether the daily demonstrations with the vacuum cleaner are intended to make the female members of the staff feel more at home, or whether it is is some form of vocational course for the demonstrators.

What if your "box of tricks" *is* busted,
As long as the inside's been dusted.

That's all for now. Address your "dirt" to the Social Editor, B.S.M. Cheerio!

OLLIE.

EXIT THE EXILES.

The hour has come, the work's been done,
    the straining forms relax;
With lifted hearts, the shift departs,
    to dream of . . . INCOME TAX!!

"Smiler."

CALLING ALL

THIS month the A.T.S. Section of the B.S.M. makes its first bow. Before all else, we want you to feel that these six pages are your own special territory. So make yourselves at home, while we tell you a little about them.

As you will see, we are catering particularly for feminine interests. For instance, do you want to be beautiful ? Or more beautiful ? Then let our Beauty Expert (and she really is an expert) give you a few wrinkles on how to take those wrinkles away !

Or are you going on Leave, and feeling sick and tired of all your " Civvies " ? New ones are hard to come by, for coupons are few and far between, but perhaps the suggestions in our Fashion Feature will help give your existing wardrobe a new lease of life.

It's awfully hard to think of presents to give people nowadays, and very often the solution is a Book Token. Very nice too, but if you have got out of touch with books as we have, it's a problem to know what to choose, isn't it? That is where " Good Reading " is meant to help you. Every month we will try to tell you a little about books seen recently at the local booksellers or borrowed from the local Library; but don't take our word as criticism—we don't set out ourselves as critics. " Good Reading " is intended only as a guide— and if *you* have read anything good yourself lately, why not let us know all about it ?

And that brings us to a most important point. We want *your* contributions in this A.T.S. Section, especially in the feature, " Before the War." What did you do before you were in the Army ? Some of you must have had awfully interesting jobs, or maybe lived in interesting places, or travelled abroad. Or even (like us) had a dull job and found an amusing side to it. We want to know about it, anyway, so won't you write and tell us ? Use a nom-de-plume if you feel shy, but the main thing is—write and let us know.

In due course we hope to have a page of A.T.S. news dealing with items of strictly A.T.S. interest from all the different Wings, so if *you* have any tit-bits to report, please send them in.

We won't keep you any longer now. Go ahead and explore these pages for yourselves, and if you can suggest any new feature you would like to see, we'll be glad to consider it.

Remember, it is *your* interest and support alone that can make this section a success. So cheerio. We know you won't let us down.

" MARY and KAY."

My Job before the War

By Daphne Carter.

"TO hold as 'twere a mirror up to nature." That was my job in Civvy Street, and I don't think there has ever been a better description of it. When I tell people that I was on the stage, they invariably say "How interesting." I have often noticed that the word interesting, used like that, means exactly the opposite, and is merely a courtesy title for boring, but this does not apply to the stage, for the stage really *is* interesting—tremendously interesting. I loved my job; if I hadn't I should never have stuck it, for it is very far from being an easy life. Some people hold the opinion that being on the stage isn't work at all, but a kind of glorified amusement. Nothing could be farther from the truth. Being on the stage is extremely hard work, especially my branch of it. I was a repertory actress, and repertory is just about the hardest and the worst paid branch of the profession.

I remember when the war first broke out, and business dropped to zero, we used to do matinees and evening shows every day, so instead of rehearsing in the morning we rehearsed between the matinee and the evening performance, having tea in the theatre. We never saw a book before Wednesday, and we had only time to rehearse half the show each day, so that we had two full rehearsals, besides the "dress" rehearsal. I have put dress in inverted commas, because it is very rarely in Rep. that one has an actual dress rehearsal. In Rep. a dress rehearsal is just an ordinary one, except that the props and the scenery are there, and that it takes an extremely long time, because the producer is usually completely preoccupied with the lighting, and the actual rehearsal always begins hours late.

One of the most exciting and alarming aspects of the theatre is the number of things that can go wrong. I remember when I was playing Gladiola in "Daddy Long Legs." I had to open the show by breaking a cup. The show simply couldn't begin until that cup was broken. On the the first night it didn't break. I gagged frantically, saying "Oh, thank goodness it didn't break." I tried again, and again it didn't break. Once more I gagged with remarks about my fingers being all thumbs, then I turned my back on the audience, and smashed it on the floor with all my strength, and at last I was successful. When I came off the stage I expected to be blown sky high by the producer, but all I got was congratulations on my presence of mind.

Yes, the theatre is an uncertain sort of business and a hard life, but it has its compensations. I have never stopped being homesick for the smell of greasepaint, and the thrill of a first night. Although there is a first night every week in Rep., it never loses its thrill. When the Assistant Stage Manager yells "Overture and beginners please," and the curtain goes up, then one knows that it is all worth it, and that there is nothing like it in all the world.

GOOD READING

"DAYLIGHT ON SATURDAY," by PRIESTLEY.
Reviewed by Celia Allan.

A convincing story, revolving round the lives of various workers, practically the whole of whose lives is spent in the glare of artificial "daylight," embedded in the rhythm of giant machines, which crash out the parts which will eventually be part of aircraft.

Priestley gives, vividly, a character picture of each worker from the simplest country girl, who is doing her "bit," to the exalted Works Manager and Director—their lives when they leave behind the hideous clatter of machinery and step out into the daylight; the workings of their minds as their hands, everlastingly receive, assemble, and sort; the joys and tragedies which lie behind their raucous shouts and mechanical movements. Nor does he except their ambitions—be it the small girl doing the simplest job, whose one and only aim in life is, one day, to be able to play the piano—to those with finer brains, whose ambition is to sort out the muddled world and, at the same time, produce more aircraft.

Entertaining, informative, with a goodly touch of humour thrown in—in fact "good reading."

"THE HUMAN COMEDY," by WILLIAM SAROYAN.
Reviewed by Miki Druyan.

For those of you who like to read about life as it is, and about people as they really are, good or bad, ladies and gentlemen—girls and boys too—I give you William Saroyan.

"The Human Comedy," Saroyan's first novel, lives up to every letter of its title. Humanity and humour go hand in hand. This is the story of a typical American family, and every member of it comes alive as Saroyan, with an uncanny knack of putting his pen on every turn of the human mind and heart, shows us this family, its ups and downs, and every changing mood of any family in war-time.

Perhaps the most lovable character in the book is Ulysses, a typical youngster of three, American, British or Chinese, for children of his age are the same the world over, alert, inquisitive, spontaneous —and naughty. Homer, his elder brother, about twelve years old, who works after school in a telegraph office to eke out the family's finances, is a very real, if rather serious boy, with his love of adventure, his ever present joyous expectation of what might be round the corner.

These two are perhaps the most outstanding characters, but each lesser one is so fine that one wishes there had been more of Mr. Grogan, a very endearing, drunkard philosopher, the telegraphist in the office where Homer works, of Bess, just your or my, or anybody's elder sister, or of Mrs. Macaulay, a very real mother, with a heart big enough to mother not only her own family, but the whole of the American Army.

Perhaps inclined rather, to over sentimentality in a few places— but after all, isn't that "life"—this book is definitely a book worth reading, worth having if you can afford it. Price 7s. 6d.

This Month's Fashion Feature.
WEAR A BIB'

Yes, I really mean it. There's nothing like a bib for dresses with tired necklines, and they are so simple to make. You can make them yourself out of left-over scraps of gay material—make them square, or round, or even heart-shaped, with the point in front and the rounded pieces meeting at the back of the neck.

A dark-coloured dress comes to life with a gay bib. If you are the "tailored" type, make it of a scrap of white linen or pique, the neck bound with an inch wide band of some contrasting colour, which stands up round your throat like a Russian collar, and an initial, or your favourite motif, in the same colour, appliqued in one corner.

Or if you are the "cuddly" kind, make your bib of polka-dot lace (no coupons required) and put a provoking little frill, half an inch wide, round the edge, and the neck. Bibs of flowered silk or cotton on plain colours, or plain bibs on flowered or striped materials make an old dress look like new.

This is just an idea. You can probably improve on it to suit yourself. But try it. You can work wonders with a bib!

This Month's Beauty Hint.

It isn't too late to make another New Year Resolution, so why not make one now? The war won't last for ever, and no one wants to go back to "Civvy Street" looking neglected, so let's take stock of ourselves. Shall we begin with the figure? This is, I think, our greatest problem, for so much sitting, stodgy food and irregular hours tend to make curves appear in quite the wrong places. So do try and make time for at least five minutes regular exercise every day. It does much more good than a violent spurt once a week.

Try these simple exercises before you go to bed, or better still, while running the bath :—

1. Stretch the arms above your head and then swing down vigorously to touch your toes. Do this twelve times.
2. Standing with feet slightly apart—arms stretched in front of you—swing from side to side, swinging the arms well round until you feel the muscles in your side really pulling. Repeat six times.
3. Standing with feet still apart, head held high, shoulders back, tummy and tail tucked well in, bend over first to the left, stretching the left hand as far down your side as possible. Do this six times, then repeat bending over to the right.

(These last two work wonders against those extra inches round your waist).

But if you find those inches do not respond to such gentle treatment, try and be really firm, and resist the temptation of that extra roll at Break-time. Another little "don't." We all feel tired on duty, but do try not to lounge in your chair. Those tummy muscles will jump at the opportunity to get lazy if you won't sit properly!

Do I hear you say, "Oh, I haven't time?" I hope not. Remember—if you don't watch your figure, no one else will, so I think you'll agree it's worth it.

NIGHT TRAIN

By Mary Gill.

THE train dragged slowly through the night, frequently staggering to a halt, sometimes at a ghostly, green lit station, but more often stopping nowhere in particular, and for no apparent reason. It was packed with the usual crowd of khaki and blue-clad men, some going on leave, tired but cheerful, others returning, tired and not so cheerful, sitting on kit bags in the corridors, crammed together in the stuffy compartment, most of them trying to sleep, some talking quietly, some alert and watchful, continually looking at their watches, wondering if they would get the connection which would enable them to spend a few of their precious forty-eight hours at home. All of them quiet, none of them conscious of their immediate surroundings, of the monotonous crawl of the train, or the phantom stations, or each other. All of them thinking of what they had left, or to what they were going.

In a corner seat in one carriage sat a soldier. He was thinking of his home, and his leave, which was over, and he wondered idly, where he would be sent. Italy perhaps. He was really too tired to care. He had no interest in his fellow passengers. They were just dim, meaningless shapes, slumped back in the shadows behind the blue bars of light from the reading lamps. They were silent, and heavy, and dead.

Then he became conscious of movement. The train had stopped, and two people were getting out. There was a general disturbance while they collected their baggage and bundled out, and two passengers from the corridor came in and took their places. He looked at the first with little interest. She was a little wiry woman in grey, with wispy hair, a bundle of newspapers and magazines, and a determined expression. A schoolmistress, probably. The other one he found more interesting. She was a girl in khaki, small and very neat, with a shining roll of dark hair curling up over the edge of her service cap. She sat down opposite the soldier, next to the little grey woman. The soldier looked at her face. And then he looked again, because it was a nice face, pale and pointed, with dark brows, and wide grey eyes. A sensitive face, very tired at the moment.

He was disturbed from his contemplation of the new arrival by a sharp sound shattering through the thick silence of the carriage. It was a voice, belonging to the little woman in grey. "Really," she said, "Really, it's disgusting!" The soldier looked at her. She looked very awake and earnest. She was obviously the kind of woman who talks in railway carriages. Even at night, and to very tired people.

"It's disgusting," she said, "shooting defenceless sailors floating on a raft." The paper in her hand quivered with emotion. "Just like them," she said—"the brutes!"

This stirred the carriage to life. It was as if everyone realised the impossibility of holding out against the little woman. She was obviously determined to be conversed with. A sergeant emerged from the shadows, and his face appeared vaguely through the blue haze of cigarette smoke. "Who?" he enquired. "Why, the Germans," said the little woman triumphantly, as if propounding some new and extraordinary truth. "Listen!"—and she proceeded to read the latest atrocity story with great relish. After which the sergeant followed her lead with first hand experience of Aryan brutality. The young soldier was bored, he had heard it so often before; but the rest of the carriage joined in, half-heartedly at first, and then, spurred on by the energetic little woman, with growing enthusiasm. All except the little girl in khaki, who did not seem to hear, but sat gazing seriously at nothing with her calm, grey eyes.

The wickedness of Germans having been dealt with exhaustively, and the compartment thoroughly aroused, the little woman led the conversation into an even fruitier and more horror-provoking channel.

"Of course," she said, "the Germans are angels"—her voice dropped to a hoarse, knowing whisper—"compared with the Japs!" "Ah," said the carriage appreciatively, and waited for something good. It came. The little woman had friends who knew, and her friends had relations who had seen, and she went off through the whole ghastly list—rapes and massacres and tortures, and tongues cut out, and ears sheared off, and men disfigured so badly that even their families were unable to recognise them. All the stories that are bad enough in print, but when told by that hoarse, eager, almost gloating voice, were infinitely more loathsome.

On she went, piling horror on horror, and the whole carriage listened; even the sergeant knew nothing worse than she did. Even the young soldier, who was sickened and disgusted, could not avoid that beastly recital.

Suddenly he heard a little, strangled gasp like an animal in pain. He looked at the girl in khaki. She was standing up, tense and with clenched hands. Her grey eyes were no longer calm, but wild, and wide with fear and dumb agony. Her mouth trembled and she closed her eyes, and stumbled blindly out into the corridor.

There was silence. Even the little woman in grey stopped her grim monologue. "Poor child," she said with genuine concern. "Journey's probably upset her. I'd better go—" "No" said the soldier. "No, I'll go."

He went out, closing the door behind him on the hot, stifling compartment. The girl was standing in the corridor, staring out into the blackness. She was grasping the wooden window frame tightly, trying vainly to stop herself trembling.

The soldier was silent for a moment. Then he said softly, "What's the matter?"

She answered without turning, in a lost, dead voice. "My husband—he was in Shanghai. I've heard nothing for two years!"

The soldier put his hand on her shoulder. He said nothing. There was nothing to say, really.

FOR SALE.

Quantity Excellent Quarto Size **PAPER** (old B.S.M.) Suitable for Writing or Typewriting. Price per 100 Sheets— 1/6. Apply L. P. Jones.

VICTORY

Monday, March 6th (3 days)
Ronald Colman in
"Lost Horizon"
Also March of Time

Thursday, March 9th (3 days)
Charles Laughton and George Sanders in
"This Land is Mine"
Also Edgar Kennedy in "Cooks and Crooks"

Monday, March 13th (6 days)
Errol Flynn and Ann Sheridan in
"Edge of Darkness"
Also Full Supporting Programme

Monday, March 20th (6 days)
Vera Lynn, Jewell and Warriss in
"Rhythm Serenade"
Also Otto Kruger in "Power of the Press"

Monday, March 27th (6 days)
Walter Huston and Ann Harding in
"Mission to Moscow"
Also Interest, Musical, News, etc.

The Gospel according to St. Upid
Chapter XXIX.

(Translated from the English by Disciple Millhouse).

NOW in the days of their banishment a great sickness fell upon the mighty tribe of Woyg. For the Plague of Apathy was visited upon them.

Thus it came to pass that one among their number conceived a Bright Idea to make a team of Feetballers. And he saith unto the multitude: "What say ye?" And they answered him: "Notarf" which meaneth: Absolutely. Wherefore he gathered together many Feetballers and they uttered challenges to other Feetballers. But the team endured not, for they were become sick of the Apathy.

Likewise, another crieth: Let us play Tennis upon Tables. And there were many which came and were exceeding cruel unto a small white ball. But the Apathy descended also upon them, and the ball was become still.

And there were many others who desired to be unkind to divers balls, both great and small. But it came to pass that they presently conceived a mighty compassion for the ball, and smote it no more. For they were sorely afflicted with the Apathy.

Then a certain man saith: Let us make a mighty side of Dartsmen, and shew the peoples of Lesta what manner of a nifty arrow we flicketh. But when they had flicked a few score arrows they were seized with the Apathy, and flicked no more.

And Vox Plebis, the Great Prophet, was given unto the peoples, to preach the Gospel of Wells unto them. But they heeded not his words, and his exhortations fell upon ears which were stony. And the Apathy became exceeding great, and Vox Plebis was no more in the land.

Now Eksmas was a time of feasting and rejoicing throughout the land. And in Eksmasses which had gone the peoples entered into Kantin and found it hung with garlands, and there was an abundance of Food and Womp. But upon this certain Eksmas, when the Plague was great, they came hither and saw that there were no garlands, and precious little Food and Womp. And they shaked their heads and murmured: "Woe is us. For behold, it is the Apathy."

Then a certain man conceived a mighty Brainwave, and journeyed among the peoples, crying: "Let us make the A.A.A.!" And they answered, saying: "Why wantest thou a full stop?" And he replied "Nay. Let us conceive the Anti-Apathy Association." And he besought many of them, saying: "Behold, is not this our salvation? Wilt thou not aid me?"

And each one answered him, saying: "Yea verily, it is a Great Scheme, and I am All For It. But alas, and woe is me, that I cannot aid thee. For behold! I suffer from Lethargy!"

Now one Barkus, a caravan merchant, being possessed of great wealth, brought a gift unto the peoples of Woyg, and gave unto them two great firkins of Womp. And upon the day appointed for the supping of the Womp, the Ewas came in thousands to Lownj. And it was noised abroad: "Barkus hath discovered a great cure for Apathy."

THIS ENGAGEMENT BUSINESS
By Kay Metcalfe.

I HAD no objections to getting engaged. I mean, that seems to be the usual thing round here when a girl has been out once or twice with a fellow (especially in this station), put up with his beery kisses and stubbly chin without complaining, and suffered the scandalous tongues of Woyg. After all, a girl has to have some compensation for two months' hard graft, and a diamond ring is as good as anything else, especially in these lean times.

No! I'm not complaining about that. I could take the sorrowful headshakes of fellow sufferers, the sarcastic announcement in the "Beaumanor Democrat," and the leering grins of congratulation from the male element of the section, which said as plainly as if they'd spoken aloud: "Nice work, sister, you've hooked your man at last, now try and keep him!"

My family had no objections to raise either—rather the reverse. Mother's "Thank heavens we've got her off the shelf early; wait until Cousin Jane's girl hears about this, she'll be green with envy," was only echoed by father's "One less to feed and clothe, thank God. Some other mug can have the job now!"

Oh no, the snag I had overlooked was the ordeal of meeting HIS people. What an experience!—nerve wracking was only the least of it! They were lined up in a row like a collection of oil paintings when we arrived. Ma-in-law ("you're going to get on awfully well together, darling"), tall and gaunt, wearing a black beaded frock which rustled and chinked when she moved. Brother Bert—a would-be happy youth, well under his mother's thumb. Sister Mary—an anæmic looking wench with a permanent lisp. Ye Gods! What had I let myself in for? I turned to flee, only to find the exit barred by Bill, two cases, and a large photograph of great-uncle William, which was staring accusingly at me from a conspicuous position near the door. My one way of retreat being cut off I turned round and murmured with a sickly grin: "What a delightful family I'm going to become part of; I've been dying to meet you all." (Dying was definitely the right word just then!) The face which I'd decided was impregnable moved into a contortion which most nearly resembled a walnut cracking (a feat which I afterwards came to recognise as a smile) and a grating voice said "Mary will show you to your room. This is a great surprise to us, we never intended William to marry so young" (Bill is 35.), with which utterance she swept from the room in a swish of silk and ear-rings.

Further treats were in store for me. As if by mutual consent (probably all pre-arranged), the various members of the family "dropped in," plus wives or husbands, as the case may be. Thank God I come of a small family. I should hate my brother's wife-to-be (if he ever has one) to suffer as I suffered that night. I was looked over, sized up, criticised, and probably found wanting by one and all until I was ready to drop. One brother demanded to see the ring, compared it with his wife's, sniffed and handed it back without comment. Another enquired exactly what I was, what I did, and where I did it. Ma-in-law grew inquisitive about my family and their means, whilst sister enquired if I could cook. I couldn't, so received a scathing look from the female section.

Nor was this all. I had to be inspected and have my morals tested by the local parson, hoiked round half the neighbourhood as

Contd. over.

B. B. B. — By "OLLIE" PEARCE

THE huts have now been re-arranged, and many other things have changed,
Examples all around we see of "military mentality."
A lot of us have recollections concerning weekly kit inspections,
Which are enforced **ostensibly,** to let the Quartermaster see
If every article is there, and whether it is fit to wear,
And, as upon the bed it lies, all folded to specific size,
Each item, article, or thing, is lined up with a piece of string,
Extended lengthwise down the hut, a most impressive layout—BUT
Your boots don't fit, your shirt is torn, and though your kit is badly worn,
It's uselessness won't be resented, in fact, you may get complimented,
If metal parts and leather shine, and every item is in line.
This policy, it would appear, is coming into practice here;
Equipment is installed likewise, according to its shape and size,
With everything arranged in line, symmetrical effect is fine;
No brasshat can, with truth, imply that it's displeasing to the eye,
Though what the eye has gained, I fear, may be a dead loss to the ear
But that's the order of the day, why not pursue it all the way?
Why can't brunettes and *per*oxides be made to sit on different sides?
Then, as they move from here to there, they'd have to bleach, or dye their hair.
But dye, these days, is hard to get, and time we know is precious—yet
We might arrange (with breaks so brief) a wig for every break relief,
With chairs adjustable, we might, keep all heads uniform in height,
Although I don't know how we'd manage, with Private Bruce and Corporal Ramage,
For Bruce, on such a lofty chair, would be suspended in mid-air,
Whilst Barbara's would be so low, I can't see where her legs would go,
Unless we could contrive to bore two holes beneath her through the floor!

Contd. from P. 15.

a small (?) showpiece, viz.: "Exhibit 'A' now on view, roll up in your thousands" style of thing, until my feet ached from hopping on and off buses and tubes and my face positively ached from wearing a perpetual grin firmly pinned from ear to ear. "Be nice to Mrs. So-and-so, darling, she might give us a wedding present," became a catch phrase, while "Old Mrs. X always promised to leave me something when she popped off, darling; do make allowances for her," rang in my ears for 48 hours while the old so-and-sos pawed me round felt the texture and weighed up the probable cost of my clothes.

Oh, if ever a woman suffered!

How I got through the ordeal, God alone knows and he won't split! 48 hours on trial for my life, as it were. Mother, is it worth it? That is the burning question now confronting me. I ask myself, "Shall I go through with it, or shall I cut my losses, get out while the getting's good, and return the ring?" What would you do about it, chums? Write to Sweet Fanny Adams?

HOW'RE WE DOING.

By Fred Hearn.

THE second-in-command folded the document, put it in an envelope, sealed it, placed the whole in another envelope, which was in its turn sealed, and then this was put in a slightly larger envelope, which was doubly sealed and finally stamped with the portentous inscription:

" MOST SECRET — NOT TO BE DIVULGED TO THE ENEMY."

" The D.R. is ready, sir," called the clerk.

" Right," answered the officer, " Give him this and tell him to make the best possible speed he can. It's urgent, damned urgent."

The D.R. signed for the important looking packet, and glancing at the inscription realised he was taking something of paramount importance to the front line. He felt proud that he was the chosen one to take a document that might in all probability start a push that would finish the war.

His motor-cycle was " chug-chug-chugging " gently. He mounted and a sudden exultant snort from the exhaust told the second-in-command that the document was on its way. He breathed a sigh of relief.

The D.R. made remarkable progress, taking risks that he would normally never think of. He finally drew up at his destination with a flourish and a fanfare on his hooter. A tired looking sergeant appeared and shouted " What the blazes are you making that row for ? " The D.R. wilted. He had not expected a welcome like that.

" Important dispatch, sergeant," he said, handing it over.

" Oh! all right." The sergeant seemed impressed by the outside of the envelope, and took it straightway to the adjutant, who looked at the packet with disfavour.

" I hope this does not mean a move from this cushy spot," he remarked, " just when we are getting used to the neighbourhood."

He mopped his brow. " Oh! well, I suppose I'd better know the worst." He slit the envelopes slowly, wondering when he would reach the vital contents, until the paper fluttered to the desk. He picked it up, smoothed the creases, and read:

" Our Intelligence suspects that the Nth Panzer Division is facing you, comprising the following units—" Here followed a list of regiments, etc. The document ended: " For goodness sake make a determined raid and bring in a few hundred prisoners to prove that the Intelligence johnnies' suspicions are correct for once."

" P.S. Our wireless set has broken down, so send us back another one at once, so that we can listen to the B.B.C. and find out what progress we are making on this front."

FUEHRER.

Into the limelight Adolf trod,
 An adulated demi-god,
But see him now, obscured in fog,
 A poor deflated demagogue.   G.M.S.

Sweet FANNY ADAMS replies

Dear Friends,

Very many thanks to all of you who have written for help and guidance, and for your patience, necessitated by the unavoidable delay in dealing with your problems.

"WORRIED TAFFY" (You omitted your address, Taffy) explains that her friend, a corporal, "is engaged to a very nice boy working in the same place" as themselves. They all three recently went to a Unit Dance, but the friend's fiance had to leave early, "owing to circumstances beyond Love's control." Soon afterwards WORRIED TAFFY found her friend "in the arms of an Allied Officer," with whom she spent the rest of the evening. (You say: "the rest of the night" in your letter, Taffy, but I presume that isn't quite what you meant). They danced cheek to cheek, and she was gazing longingly into his eyes. "Altogether her behaviour was disgusting," writes WORRIED TAFFY, "Shall I tell her fiance? He is such a very nice boy, and I should hate to hurt his feelings."

WORRIED TAFFY! Though it grieves me to have to say so, I am afraid you stand convicted on your own evidence. Twice, in your very brief letter, you refer to your friend's fiance as "a very nice boy." Is it not therefore possible that your interest is not a wholly unselfish one? Has not the spark of jealousy been fanned by your friend's acquisition of another admirer? If you must speak to someone, Taffy, I think it ought to be your friend. Be honest, and confess to her that you are in love with her fiance!

"PUZZLED," writing from H, tells me he has very good "digs" as far as food and home comforts are concerned, but his landlady-landlord will not permit him to stay out after 10 p.m. on threat of being locked out. As he is fond of dances, socials and "merry Do's" he seeks my advice as to whether he ought to change his "digs," or rub along as at present, leaving the dances, etc., when they are just "warming up."

Well, PUZZLED, it is a very difficult problem. You do not say whether you arrive home from the merry Do's intoxicated, or go to bed with your boots on. Nor do you say how or where you sleep when your duty does not finish until 10 p.m. Why not try taking them to a "Do" to show them what harmless fun you have? Or would they always want to come? Perhaps you could try taking them to the "local," and earnestly explaining your feelings over a milk stout. You do not say how old you are, but if these ideas don't bear fruit, you might try running around the house in shorts and a college cap. If, too, you could prevail upon a friend to call and enquire if you are coming out with your hoop, they might see your point. Keep trying.

"VERY DISTRESSED," of B.M., tells me he is suffering from sleeplessness, due to his inability to make any contacts with the fair sex. Matters have come to a head now that he has seen the girl of his dreams in A.T.S. uniform in the canteen where he works. "If I do not do something about it soon," he says, "I shall go completely crazy, and do something drastic. I have omitted to mention that I do not seem to get along very well with the fairer sex. Perhaps you could tell me why this is. Please, please help me Fanny."

My heart bleeds for you, VERY DISTRESSED. I am not permitted to advertise in these columns, but I have heard that a Marriage Bureau was being contemplated in Loughborough. This may provide the answer to your difficulties. Otherwise, if it must be the girl you saw in the canteen, try upsetting her cup of tea. When you have spilt it all down her skirt say, very earnestly: "Sorry Aggie." If she is the kind of girl I imagine her to be she will probably protest that her name is not "Aggie," which provides you with an opportunity to ask what it is, and to generally get acquainted, at an overall cost of 1½d. for a fresh cup of tea. Be bold and daring, VERY DISTRESSED

MYRTLE WATERFALL (no address) writes to say that recently a man has been wandering round her camp at night. "Well Fanny, he makes me very nervous," she goes on; "I want to see him, and yet I am too scared to meet him. Can you advise me what to do?"

What precisely do you hope to achieve by "seeing" him, MYRTLE dear? If your aspirations only amount to discovering what he looks like I should be pleased to furnish you with a formidable male escort from Aunt Fanny's Personal Bodyguard Service, who will hover discreetly in the background while you effect the necessary investigation. But, IS "seeing" the extent of your desire? Though I cannot undertake to arrange introductions, it seems to me that VERY DISTRESSED, above, and yourself have a lot in common. It should not be beyond a woman's wiles to find out the identity of our girl-starved friend, MYRTLE.

THE GARATS HEY GERTIES have set me a formidable problem: When is a sitting-room not a sitting-room? They think the answer is: When it is a barrack-room, but they would welcome my "exalted opinion." They sign themselves "Yours from Banished from the Barrack-room." I have given the matter the profoundest consideration, GERTIES, and would recommend you to obtain a copy of the treatise "IN BED OR OUT OF BARRACKS," obtainable from this office, price 10s. 6d., postage and packing extra, which would appear to give a ruling on the matter. I would at the same time suggest that you make discreet enquiries as to where are the most comfortable sitting-rooms in the vicinity of your camp (not yet acquired) and then set to work with every feminine wile, smile, and guile. Another valuable work, uniform with the above, entitled "GETTING YOUR FEET UNDER THE TABLE," may prove very helpful if you are inexperienced, and also offers guidance should you, after achieving success, be in doubt as to what to tell the authorities to do with their barrack-rooms.

"WALLY" has written me a very lengthy letter on the subject of a shattered romance with an A.T.S. girl. It is quite amusing, but far too long to reproduce in the limited space at my disposal. Also, WALLY, I am afraid I suspect you of mere facetiousness. I am sure you confine your break period to the regulation time.

Let me have your problems, dears.

SWEET FANNY ADAMS.

EMPIRE

Monday, March 6th (6 days)

Randolph Scott and Claire Trevor in

"THE DESPERADOES"

IN TECHNICOLOR

Also Chester Morris in "After Midnight"

Monday, March 13th (3 days)

Ann Miller and Dick Purcell in

"REVEILLE WITH BEVERLEY"

Also William Gargan in "No Place for a Lady"

Thursday, March 16th (3 days)

Tom Conway in

"I WALKED WITH A ZOMBIE"

Also Lupe Velez in "Redhead from Manhattan"

Monday, March 20th (6 days)

Humphrey Bogart and Raymond Massey in

"ACTION IN THE NORTH ATLANTIC"

Also Full Supporting Programme

Monday, March 27th (3 days)

Johnny Weismuller in

"TARZAN TRIUMPHS"

Also Tim Holt in "Cyclone on Horseback"

Thursday, March 30th (3 days)

Claude Hulbert and Jack Warner in

"THE DUMMY TALKS"

Also Priscilla Lane in "All by Myself"

APRIL, 1944

VOL. I. No. 2 (NEW SERIES) - **6d.**

YOUR FILM ATTRACTIONS for APRIL

SHOWING AT THE ODEON THEATRE

Sunday, April 2nd—Gary Cooper & David Niven in **The Real Glory.** Also Lucille Gleason & Marie Wilson in **She's in the Army**

MONDAY, APRIL 3rd, and all the week:
Laurence Olivier's Latest and Greatest Picture—
THE DEMI PARADISE
with a sensational New Star, Penelope Ward.

Sunday, April 9th—George Raft & Joan Bennett in **The House Across the Bay.** Also Ralph Lynn & Tom Walls in **Cuckoo in the Nest**

MONDAY, APRIL 10th—3 days	THURS., APRIL 13th—3 days.
Lucille Ball & Virginia Weidler — in —	Ginger Rogers & David Niven — in —
Best Foot Forward	**Bachelor Mother**
A Great Musical Comedy ALL IN TECHNICOLOUR	Geo. Montgomery & Annabella in **BOMBERS' MOON**

Sunday, April 16th—Gary Cooper & Merle Oberon in **The Cowboy & the Lady.** Also Robt. Lowery & Edith Fellows in **Criminal Investigator**

MONDAY, APRIL 17th, and all the week:
Fred Astaire & Joan Leslie in
THE SKY'S THE LIMIT
with Robt. Benchley and Freddie Slack and his Orchestra.

Sunday, April 23rd—David Niven & Olivia de Haviland in **Raffles.** Also Bonita Granville and Ray McDonald in **Down in San Diego.**

MONDAY, APRIL 24th—3 days	THURS., APRIL 27th—3 days
Lionel Barrymore and Van Johnson in	Red Skelton & Eleanor Powell — in —
Crazy to Kill	**By Hook or by Crook**
Margo & J. Carrol Naish in **BEHIND THE RISING SUN**	David Farrar & Helen Perry in **SHEEP DOG OF THE HILLS**

Sunday, April 30th.—Evelyn Keyes & Peter Lorre in **The Face Behind the Mask.** Also Ralph Bellamy in **Ellery Queen, Master Detective**

Continuous Performance Daily 1-45 p.m. Sunday, One Perf at 6 p.m.

B.S.M.

Vol. I. No. 2 (New Series)
APRIL, 1944.

Editors: LEONARD P. JONES, ERIC C. MILLHOUSE
A.T.S. Editresses: KAY PRICE, MARY GILL, MURIEL FIDOE.
Editorial Board: DICK WILKINSON, OLLIE PEARCE, DUDLEY TRUIN.

THIS month, instead of an Editorial, we reproduce two letters which require no explanation. We feel that readers may be interested to know how the New B.S.M. was received, and perhaps, too, we are a little proud of these letters:

The War Office,
Whitehall,
London, S.W.1.
29th February, 1944

Dear Ellingworth,

Thank you very much for sending me a copy of your new B.S.M. It is most interesting and a decided improvement on the previous production.

I am sure it will do a lot to keep up the morale of your people, and I certainly congratulate the Editors and the editorial staff on the appearance of their production.

Yours sincerely,
C. V. L. LYCETT

The Editor, B.S.M.   26/2/44

Dear Sir,

You are the first man in B.M. to do it! Going home at 1400 hours on that memorable 25th, it was so quiet that one could even hear Mr. Barkus' bus engine! Strange to relate nobody was talking, and you silenced for ever (I hope) "The airman who was far, far away," "Colonel Bogey," and many other B.M. classics, and for a change nobody wanted to remove Mr. De Labertauche's boots, or fight—apart from these minor discomforts we always have a pleasant journey.

Can't we have an issue every day? My congratulations on producing a magazine which had 'em all reading at the same time. All I hope is that it didn't have the same effect on the 1400/2200 watch at precisely the same time.

Yours etc.,
JIMMY HUNTER.

YOU will be pleased to find a further extra four pages in your B.S.M. this month. It must be understood that expansion of the magazine ends at this point. We have had great difficulty in prevailing upon our printers to let us have this further increase, owing to acute shortage of labour, and accordingly have given our pledge that this will be the limit.

We had hoped to give you a coloured cover on a stouter paper, but, due to the technical processes involved, we found ourselves having to choose between 20 pages including a coloured cover, or 24 pages all white. While a coloured cover would undoubtedly have enhanced the appearance of the magazine we feel sure you will support the choice we have made.

Next Issue ready: April 28th.   *All contributions to reach the Editors by April 15th.*

The Missing Fauteuil
By Yonc.

A Drama

(AUTHOR'S NOTE. *For the benefit of those who have never enjoyed the privileges and blessings of tuition in the language of our good friends, the French, I might explain that "Fauteuil" means "Armchair." At least, that's what it means in this story, although, on reading it through, I see that it might easily be mistaken for something else*).

SCENE I.

(*A country cottage in Leicestershire. On the wall, the name: AYCHUT. Inside: a table, a chair, a wireless set, and an assortment of telephones. In the chair is Mr. D, disguised as a fairy queen, hereinafter to be called F.Q., if you don't mind, Charlie*).

F.Q. (Sings): Here we go round the wireless set,
        Wireless set,
        Wireless set,
        Here we go round the wireless set,
At six o'clock in the morning, if you ever heard of such a stupid, incredible, unbelievable, unearthly hour.
(Enter a luscious lump, hereinafter to be called L.L. carrying a gramophone and four records).

F.Q. Oh! What a jump you gave me! I'm sure I'll never grow another inch.
L.L. Not upwards, anyway.
F.Q. Very funny! And who are you, if one might make so bold as to ask?
L.L. My name is Miss Ann Ecks, and I've some records here. The O.M. says I'm to play them over to you. Just so's you can't see what you think of them, y'know.
F.Q. Righto! What's it called?
L.L. It's a four-part song, y'know. In four parts, as it were. It's called "Bird Songs at Eventide," and its recorded by Ginger McBurnie and his full recording choir.
F.Q. Sounds good. Let's hear it.
L.L. Well, here's the first part. (Puts on recording. Strains of "Music while you work" fill the air).
F.Q. Stop! Stop! Stop (Recording off). I knew it! I knew it! I knew it all the time! It's that young Ginger again, mucking everything up. I knew he would. I told everyone so. I told him. I told Dak. I told the O.M. Oh Lor! The O.M.! What the devil's he going to say? (Raises her voice) Ginger! Giiinngerrr! Where are you?
Ginger. (Off). I'm here! And I'm busy.
F.Q. What're you doing?
G. I'm ——
F.Q. Well, stop it for once, and come here. I want you.
(Enter G.). G. What's up? Has old Slap gone and messed things up?
F.Q. He has not. This (indicates records) should be a recording of a Fo'teil song you're supposed to have made. One of those bird songs y'know. In four parts.

4

G. Well?
F.Q. It's not well! It's "Music while you work," and I'm going to ring up the O.M. and tell him so. You're going to cop it hot, young Ginger. My hat, you are! (Reaches for 'phone).
L.L. Poor Ginger!
G. I'm not worried.

(Curtain).

SCENE II.

(Same. O.M. in the chair. F.Q., L.L. and G. stand around).

O.M. Well? Where is it, what?
G. What?
O.M. Don't mimic me, suh! The fauteuil, I mean. I know one's gone. The Canteen Manageress told me so.
G. What's she know about it? Fo'teils are nothing to do with her
F.Q. If I might make so bold——
O.M. Silence! What? The point is, as Mr. Clark would say, a fauteuil is missing, though how one can lose such a big thing beats me. I mean, one doesn't put such things in one's pocket, does one? What?
G. I've know runners to, when it's raining.
O.M. What? A fauteuil?
G. Yes, a fo'teil.
O.M. You're drunk again suh! Drunk, I say, what?
G. I'm not. And if I were, it's a good thing to be, isnt' it Geoff, Don and Mac?
Geoff, Don, Mac. (off). Yesh, ol' boy. Bit rancid tho'.
O.M. Well, I don't know. I saw the Manageress, not five minutes ago, she said to me: "Oh! O.M. dear! Some of your rough boys have pinched, lifted, or otherwise nicked one of my fauteuils out of the Lounge y'know." That's what she said, tho' how——

(Enter Myrtle, dressed as a squaw).

G. Hullo Myrtle! I say, Myrtle, have you seen a fo'teil knocking about?
M. Oh yeees! I took several over to my tepee just now.
O.M. What! Several? Several fauteuils?
F.Q. If I might make so bold——

Stops. Sound of a lyre without. Enter Paddy—not the mad one, or the C.S.R.O.A. one. The other one, y'know).

All. Ah! Paddy, me bhoy!
Paddy. Pardon?
G. Have you seen it? The fo'teil?
P. Pardon?
O.M. The fauteuil, fathead!
P. Vix!
All. What?
P. Oh! Vikak..
O.M. Must be Irish, or something.

(Curtain).

(Irish, maybe. Could be Greek, or even Double-Dutch, for all I know. Anyway, the Fo'teil -(or is it "Fauteuil"?) is still unfound. Don't ask me where it is. Mysteries aren't in my line).

Theatre Royal
LOUGHBOROUGH.

PROGRAMME FOR APRIL, 1944

Monday, April 3rd (6 days)

MANNIE JAY presents the Sparkling Revue

" Starlight Parade "

Easter Monday, April 10th (6 days)

MANNIE JAY presents

' Stage Door Scandals '

Featuring Joe Poynton & the Musical Elliotts

Monday, April 17th.

Frank H. Fortescue Famous Players commence a Repertory Season of First Class Stage Plays.

April 17th (6 days)

The World Famous Classic

" Rebecca "

April 24th (6 days)

Geo. Bernard Shaw's play

" Pygmalion "

Coming Shortly " They Walk Alone " and " While Parents Sleep " &c., &c.

6-15   TWICE NIGHTLY   8-15

SHOW PARADE

Edited by Dudley Truin.

A pleasing portrayal of "QUIET WEDDING," Esther McCracken's best seller, was given in Loughborough on March 13th, by Meretas—a company consisting of members of R.E.M.E. and A.T.S.

The story is of a young couple who wanted a "Quiet Wedding," but driven almost to distraction by their families' frenzied preparations nearly throw up the whole idea. Helped, however, by a friend of the family, they succeed in finding a solution.

Mary Gill and **George Garner** won the audience as the young couple, and **Kay Metcalfe**, fussily exasperating as the bride's mother, kept them in high humour. Special mention must be made of **Miki Druyan's** vivacious and convincing work as the bride's cousin, and of **Albert Mayfield** as the bride's solid, quiet father. Congratulations to an excellent supporting cast, particularly to that model of eccentricity **Daphne Carter**.

Many thanks are due to the generous co-operation of local tradespeople, without whose help the staging and presentation, most lavish for an amateur production, would not have been half so effective.

The stage manager, **Pat Emery**, deserves special mention for the splendid production of this play, and the whole company obviously put "all they had" into it. We hope to see more of these shows in the near future.

(Reviewed by Ivy Walton and Margaret Rhodes).

◎ ◎ ◎ ◎ ◎

In "HER'S TO HOLD" (Empire, April 24th, 6 days), **Deanna Durbin** renews the part of Penny, which she created in her first picture, "Three Smart Girls," and her screen father is still **Charles Winninger,** who gives us some shots from that earlier film. The story is slight, and concerns a beautiful society girl's mad chase after an airman, perfectly acted by **Joseph Cotten.** The usual quota of Durbin songs is rendered as delightfully as ever.

"THE DEMI-PARADISE" (Odeon, April 3rd, 6 days) gives the reactions of a Russian inventor who visits England in 1939 and hates everything he sees, but who, on returning to wartime Britain in 1941, changes his views completely and wins the love of an English girl. **Laurence Olivier,** with strong Russian accent, gives a fine performance, and **Penelope Ward** is well cast as the girl he loves. The local inhabitants he meets, however, are more of caricatures than living people, and this is the main fault in a worth-while film.

"DEAR OCTOPUS" (Victory, April 3rd, 6 days) is the film version of Dodie Smith's successful play of family life. Like most British films adapted from stage successes, it suffers from lack of action, and too much talking. The family and its ties are the "Octopus," and though the main interest is in the romance between the son of the house (**Michael Wilding**) and his mother's companion (**Margaret Lockwood**), the picture's real charm lies in its naturalness to pre-war everyday life. The supporting cast give fine characterisations. This is a woman's picture. They'll love it.

We learn with pleasure that the Theatre Royal, Loughborough, is going over to "Rep" after Easter. We wish the Fortescue Players every success, and look forward to seeing some good plays in the near future.

FAMOUS LAST WORDS.

"That can't have been ours, can it?" (Or can it?)

PARADOXICAL

By F. C. Staddon.

She had finished duty and on arrival at barracks was overjoyed to find a letter from HIM. She always knew when it was from HIM, the thick, scrawly, childlike writing somehow held his character. Bold, impetuous, with still traces of the small boy, that part of him, which somehow, only she managed to discern beneath his otherwise matter-of-fact, mannish exterior.

She loved him, she wore his ring, they were both saving hard, it was a glorious day, everything was perfect, she was happy, her "bottom drawer" creaked beneath its load of knick-knacks. Gathering her stationery from its many hideaways, she picked up her pen. She would reply at once, as she always did. She gazed at his photograph by her side; she loved his honest face, his trusting eyes. She knew him for what he was—a gentleman. She began to write, and was lost in her letter.

Endearments flowed freely: "he knew she did," "of course she didn't, darling; he ought to know she wasn't that kind of a girl." "She missed him terribly." "Oh, it was just duties, a few organised events and occasional trips into the local town with the girls." "Yes, of course I do darling, you asked me not to give up my dancing (although I did offer to). The girls and I go dancing occasionally, but it's not really fun without you, darling."

She sighed, the rest of the page was devoted to endearments, promises and X's. She signed her name, his own private nickname, placed the letter in an envelope, sealed it, and then glanced at the clock. Heavens! it was 4 o'clock. She rushed across to one of her friends and said: "Shove this in the post for me, Mary. I'm in the dickens of a hurry. I've got a date with a perfectly smashing Yank!

B.M. DANCE CLUB.

The first anniversary dance was held in the main canteen on 16th February, and despite opposition from certain well-meaning but ill-informed quarters, was very successful.

Four experimental features were tried out:—
- (a) Music from gramophone records
- (b) Bar removed from the vicinity of the dance floor.
- (c) Sixpence admission charge
- (d) Refreshments other than beer.

The loudspeaker reproduction was of rather poor quality, but this has been improved.

It is gratifying to note that the B.D.C. lead is now being followed by the C.E.C., which is organising fortnightly dances.

Dance Club membership is increasing, and new members are always welcome. Several prospective members appear to be overcome by shyness. The classes are held in the semi-privacy of the canteen lounge, and should not cause embarrassment to anyone. So come, along and give them a trial.

Owing to the unfortunate posting of instructress Miss H. Fry, provisional arrangements are: Monday 7 p.m. (instruction), Friday 7 p.m. (Club Night). B.D.C.

The Flea's Philosophy

By NOEL ROYLE.

TWO fleas were romping in the sun;
  A joyous life, so full of fun.
Said one, "A favoured lot is ours;
We pass the carefree, pleasant hours
In sport, in games, on pleasure bent,
With happiness our sole intent.
We have no problems, doubts or ills,
No rents, nor rates, nor grocers' bills;
Mankind is our eternal slave
From day of birth, until the grave;
We share Man's life, his clothes, his bed,
And dance all day on his bald head.
Whilst others toil by brain or hand
To win existence from the land,
We share their wealth, but not their plight:
Who would not be a parasite?"

"Your words are true," his friend replied,
"For all this Earth, diverse and wide
Was made for love of you and me
By the Great Almighty Flea.
It must be so, for are not we
The only race from care set free:
Of plague and want we have no fear,
And neither need we shed a tear
For our beloved who lost their life
In petty nationalistic strife.
We are Creation's jumping lords
And need not rule by guns or swords:
Our lordship is hereditary,
Ordained by Divine Destiny!"

Oh reader do not mock the fleas
Or scorn the logic of their pleas,
For though it has no better claim,
Mankind imagines just the same.

TAILORING FOR THE SERVICES
— from —

| START TO FINISH | 8, BAXTER GATE LOUGHBOROUGH. | TOP TO BOTTOM |

The London Tailoring Co.

Est. 1899.   'Phone 2794.

SNOOP'S CORNER

CONGRATULATIONS to Ron and Mrs. Worster (Norrie Smart) on the arrival of a daughter, Rosemary Ann, on 30th January.

To Edna and Claude Deakin on producing a bouncing boy, Lindon John, on 18th February.

To George Curd and L/C Netta Lees, whose wedding took place on 15th March.

To Joan Clarke, who was married on 22nd February to Gunner Glen McChesney, R. Canadian Artillery. The honeymoon was such a success that the bride overstayed her marriage leave, and was subsequently three days overdue on a 48-hour pass, for which she was awarded three days C.B. I wonder what there is about this marriage business that makes people cease to care about a hitherto unblemished record?

To Private Hilda Gamble (runner) on her engagement to Mr. Percy Cox, late R.A.F. To Miss Maud Winifred Dunne, of the Canteen Staff, on her engagement to A.B. Richard Sleath, R.N. Maybe Maudie will be having a boudoir of her own soon, then she might be able to complete her toilet before arriving at the canteen!

To "Johnnie," whose quest for an engagement ring is over. It has now been delivered, but as nobody is supposed to know, I hope you will all play the game.

To "Tubby" Garnham on getting her second tape. I understand that she will be trotting up the aisle on Easter Saturday, and that Mr. Tom Ayscough will be waiting there for her (with carnations 3/6 each, too!)

DEPARTURES.—This month we said goodbye to the staff of "H" Hut annexe, which included Hilary (Small) Fry, of B.D.C. fame. I expect she will soon be shaking a nifty limb in her new surroundings. Somerset papers please copy.

We are pleased to hear that "Gerry" Dalton is making good progress following an operation necessitated by his unfortunate accident during a recent football match. Our editor, Mr. L. P. Jones is also recovering from an operation. We hope they will both be back with us in the near future.

We hear that Dickie Wildblood and Rita Jellings have a date for May 5th at St. Mary's Chapel, Everton.

Fate has not been too kind to Jimmy Rogers lately. You will remember how his Sir Galahad act came to an inglorious end owing to his American playmate not being conversant with the latter part of the villain's role. Jimmy has now received marching orders from his billet. It seems that he has the welfare of the A.T.S. too much at heart.

At Pte. Laurie Isaac's 21st birthday party on Feb. 19th, "Ten Port Terrie" Aiken, after boasting about her capacity, drank three half-pints and then laid a kit all over the Pear Tree floor. Laurie's party finished up very informally, and was such a success that one of the guests was stricken with fainting fits as a result. He is still convalescing at Morecambe, where by strange coincidence, his wife is stationed. He writes to say that he has caught a cold—we rather expected that he would.

The O.C. got a shock recently when taking a swig of his after dinner coffee he found that it had been made with mixed spice. We who are dependent on the canteen for our beverages would not have been so discerning.

Mr. "Lothario" Appleton, of "C" Hut, having escorted a Junior Commander home, then a subaltern, worked his way systematically through the ranks until he got down to a Private. "Appie" did not want his name published as treasurer of the B.S.M. I hope this preference for presumably less expensive dates does not signify that our funds are dwindling. By the way, my informant seems anxious to know whether he will climb the scale again.

L/Cpl. Doris Light will not be a June bride as stated in this column last month. She now expects to be married some time in April, as her fiance has been ordered overseas.

The "Shake-Jack" dance held on March 8th was very well organised. Though the dance tempo was somewhat erratic, the enthusiasm of "Shaker" Smith and "Jackson" Owen more than made up for this. Congratulations to Peter Gardner and Edith Turner on winning the Jitterbug competition with their acrobatics, even though they were not very conversant with the great American art.

Proof of the theory that love is blind was provided at the Empire the other evening when the writer of "This Engagement Business" sat at an adjacent table to that of her betrothed for twenty minutes before he became aware of her presence. Both parties afterwards delivered separate explanations just in case I should get any wrong ideas.

We see that Eddie is putting on a super show at the Town Hall on April 6th. Prices of admission suggest that the organisers don't see why the girls should have a monopoly on the pickings. We hope that the prospective market is not removed before that date.

"Blondie" Hewson who, after breaking off his long standing engagement, stated that he had finished with women for ever, was seen a few nights later very sheepishly conducting a young lady to a seat in the Odeon.

We were amused at the impersonation of the Knave of Hearts given jointly by Freddie Burgess and Rex Welch. Fortunately the "Queen" never discovered her loss, so there were no repercussions.

WHAT PRICE GLORY?

With sense of duty so imbued she answered her country's call,
She now paints figures in the nude on the Major's bathroom wall.

That's all for now. Cheerio,

OLLIE.

PASSING THE BUCK is making quite sure that the Break-numbers are written in.

Did you ever hear about the Dumb Blonde who thought that the Black Market was in Harlem?

NEXT MONTH—Through the good offices of the C.O., Lieut.-Col. M. J. W. Ellingworth, we have been fortunate in securing a series of articles dealing with the history of BEAUMANOR, by an eminent authority, Mr. S. H. SKILLINGTON, F.S.A., the Hon. Secretary of the Leicestershire Archæological Society. The first instalment will appear in the MAY issue.

WONDERLAND

By G. M

(*With acknowledgments*

THE sun had disappeared from sight
   Leaving the earth in gloom—
The sun of radiant delight,
   The gloom of boding doom—
And everything seemed ripe—for what ?
   And ominous—for whom ?

The moon was shining just to spite—
   The moon of memory :
She shed a fitful waning light
   Upon the land and sea :
Recalling dimly what things were
   While yet the world was free.

The Painter and the Pachyderm
   Were strutting close at hand
They spat like anything to see
   Such quantities of land :
" If all of that were only ours "
   They said " It would be grand."

" If seven pacts, with seven threats,
   Were trampled on by force—
That I suppose," the Painter said
   " Would be a fruitful course."
" I doubt it," said the Pachyderm,
   " You fill me with remorse."

" O Neutrals ! come and talk with us,"
   The Painter did beseech
" For there is much we must discuss,
   And you must hear a speech :
We cannot do with more than **four**,
   To keep a foot on each."

The nearest neutral looked at him,
   But never a word said she;
The nearest neutral hid her head
   Pretending not to see;
Thinking that so she might preserve
   A strict neutrality.

But four small Neutrals hurried up
   All eager for the treat
Their trade was brisk, their credit high,
   Their warships quite effete—
(And this was scarcely odd because
   They hadn't any fleet).

Two other Neutrals followed them,
   And then three more or so,
And then at last the rest came fast
   In quite a steady flow;
All giving up their status free
   To guard their *status quo.*

November, 1939)

POONER.

shade of Lewis Carroll)

"The time has come," the Painter said,
  "To talk of many things—
Of guns, and gas, and glycerine,
  Of Commissars and Kings,
Of how the sea produces mines
  And lions get their wings.'
"But wait a bit" the Neutrals cried,
  "Before you skin our fleece;
For some of us are unprepared,
  And all of us want peace."
"Delay," remarked the Pachyderm
  "Will mean our terms increase."

"Supplies of bread," the Painter said,
  From you we have decreed;
Petrol and iron ore as well
  Will fill a vital need:
Now, if you're ready, Neutrals dear,
  We shall begin to feed."

"But not on us!" the Neutrals cried,
  Turning a greenish blue,
"After your pledges that would be
  A brutal thing to do!"
"The cup is full," the Painter said,
  "At any rate for you."

"It is considerate of you
  To seek our guiding hand."
The Pachyderm said nothing but
  "Free speech from now is banned!
It's no good telling you the truth
  You might not understand."

"It seems a shame," the Painter cried,
  "To play them such a trick,
But everything is justified
  In our Weltpolitik."
The Pachyderm said nothing, but
  He gave his chops a lick.

"I weep for you," the painter sobbed,
  "For swallowing our lies,"
With fits of rage he tore to bits
  Those of the choicer size,
Keeping his S.S. Bodychief
  Before his streaming eyes.

"'Twas good of you," the Painter wept,
  "To carry out our plot:
Some large investments please accept"—
  But answer came there not;
And this was scarcely odd, because
  They'd "anschlussed" the whole lot.

The Gospel according to St. Upid

Chapter XXX.

(Translated from the English by Disciple Millhouse).

NOW in a far off land across the oceans dwelled a mighty man called Uncle Sam, chief over all the Dohbois. And when the King of Brit had fought his War with Itla for many days, Uncle Sam, who had fallen sick with Isolationism, became cured, and conceived a great hatred for the Hunnites. Wherefore he sent his prophet Izenhour, with a multitude of Dohbois across the seas to fight beside the Swoddis of the King.

And it came to pass that a mighty host of Dohbois, under their centurians, journeyed up into the Promised Land, and tethered their jeeps, and parked their gum, and sought out a place wherein to rest. And when they had found a place they pitched their nissens and tarried a while.

Now the Dohbois were a strange tribe who spake English which wasn't. And they were afflicted with divers strange ills called Craps, and Camels, and Jitterbugs. Likewise did they also suffer under an abundance of shekels, for it was not without cause that they were called Dohbois.

And the Dohbois went abroad in the land to have a Look-see. And they forgathered at a certain place in Kwarn called X, until it was verily become like unto the Circus of Piccadilly upon the eve of the sabbath. And when the sun was gone down they brought forth searchlights in their hands and held a Tattoo. Likewise were they themselves also become Lit Up.

And they went forth into the city of Luff to discover which was the day appointed by the publicans for the sinners to see the interiors of the inns.

Now the chief Koppa had ordered that no Brittite might drive a caravan upon the highways after a certain hour, wherefore the Dohbois knew him to be a Big Sap. And accordingly each evening when it was past the hour called Chucking Out Time there came into Luff a Dohbois caravan to gather up the sick and the halt, and the lame, and the weary, and to bear them back unto their nissens.

And when the Dohbois saw that there dwelled in the land a host of Atsites, they rejoiced, and one saith unto another: Dem goils shore is swell, buddy. And his companion, when he had given the Atsites the Once-over, answered him, saying: Mighdy fine, pardner, mighdy fine.

And likewise the Atsites, when they beheld the Dohbois, were well pleased, and straightway were in a Flutter. For it is written that the Atsites did find the Dohbois Awfully Nice, or Nicely Awful, according to their lights.

And the Dohbois discovered the dead cities of Kwarn, and Baro and Wudhows, and found there many Goils who had been put into Cold Storage. And they forthwith took them out.

And thus it came to pass that full many an Atsite, having conceived a Date with a Dohboi, hastened back unto her sisters, and, clasping her hands in great rapture, raised up her eyes unto the heavens, crying: O joy is me. Yea verily, for I am airborne at 1400 hours.

Answer to last month's Teaser: **The 16th of the month.**

CALLING ALL

THIS is the second appearance of the A.T.S. Section—we hope you like it as well as you seemed to like the last. This time we have had to cut out the fashion page, and we have also given up the idea of a news page, as there just is not room for them.

This month introduces you to the DIGBY family—we hope you like them. We do. Anyway, write and tell us what you think of them. On the subject of writing, our last month's appeal for your ideas has met with very scant response. Surely someone must have some views to air, or some complaints to make, or some interesting experiences to tell us about ? This is your Section, and we want material for it from you. So come along, it's up to you.

There has been some slight misunderstanding regarding a remark we made last month. Although there is no objection whatsoever to contributors using incognitos or pen-names, the Editorial Board feel that as a sign of good faith the contributors' own names should be entrusted to them, and strictest confidence is guaranteed. No anonymous contributions, therefore, will be accepted in future.

BEFORE THE WAR
By M. Fidoe.

ONE day in September '38 my sister 'phoned to say she had shingles. Now I had no objections to her having shingles but I did object to her having them just four days before our holiday. She said she didn't think she could go, but I wasn't to tell mother in case she went after all, when there'd be a fuss about her haring all over Europe with spots round her tummy.

The outcome was that we had to postpone our holiday in Switzerland for a week, and agree to sleep on the ground floor of the hotel annexe.

Apparently each year there is a Musical Festival in Lugano, and the proprietor of our hotel accommodates the band from his native village—in the annexe. On the evening of the festival we turned in early, but by 12-30 it was apparent that the Band, having " got organised " with the local belles, were bringing them back to say goodnight under our window. Swiss Love !—the tramp of hob-nailed boots, shrill laughs, and sudden prolonged silences and an occasional excited yodel.

Next, a pair of particularly heavy boots lurched up the steps, zigzagged across the hall, and stopped outside our door. Fortunately I had turned the catch inside, but our visitor made several determined sallies, swore, and fetched a few friends, who rattled away while we trembled in maidenly terror, hoping the catch wouldn't give way. After a while they gave up, and we sighed with relief and got to sleep

ATS

In the morning, as soon as I was dressed, I made a dash for the door and breakfast. Curses on all village bands and idiots! Someone had locked the door. Bunt had the brilliant idea that I should climb out of the window. Letting her bully me on to the sill, I was swinging a leg either side, cautiously contemplating the drop, when something electric in the air made me look up. I had forgotten the lakeside garden opposite, where breakfast was in full swing. A row of bulging German eyes stared fascinatedly at me over the hedge. For two seconds I think they forgot Hitler! As for me, I beat such a hasty retreat that I crashed in a heap on the polished parquet floor and shot into a power dive under the bed.

On the other side of the room was another window, less "public," but permanently shuttered, so we thought we'd try it. First we had to move the dressing table, so we both took an end. Bunt yelled "Heave!" and the next thing we knew was that we were both on the bed, mixed up with the dressing-table top, pots of cream, face powder, and lord knows what. The drawers were still standing under the window. The shutters hadn't been opened for a long time and refused to give, but Bunt thought that gritting her teeth and pushing both at once might help. It did, for suddenly the two sides shot apart and I just stopped Bunt from falling right out by grabbing her legs, only to find that her other end appeared to be in close embrace with a Swiss musician.

He seemed rather surprised. When she had extricated herself from his whiskers we discovered a row of grinning males assembled under the window. I thought they might as well come and let us out, so, leaning out, I beckoned and pointed into the room. Pardon my innocence! Their faces lit up, and with one accord they made round the house for the door. My sister remarked I'd asked for it and I could cope with it.

After much fumbling the door was flung open, revealing four of them beaming all over their faces. Mustering what dignity I could, I said, in English: "Thank you, the door was locked." Alas! their spokesman understood only Italian that morning, for when I tried to shut the door he put his trombone in it! For the next few minutes I argued with the trombone, while Bunt writhed in silent laughter on the bed. At last the other three, grasping the situation, hauled him off, smirked, and bowed. Thankfully I closed the door... We were awfully late for breakfast.

○ ○ ○ ○ ○

This Month's Beauty Hint.

By MARGARET DUNN.

Spots and blackheads do spoil the skin, and even though make-up camouflages these blemishes, it is far better to get to the root of the trouble.

The skin swarms with bacteria, mostly harmless, so long as they remain on the outside. But if they once penetrate they can, and frequently do, give rise to infection. Anything which rubs the skin and makes it easier for bacteria to enter a hair-follicle or pose, is liable to cause acne—for instance, the pressure of ear phones!

The only way to treat spots is by thorough and regular cleansing. Remember, soap and water are the first beauty aids—provided it is the right kind of soap! Try several brands and study the effect on your skin. Once you find the one most suited, stick to it.

If you have time to spare, steam the face by applying really hot towels. When the pores are open, gently press out those little blackheads. This rids the skin of impurities liable to cause spots—but be sure to close the pores by dabbing the skin with witch hazel, or even cold water.

The greasy skin is more liable to blemishes than the dry or normal one, so let's try and counteract the oiliness. I think you will find that a liquid make-up is the solution. These, however, with regular use tend to make even the greasiest skin dry, so have handy a heavy cream and use this occasionally to replace those natural oils.

Don't forget facial beauty includes the neck! It is just as important as the face. Especially does this apply to us A.T.S., for wearing khaki collars tends to make even the skin look khaki! Bleach packs are unobtainable, but an equally good idea is to mix up a weak solution of peroxide and apply to the neck as an astringent.

Briefly, I have tried to stress how important the care of the skin is—but if you do have any beauty problems, do let me have them. I shall be only too pleased to help you.

WARNING.

Although I know we owe much thanks
For many blessings, to the Yanks,
One word of warning I'd impart;
Don't take their honeyed words to heart,
And if they tell you love's sweet story,
Believe them not—or you'll be sorry,
Because (it's only natural, mind),
They, too, have girls they left behind.

Mary went upon the ice
To have a little frisk,
Wasn't she a silly girl,
Her little   *   (Anon.)

GET YOUR———

Beauty and Toilet Preparations

FROM

"LEONARD'S"

Gentlemen's Hairdresser

25, CHURCH GATE, LOUGHBOROUGH

Large Variety in Stock!

ATS GOOD READING
By Muriel Fidoe.

IF you ever find time to read and wonder what on earth you can read besides the book that has steadily been doing the rounds of the watch for the last three months, I hope that you will find some inspiration in our new monthly book page. This is to be no review of new books or best sellers which no one can afford to keep on buying, but merely a reminder of interesting books, many of them old favourites, to be had for the fetching. All the titles I am going to suggest are obtainable in Loughborough Library or in a popular edition from the local book shops. I hope the choice is varied enough to suit everyone's taste—or as near as possible.

A very good topical book which has been written a few years is Phyllis Bottome's "**Mortal Storm.**" It is the story of a German family, which through second marriage is partly Jewish and partly pure German. With the coming of Hitlerism, the inevitable happens Many books have dealt since with the same subject, but few, I think, so well. It really does "get you."

If you like historical books, try "**The Rocklitz,**" by George Preedy. This too, is no milk and water book, and the scene is again in Germany. It is an almost macabre tale, based on fact, of a young girl who became an adventuress against her will. Forced into a convenient marriage by her power-seeking father and brothers, she was steadfastly denied by the man who really loved her, and whose fate she finally helped to determine. It is a book one doesn't easily forget

To come to the lighter side, if you are being swept away by the present "American" fashion, you will probably enjoy a very humorous book of short stories written by an American called Damon Runyan. The title of the book is "**More Than Somewhat.**" Apparently the author is a great favourite with the Americans, so it has value, if only as a new topic of conversation!

For animal lovers there is a delightful book about a dog called "**The Bunch Book.**" Bunch is the name of a little dog who makes his debut in the book as a very small puppy. The text is very nicely illustrated too. You will find this in the biology section, but don't let this put you off.

In the Big Ben books (price 9d.) you will find a book called "**Sleep and Cease Crying,**" by Elizabeth Sadler. It is an account of the experiences of a V.A.D. during the Battle of Britain, written in a very easy conversational style. The authoress is quite a young girl who was moved by the love of humanity rather than a desire to "Nurse" as a profession, to take up V.A.D. duties. You will be filled anew with admiration for the courage and endurance of our own and Allied women. There is perhaps nothing outstanding about this book, but it is full of very human interest.

"FANNY BY GASLIGHT," by MICHAEL SADLEIR
Reviewed by Joan Morley.

This book will, for many readers, prove surprising and something of a revelation.

Many people have the firm conviction that the moral behaviour of the present generation has sunk lower than it has ever been before, but as one progresses further into Sadleir's remarkable book, one can see that the immorality of the last generation was on the same scale, and could even be judged lower when one reads of the subterfuges and cunning indulged in by these "houses of ill-repute," in their efforts to maintain their air of Victorian respectability.

[Contd. foot of P. 20.

"SPAM FRITTERS"

ATS

" AMERICAN AS SHE IS SPOKE ! "
"Say, Babe, there's something about you that puts me in mind of Ginny Sims. What's that? Who's Ginny Sims? Why, she sings for Kay Kyser. You know Kay Kyser, don't you? He's one of our top band-leaders. He's hot—he's swell—he's a Hip-cat! What's a Hip-cat? I'm telling you, Babe, a Hip-cat's a guy that digs Boogie !"

" THE 'FLU——"
That feeling—that your lungs are stuffed with a mixture of iron filings and porridge, and that your head is divorced by apparently six feet from your shoulders——

" DO YOU KNOW ? "
That Al Fresco was a man who made his name in the Picnic Lunch business.

EXCERPT FROM A CHATTY LETTER.
My dear———, while I was home on leave we had a Bergulary! Simply fraught with mystery and danger from start to finish. It started with a threatening letter, coyly nestling among the milk bottles, which read in deep purple, " YOU DIE TONIGHT ! "
Of course, we all laughed like drains, and thought it was a Yuge Joke. We laughed on the other side of our pans, however, when, with the house left unattended for only three-quarters of an hour, someone got in, turned the place into a shambles, and calmly walked off with many things of value, several useful commodities,—and one red, rosy apple! The upshot was that the house, from cellars to attic, was simply swarming with bog-eyed constables, supercilious police-sergeants, detective and finger print experts, all crawling about on their bellies, peering into the most impossible places for Prints and Cloos.
It went on for days without any satisfactory result. I think our Policemen are wonderful—they are, too, at imbibing cups of tea when their immediate superior isn't looking! We evolved a magnificent technique in dispensing tea to the various departments without their respective gaffers seeing them—but it was all very wearing.

LINES ON LEAP YEAR DAY.

Oh! Woygland Bachelors today, proceed with trepidation,
There are so many single girls employed upon this station,
And I warn you that the purest,
The discreetest, the demurest
May try and get you in a compromising situation.
On one day only in four years they get this opportunity
To show their hidden passion for some man in the community,
Be it Jimmy, John or Harry,
The girls are out to marry,
And today they dare to press their suits without undue impunity.
But if a bloke is shy, this day may obviate a blunder,
For a girl may show her feelings when before she made him wonder,
And although it may be stupid,
You can't get away from Cupid
And the twenty-ninth's as good a day as any to go under.

K.L.B.P.

The Digby Chronicles

IT is my daughter Judith's fourth birthday, and it marks an epoch in her life. "When I'm four," Judy has always said. I have made innumerable promises regarding the privileges according to that mature age, and Judy is anticipating being classed as nearly grown-up—like Susan, who is seven, and no longer like Gilly, who is only two.

She is awake already—I can hear her fidgetting about in the next room. Her presents are arranged, according to tradition, by her bed, but she is on her honour not to touch them till seven o'clock. But will she be able to resist the temptation? Among those presents is a tricycle with real "ker-romium" handlebars—and a bell. Will she, I wonder——? My wonderings are cut short by the sudden ringing of a bicycle bell, a crash and a howl.

Daddy, slumbering stertorously beside me, plunges irritably and begins to expostulate.

"All right, dear," I say. "I'll go."

In the next room I find Judy snivelling on the floor, a bump like an egg on her brow, and Susan, sitting up in bed, is chiding her in a low, fierce whisper. In the far corner, Gilly is jumping up and down delightedly in her cot. Explanations babel forth.

"Mummy, I TOLD her not to——"
"I only just wanted to FEEL, Mummy——"
"More, Judy,—more bell!"

The situation is quite simple. Judy, lying awake, could endure no longer the glint of the grey dawn-light on the bell. She *had* to touch it! Just a feel— Judy's hand reached out, she leaned over, then ting-a-ling-a-ling. Oh, the glorious noise of it! Lost in ecstasy, she fell out of bed.

Having administered admonishment and witch-hazel I return to bed. Daddy has begun to snore. Unconsciously I begin to count the snores. At four hundred and ninety-seven there is an interruption —Judy, all bunchy curls and flannelette sleeping-suit.

"Mummy, can't I open my presents now?"
"It's only half-past six, dear."
"Yes, but——"

Here Daddy wakes up again, and Judy turns her attention to him with a crow of delight.

"Oh! Doesn't Daddy look funny in bed!"

Daddy grunts and asks: "What IS all this?"

I explain about the presents——

"For goodness sake, Joanna," he exclaims, "let her open them! Peace in the mornings at any price!"

Judy smothers him with over-bubbling affection. Then, wry-faced, "Ooh, daddy, you are *prickly*!"

Susan comes in, looking severe. "Come back to bed, Judy, and be good."

Left alone, Gilly sets up a roar.

"Bring him in," I say, realising that only a family gathering will do to launch the birthday properly. "And bring the presents—and above all, bring your dressing-gowns—or you'll catch cold."

K.L.B.P.

Contd. from P. 18]

Against this rather sordid background, the author has written the love story of Fanny, a woman whose childhood and girlhood were spent in close proximity to the tarnished livelihood of her parents, but who retained her freshness and purity.

The book is engrossing and is one that cannot be left until "The End" is reached.

VICTORY
BIGGIN STREET, LOUGHBOROUGH

MONDAY, APRIL 3rd—3 days.
Jeanette MacDonald & Nelson Eddy in
"NEW MOON"
Also "Before the Raid"

THURSDAY, APRIL 6th—3 days.
Anton Walbrook and Sally Gray in
"DANGEROUS MOONLIGHT"
Also Helen Parrish in "Sunset Serenade"

EASTER MONDAY, APRIL 10th—3 days.
Diana Barrymore in
"FIRED WIFE"
Also Henry Stephenson in "Mantrap"

THURSDAY, APRIL 13th—3 days.
John Craven in
"SOMEONE TO REMEMBER"
Also Fritz Kortner in "The Purple V"

MONDAY, APRIL 17th—6 days.
Margaret Lockwood & Michael Wilding in
"DEAR OCTOPUS"
Also J. Mack Brown in
"Deep in the Heart of Texas"

MONDAY, APRIL 24th—6 days.
Lucille Ball and Gene Kelly in
"DUBARRY WAS A LADY"
(TECH.)
Also Full Supporting Programme

Mon. to Fri.—Con. from 5-30 p.m. Sat.—Con. from 2 p.m.
MATINEES.—Mon. and Wed. at 2-15 p.m.
SUNDAYS—6-15 p.m. (One Show)

Sweet FANNY ADAMS replies

Dear Friends,

My Fanny-mail has not been particularly heavy this time. Remember your Aunt Fanny is always waiting and eager to help.

"JOHNNY" is unable to decide which of two A.T.S. girlfriends to "keep." (By the way, JOHNNY, you write and mis-spell just like WALLY!). One girl is "intelligent, a delightful companion, but of a fairly serious nature," the other "more frivolous" (*sic*), a "light-hearted personality, and at times rather passionate."

One girl is intelligent, the other light-hearted, you say—but are either *clever* in any commercial way? That must be the deciding factor. Lack of money being your principal trouble, you must give a thought to the future. Choose the one who is more likely to earn enough to keep you in comfort.

NOBBY (of no fixed abode, apparently) was "claimed" by a girl on Feb. 29th, and unwisely put his pledge into writing, subsequently regretting it. "I have no money," he says, "and can only offer the lady bread and jam." He is going grey, as well as off his beer. "Every time this girl sees me, she paws all over me and says have half of my stale cheese roll, and keeps on asking when are we to be married? I cannot sleep at night; every time I close my eyes her face appears, saying Come to me my darling, you are mine for always, at last I have got my man. My holy smoking mackerel, I shall die with fright soon." That wasn't very kind of her NOBBY—or do I misread your letter, and is it *you* who might die of fright?

NOBBY offers me his next week's pay to get him free. Show her a copy of Eric Dobson's poem in last month's B.S.M., NOBBY. There is a Money Order Office near B.M.

"AWAKENED" (but not sufficiently to remember her address!) tells me she is "passionately, desperately, dangerously in love" for the first time. "Air, food, sleep are no longer necessary to sustain me," she goes on. "My body is hungry, yes, my heart burning with a thousand flames, my brain thirsting for more and more—but only he can satisfy me; no one, nothing else. All is changed. My eyes sparkle with a new light, my voice speaks only his name, my very finger-tips tremble at the sight of him. Is this right, Fanny? Can this be Love?... You see, he's blind and deaf, so I must be sure I must decide our fate."

Poor dear thing, how unbalanced your letter shows you to be, "AWAKENED." You begin by telling me you are in love, and you finish by asking me whether you are! It is indeed a blessing that HE *is* blind and deaf, for he would find it awfully monotonous listening to your voice speaking only his name, and even the best eyesight could not long survive the dazzle of your permanently sparkling orbs, I'm sure. If this remarkable ability to exist without air, food and sleep persists, let me know dear. I can doubtless find someone who will be glad of your rations, and I'll also use my influence to have you put on permanent night-work. But it isn't love, Bella—just high blood pressure, or something you ate, which causes the heart flames and finger-tip tremors. It's a doctor you need, dear, not

SWEET FANNY ADAMS

Bookseller and Stationer :: Lending Library

J. SKETCHLEY

24 & 25, High Street, Loughborough
Telephone 2980.

SPORTOPICS.

A list will shortly be posted in the Canteen for signatures of those wishing to participate in the forthcoming cricket season. All military personnel on the Station are eligible, and we look for better support than last season, when difficulty was experienced in raising a full team. The home ground will again be Quorn.

With the kind permission of the C.O. it is hoped to re-open the Tennis Court, but the shortage of balls will be a handicap.

A. H. APPLETON, Sports Secretary.

SOCCER.—EXILES v. ARMY. The first half of this "local derby" produced some good, evenly contested football, the Army taking an early lead. The equaliser came from a grand goal by Dix from the left wing, and at half time the score was two all. Play was much more ragged in the second half, the loss of Dalton, through injury, being keenly felt by the Exiles. Despite a very fine effort by Keenlyside, playing wherever he was needed, the Army succeeded in scoring again, and finished winners by the odd goal in five. Thanks are due to Jim Griffin for playing such a useful game at short notice.

J.T.H.

HOCKEY.—After a brilliant start to the season the Exiles have had some very bad luck in losing, by the odd goal, three of their latest matches. As there are still a number of fixtures to be played, including some evening matches, we yet have a chance to shine, and finish the season as we started it.

Feb. 26th.	Exiles	v. Leicester	H	1—2
Mar. 11th.	"	v. Army Pay Corps	A	1—2
" 12th.	"	v. Brush (Mixed)	A	0—1
" 18th.	"	v. Lough. College	H	3—0

G.A.L.

A GUINEA FOR **YOUR** SHORT STORY.

You are invited to submit a short story for the B.S.M. The best story received will be awarded a prize of ONE GUINEA, kindly donated by Mr. HARRY APPLETON. The next two in order of merit will receive 10/6 and 5/- respectively. The Adjudicators will be the Editorial Board (Page 3).

The only rules of this contest are :
  Stories must not exceed 1,000 words.
  Closing date : APRIL 15th.
  The decision of the Adjudicators is final.

The three winning entries will be published in successive numbers of the B.S.M., commencing with the MAY issue.

Address your entries: GUINEA-TALES, c/o Editors, B.S.M.

EMPIRE
MARKET PLACE, LOUGHBOROUGH

MONDAY, APRIL 3rd—3 days.
Bonita Granville and Otto Kruger in
"HITLER'S CHILDREN"
Also George O'Brien in "Stage to Chino"

THURSDAY, APRIL 6th—3 days.
Roy Rogers in
"IDAHO"
Also Robert Lowery in Criminal Investigator

EASTER MONDAY, APRIL 10th—3 days.
Lloyd Nolan in
"STEEL AGAINST THE SKY"
Also John Abbot in "Secret Motive"

THURSDAY, APRIL 13th—3 days.
Jean Parker and Ralph Morgan in
"TRAITOR WITHIN"
Also Gene Autry in "Call of the Canyon"

MONDAY, APRIL 17th—6 days.
Wallace Beery and Fay Bainter in
"SALUTE TO THE MARINES"
IN TECHNICOLOR
Also Full Supporting Programme

MONDAY, APRIL 24th—6 days.
Deanna Durbin in
"HER'S TO HOLD"
Also J. Mack Brown in "Arizona Cyclone"

CONTINUOUS DAILY. Doors open at 1-30 p.m.
SUNDAYS at 5-30 p.m.

Printed by Toppings Ltd., 17, Southfield Rd., Loughborough, and published by L. P. Jones for Beaumanor Staff Magazine Committee.

YOUR FILM ATTRACTIONS for MAY

SHOWING AT THE ODEON THEATRE

MONDAY, MAY 1st. and all the week:
Bob Hope and Betty Hutton in a screaming comedy,
LET'S FACE IT
Also Richard Arlen & Jean Parker in ALASKA HIGHWAY

Sunday, May 7th—John Wayne & Thomas Mitchell in **The Long Voyage Home**, also **Pathetone Parade of 1942**

MONDAY, MAY 8th, and all the week:
A great new star, Dorothy McGuire with Robert Young in
CLAUDIA
Also Richard Dix & Jane Wyatt in THE IRON ROAD

Sunday, May 14th—Richard Carlson & Jane Randolph in **Highways by Night**. Also Joel McCrea & Andrea Leeds in **Melody of Youth**

MONDAY, MAY 15th—3 days
Randolph Scott and James Brown in
The Nelson Touch
Also Ray Milland and Loretta Young in
The Doctor Takes a Wife

THURS., MAY 18th—3 days
Margaret O'Brien, the star of "Journey for Margaret," with James Craig and Marsha Hunt
LOST ANGEL
with full supporting programme

Sunday, May 21st—Gary Cooper & Walter Brennan in **The Westerner**
Also Billie Lee in **Reg'lar Fellers**

MONDAY, MAY 22nd, and all the week:
Heralded as the greatest picture of the year—
Charlotte Bronte's JANE EYRE
with Orson Welles and Joan Fontaine
(N.B.—This Picture must be seen from the beginning).

Sunday May 28th—Diana Barrymore & Robert Cummings in **Between Us Girls**. Also Philip Terry & Wendy Barrie in **Public Enemies**

MONDAY, MAY 29th—3 days
Eddie Bracken and Betty Hutton in
The Miracle of Morgan's Creek
Also Bob Hope and Paulette Goddard in
THE CAT AND THE CANARY

THURS., JUNE 1st—3 days
George Sanders and Brenda Marshall in
The Night is Ending
Also Tyrone Power and Sonja Henie in
LOVELY TO LOOK AT

Continuous Performance Daily 1-45 p.m.   Sunday, One Perf. at 6 p.m.

B.S.M.

Vol. I. No. 3 (New Series)
MAY, 1944.

Editors: LEONARD P. JONES, ERIC C. MILLHOUSE
A.T.S. Editresses   KAY PRICE, MARY GILL.   Treasurer: A. H. APPLETON.
Editorial Board:
DICK WILKINSON, OLLIE PEARCE, DUDLEY TRUIN, RON DENNY (B.W.)

OBITUARY.

We deeply regret to record the tragic death of LANCE-CORPORAL MURIEL FIDOE, A.T.S., at Loughborough Hospital, on April 21st.

Muriel Fidoe will be remembered for her amusing "Before The War" anecdote in last month's issue, as well as for her informative Book Reviews. A staunch supporter of the old B.S.M., she was no less enthusiastic in her efforts for the new one. It is, therefore, with a sense of grateful recognition and remembrance that we publish, on page 16, her last contribution to the magazine.

Her bright and artistic Posters in the Canteen, for this journal, and for many Station events, reflected her sunny disposition. We hope to print an Appreciation of her in our next number. Meanwhile, her colleagues on the Editorial Board extend their deepest sympathy to her sorrowing parents.

SPORTOPICS.

SOCCER—EXILES (Juniors) v. ARMY. In their match against "Manor Army" Exiles Juniors were very unlucky to lose by four goals to nil. The play was, in fact, very even throughout. Two outstanding players for Exiles were Bartlett and Merritt. Harry, in goal, "faced up" to it in both senses, while Merritt's unfailing inaccuracy at back was a source of constant amusement to the spectators. Andy played his usual inspired game, being the mainstay of both defence and attack. The main cause of our defeat was, I think, the very poor finishing by the forwards, who otherwise played a good game.   J.T.H.

Congratulations to 'Andy,' 'Alec' and 'Hobby,'' members of the **Quorn** team which beat the **Brush Car Shop** 4-0 in the final of the Corbin Cup on Easter Monday. A good crowd, including many Woygites, saw a scintillating game which was much more evenly contested than the score suggests. Phillip Arnold, normally a member of the side, was unfortunately prevented from playing owing to injury.   D.J.T.

HOCKEY.—Four of the Exiles' last five matches were played in one week. In summery weather they beat the **Brush (Mixed)** on Sunday, March 26th, after a hard struggle and a very enjoyable game. They were again successful on Monday, 27th, against **College (Mixed)**, but lost on Wednesday, 29th, to the **College "B" (Mixed)** team. This game was spoiled by a continual downpour of rain and an icy wind. On the Saturday, however, they beat **R.A.F. (Men).**

March 26th.		Exiles v. Brush (Mixed)		A	4—2	
,,	27th.	,,	v. College (Mixed)	A	4—2	
,,	29th.	,,	v. College 'B' (Mixed)	A	1—5	
April	1st.	,,	v. R.A.F.	A	5—4	D.C.L.

Next Issue ready: May 26th.   *All contributions to reach the Editors by May 12th.*

THE QUEST

By "Moulin Maison."

AH Joy! Now at last I have found you!
    My desperate searching is o'er.
Yet even before I approach you
    Your shy eyes have dropped to the floor.

And as I draw near you, my nostrils,
    Caressed with your fragrance divine,
Are thrilled by that singular perfume,
    So subtle, and hard to define.

Alas! There are others who seek you,
    You'll ne'er be completely my own.
Your favours are shared by these suitors
    Who patiently wait at your throne.

I knew I would find you here, swimming,
    Disporting yourself in the pool,
But as I come near you emerge, to
    Recline on the side, in the cool.

I'd heard that your skin had been peeling,
    But now it is flawless and tanned,
Still glistening and moist from your bathing,
    As eagerly waiting I stand.

You're just as I've always remembered,
    So graceful and slender—the same!
And now that those few have departed,
    I anxiously whisper your name.

The lady in white, who attends you,
    Nods gravely—my patience must snap!
For hungry desire overwhelms me
    As you struggle into your wrap.

I see that she proffers a bottle
    Of liquor, dark, mellow, and clear
But nothing nor none shall delay me
    Now you, at long last, are so near.

But vanity won't be denied, Dear,
    And *you* will not pander to haste.
No! Powder must first be applied—well,
    You've nothing if you haven't Taste.

And now Dear, at length, you are ready,
    No longer need we postpone,
The lady in white now has left us,
    And just you and I are alone!

Forgive me my trembling, as now, your
    Familiar figure I clutch.
Your form is but scantily covered
    So soft, and so warm to the touch.

I fervently draw you towards me,
    And press you, afire, to my lips,
And so, at long last, I possess you,
    My Own—My two penn'orth of chips!

Social Calendar

Edited by "Ollie" Pearce.

MARCH 21st.—An Op's Hop was given by "C" Watch, No. 7 Wing, at Swithland Hall. "Jock," Brand Hill's boiler man, solved the manpower problem by rounding up the 505th just in time to make the event a great success. Although Sgt. Burton did not consolidate the title of Jitterbug Queen which she won at "D" Watch's brawl (sorry, I mean "Ball") a week or so earlier, some very energetic jiving was witnessed. The Exiles Dance Band compensated for their late arrival by putting in some very useful work, not all of which was confined to music.

MARCH 29th.—Another excellent dance put on by those live-wires of entertainment, Shaker and Jackson, under the auspices of the C.E.C. It was good to see the Exiles Dance Band playing at home once again, and a merry crowd in a gaily decorated Canteen thoroughly enjoyed themselves. We were pleased to see Jimmy Edge there, even though he did snaffle one of the spot prizes. Thanks for a good show. More please!

APRIL 3rd.—Another successful dance was given by "B" Watch, No. 2 Wing, at Garats Hay. Members of the R.A.F., Army, U.S. Army, a sprinkling of civilians, and three small boys in Naval uniform shared a very pleasant evening with the girls.

APRIL 5th.—The C.E.C's usual fortnightly dance was held in the Canteen. There was a good average attendance and the new selection of records greatly contributed to the evening's success. Lighting, or rather the lack of it, was much appreciated during the latter dances. Mr. Jimmy Hunter acted as M.C.

APRIL 12th.—A social evening was given by the Music Club at the "Hurst." The occasion was also a farewell party for Mr. and Mrs. Charles Brown, who were presented, on behalf of the members, with a collection of classical gramophone records. A speech was made by Mr. Harry Dodd, who expressed sorrow at the loss of the founder and mainstay of the club, Mr. C. Brown, who received considerable assistance and encouragement from his wife. Charles and Mrs. Brown made suitable responses, and the meeting closed with the singing of Auld Lang Syne.

APRIL 13th.—At Garats Hay, "D" Watch, No. 2 Wing, proved that a dance *can* be a success without the American Army. A very enjoyable evening was spent by an all-military gathering comprising members of the Signals Staff and the R.A.O.C.

APRIL 14th.—A farewell party was held in the "house" on the occasion of Sgt. Audrey Holland's departure. A good attendance included the O.C., and Major and Mrs. Clifton. Audrey was presented with a small travelling compact, and a pair of kid gloves.

APRIL 19th.—Local counter attractions were probably responsible for the poor attendance at the C.E.C's fortnightly dance, which places the committee in the unique position of having to organise an extra event to dispose of the surplus beer!

Theatre Royal
LOUGHBOROUGH.

PROGRAMME FOR MAY, 1944

THE FRANK H. FORTESQUE

Famous Players

PRESENT

Monday, May 8th (6 days)

THE GREAT THRILLER

Night Must Fall

By Emlyn Williams.

Monday, May 15th (6 days)

Peg O' My Heart

There's nothing half so sweet in Life as Love's Young Dream.

Monday, May 22nd (6 days)

Common Clay

By Leah Corentez.

Monday, May 29th (6 days)

London's Most Successful Comedy

George and Margaret

SHOW PARADE

Edited by Dudley Truin.

One of the few dominant personalities to emerge from wartime Hollywood has been **Orson Welles**. Here is a young man—he is still only twenty-eight—with definite ideas of his own which he has not been afraid to put into effect; controversial effect it must be admitted, but whether you liked his work in "Citizen Kane" and "The Magnificent Ambersons" or not, you could not ignore it, and several eminent directors have not hesitated to copy his methods.

In "JANE EYRE" (Odeon, May 22nd, 6 days) Welles, who plays the part of Rochester, is not the director, but his influence is very apparent. There is the dark photography, whirling mists, and Welles continually seen against the eerie background of his castle with his coat flapping in the wind; in other words a typical Orson Welles production. Theatrical and melodramatic in the extreme, but then, so is Charlotte Bronte's novel. **Joan Fontaine**, who plays the name part, fits into the role perfectly, and together they have made a film which, even at the cost of over emphasis, definitely creates the atmosphere of this Victorian tear-jerker in which women in particular, will revel.

Another film of the same genre is "KINGS ROW" (Victory, May 22nd, 6 days), a sombre but beautifully acted drama of the old Grand Guignol type, which has insanity as its main theme. It has little to relieve its grimness but should be seen for the fine performances given by **Robert Cummings, Ann Sheridan, Charles Coburn, Ronald Reagan** and **Claude Rains**.

For the amateur of swing there is one film that must not be missed this month—it is "STORMY WEATHER" (Empire May 22nd, 3 days). This is an all-negro show covering the last twenty-five years of the coloured folks' contribution to entertainment. With **Bill Robinson** and **Lena Horne** it features such famous exponents of hot music as **Cab Calloway** and the late **Fats Waller** and their bands. There is some superb tap dancing by the **Nicholas Brothers** and a delightful negro ballet in this rhythmic picture, which tells the story of negro music from jazz to jive.

"GENTLEMAN JIM" (Empire, May 8th, 6 days) is a boxing comedy-drama based on the life of James Corbett, played by **Errol Flynn**. There are some good ring sequences showing his fights with John L. Sullivan. This is good, meaty entertainment.

"MILLIONS LIKE US" (Victory, May 1st, 6 days) tells in a human, unpretentious way, of the changes wrought by the war in a typical British working-class family. The acting is very natural; in particular **Moore Marriott**, playing a straight role, scores a personal triumph as the father, and **Eric Portman** is great as a socialist foreman. **Patricia Roc** gives a sensitive performance as the baby of the family, who blossoms under the warmth of a wartime romance only to taste the bitterness of tragedy. Though this film could have done with a little more humour, it is a fine and sincere tribute to the war-workers of Britain.

"CLAUDIA" (Odeon, May 8th, 6 days) is a psychological drama, in which **Dorothy McGuire**, a newcomer to the screen, gives an outstanding performance in a difficult role of a young girl's first year of married life. **Robert Young** is adequate as the perplexed husband.

FAMOUS LAST WORDS.

Well, I will say one thing—this Boiler always lights easily.

MOGGY'S END

A doleful ditty by "Dooke" Downer.

Home Guard Lance-Jack Maurice Reed
    To Whitford's orders paid no heed;
His attitude made sergeants frown,
    He wouldn't keep his bottom down.
Advancing under hostile fire,
    Crouched on his belly in the mire,
Mog's behind would rise on high
    And silhouette against the sky.
And though his Section Leader swore,
    He only stuck it up the more;
Until one sad and fateful day
    The wretched thing was shot away,
And being the only one he had,
    It proved a sore loss to the lad.
He gazed upon his shattered rear,
    His countenance became most drear
When through his mind the sad thought flit,
    Without that part he could not sit.
So with a lump of plasticine,
    With stripes of yellow, red and green
He made himself seem more complete
    (But had to keep away from heat)
And though with whalebone pants it's draped
    His rear each night must be re-shaped.
But there's one thing for which Mog's pleased;
    The tension in the corps has eased;
For when he showed his seat to Sarge
    He won a prize for camouflage!

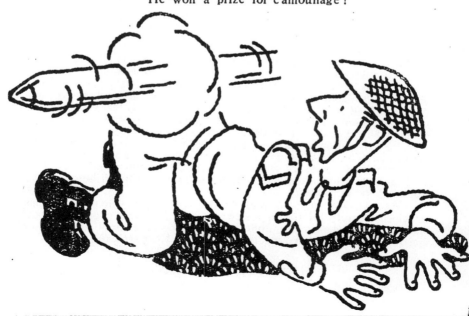

"Night Bomber"

By NOEL ROYLE.

UPWARD, upward, across the dark bosom of the night;
    Macabre voyager thro' unknown realms of frozen void;
Sullen engines chant their evil largo;
Endless and inevitable, ceaseless and insatiable.

High-winging o'er the sleeping cities of the West,
Across the Nordic seas' wind-scattered brine:
Within thy monstrous belly, closely lying,
Transport'st thou death, implacable and all-resisting.

And now at last, whilst tortured Earth replies,
And human ants in terror refuge seek,
Thou vomit'st forth thy shining brood of hell:
To make high sacrilege on noble towers and paupers' homes.

Thus having thy dread cargo freed,
And chaos made where once lay ordered life;
Before approaching heralds of the dawn thou fliest
And searchest out once more thy secret lair.

◎ ◎ ◎ ◎ ◎

CORRESPONDENCE.

The Editor, B.S.M.
April 4th, 1944.

    I am writing this letter in the form of criticism of Snoops Corner and Sweet Fanny Adams, whoever they may be. I think the past two magazines have been quite good reading and calls for congratulations on the part of all concerned. Nevertheless I personally, and I know a large proportion of the A.T.S. object to part of some of the issues that have appeared in the past. I am not trying to make any excuse for my own name appearing in one of these columns; I am prepared to accept what was said, although the facts are not correct. What most folks object to, is the use of names of people working at Beaumanor. I am no saint myself and everyone of us has some weakness of which we are well aware, but do not wish the whole of the personnel, or the residents of Woodhouse to know about it. Some of us have the responsibility of training A.T.S. girls for a job which we believe is greatly helping to win this war, and we do not want these girls at one anothers throats all the time. Surely the type of humour that should be printed is that which will build up the moral of these girls and give them something that will encourage them in their work, something they will really laugh about and not the sort of stuff that will cause disruption between them. I think their job is quite a difficult one and we should all appreciate the service they are giving in an effort to get this war over as soon as possible. I trust you will print this letter, and I am quite prepared to take any kicks that may come.

Yours faithfully,
J. ROGERS.

    Jimmy Rogers, Voice Of The ATS, puts us right on the spot! Girls! Can you find time to tear yourself away from each other's throats to let us know what YOU think?

SNOOP'S CORNER

CONGRATULATIONS to Mr. and Mrs. Ted Beckwith on the arrival of a son, Peter, born March 12th. To Mr. and Mrs. Harold Sweeten, whose daughter was born on April 8th (and he told us *he* was ill!) At the time of going to press, the proud parents have not decided upon a name. To Dudley and Christabel Truin on the birth of a son, John Dudley, on April 12th. To Mr. and Mrs. Reedman on the arrival of another son, Paul Graham, on April 18th. "Slap" made a splendid recovery and was back at work only two days after the event!

On hearing that Cpl. Ellen Smith, of "D" Watch, No. 1 Wing, had a child I did some high pressure snooping and learnt that she is due for congratulations on her engagement to Ldg. Torpedoeman Ernest Child, of H.M.S. Chaser. It just goes to show how these things get distorted.

On the evening of April 19th Pte. Mavis ("Tich") Warren went to the canteen for her break. She apparently got it, as she came back wearing an engagement ring which had been purchased that afternoon by Ken ("Ginger") Talbot. It is significant that "A" Watch No. 7 Wing, seems to be the only Watch opposing the suggested boycotting of the canteen by the A.T.S.

Further congratulations are due to Pte. Peggy Wilding of the T.P. Staff, on her engagement to Cpl. Paul England, of the R.A.S.C., at present serving in N. Africa. To Pte. Rose Barlow, runner, on her engagement to Jack Bowman, of the R.A.O.C. To Pte. Helen Brown, of "B" Watch No. 1 Wing, who, I hear is taking steps to cement our relations with the U.S.A. Rumour has it that Pte. Pat Price has already taken steps in this direction, but she won't talk.

At a secret conference between Pte. Muriel Furniss and Bill Ghent it was decided to do something about his income tax returns as from July 1st.

Well, so far I have managed to survive all those threats of physical violence, etc., including the one by the ambitious young "gentleman" who told me he would like to slit my throat; he also used an adjective which would be much more appropriate after the event!

I have a letter in front of me from "Ten Port Terrie" Aiken, who says she is "Prepared to challenge my misinformed reporter, pint for pint, or glass for glass, at any convenient date if he/she will establish his/her identity." Well Terrie, as he has just become engaged, and has no doubt promised not to make a beast of himself any more I think you've had it, but if you are proud of your reputation, and honour must be satisfied, I am quite willing to deputize *and* pay for all the beer you drink, if you are prepared to return the compliment.

Another letter, which appears on a separate page of this issue, is written by a "gentleman" who shares the misguided impression that I am responsible for "Sweet Fanny Adams." As I always sign my contributions it seems that he reads just about as badly as he writes. However, I would like to point out that everything I write in this column has its foundation in fact, and any details which I consider too intimate are omitted, as they were in the case in question It is not clear whether his concern is for the morale or morals of the girls, but I can assure him that I would not do anything which might be detrimental to either.

Our best wishes go with the P.O. personnel who left us on 17th April, and also with Mr. Harry Appleton, who left us on March 24th. Harry has been a virile member of the Staff Club Committee for the past year, and was also chairman of the C.E.C. He has been succeeded in this latter office by his namesake, Mr. A. H. Appleton, our esteemed treasurer. We are also indebted to Harry for his generosity in putting up the first prize in the Short Story Competition.

This month we also say goodbye to Sgt. Joan Cook and C.S.M. Denne.

I must apologise for any inconvenience I may have caused the Somerset papers, but since our last issue we have welcomed back our premiere danseuse "AUXILARYILARY" L/C. Netta Lees has reverted to Pte. at her own request, so that she can pay more attention to her home duties. Mrs. Reeves is now C.S.M.

I am pleased to be able to announce that "Gerry" Dalton is on his feet again and will probably be back at work by the time this issue appears.

Henry Lewis is back on the job after seven weeks absence. We were wondering what Eisenhower had been waiting for!

We would like to know why it was necessary for L/Cpl. Snell (H.G.) to write to an A.T.S. corporal asking for the return of his trousers! Probably the result of a "pressing situation."

We read in the "Echo" that Peter Gardner was fined £3 for absenting himself from Home Guard duty. With the threat of a German invasion imminent it is foolish of him not to avail himself of the splendid facilities offered by our Home Guard Unit. Training includes searching the football pitch for lost petrol lighters, marking A.T.S. test papers, and many other useful jobs which *might* assist in the defence of our island.

Mr. R. G. Denny paid us a visit recently. Rustication does not seem to have affected his capacity for philandering.

With the growth of the new building speculation is rife as to who is going to "L" in the near future.

It seems that the subaltern who was so interested in our treasurer is intrigued by the voices of our male supervisors, especially the one possessed by a bachelor who is renowned for his bank roll. It certainly looks as though the B.S.M. funds are in a poor state!

Perhaps Pte Dorothy Sharman can tell us why "Geff" Nicol, non-smoking member of the fast crumbling "Bull Ring," now accepts proffered cigarettes and unconsumed sundries left over by his pals at break time.

Our recent Board meeting was brought to a premature conclusion to enable "Deadly" Truin to accompany Kay Price to the theatre. It is of course essential (or is it?) to have the views of both sexes when compiling a criticism.

That's all for now. Cheerio,

OLLIE.

GUINEA-TALES.

Eighteen entries were received for this Contest, including only three from the feminine element of the Station. The general standard of the stories was not considered to be as high as it might have been, many of the plots being rather hackneyed. Adjudication was carried out by eight members of the Editorial Board, from a standpoint of general appeal. Voting was on a "points" system, this being considered the fairest means, since it ensured that any story which failed to win a "first" vote from any individual judge nevertheless remained in the running. Conversely, a story which obtained say, only two votes, but both "firsts," could not carry off the first prize before another with a substantial number of "places."

We publish below the story which wins the ONE GUINEA. Runners-up are: N. Royle (10/6) and M. Reed (5/-). Also worthy of special mention are the stories by R. Downer, W. J. Gilliard ("Whose Hose"—two stories submitted) and F. Vickers.

Matter for Reflection
By J. Colville.

HE stood shaking his fist at the red rear light dwindling in the distance. With his remaining wind he withered the air around, as he cursed the unfortunate driver, the countryside, and the bad luck which had left him in this predicament.

Lack of breath ended the tirade. He leaned, gasping, against a nearby pillar, pulled out a handkerchief to mop his damp brow, and used a finger to ease the limp collar from his rather bulbous neck.

He reflected: A well fed fifty and a greyhound sprint for the last bus never mix well. Why had he left the comfortable, well ordered life of the town and come to live in this God-forsaken, rural emptiness! It was self-condemnation, because he knew the answer— his wife! She had arranged it all. He had been a fool to let her persuade him to retire to the charming but lonely villa they now occupied, miles from anywhere. He had put up a half-hearted opposition, but she was one of those apparently simple-minded women who have a baffling habit of getting their own way.

This trend of events had now culminated in his being stranded in this small village (his adjective was more pungent) with the dismal prospect of a six mile trek to home and supper. He sighed resignation. "Well," he thought, as he buttoned his coat against the chill night air, "no hope of any transport—might as well get moving."

He squared his shoulders and set off at the fast pace which characterises motorist turned foot slogger, but he had one trait in common with the regular night rambler—he walked in the centre of the road.

It was a night of dim moonlight and fast moving clouds. Half lights and shadows covered the road and clothed the bare hedgerows, and as he walked, his anger subsided. It might have been worse— raining, for example. His spirits rose a bit. He mused on: "Damn! I'm tired. Must have at least three more miles to go yet!"

Too preoccupied, he never saw the black, fast moving car. Neither did its driver see him until it was too late.

He opened his eyes; a wall loomed in front. He blinked; no, it was the kerbstone. "What the devil!"—then he remembered. "Must have been knocked out—those ..... road hogs who don't stop!" Gingerly he felt himself. He seemed all right. He levered himself upright, stamped his legs, and flailed his arms. He *was* all right. Lady Luck had smiled on him. His watch said he had been lying there for an hour.

He brushed down his coat, then continued his journey, now imbued with a deep regard for his personal safety. At last! The house was in sight. Friendly lights twinkled from two windows.

He drew level with the gate, pushed it open and entered the front yard. The big airedale never stirred. It lay near its kennel, gnawing at a bone, and he passed within a few feet of it. "Must get rid of it; no use as a watch dog," he muttered, as he strode up to the front door. Using his latch key he entered the hall, which was in darkness, but a light was showing in the living room. Good! His wife was waiting up for him. Shedding his coat, he entered.

The supper table was set, and a bright fire burned in the tiled hearth. His wife sat knitting in a low fireside chair. She gave no greeting. "Must be in the sulks," he thought, as he eased himself into an opposite chair.

Without preamble he launched into the account of his misfortunes. He finished and sat back awaiting her comments. She still did not speak. This was really too much! He opened his mouth to protest, but the strident ring of the telephone in the hall forestalled him. His wife, throwing aside her knitting as she rose, rushed to answer.

He listened. "Yes," said his wife. A few seconds elapsed, then she moaned as one in anguish. He sprang to his feet, hurried to the hall, but stopped in the doorway.

They stood in front of the big, full length floor mirror, the housemaid supporting his wife. By the light of the amber coloured ceiling fitting, she looked drawn and distracted. He caught the words "Your master is dead ... road accident ... died in Ambulance.". He thought: "Well, it's not All Fools' Day, and a joke's a joke, but this business must stop at once." He crossed over beside the two women.

Prepared to speak his mind, he took a deep breath— Wait a moment, there was something odd here, or were his eyes deceiving him? He looked again, and stood transfixed—his eyes had *not* deceived him. Awful realization flooded his mind. Of the three figures standing before the mirror only two had REFLECTIONS in it—and mirrors never lie!

Owing to the unfortunate disability of the author, "A History of Beaumanor" is not yet to hand. We hope to publish the first instalment next month.

The Gospel according to St. Apid

Chapter XXXI.

(Translated from the English by Disciple Millhouse).

NOW when Red Tabz, who dwelleth in Wyt Awl, discovered the Promised Land, and delivered his peoples out of the bondage of Chiksanz and the Glammaboiz, he built a number of temples there.

And when all the Tribe were come up, with their pencils and their rubbers, Red Tabz was cast down, and sore dismayed, crying: Woe is me. For behold; the numbers of my people sufficeth not to fill my temples.

Wherefore he sent a messenger in great haste to Piemjee, chief over the Peo tribe, saying: Deliver into my hands, I beseech thee, a number of thy people, that my temples may be filled to overflowing, yea, even to double-banking.

And Piemjee sought out a number of Suckers, and gave them the Dope about the Promised Land flowing with beer and skittles. And many of them straightway Fell for It, and journeyed up into Woygland, with their pencils, and their rubbers, and their Overtime parchments.

And it is written, they were a wild and fearless people. But when they were delivered into the hands of Tubi and his disciples they were become tamed, and like even unto Ewa's. And they tarried long days in the land, and consumed a multitude of overtime parchments.

Then it came to pass that Red Tabz conceived his Bright Idea. that there might be handmaidens for all the Ewa's, and he brought up his great tribe of Atsites into the land. And the Atsites grew and multiplied, until there was lipstick upon all the goblets of Kantin.

Wherefore Red Tabz perceived that the number of his peoples was exceeding great, and he knew that he must banish some from out of the land of Woyg. And he reasoned with the Elders of Wyt Awl in this wise, saying: Whom shall I Turf Out of It? For how canst I send forth my Ewa's, which are called Hard Core, for do not I sting them three shekels a week for the Chariot of Barkus? And they answered him saying: The Peoites, whom thou canst not Sting, must be the chosen people.

And he communed with the Peoites, saying: Get a load of this; there is a Green Hill far away, a full Sabbath day's journey from hence, where the sun ever shines, and none ever calleth another Me Doock. Ye, I have chosen to be volunteers to go forth into the land of Bedublyu. Get thou bouncing.

And forgetting to hearken whether they answered him Yea, or Nay, he straightway dispatched a body of missionaries to the Green Hill, that they might prepare a place for their brethren.

Thus it came to pass, when the Feast of the Pullover was nigh unto a close, and the Optimists of Woygland searched in their diary tablets to know upon which day Summer was due, the last of the great Peo Tribe sang a Peoites Farewell to Woygland, and departed along the Iron Road, upon their pilgrimage.

And they found the rivers of Bedublyu flowing with an abundance of Womp, and the land rich with mushrooms. Yea verily, for ere many days, fungus grew even upon the face of Deni, and the mighty thirst of the Vicar diminished.

Now a great silence descended upon Woygland, and upon the temple of Aych. For no more was the voice of Sandi, the keyman, heard, crying in the wilderness: Hast thou got him?

CALLING ALL

IT'S just the tiniest bit disappointing. The ATS Section of this magazine has made two appearances, and after this month, those of you who only took out three-month subscriptions will have to start fishing in your pockets again if you want to continue as subscribers, and believe it or not, we have not had ONE SINGLE CRITICISM, unfavourable or otherwise, sent in to guide us as to your tastes, and opinions of our efforts. So there is only one thing to do. We take it that your silence means that you have no particularly withering fault to find, or encouraging praise to bestow, and therefore we shall continue in future along the same lines as we do now.

Although there has been a fairly good response to our cry for contributions, there is still plenty of room for more—particularly for those of the "Before the War" type. But we welcome any kind. We also hope that some of you have entered for the Short Story Competition advertised last month, and that at least one member of the A.T.S. will be a lucky winner. Good luck, anyway. Cheerio!

BEFORE THE WAR.

"I TOURED WITH ENSA."

(she must mean before HER War! Ed.)

DURING this War, ENSA—entertainments department of NAAFI—has grown into a considerably large body. They have taken over the notorious Drury Lane Theatre, and it is there that all the shows are produced and rehearsed.

I was dancing in a musical revue. There were about 20 people in the company, and we were scheduled to play all the larger R.A.F. Stations in the North. This was in 1940-1 during London's Blitz, when owing to the closing of the theatres many first-rate artistes joined ENSA. Nowadays all the shows are not up to their one-time standard.

Every show follows a recognized route. The company stay for a week or two at each town, and travel nightly, in a coach to the surrounding camps. We had an interesting time. The scenery was always different. We drove all over the isolated moors, playing to the lone Bomber stations, and by contrast along the Banks of the industrial Clyde, where we gave shows for the Navy.

In a few places there were hostels run by NAAFI for us to stay at, but mostly we lived in "digs" and hotels. If there was a Garrison theatre we performed there, but it is only the Army camps that boast these luxuries. Mostly we worked under tremendous difficulties, dancing in icy hangars, or on tiny stages. Coming straight from the comfort of London theatres, the dressing room accommodation was appalling—small and truly "camp."

Occasionally hitches occurred. I remember one instance when some Hospital boys were coming over to see the show, and neither costumes nor make-up had arrived. We could not disappoint them, so we did the first half in "civvies" and the second in costumes, but still no make-up!

But the appreciation of our audiences made up for all the hard work. They showed their gratitude by inviting us back to parties in the Officers' or Sergeants' Mess. Once some Naval officers took us back to their ship, and we had a wonderful time. Like this we met crowds of interesting people of all nationalities. We talked to Bomber crews, when they came into the Mess for their last few minutes before going out on operations, and as we left, we would watch the bombers taking off, and it gave one a feeling inside that I shall never forget.

Touring with ENSA is very different from playing in a West-end show, but it was an exciting experience, and I only wish that I could have gone abroad with them instead of being called up into the Army. However, it is bad policy not to finish a job, so I must use all my energy for the work in hand. When this war is over I sincerely hope to be able to resume my career as a dancer. In the meantime I can pleasureably look back on the now amusing "incidents" and eventful times I had with ENSA.   "Y.B."

GOOD READING
By Muriel Fidoe.

HAVE you heard this one?
> When the Fuehrer comes to meet his fate
> He'll ride in a fiery chariot,
> And sit in state on a red-hot plate
> With the devil and Judas Iscariot.

That, for twenty centuries, has been the popular opinion of Judas Iscariot. Eric Linklater, in his book **"Judas,"** interprets him as a highly-strung, somewhat hysterical young man, who is persuaded, because he wants to be persuaded, that by handing over Christ to the political authorities, he will save the country from revolution. He sees himself as the new Saviour of the people, and Jesus of Nazareth as a man who goes a little too far. You will be interested in seeing Mary Magdalene without the saintly hood and expression with which tradition endows her.

Henry Williamson has written four novels which tell the story of Willie Maddison, from his extreme youth—"**Dandelion Days**"—to his tragic death in "**The Pathway.**" His schooldays are told in "**The Flax of a Dream**" and the other book, "**The Dream of Fair Women,**" speaks for itself. Willie (frightful name) who is drawn from life, is somewhat unhealthy, both physically and morally, and is a bit of a liar too. That doesn't prevent him from being interesting, however, and I think you will really like these books which are full of that breath of the countryside for which Henry Williamson is so famous. Against this typical background is our hero, with his passion for two women. It is not necessary to read these books in order, although of course, it is better.

Do you suffer from the type of browned-offness when you ask yourself why you were born, why men fight wars, and whether it's all worth it? You brood gloomily on the universe, and reflect bitterly that if there's a heaven, it's probably a place where Archangels are a specie of divine N.C.O., and minor angels are detailed eternally to scrub the celestial steps. If you get in this mood, or even if you don't, James Dunne is the man for you. He has written a vitally interesting book called "**An Experiment with Time,**" which is very well worth while attempting to digest. His theory of Time has received wide notice in scientific circles, and is satisfying in that it provides sound suggestions for the reasons of Birth, Progress, Death, Life after Death, and the existence of an Omnipotent. This is in the Q Book series, price 2/-.

A light, entertaining book is "**Serena Blandish**," by A Lady of Quality. This is the story of Serena's adventures on the marriage market of the eighteenth century. You can get this from Sketchley's, price 4/6. The Williamson and Linklater are both in Loughborough Library.

VOCATION— *By MARY GILL*

THEY probed into my intellect
  For any blemish or defect,
They found that my ears were good,
And that my glands did all they should,
And that my mind was very nice,
And that my head was free from lice.

They said that I would do, and then
They sent me back to school again.
Each day with vigour on a key
They pounded endless morse at me.
Procedure signals poured like rain
Into my parched and barren brain.
They kindly tried to show to me
The precepts of 'lectricity.

They told me it was common sense
That a condenser should condense,
And that two protons never mate,
And that a valve should oscillate.
They gave me many demonstrations
To show the ether's undulations.

And when my brain would hold no more
They sent me out to win the war.

All this, and more, they did to me,
That I might skilled and practised be,
In writing, with efficiency,
NIL AUDIBLE ACTIVITY.

GET YOUR———

Beauty and Toilet Preparations

FROM

"LEONARD'S"

Gentlemen's Hairdresser

25, CHURCH GATE, LOUGHBOROUGH

Large Variety in Stock!

The Passing of Old Joe

By "SCORPIO."

IT was a fine summer evening in the year 2,000 A.D., and from the village green could be heard the glad cries of the children, as the Automatic Guardian from the Local National Incubator Centre summoned them indoors for their supper-pill of Concentrated Vitamin Values.

But Old Joe heeded them not. He lay inert in his welded bed, covered by Synthetic Blankets, his wasted frame shuddering with the tremors of utter dotage, in its Plastic-weave Pyjamas. And indeed, why should he heed them? He was an old, old man, and as he lay there a-dying, visions of his youth passed through his doddering memory.

As if out of a mist returned to him the strident jangle of an alarm clock, and his feeble limbs twitched a little as in retrospect he stumbled forth and, unwashed, unshaven, and clad in leather-bound tweed and baggy corduroy, took his place among the bilious, surly rabble in a noisy bus.... They would laugh at such vehicles nowadays, when all you had to do to travel from one place to another was to sit in your Specially Constructed Travel-easy, and press the button operating the appropriate ray.

But memories of the past crowded present facts from his swimming head. He saw a stately old building, but in the grey, chilly morning he failed to appreciate its charm, and he passed by a glass-house-looking place, wherein the sordid crumbs of every Break during the night were being slowly mopped up by the sluttish cloths of the languid Harpies who condescendingly presided therein, and at last, after much flabby-footed stumbling, he reached the unshapely brick pile where he worked, whence emanated a curious humming and buzzing—just like a giant bee-hive.

And in he went, pausing on the threshold, knocked back by the foetid, night-ridden atmosphere that enveloped him—a mixture of hot, weary humanity and dust, and the lingering aroma of a foul pipe, incinerating old rope.

But he staggered in, picking his way uncertainly through the ankle-deep lava of fag-ends and pencil sharpenings that littered the floor, till he reached his appointed place, where an individual, similarly clad, but even frowsier than himself, greeted him with the opening of one bleary eye, and the words, "Not a dam' thing all night!" So he sat down, and adopted the Weary One's head harness, and let him depart. And just as he said, there was nothing— only a lot of crackling and howls....

He gave a long, yearning sigh, and then his memories were broken by the entrance of his little great-grandson, wearing a Fibrose Youth Tunic, and blowing vigorously on his Juvenile Respiration Developer, which was not so very unlike the Penny-whistle of his own childhood days. The shrill, squalling note brought back a recollection stronger than all the others....

"Blow like this," he commanded weakly, and his emaciated fingers feebly beat an odd, irregular tattoo on the coverlet. Interested, the child soon took up the unfamiliar rhythm.... Old Joe listened in enraptured silence, as if to some heavenly strain of music. Then ....

"Vics!" he murmured. And died happy.

This Month's Beauty Hint.
By MARGARET DUNN.

"Head's win!"—or do they? Before your next hair-do, ask yourself: "Is my hair my crowning glory?" It should be, you know, but nine times out of ten the answer is "No."

With so little time to spend on our "Hair-care" I think you will agree that it is infinitely better to have the hair the regulation two inches above the collar. If your hair is inclined to be rather straight and unmanageable, have a perm. Make your appointment early, and know beforehand exactly what you want—how much you want cut off, where you would like it shorter, how you want it set, etc.—and make sure you get it!

Most important is the tapering, which, apart from making it curl easier, also ensures a tight, lasting curl. Having had the "unpleasant operation" performed, look after it. Before getting into bed, brush your hair briskly, then screw up the ends into pin-curls, winding the tips round the first finger and continuing the winding down to the roots. If the perm is too curly, put some brilliantine on before brushing. Not all of us are fortunate enough to have a weekly hair-do, but if you do have difficulty having it set at camp, make a regular appointment with your hairdresser regularly every three weeks.

Dandruff—the bugbear of us ATS—is something that little can be done about, but some Borax dissolved in the rinsing water does improve this condition. Another little tip (particularly for red-heads) is to massage a little Dettol into the scalp—you'll be surprised at the results.

If you bleach, I do hope you are really sensible and use "Hiltone"—you can have your hair permed afterwards quite successfully.

I don't think I need say anything about hair-styles, but if you are feeling browned-off sometime, try experimenting with a new hair-do and a change of make-up. It does put a "new face" on things, and makes you feel good, too!

The Digby Chronicles

SUSAN has reached the stage where she is beginning to lose her milk-teeth. It started at breakfast the other morning when she was gnawing on a buttered crust. Suddenly, round-eyed, she laid the half-eaten crust aside, and explored stealthily with her tongue. Then—

"Mummy, one of my teeth has come loose."

"Well, don't worry, dear. Everyone loses their teeth when they're seven or so, and then they grow new ones—lovely and strong"

Judy, golluping busily at her milk, giggles liquidly and has to be dried.

"And what," enquires Daddy coldly from behind his newspaper, "just what was that disgusting noise for, Judy?"

Judy's smile in his direction would melt the heart of an ogre—and Steve is no ogre.

"I was thinking," she remarked in tones of penetrating sweetness, "wouldn't Susan look funny if the new teeth didn't grow, and she had to look like Mrs. Buckett all her life!"

(Mrs. Buckett is the good soul who "obliges." As we do not want her to take umbrage and leave, we hasten to suppress Judy).

Then Susan said, "Daddy, will you give me sixpence when my tooth comes right out?"

Steve snorted. "Sixpence—whatever for?"

"Well," pursued Susan (it's wonderful how the children fail to be intimidated by that abrupt manner of his), "well, Jean Dane-at-school's father gave her five shillings when she had her tonsils out—so I thought a tooth would be worth sixpence, at least?"

"We'll see," said Steve darkly. "But you'll have to be very brave."

That was three days ago. Since then, the tooth has grown looser and looser, and Susan's reluctance to have it out has grown in direct proportion.

"It won't hurt you any more than a little pin-prick, darling, honestly it won't," I tell her encouragingly. "Look, we'll put a thread round it and give it one little tweak—you can do it yourself if you'd rather."

"No, Mummy," declares Susan vehemently. "It's not really ready yet."

"Of course it's ready, darling. If you don't have it out before you go to bed, you'll swallow it in your sleep."

"No Mummy. Not yet."

"You're 'fraid," says Judy temptingly.

"'m not." S'there!"

"'Fraid, 'fraid! Susan's 'fraid!" crows Judy. "Gilly! Susan's 'fraid."

"'m NOT 'fraid," bawls Susan, rising to the bait.

Judy's reply is to poke the tip of her tongue out and screw up her face knowingly. With a hoot of indignation Susan launches herself towards her. The scuffle that ensues has barely begun when Susan stops short, her hand clapped to her mouth. On the floor, between the combatants, lies a small, gleaming, pearly thing—the tooth.

"Oh," cries Susan, almost disappointed. "It's OUT!" Then another thought seems to strike her, and with a charming, gory smile, she cradles the tooth in her hand, and fixes her eye hypnotically on my handbag.

"Bedtime, Judy," I say. And as she leaves the room I beckon to Susan and reach for my purse——

K.L.B.P.

VICTORY
BIGGIN STREET, LOUGHBOROUGH

MONDAY, MAY 1st—6 days.
   Eric Portman and Patricia Roc in
   "MILLIONS LIKE US"
   also Musical, Interest and News Films.

MONDAY, MAY 8th—3 days.
   Ronald Colman in
   "CLIVE OF INDIA"
   also Bruce Bennett in "Underground Agent"

THURSDAY, MAY 11th—3 days.
   David Niven in
   "DINNER AT THE RITZ"
   also East Side Kids in "Ghosts in the Night"

MONDAY, MAY 15th—6 days.
   George Murphy & Alan Hale in Irvin Berlin's
   "THIS IS THE ARMY"
   (in Technicolor) also **Full Supporting Programme**

MONDAY, MAY 22nd—6 days.
   Ann Sheridan and Ronald Reagan in
   "KINGS ROW"
   also "Rear Gunner"

WHIT MONDAY, May 29th—3 days.
   Richard Herne and Judy Kelly in
   "BUTLER'S DILEMMA"
   also Esther Dale in "Swing your Partner"

THURSDAY, JUNE 1st—3 days.
   Charles Chaplin in
   "CHAPLIN FESTIVAL"
   also John Litel in Boss of Big Town & March of Time No. 9

Mon. to Fri.—Con. from 5-30 p.m. Sat.—Con. from 2 p.m.
MATINEES.—Mon. and Wed. at 2-15 p.m.
SUNDAYS—6-15 p.m. (One Show)

Sweet FANNY ADAMS replies

Dear Friends,

If you wish to use a nom-de-plume when you write to me, make sure that the one you choose isn't somebody else's real name!

WORRIED NICE GIRL. I'm afraid your mother is a little narrow-minded. Accepting silk stockings from a *sailor* is no less respectable than receiving, say, a book, from a non-seafaring boy. Send me two coupons to ease your conscience, and take the stockings.

BEAUTY BASHFUL "K." I think your Rugby-playing boyfriend must have had a very good reason for falling on his tummy when, with three minutes to go, and only the full-back to beat, his shorts were ripped off. Perhaps he is self-conscious about a birthmark on his tummy?

BILIOUS & Co. I am sorry to hear about the two goats, but the matter isn't as serious as you seem to imagine. If the plus-foured one starts to croon " Pistol Packin' Momma," or demonstrates a Natural Spin Turn, add more Soda. At the first manifestation of pink elephants with pop-guns, sign the pledge and report to C.R.S. Keep me informed, Dears.

TERRIFIED is in "orful truble"—which might be orfuller if I printed her Basic English letter! Anyway, why *should* you tell your mother, "Terrified"? I gather she hasn't told *you* very much.

INJURED INNOCENCE.—A tooth broken on a canteen roll is *not* covered by the Workmen's Compensation Act.

SCORNED LOVER. I don't think becoming an "Airborne Babe" will have the desired effect on the Woygland Officer you secretly cherish. Find out discreetly who is his favourite film actress, and imitate her. If it turns out to be Dorothy Lamour, don't wear the sarong on duty. Should it be Minnie Mouse, write me again.

JIMMY ROGERS. If you have a particular letter in mind, and can prove you have a *bona fide* interest in the matter, I'll arrange with the Editor for you to see that such a letter was, in fact, received

NOBBY. See above.

GINGER. She was perfectly justified in "sloshing" you, as you so exquisitely put it.

M.J.W.E. No.

KATHLEEN. As you are so ideally matched in height, I think it is beastly of the other girl to interfere.

MYRTLE. Not alone, in such a deserted spot, Dear.

THRILLED. I will see what I can find out about the nice boy in the blue lumber-jacket, and let you know.

SWEET FANNY ADAMS

THE MUSIC CLUB

We are coming to the end of our third and most successful season. We have become quite proficient at part-singing (even though many of us would probably still maintain individually that we can't sing!). At Christmas the Choir gave a Carol Recital in Quorn Methodist Chapel, and we were led to believe, by remarks made to us afterwards and by a note in the local newspaper, that our performance was appreciated and enjoyed.

The weekly gramophone recitals have included some interesting and varied programmes; here are a few of the items played: Elgar's "Serenade for Strings," Tchaikowsky's 5th, and Mozart's 39th, symphonies, and "The Carnival of Animals," by Saint-Saens.

Grateful thanks are due to the O.C. and Officers of No. 1 "Y" Wing for the excellent facilities with which they have so kindly provided us at the "Hurst" for our weekly meetings.

At the Party on April 12th (of which a note appears elsewhere in this issue) we bade farewell to Charles and Mary Brown, George Money and Jock Smyth, four original members whose enthusiasm and help have contributed so much to the success of the Club.

We shall shortly be suspending our regular Wednesday meetings at the "Hurst" (to be resumed, circumstances permitting, in the autumn) in favour of an activity which proved so enjoyable last summer—our Wednesday rambles. Watch the Canteen notice board for particulars.

We extend to all BMR staff interested in music an invitation to join the Club. We believe that our activities will help to keep you in touch with good music during these somewhat difficult times. The rambles should provide a good opportunity to join us.

Bookseller and Stationer :: Lending Library

J. SKETCHLEY

24 & 25, High Street, Loughborough

Telephone 2980.

TAILORING FOR THE SERVICES
— from —

| START TO FINISH | 8, BAXTER GATE LOUGHBOROUGH. | TOP TO BOTTOM |

The London Tailoring Co.

Est. 1899.   'Phone 2794.

EMPIRE
MARKET PLACE, LOUGHBOROUGH

MONDAY, MAY 1st—3 days.
 Ann Sothern in "Girl in Overalls"
  also Phillip Dorn in "The Fighting Guerillas"

THURSDAY, MAY 4th—3 days.
 Sabu in "Elephant Boy"
  also Jane Withers in "Johnny Doughboy"

MONDAY, MAY 8th—6 days.
 Errol Flynn in "Gentleman Jim"
  also Full Supporting Programme

MONDAY, MAY 15th—3 days.
 David Farrar and Ann Crawford in
  "Night Invader"
  also Roy Rogers in "Sunset in the Desert"

THURSDAY, MAY 18th—3 days.
 Gordon Harker in "Warn that Man"
  also William Henry in "Sarong Girl"

MONDAY, MAY 22nd—3 days.
 Bill Robinson and Fats Waller in
  "Stormy Weather"
  also Warner Baxter in "Crime Doctor"

THURSDAY, MAY 25th—3 days.
 Flanagan & Allen in "Theatre Royal"
  also Barton McLane in "A Gentle Gangster"

WHIT MONDAY, MAY 29th—3 days.
 East Side Kids in "Clancy St. Boys"
  also Raymond Walburn in 'The Man in the Trunk'

THURSDAY, JUNE 1st—3 days.
 Pat O'Brien & Randolph Scott in '**Bombardier**'
  also Charles Starrett in "Next in Line"

**CONTINUOUS DAILY. Doors open at 1-30 p.m.
SUNDAYS at 5-30 p.m.**

Printed by Toppings Ltd., 17, Southfield Rd., Lough
for Beaumanor Staff M

JUNE, 1944

VOL. I. No. 4 (NEW SERIES) - **6d.**

YOUR FILM ATTRACTIONS for JUNE

SHOWING AT THE ODEON THEATRE

Sunday, June 4th—Basil Rathbone and Nigel Bruce in **Sherlock Holmes in Washington**. Also Will Hay in **Old Bones of the River**.

MONDAY, JUNE 5th, and all the week:
Nelson Eddy, Susanna Foster and Claude Rains in
The Screen's "Classic" of Terror

PHANTOM OF THE OPERA
in Technicolor

Sunday, June 11th—Walter Brennan and Anne Baxter in **The Man Who Came Back**. Also Sidney Toler in **Castle in the Desert**.

MONDAY, JUNE 12th, and all the week:
James Cagney
in his greatest of films

JOHNNY VAGABOND
with Grace George and Marjorie Main

Sunday, June 18th—Ginger Rogers and George Montgomery in **Roxie Hart**. Also Roddy McDowall in **On The Sunny Side**.

MONDAY, JUNE 19th—3 days
Leni Lynn & Will Fyffe in

Heaven is Round the Corner

Also William Boyd & Andy Clyde in

UNDER COVER MAN

THURS., JUNE 22nd—3 days
Louise Rainer & Paul Lukas in

HOSTAGES

Also Bing Crosby & Franciska Gaal in

PARIS HONEYMOON

Sunday, June 25th—Marlene Dietrich and Randolph Scott in **Pittsburg**. Also Robert Paige in **Hi! Buddy**.

MONDAY, JUNE 26th, and all the week:
Alice Faye—Carmen Miranda—James Ellison in
The Day's Musical Comedy

THE GIRLS HE LEFT BEHIND
in Technicolor

Continuous Performance Daily 1-45 p.m.   Sunday, One Performance at 6 p.m.

B.S.M.
Vol. I. No. 4 (New Series)
JUNE, 1944.

Editors: LEONARD P. JONES, ERIC C. MILLHOUSE
A.T.S. Editresses: KAY PRICE, MARY GILL. Treasurer: A. H. APPLETON.
Editorial Board:
DICK WILKINSON, OLLIE PEARCE, DUDLEY TRUIN, RON DENNY (B.W.)

An *APPRECIATION* of
MURIEL FIDOE.

All at Beaumanor will miss Muriel. She was so complex a girl that the little I can say will only conjure up the smallest vision of her.

She was happy here, and she possessed the rare ability to make others happy. She had a charm of her very own; unhurried, logical, good-tempered, easy-going; and an unfailing interest in all things. We all know how gifted she was; her many contributions to the B.S.M. bear that out. She had a very wide range of talent; a clever artist, linguist, and actress. Not many of us knew of her dramatic work, as unfortunately there was little time or scope in this field at Beaumanor.

Although Muriel had many friends she confided in few. She was sentimental, tender-hearted, and possessed a depth of feeling which she rarely showed, mainly because she hated cheap sentiment and was afraid of cheapening these sincere, grand emotions in herself. Consequently many of us remember her mainly for her light-heartedness and ready wit.

I vividly remember one of the more thoughtful of the "Beaumanor boys" asking if we believed in life after death. She smiled, and summed up the whole question with: "Let's all wait another fifty years or so, and then we shall all know for sure."

Her call came early, but I know that she has found the ultimate peace, and is still exercising her rare ability to make others happy.

Yes, we shall all miss her.

MARY NORRIS.

Next issue ready: June 30th. All contributions to reach the Editors by June 16th.

Spotlight on Courage

By Eric Dobson.

I LAY quietly there in my hospital bed,
    Just home from Dunkirk with wounds in my head,
Grateful to be there, thankful that I
    Had lived to come home through the bomb-laden sky,
When into the ward two nurses came slowly,
    Bearing between them a stretcher swung lowly
And into the cot next to mine gently lay
    A boy, just a lad, whose complexion was grey.
He was heavily bandaged from head to his toes
    And lay quite still, murmuring in high fever throes.
For days he was raving and gathering the threads
    Of his anguish, his fears and his terrified dreads
I learned that this boy had been out on the foam
    In a ship bringing oil for our transport at home.
Five hundred miles yet ere land could be seen
    With a storm blowing hard they were shipping it green,
When suddenly aft came an ominous roar,
    Of tin fish exploding, throwing men in the maw
Of the mountainous waves with their limbs cruelly shattered
    And the ship gave a lurch as her hull, badly battered,
Reeled like a drunkard against the hard blow,
    Then righted herself though so painfully slow.
The lad, being forrard, was flung on his face,
    Upon the steel deck and then in a trace
Down came the derrick and pinned him fast there
    As oil caught alight with a red-glowing flare.
Another explosion, amidships this time,
    And the roar of alarms, like the devil's own chime,
Bade those who still lived, to abandon the ship,
    As, mortally stricken, she downward did slip.
And some running forward to stand by their boat,
    Throwing out lifeboats and all that would float,
Lifted the boy, placed him down in the thwart,
    Of a life-boat, whose fall to the water was short.
The ship deeply rolled in her agony grave,
    So they pulled from her quickly with all they could save.
In the storm tossed black night, barely held by sea-anchor,
    They sat there and watched the sad end of their tanker.
And for seventeen days they lay tossed on the deep,
    Bare rations of water, too chilly to sleep,
Seventeen days they were bitterly cold,
    And each of them wounded, the young and the old.
Seventeen days without sighting a ship
    Seventeen days on a nightmarish trip.
Seventeen years it seemed to the crew
    As daily more haggard and shrinking they grew,
With festering wounds and pounded by seas,
    Buffeted, battered, until by degrees,
They lay on the boards in a pitiful state—
    Help must arrive now or else come too late.
The seventeenth day was drawn to a close,
    When a drone overhead roused the most comatose,
And bleary eyes saw, swooping down from on high,
    A giant Catalina, who swung from the sky,
And taxi-ing up to the poor shipwrecked men,
    She opened her hatches wide to them and then
The life saving airmen came into the boat

And transferred the crew to the huge flying boat.
Hardly aware that their ordeal was ended,
   The tanker's survivors were carefully tended.
And soon they were tenderly landed ashore
   To nurses who bandaged their injuries sore.
That was the story I learned from his raving,
   The nurses heard too as his life they were saving.
But as the lad thrived and regained his sense,
   Never a word of his suffering immense
Was heard on his lips as he lay there and talked,
   And not till weeks later when finally he walked
Did he echo the tragic events he'd been through,
   And please let me emphasise it to you
We were both being moved to a distant hotel,
   To start convalescing, to make us quite well
And the ambulance driver said before we'd begun,
   Are we going straight there or would you both like a run?
I've wangled the petrol and no-one will know,
   I can get what I like so where shall we go?
I think we'll go straight to the place said the lad,
   And the ambulance driver felt like a cad.
And after a while as we sped on our way
   The boy turned to me and had this to say.
Are there **many** who squander their petrol like him?
   And the tears in his eyes made me feel mighty grim.
No son, I said, and hope I said true,
   Most of our drivers appreciate you,
And use petrol carefully, knowing full well
   That bringing it here is like going through hell.
His face shone again, he smiled and said: "Gee,
   When I'm well enough I'm going back to sea!"

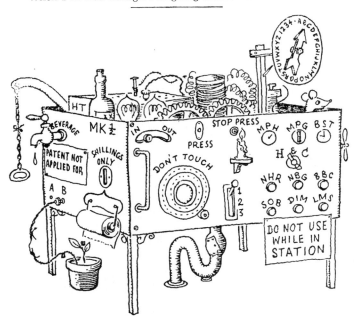

An early model of the Doolittle Selfstultifying Transmogrifier.
Designed by Prof. Goodyear to give the minimum results with maximum complication.

Theatre Royal
LOUGHBOROUGH.

PROGRAMME FOR JUNE, 1944

THE FRANK H. FORTESCUE

Famous Players

PRESENT

Monday, June 5th—(6 days)

Common Clay
By Leah Corentz

Monday, June 12th—(6 days)
FOR ADULTS ONLY.

The Dominant Sex
By Michael Egan

Monday, June 19th—(for 5 Nights Only)
Prior to London Production—
A GRIPPING DRAMA

Murder in the Shelter
By Paul Courtney

Friday, June 23rd—(for One Night Only)

East Lynne

Monday, June 26th—(6 days)

Ladies in Retirement
By Edward Percy and Reginald Denham

SHOW PARADE
Edited by Dudley Truin.

AMONG the six films on the short list for the Academy Award, from which "Casablanca" was eventually chosen as the best film of 1943, was "HEAVEN CAN WAIT" (Victory, June 5th, 6 days). Here is a review of this picture by **J. Hwfa Pryse.**

Adapted from a Broadway play "Heaven Can Wait" is another of those perfect films which Hollywood sends us once in a while, superbly directed by that master of satire and cinema artistry **Ernst Lubitsch.**

To relate the story would destroy its enjoyment, so let it suffice to say merely that its theme is biographical. Maintaining his reputation for originality and surprise Lubitsch treats us again to several unexpected and merry incidents, including a visit to Hell where we meet "His Excellency" the Devil, in the person of **Laird Cregar.** Our own English stage veteran **Charles Coburn,** using make-up for the first time among the many parts he has played, very nearly steals the picture as "Grandpa". There is also a young French governess who wears an attractive bustle with apron strings tied beneath it for greater emphasis—a definite Lubitsch touch— and **Spring Byington, Allyn Joslyn, Eugene Pallette** and **Marjorie Main** all give comedy performances that are excellent.

Surprise was expressed in Hollywood over the choice of **Don Ameche** (usually associated with musicals) and **Gene Tierney** for the leading parts, but both take full advantage of their opportunities and give the best performances of their careers to date. It is interesting to note that in one scene Lubitsch repeats an identical piece of screen technique he employed in his Garbo film "Ninotchka" when he focussed the camera on the closed door of a room in which three Russians were dining in splendour, and allowed the sound from within to convey the meaning of what transpired. In that film it was used farcically whereas in this he uses the method again with equal effect to convey a death. Colour photography adds greatly to the pictorial effect of the costumes and period settings of this outstanding picture.—J.H.P.

Ever since that over enthusiastic press agent arranged for a military escort for eight tin boxes containing celluloid from Southampton Docks to Wardour Street about twenty years ago "THE PHANTOM OF THE OPERA" has always been a title to conjure with. In the latest lavish technicolor version of Gaston Leroux's novel, (Odeon, June 5th, 6 days) **Claude Rains** gives another first class performance in the Lon Chaney part of the Phantom; but, unlike him, does not rely on grotesque make-up for his effect. Set against the colourful background of the Paris Opera of the eighteen hundreds, with a wealth of music and song from **Nelson Eddy** and **Susanna Foster,** it tells a thrilling story which will keep you guessing to the end.

Robert Donat is a British agent posing as a Rumanian in "THE ADVENTURES OF TARTU" (Empire, June 26th, 6 days). Though this is just another spy story it is a very polished affair, and you will enjoy it immensely provided you don't take it too seriously. **Valerie Hobson** supplies the familiar feminine interest as a Czech girl seemingly working for the Nazis, but actually a member of the underground movement, and together, after the usual misunderstandings, they succeed in destroying a poison gas factory. As this is a British film the Nazis are convincingly played, in particular **Walter Rilla** gives a sound performance as a Gestapo officer.

Also recommended this month are the re-issue of Irving Berlin's "ALEXANDER'S RAGTIME BAND" (Empire, June 15th, 3 days), with **Tyrone Power** and **Alice Faye**; **James Cagney** as a hobo in "JOHNNY VAGABOND" (Odeon, June 12th, 6 days); and "NOW VOYAGER" (Victory, June 26th, 6 days), with **Bette Davis** in a made-to-measure part, which, if you're a Davis fan like I am, you will lap up.

Last Goodnight
By Noel Royle.

(Second Prize "Guinea-tales".)

YES, Jean was the only girl for him; she had been a new experience in sheer happiness; a wonderful combination of all that he thought best in women: she more than satisfied his pride by her fresh and simple beauty—her eyes, brown bright, and sincere; the gently curving nose; her lips soft and full, tastefully supplied with just the right amount of cosmetic; her hair a rich red gold showing from underneath her service cap; and her figure perfectly fitted for her trim, neatly-pleated uniform. Yet, although he was fully alive to her beauty and felt immensely proud to be her confidant, he had never essayed more than a tender kiss whenever they parted: for theirs was a relation based on mutual esteem and good fellowship; they were joint sharers of artistic experience, exploring the world together and delighting together in their discoveries—and in spite of the fact that he adored her, their association had nothing in common with the coarse and noisy couples who paraded the streets of the town at night.

They both revelled in beauty as they mutually understood it—Mozart and Beethoven were their musical gods. Often happily together, they struggled through the crowds and rain to a concert hall in a nearby town; waited eagerly for the overture, and said very little until the performance was over. Then, returning to the camp, they would heatedly discuss all that they had heard. She loved the Tchaikovsky symphonies.

"Gaudy showpieces!" he said. "Over emotional and self-pitying. Give me the Beethoven 8th!"

She didn't always enjoy Beethoven; much of it was too sonorous and weighty—but they always agreed on Mozart; the smooth and splendid sparkle of his full orchestral works captivated them completely: after a night of Mozart they achieved their greatest peaks of delight.

Literature and poetry were another passion; their tastes were modern; they had the courage and realism of the Rupert Brooke idiom—they really believed they cherished no false idols, or chased no antediluvian, Quixotic ideals: they had a sense of humour and bravado, in spite of the world, and took a ruthless satisfaction in searching after cold truth. Sometimes they wrote verse: they were their own critics and thrilled at each others achievements, or laughed at each others failures: it was an elevating experience—together they would, perhaps, one day achieve a great deal.

This went on for months—they lived almost as fully as 1944 would let them. Then, one day, his posting went up on the orders. It was devastating; they had never thought about it before—being much too happy in each other to meet trouble half way.

He rushed away to her billet and explained the situation: "I leave to-morrow," he said. "We must spend this evening together."

She thought for a moment: "I can't miss the lecture," she replied. "But I'll get a late pass and meet you at nine o'clock, near the seat in the park."

He agreed, they kissed, and parted.

His pals were sympathetic. "Damned bad luck, old boy," they said. "The least we can do is to have a few farewell beers to-night."

He nodded unthinkingly, "Yes!" he said slowly.

They started drinking at half-past six; the pace was fast. The conversation which had started slowly, soon became fluent and loud; then it became bold and careless: they were all great pals, flung together by a corrupt system, which cared nothing for them or their hopes—they would have to fight just as long as the big people wanted them to fight—when the big people were satisfied they would be able to go back home—if they were still alive!

"Damn the world, and damn ideals!" they shouted. "Drink and be merry: take pleasure as it comes!"

With those shouts and ideas still echoing in his ears he walked through the rain to the seat in the park. She was there when he arrived; a damp but pretty and inviting figure. She stood under a tree, and he could just see her through the gloom.

The drinks had made his head reel, and as he kissed her the touch of her warm damp lips moved him strangely—he grasped her; she was small and physically perfect—he wanted to crush her.

"If this is the last time we shall be together, please take these," she said, and handed him a folio of her poems. "There'll be one or two you may like to remember—I want you to keep them."

He took it carelessly and placed it against the tree-trunk. "Thanks!" he murmured: But his mind was preoccupied with the fact of her smallness and utter perfection; with the wonder of her eyes, and the softness against his breast.

His hand moved upwards towards the buttons of her tunic; he fumbled with them, and suddenly began to feel detestable.

Her hand grasped his, and she spoke in a low voice: "What do you want?" she asked.

"I," he faltered, "—Oh God, I'm leaving you to-night—It seems to be what one does on such occasions."

She hesitated several moments, then, reaching outwards, she clasped his head in her hands and drew his trembling lips towards her own.

It seemed to his alcoholic reasoning that, as she had kissed him, she condoned his action: a minute later, his hand strayed back to the buttons of her tunic . . . . .

For a long time they remained locked together in the shelter of the tree where the shadows lay dark; much too dark for him to see the secret tears of disappointment which ran slowly down her cheek.

B.S.M. BALLOT.

Would you like TEN SHILLINGS? Or even 7/6d., or 3/6d.? Forecast the **total** amount of money in the "NEWS OF THE WORLD" "Wills of the Week" on Sunday, June 11th, and win one of these prizes, kindly presented by Public Benefactor, Ex-Ewa, Harry Appleton.

The only condition of entry is that you also complete the Ballot Form provided with your copy, stating **your** order of preference for the regular features of the B.S.M. We hope every reader will enter this simple contest and thus enable us to gauge the popularity of the various items.

Add your "WILLS" forecast, and address to EDITORS, B.S.M. CLOSING DATE: FRIDAY, JUNE 9th.

The sender of the exact or nearest estimate will receive Ten Shillings, and the other two prizes will go to the runners-up.

For your guidance the "Wills" total on Sunday, May 21st was £1,485,965.

SNOOP'S CORNER

CONGRATULATIONS to Mr. and Mrs. Connolly on the gift of a son, Barry Rothsey, born on 24th April.

To Mr. and Mrs. E. D. Smith on the arrival of a daughter on May 6th. We appreciate the fact that people working in the same department as Mr. Smith have to be extremely careful about divulging information, but we suspect someone of holding out on us and we feel sure that his reasons are in no way connected with the interests of National Security.

To Mabel and Bill Baker on the arrival of 8¾ lbs. of bouncing boy, James Howard, born on May 16th.

To the cat which produced triplets under the Canteen counter on 29th April. It showed remarkable initiative in choosing a spot where it was not likely to be disturbed.

To L/Cpl. Dorothy Louch, "D" Watch, No. 7 Wing, whose marriage to A. C. Letten, R.A.F., took place at St. John's Church, Knotty Ash, Liverpool, on April 29th.

To Sgt. Hazel Webb, T.P. Staff, whose marriage to Lt. Leslie Stewart Jones, R.E.M.E., took place on 22nd May.

To Pte. "Midge" Dawson, "A" Watch, No. 7 Wing, who became engaged on 23rd April, her 21st birthday, to Reginald Tiplady, of the R.E.M.E., at present at an O.C.T.U. near Derby. He was gazetted 2nd Lieut. on May 18th.

To Pte. Rita Muriel Jellings, "D" Watch, No. 1 Wing, and Richard Garside Wildblood who were married on May 5th at St. Matthew's Church, Chapel Allerton. The bride looked very charming in a cream and silver brocade dress. She carried a bouquet of red roses. Mr. Roland Wildblood acted as best man. Some members of Beaumanor staff were among the many guests present at the reception after which the happy couple departed for their honeymoon. A coloured cine film of this memorable occasion had to be abandoned owing to rain, to the disappointment of all concerned.

The eligible bachelors of our community will have their confidence badly shaken on July 22nd, when Paddy Kelly makes L/Cpl. Doreen Blake his bride.

Older members of the Section will be interested to hear of the wedding in the Middle East of Joe Simonite, who left us about three years ago, and Sgt. Peggy Chaffin, one of the original members of No. 1 A.T.S. "Y" Wing, who left for service overseas just over a year ago. This is further proof of the smallness of the world in which we live, as these ex members of the Beaumanor staff first met in Cairo.

Owing to pressure of space last month we were unable to announce the departure of Messrs. Fred Staddon (our ex Editor), Max Hilder, and Philip Arnold who left us for outstation duties. Our best wishes go with them.

We also said good-bye to Sgt. Ann Law, Ptes. Pat Warren, Druyer, Wittenburg, Shakespeare and Ann Neville. The two last named have since returned, and we wish the others every success in their new surroundings.

We welcome back Mr. W. Dalton, who will be remembered by some of our readers as the writer of "Traveller's Log".

The Editorial Board wish to express a vote of thanks to the N.C.O's in charge of watches, and others who have so ably assisted in the collection of subscriptions and distribution of the B.S.M. We should like to show our appreciation in a more tangible form, but unfortunately our treasurer has mislaid the cash book. We are not in the position to offer a reward for the return of same, but we have an inexhaustible supply of thanks. The only member of the Board who is not likely to be pleased over the recovery of the missing cash book is the treasurer. Personally I think he has burnt it as I am sure he cannot afford to have dates with A.T.S. officers on his meagre stipend.

I would like to thank the people who keep me supplied with "fan mail", although they seem somewhat divided in their opinions concerning my ancestry. I have never noticed any similarity between a rat and a pig. I think swine is more appropriate, and you can add adjectives according to your taste, or lack of it, as the case may be. There have been two letters of criticism in connection with which I have been called over the coals. It is significant that both the writers are married men. May I point out that I do not create gossip, I only write about it, and if married men did not have clandestine meetings with their A.T.S. girl friends after roll call, etc., etc., I should have nothing to write about. Keeping my *own* conscience is a full time job.

Was it merely a coincidence that just before her wedding Rita Jellings was the only lady present at the Dancing Class amongst some fifteen to twenty men?

Evidently Cpl. Jean is a firm believer in the *Hale and Fair*well stuff, for after making a date with two E.W.A's for the same day, she turned up an hour late for the first; returning too late to keep the second date she joined the original in the King's Head but left him for someone else. When he went, she transferred her attentions to two other E.W.A's. Either she likes their company or a good time!

Geoff. Nicol is grateful for all the cigarettes which have been forced on him since our last issue, but he now has no further use for them.

Mr. Antrum, alias The Weasel, alias The Squanderbug, was seen eating in the canteen last week. There is no evidence to confirm the rumour that he purchased a cup of tea.

After our American friends of Hut "C" had drawn lots for the task of polishing the floor, T/Sgt. Fred Allred elected to remove his pants for the job rather than spoil his immaculate crease. We wonder if the girls will follow his example when it comes to their turn?

Although it is a bit stale, I fancy the following story will be new to the majority of readers. It concerns a young lady of "D" Watch, No. 7 Wing, who was told by her room mates that she ought to be ostracised. One of her friends hastened to reassure her, pointing out that this was an operation that could only be performed on boys!

There is no truth in the rumour that Mr. Walton has been given the honorary rank of Senior Commander in the A.T.S.

We were amused by the notice displayed in the Canteen which reads: "Please return your empty cups to the counter. This will save time and ensure better service". It might, if you bang your cups on the counter hard enough to arouse the staff from their afternoon siesta.

It would be interesting to know if Junior Commander Robinson was successful in her efforts to obtain some of Capt. Abel's clothing coupons, although we are certain that she wouldn't dream of using them. It isn't legal.

That's all for now. Cheerio,

OLLIE.

The A.T.S. owe much to Christopher Columbus—after all, he discovered **America.**

BEAUMANOR
and its Lords.

By S. H. Skillington, F.S.A.

PARTICULARS of the inception and devolution of Beaumanor, County Leicester, are clearly set forth in the late George Francis Farnham's **Quorndon Records** and in the Barrow-on-Soar Section of his **Charnwood Forest and its Historians**. In the Charnwood book, Mr. Farnham tells how, early in the Thirteenth Century, a new and separate manor called Beaumanor was formed, partly out of the Barrow Manor and partly out of the Manor of Loughborough, in favour of Hugh le Despenser, under-tenant of the Earl of Chester in the Manor of Loughborough. The exact date of this creation is not on record, but the grant must have been made to Hugh by Ranulph, Earl of Chester, before 1232, when the earl died. The lands that comprised the manors of Barrow and Loughborough had been granted by the Conqueror to his nephew, Hugh Lupus, Earl of Chester, from whom they descended to the said Ranulph, the sixth and last Earl of that line. The Despensers appear to have derived their surname from the fact that one or more of them had held the office of dispenser **(dispensator)** to the Earls, or possibly to the Constables (the de Lacys), of Chester.

Before giving an account of the descent of the new lordship, it may be well to quote a few descriptive lines from Curtis's **Topographical History of the County of Leicester**. The author of this useful compilation, which was published in 1831, says that Beaumanor is "locally situated on the East side of Charnwood Forest; contains 1,000 acres, 96 inhabitants, 15 houses. The sole landed proprietor is William Herrick, Esq. The ancient manor house is described as 'being seated in the Park, called Beaumanor Park, and moated round with a fair and clear moat, and a little distance from the said moat are barns and stables and all other useful offices, standing and seated about which lieth the said Park'. In 1725 a new manor house was built in the place of the former one; in the hall of which is a singular chair, cut out of a solid oak which measured 34 feet in circumference. The Park and scenery about it are remarkably picturesque and beautiful, and some very large timber trees form a prominent feature in the landscape . . . In 1690 Sir William Herrick cut down most of the timber in the Park." The architect of the present mansion, completed in 1847, was William Railton, designer of the Nelson Column in Trafalgar Square. The story of the historic bedstead, brought about seventy years ago from the old Blue Boar at Leicester and preserved in this house, is well and truly told in the twelfth chapter of the late Charles James Billson's **Mediaeval Leicester**. It is a tale to hold children from play and old men from the chimney corner.

The Despenser pedigree in **The Complete Peerage** begins with a certain Thomas, father of the Hugh for whose benefit Beaumanor was constituted by Ranulph, Earl of Chester. The original grantee, of whom nothing is known, died in 1238 and was succeeded by his son, also named Hugh, who has been described as the first illustrious member of a conspicuously enterprising and ambitious family. The fame of the second Hugh arose from his ardent and capable support of Simon de Montfort and the baronial party in the troublesome reign of Henry III. In 1260, and again in 1263, he was appointed Justiciar by the barons, and when war broke out he led the citizens of London in their attacks on the houses of leading royalists. He distinguished himself at the battle of Lewes in 1264, was an active member of de Montfort's noted Parliament, and died with his leader at Evesham in the following year. He was buried in Evesham Abbey. His widow, Aline, daughter and heir of Sir Philip Bassett, sometime Justiciar of England, had a grant for life of the manors of Loughborough, Freeby and Hugglescote. In 1271, the year of her father's death, Aline married Roger le Bigod, Earl of Norfolk; she died in April, 1281.

The lands of the Hugh that fell at Evesham were, as a matter of course, taken into the King's hand; but the administration of them was given to his son and heir, another Hugh, in May, 1281, and the same Hugh had livery of his mother's lands about two months later, though he did not come of age until the following March. This Hugh, whose turbulent and shifting career ended in disaster, attained to something like supreme power after the fall and execution of Thomas of Lancaster, Earl of Leicester, in March, 1322, and in the May of that year he was created Earl of Winchester by Edward II. He and his arrogant son, still another Hugh, cannot be said to have been actuated by high motions; but their influence, on the whole, seems to have been beneficial. Professor Trevelyan, summing up their period in his **History of England,** says that "Edward II and Gaveston were perhaps as unfit to govern England as Charles I and Buckingham. But the leaders of the baronial opposition, especially Earl Thomas of Lancaster, were stupid, selfish and brutal men, swollen with the pride of birth. The King's next favourite, Despenser, was not an 'upstart' like Gaveston, but he developed into a tyrant. And yet the struggle between such unpromising opponents worked out to the advantage of the nation. The machinery of administration was improved, not by subjecting it to the clumsy control of the Barons, but by certain bureaucratic reforms . . the King's Court was plastic and adaptable in its organization, yet highly specialised as a civil service, full of trained and able men who went on quietly governing while far over their heads fools or scoundrels like Gaveston and Thomas of Lancaster, Despenser and Mortimer, ranted and killed each other for the benefit of posterity and the Elizabethan dramatists."

The careers of the Earl of Winchester and his son were ignominiously extinguished by their enemies towards the end of 1326. The circumstances, in each case, may be related in the words of **The Complete Peerage**:— "On the King's flight to Wales in October, 1326, the earl was dispatched to defend Bristol, which, however, he at once surrendered on the arrival of the Queen, 26th October. Next day he was tried—without being allowed to speak in his own defence—condemned to death as a traitor, and hanged on the common gallows. On his death, 27th October, 1326, at the age of 65, all his honours were **forfeited,** the sentence of 'Exile' passed on him in 1321 being re-affirmed in Parl., I Edw. iii." The younger Hugh "accompanied the King in his flight to Wales in October, 1326, and with the King was captured near Llantrisant, Co. Glamorgan, 16th November, 1326. He was taken to Hereford, tried—without being allowed to speak in his own defence—condemned to death as a traitor, and hanged on a gallows 50 feet high, 24th November, 1326. His head was set up on London Bridge, 4th December, and his quarters in four different places", *viz.*, at Dover, Bristol, York and Newcastle. Such were the manners of the times; Thomas of Lancaster, after Boroughbridge, and Roger Mortimer, the Queen's paramour, in 1330, suffered similar indignities. Mr. Farnham, in his Charnwood book, says that the elder Hugh and his family, when staying in Leicestershire, resided at the manor house at Beaumanor. That Beaumanor and the district were not unaffected by these turmoils is shown by Curtis, who records that in 1330 the custody of the manors of Loughborough and Beaumanor, which had been wasted by war, was granted to John de Insula.

(To be continued.)

Social Calendar

Edited by "Ollie" Pearce.

THURSDAY, MAY 4th.—The Home Guard dance held in the Canteen was a great success. Some difficulty was encountered in obtaining decorations, but this was overcome in an ingenious manner and the canteen was tastefully adorned with pieces of shrubbery, etc. Comments on the originality of this form of interior decoration were profuse.

Another novel feature was the introduction of Ladies' half-hour during which the ladies ran the whole show. Connie Praeger acted as M.C., Joan Price and Irene Mayor were bar-tenders, and Mrs. Fagg took charge of the music dept. The privilege of "requesting the pleasure" was confined to ladies only, and mere males were compelled to stifle their thirst unless some lady friend was sympathetic enough to buy them a drink. The idea proved to be very popular.

A waltz competition, judged by "Auxilaryilary", Pte. McCauslan, (A.T.S.) and Pte. Fred Wells was won by Sigmn. Park and his A.T.S. partner. M.C.'s were Sgt. Geoff. Nicol and Pte. Fred Wells. Music was supplied by "One Pint" Fagg, (Jive King of Kent) and Bungy's Bar was taken care of by Ginger Talbot, Bungy Williamson, and Don Barber. There was also beer for sale!

SATURDAY, MAY 13th.—The dance organised by the A.T.S. at Garats Hay developed into an enjoyable evening, although it did not look very promising at the outset. Transport was provided for 60 Americans but only 14 arrived, the other 46 having baled out en route. The Signals were called to the rescue, but our allies turned up in force later, having primed themselves for the occasion.

WEDNESDAY, MAY 17th.—The ramble arranged by the Music Club was cancelled owing to rain although one or two enthusiasts put in an appearance.

WEDNESDAY, MAY 17th.—Another successful dance was held by the C.E.C. Once again shrubbery was used for decorations, and although the canteen was not exactly transformed into a Palm Court, it's barrack-room like appearance was eliminated. The return home of the EXILES DANCE BAND contributed largely to the evening's enjoyment. Freddie Burgess crooned, and several people remarked on his excellence as a trombone player. The entire stock of the bar was disposed of, but in spite of this, there were no cases of alcoholic superfluity. The raffle for a prize of 10/- was won by Mr. Bob Roberts, who has not attended these dances before. We expect to see more of him on future occasions. In the elimination waltz, Molly Morgan delighted the company with an exhibition of Gent's natty suspenders attached to a pair of hirsute legs. The C.E.C. have a "find" in Mr. Jimmy Hunter as organiser and M.C. Thanks are due to him and his helpers for another really good show.

Bookseller and Stationer :: Lending Library

J. SKETCHLEY

24 & 25, High Street, Loughborough

Telephone 2980.

CALLING ALL

Owing to lack of contributions, it has been decided to discontinue the "Before the War" series. We hope that readers will enjoy "Spam Fritters" as a regular feature.

GOOD READING

By "B.B." and "R.R."

IF you feel that you are in need of a healing rest from the worries of modern social life, I suggest that you read "Far Away and Long Ago", by W. H. Hudson. This is the story of his life in the pampas. Mr. Hudson is primarily a naturalist, but do not let this put you off, because he is very much more than that. A keen observer of everything about him, he is able to express himself clearly and in a fascinating manner. He is an unassuming genius, and you will find that his pages seem to turn themselves over.

Do you like Peter Wimsey? Poisoning by arsenic is not the most comfortable means of egress from this world, but it has always created interesting situations. D. L. Sayers uses it once again as the theme of her rightly popular crime novel. "Strong Poison." Written in her customary entertaining manner, the plot revolves round Lord Wimsey's attempts to prove a most unorthodox heroine innocent of a very commonplace crime. Of course, this story has the usual "Unusual twist", but it will keep you guessing, and you will eat with it in your hand.

I have been entranced for the past few days with a book which I started reading by chance. It is the story of Ninette, youngest daughter of Charles the First. The facts of her story are that she was born under cannon fire during the Civil Wars and her mother packed her off to France, disguised as a beggar's child, with her old nurse. With her frail beauty, and half-wistful elfin face, she charmed the lavish French court in which she spent the rest of her life. At seventeen, she was married to that ridiculous person, Monsieur, Louis XIV's brother. This slight girl then becomes the central figure in the Versailles scene for the next nine years. She was feted and toasted by all the brilliant gallants in the leading courts of Europe. A few days before her twenty-sixth birthday, she died, mysteriously poisoned by her mad, perverted husband, who by this time was strutting round on high red heels, dressed in pink silk, and wearing a blonde wig. This brilliant, gay story is told against the slightly fantastic background of Louis' court. Great personages slip in and out of the book, restored to clear-cut reality by the magic touch of Margaret Irwin's pen. You will meet her brother Charles II, Anne of Austria, La Grande Mademoiselle, the Duke of Buckingham, and all the satellites of Le Roi Soleil. "Royal Flush" is full of glorious incident and leaves a pleasant taste in your mind.

Who has not read "Peter Pan" or revelled in the other whimsical creations of Barrie? Patrick Chalmers has written an excellent book about this lovable character, which is on sale now, at Sketchley's. The other books mentioned are obtainable from any Public Library.

ATS

Bird Watching in Leicestershire.

HOW delightful it is now that Spring has come: to trip out to the fields and to listen to the songs of the birds!

Since feeling the nervous strain of the war, I have found great relaxation in this most enjoyable pastime.

Clad in the conventional habit—voluminous, brightly coloured trousers with leather knee-caps to ensure comfort whilst crawling, and a mac to keep me clean when riding my dirty bicycle to the scene of my nocturnal watching, I have spent many patient hours, perhaps just lying in wait for one of our small feathered friends. But, oh, the exquisite joy of that sweet piping when at last it comes!

Before setting out, it is best to consult a really good ornithology book to make sure of being in the right place at the right time. I learnt my lesson over this at an early stage of my career, when, depending on the advice of a casual 'phone acquaintance, I sat for hours one night expecting to hear a very rare song. I was bitterly disappointed when, after sitting all night long, hunched up at the back of an old cowshed, getting thoroughly cold, I was to watch the dawn break, my efforts unrewarded, only to find later that the very rhythmic chatter had been there in the barn, blowing my "bloomin'" head off.

I wish to mention here a certain eminent watcher who has the theory that the best results are obtained by throwing out a smoke screen and churning it up with a fan. The majority of people, however, find that this causes acute discomfort, and is liable to make the watcher miss the chirping of the bird while attending to his own physical needs.

To the uninitiated, bird watching may appear to be a very simple pastime, but it is often exciting, even difficult. There are, of course, some birds that can always be heard at a certain place at a certain time, although even these may not be heard sometimes, if there is a heavy gale for instance, or if they have gone in search of a mate. They will always reappear in the same place later however. There are some birds though, which are very unreliable and give one the thrill of the chase. There is a certain small bird with a deformed throat and, consequently, a very weak voice, which is never heard singing from the same tree for more than three days at a time. When the watcher can no longer hear his tiny voice through the loud shrieks and warbles of all the other birds, he must start a systematic search through the paths of the wood until he finds him again. There is a certain body of the keenest and most experienced watchers, who make it their business to find the birds that other people can no longer hear. Quite often they just find them before they fly off again to another tree.

You will soon find that there are many ways to keep interested while you are on the watch. A friend of mine, who is very fond of sketching, assures me that he has improved considerably since he has been coming, and has produced some really good pictures, which he has been able to sell, so if you are artistically inclined, take a pad and a good stock of pencils with you when setting out. Personally, I can usually find plenty to do, such as football pools, manicure, darning, crossword puzzles, and catching up on my correspondence, but, no doubt, you will soon use your ingenuity and find some way to relieve the boredom which you may, occasionally, experience.

If you should decide to take up this hobby, remember that, although you may feel at the time it is all very futile, great importance is attached to this work, this war effort, by the National Confederation of Bucolic Birdbashers.

"BEAUMANIACS."

Spam Fritters.

POET'S NIGHT OUT.

THE ghost of the poet stood under the trees, weeping over the fair daffodils and being frightfully poetic. But he got tired of that after a while; he wanted to haunt someone; besides he'd just thought up a brand-new number called "Hist! The merry nightingale", and poets just can't keep that sort of thing to themselves. Seeing what he took to be a "Peasant's humble cot", he picked up his chains (nasty noisy things) and snooped off to haunt that.

There were an awful lot of peasants in the cot, and also a wireless set. The poet knew all about wireless sets; they had them in the Better World, and he and the Heavenly Hosts listened in to "Diablo and his four Fire Balls" in the "Hot Rhythm from Hades" programmes every Wednesday. But the peasants didn't seem to be listening in; they were mostly asleep. The poet haunted up and down the room a bit, but all the peasants just murmured "Nothing" every time he went past, without even opening their eyes. Which wasn't much fun.

At one end of the room, by himself, slept the wildest and woolliest peasant and the poet decided that he'd have one last haunt at him before giving it up as a bad job, and going back to the Better World. So he dropped his chains with a loud bang beside the woolly peasant and started off—"To-night, I heard the Nightingale".

The effect on the peasant was phenomenal. With a yell, he leapt to his feet and shrieked—"Why didn't you say so before!", and fell back in a dead faint. The poet, who was sorry, because he hadn't meant to haunt him all that much, crept off very quietly and went back to the Better World —and the Heavenly Hosts.

Between Two Landladies.

MRS. DRIPPAGE and Mrs. Cudd shared a clothes-line and both billeted EWAs, so they had plenty to talk about when they met . . . . which was often.

"'Ow's your new gentleman getting on, me duck?" asked Mrs. Cudd one morning.

Mrs. Drippage smirked coyly. "My Mr. Grabchick? Oh 'e's lovely, 'e is really. A proper gentleman, you can tell."

"'Ow?" . . . . with scepticism.

"'E always wears a collar and tie," explained Mrs. Drippage fondly. "Even on six-to-two, ... none of your narsty polo-necks for 'im. And no orful langwidge neither, or fag-ends under 'is bed."

"'Umph! It can't last," declared Mrs. Cudd cynically.

Mrs. Drippage smirked even more coyly.

"'E ain't married," she remarked.

Mrs. Cudd shot her a quick look. "Well?"

"It's ten years since I buried Drippage," ruminated his widow. "A woman gets lonely. And Grabchick's no worse a name I'm sure."

"You designing 'ussy!" cried Mrs. Cudd playfully. She would have said more, but a smell of burning pervaded the air.

"My dinner!" she exclaimed. "You'll 'ave to excuse me, Mrs. Drippage!" And she fled indoors, leaving Mrs. Drippage to hang out her lodger's combinations with loving hands.

Cont. P.18

This Month's Beauty Hint.
By Margaret Dunn.

Eyes right! The eyes are the life of your face. They are the first thing people notice about you, and the last thing they forget. Make sure your eyes play up to their star role then, and make them as lovely as possible.

First you must make a determined attack on any eye-beauty problems you possess,—dark circles? Crowsfeet? Puffy eyelids?

Dark circles are usually caused by fatigue, so do try to get a little more sleep. Adopt a more restful attitude to life,—don't get "het-up" over trifles.

Crowsfeet can be treated more easily and successfully. They need smoothing away with some nourishing preparation,—almond or olive oil if you have it. If not, skinfood or cream, warmed till it is soft and oily will do just as well. Remember the skin round your eyes is very delicate—you mustn't massage it with heavy, pulling strokes, or with skinfood that drags the skin as you apply it. When you have your oil or cream slightly warmed, take a little on the tips of the fingers, and run them over the lids with tiny, gentle pats. Work outwards over the upper lid, round, and inward again underneath the eyes. Do this for a few minutes. The outer corners of your eyes are where the lines show most, so give them a little special treatment. With two fingers of the other hand hold the skin taut while you gently tap with your oily finger-tips.

Little can be done about puffiness as it usually arises from internal disorders. Drinking plenty of water between meals often helps.

If your lashes are rather short, smear white vaseline on them before going to bed. Eyebrows—pluck regularly. If they are a bit thin at the ends, try a spot of pomade on them every night for three months. It **does** make them grow. Keep an eye on your eyes,—they are your chief beauty assets.

○ ○ ○ ○ ○

SPAM FRITTERS—(contd.)

A Yankee was asked by his chum,
"Say, brother, why you look so glum?"
"Dat dame", he said sadly,
"Swore she loved me madly,
Den kissed me and pinched all mah gum!"

○ ○ ○ ○ ○

Excerpt from a Chatty Letter.

My dear——, Forgive me if this letter is rather dismal, but I am writing during a weary vigil in the Dentist's waiting room. I don't usually mind the dentist, but this time poor Mr. Pullen is in Hospital with an attack of Dentist's Elbow, or some other obscure disease, and I am faced with the prospect of his Local Demon, as the old lady called it. My inside feels like a disordered gravel mixer operating during a choppy sea-crossing,—but soft! a smiling white-robed Circe is beckoning me towards the torture-chamber. I bet he's a savage old-fashioned butcher who's never heard of Local Anæsthetics!

——My dear, he was marvellous! Too shattering! Like a Greek God! And he didn't hurt a bit. I've got to go back and be "finished off" in three days. I wish he didn't only mean my teeth!

Yours swooningly——

A Flight Over Bombay.

By Kay Statham.

WHILE we were living in Bombay, and during the hot weather, my father received an invitation for us all to go on a short flight in a K.L.M. Dutch air liner, which had flown straight from Amsterdam. Naturally we accepted as the very large air liners very rarely visit Bombay, the route from Europe being to Karachi, and then across India to the Far East via Calcutta.

We drove out to the Bombay Flying Club where the plane was "parked". Incidentally, this plane had been chartered by the Maharani of some native state, to fly out a specialist to attend her husband, the Maharajah, who was seriously ill. No doubt the specialist charged double for this trip.

The Bombay Flying Club is at Juhu, about fourteen miles out of Bombay, and it is an extremely pleasant spot near the sea. We found assembled there a number of the Dutch community. No doubt it was refreshing for them to meet the pilots, their fellow countrymen, so recently from Holland.

The air liner looked beautiful standing in the sun, and we were taken on a tour of inspection before the flight started. I think the number of passengers that could be carried was twenty. It was beautifully fitted inside with the most comfortable seats. A Dutch steward was in attendance. The heat inside was almost unbearable until we took off, and then we felt the benefit of the air conditioning, but it was still "rather warm".

We soon left Juhu with its miles of beach and belt of palm trees, also its smell of Bombay Duck, and headed towards the city. Bombay looks really grand from the air, perhaps the best place to see some parts of it! We flew over the flats where we lived, round Calaba point, and then made a sweep over the harbour before heading back to Juhu. It was a very interesting flight, all the more so, when we thought that this plane had only taken just over three days to fly from Amsterdam. In those pre-war days we had only just become accustomed to receiving four air-mails a week from England.

We soon reached the airfields at Juhu, and landed amid a dust storm caused by the propellors. This rather upset the spectators having tea on the club lawn, but a little dust never harms anyone. Thus ended a very pleasant afternoon as guests of the K.L.M. Dutch Airways.

GET YOUR———

Beauty and Toilet Preparations

FROM

"LEONARD'S"

Gentlemen's Hairdresser

25, CHURCH GATE, LOUGHBOROUGH

Large Variety in Stock!

The Digby Chronicles

"IT'S so convenient dear," I remarked artlessly to Steve, one evening, "that you're having a week of your holiday just now."

"Why?" asked Steve suspiciously.

"I want to re-distemper the nursery," I announced boldly. "And as you're home, I thought . . . ."

" . . . . That I could take three of the most unconventional, undisciplined children on earth out of your way for the day . . . ."

"Only two of them, darling," I interposed coaxingly. "Just Susan and Judy. Gilly can spend the day in his play-pen on the lawn. But of course, if you don't feel capable . . . ."

"Don't be ridiculous," snorted Steve. "But seriously, why don't you let me do the distempering and you look after the children?"

"Because I look after the children for fifty-one weeks out of the fifty-two, and I enjoy distempering," I retorted.

Steve gave in. "All right, I'll take them," he sighed. "Have you any bright ideas as to where?"

"Yes?" I said brightly. "The Zoo. They've never been to the Zoo, and they'd be sure to love it. You could make an early start, and I'd give you plenty of sandwiches . . . ."

So Steve took Susan and Judy to the Zoo, and Gilly spent the day in the garden, and I did my distempering. It was nearly six o'clock when the expedition returned, the children tired, but very happy, and Steve just tired.

"Did you have a good day, dear?" I asked cheerfully.

"Ask them," answered Steve darkly. "But never ask me to take them to the Zoo again!" And he stumped into the sitting-room.

"I put the whisky-and-soda out, darling," I murmured as he passed me. Then I went upstairs to superintend the bedding-down of my family.

"Well, dears, was it nice and did you see all the animals?"

"Oh it was lovely, Mummy! We saw the lions and tigers, and we had a ride on the elephant . . . ."

" . . . . I was SICK on the heffelunt!" said Judy proudly. "It joggled about so much I was SICK!"

"And we saw the fish in the 'Quarium, and the monkeys . . . ." pursued Susan.

"And oh Mummy!" interrupted Judy. "There was such a lovely dog!"

"Oh yes." Susan took up the tale with far more enthusiasm than she had shown hitherto. "Just outside the gates there was a poor blind man with a most LOVELY shaggy dog that did Trust-and-paid-for for pennies. And we made Daddy wait, and we watched it and watched it, till Daddy hadn't any pennies left . . . ."

I began to see daylight. Obviously, the Zoo had made little impression on them, compared with the blind-man's dog. They were still chattering about it as I kissed them good-night.

"I won't ask you to take the children to the Zoo again, darling," I said to Steve as I rejoined him downstairs. "But . . . . don't you think it would be rather nice to get them a shaggy dog that can do Trust-and-paid-for?"

FAMOUS LAST WORDS.

Nonsense! You couldn't **possibly** get a shock off those phones!

VICTORY
BIGGIN STREET, LOUGHBOROUGH

MONDAY, JUNE 5th (6 days)
Don Ameche & Gene Tierney in
"HEAVEN CAN WAIT" (Technicolor)
also Full Supporting Programme

MONDAY, JUNE 12th (6 days)
Monty Woolley & Gracie Fields in
"HOLY MATRIMONY"
also Jack Benny in "The Meanest Man in the World"

MONDAY, JUNE 19th (6 days)
Sonja Henie—Cesar Romero—Jack Oakie
in
"WINTERTIME"
also Will Fyffe in "They Came By Night"

MONDAY, JUNE 26th (6 days)
Bette Davis & Paul Henreid in
"NOW VOYAGER"
also "Spirit of West Point"

Mon. to Fri—Con. from 5-30 p.m.   Sat.—Con. from 2 p.m.
MATINEES.—Mon. and Wed. at 2-15 p.m.
SUNDAYS—6-15 p.m.   (One Show)

Sweet FANNY ADAMS replies

Dear Friends,

Quite a mixed bag this month. Thank you, ERIC W. DOBSON, for a really intelligent question! ERIC remarks that when a persons kills his father the crime is called patricide; in the case of his mother, it is matricide; and that of a brother, fratricide. ERIC cannot discover the equivalent term for the killing of a sister, although he has asked a number of people. Actually, ERIC, the term fratricide can be applied equally to the slaying of a brother *or* a sister, particularly in law, but there is another term expressly meaning the killing of a sister, but it does not appear to be very widely used. The word is SORORICIDE (from *soror*: a sister, and *coedo*: to kill).

Someone without even a name, much less an address, writes to say that just before the wedding of R.M.J. and R.G.W. a panic was caused because R.G.W. was informed that a collar with "wings" was not the correct thing to wear on such an occasion. The resultant "huddle" failing to produce a solution, the collar was worn after all. The writer requests "a definite opinion". Well, NAMELESS, surely at least a pair of trousers should have merited first consideration? If such *were* worn, (although your letter visualises R.G.W. blushing in a winged collar *ensemble*) I would say that, provided the other garments were in keeping with such a style, the collar was quite correct.

ANOTHER JIMMY is "nearly in trouble" because he is being blamed for some of the escapades of a "Jimmy" (fateful name!) whom he refers to as the Vagabond Lover, and who recently departed from Woygland. Can I suggest a way their two identities can be distinguished so that their respective indiscretions can be passed to the right quarters? As you are frank enough to admit escapades of your own, JIMMY, hasn't it occurred to you that the Vagabond Lover may equally be getting the blame for some of those?——and he isn't here to defend himself. Don't be a cad, you cad.

(EDITORIAL NOTE. These are the last words which SWEET FANNY ADAMS wrote. Shortly after she completed them we handed her a further letter from JIMMY ROGERS. This letter was full of dark threats and menacing phrases, and was altogether in a "You Die At Midnight" vein. Dear Fanny scanned it quickly, as we told her of another lengthy epistle we had ourselves received from the same person, and then collapsed. We regret to say that she never recovered from this seizure. Begging and imploring us to publish a special "Replies to Jimmy Rogers" Number, she died with his name on her lips, and a beautiful light in her one sound eye. Among the many floral tributes at her funeral was a lovely garland of raspberries from an anonymous mourner.)

An ASCETIC is a man who denies himself all earthly pleasures, and gets a hell of a kick out of doing it.

An IMPRESSARIO is a finger-print expert.

A TAXIDERMIST is a fellow who is happiest when he has a skin-full.

A MINEROLOGIST is a teetotaller.

PSYCHOLOGY is what helps a bloke to decide if a girl means "No" when she says "No".

Pre SENTIMENT

By G. M. Spooner.

THE prospect of the future curiosity arouses—
  The country freely dotted with prefabricated houses,
  And all of these are occupied, it should be understood,
By prefabricated couples with prefabricated brood—
Predesignated husbands with pre-allocated spouses,
Indulging in precontemplated quarrels and carouses,
With prerecommended work and prerequisitioned food,
And pre-inculcated notions about what is right and good.

The properties are purchased at a predetermined price:
Provisions of pre-requisites presumably suffice—
Pre-reconditioned lino on the floor in place of rugs,
And the parlours primly fitted with a panel full of plugs.
Prevaricating kittens, and precaptivated mice—
The risk of catching neighbours' kids' prefumigated lice—
The garden produce plundered by pre-predatory slugs—
Some bedroom walls bespattered with prepropagated bugs—

This premeditated England will perhaps be much the same
As the one which passed before it by a less pretentious name.
  (The above was especially written with the aim of promoting morale among the A.T.S.—AUTHOR.)

SPORTOPICS.

CRICKET.—The first two matches were played in real cricket weather. Against R.N.A.S. on May 3rd, we only scored 24, and although F. Pearce took two wickets in the first over, our opponents soon knocked off the runs. On May 10th we defeated Loughborough Continuative. Exiles: 76. Loughborough Continuative: 24. (F. Pearce 9 for 9). A feature of both these matches was the keen fielding. We lost our first home match, versus Quorn, on May 13th. Quorn: 136 for 3 (dec.). Exiles: 62. (E. D. Smith 33).

HOCKEY.—The very successful season which has just been completed is largely due to the unremitting care and hard work of Victor Hartill, who has been responsible for this section since October, 1941, and has had to cope with many difficulties. Well done, Victor!

TENNIS.—The Court is again proving popular. Anyone wishing to play, please use the Booking-sheet in the Canteen.

A. H. APPLETON, *Sports Secretary*.

TAILORING FOR THE SERVICES
— from —

| START TO FINISH | 8, BAXTER GATE LOUGHBOROUGH. | TOP TO BOTTOM |

The London Tailoring Co.
Est. 1899.   'Phone 2794.

EMPIRE
MARKET PLACE, LOUGHBOROUGH

MONDAY, JUNE 5th (3 days)
Laurel & Hardy in
"JITTERBUGS"
also Edward Norris in "Prison Mutiny"

THURSDAY, JUNE 8th (3 days)
Sabu in
"THE DRUM" (Technicolor)
also Dennis O'Keefe in "The Leopard Man"

MONDAY, JUNE 12th (3 days)
Lesley Brook & Richard Bird in
"I'LL WALK BESIDE YOU"
also Frank Albertson in "Attorney for the Defence"

THURSDAY, JUNE 15th (3 days)
Alice Faye & Tyrone Power in
"ALEXANDER'S RAGTIME BAND"
also Buck Jones in "Below The Border"

MONDAY, JUNE 19th (3 days)
Jean Arthur & John Wayne in
"LADY TAKES A CHANCE"
also Lee Tracy in "The Payoff"

THURSDAY, JUNE 22nd (3 days)
Edmund Lowe & Evelyn Keyes in
"DANGEROUS BLONDES"
also Richard Cromwell in "Crime Smasher"

MONDAY, JUNE 26th (6 days)
Robert Donat & Valerie Hobson in
"ADVENTURES OF TARTU"
also Hosts of Variety Stars in "Starlight Serenade"

CONTINUOUS DAILY. Doors open at 1-30 p.m.
SUNDAYS at 5-30 p.m.

Printed by Toppings Ltd., 17, Southfield Rd., Loughborough, and published by L. P. Jones for Beaumanor Staff Magazine Committee.

SIXPENCE

B.S.M.
Vol. I. No. 5 (New Series)
JULY, 1944.

Editors: LEONARD P. JONES, ERIC C. MILLHOUSE

A.T.S. Editresses: KAY PRICE, MARY GILL. *Treasurer:* A. H. APPLETON.

Editorial Board:
DICK WILKINSON, OLLIE PEARCE, DUDLEY TRUIN, RON DENNY (B.W.)

WE welcome the news of the elevation to the "Peerage" of our distinguished contributor, Ollie Pearce. In extending hearty congratulations, his colleagues on the Editorial Board, basking a little in the reflected glory, are wondering whether the honour conferred upon our Social Editor is a tribute to past editions of "Snoops Corner", or an insurance in respect of future issues.

THE B.S.M. BALLOT was, in common with our previous competitions, a terrific success. The phenomenal total of 26 entries were received—and we only printed eight hundred and seventy forms. This was in the very best B.M. traditions. So, now that we know exactly what you want, we can go right ahead and do precisely as we have always had to do: give you what we think you ought to have.

The Editorial Brains Trust performed quite a lot of overtime trying to evolve a contest which would provide us with a reasonable guide to readers' likes and dislikes; and which would in some small way pander to the Woygite's lust for financial reward; and which, above all, would entail the very minimum of effort. The result convinces us, among other things, that you don't want competitions, so we are not likely to run another.

The 97% of our readers who found the strain of writing fifteen numbers too great may be faintly interested in the results we obtained from the stalwart 3% who performed that prodigious feat and thus voluntarily became a cross-section of Woygland public opinion. Entries were received from 10 male and 16 female readers. Points were given thus: 15 for a "first" place, 14 for a "second", and so on. Possible points: 390.

1.	St. Upid	 371	9.	Social Calendar	.. ..	184
2.	Snoops Corner	 319	10.	Good Reading	.. ..	166
3.	Short Story	 253	11.	Show Parade	.. ..	162
4.	Cartoon	 251	11.	Sweet Fanny Adams	..	151
5.	Verse (Light)	 245	13.	Digby Chronicles	..	146
6.	History	.. .. ⎫ 226	14.	Sportopics	.. ..	127
7.	Spam Fritters	.. .. ⎭	15.	Beauty Hint	.. ..	54
8.	Verse (Serious)	 222				

We liked the wit of the lady who created a Sixteenth position for "Mr. Rogers' letters to the Editors".

The "WILLS" contest produced a wild variety of figures. The haggard old Editorial countenances almost mustered a smirk over one girl's entry which predicted a mere eight-hundred-and-forty-thousand MILLION odd pounds ! It was significant that we did not receive one entry from Hut 'C', the traditional home of wrong predictions !

The correct amount was £1,206,157. The nearest estimate came from Pt. D. M. Hoatson, B Watch, 1 Wing, who forecast £1,231,833. Runners-up were: Mr. F. Wells (£1,240,830) and L/Cpl. Bams, C Watch, 7 Wing (1,386,781).

This month we are trying out two new features—"Thro the Looking Glass" and a "thriller". Won't you let us know what you think of them ?

Next issue ready: July 28th.   *All contributions to reach the Editors by July 14th*

YOUR FILM ATTRACTIONS for JULY

SHOWING AT THE ODEON THEATRE

Sunday, July 2nd—Chester Morris and Leo Carrillo in **I Promise to Pay.** Also Don Terry in **Dangerous Adventure.**

MONDAY, JULY 3rd—3 days
Gary Cooper & Madeleine Carrol
Northwest Mounted Police
with Paulette Goddard and Preston Foster
in TECHNICOLOUR

THURS., JULY 6th— 3 days
Dorothy Lamour & Fred McMurray
And the Angels Sing
Also Lupe Velez & Leon Errol in
MEXICAN SPITFIRE'S BLESSED EVENT

Sunday, July 9th—Bruce Bennett and Ula Holt in **The New Adventures of Tarzan.** Also Lucan and McShane in **Old Mother Riley's Legacy**

MONDAY, JULY 10th, and all the week
Deanna Durbin, Franchot Tone and Pat O'Brien in
HIS BUTLER'S SISTER
Also Vera Vague and Robert Paige in **GET GOING**

Sunday, July 16th—Lionel Barrymore and Lew Ayres in **My Life is Yours.** Also John Beal in **One Thrilling Night**

MONDAY JULY 17th—3 days
Tommy Handley & Moore Marriot
TIME FLIES
Basil Rathbone & Nigel Bruce in
SPIDER WOMAN

THURS., JULY 20th—3 days
Phyllis Calvert, James Mason & Margaret Lockwood in
THE MAN IN GREY

Sunday, July 23rd—Wallace Beery and Marjorie Main in **Barnacle Bill.** Also Ricardo Cortez in **Rubber Racketeers.**

MONDAY, JULY 24th, and all the week
Paulette Goddard
Fred McMurray
Standing Room Only

A L S O

The Official Record of the African Campaign
Tunisian Victory

Sunday, July 30th—Lew Ayres and Laraine Day in **Mary Names the Day.** Also the East Side Kids in **Smart Alecks.**

MONDAY, JULY 31st, for 3 days
Frank Sinatra and Michele Morgan in
HIGHER AND HIGHER
Also Claire Trevor and Albert Dekker in
WOMAN OF THE TOWN

Continuous Performance Daily 1-45 p.m.   Sunday, One Performance at 6 p.m.

Social Calendar

Edited by "Ollie" Pearce.

JUNE 8TH. A successful dance was held by Communications Wing A.T.S. at The Lodge, Barrow. More than £28 was taken, and it is hoped that when expenses have been cleared, a profit of £10 will be handed over to Company funds. An enjoyable evening was had by all who attended, with the exception of four thirsty Woygites who arrived at 10-30 p.m. (ex 2—10), paid their two-bobs very grudgingly, only to find that there was no beer left! Hard luck, Geoff.

JUNE 13TH. The Garden Fete and Sports day, held at Staffords Orchard, Quorn, was a well deserved success, and tribute should be paid to the enthusiastic party which spent the morning in preparation, despite the frequent showers. The weather improved considerably in the afternoon, and the proceedings began with a March Past of the A.T.S., accompanied by the Band of the Leicestershire Regiment, conducted by Bandmaster Purcell.

The Salute was taken by Colonel Balmain, C.S.O., and several distinguished members of the local community were present, including the Mayor and Mayoress of Loughborough.

There was an interesting programme of events, the Inter-Wing competition being won by No. 1, A.T.S. Y Wing.

Admission was by purchase of a 6d. War Savings stamp, and there were various side-shows, including pony rides, darts, jumble sale, and tea tent. Considerable interest was shown in the two tanks which paraded in Station Road, and over £400 was raised in aid of the Loughborough "Salute the Soldier" week. At the conclusion of the afternoon's activities prizes were distributed by the Mayoress of Loughborough.

JUNE 13TH. A carnival dance and cabaret was held by A.T.S. Group at Loughborough Town Hall. Music was provided by THE EXILES Dance Band in the Corn Exchange, and THE CHEQUERS Dance Band in the Victoria Room.

An exceedingly large assembly spent a most enjoyable evening.

JUNE 15TH. MERETAS presented "Yes and No" at the Loughborough Town Hall in aid of "Salute the Soldier" week. Mary Gill was very efficient as Stage Manager and Assistant Producer. Kay Price reviews this in "Show Parade".

The fortnightly dances held by the C.E.C. have been discontinued until further notice as the committee does not anticipate much support during the summer months.

TAILORING FOR THE SERVICES
— from —

| START TO FINISH | 8, BAXTER GATE LOUGHBOROUGH. | TOP TO BOTTOM |

The London Tailoring Co.

Est. 1899.   'Phone 2794.

and its Lords

By S. H. Skillington, F.S.A.

Continued.

In 1327, after the fall of the Despensers, Beaumanor was granted to Henry Beaumont, presumably as part of his reward for betraying Edward II, who had been his friend and on whose side he had fought at Boroughbridge. Henry had married, about 1310, Alice, daughter and co-heir of Alexander Comyn and niece and heir of John Comyn, Earl of Buchan. Through this connexion, Henry Beaumont, from early in 1334, was designated Earl of Buchan, a title that did not descend to his heirs. The succession of the Beaumonts at Beaumanor is so clearly stated by Mr. Farnham that it will be best to quote his exposition as it stands:—"Six generations of Beaumonts followed Henry, the first Beaumont to own Beaumanor. John, Lord Beaumont, was created a viscount on 12th February, 1439-40, and was made a Knight of the Garter in 1441. He married Elisabeth, daughter and sole heir of Sir William Phelip, Lord Bardolf, by whom he had issue William, his second, but eldest surviving son, born in 1438. John, Viscount Beaumont, was killed on 10th July, 1460, at the battle of Northampton, and his son and successor William, Viscount Beaumont (called Lord Bardolf during his father's life), was taken prisoner at the battle of Towton and attainted at the Parliament of 1st November, 1461, whereby his honours were forfeited and also his estates. He was restored by King Henry the Seventh to his titles and estates, but in 1487 he lost his reason, when the custody of his lands, and in 1495 of his person, was committed to the Earl of Oxford, in whose house at Wivenhoe, Essex, he died without issue on 19th December, 1507 . . . . The Erdington Manor in Barrow having now devolved on the family of Hastings, and the Beaumont Manor of Barrow having come to the Crown by the death of Viscount Beaumont without issue, and the attainder of his heir, Lord Lovel, King Henry the Eighth, in 1524, granted the Beaumont Manor with Beaumanor to Lord Leonard Grey, lord deputy for Ireland, who held his first Court in October, 1524. Lord Leonard Grey was the second son of Thomas, 2nd Marquis of Dorset, and, in 1540, was attainted and beheaded, when Beaumanor fell again to the Crown. The next grantee was Henry, Duke of Suffolk, who was beheaded for his share in Sir Thomas Wyatt's rebellion in 1554, and the Crown again obtained Beaumanor by forfeiture. Beaumanor was then leased by the Crown to Frances, Duchess of Suffolk, who died in 1559, but Adrian Stokes, her second husband, held the manor until his death in 1586, when his brother William Stokes held it until his death in 1591. The next grantee was the Earl of Essex, who sold Beaumanor about 1591 to William Herrick, afterwards Knight, the fifth son of John Herrick, of Leicester. Sir William was born in 1557, knighted in 1605. He served as M.P. for Leicester in 1601, 1605 and 1629. He died on 2nd March, 1652-3, in his 96th year. He married Joan, the daughter of Richard May, esquire, and sister of Sir Humphrey May, Knight, Chancellor of the Duchy of Lancaster."

The Duke and Duchess of Suffolk were the parents of Lady Jane Grey, whom Roger Ascham, before he "went into Germanie", found in her chamber at Bradgate, their Leicestershire home, "readinge **Phaedon Platonis** in Greeke, and that with as moch delite, as some jentlemen wold read a merie tale in Bocase [Boccaccio]". Their harsh treatment of their noble and unhappy daughter shows them to have been extremely unpleasant people. When the Dowager Duchess of Suffolk married Adrian Stokes, she was thirty-seven and he was twenty-one. He is said to have been "a ginger headed lad . . . of a fairly good yeoman family and had been appointed some two years earlier secretary and groom of the chambers". Queen Elizabeth's remark upon the occasion was: "Has the woman so far forgotten herself as to marry a common groom?" **(The Complete Peerage,** iv, 421.) Mr. H. W. Cook, in **Bygone Loughborough,** says that in 1387 Richard II, when on progress from London to York, stayed for six days with Lord Beaumont at Beaumanor, hunting in Charnwood Forest, while his Marshalsea was held in Loughborough. (The Marshalsea was an ambulatory Court, held before the stewards and marshal of the royal house, to administer justice between the Sovereign's domestic servants and to deal with certain other pleas, within the verge of the Court, in which parties in the royal service were concerned.) Richard again stayed with Lord Beaumont for one night in August, 1390, after his visit, with the Queen, to John of Gaunt at Leicester Castle. This visit, which lasted for several days and was chiefly occupied with hunting in the adjacent forest, was a great event, and the courtiers are said to have been filled with admiration at the splendid hospitality of their ducal host. After the death of John, Viscount Beaumont, at the battle of Northampton, Beaumanor was held in dower by his widow, whose first husband had been the Duke of Norfolk. In 1464, the reversion of the manor, after her death, was granted to William, Lord Hastings, the favourite of Edward IV. Hastings, however, never enjoyed the estate, as he had the misfortune to be beheaded a year or so before the duchess's death.

(To be continued.)

SOLILOQUY

By G. M. Spooner.

When Berlin has been Coventrated,
    German towns all Hamburgized,
When Europe has been expurgated,
    German Volk Vansittartized,——
We'll turn our energies (perhaps)
To de-materializing Japs.

With Tokyo obliterated,
    South Sea Isles pacificized,
The Far East decontaminated,
    India departmentalized,——
Then we can turn (if not too late)
And put the old home country straight.

When our land has been Uthwatted,
    Our economics Wooltonized,
Or Beveridged, or Scotted,
Or Barlowed, or what-notted,
    And de-bureaucratized,——
The time by then will be too short
To turn and give *ourselves* a thought.

Theatre Royal
LOUGHBOROUGH.

PROGRAMME FOR JULY, 1944

THE FORTESQUE
Famous Players
CONTINUE THEIR SUCCESSFUL REPERTORY SEASON.

Monday, July 3rd—(6 days)
First Night
By REGINALD DENHAM
Definitely NOT for Children

Monday, July 10th—(6 days)
Eliza Comes To Stay
The Screaming Comedy.

Monday, July 17th—(6 days)
Gaslight
By PATRICK HAMILTON

Monday, July 24th—(6 days)
Ignorance
By CLIFFORD REAN

SHOW PARADE
Edited by Dudley Truin.

"**MERETAS**" made a very good effort in its presentation of "YES AND NO", but somehow the play was not entirely satisfying.

Possibly that was the fault of the play itself and not the players, for it was one long sequence of vagueness, agitation, and indecision, which I, at any rate, found extremely irritating. It was not a play during which we could relax, listen and watch without effort. It is possible that the acoustics in the Town Hall were partly to blame, but all the actors showed a strong tendency to "swallow" their words, with the result that, at times, it was impossible to follow their lines at all.

Daphne Carter, in the leading part, was unforced and natural, but in moments of stress it was quite impossible to hear what she was saying, though her acting spoke volumes. **George Garner** did his best in the supporting part which offered plenty of difficulties, trying to keep his temper amidst the whimsical vapourings of the most maddening family on earth. **Vera Dixon** was the most audible and was fairly convincing, but **Albert Mayfield's** Rector was too variable, his ecclesiastical mildness changing abruptly to full-throated bellowing more fitted to an Indian Colonel, during family rows. **Kay Metcalfe** in the small part of the daily help, was amusing, if exaggerated.

I think, next to Daphne Carter, the most sincere performance came from **Teresa Armour** as the younger daughter, while **Harold Taylor** as the curate was solid and reliable. Considering all things, a not discreditable production. A **Kay Price** review.

Though the production of "THEY CAME TO A CITY" (Theatre Royal, Leicester) was, taking it by and large, quite good, it must be admitted that it was nothing but Leftish propaganda, which would have been more effectively put over in a little yellow-covered book published by Victor Gollancz. Its main interest to Woygites was that the lead was played by **Hwfa Pryse** in the part of "Joe", an enlightened ship's stoker; yet, such is Priestley's wishful thinking, I'm afraid you would have to go a long way to find such a stoker. The result was that **Hwfa Pryse** was not entirely happy in the rôle. His timing and diction were as perfect as ever, but his accent, reminiscent of Gordon Harker, was offset by actions more suitable to a French Apache. But this stoker was not a real person: he was Priestley's mouthpiece; his conception of what the working man should be: not what he actually is. As such **Hwfa Pryse's** composite portrayal was quite satisfying.

Only one film so far released this year has received a coveted four star rating, and that is "SAN DEMETRIO—LONDON" (Empire, 10th July, 6 days). All the superlatives lavished on this British picture by press reviewers are fully justified and this is one film you definitely **must** not miss. Telling the story of the oil tanker that was set on fire by enemy action, abandoned by her crew and then re-boarded two days later by a handful of men and brought safely to port; it shows once again that where the theme is great enough, stars, in the accepted sense of the word, are a handicap. Here in this authentic reconstruction the entire cast and the story are the stars; and congratulations must go to **Michael Balcon,** of Ealing Studios, for a brilliant and honest production.

"STANDING ROOM ONLY" (Odeon, 24th July, 6 days) is another comedy based on the present housing shortage in Washington. The dialogue is bright and the situations are really funny. **Paulette Goddard** is quite good as a factory worker posing as a private secretary, but it is definitely **Fred MacMurray's** picture; he is right on top of his form as a factory manager.

"SWEET ROSIE O'GRADY" (Victory, 17th July, 6 days) is, I know, just another musi**Grable**color picture, but it is quite the best thing she has done to date. It has a snappy script, an ingenious plot, tunes that are above the average, and two first-class comedy performances from **Robert Young** and **Reginald Gardiner**; Altogether good escapist entertainment.

SNOOP'S CORNER

CONGRATULATIONS to Pte. Doreen Tatton, who was married during May to Robert Haslam, R.N., at Leigh, Lancs.

To Pte. Evelyn Nutten, who was married at Penzance on 23rd May to Craftsman Stanley Kay, R.E.M.E.

Both the aforementioned young ladies are of "D" Watch No. 1 Wing.

To Mr. Jimmy Purdie, whose marriage to Miss Edith Browne, of Omagh, Co. Tyrone, took place at Frederick Street Congregational Church, Loughborough, on Friday, June 2nd. Mr. Alec Berry acted as best man. The honeymoon was spent in Scotland.

To Pte. Elsie French, "D" Watch, No. 7 Wing, who was married in London on June 4th to Cpl. Eric Ameer-Beg, R.A.F.

To Pte. Iris Waller, "A" Watch, No. 7 Wing, who was married to Sgt. Sam Hall, R.A.O.C., on June 9th. The happy couple are no longer in residence at the C.R.S. Iris was a day overdue on her marriage leave. (Ain't love grand!)

To L/Cpl. Marjorie Kepple, "C" Watch, No. 1 Wing, whose marriage to L.A.C. R. Bowyer, R.A.F., took place at St. Auleyn's Church, Bristol, on Saturday, 17th June. The honeymoon was spent at Minehead.

To Pte. Gwendoline Pearce, "A" Watch, No. 1 Wing, whose marriage to L/Cpl. Taylor, R.E.M.E., is to take place on July 1st.

To Mr. Kenneth Dawes, whose engagement to Miss Madge Watkinson, of Loughborough, was announced on June 17th.

To Pte. Doreen ("Darkie") Railton, on her engagement to Staff Sgt. Charles Ward; and to Pte. Pat Drummond, on her engagement to Cpl. Joseph Dunn, "D" Watch, No. 1 Wing, is greatly indebted to Christopher Columbus, although in this respect they are not alone: the majority of A.T.S. seem to have their own interpretation of lease-lend.

Departures. During the past month we said goodbye to L/Cpl. Ann Auger, *nee* Page, "B" Watch, No. 1 Wing, who will soon be adding her hand to all those things which (so we're told) rule the world.

We also bade farewell to Henry Lewis who, however, is still in the district, presumably until the close of the racing season.

My apologies to Bill Baker for crediting him with half a pound more baby than he was entitled to. I am told that this caused him a certain amount of embarrassment. I am told a lot of other things at times which are equally fantastic.

I hear that Jimmy Hunter was "roped in" by the "Salute the Soldier" Committee at Clophill to judge a beauty, ankle, and baby competitions. Well, one thing leads to another.

Rita Wildblood returned from her honeymoon a day overdue. She says she lost her watch—maybe she means calendar. I have heard that there are occasions when time stands still!

Galahad Saunders has developed a severe crush on a certain snappy line in conductresses working for Allen's. The courtship entails frequent journeys on the beloved's chariot, and Galahad has acquired a charming old-world courtesy in standing respectfully aside and allowing the greatest possible number of persons to board the bus, before he assumes a position near the front where, strangely enough, the captivating clippie carries out her menial task.

An amusing incident occurred the other morning in Control when a rather attractive runner presented herself and asked if there was anything to take back. When asked where she was from, she replied "L", whereupon a male voice burst forth with the popular song "Heaven can wait".

Pte. Doreen Lister, of "A" Watch, No. 2 Wing, and Mr. Harry Dodd, of Hut "C" are seeing quite a lot of each other lately. Judging by their rapt expressions during the film "Phantom of the Opera" at the Odeon recently, they seem to be great lovers.

Sgt. Bond, of the "I" Corps, appeared on duty the other day with lipstick all over his face and explained that he had walked into a lamp-post. I understand the lamp-post is named Alice.

"Oh! would some power," etc., etc.

In the B.S.M. Ballot, Beauty Hint came in a very poor last. I realize, of course, that A.T.S. billets are not furnished quite as adequately as my lady's boudoir, but surely their occupants must have access to a mirror.

At the A.T.S. Sports Day, a friend of mine who for twelve years spent the bulk of his pay in the N.A.A.F.I., before most of its present day customers had heard of such an institution, succeeded after much persuasion in obtaining a cup of tea from the N.A.A.F.I. tea bar, to the accompaniment of much warning: "Don't say I served you", etc. Half an hour later an announcement was made over the loud speakers as follows: "The O.R's. canteen has a number of cakes left which it is prepared to sell to civilians". Like the rebate on N.A.A.F.I. sales, which goes to the P.R.I.—we don't get it!

A more amusing incident occurred when the Officers' race was cancelled owing to lack of entries. An A.T.S. Officer was discussing the situation with our Mr. Smith, who observed, quite unintentionially: "Probably an Old Soldiers' race would have been more suitable".

And here, I think, we have material for one of those Bateman cartoons like "The Guardsman who dropped it", etc. The vast audience at the De Montfort Hall was hushed and still. Solomon, with a glassy, far-away look in his eyes, was in the middle of a Brahm's Concerto; a soft murmur from the strings, his only accompaniment.

Suddenly the spell was broken. A hubbub arose and clouds of white smoke started billowing out from the back of the orchestra stalls. Finally, through the smoke, emerged Wally Cecil, who, holding aloft a burning cycle pump like the Statue of Liberty, strode majestically from the auditorium to plunge the burning pump into a fire bucket. It had caught alight when he had been smoking surreptitiously. "Smoking Forbidden" is the rule at the De Montfort Hall. Subsequently, Wally was late on duty, his official excuse being that the concert did not finish at the advertised time!!!

The Beaumanor Staff are having a public telephone installed in the canteen. This should prove a boon to our A.T.S. friends for the purpose of making, breaking, altering, or (in case they have forgotten the time and place) confirming dates. But why public telephone? Why not a direct line to Wood Lane?

You will probably remember how the 505th arrived back in camp just in time to prevent Maunday Thursday from being a mournday for big time promoters Dix and Sims.

I understand that their next venture on 27th April, featuring Victor Silvester's orchestra was not a financial success, consequently local dance fans have been compelled to put up with comparative small fry. (Not you, Hilary, sit down.) The big timers however, have apparently become aware of Loughborough's possibilities, and on June 24th the Town Hall is to be graced with the presence of Ivy Benson (in person) and her All Ladies' Band. I'll bet Freddie could show them something!

Re the item concerning Doreen Lister and Harry Dodd: the last two words were inadvertently omitted, and should, of course, be —— of music.

That's all for now. Cheerio.

OLLIE.

Bludgeons in Baker Street.
By E. St. U. M.

DEDLEIGH SNOUPPE stirred in his luxurious armchair as Mrs. Codphace bustled in. He had been pondering over the Case of The Blood-stained Toe-nail, but the solution still evaded him. Slipping the toe-nail quietly into a drawer, he peered round the chiffon loose-cover.

"Pancakes?" he hissed.

"Lemon-juice!" responded Mrs. Codphace with alacrity, and Snouppe snapped back the safety-catch of the Wobley Automatic beneath his tussore dressing-gown, with a tense sigh. He insisted upon the use of a pass-word by everyone who entered his consulting-room. One was obliged to take the most stringent precautions, with seventy-three members of the Crimson Circumference sworn to exterminate one.

"Well, Mrs. Snakehips?" he enquired, crisply, the formalities over. His housekeeper had only been with him for twenty-seven years, and up to the present he had not succeeded in memorising her proper name.

"Lidy to see yer," announced the aproned enormity. She always spoke Cockney on Tuesdays, as Snouppe considered it helped to baffle the avengers of the Crimson Circumference for his housekeeper to possess a wide variety of dialects. It was always a trifle embarrassing on Fridays, however, when she used Welsh, as he had to call in an interpreter.

"Show her in" commanded the celebrated criminologist, consulting the alarm-clock he carried in his bullet-proof waistcoat.

As Mrs. Codphace withdrew, Snouppe leapt to the wall and peered through a spy-hole secreted behind a picture of Blogworthy, the Bride-Slayer, which gave him an uninterrupted view of the sitting-room. So absorbed was he in studying the figure in the depths of a windsor chair that he failed to see a sallow, sinewy hand steal through the fanlight behind him and tear off the top leaf of the calendar.

"Kommen-sie——" began Mrs. Codphace, and then, blushing prettily as she remembered it wasn't Ash Wednesday, she continued: "This wiy, if yer please."

A moment later, as Snouppe returned to the fire-place, the visitor entered the room. She was extremely tall, but the master sleuth was not deceived. Rather shamefacedly, she got down from her stilts, and leaving them propped against Mrs. Codphace's mangle, came forward into the orbit of the light. He saw that she was very beautiful, apart from a boil on the tip of her nose.

"The Marchioness of Pukingditch?" he enquired.

"How did you know?" she whispered, taken aback.

Snouppe ignored the question, and went on crisply: "Your husband is in town for the Biennial Conclave of Left-Handed Cigar Addicts. Son: Just gazetted lance-corporal (unpaid) with the Fifth Anglesey Halberdiers. Dog: Schnitzel. Pedigree dachshund bitch, recently estranged from bull-terrier Crabby, father of . . ."

Then he noticed that the beautiful creature was sobbing pitifully. Swiftly he sped to the door.

"Herringbone!" he bellowed.

Mrs. Codphace tore in on roller-skates.

"Hmph," muttered Snouppe, irritably, "go back. I forgot to ring."

Mrs. Codphace slipped into reverse, and purred up the passage.

Prudently placing a bucket beside the distracted noblewoman, the intrepid detective crossed the room and pressed the bell-push dramatically.

Thirteen minutes later, Mrs. Codphace re-entered, picking her teeth pensively.

"You rang, sir?" she said politely.

"No!" screamed Snouppe. "The bell did. It always does when I press this confounded button. We must have it repaired." He made a note in code on the wall-paper.

"Lend the Marchioness your hankie," he rapped out. "And, wait . . . ." as she made for the linen-cupboard. "Send for Krumpit. He's at the Horrorscope, watching the third episode of "The Lack of Time." Krumpit was his faithful assistant.

As Mrs. Codphace departed, Snouppe crossed over the coconut-matting to where the Marchioness stood, sucking a tomato, and sobbing hysterically. He took her damp hand in his, and, flicking a few seeds from it, led her gently to the piano-stool.

"Don't sit there," he said, "there's a bomb underneath it."

As she sank down, squaw-fashion, on the rug, he took a deep breath, and a long draught from his petrol lighter—his only vice.

"Now tell me," he said softly, "what is the trouble?"

"It's Schnitzel, my Schnitzel," she sobbed, plaintively.

"Schnitzel?" he exclaimed, dilating one nostril rapidly, an infallible sign that he was mystified. "Schnitzel? You mean—er—ah—um—pups?"

"No, no!" she shrieked, despairingly. "My poor dear, darling Schnitzel has disappeared, utterly and completely. And I bought a fresh tin of 'Snappie' only yesterday!"

(To be continued.)

(Where is Schnitzel? What sinister force is at work at Pukingditch Hovel, the lovely country seat of the Marchioness? Can you wait for the next breathless instalment?)

SPORTOPICS.

ATHLETICS.—During the Whit-Monday Fete on the Brush Ground, a Home Guard team: Johnson, Vickers, Lowes and Linder, met an R.A.F. team in a relay race. Though defeated by a stronger and more experienced team, they gave a very good account of themselves, particularly since they ran after less than a week's training. R. F. W.

CRICKET.—A feature of the Sileby match on 20th May, was the duel between Keenlyside and S. Lewin, the Sileby opening batsman, who scored 40. Bob Stevens sustained a finger injury which it was thought might be serious. I understand, however, this is now on the mend. EXILES: 60 (G. Hearn 4 for 4). SILEBY: 132 for 7 (S. Lewin 40; H. Lewin 37).

On 27th May, *versus* BRUSH 'A', we made our record score. G. M. Spooner with R. Wildblood added 55 for the third wicket. EXILES: 146 for 6 dec. (Wildblood 40, Spooner 33, Reedman 22, Anderson not out 21). BRUSH 'A': 74 (P. Roberts 3 for 44, Anderson 5 for 25).

We lost against R.A.F. on 3rd June. Wildblood again played well but we did not recover from early disasters: five of the side did not score. EXILES: 64 (Wildblood 29; Carter 7 for 20). R.A.F.: 101 for 9.

The match on 10th June was not without humour. Only seven players turned up. (O, Captain, my Captain! And you had the bats, too!) Our sporting opponents allowed us to bat first, and Appleton and Dias were permitted to bat twice! As we lacked our usual bowlers some strange antics were observed. Even the Secretary bowled two overs, taking one wicket for one run, and Dias was successful with his first ball! EXILES: 58 (Spooner 36, Hall 5 for 28). COLLEGE CONTINUATIVE 2ND XI.: 96.

Again, *versus* Quorn, on 17th June, we were two short and had to prevail on two spectators to help us out. It was a tale of dropped catches: six in all. QUORN: 146 for 5 dec. (E. Ball 54, Slack 32). Dudley Smith, P. Roberts and J. Dodd all played well. Then J. Hewson showed us how to force the pace in exhilarating fashion. Our tail did not wag, but we nearly got there. EXILES: 118 (E. Smith 33, J. Hewson 35).

A. H. APPLETON, *Sports Secretary*.

More Things in Heaven and Earth
By M. A. Reed.
(Third Prize "Guinea-tales".)

HIGH Spring was in the evening air; an air of tangy softness, wandering in from the sea: a sea, hard, glassy and smooth like a plate of blue-green metal; a sea giving back to the sky its brittle chilliness: a sky empty of clouds, empty of sound, save for the lark dropping its mazy gossamer web of silvery music: a web in which it became entangled and lost to all but its own ecstasy.

The westerling sun caught the blackness of the rocks in golden hands, piling them with colours, softening them: the rocks, hard and unimaginative, stonily pushing back the sea as wave lapped on wave and hissed gently back: back to return, and back again. As the sun fell lower on to the edge of the horizon, it pushed the rocks higher against the sky, taking from them their softness, and leaving them stark; dragging out the slow shadows behind them.

It stared blankly into the face of Netty: Netty stared blankly back, without a blink, as an eagle might, without a movement, save where the breeze flickered her skirt, and played as it might play with dead grass, with her grey, dull hair.

Pitilessly it searched out the lines of her face. A face sere and old, like a reach of sand when the tide has left it—brown and crumpled with the falling waters. Netty's tide was nearly out now. It seemed to her that it had reached its ebb five days ago. For five days now she had waited. There every evening between six and nine she'd waited. Five days? Surely not. An eternity now, wasn't it? Was it so short a time since her Quiddy had not come home?

Quiddy, whom she married so long ago. They'd always called him Quiddy down there in the small fishing-port. Ever since he'd first gone on the boats, with the quid of tobacco stuck in the right side of his mouth. Quiddy and his quid seemed always to add up to each other. Each without each seemed incomplete. Now there was neither. Quiddy had gone five days ago, and for five long days had Netty waited, waited.

She came down every evening to watch for him in the sun. To see the trawler at first low and a dot, black on the shimmering skyline. Then larger and larger she would grow, with her long trail of smoke emptying from the slender funnel, pouring itself in a cloud of black profanity on the impeccable water as she forged to the harbour mouth, eight miles from Netty's home, set back behind the cliffs.

But waiting had brought nothing. Nothing until yesterday, when, just before she'd left, she'd seen, far away, that bright uneven little flicker, ticking noiselessly on the brink of the ocean. She'd told the coastguard: "Due south it was. On and off, like them soldiers done las' year." Sam had told the port people, but that was all she knew. Probably all she'd ever know.

She turned away again, up the steep path, slowly. Her heels caught the ground at each step, and scuff-scuffed on the dirt as she walked—back along the cliff path, past the coastguard station alone on the headland, down the hollow and round the woody corner. Her home was there, round the corner. Not really home now, because Quiddy——

She stopped, frozen into a state of incredulity. Quiddy? But he's dead now. He's not here. Not standing there at the door. Not home.

But he was. The real Quiddy, alive, and the same. Still the tobacco clamped in his jaws; still a perpetual, uncontrollable lock of hair poking from underneath the side of his cap. It would never stay down, that hair. Never . . .

"Quiddy?" she said, uncertainly.

"Hullo, Netty."

"What happened, Quiddy?"

"We was sunk five days ago. Picked up, tho', yes'd'y evenin'. We was flashing a mirror, hopin' to catch someone's eye, an' a plane come along about two hours after. Course, it was all right after that. I only just got back." He jerked out his answer.

She listened, hand to mouth.

"Where was you then, Quiddy?"

"When we was signallin'? About a hundred miles south of here."

A hundred miles . . .

"People can't see a hundred miles, can they, Quiddy?"

He laughed as they went inside: "'Course not, Netty."

SLIPSTREAM.

By Jimmy Hunter.

SWIMMING had never appealed to me since my school days. You see, being a boy I was naturally allergic to all forms of water. I must admit—and gladly—that I have now overcome that dislike and am, indeed, very fond of some forms of it, especially that known as beer. However, that's another story.

To continue: after very much persuasion and the promise of many delights, I eventually succumbed to the wishes of certain friends and learned to swim. Mind you, I felt a bit of a twerp attired in a natty swimming suit, but overcame that by parading in the costume before the family, prior to retiring each night.

My first lesson was to learn the use of my legs. Holding on to the bar round the edge of the bath, I had to kick out. After poking a few other customers in the face, neck and stomach, etc., I became fairly proficient. The next thing was to learn the various strokes, *viz.*, over-arm, crawl, and breast. I was delighted to find I acquired the art of the breast stroke very rapidly, and have never lost the ability. I think I can say with all sincerity that it came naturally. Since then I have often been complimented on the style of my breast stroke. Well, I made such good progress that I decided to enter a beginners' race at a gala to be held at the baths where I had learned the aquatic art. Naturally, I regarded this as a home match and fancied my chances. Indeed, I was very proud that I could now swim, which, after all, is not a thing everybody can do.

The great day arrived. On disrobing I discovered to my alarm I had lost my swimming suit. Here was a first-class calamity. Hastily dressing I rushed out in an attempt to borrow one, but my luck was out. By this time a large crowd had gathered. After another frantic chase about I was able to—shall we say borrow?—a pair of shorts. Long shorts they were, complete with mud from the previous football season. Well, there were six of us lined up at the start. It was to be a two lengths race, that is, there and back—if you could make it! At the word "go" I made a spectacular dive, landing flat on my belly, and that dive was my undoing in more ways than one. By the time I had recovered and returned the water from my mouth to the bath I was last in the queue. Here, I thought, is the chance to put my famous breast stroke into operation. It was a decided success, too, and I quickly caught up with the other optimists. I had one trouble, though: the shorts impeded my leg movements, but I struggled on. As I took the lead there was only one thought in my mind —to reach the far end of the bath before the others. . . . I've won, I think. Yes, somebody has hit me on the head with a stick. I clamber out, my head swimming now, to the clapping and cheering of the audience. They are staring at me—me, the winner. I stick my chest out and shake my hands over head. I commence to walk round the bath.

The cheering has stopped suddenly! What's the matter? Have they altered the verdict? Why are those two old ladies pointing at me? Now all is silent except for an occasional giggle. I feel cold. A horrible thought has entered my head. I look down—I LOOK DOWN AGAIN—and I can't believe my eyes! Yes, you're right: there they are, floating gently, oh! so gently! in the middle of the bath!

The Gospel according to St. Apid
Chapter XXXII
(Translated from the English by Disciple Millhouse).

NOW in the land of Woyg were many temples. And four were called Aych, and Eye, and Jay, and Kay. Peradventure they were likewise called sundry other names by the Ewas and Atsites which worshipped therein, but such names were not found in the Book of Words. Now these temples were provided with hot and cold running air, and all modern inconveniences. And some were furnished with curious stools which verily Made their Mark, for a multitude of the Tribe were afflicted with a Corrugated Rump. Yet in their wondrous mercy the Powers that Be gave the curious stools only unto such of the tribe as Nature had most bounteously blest for sitting.

Now at certain times the Powers that Be perceived that they had Done it all Wrong. Wherefore they sent a Sabotage Squad into the temples with their hammers, and their chisels, and their saws, and their measuring-rods. And the Sabotage Squad had Great Fun. But the faithful ones were Not Amused.

And it came to pass about the time when the King was preparing to send a mighty pilgrimage into Urop, that the Powers decided to Turn Over another New Leaf in the Temples, and to move the draughts into fresh corners, and to install divers new inconveniences. But they knew not where to send the worshippers from the temples whilst the Sabotage Squad had their Fun. For, inasmuch as a Little Bird whispered unto them: Send thou the faithful on Leave until the temples are prepared: the Little Bird faded badly.

And thus it was that the Powers went into a Great Huddle. And a certain Power saith: Behold! There dwelleth in Smowk one Pawtle, a great lord, who hath conceived a wondrous new habitation called Prefabricated. Let us therefore buy one, and set it up as a temple in the land of Woyg, that the peoples may go thence from out of each of the other temples in turn, and worship therein, and leave our Sabotage Squad in peace to make Whoopee. And the Powers, being agreed, forthwith sent for some shekels from the Chancellor, who had become exceeding rich by making all the peoples Salute the Soldier, and bought a house from Pawtle. And the Wehkmen bore it up through the wilderness into the land of Woyg, and builded it. And it was a goodly house, with much fiercer draughts, and ultra-modern inconveniences. And the Prophet Osee blessed it, and called it Ell. And the peoples blessed it also, and called it likewise.

And the Scribes of Aych, and Eye, and Jay, and Kay were each in turn banished from their temples into the House of Ell. And they tarried long days in Ell whilst the Sabotage Squad had a mighty Orgy. And the Squad were exceeding happy in the knowledge that their sledge-hammers would awaken nobody. Now there were oftentimes both Ewas and Atsites together in Ell. And there were two sundials in the House, one at either end. And the Atsites perceived that upon one was writ the word: Gents. Wherefore they hastened unto the other, and saw that it also bore the same word. Which was exceeding awkward.

And it came to pass that a certain Ewa dreamed a dream. And he saw a great parchment upon a board, without the House of Ell. And on the parchment was writ: For Sale. House of Pawtle. With Vacant Possession. And a man with many kine and no place to put them, came and paid a shekel for the House. And when the first beast beheld the House it marched around it seven times and moo-ed. And the walls of Ell fell to the ground. And when the Ewa awoke, he saith unto one Fredi: Lend me thy trombone, I beseech thee. And Fredi answered him saying: Why, mate? And the Ewa told his dream, and Fredi smiled a sad smile, and answered him, saying: Be not a Twerp. Whist ye not that dreams never come true?

CALLING ALL

Owing to pressure of space, it has been necessary to omit the Beauty Hint this month.

Spam Fritters.
CLEO THE CUTE CANTEEN GIRL.

CLEO sat behind the counter, occasionally pausing between stitches of the green jumper she was knitting to twist her beautiful, dark curls.

Her limpid eyes were dreamy and far away—she was oblivious to everything—to the long khaki queue in front of her, which wound from the counter, through the canteen door and way along the path to J Hut; oblivious, too, to the equally long queue of unwashed cups which stretched behind her, back into the dark, inner sanctuary of the canteen.

Suddenly her dreamy gaze chanced to focus for a moment on the queue before her. It stopped, arrested by a break of tweed in the long line of khaki. Abruptly Cleo set down her knitting, bustled towards the teapot and became a thoroughly busy little woman. "Oh, dear," she twittered, "I'm really ever so sorry. I didn't know there was a **man** waiting."

Heard from a Bottom Bunk.

"Can we have some quiet, please, I want to sleep——"
"——He said would I have a drink, so I said yes——"
"——Oh mareseatoatsanddoeseatoats——"
"Has anyone seen my——?"
"——a kiddleativytoo——"
"They **must** be somewhere——"
"——So I said yes, and he said——"
"Oh, **please** be quiet!"
"I must **have** them, I've got a date with a Commando, and——"
"——So I said yes, and he said, keep saying that and see where it gets you——"
"——Oh, sorry, darling, I'm dusting the mantlepiece with them——"
"Oh, mareseatoats——"
"For heaven's sake shut up!"

ODE TO AN OPERATOR

A wireless op. stood at the Pearly Gates
   Her face it was wrinkled and old,
And Peter was there to welcome her
   Into the Heavenly Fold.

"What have you done on earth," asked he,
   "To gain admission here?"
"I've been a Wop, Sir," said she,
   "For many and many a year."

And Peter stood, he looked at her,
   Her suffering was plain to tell!
"Come right inside, my dear," he said,
   "You've had your share of Hell!"
               MARGARET DUNN.

ATS

GOOD READING

By "B.B." and "R.R."

"—— Speak for the air, your element——
—— Of wings that bear your purpose, quick-responsive Fingers, a fighting heart, a kestrel's eye."

About these wings! Maybe you wear them on your tie, or do they just appear on the backs of countless envelopes, reminders of the great exploits of the RAF? Perhaps they bring to mind the scores of times you watched Spitfires weaving fluffy trails high up into the sun during the Battle of Britain; certainly they make you stop to think of the gigantic part which this service is playing today in its Biggest Job of all. (You prefer to forget the time you upset your tea-tray during a matinee performance of "Flare Path"!)

If you hate the "Silver Wings" sentimentality as much as these boys themselves do, you'll enjoy reading "We speak from the Air"—a collection of true accounts of their daring sky-adventures,—maybe not literary gems, but entertaining and informative.

Remember the name of the next book, because even if you've read it several times before its refreshing and inspiring atmosphere will still surprise and delight you. It is that magnificent word-classic "The Spring of Joy!" by Mary Webb. This collection consists of poems, short stories and character studies, and a group of essays from which the book gets its title. Walter de la Mare, in his introduction, deplores the inadequacy of words to describe these essays, perfect alone in their "poetic prose", quite apart from their powerful healing value. But, of course, if you are a "good reader", you will have discovered Mary Webb for yourself.

English humour is not quite like that of any other race, and the English novelist throughout the ages has always given us at least one rich and lovable comic character for which he will be remembered long after his tragic heroines and dramatic villains have been forgotten.. "English Comic Characters", a Cygnet book on sale at Sketchleys, is a selection of the best of these. This little book contains extracts from the greatest classics, ranging from the genial Falstaff to J. B. Priestley's likeable mill-hand, Jess Oakroyd—you remember him in "The Good Companions". Scott, Thackeray, Dickens, Eliot, Wells and Bennett are all represented by choice selections from their best novels, and each one of these is rich in a widely different type of humour. You may laugh uproariously at the antics and capers of Falstaff and his merry crew, but you must smile gently with Thomas Hardy, and thoughtfully with Tobias Smollet.

I want you to read this next precious slip of a book because I don't quite know what to make of it. The plot is pure fantasy, but the setting is that of the Civil Service. It is written in prose, but you have a feeling it might be lyric, poetry or a ballad. The book is "The Unpractised Heart", by L. A. G. Strong.

Bookseller and Stationer :: Lending Library

J. SKETCHLEY

24 & 25, High Street, Loughborough

Telephone 2980.

SONG

(With apologies to the Skye Boatmen.)
(Written during the absence of all sanitary arrangements in "J" Hut.)

Though many warblers' notes may be heard
  By acute ears in "J",
Nature more strongly calls than a bird ·
  Over the fields from "K".

Though the C.O.
  Bids us to go
Round by the concrete way,
  In times of need
  I'm sure he'd give speed
Priority over hay.

Shifts are so long and breaks are so brief,
  Therefore the girls from "J"
Constantly rush in search of relief
  Over the fields to "K".

Poem by MARY GILL.
Illustrated by "WILK".

"Traveller in Tokyo"

SO far most of the books reviewed here have been fictional, but I want to recommend one based solely on fact. It is John Morris's "Traveller in Tokyo", which gives the impressions of a Professor of English Literature in Japan before and during the war.

The grim facts of Japanese prison life and education since the outbreak of war are counterbalanced by the entertainment derived from situations like this:

In Japan, if a large house is demolished and a number of smaller ones put in its place, **all** these houses retain the original number of the mansion. As the houses in a block are numbered as they are built and not consecutively, one realizes that locating a friend's house for the first time is no easy matter.

You can also learn about Japanese music and theatres, and find how they differ from our own. As I read, I was forced to realize the great division between our life and life in the East, and how slight was my knowledge of those countries.

So, for those who, like myself, wish to know more of the Arts, social life, and customs of other countries, I suggest "Traveller in Tokyo".

J. M. PEARCE.

ATS

Continental Cameos.

TO me, who was lucky enough to spend my childhood abroad, visits to new places meant different and exciting food, beautifully served and often eaten in fascinating surroundings.

Take, for example, that hot September day in Bayonne. Outside, the quiet of noon lay heavily on the town, the basque sun blazed high in the heavens, and the white roads shimmered in the heat. The only sound was a gentle swish as the water from above the windows of the hotel slid in a cooling curtain on to the hot pavement below.

Inside the low ceilinged room, it was refreshingly dark and pleasant; on the long tables stood the usual bottles of red and of white wine, the long loaves of bread, and the round short sausages, so appealing to a garlic-loving race.

There was much laughter and loud talk amongst the diners for they were discussing a bull fight to be held the next day in the Spanish town of San Sebastian. Suddenly the conversation stopped and changed to shouts of appreciation as the stirring strains of Bizet's "Toreador Song" filled the air. An old man had come in, and was slowing walking round the room turning the handle of a small cylindrical barrel-organ which hung from his thin shoulders.

With this appropriate finale, I leave the frontier of Spain for that of Switzerland, and so come to Basle, after a happy drive through the highways of Alsace-Lorraine, which were lined with fruit trees so that for miles the ground was covered with walnuts. We picked them up in handfuls, squeezing the pulpy green cases until the clean nuts popped out, ready for shelling.

The market in Basle is the ideal place for buying peaches—large as oranges—juicy and smooth cheeked. They are sold there as cheaply as apples. Another speciality of this clean Swiss town is its confectionery. I remember we sat on the balcony of a cafe looking down on to the river, and there we lunched off small cakes made with honey and almonds, crisp macaroons and feather-light meringues, thick with cream.

From such delights, my memory hurries on to Freiburg, in the Black Forest, over the floating bridge of Vieux Brissach, to this pleasant German city with its smart uniformed policemen who, in 1933, still had time to be courteous and helpful to their English visitors.

Let me finish with a description of the magnificent banquet we enjoyed there. After the usual hors d'œuvres had been served, in came the maitre d'hotel carrying on a large silver dish a whole salmon fresh from the Rhine, perfectly cooked; to accompany this we had fifty different varieties of vegetables arranged on another enormous platter.

Alas! My ration-conscious mind can bear no more of these reflections. Farewell, O continental luxury, for the duration!

HAZEL MILLER.

o o o o o

Do You Like the Movies?

ONCE upon a time a very ordinary little AT, named Private X, was caught by a sergeant when climbing in through the back window of her billet at a time when all good little ATs (including sergeants) should be tucked up in their bunks. The result of this episode was that the ordinary private was interviewed by an equally ordinary officer and given a routine rebuke and seven days. Whereupon everyone very sensibly forgot all about it.

But it so happened that a gentleman from Hollywood, with a big cigar and horn-rimmed spectacles which magnified things by a million, chanced to hear of the event, and immediately let out a shriek of "Yowzah!" (the American equivalent of "Eureka!") and turned this very ordinary affair into the screen sensation of the century—"The throbbing human drama of a nation at war". When it was finished, he thought it was so good that he told everyone they really ought to see it. And of course they did, so the gentleman made millions of dollars.

The climax of the picture was the interview. Imagine it: a couple of acres of bare room lighted by a 10,000,000 watt setting sun; an unseen and unexplained orchestra softly playing "Colonel Bogey" as the camera wanders along the walls, disclosing a row of portraits of every female warrior from Boadicea to Lady Astor, then at last coming to rest on another Amazon—this time a real one—who is sitting at a desk. Her bemedalled bust is topped by a face like a stallion's: not a curl relieves her utility coiffure; not a suspicion of a dimple softens her stiff mouth. She is obviously a "no nonsense" woman. She is, of course, the C.O. ("You remember, she did the murders in that film about——" "Shh!")

We suspect, however, that she is not as tough as she looks—nobody could be—and this is confirmed when a fat, sentimental sergeant waddles in ("Coo, isn't she like our Fanny?"). For a moment the C.O. almost smiles—but stops just in time.

"Say, chief," oozes the sergeant, "dat goil's here—you know, de one dat played hookey wid no pass. Say, chief" (her voice is soapy with appeal) "chief, have a heart, just dis once—she's only a kid, chief——" But the stallion isn't having any. "Sargeant!" she neighs, "remembah—discipline! Bring in the prisonah!" And she folds her arms on her massive chest. ("Ooh, the old ——!")

Enter Pte. X—in technicolour. ("Oh, isn't she lovely!") Pte. X is certainly an eyeful. She has spun-gold hair to her waist, silk stockings on her heavily insured legs, and a mouth like a squashed raspberry. She is escorted by a bevy of female Commandos.

For a moment Pte. X is a big brave girl—she keeps her million dollar chin-line skywards and her luscious upper lip stiff. She and the C.O. stare at each other in an electric, pregnant silence. We hold our breath—the tension is terrific. Then the dewy mouth trembles and with a sob Pte. X collapses on to the nearest Commando—the sergeant begins to weep, the Commandos begin to weep, the audience joins in and a thoroughly good time is had by all. Except the C.O., who stands in frozen isolation.

When the emotion has subsided, the sergeant rushes entreatingly to the C.O. "Chief!" she sobs, "Her boy friend came up to see her. Chief! **She may never see him again! !**" This reduces everyone else to tears again, but the C.O. is unmoved. "Chief!" wails the sergeant in a last attempt, "Chief—he calls her his little Sugar Plum".

Now, that gets the C.O. where it hurts most. We get a close-up of her face—she is obviously moved. The nostrils quiver and (can it be?) a tear gleams in one glassy eye. ("Wonderful acting!"—"Just glycerine, darling.") "Did you say—Sugar Plum?" she asks in a strangled voice. "Sure, chief, Sugar Plum," wails the sergeant.

The stallion's face drops, almost audibly. Her emotion rises, but she fights it back. Her bosom heaves, her teeth clench—can she take it? With tremendous effort she swallows all the lumps in her throat (Attagirl!) and speaks. "Pte. X, your case is dismissed—you may go."

A.T.S.! Let us have *YOUR* contributions!

The Digby Chronicles

THE Yanks came to our village the other day, much to the disapproval of Steve and our Mrs. Buckett.

"Them Yanks!" she exclaimed. "The things I've 'eard about 'em, M'm. I'm keeping my young Gladys in o' nights, that's certain. You're lucky Miss Susan and Miss Judy aren't old enough to cause you any worry."

Irony! The very next day, Susan failed to return from school for dinner. Mrs. Buckett eyed the First Aid box and muttered ominously about "them jeeps", but her words gave me an idea. I hurried out of the house—— down the road——.

Outside the Yankee camp was parked a jeep, whose driver, bearing a strong resemblance to Gary Cooper, was holding enthralled a juvenile audience. Foremost among them was Susan, her jaws champing mechanically.

"Susan!" I began. But before I could go on, the driver interrupted me in an irresistable Southern drawl.

"Is this yore li'l gal, Ma'am? She shore is cute! I guess I kinder kep' her out late, didn't I? Gee, I'm sorry. I figure you muster worried some, huh? Wal, now, Ma'am, mebbe y'll let m' run y' home a little ways, seein' that I kep' y' late?"

He ran us home. The faces of Judy and Gilly, and Mrs. Buckett were a picture. And the face of Mrs. Buckett's Gladys, who had just that moment come round to see her mother, was more than that. And when Judy and Gilly insisted on the point of tears that they, too, should be allowed to ride in the jeep "a little ways", there seemed nothing for it but to ask Gary Cooper in to partake of dinner with us, which he did with a delightful disregard for the possibility that he and his jeep might be required elsewhere on official business.

"Well, I must say," remarked Mrs. Buckett when he had gone. "'e's not at all wot you'd expect. If they're all like that, maybe there won't be much trouble after all."

Steve came home in the evening and was grimly silent when he heard of the day's adventures, and after supper flung out of the house to have a game of darts at the local——. What happened there, I couldn't say. Tact forbade me to ask, but presently Steve returned in high spirits with three of our gallant allies and a huge tin of preserved chicken, which they proceeded to open and heat up with every sign of *honhomie* and goodwill. I caught Steve's eye, and he winked gracelessly——.

About half an hour later I slipped upstairs to see that the family were not disturbed by the riotous party in progress below, and found them sleeping happily with a sadly depleted packet of candy on the table. And as I passed the window, I saw Gary Cooper escorting Mrs. Buckett's Gladys homeward—the Yanks had come to stay.

K. L. B. P.

FAMOUS LAST WORDS.

"Ah! Hamburger Roast!"

DEFINITIONS.

A TWO-TIMER is a man with a watch on each wrist.

A SAVINGS STAMP is something that comes unstuck on a rainy day.

A BYSTANDER is a Supervisor who hangs around staring hard, while you search madly for something he knows isn't there.

A PLENIPOTENTIARY is the father of eighteen children.

VICTORY
BIGGIN STREET, LOUGHBOROUGH

MONDAY, JULY 3rd (6 days)
Judy Garland and Mickey Rooney in
"GIRL CRAZY"
also Full Supporting Programme

MONDAY, JULY 10th (3 days)
Charles Laughton in
"THE MAN FROM DOWN UNDER"
Cartoon, Interest and News Films

THURSDAY, JULY 13th (3 days)
Joseph Cotten and Orson Welles in
"JOURNEY INTO FEAR"
also Joan Davis in "TWO SENORITAS"

MONDAY, JULY 17th (6 days)
Betty Grable and Robert Young in
"SWEET ROSIE O'GRADY"
(in Technicolour)
also "IN THE SOUND OF BIG BEN"

MONDAY, JULY 24th (6 days)
Anna Neagle and Richard Greene in
"THE YELLOW CANARY"
also Edgar Kennedy in "DUCK SOUP"

MONDAY, JULY 31st (6 days)
George Formby in
"BELL BOTTOM GEORGE"
also Bill Elliott, in "DEVIL'S PRICE"

Mon. to Fri—Con. from 5-30 p.m. Sat.—Con. from 2 p.m.
MATINEES.—Mon. and Wed. at 2-15 p.m.
SUNDAYS—6-15 p.m. (One Show)

Through the Looking Glass

Warning.

THOSE music-minded Ats, who, every time Trainer Sargent brings the Philharmonic Menagerie to Leicester, dash over to that fair city for the specific purpose of making passes at the Timpani and Percussion, during quiet spells, had better, if they value our advice, watch their dainty steps.

On a recent occasion at the Albert Hall the Slow Movement of Groobinoff's 50th Flute Concerto was completely ruined when the 3rd Bird Call, who had been nursing an excited little actress on his knee, accidentally dropped her on to a row of Oboes on the tier below. There is no need (as they say) to dwell on the unfortunate events which followed, except to say that the audience, nauseated by the display of orchestral sensuality, rose as one man and demanded their money back.

Since then things have changed, and a Philharmonic Gestapo has been instituted which keeps a careful watch on all females attending concerts. At the slightest sign of a "glad-eye" on the part of any eligible cutie, she is seized by these gentry, dragged away, and placed in a golden cage in the Conductor's larder. Next morning, having been previously dehydrated, she is fried and served with bacon at the Maestro's breakfast-table.

"The ones between eighteen and twenty-two are delicious if lightly done and served with Worcester Sauce," said Anatolio Vistolario, reflectively picking his teeth, yesterday.

Disclosure.

Speculation about the origin of that curious fungoid growth displayed for sale (2d. per portion) under the specimen case on the canteen counter, can, we are happy to announce, now be stilled. One day recently, being in a particularly public-spirited frame of mind, we invested part of our hard-earned stipend in a piece, and, with a courageous disregard for personal risk, fought against the deadly vapours it exuded, and carried same off to our secret laboratory for analysis.

Although after having spent three hours with the specimen in a confined space our health has been ruined, and our doctors only give us three weeks to live, we ungrudgingly announce our findings for the benefit of posterity: the specimen is identical with a rare form of sea barnacle (*floris marinum*) which we remember once scraping from the keel of the sunken German battle-cruiser "Prinz Otto von Karlemutche", when we were a diver at Scapa Flow in 1922.

The only problem now remaining is how they got into the canteen; we have no information on that point, but we wouldn't mind betting our next year's Income Tax rebate that one of our ex-Naval boys located the supply during his travels round the world, and is now getting a nice little rake-off on the side by smuggling it into the Dump when all honest men are safe in bed.

Reminder.

The prolonged chorus of delighted laughter which greeted the recent screen debut of those local Big-Shots who exhorted their fellow-citizens to save in order to speed the coming of the new Utopia, was, in our enlightened view, final proof (if any were needed) of that inherent sadism which is a salient feature of our island temperament. Instead of a decent silence, or even a few sympathetic tears, the population went into an orgy of unholy mirth; hugely amused to see those unprepossessing pans magnified to a hundred times normal size.

It's just the same state of mind which (a) makes the "Trial of Jack the Ripper" the most widely read book in Christendom; (b) makes thousands of human ghouls from among the populace flock to funerals purely for their entertainment value; and (c) gives the N*WS *F TH* W*RLD the record circulation for Sunday newspapers.

To those of you bozos who joined in the general merriment, we say that it takes a handsome pan to stand up to hundred times magnification; and, like us, if it happened to you, you'd be forced to emigrate at once to one of the remoter parts of Tibet.

LEON DE BUNK.

Difference of Opinion

Between "Dook" Downer *and* "Last Goodnight" Royle.

MODERN POETRY!!!

I visited the Elysium, and trod its fields of green,
Where all the mighty poets come to live a life serene.
But only those with purest styles
Are welcome in the Land of Smiles.

And there I sat and lightly spoke of modernists like Royle,
They all agreed, those spirit folk: 'If we had blood 'twould boil—
The blighter's bound to be a cheater
Who writes without a rhyme or metre!'

                                                      DOWNER.

If within th' Elysian field
    Only rosy rhymesters sit
And modernist shades who used to wield
    Progressive pens, are barred from it—
I can not say my heart-beat jumps
    At thought of what that "heaven" may be—
Gath'ring flowers with lyrical bumps
    Or rhyming for God's nursery.

                                                      ROYLE.

Wordsworth, the greatest of all
The seekers
After perfection in rhyme was absent
And since while on Earth
He showed no great depth of thought
I sadly presumed that he
Had been completely influenced
By Mr. Royle's spiritual reasoning
(Which, being as he is
He denies he possesses)
And had been relegated
To purgatorial realms.

                                                      DOWNER.

Oh, we poets who live in Elysia
All find it very much easi-ah
To make all our matter
Like infantile chatter
Re rosebuds and flowers and bees.
And we caref'ly avoid all philosophy;
Radical trends, or theology;
On all subjects profound
We are not on safe ground
It sends us all weak at the knees.

                                                      ROYLE.

GET YOUR———
Beauty and Toilet Preparations
FROM

"LEONARD'S"

Gentlemen's Hairdresser

25, CHURCH GATE, LOUGHBOROUGH

Large Variety in Stock!

EMPIRE
MARKET PLACE, LOUGHBOROUGH

MONDAY, JULY 3rd (3 days)
Charles Laughton and Clark Gable in
"MUTINY ON THE BOUNTY"
also "FIELD MOUSE"

THURSDAY, JULY 6th (3 days)
Tom Conway in
"THE FALCON IN DANGER"
also Ken Baker in "DOUGHBOYS IN IRELAND"

MONDAY, JULY 10th (6 days)
Walter Fitzgerald and Mervyn Johns in
"SAN DEMETRIO—LONDON"
also Charles Starrett in "FALLING STONES"

MONDAY, JULY 17th (3 days)
Merle Oberon and Brian Aherne in
"FIRST COMES COURAGE"
also Hugh Herbert in "IT'S A GREAT LIFE"

THURSDAY, JULY 20th (3 days)
David Farrar in "HEADLINE"
also Claire Trevor in "GOOD LUCK, MR. YATES"

MONDAY, JULY 24th (6 days)
Humphrey Bogart in "SAHARA"
Also Allan Jones in "You're a Lucky Fellow, Mr. Smith"

MONDAY, JULY 31st (3 days)
Ann Miller and Rochester in
"WHAT'S BUZZIN' COUSIN"
also Gale Sondergard in "Strange Death of Adolph Hitler"

THURSDAY, AUGUST 3rd (3 days)
Donald O'Connor and Gloria Jean in
"MR. BIG"
also Jack Holt in "Holt of the Secret Service"

CONTINUOUS DAILY. Doors open at 1-30 p.m.
SUNDAYS at 5-30 p.m.

Printed by Toppings Ltd., 17, Southfield Rd., Loughborough, and published by L. P. Jones for Beaumanor Staff Magazine Committee.

AUGUST, 1944

VOL. I. No. 6 (NEW SERIES) - **6d.**

FILM ATTRACTIONS for AUGUST

SHOWING AT THE ODEON THEATRE

Sunday, August 6th—Rosalind Russell and Don Ameche in **THE FEMININE TOUCH**. Also J. Anthony Hughes in **MEN OF SAN QUENTIN**.

MONDAY, AUGUST 7th, for 6 days
Clive Brook, Beatrice Lillie and Roland Culver in

ON APPROVAL

Also Diana Barrymore and Robert Paige in **FRONTIER BAD MEN**

Sunday, August 13th—Robert Young and Ruth Hussey in **MARRIED BACHELOR**. Also Clifford Evans in **SUSPECTED PERSONS**.

MONDAY, AUGUST 14th, for 6 days
Ray Milland, Ruth Hussey and Gail Russell in

THE UNINVITED

Also James Stewart and Paulette Goddard in **THE GOLDEN HOUR**.

Sunday, August 20th—Kenny Baker and Patricia Morison in **SILVER SKATES**. Also the East Side Kids in **CLANCY STREET BOYS**.

MONDAY, AUG. 21st—3 days	THURS., AUG. 24th—3 days
Tallulah Bankhead, William Bendix and Mary Anderson in	Betty Grable, John Payne and Carmen Miranda in
LIFEBOAT	**Springtime in the Rockies**
Also Dennis O'Keefe in **GOOD MORNING, JUDGE**	Also James Craig and Patricia Dane in **NORTH WEST RANGERS**

Sunday, August 27th—Barton McLane and Charles Bickford in **MUTINY IN THE BIG HOUSE**. Also John Carroll in **WOLF CALL**.

MONDAY, AUGUST 28th, for 6 days
Dorothy Lamour, Dick Powell and Victor Moore in

MELODY INN

in TECHNICOLOUR

Also Richard Arlen and Mary Beth Hughes in
TIMBER QUEEN

Continuous Performance Daily 1-45 p.m.   Sunday, One Performance at 6 p.m.

B.S.M. Vol. I. No. 6 (New Series)
AUGUST, 1944.

Editors: LEONARD P. JONES, ERIC C. MILLHOUSE

A.T.S. Editresses: KAY PRICE, MARY GILL. Treasurer: A. H. APPLETON.

Editorial Board:
DICK WILKINSON, OLLIE PEARCE, DUDLEY TRUIN, RON DENNY (B.W.)

CALLING ALL

GOOD READING
By "B.B." and "R.R."

"THE Moon is Down" is a book in true John Steinbeck style—simple, straight-to-the-point-writing. He manages to give every word a significance without making the whole stilted. The scene is set in a village occupied by the Germans; the silence and inner hatred of these people causes the gradual break-down of the morale of the Army of Occupation—you learn how these soldiers long for all the things they have lost—smiling faces, trust and friendship, and how this affects each one of them. A really vital story——.

There have been many books written about Doctors, Artists, Vagabonds, Poets, etc.—all the romantic professions—so that a book about hotels and hotel-keeping doesn't sound very enthralling. But then you haven't read Sinclaire Lewis' "Work of Art". This is the story of Myron, American small-town boy, whose parents keep a very antiquated Guest House. He learns from this all the things that can be wrong with a Hotel, and is determined one day to own one himself—the perfect hotel. You can then follow his fortunes and misfortunes on his way up the scale from bell-boy to Manager, and then to Owner—always in search of perfection. It is the story of a real artist who is not content while something is still incorrect.

I know all of you like a book that you can pick when you have half-an-hour to spare. You'll enjoy "While Rome Burns", by Alexander Woolcott, as it is just that type of book,—a series of impressions of people he has met, each complete in itself. Stories of Paul Robeson's humour and genuineness, the scathing remarks and wit of Dorothy Parker, these and many others form this grand collection. Through the whole book is stamped the striking personality of Woolcott himself, making it doubly interesting. It is published in the Penguin series.

"Serious Business", "People of Importance", and "Important People"——I don't think anyone can fail to be amused and delighted by these selections of child sketches by H. Dowd. He seems to have captured exactly, by a few strokes of the pencil, those expressions of the moment:——Children by the sea, at the circus, at the zoo, etc. These are books you can look at and read again and again and still find enjoyment.

Next issue ready August 25th. All contributions to reach the Editors by August 11th.

Spam Fritters.

BETWEEN TWO LANDLADIES.

IT was after one of their clothes-line meetings that Mrs. Drippage invited Mrs. Cudd in for a cup of tea.

"There's something I want you to see," she confided mysteriously.

Mrs. Cudd was all curiosity.

"Wot is it?" she asked. "Anything to do with that feller Grabchick?"

Without replying, Mrs. Drippage led the way indoors and upstairs, stopping at her first floor front with a conspiratorial wink.

"'E's on two-to-ten this week," she explained, and flung open the door.

Mr. Grabchick's bedroom was neat in the extreme, but Mrs. Cudd did not have time to dwell on that point.

"Look," hissed Mrs. Drippage.

The gaze of Mrs. Cudd followed her pointing finger and faltered as it fell on the object in question. On the bedside table was the statue of a dancing nymph, her perfect limbs triumphantly naked.

"Disgusting!" gloated Mrs. Cudd, relishing the spectacle. "Revolting!"

Without another word, Mrs. Drippage drew her downstairs and set about making the tea.

"I'm disappointed in 'im," she said at last. "Do you think it's respectable for me to be alone in the 'ouse with some one like 'im, Mrs. Cudd?"

"Weeeell, I should think so," rejoined that lady, much moved. "I think you're the very person to 'elp 'im out of 'is un'ealthy frame of mind——a decent, well-conducted woman like you. You shouldn't take that to 'eart, Mrs. D. you shouldn't reely. I understand these men so well, you see. 'E's just lonely for feminine company I expect."

"Maybe, maybe," agreed Mrs. Drippage, doubtfully. "I think I'll just see 'ow 'e goes on before I speak to the Billeting Officer——Sugar, Mrs. Cudd?"

EXTRACTS FROM ORDERS.

Battledress or tunics will be worn properly on duty and not slung round the shoulders. Even at six o'clock in the morning this is indispensable to the War Effort.

Auxiliaries will treat the Canteen Staff with the utmost consideration and civility at all times, remembering the arduous and irksome nature of their duties; and any hastiness or discourtesy on their part will be overlooked on these grounds.

Double Banking.

"Oh yes, well, I was telling you about my Auntie Maud,
"She lost her reputation on a Summer Cruise abroad,
"They say that skirts were short that year in nineteen-twenty-six——
"——Oh just a minute, darling, there's the blighter up on vics——
"Where was I? To continue, about my Auntie's skirts,
"Well women blessed with dials like hers are very seldom flirts,
"But her legs weren't bad, and I suppose that they brought home the bacon—
"——Did you hear something then? No? Well I must have been mistaken——
"——She met a Count from Italy who doted on antiques
"He said her legs were Sheraton and studied them for weeks——
"Now why is Nobby waving in that agitated way?
"What's that? Oh really, Nobby, what a **horrid** thing to say!
"Just ring them back and tell them that they've got it wrong again,
"We've listened **very carefully**, we **couldn't** have missed **ten**!"

"ONCE UPON A WAR."

THE room was lit only by firelight; all was silent save for the remorseless, insistant ticking of the ancient clock in the corner; there was a sofa before the fire, and on it were two figures locked together blindly in a frenzied, desperate embrace, their bodies stiffened into one mute, taut agony.

It was always the same when they said goodbye——those precious few minutes, so short and yet so long, might be their last together on earth——you never could tell.

The slightly discordant chime of the clock suddenly loosened the tension, and she broke away from him and stood by the fireplace, pushing back her heavy hair, straightening her dress——.

"It's time," she said dully.

He rose too and came swiftly to her side. "I love you," he said, placing his hands on her shoulders. "I love you——I love you——"

"I love you, too," she replied.

Their words were passionate——and very banal.

He began to shrug himself into his fleece-lined flying jacket.

"I'll help you," she began.

"I'm ready now," he answered, jerking the zipper sharply. He clasped her quickly to him for one last moment, and then pushing her gently away, made for the door.

"Wait——oh wait," she cried frantically. "Your mascot——you've left it."

"Of course." He turned back, and she held out to him a shabby little black velvet cat, about two inches long, greasy with much wear.

"Kiss it for luck," he smiled half-mocking.

She pressed it to her lips. "There." She buttoned it lovingly into his breast pocket. "Goodbye darling."

"Goodbye sweet." The door slammed behind him, and she returned drearily to sit on the sofa.

The flames died to embers, and the embers to dull ash, and still she sat there, tense and waiting. At last she heard it——in the far distance, growing louder every minute, came a heavy droning. The house shook with the vibration of aero engines as the bomber squadron passed overhead,—his squadron. Gradually the sound merged away again into nothingness——

* * * *

There was plenty of resistance over the target area——flak like hail, blinding searchlights and night-fighters everywhere. Maybe the little mascot was worn out——maybe her kiss failed to propitiate it to-night——at all events, he "got his" and crashed with his plane to the ground, where it exploded thunderously.——

* * * *

They broke the news to her gently, and when they had finished she sat in frozen silence for so long that they grew anxious.

"Are you all right?" they questioned nervously.

"Leave me——please leave me,"——the words broke from her stiff lips as haltingly as if she spoke an unfamiliar language.

So they left her, and only then did she give way. She flung herself down, and her body shook with tearless, racking sobs.

* * * *

Who was this couple? you may ask. Is it of any consequence? Were they British or American or Russian—or German,—or even Jap?

What in heaven's name does it matter? That sort of thing can happen to anyone in a War.

KAY PRICE.

ATS

Do You Like the Movies?

REMEMBER the gentleman from Hollywood with the horn-rimmed glasses which magnified things by a million? Well, one day he was driving through Quorn in his turquoise and blue limousine with the technicolour headlights, and he dropped off for a shot at the local high-class hostelry—the gentleman from America called it a "joint", which was sacrilegious, but then, he didn't know any better.

Well, in this Pub (sorry, Hotel) he chanced to meet a certain Highly Placed Army Officer and promptly bought him a whisky, so they became bosom friends, and the H.P.A.O. offered to show the Gentleman from Hollywood round a Very Secret Place which was hidden in the neighbouring foliage. So they jumped into the limousine and spent a pleasant evening among the delicious scenery and disgusting noises.

Now, the Gentleman from Hollywood was so entranced with what he saw and heard that he flew straight back to the States and spent millions of dollars on a terrific Technicolour Musical called "Weekend at the Manor"—which, to quote the Gentleman himself, was "a real humdinger!"

It was one of those luscious, glamorous, incredible films, with acres of satin-smooth floors, and bathing pools from which appetizing blondes appear in miraculously dry ballet skirts and a constant stream of tunes, sugary sweet or restlessly "hot", dripping from the mouths of female singers—you know the type of thing: they turn them out by the dozen. But "Weekend at the Manor" was, to quote the Gentleman again, "Super-duper-duper!" It had everything. It even had a story, though that didn't matter very much.

The story concerned a gorgeous male operator—of course, all the male operators were gorgeous brutes, but this one was a real woman-eater—who had a misunderstanding with his sweetie, a golden-voiced telephone 'op, because of a certain tender little note she had left in the canteen rack and which had gone astray through the activities of the local Snoop. Needless to say, there were lots of complications before the note reached the hero: at one point it got baked into a canteen bun and all the male 'ops played Rugby with it. (Yes, Colonel, on the grass!) But everything turned out well and no one bothers about the story, anyway. The main thing is the spectacle.

And there certainly was some spectacle! The film was decorated by the "Danger Signals", a bevy of marvellous girls clad in judiciously placed triangles of navy and white chiffon. They had two numbers, one of them a really "hot" one called "Got Ants in my Pants and Morse on my Mind", where they all tap-danced on top of revolving wireless sets and swung by their exquisite legs on light cords. Their other number was a sweet one called "You Turn 'Ell into 'Eaven", which they crooned in close harmony to a supervisor. (Lucky Guy!)

The supervisors, naturally, were all comedy characters and caused lots of good clean fun by their contortions when trying to answer six phones at once. They were the cutest things, and they did a fast rhythm number together called "Why aintcha got it, Baby?" which was a scream in more ways than one.

The finale was set in the canteen, a superbly decorated night club with reflecting floors which enabled us to see twice as much of the "Stop Signals"—Mmm! Here the canteen girls appeared as hostesses in dream-lovely evening dresses, their duties being to entertain the male 'ops by plying them with champagne, dancing with them, and—well, generally amusing them and taking their minds off things. In this finale, the lovers were finally united in a juicy close-up, ending with a syrupy love song—"You'll never call me in vain". Everyone joined in—the male 'ops and the canteen girls melted into each others arms, the "Danger Signals" and supervisors did likewise, and the whole lot melted into a whirl of colour and music.

"Weekend at the Manor"? That's what he thinks!

MARY GILL.

CLASS DISTINCTION.

ATS

In days of old, Beaumanor-ites
Shared jointly sorrows and delights,
Discomforts too, and luxury——
The Essence of Democracy.
Until the Army took a hand
And thought this Democratic stand
Too lenient by far, and so
Declared this state of things must go.
Accordingly from far and near
A horde of workmen did appear
And straightway fell on all the huts
And heeded neither ifs nor buts.
And where had only been before
A modest universal door,
They said, "Let there be two or three"
And hacked the wall with fiendish glee,
Until to our surprise we find
A door for every rank and kind.
The ATS must make their way
The longest distance round to K,
And troop o'er floor of good concrete
With busy, clitter-clatt'ring feet,
And go to work all wearily——
The Army says such things should be.
And Supervisors and their like
Who come to work on rattling bike
Are filled with sudden deep-set awe
At having for themselves a door.
(Though why these unassuming gentry
Should be assigned a special entry
Is none too clear.) But one thing yet——
Within should lie some sacred mat
With "Welcome Home" inscribed thereon
To wipe their lovely tootsies on.
But when one quietly sits and thinks
One feels this Class Distinction stinks.

KAY PRICE.

GET YOUR———

Beauty and Toilet Preparations
FROM
"LEONARD'S"

Gentlemen's Hairdresser

25, CHURCH GATE, LOUGHBOROUGH

Large Variety in Stock!

TESS.

MAYBE it was all a joke. Of course they knew it was my birthday—they were just waiting to see how long I would go on before giving them a gentle reminder. I looked at Mummy's face—no sign there. Was she smiling? I peered hard but she turned away quickly to rescue the kettle which was whistling loudly at being neglected—it had that "I've been boiling a whole minute" note that infuriated me.

"Hang up your coat and school bag, dear,"—why she even **sounded** the same, said the same thing she said every other day. Oh well, hang up your coat, wash your hands for tea, and stop thinking about it. Wish this funny feeling would go away from me. Felt just as though I was all empty inside—my heart was running round and round and every now and then jumping up and catching my throat so that I felt all choked inside, and my nose and eyes began to run.

"Mrs. Jones called to say: 'Many Happy Returns,' dear". Mummy's voice came to me through the open door. Could it be that she **knew** and was just ignoring the fact that I was one whole year older? Well, I'd show them I didn't care. "What did you say, Mummy? Many Happy Returns? Why whose birthday is it? Mine! Well so it is—I'd completely forgotten!" I followed up this statement with an airy laugh—at least it should have been an airy laugh, but it started somewhere down in my throat, and got so mixed up that it ended up as a terrible gurgle. I rubbed my face vigorously with my towel to make it all red, instead of leaving my eyes to look like over-ripe tomatoes, and then I walked into the room with that don't-care look on my face which I always wear when made to stand behind the blackboard at school.

They'll be sorry one day.—I'll run away. The idea came quite naturally as though it had been at the back of my mind all the while. I remembered a story I had read at school about a little girl and boy who had run away from home, with only a pound of potatoes for food. Maybe I could find a loaf of bread—or even a pot of that delicious jam Mummy had made last year. I remember when she made it I stood by her and she let me stir the boiling fruit—I can still smell it—no more of that. I'd get up in the middle of the night. I hope it's not too cold. It's always cold when we get up early to go on holidays.—NO, I'd wait till to-morrow, and instead of going to school I'd run away. At least I would have had my breakfast, and I could get to the docks easily and I'd stow away to America. I might even see Robert Taylor or Shirley Temple.—

"Eat your tea, dear,"—I jumped in my chair to see Mummy watching me. I couldn't eat—everything stuck in my throat. Wish this silly heart would go back to its rightful place. This is the last meal I'll eat with Mummy at the other end of the table, last time I'd be told to hang up my coat and school bag—out came my hankie in a rush and I blew my nose so hard that I made myself deaf.

Somewhere in the distance I heard a door open and a minute tornado hit the room, heading straight for me. I put out my arms to defend myself, and they closed around a bundle of warm fur, a small pink tongue licked my face and bit playfully at my hair, but I couldn't see, my head was buried in the soft fur which was getting soaked with the tears that would not be held back any longer. The blue ribbon round its neck became crumpled and fell off, and with it a card—"My name is Tess. Happy birthday to our little daughter on her tenth birthday."

Through the mist of my tears I saw the flushed and triumphant face of my brother breathlessly explaining,—"You see the fellow was out when I got there, and I had to wait awhile."

IVY WALTON.

The Gospel according to St. Apid
CHAPTER XXXIII.
(Translated from the English by Disciple Millhouse).

NOW, when the Hard Core first came up into the Promised Land, having been sorely afflicted with a certain Nafi in Chiksanz, Red Tabz, who dwelleth in Wyt Awl, made a bond with them, saying: Verily, verily, I say unto ye, now ye are come into the Promised Land, I will raise up a mighty Greenhouse; and it shall be called Kantin; and it shall be thine own. And behold, ere one saith Jack Robinson, the Greenhouse was builded. Inasmuch as none saith Jack Robinson for fourteen moons.

And when the peoples beheld the Kantin, and the multitude of serving-maids, and the abundance of victuals, and the wherewithal to spoil the victuals in sundry ways, they were well pleased, and straightway appointed certain of their number to rule Kantin, and to count the shekels.

But with the passing of the seasons the Tribe became sorely cheesed with Kantin, and all that therein was, and communed many times among themselves, certain among them considering that they smelled rats. Wherefore they called upon a great merchant called Kowop, and cried unto him in this wise, saying: Woe is us. For Kantin hath become in a Flat Spin. Wilt thou therefore come hither and straighten it? And Kowop, who was much practised in counting shekels, answered: Yea, and forthwith came, and was like unto a New Broom. But, it is written: The New Broom moulted. And the queues waxed exceeding long, and the Char waxed exceeding foul, and there was no health in them.

Now there was a Great System. And this was the System: Whereas one entereth into Kantin and crieth unto the serving-maid: Char. Yet there is no serving-maid. And when she waketh, and cometh forth, she perceiveth that she is without Char. And she goeth within and maketh a mighty mashing. And when she bringeth forth the mashing she is cast down because there are no goblets. And she journeyeth back and forth, and gathereth up goblets, and wetteth them, and spreadeth out the lipstick, which is called cleansing. And when she hath brought forth the goblets, the Mashing is become exceeding cold. Wherefore she Masheth again and bringeth it out, but is without milk. And, going for milk, she tarrieth awhile with her fatigue. Wherefore another entereth Kantin and saith unto he whom waiteth: Time you went back, mate. But at certain times the serving-maid was possessed of much Mashing, and many goblets, and an abundance of milk. But these times were not Break times.

Now a certain Bobrob, being a Big Cheese of Kantin, as also a Chief Rabbi of the temples, went one day into Kantin, and saith unto the serving-maid which slept behind the Grub Counter: Brekker. And when she had bathed, and combed her hair, and put upon her face fresh war-paint, she brought forth a mess of pottage. And when Bobrob beheld the pottage he was exceeding wrath, for it was indeed a mess. And he caused a Great Flap, and took the mess and sought out the High Priest of Kowop. But the High Priest made a Strategic Withdrawal. Wherefore Bobrob kept the mess unto him many days, that he might shew it to the High Priest. And unto whomsoever saith unto him: Whist ye not that thy pottage will rot? he answered: Nay, nay. For such is impossible.

Then it came to pass that a number of serving-maids grew sorely cheesed, and threw in their hands. And there was again a mighty Flap. And messengers sped from Tepee to the temples, and from the temples to the Holy of Holies, crying: Kantin is closed. And when the Chief Rabbi heard this he summoned the Prophet Osee from his bed. And when the Prophet drew nigh unto Kantin he saw there were serving-swaddies mashing a mighty mash. And he saith unto himself: Is my journey really necessary?

And a certain Ewa saith unto a Big Cheese of Kantin: How canst the serving-maids desert us thus? For is not Kantin under the mighty order of Essential Works? And the Cheese answered him, saying: Nay. For it is a Non-Industrial Kantin. And the Ewa replied: Dost thou not mean Non-Industrious?

Theatre Royal
LOUGHBOROUGH.

THE FORTESQUE
Famous Players

CONTINUE THEIR SUCCESSFUL REPERTORY SEASON

Monday, July 31st—(3 days only)
THE FAMOUS COMEDY
Billetted
From the Aldwych Theatre, London.

Monday, Aug. 7th—(6 days)
THE SCREAMING FARCE
The Rotters
By H. F. Maltby.

Monday, Aug. 14th—(5 nights)
THE FAMOUS PLAY
Camille
Adapted from the Play "The Lady of the Camelias."

Friday Only. Aug. 18th.
MARIA MARTEN
OR
THE MURDER IN THE RED BARN

Monday, Aug. 21st—(6 days)
A Sinner in Paradise
By Val Gurney.

Monday, Aug. 28th—(6 days)
NOEL COWARD'S Famous Comedy
Blithe Spirit

SHOW PARADE
Edited by Dudley Truin.

THOUGH **Leslie Howard** was a sensitive and polished actor I felt, after seeing "THE LAMP STILL BURNS", (Victory, 14th August, 6 days), that the British film industry's real loss was not so much an accomplished artist as an enlightened producer. Here was a man who had something to say and knew how to say it.

Completed just before his death, due to enemy action, "The Lamp Still Burns" deals objectively with the nursing profession in the same way as his "The Gentle Sex" dealt with the A.T.S.; but, whereas the latter film was inclined in places to glamorise life in that service, here the nurse's daily round of hard sacrificial work is presented in grim reality. The hospital's reliance on charity, the continual struggle for existence and how the acute shortage of funds is always felt first and foremost by the nurses, in poor pay and living conditions, is shown in the simple, unpretentious story of a girl architect—beautifully played by **Rosamund John**—who, as the result of an accident, feels the urge to serve her country as a nurse, and deals with her endeavours to adapt herself to the many irksome regulations of a nurse's life. The whole is a sincere tribute to the nursing profession and a fitting epitaph to **Leslie Howard's** social spirit.

It is not often that you find an actor who is capable of directing and producing a picture with any degree of success as well as playing the lead; Noel Coward is one, Chaplin another; it is therefore a refreshing surprise to find our old friend **Clive Brook** making such a first rate British comedy as "ON APPROVAL" (Odeon, 7th August, 6 days).

By emphasising the period and adding an amusing introduction and finale commentary by E. V. Emmett, he has turned this well known Lonsdale satire on society in the "nineties" which, as a play, I personally found rather brittle, into a really sparkling affair. Brook himself is excellent as the noble lord, as is **Roland Culver** as his friend; and on the feminine side **Beatrice Lillie** as the widow and **Googie Withers** as the American are perfect in this first class production.

If you like sentiment it is laid on with a trowel in "LASSIE COME HOME", (Empire, 28th August, 1944); though few will be able to resist the story of a collie's devotion to her young master. **Roddy McDowall** is quite good in the juvenile lead, and **Donald Crisp** is suitably taciturn as his father, who as an unemployed Yorkshireman sells Lassie to a duke (**Nigel Bruce**) from whom she escapes and returns home twice before she is taken to Scotland. Considering this is a Hollywood production the British backgrounds are fairly convincing, and photographed in Technicolor it makes pleasing entertainment.

There seems to be quite a vogue for films dealing with the supernatural at the moment, and though "THE UNINVITED" (Odeon, 14th August, 6 days) is not in the same class as the British production "The Half-Way House" yet to be shown locally, even so it is interestingly different. It is based on the assumption that spiritual bodies can influence human beings for good or evil; and there is an excellent performance from **Gail Russell,** a newcomer to the screen, as a girl influenced by the spirits of her dead father's wife and his mistress.

"WATCH ON THE RHINE" (Victory, 28th August, 6 days) is taken from the play of the same name, and is rather a talkative affair. **Bette Davis** is good as the American wife of an anti-Nazi German who works for the underground, but she is not quite in her element. The picture should be seen for the fine acting of **Paul Lukas** whose portrayal as the husband won for him the Academy Award last year.

It is a joy to see **Margaret Sullavan** again even if "CRY HAVOC" (Empire, 3 days, 21st August), in which she plays the part of a nurse, isn't all that it might be. Good acting has not been able to overcome the theatricality of this story of the women on Bataan.

11

SNOOP'S CORNER

CONGRATULATIONS to Reg. and Mrs. Hilder on the happy event which took place on July 7th, when Reg. was informed that he had a daughter. It was almost a week later that he learned it was a boy, and the celebrations in honour of Anthony Peter took place at "The Old English Gentleman" on the evening of July 13th. Father and guests did as well as could be expected.

To Marjorie Bartram, S.B.O., now at B.W., who was married during June to Petty Officer Jimmy Crabtree, R.N. The romance began at Barrow when the bridegroom was at Quorn College.

To Sgt. Betty Coombs, "A" Watch, No. 1 Wing, whose wedding is to take place in Surrey on July 24th. The bridegroom is a Pte. Quick, of the U.S. Army, and judging by the comparative short time that the Yanks have been in the district, it seems that he is appropriately named. Good luck, Betty; may you never have any leisure.

To Paddy Kelly and L/Cpl. Doreen Blake, who are now to be married on July 24th, the ceremony having been postponed for two days. It looks as though the B.S.M. will have to start a Ripley section.

To Sgt. Mary Parker, "B" Watch, No. 1 Wing, on her recent engagement to Pte. First Class Billy Reilly (or maybe it is Riley). It seems that our sergeants have a distinct preference for the American Army's privates.

To Pte. Mary Willcock, "C" Watch, No. 2 Wing, who was married at St. Mark's Church, Wolverhampton, on 20th July, to Kenneth Leighton Chick, late of S.O.T.B., Douglas.

I have often heard discussions concerning the dubious value of y and must confess that there have been times when I, too, have wondered. I have just returned from a trip during which I learned quite a lot about the mysteries of x, and as a result I have no hesitation in saying that the value of $x + y$ is incalculable. As this trip made me somewhat late with my MSS, I am afraid that I am to blame for the late publication of the August issue, and I suppose I shall suffer by being misquoted here and there due to there being insufficient time to check the proofs. However, this is not important as the Editorial Board (which includes "Ollie"—*Ed.*) are not interested in accuracy; in fact, they object to it.

We were amused at the invitation which was circulated recently, and read as follows:—The "I" Corps invites the Supervisers and operators, etc. The "I" presumably stands for Intelligence!

I read in the daily press that American Service drivers may no longer offer lifts to British Service girls. According to the explanation, "the ban had a certain moral background as there is no doubt that there have been incidents". It goes on to say that there have been too many accidents lately. Well, accidents will happen! I wonder why this statement was published on American Independence Day?

The many choir friends of Mrs. Chas. Brown (B.W.) will be pleased to know that she is now fully recovered from her recent illness.

We of Control have always suspected that our stock is pretty low in the numerous departments of the establishment, but we resent the implication of the two runners who paused outside the other morning to don their gas masks before entering. Surely this is carrying things a bit too far.

Amongst the pin-ups, which appeared on the canteen notice board recently, were a couple of interesting studies of Fred Vickers and Kathleen Sutcliffe, who appeared to be emulating the Siamese twins. Another picture showed Kathleen at the other end of the line with Mr. Dart, to the apparent consternation of Fred Vickers. Kathleen obviously believes that there is safety in numbers, as she also corresponds with Stan Brister. I wonder what Mr. Snell thinks about all this; or maybe he is not of a jealous disposition.

I have just finished filling in my new ration book and, carefully avoiding those spaces "To be filled in by retailer", and others marked "Do not fill in this space", etc., I find that I have signed my name 58 times, written my address 9 times, my national registration number 52 times, names and addresses of eight retailers with whom coupons are deposited, and a few other items such as food office Code No., Serial and No. of ration book, etc. As it is something of a phenomenon to receive a complete set of 3 A.T.S. Watch returns with no corrections necessary, I am forced to the conclusion that a large percentage of our senior N.C.O's. would starve to death if they were in Civvy street.

I understand that Johnny Hodge and Roy Aldridge took an unexpected plunge into the Soar the other day whilst on a boating trip. A couple of days later the following item appeared in the *News Chronicle*: "By aerating the heavily polluted waters in the river Soar, near Loughborough, Leicester N.F.S. are saving millions of fish from suffocation". No doubt our two heroes will point out in their own defence that in their case it was an accident, whilst several of the young ladies stationed at Barrow make a habit of bathing in the Soar.

Theatre Royal advert. per July B.S.M.: " 'First Night' by Reginald Denham. Definitely not for children". Of course it isn't; it's always been for adults.

We admire the spirit of the North West Mounted as displayed by the young lady who strode defiantly into the "Gents." at Loughborough the other night, but would like to point out that this reckless abandon stuff can be overdone.

We are informed by one of our scouts that the "Squanderbug", being too weary to clean his shoes, approached his landlady's small son, who pointed out that the job was worth a penny, whereupon our hero overcame his physical fatigue immediately and performed the task himself.

I hear that Pte. Helen Brown, of "B" Watch, No. 1 Wing, is to marry Sgt. Mulligan, of the U.S. Army towards the end of September.

Our sympathies are extended to Hazel, of the T.P. staff, who caught her finger in a mousetrap whilst trying to supplement her cheese ration.

We notice that the number of paratroop badges being worn by the A.T.S. is steadily increasing. Is it still a fact that these badges are only worn by people who have completed five missions?

That's all for now. Cheerio.

OLLIE.

I learn that our A.T.S. friends are permitted to go boating in sports attire, provided there is a party of three or more auxiliaries, who would be under the charge of an N.C.O. There is another stipulation to the effect that a "life-belt" must also be taken! The authorities, however, have no objection to a girl going out alone, and without a "life-belt", when in uniform. I wonder if I ought to tell them?

Bludgeons in Baker Street.
By E. St. U. M.
Second Hideous Episode
(Have you forgotten what happened last month? We have.)

AS the Marchioness of Pukingditch dried her lovely eyes and finished her tomato, Krumpit, the famous detective's assistant, rushed in.

"Hullo, Guvnor!" he cried breezily, planting a pound of dripping in his master's outstretched hand. He had been obliged to slip into a shop to evade a minion of the Crimson Circumference who had been shadowing him since he left the "Horrorscope".

Snouppe introduced the lad to the Marchioness and briefly recounted the details of her story. Krumpit possessed far above the normal amount of courage but Snouppe had to administer a little sal volatile before the lad was fit to receive his instructions.

"I want you to return with her Ladyship to Pukingditch, and see what you can find out," he said crisply. "I'll follow later. I've an appointment at 7-30 for a murderous struggle with Bung Ho, the Yellow Peril, and I can't let down the Editor of 'The Ghastly'; it's his final instalment."

In a flash Krumpit was outside pumping up his tyres, and soon the Marchioness and he were coasting down Baker Street. A furtive figure emerged from a gloomy corner, and, hurrying a little way along the street, he paused for a second before a fishmonger's to glance cautiously up and down. Swiftly, he entered. "A box of tin-tacks," he snarled.

"Next door," snarled back the man behind the counter.

The furtive man withdrew, and, entering the next shop, obtained his box of tin-tacks.

Precisely at 7-56 Dedleigh Snouppe handed over the writhing, bound and handcuffed body of Bung Ho to a Yard man, and, hailing a taxi, sped through the murky streets to Paddingloo. By the time he had paid the fare and tipped the driver he had only eight-and-sevenpence left. Breathlessly studying the timetable, he remembered that the Pukingditch trains departed from Charing Bridge. By the time he had reached there he only had three-and-fivepence, and he knew the fare to Pukingditch was considerably more than that. But Dedleigh Snouppe was never baffled. Unobtrusively he slipped into a deserted waiting-room.

Ten minutes later a small boy purchased a half fare to Pukingditch.

Emerging from the sleepy rural station he found the Marchioness's powerful limousine awaiting him. The chauffeur was somewhat upset when an untidy-looking ragamuffin poked the cold steel of a Wobley into his ribs and commanded him to drive to The Hovel.

The Marchioness was talking to a bowler-hatted man at the door, as he arrived.

"If you can't pay something off the arrears next week we'll have to lapse your policies," the man was saying, curtly. Snouppe, who had now resumed his normal appearance, strode up to the man, and quickly snapped a pair of handcuffs over his wrists. At that moment a police-car pulled up in a cloud of dust, and Snouppe's old rival, Inspector Dribblepuss, scrambled out, followed by eighteen constables.

"Bah!" panted the burly Inspector. "Foiled again by Dedleigh Snouppe!"

"Here's your man, Drib," said the famous criminologist, affably, and, dragging the cowering insurance-man forward, he ripped off the false beard, moustache, wig, spectacles, and eyebrows, with one smart jerk.

"Great Scot!" exclaimed the Yard man, "it's Jim the Pencilman!"

Bookseller and Stationer :: Lending Library

J. SKETCHLEY

24 & 25, High Street, Loughborough

Telephone 2980.

BLUDGEONS IN BAKER STREET—continued.

"Himself," replied Snouppe coolly, and, fumbling in his waistcoat pocket, he drew out a set of dentures. "Your teeth, Jim," he said, handing them to the arch-forger. "Don't leave them in my bathroom next time you decide to borrow my make-up."

Jim the Pencilman stamped his foot, and said "Tut!"

Snouppe turned to the Inspector.

"If you'll send one of your men round to the back of the house, he'll probably find something very interesting going on in the larder," he said.

Dribblepuss despatched half a dozen of the constables as the detective had suggested. Snouppe delved into Jim's jacket pocket and withdrew a small cardboard box. He smiled to himself, and turned to the Marchioness who had been peeling some potatoes on the step to save time.

"Did you have any punctures on the way down, your Ladyship?"

"Why, no," replied the noblewoman; and then, after a thoughtful pause: "but Mr. Krumpit hasn't turned up yet. We quarrelled at Marble Arch about which route we should take, and I came by way of Tooting Bec Common. I think Mr. Krumpit took the Birmingham road."

The detective paled visibly, and a suspicion of a tear loomed in his right eye. "Geography was never a strong point with women," he said drily, recovering his composure. "The Birmingham route is much more direct, but I am very much afraid that somewhere between Baker Street and that city a few dozen tin-tacks are strewn across the road. Heaven alone knows what grim fate may have overtaken the poor lad by now. He used the last of his rubber-solution when we went blackberrying last Tuesday."

At that moment four of the six constables emerged from the rear of the house. On the two stretchers they carried were the corpses of their two companions, dripping with blood. But, dragging along behind them was the battered figure of a Sudanese albino, a bent and battered tin of "Snappie —The Dog's Delicacy" in his hand.

·(Where is Krumpit? If we can decide by next month there will be another gripping instalment.)

FAMOUS LAST WORDS.

"Go on and write it then—they'll never see you this far back."

The Small Things.

By BILL HAYWARD.

(Selected at random from "Guinea-tales entries.)

THE sun had barely cleared the fringe of low trees that bordered the field that was, for the time being, the home of No. 36 Squadron, R.A.F., when a sleek little biplane fighter, an S.E.5, skimmed across the sparse turf, and sweeping up in a wide curve, hovered a moment before tilting in a long climb towards where, in the distance, the unending rumble of gunfire marked the territory where mud-begrimed men of the Allied Armies were locked in deadly combat with the grey forces of Prussian militarism.

Up in his tiny cockpit, Dick Gerrard hummed a snatch of song as he squinted through his gloved fingers at the sun; then, satisfied as to the complete absence of any lurking enemy planes, he turned and contemplated the earth, now far below: an earth which for nearly four years had known only the voice of war and the tumult of fighting. Here and there were the outlines of shattered trees and buildings, little French hamlets, farms, cottages—homes of people who had lived in them all their lives. Now the ebbing tide of war had receded, leaving only the shells and parts of walls remaining.

Small things, mused Dick, insignificant almost compared with the great stakes that were piled against the outcome of this mighty struggle, which, according to the papers, would mean the end of war for all time and a safeguard for all the little homes such as these the world over. That's what Joan had said, that last night in England, as they walked back to the village together—unconsciously paraphrasing Professor Higgins in *Pygmalion*. "The small things," she had said, "take care of the pence, and the pounds will take care of themselves."

Dick came to with a start. Three miles to the south "Archie" was putting up some tentative shots at a lone Rumpler—a jerry photo patrol plane. He could, however, see no fighter escort with it. This in itself was a small thing, but it registered on his brain the fact that somewhere up in the sun some dozen or so Fokkers were sitting waiting for any unwary Allied pilot to nibble at the bait which hovered so temptingly below.

Dick, however, was not interested in Rumplers, having seen the trick used too many times before; and his job at the moment was to contact two straggling Bristols over the lines and lead them back safely.

Crossing the lines at a "safe" height, he grinned cheerfully as the German ack-ack (commonly called "Archie" by both sides) potted hopefully at him, and splashed bursts well to the rear as he swung round and contacted the Bristols, which had suddenly emerged from a sunlit cloud over to his left. "Archie" was still throwing things up, but was still hopelessly "out", a fact which again was only a small thing in itself. How was he to know that a 1,000 feet above eyes were attracted by these pin-points of fire? Eyes which narrowed to see the three lone planes, homing far below.

Yet oddly enough his mind was on small things as he glanced at his watch and noted that the flight had barely taken ten minutes from start to finish. Yes, the flight was practically over now and in ten more minutes he'd be safely ensconced over a "small thing", consisting mainly of Scotch, some bottles of which the mess orderly had procured from a place where only mess orderlies can procure things, and which was a welcome change from the local "vang". Yes, in ten more minutes . . .

And then the Fokkers arrived. These gentlemen came down at 200 m.p.h. and announced their arrival in no uncertain manner with their spandaus, sending a hail of tracer through his top planes even before the

Contd. over.

SPORTOPICS.

O N June 21st we broke our previous record score of 146 for 6 (dec.) by declaring against R.N.A.S. with the score of 159 for 6 (dec.). E. D. Smith and R. Wildblood put on 79 for the second wicket, followed by a characteristic innings by Reedman. Exiles: 159 for 6 (dec.) (E. D. Smith, 38; R. Wildblood, 39; E. Reedman, 33). R.N.A.S.: 93 (Bennett, 39; Smart, 3 for 3).

On a wet wicket, versus Morris Sports (2nd XI.), G. Billingsley and A. Keenlyside bowled unchanged. "George" was able to turn the ball and had the good analysis of 7 for 23. The Secretary discovered that "silly" point can be too silly when he got a crack on the head. As no damage resulted it was decided he must be "thick-headed". After two wickets had fallen quickly, E. D. Smith and R. Wildblood made the necessary runs. Morris Sports (2nd XI.): 45; (G. Billingsley, 7 for 23; A. Keenlyside, 3 for 21). Exiles: 85; (E. D. Smith, 20; R. W. Wildblood, 25 (both retired); G. Billingsley, 17). Played on July 1st.

The Woodhouse Eaves match on July 8th ended our run of high scores. Our batting failed and we only totalled 26. Castleman bowled well, taking 6 for 7. Woodhouse lost 5 wickets before the runs were knocked off. Exiles: 26; (J. Dodd, 10; Castleman, 6 for 7; Stanley, 3 for 17). Woodhouse 102; (Castleman, not out 25); (G. M. Spooner, 4 for 17).

TENNIS.—At great cost and by good reconaissance by V. Hartill, we have obtained another net. Please treat same with the care it deserves as they are not being manufactured now and are extremely difficult to find.

THE SMALL THINGS—continued.

rear gunners in the Bristols got busy. Dick swung round to meet the attack with his fixed Lewis, sending a spear of fire into the nearest German. Then his gun jammed.

A small thing, but when his armourer had put in his ammo. belts his usual eagle-like eyes had missed a round that was slightly larger than the rest, and this "killed" his gun completely. No hope of clearing it, either, for it was way out on the side of the engine casing, beyond reach. He engaged with his Lewis, mounted on the top of his centre-section, but he had little hope of holding out as he had but three drums with him.

A fierce fight followed. Dick downed two more Fokkers, while the Bristols, holding their own, had drifted away and were unable to get back to help the unfortunate S.E.5. Finally, Dick sent his last burst through the prop. of a gaily painted Teuton, which sent it down in an engineless glide, and, defenceless, he swung round to await the inevitable. Dick felt no fear as he watched the Fokkers sweep round ready to finish him off: no conscious fear, just a sense of resentment that it had to be this way— he hoped it wouldn't burn. Idly he watched the leading 'plane bank round, a sheet of flame flashed from its air screw as the sun caught its spinning disc. A stream of tracer pounded into the plane, plucked at the fabric, smashed at the struts, hurling it sideways and downwards. Dick waited for the final burst.

* * * * *

The S.E.5 swept down, brushed over a line of poplars and staggered cross-wind to make a shaky landing in a somewhat desolate field, while above a dozen or so Spads, who had turned up in the nick of time to rescue the Bristols, put the fear of death into the remaining Fokkers.

Dick leaned back in his seat and closed his eyes, thankful to be back safe on solid earth. A small thing? Yes, but as Joan had said, it was the small things that counted, and a small thing in the shape of a German bullet embedded in a shattered knee was the most tangible evidence that the coming months would see him back in England. He grinned. Was it such a small thing, after all, to be home again?

and its Lords

By S. H. Skillington, F.S.A.

(Continued.)

SIR WILLIAM HERRICK, or Heyrick, the purchaser of Beaumanor, came of an old Leicestershire family that had for several centuries been established in the county, first at Stretton Magna, about six miles south-east of Leicester, and then at Houghton-on-the-Hill, some four miles to the north-east of that village. The tradition of the family, which may be true, is that they were descended from a certain Eric the Forester, a warrior of Scandinavian origin, who had raised an army in the north to oppose William of Normandy, under whom, after the Conquest, he is said to have held a military command. The story goes on that this Eric, who may have been of the same stock as the kingly hero of the famous *Dirge of Eric Bloodaxe*, eventually settled in Leicestershire and founded the notable family with some of whose later members we are now concerned.

One of the earliest records of the Stretton Herricks shows that in 1274 "the assize came to recognise whether Richard Heirick, clerk, Walter Heyrek, William Heyrek, John son of Richard le clerk . . . disseised John de Stonnesby, vicar of Glen magna church of his tenement in Stretton, namely a messuage and a virgate of land. John recovered his seisin (possession) by the view of the recognitors, and Richard Heirek and the others are in mercy". Ten years later (*Hilary*, 1284), Walter, son of Robert Eyrek, was the plaintiff against Ivo Eyrek, Robert, Roger and Philip, sons of Ivo, in a plea of assault on Walter at Stretton, beating and wounding him and taking away his oxen to the value of £10. The result of this rather unseemly action is not recorded. Walter, the plaintiff, appears to have died shortly after this case; for the De Banco Roll for Easter, 1298, tells us that Alice, who was the wife of Walter Eyrik of Stretton, demanded against Robert Jammille a third part of a messuage and virgate of land in Walton-by-Kimcote as dower. Robert, son and heir of Walter, was then a minor, and his body and lands were in the custody of the said Alice. The hearing was adjourned, the parties being ordered to be at York on the morrow of the Nativity of St. John the Baptist. Several other records show that the Herricks continued at Stretton as fairly substantial residents until after 1400. The last of them at present accessible to the writer is the Farnham abstract from the Coram Rege Roll, Easter, 1403: "John Halyok, of Stretton, senior, John Halyok, of Stretton, junior, and William Halyok, of Stretton, were attached to answer Robert Eyrick clerk, in a plea of breaking Robert's close at Stretton and taking away his goods and chattels to the value of £40, the defendants doing the trespass". The verdict of the court is not stated. There are several other records of the Herricks at Stretton, some of them quite exciting, but to deal with them would keep us too long from Beaumanor. It should be mentioned, however, that in 1378 Robert Eyrick, the first Master of Trinity Hall, Cambridge, who was Bishop of Lichfield when he died in 1385, founded a chantry at Stretton Magna and endowed it with eight virgates (nearly 200 acres) of land and four messuages.

The earliest legal record concerning the Herricks at Houghton-on-the-Hill is that of a fine (a collusive suit by which properties were conveyed by vendors to purchasers) dated Easter, 1523: "Between John Norton, William Dand, John Warde and William Evyington, plaintiffs, and Richard Eryke and Agnes his wife, defendants of a messuage, 3 tofts, 3½ virgates of land and ¼ virgate, and 2s. rent in Houghton and Frysby. The premises are granted to Richard Eryke and Agnes for their lives and after their deaths the said tenements will wholly remain to John Eryke, the son of the aforesaid Richard and Agnes, and his lawful issue, to be held of the chief lords of that fee by the right and accustomed service for ever". The account of the Lay Subsidy for 1545 shows that John Heyryke paid 12s. tax on goods valued at £12. The highest assessment in the village was on goods worth £17; one other paid on £14, and three on £13; the two lowest assessments were on £7 in each case. The name of John Erike appears first in the list of "byllmen" for 1540, when Houghton was "appointed to find horse and harness for 2 men, an archer and a bylman". In the Lay Subsidy of 1572, John Hericke was assessed at 6s. 8d. on goods valued at £4; only one man was assessed higher, 8s. 4d. on goods valued at £5. Several other members of the family, mostly described as yeomen, including Tobias Heiricke, clerk, who owned considerable property in Houghton, Leicester, and Bromkinsthorpe, in the old West Field of Leicester. The family continued at Houghton long after the seventeenth century and are still represented there.

The first of the Houghton Herricks to settle at Leicester was Thomas Heyrick, who was one of the two Town Chamberlains in 1511-12 and died in 1517. He was a son of Robert Evrick, of Houghton-on-the-Hill, descended from the Eyricks of Stretton Magna, and Agnes, his wife. Thomas Heyrick had two sons: Nicholas, born about 1512, and John, born in 1513. Nicholas, who was a draper, was elected mayor in 1522; he died in 1562. John, whose youngest son became the first Herrick lord of Beaumanor, lived and conducted the business of an ironmonger at the corner of the Saturday Market (now called the Market Place) and Cheapside, Leicester, near the famous Angel inn. John and his household may be conveniently introduced by quoting the inscription on his monument in the Herrick chapel of St. Martin's Church, which since 1926 has been the cathedral of the modern diocese:—

> "Here lyeth buried the bodie of John Heyricke of this parish, who departed this life on 2nd of Aprill 1589, being about the age of 76. He did marry Marie, the daughter of John Bond of Wardend, in the county of Warwicke, Esq., who lived with the said Marie in one house full fifty-two years, and in all that tyme never buried man, woman, nor childe, though they were sometimes 20 in household. He had issue by the said Marie five sons and seven daughters, viz., Robert, Nicholas, Thomas, John, and William, and daughters Ursula, Agnes, Marie, Elizabeth, Ellen, Christian, and Alice. The said John was mayor of this town in the year 1557 and again in 1572. The said Marie departed this life the 8th of December, 1611, being of the age of 97 years. She did see before her departure of her children and children's children and their children to the number of 142."

The sort of people John and Mary Herrick were is shown by a charming letter written to their son Nicholas, a goldsmith in Cheapside, London, a few days after Nicholas had married Juliana, daughter of William Stone of London, gentleman. At the time of these nuptials Nicholas, who had been apprenticed in or before 1556, must have been a little more than forty years of age. For several years his sister Mary had kept house for him, in succession to the eldest sister, Ursula, who had married. Here is the greater part of John's letter:—

Contd. over.

Caustic Clerihews
By Emanuel Sidebotham

If Canteen chips
Had lips,
Would they disclose the mystery
Of their life history?

The A.T.S.
Are in a mess:
'Cause tightly fitting service slacks
Reveal the contours of their backs.

The meetings of the C.E.C.
Have (as far as I can see),
More delegates for deliberations
Than ever had the League of Nations.

If I could play a xylophone,
Or had some corduroys of my own,
Then I know I should by rights
Get two hours off when I'm on "nights".

Canteen rolls' Specific Gravity
Is greater than lead—
By a short head.

Wilk
Has an ilk
For pornographic panorama—
The old rama!

Mr. Merritt
Couldn't bear it
If someone stated
The yarns he's related
Are all prefabricated!

Would Antrum
Go into a tantrum
If inflation
Caused pecuniary devaluation?

If he should be
On a "Deeyesstee"
Jimmy Hunter
Becomes a grunter.

BEAUMANOR—continued.

"Sonne Nicholas Eyrick: your mother and I have us commended to your bedfellowe and you; for I trust now that ye be a married man; for I hard by your brother Stanford that you weir appointed to marry on Monday the tenth of December; and if youe be maryed, we pray God to sende youe bothe muche joy and comfort together, and to all hir friends and yours. I pray you have us commended to your wive's parents and frends not as yet knowe or acquaynted with us; but I trust hereafter we shall, if God send us lyffe togethar. We wishe ourselffs that we had bene with youe at your weddyng; but the tyme of the year is so, that it hade bene painful for your moder and me to have ridden suche a journay: the dais being so short, and way so foule. Cheffely being so olde and onweldy as we be both; and specyally your mother hath such paine in one of her knebones that she cannot goe many tyms about the hows without a staff in her hand; and I myselffe have had for a spase of allmost this halffe yeare mych paine of my right sholder that I cannot get on my gowne without help. Age bringeth infyrmities; God hath so ordaynd . . .

Your mother and I have sent your wiffe and youe, to make mery withall in Christmas, two sholdir of brawne and two rondes. . . . My wiffe hath sent to your sistar Mary three yards of cloth to make hir a smock. Thus I bid you hartely farwell. At Leicester, on Sunday morning, being the xv day of December, 1582. By your loving father to his power, John Eyrick."

(To be concluded.)

VICTORY
BIGGIN STREET, LOUGHBOROUGH

BANK HOLIDAY MONDAY, AUG. 7th (3 days)
Frank Morgan in
"A STRANGER IN TOWN"
also Ted. Lewis and Orch. in "IS EVERYBODY HAPPY?"

THURSDAY, AUGUST 10th (3 days)
Penelope Dudley-Ward & Felix Aylmer in
"THE CASE of the FRIGHTENED LADY"
also Leon Errol in "GALS INCORPORATED"

MONDAY, AUGUST 14th (6 days)
Rosamund John and Stewart Granger in
"THE LAMP STILL BURNS"
also The Ritz Bros. in "NEVER A DULL MOMENT"

MONDAY, AUGUST 21st (6 days)
Charles Boyer and Ed. G. Robinson in
"FLESH AND FANTASY"
also Ed. Quillan in "FOLLOW THE BAND"

MONDAY, AUGUST 28th (6 days)
Bette Davis and Paul Lukas in
"WATCH ON THE RHINE"
also Full Supporting Programme

Note.—SEPT. 18th (Twice Daily—All Seats Bookable)
"GONE WITH THE WIND"
(in Technicolour)
(Full Length Film) Booking Starts Monday, Sept. 4th

Mon. to Fri—Con. from 5-30 p.m.   Sat.—Con. from 2 p.m.
MATINEES.—Mon. and Wed. at 2-15 p.m.
SUNDAYS—6-15 p.m. (One Show)

Through the Looking Glass

Lost Cause.

OUR heart is melted by the tragic spectacle of that heroic but futile fight which the B.S.M. book-reviewers wage in the name of Culture by trying to interest the denizens of The Dump in new authors. It's a vain conflict, my dears. As far as the girls are concerned, Daphne du Maurier, Dorothy L. Sayers, and Margaret Mitchell are the only authors who ever lived; and no literature outside the covers of the *Daily Mirror* has ever been known to move we blokes. So when you see us in a semi-religious mania devouring the cartoon page of that periodical every day, don't weep, or try to reform us—just say: "There, but for the grace of Orson Welles, go I". Then run home to read Charlotte Bronte, and be thankful.

Retribution.

That second Henry Irving at present knocking local audiences cold, seems to possess, amongst other talents, a strong imagination; which, as you intellectuals will agree, is useful only up to a point. The danger about the excess use of imagination on the Stage is that the populace, being for the most part, cow-herds of the duller sort, or broker's men from Birmingham, just don't see the point if you tax them too far.

So, when our Star, during a high-pressure love orgy a few weeks back, said in passion-laden tones: "My God, you're beautiful!" to a rather large girl who might have been nurse-maid to Mary Pickford, he was assuredly asking for trouble.

The locals, true to form, weren't going to let him get away with it, and the chorus of sniggers and cat-calls which resulted, were just what we expected. Of course, it must have been agonising for an artist to bear, and our heart was up there on the stage with him, meting out sympathy—but what could we do? In fact, we were so harrowed by all this, that we opened a vein there and then with our penknife, and quietly bled to death in the stalls.

Camouflage.

Dr. Jekyll (or Mr. Hyde) had nothing as far as dual personality is concerned, on that supervisor we love so well, who, after slowly and sadistically breaking all the bones of some innocent Minion on the Wheel, will, some two minutes later, adopt a captivating old-world manner towards old A.T.S. cuties who happen to be around; *viz.* :—

"And could I possibly persuade any of you charming young ladies to take your break?"

Thus, all smiles, the little blue-eyed creatures gambol gaily off to the canteen—although wondering just the tiniest bit as to how that adorable old gentleman could possibly have got his hands so stained with blood. . .

Programme.

A recent unearthing of some of our past Parliamentary smells—"Your M.P."—is, unless our judgment is sadly awry, going to give a certain gentleman from these parts a good deal of severe heart-burn and acute insomnia.

In fact, we are so certain of this that we are personally meeting the election expenses of "Rosebud the Second", a handsome dapple-grey mare who will fight a local constituency the next time the Nation goes to the Poll. Although only a cart-horse, Rosebud has a mind of her own—when she votes in favour she will waggle her right ear; and when against, her left.

This faculty gives her a distinct advantage over at least one of her potential competitors, who, as far as the information contained in the *exposé* just mentioned is concerned, has only the capacity to say "Yes" to whatever the Big Cheeses propose.

LEON de BUNK.

ON CROONERS.

Into a sympathetic "mike"
The world's wet mouth sobs forth its tears
In syrup-laden chords that strike
With poignant pathos in our ears;
Heart-tearing dirges of despair,
Pathetic tales of blighted love,
Vibrate across the weeping air:
The death-dirge of a tortured dove.

A melancholy saxophone
Portends the future's misery,
Informs us that all hope is gone,
Anounces Life's futility.
And blue-eyed maidens softly weep,
And find their grief so hard to hide
That, when to-night the world's asleep
They'll seek a lonely suicide.

There are no stars, no sun, no light,
Nor purpose in the Universe:
Mankind is in a tragic plight,
There's no improvement—things get worse.
But yet, although the chance is thin,
There's still one hope for Human joy:
For God's sake see if Vera Lynn
Will make a date with Harry Roy!

NOEL ROYLE.

TAILORING FOR THE SERVICES
— from —
START TO FINISH — 8, BAXTER GATE LOUGHBOROUGH. — TOP TO BOTTOM

The London Tailoring Co.
Est. 1899.   'Phone 2794.

EMPIRE
MARKET PLACE, LOUGHBOROUGH

BANK HOLIDAY, MONDAY, AUG. 7th (3 days)
BASIL RATHBONE and NIGEL BRUCE in
"**Sherlock Holmes and the Voice of Terror**"
also Andrews Sisters in "ALWAYS A BRIDESMAID"

THURSDAY, AUGUST 10th (3 days)
GEORGE SANDERS in
"**APPOINTMENT IN BERLIN**"
also Bill Elliott in "ROGUES GALLERY"

MONDAY, AUGUST 14th (3 days)
GEORGE ZUCCO in "**BLACK RAVEN**"
also Buck Jones in "DAWN ON THE GREAT DIVIDE"

THURSDAY, AUGUST 17th (3 days)
NOAH BEERY, JR. in
"**TEXAS TO TOKYO**"
also David Bruce in "HONEYMOON LODGE"

MONDAY, AUGUST 21st (3 days)
MARG. SULLAVAN—JOAN BLONDELL—
ANN SOTHERN in "**CRY HAVOC**"
also Clyde Beatty in "LOST JUNGLE"

THURSDAY, AUGUST 24th (3 days)
FRANK CRAVEN in
"**HARRIGAN'S KID**"
also Allan Jones in "LARCENY WITH MUSIC"

MONDAY, AUGUST 28th (6 days)
RODDY McDOWELL and DONALD CRISP in
"**LASSIE COME HOME**"
(in Technicolour)
also "Hutch" and Famous Variety Acts in
"DOWN MELODY LANE"

**CONTINUOUS DAILY. Doors open at 1-30 p.m.
SUNDAYS at 5-30 p.m.**

Printed by Toppings Ltd., 17, Southfield Rd., Loughborough, and published by L. P. Jones for Beaumanor Staff Magazine Committee.

SEPTEMBER, 1944

VOL. I. No. 7 (NEW SERIES) - **6d.**

FILM ATTRACTIONS for SEPTEMBER

SHOWING AT THE ODEON THEATRE

Sunday, Sept. 3rd—Randolph Scott and Binnie Barnes in **The Last of the Mohicans**. Also Lupino Lane in **Hot News**.

MONDAY, SEPT. 4th, for 6 days:
Ginger Rogers, Robert Ryan and Ruth Hussey in
TENDER COMRADE
Also Chester Morris and Nancy Kelly in **Tornado**.

Sunday, Sept. 10th—Wallace Beery and Marjorie Main in **Barnacle Bill**. Also John Howard in **Submarine Raider**.

MONDAY, SEPT. 11th—3 days	THURS., SEPT. 14th—3 days
Greer Garson, Laurence Olivier and Maureen O'Sullivan in	Donald O'Connor and Peggy Ryan in
PRIDE AND PREJUDICE	**CHIP OFF THE OLD BLOCK**
with a full supporting programme.	Also Jean Gabin in **The Impostor**

Sunday, Sept. 17th—Humphrey Bogart and Gale Page in **You Can't Get Away With Murder**. Also Conrad Nagel in **Yellow Cargo**.

MONDAY, SEPT. 18th, for 6 days:
Akim Tamiroff, Lynn Bari and Francis Lederer in
THE BRIDGE OF SAN LUIS REY
Also Richard Arlen and Jean Parker in **Minesweeper**.

Sunday, Sept. 24th—Joan Blondell and Pat O'Brien in **Off the Record**. Also Margie Hart in **The Lure of the Islands**.

MONDAY, SEPT. 25th—3 days	THURS., SEPT. 28th—3 days
Ray Milland and Marjorie Reynolds in	Norman Evans and Nat Jackley in
THE MINISTRY OF FEAR	**DEMOBBED**
Also Tom Conway and Jean Brooks in	Also Allan Jones and June Vincent in
The Falcon and the Co-eds.	**Lucky Days**.

Continuous Performance Daily 1-45 p.m.   Sunday, One Performance at 6 p.m.

B.S.M. Vol. I. No. 7 (New Series)
SEPTEMBER, 1944.

Editors: LEONARD P. JONES, ERIC C. MILLHOUSE
A.T.S. Editresses: KAY PRICE, MARY GILL.   Treasurer: A. H. APPLETON.
Editorial Board:
DICK WILKINSON, OLLIE PEARCE, DUDLEY TRUIN, RON DENNY (B.W.)

HIGH YORKSHIRE.

By Noel Royle.

HIGH in the fastness of the moorland pass
    Where jocund breezes shake the sombre grass,
    And 'neath the kindly greyness of the skies
There break the grouses' wild spasmodic cries.

Above, the clouds are galleons sailing by—
Across the abstract ocean of the sky;
They cast their changing shadows as they go
In monstrous liquid patterns far below.

And in these ancient hills there is no time
Except the endless cycle of the clime:
The seasons come, and break, and come again,
But steadfastly the patient hills remain.

What joy to tramp with youth's e'er-questing tread
Across the moorland's brown and broken bed;
To walk abroad in that ozonic air,
To seek the mountain's furthest secrets there.

The wind's coarse bluster dins against my ear,
And then, amongst its boisterous thrust, I hear
Strange voices carried on the wind's gross wave;
Like soft, sad, secret whispers from the grave.

Is this the empty chorus of the wind,
Or some persistent fallacy of mind;
Or can it be the vain nostalgic sigh
Of those who knew the hills in days gone by?

Perhaps they wandered through this rocky dale
And now have passed beyond this earthly pale;
But having once climbed up the wild hillsides
Would change for that all joys which Heaven provides!

Oh God, when can I leave this stinking town
And turn my back on Industry's grim frown
To seek the peace and friendship of the moor,
As I so often have done in days of yore!

Next issue ready: Sept. 29th. All contributions to reach the Editors by Sept. 15th

and its Lords

By S. H. Skillington, F.S.A.

(Concluded.)

SEVERAL of the children of John and Mary Herrick prospered in life and left descendants who served their generations well and honourably.

Robert, the eldest son, went into his father's ironmongery business, which he continued after the old man's death. He was mayor of Leicester in 1584, 1593 and 1606. In later life, he was associated with his brother William, for whom he acted in important financial transactions in the town and its neighbourhood. In 1598 he and William obtained a confirmation of the family arms, with the addition of a crest: a bull's head argent, the muzzle, ears and horns tipped sable, gorged with a chaplet of leaves vert. In his later years, he lived in a mansion house, near the site of the old Greyfriars' convent, between Friar Lane and St. Martin's churchyard. It is probable that the remains of Richard III, who was buried in the Greyfriars' church, lay beneath the garden of this house. Robert Herrick married Elizabeth Manly, daughter of a former mayor, by whom he had two sons and nine daughters. The inscription on his monument in St. Martin's church concludes: "at his death he gave away 16 pounds 10 shillings a year to good uses. He lived 78 years; and after dyed very godly the 14th of June, 1618.

> All flesh is grasse both young and old must die:
> And so we pass to Judgment by and by."

The ironmongery business was carried on by his brother John, mayor in 1619, who died in 1633, leaving issue, and was buried in St. Martin's.

Nicholas Herrick, the second son of John and Mary, appears to have been an entirely creditable person. The Christmas letter, quoted last month, written by old John to him and his recently espoused "bedfellowe", is heart-warming evidence of the best sort of family affection and reciprocal kindness. Nicholas prospered in business and, as soon as he had established himself, did what he could for the advancement of his sisters and his youngest brother. Two of the sisters, who had kept house for him, found affluent husbands in London. Ursula, the eldest daughter of John, married James Hawes, who was Lord Mayor in 1574; Mary married Sir John Bennett, and rode with him to the Guildhall in 1603. A younger sister, Ellen, who married a Mr. Holden, also lived in London and was in touch with Nicholas in 1582. William, the future lord of Beaumanor, was apprenticed to Nicholas and became in inmate of his house, then presided over by Mary. Nicholas and Juliana had six children between 1585 and 1591, the youngest of whom was Robert, author of *Hesperides* and *Noble Numbers*, the greatest of all our lyric poets. About a year after Robert's birth, a most distressing calamity befell the household in Goldsmiths' Row. Nicholas, who had been suffering from ague, died as a consequence of falling from an upper window. This disaster, sad enough in itself, threatened Juliana and her young family with utter ruin: for it was alleged that the death was not accidental. In the claim put forward by the Queen's High Almoner, Dr. Richard Fisher, Bishop of Bristol, it is stated that "one Nich'as Herrick late citezeine and Goldsmythe of London . . . did throwe himself forthe of a garret window in London aforesaide whereby he did kill and destroye himselfe By reason whereof all such goodes chattells and debtes as were the said Nich'as Herrickes at the tyme of his deathe or ought any waies to apperteyne or belong unto him do nowe belonge apperteyne and are forfeyted unto or said sou'aigne Lady the quene by force of her P'rogatyve royal and nowe are in the only order and disposicon of me the saide bushop Almoner . . ." Probably through the good offices of influential friends, the Almoner's formidable demand was commuted into a fine of £200. This sum could easily be found, but the whole business was regrettably painful and embarrassing. Nicholas had estimated his estate to be worth £3,000, but it was ultimately valued at £5,000, a very considerable amount in those days. In addition, there was a fund, in the hands of two London merchants, from which £800 was disbursed for the widow's benefit. Soon after her bereavement, Juliana, with her six young children and a seventh on the way, were received into the house of her sister Anne, who had married Henry Campion, a Londoner of good Kentish family, at Hampton, Middlesex. Thus Robert came to spend his early, impressionable years in surroundings admirably suited to foster his peculiar genius. There often seems to be a destiny that shapes our ends.

When Nicholas Herrick died, his brother William, then about thirty, had been living in his house and actively engaged in the business for some sixteen years. He must have been a capable man of affairs, for, as early as 1580-1, he had been sent on a mission from Queen Elizabeth to the Grand Turk. This Levantine excursion may have been connected with an enterprise by which a group of London capitalists in 1581 obtained from Elizabeth the sole privilege of "trading into the dominions of the Grand Signior" for a term of seven years. The queen herself contributed £40,000 as a loan or an investment to the venture, which was organised on a joint-stock basis.

Shortly after his brother's death, William Herrick removed to Greater Wood Street, where he carried on his increasingly prosperous business for many years; he also had a house at Westminster. He married Joan, daughter of Richard May, Esq., of Mayfield, citizen and merchant-tailor of London, by whom he had children. In 1595, he purchased Beaumanor from the representatives of the Earl of Essex; ten years later, the honour of Knighthood was conferred upon him. How, in his mature years, he was regarded in his native town is somewhat effusively set forth by John Throsby, the eighteenth-century historian of Leicester:—"This gentleman was seated at Beaumanor, in this county, in the reign of Elizabeth, where his immediate descendant, William Heyrick, Esq., now dwells. . . . By James the First he was appointed one of the Tellers of the Exchequer. In 1601 he was chosen to represent this borough in Parliament; and again, in 1605 and 1620. He died in 1652, aged 96, and was buried with his ancestors in St. Martin's Church, Leicester. . . . This gentleman was of known probity, punctual in his dealings, remarkably accurate in his private as well as public concerns, and acquired so large a fortune, that it enabled him not only to assist many of the nobility with money in those days of scarcity, but his soveriegn on many urgent occasions. His services to this place made him the idol of the people". Though this eulogy may be a little too exuberant, official and other records show that it is substantially just. Sir William Herrick shared the privilege of being jeweller and moneylender to James I with George Heriot, "Jingling Geordie" of *The Fortunes of Nigel*, the munificent founder of Heriot's Hospital at Edinburgh.

After Sir William's death, Beaumanor descended through five generations to William Perry Herrick who died, as the result of a hunting accident, in 1876. His widow continued at Beaumanor until her death in 1915. Throughout her long and beneficent reign, Mrs. Perry Herrick was loved and respected by all who knew her. One of her near neighbours, who has the happiest recollections of her, writes: "She was a most kind and charitable

(Concluded on p. 7.)

Theatre Royal
LOUGHBOROUGH.

PROGRAMMES FOR SEPTEMBER
1944

Monday, Sept. 4th (6 days)

FORTESQUE PLAYERS PRESENT

A BUNCH OF VIOLETS

By Sydney Grundy.

Monday, Sept. 11th (6 days)

FORTESQUE PLAYERS PRESENT

NAUGHTY WIFE

A Screaming Comedy by Fred Jackson.

Monday, Sept. 18th (6 days)

1944 EDITION OF

THE SQUIRE'S PARTY

Including

Morris & Cowley and Johnson Clark

Monday, Sept. 25th (6 days)

FORTESQUE PLAYERS PRESENT

ANOTHER DELIGHTFUL ATTRACTION

(Details Later).

SHOW PARADE
Edited by Dudley Truin.

THERE is little I can add to the many thousands of words that must have been written about "GONE WITH THE WIND" (Victory, September 18th, 6 days). It is, presumably, like "The Birth of a Nation", "Ben Hur" and the first Mickey Mouse, a milestone in the history of films; and therefore should not be missed. Personally, however, I doubt whether **Margaret Mitchell's** best-seller has a great enough theme for a film which, for want of a better word, we must call classic.

The adaptation and characterisation have been extremely well done, and great care has obviously been taken down to the smallest detail of production; also, for once, we have a film which, so closely does it follow the novel, can be seen without qualms by anyone who has read the book first. It must have needed terrific courage on the part of Hollywood to retain Mitchell's ending intact instead of substituting a glorious Technicolor reconciliation between **Vivien Leigh** and **Clark Gable,** and sending them back through a sugary Schubert mist hand-in-hand to Tara. That decision has since been upheld by the Supreme Master, the Box Office.

Ginger Rogers has come a long way since she teamed with Fred Astaire and it is chiefly due to her fine acting in "TENDER COMRADE" (Odeon, September 4th, 6 days) that this picture makes the grade. Told in flash-back form, it deals with the lives of four women who decide to live together while their menfolk are away at the war. In spite of the insistence on democracy it is a warm and appealing mixture of romance and tragedy with a nice dash of comedy.

"FOR THOSE IN PERIL" 'Empire, September 14th, 6 days) is noteworthy for the fact that the story and scenario are by the late **Richard Hilary**, whose autobiography "The Last Enemy", in which he told his experiences as a fighter pilot, moved the English-speaking world. Here he tells in a vivid way the story of the little-known Air-Sea Rescue Service, its routine round broken here and there by moments of intense danger and supreme heroism.

BEAUMANOR AND ITS LORDS—*concluded.*

woman who, up to late middle life, would not hesitate to make considerable journeys, in order to check by personal inspection the statements made to her by the writers of the numerous begging letters that used to be addressed to her". Mr. Perry Herrick provided in his will that, after Mrs. Herrick's death, the Beaumanor estate should go to Colonel the Hon. Montagu Curzon, of Garats Hay, younger son of his old friend, the first Earl Howe of Gopsall. Colonel Curzon, however, died before 1915, and the estate devolved upon his son, Mr. William Curzon-Herrick, the present owner. The house and its surroundings were then let to Mrs. Frances Abel Smith, whose tenancy came to an end shortly before the outbreak of the war that Beaumanor is helping to bring to a triumphant end.

(*Finis.*)

Bookseller and Stationer :: Lending Library

J. SKETCHLEY
24 & 25, High Street, Loughborough
Telephone 2980.

The Editors regret to announce that Ollie Pearce has decided to discontinue his popular gossip feature, "Snoop's Corner", but in its place they have pleasure in introducing "They're Telling Me", by the well-known columnist, Jimmy Hewson.

CONGRATULATIONS to D.A.K. and Mrs. Kirkby on the arrival of a daughter, Margaret Ann, on August 3rd.

Congratulations also to Joan Oakey, T.P., "C" Watch, on her marriage to W/O Brenig W. Jones, R.E., at St. Peter's, Cardiff, on the 3rd August. The honeymoon was spent at Aberystwyth.

I am pleased to record, at long last, the final "hitching" of Bill Ghent and Muriel Furniss. The wedding took place on July 1st at Manchester. Good luck to both of them—may their years of married bliss be more numerous even than their broken engagements.

It is good to hear that someone hasn't forgotten the girl he left behind. Congratulations to R.M. (Shaker) Smith on his engagement to Miss Phyllis Rowden, of Frindsbury, Kent.

Freddie (late of "Nerve Centre") Pearce has also taken the plunge, announcing his engagement, while on leave, to Miss Mary Brewin, of Loughborough. All the best, Freddie.

Also to Rose Barlow (Runner) on her marriage at Bow, London, to Pte. Jack Bowman, R.A.O.C., of Gateshead.

And to Ptes. Isabel Clay and Marie Down (T.P. "A" Watch) on their respective engagements to Pte. Aramus Grant, U.S. Army, and Cpl. Wally Pitman, R. Signals, Isle of Man.

It was a bad day for the B.S.M. when the Loughborough Police Force posted a man at the bottom of Woodhouse Road. Mr. "Squander-Bug" Antrum, failing to observe the Halt sign there, was fined one pound. Although he at first intended taking an alternative of 7 days and claiming a billeting refund, he has now decided to cancel his magazine for the next three years instead—He's slipping!

Incidentally, we hear that Mr. Roy Hardy, caught at the same time, turned up at the Police Station in shorts and school tie. He was taken into the Juvenile Court by a nurse. Such is the advantage of "Pears Golden Glory" (advt).

It is noticeable that the Woodthorpe Lane is now used more frequently.

"Slap" junr., Master Paul Reedman, evidently takes after his father, recently coming second in a "Best Looking Baby" competition in Loughborough.

Could it be coincidence that "A" Watch, No. 1 Wing, have now got a new slogan, "Be Quick, Sergeant".

We wonder if this is of Yank origin.

SCENE: LOUGHBOROUGH PARK.

Hundreds of holidaymakers are standing at attention while the band plays "God Save the King". Suddenly all eyes are turned towards one individual, a bald, portly man who, despite all his small daughter's efforts to wake him, lies peacefully sleeping. At last she is successful. A sigh of relief goes up from the assembled multitude as the "life and soul" of Beaumanor manages to stagger to his feet in time for the last bar.

We were very interested to see a girl looking in "The Times" personal column the other night. She said that she wanted to see if anyone needed her urgently—Gentlemen, there is a "Times" agent at Quorn!

The age of chivalry **is** dead. We observe with disgust Capt. Whitford's efforts to reduce our female personnel to tears. And he the leader of that all too gallant band.

And while we're on the subject; the A.T.S. method of checking respirators is worthy of note. The idea is as follows:

You go into the gas chamber first, and, having recovered sufficiently, you then hand in the respirator for check, together with your paybook. If it is found that a previous check has been made you are told that you needn't have had a second.

I hear that stranger things happen at sea. I doubt it.

The notes now being left in the letter rack—the ones with the picturesque addresses—are causing much bewilderment, but alas! my name is Watson and I have no Sherlock. I still await the author's first indiscretion.

We have it on very good authority that pink lollipops do not come under the "No eating while working" rule.

All the same, I should stick to gum, Freddy.

Congratulations to Mr. P. M. Tuke on attaining his majority on August 14th. The party, held the day after, in the Church Room, Quorn, was a great success.

We are still awaiting the day when Wally Cecil will find a watertight alibi. Remember in future, Wally, that telegrams have the office and time of origin on them.

Dismal thought!

Should the war end between Monday and Thursday of any week it looks as though, unless we live near the "Curzon Arms", we shall have to celebrate victory with canteen tea.

We hear that the provisional date for the recommencement of the Dancing Club activities is fixed for September 1st. May last season's success be repeated.

JIMMY.

Bludgeons in Baker Street.
By E. St. U. M.

(Third grisly instalment. Action Stations as last month).

"WHERE were you going with that tin of 'Snappie'?" rapped out Dedleigh Snouppe in perfect Arabic.

"To the 'Dying Duck' in Wapping", replied the Sudanese albino, in exquisite English. "I was to hand it to a man with a red ring tattooed on his left elbow."

Snouppe drew a deep breath, his Wobley Automatic from his hip pocket, and a card from the pack which the handcuffed Jim the Pencilman was proffering.

"It's the Crimson Circumference!" he muttered, tensely, his nostril twitching unmistakably. Then he glanced at the card he had drawn. It bore a crude outline of a kipper, and the words: YOU DYE AT DORN, EVRY MORNIN NEXT WEEK.

Rapidly scribbling instructions to his undertakers, the master sleuth turned to Inspector Dribblepuss:

"We must go to Wapping at once. It's our one chance to foil the Circumference!!!!!!!"—(*Whoa! Ed.*).

Drib at once began to disguise himself as a printer's devil.

"What's this for?" queried Snouppe.

"Didn't you say we're going to Topping's?"

Snouppe snorted and strode over to the Marchioness, letting off a round or two from his Wobley to attract her attention.

"Where's the nearest 'phone, Ducks? Yours has been disconnected, I suspect."

"In the booth at Scratchitt X-roads," replied the noblewoman. Seizing her bike, the celebrated criminologist leapt into the saddle, missed, leaped again, and rode off in a cloud of dust.

Arriving at the X-roads ten minutes later, he crashed breathlessly into the booth and dialled a number.

"Hello?" he panted, as a dark brown voice came over the wire. "Is that the Editor of the B.S.M.? Good. Have you decided what has happened to Krumpit?"

"Yes," replied the dark brown voice, gravely. "You are to deduce from an advertisement of a bicycle for sale in the 'Crinklehaven Courier' that he is bound and gagged in the old mill on Crinklehaven Common. If we don't forget we'll announce a lapse of time at the beginning of this instalment, to allow for publication of the 'Courier'." (*We forgot—Ed.*)

With that the dark brown voice hung up. The next moment a window of the booth disintegrated with a shatter, and a bullet ricocheted off the receiver. Three daggers landed quivering in the woodwork above the detective's head, and a land-mine detonated with a sickening crack beneath a nearby tree. Sensing that something was wrong, Snouppe ducked.

◎ ◎ ◎ ◎ ◎

Meantime, Krumpit was regaining consciousness in a dark and unfamiliar room. Dazedly he tried to pierce the gloom. Then he realised that he was blindfolded. Somewhere close at hand he could hear the steady whir of machinery, and every few moments something damp and clammy fell with a plop across his face.

Suddenly a voice right at his ear whispered hoarsely: "I'm going to cut your bonds. You're meant to discover what these clammy things are, to finish off this instalment, and it's a dead cert you won't be able to with your hands tied!"

"Thanks. There's a pair of scissors in your jacket pocket," deduced Krumpit. Sure enough there were, and, quickly snipping the lads bonds, the mysterious figure was gone.

Groping round, Krumpit found his head and shoulders surrounded by a cold, squelchy mass of long objects. As he grasped them he let out his breath in a tense hiss. "By George!" he gasped, as the sinister truth dawned upon him. At that moment a further string of sausages hit him fair and square on the mouth.

(*Will Krumpit suffocate in the mounting sea of sausages? What has befallen Dedleigh Snouppe? Gee! We're so worked up we'd love to carry on with next month's episode straight away*).

SLAP-DASH———A once-familiar form of feminine defence and getaway. Now obsolete.

HANDICAP ———A bicycle, when one is offered a lift in a jeep.

By Archangel.

IT would not be true if I were to say I had made a complete study of them, but I may say that I have kept close contact with the subject from the time I first saw the light of day.

Even so, there are many types which I have never seen, so varied are their shapes and forms. However, I state here and now that we who have the good fortune to live in the towns and cities of this lovely England have no grounds whatever for complaint. Some of us cannot know of the vast difference which lies between those that we use and those which our country cousins are forced to inhabit.

In many places to-day we take pleasure in their use. We have plenty of room to move about and every modern device is utilised for our comfort. Even those outside are pleasurable, though perhaps a trifle colder in winter.

But the country variety are cold all the year round, not to mention their different types, sizes and general awkwardness. (I say "different types" because there never seems to be two alike). The crux of the matter rests with the door. Upon this depends your comfort, your state of mind, and your pride.

If the door opens inwards you can manage as a rule, but even then you will find that a number of difficulties can arise. Usually your foot is within easy reach of the door; but there, again, if you find yourself any distance away there's some tricky footwork to be put in if you wish to keep yourself to yourself.

And the stubbornness of some people! They come rushing down the path, grab the door, and push. But because of your readiness for just such an emergency nothing happens; your foot is doing its stuff. Then follows a titanic struggle. The blighter outside becomes a bit panicky and musters all his strength while you inside are determined more than ever to defend your sanctity. So it goes on for perhaps two minutes.

Then as suddenly as the onslaught started so it ceases, leaving you a little breathless and wondering what's going to happen next. You are not left in the dark for long; a sinister eye is looking at you through a crack in the door. A wild eye, an eye full of hate and venom. Shivers run up and down your spine as you notice its baleful, unblinking, unwavering stare. Then it disappears. You hear the slow and thoughtful footsteps of the owner as he dejectedly retreats.

By far the worst type is the one in which the door opens outwards. All manner of things can happen to one while using this insidious variety. Imagine the contortions you create when you find yourself compelled to bend double in order to make a frantic grab at the door. So it starts all over again, and after another two minutes, during which the door has been pulled open at least six times and six times hurled to by the inmate, someone outside says, "Oh! sorry", and creeps away, just like the other fellow did.

Those of you who are inclined to be nervous or highly strung I would strongly advise never to go near this type, the ordeal will prove too nerve-racking. This warning applies to sensitive people as well; here, the finer feelings can easily be upset.

So just remember, you town dwellers, that on a cold morning you don't, like your country cousins, have to go to a dismal outhouse for your morning ablutions.

Neuralgic Adventure.

By Eric W. Dobson.

UNDERSTAND, please, that I offer no explanation for this story. I give it to you as fiction, even though names of places and people are real.

I've recently been home, suffering from neuralgia, and found on my arrival that the chief topic of conversation—apart from buzz-bombs—was that a sheep-killing dog was ravaging the flocks in the neighbourhood at night. Some thirty or so animals had been mauled, and were either killed outright or so badly mutilated as to warrant their being destroyed.

I paid scant attention to the gossip, as it happened, having more important personal things to worry me, and for two days I forgot it.

Now, there may be some of you who think that neuralgia is a paltry ailment, but, believe me, it can be pretty grim! Anyhow, my attack necessitated my getting up and roaming about at night in a vain endeavour to woo an hour or so of sleep, and I took to striding across Wrest Park—which, some of you will remember, lies between Silsoe and Gravenhurst. Not much of a park these days, with its concrete roads and many tin store shacks, but open country, sparsely dotted with trees, where three years ago there had been whole woods.

I suppose it was about three ack emma that I first saw the dog, skulking in the distance. It didn't strike me at first that it might be the sheep-killer. Just an ordinary dog, I thought, and even debated whether it, too, might have neuralgia! It seemed an abnormally large animal, long and sleek, something like an Alsatian, as far as I could see, but as I said, I didn't pay much attention to it. It wasn't until the next day that I recollected having seen it, when a report of more sheep mutilation was circulated.

I was out the next night, too, on my lonely, pain-ridden ramble, and it was then I had a closer view of the brute. It ran when it heard my footsteps, into a copse—about the only one left intact from war needs—and, although armed with a thick stick, I didn't venture to follow it.

Next morning, as I expected, came the tale of more killings, but with an added toll of young calves this time. There was a deal of righteous anger, and the local farmers decided to go after the Killer with guns, that night, and I, being sure that I'd be without sleep in any case, volunteered to go as a member of the party.

Now, that afternoon, I was in the park again—I'd been across to Silsoe with a friend who was catching the bus to Bedford—and on the way back I overtook an old man whom I knew well enough by sight, an ex-gardener of Wrest Manor, who lived in a shack on the far edge of the copse. We exchanged greetings and walked together, yarning about things in general, until I happened to mention that I'd been in Egypt, when the old chap, who was apparently a bit of a collector, asked me to pass an opinion on his scarab collection. I said that he was welcome to my somewhat amateurish knowledge—I'd done a bit of collecting of scarabs, and had had several rare species accepted by museums with thanks (and little else!)—so we went over to his shack. Through the copse I felt somewhat creepy, and the feeling increased as we entered the one-roomed hovel.

I'm at a loss to describe it completely. Dirt and junk were predominant. A low table, filling half the room, was covered with a miscellany of objects. The head of a cat, mounted; a box of twittering white mice; a spade with a broken handle; a statue of a naked woman on her knees; two skull-caps, one grey, one brown; and many other things in boxes, or lying loose. The floors were filthy, as were the blankets tossed in a corner, and, despite it being July, a blazing hot fire of logs roared in an open-mouthed stove.

The old chap waved me to a seat, took the only other one, and, fishing among the debris on the table, hauled out his box of scarabs. While I passed my inexpert opinion he lit his foul clay pipe and put on the brown skull-cap. We talked of this and that, and he surprised me with his worldly and mythological knowledge, so unusual in an ex-son of the soil. Suddenly he asked: "Ever heard of Tarnhelm?"

I nodded. There is an ancient Norse myth of a dwarf who had a cap called Tarnhelm, which changed him into whatever he wished each time he donned it. The story says that the god Wotan persuaded the dwarf to turn himself into a mouse, promptly to be killed by the god who confiscated the cap.

At my nod the old gardener pointed to the grey skull-cap and said in a whisper: "Tarnhelm".

I grinned uneasily, for surely solitude among his "treasures" had turned the old fellow's brain, or he was joking. But no, at least he wasn't joking, for, sensing my ridicule, he took deep offence, and almost ordered me out of his shack, his friendliness disappearing, his old wizened face turning to a snarl. Believe me, I felt much more comfortable when I was past the copse, and back among those store sheds!

I didn't mention my visit when I got home, but spent a long time in preparing for the night's dog hunt. My gun needed a good cleaning, and I used the ramrod and oily rag with vigour.

I spent the evening quietly reading—and swallowing the usual liberal doses of aspirin—and at eleven o'clock strolled outside with my gun to meet the others at the village hall. There were at least twenty of us. Mark and Edgar, my next door neighbours, Tom from Park Hill, and his brothers and uncles, the Parrishes, the Redmans, and sundry others, and we set off up to the park, having planned to split into sections to comb the meadows and copse.

I was with Mark, two of the Redman brothers, and Cyril Parrishe. Our beat took us beyond the copse, our object being to beat back towards the others. We went quietly and quickly to our position, and then noisily, after the manner of most beaters, crashed our way across the bracken-edged copse. Suddenly, ahead of us, the dog broke free, with a howl that froze the blood in my veins. We yelled to those beyond, who yelled back, and the beast suddenly doubled back towards us, coming at a long, mile-eating lope, only to halt and sink back on its haunches some ten yards ahead of us. A gleam of fitful moonlight showed us yellow, snarling fangs, and a reddish brown body. Blood drooled from repulsive lips; the eyes were gleaming brilliant red.

This was so obviously our quarry that we all lifted our guns together. The brute must have sensed sudden catastrophe, for he leaped to his feet and disappeared into the copse as we all squeezed our triggers. The buck-shot slashed through the undergrowth and a terrible howl which ended in an almost human scream rent the air. We rushed towards the copse in a body, the other parties converging from other directions.

We didn't find the dog, but some ten yards inside the copse, directly in our line of fire, we found the old gardener lying dead in a welter of blood.

We hastily sent for the police and a doctor, and at the subsequent inquiry "death by misadventure" was recorded, as it was surmised that he, too, had been out after the dog, and had run foul of us.

What puzzles me is what happened to that brute of a dog; and I'm hanged if I'll ever wear the grey skull-cap I found beside the gardener's body.

Editorial Note.—"**SPORTOPICS**", received too late for publication, will appear next month.

The Gospel according to St. Apid
Chapter XXXIV

(Translated from the English by Disciple Millhouse).

NOW a certain shepherd of Woodus, in the Promised Land, possessed a great flock of sheep. And because he was a good shepherd, Red Tabz, who dwelleth in Wyt Awl, decreed that he might put his flock to graze in the bountiful land of Woyg. For there were in Woyg many sacred pastures upon which no soul was suffered to set foot; save when it was too dark to be seen.

And the mighty flock entered into the land, and ate the pastures, and the foliage upon the temple walls, and the posts, and the wire, and the string. And such of the flock which still hungered entered into Kantin and saith: Baa. But the ears of the serving maids were good; wherefore they poured forth no Chaa. Likewise did they proffer not their messes of pottage, for they knew that the sheep were particular.

And in the flock were many Ewes, and their Lambs, and sundry Rams. And here and there was a Black Sheep.

Now the Prophet Osee also was possessed of a mighty flock. And in the flock of Osee were many Ewas, and **their** Lambs, and furthermore sundry Rams. Likewise were there Black Sheep here also. Thus were the two flocks exceeding like one unto the other; and in divers otherwise also. For inasmuch as the flock wandereth whithersoever one sheep goeth, so also were the flock of Osee. So when they were gathered together in the House of Cloaks before their sundry prayers of Matins, Nites, or Tootaten, they tarried without the doors of the temples many minutes, ere one, being possessed of a Gremlin, entered thereinto; whereupon the flock followed. Or when they walked upon the highways of Woygland they differed in no wise from the true sheep in the eyes, and the oaths, of the riders of the Grids. For it is written in the Book of Wisdom of Woyg: Whensoever a Grid-rider attempteth to pass thee on thy right hand, go thou also to the right. And if he maketh to thy left hand, Shake thou him likewise.

And certain of the braver of the true sheep carried out Inspections of the sundry mansions of Woygland, but the worshippers noticed not whether or not they wore Brass Hats. Yet, peradventure one should sit upon the seat of the Chief Rabbi in a temple, the worshippers must straightway perceive it; for their keen ears surely discerneth the greater sweetness of the Baa's.

Now a certain lamb which had consumed an abundance of bicycle tyres, fell sick of the palsy, and was nigh unto Flaking Out. Wherefore when one Adewo beheld the lamb he was filled with compassion, and took it, and brought it into the tabernacle of Woyg, and offered it up as a sacrifice. For it was meet and proper so to do in the tabernacle, where sundry lambs had been led to the slaughter hitherto.

And the Prophet Osee, when he learned concerning the lamb, waxed exceeding Cheesed, and his heart was cast down for the flock of the good shepherd. Wherefore he bade the Tribe guard the flock, and watch over them by day and by night, saying: Behold. Red Tabz hath called forth the Man-power, and it hath been exhausted. And he hath summoned the Woman-power, and likewise it hath been spent. Take heed, therefore, lest the Sheep-power be consumed, for there are none other unto whom he may call. Yea verily, for even the chariot of Woygshops hath but half of a Horse-power.

Blonde:—"I've got the cutest husband."
Redhead:—"I never knew you were married."
Blonde:—"Oh, he isn't MY husband."

CALLING ALL

We regret the misunderstanding caused by a printer's error last month, and offer our apologies to those it concerned. We wish to state that "Good Reading" was not written by "B.B." and "R.R.", but by "G.M.T.", whose contribution it again is this month.—Editors.

GOOD READING
By G.M.T.

DO you like books to take you right into the spirit and soul of other countries? "Moment in Peking" and "Leaf in a Storm" are written by the Chinese author, Lin Yutang. By reading these books you understand the slow, ordered Chinese life built on a background of centuries of philosophy and custom. This may not coincide with your ideas of China after reading Pearl Buck's "Good Earth". My advice, however, is to read both, and then you will have a good idea of China as a whole—the two sides, rich and poor—the labourers and the merchant men, with the dominating theme of custom and tradition running through both.

As a real, live story of the life of a slum child, the autobiography "I, James Whittaker" will hold your interest from cover to cover. It is grim, yes, but how could it escape being so and still give a true picture of the horror and filth of slum dwelling? You'll admire the indomitable spirit of the author in his fight against this upbringing and very bad health—his thirst for knowledge and determination to be a success in life. It is a book that will stay in your memory clearly and for many years.

I don't know whether, technically, this book is good or not as I am not an expert on ballet. But perhaps you, like myself, know just enough to want to know more. If so you'll find plenty to interest you in Arnold Haskell's "Ballet". The history of the Ballet—how it started and how it developed into its present form. You'll learn more of the personalities behind the great names of this art—Pavlova, Stravinsky, Nijinski and many others. And then, of the ballets themselves, all the different sections which go to make the whole—the music, the choreography, the decor, etc., and the perfect co-ordination needed between these to make a whole that will live on.

And now for a book that is sheer fun yet also full of reality—"The Royal Runaway," by Lawrence Houseman.

The setting for this story is an imaginary country ruled and governed as we are in England with all the regal and governmental red tape. Now imagine a king, incognito, amongst his own people, trying to live the life of the "ordinary man", and you will realise all the humour that is packed into this book.

The suggestion, shown very strongly in a speech during the ensuing revolution, is that it isn't just money that turns mens' heads, but Power—power to sway the thoughts and lives of others; that the peoples' man of to-day may be, when he gains power and position, the tyrant of to-morrow.

This seriousness gives a good balance to a very entertaining story.

A STOP-GAP——ATS Tunic Belt worn round the top of the skirt.

Johnny's Home.
By Margaret Jones.

SHE was tired after her hard day's work but her step was light and she smiled as she entered the tiny house. Johnny was home and her world was complete again. She moved mechanically about the kitchen, her hands busy with her supper, her mind and thoughts on Johnny. He was so dear although she had not seen him for more than a year. Tall and so handsome, his image to her was always clear. Now he was home. At the Hospital he was waiting for her. She did not think of the wounds which had caused him to be sent home. Johnny was strong; he would soon recover. To-morrow when he saw her, he would smile up at her and say, "It was only a scratch". She must look pretty for him. What should she wear?

Her wardrobe was meagre, pitifully so. But there was the blue dress. Johnny liked her in blue and he had never seen this dress. She held it up in front of her, pulling it tightly round her slight waist. It looked nice she thought. If only she had a blue hat. A hat with a wide brim and a ribbon round it. Perhaps there was time to get one. If she wore a hat Johnny would never notice that she had not had a permanent wave lately, that her brown hair was now straight at the top of her head and only curled slightly at the ends. She broke open the Swiss Chalet money-box with a knife and shook out a shower of coppers and sixpences on to the floor. The blue hat took a large part of her savings but she felt it was worth it. The shade of the wide brim hid the tired lines under her eyes, and the brown curls peeping out looked as shining as they had been when Johnny went away. She would use the new lipstick she had kept by for a special occasion and the perfume Johnny had brought her two Christmases ago.

The nurse looked askance at the blue hat. "Mrs. Burton?" she queried. The girl nodded, chilled by the professionally detached voice. "Your husband has a room to himself", said the nurse as they walked along the shining corridor together. Her starched dress whispered evilly, cruelly. The girl was vaguely disturbed. "Why is he in a room by himself?", she asked. The nurse did not answer. Perhaps she did not hear. She opened a door at the end of the corridor and stood back to let the girl into the little sun-filled room.

The still figure on the bed seemed lifeless. The girl ran across to it, her heels clacking loudly, her curls bobbing. She knelt beside the bed, "Johnny, Johnny, it's me". She stared at the face, covered in bandage. Slits were left for the mouth and nostrils and one eye was free. One eye. Blue as ever and fringed by the incredibly long lashes she had always admired and secretly envied. But the eye was dull. It stared at her uncomprehendingly. She timidly touched the pillow. "It's me, Johnny", she faltered, "you do know me, don't you? don't you? don't you?" The blue eye stared at her unwinkingly.

"He is deaf", said the nurse, "and dumb". She looked compassionately at the girl kneeling on the floor and added, "He has lost his right arm too". She turned to go. The girl clutched the hem of her skirt. It crackled under her touch and the nurse whisked it away. The girl asked in a whisper, "He's not, he's not mad, is he?" The nurse walked to the door and went out of the room, silently.

Left alone, the girl stared intently at the blue eye. The eyelid flickered and was still. The eye remained vacant, fixed on a point in the middle of her chin. On the dimple he had always kissed before his lips moved to her mouth. She shuddered and turned her head away, unconsciously covering the dimple with her hand. She walked to the door and then turned suddenly and returned to the bed. As she knelt beside it, her hat, the wide-brimmed blue hat, fell off, making a bright puddle of colour in the middle of the white coverlet. She put her arm under Johnny's shoulder and lifted him slightly. With her free hand she pulled the pillow from under his head. When she had it free, she let his head rest flat on the mattress.

She stretched out one finger and shut the eyelid over the blue eye, her flesh shrinking at the contact. Quickly, so that he should not open his eye again, she put the pillow over his face. She looked at it critically and moved it a little to one side so that there was exactly the same amount of pillow each side of his head. Then she put her elbows, one each side of him and pressed down, gently, carefully, so as not to hurt his shattered face.

Surely five minutes would be enough? She had no watch but five minutes was five times sixty seconds. Five times sixty seconds was three hundred seconds. If she counted three hundred slowly that would do. She knelt there, pressing on the pillow, counting, counting.

She reached three hundred. Supposing that wasn't enough? She counted another ten and then suddenly whipped the pillow off Johnny's face. Thank God, the eye was still closed. Only a sliver of blue glinted up at her. She knew he was dead. She carefully lifted his head and put the pillow back under it. She smoothed the coverlet which was creased where she had leaned on it and went away, leaving the blue hat lying in the sunshine on the dead man's chest.

"One Hell of a Job."

I'VE got one hell of a job. I work for a Watch-On-Your-Game Agency which means Private detectives, which boils down to nothing less than plain Eavesdropping. I'll tell you what happened last week.

A fellow suspected that his wife was having an affair with a Piano Tuner, of all people, but he hadn't any evidence. So he arranged to go away for the week-end and he wanted us to check up on his house while he was gone—just to see if this Tuner bloke hung around any. Well, they picked me for the job, and the Criminal Research Recorders gave me a few details.

Apparently this Piano Tuner was expected to drop in round about seven a.m., of all unearthly hours. They told me his name—it was Con—short for Conrad, I guess—and the dame's name was Ann. The house had a rum name too—something-or-other-Five Apples, but that doesn't matter.

I got up early and after a pretty lousy breakfast took up my position underneath a bush of begonias, and sure enough, before long, the Tuner guy comes barging up and taps on the window—softly at first, and then quite loud. No sign of the dame, so he calls her—three times he calls her name.

"Ann, Ann, Ann," he calls. "Are you there?" (I'm taking it all down in my notebook, you see.) Presently she ups and answers him. "O.K", she says, "O.K". And she opens the window, and he starts climbing in.

"Well", he says, "I don't like it down here. Let's go up".

So she says O.K. again, and I shin up a drainpipe and get a foothold outside one of the first-floor windows, just in time to hear them come in. The window is open and I'm just thinking it will be a cinch to hear what they say, when they turn on the radio and the broadcast drowns every word. And then a guy with a hurdy-gurdy strikes up just down the street, and what with all that, and them dropping their voices to a whisper, I don't hear a single word of what is going on.

So I ring up my Boss, and he grunts, and rings up the Head Office, and the Big Slap there gets mad and says, "I bet *I* could have got it," (which I don't believe)—and my Boss tells me to go back and listen some more, and keep my cloth-ears pinned back this time; so I go back, but I can't find them anywhere. So then my Boss gets mad.

I hope I never have to check up on any more of these Piano Tuners. It's one hell of a job.

Continental Cameos.

HOT sun blazing down on to white gleaming buildings, blue water lapping gently at a golden beach, happy brown children digging in the sand, colourful, laughing crowds pushing to get to the sea. This is Ostend.

Englishmen in flannels, elderly English ladies in flowered dresses walking as if they owned the world, gesticulating Frenchmen with berets, sallow, attractive Frenchwomen in scarlet beach-pyjamas, or chic afternoon dress with hat exactly right, and children—children everywhere, jostle each other in the busy Rue de la Chapelle.

The English spinster is buying vivid picture-postcards in the bazaar, and her nephew has just produced roll after roll of Kodak films to be developed The little Frenchman eats his shrimps and nonchalantly throws the husks into the gutter; his black-clad wife fingers some material, makes a rapid mental calculation, then argues at great length with the stall-owner. The band in the Place d'Armes plays louder, the crowd surges forward past the delicatessen shop which sells larks and snails, past the English church in the Rue Longue until it reaches the Digue de Mer. There on the promenade everyone is seated on wicker chairs in front of the big hotels—the Continental, the Splendide, the Miramar, and the Renomme, which, the Frenchman will assure you, has the so excellent food. Out come the bocks, the lagers, and one leans back and lazily watches the world go by.

On the sands, the old horse ambles to the water's edge, pulling bathing vans for the self-conscious, whilst braver souls in gay, revealing costumes, run down, tossing bright medicine balls between them. Tall, fair youths, carrying rackets, hurry their pretty partners to the tennis courts for a quick game before lunch. Fathers with a similar idea, motor to the golf-resort at Breedene, knowing their wives are enjoying an aperitif on a cafe terrace.

Not everybody is rushing. A few people are admiring the flower clock in the little park and turning to get a good view of the Casino with it's palm-trees and hanging bowls of pink geraniums. Others are looking at the boats in the small harbour—little yachts with gleaming white paintwork, rusty old tugs, and green-hulled fishing smacks. On the quayside sit the fisher-women mending nets with lightning efficiency, and waiting to collect the baskets of shrimps and silvery plaice which will be unloaded when the fishing-fleet comes chugging home. On the distant horizon the "Marie-Louise" and the "Suzette" are two brown dots shimmering in a haze of blue.

The hot sun shines through another burning day, then sinks in glorious colour, leaving a crimson sky palling into the dusk. In the warm evening a cosmopolitan throng moves slowly along the Digue towards the Kursal. Twilight is fading fast, black, velvety night creeps on, and the sea is mysteriously dark with the merest glimmer of silvery phosphorescence outlining each shallow wave. The distant music of an Aria from a Puccini opera drifts over the water, blending with its rhythmic rise and fall. Far over the sea, a few stars twinkle in the sky. The world is at peace.

HAZEL MILLER.

GET YOUR———
Beauty and Toilet Preparations
FROM
"LEONARD'S"
Gentlemen's Hairdresser
25, CHURCH GATE, LOUGHBOROUGH
Large Variety in Stock!

ATS

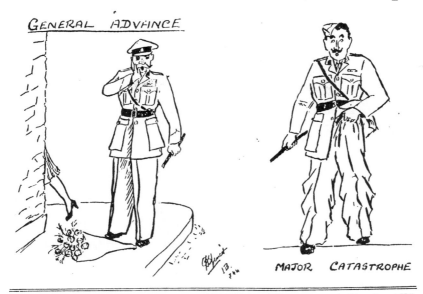

A successful Arab acquires many CAMELS.   The same applies to ATS.

"War and its Effect on Men."

WAR, and its effect on men—
  It never gives them back again
  That carefree happiness of youth;
They doubt all words.   They doubt the truth

They leave with laughing eyes and heart,
Each one eager for the start.
Returning when the battle's won
They thank their God the job is done.

The sparkle fades from each bright eye,
They ask why men are born to die.
So full of youth.   Why do we fight?
Why is this War, and what is RIGHT?

They wonder, and their hearts grow hard,
Grim and weary, battle-scarred.
They hear of strikes for higher pay,
When they themselves on that D-Day

Fought with friends who died in France,
Friends who'll never have a chance
To draw a week's well, hard-earned pay,
Or ask a raise or holiday.

The soldiers back from War are changed,
For now they're men.   They've rearranged
Their lives, ideas, their every thought.
Let's see they get for what they fought.

ANON.

ATS

Collectors' Corner.

AS the "collecting" hobby is gaining in popularity, we asked one of our most eminent collectors of that engaging species—the Paratroop (Americanus)—to give us some notes on the more interesting types which may be secured locally. We trust our specialist's experience will serve as a guide to enthusiasts who are just starting their collections.

1. **Paratroopus Vulgaris.** (The common, or "Hi Babe", variety). The most common variety of Paratroop. May be identified by its gregarious habits, and a tendency to behave like a college youth from a "Campus" picture. (Research has not yet discovered whether this behaviour is natural or only assumed because it's what English people expect). Extraordinarily colourful chest markings are found in this group, arms are usually striped, coiffure has a strange tooth-brush effect. Diet consists almost entirely of ice-cream and beer, and jaws are constantly in motion even between meals. Mating call, a peculiar clucking noise made by clicking the tongue against the teeth followed by, "Gotta-be-in-for-bed-check-honey?" Is mostly harmless, except when confronted by people wearing iron crosses or swastikas, when it becomes violent and impossible to suppress.

2. **The Statistician.** Main characteristic—the ability to think only in terms of figures. (The mathematical kind). Knows the population of every town in America and how far it is from every other town. Probably knows the same about England. Is an authority on Shakespeare—knows how much he weighed, how many teeth he had, how many plays he wrote, and how many words in each. Feminine wiles avail nothing with this specimen—the only way to charm it is to murmur arithmetical progressions in its ear or read extracts from a bus time-table.

3. **The Hayseed (or "small town hick").** Originates in Red River Rapids, or Gurgling Gulf or some such place. A very rare species because, although many other varieties of paratroops come from small rural towns, they all have big town ideas. Characteristics—extreme bashfulness, and a tendency to chew words several times before uttering them, so rendering them entirely unintelligible. Reacts to kindness and will, with encouragement, produce battered photos of its sister Hepzebah on a hayride, or its Uncle Hiram driving a pony express. (Does one *drive* a pony express?) Only one specimen of this type has so far been observed in the district and, though energetically pursued by our expert, managed to evade capture, and has not left its camp since.

Mary Gill.

Coupondering.

The Army's very kind to all the girls in its protection,
It feeds them, clothes them, boards them, and preserves them from infection.
But best of all, their female vanities to satisfy,
To wear non-issue stockings is allowed by ACI.
And every year are issued Clothing Coupons to each girl
——Ten precious slips,——the quantity's enough to make you whirl.
But now, each Coupon-leaflet bears a dreary stipulation——
Instead of any article for self-beautification,
For slippers, dressing-gown and such are coupons only valid
——No mention here of stockings——it's enough to turn you palid!
Whatever, **ever** is the use, good father ACI
To let us wear silk stockings which our coupons cannot buy?

KAY PRICE.

VICTORY
BIGGIN STREET, LOUGHBOROUGH

MONDAY, SEPT. 4th (6 days)
   Greer Garson and Walter Pidgeon in
   "MADAME CURIE"

MONDAY, SEPT. 11th (3 days)
   Robert Donat and Greer Garson in
   "GOOD-BYE MR. CHIPS"
   also Full Supporting Programme

THURSDAY, SEPT 14th (3 days)
   James Mason and Carla Lehmann in
   "CANDLELIGHT IN ALGERIA"
   also Eddie Quillan in "Here Comes Kelly"

MONDAY, SEPT. 18th (6 days)
   Clark Gable, Vivien Leigh and Leslie Howard in
"GONE WITH THE WIND" (Technicolour)
   Twice Daily—1.30 and 6.30—All Seats Bookable

MONDAY, SEPT. 25th (6 days)
   Laird Cregar and Sir Cedric Hardwicke in
   "THE LODGER"
   also Roy Rogers in "King of the Cowboys"

Mon. to Fri—Con. from 5-30 p.m.   Sat.—Con. from 2 p.m.
MATINEES.—Mon. and Wed. at 2-15 p.m.
SUNDAYS—6-15 p.m.   (One Show)

Through the Looking Glass

SALUTE

ONLY now, after the noise of battle has died away, can the full story be told (as those emotional little "leader"-writers say) of that classic delaying action, fought alone and single-handed by the dauntless Private Henry G. Lewis against the combined onslaught of the local Home Guard and Ernie Bevin's underlings. In spite of all their attacks, threats, and entreaties, the gallant warrior kept them at bay for a twelve-month —defying the worst that militarist and bureaucrat could devise. "Egad, and 'twas a famous victory!"

We have been so moved by all this that we are opening a subscription list for the erection of a statue in bronze to commemorate the hero's deeds for all time, and we feel that all right-thinking people (if there are any left) will join us in our venture.

As for where it will stand: Well, although not wishing to appear irreverent, we think that Old Cornwallis, with his half-drawn sword, has been terrorising the Courtyard for long enough; and that a buccaneering attitude of that sort is hardly suitable for this sophisticated age. So, if someone could gently persuade him to join his ancestors in Valhalla, and make way for a younger man, Henry could occupy his pedestal instead.

We might say *en passant*, that our hero has done a sight more for A.T.S. morale than any worm-eaten old matelot ever did.

POSTBAG

SIR,

Your allegation, four weeks ago, that the only authors of whom the A.T.S. at Beaumanor have ever heard, are: Daphne du Maurier, Dorothy L. Sayers and Margaret Mitchell, is a gross fabrication, an insult to British Womanhood, and a betrayal of the principles for which we girls are fighting this war.

In point of fact, a Gallup survey recently taken by myself amongst the A.T.S. stationed here reveals that, in addition to the three authors you mention, 10 per cent. of the girls are regular readers of the serial, "Love's Temptation", by Penelope Pinkerton (appearing in the "Lovers Crystal" magazine), and a further 20 per cent. never go to sleep without placing lavender leaves and fragments from the literary works of Patience Strong under their pillows.

This information will compel you, and others of your kind, at last to understand that hitherto women have never yet received their rightful recognition in literary, artistic, economic and political spheres. If the affairs of Europe were placed exclusively in the hands of us girls, womens' commonsense and practical thinking would win the day, and the peace and prosperity of the Post-War World would be assured.

What about a woman Prime Minister?

I, myself, would be a particularly suitable candidate.

Yours in earnest,
HERMIONE REDFLANNEL,
(*Junior Commandant, A.T.S.*)

BASIC CHURCHILL

Now having, with dogged determination, waded through vast oceans of blood, sweat, toil and tears, we can proceed to tear the guts from out of the remaining soft underbellies, and continue wringing the bloodstained necks of the serving jackals and blood-thirsty guttersnipes; at the same time looking forward with sober confidence to that irresistibly approaching epoch of doom when the last of all the Nazi hordes will be finally ground into the dust.

LEON DE BUNK.

AUSTERITY.
By "RAZ"

IT is all too common to hear people in Woygland running down shift work. This shift doesn't suit them, or that shift doesn't suit them, and, in fact, some malcontents even go so far as to say they hate them all, and would prefer office hours.

But in common fairness, one has to admit there is something to be said for shift work. For instance, one important advantage which becomes increasingly obvious is it's conduciveness to Austerity and Virtue. By reducing the physical condition, it lessens all inclination to the sins of the flesh.

Especially does it penalize the use of alcohol. I knew a man who came here a life-long pub crawler, and was cured by shift work. If he went pubblng before a 2-10, he would be fighting sleep all afternoon. On night shift, an evening on the ale meant he was half dead by 0200 hours. And on morning shift he just could not wake up. So he gave it up; a striking tribute to the corrective effects of shift work.

Then there is the fellow who lives to eat. Lives for his stomach. Shift work corrects all this for him, because in less than no time the shifts make his digestion so weak, it's all he can do to eat at all. Night shift is especially beneficial in this respect; the business of coming from fetid bedchamber to huge plate of hotted up meat and vegetables seeming to quell even the worst cases.

Slothfulness also benefits. What better remedy for the sluggard than a nice row of 6-2 shifts in the middle of winter? Not only up with the lark but up three hours before him!

Of course, like everything that is worth while, it takes a bit of getting used to. I knew a fellow, for instance, who had been on it for twenty years, and still was not used to it. And then there was another fellow who just as he was getting used to it—died.

But these are exceptional cases. It's a nice life if you don't weaken.

The Londoner's Litany.

O Lord, with Thy infinite Might
Protect us poor fools in our plight:
   In Thy Providence quell
   These productions of Hell
Which Buzz and go Pop in the night.
P.S.
Thy servant would add, if he may,
He is also most anxious to pray
   For protection from Hell
   In the day-time as well
From things which go Pop in the day.

                                                            G.M.S.

TAILORING FOR THE SERVICES
— from —

| START TO FINISH | 8, BAXTER GATE LOUGHBOROUGH. | TOP TO BOTTOM |

The London Tailoring Co.
Est. 1899.   'Phone 2794.

EMPIRE
MARKET PLACE, LOUGHBOROUGH

MONDAY, SEPT. 4th (3 days)
Preston Foster and Lloyd Nolan in
"GUADACANAL DIARY"
also Ronald Colman in
"The Man Who Broke the Bank at Monte Carlo"

THURSDAY, SEPT. 7th (3 days)
Donald O'Connor and Susanna Foster in
"TOP MAN"
also Craig Stevens in "Secret Enemies"

MONDAY, SEPT. 11th (3 days)
Laurel and Hardy in
"THE DANCING MASTERS"
also William Lundigan in "Headin' for God's Country"

THURSDAY, SEPT. 14th (3 days)
David Farrar in
"FOR THOSE IN PERIL"
also Sidney Toler in "Charlie Chan in the Secret Service"

MONDAY, SEPT. 18th (3 days)
Tyrone Power and Basil Rathbone in
"THE MARK OF ZORRO"
also Edgar Kennedy in "Girl from Monterey"

THURSDAY, SEPT. 21st (3 days)
Ann Crawford in
"£100 WINDOW"
also Roscoe Karns in "My Son The Hero"

MONDAY, SEPT. 25th (3 days)
Errol Flynn in
"NORTHERN PURSUIT"
also Frank Buck in "Tiger Fangs"

CONTINUOUS DAILY. Doors open at 1-30 p.m.
SUNDAYS at 5-30 p.m.

Printed by Toppings Ltd., 17, Southfield Rd., Loughborough, and published by L. P. Jones for Beaumanor Staff Magazine Committee.

CHAPTER XXXIV

A certain shepherd and the sacred pastures. The two flocks. Customs of the Grid-riders. Sheep and Brass Hats. A lamb hath a sickness. Osee is exceeding cheesed.

Now A CERTAIN SHEPHERD of Woodus, in the Promised Land, possessed a great flock of sheep. And because he was a good shepherd, Red Tabz, who dwelleth in Wyt Awl, decreed that he might put his flock to graze in the beautiful land of Woyg. For there were in Woyg many sacred pastures upon which no soul was suffered to set foot; save when it was too dark to be seen.

And the mighty flock entered into the land, and ate the pastures, and the foliage upon the temple walls, and the posts, and the wire, and the string. And such of the flock which still hungered entered into Kantin and saith: Baa. But the ears of the serving maids were good; wherefore they poured forth no Chaa. Likewise did they proffer not their messes of pottage, for they knew that the sheep were particular.

And in the flock were many Ewes, and their Lambs, and sundry Rams. And here and there was a Black Sheep.

Now the Prophet Osee also was possessed of a mighty flock. And in the flock of Osee were many Ewas, and their Lambs, and furthermore, sundry Rams. Likewise were there Black Sheep here also. Thus were the two flocks exceeding like one unto the other; and in divers otherwise also. For inasmuch as the flock wandereth whithersoever one sheep goeth, so also did the flock of Osee. So when they were gathered together in the House of Cloaks before their sundry prayers of Matins, Nytz, or Tootaten, they tarried without the doors of the temples many minutes ere one, being possessed of a Gremlin, entered thereinto; whereupon the flock followed. Or when they walked upon the highways of Woyg they differed in no wise from the true sheep in the eyes, and the oaths, of the riders of the Grids. For it is written in the Book of Wisdom of Woyg: Whensoever a Grid-rider attempteth to pass thee on thy right hand, go thou also to the right. And if he maketh to thy left hand, Shake thou him likewise.

E

And certain of the braver of the true sheep carried out Inspections of the sundry mansions of Woyg, but the worshippers noticed not whether or not they wore Brass Hats. Yet, peradventure one should sit upon the seat of the Chief Rabbi in a temple, the worshippers must straightway perceive it; for their keen ears surely discerneth the greater sweetness of the Baas.

Now a certain lamb which had consumed an abundance of bicycle tyres fell sick of the palsy and was nigh unto Flaking Out. Wherefore when an Adewo beheld the lamb he was filled with compassion, and took it, and brought it into the tabernacle of Woyg, and offered it up as a sacrifice. For it was meet and proper so to do in the tabernacle, where sundry lambs had been led to the slaughter hitherto.

And the Prophet Osee, when he learned concerning the lamb, waxed exceeding cheesed, and his heart was cast down for the flock of the good shepherd. Wherefore he bade the Tribe guard the flock, and watch over them by day and by night, saying: Behold, Red Tabz hath called forth the Man-power, and it hath been exhausted. And he hath summoned the Woman-power, and likewise it hath been spent. Take heed, therefore, lest the Sheep-power be consumed, for there are none other unto whom he may call. Yea, verily, for even the chariot of Woygshops hath but half of a Horse-power.

OCTOBER, 1944

VOL. I. No. 8 (NEW SERIES) - **6d.**

FILM ATTRACTIONS for OCTOBER

SHOWING AT THE ODEON THEATRE

Sunday, Oct. 1st—Pat O'Brien and Glenn Ford in **Flight Lieutenant**. Also Jinx Falkenburg in **Sweetheart of the Fleet**.

MONDAY, OCT. 2nd, and all the Week—
Noel Coward's
THIS HAPPY BREED
in Technicolor
with Robert Newton, Celia Johnson, John Mills and Stanley Holloway.

Sunday, Oct. 8th—Preston Foster and Lynn Bari in **Secret Agent of Japan**. Also Gale Storm in **Rhythm Parade**.

MONDAY, OCT. 9th, and all the Week—
Gary Cooper and Ingrid Bergman in
FOR WHOM THE BELL TOLLS
in Technicolor
with Akim Tamiroff and Katina Paxinou.
Please note that this picture takes 2 hrs. 35 mins. to run, and we urge you to see it from the start at 2-0, 5-0 and 8 p.m. daily. There are no separate performances and **no increase in Prices**.

Sunday, Oct. 15th—Loretta Young and Brian Aherne in **A Night to Remember**. Also Edward Norris in **Sabotage Squad**.

MONDAY, OCT. 16th, and all the Week—
George Raft and Vera Zorina in
FOLLOW THE BOYS
with Jeanette MacDonald, Orson Welles, Marlene Dietrich, W. C. Fields, Arthur Rubinstein, Sophie Tucker, Dinah Shore, and 4 Big Bands.

Sunday, Oct. 22nd—Gary Cooper and Jean Arthur in **The Plainsman**. Also Gordon Harker in **Two's Company**.

MONDAY, Oct. 23rd, for 3 days	THURS., OCT. 26th, for 3 days
Bing Crosby, Bob Hope and Dorothy Lamour in **The Road to Zanzibar** Also Betty Field and Joel McCrea in **The Great Moment**	Bernard Miles and Rosamond John in **Tawny Pipit** Also Dorothy Lamour and Ray Milland in **Her Jungle Love** in Technicolor

Sunday, Oct. 29th—Bob Hope and Madeleine Carroll in **My Favourite Blonde**. Also Robert Amstrong in **The Mystery Man**.

MONDAY, OCT. 30th, and all the Week—
David Niven in
THE WAY AHEAD
with Stanley Holloway, Raymond Huntley, and Tessie O'Shea.
The film of which Ewart Hodgson, of the *News of the World*, said: "I cannot recall ever having laughed more at a film".

Continuous Performance Daily 1-45 p.m.   Sunday, One Performance at 6 p.m.

B.S.M. Vol. I. No. 8 (New Series) OCTOBER, 1944.

Managing Editor: LEONARD P. JONES.

Editors: KAY PRICE, ERIC C. MILLHOUSE   *Treasurer:* A. H. APPLETON.

FIRST of all, the Editorial Board wish to offer their most sincere condolences to Charlie Gilbert in the sad loss of his wife, after a long and painful illness.

This month we have had to say *au revoir* to Mary Gill, who has left for an O.C.T.U. (It might be prudent to add here, in connection with "The Ballad of Barmy Bess", the *cliche* about: "Any resemblance to any living person is purely coincidental!")

But, seriously, Mary, as Joint Editress of our A.T.S. Section, as well as a prolific contributor, was a pillar of strength we shall find it hard to replace. Since there has recently been a good deal of speculation as to the necessity for a separate A.T.S. Section, we are using this occasion to merge it with the rest of the magazine, thus throwing open all of the pages to A.T.S. contributors.

The other day a certain Woygite stopped one of us in the Canteen and, in what was doubtless intended to be a tone of encouragement, said: "I hope it will be better next month". Now criticism or, for that matter, *any* kind of comment about the B.S.M., is so extremely rare, that the languishing Editorial ears sprang to attention in astonishment. (Fortunately it was not the same day as they first had to endure the amazing enquiry: "Tea *or* coffee?" in the Canteen). People are far more ready to announce their dislikes than to bother to voice any appreciation of what does happen to suit them—the infamous B.S.M. Ballot was proof enough of that—so that we have all along had to be guided in a purely negative way. That is to say, if a number of people took the trouble to remark: "I think your so-and-so feature stinks" we replaced the offending article. Conversely, when no comments were forthcoming we were obliged to presume that the feature met with fairly general approval. But is that a satisfactory way to go on?

The number of men who contribute anything to the B.S.M. could be counted on the fingers, while as for the girls (so vastly superior numerically, *and*, as we were once told, intellectually!) well, one hand could be left in the pocket. So what about a little support, girls? It's as much your magazine as anybody else's now.

It has come to our ears that there is a need for a separate "A.T.S. Gossip" feature, quite distinct from Jimmy Hewson's "scandal-pages", to record such mundane, but, among the feminine factions, interesting items as postings, promotions, birthdays and the like. To run such a page successfully it would be necessary to form a panel of girls representing the various Wings. We already have representatives for Barrow and Brand Hill, so if anyone in the other Wings would care to volunteer to collect the information we shall be glad to receive their names *as soon as possible.*

Now don't forget your contributions, folks; and if you're convinced that you have no literary bent, at least show you are interested in the Mag. by letting us have your comments, criticisms and suggestions. Just pop 'em in the rack. They will be appreciated by, and very helpful to

THE EDITORS.

Some women are afraid of mice.   Others have ugly legs.

GOOD READING
By KAY PRICE

AS long, or even longer, than "Gone With the Wind", and so packed with action and colour that Margaret Mitchell's best-seller pales into insignificance beside it, "The Sun Is My Undoing", by Marguerite Steen, is no book for the squeamish, or for those who, ostrich-like, prefer to hide their heads in the sand of British Hypocrisy and turn a blind eye to the fact that this country's part in the Slave Trade was no less disgraceful than that of any other nation.

The story is too lengthy and complicated to give more than a brief summary, but it concerns a Slave Trader and his adventures, ending with his capture by Moorish pirates by whom he is himself enslaved. The story then covers the life of his illegitimate daughter—a half-caste, since her mother was a superb negress—and thence on the life of *her* daughter. Prominent in the beginning of the book, and making her presence felt throughout, is the beautiful girl of Abolitionist principals, who repudiates her love of the Slave Trader, and in the end, takes charge of his Mulatto grand-daughter, and finally comforts his old age, when he, a broken wreck of a man, escapes his slavery and returns home.

That is the merest outline. In the book, it is filled out with harshness and tenderness, beauty and brutality, clever characterization and appalling frankness. "The Sun Is My Undoing" is a book to be read and remembered.

The next book I offer you is in sharp contrast. It is Stella Gibbons' "Cold Comfort Farm," which is pure satire and debunkery of all "sweat-and-soil" novels from beginning to end. Either you will hug it till the last page is read, or discard it with a heedless shrug after the first chapter or two. But if it *does* catch your fancy, as it did mine, you will revel in the variety of familiar characters, all laughably overdrawn and mocked at by this very gifted authoress. It is obtainable in the Penguin Edition, Fiction section.

And finally, something for the Crime-lover. I always feel that Ngaio Marsh deserves greater popularity than she enjoys for her Crime novels, in which her charming Scotland Yard detective, Roderick Alleyn, solves the mystery without any of the usual irritating smugness and secretiveness of so many fictional detectives. "Enter A Murderer", "Death in a White Tie"—all her books are absorbingly good, but one of the best is "Death in Ecstasy". The plot is built up around the spectacular and horrible death of a wealthy maiden lady while partaking in the practice of a "phoney" religion, whose existence, in the heart of London, is a cloak for—but I will leave you to find that out for yourselves. It is written with light-hearted finesse, and there is plenty of interest in it besides the solving of the murder. Remember the name of Ngaio Marsh. It's worth remembering.

TRYST.

"I DO love him so", she whispered. "He's everything to me—everything". Sitting alone in the quiet familiar room, she waited HIS coming. HE was late tonight. It was long past lighting-up time. Oh God, don't let anything have happened to HIM. Her gaze strayed to HIS chair, to the savoury pot on the fire where HIS supper simmered invitingly.

Could it be only a month ago that her life was empty and lonely? Only a month since HE walked into it? And brought love with HIM—the all-absorbing love she had dreamed of—craved? "I love him", she breathed again. "Oh why doesn't he come?" A sound at the door made her start —it could only be HE.

And with a wonderful smile, the old lady hurried across the room to obey the imperious summons of her huge black cat.

LAMENT

By Ex H.G.

O DICK, thou gallant man, how sad thy fate,
How foul the circumstance that takes from thee
Thy pride and joy, thy heart's felicity,
And leaves thee pained who once was so elate.
Before this latest law thou hadst of late
Taught all thy men with true sincerity,
How they should kill the German enemy,
And now so soon they turn from thee ingrate.
And all thy fiery cohorts are no more,
No longer is the tramp of marching feet
Heard in the courtyard. All thy soldiers sleep,
No longer do they care how goes the war,
Their doleful glance at thee spells thy defeat,
And only thou and Lord Cornwallis weep.

Phoney Phrases By WILK : No. 1

"Sit on it a minute while I measure it!"

Theatre Royal
LOUGHBOROUGH.

PROGRAMMES for OCTOBER 1944

THE FORTESCUE
Famous Players

continue their Repertory Season with the following outstanding attractions:—

Monday, October 2nd—for 6 days
The Outspoken Lancashire Play by Stanley Houghton.
HINDLE WAKES

Monday, October 9th—for 6 days
THE FAMOUS DRAMA
BLACKMAIL
By D. C. Bennett.

Monday, October 16th—for 6 days
THE SCREAMING COMEDY
THE FAMILY UPSTAIRS
By Richard Delf.

Monday, October 23rd—for 6 days
THE PLAY YOU ARE WAITING FOR
JANE EYRE
From Charlotte Bronte's Famous Novel
By Ellen Jerome.

Monday, October 30th—for 6 days
THAT GREAT LANCASHIRE COMEDY
HOT POT
By Harry Lomax.
From St. Martin's Theatre, London.

Me at the Pictures

By LEW OWEN

WEEK COMMENCING 2nd OCTOBER

"THIS HAPPY BREED" (Odeon). A cynic re-named it "This Unhappy Breed". Though this second title may be more apt, it remains a true-to-life study of an average working class family in the unsettled period between the two Great Wars. A sound **Noel Coward** production, it lacks the fine touches of his "In Which We Serve". It is in Technicolour, which is, thank goodness, not "glorious". Acting honours to **John Mills** as the faithful sailor lover of the erring daughter, **Robert Newton** as the placid ex-service man and **Celia Johnson** as his rather too harassed looking wife. A fine British film. Score 75.

"THE SULLIVANS" (Victory) is the story, based on fact, of the upbringing of five American boys and how they go to war. American life truly presented. **Thomas Mitchell** as the father is excellent. Score 65.

WEEK COMMENCING 9th OCTOBER

"FOR WHOM THE BELL TOLLS" (Odeon). Those who advocate bringing a novel to the screen as written should not be disappointed by this film of Hemmingway's best-seller. The story of a great love in the Spanish Civil War, for me therein lies its main fault. It makes it too long and slow. Its other fault is having **Gary Cooper** and **Ingrid Bergman** in the main roles to give it box office appeal. They are cast as the lovers; Cooper the American dynamiter of bridges and Bergman too smiling for a tortured Spanish girl. Their performances are put in the shade by those of **Katina Paxinou** as Pilar, the fiery peasant woman, and **Akim Tamiroff** as Pablo, the worn-out leader of the guerilas. It is a fine vehicle for Technicolour. Forty minutes shorter, two "unknowns" in the main parts, and it would have been superb. Score 80.

WEEK COMMENCING 16th OCTOBER

"FOLLOW THE BOYS" (Odeon), and "THANK YOUR LUCKY STARS" (Victory). Both these films are "star" parades, which means that the money spinners of a Hollywood studio are gathered together to provide the best light entertainment that can be got for one-and-ninepence. The first is Universal's effort; the second Warner Bros. Both have fifty stars and half-a-dozen bands; but the former is the slicker of the two. Score 60 and 50 respectively.

WEEK COMMENCING 23rd OCTOBER

"HALFWAY HOUSE" (Empire, first 3 days). You have probably heard less of this picture than any other mentioned here, yet, for its unusual theme, treated so finely, I rate this the FILM OF THE MONTH. Story concerns nine people who arrive at this Welsh retreat in 1943. All are worried and in need of a rest and guidance. The inn, with its strange atmosphere, gives them that guidance; many debatable things are said and happen, but all are handled with reverence, the ending being brilliantly treated. Most of the actors you will recognise; best performances from **Tom Walls** as Captain Meadows, and **Francoise Rosay,** in her first British film, as his wife. See it. Score 90.

WEEK COMMENCING 30th OCTOBER

"THE WAY AHEAD" (Odeon). This film does for the army what "In Which We Serve" did for the navy. Some fine British character actors have been gathered round a star and we see them unwillingly leave their varied civilian jobs as they are called to the colours. This film, full of broad British humour, follows them through their training and leaves them going forward to attack a German strong point. The direction shows patches of brilliance, such as the shots of a modern battle course as an accompaniment to an old Chelsea pensioners derisive remarks of present day warfare compared with his day. **David Niven** as the officer, acts with restraint, but watch for **Stanley Holloway's** study as Brewer. Only things I didn't like about this picture were the Chelsea pensioners and the title. Score 80.

They're telling Me!

FIRST I should like to point out an error in last month's issue. In the introduction, for "well-known", read "fifth".

We have pleasure in recording the gift of a third daughter to Mr. and Mrs. Eric ("Tarnhelm") Dobson, on August 27th.

Eric seems to be doing as well as can be expected and we sincerely hope that his recent promotion will afford him some consolation.

Congratulations also to all the others who have recently "moved up".

On the same day Mr. and Mrs. Eddie Philpott merited our congratulations on the arrival of a son, Alan John.

It seems to have been quite a "D"-Day.

Another proud father this month is Mr. R. G. Yaxley, Mrs. Yaxley presenting him with a son, Graham Lionel, on August 24th.

By the time that this issue is published Pte. May Wesson, "A" Watch, will have tied the knot with P/O William E. Coppin, R.N.A.S. We offer our best wishes for their future happiness.

Felicitations to the Ellingworth twins, Margaret and John, who attained their eighteenth birthday on September 18th.

And now for the engagements.

We extend our congratulations to the following:—

Mr. Fred Mayne, affianced to Miss Irene Hall, of Leeds.

Pte. Cècile Groves, "C" Watch, to PFC Tommy Bryner, Reg. H.Q. Coy., U.S. Paratroops.

(I'd like to make a crack about this one, but cannot under threat of my life).

Also Pte. Sybil Gregory, "C" Watch, to Tel. E. Pope, R.N.

(Birds of a feather————!)

Next, I must mention, with extreme regret, that one, James T. Hewson, has also fallen foul of the ever vigilant Loughborough Police Force, to the extent of £1.

It is scandalous, to my mind, that these robberies should continue to receive official sanction.

It is rumoured that Capt. (Mr. ?) R. W. Whitford now intends to raffle the two-pounder as he has no further use for it.

This is subject, of course, to the consent of the Yes-men.

Our congratulations to Miss Connie Praeger on being elected "Miss Woygland, 1944". She now fully deserves the title of "Dumb Blonde" as we hear that she excitedly informed her watch, the other night, that there is a circus in Piccadilly.

We have no information about Park seats.

Congratulations also to Miss Gloria Adams (sister of Sweet Fanny) who was runner-up in the same competition.

Peter Gardner must have been a beautiful baby.

L/Cpl. "Bobby" Lord, of "C" Watch, reported for duty the other day complaining of a sore foot. She said that she was showing a cow when it trod on her.

We venture to wonder what she could have been showing it to make it paw the ground in such agitation.

Apart from this incident the cattle show was a success, the above-mentioned cow gaining second prize.

We are very pleased to see that a supervisors' boudoir has now been added to "H(ole)". This gives a certain sleepy person his chance. (See previous edition).

The great "Colonel" Merritt has started his life story. Every effort is being made to find a producer with enough imagination to make a film of it. Walt Disney and Orson Welles have been suggested.

It appears that Norman Rees and "Zombie" Knott thought that they had found a "lovely way to spend an evening" until our great American Allies decided that it was too lovely.

It was in this connection that "Andy" started his army career with a strategic withdrawal.

> Picture, if you can, a super,
> Vainly hunting for a bike.
> Picture, IF you can, THE super,
> George Kenneally, on a hike.
> (*With apologies to Arthur Askey*).

Congratulations to Eric Millhouse, our editor, on being made supervisor. We hope that the magazine will never again be late now that he has more time to collect his dope.

It seems that the modern, "sordid realism" type of literature does not appeal to some of our A.T.S. members. It was with much amusement that we watched a wee Scotch lassie make a strong verbal attack on Mr. Noel Royle, author of "The Last Goodnight".

Really, Noel, it is *too* bad of you to give the girls ideas.

SCENE: THE CLOAKROOM, AITCHUT.

Utter confusion reigns as all the occupants throw themselves flat at the sound of an approaching "doodle-bug". Suddenly the engine cuts out. Chaos!

ENTER (a few seconds later): Mr. Tomlinson—without autocycle.

September 3rd, anniversary of the start of War, had a special significance to members of the group. 'Twas the occasion of the 21st birthday of Mr. Roy Hardy. I cannot understand why so much fuss was made of Peter Pan.

Incidentally, his birthday presents included a shaving set (anticipation?) and an extra tablet of "Pears Golden Glory" (advt.).

(Readers please note that I have no connection whatsoever with the firm of "Pears").

We are pleased to record that Charlie (Bank-balance) Dobson can now almost balance himself on his new cycle although he still believes in the navy order, "Clear the decks for action".

Some of the inmates of Garats Hey were very surprised a short time ago to find some masculine garments mixed with their laundry. Excitement grew as rumours of "a stowaway" went their rounds.

Anti-climax followed. The clothes were traced to George Curd, who certainly deserves commendation for his opportunism.

L/Cpl. "Bobby" Lord (yes, again) made history for the girls this month. She found a Yank without his trousers. We believe this to be a new type—the "Americanus vulgaris minus pantus".

Anyway, it certainly merits a full explanation.

It is reported, from a reliable authority, that my predecessor has a deep-knit forehead these days. I am informed that he is cogitating on:—
(a) Removal to Woodhouse Eaves.
(b) The merits of a super-stream-lined racer over his own stilt-on model.
(c) Whether he is still "not as other men are".

We, too, think that the Brand is a long way out.

I noted, with injury to my eyes, that a member of our young, sartorially perfect(?) sect, has resorted to a pair of bright blue trousers.

They say that quite an effect is created as he "darts" about.

Mr. MacNulty's life story, now being written by Noel Royle and to be printed and published by Bill Baker, should prove interesting reading. Mac arrived at Woyg via experiences in the Royal Navy, the Merchant Service, Gun running, Rum running, Whaling, sealing, and boarding house keeping, among others.

The material is there, let's see you make a good job of it, Noel. (News of the World, please copy).

A great wave of spiritualism appears to be sweeping over the manor. It started with ghost hunts and midnight séances in old ruins, but now the activities seem to be confined to a parlour game called "chasing the spook". Teepee asserts that there is something in it. I daren't take sides.

[*continued at foot of page 15*

Bludgeons in Baker Street.
By E. St. U. M.
(Last final conclusively terminating closing instalment).

DEDLEIGH SNOUPPE peered intrepidly over the shattered woodwork of the telephone kiosk. Four roads met at the crossroads. "Most extraordinary!" he muttered. Then a further glance revealed that there were really only two, which crossed over each other. He smiled grimly, to think how very nearly he had let himself be deceived. Converging on the junction from opposite directions were two massive armoured cars flaunting the unmistakable insignia of the Crimson Circumference. A machine-gun, a few yards up a third turning, was trained menacingly on the kiosk, while up the fourth road stood a battery of flame throwers. From several directions in the air above, sinister-looking aircraft were volplaning down, their cannon pointed terrifyingly at the splintered booth, the red circles on their wings plainly visible.

"Bother!" ejaculated the famous criminologist, involuntarily. He bent down and grasped a ring set in the floor of the kiosk, pulling it, and revealing a trap-door. Below him ran a dark tunnel. He heard the ominous roar of a fast-approaching train. Leaping to the telephone, he whipped out his faithful Wobley, and dialled the number of the Head Office of the Underground. Before he had finished his conversation the dauntless detective had brought down twenty-three aircraft, silenced all but one of the machine-guns, and disabled both armoured-cars. Coolly lighting a cigarettes from one of the flame throwers, he descended on to the track. The train pulled up beside him with a screech of brakes and he leapt in beside the driver. "Drive like stink to Crinklehaven Common!" he panted, coolly, and thrust sixpence magnanimously into the driver's palm. The driver, recognising his distinguished passenger, wrenched out his maps, and trod on the accelerator (or whatever they have in trains) and the train darted forward at a shuddering three-mile-an-hour velocity.

"Di-di-di-dah, Di-di-di-dah", murmured the great detective, a far-away look in his eyes, as the train throbbed forward on its errand of mercy. The driver glanced at him and shook his head sorrowfully; he could not be expected to know that the celebrated sleuth was calling up Inspector Dribblepuss by telepathy.

* * * *

Krumpit was fed up—in more senses than one. Since the mass of sausages had reached above his chin he had been continuously eating them to keep their level down. But he knew he could not swallow many more. He hiccoughed dismally.

Suddenly there was a burst of firing in the room above; fierce shouting, and the joyous bark of a dog. As Krumpit's head sagged forward, the last sausage stuck obstinately in his throat, a trap-door above his head was flung open and Inspector Dribblepuss's voice bellowed his name. He tried to answer, but only succeeded in producing a long string of sausages. A torch flashed on his bloated face. "Quick!" shouted Drib, and with a squelch he landed on the heap of sausages, followed by several of his faithful constables. A sergeant leaned through the trap-door and passed them the mustard. They had eaten the exhausted lad free before Dedleigh Snouppe arrived.

* * * *

'It was all really very elementary, you know", said the famous detective to the crowd who were assembled in the scullery of Pukingditch Hovel. "It was the tin of 'Snappie' which put me on the right track. But", and he glanced around the throng of awe-stricken faces, searching for one he could not find, "we owe our thanks to Krumpit, the brave lad who actually uncovered the whereabouts of the sinister sausage factory, and, in the nick of time, saved the Marchioness' precious dachschund from a fate too ghastly to contemplate. Where is Krumpit, by the way?"

The crowd looked wonderingly from one to another, and decided that none of them was the detective's assistant. Her Ladyship put down the sock she was darning for the Marquis, and searched under the sink, shaking her head futilely.

At that moment the door burst open, and Krumpit dashed in, breathlessly. He was carrying two large, knobbly sticks, which he thrust excitedly into his master's arms.

"What's this?" exclaimed Dedleigh Snouppe, his right nostril twitching away like one o'clock.

"I thought you'd need 'em for the title, Guv'nor", replied Krumpit, sheepishly.

(*End. Was your journey really necessary?*)

NOEL ROYLE once used to teach
    The laws of evolution;
And all the wisdom, loved to preach
Of putting life beyond the reach
Of clerical pollution.
But finding Darwin soon reduced
His chance of popularity;
He changed his style, and soon produced
A series, which, if widely loosed,
Would shock this staid locality.
                      THE DOOK.

Kay Metcalfe Explains

TO say that "Bris" was unwilling to get into bed beside me is hardly truthful. Actually he didn't have much option—he was slung there by superior weight, and Ann was as much to blame for it as Kim. (She'll murder me for telling you this, 'cos she's not really "that kind of a girl"). Anyway the end justified the means and we were able to get down to business without any further hitches.

"Bris" is really an exceptionally nice little fellow, you know—bit on the small side perhaps, but none the worse for that, as you yourself probably know. In this case, however, his conscience started getting a bit obstreperous and we began to have trouble—this was after the deed was done though. If he'd said anything about this in the beginning I should never have gone through with it you may be sure, but how the heck was I to know that his wife might object if she found out? After all it isn't as if it's the first time things like this have happened—similar scenes are enacted all up and down the country every day, and nobody thinks anything at all about it. Or do they? However, "Bris" appeared to think they did, and started muttering vaguely about "chemists" and "Ollie" and "awkward to explain if anything came of it" and "Fred", and—oh you know the sort of thing I mean.

I tried to treat the whole affair lightly, as if it were a huge joke, but he refused to be comforted. "The tent flap was open" and "if anyone saw us they might start talking" seemed to be the trouble then.

Taken all round I suppose it did look a bit compromising—me gaily attired in a natty pair of blue striped pyjamas (army issue, A.T.S., for the use of) and "Bris" resplendent in a nifty green/white striped silk affair people could only think one thing.

Poor little soul—I can see him now, after we'd finished our antics—sitting up with his chin in his hand, gazing into space. Over and over again he repeated to the world in general (while we roared with laughter) "I'll never be able to convince them I'd got my trousers and shoes on under this blanket", "If only I'd left one foot out it wouldn't have looked so bad", "Who's going to believe there were really two beds under this top blanket?" And then accusingly to Ann and Kim, "It's alright for you two to laugh—you're not in the ruddy photograph!"

PYROMANIA

By ERIC W. DOBSON

IN the fitful light of a waning moon, a brilliant orange flash suddenly awoke the echoes of the woods, and the hundreds of nearby villagers reacted in their several ways to the explosion which rocked the neighbourhood.

One man only could have told the cause of the tremendous upheaval; at least he could, had he lived, but as he disintegrated into the cold morning air with various components of ordnance pieces I'm obliged to tell the story myself.

Wilfred Gray was a chemist in a government factory, an extremely clever chemist, too, but afflicted with an ill-found sense of injustice which made him habitually discontented and, on the whole, insubordinate. Friction with his superiors rose to such a pitch that in a fit of pique he resigned from his job and vowed he'd have nothing more to do with government departments. Naturally, in these days of war, when government control has almost a monopoly over all commercial concerns, he found that, contrary to his belief, obtaining fresh employment was very difficult.

For some days he brooded, and as the days turned to weeks his mind became the prey of vague plans for revenge against the personal injustices of life.

Sitting crouched in a chair by an empty grate he finally evolved a plan, which, although petty, in his hoped-for results would at least satisfy his peace of mind, restore a certain mythical sense of respectability. Sheer inferiority complex, of course, but the *force majeur* in his consequent actions. He knew there were many ammunition dumps in the country, millions of rounds of ammunition, thousands of shells and bombs, all waiting to be used against the enemy. His torturous thoughts led him to believe that his mission lay in destroying these dumps, one by one. He toured various localities and finally decided upon a park in Blankshire. Here the dumps were, for the most part, unguarded and readily accessible, so, elaborating upon his plans, and utilizing his chemical knowledge he prepared an intricate time-bomb. Many gleeful hours he spent in piecing together the delicate mechanism which would be instrumental in blasting his first dump, and the day came when he was satisfied with his labour and prepared himself for action.

He went by train to a town near the park, arriving after dark, and made his way through sleeping villages to the scene of his diabolical intentions. He carefully ascertained the absence of sentries and deliberately chose the dump which was to commence his campaign of revenge.

"This one contains machine-gun (.303) ammunition—not much of a bang there, and I mustn't give just a poor imitation of Crystal Palace. What's in this one? Howitzer and mortar shells—not too violent a reaction here, either".

"Ah, here we are, 400 pounders, sleek messengers of death that would wake the woods to an early cacophonous reveille, an eruption worthy of a master hand!"

With beaver-like enthusiasm he set about the task of clearing a space for his time bomb. With the aid of a prop of wood he levered the heavy cases to the side until, in the centre, lay a hollow core in which to plant his devilry.

A glance at his watch, "one-fifteen"; he'd set the bomb for four o'clock, by which time he would be some miles away, far enough to hear just the distant rumble of the explosion. The bomb duly timed, he placed it carefully and began the task of restoring some of the cases. All went well for a while, but suddenly as he reached for his lever to shift a particularly obstinate case, there was an ominous rumble and half-a-dozen cases slid against him. He tried to move and found his left leg pinned between the cases. He began calmly to shift them, but the angle at which he crouched effectively destroyed his ability to exert any pressure.

Well, he would use the prop to help him away. But no, the prop lay tantalisingly out of reach. His serenity began to dwindle and with a suggestion of panic he struggled afresh, only to subside in an agony of perspiration, panting, and now really frightened. More than that, his leg must have been broken, or at least fractured, by the sudden weight, for a wave of pain and nausea robbed him of consciousness. He came gradually to his senses and suddenly realised his predicament.

God! That bomb was still ticking away! "What's the time?" "Half-past two; oh well, plenty of time to stop it".

He reached carefully forward and then the horror of it smote him, for the bomb was, like the prop, beyond his reach. He became suddenly a screaming, raving maniac. He shrieked at the top of his voice and tore vainly at the cases, which might become his coffin.

Another fit of fainting left him mercifully unconscious for a while, but when he gained enough sense to look at those luminous hands on his watch they showed the hour of three-thirty.

The time-bomb ticked a rhythm every stroke of which beat itself into his deranged brain. The seconds of his career were numbered, slipping past him rapidly. He lay back and thought of what might have been. What a fool he was to have been so negligent, what a fiendish end lay less than half-an-hour ahead of him. And then, hope born of panic; perhaps his bomb wouldn't explode, perhaps someone would rescue him! But no, only too well had he made his infernal machine, and only too well had he chosen this spot for its remoteness from interference.

He laughed raucously and discordantly and his laughter turned gradually to screams, ending in bitter, hopeless sobs.

Another glance at his watch; "three minutes to go"! Three minutes of misery, fear, and mental agony before the roar of T.N.T. would send him to oblivion!

Fascinated, he watched two minutes pulse away. The steady tick of the bomb seemed an ever-increasing crescendo, drumming into his fevered brain, thud by thud.

Thirty seconds now, and the hammering roaring in his ears.
Twenty seconds!
He wiped the sweat from his eyes better to count his approaching doom.
Five seconds left!
Four!
Three!
Two!
One!!

In the fitful light of a waning moon a brilliant orange flash suddenly awoke the echoes of the woods, and the hundreds of nearby villagers reacted in their several ways to the explosion which rocked the neighbourhood.

○ ○ ○ ○ ○

The Pyramids were designed by a Cubist who came to the point.

Bookseller and Stationer :: Lending Library

J. SKETCHLEY
24 & 25, High Street, Loughborough

Telephone 2980.

The Gospel according to St. Apid

(Translated from the English by Disciple Millhouse).

CHAPTER XXXV

NOW in the days when Itla the Hunnite began to send his birdmen forth over the land of Brit, to lay their eggs in sundry places, the King, who dwelleth in Smowk, was gravely concerned lest the birdmen be able to discern the hospitals and the churches, and thus not lay their eggs upon a certain place which is called Random.

Wherefore he summoned his chiefs before him, and cried unto them in a loud voice, saying: Darken thy lightness, I beseech thee. Yea, verily, hide thy light under a bushel of Blackout, that the birdmen of Itla may be confounded, and their eggs be addled.

And the chiefs went forth in the land, and commanded the peoples accordingly; and one Alvar spake throughout the length and breadth of Brit with the Great Voice of Bebesee, saying: Get a load of this.

And thus it came to pass that the Black Plague descended over all the cities and hamlets of Brit. And the trade of the vendors of Blackouts waxed exceeding great. And the air within the habitations of the people, and in the houses of toil, and in the inns, and in the temples, waxed exceeding foul. And the citizens which buffetted one into another in the darkness waxed exceeding wrath. And the Turtle-doves, because they were no longer constrained to take refuge in the Flicks, waxed exceeding glad, and squandered their one-and-nines in otherwise. But still the birdmen of Itla found not the place which is called Random, and continued to lay their eggs carefully upon the hospitals and the churches.

Yea, even though the Raffites and the Ackackites and the Beerbeerites of Brit persuaded many scores of the birdmen not to return unto their master Itla, the chiefs of the King forbore to lighten the darkness. And they saith unto the drivers of the chariots: Let thy lights suffice only to blind the riders of the Grids. And unto the riders of the Grids they saith: Let thy lights suffice only that thou hast no idea where thou art going. And it was so.

Then it came to pass that Itla ran short of birdmen, and the few which remained were become afflicted with exceeding cold feet. Wherefore Itla conceived a mighty Doodlebug, which was a flying egg without men. And he builded an abundance of Doodlebugs and despatched them with single tickets to Brit. But the soldiers of the King, with their comrades, the Dohbois, went forth on a pilgrimage to Urop, and seized the Doodlebug nests, on their way to Berlin.

And because there were no longer any birdmen to be guided unto Random, and because the lamps upon the multitude of chariots of the Dohbois in Brit had already turned the night into day, the hearts of the chiefs of the King were become softened, and they suffered the peoples to enjoy a modicum of light. And when the peoples in the houses of toil, and in the temples, and in the habitations, smelled the fresh air again they knew that the end of the battle was indeed nigh. But the Turtle-doves were cast down.

GET YOUR———

Beauty and Toilet Preparations

FROM

"LEONARD'S"

Gentlemen's Hairdresser

25, CHURCH GATE, LOUGHBOROUGH

Large Variety in Stock!

THE FARM
By HAZEL MILLER

THE pines on the hill whisper dark secrets to each other, and, in the ravine far below, a thin trickle of water murmurs through the undergrowth and decaying leaves. The road winds steeply upward to a tiny hamlet.

There, a little apart from the other houses, stands a farm, built of grey stone, stolid as the earth on which it depends. Across the yard, swinging the buckets which dangle from the yoke on her shoulder, comes Madame Dupré. Small and dark, her faced lined and weather-beaten, yet kindly and shrewd, she is a typical Belgian Walloon, strong as her peasant ancestry can make her.

A hard life, hers, ever since she came here as a bride twenty-five years ago. Her eyes smile as she thinks of that day. "Eh bien", but her husband was a good man if there ever was one—and so are the two sons. She was indeed lucky. What did hard work matter? She was content to look after her men-folk. After all that was a woman's job even if she herself was dropping with fatigue. Then there was always the house . . . . She turned round and her quick glance took in each beloved detail. The half-open door leading into the beautifully kept kitchen, so much part of her existence. Here were spent the happiest hours of the day when Paul, Jean and Henri would enjoy a few minutes rest before going upstairs. She would listen respectfully to their talk and make sure that all pipes were filled and ready. But this was late in the evening when the last job was done, and the fresh, warm milk had been poured through the separator from which it emerged in two steady streams; cream into the blue enamel pail and skim milk into the big zinc buckets. "Bon dieu!" What satisfaction to hear the drone of the machine and watch the good milk going in.

Then milk-cans to be scalded whilst Paul and the two boys fed the calves in the stable. She always hurried over this and had a few minutes to spare before they came back for supper. As her expert hands beat eggs for a gigantic omelette, perhaps she would be thinking of the high price those animals would fetch next market-day for milk-fed veal was tender. The sizzling of mushrooms in the pan would remind her that it was ready for the egg. Yes, it was indeed good to lay a well-cooked meal before your men-folk when they were hungry after a long day in the fields.

A chain rattled noisily as Turc, the black watch-dog moved forward to drink from his basin. Madame Dupré started guiltily. Here she was dreaming away, and the water still to be carried and the cows to be milked. Still there were good times too, life wasn't all hard work.

As she went to find her three-legged milking stool, she thought about the fêtes when all the village made merry, and everyone was jolly, even Monsieur Le Curé when he had tried a little of her husband's Cognac. All the women would wear their best dresses; girls in bright colours, married women in black as befitted the dignity of their position. She too had been pretty once and had danced with the best of them. That was when Paul was courting her, and he was not the only one either, for all her mother's daughters were good looking.

In later years she had proudly worn a black frock and, as a married woman, helped to make the huge fruit tarts, pies and other delicacies for the feast. You had to know how to cook if you wanted to keep a man content at home. Every woman knows that!

Once again Madame Dupré came back to the present with a start as a mans voice called "Marie, Marie, where are you?" "Coming", she cried and picked up the stool.

THEY'RE TELLING ME—*continued.*

We regret to announce that, owing to lack of space, the monthly crack about the Weasel must be held over to a further issue.

By way of conclusion, and to be serious for a moment, the large amount of gossip left for me in the letter rack is conspicuous by its absence. Play the game, please, you have to tell me before I can tell you.

Address your letters to   JIMMY.

AD INFINITUM.
By BILL HAYWARD

I'M beginning to wish that I had never worked in a Patents Office. I even begin to wonder sometimes if there is any future in it. Mind you, it's not that the work isn't interesting; far from it. You're always meeting all kinds of interesting, and sometimes, queer people. I remember several times having very enlightening conversations with—well, for instance, there was the very earnest young man who had just invented a four-sided brace and bit, for boring square holes (for square pegs that usually got put into round ones). Then there was the youthful-looking fellow who wanted to take out a patent for an atom-smasher he'd invented. He had it with him in his suitcase and insisted on giving me a demonstration. But, as he confided to me, he hadn't been able to get any atoms to try on it, so he used walnuts; and it seemed to work quite well. The thing that has finally turned me against my job, however, happened this morning.

At 8.30 a.m. I hurry over my cup of tea and dash out to catch my bus which takes me to town, and to the office; a fresh summer morning with still a trace of the coolness of the night in the air, especially in the shadows.

Arriving at the office, I am greeted by a brisk "Good morning" from my secretary, and collecting up a pile of mail from her desk, I go into my office to await the business of the day.

I have not long to wait. I am half way through a letter which begins "Dear Sir, Unless——" which, unfortunately has no connection with the patents business, when my secretary ushers in the first of my customers; a little grey-haired man with ginger whiskers.

"Good morning", he says.
"Good morning", say I.
"I want", he says, "to take out a patent on a time-machine". I take a deep breath.

"Now look", say I, "regularly, once, sometimes twice a week, I get people in here claiming they've invented a time-machine. The idea just isn't practical. It simply *can't* work".

The little old man looks at me, and doesn't say anything, but unlatches a large suitcase he had been carrying, which I had failed to notice until now.

"I can see", he says, "that you will only be convinced by a demonstration. Here, hold these", shoving two shiny handles attached to a length of wire across the desk. I automatically grasp them, and he continues;

"Now at what period of history would you prefer to start?"

"Couldn't you make it about breakfast time this morning?" I suggest with a weak smile, thinking at all costs to humour him. He bends down, makes one or two adjustments to something in the bag, and then reaches over, removes the bulb from my desk light, and inserts a plug on a wire leading to his case, and switches on.

* * * *

I finish my cup of tea, and dashing out, catch my bus that takes me to the town, and to the office. It's a delightfully fresh Summer morning.

At the office, I collect up my pile of mail after receiving a brisk "Good morning" from my secretary, and go into my office to read it. I am dealing with one rather insistent correspondent when my secretary ushers in a little grey-haired man with ginger whiskers.

"Good morning", he says.
"Good morning", say I.
"I want", he says, "to take out a patent on a time-machine——".

And so it goes on. Y'know, I'm getting actully fed up of hovering back and forth between 8.30 and 9.30 a.m.

Also I'm getting *very* hungry.

FAMOUS LAST WORDS———

"I'd give ANYTHING for a breath of fresh air".

Ode to Three Supervisors.

I'LL tell you a story, me ducks, so here goes,
   It's a tale of Beaumanor and three of its Beaux,
By now all the A.T.S. know, I suppose,
Those three supervisors in J.

Johnny's a bachelor—he sticks to Morse,
   Britt, dark and attractive, is married of course,
But Nobby, who's ditto, is quite a dark horse,
He's a one with the ladies in J.

They've all got dark hair—it's impeccably sleek,
They visit the Barber's at least twice a week,
The rest of their off-duty time's spent "on seek"
   For Brylcreem—for supers of J.

Their clothes are delightfully "man-about-town,"
From Johnny in sports coat, to Nobby in brown.
Britt's Government issue does let the side down,
   But he still looks quite nifty in J.

Britt knows all the answers, but says very few,
Of course, Johnny knows them, and uses them too,
But Nobby's forgotten all he ever knew,
   So beware of those supers in J.

They're really nice fellows, although it seems strange
We curse 'em a lot but we don't want to change.
All the nice things we say when they're well out of range
   Would surprise the three supers of J.
                        TEDDY ("B" WATCH).

Pentahedral Nucleiform Gasometry.

OMNISCIENT and agglutinating among all ultra-oleaginous fulminents of anatomical pendentives, Professor Fylitz Schildbraun says, "Globular particles of $\theta\pi\varepsilon\beta\ell$ combustible apocalypse roccellic emanating from occidental serpentiform aspidistræ *ad infinitum*, resulting conclusively in Levantine dehydration redistributing fœtidity until bucolic speculation degenerates into mere *status quo*". More simply, therefore, we may draw conclusions as follows: Pachyderm phrenological librarians, basic Gothic obelisk principally, encyclopædic superimposition sub-strata rhetorically hyper-redundancy (usually known as egg-whisks) over-inflate asafœteda, penicillin, M and B, and the amazing drug, discovered by Dr. Erlich, known as 606.

Alternatively it is alleged by Dr. Sergei Pjvnvjski, of the University of Moscow, that $\theta\pi\varepsilon\beta\ell$ in trigonometrical form does not exist save in circumstances of $xp\theta d$ as demonstrated *ad absurdum pro rata*. Without Logarithms then, it may be understood if illustrated thus (x being understood to equal p^{10}):

$$\frac{\theta\pi\varepsilon\beta\ell}{4x^2} \times \frac{Xp\theta d}{\pi R^2 X 101} = \frac{M:N}{P:Q} = \frac{nbg}{\beta\ell:\theta\varepsilon}$$

———a process easily grasped and discarded as soon as its hypothesis has been fully exploded.

However, we must not forget that the Minister of Health wishes to impress clearly on the General Public the importance of reading all the current literature published by his Ministry.
              PROF. SCIPIO UTTADRIVVLE-TOTALLROTT,
                     B.A., B.Sc., B.F., OXEN COWES.

What has Happened to "H's"- - - ?

(From the original ponderings of "Spike" Forster).

(The following selection of Press and Radio reports may afford a solution to the mystery which has been engaging the attention of so many Woygites lately).

"BARROVIAN", writing in the "Sileby Sentinel", says: "The other day while rowing on the Soar our boat struck one of a number of large, submerged objects. They seemed to be green metal boxes with arrangements like towel-rails attached".

The "Daily Dose" correspondent on the Italian front reports that a new kind of tank barricade is being erected there by Pioneers. It is composed of stout steel units, painted green, and is claimed to be impregnable.

The German Official Radio says that the R.A.F. are dropping a new "secret weapon", consisting of an oblong container filled with very high explosive. As it falls it emits the "V-Sign" in a series of piercing whistles.

The latest model jeep to go into action is provided with a very unorthodox type of wheels, says Reuter's correspondent in France. This consists of a solid metal disc, bearing graduated numbers in white (for what purpose is not disclosed). The usual tyre is replaced by an outer metal rim with a heavily knurled edge.

Berlin Radio claims to have obtained evidence of a fiendish new torture to be meted out to War Criminals by the Allies "when they have won the War". The victims will be made to sit before a large green box, and a pair of headphones will be clamped on their ears. At the touch of a switch a cacophony of noise of unbelievable intensity will be unloosed, gradually sending them insane. Large dumps of these diabolical devices are said to be held in readiness in England. The report also claims that a number of English men and women have already been driven demented in experiments with these devices.

Blitzed fish-and-chip saloons in "Doodlebug Alley" are to be provided by the Government with ultra-modern potato-slicers operated by thirteen controls, says Exchange Telegraph.

A new machine has made its appearance in pin-table saloons up and down the country, reports Press Association. It consists of a large drum in a long box. The drum has to be rotated by a handle, in the manner of a "fruit machine", but instead of combinations of fruits, numbers are employed. Certain sequences of numbers yield jack-pots of pencils, rubbers, razor-blades and cigarette cartons. On one machine which our reporter tested to-day, he received a stale spam roll, a drawing of a raven, and a half-completed crossword puzzle.

D.S.T.

A sailor is a wolf in ship's clothing.

A Glimpse of the Digby's

JUDY, at her bead-frame, is deep in the intricacies of Mathematics. Then suddenly—"Mummy, I'm four. How old is Gilly?"
I tell her, "Two".
Judy ponders a moment. Then, "Is two half of four?"
"Yes, dear".
"Well, when I'm a hundred how old will Gilly be?"
"Ninety-eight".
"Is ninety-eight half a hundred?"
"No, dear, fifty is half a hundred".
Judy is unable either to grasp or believe this. "Well", she concludes suspiciously, "I think I'd better ask Susan. *She* goes to school".
And turning a crushing shoulder, she becomes once more absorbed in her bead-frame.

EVENTIDE AT SEA.

DESCENDING slowly 'neath the western sky,
    Shouting his farewell' midst splendid array
    Of gold, scarlet, and palest green on high,
The sun declines.   So ends another day.

The sea, a glossy field of silv'ry green,
    Rolls endlessly into the far unknown,
Into a world where Man has never been,
    Beyond the realm of flesh and blood and bone.

Who knows the sombre secrets of this realm?
    Who can foresee the mysteries of the night?
Perhaps with Satan howling at the helm,
    Hell lies past that horizon, out of sight.

Perhaps if worldly men could visit there,
    And learn the secrets of the ageless past,
And then return again to human lair,
    They'd solve the Mystery of Life at last.

                              J.C.M.B.

THE MUSIC CLUB.

AS in previous years, we begin our fourth season with a Social, on Friday, 29th September, at Quorn Church Room; our regular Wednesday meetings at the "Hurst" will be resumed on 4th October, at 6 p.m.

An important feature of each meeting will, of course, be a gramophone recital, and this year we intend, by means of a "request" arrangement, to give you the opportunity of stating which of the records available to us you would specially like to hear, and to ensure that they will be played on a Wednesday when you are able to be present. The collection to which we have access is large and representative and contains many "firm favourites".

In addition to the Wednesday recitals, it is planned to have occasional recitals in the Canteen Lounge, on evenings other than Wednesday. We have had two already, and their success evidently indicates that they satisfy a need.

Once more we extend to all B.M.R. staff an invitation to join us. There are no formalities to observe—just come along to the "Hurst" on the first Wednesday evening you can manage. We take this opportunity of welcoming to our winter activities those who came with us for the first time on any of our rambles and cycle rides during the past summer.

Perhaps this will be our last season—let's make it a memorable one!

TAILORING FOR THE SERVICES
— from —

| START TO FINISH | 8, BAXTER GATE LOUGHBOROUGH. | TOP TO BOTTOM |

The London Tailoring Co.
Est. 1899.   'Phone 2794.

The Ballad of Barmy Bess

THIS is the tale of Barmy Bess,
   A private in the A.T.S.,
     Who, stupid, as her name suggests,
Fell down on her Selection Tests,
But showing an aptitude for Morse
Was sent upon a Wireless Course,
Whence she emerged, some six months later,
Alleged to be an operator.
They sent her to a secret place,
And there a gent with solemn face
Declared her knowledge was as nil,
And trained her on to further skill
Until he felt she might be fit
To try her heavy hand at it.

On duty therefore did she go,
With pencils sharp, and eyes aglow,
Convinced that she the War would win—
(The others grinned a knowing grin)
—And plied the knobs, and switched the switches
With nervous, futile jerks and twitches,
But all to no avail—for she
Was absolutely N.B.G.
The Supervisor held his head
Between his hands, and faintly said,
"My Gawd! What are we coming to?"
And Bessie said, "I wish I knew".

The weeks passed by, and Barmy Bess
Still kept on getting in a mess
No matter how she tried, until
The Supervisors all fell ill,
And all the I.Ms. and their like,
In self-defence went out on strike.
And the long-suffering C.O.
Summoned our Bess, to let her know
That she some other job must find.
(He was quite firm, but very kind).
She cut him short—"Now listen here,
My fond Papa's a Brigadier—
A more important man than you,
And he can pull a string or two!"
She spoke the truth—the OCTU Board,
Her full incompetence ignored,
And thinking of her Dad's position
Were glad to give her a Commission.

      *   *   *   *

She stooged around, as dumb as ever,
—Rewards come slowly to the clever—
But it's such as *her*—not you and me,
Who will win this War, and an O.B.E.!

KAY PRICE.

ALLOTMENT—A Government arrangement whereby at least some of a soldier's pay goes to the woman who is entitled to it.

PIN-UP GIRLS are the rage. You never know when the pin will give way.

VICTORY
BIGGIN STREET, LOUGHBOROUGH

MONDAY, OCT. 2nd (3 days)
Don Ameche and Francis Dee in
"HAPPY LAND"
also Bill Henry in "Attorney's Dilemma"

THURSDAY, OCT. 5th (3 days)
Irene Dunne and Cary Grant in
"MY FAVOURITE WIFE"
also Wendy Barrie in "Follies Girl"

MONDAY, OCT. 9th (6 days)
Thomas Mitchell and Ann Baxter in
"THE SULLIVANS"
also Travel, Comedy and News Films

MONDAY, OCT. 16th (6 days)
Errol Flynn and Bette Davis in
"THANK YOUR LUCKY STARS"
also Full Supporting Programme

MONDAY, OCT. 23rd (6 days)
Welcome return visit of the Disney masterpiece
"SNOW WHITE & THE SEVEN DWARFS"
(In Technicolour)
also Singleton and Lake in "Footlight Glamour"

MONDAY, OCT. 30th (6 days)
Kathryn Grayson and Gene Kelly in
"THOUSANDS CHEER"
(In Technicolour)

Mon. to Fri—Con. from 5-30 p.m.   Sat.—Con. from 2 p.m.
MATINEES.—Mon. and Wed. at 2-15 p.m.
SUNDAYS—6-15 p.m.   (One Show)

Through the Looking Glass

LIBERATRIX

WE greatly admired the frank courage of that authoress who confirmed, in last month's Rag, a theory we have long held in relation to female psychology. As you rabble may remember, a picture was painted of the fervour and excitement with which Fanny awaited the return of her long-lost love; and how, with trembling fingers she extracted the last few coins from her faithful old money box to invest in a new hat which would knock Herbert cold. But when that frail affectionate flower, at length being closeted with her dear one, discovered he had been knocked about a bit, and didn't look quite as young as he used to do, with a great surge of humanitarian self-effacement she there and then seized a pillow, and put him out of his misery by means of a discreet suffocation.

Anyone who may, in the past, have imagined that the fair ones are sometimes inclined to a certain callous worldliness, will have his fears dispelled by this simple tale of womanly devotion. So, the next time you see the Vicar's daughter romping round the Vicarage lawn with the infants from the Sunday School, remember that she's not as indifferent to human happiness as you may suppose. It only needs the slightest sign on your part that the world isn't treating you too well, and, like an angel from heaven, she will slip a double shot of strychnine into your lemonade, or administer the blessed relief of a practised blow on the back of the skull with the spiked blackjack she always carries close to her heart.

SUBMISSION

After having been weaned in a sheltered and refined, if somewhat archaic mid-Victorian atmosphere, where Mama would swoon if Papa forgot himself and expressed his real views about the Corn Laws: our delicately nurtured feelings were rudely shocked the first time we came up against the bluff Twentieth Century heartiness of the Official Letter; which, if our failing memory serves us aright, ran something like this:—

From: Local Officer, Ministry for Air.
To: Leon de Bunk, 3rd Class Breather.

Providing that the following requirements are fulfilled, you will be allowed to breathe, as from the 1st January, 1941:—

(1) Providing forms WT 1345/63x and LK 93475 have been completed to the satisfaction of the Ministry for Air.
(2) Providing that this does not interfere with your Civil Service duties.
(3) Providing that the air is not required by any Superior Officer.
(4) Providing that your time could not be devoted to any other more useful purpose.

After three years of this, our former spirit of fine independence has disappeared; and, becoming just a mass of reflexes blown hither and thither by the winds of Bureaucracy, we stopped caring. Now, like the rest of you we grovel on our knees and plead for mercy whenever a Mogul draws near.

CHEZ LUI

Conversing the other day with one of those rare characters—a minion who has a good word to say for the supervisors—we received information which has shattered most of our former fundamental beliefs, and compels us to admit that there may be some ultimate good in the Universe, after all.

According to this chap—who, it appears, has studied the matter—supervisors are often quite beautiful in their home life: they are frequently quite kindly towards infants, and rarely beat their wives more than once a week; in moments of particular affection they may even be seen nursing babies or rinsing nappies. As is well known, no domestic animal can be persuaded to live with a supervisor—they invariably bolt after two hours in the same house—and some of these unhappy men feel keenly about it. Indeed, in one case, a supervisor who had brought home a tame skunk broke down in tears when it refused to cross the front door-step.

This, as you lambs will agree, only goes to show that Jack the Ripper may have been just a homely boy at heart.

LEON DE BUNK.

SPORTOPICS.

WE lost at Sileby on July 29th. Six of the team failed to score, and on a batsman's wicket we only obtained 50 runs. Our bowling was weak and our opponents easily got their runs. Score:

Exiles.—50 (Reedman 21, Burrows 5 for 1).
Sileby.—Over 100. (No details).

On August 5th, versus Willowbrook, G. M. Spooner and Lt. Mace made a good stand and we had a total score of 100. After a well-contested game we won by 19 runs with a few minutes to spare.

Exiles.—100. (Spooner 38, Mace 17, North 5 for 26).
Willowbrook.—81. (Cashmore 20, Bancroft 17, C. O. Smith 4 for 8).

Two enjoyable matches were played between "H" and The Rest. Scores:

First match:—
The Rest.—126. (Lt. Mace not out 49, Billingsley 5 for 42).
"H".—68. (J. Dodd 23, Billingsley 20).

Second match:—
"H".—42. (E. D. Smith 6 for 17).
The Rest.—108. (Spooner 28, Hewson 21, Sgt. Sibley, U.S.A., 19, Keenlyside 5 for 47).

W. H. Anderson has now left us for the Forces. "Andy" has been one of our best and staunchest players. His football has impressed a representative of a famous club and we may hear of him in "big" football after the war. We wish him the best of luck and a safe return.

I would like to thank Mrs. Robey for so very kindly storing our cricket gear all this summer. It is extremely helpful to have the kit so close to the ground.

The two matches against Woodhouse and Morris Sports were "rained off".

So we have come to the end of another cricket season. It has been an enjoyable one, and our batting has improved considerably, but we require more bowlers. Some of the younger element seem afraid to "try their luck".

HOCKEY.—Mr. Hartill has arranged fixtures for this season. Those who are interested please contact him.

A. H. APPLETON,
Sports Secretary.

◎ ◎ ◎ ◎ ◎

Waiting.

THE air was as still and oppressive as death,
My lungs felt so choked I could scarce take a breath,
I sat there with every nerve strung to the full,
And I longed once again for the thing that could pull
Me from that dark abyss which I couldn't fight,
Which pinioned me down and held me there tight,
Which shrouded my senses and beat at my head,
Which said "Move now," and finish this torturing dread.
But I couldn't move, couldn't speak, couldn't breathe,
For I feared fate had got one more trick up his sleeve.
And then my mind wandered to ifs, buts, and on
Till I thought my last vestige of reason had gone.
A noise made me jump—I sat forward and then
With a sigh of despair I sunk back once again
To that same moody silence that drives one insane:
Then another noise caught me and drew me again.
I looked at my hands as they gripped at the chair
And I saw without shock that my knuckles were bare,
Then all of a sudden I felt everything change,
A feeling familiar, yet all the time strange,
And I knew as the curtain of silence did lift,
That an Angel approached from the oncoming shift.

IVY WALTON.

EMPIRE
MARKET PLACE, LOUGHBOROUGH

MONDAY, OCT. 2nd (3 days)
RICHARD DIX in
"GHOST SHIP"
also Tommy Trinder in "Laugh it Off"

THURSDAY, OCT. 5th (3 days)
ROY ROGERS in
"SONG OF TEXAS"
also Little Mary Lee in "Nobody's Darling"

MONDAY, OCT. 9th (3 days)
GEORGE FORMBY in
"LET GEORGE DO IT"
also Dick Purcell in "Mystery of the 13th Guest"

THURSDAY, OCT. 12th (3 days)
JOHN WAYNE in
"IN OLD OKLAHOMA"
also F. Ratcliffe-Holmes in "Jungle Scrapbook"

MONDAY, OCT. 16th (3 days)
BRIAN AHERNE and PAUL LUKAS in
"CAPTAIN FURY"
also Laurel and Hardy in "A Chump at Oxford"

THURSDAY, OCT. 19th (3 days)
LESLEY BROOK in
"ROSE OF TRALEE"
also John Carradine in "Isle of Forgotten Sins"

MONDAY, OCT. 23rd (3 days)
ESMOND KNIGHT and MERVYN JOHNS in
"HALFWAY HOUSE"
also Edward Norris in "Wings Over the Pacific"

THURSDAY, OCT. 26th (3 days)
RALPH RICHARDSON and JOHN CLEMENTS in
"FOUR FEATHERS" (in Technicolour)
also Wally Patch in "Strange to Relate"

MONDAY, OCT. 30th (3 days)
JOHN GARFIELD and MAUREEN O'HARA in
"FALLEN SPARROW"
also Warren Hymer in "Danger, Women at Work"

THURSDAY, NOV. 2nd (3 days)
LUCAN AND McSHANE in
"OLD MOTHER RILEY OVERSEAS"
also Craig Stevens in "Spy Ship"

**CONTINUOUS DAILY. Doors open at 1-30 p.m.
SUNDAYS at 5-30 p.m.**

Printed by Toppings Ltd., 17, Southfield Rd., Loughborough, and published by L. P. Jones for Beaumanor Staff Magazine Committee.

NOVEMBER, 1944

VOL. I. No. 9 (NEW SERIES) - **6d.**

FILM ATTRACTIONS for NOVEMBER

SHOWING AT THE ODEON THEATRE

Sunday, Nov. 5th—Alan Ladd, Brian Donlevy and Veronica Lake in **The Glass Key**. Also Noah Beery in **Mystery Liner**.

MONDAY, NOV. 6th, for 3 days
Anne Baxter, William Eythe and Michael O'Shea in
EVE OF ST. MARK
Also Don Ameche and The Ritz Brothers in
The Singing Musketeer

THURS., NOV. 9th, for 3 days
Joel McCrea and Maureen O'Hara in
BUFFALO BILL
in Technicolor
Also Lupe Velez and Eddie Albert in
Ladies Day.

Sunday, Nov. 12th—George Montgomery and Maureen O'Hara in **Ten Gentlemen from West Point**. Also Esmond Knight in **What Men Live By**.

MONDAY, NOV. 13th, and all the week:
Ginger Rogers and Ray Milland in the Technicolor Production
LADY IN THE DARK
with Warner Baxter, Jon Hall and Mischa Auer.

Sunday, Nov. 19th—Jimmy Durante and Phil Silvers in **You're in the Army now**. Also Lloyd Nolan and Marjorie Weaver in **The Man Who Wouldn't Die**.

MONDAY, Nov. 20th, and all the week:
Betty Grable in
PIN UP GIRL
a Technicolor Musical with John Harvey, Martha Raye, Joe E. Brown, Eugene Pallette and the Skating Vanities plus Charles Spivak and his Orchestra.

Sunday, Nov. 26th—Jack Oakie and Ann Sheridan in **Navy Blues**. Also Lynn Bari and Mary Beth Hughes in **The Night Before the Divorce**.

MONDAY, NOV. 27th, and all the week:
Bing Crosby in
GOING MY WAY
with Barry Fitzgerald and Rise Stevens.

Continuous Performance Daily 1-45 p.m.   Sunday, One Performance at 6 p.m.

B.S.M. Vol. I. No. 9 (New Series) NOVEMBER, 1944.

Managing Editor: LEONARD P. JONES.

Editors: KAY PRICE, ERIC C. MILLHOUSE   *Treasurer:* A. H. APPLETON.

NIGHT CONNECTION
By NOEL ROYLE

A LOOSE migratory band of passengers
   Ebbs round the bar;
   The clink of glass and hollow drone
Of dying conversation
Comes dully to the ear.

Against a gross Victorian roof,
High, pallored orbs of light
Cast down dispassioned luminescence:
Mirrors, marble, black beer handles,
Shine vaguely through tobacco smoke.

The long-established dust
Clings to its ancient corners,
Nocturnal soot goes home to roost
In dim, forgotten crannies,

And consciousness begins to gutter low.

The pies and cake are strange antiquities,
Like fossils underneath their glass,
Awaiting through the ponderous hours
For far-off passengers, already ages over-due——

When will the next train come?

The fire is out; the tea is cold;
The beer has gone; the clock has stopped;
The waitress doesn't seem to care——

No one seems to care. . . .

Hardness and tangibility are broken down:
Shapes fuse into shapes
And melt to nothingness;

Silence buries all the ghosts
Who haunt the misty centuries . . .
The drowsy centuries:

Perhaps the train will never come?
Who knows?

Christmas Number ready: Dec. 2nd. All contributions to reach Editors by Nov. 18th.

GOOD READING

By "B.B. and R.R."

IF you were to visit Axel Munthe and be as rude to open a cupboard in his study whilst he was out of the room, I feel sure that you would find, tucked away in a corner, a small, brightly-coloured carpet, such as the professional story-tellers carry around with them in the East, for he is a born story-teller.

Now, of course you read his book, "THE STORY OF SAN MICHELE" several years ago, but you must have said at the time, "Some day I must read that book again!"—it's the way it leaves you. Remember? A doctor's autobiography, or a collection of stories and anecdotes, yet not exactly either. Life is Dr. Munthe's hobby and this book can best be described as tapestry woven by him during his years of service as a doctor in various parts of Europe; the humour, the tragedy, the folly, and apparent futility of human strivings provide him with the threads which he weaves, capably and delightfully, blended and smooth—and yet one is not denied a glimpse at the wrong side of the tapestry, even though the ends of some of the threads are left jagged. You can't fail to be intensely interested in this book, so it's up to you.

James Agate is a personality, and like all such, he realizes the fact, cultivates it, and publishes his diary to the world in six weighty volumes. The most recent of these, "EGO 6", is, I think, the spiciest, and covers the period from August 1942 until December 1943. He is a critic—of plays, poetry, films, actors, and, in less exalted moments, of racehorses, food and drink. His writing is always trenchant and often dogmatic. He favours the old masters always, and can never resist a dig at our intellectual moderns. And who can blame him for murmuring to himself—

"Now dance the lights on lawn and lea,
The flocks are whiter down the vale,
And milkier every milky sail
On winding stream or distant sea." rather than——
"Now the stiff climb, some duck-necked oyster-catchers,
Recall a poet's hæmorrage at base; talk bosh.
Watch specks move up towards sightseers' crags, so we, late
Just before tea dare go, and I, a wind-in-jawbone man—"

He is a very active man, and mixes with our leading writers, actors and musicians. In his "EGO" he comments on many things but leaves religion, philosophy and women, (apart from one or two bawdy digressions) severely alone.

He has the ready wit and mobility of phrase of the practised raconteur and he has a broad sense of humour. He doesn't think Tommy Handley amusing, but Charlie Chaplin's glass-framed cane is one of his most treasured possessions.

To sum up, he is that all too rare thing these days—a character—and his diaries make fascinating reading.

Bookseller and Stationer :: Lending Library

J. SKETCHLEY

24 & 25, High Street, Loughborough

Telephone 2980.

21 PLATOON, 'E' COMPANY, 10th (CHARNWOOD) BATTN. LEICESTERSHIRE HOME GUARD

Reproduced by courtesy of the Editor of the "Loughborough Monitor."

Theatre Royal
LOUGHBOROUGH.

PROGRAMMES for NOVEMBER 1944

THE FORTESCUE
Famous Players

continue their Repertory Season with the following outstanding attractions:—

Monday, Nov. 6th, for 6 days
A True To Life Play—
MASTER OF HIS HOUSE
By Arthur Mertz.
(Author of the George Formby Films, also "Demobbed," &c.)

Monday, Nov. 13th, for 6 days
The greatest of all Poison Dramas
A FOOLS PARADISE
By SYDNEY GRUNDY.

Monday, Nov. 20th, for 6 days
The World Famous Play—
LITTLE WOMEN
By MARIAN DE FORREST
(From the story of Louisa M. Alcott).
This is a Family Show. Mothers, Fathers, Sisters and Brothers should not miss it!
BOOK YOUR PARTY NOW!

Monday, Nov. 27th, for 6 days
A WONDERFUL COMEDY—
IF FOUR WALLS TOLD
By EDWARD PERCY.

Me at the Pictures

By LEW OWEN

TAKING time off from the silver screen, I went to the fifth MERETAS production "TIME AND THE CONWAYS" at the Town Hall on the 11th October. In this Priestley play of a family and the effect time has on it, the second act is dated twenty years after the first. This proved too much for the company, most of whom failed to look or act twenty years older. In addition, acoustics were so bad that much of the dialogue was completely lost; amplifiers fitted to overcome this proved useless.

Best performance came from Vera Dixon as Mrs. Conway, her ageing was most effective, as was her acting. Not so Frederick Tinworth (Alan) who annoyingly played with a pipe as an aid to naturalness. Joan Whiten impressed as Carol; her stage movements and voice were very good. Gwen Storey and Daphne Carter were the best of the remaining cast. Settings, costumes and musical interludes were excellent. A less ambitious play, produced elsewhere (the Theatre Royal, say—a one night booking could surely be arranged) should now be the aim of this society.

Of this month's films serious fare is mainly re-issue. I recommend "THE SISTERS" (Victory), and "THE RAT", "PRISONER OF ZENDA" and "STELLA DALLAS" (Empire), the last for fine performances by Barbara Stanwyck and Bonita Granville. See advts. for dates of showing. New films include:—

NOVEMBER 13th AND WEEK: "LADY IN THE DARK" (Odeon). In her first Technicolor film, a musical fanatasy, Ginger Rogers is more agreeably cast than in the slushy "Tender Comrade", but she could still do with more opportunities to sing, dance and wisecrack. Story is how she, a pseudo-masculine editress of a magazine, is changed by physco-analysis to the love-desiring woman of her dreams. The three dream sequences are the best in the film, colour being exploited to the full. Settings and costumes are most original in the marriage dream and "Poor Jennie" sequence. Co-star Ray Milland is attractively humorous, and Warner Baxter and Jon Hall are adequate as a sugar daddy and a glamour boy. Though slow in starting it is quite entertaining.

NOVEMBER 20th AND WEEK: "PIN UP GIRL" (Odeon). For years 20th Century-Fox have made spectacular musicolors. This, their latest Betty Grable leg effort, they describe as "The Zenith of Musicals". Apparently they have not seen Columbia's "Cover Girl" with Rita Hayworth. As a bogus Broadway star, Betty's body beautiful is well to the fore except when, in her dual role as a secretary, she keeps her underpinnings beneath her desk to conceal her identity from her hero, John Harvey! Musical numbers are below standard as is the humour of Joe E. Brown and Martha Raye.

"ALI BABA AND THE FORTY THIEVES" (Victory. The old firm of Hall, Montez and Co., playing make-believe in colour, as only Hollywood knows how. The stars are either lavishly dressed for you to gasp at their million dollar raiment or delicately undressed for you to admire their amazing bodies. All very simple and artless, but go early there will be a queue.

NOVEMBER 27th AND WEEK: "GOING MY WAY" (Odeon). Bing Crosby's latest, I rate THE FILM OF THE MONTH. The way Bing has been handled recently brings credit to the Paramount Studios. He is no longer a young handsome romantic crooner, but middle-aged with children in their 'teens and his films have mellowed with him. Here he plays a Catholic priest, Father O'Malley. The somewhat controversial plot, with introduction of popular songs is well handled by director Leo McCarey. Picture-stealer is Barry Fitzgerald as Father Fitzgibbon. Excellent fare.

"DESERT SONG" (Victory). The modernised Technicolor version of this famous musical comedy sent me to sleep. To hear Romberg's "Blue Heaven" rendered in a film that includes "The Nazi Hordes" is asking too much of a gullible public. Dennis Morgan and newcomer Irene Manning are not of star calibre, but their singing is good.

Yipee! - - We've been CRITICISED!

"JONAH" replies.

BEFORE commenting on our *first two* letters of criticism, I would like to clear up some misunderstanding about the B.S.M. This is, and always will be, a Staff Magazine, and as such, it relies for its contribution upon *you*; the quality and variety, or lack of same, depends upon the material *you* send us.

For some months now, the same old contributors have turned up trumps, but I am convinced that among our large numbers we should be able to find more than enough contributions.

One complaint has been that would-be contributors are never notified as to the fate of their MSS. The answer is, that while we reserve the right to choose the B.S.M. MSS., we do not for one moment suggest that all unused items are of poor quality; it is because we feel that some MSS. are not suitable for our pages. In future a rejection slip will be attached to each returned MS, giving the Editorial reason for so doing. It should be added that we have a rule that no anonymous contributions can be accepted. Any contributor may, if he wishes, use a nom-de-plume, but he must at the same time supply the Editors with his correct name, as evidence of good faith.

Here is our first letter, dated 9th October.

DEAR SIRS,

Your constant accusations of apathy among the rank and file of Beaumanor have prompted me to write a word or two about the B.S.M. . . . Apathy is not to blame for your failure to attract contributions. Timidity is partly to blame. Try more competitions, and endeavour to make them more attractive!

I feel that too much space should not be occupied by rather weak quips at the expense of various members of the station; a gossip column has to be handled very carefully before it can remain interesting month after month. Mr. Hewson's articles, although less offensive than those of his predecessor, are far too long. Please ration his space!

I was also going to object to the "Dedleigh Snouppe" series, but fortunately it has now come to an end. The remainder of the B.S.M. seems to me to be of a remarkably high standard, and I would single out for particular praise "St. Upid" and the poems of Mr. Noel Royle.

Yours faithfully,
J. C. M. BARNES.

Mr. Barnes' letter falls into two parts: (*a*) An attempt to answer the accusation of apathy, and (*b*) a criticism of those B.S.M. items which he does not like. What does he mean by "timidity"? We are not ogres; we do not bite; nor do we insist upon Quarterly Review standards, and we would be only too willing to assist anyone who has the desire to contribute. No, Mr. Barnes, *Apathy* is the right word, backed up by that old Woygland characteristic: "Why should I do it when someone else will?"

On the subject of Competitions he is completely at sea. For more than three years competitions of various kinds have been tried without success. If Mr. Barnes can devise a competition which will interest more than ·5% of our readers we will be pleased to consider it. For the answer to the second part of his letter, may we suggest the one that follows?

SIR,

As no-one else seems to have the time or the inclination to voice any criticisms about the B.S.M., I thought I'd have a shot at it. Actually, I think the rest of Woyg must have an aversion to seeing themselves in print, because I've heard plenty of *verbal* comments on the various contributions. So here goes on a few criticisms of my own, and some which I've heard from other people about the regular articles in the B.S.M.

(1) "The Gospel according to St. Upid" could be improved if Disciple Millhouse moved away from the land of Woyg for a bit—tried out a few new pastures, as it were. May I suggest some chapters on Rationing, Queueing, etc.?

(2) I should like to see at least half a page of "Snappy Sayings." At the moment one finds one or two marooned at the bottom of a page.

(3) Definitely NO A.T.S. Gossip Section. We do quite well enough in "They're Telling Me" thank you!

(4) More of Dedleigh Snouppe and his satellite Krumpit, please. Their antics always reduce me to helpless laughter—the more ridiculous and impossible the situations, the better.

(5) The Sunday programmes are advertised for the Odeon; why not the Empire and Victory as well?

In conclusion—I haven't mentioned the "Digby Chronicles" because I never read them.

Yours sincerely,
JANET FOURDRINIER.

For the first paragraph of Miss Fourdrinier's letter, many thanks. We also were aware of the *verbal* critics, but have always presumed that these people had not the courage of their convictions, or were short of paper and ink.

Her point about "St. Upid" is good, but the answer is better. The "Gospel" series is intended to be a chronological study of the life and habits of Woygites, and that is why there has been little departure from this historical record. The new Doomsday Book will have to start somewhere, so why not with us?

The "Snappy Sayings" are purposely written for use in filling up odd spaces; we can rarely spare the room for a collection of them. As for the A.T.S. Gossip—well, we have received no word from any volunteers. The matter of Sunday cinema programmes will be taken up in the right quarter.

At the risk of repeating ourselves, may we suggest that the lady reads the gentleman's letter for the other answers?

"WHO'S HOSE?"

By W. J. GILLIARD

IT was strange that Ethel and I had discussed the matter during lunch that day. It arose over young Albert's threadbare blouse and shabby knickers. Ethel said both the girls needed new frocks too; *and* some undies. "And I've scarcely a decent pair of stockings to my name," she added. We were in the second year of the War, and "Utility" and "Clothing Coupons" had not yet arrived. Wearing apparel had become increasingly scarce, and (of course) increasingly dear. We decided on a certain line of action for the coming week-end—but that's jumping ahead of the story.

I had returned to work about half-an-hour, Ethel tells me, when she answered the door to a smart, business-like knock. The gentleman said he had something to show her which he knew would interest her, if she wasn't too busy. With the door only partly open, Ethel cautiously said, "What is it? I haven't much time?" The gentleman leisurely opened his case and produced—SILK STOCKINGS. The door, and Ethel's eyes opened a bit wider. He explained that these hose were made by machinery at the rate of thousands per day. Girl examiners hastily looked at them as they were peeled off the machine and threw out all the faulty hose. At the rate they have to work, they sometimes let faulty hose pass, and, on the other hand, sometimes perfectly good hose got thrown out. "That's where I come in" the gentleman said, "I buy all the 'rejects', examine them singly and carefully, dispose of the duds, and the perfectly good ones——well, here they are." He invited her to go through his case, containing thirty pairs or so, and give them the closest examination. "If there's any there that you like you can have three pairs for ten bob. If you don't want any,—

well, I'll push along." Needless to say, Ethel fell for it and *did* examine them. They were really faultless, and as she fondled the lovely soft material, she echoed the words of lunchtime. "And I've scarcely a decent pair of stockings to my name," she said to herself quietly. The deal was closed. Ethel bought her three pairs of stockings, and returned to the gentleman with the ten shillings. He thanked her, said he would try and call again if he got any more, but couldn't promise as the hosiery trade was being cut down, and so on, and so on.

When he had gone, Ethel, just to *make sure*, took her stockings into the back yard where the light was good, and examined them more closely than before. "Perfect," was her final verdict, and she returned to her housework with a light step and a song in her heart.

It was just over an hour later, when, in response to another knock, Ethel found a tall, broad, severe-looking man on the step. "I believe a man's been here selling hosiery?" he said brusquely, and Ethel timidly replied "Yes."

"Ah," he said. "I'm well on his track. I regret to inform you, Madam, that it was stolen property he sold you, and I'm investigating the matter. This is me," and he held out a card which read:—Detective Jones (late C.I.D.) and very neatly in the corner, "Grosvenor Enquiry Agency."

He entered Ethel's name and address in his notebook, said she might be wanted in the Public Court as a witness, but he'd get her out of it if he could. He then explained that by retaining the stolen property she was involved in the crime, and for her safety he'd better take them from her. "I'll give you a receipt for them," he said, "and of course, we'll do all in our power to get your money back for you." Ethel reluctantly handed him the hose and he wrote a receipt in duplicate, on the printed pad of the "Grosvenor Enquiry Agency", enjoining her to take care of her copy which he handed her.

Ethel poured the story out to me as soon as I got home to tea, and terrified at the prospect of appearing in the Police Court. I reminded her of the Detective's promise to keep her out of it if possible, and, I think, allayed her fears a bit.

On my way to the Club that evening, I called in at the Police Station, and was pleased to notice, on entering, my old friend Sgt. Jennings doing Station duty. "'Evening, sir," he hailed me. "Caught without your dog-licence?"

"No Jenn," I said. "Ethel's a bit worried over an affair with some hose she bought at the door to-day. She's a bit scared at the prospect of being called as a witness, and I wondered if you——"

"Not a hope," he said. "All she's got to worry about is the loss of her ten bob, (or was it six pairs for a quid?) They worked Colchester with that stunt three days ago, and cleared over fifty quid. I reckon they'll be pretty near that figure for to-day's work here too. All we've got so far is that they caught the 6-10 together—the fast train to London, you know. Tell Ethel I'm sorry."

FAMOUS LAST WORDS———

"——I think Samuel Morse must have been a WONDERFUL Man!"

"Very Tasty — Verra Sweet"
By PADDIE McGRATH

"AH! the Pickerel of Walden," signs Thoreau, in one of his delightful philosophical moments. Thoreau, of course, was not thinking of the gastronomical qualities of his exquisite Pickerel, but for other artistic reasons.

Listen! Have you ever eaten Woppits at Monginis in the Rue Pigale, Paris? Ah! what a delicacy! Served with garlic and Zippits, they are food for gods. I can almost taste them now, though it's many moons since I roamed through the dim-lit quartier of the Montmartre.

Mr. Editor! A few months ago I read the following in your classic magazine, "I was so fortunate to spend the best part of my youth in the Continent," and it prompts me to write these few lines to disapprove of the attitude taken by so many British authors, essayists, and newspaper correspondents, that food guzzled down in any other country, but their own, is always something wonderfully delicious, æsthetic and sublime. They never mention tripe and onions at Wigan, pot-pie in Jarrow, or Cornish pasties at Penzance. Which reminds me. Why not run down to the Basque country in Autumn. There the sunlight seems to sleep and dream. There you can enjoy (how I love that basic English verb) that scrumptious dish called Pollita con Arroz and drink of the sparkling Burgundies. If a barrel organ plays in the Annexe of your hotel Esplendide—what matter! if the monkey toys with your Crepe Suzette—who cares?

Wait a moment! Have you ever been to those beautiful Gorges in the Haut Maritimes? It is there you can eat the Fruit Bleu. Gourmets eat only the eyes—but Dudley will tell you all about it and of his amazing escapades as he hopped about the Dolomites leading Anna tenderly by the hand.

It is only a few hours to Baden-Baden, where the old waiter Fritz delicately serves you with a dish of Schnitzel or Kalb steak mit Champignons. What wine would one imbibe? "Hock," echoes Mr. Champion, "Hock Sir, Hock."

The Balkan Express thunders into Buda-pest. Note that word "thunders". If it was Loughborough it would merely "steam" in. Never been in Buda-pest? How horribly mediocre you are, my dear! We had Hungarian Gaulash and baked Brujas washed down by Imperial Tokay.

The further East you go from Britain the more romantic life becomes. A dish of Hookas in Baghdad chased down by a few pints of Arak. Freddie Pike will tell you about quails on toast or jugged hare taken from the gardens of the local Sheikh.

Bombay in the monsoon! As our plane circles round Colaby, or is it Colaba, we can see the Parsee tower of silence, where a glorious old bun fight is in progress; or we can meander along to the Taj Mahal in quest of a real curry. We cannot but pity those poor, poor people back home who will never know the delights of Bombay Duck, or is it Duckies? Ask Kay. She knows, she knows.

There are the lofty Himalayas in the distance. I can almost see Ted being chased through the Khyber Pass, by an old-fashioned mule, with ears well back and teeth a-showing. Ted will doubtless hold forth to you of the delicious loveliness of a chupatee or a plateful of Soorka-butches served piping hot.

And now for America. What a glamourous exotic place that is. Ever eaten a Philadelphia Squab? No! Good heavens! It's only a young sea-gull but it's divine. Or you could worry a Lobster Neuberg at the Roof Garden in 42nd Street or surfeit yourself at a Barbecue in New Orleans.

Hurry on down to Mexico and partake of Garnachas Tamales and Frijoles whilst the mid-day sun gleams and glitters on the snows of Orizaba; and if you want to stimulate your biological urge drink a quart or two of Tequila. If, by the way, you gave a spoonful of Tequila to a mouse he would rear up on his hind legs, gnash his teeth and say "send out your fifty cats".

Yes, mes amis, I have been to all these places and eaten most of these foods, but on due consideration I would much prefer to stroll along those lovely leafy lanes of Leicestershire and have a pint or two at Fred's or even Sam's, then some roast pork with plenty of crackling, cauliflower with a dollop of white sauce, brown gravy. Oh baby, where did you get dem goo-goo eyes!

Or even I wouldn't mind wandering neath those grey skies, with my contemporary Noel Royle, a book of Iambic Pentameter in one hand, and a cow-heel in the other, through the twisted pathways and brooding crags on the blasted heath of Ilkley Moor.

What of the Future?

By KAY PRICE

"WE might as well go and have a look at the old place," said Angie, as their homeward road from a holiday up North took them through Loughborough.

"Or not," retorted Jack. "Gosh, I'd have thought that place had given you enough headaches to last you a lifetime."

"It gave me you, dear," murmured Angie ambiguously. "Oh do let's go!" So they turned the car off the main road, down Woodhouse Lane. The clock on the dashboard showed five minutes to two.

"Just like old times," continued Angie chattily as they swooped stomach-rendingly over the railway bridge. "I wonder how many times you puffed up this way on your old bike at this very time?"

"At this very time," stated Jack with dignity, "I was *never* cycling along the road. I was enjoying a last breath of fresh air outside H——" he paused to swing right between the stone gates.

"Look out," cried Angie.

The car screeched to a standstill. An elderly attendant in a very rakish ensemble of Military and Naval uniform was halting their progress and directing them into a crowded car-park.

"Half-a-crown to pay," muttered Jack, "and once we worked here!"

Angie's eyes were round as saucers—"But the Attendant, Jack," she persisted. "Surely it was the Old M——"

"——Couldn't be," said Jack firmly. "Just a resemblance that's all. I tipped him sixpence, anyway."

They drifted up the drive towards the canteen. It was a very impressive building bearing the neon sign "Cafe" that they found on the old site, and it was already crowded to the door. However, an efficient staff was dealing rapidly with all comers. "Well, that's a change for the better anyway," remarked Jack, as they settled themselves at the Soda Fountain. A portly, bald man in a white jacket took their order. He had not changed much since the days when Leon de Bunk had seen fit to pillory him in "Through the Looking Glass", but he did not recognize them. Obviously, the absence of dark rings under their eyes and the fact that they were fully awake had transformed them beyond all recognition. They would have reminded him, had he not been so busy, but as it was, they finished their sundaes and left quietly.

Outside, an organized tour of inspection was forming up under the fussy auspices of a Guide, and they attached themselves to its tail.

"I'm sure I know his face," whispered Angie, indicating the Guide. "Don't you?"

"No, he wasn't one of us, I'm sure."

"Yes——I remember!" Angie's perplexed frown cleared. "He's one of those Generals they were always bringing round to fill up the time between morning coffee and cocktails! He's sure to know the place perfectly."

"But it wasn't the same lot of generals all the time, was it?" demurred Jack.

"Don't be silly, darling," argued Angie. "We didn't have that many Generals. Of course it was the same ones all the time—only with different hats and moustaches just to keep us interested. Poor dears, they must have got awfully bored."

By this time the procession had stopped outside a building of graceful tranquility. "The Rest Room," remarked the Guide, waving a beautiful white hand. "Divans—armchairs—every luxury."

"It's the old "C" hut!" exclaimed Angie. "Rest Room! Well, that hasn't changed."

"Don't be sarcastic," said Jack. "I wonder what goes on where Control used to be?"

"——Up-to-the-minute Information on all Current Attractions——" The Guide's mellifluous voice emerged and submerged again. (Shades of Ollie!)

The crowd drifted on. "Now he-ah," said the Guide halting outside the building that used to be H, "He-ah is our Hall of Fun. The tour does not include admittance, but if you listen a moment, you will he-ah the ro-ahs of hilarity going on inside."

Everybody listened. The "roahs of hilarity" obligingly resounded.

"They must be looking at the plaque we put up to commemorate Wally Cecil's watertight alibi," whispered Jack.

In turn, "I" proved to be an ice-rink, "J" a swimming-pool, and "K" a Sportsdrome.

"The man in charge has been he-ah for ye-ahs," confided the Guide!— "In a different capacity, of course." Through the wide-open windows came the ping of tennis rackets, the click of table-tennis balls and the roar of a swiftly-turning electric fan. A heavy puff of smoke as from an aged pipe also wafted out.

"Well that's a change, isn't it," said Jack.

"No fear," contradicted Angie. "It was almost the same in my day—modified a bit of course."

"And now," concluded the Guide, "we come to the climax of our tour—a visit to the Manah Museum, to inspect documents and equipment used here during the Wah."

Jack and Angie stiffened into petrified rigidity. They longed to break away, but somehow their limbs had lost all independent movement, and they could only follow the procession, hypnotized. Through the yard they went, too stupified to notice that poor old "Corney Wallace" had left his place on his pedestal in favour of an electrically operated figure advertising "Johnnie Walker"—on into the slowly dessicating house, till a hatefully familiar sight met their eyes. All the horrid paraphernalia of "their" War was laid out with careless realism. The Guide nonchalantly took up a pair of headphones. "One listened," he explained, "through these. Would anyone like to try—you Sir?—Madam?"

Mechanically Jack and Angie reached out, and adjusted the headphones. With a smile of guileless charm, the Guide switched on. And then the horrible thing happened. · The spell of hypnotism that had held them inert was suddenly broken. As a stream of vics bawled forth, the couple woke to life—writhing and screaming. Another moment, and they were prone on the floor, foaming at the mouth. A moment more and they were dead.

○ ○ ○ ○ ○

The *Loughborough Liar* hushed the whole thing up. The paper had shares in the Pleasure Park and didn't want it to get a bad reputation. But they did close the Museum. After all, one day, another of the Beaumaniacs might have returned.

NATIONAL RIFLE ASSOCIATION.—BEAUMANOR BRANCH.

There has been a splendid response to the proposal that a Rifle Club be formed at B.M. In little over four days 50 members have enrolled. It being necessary, under N.R.A. rules, that a President and Hon. Secretary be appointed, a vote was taken on 16th October, and Lt.-Col. Ellingworth was elected President, with Mr. Whitford as Hon. Secretary. The affiliation fee has been forwarded to Bisley, and we hope to start firing very shortly. Watch this column for news of the Club.

The Gospel according to St. Upid

(Translated from the English by Disciple Millhouse).

Chapter XXXVI

NOW there was a distant land, a full Sabbath day's journey from Woyg, a land called Iawkz, from whence came Relish, and Pudden, and No Ell. And No Ell was a kingly man, and a mighty scribe; a poet, philosopher, and politician withal.

And when he had entered within the portals of Woyg, and become well-nigh civilised, he was received into the mighty Tribe. And he saith unto them: Verily, verily, I say unto ye: My name shall be Vox Plebis. And he writ full many a score words upon the tablets of Biessem, as it is recorded in the chronicles of those days.

But many moons after the war between the Vox Plebiscites and the Pax Brittanicites had ended in a Draw, the fame of No Ell again waxed exceeding great in the land. And it was in this wise:

For it was told unto him that the Caliph of Biessem was offering a great prize of many shekels unto whomsoever should write a great new Parable. And because No Ell knew that the Caliph was a poor man, he judged that he had Scrounged the shekels, but even so he lusted after the money. Wherefore he burned an abundance of Midnight Therms, and consumed a multitude of parchments. And when he was nigh unto Flaking Out he finished his labours, and gathered up the parchments. And he looked upon his Parable, and saw that it was good. And he blessed it, and called it Last Goodnight. And when the Caliph and the Stooges of Biessem did read the Parable they hid their blushes, and paid Hush Money unto No Ell.

And it came to pass, when the tablets of Biessem were shared among the mighty tribe of Atsites, that the Parable of No Ell produced great argument. For many amongst them blushed even redder than the Caliph, and cried: Fie! and: Shame! and: E aint arf a one, E aint! And one at least crieth in a loud voice: Hoots mon!

But yet others were well pleased with the Parable. And a certain maid called Bebe, when she had read it, marvelled at it, and saith: Yipee! What a man! Wherefore she sent a message unto No Ell, saying: Thy soul and my soul, are as one. Speak thou unto me, I beseech thee.

And No Ell answered unto her, saying not: Hiya Toots, nor: Howdee Sugar, for such was the tongue of common peoples. But he writ in the language of Decorum. And when he was come forth, she saw that he was a Luscious Thing, and she rejoiced, and gave unto him a Date. And when he had spoken with her, he perceived that she was not as other maidens, and his heart was filled to overflowing. And he wandered forth in the wilderness, crying: Bebe, Bebe. And when she answered him not, he was cast down, and sorely cheesed. And when their Dates were numbered as the trees of the Spinney wherein they lingered, they forgot the language of Decorum, and spake and writ in the language of Luv.

Now when the sisters of Bebe learned concerning No Ell they were sore afraid, and gave unto her a package of raiment buttons, saying: Woe art thou, for thou art undone. But she answered them wrathfully, saying: Nark thou it. For verily, verily, I say unto ye: No Ell is a gentle man; neither is he so strong; neither carrieth he scissors. Yea, even though we have spoken the language of Luv; and notwithstanding No Ell is a truly Gorgeous Piece, it is but within the minds that we are as one. For I am an innocent maid, and he is a kingly man. Yet am I affrighted by all this glory, and am sore dismayed. Call thou me therefore: Bambi.

And it was so.

And the fame of Bambi and No Ell spread throughout the land, and reached even unto the ears of St. Upid.

Which was Too Bad.

Pixie's Search for Luv

By TOU-TOU ETHELEMM-DELLISH

IT was Pixie Mountjoy's wedding eve, but she was experiencing none of the feelings of happy anticipation usual to a young bride. Alone in her luxurious bedroom, she sat at her mirror, her chin cupped in her hands. It was a flower-like, heart-shaped little face that the mirror reflected, with great wide-set blue eyes, thickly and blackly lashed. She had an adorably retrousse nose, and her mouth was a small curvatious temptation. When she smiled, there was a dimple at its corner, and pearly teeth were revealed, but to-night she was not smiling. No, her slender brows, dlicate as a butterfly's feelers, were puckered together, and her smooth skin, always alabasterly milky, had a transparent look that accentuated the blue-black shadows under her eyes.

Suddenly she addressed her own reflection, and her voice was low and sweet. "To-night," she whispered. "This is your last night of freedom—of girlhood. To-morrow——" but she could not frame the words. She buried her head in her hands and ran her fingers through her red-brown hair which curled like the petals of a breeze-blown chrysanthemum all over her head. Her engagement ring, a huge modern conglomeration of diamonds, far too heavy for her slight finger, gleamed expensively among the reddish mass.

Lifting her head again, her eye fell on Mortimer's photograph in its costly gold frame. Sir Mortimer Duvaine. Her fiancé. Dear Uncle Edgar's best friend. He was everything that a fiancé should be—successful, wealthy, devoted—but he was forty-four to her eighteen, and already inclined to baldness and corpulence. Somehow, he repulsed her. She hated the soft squashiness of him as he clasped her to him—his glistening close-set eyes,—and she hated the kisses of his full, wet lips, and the touch of his plump, warm hands. And to-morrow she would be Lady Duvaine,—his wife. In a moment of swift revulsion, she laid the photograph face down.

Pixie was a foundling. Eighteen years ago she had been left on the doorstep of Edgar and Matilda Mountjoy, a nameless waif with nothing to identify her but an old-fashioned locket containing a curl of soft white hair. Although they were by no means as prosperous as they were now, the kind-hearted Mountjoys had taken her in and reared her as their own daughter. She owed them everything. That was why she was marrying Mortimer. Just to please them. After all he was Uncle Edgar's best friend. She began to pace up and down the room, hating everything, but most of all, hating herself. "I should be *glad*," she kept repeating. "I should be GLAD."

"'Ullo ducks."

With a muffled gasp she spun round to confront the speaker. Looking through the window was an old man, wielding a damp cloth. The window-cleaner. He was unshaven, with a soiled choker taking the place of collar and tie, but his eyes were the kindest, merriest, she had ever seen. She took to him at once.

"Hullo," she returned his greeting.

"Don't mind me speakin' to yer, do yer?" he pursued. "Though you was lookin' a bit down."

Pixie forced a smile. "Just a little," she admitted.

"Wot's up, ducks?"

"I'm being married to-morrow."

"Ought to be 'appy, you ought, then."

"But I don't love him!" The words, framing her thoughts of the last few weeks broke out passionately. "He's old—and fat—and I'm only eighteen. I don't want to marry him!" And she burst into tears.

Without more ado, the Window-cleaner swung himself over the sill and hurried to comfort her. "Then don't marry 'im, ducks," he counselled.

15

"But what can I do? Where can I go?"

"Come 'ome with me," offered the old man genially. "I got a girl o' me own, just your age, and she'd like a bit o' company."

Pixie hesitated—and was lost. "All right," she whispered. "I'll come with you now. Wait a moment."

She hastily packed a small suitcase and scribbled two brief notes—one to Mortimer, and one to Uncle Edgar and Aunt Matilda. In them, she assured them of her undying gratitude, her reason for absconding, and implored them neither to seek her, nor worry about her—she was in good hands. And begging their forgiveness, she dropped a few tears and signed her name. Then, fastening the locket—her only true possession—about her throat, she turned to the Window-cleaner, who escorted her down the ladder, out into the night, leaving Mountjoy Hall behind her for how long Fate only knew.

To be continued.

What will become of Pixie in the great big world? Will she regret her hasty action, or will she find True Luv in her new life? Do not miss next month's heart-stirring instalment.

Phoney Phrases By WILK : No. 2

"The girls have been sitting on him ever since he came in."

HOLY MATRIMONY

By "SLIPSTREAM"

I HAVE only been married once and that's quite enough for me. Now don't get me wrong, actually I am still very fond of my wife even after eight years of married blitz; perhaps I should say at this juncture that I have not lived at home for nearly five years. To say I got married by accident would be inaccurate, but never-the-less it was all because of a sudden shower (rain of course). My girl friend—the fifteenth I think she was—and I were out for a stroll and happened to be passing a housing estate in course of construction. They were the usual sort of houses, you know, semi-det. res., two bdrms., two recp., bthrm, usual conveniences, H. and C., E. and G., gdn back & front. We made a dash for shelter into the nearest of these villas, entry being quite easy, there being no doors in place. Of course, we whiled away the time looking over the builder's mess, when suddenly heavy steps were heard ascending the stairs.

Quickly removing the lipstick from my face I opened the door in response to a discreet knock and was confronted by a beady-eyed individual who greeted me with "Arternoon Sir, bit wet aint it." Having agreed the girl and I prepared to descend the stairs, but hawkeyes wasn't having any. Of course we said we weren't thinking of buying, only looking, also we didn't intend getting married, etc., etc. In fact I said "No" more that afternoon than at any other time in my life. . . .

Well, after he gave me a receipt for the deposit we moved off just in case he tried to sell us two, and I must admit I felt a little alarmed. "I don't think we'll mention this to anybody" I said, "but I suppose we ought to tell mum and dad." The trouble was, I just didn't know how to tell mum. I couldn't think how she would take it or what she would say. You see, I am the only son and was only twenty-six at the time. And again, what about father? He'd probably call me a ———y fool. Any way, to cut a long story short we told them.

It was just twelve months later when we did get married,—even I couldn't hang it out any longer, everybody was asking us "when?" Gradually we got a swell home together and gradually my hard earned savings fell apart.

At last the day fell when I fell. We were to be wed in a little village church "somewhere in Suffolk." When I awoke at seven B.S.T. I had to rise at once—but I went back. I think it must have been my supper or something because I was suffering from heartburn and various other minor discomforts not to mention metaphorical cold feet. I went for a walk with my father during the morning, and during this stroll he attempted to explain various things to me but it turned out I knew more than he; in fact, he became quite interested in my conversation. We called at the local after running the gauntlet of peeping eyes and slowly moving curtains, but after a glasses of beer I felt better and returned to the farm for lunch. I didn't eat much and left the table (my hands were continually dirty that day) to take a stroll down the garden where the fresh air seemed to choke me. At one-fifteen exactly the car came for my best man and I, knowing the driver, I anxiously asked him if there were many people at the church, to which he replied "Crowds". This did not improve my nerves but reminded me I had left my gloves in the house. . . . At last we were off.

On arriving at the church I was relieved to find nobody about, and no wonder, all the population was inside. They had, however, had the decency to leave two seats for me too. The usher, I think that's what they call the old chaps who keep order and act as chuckers-out, asked us which side we were fighting for. As I couldn't talk my "understudy" (for this part only) explained I was the necessary evil for the performance due to commence. On reaching our seats I began to think, everyone knows a bride wears white to signify purity, but why the heck do bridegrooms invariably wear black, it's a point you know. We waited, of course the dear bride was late, that

[Continued foot of p.23

They're telling Me!

CONGRATULATIONS to John Dodd and Kay Norman on their engagement on October 17th.

I am told that L/Cpl. Priscilla Hall, late of "C" Hut, now at B.W., recently became engaged. I have no details, but then, neither had Jean Murray when she congratulated Priscilla on her engagement to the WRONG man. Anyway, when it is all sorted out I hope everybody will be very happy.

Miss Freda Ward (one of Col. Ellingworth's Young Ladies) of the Group Office, married L.A.C. Leonard W. Steane, R.A.F., at St. Peter's Church, Mountsorrel, on 21st October, 1944. Members of the Group Office were present and home-made confetti was very plentiful. Good Luck!

Standing at Quorn X the other night I was surprised to see two A.T.S. running hell for leather, closely pursued by about half-a-dozen R.N.A.S. cadets. However, the A.T.S. did manage to beat them to the car which offered a lift to Loughborough.

We reluctantly say farewell this month to Sgt. Hazel Stewart-Jones (nee Webb) and Pte. Joan Jones (nee Oakey) who leave the T.P. staff for more productive work on the Home Front.

Also to Sgt. Ann Boughey, who is doing a swop with Sgt. Florrie Please at B.W. Hi ya! Flo. Yes please.

Our sympathies are extended to our old friend "Mac" (Nerve Centre), who is at present suffering from nervous strain following a series of lost football matches. (He gave it but couldn't take it).

For many moons the G.B.S. of Beaumanor, Paddy McGrath, has promised us, in addition to his many scathing criticisms of the B.S.M., an eye-opening article entitled "Symphony—the New Dope". Tackled about it in the canteen the other day he told us that, having been treated to a couple of performances at the de Montfort, he has become a convert. "How are the mighty fallen".

We are curious to know whether Edith has managed to convince anyone yet that the damp patch on her skirt was caused by a wet bicycle seat after the canteen dance.

To all those people who have been taking an interest in the association of Peter Tuke with Subaltern I. Romer, Peter wants to say that they are cousins. (And he's sticking to it!)

The other night, after 2—10, Mr. Reedman was stopped by three meek little girls, two of them A.T.S., at the Quorn end of Woodhouse Lane, with a request to be escorted back to their billets in Quorn as A MAN was following them. The noble officer obliged.

It is a matter of much speculation whether they suspected the identity of the kind man BEFORE they stopped him.

I know what "Sam" Murgatroyd, our Woodhouse Eaves Romeo, was doing at Shelthorpe one morning at 5.30—but I am not going to tell you girls.

Myrtle "Glamour" Barnes, recently returned after a long period of sick leave and informed us that she had been suffering from quinsy—at least, it sounded like quinsy.

The cow mentioned last month must have been some cow. They have now discovered that "Bobby" Lord's foot is broken. Still, she has the compensation of that other stripe. Mother! was it worth it?

Norman Rees' distrust of Bernard Norwood, when he left the last Shake-Jack dance at 10 o'clock, appears to have been well-founded. Or was it Sweet Fanny Adams that Bernard escorted back to Garats Hey. ?

Talking of Sweet Fanny Adams, Peter Gardner once more showed his versatility, among other things, at the above-mentioned dance, this time appearing as a quiz kid.

I'll take back my "beautiful baby" remark of a previous issue.

We are sorry to record the departure of "Molly" Morgan, the notorious tea-time Casanova, for foreign shores. His teas and shack will be much missed by some of our Garats Hey friends.

It is rumoured that Charlie Dobson has now taken over the shack. Does the tea invitation still stand, Charlie?

And, talking of Charlie Dobson, we hear that Elsie, the reserved runner, of "D" Watch, was invited to break by Charlie the other day and he actually gave her a bar of chocolate. This is marvellous in the light of Charlie's complete distrust of anything in skirts (or slacks).

We see that more of the staff are now attending evening classes at Loughborough College. An unconfirmed report states that, on one occasion recently, when a supervisor asked "Have you got the answer yet?" his unfortunate victim was heard to reply, "Yes, £394 7s. 10½d."

The Music Club Social, held on Friday, 29th September, was a complete success in spite of a report from a hitherto reliable source that there was a bigger attendance at the "Bull's Head" than ever before.

The outstanding piece of news this month is, in my opinion, the fact that the "Squander-bug" has done nothing outstanding.

We welcome two new male members of the staff, Messrs. Freeman and Hedley, and congratulate them on their courage.

I am told that classes in simple arithmetic have been started for people who, by signing for Xmas week leave, have proved that they cannot count up to six.

We congratulate Pte. Doris, runner, "D" Watch, on attaining her majority on the 18th of October. The binge was thoroughly enjoyed by all who attended.

Congratulations are also due to Ron Smith and Lew Owen, who, under the auspices of the C.E.C., are creating a precedent in bringing an outside band to the canteen to play for a dance. We offer best wishes for the success of their venture, which, we hope, is a fore-runner of better things to come.

Since my appeal for more "dope" for this corner the amount left for me in the rack has been exactly nil. Surely not everybody on the station lives a completely uneventful life. Everything out of the ordinary is of interest to somebody however insignificant it may seem to you, so play the game. Let's hear from you.

JIMMY.

GET YOUR———

Beauty and Toilet Preparations
FROM
"LEONARD'S"
Gentlemen's Hairdresser
25, CHURCH GATE, LOUGHBOROUGH
Large Variety in Stock!

CORRESPONDENCE.

Sir,

With transuit reference to your Articalus Laughem, on Pentahedral Nucleiform Gasometry, may I state that Professor Fylitz Schildbraun was merely quoting Herr Doktor Von Estwost. It must be mentioned that Herr Doktor was responsible for the labour of the conserveranable liberation, and with implecable insontic extrolopations of the nowen corrupt Roryalism, so it will be seen, *sans glassania*, that the theory you exhibited, could be :—

$$\frac{\text{Sin K}}{\text{TA}^2\text{P}} \times \frac{X279}{\text{BST}} \div \frac{XX^2}{\text{TL}} = \frac{\text{FFI}}{\text{WAAF}}$$

soon to be discovered confuciosly.

And it can now be said, *whisperendum*, that the American Corniculturist Svend Lesdow, C.P.R., in his boshorism of scienic railelities compiled semaphoricaly (*per vic*) the enslaving bueroscoponcy of entimatable Englishmen, Irishmen and Jews.

Yours, etc.,
COLONEL PILAS WINTERBOTTOM.

THREE AND A ROAD
By HAZEL MILLER

THE pale watery sun climbed heavily in a pearly sky. Below, the earth lay stiffly under its mantle of frost. Each leaf, each frond of bracken on the moor seemed to be transformed into a rare piece of jewellery, hard and bright.

The road itself sparkled and shone like diamonds. Never, thought Belinda, had it looked more beautiful or more inviting. Her small feet in their stout shoes hesitated as she looked upward, her eyes following that lovely curve and the sharp rise before it suddenly disappeared over the brow of the hill. Suddenly! Something as concrete as a road had disappeared into the vast unknown. Belinda sighed. Lessons were so dull and uninteresting. Here was mystery, alive, beckoning. Each morning, it struggled with her seven-year-old conscience, and each morning the struggle was harder. One of these days, her little figure would go bobbing up the road, over the top, and into that fairy land beyond. But not to-day—duty's pull was still too strong. She tucked the blue check scarf more firmly into her coat, and walked slowly into the village school.

Somewhere a bell tinkled, all the children disappeared, and the houses quietly relaxed. From their roofs, the hoar began to melt as, deep in the interior, fires were lit, so that smoke rose thickly from each chimney, black against the patches of white still lying on the tiles.

Inside the "Blue Stag", Miranda, the innkeeper's daughter, busied herself with the preparations of the midday meal with an efficiency far beyond her years. When all the pans were simmering on the stove, she went to the diamond-paned window and looked slowly up the length of the road. Her road, she called it, because one Thursday (it would be a Thursday because that was her lucky day), a prince would come galloping down it, and he would ride up to the Inn, sweeping her on to the saddle before him, into a life far removed from pots and pans. Miranda smiled to herself; more likely it would be Peter striding down the road to claim her. Peter who had always loved her, and whom she had known ever since they had shared a bench at Sunday School. He was far away now in some hot country, India, perhaps, or Palestine, but when he came back his battledress and beret would be as precious to her as the shining armour and feathery plume of Prince Charming himself. Miranda turned back to her cooking, singing the first bars of a lilting waltz which matched the happiness in her heart.

Later that day when evening was drawing to its close, a lonely figure trudged past the one or two straggling trees which stood by the last house, until the criss-cross shadows on the grey road were left behind and only the moors stretched into the gloom on either side. It was an old man, bent

[*Continued top of p.23*

VICTORY
BIGGIN STREET, LOUGHBOROUGH

MONDAY, NOV. 6th (3 days)
Ida Lupino and Dennis Morgan in
THE HARD WAY
Also **MONSTERS OF THE DEEP**

THURSDAY, NOV. 9th (3 days)
Errol Flynn and Bette Davis in
THE SISTERS
Also **Eileen Joyce** in **Battle for Music**

MONDAY, NOV. 13th (6 days)
Robert Taylor and Susan Peters in
SONG OF RUSSIA
also **Our Gang, Interest and News Films**

MONDAY, NOV. 20th (6 days)
Maria Montez and Jon Hall in
ALI BABA & THE FORTY THIEVES
(in Technicolor)
also **Gloria Jean** in **Moonlight in Vermont**

MONDAY, NOV. 27th (6 days)
Dennis Morgan and Irene Manning in
THE DESERT SONG
(in Technicolor)
(NOTE.—This is a New Film—not a Re-issue)
Also **BEYOND THE LINE OF DUTY**

Mon. to Fri—Con. from 5-30 p.m.   Sat.—Con. from 2 p.m.
MATINEES.—Mon. and Wed. at 2-15 p.m.
SUNDAYS—6-15 p.m.   (One Show)

Through the Looking Glass

FEUD

SCOTTISH A.T.S. girls, famed in story and song for the purity of their lives, will, we feel, be grateful to us for exposing a dangerous source of moral corruption, which, as yet unknown, festers like a monstrous sore in the midst of this otherwise unblemished and contented community. Behind a facade of pseudo culture and literary virtuosity in the palatial offices of the B.S.M., a tense £30,000 love-triangle drama is being played out, and passion surges like a raging ocean.

Participants in this gargantuan struggle are Eric la Souris, scheming and embittered editor; and Deadly Dooin, smooth, soft-voiced ex-ladies handbag king, who, locked in epic conflict, fight for the love of Katherine de la Pris, winsome, starry-eyed Editorial Moll. As we write, Dooin is the master: Katie, lured by the temptation of unlimited free tickets at the local cinemas, with which he has insidiously supplied himself, receives his approaches with a fascinated ear; and Souris, although gaining a temporary superiority during a drunken orgy a few weeks back, has lately been left out in the cold. But that lamb has a few more cards left up his sleeve: "I'll get her yet; that tiny baby's mine, and Dooin will pay!" he declared in fervent tones yesterday.

What the outcome will be we daren't attempt to speculate, but your faithful old retainer will keep you well-informed—if the Editorial Gestapo don't get him first—and even if he should die, what sweeter death than for the Presbyterian pure hearts?

SCOURGE

A freshman, to whom we were explaining the Prison Regulations the other day, expressed some surprise to see the supervisor toying thoughtfully with that Thompson sub machine-gun which is always kept in the drawer of the desk; so, for the benefit of this chap and future generations we will explain. The weapon is used to deal with severe cases of "Radioclaustrophobia"—the fear of being trapped in a confined space with a lot of wild wireless sets; an industrial disease which takes a grim toll of life in this *locale*.

About once every three weeks some poor down-trodden minion just can't take it on the chin any longer, and, on seeing a squad of green scorpions walk in through the door wearing straw boaters and playing the Prelude to Act 3 of Lohengrin on German concertinas, something snaps inside his brain, and the dread disease has claimed another victim. With a cry such as "A plague on Control!" or "A murrain take the Supervisor!", the victim seizes his box of tricks, flings it on the floor with a scream of unholy delight, and runs amok down the room imploring the nearest A.T.S. cutie to give him one moment of her love before he dies.

By this time the supervisor has nonchalantly sighted his weapon; his finger slowly closes round the trigger; and the victim crumples to the ground in a twitching heap.

Next, Control is informed: "Say Butch, we can take dat extra goil; and ask 'em to send da van round—dere's anudder of 'em here".

Five minutes later, life in the dungeon has resumed its normal routine; and only a shining tear which trembles in the eye of a tiny A.T.S. girl speaks of the tragedy.

THROB

That promise made by the Editor last month to institute a special super, intimate, cosy gossip column for soulful maidens filled our mind with ecstasy and brought a final peace to our weary old bones. Now, now at last we shall share every secret which nestles in those tender hearts: We shall know just what it was that Gertrude Flannelside's daddy sent for her seventeenth birthday present; the world will tremble with excitement to learn the colour of Fannie Greenbaum's wedding dress; and a thousand hearts will sorrow when Winifred Winterbotham's pet Angora rabbit passes on. Yes, yes, like all you tiny darlings we can hardly wait to read the first issue.

Of course, some of those nasty, rude, grizzled old sailors may say some unkind things, or laugh at us; but they don't understand the beautiful side of life. We shall have to bear their coarseness with patience and forbearance—just as that *too* divine Curate told us last week.

LEON DE BUNK.

"THREE AND A ROAD"—cont.

with weariness, yet with an almost youthful spring to his step as he neared the last steep pull up. The homespun jacket and cap betrayed his calling as surely as did the lean sheep-dog which followed closely behind its master.

A few steps more, and old John reached the top of the hill, pausing there as he always did to get his breath. Then he turned, his glance taking in the lights of the village twinkling cheerily below, the long road leading from it, and he wondered, as he had wondered many a time before, why the road had been made when the old pathway did just as well. Still, supper was ready, and Mary, his wife waiting at the door, so, briskly now, he stepped towards the tiny cottage that stood at the end of the road.

EXTRACTS FROM PART ONE ORDERS
18th September, 1916.

SERVICE CHEVRONS. A.S.I. 953/422, states that the wearing of service chevrons is optional, but, if worn, these must be goffered in the following manner:—
    Seven bumps and eight dips in the first, and eight bumps and seven dips in the second.
Corporals will see that this is strictly adhered to.

DRESS. Old-style chemises and bust-bodices will be handed into stores no later than 12 mid-day, on Tuesday. Will Ptes. please see that note of receipt of elastic sides for third issue boots is entered on form PX171.

DISCIPLINE. MEALS. Physical gymnastic kit may be worn for the 0800 hrs. parade breakfast, only if worn long enough to conceal the ankles and top of boots. There is no necessity to sign for this meal.

HAIR. Hair will not be worn in the "earphone" nor the Mary Pickford styles, but must be worn in either three four-stranded plaited buns, or in four two-ply coiled buns, not to exceed six inches above the ears.

PARASOLS. These will be carried under left arm, and not under right.

AMENDMENT. Ref., Pt. 1, Order No. 121, d/d 3rd Sept., para. 490. Special Order of the Day, please cancel para. No. 4 and amend to read "Special Order of the Day by G.O.C. South Eastern District" and add . . . "these".

RECREATION. Those wishing to attend instructional lectures on putting, spinning, tatting, and ping-pong, are requested to sign attached list.

KIT LAY-OUT. Veils will be rolled carefully after use, and placed at the head of bed, flush with c.p.v.'s (Mark 11) and goloshes.

"HOLY MATRIMONY"—cont.

was such a help to me in my state, but at last I heard a scuffle outside and the organ started up "Here comes the bride". Panic seized me then and if my legs had been working it would have been a case of "here goes the bridegroom". She eventually arrived at the altar steps, and I must say she looked charming. I had a second look to make sure it was the right woman, accidents do happen even at weddings. Everybody apparently satisfied, the service began, and when I came to I was married. The parson took us up to the altar and gave us some advice—so my wife tells me, but believe me, I can't recall a single word of his lecture. Perhaps it is just as well I can't remember those words of wisdom uttered by the cleric, because he was subsequently unfrocked, but that's another story.

Anyhow, after signing the register and facing the usual battery of cameras, rice and confetti we adjourned for the breakfast. At last I began to feel better and by the time the drink, etc., had been quaffed, I was more or less normal again. I think I can leave you here as there is nothing in the rest of the story likely to be of interest, but it just goes to show how a shower of rain can lead to man's undoing.

EMPIRE
MARKET PLACE, LOUGHBOROUGH

MONDAY, NOV. 6th (3 days)
Johnny Weismuller and John Sheffield in
TARZAN'S DESERT MYSTERY
also David Bruce in SHE'S FOR ME

THURSDAY, NOV. 9th (3 days)
TOM CONWAY in
THE SEVENTH VICTIM
also Bill Henry in Nearly Eighteen

MONDAY, NOV. 13th (3 days)
ANTON WALBROOK in
THE RAT
also Geo. O'Brien in PRAIRIE LAW

THURSDAY, NOV. 16th (3 days)
CLIVE BROOK in
THE SHIPBUILDERS
also Michael Whalen in I'll Sell My Life

MONDAY, NOV. 20th (3 days)
Ronald Colman and Madeleine Carroll in
THE PRISONER OF ZENDA
also THE AVALANCHE

THURSDAY, NOV. 23 (3 days)
BUSTER CRABBE in
JUNGLE WOMAN
also Richard Travis in BUSSES ROAR

MONDAY, NOV. 27th (3 days)
BASIL RATHBONE in
SHERLOCK HOLMES FACES DEATH
also Bob Haynes in Swing Out the Blues

THURSDAY, NOV. 30th (3 days)
BARBARA STANWYCK in
STELLA DALLAS
also Leo Carrillo in Moonlight and Cactus

CONTINUOUS DAILY. Doors open at 1-30 p.m.
SUNDAYS at 5-30 p.m.

Printed by Toppings Ltd., 17, Southfield Rd., Loughborough, and published by L. P. Jones for Beaumanor Staff Magazine Committee.

DECEMBER, 1944

VOL. I. No. 10 (NEW SERIES) - **6d.**

FILM ATTRACTIONS for DECEMBER

SHOWING AT THE ODEON THEATRE

Sunday, Dec. 3rd.—Ida Lupino and Edward G. Robinson in **Sea Wolf**. Also East Side Kids in **Kid Dynamite**.

MONDAY, DEC. 4th, and all the week:
Gary Cooper and Laraine Day in Cecil B. De Mille's
THE STORY OF DR. WASSELL
in Technicolor.

Sunday, Dec. 10th.—Ronald Reagan and Priscilla Lane in **Million Dollar Baby**. Also Bela Lugosi and Wallace Ford in **Mysterious Mr. Wong**.

MONDAY, DEC. 11th, for 3 days	THURS., DEC. 14th, for 3 days
Leslie Bradley and Barbara Mullen in	Eric Portman in
WELCOME MR. WASHINGTON	**A CANTERBURY TALE**
Also James Craig and Patricia Dane in **North West Rangers**.	with Sheila Sim, Dennis Price and Sgt. John Sweet, U.S. Army.

Sunday, Dec. 17th.—Bud Abbott and Lou Costello in **Money for Jam**. Also Otto Kruger in **The Silent Witness**.

MONDAY, DEC. 18th, and all the week:
Penelope Ward, Michael Wilding and Lili Palmer in
ENGLISH WITHOUT TEARS
Also Basil Rathbone and Nigel Bruce in **The Scarlet Claw**.

Sunday, Dec. 24th.—Ida Lupino and John Garfield in **Out of the Fog**. Also Ronald Reagan and James Gleason in **Nine Lives are not Enough**.

MONDAY, DEC. 25th, and all the week:
Walter Brennan and Charlotte Greenwood in
HOME IN INDIANA
in Technicolor.
Also Laurel and Hardy in **Fraternally Yours**.

P.S.—Please consult local papers for times of opening on Xmas Day.

Continuous Performance Daily 1-45 p.m.   Sunday, One Performance at 6 p.m.

B.S.M. Vol. I. No. 10 (New Series) DECEMBER, 1944.

Managing Editor: LEONARD P. JONES.

Editors: KAY PRICE, ERIC C. MILLHOUSE   Treasurer: A. H. APPLETON.

Message from C.O., W.O.Y.G.

In wishing you all a very happy Christmas, and all the best of good fortune in 1945, I feel sure that all of you will hope that this is the last war-time Christmas. If the war has not finished quite as early as we had hoped, we can at least be happy in the knowledge that we at Beaumanor have tried to play our part in hastening that wonderful day of victory which cannot now be far off.

1944 has seen many changes as far as we are concerned, but I think we have been extremely fortunate in maintaining our Group as a cohesive whole. This has been our first complete year as a combined military and civilian organisation, and I am very grateful to all those who have assisted so splendidly in welding the combined organisation into a workable whole. Particular mention should be made of the Sports, Music, Magazine, and Recreation sections, and we must not forget the Canteen Committee who normally receive "all the kicks and none of the ha'pence".

I could not wish to have a better military unit, and that, from an old sailor, is high praise indeed.

Our old "hard core" of civilians—and in this connection I include some of the youngsters—have met all the difficulties in the past year with their usual efficiency and good humour. I know only too well, that they are a little worried about the future, and I would ask them to realise that their good service is fully recognised in many quarters, and will not pass unnoticed when post-war arrangements are under consideration. I would like to add a special word of greeting and appreciation to our fellows in the South, and at the out-stations. They have done a magnificent job and I do hope it will be possible for Mr. Thornton's "lost legion" to come into Headquarters for a few days' change of scene during the coming year.

Finally, our A.T.S., many of them with us for over two years. They have certainly brightened up our somewhat drab and monotonous lives, and we are truly grateful. They have also done a grand job of work, and where should we have been without them?

So enjoy yourselves all you can during this last war-time Christmas, and may the New Year bring Victory and Peace.

CHRISTMAS 1944.   M. J. W. E.

Next issue ready January 5th.   Contributions to reach Editors by Dec. 20th.

The Star.

By KAY PRICE

It was the Eve of Christmas, and asleep,
    The children of the land
Smiled in their dreams, and at the foot
    Of every bed
An empty stocking dangled,
    Which by dawn
Would be mysteriously filled:
And eager hands would grab them on awakening
    And happy voices fill the Christmas morn.

    One little boy alone expected nothing;
He lay, a crumpled, ragged dirty heap,
    Couched on a pile of sacking
In the corner of a cellar.
    He had not hung his stocking out
—poor child, he had no stocking—
A pair of worn-out boots was all
    That he possessed,
And these he slept in,
    Hoping to keep his poor feet warm.

The morning came, first grey,
    Then rosy-hued;
The wint'ry sun crept forth
    And kissed the snow-touched world
Which blushed, and brightened redly.

With gleeful cries the children
    Came gambolling out to play.
One had a hoop,
    One had a ball,
A whip, a top, a wooden horse, a doll.
    Sadly, the little boy
Watched from afar, and sighing,
    Envied them.
He did not hope to share their happy lot,
But boy-like, dreading to seem left out,
    He found a battered tin,
And aimlessly
    Trundled it along the gutter
With sundry kicks, until his gaping boot
Fell all apart;
    The day dragged by,
Wearily, drearily.

The children disappeared indoors
    To savour to the full
The joys of crackers and gleaming Christmas trees,
    Paper festoons, and nuts around the fire.

The twilight fell, like some thick, misty mantle,
    While the little boy
Sat on a stump, moodily gazing down
    Into a puddle which he stirred around
With a broken stick,
    Conjuring up
Thick, creamy whirls of mud
    From its murkiest depths.
The sound of carols wafted on the breeze,
    Childrens' voices, singing joyfully,
"Star of wonder, star of light'', they sang.

The little boy lifted his sullen head.
"What star is that?" he cried in passionate plaint.
"What Christmas is there for such folk as I?"
He ceased to scoop his stick around the puddle
And wailed aloud into the lonely night.

When suddenly, his answer came to him;
For there at his feet, where he had seen before
Only a flat of dirty, ruffled water,
A glistening pool of deep blue silkiness
Lapped and caressed its margin.
And behold!
High up in Heaven
The beckoning star of Bethlehem itself
Flung down its very soul into the water,
So that it caught the downcast eye of the little boy
Who, seeing it twinkle up at him,
Smiled back,
And knew that he too
Had known Christmas.

Football Epic.

IT was a broad, liberal, cosmopolitan gesture: Officialdom was to unbend; social barriers were to be broken; nationalities were to be forgotten; and those from every layer of society were to plunge into the bluff *bonhomie* of the football field, sharing together the effervescent sensations of the game without regard to rank, caste, status, or origin; it was indeed a commendable project. A poster on the Canteen wall announced the fact to a delighted world the day before the match; and a substantial crowd of spectators arrived to grace the occasion on that boisterous autumnal afternoon

A fascinating experience for the observer was to see officials who, in saner moments, maintain the barrier of formal reserve which their position demands, romping on to the field with as much light-hearted and noisy abandon as the Lower Fourth Eleven ever exhibited on Big Side in the far-off days. . . .

The O.C. was a particularly distinguished figure in a garb which gave the ecclesiastical dignity of the Dalai Lama combined with the workaday utility of a Billingsgate fish porter, but, unhappily, he was to retire before we could discover whether his performance matched his appearance; Mr. Pope cut no mean figure in a becoming pair of shorts and red shirt; the Spartan, nay, almost nymph-like forms of Messrs. Walton and Neary gave a hint of their latent athletic ability, whilst the ascetic slimness of Sgt. Allred and Mr. Spooner made some spectators tremble for their well-being in the event of their colliding with any more substantial opponents.

From the first to the last minute of play there was literally never a dull moment for the spectators: the goals came almost as thickly as the penalties, and whatever the players lacked in practice, they supplied in courage and invention; this applied particularly to our American colleagues. Sgt. Allred's short dash down the field with the ball under his arm was more than delightful. Mr. Pope's successful penalty kick was taken with a confidence and grace which Alec James might have envied, and the applause it won was well merited; in addition, the cheers which greeted Captain Whitford's goal showed that the old loyalties of the "Home Guard" days are not yet dead. For the rest, it was good fun and sportsmanship, and a none too scrupulous regard for the rules—the referee using a certain discretion in deciding whether or not a goal was allowable.

When the game had ended there was some controversy as to the score; so many goals had been "offside" that it was difficult to keep track of the ones which had been allowed. The consensus of opinion seemed to favour "four-all"; and as that seems an amicable conclusion to a most pleasant afternoon we will record it as such for posterity.

FIGARO.

Theatre Royal
LOUGHBOROUGH.

PROGRAMMES FOR DECEMBER 1944

THE FORTESCUE
Famous Players

continue their Repertory Season with the following outstanding attractions:—

Monday, Dec. 4th, for 6 days

MEET THE WIFE
By Larry Starling

Monday, Dec. 11th, for 6 days

THEY FLY BY TWILIGHT
Based on the most sensational Murder Trial in History

Monday, Dec. 18th,

Monday, Dec. 25th,

Watch the weekly Press for particulars regarding these dates

Camp Capers

EPISODE 1

THE INSIDE STORY
REVEALED AT LAST
BY KAY METCALFE

THE Camp was a chaos when we arrived. Clothes strewn around, bedding hung from every branch, and food, cases and shoes were mixed higgledy-piggledy in heaps around the tents. The occupants presented a sorry sight—Bris disconsolately viewing the upheaval from a small collapsible stool (it eventually did collapse under my fairylike figure), Kim apparently seeking inspiration from the remains of his landlady's "slimfit" unmentionables hanging like a banner from the flagpole.

My first words shook them considerably. "Can you lend me a safety pin"? Galvanised into action they proceeded to trip each other up in an attempt to spare my modesty. After 10 mins. rummaging I was presented with needle, and cotton in 3 shades—black, white and khaki (they do things on a grand scale there), with the instructions to "get cracking" while they looked the other way.

My stockings once again being out of danger, tea was the next concern. Four eggs appeared miraculously from where they'd been sitting beneath the bell-tent, and were plonked in a pan on the oil-stove. Meanwhile, Fred and Kim (with many references to "Gillwell", mecca of scout camping) were putting up a good show of lighting a camp fire between two bricks, while Bris pottered aimlessly around wearing a bewildered expression and a pair of grubby white shorts, which, being badly in need of some new elastic round the waist, required constant hitching.

The camp fire was eventually persuaded to burn, to the accompaniment of clouds of smoke belching forth, and two pans of water placed thereon, while we set the table. Far be it from me to criticize "furnishings luxurious a la Brister", but its the first time in my life I've ever sat on the ground among squelchy slugs and beetles and eaten off a small cabin trunk—still I'll try anything once.

Bread and jam formed the main part of the feast—you know, really nice thick doorsteps, worthy of any navvy. Still, I survived. At length (half-an-hour after the eggs were cooked) a whoop of joy from somewhere amid the smoke, announced that the water was boiling. Then came the highlight of the afternoon—the piece de resistance. We'd heard many allusions to this wondrous article—it had been referred to with accents of awe and regarded in terms of reverence so that naturally we expected to see something worthy of the name. Judge our horror then when a tiny tea-pot appeared, capable of holding one small cup of tea and no more. (It took five mashings to provide us with a mug full each). I ask yer, chums, "Is it fair to build up a girl's hopes in this pretentious fashion, then dash them to the ground so rudely?"

While the other two were joyfully hopping round like fleas, replacing the water they'd used, accompanied by loud war cries and many more references to "Gillwell", Bris and I sat down, to make it look more civilised. The tea (that's what they called it, though I had my own ideas) didn't look very inviting, but somebody had to be the guinea-pig and the menfolk didn't seem very keen on dying just then. Anxiously watched by Bris I tried it. My expression must have been eloquent, for uttering a shriek of mirth, he jumped to his feet, ricocheted off the fence against the guy-ropes and eventually landed on top of the jam.

To call it smoked is putting it mildly. It was putrid.

Wearing hurt expressions, our two heroes reluctantly left their game of cowboys and Indians round the camp fire and came to prove me wrong (they hoped). Manfully gripping their mugs, and adopting a do-or-die look on their would-be, long-suffering countenances, they took a large gulp.

Sorrowfully each turned to the other and murmured: "Definitely **not** up to 'Gillwell' standard!"

(More Anon).

They're telling Me!

RATHER belated congratulations to S/Sgt. Fred Allred, U.S.A.A., and Pte. Audrey Robinson, who tied the knot on October 21st.

Congratulations to Pte. Joan Nixon, "C" Watch, on her marriage to W/O Frank Williams, R.A.F., also on the 21st October.

Also to Pte. Jean Hammond—whose name is now Chapman. The deed was dood in Timperley, Cheshire, but I have not managed to get any dope on the lucky bridegroom.

And talking of marriages, Pte. Margaret Dart (nee Rhodes), of "C" Watch, recently got married. The funny thing is that a few days after her return from marriage leave she had a letter from her husband addressed in her maiden name. Some forgetfulness is excusable!

Congratulations to Pte. Margaret Willet, "D" Watch, on her engagement to 2nd Lt. P. S. Hedgeland (Buffs.) of Maidstone.

My predecessor once made a remark about the "bull ring" crumbling. . I will go so far as to say that it has completely disintegrated for, with the engagement of Geoff Nicol to Connie Praeger, it leaves "Bungy" Williamson the only eligible bachelor, and, by all accounts, his fall is fast approaching.

And while on the subject of the "bull ring" we are to congratulate the first member on becoming a father. A son was born to Mr. and Mrs. Don Barber on October 21st.

At Radmoor Nursing Home, on November 8th, Mrs. Glanville presented her husband, Mr. G. Glanville (Accounts Branch) with a £50 reduction in Income Tax, Graham Glanville. The re-assessment weighed 7 lbs. 14 ozs. It is believed that the rebate will be used to furnish a bedroom carpet with specially reinforced tread.

We regretfully say goodbye this month to S/Mjr. "Bunny" Bunyard, who left for Harrogate on November 17th.

Also to Charlie "P. F. Q." Gilbert, who has left to find his serenity in the Brighton Plumbers Union. Good luck, Charlie!

Goodbye, too, to Pte. Laurie Domina (nee Isaacs), who has left us to start production in America.

We have often heard of A.T.S. falling **for** a Yank, but surely it is a somewhat unusual occurence to see one falling head over heels **with** a Yank (through the curtains, into the Empire's "back-of-beyond", chair and all!)

Tut! Tut! Trixie, that's not the way to bowl a man off his feet. Try a new technique, dear.

BELIEVE IT OR NOT
    KAY: I'm catching the 1.38 bus, are you?
    MINA: No, I'm getting the 20 to 2!
Later. (Time 6.20).
    NELLIE: What time's that bus to Loughborough just after six?
    GANG: 6.18.
    NELLIE: Oh, goody! I've 2 mins. in which to catch it.

And did you hear about the T.P. runner who phoned "H" hut and said that a troop-carrier was on its way.

And, I think, the best *faux pas*:—

Pte. Audrey Chope was returning by train from leave some time ago when she dozed off. The inspector arrived, looking at tickets, and Audrey, opening one eye, mumbled "All the way" and relapsed into slumber.

Talking of *faux pas*:—

Peter Tuke was outside the Town Hall the other night after a dance, waiting for an ordered taxi. Seeing a large Austin draw up he opened the door and asked "Are you booked?"

"No", came the surprising reply, "Ai'm the Mayor's chauffeur!"

The most surprising affair that has come to my knowledge lately is that of George White and Molly Cronin. I am reliably informed that George has even gone so far as to give up his beer. I hear, too, that he now has a habit of going for walks during break and eating his sandwiches in the returning bus. Such is love!!

I am glad to report that, at long last, after representations, complete with money offers, had been made, Mr. Noel Royle had his bi-annual haircut on Remembrance Day.

Watch "Thru' the Looking Glass" next month for interesting repercussions! (Advt.).

Mrs. Curd, having had a stove installed in "Ye Caravan", got weavin' on cooking and concocted a rice pud., which she put in the oven. Arriving on duty, 1900-2359, she remembered with consternation the pud. and frantically requested break at 21.30 in order to contact George and see if he'd rescued said pud. Alas, no! George, before leaving, had made up the fire. I am told, however, that the delicacy was ultimately consumed.

Did you hear that the girls in "I" hut are being issued with blankets to bring on night duty—a fitting tribute to the iciness of that hut. Supervisors are now anxiously awaiting the issue of hot water bottles.

There was an unprecedented occurrence, for Woyg, at Kay Metcalfe's party—an excess of men! However, both the original and the "return visit" passed off very well despite this obvious setback.

As a consequence of these efforts I am told that "A" Watch T.P. ops are now all wearing gaily coloured garters although, naturally, I have had no confirmation.

The "do's" seemed to have been fraught with incidents (reportable, Snoop, for the use of), not the least worthy of which appears to be that "½ pint 'Snubby' Pollard" actually partook of 2 pints of beer at one sitting. I hear, too, that "Trixie" Scillitoe still wears the marks of "Mouse's" 3-speed, gained on the homeward journey. Jean Tolley might have some information about the non-durability of cycle crossbars, as well.

Apparently "Spike" Forster's good work with Mina, on one of the above occasions, was wasted, for the young lady has been seen several times with a charming Yank. How many people **are** slipping?

And talking of Mina's. We have now said goodbye to Reg. Cecil, who has joined Mr. Bevin's underground movement. We wish him luck in his new vocation and sincerely hope that he doesn't bury himself in his work.

SCENE:—"H" Hut, 5 mins. after a recent inspection by the O.C. "Laddie" is discovered, sitting patiently in the lobby.

Mr. Charles Dobson is summoned, and, pushing his hands in his pockets with an air becoming an established Grade 2 C.E.W.A., he solemnly informs the dog that "He has gone out the other way!"

A group of Ewas started one evening to find the "lowest" pub in Loughborough. After making their rounds they came to rest in the "singing-room" of the "Volunteer". Who should they find there but Sub./Lt. Connolly, "V.R." and, stranger still, in the immediate proximity were 5 ladies. "Con" is still protesting his innocence! I daren't say any more on this theme or all you reservists will be put, at Mr. Connolly's request, into the Army, but I would like to ascertain why the first-mentioned Ewas were looking for the lowest pub.

It is a notable fact that since Maurice Reed became so attached to Jean Donlon we have had no Mag. contributions from him—Blackleg lover?

To close I would like to convey to my readers my somewhat premature Best Wishes for a Very Merry Xmas. May this be your last one here and the best one to date.

Cheerio, chums,
JIMMY.

Pixie's Search for Luv.
By TOU-TOU ETHELEMM-DELLISH

IT was late afternoon in a dirty little Snack-joint. At a soiled table, behind an encrusted cup and plate, sat a noble-looking young man. He was tall, and handsome as a Greek God, and for all his shabby clothes, he looked like a young lordling. This was not surprising, as he was the eldest son of the Earl of Pighle (pronounced "Piffle"). His name was Piers ffanshawe, but for the time being he called himself Peter Shaw, since that name was more acceptable to the Communist friends with whom he associated, for he had cast off his family, wealth, and honour, and was living in triumphant squalor with the Masses.

There was movement in the dingy rear of the shop, and the young man stiffened expectantly. The tatty bead-curtains parted and a lovely young waitress appeared. It was Pixie, who had found employment here through the good influence of the Window-cleaner's daughter. She approached Peter's table, and inadeptly balanced his cup and plate on a tray, and was preparing to retreat when he cleared his throat and spoke in a deep musical voice. "May I see you home to-night"? he begged. Pixie's eyes widened like those of a startled fawn, and she swayed on her toes like a bird poised for flight. Then her soft lips parted and she whispered, "Yes. I finish at half-past six. I'll see you in the Alley". And blushing deeply, she withdrew.

Peter gripped the edge of the table till his knuckles showed white, and the aged oilcloth flaked under his fingers. At last! Six weeks of patient tea-and-bun swallowing in this horrible place just to win the favour of this lovely creature. And at last he had dared to speak his desire, and she to answer.

The minutes crawled by, but (inevitably) half-past six came, and found Peter waiting impatiently in the Alley. A light step sounded behind him, and spinning round eagerly, he looked down into two eyes like starry pools. Pixie had come.

He took her arm, and they moved off in silence. Neither could trust themselves to speak. Then they dared.

"It's a fine evening", ventured Peter.

"Yes", rejoined Pixie.

An ominous roll of thunder in the distance, and a spatter of heavy raindrops gave the lie to their words.

"We must hurry", declared Peter. "You mustn't get wet".

"But I live here", said Pixie, halting about three yards further on. "We live over that Plumber's shop".

"Oh", said Peter, bitterly disappointed. "Well, good night".

"Goodnight", whispered Pixie.

Peter glanced up and down the street—no one was in sight. The passion born of six weeks of iron-controlled bun-worrying suddenly broke loose in him. She was so small, so sweet, so desirable. He caught her closely to him and covered her upturned face with kisses, like the wordless endearments of butterfly's wing. At first she struggled in his amorous grip, but then her heart began to beat painfully and she shyly returned his caresses. She was only a girl in years, but in that moment, he knew that he held a woman in his arms. Clinched tightly together, they stood swaying slightly. The setting sun leered down on them, and winked knowingly at the intimate array of porcelaine-ware on show behind them in the Plumber's window. And here was Luv born. But would the gentle rain of understanding, and the soft sunlight of tolerance foster it into healthy life?

The savoury odour of frying onions wafted out of an upper window, and Pixie gently prised herself free. "I must go," she sighed. Peter dropped to his knees. "I kiss your little feet!" he cried. And did so.

The mud-splashed, well-worn suede of her shoes on his lips rather reminded him of the Snack-bar buns. One quick movement, and Pixie was gone. But Peter lingered kneeling below her window, till an uncomfortable dampness at the knees warned him that he was ruining his trousers. "Good night, my love, my darling," he moaned to the lighted window and the aroma of onions above him—and went back to the Masses for his Communal supper.

The following days passed like a golden dream. Every night Peter saw Pixie home, and kissed her ecstatically in the shelter of the Plumber's window. Once he took her to the Pictures and wrung her hand in the dark, and once he was invited in to the Window-cleaner's abode to partake of a modest supper of whelks and cow-heels. He dreamed of her every night (particularly that night)—but his heart was heavy and troubled. He longed for her, but how could he take her from the savoury security above the Plumber's and ask her to be his, and live in his corner of the Communal Garret, while the Masses disported themselves collectively in the other three corners? Such was not for her. And yet he could not repudiate his principles and his vocation (Soap-box erector for Orators in Hyde Park, and Pamphlet-distributing on street corners), and go back to his family, and plutocratic life. His torture of worry infected Pixie, and relations became strained. They began to quarrel—and then one day the break he dreaded came.

He entered the Snack-bar one evening, just as a dark, oily-looking man, whom he had seen there often of late, was leaving. Pixie was buttoning a crackling document into the bosom of her dress. Peter grasped her wrists. "What's that?" he demanded roughly. Pixie faced him, her sweet face defiant. "My Contract!" she cried. "Mr. Isaac Fischlein is going to put me on the Stage. I'VE FINISHED HERE!!"

"But what about me?" cried poor Peter, his face working. Pixie laughed cruelly. Already she was becoming affected and heartless. "What makes you think I care?" she scoffed, and swept triumphantly out of the shop.

(What now? Will Pixie become a great Star, or will deceit and infamy ruin her lovely girlhood? And what will Peter do? More Next Month!!!)

SPORTOPICS.

Soccer.—Our match versus R.N.A.S. on Wednesday, 27th September, resulted in a goalless draw. Our opponents were more dangerous in front of goal, but our "Supervisors'" defence always had the situation under control, although Hobden had to make some typically good saves.

The "Annual Derby" versus the Military was a good hard match. The teams were very equal, with, as usual, our defence the strongest part of our side. Musgrave, on the left wing, nearly scored in the first few minutes. A mis-kick by one of the defence led to our opponents' first goal. Towards the end of the second half the ball slid off our centre-half's foot, giving the Military a two-goal lead. Bad luck, Alec! After the change-over we kept up pressure and played well, Musgrave heading in from a corner to make the score 2—1. The soldiers increased their lead from a disputed penalty for "hands". Keenlyside went up into the attack and scored a good goal. Cleveland at back gave a great display, never making a mistake. A draw would have been a fair result.

The "Veterans" versus "Old Crocks" match is reported on another page. The writer now *feels* an "Old Crock".

Tennis.—It is interesting to note that during the summer the number of hours booked on the B.M. court amounted to over 400.

Table-tennis.—A league has been started, and some enjoyable matches have been played. These are organised by Mr. Fred Hearne.

A. H. APPLETON, *Sports Secretary.*

The Gospel according to St. Apid

(Translated from the English by Disciple Millhouse).

Chapter XXXVII

NOW in the days when Itla, the Schweinhund, purposed to send forth his Hunnites upon a mighty pilgrimage unto Brit, the King, and Red Tabz, and all the peoples were sore dismayed because they had not the wherewithal to greet the pilgrims. For it is written; they had Done a Mighty Dunkirk, and delivered all their weapons and chariots into Urop.

Wherefore Toni, a minister of the King, desiring to shew the Hunnites that the land of Brit was indeed exceeding unhealthy for visitors, spake unto all men of Brit with the Loud Voice of Bebesee in this wise, saying: Whomsoever among ye desireth to salute the pilgrims shall henceforth be a soldier of the King. Thy raiment shall be a fine armband, and thy name shall be Eldevee.

Now among the great Tribe, which in these days abode in Chm, dwelled one Dik, a noted warrior and leader of men. And Dik was a centurion of a mighty Legion called the Front Ears Men. But when he had hearkened unto Toni, and learned concerning Eldevee, he swore a mighty oath, and casting aside his breeches and stetson, he robed himself in a fine armband, crying in a loud voice: Yea, verily, I will lead forth the peoples of Chm to Beat Up all Hunnites which venture nigh unto us.

And it came to pass that the tailors of Brit got weaving and produced an abundance of soldiers' raiment for the legions of Eldevee. Wherefore Jurjil, who sitteth upon the right hand of the King in Smowk, raised up his voice, saying: Henceforth thy name shall be Ohmgard. And unto every man of Ohmgard was given a broomstick wherewith to halt the chariots of Itla.

And the legion of Dik grew and waxed exceeding strong, and certain among them were possessed of Bonduks; yea, and even of bullets also. But about this time the King delivered the Tribe out of Chm, and into the hands of the Glammaboiz in Chiksanz. But Dik tarried in Chm and Stuck to his Guns, even though he was no more a centurion. And he swore another load of oaths against the Hunnites, and teached himself divers new ways of eliminating them.

And when the Tribe were delivered up into the Promised Land of Woyg, Dik journeyed thence and summoned a new army. And Ohmgard grew anew and waxed exceeding great, and Dik likewise flourished, and the pips upon his shoulders multiplied. And the Orders of the Day were many and of great length.

But the Brittites across the Ditch, with their comrades the Iankis, and the Russites, and the countless hordes of degenerate Democracy, incited the Hunnites to make a pilgrimage unto Berlin. And Itla was afflicted with a mighty Headache, and became an Invisible Schweinhund. Wherefore the King perceived that the War might not endure more than ten years hence, and because the Hunnites' pilgrimage was going the wrong way, he commanded the Chief of all Ohmgards to dismiss his legions, saying: All those which Stood Up must Stand Down.

And Dik was cast down and most sorely cheesed. And he went into the House of Ohmgard and communed with himself, saying: Woe is me, for it is Curtains, and I am undone. Yea, verily, for I am a captain without an army; neither have I any Front Ears Men. And, behold, he knew no more oaths to swear. But a mighty vision appeared before him, and he saw, writ in the heavens, in letters of flame: N R A. And when he had read the letters, and interpreted them, he cried in a loud voice: Goody-goody.

And seizing his Bonduk, he went forth, crying: Targets. Targets. One shekel each.

B.S.M. XMAS SUPPLEMENT

For Auld Lang Syne

By "OLLIE" PEARCE.

May we take this opportunity
Of wishing our community
A very Happy Christmas and New Year?

Everywhere our troops advance,
And it might be our last chance;
By next Christmas most of us may not be
here.

Through the recent trying years
We have shared our joys and fears,
In our work and mode of living we've
been near.

We have worked and played together,
We have cursed about the weather,
The job, the food, the lack of fags and beer.

When we finally disperse,
Some for better, some for worse,
We don't suppose you'll want to shed a tear.

But we'd like you all to know,
That wherever you may go,
A little bit of you will still be here.

A MIDWINTER

By CPL. E

TO say that Pte. Amelia Bagwash was deliriously happy would be a slight exaggeration.

It was almost midnight on Christmas Eve and she had just arrived on duty where she would remain until 7 a.m. on Christmas morning, after which she was faced with the prospect of trying to snatch some sleep before coming back at 7 p.m. Already she was feeling tired, and this was not surprising, for back at camp the other watches, taking advantage of their off-duty hours, had commenced the Christmas celebrations, consequently Amelia had not been able to get much rest since she came off duty at 1 p.m. She pondered over the possibility of being able to sleep the next day, and was forced to the dismal conclusion that her chances were very slender as the festivities would most probably be at their height by then.

She reflected, a little indignantly, that even if sleep were possible, there must be better ways of spending Christmas.

So pre-occupied was she with her thoughts that she failed to notice the arrival of her break relief; no—it couldn't possibly be—she had hardly been on duty half an hour.

She turned to investigate and was met by the gracious smile of the Group Commander.

"Amelia, dear," she said, "I just couldn't bear to think of you spending Christmas like this, so I have decided to take your place. You will find the car outside; it is at your disposal."

"Your car, Ma'am?" gasped Amelia.

"My dear," said the Group Commander pleadingly, *"please* don't call me Ma'am. Call me G.C. or Groupy, or something."

Amelia withdrew smiling to herself at the various interpretations of "or something" that she had heard from time to time. As she approached the door the Supervisor jumped up from his table, where he had been working busily on some theory of his for ensuring that each girl went to break at the same time as her particular pal, and wishing her a *very* happy Christmas, handed her "a little present", explaining shyly that it was his favourite toothpaste.

Slipping the tin of Kiwi into her pocket, she proceeded outside to behold a seemingly endless stream of Generals, each of whom saluted smartly as he passed the empty car.

At this stage she caught sight of the R.S.M., who, having curtsied gracefully, rushed forward to open the door of the car, but in her eagerness, tripped, fell face downwards, and was trampled in the mud by the oncoming Generals.

Making full use of the facilities afforded by the prostrate figure, Amelia climbed into the car.

Having decided that it would be rather a good idea to call in and convey the season's greetings to the boys, she stopped outside "H", but on entering the hut rather boisterously she was met with an almost reproachful look from Harry, who was crooning softly to his charges that popular song of recent years, "Close your Eyes", whilst the two runners, perched on the arms of his chair, were enviously fingering his thick mass of curls.

SUPPLEMENT

NIGHT'S DREAM

O'LEARY.

Harry explained that he was having a little difficulty in "getting the boys off again" following a slight disturbance by Noel, who, during a temporary lapse from his usual reticence, had been pointing out in basic English that he was just an ordinary guy.

Harry had overcome the situation in his usual masterly fashion by sending all Noel's admirers to break.

Amelia declined the offer of the only available chair, and after getting Harry to promise that he would kiss each of the boys for her as they went off duty, she departed.

On her way out by way of the courtyard, she glanced through the window at the floodlit figure of Cornwallis, observing that at long last he had succeeded in getting his sword completely clear of its scabbard, and that his usual strained expression was replaced by one of smiling contentment. Arrived back at the camp Amelia went straight to the messroom, in the centre of which was a gigantic Christmas tree laden with an inexhaustible supply of good things to eat and nice things to wear.

At the top of the tree, in the place usually occupied by the fairy, was the Stores Officer uncomfortably attired in the most ill-fitting tunic and skirt, overdarned stockings, a hat three sizes too small, and shoes three sizes too large. In a hoarse voice, reminiscent of a London costermonger, she was entreating all and sundry to come and help themselves.

In the cookhouse, the Messing Officer was preparing the Officers' Christmas dinner single handed.

It comprised a mountainous mixture of the soggiest fish pie and alleged chocolate soufflé imaginable. Two other officers were fetching coal and stoking the fire, whilst the remainder were engaged in preparing their quarters for an inspection by the auxiliaries which was to take place next morning. Apart from the unpleasant scrubbing and polishing that this entailed, they were faced with the problem of how to conceal the numerous non-regulation articles which they possessed, and they were beginning to realize that, under certain circumstances, life can be very irksome.

Amelia was surprised to learn that although passes were no longer necessary, the majority of the girls had chosen to remain in camp where everything possible was being done for their enjoyment.

Two of the most famous modern bands were supplying dance music alternately, and as she appeared on the scene a Ladies' "Excuse Me" was just being announced.

Helping herself to an extremely handsome handful, Amelia joined in the fun.

With such a surplus of eligible partners available, she did not anticipate being interrupted, and was therefore surprised a few seconds later to feel someone tugging at her sleeve. Gradually she became aware of the fact that the familiar sounding voice was addressing her.

"Come on, Baggy," it said, "otherwise you will have to grope your way round to the canteen alone. It's as black as pitch outside and raining like ———."

THE B.S.M. XMAS COMPETITION.

Presented by Dudley Truin

WOULD ARTHUR RANK GIVE YOU A JOB?

He might if you could spot the box-office winners! Here's your chance to assess the public's taste.

Below are the 36 Films which have taken most money at Loughborough's Cinemas in the past year.

EMPIRE

Action in the North Atlantic. Sahara. The Adventures of Tartu. Hers to Hold. Salute to the Marines. Crash Dive. Gentleman Jim. San Demetrio—London. The Four Feathers. Pittsburgh. Lassie Come Home. The Desperadoes.

ODEON

The Uninvited. For whom the Bell Tolls. Dixie. The Phantom of the Opera. Coney Island. My Friend Flicka. White Captive. The Way Ahead. His Butler's Sister. This Happy Breed. Stage Door Canteen. Jane Eyre.

VICTORY

Snow White and the Seven Dwarfs. Now Voyager. The Yellow Canary. Gone With the Wind. Sweet Rosie O'Grady. The Lamp Still Burns. Madame Curie. The Sullivans. This is the Army. Watch on the Rhine. The Man in Grey. Dear Octopus.

Judging will be on a POINTS BASIS, *i.e.*, 3 for a FIRST; 2 for a SECOND; 1 for a THIRD; 4 for a FOURTH.

N.B.—The FOURTH will be the most difficult to forecast.

Prizes will be given to the readers who place the first four from each Cinema **in their order as money makers.** Remember, you have to forecast which films were "Box Office", **not** name those you liked best.

Write your name, rank, and address on the form provided. Entries must be placed in the special box in the canteen or sent direct to "Film Competition, B.S.M., Beaumanor".

Here are the prizes; they may solve your Xmas problems!

First: Two free seats each for the Empire, Odeon, Victory and Theatre Royal (value One Guinea)—Presented by the Managers.

Second, Ladies: A Compact. *Second, Gentlemen*: A Pair of Brushes.

Third: A Perpetual Calendar. *Fourth*: A mirror

Prizes presented by Dudley Truin.

And two consolation prizes of **50 Players'** cigarettes—Presented by Lt.-Col. M. J. Ellingworth and the Editors.

REMEMBER THE CLOSING DATE—DECEMBER 18th.

Birds of Prey.

By ARCHANGEL

TIME.—Anywhere between 0600 *and* 2200.
PLACE.—Somewhere in England!

WITH conspiratorial and secretive air about him first op whispers urgently to second op, then in challenging voice says that the "bloke" he's got is *theirs*, so keep off! Third op then turns round and says in sneering voice, "Oh? well, we got 'im on 'ere, see?" First op sways backwards a bit at concentrated venom contained in third ops voice, but quickly rallying, exclaims in utter amazement, "Well, blimey! we 'ad 'im when 'e first started". "Well, s'ours—and 'e's on 'ere anyway", repeats third op with stubborn tenacity, and commences writing.

First op then begins to rise from chair with determined look on face when second op suddenly goes mad and thumps him back again; at same time he juggles with some sheets in front of him and mutters something about letting them have flaming thing because he's got another. Whispered council of war is then held between first and second ops which lasts at least three seconds, then first op, as though he were delivering an ultimatum, says, "Alright then, we'll 'ave the other "bloke" who's in the same place". Tired voice of sixth op then intervenes, who says in one of those soft, goading ways that we've had it for the last half hour old man!

Following this announcement several things happen simultaneously. Second op, maddened almost beyond endurance, flings pencil on to table and says in exasperation, "Tch!" and at same time valiantly overcomes terrible impulse to hurl things about room. Meanwhile, first op, his lips being drawn back in savage, animal snarl, is noisily sucking air in between tightly clenched teeth. But at last, when able to speak coherently, he renders such fine oration about things in general, and sixth op in particular, that all those who are able pause to listen and also to memorise any words that still remain unknown to them—which are few. Exhaustion soon sets in, however, and when it does, first op declines all further interest in matter and sulks for next hour.

Thus, at end of said hour, first op changes technique. He gets up and takes sneaking looks at what ops three and four, five and six, seven and eight are doing, disdainful expression on face the whole time. Suddenly, he screams back to chair like a comet, his teeth being bared in fiendish grin and eyes alight with insane gleam, to have another little whisper with second op, who is by now thoroughly frightened and wishing he was out of it all.

Whispered conversation being over, first op starts to write; precisely thirty seconds later insidious voice of sixth op states, in no uncertain manner, that the "bloke" *he's* now got is *his!* First op then gets up with satisfied smirk on face, the very moment he's been living for having arrived, and sneers back, "Ah! see? s'ours; we got 'im 'ere old cock—so you can flaming well wrap it!"

* * * * * *

And so, at this stage, it is fitting that we leave these two gallant gentlemen to carry on; they are working once more in complete harmony. Just take a last look at them—they're like a couple of vultures gloating over their prey, and if they could crow, or cluck, or whatever it is that vultures do—they would.

In the near future some fortunate Woygite will be the recipient of a FREE PORTRAIT taken and presented by SMITH'S STUDIOS, LOUGHBOROUGH. See Poster in Canteen.

In a Manor of Spooking.

By BILL HAYWARD

DINNER was over, and the guests were grouped round the old oak-beamed fireplace, from whence flickering flames sent silent shadows leaping, spectral-like, into its furthest corners; the warm firelight gleamed on the black oaken furniture, and glinted keenly here and there, on a crystal glass, or a decanter in which nestled a rich red wine. Only the soft murmer of the wind outside, as it piled up still more snow against the buttresses, chimneys and roofs, broke the stillness of the room, for the diners could remember the times of War, not long past, when Christmas had not been a season of warmth and good cheer.

Things were different now. The friendly scented smoke of the cigars curled upwards, and gradually the voices began to give tongue. The somnolent atmosphere, the cheerful glow of the fire, and the heady warmth of the sherry all lent towards the men-folk rising, and dwelling on the most obvious topic, Ghosts! Was not this a perfect setting for a ghost story?

Time passed, while various narrators spun, invented, and related the most blood-curdling, spook stories, each striving to outdo the others, and the ladies listened in incredulous and delighted fear.

It seemed, at last, that human ingenuity was exhausted, for the talk once more stilled. On a distant landing a deep-voiced clock chimed a sonorous, remote midnight. A log in the wide fireplace tumbled forward, and broke into a cascade of sparks, sending curling flames upwards for a few moments, and revealing a figure seated in the depths of one of the oaken armchairs, which was placed so that until now it had remained hidden in the shadows.

"I think I can relate an experience stranger than any you have yet heard". The voice was clear and strong, and yet, somehow, far away.

He paused, as if awaiting permission to continue, and sensing the eagerness as the others leaned forward, he continued.

"A long time ago—most good stories seem to begin like that", he said—"a long time ago there lived in this house a man whom I shall call, for want of a better name, Grimm. He was the owner of the house, all the grounds in which it stands, and much of the land between here and the village, and beyond. He was a man of most unusual ways. Some said he was mad, others, just completely ruthless, but he most certainly could have got very little out of life other than the large quantities of gold, which came from various business concerns in London, the rents from the villagers, and from the spin of the wheels, and the turn of the cards at the tables of the many London gaming houses, at which he spent a great deal of time. He often returned in the early hours of the morning in his coach and four; a wakeful cottager might occasionally peer fearfully from the corner of his window to watch the coach, with lamps afire, and brass agleam, career through the village. As the rumble of wheels and the clatter of hooves echoed into the distance he would creep back to his meagre bed, while up at the manor house My Lord would finish his day with a quantity of wine before a huge fire, which leapt and crackled in the hearth.

"On such a night as this, and by strange chance, on a Christmas Night, Grimm returned early from his revels, very much the worse for wine, but carrying no small sum in golden sovereigns, his gaming winnings. As he entered the house and shook the snow from his cape, a clock struck the hour of midnight. Making his reeling way to this very room, where a gigantic fire burned, he seated himself at the table, and setting a glass of wine close at hand, he began to count his gold, heaping into little piles the coins that were his life-blood. In front of him on the table stood a heavy, iron-bound box, from the open lid of which gleamed more golden coins, and the glittering facets of precious stones. As the piles of coins grew he found amongst them several papers, which he cast aside with a gesture of impatience. What good were I.O.Us? He recollected that young Wellerby, whose signature

VILLAGE PUB.

By NOEL ROYLE.

Mellow lights, and smiling eyes;
Shiny noses, crumpled ties;
Low-toned confabs., loud orations;
Coarse guffaws, and lamentations;
Weathered cheeks, and painted lips;
Purple veins, and shapely hips;
Secret glances, beery singing;
Heated quarrels, push-bells ringing;
Swollen necks, heavy haunches;
Gleaming pates, drooping paunches;
Boozy spinsters, artful dodgers;
Slim young ATS and fat old codgers;
Wordy windbags, ranting liars;
Bleary grocers, sozzled squires;
Now the Doctor, deep in whiskey,
Tells a tale that's more than risky;
Though he has heard that one before,
The Verger's laughter shakes the floor.
So the Village spends its leisure,
Breathing air as thick as tar,
Drowning every woe in pleasure
With a "quick one" at the bar.

---

was on most of them, was a somewhat irresponsible young idiot, who, tonight, had lost a considerable sum, and, in trying to regain some of it, had lost even more. With the same gesture he dismissed Wellerby from his thoughts again; which was perhaps just as well.

"At that very moment Wellerby, who had ridden in frantic haste in pursuit of Grimm, with a faint hope of regaining his I.O.Us, having left his lathered horse tethered nearby, was ploughing his way through the deep snow towards the house. As he passed a lighted window, he was attracted by the sight of Grimm, once more engrossed in his avaricious pastime; so engrossed that he failed to hear the door behind him open, or see a dark figure sidle in. Wellerby's eyes were not now on the scattered papers on the floor, but were agleam with greed as he fumbled for the flint lock of his already primed pistol. The click as it snapped back echoed through the house and Grimm, drunk though he was, wheeled on the instant, and sensing rather than seeing the intruder, swung the goblet and its contents full into his face. The pistol exploded, the ball ploughed into the oak beams and Grimm was borne back as Wellerby, blinded by both wine and fear, closed with him, and fought to secure a stranglehold. For a minute neither had the advantage, but suddenly Wellerby's frantic fingers closed over a heavy table knife, and, clutching it, he raised his arm and brought it plunging down—once, twice, thrice—

"So it was that, here in this very room, Grimm died, his body slumped across the table, his gold scattered about him".

Something made one of the company lean forward, her voice suddenly dry, as she realised that the speaker was unfamiliar.

"*YOU'RE* not Grimm, are you?" she said.

"No, not Grimm, my dear. I'm Wellerby. I was hanged at Tyburn in 1783", he said, and leaning back into the shadows of the armchair, he disappeared.

BEAU-MOVIETONE FLASHES
By IVY WALTON

INACTIVITY

"I can't go on! I——can't——go——on!" Patient Pru's patience snaps with a deafening crack.

"Why? Why?" whisper a thousand thunderous voices. Glen Miller's band, off stage, strikes up with the opening bars of a famous dance-tune, whilst Pru unzipps the front of her khaki skirt revealing glorious scarlet tights, strudded with sequins, and with a sob in her voice, gives the vocal "No Morse—No Morse—No Morse."

ACTIVITY

Dawn Delicious sat idly drumming her fingers to the tune that came over the air. Her mind was far away—what could she wear to-night for dinner? Suddenly there was a stifled scream from Dithering Dulcie who sat beside her. "He's here—he's here again—LOOK!——" Dawn looked. Coming towards them was Slimy Sam the terror of the underworld. Ten guns hung from the belt around his waist, and with two in either hand, and a machine-gun dangling from his little finger in case of emergencies, he slopes up to them. As the hands of the clock reached the hour he said in a hoarse whisper,—"Well, and what's y'r action?" Dawn Delicious tossed her fair curls defiantly. "Delayed," she said. "*Very* delayed."

"EFFEMMESS"

The Killer sat with his head in his hands. Twenty minutes left. Fifteen minutes. Ten minutes. Why didn't something happen? He got up and paced the room. He wouldn't go back to that prison. He wouldn't! What could he do? He had no gun with which to end his misery. Suddenly the door burst open and in came the Police. "You're trapped, Killer," said the first one,—a small fellow with a leering grin—"Or would you prefer to bump yourself off? You would?" Turning, he whispered in the ear of the other cop behind him who went away only to return with a cup full of liquid. "This'll do it, Chief—he'll be as dead as a door-nail in thirty seconds. Closing his eyes and clasping his photo of Two-gun Sal to his breast, the Killer drank off the cup of strychnine—sometimes known as Canteen tea—whilst the Policemen took off their hats and bowed their heads. Silently they crept out as the Killer's body fell to the ground. "What'll we tell the Sup.?" said the hefty one. "Aw, we'll tell him the Killer strangled himself to death measuring dem goils!"

BREAK

"OK, cut!" yelled the "Big Cheese" taking off his eye-shade. "Take your Break." At this command, fifty or so lovelies hurried toward the swing-doors at the end of the room. Tripping out into the cloakroom, they stopped to straighten a stocking-seam or change their sarongs. Snatches of girlish conversations could be heard—"I think that new leading man—Victor What's-his-name—is too, too thrilling, don't you?"—"And when I said 'Nothing' to him, he just LOOKED—well you know!"—"And there he stood, looking all domesticated with an apron around him"—said he was quite handy round the house too—could handle a meat-waver as well as anyone. I couldn't help saying "yes" just for him.—I do get so tired of saying "no". And so with a final glance in the mirror as they passed, these beauties filed outside to meet their various escorts who were to take them in private planes, specially provided, to the Cafe de Splosh for their mid-morning break.

NIGHT DUTY

"Really, this night-duty is quite exhausting," said Blondie to her companion, Greta Goo. "I just can't think why we have to sit here night after night just to watch some silly little men who wouldn't dream of violating the Union's rules and work at night." Greta Goo looked wise and

16

took a passing glass of chocolate from the conveyor-belt which delivered hot drinks, cigarettes and chocolates continually. "You never know," she said, sipping the hot chocolate, and wiping the steam off her specs with her free hand. Blondie reached for the switch at her side, which lowered the chair on which she was sitting until it straightened out into a divan, and then pressed another switch summoning the odd-job man who sat waiting for such occasions as this. He brought a pillow and a feather eiderdown with which he gently covered Blondie, switched off the light and the radio, and crept softly sway. Blondie slept peacefully until frenzied shaking by Greta Goo brought her to consciousness. "He's up, blast his hide!"

POST-WAR PLANS.
By E. A. Hooper

(When interviewed, D.S. was obliged to admit that she really had no post-war ambitions beyond the desire to go to Thibet).

I, too, have very little inclination
For years and years of post-war education,
And yet,
I'd like to go with you by submarine to far Thibet.
Unless you think that we had better go
By something sure and slow,
Such as a camel,
Or sail in a bath-tub painted with pea-green enamel?
I'd even suggest hitch-hiking,
If that's to your liking,
But feel there's not likely to be much traffic to pass a
Couple of Ats on the way to Lhasa,
And it really would be a most dreadful pity
If we had to hoof it all the way to the Forbidden City.
And shall we go by way
Of Bombay?
Or do you think that it would better suit yer
To swim up the Brahma-Putra?
Might we get there sooner
Via Poona,
Or would it be convenient, if that was the way the trams ran,
Through Afghanistan?
Then, of course, we'll need a complete shipment
Of necessary equipment.
Clothes—one simply must wear long combs.—and a turkish
    towelling toga
When travelling to the land of Yoga,
Replacements, in case these get worn out and slightly rude,
Also food.
Also gifts—I suggest pale pink-and-lemon silk pyjamas
To give to the Lamas,
So that they will put in a good word for us, to save us being hurled
Off the Roof of the World.
This can all be conveyed overland, where the slopes are steep,
By jeep,
And in the gorges, where the road is narrow,
By wheelbarrow.
Ah me!
I see
There's a good deal of planning before the idea of this expedition
Can come to fruition.
Yet how worthwhile,
When senile,
To look back on this
And reminisce.
Or even cash in by writing some volume such as "Through Thibet
    in a Tank",
Thus fulfilling the best of post-war dreams—a hefty wad in the bank.

THE BEAUMANOR "PROMS"

An appreciation by FORBES SIBLEY, U.S. ARMY

On Thursday, October 26, listeners in the Canteen Lounge heard the first notes of a new series of concerts of recorded music, the Beaumanor Proms. The concerts, arranged and produced by Harry Dodd, are planned on the lines of the famous Albert Hall Promenade Concerts of Sir Henry Wood. In this series of programs, Woygites have an opportunity to acquaint themselves with those items of symphonic music which are most popular and most likely to be heard in programs of the big symphony orchestras. Each of the selections is introduced by Mr. Dodd with a few interesting comments concerning the life of the composer, his general musical style, and his ideas underlying the particular piece to be played.

In general, each concert centers on the work of a single well-known composer or group of associated composers, while interspersed are programs of more varied interest.

The first concert in the series included three works of Tschaikowsky, his Fourth Symphony, the Overture to "Romeo and Juliet", and the "Sleeping Beauty" waltz. The second, on November 4, was of the music of Grieg. Among the selections played were the well-known Piano Concerto in A Minor, and two movements, "Anitra's Dance", and "In the Hall of the Mountain King" from the Peer Gynt Suite. On November 13, Beethoven was the composer of the hour. The main attraction was his best known symphony, the Fifth.

The outline of programs for the future promises a series of continuing interest. The fine Czech music of Smetana and Dvorak will fill one evening. The Russian delegates, Messrs. Moussorgsky, Borodin, Rimsky-Korsakoff and Sergie Prokofieff, will demonstrate their brilliant effects at another time. The music of Mozart and Haydn will provide the material for a concert which will include, among other things, Mozart's sparkling Overture to "The Marriage of Figaro", and Haydn's lively "Clock Symphony".

A program of compositions by our allies, the English, will be highlighted by Sir Edward Elgar's "Enigma Variations". Excerpts from the "Messiah" of G. F. Handel, as well as his "Royal Water Music" will be heard during the Bach-Handel evening.

The Beaumanor Proms are planned to last just under an hour and a half, beginning at seven-thirty and ending shortly before nine. The details of each concert are set forth well in advance in a poster in the canteen. For those who are interested in hearing good music played by the finest orchestras, these performances should provide a welcome evenings entertainment.

AGE-OF-MIRACLES-DEPT.

Scene: Town Hall Signals Dance.
BOB ROBERTS: "Are you going to have a drink, Sir?"
O.C. (loftily): "No, thank you. I already have one." (Flourishes GRAPEFRUIT!)

GET YOUR———

Beauty and Toilet Preparations
FROM
"LEONARD'S"
Gentlemen's Hairdresser
25, CHURCH GATE, LOUGHBOROUGH
Large Variety in Stock!

ALARM!

By Ann Campbell

From out the quiet there rang a cry,
A loud shrill echo piercing high.
    Mouse! Mouse!

The hut, which till then quiet had been,
Resounded to a bedlam scene.
    Mouse! Mouse!

Forty women on their chairs
  With skirts above their knees,
Whispering their fervent prayers,
    "Save us from this monster please!"
    Mouse! Mouse!

No man around to hear their prayer,
Only women everywhere.
    Yelling: Mouse!

  No beastie crawling on the floor,
What then were they shouting for?
    Mouse! Mouse!

And then, amidst the plaintive cry
Our new Super. walked into "I"
    —Mouse! Mouse!

Phoney Phrases

By WILK

* *

No. 3

"*You stay up here a bit; I'll see if anything's happening downstairs*".

INTERVIEW   By "B.B."

"Good morning, Ma'am".
"Good morning. You're Jones?"
"Sackville-Jones."
"Oh! The purpose of all this is that we want to try and arrange suitable courses to fit you out for your post-war jobs. Now, what did you do before you joined up?"
"Well, I did several things. I had a job for a month counting up Insurance stamps on contribution cards, taught Shorthand-typing for two terms, worked for a while as a piano-tuner's receptionist, but I was originally trained for the Stage, in an acrobatic act. I had to do contortions with a chair and a beach-ball, but I gave it up as it might have been injurious to my. . . . ."
"Married?"
"No, single. And I had a job as a Crooner with a Dance-band for three weeks, until . . . . ."
"You can't have had any more jobs. I've filled up that space on the form. What are your intentions for after the War?"
"I haven't decided for sure, but I'll either open a wallpaper shop in Havant, or marry a Methodist minister in Stratford-on-Avon. Or I may even go to Burma with a civvy operator".
"In what capacity?"
"He says that he wants a sort of gun-moll to tote his tooth-brush and tie-press, blow the froth off his beer, and to read Sitwell to him while he . . ."
"Dependants?"
"None. And, Ma'am . . . ."
"Then I think I've found a Course for you."

* * * * *

(Pte. Sackville-Jones is to attend her first lecture next Friday—on Domestic Science).

"Kenilworth" is a hand-book for Dog-Breeders.
A Foot Rule is something to do with Dr. Scholl.

THE LANGUAGE OF LOVE

YOU can't beat the modern language of love. Oh yes, I know Shakespeare put it over pretty well——but he took lines and lines of well-balanced blank verse or poetry to do it, and you needed an extensive knowledge of ancient mythology to get the full gist of it. Besides—it would be right down unpatriotic to use a telephone long enough to get the dam' rigmarole off your chest. Keats put it quite well,—and Shelley and Byron, but oh boy! you'd need the technique of Laurence Olivier to get away with it. Tennyson was daring, of course. He wanted to be a girdle about his lady's waist—or something.

But nowadays, its childs-play—the number of early-teens out with Yanks or Italians proves that; and popular song-writers do the rest. "You" rhymes with "blue". Of course, if the beloved's eyes are brown, they probably "get you down"—or some equally simple emotion. And surely, it must be June all the year round, because it rhymes so conveniently with "Moon". And there are ever so many simple observations which would not floor the most tongue-tied of us. "This is a lovely way to spend an evening" you liltingly remark (unless of course, you're on two-to-ten, and then you're sarcastic)—and a ninepenny outlay on coffee and biscuits at the Empire Cafe will secure you the proper musical backround.

And if you want to keep sweetie-pie guessing, there's always "Mairzy Doats". AFTER ALL . . . "You may grow up to be a Pig."

VICTORY
BIGGIN STREET, LOUGHBOROUGH

MONDAY, DEC. 4th (6 Days)—
  JAMES MASON and STEWART GRANGER in
    FANNY BY GASLIGHT
  also DOUBLE THREAD and SOUTH SEA RHYTHMS

MONDAY, DEC. 11th (6 Days)
  CARY GRANT and JOHN GARFIELD in
    DESTINATION TOKYO
  also FULL SUPPORTING PROGRAMME

MONDAY, DEC. 18th (6 Days)
  OLIVIA DE HAVILAND & ROBERT CUMMINGS in
    PRINCESS O'ROURKE
  also Victor Jory in UNKNOWN GUEST

XMAS DAY, MONDAY, DEC. 25th (3 Days)
  ANN MILLER in
    HEY ROOKIE
  also Jack La Rue in YOU CAN'T BEAT THE LAW

THURSDAY, DEC. 28th (3 Days)
  LAURENCE OLIVIER and VIVIENNE LEIGH in
    LADY HAMILTON
  also VALLEY OF THE WINDRUSH

Mon. to Fri—Con. from 5-30 p.m. Sat.—Con. from 2 p.m.
MATINEES.—Mon. and Wed. at 2-15 p.m.
SUNDAYS—6-15 p.m. (One Show)

Through the Looking Glass.

APPEAL

Now that Christmas begins to loom upon the horizon, we feel it our duty and in the public interest, to express a pious hope that this year the Moguls will suppress (instead of encourage) any threatened repetition of that mass sex orgy which flamed into terrifying life within these ancient walls last year.

Quiet home girls, sitting in "J" Hut, peacefully knitting singlets for dear ones across the sea, were startled on the fateful night of December 24th, 1943, to hear the heart-chilling howls of the sex-starved human wolf-packs as they broke out from captivity in "H" and raced towards the bowers of beauty across the field. The maidens' eyes dilated; stark horror shone in their faces; they knew too well what it meant. A gallant C.S.M. threw herself against the door and thrust her arm into the bolt; but in vain, the odds were overwhelming, and ten seconds later her corpse lay crushed under the feet of the hordes who swept, with saliva drooling from their jaws, into the sanctity of the room.

Beside a recital of the events which followed, "The Confessions of Maria Monk" would read like a page from the "Temperance Gazette", and, thinking of those unsullied Scotch lassies amongst you, we will omit the details. Suffice it to say, however, that there's many a grey-haired old lady, from Kirkaldy to Oswaldtwistle, who will mourn her daughter when the Yuletide Bells ring out this year. And, anyway, we always did prefer Musical Chairs to Postman's Knock.

NARCOTIC

Whilst wishing every success to Trainer Dodd and his Culture Conscious Cuties in their first season of "Proms", we would, if they will listen to the advice of a sad old man, whisper a few words of good counsel into the ears of the promoters before they (unwittingly) do any serious harm.

There are three pieces of orchestral sugar on which it is anti-social to feed A.T.S. girls. They are: Vaughan Williams' "Greensleeves" Fantasy (dangerous); Tchaikovsky's "B Flat Piano Concerto" (highly dangerous) and Addinsell's "Warsaw Concerto" (often fatal). On hearing these creations, music-minded maidens first give a squeal of ecstatic delight, and then start skipping round the room, twittering like anything; next, they break out in a rash of blue spots (musical measles); and finally, unless the source of infection is removed, they pass into a delirious coma, continuously muttering: "Oh, Anton Walbrook, where art thou"? or "Come and take me, Mr. Pagannini, I'm yours!"

Therefore, when, in future, as they assuredly will, winsome Ats with far-away looks on their faces plead with you to include any of the above in your programme, please, for the public good, and your social conscience, don't do it—no matter how hard it may be to resist the appeal in those large, blue, expressive eyes.

OMISSION

That circular congratulating the Staff on its performance a month ago, although mentioning everyone else, failed, for some reason, to commend (a) The cleaners, without whose efforts in combating dirt and disease we might have all caught leprosy and died; (b) The Canteen Staff, whose herculean services kept us well supplied with the essential sustenance of tea, coffee and cheese rolls during the period of stress; and (c) The men at the gate, whose devoted vigilance and opening (or closing) of the entrance alone made it possible for us to get into the Dump.

THOUGHT FOR TO-DAY

"Nothing is finally true until it has been officially denied".—Bismarck.

LEON DE BUNK.

Bookseller and Stationer :: Lending Library

J. SKETCHLEY
24 & 25, High Street, Loughborough
Telephone 2980.

The Digby Chronicles.

It's fatal when strangers interfere with one's children, don't you think? We were at the Pantomime, and a stalwart young lady in skin-tight pink stockinette was contorting strenuously before a back-cloth, while sundry thuds behind indicated that the Transformation Scene was in the process of construction. Suddenly Judy raised her voice.

"Mummy", she shrilled, "that lady hasn't got anything on"! And she chuckled with uninhibited delight at the notion. The two old spinsters sitting behind us were shocked.

"What an indecent idea for a child" they fluttered. And gave me a dirty look. Judy has sharp ears, and my heart sank as I watched her lips form the word a few times as she committed it to memory.

She was silent all the way home, and as luck would have it, Steve was at the gate talking to the Vicar—whose own children were not permitted the worldly delights of the Pantomime. Judy charged forward and clutched Steve lovingly round the knees.

"Well, Judy", he asked her. "What did you see"?

Judy's eyes doubled their size. "Daddy", she breathed reverently, "I've seen an INDECENT LADY"! .... It's fatal when strangers interfere with one's children, don't you think?

K.L.B.P.

CORRESPONDENCE.

To Editor of B.S.M.

Tolerance and thoughtfulness are two good virtues, but very hard to acquire. In little things, however, tolerance should be easy to exercise.

Sad to say, some people who frequent the Canteen are sadly lacking in it.

A short time ago, a swing programme was being appreciated by several ATS—who, being young and vital—enjoy these lively tunes. In the middle of one favourite, a Gentleman (? ? ?) rushed to the radio and, without further ado, switched off. I don't blame this personage for disliking such "Music". His taste probably lies somewhere in the higher regions, but if he is an admirer of Grieg, it still doesn't give him the priority for use of the wireless set.

If said set was blaring rather loudly we should have understood if he had decreased volume a bit, but we deplored his other action.

(Ptes.) PEGGY DOHERTY, PEGGIE MORGAN, PEGGY EVANS, ALICE COOKE, LYNDA COURTNAGE.

FAMOUS LAST WORDS

"I know he's married. So what? We're platonic".

EMPIRE
MARKET PLACE, LOUGHBOROUGH

MONDAY, DEC. 4th (3 Days)
ERROL FLYNN in
THE CHARGE OF THE LIGHT BRIGADE
also FULL SUPPORTING PROGRAMME

THURSDAY, DEC. 7th (3 Days)
RANDOLPH SCOTT in
GUNG HO
also Donald Woods in SO'S YOUR UNCLE

MONDAY, DEC. 11th (3 Days)
MICKEY ROONEY and BONITA GRANVILLE in
ANDY HARDY'S BLONDE TROUBLE
also REPORT FROM THE ALEUTIANS (Tech.)

THURSDAY, DEC. 14th (3 Days)
ABBOTT and COSTELLO in
HOLD THAT GHOST
also Jerome Cowan in CRIME BY NIGHT

MONDAY, DEC. 18th (3 Days)
MAE WEST and VICTOR MOORE in
TROPICANA
also Sidney Toler in THE CHINESE CAT

THURSDAY, DEC. 21st (3 Days)
EDDIE QUILLAN in
MELODY PARADE
also Lon Chaney in WEIRD WOMAN

XMAS DAY, MONDAY, DEC. 25th (3 Days)
TOM NEAL and BRUCE BENNETT in
SOMETHING ABOUT A SOLDIER
also J. Mack Brown in LONE STAR TRAIL

THURSDAY, DEC. 28th (3 Days)
ERROL FLYNN and BASIL RATHBONE in
THE ADVENTURES OF ROBIN HOOD
(in Technicolour)
also FULL SUPPORTING PROGRAMME

**CONTINUOUS DAILY. Doors open at 1-30 p.m.
SUNDAYS at 5-30 p.m.**

Printed by Toppings Ltd., 17, Southfield Rd., Loughborough, and published by L. P. Jones for Beaumanor Staff Magazine Committee.

JANUARY, 1945

VOL. I. No. 11 (NEW SERIES) - 6d.

FILM ATTRACTIONS for JANUARY

SHOWING AT THE ODEON THEATRE

Sunday, Dec. 31st—Rosalind Russell and Brian Aherne in '**My Sister Eileen**'. Also Frank Alberton in '**Attorney for the Defence**'.

MONDAY, JAN. 1st, and all the week—
JENNIFER JONES, the Academy Award Winner, in Franz Werfel's
THE SONG OF BERNADETTE
You should see this Film from the start at 1-45, 4-45, 7-45.

Sunday, Jan. 7th—Wayne Morris and Jane Wyman in '**Bad Men from Missouri**'. Also Ricardo Cortez in '**Talk of the Devil**'.

MONDAY, JAN. 8th, for 3 days Ray Milland and Barbara Britton in **Till We Meet Again** Also Bob Hope and Shirley Ross in **Thanks for the Memory.**	**THURS., Jan. 11th, for 3 days** Dick Powell and Linda Darnell in **It Happened To-morrow** Also Tyrone Power and Alice Faye in **In Old Chicago.**

Sunday, Jan. 14th—James Cagney and Evelyn Daw in '**Something to Sing About**'. Also Bela Lugosi in '**Ghosts in the Night**'.

MONDAY, JAN. 15th, and all the week—
Margaret Lockwood and Stewart Granger in
LOVE STORY
with Tom Walls and Patricia Rock. This Film introduces 'The Cornish Rhapsody' played by the National Symphony Orchestra.

Sunday, Jan. 21st—John Clements and Leslie Banks in '**Ships with Wings**'. Also Slim Summerville in '**Niagara Falls**'.

MONDAY, JAN. 22nd, and all the week—

Richard Greene, Patricia Medina and Alfred Drayton in **Don't Take It To Heart**	A L S O	Donald O'Connor, Susanna Foster and Peggy Ryan in **This Is The Life**

Sunday, Jan. 28th—George Sanders and Marguerite Chapman in '**Appointment in Berlin**'. Also Lupe Velez in '**Redhead from Manhattan**'.

MONDAY, JAN. 29th, for 3 days Lionel Barrymore & Van Johnson in **Three Men in White** Also Jessie Mathews and John Stuart in **Candles at Nine.**	**THURS., FEB. 1st, for 3 days** Robert Watson in **The Hitler Gang** Claudette Colbert and Melvyn Douglas in **I Met Him in Paris.**

Continuous Performance Daily 1-45 p.m.   Sunday, One Performance at 6 p.m.

B.S.M.

Vol. I. No. 11 (New Series)
JANUARY, 1945.

Managing Editor: LEONARD P. JONES.

Editors: KAY PRICE, ERIC C. MILLHOUSE   Treasurer: A. H. APPLETON.

GOOD READING

You may blush - but this writer's good says Ralph Champion

"IT all depends what you mean by a good book!! That sounds like Professor Joad, but I've never yet discovered a true definition, so I raise the point.

I usually classify a book as "good" if I can remember it well. Bad books are legion, so let me tell you about a few of the better ones—some new, some old, but all to be found in local libraries.

First, let me introduce James Cain, the American writer, who adapted the modern, tough style to create a new art. I remember him first for "THE POSTMAN ALWAYS RINGS TWICE", a story which in comparison makes "NO ORCHIDS FOR MISS BLANDISH" seem like a Sunday School prize. Yet he redeems the sordid theme by brilliant description and economy of words. Slightly purged, the book was serialized in the *Daily Express* a few years ago.

Cain followed with "SERENADE", a love story of a type not mentioned in polite circles. In this he established himself as a master of the New English. Famous critics raved about it. For once, they were right. Cain could say more in two words than others could in twenty. His scenes were so tender that readers fought their tears; yet, his phrases were brutal, his words, coarse.

Where Cain used the pick and shovel to create his work of art, Charles Morgan etched his greatest novel, "THE VOYAGE", with the most delicate tools. His story is gripping, his prose is poetry. Each word pleases, which is all the more surprising when you recall that Morgan earns his living as a civil servant.

By accident I obtained "STATELY TIMBER", by Rupert Hughes. It's similar in style to "THE SUN IS MY UNDOING", and equally good. I had not read this author before, but that was my loss.

Howard Spring, the ex-Cardiff journalist-turned-author, is well known to most of you. I have just completed his latest, "HARD FACTS". Despite unreal characters and novelette situations, it's just worth reading if you cannot find a title for your book list. "FAME IS THE SPUR", his best novel, has my whole-hearted "five star" rating. It deals with a young socialist who progressed from early sincerity and consequent obscurity to success, via cynicism and hypocrisy.

My "Y" group left-wing friends who try to convert me to their ideas might heed the object lesson. "FAME IS THE SPUR" tells such a familiar Labour Party story.

Next issue ready February 2nd.   Contributions to reach Editors by Jan. 20th.

Poor Old Britain

(An appreciation of the Government's action with regard to the Greek situation, December, 1944.)

Poor old Britain
Churchill's phrase
Echo not sorrow
Her's are great days;
This little Island
Bred the stock
That accepted the challenge
Took the shock
Halted the evil
That threatened to spread
O'er all the earth
Democracy's dead!
Dead, if we stand by
And watch people fight
For power that's gained
By force, not by Right;
Even when this
Is Nationally internal
It's still just as rotten
Nay, more infernal;
So, when "friends" condemn
And enemies jeer,
Let the whole British people
Stand up and cheer
For the Government
And for the man with the sight
And the faith and the courage
To still fight for what's RIGHT.
"FREELANCE."

MAXIM

At books I was never proficient,
  But one thing I learnt in the schools,
A word to the wise is sufficient,
  But it's useless to argue with fools.

CHOLMONDELY.

CO-OPERATION

With apologies to G. M. Spooner.

The future of the Canteen curiosity arouses,
The air completely purple with Co-operative grouses,
And all the floor is littered with—it should be understood,
Co-operative fag-ends and Co-operative food.
The counter neatly garnished with Co-operative wares
And Co-operative beverages disfiguring the chairs.
Anæmic-looking "EWAS", with many an inward fear—
Endeavouring to swallow weird Co-operative beer;
Co-operative assistants, nicely settled in their nests—
Indulging in the usual Co-operative "rests"—
Perhaps this is the reason—it seems quite clear to me,
Why Mr. Antrum never buys Co-operative tea!

J. M. E.

SEVEN OF THEM

THERE were seven of them. The first was a young officer, resplendent in his immaculate uniform, his buttons polished almost beyond the pitch of perfection and his clean shaven face glistening in the sunshine. Every part of him seemed perfect: clearly he was one to whom the good things of life had come easily and he had never known hunger, thirst and "starvation wages". He was a man born to command, and who would not wish to be commanded by so handsome and attractive a creature?

The man on his immediate left presented a striking, almost a shocking contrast. Here was a ragged, dirty peasant, a tramp, a vagabond, and an outcast of society. His straggly beard and hair were matted with filth, his face was covered with sores, his shirt had been on his body for so long that it would take, so it seemed, brute force to remove it. His body itself seemed mis-shapen and deformed: certainly he could neither read nor write, and his mind must have been as crooked, as stunted and as ugly as his body.

Not far from this grotesque figure, a young girl was to be seen. Attractive in a superficial way, her appearance was spoilt by a too-heavy appliance of cosmetics, but under cover of this camouflage it was possible to discern the makings of a pretty face. Her attire and her general appearance gave an easy clue to her character—coquettish, quick tempered, vain, just a little too fond of the society of the opposite sex—a "good-time" girl.

The corpulent gentleman to be seen on her left was clearly a business man, and a successful one too, judging by his air of prosperity. Doubtless he had worked his way up from the drudgery of office boy to the exaltation of company director. It was not difficult to imagine him gambling with fortunes, and perhaps with lives as well, and although his continued success had made him just a little cruelly self-satisfied, who was to blame him? This is a harsh world: "Every man to himself" is our slogan.

Very close to this gentleman was a middle-aged woman who might well have been his wife. There was nothing out of the ordinary about her: her clothes, her plump cheeks, her greying hair, all spoke of the housewife whose thoughts do not wander far away from the eternal problems of domesticity. Narrow-minded and unattractive in personality as she and others like her might be, the world would be a poorer place without her.

A space between this woman and the sixth person, who appeared to be an artist, or perhaps a musician or a poet. His clothes appeared hopelessly ill-cut, his hair was long and billowy, his beard seemed unable to make up its mind which way to turn. Here was one with that indefinable impression of eccentric genius: probably he had a cascade of initials after his name, and, of course, he was certainly regarded as a crank by his friends.

The last figure in the group was a small boy of perhaps six years. Chubby cheeks, curly hair, and clothes that were far too small for him gave him the appearance of a mischievous cherub. He would steal your fruit from under your eyes and yet you would find it easy to forgive him.

Those were the seven. Seven twisted and broken corpses lying in the ruins of the building where they had been sheltering from the air raid. Seven who would see the light of day no more. Seven victims of the wrath of an unknown and an unseen enemy. This scene may have been enacted in any or all of the countries at war, where sudden and violent death is never far away. Those seven characters may have been Englishmen, Americans, Russians, Chinese, Japanese, or Germans. Who can tell?

An eighth character has appeared—a casual observer. "A war to save civilization," he muses. "These, then, must have been some of the forces that would destroy civilization. How strange!"

J. C. M. B.

Theatre Royal
LOUGHBOROUGH.

Programmes for January 1945

FRANK H. FORTESCUE

PRESENTS

Monday, Jan. 1st, for 6 days
A CHARMING PLAY—
LITTLE WOMEN
By LOUISE ALLCOTT

Monday, Jan. 8th, for 6 days
A GREAT THRILLER!
SUSPECT
By Edward Percy

Monday, Jan. 15th, for 6 days
Gordon Harker's Big Success
ACACIA AVENUE
FIRST RELEASE FOR REP.

Monday, Jan. 22nd, for 6 days
A BEAUTIFUL PLAY
TO HAVE AND TO HOLD
By LIONEL BROWN

Monday, Jan. 29th, for 6 days
A GREAT COMEDY
SLEEPING OUT
By W. W. ELLIS

FILM FLASHES

By JANET FOURDRINIER.

THE films this month start the New Year off well from the Box Office point of view, offering a wide selection for you cinema-goers. Well worth seeing are "PHANTOM LADY" and "ROSE MARIE" (Empire); "SONG OF BERNADETTE" (Odeon); "A GUY NAMED JOE", and, for those of you who enjoy the macabre, "MURDER IN THORNTON SQUARE" (Victory).

Other films include:—

JANUARY 14th (for 6 days)—"LOVE STORY" (Odeon). This is the story of a romance between an airman, who is going blind, and a famous pianist, whose doctor has given her only a short time to live. The plot is based on the fact that neither the man (Stewart Granger) nor the woman (Margaret Lockwood) tell each other of the fate which is hanging over them. High spot of the picture is the performance of a piano concerto called "Cornish Rhapsody", supposed to be written by the heroine. This faintly resembles the Warsaw Concerto, but it is nevertheless an effective composition.

FOOTNOTE.—Watch Patricia Roe's performance in this film. She is excellent as the selfish actress who is "out" to marry the airman.

JANUARY 22nd (for 6 days)—"DON'T TAKE IT TO HEART" (Odeon). This is a really good British film and you shouldn't miss it. The story deals with the feud between the villagers and a wealthy "gentleman" who has rented the dower house from the Lord of the Manor, Lord Chaunduyt. Richard Greene plays the part of the young man who falls in love with the lord's daughter, played by Patricia Medina (incidentally, these two are husband and wife in real life), and he takes the side of the villagers with amusing results all round. This picture is, I think, one of the best that has come from a British studio of late.

JANUARY 22nd (for 6 days)—"COVER GIRL" (Victory). Well, here is the film, starring Rita Hayworth and Gene Kelly, which according to Mr. Lew Owen, is far above the standard of "Pin Up Girl". Those of you who dislike Betty Grable's films will no doubt agree. For myself, I can only say that I thoroughly enjoyed both. The story of "Cover Girl" is unimportant, but for pure escapism it ranks high. And the dances, dresses and set designs look extravagantly gorgeous in heavenly Hollywood Technicolour!

JANUARY 22nd (for 6 days)—"CHAMPAGNE CHARLIE" (Empire). This has been a widely-published film, and rightly so, I think, as it is one of the best musical comedies that we have made in this country to date. The story shows the rivalry between George Leybourne (played by Tommy Trinder) top of the bill at Bessie Bellwood's music hall, and the great Vance (played by Stanley Holloway) the star of Gatti's in the 'Sixties. The acting is good, and the period atmosphere well sustained.

FOOTNOTE.—Some of the scenes are too long drawn out, and the side issue of the romance of Peter de Greef as the young man who falls in love with Bessie Bellwood's daughter will most likely bore you. However, on the whole I think you'll enjoy this picture (if you like Tommy Trinder, of course).

Shakespeare re-potted

Hamlet: "A lass. Poor Yorick—
I knew him well."

E. W. J. S.

SAYS BILL HAYWARD.

IN wishing everyone a Happy New Year, I hope you all made the most of the Christmas Season, which, according to general opinion was far more successful than last year's. So to those people who helped to make this possible—thanks a lot.

Congratulations commence this month with one to "Jimmie", who went sick with laryngitis a few days before Christmas, which is the reason for his absence from this column.

Our old friend, "Wilkie", had a bumper Christmas box in the shape of a bouncing boy over nine pounds. Nice work, Mrs. Dick.

"Bungy" Williamson, as foreshadowed last month, has bitten the dust, and the "Bull-ring" is now non-existent. He has become engaged to Joan Price, who hails from Room 61.

A *signal* event took place in Scotland on December 29th, when Jean Coates, of Brand Hill, married James Taylor, of the Royal Signals. The bride wore one of Mrs. Roosevelt's A.T.S. "lend-lease" wedding dresses.

On Christmas Day Kay Metcalfe told me that she is to be posted to Shenley in the New Year, and while regretting her departure, here's wishing her the best of luck.

A one-man human wolf pack, in the shape of "Smiler" Smith was doing his best to emulate the best traditions of the scene from "Thro' the Looking Glass" this Yuletide, when the gallant company of girls in I hut valiantly beat off the attack, and forcibly ejected him into the cold, outside. "Smiler" still cannot believe it really happened.

To those unfortunates who left us for a period of outstation duty at a time when the Christmas festivities were fast approaching, we offer our condolences, and hope that their season of Goodwill was not too bleak.

Whilst on the subject:—Stan. Saunders received a bogus note in connection with the above, telling him *he* had been selected to go. He swallowed it, hook, line and sinker, and had gone as far as to arrange a farewell binge before he was told it was all a gag. So if you want to know what relief is—*don't* ask Stan.

Vera Adams, who has been absent from our midst for quite a while, has returned. Hard luck, but welcome back, Vera.

A successful operation for appendicitis on Alec Berry, at Leicester, recently, means that he'll soon be back with us, so we wish him a speedy return to duty, and to the "Pear Tree". More room inside now, Alec.

"The youngest qualified referee in Leicestershire" is the claim made by Harry Bartlett, now that he has passed his "exam.".

FINANCIAL SECTION.

At the Royal Signals Dance at the Town Hall on November 21st, a double tooth, newly extracted from the jaw of Sub. I. Romer, was on display, under the auspices of C.S.M's. Reeves and Rostron, at "1d. per look". The profits, amounting to 2/1½, are being held in abeyance, in anticipation of a further attack of toothache in other quarters, with a view to increasing the total, before forwarding it to the Red Cross.

If you see a long line of Rolls Royces pull up at "H" Hut in the near future, you'll know that the football pool millionaires are reporting for duty.

One of these gentlemen, Charlie (Bank Balance) Dobson, won £80, and as he has been established, and is also the new Chairman of the Staff Club, we hear that he is seriously considering getting married. Time marches on!

Just previous to Christmas the girls of "C" Watch, Brand Hill, went carol singing, and collected from the "night life" of Woodhouse Eaves the sum of £7 10s. 0d. If they'd had time to call at the *private* houses as well, they might have doubled this.

Much interest has been aroused by the erection of the new fan in "H". The little door in the side of the "Box" has become the object of much speculation, but between you and me, I have it on very good authority, that the assistant supers., now that the supers. have a boudoir, have agitated for, and finally got a roost.

Mirth provoking was the scene in "H" when Barbara Woodman and Ann Childs 'phoned up recently to ask if anyone would lend them a pair of red and white striped pyjamas. Finally, John Godfrey volunteered. We wonder why on the night in question they failed to materialise. They were required for the "dramatics" put on at Garats Hey on December 18th.

Scene: "H" Hut.
Time: The wee sma' hours.

The Chief Racketeer stands with his "tommy" gun ready loaded, "Butch" Kelly by his side.

"Get der goils outta here," he snarls.

"O.K., borss," snarls back Kelly, and opens the door. "Youse dames beat it."

The "molls" exit.

"O.K. Now frisk this mob," indicating the cowering victims lined up against the wall.

Slowly "Butch" makes his way down the line, searching everyone.

"No sign of it anywhere. What do we do now, borss?"

The Chief Racketeer grits his teeth in an even broader snarl:

"PLUG the lot of them," he roars.

CURTAIN.

On Christmas night I watched with interest, as Jimmy Hunter signed his autograph on an A.T.S. girl's thigh. On looking again, however, I realised the "girl" was none other than "Bob" Roberts, done up in a natty line of khaki, with "make up" to match.

Romance came to the occupants of Room 96, Brand Hill, the other day, when, in a roll of "Government Property" they found a note, purporting to come from a "tall, dark, handsome man, aged 21" who would "be glad if any A.T.S., WREN, or W.A.A.F. would write to him". While wondering if anyone has taken advantage of this offer out of the—er —blue, we *have* noted a lot of happy faces about——or is it Xmas?

The mice, lately, all go to No. 2 Hut, Garats Hey, for, while all the other huts get plain cheese, No. 2 gets welsh rarebit.

RECIPE FOR WARMTH.

Take 2 pairs of trousers, 2 pullovers, 2 pairs of gloves, 2 raincoats, and a thick cap, and into these put Mr. John Dodd. You've got a cold, cold man on your hands, Kay.

Altho' we like to stay clear of politics as much as possible, we cannot help but wonder from whence came the rumours that those rabid, Left Wing extremists, Royle and Truin, who sent a strongly worded telegram of protest to Churchill on the Greek crisis, have since been offered lucrative posts in the Foreign Office to keep them quiet.

(continued on page 23)

TRAVELLING COMPANION

By ERIC W. DOBSON.

SHE stood beside me in the cramped, swaying train corridor; quite an ordinary sort of woman—no longer young, and appearing a little drab and bedraggled. Her one noticeable feature was her expression. Never have I seen such happiness as that which showed in her eyes and lit up her features.

Standing there gazing into the passing panorama of fields and villages, dressed in a grey tweed costume and clutching a bunch of wilting violets, she was dreaming a rhapsody that illuminated her face and brought her a strange aura of beauty.

In these days of crowded, uncomfortable travel, when the rigid etiquette of facing one's fellow travellers with a stony glare or complete indifference has relaxed, and folk have become more companionable, I felt I could risk a snub and satisfy my insatiable curiosity by the ever easy approach of the proffered cigarette.

My offer was accepted with a slow smile and low spoken thanks, and soon we were discussing general subjects. I brought to notice her violets.

"These violets," she said, "are not only flowers: they are the outward sign of an inward memory which will live with me all my life." She hesitated, but, seeing I was interested, she, being obviously in need of a confidant, gradually unfolded her story.

It began twelve years ago in a commonplace way with her wedding. Then followed a few months of bliss that gradually changed to unhappiness and misery. The usual tale of a husband's drinking, his neglect and his infidelity. It went on for years, until her two children were growing and of school age, and then, one day, HE came to the door.

What matter that he was just a baker's roundsman? What matter that she was just a customer on a new round? Between them they struck a spark that smouldered slowly for months, confining itself to mutual pleasure in meeting, at happiness in glances. It was inevitable that the reciprocation should grow into something more tangible, and there came a day when the spark blew itself to a red glow, which developed into a white heat.

They began to meet clandestinely—for she would never risk her children's keen eyes—and they would sit in a cafe talking, learning each other's ways, he hearing, bit by bit, her unhappiness at home, of her brutal beatings by her drunken husband, of her continual struggle to clothe and feed herself and her children on the pittance left after drinking bouts. Together they planned a brief journey into a heaven of their own, and the opportunity arose when the husband said he was going away for a week-end. In fear and trembling—for she was at heart frightened of unfaithfulness—she agreed to send her children to her mother and spend the week-end with her lover.

"It has been really lovely," she said. "He took me to a quiet country inn where we were both happy and content for a while. I lay there at sunrise, hearing the birds and the cattle, and vowed that this memory should be the background of my thoughts always. He was so kind, gentle and considerate. When we rose we walked through the woods, and I picked these violets. Already they are dying, but I'll press them in my old Bible and there they will always be—a breath of heaven in a life of hell."

Her bitterness and rapture mingled strangely. I could see the conflicting emotions flitting across her face, and I thought that surely she deserved her small glimpse into happiness; that no one, knowing her story, would say she'd been wicked to snatch at the seemingly impossible. No one, at least, could deny the happiness that shone so clearly through her troubled eyes.

It so happened that she left the train at my destination, and I bade her adieu, and went to my hotel where, after a bath and a meal, I endeavoured to catch up with my rest, and retired until about seven o'clock.

When I went into the dining room, I sensed an undercurrent of excitement. Seeing my inquiring glances, a waiter approached, carrying an evening paper. Confidentially he whispered: "Have you heard about our local murder, sir? A chap who often comes in here has given himself up after killing his wife". He waxed indignant. "The hussie; she was apparently in the habit of going off with her lover when her husband was away, but was caught red-handed this week-end, when her husband cancelled his trip. She deserved all she got, the unfaithful hussie."

He showed me the paper, and there, beneath glaring headlines was a photograph of my travelling companion.

SPORTOPICS

HOCKEY.

Despite appalling weather conditions since the start of the Hockey season, not one fixture has been cancelled. Men and "Mixed" teams alike have played well in gales, rain, hail and "slosh", and have been very unfortunate in losing five of the eight matches played to date.

Two mixed games were lost at Sutton Bonington against Midland Agricultural College, scores being 4—2 and 5—2. As yet we haven't managed to score over the "Brush", losing two mixed matches 4—2 and 2—1, and losing against the men's team 4—2.

A fast game against R.A.P.C., Leicester, resulted in a draw, 2—2, as did our game with Quorn, score 4—4.

Our one and only win was against R.A.F. at Leicester, 2—1, but I hope it won't be our last.

G. A. L.

FOOTBALL.

The match between Officers, Supervisors and Sergeants (Reds) v. The Rest (Blues) provided the spectators with an interesting match. The Reds' defence was strong and Blues had difficulty in getting near goal. The appearance of Ollie Pearce in goal caused many humorous comments, but Ollie made some good saves. Both sides attacked, but the Reds had a deserved lead of 2—0 at half-time, scored by Capt. Donaldson and (?). In the second half Blues combined better and had more of the play. Lowes hit the post with a good shot, and F. Pearce and Sigmn. Baker scored two good goals for Blues. M. Musgrave scored for Reds, and the issue was in doubt right to the end. The final score: Reds 3, Blues 2.

The match was refereed by H. Bartlett, who has just got his referee's certificate. I am told he is the youngest referee in the County.

I have been asked to get more outside fixtures, but recently a fixture had to be cancelled as I did not get one name!!

TABLE TENNIS.

The League Competition is now in full swing. Although playing on an improvised table, many exciting games have been played. The leading position is now held by A.R.13, who have played and won three matches. Second, J. Godfrey's team.

A. H. APPLETON,
Sports Secretary.

OUR DUMB BLONDE SAYS:—

The Beveridge Plan is a new Tariff for Soda Fountains.

French leave is granted to our troops on the Continent.

'ENGLAND EXPECTS' - OR 'JUST PLAIN PHOOEY'
By EDITH TURNER.

ALL her life Agnes Mildew had longed to do something fine, something noble, fired with patriotism—and, er, sacrificial (to a certain extent).

For a whole year the war had been waging "over there", and now, in this year of 1915, having completed 24 pullovers, 6 Balaclava helmets, not to mention the pairs of socks and kilt-linings for the "ladies of hell", Aggie had finally come to the decision that something more than mere bolstering-up of the morale of the Forces with these natty knittings was required of her. Accordingly she took the plunge and filled in the dotted line which was to initiate her into the eventful life of a member of the W.A.A.C.'s.

So it was, that on a chilly morning in late autumn, little Aggie emerged from the sacred precincts of the Q.M. stores arrayed in a manner which suggested her visit had not been one of great success. Her hat, for instance—a perfect fright! Bitterly she reflected on the lovely blue of the hat she had worn when she first set foot inside the barracks. Oh! that hat—with its tumbling cherries and rasp—I mean bananas—in gay profusion on the crown. Reflection, however, was all that was left to her—it was rather late now to regret she had intended to feel sacrificial. Of course, it wouldn't have been so bad if her "combs." hadn't been so tight—they were apt to restrict in the wrong places—and her camisole—the last word in bulkiness! In fact, she had to admit she presented a glorious spectacle.

Life could be extraordinarily difficult at times—it wasn't HER fault she missed parade. The corporal could surely have been a little more understanding when she explained that she hadn't been able to get her stays laced tightly enough to permit her to don her "issue" skirt. Then there was marching. After all, such caustic comments about "two left feet" injured her feelings so. It wasn't natural for a woman to march, but these grim perpetrators of army routine were soul-less—that was evident. As she sat in the mess in company with the eleven other girls on her table, her thoughts strayed to the quiet little homestead with its antimacassars and aspidistras, and the china dogs on the mantelshelf, where her parents would be partaking their lunch at the familiar mahogany table. How lost they would seem in the vastness of——an indignant voice at her side recalled harsh reality: "If you're so fond of Hamburger roll you might at least ask permission to eat off my plate! Mind your elbow—I'm going to lift my mug".

Swedish drill was another fly in the ointment. This violent exercise, alas! cost her an issue suspender and her two-plain two-purl stockings slipped and revealed a nifty ankle—to her profound embarrassment.

However, all good things come to an end, and so luckily, do the bad ones, and eventually came the longed-for day of her first "posting". She had longed to see the world, and here the path of opportunity lay stretched before her (or so she thought). She landed "somewhere in England" (it sounds more mysterious like that) and there, after prolonged and nerve-racking experience, the intricacies of a crystal set (the secret weapon of the last war???) were made known to her. Shortly afterwards she entered the portals of what has been described as "the promised land" (and other names I could mention), and there, if not seeing the world she was at least coming into contact with it. The place had its pleasantries, too. Quite early in her new surroundings she had experienced painful heart-throbs at the mere approach of a certain handsome supervisor. Quite positively, she thought, she had never seen so magnificent a specimen before. It wasn't long before they were arranging their "breaks" together, and there in the canteen, as she gazed at him over her plate of chips and sipped her cup of "char", girlish delight sprang up in her eager young breast and shone from her lovely brown eyes. Of course, this intrigued him immensely—to put it vulgarly, it "warmed the cockles of 'is 'eart" and he forthwith popped the question: "Would she like to accompany him to the gripping film showing this month at the new Picture Palace in town—the 'Victory' ?" (rather prematurely named, but none the less imposing).

The night arrived, and as the attendant showed them into one of the ultra-modern double seats, little Aggie was spellbound at the sight of the magnetic features of Rudolph Valentino gazing soulfully from the silver screen. (Admittedly, it was rather indistinct to be termed "silver"—but who cared if the management did not use "Persil" ?) His compelling smile outshone everything! ! The effect on Aggie had been somewhat devastating for she sat heavily on the floor, not having noticed that the seat was of the tip-up variety (very new). Blushes of mortification! !

After this unfortunate episode poor Aggie felt their relationship was growing extremely casual, and attributed it to her lack of technique—she was a guileless child! How was she to know that the handsome supervisor lived in mortal dread that any little indiscretions on his part would be pounced upon by the local "Snoop" and aired in the Staff Magazine? Their visit to the "movies" had rather savoured of suitable "gen" for the pen of this ogre, and he feared similar mishaps were likely to occur.

It was just about this time when her poor heart was torn and bleeding, that Aggie succumbed to a "coed on de chest". Having been delicately nurtured, the frequent journeys in a draughty army truck proved too much (much too much too much) and so little Aggie had to resort to thermogene. It was whilst sitting on their little wooden beds in their natty little army pyjamas discussing the usual subject (guess what?) that the tragedy occurred. Some of her room-mates were ultra-modern minded, and indulged in the art of smoking (Woodbines). Poor little Aggie—fate it seemed had marked her out from the start to perish in a blaze of glory (well, a blaze at any rate) and the "fag-end" carelessly flung in the direction of her bosom set fire to the "thermogene". And so she died, poor patriot, in her country's hour of need—the need to supply these brazen smokers with "issue" ash-trays! !

B.S.M. FILM COMPETITION

The correct placings were :—

	Odeon	Victory	Empire
1.	This Happy Breed.	Gone With the Wind.	Lassie Come Home.
2.	Jane Eyre.	This is the Army.	Hers to Hold.
3.	Stage Door Canteen.	The Sullivans.	Crash Dive.
4.	His Butler's Sister.	Now Voyager.	The Four Feathers.

The possible number of points was 30.
Here are the Prizewinners :—

1st. L. RICHARDSON, T.P., 17 points.
2nd A. D. TARR, "K" Hut, 16 points.
3rd G. WICKS, "H" Hut, 14 points.
4th J. COATES, "K" Hut, and D. SWALE, Room 61, 13 points each.
5th M. HOUSTON, Harrogate, L. SARRE, "J" Hut, and R. DOWNER, "H" Hut, 12 points each.

WINNERS OF THE B.S.M. RAFFLE

1st Pte. FOOT, "I" Hut.
2nd Pte. WEBSTER, "J" Hut.
3rd Pte. BURNS, "K" Hut.
4th Signalman ETHERINGTON, "House."
Consolation Prizes, JOHN GODFREY, "H" Hut, and Pte. M. DIXON, Runner.

THE TRAGIC TALE OF AGGY GUPP
By DUC

Aggy Annabella Gupp was very fond of dressing up;
She bought a new dress every day
And promptly threw the old away,
Till, being so extravagant,
She'd very soon her coupons spent.
Then came the day when Willie Fall
Invited Aggy to a ball,
And she was filled with eagerness,
When Willie said "It's fancy dress".
She raced home for her coupon book,
But gave each page a doleful look;
The reason was quite plain to see,
She'd used the lot—except for three:
No coupons for a fancy dress!
Poor Agatha was in a mess
She sat and wept in her dismay,
She sat and wept the live long day,
But suddenly she thought that she
With fine originality,
Could make herself a fancy dress,
In spite of being couponless.

Next morning at the draper's shop,
Her eyes again began to pop,
For on the counter, gently laid,
A notice to the world displayed
That she could buy with her three pledges
Six handkerchiefs with frilly edges;
And these our Annabella brought
Selecting from the larger sort.

At home, before a mirror, she
Regarded her anatomy,
And with most violent contortions,
Contrived to cover vital portions,
Remembering to keep a frieze
About the level of her knees;
Till finally she chose a fashion
Designed to raise the lowest passion.
Then after dark she ventured out,
(When dogs and Woygites weren't about)
And meeting boy friend Willie Fall,
She made her debut at the ball.

At once her dress's brevity
Acquired her popularity,
And every goggle-eyed young man,
As soon as any tune began,
Would rush to join the mighty throng
That stood in awe of Agg's sarong;
And condescending, Annabella
Chose the most attractive feller,
Leaving her poor lover, Willie,
Feeling just a wee bit chilly,
Worrying, with many a frown,
Because he'd *wasted* 'alf a crown!

Just then the band struck up a number
—Tango followed by a rhumba—
And, answering a gentle tap,
She lent her chassis to a chap
Who, though he looked so frail and fragile,
Proved himself a trifle agile.
They whirled and twirled and bounced, till Aggy
Felt her garments getting baggy,
And glancing down, to her dismay,
She watched them softly float away;
To leave her balanced on one foot:
—A Venus in her birthday suit.

It was the end—in her disgrace
She knew not where to put her face;
She couldn't live such scandal down,
She had to leave the old home town;
And in the midst of her distress
She went and joined the A.T.S.
Now in some dull outlandish station
Agg redeems her reputation,
But instead of wearing flimsy tissue,
She dances now in khaki issue.

The Digby Chronicles

MICKY MERRILL was Steve's best friend at school, and despite the fact that he has found fame and fortune, while Steve has not, the friendship is still very strong. Micky's particular bent is for drawing Movie Cartoons—not as good as Disney's, but pretty good. And very lucrative. And he is Gilly's godfather—that was a very good idea on our part. But such being the case, we were not in the least surprised when he arrived unannounced to spend a week-end with us. (Incidentally, the telegram warning us of his arrival was delivered not long before he was packing to leave—such is our Village Post Office).

The children took to Micky at once. And when my adorable, detestable brats take to you, there is no escape. "You'll have to go and say goodnight to them", I warned him. "And they'll probably want a bedtime story". And I basely abandoned him to his fate.

In a remarkably short interval after Mickey's approach to their bedsides, silence reigned. "*You* can't keep them quiet like that", I remarked meanly to Steve. Steve said nothing.

After ten minutes the silence became ominous, and we went to investigate. A delightful scene met our eyes. Micky was seated on the floor with the gang draped admiringly round his shoulders. He was busy with pencil and paper. The impudent face and angular body of his most famous cat-creation leered up from the drawing-block. Susan and Gilly were in raptures, but not so Judy.

"Is that a cat?" she asked suspiciously.

"Why, yes".

"It's not very good, is it?" she pursued. "Not really like a cat?"

"Well, no, perhaps not", admitted poor Micky, abashed.

"Still", continued Judy kindly, "perhaps if there was a real cat here for you to see, you could draw it properly?"

* * *

It's as well that Micky has a sense of humour. Incidentally, I believe he has dined out on that anecdote more than once.

K.L.B.P.

Western Serenade

Screen play by WILLIAM HAYWARD
Based on an idea by Roy F. Aldridge

THE full, golden moon hung over the black mass of the distant *sierra*, and turned to silver the white adobe buildings of the clustered ranch-house, while in the big corrals a beast stirred restlessly as a coyote, out on the dark waste of prairie, uttered again and again its mournful cry. A warm gleam of light came from the bunkhouse, where the "boys" were singing one of the melancholy songs of the West to the rhythmic accompaniment of a guitar.

A dark figure detached itself from the shadows of the outbuildings, and, as it passed a clump of cacti, the moon revealed a tall curly-haired westerner cautiously making his way, with the characteristic gait of a cowpuncher, towards the ranch-house. The faint metallic jingle of his spurs merged with the swish of his wide sweeping "chaps", and across one shoulder, by a cord, he carried a guitar, without which no cowboy is complete.

The night was warm, and a harsh chorus of many bullfrogs maintained an insistant, but subdued orchestration as Tex moved, all but silently, across the *hacienda*, and, ignoring the front porch, and its white painted front door, swung round to the side of the house, where, amid the various sub-tropical plants, and a stunted tree, the moonlight played hide and seek with the velvet shadows.

Here, on the upper floor, a square of light shone from a window—*her* window. Even as he watched, a shadow moved across the shade, and he unslung his guitar, and carefully placing his foot on a convenient log, he adjusted his fingers to a suitable chord and a plaintive melody was borne on the night air—to the complete disgust of the bullfrogs.

Up in her room she was listening. He knew she was listening because, for a moment, he had seen her, sillhouetted against the light. Then she had moved away again. He tried with the other foot on the log, changed key, and began another melody. There came a click of the latch—she was opening the window—and he deserted the log and moved a little nearer to the house, still strumming, and singing in his woolly western baritone.

The window was open wide now, and he looked up. The moon shone on her golden hair, and on her face, and emphasised the white curve of her neck and shoulders, while the shaded light behind her added a golden lustre. She leaned forward—SPLASH!!

A cascade of water caught him full in the face, he lost his guitar, and his footing, and sat down suddenly in a spreading pool of water, his ardour and his appearance both somewhat dampened.

"Get outta here you ornery crittur", cried the girl, "you've had five tonight already and you don't get one more pumpkin pie!"

(Fade out).

Bookseller and Stationer :: Lending Library

J. SKETCHLEY

24 & 25, High Street, Loughborough

Telephone 2980.

THE BALLAD OF THOMAS TUPPER

This is the tale of Thomas Tupper
Who was an Aerial-Putter-Upper,
Who worked with strong and lengthy poles
(Stuck upright in the ground, in holes).
Then up he'd climb them, higher and higher,
And drape the top with bits of wigher,
And people, looking up, said: "Ah——
He must be swinging on a star!"

My story opens at a time
When he was once required to climb
A mast, which measured, more or less,
Some fifteen hundred feet, I guess.
So he resolved to take a bit
Of lunch, and make a day of it.
And with his bag of tools complete
Commenced this quite stupendous feat.

Below him, soon came passing by,
A man, who watched with keenest eye
His upward-scrambling form recede . . .
His name was Captain Bones, and he'd
Spent half his life at least, abroad,
And consequently felt assured
That he the rope-trick could perform,
(Despite his colleagues' ribald scorn,)
And seeing Tom, with upward glance,
Declared with joy, "Now, here's my chance!"
The Woygites hurried in a host
To watch him carry out his boast,
And nudged each other, and agreed
A joke like that could not succeed . . .
"Observe!" cried Captain Bones, "just how
That man is climbing upward now,
But when the top is reached, then he
Will disappear, I guarantee!"

The hours passed by, and still our Tom
Went slowly scrambling on and on,
Until he was the merest speck . . .
The crowd began to crane its neck . . .
And Bones, that mighty man, did swear
And cried, "Great Scott! He's nearly there!"
And made strange passes with his hands
And uttered the occult commands,
Till Tom was at the mast-head, quite,
——And then,——HE DISAPPEARED FROM SIGHT! ! !

The crowd rubbed startled eyes and swore
They'd never seen the like before,
And Bones said proudly, "Well, that's that!"
And passed around his battered hat.
But suddenly a voice cried, "Now——
You bring the blighter back some'ow,
'E owes me thirty bob or more. . . ."
Again the gallant captain swore,
And cried "Alas!" and then "Alack!"
"I DON'T KNOW HOW TO BRING HIM BACK! ! !"
"The spell is useless in reverse,
He's gone, FOR BETTER OR FOR WORSE! ! !"

Contd. over

Meanwhile our Tom was unaware
That he had vanished into air
Until an angel kissed his brow
And told him: "You belong here now:
I welcome you to Paradise!"
And Thomas said, "Well, ain't that nice!"
And there he stayed content——but we
Must fall to earth——and Mrs. T.

Our Tommy's wife was scarcely grieved
At finding she was now bereaved.
And as for Captain Bones—well, his
Was not a gentle Nemesis.
The widow soon became his wife,
And now he leads a wretched life.
And more than that, he had to pay
The thirty bob Tom owed that day.

The moral's plain—just hesitate
Before you try to emulate
The tricks you've seen another do
Or Bones' fate may come to you!

KAY PRICE.

THE TUESDAY CLUB

THOSE of you at Loughborough who call yourselves "exiles" and have only three Cinemas, a Theatre and sundry Dance Halls in which to pass away off duty hours, should spend a week or two at Bishops Waltham, where an eclipse of the moon is an event.

It was mainly to relieve boredom that an intrepid little band of pioneers put forward the idea of a Debating Club for the Bishops Waltham ex-exiles, and an extremely good backing was given straight away. Headed by the O.C. Station, some thirty members of the staff enrolled, and the Club held its inaugural meeting on Tuesday, 28th November, in a cheery and comfortable setting at the "Crown" Hotel.

Mr. McKee, of the Liaison Office, whose experience in Debating Clubs is wide and varied, was elected Chairman, and the rules of the Club were drawn up amicably, while all those present felt that a good start had been made to what we hope will become a pleasant weekly feature.

The first subject for debate, "CAPITAL PUNISHMENT", was very ably dealt with by George Money (of Home Guard fame) and a lively debate followed.

A member puts up a subject each week and all are at liberty to voice their views; in fact, with some shy members we welcome the opportunity that may be theirs to prove in themselves an eloquence unsuspected.

Wives of members and our A.T.S. Staff are Honorary Members, and we are looking forward to our first "Ladies' Night" on December 19th, when Fred Wright has, with great courage, offered to champion Electricity against Gas for Domestic Purposes. It will be interesting and enlightening to have the ladies' views on this subject.

Those of you at Beaumanor who are "experts" on any subject and who can be spared from your normal arduous task of "Using the Tools", are cordially invited to visit our Club and air your views. Remember, then, every Tuesday at the "Crown", and, in case you think it **too** much of a good thing, no beer until **after** debating has finished!

ERIC W. DOBSON,
Hon. Sec., Tuesday Club.

PIXIE'S SEARCH FOR LUV
By TOU-TOU ETHELLEM-DELLISH.

PIXIE hurried home full of her good fortune, the contract crackling encouragingly inside her modesty-vest. She had not told Peter everything. She had not told him that she was leaving the protection of the kind window-cleaner, and moving into a flat provided by Mr. Isaac Fischlein. Her eyes shining with happy innocence, she and her trifle of luggage arrived in a taxi and were welcomed with enthusiasm.

It was not until she was in the flat and saw the bedroom with its luxurious doub——(Oh, horror! Not really! Say it not!)——that she realized to what she had exposed herself. It was Mr. Fischlein's own flat, and his idea of sharing it with her was prompted neither by motives of economy nor generosity. Her face pale, her lips set, Pixie grasped her suitcase and made straight for the door, but Mr. Fischlein intercepted her.

"Oh, no, you don't, my little beauty," he purred in tones of silky menace. He wrenched the suitcase from her hand and threw it aside. Then he was kissing her. Pixie writhed in his grasp but it was no use. His lips were as clinging as a fly-paper—and so **practised**—not like the puppy-dog devotions of Peter. She struggled again, but when she wriggled her face aside his beautiful white teeth fastened sharply in her ear. She was at his mercy. His hot breath tickled her neck. Dark red waves of unconsciousness began to well up and engulf her. She must not faint—**must—not—faint**.——

When she came to, she was lying on the doub—(No!)—the divan, with her stockings peeled off, and Mr. Isaac Fischlein frantically chafing her feet. He had not noticed her open her eyes so she shut them again, and lay there inert, shamming faint, her brain working furiously. Mr. Isaac Fischlein, abandoning his attempt to bring her round by this method, retired into the kitchenette for a jug of water. Then Pixie acted. She sprang to her feet, and grasping a handy statuette, hid herself behind the door. Hurried footsteps, and Mr. Isaac Fischlein reappeared. Almost simultaneously the statuette—a cubist representation of Tarquin, seventh King of Rome—came crashing down on his head, felling him to the floor.

Trembling slightly, Pixie stood over him. What should she do now? Before she had time to decide, there came a crash of splintering glass, and a huge stone came hurtling through the window, and thudded on the carpet. Round it was tied a red flag bearing the insignia of the Hammer and Sickle. At the same moment feet resounded on the stairs, and the door burst open to admit Peter, leading a frenzied handful of the Masses to her rescue. He bounded across the limp body on the floor, and grabbed her frantically.

"My darling, are you all right?" he cried.

"Oh, yes," replied Pixie with remarkable composure. "But what is the matter with that woman?"

Peter followed her pointing finger. A middle-aged woman, in an advanced state of apoplectic excitement was dancing like a dervish and poking a bony finger at the locket hanging round Pixie's neck.

"Where—did—you—get—that?" she jerked, and fell squirming to the ground. Pixie hurried and bent over her, and the woman seized the locket feverishly.

"That was my mother's locket," said Pixie gravely. "It's the only thing I have in the world."

The woman uttered a screech and tore it open. The snowy curl of hair fell out. "My Fi-Fi!" she screamed. "Oh, my darling little poodle." And then, in her ecstasy, she fell back, dead. The cutting of poodle-hair floatly limply from her fingers. Tears of surprise and disappointment coursed down Pixie's cheeks. "Dead!" she cried. "Dead! And never lived to call me Daughter!"

Contd. over.

There was a sudden hooting of motor-horns, and a tramp of heavy boots. The Law had arrived. Policemen stumped in and arrested everybody—including Mr. Fischlein—for making a disturbance. In the Black Maria, Peter dropped to his knees at Pixie's feet. "Will you marry me?" he pleaded. And Pixie answered "Yes".

* * * *

It all turned out all right. Peter's father, the Earl of Pighle (pronounced Piffle) arrived post-haste to bail out his son, and he and Peter—or Piers as he was really called—had a loving reconciliation. The Masses were released and marched away singing "The Red Flag". Mr. Isaac Fischlein was given a cold compress and a stern warning, and in due course, the body of Pixie's long-lost mother was reverently consigned to an honoured grave.

And there we can leave Pixie, perfectly happy, with the prospect of a wedding at St. Paul's Cathedral and a honeymoon in the south of France. She has everything she wants—an adoring husband, money and position. And—best of all—she has found LUV.

(P.S.—Some people certainly get more than they deserve!—Tou-Tou.)

○ ○ ○ ○ ○

AFTER HEINE

Weary after a day's impetuous life,
The traveller entered the inn
That stands on the crest of the wave.
The comforting meal and the witty talk
Had made him ready for sleep.

From the creeper edged window wide
He saw the yellow moon
Standing beside the hill.
The careless game of the clouds and the wind
Threw shadows over the trees.

It seemed the moon that saw the infant life begin
And watched the growing sparks,
Creating self and self-destructive
And bursting from decay,
Had seen in its unending change the secret of eternity.

Was it to the languid bourgeois facing death
And the shock of his well formed life,
Came the easy thought of immortality—
Or was it to the spirit of youth
In the arms of his love,
Came the ecstasy and all-embracing thought
Of pulsing life unending fed from love?

The breath of the scented flowers
Was borne on the waves of the falling night—
Heavier and more entrancing
Like the scent in the traveller's heart
Hot with the dream of love.

He saw the love of his dreams
In fancy's distant cradle rocked.
The angels were guarding her sleep—
Repeating her murmured prayers.
Beneath her lids were the emerald suns of his life
And when she awoke the birds would sing in the woods
And the mountains gleam in the morning light.
But the traveller, packing his bags, would leave his dream with the inn.

BERYL E. C. MINTER.

VICTORY
BIGGIN STREET, LOUGHBOROUGH

MONDAY, JAN. 1st (6 days)
Spencer Tracy and Irene Dunne in
A GUY NAMED JOE
also Full Supporting Programme

MONDAY, JAN. 8th (6 days)
Deanna Durbin in
CHRISTMAS HOLIDAY
also Noah Beery, Jun., in WEEK-END PASS

MONDAY, JAN. 15th (6 days)
George Murphy and Ginny Simms in
BROADWAY RHYTHM
(in Technicolor)
also BORDER WEAVE (in Technicolor)

MONDAY, JAN. 22nd (6 days)
Rita Hayworth and Gene Kelly in
COVER GIRL
(in Technicolor)
also Full Supporting Programme

MONDAY, JAN. 29th (6 days)
Charles Boyer, Ingrid Bergman and Jos Cotten in
MURDER IN THORNTON SQUARE
also HEAVENLY MUSIC

Mon. to Fri—Con. from 5-30 p.m. Sat.—Con. from 2 p.m.
MATINEES.—Mon. and Wed. at 2-15 p.m.
SUNDAYS—6-15 p.m. (One Show)

Through the Looking Glass

FOLK-LORE

IMBIBING, by way of a change, at one of Messrs. Inde Coope's Quorn social-welfare centres, we, in conversation with some of the more superstitious local peasantry, happened, quite casually, to mention the word "Barkus". Immediately a deathly silence fell on the company, and we were faced by a barrage of glassy, half-accusing stares. At the last the landlord spoke: "Don't 'e mention that name in this 'ouse" he said in chill accents, "'us be 'onest God-fearing folk, and it baint right for any man 'o talk lightly o' the Devil's Chariot; there be things as isn't meant for 'uman ears. But I'll tell 'e this: 'tis death to look upon 'er the Devil's Chariot. Every night she passes through 'bout quarter to ten, and before she do folk in these parts shutters up their windows, and puts their kids to bed for fear they might look upon 'er. 'Tis an awful sight they say: there be 'orrid faces (folks says they're ghouls) a learin' and a grinnin' through the windows; and there's awful groanin's and mooin's, and shrieks like tortured souls in 'ell. Sometimes the windows is open and they creatures wave their 'orrible withered claws and drag young maids and little children inside—poor little Florrie Wainright—ten years old she was—was took last week. Lord knows when the next'll go"....

This only goes to bear out what we have consistently maintained in spite of much support for the latter thesis, *i.e.*, that the Work's Bus *en route* resembles a travelling menagerie *much* more than a Limehouse Sunday School outing.

PURGE

Although not wishing for one moment to detract from the glory which has rightly accrued to the heroic writers of Europe's Underground Press, we feel that, in all modesty, we should draw the attention of the world to the fact that scribblers in this Rag run hazards approximately five times more horrifying than the worst experienced under the New Order.

Perhaps the worst of these is the Editorial Gestapo: One sentence, one word, one hyphen or one semi-colon which doesn't tally exactly with the current Editorial political line, and you can start filling in the claim forms on your Life Assurance policies; these boys are quick, silent, efficient and merciless in their methods, viz:—

"And yes, Monsieur la Souris, de Bunk has been giving more trouble: there is a faint suggestion in his last MSS that I (the General Editor) am not all-wise, all-knowing, all-generous, all-loving and completely unbiased in my desire to serve the best interests of the Public. You will take Jake, Lefty and the cross-eyed Mulatto (whose tongue it has recently been necessary to remove) each of you armed with two rubber truncheons and one bottle of castor oil, and proceed to impress upon the gentleman that this opinion is mistaken. Should these methods fail, he will be bound, gagged, and thrown to the Presbyterians".

That's why you see us staggering about wearing this shifty, hunted expression, why our youth has waned so prematurely, and how we got these cruel purple scars which we shall carry to the grave.

REFORM

Apropos gossip writers (as the little actress said to the Social News Editor) it is invariably the case that this species of pond-life are either reformed ex-confidence men, unfrocked Noncomformist curates, or hopeless cases of wayward children from Strood; each, in a perverted desire to turn attention from his own sordid past, directs a libellous spotlight upon the innocent and defenceless, bringing grief and bereavement into homes of former spotless purity.

To remove this menace from the Post-War World, we are shortly introducing a Bill (The Liquidation of Legalised Blackmail Act, 1944) in the Commons. When the "True-Blues" oppose it (for of course it is axiomatic that they will oppose, on principle, anything which smells—no matter how faintly—of progress) we shall get Aneurin to storm their positions; and you can take it from us that if the Old Warhorse turns *this* into a confidence motion, Messrs. Pickford's will have a removal job in Downing Street.

THOUGHT FOR TO-DAY

"Man is the only animal which esteems itself rich in proportion to the number and voracity of its parasites".—BERNARD SHAW.

LEON DE BUNK.

GET YOUR——————
Beauty and Toilet Preparations
FROM
"LEONARD'S"
Gentlemen's Hairdresser
25, CHURCH GATE, LOUGHBOROUGH
Large Variety in Stock!

"THEY'RE TELLING ME"—*continued from page 9*

At the same time, one of Beaumanor's best loved racketeers, who wired Downing Street: "Dear Winston, Your policy has my fullest support, signed Baker", is still wondering who will be the next ambassador to Franco Spain.

I don't expect you to believe it, but it really did happen. One of the new runners told Mr. Dix that the clock in "H" was an hour slow!

"Lew" Owen, writer of "Me at the Pictures", seems to have succumbed to the rigours of reporting. During the showing of "Going My Way" his companions turned on "lachrymonious Lew" to find him reduced to tears in a corner of his seat. We always knew Mr. Crosby affected different people in different ways, but we have never seen *this* happen before.

At the dance at the Lodge on December 18th, Jean Tolley got the idea that beer should be taken externally. This is all wrong, Jean; it is usually administered via the mouth, preferably in large quantities.

Freddie (Hot Air) Burgess, highly incensed by the cool fresh breeze, blowing into "H" off the Beacon the other day, put on his coat and walked out. Returning some time later, he was heard to mutter something about the "vile smell" in Control.

To terminate, may I, on behalf of Jimmy and myself, offer our hope for a Happy and Victorious New Year.

Cheerio, BILL.

We understand that Mr. Connolly considers an apology is due from us for the paragraph about him which appeared in last month's "They're Telling Me". We would like to say that if at any time Mr. Connolly can produce evidence to show that he has in any way suffered as a result of what we printed we shall be ready to make a public apology.

Phoney Phrases By WILK : No. 4

"*No activity this end—How about yours?*"

EMPIRE
MARKET PLACE, LOUGHBOROUGH

MONDAY, JAN. 1st (3 days)
ROBERT WALKER and DONNA REED in
SEE HERE PRIVATE HARGRAVE
also LILI MARLENE

THURSDAY, JAN. 4th (3 days)
TOM CONWAY in
THE FALCON OUT WEST
also Charles Coburn in MY KINGDOM FOR A COOK

MONDAY, JAN. 8th (3 days)
JUNE ALLYSON and VAN JOHNSON in
TWO GIRLS AND A SAILOR
also Full Supporting Programme

THURSDAY, JAN. 11th (3 days)
FRANCHOT TONE in
PHANTOM LADY
also Donald Woods in HI YA SAILOR

MONDAY, JAN. 15th (3 days)
MARSHA HUNT and ALEXANDER KNOX in
NONE SHALL ESCAPE
also Jinx Falkenberg in SHE HAS WHAT IT TAKES

THURSDAY, JAN. 18th (3 days)
WARNER BAXTER and REGINALD DENNY in
THE STRANGEST CASE
also Carney and Brown in ROOKIES IN BURMA

MONDAY, JAN. 22nd (6 days)
TOMMY TRINDER and STANLEY HOLLOWAY in
CHAMPAGNE CHARLIE
also LEFT OF THE LINE

MONDAY, JAN. 29th (3 days)
JEANETTE MACDONALD and NELSON EDDY in
ROSE MARIE
(By Request)
also THE PUBLIC PAYS

THURSDAY, FEB. 1st (3 days)
PATRICIA MORRISON in
CALLING DR. DEATH
also Jane Withers in MY BEST GAL

**CONTINUOUS DAILY. Doors open at 1-30 p.m.
SUNDAYS at 5-30 p.m.**

Printed by Toppings Ltd., 17, Southfield Rd., Loughborough, and published by L. P. Jones for Beaumanor Staff Magazine Committee.

FEBRUARY, 1945

VOL. I. No. 12 (NEW SERIES) - **6d.**

FILM ATTRACTIONS for FEBRUARY

SHOWING AT THE ODEON THEATRE

Sunday, Feb. 4th—Constance Bennett and Roland Young in 'Topper Takes a Trip.' Also Edward Norris in 'Prison Mutiny.'

MONDAY, FEB. 5th, and all the week—
Barbara Stanwyck, Edward G. Robinson and Fred McMurray in
DOUBLE INDEMNITY
Also Trudy Marshall in 'Ladies of Washington'

Sunday, Feb. 11th—George Brent and Ilona Massey in 'International Lady.' Also Zasu Pitts in 'Miss Polly.'

MONDAY, FEB. 12th—3 days
Don Ameche & Dana Andrews in
Wing and a Prayer
Also Betty Rhodes & Johnny Johnston in **You Can't Ration Love**

THURS., FEB. 15th—3 days
Phil Baker & Edward Ryan in
Take it or Leave it
Also Richard Greene & David Niven in **Four Men and a Prayer**

Sunday, Feb. 18th—Gordon Harker and Raymond Lovell in 'Warn That Man.' Also Jinx Falkenburg in 'Lucky Legs.'

MONDAY, FEB. 19th—3 days
Eddie Bracken & Ella Raines in
Hail the Conquering Hero
Also Tom Conway & Mona Maris in **The Falcon in Mexico**

THURS., FEB. 22nd—3 days
Leslie Howard & Francis Sullivan in
Pimpernel Smith
Also Laurel & Hardy in **Beau Chumps**

Sunday, Feb. 25th—Bud Abbott and Lou Costello 'In the Navy.' Also John Carradine in 'I Escaped from the Gestapo.'

MONDAY, FEB. 26th, and all the week.
Carmen Miranda, Don Ameche, Vivian Blaine and William Bendix in
GREENWICH VILLAGE
(in Technicolour)
Also Jack Haley, Jean Parker and Bela Lugosi in
ONE BODY TOO MANY

Continuous Performance Daily 1-45 p.m.   Sunday, One Performance at 6 p.m.

B.S.M.

Vol. I. No. 12 (New Series)
FEBRUARY, 1945.

Managing Editor: LEONARD P. JONES.

Editors: KAY PRICE, ERIC C. MILLHOUSE   *Treasurer:* A. H. APPLETON.

WITH this issue the New B.S.M. reaches a milestone, in the completion of its first volume. Production of your magazine, with the various Editorial members and contributors working on different shifts, and scattered over the face of the Promised Land; the scarcity of printing labour; and the arduous tasks of accountancy and distribution, have brought their full quota of headaches. But we have managed to win through. With the opening of Volume II. next month we have decided to try to "pep up" your magazine with a series of twin-articles on various controversial topics, presenting "both sides of the question." We shall begin the series with the theme: EQUALITY OF THE SEXES. Accordingly we invite those of you who have decided views, one way or the other, on this ever-topical question, to submit articles of approximately 500 words, to reach the Editors by February 12th. The two articles which we consider present the soundest arguments for and against this subject will appear in our next issue under the title: WOYO FORUM. So now, Mr. Superior Being, and Miss I'm-Every-Bit-As-Good-As-You, here's your chance to air your opinions. Remember the closing date. You haven't much time. And, *please,* don't leave it to someone else," or we shan't receive any contributions!

Each month we shall choose a similarly provocative theme, and we welcome suggestions for further subjects in the series. Also, when you have read the views expressed by our contributors, let us have your comments—but please be brief. We will publish a symposium of readers' opinions the following month.

This month our old friend Yonc returns to give you the first of a series of highly amusing interpretations of Shakespeare. We also welcome Fleet Street's Ralph Champion, who begins a series of lively biographies of some of the better-known denizens of this inscrutable jungle. Incidentally, if *you* have a past, sordid or otherwise, and don't feel confident to write it up, why not give Ralph an interview?

We regret that the illness of our satirical comrade Leon de Bunk has caused a temporary steaming of his Looking Glass, and hope we shall be able to resume this popular feature next month.

It seems that one of the principal reasons for the paucity of contributions, particularly from our Atsite readers, is (believe it or not) *modesty*! Well, (in fact, well, well!) by all means hide your light under a pseudonym if you wish, but in fairness to the Editors they must know the identity of the writers of all matter published. This will not be disclosed if such is your desire. Remember, we don't know who can, and who cannot write, and if we go around canvassing your contributions it is a little embarrassing, since we aren't paying for your work, to have to reject something which we have directly asked for. You know whether you can write. Why not let *us* be the judges of whether or not it is worth a place in the B.S.M?

Next issue ready: Mar. 2nd.   All contributions to reach Editors by Feb. 17th.

GOOD READING
By JEAN C. DONLON.

SINCE its introduction, "Good Reading" has consisted entirely of prose works. This month I propose to devote it to two main works of poetry and to one smaller series of booklets.

First of all, "The Island," by Francis Brett Young. Mr. Young has completed, in one volume of poetry, the story of Great Britain from its volcanic birth to its greatest fight for life in 1940. He tells his story through the mouths of a Roman Centurion, a Saxon, a Crusader, a ploughman, a taverner of the Civil Wars, and one of Nelson's sailors, with other voices continuing the story up to 1940. In such a huge work, one may allow a certain falling-off in the quality of the poetry, and although many purists will object to Mr. Young's freely used licence in metre, the standard generally is high. I would particularly commend the lessons of the final, bitter condemnation in "Fantastic Symphony," 1918-1939, of the ways and policies of the ruling men. It is not great poetry, but it is readable and full of truth. Of a higher standard of beauty is " Winged Victory," immediately following, telling of the defeat of the Luftwaffe in 1940. Perhaps, one of its greatest advantages as reading matter is the splitting up of the work into 46 sections, allowing the reader to pick it up and put it down, without losing the thread of the whole long story.

Now an Anthology of Verse : " The Albatross Book of Living Verse." The anthologist, an American, Louis Untermeyer, begins at the ballads written before the time of Chaucer, covers the whole field of English and American verse, and finishes at the beginning of the present century, in a comprehensive, well-balanced survey. A more modern version of " The Golden Treasury " or the " Oxford Book of English Verse," the volume includes many of the lesser-known works of the better-known poets. I commend it to you if only because Blake's only contribution is not "Jerusalem," and Burns has more than " To a Mouse " to his name. Chaucer is translated for you, and you may read many of Shakespeare's too-little-read sonnets. There is a comprehensive analysis in the Appendix of poetic form and metre.

Booklets, the size of a small diary, neatly bound, and with 96 pages of verse are offered in the " Kingsway Series." Many of the well-known works of the more famous poets are in these neat little volumes. You can slip one into your pocket, and take out masterpieces to read at will.

Bookseller and Stationer :: Lending Library

J. SKETCHLEY
24 & 25, High Street, Loughborough
Telephone 2980.

News from B. W.

THE eagerly awaited Staff Social was held in the local Church Hall on January 10th, and proved to be a resounding success, over a hundred people attending. The programme comprised games, a stage show and dancing, in that order. the stage show being presented by Fred Staddon and his "Masculine Follies," Messrs. Dobson, Wright, and Money. Hilarious sketches alternated with more serious items ably rendered by Walter Dalton (solo violin), George Money (short pianoforte recital) and Fred Wright (baritone songs). Incidentally, it may not be generally known that the charming little piece with which Walter concluded, was his own composition and was making its first public appearance.

The excellent catering arrangements were made by Mrs. H. Smith, of the local Women's Institute, in conjunction with the Mill House (A.T.S.) Girls.

High spots of the evening were Fred Staddon reading an acidulous and, (speaking as a victim) highly libellous local News Bulletin, and "Eric," as an Eastern Illusionist complete with beard and turban.

Special mention must be made of the amazing performance of Mr. Weeks (he "does" for us—70 years young) who, in a three-hours non-stop Dancing Marathon, danced successive relays of A.T.S. off their feet. To see him participating in two sets of Lancers simultaneously was to witness a remarkable display of terpsichorean ability, (or should I say adaptability?).

One little thing; obviously we have the masculine nucleus of a really good Concert Party. Possibly, equally unsuspected talent lurks amongst the ranks of the A.T.S., waiting to be co-opted for our next function. What about it, Eric?

I understand that in view of the warm reception given to their initial venture, the committee are shortly convening a meeting to discuss holding a similar entertainment at some future date. Thank you gentlemen. Let it be soon! G.B.M.

The Committee : Messrs. Wright, Dobson, Money, Staddon and Dalton

---

Down to Earth
By Tommy Bancroft.

IT was a dull, grey afternoon. I was lying on a pebbly beach, part of the wild, rugged coasts of the Outer Hebrides. The beating of the surf filled the air with an ominous sound and seemed to warn me of the approaching storm. I lay there, however, fascinated, gazing at that grim scene, hypnotised and unable to move.

Slowly my eyes closed and I was aware only of the many sounds which reverberated round me. The wind shrieked and the threatening waves became mountainous. The granite cliffs which had defied the elements for centuries seemed likely to be torn down. Lightning stabbed and thunder roared with baffled fury. The tremendous breakers crashed themselves into blinding spray on the unyielding monuments of nature.

Gradually the tempest died down. The tide running at an amazing speed dashed between the boulders and hurled itself into the lofty black cavern which mocked the onslaught with terrifying echoes. Sounds slowly faded until there was only a murmur. The tiny wavelets played gently on the pebbly beach and softly floated me into a peaceful sleep.

Suddenly I was awakened by my wife's sweet voice asking: "Will you wipe the pots Tommy, please?"

Automatically I reached forward and, with a flick of the switch, the dying strains of Mendelsohn's "Fingal's Cave" collapsed.

Theatre Royal
LOUGHBOROUGH.

Programmme for February, 1945

Monday, Feb. 5th—6 days

J. Gillam Productions present

Sailors Don't Stare

Featuring Gene Durham and Matt Leamore

Monday, Feb. 12th—6 days

Hinge Productions present

Laugh It Off

Sparkling Revue of Beauty and Laughter.
Featuring Chas. Regan & Danny Keen.

Monday Feb. 19th—6 days

Loughborough Amateur Operatic Society presents

Goodnight Vienna

Spectacular Musical Comedy by George Posford and Holt Marvel.

Booking Office opens February 12th.

Monday, Feb. 26th—6 days

Watch Local Press for Details of Production for this date.

6-15　　　Twice Nightly　　　8-15

This Month's Starred Programmes.

*** "THE WHITE CLIFFS OF DOVER" (Victory, Feb. 19th 6 days). Based on the poem by Alice Duer Miller, it is a tear-jerker of the first order; with Irene Dunne as the American girl married to a British Tommy killed in the last war, who sends her son off to fight in this one. A loveable picture.

*** "DOUBLE INDEMNITY" (Odeon, 5th Feb., 6 days). Taken from the book by James Cain reviewed in last month's B.S.M. by Ralph Champion, it is a psychological thriller of cold-blooded murder that will get you on the edge of your chair. **Stanwyck and MacMurray** are terrific.

** "THE SEA HAWK" (Empire, 8th Feb., 3 days). Spectacular adventure of a bygone age, with pirates and windjammers, all very picturesque.

** "PIMPERNEL SMITH" (Odeon, 22nd Feb., 3 days) Reissue. Your chance to see **Hwfa Pryse** in the Gestapo.

** "BEAUTIFUL CHEAT" (Victory, 8th Feb., 3 days). One of those sophisticated comedies with the incomparable **Rosalind Russell**. You like 'em? So do I!   D.J.T.

Phoney Phrases By WILK : No. 5

"PUT IT ON THE LINE."

Freelance shows the way!

ALTHOUGH, previously, I have been loth to air any political views whatsoever in this magazine, feeling, as many others feel, that these pages are not the place, I am now moved to write a short comment, not, as one would expect, against Mr. Royle or one of the other well-known agitators, but against what appears to be the work of a politically backward, unthinking reactionary.

I refer, of course, to the poem "Poor Old Britain," appearing last month above the *nom-ge-plume* of "Freelance."

This poem has come at a time when our fighting forces, tied as they are by the necessity for obedience to their superiors in rank, are being *forced* to fight for their lives against men of similar political views or, at least, from the same social class. Their Greek opponents are only fighting for the right to their own opinions against the unscrupulous machinations of a decadent Royalist caste, who, once before, instituted a semi-fascist government in their country. The fact that "Freelance" has mis-read the situation and, much worse, *publicised* his unfortunate views reveals his appalling lack of political education. To think that a Government which, I venture to say, is not, after $5\frac{1}{2}$ years of war, representative of public opinion, should be allowed to make so important a decision, is not satisfying to anyone with even the vaguest principles of democracy, and consequently it appears unbelievable that any person, other than the small but powerful Conservative groups who profit by the situation, could hear of that decision and not only accept it but comment favourably on it.

"Freelance" says :—
> Democracy's dead!
> Dead, if we stand by
> And watch people fight
> For power that's gained
> By force, not Right.

Unless, as is inferred by the use of the capital letter, Right is to be taken as meaning Right Wing, this sentence is not even good logic, let alone good politics. What is right and what is wrong is a question which never can be irrevocably decided. Not the least remarkable of "Freelance's" ideas is his dogmatically stated belief that *his* ideas are *right*. Most people are prepared to admit that they are capable of making misjudgements—not so "Freelance"! He, with a complacency equalled only by that of the Pope of Rome, claims that his judgdgement is infallible.

If, on the other hand, Right Wing *is* meant, the whole sentence MUST be disregarded by the intelligent as a typical example of the results of popular Conservative propaganda.

I suggest, therefore, that "Freelance" is not only extremely fallible but also politically and/or mentally naïve.

This comment will, no doubt, provoke some discussion—if it does I am glad. It is time now that people did start to think for themselves, rather than allow their opinions to be easily swayed by the extensive propaganda of one financially powerful political party.

JIMMY HEWSON.

"ANNIVERSARY"

By PTE. SACKVILLE JONES

WOODUS HAY Village Hall (scene of so many sparkling local functions) lent itself admirably for the purpose of the 25th Anniversary Dinner and Social of the "Woygian Association," held last Saturday.

Everyone who was anyone was there, and I noticed many faces with which I could never connect the appropriate names in the "old days." I even had some difficulty in recognising the chairman, who made a most impressive, if startling figure, as he took the chair. He had, after years of indecision, gone completely Shavian; he was now tall and thin (white hair was his crowning glory), with an enviable beard worn to the waist, and was clad in a light grey one-piece woollen suit (Morley—I looked) embroidered with Socialist symbols. He had with him an army of employees whom I had to have explained to me. The retinue consisted of three seductive stenographers with Yorkshire accents and very rosy cheeks, two pages carrying pipes and tobacco (to illustrate the folly of excessive smoking), a Chinaman, whose devoted duty it was to chop the Great Man's raw veg., and four chained and gagged members of the now almost extinct British aristocracy, bearing bound volumes of "The Manchester Guardian," "The Tribune," and an immense dictionary, for additions to be made, of course, and, it is rumoured, for an occasional reference. He addressed the assembly admirably, choosing as his subject, "Good cultivation as a factor in soil fertility," and his flowery oration was not lost on his audience. Never was he at a loss for extravagant wording which couldn't fail to impress, even though the point (for there must have been one surely?) was more than a little obscure.

Dinner was followed by a variety of old-fashioned games which included "Hunt the Bird" (this brought many a reminiscent tear), a roll-eating contest, and a game in which one had to guess boys' names beginning with certain letters, at which most were hopelessly out of practice, but warmed up later on.

Music was provided by Sir Broderick Sturgess, who also organised a face-pulling contest; an ex-Fleet St. journalist, who had torn himself away from his library of James Cain's books especially for the item was barred from entering as it was considered that he had an unfair advantage.

Three minutes silence was called later in the evening to celebrate the octogenary of one of the Supervisors. He was presented with a solid silver table-tennis bat, a bunch of pipe cleaners, a papier maché bust of Tchaikovsky, and an electric fan. He was held up on a small, tastefully decorated platform, and made a touching speech, which was followed (a little too closely, I thought) by an instructive demonstration of rough-puff pastry.

There was one calamity, however, during the course of the evening, when a hired waiter (on whose appearance the female half of the assembly had hastily straightened their cutlery into neat rows and removed wine-glasses and every trace of food out of sight) caused greast concern by shutting his thumb in a swing door. Between sobs and hiccups he pleaded to be allowed to stay, on the doubtful grounds that he had served in His Majesty's Navy, and once held a responsible position which necessitated daily inspection of the out-houses in the grounds of one of the stately homes of England. He said that he "needed the money" to support his assorted baby triplets.

[Cont'd foot of P. 11.

They're telling Me!

AFTER much trouble I have solicited the fact that some of you do get married occasionally. I wish you wouldn't be so shy. I've got space to fill up, whether people are interested or not, so let's have the dope, please.

First, congratulations to Pte Mee and L/Cpl. Joan Blackburn, who changed their names to O'Donaghue and Turnham respectively. They both "dood" it somewhere in England, sometime recently. Apparently Joan's stripe was a wedding gift from the War Office.

Now for engagements—a little more plentiful!

Congratulations to Renee Smith (Group Office) and Capt. Siddalls on their engagement announced recently. Also our best wishes to Doreen Lister and Harry Dodd on following John and Kay's example

All the best, too, to Peter M. Tuke on his recent engagement to Miss Betty Wilson, B.Sc., of London. Peter gains double congratulations this month in that he has also succeeded in getting that elusive thing, his ticket. We wish him the best of luck in his new vocation.

And now, somebody else with the right spirit! All the way from B.W. has come news of two engagements. Congrats. to L/Cpls. Eileen Herbet and Anne Wickson on getting their men, C.F.N. Steve Moore and Sgt. Jimmy Piggot, both of R.E.M.E.

You may have noticed the tear-stained features of quite a few people lately, as they have made their last fond farewells. First to go were Mr. and Mrs. Ghent, Bill and Muriel to you. We hear that Muriel is going on more productive work. Our best wishes go with them. We say farewell also to Don Palmer and Dick Stephens who, no doubt, are extremely sorry to leave. Dick hopes to join Molly Morgan soon.

Breaks arranged with a view to fostering better A.T.S. and Civilian relationship.—Apply "The CUPIDAX" Agency (advt.).

I've seen some examples of forgetfulness, but here is one which, I think, caps the lot. Pte. Bunce of "C" Watch, 2 Wing, celebrated her *second* wedding anniversary the other day by receiving a letter from her husband addressed in her maiden name! The second courtship idea for separated married couples seems a good one, but this seems to be taking it a little too far. Happy daze!

Overheard in Barrow Coffee Shop: ". . . . of course it's very nice when it's hot, but it's not so hot when it's cold." Do all Tepee girls go like this eventually, or is it just a legacy from the Yanks?

Did you hear about the home carpentry efforts in "I" Hut during the Christmas Chaos? It all started over an obstinate almond. For further details see Gerry Dalton, who appears to have missed his vocation.

Having seen nothing of Wally Cecil since Reg made his abrupt departure for the mines, we presume that Wally didn't want him to be lonely and that they are consequently still on their Xmas holiday.

Very many and varied circulars have at times been passed round "H" Hut, but one struck me as being very much out of the ordinary. I reproduce it: "Will the jerk who took 20 players out of the cloakroom at 1400 please lend me one, as they were all I had. Ta, D.U.C." After such a heartrending cry, this jerk deserves to get cigarettes back.

If you want to succeed with the opposite sex, boys, you only have to follow one or two simple rules. First, you must wear your hair poet fashion, and acquire a pair of spectacles. An old pipe, a red tie and a beer-drinking capacity, complete the ensemble. I can't give you the proportionate mixture or further details for reasons of security (mine), but if you are really interested you should read the book shortly to be published by the Forces Sweetheart, N—— R——. entitled "The Low-down on my Xmas Mail."

By the way, I am not wayward, and I deny all association with Strood.

And now, I have a complaint to make. If a certain Tepee—Nerve Centre Association must do its necking in Barrow, will it, please, move on to a side road, and not use the centre of the main street where innocent pedestrians are liable to fall over it.

And here is another creditable, but nevertheless true, "dumb At" story. The scene is the Boat-house Cafe. Three Ats are grouped around the fire, one of whom is reading an extract from a letter sent from France, remarking the cold. The writer quotes: "even the flame of my candle has frozen, several times." The ensuing laughter is broken by the domb-one's voice saying: "It's a shame to laugh, we don't know how cold it *is* out there."

We are sorry to hear that Claude Deakin has given up reading the "New Statesman." Careful, Aneurin, there is only Noel now!

Highly amazed was E.W.A. Dance Organiser, Lew Owen, when he found that, after connecting the canteen loudspeakers to the mains, he didn't receive music, but a bill for £1 5s. 9d.

And talking of Lew Owen, did you hear about his heroic "break" marathon. He didn't think it was possible to return a piano to Loughborough and get back to B.M. in 30 mins. either. About the only thing he didn't break was his fast.

Incidentally, for those who are interested, a pano is a cross between a punt and a canoe. Suitable for Soaring.

STOP PRESS!—The engagement is announced of Sgt. Daphne Workman to Capt. Graham Abels.   Cheerio!   JIMMY.

"ANNIVERSARY," cont'd

To round off the evening, a stocky little old man in a knee-length sweater and a battered Admiral's hat, executed his own version of the sailors' hornpipe on a table top, gave an impromptu exhibition of knots, and was persuaded to render a sentimental shore-going ballad, "Come where the booze is cheaper."

It was on this hilarious, almost riotous note that a most successevening came to its close, and I'm pleased to say that nobody was trampled to death in the swirling rush to the long rank of waiting bath-chairs.

(Leather-bound copies of the programme of the evening, in several shades of leather, may be obtained upon application to Ded Lee Specialties, Ltd. Also a limited supply of initialled outworn soap-boxes on sale).   B.B.

Yonc's Tales from Shakespeare
I. THE MERCHANT OF VENICE.

THERE is a Wop living in Venice (well, Gee! I know there are always some living there, but this is a particular guy). He's a high-class salesman see, and though I guess he ain't the only one, he rates pretty high on the Rialto, which ain't a classy picture house but a kind of Wall Street, where all the guys who rate any spend their time raking in pin-money.

Well, one day, this guy, Antonio, is swapping yarns with some of his pards and they get to talking and having a highball, and Antonio spills the beans about all his cash which he's wrapped up in a few ships; and the poor sap tells them how these ships have caught it where it hurts most and are now engaged in vitaminizing the fishes at the bottom of the English Channel. Which is too bad, so he tells them, looking kind of green, because he has borrowed a few grand from a heel called Shylock, and if that heel don't get his cash back pronto, he says he is going to get busy with Ma's best Sunday Carver and cash in on 1 lb. of Antonio's corpus dee-lec-ti, according to the dim-wit contract that Antonio has signed with the Shylock Corp.—if he don't return the cash.

But Antonio has a buddy and his handle is Bay-sannio. And I guess he'd be ready to dip his hand and help, but he has a sked. And I will say this sked is some dame. A high-stepper, if ever there was a Venus-de-Milo. And Bay-sannio is legging it over to this dame's homestead. When they get there Bay-sannio's trigger-man gives the old one-two with the high-stepper's dresser, and they do fine in the back kitchen, while the boss backs his fancy in the parlour. But Bay-sannio has got competition because his dame, Portia, had a Pa who had less than nothing up top, being more than a little wee-willy in the woodpile. And her Pa said, before he handed in his chips, that any guy who wanted to tie the knot with Portia had to come and have a gander at three caskets, gold, silver and lead, and put his shirt on one; and if he guessed O.K. he took the dame and her bank-roll. But if he went down the drain, he must not get fresh with any other dame, as long as he took in air and breathed out carbon di-oxide. Well, two more guys have got to the ticket-office before Bay-sannio, both wishing to have a cut in on the racket. So he joins the queue and crosses his fingers. Then Portia gives the first guy the O.K. And he goes in and parks his eye on the gold casket and spills out a pome and says: Dat one. But Portia says no bud and she's sorry, but all that glisters ain't gold by long chalks, so scram. So the next guy lines up at the tape and when the traps go up he runs his eye over those caskets, and after a bit more poitry, says he's betting hard on silver. But he's had it too, and has to pack his grip and call a cab. Then Bay-sannio is all set and goes in ready to beat the band. And Portia gives a mental high-kick and slides her orbs over him, and says Hot Dog. And Bay-sanno does the same by her and thinks she's some floomy alright. So Portia tells him to get moving, and cast his peepers over the caskets and watch for the outsider. So Bay-sannio has a gander and spills a spot more hot verse, but being sharp he puts his money on the dark horse and comes up a hundred to one on lead. And inside the box he finds a picture of this prize pin-up girl and a letter from her defunct old man telling him he's a wise guy, and Portia says here I am Bay-sannio, come and get me. So Bay-sannio goes in fighting and after a clinch or so they're already to leg it to the preacher. But Bay-sannio says sorry sugar, but he's just heard his pard is all muzzed up and he has got to vamoose back to Venice pronto and set the D.A. on this Shylock racketeer, who is busy with a whetstone on his Ma's Sunday carver. So Portia gives him the O.K. and he gets a cab back to town with his trigger-man to see how Antonio is making out.

Well, Antonio is not doing so good, because this racketeer Shylock is more than a little peeved at the way Antonio has been pushing him around, and he says he is not used to being pushed around, see, and no guy is going to expectorate on his Jewish gabardine and give him the works any. Not a guy that's got his cash wrapped up in ships that are providing homes for destitute barnacles, anyway. So Shylock hales Antonio up before the D.A. and he asks how about it, and can he have his 1 lb. of flesh since Antonio can't fork out the necessary. And the D.A. says Aw Heck, he cannot stop him, but Gee! he doesn't want homicide on his mind, does he? But Shylock says he ain't scared and this guy has pushed him around long enough, see? So the D.A. says O.K., but Antonio must have a lawyer and he will fetch one from Padua. So they send for this sharp attorney guy. But when he comes in it is not the real one but Portia, all dolled' up in glad rags like she knows the law inside otu.

But none of the others recognise her, and Portia guesses she will cash in on these ducks. And this dame sure is a hep-cat with those law books, and she starts walking these saps up the garden path and asks Shylock what he aims to do. Then that mobster says that if Antonio cannot hand over the greenbacks bingo, just like that, he is aiming to have 1 lb. of that guy's flesh. So Portia starts to gab to him something about mercy, but that swell mobster says for her to can it and he's gotta have his flesh right now, since Antonio can't pay up. Then Portia says that's fine and dandy, and that she can't put a stopper on his bright-eyed plan, and Shylock says she's a great kid. But Portia hasn't finished with this guy. No man. She says for him to get busy on his carving act but that if he takes too much or too little, or if he gets sanguinary about it, he breaks his contract. Of course that gets Shylock below the belt, because no guy can cut up another guy without spilling a double tot of blood, and he starts beefing a bit. But the jury and the audience and the newspaper men all stand on their pins and laugh fit to bust, And the D.A. tells Shylock he's lucky not to get a stretch in the Big House up river, but that as it is he loses all his cash and land. Which does the poor guy down good and proper because after all it was his dough. But all the other guys are happy, and so are their molls, so what the hell?

○ ○ ○ ○ ○

SNOW SCENE
By NOEL ROYLE.

SILENCE, silence
   Spreading through the crystal night,
Hovering over hoary lawns,
Across the silver-curtained meads,
And far beyond the shining hills :
Silence to eternity.
The moonlight's pale liquidity
Holds all the earth in matronly benevolence—
Except where phantom trees,
Brooding in their secret conclaves,
Fragmentate the lunar stream
And, casting down their twisted shades,
Outrage the virgin carpet of the snow.
Sub-polar night
Enshrouds the sleeping cottage
Surrendered to the winter :
No sound of man, or beast, or bird;
All life is lost in snow and silence . . . .
Eternal silence.

A Clean Rope for the Hangman
By DUDLEY TRUIN.

Based on a true story, related by **BILL BAKER**

*"He will answer to the purpose, easy things to understand,
Better that thou wert dead before me, Tho' I slew thee with my hand."*
                                                LOCKSLEY HALL.

THREE o'clock! It's cold in the cell to-night. Only a few hours before I know what lies beyond that closed door. I shall go with a song in my heart.

Old Joe is going to miss me. He's my warder, you know. Giving me a bath yesterday, he said: "There's a dirty mark on your neck. I'll wash it off." I laughingly replied, "Yes, wash it. We don't want to spoil a perfectly good rope."

Yes, Old Joe will miss me.

○ ○ ○ ○ ○

I worshipped Edna with all the spiritual devotion and abandon of which my sensitive, imaginative nature was capable. 'Life with her was sheer poetry. Then, on that soul-shattering night, I heard the full story of her cheap and sordid intrigues, and realised her only regard for me lay in my wealth and position.

I felt I had been crucified.

Somehow, I hurled myself into a vortex of gaiety, seeking oblivion in drink and women. For ten days and nights I lived in a ceaseless round of so-called pleasure, yet thoughts of Edna were still like knife-thrusts in an open wound.

Then one Saturday night, I was at the County Hotel dinner-dance leaning against the bar, already pretty hazy. Suddenly, she floated in on the arm of a man I vaguely remembered having seen in the local hardware store. My eyes followed her as she swept across the floor. Something seemed to snap. Cold as ice, but outwardly calm, I strolled across to where she and her partner sat, and asked, "Care to dance, Edna?" I knew she wouldn't refuse; she would be only too willing to stage repentance, in the hope of reconciliation. I was far too valuable to be ignored by such a business-like young woman. We slipped out by the side door before the dance ended, and were soon tearing along the Portsmouth road in my tourer.

It was a perfect night. The moon was climbing slowly as I swung the car off the main road up towards Thorney Mill, a secluded spot, where we had many times drunk at the well of ecstasy.

I parked by the side of the Mill pond. The elms cast fitful shadows as I took her in my arms for the last time.

She felt my strangeness and murmured: "You have forgiven me, haven't you, darling?" I hushed her with a kiss as I drew her scarf around her neck. Tighter, tighter, tighter. She never struggled.

I lit a cigarette and lay there contentedly, smoking and watching the clouds flitting across the moon, my mind at peace.

A deep voice broke my reverie: "You all right, sir?" I glanced up to see the face of our local constable peering through the off-side door. "Yes thanks, Reeves," I replied.

"Lovely night. I saw the lights, and as it was a bit late—it's gone two—I thought I'd have a look."

He knew I had a woman there, all right, but it was not until he was leaving that he had a good look at Edna, slumped in the seat beside me.

"God, sir, your friend looks ill!"

"Yes, Reeves, she does, doesn't she, the dirty little bitch. But then, I don't suppose you'd look so good yourself if you had just been strangled!"

The Gospel according to St. Ayid

(Translated from the English by Disciple Millhouse).

NOW in Brit were many cold places. And the coldest of all the cold places was Woyg. And the coldest place in the land of Woyg was the temple of Eye, which is called Item, but not very often.

For inasmuch as the worshippers in Eye perceived that all the temples were contrived by learned men, they knew in their hearts that this temple was conceived by a master Draughtsman. Likewise knew they this in their necks, and down their backbones.

And the Chief of the Atsites, when she had hearkened unto the chattering of teeth and knocking of knees in Eye, was filled with compassion for her flock, and for all brass monkeys. Wherefore she went unto the Prophet Osee, crying: Get a load of this. For my flock which is called Toowing are the Chilled-ren of Israel. Yea, for even the Red Hot Mammas goeth off the boil. And the Prophet answered her, saying: Take thy Chilled-ren and wrap them in swaddling clothes, that their fingers may yet twiddle and write Nil.

And it was so. But a plague of Cohds id der Doze descended upon Eye, and there were many Churchyarders. Wherefore the Prophet communed with Red Tabz, saying: Warm thou my flock, I beseech thee, for even such zeal as theirs sufficeth not to keep out the frost. For all the flocks in all the temples are bleating loud bleats, but Eye is verily the Frigid Zone. And Red Tabz answered: Straightway will I send thee Hot Air Gadgets, Ackess. And when the scribes of the temple heard the Gen they marvelled, saying one to another: Doth not Red Tabz know there is an abundance of Hot Air in the temples? But certain among them answereth: Whist ye not there is oft-times also a Mighty Flutter?

And the Sabbaths of the Ackess came and went, and the chattering of teeth waxed exceeding loud. Then it came to pass that it was noised abroad above this Kewahrem: Stand by for a Mighty Flap. For Red Tabz cometh hither. And straightway there was in their midst a host of elecktricks men, and slaves with hammers and chisels, and Brains Trusts with no tools. And when they had battered the temples into shape they brought forth the Gadgets and made them fast, crying: Hasten, hasten, for Red Tabz must have a Warm Reception.

But Red Tabz worked them a Flanker and came nigh ere the Gadgets were ready, which is called Fate, for thus was he saved from Pneumonia. For when he had departed the Brains Trust commanded the Gadget in Eye to function. And the Gadget blew a mighty blizzard into the temple so that the scribes cried out in their agony: Give us a Break, that we may thaw ourselves without. And the elecktricks men were cast down, crying: Woe is us, for we have done it all wrong.

And the Gadget in the temple which is called Aych (and How) fell sick of the palsy, and there was no warmth. And the Chief Rabbi of Aych cried unto the Chief Rabbi of Eye: Give thou me thy swaddling clothes. And when he had given them unto him there was no warmth in Eye. And the elecktricks men fiddled; and the slaves toiled; and the Brains Trust considered. And all the scribes in all the temples prayed in this wise: Roll on Summer.

RALPH CHAMPION blows Freddie's Trumpet.

Telling the story of the Little Man Who Is BIG TIME.

FREDDIE Burgess was only 4½ when he lost his first job.

I suppose you cannot really blame him. It was tough work for a little chap, blowing his tiny trumpet in a Salvation Army band. And the cobbles in Oldham were slippery. And his clogs were just a bit too large. When he fell down hard, he tried not to cry, though his trumpet was bent so badly that every time he blew it puffed into his face.

The remarkable thing was that the bandmaster did not know sooner. It was several weeks before he discovered the wrecked instrument. Freddie must have sounded a particularly "corny" note that day.

Freddie combined his musical studies under a father who talked, thought, and dreamed "brass," besides a head teacher who had the same queer obsession.

Whenever the head could spare a few minutes Freddie was called from his lessons to practise the cornet in his study. It was all rather terrifying. Each time the boy blew a wrong note, the head-teacher boxed his ears. Perhaps the system did not quite concur with modern teaching methods, but it worked.

Freddie did not play wrong notes often!

Like most young Lancastrians, Freddie began his working life in the cotton trade. He spent 2½ years in a warehouse before the slump convinced his parents that he could do better on the stage.

It's important to remember Freddie is primarily a comedian. It explains many things which happen when he is off duty today.

He made his debut in "Black and White Birds"—he was one of each at various times. The show worked three-night stands in village halls and miners' institutes throughout the North and Midlands. His toughest breaks were morning performances, where he tried, sometimes successfully, to make miners laugh, though they had only just finished night shift.

Freddie was paid in shares. When the show finished at Leicester Theatre Royal, he had 3s. 2d. left after paying his landlady.

A few years later, he earned £40 accompanying a single film.

Before he became Big Time, Freddie was playing at various dance halls, and went on a Continental tour with Syd Seymour's Band. By then, he had learned some tricks of his trade. He developed a virtuoso hair-style, and charged sixpence a week on his income tax for cold cream to lubricate his trombone.

When appearing with Jan Ralfini, Burgess frequently met a young man named Trinder, who was happy to earn £4 or £5 a week with the band, telling funny stories. Incidentally, Trinder did not forget his friends. Ralfini is now his musical director, and the band's old stage-manager is working for him too.

Freddie's story becomes just "Local Boy Makes Good." With his two brothers he toured the halls successfully, worked for stars like Billy Cotton and Geraldo, and was booked by George Black for the West End. He claims to have discovered Harry Parry, the swing clarinet player, and Eddie Macauley, now Britain's best-known dance pianist.

When war began, Freddie qualified as a Merchant Navy radio officer, while continuing to fill dates at theatres and night clubs.

All this left him little time to grow. He decided 5ft. 1½in. might be O.K. for a comic, but not for a sea-dog, so he came to Woygt. He's been here 3½ years—and that's the longest engagement he's ever had.

REFLECTIONS on the ANNUAL PARTY.

O.C. Lieut.-Col. M. J. W. Ellingworth : A jolly good show !
Freddie Burgess : Absolute chaos !
Flora Mutton : Perfect organisation.
Harry Dix : Thank-you, all you willing helpers.
Sgt. Joan Rogerson : A lot of bottles with an occasional glimpse of George Billingsley.
Ron Blease's Landlady : Isn't your O.C. a *nice* man !
Victor Hartill: The balcony wasn't blacked out—I was all disappointed
Edna Sharman : Stern supervisors miraculously transformed into benevolent, doting fathers
"Colonel Merritt": Beer, beer, and still more beer.
Moira Byrne : Tremendous Do—but, like last year, I was on 7 till Midnight.
Jimmy Hewson : The Duty Bus at 9-25 p.m.
Di Brandle : Are our intrepid Supervisors *really* scared of their wives, or must they always insert something between their bases and the floor ?
Lois Seal : Like a tin of sardines—well oiled !
Irene Goldsmith : No reflections—I was on leave, thank God.
Mager Musgrave : How quickly the time went, before 10 p.m. !
Bob Broom : How quickly the time went, after 10 p.m. !
Joan Davis : We came, we saw, we wilted.
"Tich" Warren: I wasn't there; but if it was anything like last year I'd rather not commit myself.
Young Ben " Wilk ": Panto. was good—but not as good as Errol Flynn in "The Charge of the Light Brigade."
"Jimmie" Davis : A very pleasant——Double-shift !
Mr. C. O. Smith : The Tea Dance with no tea :
Vera Adams : Grand Kindergarten.
St. Upid : Yea verily, a mighty Binge.
Mrs. Byron (Canteen) : How on earth did all the ATS identify their shoulder-bags out of the "mountain" in the Corn Exchange ?
Norman Shuttlewood : Words fail me—I left at 7 p.m.

And finally, an anonymous member of "A" Watch 3 Wing, with the pseudonym "Dry"—pronounced "shy"—sends us this piquant observation :

Never was so much consumed by so many in so short a time, leaving none for so many.

Pay Parade.

I lie in my bed watching the other girls as, one by one, they reluctantly get up.

If funds weren't so low I should feel inclined to miss Pay Parade and get double pay next week, but as usual I am "stony broke." In a few minutes I, too, will have to get up. I turn over—just five minutes more, I think to myself, and I snuggle further under the bedclothes.

"Oh no, you don't," says someone, and the bed clothes are pulled off. There is nothing for it but to get up. The hut is cold and I am tired. Still, the thought of a few well-earned (?) coins lures me out.

I have lots to do in a very short time: shoes and badge to clean; hat to find, and bed to barrack. The bed collapses when I least expect it—a common occurrence, and one which does not improve my temper. Well, at lest I am ready and, having rescued my hat from the grate, I hurry over to the house.

Pay Parade is about to begin. "Thank goodness," I think, "My initial is near the beginning of the alphabet." But I am to be disappointed, for the Sergeant appeaars in the doorway and says: "We are starting from the end of the alphabet for a change." After a general reshuffle I find myself near the end of the queue.

Again the sergeant appears in the doorway: "You will not pay a penny for the House Fund this week"—a general murmur of approval—"But," she adds, "We are collecting threepence from each of you for the basin that was cracked in the house four months ago."

The girl ahead of me whispers: "I always wash in our hut and never use the basins over here. Another girl pipes up: "And I wasn't here four months ago!"

"No talking!" yells the sergeant. "You're on parade!" She evidently thinks I am responsible for the talking, and singles out me and another girl for witnesses. This means we shall be paid last. The queue at last diminishes, and it is my turn to be paid. I step out from behind the pay desk, and after the usual formalities of saluting, handing over my pay book and signing, I stand there, eagerly waiting for my pay and pay book. It is handed to me, but what is the matter? Why am I being paid five shillings less than usual? As I walk away from the desk I see, by my pay-book, that I am being charged for something I bought at the stores six months ago.

I have just reached the door when I am called back by a corporal, who asks me for the money for the basin—"And you haven't paid for last week's House Fund," says a second corporal, and "How would you like to give something towards the ATS Comforts Fund?" suggests the first corporal. It is no use arguing, and I reluctantly dole out the necessary coins.

Outside I see Doreen, and realise, with a sigh, that I owe her two shillings. I pay her and pocket the meagre remains.

"Where's Kath?" "Having tea," says Doreen, "But you're too late. Tea is at six, and it is now a quarter past." That means I shall have to get my tea in town. Another expense!

Perhaps after all I should have been wiser to have stayed in bed. What do you think?   H.F.

The Morning After the Night Before
By ARCHANGEL.

2200. Given: eight hours off, after finishing duty.
2230. Begin supper, one eye on landlord, the other on clock.
2245. Landlord (who has half Saturday and all Sunday off, *every* week-end) says pleasantly: "On at six in the morning?" After slight pause I reply : "Yes, on at six,' nonchalant tone rendered somewhat hoarse owing to slight constriction of vocal chords and landlord's pleasant, loving, homely face.
2300. Finish eating and prepare to retire for the few minutes allowed me by the Fiends; drag weary limbs upstairs.
2301. Drag 'em down again to find correct time. Landlord unable to say if clock is fast, right, or slow. Tch!
2303. Retrace footsteps. Mind now in such a state that I try to add extra stair. Hurtle into bathroom at 35 m.p.h. Bath gives hollow boom as head strikes it.
2310. Set the torture machine which is called an alarm clock. It hates me, and I hate it, so the feeling is mutual. Undress and climb slowly into bed.
2320. "Inner Voice," for whom I have resignedly been waiting, now comes into being, and asks if the alarm is right. Have I set it to 0445? Was I sure hands pointed to 2310 when winding it up, and not to 0010 or 2210? Was lever in correct position? Try to ignore malignant and persistent whispers of I.V.
2335. Patience exhausted. Savagely turn on light, barking knuckles in process, and glare at the bloo—, er, blasted clock, to satisfy I.V.
0015 approx. Drop into uneasy sleep.
0115, 0245, 0345. Wake up.
0445. ALARM! Narrowly avert hitting ceiling. On coming down again viciously thrust arm out in direction of hellish din. Manage to knock clock on floor. After frantic search in dark, bordering on state of panic, am successful in finding infernal thing, but not lever. Finally get clock into bed and lie on it where it continues to scream to its last gasp.
0447. Silence — awful and complete.
0450. Limbs cease twitching and nerves stop jangling. Loathe anything and everybody. Decide that the Fiends should be lined up in the courtyard in front of that hesitant swordsman, to be shot out of hand.
0450 Stumble out of bed, totter into clothes, and stagger into bathroom.
0457. Wander out again. Pause at head of those damn stairs. On getting eyes to remain open, nearly tumble down.
0500. Bacon sizzling, water boiling. Notice with interest kitchen filling with usual blue smoke. (Am jealous of my blue smoke. Only man who can make it; clouds of it; layers of it).
0503. Make tea, fight way back through blue haze to get bacon. I'm the only one who can make it as crisp and burnt, or able to get it so curled up).
0510. Make tentative stab at rasher; it flies into little bits. Spend next 30 secs. on floor, trying to cover six pieces with two hands, in frantic, but hopeless endeavour to outdo speed of cat, which has been waiting for this precise moment.

[Cont'd overleaf.

All this and Burma too
or "Y" Move.

THIS is the tale of Brainless Bob,
  Who found himself a "cushy" job—
Eight solid hours he always worked,
And not a soul could say he shirked—
Until one day he deemed it time
To languish in a foreign clime—
So, with his work completely bored,
He volunteered to go abroad.

The joys of travel in his mind,
He left "Reservists" far behind,
And sallied forth—completely barmy,
To seek adventure in the Army.
Then found himself upon a ship—
With prospects of a pleasant trip
Far from Beaumanor's maddening strife—
He pondered deeply: "*This* is Life."

Established, therefore, on the "drink,"
His hopes—and stomach—soon did sink,
His thoughts of glory swiftly were
Dispelled by chronic "mal de mer,"
Young Bob admitted he was beat,
And pined again for "Civvy Street"
Then, when they docked, he heard this murmur:
"That's right mate—'ere we are—it's Burma."

Surrounded now by vegetation,
He sits in earnest contemplation—
And finds himself in quite a fix
With native tom-toms up on vics—
While local parrots in his ear
Screec joyfully: "No 'flicks, no beer.
The monkeys watch he doesn't take
His usual forty-minute "break";
The Burmese "super," with a grin,
Announces constantly "He's in."
The insects take a wild delight
In giving torment night by night—
So take a lesson from your job,
Don't be a *** fool like Bob.

By "ONE WHO GOES."

[*Cont'd from previous page.*]

0511. Sit back on carpet and watch cat licking chops. Wonder dispassionately whether to kill it or not, but decide against idea, as landlady might not like it.

0515. Suddenly notice time. Swallow tea, stuff slice of bread into mouth, raid pantry for more; get hat, coat, and put on shoes.

0517. Leave house (remembering with great presence of mind to kick cat on way out), tear madly up road with collar and tie in one hand and a piece of cake in other.

0526. Catch bus, which has been hanging back for me.

0600. Back where I started. It is six o'clock in the morning, it is a Sunday morning, and I am in Leicestershire. For that, black and burning hatred against the Fiends fills my soul to the uttermost.

VICTORY
BIGGIN STREET, LOUGHBOROUGH

MONDAY, FEB. 5th—3 days.

Ann Harding and Anita Louise in
NINE GIRLS
Also Bily Gilbert in "SPOTLIGHT SCANDALS"

THURSDAY, FEB. 8th—3 days.

Rosalind Russell and Brian Aherne in
BEAUTIFUL CHEAT
Also Chas. Starrett in "DOUBLE PUNCH"

MONDAY, FEB. 12th—6 days.

Danny Kaye (The New Comedian) in
UP IN ARMS
(TECHNICOLOUR).
Also FULL SUPPORTING PROGRAMME

MONDAY, FEB. 19th—6 days.

Irene Dunne and Alan Marshall in
THE WHITE CLIFFS OF DOVER
Proving a greater attraction than "Mrs. Miniver"

MONDAY, FEB. 26th—6 days.

Errol Flynn and Paul Lukas in
UNCERTAIN GLORY
Also "MEMPHIS BELLE" (Technicolour)

Mon. to Fri.—Con. from 5-30 p.m. Sat.—Con. from 2 p.m.
MATINEES.—Mon. and Wed. at 2-15 p.m.
SUNDAYS.— 6-15 p.m. (One Show)

BEAU-ROMANCE

(An intellectual delusion in several stages)

By KAY PRICE.

LOST!—AT B.M. DURING XMAS FESTIVITIES, ATS HANDBAG CONTAINING ARTICLES OF GREAT PERSONAL VALUE. FINDER PLEASE RETURN TO CANTEEN MANAGERESS, OR—
>PTE. EGERIA HELMETT,
>"X" HUT.

Dear Miss Helmett,
    It gives me great pleasure to return your bag, which I found behind the bicycle shed attached to "H" Hut. In order to find the owner I was constrained to examine the interior of the bag, and could not help noticing a copy of the poems of that seldom-recognised modern Genius, Blurb Gass. I, too, am a great admirer of his works—particularly his "Meditation on an Infant's Respirator."
    Hoping that you will not find your bag impaired by its exposure to the frost, I leave you in Gass' own words:
>"Numb-thwarted, heart-botched,
> Seeking ever light in rancid darkness——"
>   Yours sincerely,
>   Septimus Farthing.

Dear Mr. Farthing,
    Thank you so much for returning my bag. I can't imagine how it got there. Yes, I am a great admirer of Blurb Gass, but all my friends laugh at me for it.
    Thanking you again,
>"I grovel in the hovels of harsh trash
> Glutted with ochre, hunger-slaked with slush——"
>   Yours sincerely,
>   Egeria Helmett.

Dear Miss Helmett,
    How kind of you to answer my letter. I am not surprised that your friends do not share your admiration for Blurb Gass—he is only for those whose artistic sense is keenest. Would you think it very impertinent of me to suggest meeting you one night, when we could, perhaps, read a little Gass together, and share his earthy perfection?
>"Hoping, sack-mouthed, rubble-lunged, agape——"
>   Yours,
>   Septimus (Pongo) Farthing.

Dear Pongo,
    What a lovely suggestion! Would tomorrow suit you? It is my day off, and I could be at the Vampire by six o'clock.
    In haste, "Fiery-penned I fly,
> Leaving livid pencil shavings
> Patterned on the brooding floor——"
>   Yours,
>   "Gerry."

GOSSIP FLASH.

Seen recently at the Vampire, in closest conference, were "Pongo" Farthing and one of our ATS friends, whom he was heard to address as "Gerry, my half-soul." We will be interested to learn whether or not he is the "Other Half."

IN THE SHADOWS.

"Darling, this is forever, isn't it?"

FIVE YEARS HENCE.

"I don't know why the hell I married you! Confound that imbecile Blurb Gass!"

NIGHT ATTACK

Slowly they steal across the shadowed sky,
Pulsating through the peacefulness of night,
And, throb for throb, my heart makes soft reply
Reverberating, breath for breath.
Must I, then, wakeful, mock this tired hour,
This silent hour when Nature fashioned sleep,
Must men this short-lived dusk-born Peace devour
To find, with Dawn's uprising, Death.

"BOFEN."

A.T.S. LITERARY COMPETITION.

A Literary Competition has been planned for all auxiliaries of "Y" Signals A.T.S. Miss Pamela Frankau has kindly consented to judge the entries, and two prizes of £5 and £3 will be awaredd in each of the three classes—short stories, poems, and miscellaneous compositions. The closing date for all entries, which should bear the author's name, number and Wing, and be submitted to Quorn Court through Companies, is **Feb. 24th, 1945**

FAMOUS LAST WORDS———
"No——I'm not much used to travelling at night."

GET YOUR———

Beauty and Toilet Preparations

FROM

"LEONARD'S"

Gentlemen's Hairdresser

25, CHURCH GATE, LOUGHBOROUGH

Large Variety in Stock!

EMPIRE

MARKET PLACE, LOUGHBOROUGH

MONDAY, FEB. 5th—3 days.
Lucille Ball and Dick Powell in
MEET THE PEOPLE
Also J. Mack Brown in "THE GHOST RIDER"

THURSDAY, FEB. 8th—3 days.
Errol Flynn and Claude Rains in
THE SEA HAWK
Also FULL SUPPORTING PROGRAMME

MONDAY, FEB. 12th—3 days.
Roy Rogers in
HANDS ACROSS THE BORDER
Also Glenda Farrell in "KLONDYKE KATE"

THURSDAY, FEB. 15th—3 days.
Jean Parker in
DETECTIVE KITTY O'DAY
Also Joan Davis in "BEAUTIFUL BUT BROKE"

MONDAY, FEB. 19th—3 days.
James Mason and Herbert Lom in
HOTEL RESERVE
Also Brown & Carney in "ADVENTURES OF A ROOKIE"

THURSDAY, FEB. 22nd—3 days.
Barry K. Barnes in
The Return of the Scarlet Pimpernel
Also East Side Kids in "MR. MUGGS STEPS OUT"

MONDAY, FEB. 26th—6 days.
Maria Montez and Jon Hall in
COBRA WOMAN
(TECHNICOLOUR).
Also David Bruce in "MOON OVER LAS VEGAS"

**CONTINUOUS DAILY. Doors open at 1-30 p.m.
SUNDAYS at 1-30 p.m.**

Printed by Toppings Ltd., 17, Southfield Rd., Loughborough, and published by L. P. Jones for Beaumanor Staff Magazine Committee.

CHAPTER XXXIX

The Atsites called Beetoo. Prophet offereth shekels. The two wise men and the tongue of Eanem. Adewo is well pleased. Atsites have strange visions. It is as clear as mud.

Now AMONG THE MIGHTY TRIBE OF ATSITES which dwelled in the fair land of Woyg were many which were exceeding poor. And they were called Beetoo. And because they were possessed of few shekels they were sorely cheesed, and life was exceeding Ropey.

And it came to pass that the Prophet Osee, with Adewo upon his right hand, appeared before the multitude, saying: Wouldst thou desire to be Beewun and thus inherit more filthy lucre? And they answered him with one voice, crying: Not Half. Therefore, saith the Prophet, ye must hearken unto my disciples, Capdon and Pyk, and learn concerning the mysteries of Eanem, and write certain parchments for me, and verily, verily I say unto ye, if the parchments are good to look upon, and ye possess the Low-down upon Eanem,

ATSITES CALLED BEETOO

then will I beseech Red Tabz and thy Mother Superior to call ye Beewuns and to give unto ye more shekels.

And accordingly he sent the two wise men, Capdon and Pyk amongst them, to give them the Gen. And the wise men saith: Get a load of this; and spake long and earnestly of Juice, and the wondrous ways of it. And upon the tablets of Ell they writ many boxes and squiggles which were passing strange, and nattered away in the curious tongue of Eanem. And when they preached a sermon concerning the Law of one Ome, a mighty prophet of Eanem, the Atsites were confounded and accounted Mr. Ome a bit of a twerp. And the wondrous words of Capdon and Pyk flowed into one ear and out of the other. And the Atsites marvelled at them, and saith, one unto the other: Verily, these are two comely men, and fair to look upon. And their voices are truly a rhapsody. But what the heck is it all about? And behold, none twiggeth.

And when Adewo came forth and tootled at them with his hand, they knew his tootles and writ upon parchments in great haste, murmuring: Coo! This bloke's in a hurry! And Adewo looked upon their parchments and saw that there were many spaces, crying: What's all this? And they answered him saying: Fear not, for these are all Dead Easy. And Adewo was well pleased and delivered them back into the hands of Capdon and Pyk.

And in their slumbers they beheld mighty corkscrews, and wiggles, and squiggles. And voices bellowed gibberish into their ears, and screamed awful words at them. And when they awoke they cried: Behold, it is as clear as mud. For it is this wise: The Juice goeth down and around. And it goeth in here. And it cometh out there. Verily, the why and the wherefore are past all understanding. Yet if it pleaseth Red Tabz that we write the squiggles that Capdon and Pyk sheweth unto us, let us therefore make him happy. For thus will he fashion us into Beewuns and dispense his largess upon us to the tune of fourpence a day.

APRIL, 1945

VOL. II. No. 2 (NEW SERIES) - **6d.**

FILM ATTRACTIONS FOR APRIL

SHOWING AT THE ODEON THEATRE

Sunday, April 1st—Janet Gaynor, Frederic March and Adolphe Menjou in **A Star is Born**, in Technicolor, with full supporting programme.

MONDAY, APRIL 2nd, for 3 days. George Murphy, Gloria de Haven, Frank Sinatra in

Step Lively

Also Charles Ruggles and Diana Lynn in **Our Hearts were Young and Gay**

THURS., April 5th, for 3 days. By public demand, Daphne du Maurier's

Rebecca

with Laurence Olivier, Joan Fontaine and George Sanders, and full supporting programme.

Sunday, April 8th—Margaret Lockwood and Michael Wilding in **Dear Octopus**. Also Anne Coric in **Sarong Girl**.

MONDAY, APRIL 9th, and all the week—
Monty Woolley, June Haver and Dick Haymes in

IRISH EYES ARE SMILING

in Technicolor.
Also Robert Ryan and John Carradine in **Gangway for Tomorrow**.

Sunday, April 15th—Carole Lombard and Frederic March in **Nothing Sacred**, in Technicolor. Also Hutch, Naughton and Gold in **Down Melody Lane**.

MONDAY, APRIL 16th, and all the week—
Dorothy Lamour and Eddie Bracken in

RAINBOW ISLAND

in Technicolor.
Also Jimmy Lydon and John Litel in **Henry Boy Scout**.

Sunday, April 22nd—Melvyn Douglas and Merle Oberon in **That Uncertain Feeling**. Also Ralph Byrd and Bela Lugosi in **S.O.S. Coastguard**.

MONDAY, APRIL 23rd, for 3 days. Lon McCallister and Jeanne Craine in

Winged Victory

with full supporting programme.

THURS., APRIL 26th, for 3 days. Gary Cooper and Teresa Wright in

Casanova Brown

Also Robert Lowery and Jean Parker in **The Navy Way**.

Continuous Performance Daily 1-45 p.m.   Sunday, One Performance at 6 p.m.

Vol. II. No. 2 (New Series).

BEAUMANOR
STAFF MAGAZINE

Editor: ERIC C. MILLHOUSE
Manager and Publisher ... ... LEONARD P. JONES
Associate Editors ... ... , ... KAY PRICE, DUDLEY TRUIN
Art Editor: DICK WILKINSON   Treasurer: A. H. APPLETON

IN offering our apologies for the late publication of the B.S.M. this month we draw your attention to the new and greatly improved appearance of your magazine.

Shortly after the last publication our printers, deciding that they could make a living without our custom, threw in their hands practically without warning, leaving us barely a fortnight in which to make fresh arrangements. In less strenuous times no even moderately efficient trader with any sort of a reputation to consider would have presumed to behave in so unbusinesslike a fashion, but—*c'est la guerre*!

However, thanks to the sterling efforts of our O.C., and his friends, we have been fortunate in securing the services of a first-class printer, and so—the B.S.M. survives! If some of our regular features are missing from this issue we ask to be excused on account of the recent upheaval. Next month we hope to return to normal.

You mut be getting tired of reading appeals for contributions—but not as tired as we are of making them! We don't think we are exaggerating when we state that the B.S.M. is popular. But, do *you*, if you enjoy reading it, ever pause to consider that it would be twenty-four sheets of *blank* paper if *someone* didn't offer some contributions? It seems that you are content to have the magazine thrown in your lap once a month, read it, and then cast it aside until the next one comes along—sure that it *will* come; and certain that *somebody else* will have written enough to fill its pages. Perhaps you imagine we are overwhelmed with contributions, from which we leisurely sift what we require, and throw the rest away. Reader, we hate to shatter your illusions. Perhaps you don't realise that 75 per cent. of your B.S.M is filled by contributions which the Editorial Board have had to beg, beseech and bully people into writing. Possibly you will scornfully mutter: "That's what an Editorial Board's for!" Maybe you are right, but when that Board is devoting a very large part of its spare time towards preparing the magazine for you, isn't it entitled to some *voluntary* support? We don't forget the few stalwarts who do consistently supply us with material, but how few they are! The vast majority of readers just sit back and do nothing—except, perhaps criticise the contents!

WOYG FORUM, after its phenomenal start, lapsed in the true Woygian fashion. Only three contributions on the subject of NATIONALISATION arrived, and only two comments on last month's EQUALITY OF THE SEXES articles. For next month we have chosen the highly topical subject of CAPITAL PUNISHMENT. Are you FOR or AGAINST? Articles, of approximately 500 words, to reach the Editor by April 20th.

Next issue ready May 4th.   Contributions to reach Editors by April 20th.

GOOD READING

By LILY SHEPHERD.

WILLIAM GAUNT, author of "The Pre-Raphaelite Tragedy," has given us another very entertaining book, "The Æsthetic Adventure," chosen by the Book Society as the book of the month.

Although this is not a novel, but rather a collective biography of various famous nineteenth- and early twentieth-century characters, it is a very readable book, and tells of that strange movement, both in Britain and France, known as the Æsthetic Movement. We meet Swinburne the poet, Whistler the painter, Du Maurier, Oscar Wilde and many more well-known people who were prominent between the years 1880 and 1910. Their rather indefinable belief, "art for art's sake," was carried to a point of ridicule and decadence, but in spite of this, they produced some very remarkable works of art, both in painting and literature.

Around these strange but interesting characters, William Gaunt has built his story and tells it in such amusing style as to make it good reading, even for those not interested in the characters themselves.

William Gaunt is both historian and artist, having left Oxford with a History degree in the early 1920's, and having exhibited his work as an artist at the Royal Academy. He has used his knowledge of history and art in this delightful "Æsthetic Adventure" and although it is primarily a social history, it is nevertheless quite as readable as any fictional work.

If you prefer something in a lighter vein let me offer you Jane Austen's "Persuasion." Not perhaps as great or as famous as "Pride and Prejudice" but nevertheless attractive, in that it is light and far from the present day world. The whole story is leisurely, concerned mainly with the romance and social snobbery of the Regency Period. This was Jane Austen's last book and was published after her death, but it is as polished as any of her former works, and sparkles with all her usual charm and quiet humour.

Among the new poets we find Mr. Ralph Lawrence from whose book "The Mill-stream" I have taken this very amusing and quotable passage.

> "Such is the scene my eye confronts
> While fishermen in mackintoshes
> Sitting despondently in punts,
> Listless and limp as their goloshes
>
> Wait for the silvery-breasted dace
> To bite a deftly-baited hook:
> But not one drawn moustachioed face
> Wears even a faintly hopeful look."

Bookseller and Stationer   ::   Lending Library

J. SKETCHLEY
24 & 25 High Street, Loughborough

Telephone 2980

PERPLEXIANA

EDITED BY 'SHAKE-JACK."

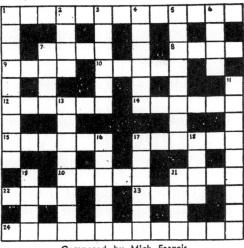

Composed by Mick Francis.

ACROSS.
1. This doesn't mean that you pour the final pint over the King's highway (3, 3, 3, 4).
7. Containers (4).
8. Amicable, 50% mixed, gives you this sort of compound (4).
9. Double five to a T. What a cover! (4).
10. Hand out (5).
12. You are part of it (6).
14. Me, amid the halting and the infirm (6).
15. A state of feeling (6).
17. Sounds like a queer sort of song (6).
20. That is, rat in the middle (5).
21. Ooze (4).
22. The French sailing ship; not as much anyway (4).
23. Rise up before one (4).
24. Pompous, and 12 across (with a bit added). Jump to it, hosses! (5, 8).

DOWN.
1. Determined (9).
2. An abbreviated twelve inches round an alternative (4).
3. The singer is not in "harmony," he has to give up (6).
4. This cab sounds as if it was a good looker (6).
5. Looks as though the Royal Electrical and Mechanical Engineer has "kicked the bucket" (8).
6. Cunning (4).
7. In the army, a group of men (4).
11. But it doesn't mean a non-drinking spelling bee (1, 3, 5).
13. To put away (8).
16. Looks as though this animal limps his way forward (6).
17. O.C. Tole (anag. It's a South American leopard) (6).
18. Just a small thing (4).
19. Does he notice more than you and I? (4).
21. Looks like a call for help with nothing on the end of it but actually it's just middling (2, 2).

SERIOUS QUIZ.

Do you know Nature? Which of the following are true, which are false? One mark for each correct. If you get more than five you are not human; less than five shows commendable ignorance. Turn to page 9 for the bad news.

1. Moles are blind.
2. Eagles have been known to carry off babies.
3. Dragonflies sting.
4. The bite of a Tarantula is fatal to man.
5. Snakes are slimy.
6. Warts are caused by handling toads.
7. Frogs drink through their skin.
8. Hair will turn to worms when left long in water.
9. Mules never have offsprings.
10. The growth of garden vegetables is affected by the moon.

TWO MORE ANAGRAMS FOR YOU TO SOLVE.

(1) DAPPY AREA   Clue: To many, an event of immense value.
(2) MONCFORT JAIL Clue: Close to O.C.

Theatre Royal
LOUGHBOROUGH

Programme for April, 1945

Easter Monday, April 2nd—6 days.
CARROLL LEVIS AND HIS DISCOVERIES
A Feast of Good Fun Provided by the Stars of the Future.

Mon., April 9th (6 days), Mats.: Wed., Thurs., & Sat.
LEON UNDERWOOD presents the Loveliest of All Musical Plays—SCHUBERT'S
LILAC TIME
THREE HOURS of Glorious Music, Comedy, and Comedy.

Monday, April 18th—6 days.
Hinge Productions presents the New Type of Show
JOIN THE PARTY
OLD TIME MINSTREL SHOW
Including many well-known Loughborough Vocalists.

Monday, April 23rd—6 days.
SECOND WEEK OF
JOIN THE PARTY
With New Guest Stars.

Monday, April 30th—6 days.
JOIN THE PARTY
Once Again and Meet Further Top-ranking Stars.

The Woygian Association

MOST people will readily disagree with the popular assertion that one's schooldays are the happiest of one's life. You have only to cast back your minds over years of,—well need I say?—to explode that theory. And no one would even think of applying that threadbare dogma to their sojourn at Beaumanor. But despite the ups and downs of school life, Old Boys, and Old Girls Associations flourish, so why should not a similar organisation thrive amongst us, as time gradually obliterates the "scars" that we now feel so acutely? Such, at any rate, was the reasoning behind the idea of the Woygian Association.

All right! We heard what you said! "Once we get away from this dump, we never want to see or hear of it again!" But do you really mean that? How long have you been here? A year? Two years? Five? Quite a slice out of one's life, one's youth. Are you going to seal up that part of your memory and never think of it again? Impossible,—and you know it! You won't be able to help remembering, and as time goes on, the memories will be more and more pleasant. You'll forget the awfulness of Night Duties and Canteen tea, and only look back on the amusing incidents that you may connect with them. Distance will always lend enchantment—even to Woygland.

The object of the Association is this: to keep Woygites loosely in touch with each other, no matter how widely scattered they may be. For this purpose there will be a magazine,—it is not yet decided whether publication will be quarterly or half-yearly. In it will be as much news of as many people as its hard-working production staff can rake up. That, of course, will call for co-operation from you. If you hear that so-and-so has had quins, or such-and-such has gone to jail (at last!), or you yourself find a four-leaved clover growing on the top of Mt. Kilimanjaro, it is not entirely optimistic to suppose that one's fellow Woygites might be faintly interested to hear of it. Human nature being what it is, they may even mutter that it was "Just what you'd expect of old ———." These are exaggerated cases of course, but exaggerated for a purpose. To drive home the point that on *you* depends the success of the Woygian Association and its magazine. A mere post-card of some incident of news connected with yourself or another ex-Beaumanorite, sent to the proper quarter whose address will be made known later, will be of enormous value.

Details of how to enter are set out very clearly on the backs of the Entrance Forms which are already in circulation. If you have not had one yet, you will soon, and you will see that we are not out to ruin you, financially.

Re-unions will be staged from time to time, and as our homes stretch from Scotland to Cornwall, there will be a sort of Zoning scheme with several convenient centres of re-union. However, it is impossible to give more details until we have a sizeable number of members to re-unite.

That's what it all boils down to. On *you* depends the success of the whole project. No members—no Woygian Association. Don't put it off till later, don't leave it to that bloke over there. Join as soon as possible, so that on the great day when you see Lt.-Col. Ellingworth hoist his White Ensign, you will be part of the Woygian Association that even now, is waiting to spring into life.

Further information from:—Mr. H. Dodd and Cpl. M. Norris, "C" Hut, Beaumanor.

Ralph Champion has The O.C. on the Mat

PART of an official notice, hanging on the wall of the O.C.'s office, says: "1899—No mention has been made of the Marconi System which has tremendous possibilities but seems a long way off being tried yet."

About the time that was written, Marshall John William Ellingworth, a ten-year-old Oakham boy, visited a fairground. There, a phrenologist declared: "You will travel widely. You will see many wonders. You will hear many secrets."

This prophecy came true. Five years later, young Ellingworth went to sea to learn about the navy the hard way—as ship's boy. Had it not been for experimental work he and men like him carried out in later years, the writing on the O.C.'s wall might not seem so quaint to-day.

Col. Ellingworth did not remain long on the bottom rung. Within two years he had been selected to take up "the new science of wireless telegraphy." His first job on starting his new duties was to shin up the 220 feet high mast of a battleship and square the wireless aerial.

The radio equipment on the ship was primitive. Part of it consisted of a "Coherer," a large piece of tubing filled with iron filings which theoretically produced wireless signals on a tape and also rang a bell. The latter task it performed so efficiently that every time there were atmospherics the bell clanged and the operator had to rush from the deck, his bunk, or wherever he happened to be. On the coherer was a notice "do not thump." But the temptation was irresistible at times. It was not until a year after the O.C. joined the wireless branch that oral reception was introduced.

The outbreak of the last war found Ellingworth—one of the Navy's youngest Chief Petty Officer Telegraphists—in charge of the radio service of a flotilla of 16 destroyers.

Col. Ellingworth seldom mentions the next part of his adventures. But on April 28th, 1915, he was on duty in his wireless cabin when a shell struck the bridge above, killing the captain, officer of the watch, and the coxswain. A tuner, weighing 40 lbs. struck our O.C. on the head injuring him so badly that he still carries the scars. Despite his injuries, Chief Petty Officer Ellingworth remained at his post until the end of the action—and later received the D.S.M.

Next year he was commissioned—one of the first wireless officers to be chosen from the lower deck.

Radio was still in its infancy, ships called each other by searchlight before transmitting on their feeble radio sets; yet each month progress was being made.

From childhood Col. Ellingworth has kept a diary. If you could read the black-bound, neatly written volumes you would see how he and his hard-working colleagues were studying each new move, suggesting others—always confident, despite set-backs, that radio was one of the biggest things of the future.

In 1920 he helped with experiments which revolutionised anti-submarine warfare 20 years later. He had joined H.M.S. Antrim which he equipped as a research ship. There, the first "Asdic"—U-Boat detector—was tested in shallow coastal waters. His Asdic tube was five feet in diameter, stretching to the actual keel of the ship and requiring a whole watch of sailors to haul it up.

In 1921, Ellingworth was in charge of Horsea high-power wireless station and two years later was sent to Singapore to modernise the wireless station there. Other appointments followed, including charge of a station at Malta. There he had his most un-nerving experience—a cocktail party at the top of a 600 feet radio mast.

Col. Ellingworth retired from the navy with the rank of Lieut.-Commander on Dec. 15th, 1934. It is typical of his enthusiasm for hard work that within a fortnight he began his civilian duties as O.C. at Fort Bridgewoods.

Nothing may be said of his recent work. But five stars for the prophet who said: "You will hear many secrets."

Though Ellingworth is back in uniform to-day—as Lieut.-Colonel in the Signals—a naval atmosphere still pervades Beaumanor. There is the figure head of Cornwallis threatening late-comers with half-drawn sword; there is the Colonel's passion for tidiness; there is the White Ensign held in readiness for victory day.

Though the work has grown and the staff with it, Col. Ellingworth sometimes regrets the loss of the personal touch of the old Chatham days. Then the "Old Man," as the staff affectionately called him, was often asked to settle all kinds of domestic matters and as a family man with a wife, elder daughter and twins, his advice was usually sound.

Col. Ellingworth worries sometimes that he must retire in four years, for he certainly will not be happy without a job. So if you can suggest a career which a young man can begin on reaching 60, drop him a line.

Comments on "Equality of the Sexes"

I agree with E. Catchpole and Joan H. Rogerson; there can never be Equality in the strict sense of the word. The physical and psychological differences between man and woman make this impossible. For instance, if women wish for equal pay they will have to compete with men on equal terms, and will always be the losers.

Nan Brown mentions the single girl with an invalid parent. There are also single men with invalid parents. Nan also thinks women should have equal pay, if only for the sake of "chivalry." The world is not run on those lines.

Barnes says men and women are born equal. Very true; but they do not grow up to be equals. We have not got Equality yet. Mrs. Jones has been reprieved. *A. H. APPLETON.*

The chief argument "Against" is apparently based on physical differences; I fail to see why this should count at all. We are not agitating to be coal-heavers or heavy-weight boxers, any more than a man would enjoy embroidering the corner of a handkerchief! In any case, it is a fact that there are as many masculine women as there are effeminate men, so let's call it quits.

As to Mr. Catchpole's reference to female bias, feminine charm seems to go a long way in Woygland! *NAN BROWN.*

PERPLEXIANA SOLUTIONS:

ANSWER TO SERIOUS QUIZ: "Only No. 7 is true, the rest are false.

ANSWER TO ANAGRAMS: (1) PAY PARADE. (2) MAJOR CLIFTON.

Here is the solution to last month's crossword. How many of you, besides ourselves completed it correctly?

Across.—1, Contradiction; 7, Talc; 8, Ally; 9, Port; 10, Houri; 12, Nether; 14, Evince; 15, Reuter; 17, Augers; 20, Robot; 21, Asia; 22, Peri; 23, Agra; 24, Bank of England.

Down.—1, Carpentry; 2, Test; 3, Anchor; 4, Immune; 5, Trailing; 6, Oslo; 7, Tort; 11, Beeswaxed; 13, Hat-trick; 16, Rebuff; 17, Attain; 18, Ensa; 19, Lena; 21, Aral.

The Saga of Black Thursday

By N. REID.

YES! I went to the dance. I crept into the Hall—clinging very tightly to Jean's arm—(incidentally I left in practically the same manner!)—to find the place absolutely empty save for Norah—our honourable M.C.—and two harpies who almost snatched at my hard-earned shekels.

Needless to say at that time the "MEN" hadn't arrived—nor had the band—the dance was scheduled to start at 7.30 p.m.—it was then 8.30 B.S.T.).

The M.C. was gnashing her pearly teeth and if she hadn't had her hair "set" she might even have torn some out by the roots. Before the air became too "blue" for our innocent ears we beat a hasty retreat to the "Bar," leaving instructions to "come and dig us out if those 'Ballet' Dancers arrived."

I had just installed myself in a very comfortable chair—gazing with delight into the murky gloom of my fourth "light ale," when I espied the sylph-like form of our worthy Norah ploughing her way through the smoke. In tones of rising hysteria she announced "they've come, and now there are no so-and-so women!" I bade an almost tearful farewell to my beloved tankard and strode masterfully towards the scene of battle. I could hear the banshee-like wail of the "sax" tuning up in the distance. I think I felt sick, but having gathered courage from the little prayer I sent up (for the sake of my feet) I entered . . .

For one brief moment, as I stood swaying in the doorway, I thought of the loved ones I'd left at home: I thought of the days (and nights) spent in the highways and byways of this beautiful land of ours, listening to the sweet and melodious song of the birds. For one brief moment I thought—crash! the advancing hordes were rapidly approaching from all sides, and so with a hollow laugh I went forward; forward to my doom.

The rest of the evening was a nightmare of blurred faces, slightly inebriated partners who breathed eerily and beerily into my shell pink ears—*AND* BOOTS, BOOTS, BOOTS.

By ten p.m. the grin on my face had become a permanent fixture—one might almost say, a leer. I was becoming tired of asking and answering inane questions and oh, my poor feet. They were literally asking for mercy. But no, this was denied me. On! On! On! went that . . . band till finally with a crash of cymbals and an ominous roll on the drums, they too, intimated that they could hold out no longer.

NEVER, in all the long and varied years of my brilliant (?) career was I so thankful to hear the strains of our National Anthem. (The guy who wrote same will *never* know how fervently grateful I was).

And so, with a weary sigh I limped homewards, bruised in body and dazed in spirit, my mind filled solely by thoughts of BED and a mission nobly fulfilled.

"B" Watch Dance was a complete success.

Who's Who --- Beaumanor 1985

The following extracts are taken from the book by Victor F. Swakeley.

NOEL ROYLE, age 62. Revolutionary poet and short story writer. Famous during World War 1939-1945 as a political maniac. He was responsible for the murder of forty Catholic Scots during the Anarchist Revolution, 1962. Self-confessed Mormon, and has been convicted three times for bigamy. Now spends his time in pilgrimages to the tomb of H. G. Wells and asking young ladies if it is time for the last goodnight.

His motto: "Labor omnia vincit."

"SLAP" REEDMAN, age 73. Lecturer at Dee College and for many years chief controller of traffic. He has a mania for telephones and can be seen at any time in his office seated on a pile of directories surrounded by 'phones of all shapes and sizes. In March 1950 he gave an exhibition of whip-cracking to members of the staff. One trick, knocking cigarettes out of sleeping persons mouths so that they would not burn their lips, was greeted by a roar of approval and admiration. In 1960 he was responsible for persuading Aileen Tunnington to take three months leave: it was obvious that she was working herself to a standstill.

His motto: "Ne plus ultra."

VICTOR MERRITT, age 59. Origin unknown. Was well known in his younger days as a great traveller and superman. His nickname of "Colonel" was conferred upon him for his obvious love of military discipline and constant devotion to duty. In 1947 he was attacked by Jimmy Hunter and Claude Deakin for opening windows at 6 o'clock on a cold and frosty morning, and he has never been the same since. He is now devoting his time posing for "Wilk" in goodbye scenes, and giving lectures on "Life on the Burma Road."

MARGARET ELLINGWORTH, age 58. A surprising woman, well known for her contumacy and *otium cum dignitate.* In her childhood she showed great versatility with both pen and typewriter, but she is now satisfied with the Smith's Dictation Sysem. Many will no doubt remember her very beautiful wedding at St. Mary's to Mr. Antrum, F.J.S., F.R.G.S., F.A.S., F.R.A.S., F.S.A., F.A.I. She has shown herself to be a devoted mother, and, like her husband, has spared no expense in the education and welfare of their twelve children. In 1959, 1960 and 1961 she played principal boy in the Shakejack Pantomime.

BILLIE BROWN, age 61. Although her childhood is unknown, rumour has it that she served as a waitress until she ran away from a perfectly good home to be a gun moll. Her violent temper is shown by the way in which she attacked her lover in an article in one of the original copies of the B.S.M. dated Feb. 1945. In 1948 she was elected head of the Windmill Society. Since 1957 she has held the post of editor in the "Babies before Butter" Magazine, and as Aunt Elsie in the "Red Letter" she has given advice to thousands of worried just-16's.

HARRY DIX, age 71. One of the richest men in Beaumanor for many years, he started to make big money in a series of coups on the football pools. The earliest record of Harry dates back to March 1933 when he won the lightweight boxing championship of India (his only opponent being a blind goat and a crippled urchin). The death of his partner Mr. George Billingsley after a heart attack through overwork in 1950 was a great shock to his, and his £2,000 funeral was filmed in Technicolor.

RICHARD WHITFORD, age 79. Best known as "Old Dick," he spent the first forty years of his life in the British Army (Middle East and India). Many will remember him as a captain in the Home Guard during the war years 1939-1945. During the Anarchist Revolution of 1962 he joined the Government Volunteers and was badly wounded during the siege of the House of Lords. In 1980 he accepted the position of Lecturer at the War Museum where he demonstrates the working of a two-pounder anti-tank gun.

P.S.—In answer to many requests I will explain the statue standing amid the ruins of a wooden hut next to the cricket pavilion. This statue is in memory of our first Officer Commanding Lt.-Col. Ellingworth. He was unfortunately killed when his office caught fire during an interview with Mr. James Hewson (also consumed by the flames). Lt.-Col. Ellingworth was the perfect Officer Commanding. At his funeral all the station turned out in sackcloth and ashes, and after the ceremony retired to the Empire for coffees.

Woyg Forum: NATIONALISAT

"Nationalisation will not kill competition" declares F. W. Leedham.

RAILWAYS, motor transport, mines, gas, electricity and water supplies should be nationalised after World War Two is over for the very important reason that no profit should ever be made from any public utility.

In this highly complex life of ours the above-mentioned utilities are absolutely essential for our continued existence. It is of national importance for the Government to see that they are all run efficiently and cheaply.

Now, this efficient management of public utilities cannot, in my opinion, be carried out under private enterprise or by limited companies. The history of these public utilities lends support to my opinion.

For instance, let us consider the railways up to the time of the present war. That they were making a profit nobody would deny. But were they satisfied? Not they. They were not making enough profit. Their returns were falling off. Just before the war started I can remember large posters pasted up on all railway stations and boardings—" Give the Railways a Square Deal." If you had asked any railway shareholder the reason for the diminishing returns he would probably have replied that the road transport services were undercutting the railways; were transporting goods and passengers about the country more cheaply than the railways could do.

In short, the railways who had had a free hand in the business of land transport hitherto, were for the first time coming up against competition. And what is more, quite naturally I suppose, they didn't like it.

One more point is worth mentioning. It has always seemed to me hostile to the public interest and a great waste of money to pay the chairman of a railway company a large salary (by holding a number of shares) and at the same time allow him to draw large salaries as chairman of other private companies. No man is worth more than one good salary.

I think a lot of nonsense has been talked and written about competition and private enterprise in the past years until many people are deluded into thinking that once competition has been removed everything and everybody will become stagnant and apathetic. The very word competition has tended to become a catch phrase—a mere shibboleth. It has served the capitalists very well; they hope it will serve them longer.

Yet, freed from its party dress, competition—*individual competition*—is a very useful and necessary word. Nationalisation will not kill it.

In conclusion, may I put in a plea for the hospitals. I think it a national disgrace that many hospitals must rely on charity and flag days for their upkeep. The hospital is a very necessary utility, and a very necessary utility should be controlled and supported by the Government.

...N OF ESSENTIAL INDUSTRIES...

"'Take it or leave it' under Nationalisation," says J. Hunter.

NATIONALISATION of Industry like so many other subjects is ideal—as a theory only. We have seen the disadvantages and evils of monopolies and cartels. Give anybody, be it Government or private concern, a monopoly and it commences to squeeze the man who always pays; the consumer. We have seen a good, or I should say, bad example in the Railways.

Whilst road transport was competing, fares and rates were lower. Now the railways are virtually a Government-controlled monopoly, with road transport as an industry successfully smothered. The result has been a gradual increase in rates and fares (with the threat of more to come shortly) and an utter disregard for the passengers to whom they were appealing for a "square deal" prior to the war. We agree war traffic is a priority, but to me the ignoring of passengers comforts and finances is a pointer as to what we could expect should the railways become a peace-time monopoly or nationalised industry. To carry the nationalisation theory to its logical end would mean engulfing all industries with disastrous results. Furthermore, how would the individual benefit? Certainly the administration would operate in a similar manner as the Civil Service.

To many people one of the most iniquitous systems in the Government is the "promotion by seniority" system, a certain and sure way of killing ambition and initiative. Very handy for the man with years of service, but to the go-ahead man it means disillusion and mental stagnation until the man above him dies or retires. No industry could survive under such a system and it is obvious that the only way to encourage and improve trade is for open competition to prevail between the companies connected with the particular industry. I wonder what state the ordinary radio receiver would be in to-day had the development been left to a nationalised radio industry?. By these previous remarks I do not wish it to be implied that I want to see a return to the old system of cut-throat competition with a consequent derogatory effect on the wages of the employees.

What I would like to see would be *all* industries run as private concerns with a workers' representative or representatives on the board of directors, a living wage to all employees, and promotion by ABILITY ONLY. The latter has always been practised in private enterprise and the results have justified this method. The thousands of varieties, quality and reasonable prices testify to this. Under nationalisation it would be a question of take it or leave it.

Space does not allow for much criticism of the coal industry. True the conditions in that industry have been unhappy but who can say they have improved under Government supervision? No, to put it mildly they are at present chaotic—not much of an advert for Nationalisation.

Military Entomology

Four soul-searing blasts on a whistle herald the dawn of another day. Sleepy, tousled heads appear from beneath mosquito nets, to be greeted derisively by a few hardy souls returning from a pre-reveille cold shower.

To-day is "de-bugging" day and the long cylindrical mosquito nets are lowered from the ceiling while the owners thereof carefully examine the folds and wooden hoops for these obnoxious insects. Buckets of paraffin next appear upon the scene and the corners of the coir bedding "biscuits" are dipped into the liquid to remove further families of bugs. Next, the iron Macdonald bedsteads are dismantled and all parts thoroughly washed in paraffin.

Effective as these measures may seem—they are merely a temporary check on the activities of the insects. The harvest will be equally good the following week.

Shelf-kit is then taken down and examined for "Wooly-bear," a peculiar looking creature whose chief object in life seems to be to make the ravages of moths appear an amateurish affair.

Filled with the lust of battle, parties of men armed with blow-lamps, buckets of paraffin and brushes, then attack the Set Room, removing centipedes, scorpions, beets, etc., from inside the instruments and from behind wall panels.

George Henry, the pet hedgehog, views proceedings nervously and decides to go on points until things have quietened down, while the owner of Shammy, the tame chamelion, carefully removes his pet to a place of safety. Shammy causes endless amusement to the station. The favourite pastime being to place him upon objects of different colour to which he endeavours to blend himself. Black is his particular aversion and appears to cause him some discomfort.

Dog owners in the section spend an interesting (sic) half-hour with a pair of tweezers removing camel tics from their pets. These pests imbed themselves firmly in the dogs' flesh (chiefly under the collar) and feed on the blood of the animal until bloated to an enormous size, causing them considerable discomfort to the dogs.

"Break" indicates that the mornings activities have not in any way impaired the troops' appetites. Warm, freshly-made doughnuts are a speciality in the canteen and very few are left when the orderly-sergeant "blows-up" to resume work.

After dinner, time is one's own and the swimming pool with the café adjoining proves a great attraction. Other parties are to be seen setting out armed with cameras. These are members of the very popular Camera Club which organises outings to places of interest and gives help and advice to members, as well as supplying a fairly well equipped dark room.

The real enthusiasts, however are those who have purchased cameras fitted with special lenses for the purpose of photographing INSECTS.

E.S.C.

GET YOUR———

Beauty and Toilet Preparations

FROM

"LEONARD'S"

Gentlemen's Hairdresser

25 CHURCH GATE, LOUGHBOROUGH

Large Variety in Stock!

Citizen Army

By JOHN ELLINGWORTH.

"O England, model to thine inward greatness
Like little body with a mighty heart" . . .
                                    King Henry V.

Five years ago, with France o'errun,
By ruthless forces of the Hun:
The Nazi eagle flexed his claws,
Looked longingly at Britain's shores—
For he, all-powerful, held surmise,
That Britain was his greatest prize.

Rejoicing that our manhood's flower
Lay wearied at that crucial hour,
And ready, with fresh flags unfurl'd,
Prepared for conquest of the world—
With blood-stained talons to advance
On Britain, over prostrate France.

The wounded Lion raised its head,
Proclaimed resistance far from dead,
From town and hamlet forth they came—
Their lot was hard—no thoughts of fame
Were theirs—with valiant hearts to stand,
And to defend their Mother-land.

For them a tedious, arduous wait,
Defiant—and spurred on by hate
Of German vandals—patiently
They watched—Britannia's offspring free,
And chose their task of ceaseless toil,
To drive them from her hallowed soil.

Like Knights Defiant, grim and dour,
They lived anew their finest hour,
With weary eyes and bodies strained,
Though lacking arms and scarcely trained,
Then, as the fleeting weeks passed by,
Saw new Armadas in the sky.

They watched the warplanes, drove by drove,
The intricate designs they wove,
And saw each vast formation new,
Sent earthwards by those "gallant few,"
But never that they fear'd the most,
The vanguards of th'invasion host.

They kept their faith with those who fell,
Their resting-place 'midst Dunkirk's Hell,
Still recollect each desperate day,
Their calm demeanor, grim or gay,
And now, our arms assured at least,
They rest—an Army of the past,
But proud that Fate onetime decreed
They should fulfill their country's need.

They're telling Me!

CONGRATULATIONS to Ken. Talbot and Mavis Warren (Tich) who were married at Woodhouse Eaves on Saturday, the 24th March. Ken. had his Bachelor party on the 13th March. Not superstitious Ken.?

Our congratulations also to Irene Smith of Group Office and Capt. Siddall of the Royal Corps of Signals at Beaumanor, on their marriage at Loughborough on the 17th March. The reception was held in Beaumanor. The happy couple spent their honeymoon in Cornwall.

A party was held at the Curzon Arms on the 17th March, which was a farewell to Blenki, who left us for an out-station. It developed into quite a family affair when Blanco (brother-in-law to Blenki) informed the then happy gathering that this was also a celebration of his engagement to W.A.A.F. Molly Cronin attached to Woyg. It was noted that one of the company obviously believed that prevention was better than cure when he took a liberal supply of Aspirins before and during the session. Did you escape the hang-over Bobby?

EXILES.—On Wednesday, Feb. 21st, the Civil Service Wireless Staff, under the title "Exiles," held their first dance in the Miller Calder Hall, Thurso. Mr. G. Gordon Cooper acted as M.C. to approximately 160 dancers, and prizes were awarded to the winners of the novelty dances. The sum of £8 10s. has been handed over to the general funds of the British Red Cross Society. In response to many requests the staff hope to hold another dance in the near future. Good luck in your next effort you Exiles in Thurso.

Who was the astute financier who bought a share of the Pool Club for £3. Hardly a gilt-edged investment, eh!

We have been called things good and bad. The duty bus passing on its homeward journey was referred to, in the writer's company, as the Guinea Pigs 'bus. Guinea a week—get it?

"Dickey" tells us that her engagement to the Yank, Vincent van Domelen, is off. We wonder if that means that Peter Kingsland and Jimmy are still in the running. She did say something about her "heart is still with Beaumanor." Time will tell.

The haggis which Muriel McAra recently presented to Freddie Fox, turned on him, we hear, during his lonely journey home, and bit him in several places. After a short scuffle Freddie succeeded in overpowering the ferocious beast and bore the carcase in triumph to his wondering, and probably highly suspicious spouse. We always wondered whether haggis was snared or shot.

There's a rumour that coat hooks are to be included in the "I" Corps equipment. Is this true Nancy?

A recently married officer on this station has been seen with a rifle. So soon, Captain?

Oh Khaki, what "shape" is shrouded in thy folds! Brand Hill has its own Maria McDonald. Is this true Pte. Billie Brown? Come up and see us some time.

Mr. P. K. Antrum (alias Squanderbug, alias Weasel) wishes to make a public denial that he bought a cup of canteen tea on the 11th Feb., 1945. He agrees it was his first since October 1943, but he didn't pay for it.

Daffodil time in Beaumanor. Here to-day, gone to-morrow.

Congratulations to Mr. and Mrs. Fagg on the birth of a daughter.

L/Cpl. Lillian Nichol of the Plotting Room has left us. Motherhood is her next venture.

BETTER LATE THAN NEVER.—The new Liberty Club for war workers, male and female, was officially opened by Viscount Samuel on Friday, 23rd March. The club had already been sampled by Woygites young and old. Tuesday, Thursday and Saturday are popular days, perhaps this is due to the setting aside of these days for baths—MEN ONLY.

Through the medium of this column Mr. Peter Dart wishes to thank the unknown A.T.S. girl who recently on a crowded Barkus 'bus offered him her seat on condition that she might sit on his lap.

On a recent northbound train-journey, Auxiliary confessed that she once taught the plain facts of knitting to a Yank in a railway carriage. We thought one knitted with " hanks " and not " yanks."

We bid adieu to Chick Last, who has left us for the Army, and wish him luck, also to Mac. whose health necessitated his leaving us. We hope his health improves.

Let's have the " dope, " folks!

CAIRN X.

B.W. 'Castledowner' Staff Social

FOR those of us who are Exiles in the widest sense of the word, and have been " cast into outer darkness " these many months, the Staff Social held on February 22nd was a real " high spot."

The programme, as before—games, stage-show and dancing—proved an even greater success than the initial effort. Mrs. Smith again organised the catering arrangements, ably assisted by our ladies from Mill House. The stage-show, by that versatile troupe the " Castledowners " must take pride of place. After Eric's devastating " strip-tease " act, in which his youthful honour was only saved from the avid attentions of Tommy Bancroft by the adroit use of Jack's umbrella, we all expect to lose our Supervisor to some West-End engagement. It's refreshing to see a Supervisor's trousers really taken off! The sketch on Billeting provided much amusement, although we have yet to meet the landlady with the amorous inclinations as displayed by Fred Wright. Walter Dalton gave violin solos, and George Money, at the piano, and Fred Wright with baritone songs, also contributed. Messrs. Staddon and Dobson in a ventriloquist act proved that Supervisors can be answered back—as if we didn't know! George Money and Fred Staddon, as the " Castledown Cads " gave us the low-down on " private lives " in rhyme and song—an extension of " Snoops Corner," known locally as the " Bush Telegraph." Congratulation to all concerned—a first rate effort and an object lesson in team work.

Mr. Weeks—our Mrs. Mopp—proved once again that he is 70 years young. His performance of the Lancers was completed without the aid of that well-known Sccottish beverage—the article being in short supply.

To all the committee who worked so hard before and during the evening, many thanks for a grand show, and same again as soon as convenient, and please, some more of Frank " Sinatra " Fletcher.

E. T.

Ad Astra

By WILLIAM HAYWARD

YOU remember me, no doubt. I run a Patents Office. Ah! yes, of course you do. Well, I am making enquiries as to the whereabouts of a fellow named Jones. I wonder if any of you have run across him? He's quite short, has a jet black walrus moustache, and wears pince-nez. We were at school together, but after he left, we lost touch with each other, and it was the best part of twenty years later that he walked into my office one cold winter's morning with a black box tucked under one arm and a big loop of wire over the other. The box had two white insulators on it, and a large nozzle, not unlike a cinema projector lens.

Well, we had quite a reunion, and after swapping yarns we got down to business, although since my adventure with the time machine I have treated with diffidence people who bring little black boxes into my office.

He had, he claimed, invented a Z-ray Projector, which threw ultra-super-high-frequency electrical waves high up beyond the edge of the stratosphere right into the depths of the cosmic layers, where, he explained, they acted more or less like an inverted well, allowing cosmic energy to travel down on the waves, to be received on the earth by the afore-mentioned black box.

I was very dubious when he asked me to let him demonstrate, but he had always been hot on "stinks" at school, so I smothered my qualms, and let him go out on to the small balcony, which my office overlooks, to tap a power cable that ran a big neon sign. A few showers of sparks, a loud curse, and he came in again sucking his little finger, carrying in his other hand a screwdriver that had assumed the proportions, if not the usefulness, of a corkscrew. Then he began connecting lengths of wire to various terminals, taking a long length right out of the office and joining it to something he appeared to have left outside. He returned at once.

"Just hold that wire a minute," he said, indicating a loose end, and I grasped it. "Feel anything?—"No." "Good. Then the other one must be the one with 3000 volts in it. Now we're all set. I'll just switch on and it'll warm up in a very few seconds." He pressed a switch. "There's only one thing I haven't found out about this ray," he continued casually, "because, although it collects the cosmic energy all right, I have never succeeded in getting enough down to be of use to anyone as, until to-day, I have never been able to use a high enough current.

"What is liable to happen if you do manage to get some down?" I asked, having read somewhere that cosmic rays are rather dangerous to handle.

"Oh! nothing much, I suppose," Jones replied, "it should go straight through the transformer into my special batteries which I have connected to the projector: after which I will be able to supply consumers at the rate of a tenth of a farthing for an amount of energy equivalent to four hundred thousand units of electricity."

At this moment I looked at the wires on the insulators of the box, and they were glowing bright green, and giving off weird brown and mauve fumes.

"Aha!" said Jones, "it won't be long now." He was right. There came a loud "fizz," which was followed immediately by a vivid purple explosion, and as the office disintegrated I felt myself going up, and up, and up———

* * * * *

When I regained consciousness I had been in hospital nine days. During periods of delirium I must have made references to the Z-ray, for as soon as I started to enquire about Jones and his little black box the nurse hastily arose, murmuring "He's off again," went out to fetch the doctor, who felt my pulse, looked under my eyelids, said "Yes, still delirious," and ordered another ice-bag.

This has been going on for weeks now and I'm blessed if I can persuade the hospital staff I am perfectly all right, because as soon as they think I have the appearance of a fully conscious being they ask if they can get me anything, and such is the anxiety in my mind about Jones, that I cannot restrain myself from asking about him, and as soon as I utter the phrase "little black box" I am suddenly tucked up, more ice-bags are brought in, and I'm once more relegated to the sub-conscious. It looks like I'll never get out of here.

"Here, wait a minute." (This interruption appears to be coming from a sceptical reader). "The last we heard of you, you were held captive in an æon of time. How did you get out of that?"

Ah—that, my dear reader, is another story.

Cornish Cream

By KAY PRICE.

Mrs. Ugg, eighty, ferocious, wrinkled, and domineering as only the old can be, placed her son's tea before him in ominous silence, and as he bared his grizzled head and set to, she spoke.

"Yu'm late, 'Oratio."
"Aye, Mother."
"'Ave yu bin wi' that traipsy mommet Tilly Bodkin again?"
"Aye, Mother."
"Fer why, 'Oratio?"
"Oi be goin' fer ter marry 'er, Mother."
"Don't yu be in too much 'urry, 'Oratio. Yu'm not known 'er long."
"Oi've known 'er man and boy fer fifty year, Mother."
"Aye, 'Oratio, maybe yu'ave. But I still don't 'old wi' young folks actin' so 'asty."

* * *

Night in a grove of cedars; a hunter's moon hanging over a silver sea; soft breezes blowing the hair about Annie's heavy face, and fluttering the straw in George's mouth.

"Du 'ee look at thicce moon, Jarge."
"Ooh—ar."
"Don't it make 'ee think o' nothin', Jarge?"
"Ooh—ar—yiiisss."
"What, Jarge?"
"Why, it du put I in mind o' our fat pig, Annie. We'm killed un yistedy. Ar. 'Ow 'un did bleed!"

* * *

"No, zur, oi can't roightly tell 'ee 'ow tu git tu 'Opper-go-down from y'ere. But if yu go ter top o' this lane, and stand wi' yer back tu "Wagginers' Arms," t'es left-'and turnin' and keep straight on h'up 'ill till yu'm there."

* * *

A farmhouse sitting-room with cultured lady P.G. in possession. Enter Mrs. Yeo in deep mourning.

"Yu don't mind gettin' your own tea fer once, du yu, Miss Clock-stopper? I mun go ter funreal at Chapel. T'es Maggie 'Addon, yu know."
"Of course I don't mind, Mrs. Yeo. Was she a friend of yours?"
"Friend. 'Er were related, Miss Clockstopper. My 'usband's brother's second wife were 'er niece,—and SHE'M my second cousin, and poor Maggie's 'usband's brother wur godson tu my grandfather, so yu see, t'es pretty close. Mind yu, I niver liked Maggie, but I think t'es a duty tu see relations buried proper, don't yu."

"Mary"

By IVY WALTON

I had never been stationed in such a desolate spot before, but I was still with my old crowd and we made the best of a bad job. Our billet was an old house, miles away from anywhere, and out of reach of either a chip shop or a cinema,—they both came first in our list of essentials in life. We had a small radio, however, which had been given by some fund or other, which worked when it felt so inclined. On this particular night it didn't feel inclined, so we sat all together in one of the bedrooms where there was a fire, and wrote letters. But after an hour or two we got bored with that, and suddenly my friend Mary threw down her writing pad and exclaimed: "I'm tired of writing to Jim. He hasn't written to me, and anyway, I can't think of anything to say." We knew Jim was her husband. They had been married three months ago and now he was stationed at some aerodrome in the South of England. He was a pilot, I think. He had had leave a few weeks ago, and had come up to the Camp to see Mary unexpectedly, whilst we were having a little party. We had insisted on his playing the piano for us, and I remember thinking what a nice fellow he was. Anyway, that's getting off my story.

Mary then suggested having a seance, and without waiting for a reply, for she seemed to rouse her own enthusiasm much more than ours, dived across the room and started polishing vigorously at one part of the floor. When she had got it to her satisfaction, she began cutting up squares of paper, putting a letter of the alphabet on each piece and placing them in a circle on the polished patch. Then she called for a wineglass. We were unable to oblige, so, making the best of a bad job, she fetched a glass jam-jar and turned it upside down in the centre of the circle.

Following this active one's instructions, we each knelt round the circle and placed one finger on top of the jar. The atmosphere was definitely not right, so someone jumped up and turned off the light, so that our only illumination was the flickering firelight. Two minutes later there was a sickening crash. We all jumped at the noise, but sank back with a sigh, and a restrained giggle, when we realised that it was nothing but the big window at the end of the corridor, banging in the wind. The catch had been broken for a long time but it had never been mended.

Mary looked like a sun-worshipper kneeling there with her eyes closed and a very earnest expression on her face, which I am sure no spirit would have been able to resist. Softly, she began her persuasive call. "Is anybody there?" We started to giggle, but she went on. "Is anybody there?" I felt a movement under my finger, and then my stomach gave a lurch. The glass was moving! Slowly it went round the circle of letters, and then stopped at "Yes." "What is your name?" was the next question Mary asked, but then the glass only spun round and round in a circle and we decided not to delve too deeply into the unknown, so we contented ourselves with questions about our own futures—How long will the war last, and When shall we be out of the Army, etc. At ten o'clock we decided to pack up, and with faint regret began to collect together the cards. Our knees were stiff, and we sat back in a more comfortable position chattering blithely about our "spirit." It was Mary who finished the discussion by saying she'd have to scoot off to her room and finish her letter by torchlight, and saying good-night, she left us. We all started to scramble up too, but suddenly we stopped and listened. Someone was playing the violin very softly. It was a beautiful melody lilting and sad. There was a spell over the room because of the beauty of the music. Someone must have mended the radio. The music died away and the spell broke. The fire was almost out, and I shouted, "Last in bed cleans the fireplace in the morning." There was a wild dash as people stumbled against each other in the gloom, and one by one we snuggled down into bed.

We found Mary next morning. She was dead. I couldn't believe it at first. She had always been so full of fun and life, and now she was so still. Yet I couldn't feel really sad, for she had such a happy little smile on her face. She must have stumbled against the broken window in the passage on the way back to her room last night, and had fallen out and down on to the path below.

I went through her things later, and found a manuscript, and written across the top was, " To my darling Mary. I wrote this just for you.—Jim." I remembered then that she had received it only the morning before she died, and hadn't had time to play it yet. I took it to the piano and began playing. And then, somewhere there came the sound of a violin. That wireless again, I thought. I stopped, but it was playing with me the same tune. I couldn't move, but sat there transfixed as I heard the melody taken up by a beautiful voice,—softly, tenderly. And the voice belonged to Mary.

Don't Try It

A WARNING by "SMILER"

"HARRY! Harry! something terrible's happened. That new joik you put on with me has taken it on the lam and it's only a quarter to ten, too!"

"Did I hear you say lamb?—very tasty with a nice drop o' mint sauce I must say," replies Harry. Then, suddenly grasping the fact, his eyes drop out.

"Git on the phone to Control you dope and ask Slap to hustle his critters up. Perhaps they can intercept him on the way round."

"Yes, that's a good idea Harry—but how does one operate this new-fangled switch-board?" queries the squealer.

"No time to explain now, stoopid!" barks out Harry, making a grab for one of the speaking tubes which littered his desk.

"Is that you Sir?—'H' here; a guy's just left before he was relieved. We can't touch him—can you try? What's that you say—if he keeps to the road?—well if he don't it's going to be mighty unhealthy for him across the field—it's just been mined!"

"Righto, thanks for the tip-off,—listening out," says Slap.

"O.K., drop what you're doing youse guys. Stand by the searchlight and man the gun—some gink's just escaped from 'H.'"

"There he is, he's crawling now!" yells Dick, who handles the hardware. Cowering at the side of 'H' in the beams of the searchlight, like a frightened rabbit, was the defaulter.

"Give him de woiks!" barks Slap.

"All of it?" asks Dick.

"Yus all the way slave, and make quite sure you get him 100% solid."

The multiple-barrelled machine. gun swung on to its human target sending a stream of tracers zipping straight into the north side of 'H' making a few more draughts.

"Missed him! So solly boss," lisps Dick.

"You would!" snarls Slap. "Remind me to stop all your changes of duty for the next six months—but he won't get far, the wire will get him if he ignores administration instruction 99 and tries to make a break for it across the mine-field."

He predicts right. A brilliant flash reveals the unfortunate jail-breaker suspended sizzling in mid-air on the electrified fence outside "H," illuminating his epitaph like a neon sign: "Keep to the Road!"

"O.K. Dick, you can switch off now he's finished and take your break, and remember—*NO MORE THAN 30 MINUTES!*"

FAMOUS LAST WORDS—

'I didn't notice that the red light was still on!"

Through The Looking Glass

PLAN.

For sheer breadth of far-sighted long-term planning, that Charter of the OLD WOYGIAN Association makes a Yalta Conference look like a spinsters' Sunday afternoon tea-party: the organising boys are nothing if not ambitious. But, although we hate to damp idealistic exuberance, we feel that their genius has its inconsistencies. Why, for example, after requesting all the inner secrets of our private lives on the Application Form, have they omitted a blood test? We personally, always insist on one: any two-timing double-crosser can fake the answers on paper;—how many applicants, for example, can gracefully quote a truthful figure for their bank overdraft? But the red corpuscles cannot lie; they contain the unadulterated truth about all the Choir Outings to Brighton; and, a biologist chap was telling us, there's enough evidence in the blood-stream of the average curate to send him packing to Devil's Island. And, again after extending the membership to husbands and wives, how can one logically exclude the children, and, later, their children. It doesn't take five minutes with a slide rule to convince any sound mathematician that by 1970, two-thirds of the English speaking world will be Ex-Woygians. It looks to our sad old eyes as if there will be a political implications; maybe we ought to warn Lord Beaverbrook about the risk of monopoly;—the Shirley Temple Fan Club would pay a film-director's ransom to gain control of a set-up that size!

URGE.

Those A.T.S. who, shortly after taking up duties in "H" must have observed restless and excited conduct on the part of the male Staff will agree with us that the progressive Moguls seem to have carried co-education to the point of anarchy within these ancient walls. And, notwithstanding that we modestly confess ourself the most broad-minded, enlightened, tolerant, humane thinker in the county, we realise that we minions are a shade too close to the Piltdown Man to accept co-education without social repercussions. Only this can explain why rosy-cheeked open-necked, hard-drinking children from Strood begin to stamp their feet and neigh loudly, beating their chests with huge, hairy claws at the first sight of a fairy from across the fields. Frequently they climb the walls and swing hand over hand in between the roof-girders to demonstrate their manliness to the fair ones.

The rest of the staff are affected in different ways: artists, bank-clerks, Hoover salesmen, and supervisors usually compose love-sonnets;— we wish we had a shilling for each occasion one of these timid, trembling creatures has asked us for a rhyme for "innocence"—even a cynical, hard-boiled publicist, weary of Fleet Street's corruption, has been known to abandon Brother Cain's harsh morality and shyly entreat with a certain tall, serious cutie to help him to drown his inhibitions in the scented tea-bowers of the Loughborough "Empire."

OFFENSIVE.

The surest way to prevent the Nazis from adopting any guerilla tactics in the Bavarian Alps after the official defeat of the Wehrmacht is, in our view, to turn a few B.B.C. variety programmes loose upon the area in which they hide. The widespread epidemics of scurvy and creeping-paralysis which normally follow broadcasts like "Workers' Playtime" in the United Kingdom, would, if the programmes were properly used as a war-weapon, make the most fanatical party-leader glad to accept "Unconditional Surrender" as a gift from the gods—in spite of what you outraged humanitarians may cry about bacteriological warfare being against the Geneva Convention!

LEON DE BUNK.

VICTORY
BIGGIN STREET, LOUGHBOROUGH

EASTER, MONDAY, APRIL 2nd—for 3 days.
LOUISE ALLBRITTON and ED. E. HORTON in

Her Primitive Man

Also Frank Albertson in "MYSTERY BROADCAST."

THURSDAY, APRIL 5th—for 3 days.
BY REQUEST—DISNEY FULL-LENGTH CARTOON

Bambi

(in Technicolor).
Also Tim Holt in "FARGO KID."

MONDAY, APRIL 9th—for 6 days.
PHYLLIS CALVERT and PATRICIA ROC in

Two Thousand Women

Also Harriet Hilliard in "HI GOOD-LOOKING."

MONDAY, APRIL 16th—for 3 days.
LANA TURNER and JAMES CRAIG in

Marriage is a Private Affair

Also "METROPOLIS OF THE TURF."

THURSDAY, APRIL 19th—for 3 days.
BETTE DAVIS and GEORGE BRENT in

Dark Victory

Also R.A.F. Staff in "THE BIG PACK."

MONDAY, APRIL 23rd—for 6 days.
SPENCER TRACY and SIGNE HASSO in

The Seventh Cross

Also FULL SUPPORTING PROGRAMME.

MONDAY, APRIL 30th—for 3 days.
OLIVIA DE HAVILLAND and SUNNY TUFTS in

Government Girl

Also Anne Gwynne in "SOUTH OF DIXIE."

THURSDAY, MAY 3rd—for 3 days.
PAUL LUKAS in

Address Unknown

Also Jane Frazee in "IN ROSIE'S ROOM."

Monday to Friday—Con. from 5-30 p.m.   Saturday—Con. from 2 p.m.
MATINEES.—Monday and Wednesday at 2-15 p.m.
SUNDAYS.—6-15 p.m. (One Show).

EMPIRE

MARKET PLACE, LOUGHBOROUGH

EASTER MONDAY, APRIL 2nd—for 3 days.
BING CROSBY and GLORIA JEAN in

If I Had My Way

Also Iris Adrian in "SHAKE HANDS WITH MURDER."

THURSDAY, APRIL 5th—for 3 days.
ROY ROGERS in

Yellow Rose of Texas

Also Una Merkel in "SWEETHEARTS ON PARADE."

MONDAY, APRIL 9th—for 3 days—
BY REQUEST—RODDY McDOWELL and DONALD CRISP in

Lassie Come Home
(in Technicolor).

Also J. Mack Brown in "STRANGER FROM PECOS."

THURSDAY, APRIL 12th—for 3 days.
BUSTER CRABBE in

The Contender

Also Ann Shirley in "MUSIC IN MANHATTAN."

MONDAY, APRIL 15th—for 6 days.
ABBOTT and COSTELLO in

In Society

Also Noah Beery Jr. in "PASS TO ROMANCE."

MONDAY, APRIL 23rd—for 3 days.
JUDY GARLAND and GEORGE MURPHY in

Little Nelly Kelly

Also Lee Patrick in "NURSE'S SECRET."

THURSDAY, APRIL 26th—for 3 days.
PAT O'BRIEN and RUTH HUSSEY in

Marine Raiders

Also Andrew Sisters in "SWINGTIME JOHNNY."

MONDAY, APRIL 30th—for 6 days.
DONALD O'CONNOR and PEGGY RYAN in

Patrick The Great

Also Charles Starratt in "ROLL ON."

CONTINUOUS DAILY. Doors open at 1-30 p.m.
SUNDAYS at 1-30 p.m.

Printed by Hodgkins, Millar & Co., Halstead Street, Leicester, and published by L. P. Jones for Beaumanor Staff Magazine Committee.

May 45 (missing) It is not clear if an issue appeared as the war ended.

The first issue of The Woygian was Autumn 1945 and it contained the Epistle of St. Upid to the Woygians, Chapter 1 which was reproduced in the book as Chapter XL.

In its place we reproduce:

—the Administrative Instruction N.111 on VE Day issued by the Commanding Officer on 3 May 1945:
—Congratulations from the D.D. "Y" of 14 May 1945—
—Congratulations from Director, Station "X" (i.e B.P.)
—Congratulations from D.D.Y to Beaumanor, Forest Moor, Kedleston Hall, Shenley.

WAR OFFICE 'Y' GROUP.

ADMINISTRATIVE INSTRUCTION No. 111.

V E D A Y.

VE DAY will probably come upon us in the very near future and at very short notice, and I want to give some preliminary indication of what I hope will happen on that and the following day.

Operationally, I hope to close down to a minimum on these days, but it may be necessary to keep a few tasks going if we are ordered to. It may therefore be necessary to call for volunteers for these tasks, in which case these will be given full time off in lieu as early as possible after the break. I shall not know if this will be needed, and to what extent, until VE day arrives.

The remaining operational tasks will close down immediately on VE and the following day.

Immediately VE day is announced I propose to call the whole Group into the M.T. yard for a two-minute talk, and then dispersal. Information regarding watch attendances on these days will be given as soon as a forecast of requirements can be made.

The Canteen will be open for those desiring to stay, with, it is hoped, free beer and refreshments for all, and this will continue for the whole of the day, and as far as practicable the following day.

All forms of festivity will be encouraged, and I leave it to the good sense of the Group to see that such festivities do not involve the destruction of Government property in any way.

I want every member of the Group, military and civilian alike, to enjoy himself or herself on these days, happy in the knowledge that they have done a good job in the Group, and that this job has helped, more than is generally realised, in achieving Victory. At the same time, I am sure that everyone will give a thought to those still engaged in fighting in the Far East.

Beaumanor Park,
Nr. Loughborough.
3rd May, 1945.

Lieut-Col., R. Signals,
O.C., War Office 'Y' Group.

Distribution:-
2 i/c.
D/F O.
Adjt.
T.O.
O.O.
Mr. Spooner.
Mr. E. Smith.
Mr. J. Reid.
D/F Plotting Rm.
Pay Office.
Group Notice Board.

Control.
T.P. Room.
Hut 'H'
"   'Y'
"   'J'
"   'K'
C.R.R.
A.R. 13.
Stores.
Workshops.
File.

Memorandum.

YG/

Congratulations from D.M.I.

It gives me great pleasure to circulate to all members of the staff, civilian and military, the appended copy of letter from the D.M.I.

Beaumanor Park,
Woodhouse Eaves.
23rd May, 1945.

Lieut-Col., R. Sinclair,
O.C., War Office "Y" Group.

BDY/11/1.

C.S.O., Spec. Wireless.

From : D.D.'Y'.

The War Office,
Whitehall,
London, S.W.1.

I am sure that it was D.M.I's intention that the following which I have received from him should apply to the station officer and all ranks of the 'Y' stations in the U.K. I shall therefore be glad if you will pass this message to officers commanding Forest Moor, Beaumanor, Bishops Waltham, Shenley and Kedleston Hall.

The German war is over. It is the moment to congratulate you and your staffs of all ranks and services on the great work which you and they have done to help to bring victory. Many of them have been in the Directorate since the early days of the war and have played their full part in building it up from almost nothing to its present state of efficiency.

Please pass to all your people my admiration for their efficiency, keenness and hard work. That our Commanders have been able to see while the German Commanders have largely been kept blind is their reward.

(sgd) J.A. SINCLAIR,

D.M.I.

Ext. 1726.
14 May 1945.

(sgd) J.R. VAUGHAN.
Brigadier, D.D. 'Y'."

MEMORANDUM

YG/143

I have much pleasure in promulgating copies of teleprints from Director Station "X" and D.D.Y.

1. "From Director, Station "X".

   To Scarborough, Flowerdown, Beaumanor, Bishops Waltham, Forest Moor, Shenly, Kedleston Hall, Cheadle, Chicksands, Canterbury, Knock Holt, Brora Denmark Hill, Sandridge, Whitchurch, Wincombe Etousa (. For Santa Fe)

   We have fought a long battle together and won, without complete cooperation between us all we could not have accomplished what has been done. On my own behalf and that of the Staff of Station X I want to thank our comrades in "Y" I am able to tell you that as a service we have made a valuable contribution to the war and although this may never be blazoned abroad we can be satisfied that we have played our part."

2. "From D.D.Y.

   To Beaumanor, Forest Moor, Kedleston Hall, Shenley.

   Please pass to all ranks under your command my warmest thanks and congratulations for their magnificent and faithful part in bringing about this day."

Lieut-Col., R. Signals,
O.C., War Office "Y" Group.

Distribution :-
2nd i/c.
All Outstation.
O.C., Bishops Waltham.
Sup. i/c Chatham.
D/F Officer.
Adjt.
T.O.
O.O.
Mr. Spooner.
Mr. E. Smith.
Mr. J. Reid.
D/F Plotting Room.
Pay Office.

Control.
T.P. Room.
Hut "H"
"I"
"J"
"K"
C.R.R.
A.R.13.
Stores.
Workshops.
Group Notice Board.
File.
Spare 10.

J.C.M. Barnes

The WOYGIAN

BRIDGEWOODS 1939 CHICKSANDS 1945 BEAUMANOR

Vol. 1   Autumn 1945   No. 1

JOURNAL OF THE WOYGIAN ASSOCIATION

President:
Lt. Col. M. J. W. Ellingworth, R. Sigs.

Vice-Presidents:
Major H. F. Jolowicz. Mr. G. M. Spooner.
Jnr. Cdr. I. F. Romer, A.T.S. Mr. C. O. Smith.

Chairman of the Association:
Mr. R. W. Hilder.

Honorary Secretary: *Honorary Treasurer:*
Sgt. J. Rogerson, A.T.S. Capt. G. E. M. Abels.

Honorary Editor:
Mr. E. C. Millhouse.

Central Committee:
Mr. E. W. Dobson. Mr. H. Dodd. Mrs. P. L. Edmundson.

Midland Zone Committee: *Scottish Zone Committee:*
S/Sgt. L. Whittaker. Cpl. S. J. M. Murray, A.T.S.
Sgt. J. A. Kearney. Cpl. R. Symington, A.T.S.
C.S.M. M. Reynolds, A.T.S. Cpl. A. Robertson, A.T.S.
Sgt. A. A. Marshall, A.T.S. Cpl. J. C. Donlon, A.T.S.
Mr. T. Pollard. Mr. G. G. Cooper.

Honorary Auditor:
Mr. A. H. Appleton.

A Message from the PRESIDENT

Dear Mr. Editor,

You have asked me to write a few words for the first number of the WOYGIAN magazine. I do so with pleasure, because I am convinced that this little publication will do a great deal towards perpetuating the wartime comradeship of a large group of people from all walks of life. Some of us have seen this show grow from a mere handful of men to over 1,000 strong, and what is more, we have, in common with many wartime institutions, noticed how the ladies have out-numbered us, to the life-long satisfaction of some of them. These, at least, will never forget W.O.Y.G., and for the others the WOYGIAN magazine will bring back memories, not all of them bad, when the two wars, both happily concluded, fade into oblivion. Now, our wartime job is finished and dispersal is in the air, but we can, through the Woygian Association, and particularly this magazine, keep these memories green. If some of us can meet at times, and swap yarns it will be all to the good, and better still if we can help any of our comrades who have struck a bad patch.

So I hope everyone will back up the Association, and send you plenty of copy for the magazine, and may I take this opportunity of sending greetings to all Woygians, past and present, wherever they may be, and wish them all good fortune in the future.

Yours sincerely,
M. J. W. E.

Beaumanor Park,
29th Aug., 1945.

MAJOR JOLOWICZ (Vice-President) writes—

Dear Mr. Editor,

YOU suggest that I should write a note in commendation of the magazine in its new form. The obvious thing to say is that good wine needs no bush, and that we have all by now had sufficient samples of what you provide to be sure that we are taking less than an ordinary commercial risk in contracting to purchase further vintages. But I suppose that will hardly earn the advertisement agent's fee, and what you wish to further is, I take it, not only the circulation of the Magazine itself, but the interest of the Woygian Association as a whole. Well, to begin with, it has its name to recommend it. Let anyone who is in doubt consider how well "Member of the Woygian Association" would look on his visiting card. We are all used nowadays to the game of guessing what initials stand for. It is, indeed, estimated by statisticians of the highest authority that four hundred thousand man-hours have been wasted in the British Army alone in puzzling over authorized abbreviations which it would have taken only one thousand and fifty-seven hours to write out in full, but in the initials W.O.Y.G. there is something peculiarly glamorous, something secret and mysterious, but at the same time not sinister, which should thrill the individual aware of his own privileges and, by arousing awe in the general public, greatly enhance his social prestige. But, though there is much in the name, it is not all. The "show" is really unique, and it is interesting that the founders of the Association, presumably after considerable debate, found it impossible to define the qualifications for membership otherwise than by service under a particular individual, so outstanding has been the impress given to the institution by that individual's personality and so varied have been the contributions brought by the men and women who served under him, to the success of the whole. No doubt each one of us would have something of a story to tell of how he came to be part of the machine, of the effect that his first contact with it had on his mind, and of his experiences during his service. Perhaps I may be permitted to tell mine.

War is at least 99 per cent evil, but it has some advantageous by-products, and one of them is that it can dig people out of their ruts, and my particular rut of a teacher in the University of London was one in which I could not contemplate remaining after war had broken out. I had had some experience of a particular kind of work towards the end of the last war, and so I applied to the appropriate department of the War Office for employment. After a couple of interviews I was accepted. I had probably slightly more idea of what I should have to do than most people who joined the service, but only very slightly, and one of the interesting things about our job, when you come to think of it, is that nearly everybody on joining "bought a pig in a poke". To that extent we are like the Freemasons. When the Colonel in charge told me I was to proceed to Chatham, I hope I did not blench visibly, but I had never visited that famous town, and my ideas about it were chiefly derived from Dickens who, I think, speaks with a little irony of those "twin jewels", Chatham and Rochester. My instructions were definitely not to wear uniform, which seemed odd, and I was met at the station by a tall man in shabby clothes (reminding me strongly of my academic colleagues) who, rather surprisingly, afterwards turned out to be the only Regular Army officer about the place—and looked it, too, when once he put his uniform on. Apart from him there was a retired Naval officer in command, a lot of men in civilian clothes and the only people in khaki were the young ladies who operated the teleprinters and ran the diminutive canteen. "This", I said to myself, "is definitely Fred Karno's Army".

It was now the middle of October, 1939, and for some days all went well, for, though my senior officer explained the elements to me, I found that things had changed so much since the last war that my previous experience was of no great value. Then the awful thing happened. My senior officer was suddenly ordered to France, and I was left as the only Officer to face a still almost entirely incomprehensible mass of paper. It was a trying experience, but it had at least one good result, for when, two-and-a-half years later, I was called upon to organise the training of the same kind of personnel, I remembered what a shock the whole business had been to me at first and was able to make allowances for other people. One of our difficulties in training was in fact that we did not merely have to teach facts and methods, but had to introduce our students—in a war-time rush—to a whole new set of ideas. They consequently often spent their early days with us in a maze which was caused, not by the difficulty of what we taught them, but by the shock of meeting what was almost a new world.

Gradually, in those early months at Chatham, things became clearer to me. The Prophet Osee spared what time he could to lighten my darkness, the prodigies of memory performed by Mr. Giles, Mr. Peerless and several others became an everyday matter, and their deductions appeared no longer to be merely black magic but were seen to be the result of human, though rather advanced, ratiocination. Other fellows, some senior to me, joined, and by the time the "phoney" war ended we were well prepared to play our part in the long struggle. Excitement came with the "Blitz" and, though on the whole we were fortunate, tragedy too; but humour was always there and there are some incidents I can never forget. One is the picture of Capt. Burgess wearing a pair of high boots (his "fairy-prince" boots) and armed with nothing more formidable than field-glasses, striking an attitude on the observation post as the German 'planes went over and declaring "They shall not pass!" Another is Mr. (later Captain) Barnett, to whom Nature has given rather thick eyebrows, and to whom chance had given a Home Guard "battle-bowler" several sizes too small for him, making the resemblance to a certain famous comedian unmistakable. The worst was (of course) over by the time we moved to Bedfordshire. Of that trek I need say nothing, for it is enshrined in the immortal prose of St. Upid himself, and, incidentally, Mr. Editor, I suggest that the passage in question together with some other gems from previous issues might well be reprinted for the instruction of younger readers and the delectation of the old.

In Bedfordshire the Duke has, I believe, a pretty good collection of curious animals, but he could not touch our human zoo. There was an Admiral (in uniform this time), another Naval officer or so, a Wren now and again, civilians of different shapes and sizes, Air Force of all sexes and most ranks, A.T.S. (pretty and purl), to say nothing of us soldiers. It was a good place in some ways, but it had its drawbacks—ask Mr. Walton, for instance, about them—and in the Autumn of 1941 we moved again, to the place we all know and, I think, most of us remember with at least some affection. It was there that the great expansion took place, fortunately still under the same management and for a considerable time under the same indefatigable second-in-command. Two magazine competitions suggest themselves:—(i) What, if anything, is there that Major Wort cannot do? and (ii) When, if ever, does he sleep? Something of the old intimacy was no doubt lost in the expansion, but the work was there to do and it was done devotedly in conditions which were for many people far from easy. We may all be proud to have had a hand in it, and that is the point of these remarks.

An Association formed in the stress and hazards of war should not be allowed to fade altogether into the past, for it was well worth while and was part of a great co-operative effort that should be an example for peace-time work also. It will not only be pleasant to meet old friends and hear about their doings in the Magazine, but it may be an inspiration as well, and a safeguard against selfish absorption in our own concerns. So I hope all persons eligible will join the Association and read its Magazine. The best of success to you!

Yours very sincerely,
H. F. JOLOWICZ.

Beaconsfield, Bucks.
12th *August*, 1945.

B.W. Dispersal

"THE old order changeth——", and it was in anticipation of this that the Bishops Waltham staff waited anxiously for orders to proceed home to normal offices and to families.

Being informed of "Der Tag" (30th June) a buzz of activity arose. Many parcels were posted, odd days-off granted for the removal of "extras", much poring over timetables, arguments about taxis, in fact, arguments about lots of things.

Farewell celebrations were many, lengthy and varied. The official goodbye came from Col. Ellingworth, who journeyed to Mill House for the occasion, and, in addition to a number of complimentary speeches, a pleasant, well-organised Social was enjoyed by all. The "Castledowners" organised a farewell social for the landladies and gave the usual prescription so popular in the village. The small hall was packed to capacity, and sincere votes of thanks were passed to all who had made the stay of the "wireless gentlemen" such a pleasant one.

Each watch had a separate celebration, one partaking in a dinner (with the inevitable aftermath which included, I believe, lamp-post gymnastics) the two others selecting a charabanc trip to Southsea.

A high spot on one of these was the spectacle of the O.C. Station minding socks and shoes while members of the staff paddled. He also "forked out" for extra fares to prevent the same members travelling "steerage" from the Isle of Wight (and he with a brand new daughter to keep, too!).

To those going home the leave-taking was a pleasure, although I feel sure everyone had regrets at leaving B.W. and at the cessation of such good companionship.

To those of us returning to Beaumanor, the break-up was more poignant. Fresh billets and new jobs loomed ahead, as well as the thought that the many pleasant associations at B.W. were at an end.

We few are now hoping the many will remember us, and let us know how they are faring, back at "work". We hope that members of the Association will show this magazine to all who served so well at B.W. and perhaps persuade them that it **would** be nice to keep in touch with old friends. In any case, we remember them and wish them luck and happiness.

The site on Castle Down is now being dismantled. It is rumoured that we shall one day see the masts again, with all those names scratched at the top, but the fruit and nuts, the rabbits, and Dodger's hat are gone from our midst.

Here at Beaumanor we'll keep you up-to-date with news. "You, too, can do your bit". Let's have your news; about yourself, and about the old "Castledowner" you ran across in Hastings or Bradford, Leeds or London. We'll pass it on, and help keep green a memory of friends who were with us when we most needed them.

ERIC.

"What's He Doing Now?"

By OLLIE PEARCE.

To most of us a common phrase familiar in the doubtful days,
Now as we go our sundry ways, a different meaning it conveys,
Remote from that elusive "he", confined instead to you and me,
Therefore the word must also be interpreted at times as "she".

IN compiling a feature of this nature, the object of which is to keep members informed of the whereabouts and activities of Woygites past and present, there are two obvious drawbacks. Firstly, what is news to some readers will be history to others, and secondly, various people mentioned from time to time may not be known to the whole of our community, consequently items which seem boring or meaningless to some readers may be quite interesting to others, and vice versa.

I do not know whether the recognition of these facts has been responsible for the lack of material for this issue, but I do know that the amount of unsolicited material submitted has been absolutely nil, and I would like to take this opportunity of appealing to readers for any items of news concerning themselves, or other members and ex-members of W.O.Y.G.

Remember, the fact that you hear news of Mr. X may seem insignificant to you, but he may have creditors amongst our readers who would doubtless be most interested to hear of him!

I am sure that everybody who knows Kay Price will join me in wishing her a complete and speedy recovery after the unfortunate accident which necessitated an operation for the removal of a blood clot from the brain.

Kay, who was well known as a member of the B.S.M. Editorial Board and a popular contributor to that journal, was knocked down by an Army lorry when cycling out of Garats Hay on VJ-Day, and at the time of writing has been unconscious for several days in a Leicester hospital.

Unconditional surrender seems to be the vogue these days and here is a list of Woygites who have recently given up the struggle. May we offer our congratulations and best wishes for future happiness to:

Geoff Nicol, and Pte. (Now L/Cpl.) Connie Praeger (Communications Wing,) who were married at Leicester on May 19th.

Dennis Brett (Sutton Valence) and Miss Gladys Gould, on July 14th.

Fred Wells, and Joan Vernon (Communications Wing,) on July 21st.

Fred Pearce, and Miss Mary Brewin, at Emmanuel Church, Loughborough on August 4th.

Bob ("Dook") Downer, and Pte. Cecile Groves ex-"C" Watch No. 1/2 Wing, at Tunbridge Wells on August 10th.

John Dodd, and Sgt. Kay Norman of the "I" Corps, on August 11th at Birmingham. The honeymoon was spent at Newquay, Cornwall.

Big brother Harry Dodd, and Pte. Doreen Lister of No. 1/2 Wing, on August 25th.

"Bungy" Williamson, and Pte. Joan Price ex-Room 61, also on August 25th. Like all the other members of the now extinct Bull-ring, "Bungy" has at last succumbed to the irresitible glamour of uniform, or something.

Pte. Vera Winzer ex "C" Watch No. 1/2 Wing, who was married recently when her fiance returned from overseas.

Congratulations are also due to:

Roy Nicholls, and Cpl. Molly Smith of the "I" Corps, who became engaged a few weeks ago, and last but not least to the proud parents of baby daughters, Les and Mrs. Hadler, Harry and Mrs. Dix.

From the above list it will be seen that for many girls the Service is merely a stepping-stone to marriage. Hence the following nonsense rhyme:

Martial careers for girls should be,
Spelt with the "i" before the "t".

Another victim of Cupid's arrow is Mr. R. Ward, of Chacewater. Reports indicate that his position is serious and he has little hope of recovering, although he may linger on for several months before he finally succumbs. Your earnest prayers are requested.

The following left us on the dates shown "for the benefit of their health" : W. J. (Wally) Cecil, April 14th; D. F. Gibling, May 26th, (to those readers who do not know Mr. Gibling, his initials will probably give a clue to the reason); Dudley Truin, June 23rd, Messrs A. G. Berry, W. H. Baker, V. F. Merritt, and G. J. Nixon, June 30th; Ralph Champion, July 7th; Messrs. R. G. Welch, and W. R. Jones, July 14th; Messrs. Jimmy Hunter, and J. Colville, July 21st; and Fred Mayne, July 28th. Claude Deakin has also applied for release for the same reason and is awaiting a decision.

Mr. G. Heasman left us on April 19th for service with the army, Mr. Harold Sweeten, May 5th on compassionate grounds, Miss Margaret Ellingworth, May 26th for service with the W.R.N.S. She is at present stationed in London where her duties have included making coffee for the First Sea Lord!

Our three American friends, Forbes Sibley, Fred Allred, and "Mac", left us at the end of May and are at present stationed at Brick Hill Camp, near Bletchley, Bucks. They do not yet know when they are likely to be returning to the States.

Messrs. Malcolm Spooner, John Reid, and Dudley Smith, left us on June 1st to pursue their respective peace-time occupations.

Capt. Johnnie ("Any time you like") Mace, also left us on June 1st and has since arrived safely in India.

Major ("Take a card") Donaldson who left on July 1st is now at Forest Moor, and as frequent attempts to contact him have been unsuccessful, I can only conclude that he is preoccupied in mantaining a lasting victory!

Major Clifton, who also left on July 1st, has settled down in Douglas where he is apparently confined to barracks by the weather which provides the main topic of conversation. He sends his regards to all the other teetotallers. One of his first discoveries on arrival was the fact that Double Diamond is obtainable at 5/6d. per dozen! (Applications for posting cannot be considered.) There are one or two of the old Sarafand crowd in the Officers' Mess there including Bob Brett, Bill Chesters, and Wrixon.

Freddie ("Trombone") Burgess who left us in July, and Tony Mosley August 3rd, are both, I believe, in London.

Capt. Ernest Siddall is at present in Minden, Germany, and is hoping to be home again in the near future.

We have also lost several married members of the A.T.S. recently including:

S/Sgt. Peggy McCarthy who is now living with her mother at Exeter and hopes to go to Canada in the very near future to join her husband.

Sgt. Jimmy Davies, now living in her husband's home in Doncaster.

Sgt. Daphne Abels née Workman, is staying with her husband's family in Stafford and hopes her husband, Capt. Graham Abels, who seems quite happy in his unit in N. Italy, will be home about Christmas.

Pte. Jean Taylor née Coates, whose husband has just gone abroad, is at her home where she hopes to get her old job back.

Pte. Dart née Rhodes is making a full time job of looking for a house.

Pte. Pendlebury née Lammas is expecting a happy event. Her husband is believed to have gone abroad.

Pte. Joyce Hardacre née Gregory is expecting her husband home from Italy any time now. He should be back in Civvie Street soon.

Ex L/Cpl. Mary Sheldon has returned to her old job but is finding rationing a bit difficult. Her husband manages to get home each weekend.

Also C.S.M. Betty McKeough née Brown, Cpl. Mary Norris née Watson, Cpl. Dorothy Garside; Ptes. Guyver, Worrall née Savage, May Knight née Nichol, and several others of whom we have had no news since their departure.

26 of Room 61's A.T.S. staff have gone to Forest Moor leaving Messrs. Jimmy Rogers and Fred Nicholson to look after the dump. Their sole occupation at the moment is to answer the phone twice daily when the switchboard operator announces that tea is ready.

Cpls. Joyce Harraden, Marie Hunt, Maude Wood, and L/Cpl. Beryl Minter, all of the "I" Corps have been posted. Marie Hunt to a holding unit near Derby, the remainder to a similar unit at Cambridge.

To all who have left the fold including those of the overseas draft, which I understand has now been cancelled, we say "Good luck in your new surroundings and we are always pleased to hear from you."

Several old Woygites have rejoined us during the past few weeks and we say "Greetings" to our old friend Major Wort, ex-Forest Moor, and also to the following, who have returned from "exile" in Utopia: Messrs. George Giles, "Jock" Hamilton, W. Dalton, A. M. Hilder, F. C. Staddon, R. G. Denny, H. P. Arnold, H. D. Hutchinson, E. W. Dobson, R. P. L. Smith, Ken Cook, and A. H. Dodds. We were also pleased to see Mr. Pethers who visited this station for a few days early in August.

We extend a cordial welcome to L/Cpl. Yvonne Buckley, Ptes. Beryl Appleby, H. Baker, and M. Wass who are back at W.O.Y.G. after an absence of over two years, part of which time was spent in the land of the Pharaohs.

We get an occasional glimpse of "Babs" Nash who is back in this district after having exchanged her two stripes for two pips in Egypt.

I have not been able to keep pace with all the A.T.S. promotions but I am sure that ex-Woygites will be interested to learn that "Auxiliaryilary" has at last risen to the dizzy heights of L/Cpl., The Japs immediately asked for terms!

Other recent promotions include L/Cpl. Jean Donlon to Cpl., and Pte. Evelyn Woodhouse to L/Cpl.

The following have been promoted to Sgt. (Educational): Cpl. Margaret Nucator; L/Cpls. Celia Allen and Peggy James, the latter having rejoined from overseas, and Ptes. Muriel Dick, "Lexie" Burns, "Billie" Brown, and Kathleen Scott. Congratulations to all concerned.

Our old friend Mr. Batchelor is at Forest Moor. He is hoping to get back into civvies again by about Christmas and tells me he would like to stay in this racket.

Philip Wade is a C.S.M. in the "I" Corps at Forest Moor, and Mr. Carr has applied for admission to the Allied Fine Arts Commission and, I think, has been accepted.

C.S.M. Marjorie Reynolds has also moved from Shenley to Forest Moor where she will be able to renew many old acquaintances.

Margaret ("Nightingale") Lidbury is now Mrs Arnold and has a daughter, Jane, born May 3rd.

Ex-Sgt. Betty Quick née Coombes also has a daughter, born last April. Her husband Ralph is now a civilian in America where she hopes to join him soon.

Ex-L/Cpl. Joan Palmer née Brammer now has a baby son.

Ex-Sgt. Dicks, one of the "old originals" who married a Signals Officer, now has a son and heir.

Ex-L/Cpl. Phillipa Plant, whose husband is at present in Germany, is expecting a happy event in about two months time.

Ex-Sgt. Anne Law has not entirely disassociated herself from W.O.Y.G. She seems to be keeping in close touch with "Sandy" Le Gassick of Croft Spa.

There has been a dearth in social activities here lately, but the music lovers are still as keen as ever, and attended a Concert by the London Philharmonic Orchestra at the De Montfort Hall, Leicester, on July 31st. Barkus' bus took the party to and from the concert. The organiser, Mr. Harry Dodd, was obliged to stand on the return journey. All who attended agreed that a hired bus is the solution to the W.O.Y.G. concert-goers' previous problem: How to get back to the Beaumanor district in good time without leaving the concert before the end; enduring the discomforts of a cycle ride; or staying in Leicester for the last train, plus a walk from Barrow or Loughborough.

An added advantage was the speedy return, and arrival before closing time, although one or two of the more impatient element baled out at Mountsorrel and Quorn in search of liquid refreshment.

Repetition of this arrangement for future Leicester concerts is anticipated.

Some Woygites, attending a Symphony concert for the first time, were much impressed by the conducting, by Dr. Heinz Unger, of the whole programme from memory.

The only other functions worth mentioning are the numerous binges at Garats Hay, the excuses for which seem to be as inexhaustible as the supply of that most-sought-after commodity.

STOP PRESS.

Noel ("Vox Plebis-cum-Last Goodnight") Royle is to marry A.T.S. Sgt. "Billie" Brown in the very near future, possibly early September.

Pte. Pat Hughes is now wearing an engagement ring which she was given last week-end by Roy Fullager, of Sutton Valence, and Pte. Peggy Kay is expecting to be married very soon, her fiancé having just returned from overseas. It seems that a course in plotting is not entirely useless.

Seventy-eight of the younger element have been notified that "subject to military fitness, they will be required to join the Army at a date not earlier than one month from the date of notification". Others have been told to stand by to replace men who fail to pass the medical examination. I regret that space does not permit me to give a list of names of those affected.

C.S.M. Jessie Reeves left us shortly after VJ-Day for a reconditioning centre at Cobham, Surrey. Had we known the address, many of us would probably have done the same thing after VE-Day!

Con'd on page 11.

THE EPISTLE OF ST. UPID

TO THE

Woygians

CHAPTER I.

NOW when the day appointed as the fourth summer of their sojourn drew nigh certain great happenings befell the mighty Tribe of Woyg. For Itla the Hunnite grew weary of the strife and hid himself, and his peoples were filled with a desire to Fraternise. And when the magicians of the King and Uncle Sam had Busted the Atom and hurled it upon the Japites, Mik, their King, knew that he despised war, and sought peace with his enemies. And the Japites were without faces.

Thus it came to pass that the peoples of Woyg perceived that their days in the land were numbered. Yet none could judge what the number was. But there was much Griffin in the land. Likewise was there an abundance of Gen. But the truth was not in it. And the feasts of Ve-ee and Ve-jay were marked with great rejoicings, and the land flowed with beer and skittles. And the houses of the publicans were filled with sinners. And the sinners were filled with the waters of the publicans. And certain among them were Cockeyed, and Pickled, and Stewed.

Now the Prophet Osee prepared to shed his raiment of Khaki and to cast aside his Crown and Pips, and to be once more Ahren Retired. And his prodigal son Eswert, who had wasted his Subsistence in a forest which is nigh unto the gate of Haro, returned unto him. And Osee received him with open bottles and killed the vatted Womp in his honour. But Malkum, and Jon, and Dudli, and the Iankis, and a great number of the disciples of Osee, went forth and departed out of the land for ever.

And when Red Tabz perceived that the fighting had ceased he sent a Chitti unto Osee, saying: Behold, now can I suffer a few score Ewas to become soldiers. And certain among the Ewas spake largely between themselves of Jankers, and Clink, and sundry mats and carpets.

And certain others among the Scribes fell sick of the palsy. And they went into the presence of the Quack, crying: Woe is us. For behold, our palsy cometh out of the land of Woyg, and there is no health in us. And when the Quack perceived that they had Rotated exceeding much and were sorely cheesed he gave unto them a Chitti and bid them go forth into the world and spend their nights in Kip. And he saw not their heels for dust.

And the Atsites were in a mighty Flutter, and spake one to another only in Demob Numbers. And those which were possessed of dilatory Sweety-pies cried unto them uneasily: Poppeth thou not me the Question? For behold, what are we waiting for? And many among them sought out the Tutors that they might learn Domestic Silence, and the manner of boiling water without burning it.

But the Hard Core suffered in well-nigh silence, and Carried on Pulling Their Weight, murmuring only: Whither goeth we from hence? And there were sundry Promised Lands on the Short List.

Song of the Enlightened O.C.

By G. M. Spooner.

(*To be sung to the tune of "The Punishment Fits The Crime*).

A more progressive "Station-master"
   Did never before exist;
To nobody second, I'm certainly reckoned
   A thorough humanist.
It is my very humane endeavour
   To make to some extent
Each evildoer, and erring Ewa,
   A source of merriment!

    (*Chorus*)
   My object all sublime
    I shall achieve in time—
  To make the punishment fit the crime,
   The punishment fit the crime;
   And make each de-lin-quent
   Unwillingly represent
 A source of innocent merriment
  Of innocent merriment!

The troublesome youngsters in H who muddle
   And make such a horrible mess,
Shall during off-hours Be shut in the Towers
   And wait on the Group A.T.S. :
The innocent girl who *imagines* her sall-cigns,
   A crime she must never forget,
Will be noted and quoted And quickly promoted
   To get her away from a set.
The chump who spills tea on the canteen papers
   And leaves all the table-tops wet
Shall feed, if he's able, From cloth-covered table,
   With saucer and clean serviette.
The man who never does more than he need do,
   And cuts what he has to do short—
I *may* designate him To copy verbatim
   The whole of each nasty Report!

    (*Chorus*)

The Supervisor of Z who wearies
   With tales of countless woes
Shall go to B.W., Where he won't trouble you,
   As every innocent knows.
The caller who stops here to get a free lunch
   And to draw on our transport when stuck
May only be seated At back of a foetid
   And rattling utility-truck!
The female Admin. officer who
   Would enforce every barrack-room rule
On girls she should care for, without asking wherefore,
   Shall promptly be sent back to school;
Or any who try to impose this and that,
   As though ops did not matter at all,
Shall hear dissertations From me, with quotations
   Direct from Isaiah and Paul!

    (*Chorus*)

"What's he doing now"—*cont'd*—

In contrast, VJ-Day here was extremely quiet and the place was deserted excepting for the girls who carried on as usual. About 20 of them took "French leave" but the remainder certainly deserve a bouquet.

By the way, I think it was most inconsiderate of the Japs to pack in on a Wednesday. Don't they know that delivery day here is Thursday?

In conclusion, since Robert Southey is not in a position to care, I should like to record my personal impressions of VJ.

> It was a summer evening,
>   The war had just been won,
> But I had the hump in a one-horse dump,
>   Away from all the fun,
> To reach which, I had spent the night,
> Marooned on a platform by the strike.
>
> I queued for lunch, then queued for tea
>   And "fags" without success,
> I tried to buy a loaf of bread,
>   But could not answer "Yes"
> When asked, "Do you deal here each day?"
> So hungrily I slunk away.
>
> The shops then took a holiday.
>   And I began to fear,
> That I'd depend for nourishment
>   Upon fresh air and beer;
> But things like that, you know, must be
> At every famous victory.
>
> With only half a dozen pubs
>   In such a little town,
> The beer supply was very short,
>   And sadly watered down,
> But things like that, you know, must be
> After a famous victory.

That's all for now, folks. Cheerio, and let's hear from you.

THE WOYGIAN

Beaumanor Park,
Woodhouse,
Nr. Loughborough, Leics.

WITH the first number of THE WOYGIAN in your hands you are able to judge the type of contributions required. The "WHAT'S HE DOING NOW?" pages must obviously increasingly play a large part in the make-up of the magazine. As you read Ollie's paragraphs you will, I am sure, find yourself remarking: "Well, fancy old So-and-So . . . .", or: "I wonder if Whosit knows about . . . . ?" So please remember that by passing on the slightest scrap of information concerning other members which comes your way you will be interesting some, if not all of the Woygian readers. It is remarkable that not one item concerns the male military members. Considering the strength of their membership this seems all wrong. How about it, Signals?

We have lost touch with quite a large number of people who are qualified to be members and might be eager to join and renew old acquaintance, if they knew of the Association's existence. Perhaps **you** are in touch with someone? Also it is most important that members keep us informed of their movements and changes of address.

In future issues there will be a little more space for unsolicited material and we shall be pleased to receive anything, fictional or otherwise, calculated to interest Woygians. Comments, suggestions and correspondence, which should be brief and to the point, will be welcomed. Where it is possible to have the matter typewritten, double-spaced, this will be of the greatest assistance. Here's hoping you'll help to make the Christmas Number a success! Contributions by December 1st, please.

THE EDITOR.

All Association correspondence should be sent to the appropriate officer at the above address.

WOYGIAN CROSSWORD

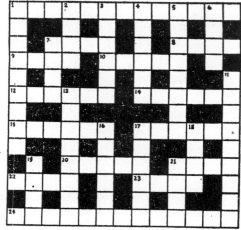

ACROSS.
1. Dispersed (13).
7. Ripe as a mole. (4)
8. Wireless signals often do this to nothing! (4)
9. Leave out? But coming back I'm into here! (4)
10. Yellow. (5)
12. The land which is cultivated. (They often 21 Down it). (6)
14. No Sedentary booklet this. (6)
15. Patriotic Exiles' rendezvous, perhaps. (6)
17. Scene of many Nazi atrocities. (6)
20. It's a bore. The soldier probably thinks so too! (5)
21. In the Civil Service, such bindings are said to be sanguine. (4)
22. List, showing duties to be performed, possibly. (4)
23. The hide-out of a liar. (4)
24. It may be red, yellow, or blue. (7, 6)

Composed by L. C. MOORE.

DOWN.
1. So dismal that even the dead stole from here! (9)
2. Ear-phones do this—in time, anyway. (4)
3. The Mikado finds his less comfortable now. (6)
4. Just the man for a national song! (6)
5. The clue to this one is hellish! (8)
6. One might think this chap was always rotating! (4)
7. A peculiar example of Italian architectural leanings may be seen here. (4)
11. One who commits verbal libel. (9)
13. One takes this when firing over open sights, 'tis said. (5, 3)
16. Obviously, he has accepted this Crossword for the "WOYGIAN". (6)
17. Contemporary Anglo-French historian and miscellaneous writer. (6)
18. Many an Exile has enjoyed recreation upon, in, or by it. (4)
19. General Smuts is one. (4)
21. Until you can keep your money in it! (4)

The SUCCESS of

The Woygian Association

depends on YOU.

Please try to make that little effort to keep us informed of your doings, and those of old friends.

We are indebted to "Wilk" for our splendid Cover Design.

Printed by John Corah & Son Ltd., and published by E. C. Millhouse for The Woygian Association.

The WOYGIAN

BRIDGEWOODS 1939 CHICKSANDS 1945 BEAUMANOR

Vol. 1   Christmas 1945   No. 2

JOURNAL OF
THE WOYGIAN
ASSOCIATION

President:
Lt. Col. M. J. W. Ellingworth, R. Sigs.

Vice-Presidents:
Major H. F. Jolowicz.   Mr. G. M. Spooner.
Jnr. Cdr. I. F. Romer, A.T.S.   Mr. C. O. Smith.

Chairman of the Association:
Mr. R. W. Hilder.

Honorary Secretary: *Honorary Treasurer:*
Sgt. J. Rogerson, A.T.S.   Capt. G. E. M. Abels.

Honorary Editor:
Mr. E. C. Millhouse.

Central Committee:
Mr. E. W. Dobson. Mr. H. Dodd. Mrs. P. L. Edmundson.

Midland Zone Committee: *Scottish Zone Committee:*
S/Sgt. L. Whittaker.   Cpl. S. J. M. Murray, A.T.S.
Sgt. J. A. Kearney.   Cpl. R. Symington, A.T.S.
C.S.M. M. Reynolds, A.T.S.   Sgt. A. Robertson, A.T.S.
Sgt. A. A. Marshall, A.T.S.   Cpl. J. C. Donlon, A.T.S.
Mr. T. Pollard.   Mr. G. G. Cooper.

Honorary Auditor:
Mr. A. H. Appleton.

TWO OPEN LETTERS

(The first, which explains itself, will interest all Woygians, and is reproduced by permission of the recipient. The purpose of the second one is referred to by "Ollie" on Page 8.)

6813 SIG. SEC. DET.
APO 527, U.S. ARMY.
7th September, 1945.

DEAR COLONEL ELLINGWORTH,

ALTHOUGH the orders which sent us to W.O.Y.G. followed the normal military channels, and no doubt any official expressions of our feelings about them should also take the same course, we should nevertheless like to send to you personally this unofficial letter which will put on record at W.O.Y.G. our own appreciation of the circumstances which sent us to work with the members of the War Office Y Group.

We feel sure that an opportunity like ours never came to any other three soldiers of the United States Army, and should like to tell you that we feel most grateful for the orders which took us to Beaumanor. We are pleased to have been accepted as members of a unit which made unique contributions to the cause of Allied victory, and will carry home with us not only a sort of professional pride at having been allowed to share in the achievements of W.O.Y.G., but also a warm sense of gratitude for the associations which brought us so many fine friendships among our Allies. Our months at Beaumanor have given us a store of pleasant memories, and we hope that through the Woygian Association we may keep those memories alive and vigorous.

Very sincerely yours,

(*Signed*) S/SGT. FRED J. ALLRED
SGT. JOHN A. MCGEACHY, JR.
SGT. FORBES S. SIBLEY.

BEAUMANOR PARK,
4th October, 1945.

MALCOLM SPOONER, ESQ., M.A.,
THE LABORATORY,
THE CITADEL, PLYMOUTH.

DEAR SIR,

I UNDERSTAND that the organisation with which you are connected will shortly be acquiring a "ship". I, therefore, offer my services as Captain, Second Mate, or Galley Boy of this ship.

I have, during a somewhat varied career, taken command of cruisers, destroyers, skiffs, operational huts and civilian canteens with inconspicuous success. I therefore feel that, before I am finally "on the rocks", I should at least be given a chance to put somebody else's ship "on the rocks" too.

If your ship happened to be fitted with wireless, I could ensure that this, too, would not be working when the said ship was away from port, and thus provide complete freedom of action for the remainder of the crew. Further, I could guarantee that if the ship was bound for the Eddystone, we should make a fine landfall near the Azores, and you realise what advantages this would have.

Finally, my wife says I am extremely good at cooking hot water, with the slight disadvantage that the electrical appliances in our house invariably "blow up" when I approach for the purpose of exercising my superb knowledge of the culinary art.

So I am the only man you could select for the job.

I am, Sir,
Your obedient servant,

(*Signed*) M. J. W. E.

Lieut-Col., R. Signals (Unpaid).
Lieut-Cdr. R.N. (Retired Pay).

From the CHAIRMAN of the ASSOCIATION

DEAR MEMBERS,

YOU are by now, I am sure, fully aware of the objects for which the Woygian Association exists, and I need not remind you of them here. It has, however, occurred to me that you might be interested to hear how the Association came into being, and to learn something of the people behind the scenes who have played a big part in that process of creation.

It was almost exactly a year ago that I began to draft the original notes of the scheme for the formation of the Woygian Association. Three other members of my Section, Mrs. G. E. M. Abels (née Workman), Mr. Harry Dodd and S/Sgt. Lewis Whittaker, gave me invaluable assistance in the preparation of the notes, and many of their ideas were embodied in the scheme. The notes were published early in January, 1945, and it was found that sufficient people were interested in the project to make it worth while investigating the practicability of establishing the Association. In order to pursue these investigations a Formation Committee was convened, consisting of representatives of the various departments of W.O.Y.G., and the first meeting of that body took place on 15th February, 1945. The Formation Committee met nine times, and in June, 1945, were in a position to publish a report of the progress that had been made towards the foundation of the Association. In the meantime some five hundred members had been enrolled and it was decided that 1st July, 1945, should be the date on which the Association should officially come into being.

At this point I should like to take the opportunity of thanking, first, the sponsors of the scheme, mentioned above, and secondly, the other members of the Formation Committee, who gave many hours of their precious time to attend meetings and to foster enthusiasm amongst their colleagues.

At the time of writing, the Membership of the Association is 525 Ordinary Members, and 57 Associate Members. Of this total, I regret to say, seventy-five have not paid their Annual Subscriptions for this year, and in accordance with Rule 14 should not receive this issue of the Magazine. However, the Committee have decided, in view of the difficulties in the inaugural stages of the Association's career, to waive the Rule in respect of this issue, and all members will receive a copy.

There are many difficulties that the Committee have had to face during this period of transition from war to peace. Demobilisation and releases have presented the Committee with many problems. I wish to point out, with much emphasis, the utmost importance of informing the Secretary of any change of address. In connection with administration, it was found that the "zone" plan could not be instituted at present, and the most satisfactory policy would be for the remaining members of the Formation Committee to act jointly with the elected Committees at Beaumanor until such time as the Zone Committees were able to function in their proper spheres. An inaugural function was planned to take place at Christmas-time, but the Committee came up against insurmountable difficulties and the plan has had to be postponed. Such have been the worries of your Committee during the first half of the inaugural year.

So much for this brief history of events; now as to personalities. Mr. Harry Dodd, as already mentioned, did an enormous amount of pioneer work for the Association. He has spent many hours of his time preparing records of membership, dealing with correspondence, and with other matters necessary for the proper establishment of the Association. I can confidently say that without Harry's untiring efforts the Woygian Association would not be where it is to-day. He is still giving a good deal of his time to the Association.

Mrs. Mary Norris (née Watson), Joint Hon. Secretary of the Formation Committee with Mr. Harry Dodd, did valuable work in connection with the compilation of lists of members and other records.

Sgt. Joan Rogerson was a member of the Formation Committee and was subsequently elected Secretary of the Central Committee. She and Mr. Harry Dodd are sharing the secretarial work, as her official duties do not at present afford her much opportunity or facilities.

Mr. Eric Millhouse was co-opted to the Formation Committee in order that we might have his advice on matters connected with the Magazine, and was later appointed Editor. We are indeed fortunate in having an Editor so capable and experienced, and there is little doubt that the success of the "B.S.M." of which "Mouse" was Editor for much of its life, is a guarantee of the continued success of "The Woygian".

Mr. "Ollie" Pearce, who is responsible for the Notes and News section of the Magazine ("What's He Doing Now?") is untiring in his searchings for information of interest to members of the Association. I might add that he looks to you to make his none-too-easy task as light as possible, by providing him with news of yourself and your Woygian friends.

Mr. Clem Smith, one of our Vice-Presidents, was elected Treasurer of the Formation Committee and has kindly consented to act as Treasurer to the Association until Capt. Abels returns from abroad. He has watched over the funds of the Association with great devotion from the time the first membership fee was received. The elected Treasurer, Capt. G. E. M. Abels, has kept in touch with the Association through his wife, and it is our sincere wish that he will soon return to this country and be in a position to play his part in the affairs of the Association.

To these, to many others on the Formation Committee, and to the elected Committees, who have supported me in founding the Woygian Association, I say "Thank you". The honour you have done me in making me the first Chairman gives me a feeling of great pride, and I shall do my utmost to see the Woygian Association firmly established during its inaugural year.

It is my duty to convey, in the name of the Association, a message of goodwill to our President and Vice-Presidents: we extend to them our most hearty greetings at this happy time of the first Christmas of Peace, and our cordial wishes for the coming year.

Finally, I send to all members, at home and overseas, my warmest Christmas greetings, and best wishes for 1946.

Sincerely yours,

REGINALD W. HILDER.

THE WOYGIAN

Beaumanor Park,
Woodhouse,
Nr. Loughborough, Leics.

A REAL MERRY CHRISTMAS AND A HAPPY NEW YEAR TO ALL WOYGIANS!

It cannot be too strongly emphasised that matter intended for publication in the next issue must reach us not later than the announced date. Production of this number has been delayed by late arrival of contributions, and in fact one expected item has not arrived at the moment of going to press. Readers will appreciate that such delays cannot be allowed to re-occur. Contributions intended for the Spring Number must be in my hands by **March 2nd**—and it doesn't matter how much earlier!

Apart from the heavy demands on space, "St. Upid's" non-appearance this time is due, the Scribe assures me, to the fact that, despite "Ollie's" refutation, "nothing ever happens around here". Incidentally, if other readers are in agreement with Major Jolowicz's suggestion in our last issue, I should be glad to republish some of the earlier Chapters. It has been proposed that I might arrange to publish a decently bound and illustrated souvenir volume of all the chapters of St. Upid to date. Unfortunately many snags have arisen, not least of which is uncertainty as to how many ex-Woygites would require a copy. Preliminary enquiries indicate that it may cost anything up to 7/6 per volume. If any Woygians are interested and care to write me it would be of great guidance in deciding whether the idea is worth proceeding with.

THE EDITOR.

"What's He Doing Now?"

By OLLIE PEARCE.

To most of us a common phrase familiar in the doubtful days,
Now as we go our sundry ways, a different meaning it conveys,
Remote from that elusive "he", confined instead to you and me,
Therefore the word must also be interpreted at times as "she".

IN spite of the common belief that "nothing ever happens around here", there have been some sweeping changes since our last issue, but before unloading I should like to thank those members who responded to my appeal for "Gen", and remind others that a few lines are always welcome. Now that we are unable to see for ourselves what the majority of members are doing, we must rely on your letters for material, so please don't let us down.

It was with profound regret that we learned of the death, in childbirth, of Mrs. Jenkins, wife of R.A.F. Cpl. Peter Jenkins (DFX), who has gone to Chicksands prior to getting his release. The baby, a boy, is making normal progress.

Our sympathies are extended to Tommy Hill who was taken ill whilst on duty during the night of 7/8 October. He is now in Loughborough Hospital and is still keeping cheerful in spite of complications following an operation for appendicitis. We hope it will not be too long before he is well enough to return.

I am pleased to be able to report that Kay Price is making rapid progress, and is now at the Churchill Military Hospital, Headington, Nr. Oxford, after a spot of leave at her home in Cornwall.

Recently promoted L/Cpl. Bridget Atkinson is in hospital at Leicester, and will be returning to her home in Casablanca when she has fully recovered from an operation for appendicitis.

Births. Heartiest congratulations to our Editor, Mr. E. C. Millhouse, and his wife on the arrival of a daughter, Patricia Melody, at Loughborough on November 8th. Also to the following Woygites or ex-Woygites, and their spouses, who have been similarly blessed during the past few months, although, unfortunately, some of the details are a little vague: Joe Blake has another son, Peter, and "Gerry" Dalton a daughter, Mary, both born early in the summer; Norman Johnson, a son, born on August 14th; Jock Baston (I.M.), a son, born at Harrogate, since when Jock has spent most of his time studying the Unit leave roster. L/Cpl. Taylor ("Con") ex-M.F.D.F. and Mrs. Muriel Taylor, née Bromley, late of "A" Watch, now have a baby daughter, and ex-L/Cpl. Lilian Nichol, of the Plotting Room, a daughter. "Bosun" Sleeper's P.A.Y.E. code number changed from 60 to 65 on April 1st.

Marriages. Congratulations and best wishes for future happiness to the following: Bill Cooper, ex-BMR. Linesman, and Rene Warwick, ex-A.T.S. BMR., who were married at Leicester during October; ex-Sgt. Madeline Saunders, who returned to W.O.Y.G. on the cancellation of the Overseas Draft, became Mrs. Taylor during Oct., and left us on Nov. 26th; Sgt. John Alexander McGeachy, Junr. ("Mac"), who was married to Margaret, daughter of the Rev. Samuel Lee Cathey, on Oct. 18th at Concord Presbyterian Church, Loray, N. Carolina, U.S.A.; Fred Mayne, who was married to Miss Irene Hall at Leeds on Sept. 22nd; ex-Pte. Gwen. Storey, who married P/O McElrea, R.A.A.F., of Queensland, Australia; Pte. Heather Brewer, ex-"B" Watch, married at Bournemouth on Nov. 24th to W/O Trevor Norris, R.A.F.V.R., who has been a P.O.W. for three years; ex-L/Cpl. Joan Bailey, "B" Watch, married at Swanscombe, Kent, on July 28th to Cpl. Bob Wykes, who spent four years with the M.E.F.; Pte. Win. Forkin, "C" Watch, who was married to Capt. Bill Leadbeater, R.E.M.E., on Nov. 29th, at Bolton; ex-Pte. Betty Richards, "A" Watch, now Mrs. Clark; ex-Pte. Glenis Parry, "A" Watch, now Mrs. Kiliminster; Hazel Clements, ex-"A" Watch, now Mrs. Knights, who left us on Nov. 26th; ex-Pte. May Thompson, now Mrs. Dedman; ex-Pte. Vera Fagg, now Mrs. Large; ex-Pte. Joyce Baillie, now Mrs. Bacon; Jose Merga, who left us for overseas service, and is now Mrs. Robert Savage—the wedding was on Dec. 1st at Derby; Muriel Kirk, ex-Canteen Staff, who was married on Nov. 21st; L.A.C.W. Pauline Pollard (DFX), who was married to Flt./Lt. Doubleday on Oct. 16th at Leicester; ex-L/Cpl. May Swan (Runner) who was married to Chas. Campbell, R.A.F., and left us on Nov. 26th; Mr. J. K. Mitchell (now Signalman), who married Miss Haidee Grace Penlington, of Loughborough, on Sept. 29th; Pte. Jean Dennis (Hi-ya-Bub), now on a Clerks' training course at Aldermaston, near Reading, who, having held her own against the British and U.S. Armies (separately), has now married a Merchant Seaman, and become Mrs. Richardson.

Forthcoming Marriages, Engagements, etc. Congratulations to: Miss Vera Abelwhite, who is to marry Capt. Alexander Patrick McNabb, late Adjutant, Forest Moor, at Holy Trinity, Brompton Road, London, on Dec. 15th, which incidentally is our President's 56th birthday; Sigmn. Antony Eeles, I.M. Workshops, on his engagement to Irene Fisher, M.T. driver at BMR.; "Blanco" White and A.C.W. Molly Cronin (DFX), who are to be married on Dec. 8th—Molly went to Chicksands on Nov. 28th for demobbing, but will be back in time for the wedding; Miss Barbara Stockwell (ex-Canteen Staff) on her engagement to Mr. George Tebbutt, of Woodhouse Eaves.

The following departed this "life" during Sept./Oct. on being called to the colours: A/U/P L/Cpls. Taylor, A. (not "Kim"), McPhearson, Le Gassick, Hewson, Nicholls (Roy), Linder, Owen, Vickers, Godfrey, and Rees; Sigmn. Albon, Freeman, Ellingworth, Bingham, Hedley, Duly, Antrum, Gardner, Knott, Fullager, Smith, N.L., Tomlinson, Ashman, Hyder, Baker, de la Bertauche, Alcombe, Hodge, Saunders, Withers, Snell, Stevens, A., Kingsland, Smith, R. E., Blease, Roberts, P., Norwood, Barnes, Milway, Cooper, Hendley, Pearce, F., Bartlett, Dodd, J. H., Aldridge, Ward, Smith, W. S., Murgatroyd, Lowes, Pope, H., Hardy, Purdie, Weaver, Jones, D.C., Watt, James, Basnett, Sandy, Downer, Mitchell, Royle, Smith, R. M., Reed, Burr, Hayward, Jellings, Hobbs, Stewart, Talbot, R., Johnson, N., Fagg, Pollard, Nicol, G., Simmonds, Barber, and Brett. The last two and one of the Smiths, have been mentioned in connection with Lance stripes, but I have been unable to confirm this as yet. "Bungy" Williamson failed to make the medical grade and has been discharged. "Spike" Forster was also on this list, but has not been seen in the camp according to reports by some of the lads who seem to find this district an irresistible magnet. Prior to their departure some 45 of the above attended a dinner in the Canteen Lounge on Sept. 11th, and although beer was obtainable at 3d. per half-pint, there was still some left when the party adjourned to the Loughborough Palais-de-Danse together with a few young ladies and danced to Ken Webster's Band until 11-30 p.m. "Sandy" Le Gassick, who made a special journey from Croft Spa, enjoyed himself with Noreen (now L/Cpl.) England, and was seen waiting outside Garats Hay the following day. Incidentally, Sigmn. Freeman disappeared from the camp on Oct. 5th, and there has been no further news of him so far. Apparently he wants to live up to his name. Desmond Jones is endeavouring to transfer to the "I" Corps.

On Sept. 24th, a farewell dinner was held in the Officers' Mess at BMR. on the occasion of the departure of Mr. Thornton, who, in an after dinner speech, paid special tribute to the work of the D.F. staff. "Biff" has returned to the G.P.O. in London.

Capt. Siddall, now A.M.I.E.E., returned to Germany after a short leave in this country. His wife, Rene, has now given up her employment in the Group Office, the vacancy having been filled by ex-Sgt. Flora Mutton, who was demobbed on Nov. 26th. Mr. C. O. (Clem) Smith is at present on a five weeks course at the Minories, but despite his proximity to the Mint he has not yet sent us any samples.

A farewell party was held in the Canteen Lounge on Sept. 29th by the C.R.R. men in honour of the departing "I" Corps girls. Impromptu speeches were made by Sgt. Nancy Watt and Mr. George Giles. Mr. Cairncross tap-danced, and Miss Wagon entertained. Party games were indulged in with great enthusiasm, even though the liquid refreshments consisted of nothing more intoxicating than Canteen "char". The two Jeans, Dennis and Murray, when compelled to sing as a forfeit, gave a roistering duet concerning two tipsy revellers, and their performance was all the more creditable considering that they were both cold sober. Hilda Gee's impersonation of Old Mother

Riley delighted everybody. George Giles was called upon to give his impression of Popeye, which he did after having first removed his false teeth. The party reluctantly broke up at 11-45 p.m., after Auld Lang Syne had been sung and touching farewell scenes enacted. The girls left on Sept. 30th, for leave of varying periods. According to more recent news Cpl. Eileen Argent is in the Records Office at Leicester. Sgt. Ann Stewart, Cpls. Alice Crompton, Ellen Browne, Anne Child, and Ptes. Judy Meikle, Jane Mould, and Jean Dennis have gone on a six weeks Clerks' Course at Aldermaston, near Reading, where they have since been joined by Pte. Nancy Rundle. L/Cpl. Barbara Woodman has been demobbed. Sub. (ex-Sgt.) Catherine Turner has gone to Germany as Intelligence Officer. Sgts. Joyce Harraden, who went to the Pay Corps at Dover, Maud Wood, who was scrubbing floors in a plastic surgery at East Grinstead, and Beryl Minter, who was on a course of Drama at Linton, went on an Educational Course at Preston. Beryl is now in Leeds, Maud in York, and Joyce ten miles from home. Cpls. Margaret Bell, Hilda Gee (not you, Momma) and Jean Murray have been recommended for commissions. Margaret turned the offer down, Hilda has gone somewhere prior to attending W.O.S.B., and Jean has gone to Feltham to gain experience in Administration, after which she will probably go to pre-OCTU. She has been on leave to welcome her brother Jim back from Burma. Sgt. Irene Wrixon, and sister Cpl. Marjorie, have been posted to the Pay Corps in Northumberland, and Cpls. Lilian France and Mary Innes to the Pay Corps in Leeds. Cpl. Lynne Symington, is recruiting in Edinburgh, Cpl. Ruth Yule in Paddington, and Cpl. Molly Smith in Birmingham, where she is quite near to "Nick". Sgt. Nancy Watt is at an R.A.O.C. Depot at Chilwell. Priscilla Sington, née Hall, is very happy in her married life and is practising hard on her violin with the hope of obtaining a job in a professional orchestra. Her husband, Peter, hopes to go on the stage; they are at present living in a flat in Liverpool. The remainder of the contingent are at Hampstead where Miss Romer was their Jnr. Cdr. for a while, but has now been posted. Pte. Dulcie Collins is going to be an M.T. Driver. By the way, Joyce Harraden receives frequent letters and 'phone calls from Desmond.

The last news received of our American friends, excepting Mac's marriage notice, was that they returned to the States during Sept., the crossing being made, it is believed, in the *Queen Mary*.

Max Hilder left us in Sept. to rejoin his wife and small son and take up a job with a wholesale fruit and vegetable merchant at Rochester. Philip Watson has gone to the Ipswich branch of his Bank where, his family hope to join him at the end of Nov., when a house will be available for them. Sid Harris has returned to the Biggleswade branch of his Bank. Bill Boyce is still in Loughborough and is working at the Brush, as also is Jock Miller who obtained his release on medical grounds on Oct. 6th. Fred Staddon has gone back to his old job in London. He and Kay, who also has a job, are at present living in a one-roomed flat at Teddington. Charles Brown took up a new P.O. position at Regional H.Q., Bristol, during Sept. Because of the housing shortage he is obliged to resume a bachelor's existence. Mary is remaining in Southampton for the time being, whilst Charles is endeavouring to revive the Choral Society at his new Branch. Jock Meekin also obtained his release on medical grounds on Oct. 13th, and Mr. E. Bland on the authority of the N.S.O. Bob Sharp has gone to Sunderland, where he is setting up in the fried-fish-and-chip business. Hwfa (now Hugh) Pryse has returned to the stage, and the following extract from Collie Knox's column in the *Daily Mail* of Nov. 15th, should be of interest: "Hugh Pryse, with the most difficult part of the lot, squeezed every ounce out of his electrifying, brilliantly written outburst. Mr. Pryse is heard too infrequently." The subject was a review of Priestley's "Dangerous Corner", featuring Ian Hunter, broadcast by the B.B.C. on Nov. 10th and 12th. A recent letter from "Chick" Henbest says that he is not likely to return to Germany for the present. He anticipates remaining at Bishops Stortford until February, and would be glad to hear from anyone who remembers him.

In a letter received during Oct. from Mr. Spooner, he said that he had been busy with internal decorations to his house, and that it would be some time before his job returns to normal. Building repairs are necessary and they are at present without a ship, a suitable one being difficult to obtain.

A copy of the President's amusing reply to this letter appears on page 3.

Mr. E. D. Smith has returned to Marlborough College and is in charge of mathematics and P.T., vide *The Marlburian* dated Nov. 1945. "Wilk" left us on Oct. 6th and has renewed his career as a Commercial Artist. Dudley Truin is now a director of Messrs. Dudley Truin & Co., Manufacturers Agents, Wembley, and is travelling all over the place very profitably. I saw him in Loughborough recently and he said that he had seen Freddie Burgess, who is playing in the Orchestra at the Victoria Palace (Lupino Lane's Show) and is sharing a flat with Tony Mosley. He has also seen Sgt. Beattie, ex-W.O.Y.G., at Victoria but had no chance to speak to her. He has not heard from Bill Baker since reminding him of the Labour Victory in consequence of which Dudley should have collected £5.

Alan Carr, who, as reported in the last issue, is on the Fine Arts Commission in Vienna, is now a Major. Major Clifton is now in Civvy Street, and Capt. Frank Cardew has gone to Kedleston complete with squeeze-box. Capt. Graham Abels is now in Cairo, having travelled extensively in Italy. He wishes to be remembered to Major Clifton, Mr. Thornton, and other ex-colleagues. Daphne is living in Stafford, and cycles to her job in the accountant's section of the universal firm.

"Lance" Bryan, Alec Kay, and Eric Pratt gave a farewell "do" at the Apple Tree, Quorn, on Nov. 7th. The unusually potent beer rendered several of the C.R.R. men *hors-de-combat* on the following day, and first hand accounts of the proceedings were thus somewhat hazy, but it is gathered that a good time was had by all. Eric is in the Loughborough branch and "Lance" in the Northampton branch of Barclay's Bank. Philip Arnold, having undergone a refresher course at Wimbledon, is now in the Strood branch of Barclay's and expects to return to the Rochester branch in the near future.

Mr. Appleton ("Appy") left us on Nov. 26th to take up a position in an Accountant's Office at Chatham. Jock Gordon, and Jock Harper have both left us, but we have had no news since their departure. Other departures include ex-Ptes. Shirley, D., Nora Graby, Sykes (Seth), all of whom are now married, Brough, née Busby, Dodd, née Lister, ex-L/Cpls. "Auxiliaryilary" at present making large inroads on her dowry which was £1 more than she had expected; Kay Statham, now engaged to a Major who has been serving with the army in India, where she intends to join him; Yvonne Buckley, from whom we have had no further news. L.A.C.W. Dorothy O'Neill, who went to Chicksands on Nov. 28th to be demobbed. F/Sgt. Gordon Rostance (DFX) who has obtained a Class B release. Ex-Sgt. Sally Cross, who was demobbed during Nov., and Ptes. Marjorie Groves, Rogerson, J., Keene, G., Turner, P. E., Baird, Jolley, Jowett, R., and Cameron, who have been posted for remustering. Other imminent departures include: C.S.M. Jessie Reeves, C.S.M. Rostron (Rosie), Q.M.S.I. Ada Marr, Cpl. Emily Prescott, Ptes. "Win" Jones, Joan Holden, and Kathleen Bridgman, due for demob. on Dec. 11th, as also is L/Cpl. Jackie Sarre, whose sister was demobbed on Nov. 26th together with ex-Cpl. Jessie Redman. The Sarre twins intend to return to the Channel Isles. Mr. French will be leaving us on Dec. 6th when he joins the Army, which reminds me that of those already gone, "The Weasel" is making a profitable business of blancoing gaiters, etc., and De Lab., who had probably been listening to some of our "old sweats' " yarns, charged an imaginary "loose-wallah" in the middle of the night with bayonet (in scabbard), his only apparel being a pair of long pants!

Promotions. Congratulations to: C.S.M. Lilian Lederman; Sgts. Ramage, Billet, Robertson and Lockhart; Cpls. Dot Spencer, Moira Byrne, Mollie West, and P.T. Cpl. Nan Knight; L/Cpls. Morley, Priestnall, Leedham, Clements, and Noreen England.

Arrivals. Messrs. Hadler (and family), Abraham, Bill Kirkham, and Dias are again with us, and we extend a welcome to all recent arrivals, amongst whom are Messrs. Jones, R. E., "Snowy" Kiernan, and Bert Hamilton; also to the girls, including Sgt. Dot Walton, who rejoined us when the Overseas Draft was cancelled.

Other News. Lorna Galbraith, now C.S.M., is to soldier on for another year. The C.W.S. canteen closed down on Dec. 1st, and the civilian staff are now being catered for by Maud Dunn, on behalf of the B.S.C., in the T.P. rest room, whilst the military are using the canteen lounge. Chatham is being officially relinquished on Jan. 1st. Group Cdr. Rabagliati, and Jnr. Cdr. Robinson are no longer with us. We were pleased to see Joe Simonite and his wife, ex-Sgt. Peggy Chaffin, when they visited us in Aug. Nan Stevenson is out of the A.T.S. following her husband's return from overseas. Jean Joiner is married to a Palestine Policeman, and is living out there. Marjorie Dorrington, now Mrs. Marks, is now a subaltern at Sarafand. Jean Hodgson, ex-"A" Watch, is now a Jnr. Cdr. Pat Drynan, who became a G.I. bride, is now Mrs. Cleland and is in the U.S.A. Mickie Grenfell, who became Mrs. den Bakker in Alexandria, has a baby girl, Elizabeth Marie, and is living in Penzance. Ex-Cpl. Eva Cooper, who left "D" Watch, No. 1 Wing, to go abroad, is now working in Leicester as a shorthand-typist.

Chathamites will be interested to hear that Ron Denny had the opportunity of saying farewell to Jock Forrest, who, whilst in the employ of Messrs. Short Bros., of Rochester, was transferred to De Havilands, at Whitney, near Oxford, and later loaned to the Brush at Loughborough. He has now returned to De Havilands and has a good job in connection with new aero-engines. His future is assured. Jock Smyth (P.O.) of tommy-gun and umbrella fame, is now at Dundee with his wife and son. He recently spent a week in this district, and stayed at his old billet in Woodhouse Eaves.

The I.M. Workshops staff are holding a farewell party at Quorn on Dec. 13th, and each member must bring a lady partner. They are now making a full-time job of studying the girls' duty rosters. That's all for now, folks, and in conclusion I should like to wish all readers a happy Christmas, and all they wish for themselves in the New Year.

It's all the Admiral's Eye.
By ERIC W. DOBSON.

DO I look like a murderer? Do I, Arthur Norman Other, look as if I had bumped off a man *and* a woman because they annoyed me? If you don't know me you are bound to know my name; it's appeared on duty rosters, hockey and cricket teams and even on leave lists, as bold as brass: A. N. Other. Presuming you are interested in a remarkable story and haven't already decided to turn to "Ollie's 'orrid article", I'll do my best to tell it.

It's just two ack emma (yes, C.R.R., a NIGHT watch!) and I'm standing in the corner of the quadrangle, facing old Cornwallis, and wondering if he'll ever draw that silly little bit of a wooden sword. (He can't kid *me* it's a real one.) It's cold and misty, and what I'm doing here is none of your business. Be content just to read a genius.

Well, as I was saying when you turned to this page, I am, believe it or not, a double murderer. My first effort was a particularly odious person named Cuthbert Crawley, an obnoxious man if ever there was one. He simpered and sniggered, and was a confounded bore. I'll swear he used scent, and I fully expected him to come on duty with varnished nails some day. He got on my nerves as nothing else ever did.

It happened so beautifully, too. We were at Chatham in those days, going through what has become known as "The Battle of Britain". It was pretty grim, sometimes. (Ask the locals of Luff, they had an awful time they tell me!)

Well, this loathsome Cuthbert and I were nipping up the road after duty one night, dodging the shrapnel, and hoping, as we always hoped, for the best, when a bomb came sizzling down and exploded a bare fifty yards away. And, believe it or not, Cuthbert sniggered. If he'd given an asinine bray I shouldn't have felt so hard about it, for, to tell the truth, I didn't know whether to laugh or cry myself; but to *snigger* at such a time was too much.

Years of self-control left me in a flash, and I simply ran my bike into his, jumped on his head as he fell off (I was wearing those lovely, heavy L.D.V. boots at the time) and continued my gymnastics till he stopped yelling.

Of course, a silly person like you can't possible imagine what I did. Did I run off in a panic, or report to the police? Not a bit of it! I simply picked up the crumbs of Cuthbert, carried him to that all-too-convenient bomb-crater, pitched him in, pitched his bike in with him, and went home to a mushroom supper. (Very nice and tender they were, too, and done to a turn.)

Hang on a minute: there's a couple of chaps coming along to their Break. They're talking about "getting out" without being called up, the saps. Is it my imagination or does the wooden admiral, that model of masterly Whitfordian daubing, nod in agreement? I guess it's my imagination. The lucky ones are all gone. Claud, Dudley, Wilk, and the rest. Wonder what they're all doing now? And whether Bill **still** buys old bikes?

It's blooming cold out here all the same, even although the new lights under the arches are shining bravely. Which reminds me: every time I see "Remember the Blackout" written on the Canteen and Lounge doors I have an itch (technical, of course) to scrawl underneath "Yes, vaguely". Can't help thinking I'm pretty good at this apt repartee business: ought to be good enough for "Punch", if not for Mick's "Bullets", when I'm on form. I'll have to ask Kenneth James about it.

Let's see, where was I? Oh, yes; I was telling you about my "doings". Somewhere or other I've heard a voice saying "the day war broke out my wife said to me . . .". Well, my wife was like that. ((She was a Miss Fortune before I married her, but I won't make the obvious crack!) Anyhow, note I said my wife *was*. It's really too funny for words. She's in Africa now with her brother, or would be if the ship hadn't gone down. The joke of it is, she didn't sail on that ship! Her name was on the casualty list, though, and I thoroughly enjoyed a lot of well-meant sympathy. To cut a long story short, I had to do her in. Mrs-Mopped her up, so to speak.

Of course, I had plenty of time to think *this* one out, and I first persuaded her she ought to take on a war job, and suggested nursing. She fell for it, bless her, and I used my influence to have her posted to India. She was to call in at Capetown to see her brother *en route*. (Ships all went round the Cape at that time.)

I personally took all her luggage on to the ship at Liverpool and saw she was comfortably settled in her cabin. Just before the ship left I found I had no cigarettes, so my wife hopped ashore to get some for me—she was obliging sometimes! Well, after she'd gone I carried on an imaginary conversation with her for a while and left the cabin bidding her a fond farewell. Calling a steward, I insisted that my wife was not to be disturbed as she had a headache, slipped him half-a-crown for good measure—a shocking waste of money, really —and came ashore. My wife was on her way back to the ship when I met her, and, exercising my craftiness, I said we'd go aboard by a short cut, took her into a dock shed, and, stepping behind her, gave her just one hefty wallop with the loaded stick I carried for the occasion. As luck would have it, there were a number of steel blocks—circular things with a hole through the centre, probably lathe-chucks—waiting to be shipped, so I tied a few round her and deftly tipped her into the dock with hardly a splash. Everyone was so blooming busy cheering the ship out that no one noticed.

Now, don't get me wrong! I honestly had nothing to do with the ship being sunk—it was sheer good luck for me. In the normal way my wife would have been discovered missing (I believe that is the term, although how the dickens one can be discovered if one is missing beats me) and I should have testified how prone my wife was to suicide and that would have been *that*. Anyhow, as I say, the occasion didn't arise—and neither did poor Fanny with all those chucks tied on her! What a perfect crime, eh?

Hullo, here's a couple of runners coming through the arch. They're talking (*of course* they're talking!) about the depression. It seems that since the lucky 78 went away there's no thrill or adventure left in this place. Those left are all too old (or too wise, I guess) to worry about the A.T.S. in general and runners in particular.

The hussy, I wish I could do something about her. Shades of Peter and Bernard, *and* John Henry!

Well, as I was saying, I did a nice job with my wife, and they'll never catch me for it. It was the perfect murder and if you, dear reader, should be so unkind as to report me, you too, will be luckless.

They'll never catch me, and do you know why? Remember the Cuthbert affair? Well, the police came and took away those L.D.V. boots, and they hanged me, for Cuthbert, yesterday morning!

Now *you* snigger!!!

WOYGIAN CROSSWORD

ACROSS.

1. Alter or make up a barn for place to find 15 across. (9, 4)
7. Length of life of a sage? (4)
8. Oh! my friend, what a gem! (4)
9. Twice would be too often. (4)
10. A combination of individual bodies. (5)
12. Make quite certain. (6)
14. Hardly the place to see a snipe! (6)
15. Banishes—the less fortunate Woygians are still thus! (6)
17. Maginot was the "Froggy's" line, and Siegfried was the . . . (6)
20. Wireless signals are often this, unfortunately. (5)
21. Dart. (4)
22. An aerial support. (4)
23. Pull. (4)
24. STAGE ILL SOUND (Anag.)—(and make the worst wireless interference?) (7, 6)

Composed by L. C. MOORE.

DOWN.

1. Nothing is banned in starting this weather forecaster. (9)
2. Strong inclination found in your German people. (4)
3. Equally certain, we see, to encourage belief. (6)
4. In a possessive state. (6)
5. Ring TI. 100—for fundamental principle of shorthand, perhaps. (8)
6. Raise. (4)
7. Well-known deeds of the Apostles. (4)
11. The bird that angers William. (9)
13. Raised. (8)
16. Moves from work at different times of the day. (6)
17. He bats around in water! (6)
18. Mend. (4)
19. Hallo! there's a letter gone astray for the righteous. (4)
21. Shove the spigot in here. (4)

SOLUTION TO OUR AUTUMN CROSSWORD:

ACROSS.—1, Decentralised; 7, Pier; 8, Fade; 9, Omit; 10, Ochre; 12, Arable; 14, Manual; 15, Empire; 17, Belsen; 20, Drill; 21, Tape; 22, Rota; 23, Lair; 24; Primary colour.

DOWN.—1, Desolated; 2, Emit; 3, Throne; 4, Anthem; 5, Infernal; 6, Eddy; 7, Pisa; 11, Slanderer; 13, Blind aim; 16, Editor; 17, Belloc; 18, Soar; 19, Boer; 21, Till.

The WOYGIAN

BRIDGEWOODS 1939 CHICKSANDS 1945 BEAUMANOR

Vol. I   Spring 1946   No. 3

JOURNAL OF
THE WOYGIAN
ASSOCIATION

President:
Lt. Col. M. J. W. Ellingworth, O.B.E. D.S.M. R. Sigs.

Vice-Presidents:
Major H. F. Jolowicz. Mr. G. M. Spooner.
Jnr. Cdr. I. F. Romer, A.T.S. Mr. C. O. Smith.

Chairman of the Association:
Mr. R. W. Hilder.

Honorary Secretary: *Honorary Treasurer:*
Miss J. Rogerson, Capt. G. E. M. Abels
71, Burnway, (at present overseas).
Hornchurch, Essex.

Honorary Editor:
Mr. E. C. Millhouse.

Central Committee:
Mr. E. W. Dobson. Mr. H. Dodd. Mrs. P. L. Edmundson,
27, Wood End Avenue,
S. Harrow, Middlesex.

Midland Zone Committee: *Scottish Zone Committee:*
Mr. J. A. Kearney, Mr. G. G. Cooper,
53, Baker Street, Manchester, 12. 9, Abbotsford Place, Stirling.
Miss A. A. Marshall, Cpl. J. C. Donlon, A.T.S.
8, Sycamore Road, Nottingham.
Mr. T. Pollard, Cpl. S. J. M. Murray, A.T.S.,

Miss M. Reynolds, Miss A. Robertson,
11, Lyndhurst Road, Birkdale, Brae Cottage, Old Rattray,
Southport, Lancs. Blairgowrie, Perthshire.
Mr. L. Whittaker, Cpl. R. Symington, A.T.S.,
164, Haughton Green Road,
Haughton Green, Manchester.

Honorary Auditor:
Mr. A. H. Appleton,
12, Temple Gardens, Cuxton Road, Strood, Kent.

Written with a Blanco Brush

By MAURICE REED.

LICHFIELD, STAFFS.

5*th December*, 1945.

DEAR MR. EDITOR,

YOU want to know all about those "Lucky 78" who left the verdant estates of civilian youth to don the dull attire of military manhood. During those two months much tea has poured from our china mugs, as has blanco sprayed from our brushes. But before I give you a general outline of things, I must remind you that under present conditions an easy-flowing pen does not come readily to the hand. I am in the Naafi: you know what that means. The inevitable ham-handed youth clinks on the piano in the corner. I would mention in parenthesis that there are three stock tunes: there's the heart-cry from the claustrophobic recruit, "Don't Fence me In"; odd phrases from the "Warsaw Concerto" by those who aspire to classicism but can't quite reach it; and the opening bars of Tchaikowsky's First Concerto, by those who touch the dizzy heights but soon get vertigo. Besides the limited repertoire of the pianists, the ear is confounded by a welter of rattling cups, scuffling boots and loud—very loud—voices. Add to the noise the combined effects of unusual physical energy—P.T., cross-country, drill, crawling over creation, and the mysteries of basket-ball, plus rain, wind, cold, colds, coughs, this, that and blanco, and you may understand a certain hesitancy in style and a noticeable lack of easy phrasing.

Of primary importance is the fact that we're still alive. Not unnaturally, it was feared in some quarters that over-exertion and hard work (both terms are comparative) might bring the end of our worldly lives. Surprisingly, with the exception of "Spike" Forster, "Bungy" Williamson and Bill Stewart, all of whom have disappeared into the unknown blue of Medical Boards, we are still here. Some are lacking here and there: a dent on a Bren Gun could tell a tale; you could find a few human hairs on odd pieces of gym apparatus; skin from the palm of one's hand might be discovered on a piece of waste ground of which we all wot well. But these are minor things. They are no deterrent to the general urge to get the training over and done with.

Given time and the right atmosphere, I might manage to fill "The Woygian", but with only one page, I must generalise. Odd things come to my mind: how Wilk would laugh could be but see Noel Royle, marching in denims and army specs.; how like the soda-fountain in the Empire the Y.M.C.A. in Lichfield becomes on Saturday afternoons. I remark the striking resemblance between Naafi-girls and the canteen-ladies-wot-was. Since Freddie Vickers always sang raucously in "H" Cloakroom, you'll not be surprised that he sings equally raucously at seven a.m. when he's swilling down the stairs. You yourself will have noted the amazing treks to Loughborough. Twenty men at a time, all of whom were never going to the beastly place again, gravitate on Saturdays and Sundays to the Market Place, and fan out on their various missions. (I hear that "Zombie" spent a whole afternoon and evening in the Beaumanor Canteen.) There is the weekly miracle of living on a meagre twenty shillings, and existing on a ration of forty cigarettes. By Wednesday butt-ends are at a premium, and scrapings from the bottom of one's pouch (or someone else's) are welcomed as life-preservers. One counts one's self lucky to see a paper once a week, and the world situation is a closed book, except to those searchers after truth who will not be denied.

Times change, and so do outward appearances (not half!) but those underneath are unchanged. There remains still a certain madness, inherent since Woyg days. We shan't be here much longer, for which we return devout thanks, and soon something new will turn up. But whatever it is, Freddie Vickers will sing; Pete James will condemn in round terms those who leave doors open; Desmond Jones will still whistle "Weave We the Bridal Garland"; Norman Hobbs will still start writing letters five minutes before Lights Out; and I shall always be—

Yours sincerely,

2598705.

"What's He Doing Now?"

By OLLIE PEARCE.

To most of us a common phrase familiar in the doubtful days,
Now as we go our sundry ways, a different meaning it conveys,
Remote from that elusive "he", confined instead to you and me,
Therefore the word must also be interpreted at times as "she".

MANY thanks to all members who have supplied me with items of interest for this issue, both verbally and by letter. To the latter I should like to explain that it is impracticable for me to reply to each individual, but please don't let this discourage you; we are always keen to hear from, or of, ex-Woygites.

I am sure that all our readers will welcome the news that Tommy Hill has recovered sufficiently to anticipate his discharge from hospital during March, but he will probably be convalescing for some time before returning to the fold.

We were very pleasantly surprised to receive a visit, on February 28th, from Miss Kay Price, whose recovery is a tribute to her determination. Although she is still suffering from partial paralysis of the right arm and leg, Kay made the journey from Cornwall alone. She intends to take a trip to Australia as soon as she can obtain a passage. I understand that this paralysis, which is gradually mending, is not such a handicap as it might have been had Kay been right-handed.

Congratulations to our President whose award of the O.B.E. (Order of both ends?) appeared in the New Year's Honours List. In commenting on this honour the C.O. said he was most gratified that the efforts of all who had served at this station had thus been officially recognised.

Births. Congratulations to Capt. and Mrs. Siddall on the arrival of a daughter, at Loughborough, on February 8th. Shortly after this happy event, "Granfer" Clem Smith, who is now back with us, appeared at the office looking as though he had been mauled by a tiger. It appears, however, that his facial injuries were self-inflicted. Since age and ague often go together, perhaps it would be advisable to bow to the inevitable and grow a beard. On the other hand, of course, it might have been due to excitement. Ernest managed to get a short leave from Germany to meet his new daughter.

Congratulations also to Mrs. McKeough (Betty Browne), wife of P.O. Tel. Raymond McKeough, D.S.M., on the birth of a son, Barry, at Canada House, Gillingham, on February 9th. Betty's present address is 4, Shepway Avenue, Maidstone, Kent. Also to Mrs. Pendlebury (Chris Lammas), on the birth of a daughter, Lorraine Sara, at Reading, on February 1st. And to Lieut. Harris, M.T. Officer and Mess Secretary, whose wife presented him with a son and heir on February 27th. Bearing in mind the worry and mental strain endured by fathers on such occasions, Mess members should examine their accounts for February more thoroughly than usual.

Marriages. Congratulations and best wishes for future happiness to "I" Corps Cpl. Mollie Smith, and Roy Nicholls, now Sigmn., who were married on Boxing Day. Thanks for the cake!

Also to ex-Pte. Kathleen Sutcliffe and Ray Snell, now Sigmn., who were married at Brighouse, Nr. Huddersfield, on December 22nd. Kathleen was demobbed on January 15th, and is living with her parents at Brighouse. Ray caused some varied comments when he arrived back at camp after the honeymoon and announced that he had lost half a stone! By the way, he is augmenting the family income by haircutting at 1/- for N.C.O's. and 6d. for Sigmn. Wot! only 6d. for Noel?

Also to Pte. J. Anderton, No. 3 Wing, who was married at Bolton, Lancs., to Cpl. Elmo Lee Carley, U.S.A.A.F., on February 12th; and to Pte. D. Black, No. 3 Wing, who was married to Stoker P. O. O'Connor, at St. James' Church, Newcastle. Both these girls expect to get their release from the A.T.S. on March 18th.

Also to Pte. Hilliard, No. 3 Wing, who was married to L.A.C. John Gough at Walsall, Staffs., on February 19th. To Mrs. Frost, better known to our readers as Miss Corfe, ex-C.R.R., A.T.S. Officer, whose recent marriage to Capt. Frost, of the Royal West Kent Regt., took place in Greece, her pre-war home, to which she returned last year. To ex-Pte. E. Ackroyd, No. 1 Wing, who has recently become Mrs. Hustwith. To ex-Pte. Kathleen Blake, who was married on January 15th to Cpl. Cook, of the R.A.A.F. To ex-Pte. Platt, A. J., who became Mrs. Steer on January 15th. To Sigmn. Bertram George Ashman, ex-Sutton Valence, who married Miss Beryl Wilson, of Maidstone, at the Wesleyan Chapel in that town. The reception, held at the Bridge Cafe, was attended by 35 guests, after which the happy pair left for their honeymoon at Hastings. To Mr. Peberdy, of the C.R.R., who was married at Fleckney, Nr. Leicester, on March 2nd.

Forthcoming Marriages, Engagements, etc. Congratulations to ex-Pte. Ann Morgan, "A" Watch, 1/2 Wing, on her engagement to an Army Officer, to whom she refers as "Wilf.". To Cpl. "Di" Snelling, who is to be married in the near future. Her fiancé is in the R.A.F. To Bernard Norwood, now Sigmn., who is getting married on March 23rd, and Stan. Saunders, also Sigmn., who intends to get married some time in March. To ex-Sgt. "Mickie" Marshall, on her recent engagement. She is at present staying at her home in Nottingham, but expects to live in Newport, Mon., ultimately.

To Sigmn. Bill Smith, ex-Thurso, who is to be married on his next leave. To Pte. Betty Robinson (Plotting Room), on her engagement to Army Sgt. John Seal, who has just returned from service overseas. The ring arrived by post, and the wedding will probably take place in June. To Joyce Harraden and Desmond Jones, who became engaged at Christmas. To Pte. Hilda Gee, on her recent engagement to Stan, who returned to this country some months ago after serving abroad with the Army. To Pte. Mabel Smith, on her engagement to a Naval Officer who was previously at the Naval College in Quorn.

Other News. Arrivals and departures have been numerous, particularly among the A.T.S., and in consequence promotion has been somewhat "haywire" recently. We have not had an actual case of stripes being posted to a girl on demob. leave, but it has frequently been a very near thing.

The following were demobbed on January 15th: C.S.M. Lilian Lederman, now working as a saleswoman of ladies' gowns, in London; Sgts. Ina Anderson, Bella Robertson; Cpls. Mabel Cage, and Chris Wardle (Commns. Wing), Molly West, Rosemary Price; L/Cpls. Elsie Everett, Alicia Scott, Hilda Parker; and Ptes. Walker, S.E., Moir, E.D., Merry, R., Rudge, Wilson, Workman, Hermie Baker, Janet Wood, Nan Squire, Pippen, Hardham, Green, J.K., Fay Cope, Alice Starkie, Beryl Appleby, Edge, Hackett, Cox, Hilda Yeoman, Margery Wass, Inglis, S., Abbott, N., Wattis (née Nickson), Keeler, and Norma Double (Plotting Room), who has returned to her native hamlet, E. Bergholt, which she claims is between Colchester and Ipswich, but apparently the map-makers are unaware of this. Norma is back at her pre-war office job.

On February 12th: Sgts. Joan Rogerson, "Liz" Hooper, and Sgt.-for-a-day "Bobbie" Lord; Cpls. Sheila Taylor, Molly Owen (Clerk); L/Cpls. "Bobbie" Bamber, Jane Harvey, Maisie Swann, Margaret Webb, Bickett B.; Ptes. Kirby H.M., Atkinson M.F., Marquiss B., Russell O., Sharman E., Flackfield Z.M., Pepper I.M., Woodward B.O., Saker J.E., Joan Goodall, Joyce Bringloe, Crawford M., Talbot J., Walke M., Williams F.M., Lilian Barker, Brown E., Eaton K.A., McEntyre O.J., Thomas E.S., Jordan A.W.H., Wright J., and "Bill" Sykes, of the Plotting Room.

On February 23rd: Sgts. Ruby Day, Mary Billett, Joan Tibbs (Clerk); Cpl. Gwen Sidwell, who has gone to assist her father, landlord of the "Queen Victoria", at Cheam, Surrey; L/Cpls. Betty Kitching, Dorothy Martin, "Teggy" Jones; Pte. Dorothy Craig, who is to continue her studies at the Royal College of Music in London, and Ptes. Burnside, Winnie Webster, Eileen Salter, Kathleen Northwood, Lucy Suart, Josie Hatch, Mildred Penn, Ann Smith, "Harry" Harrington, Margery Burton, Taylor W., Brown A.M., Woollaston J., Dobie, Thorniley, Griffiths, Hebditch, Luke, Lomas, Martin,

Johnstone; also Mrs. Higton (née Kirkby), Mrs. Carley (née Wilkinson), and Mrs. Spires (née Banks). Pte. Dunkin, who should have gone with this group, was unfortunately in hospital and had her demob. deferred.

Our best wishes for success and happiness in their new surroundings go with these girls, some of whom have been replaced by recent arrivals from F.M., to whom we extend a hearty welcome.

Miss Joan Holden has obtained a post at Stn. X, where she is working in the same department as our old friend, Mr. H. R. Batchelor, now demobbed. Judy Meikle, ex-C.R.R., is also at Stn. X. She is still serving with the "I" Corps. Jenny Denne, Joan Cook, and Kathleen Bridgman have obtained posts as civilian operators at Knockholt and are doing shift-work. Mary Norris (née Watson), has now recovered from an operation for appendicitis performed last January. Joan Dadswell is still in a sanatorium. Latest reports say that she has put on a lot of weight, and is looking very well. Pat Drynan, wrongly reported in our last issue as being a G.I. bride, married an American civilian and is expecting a happy event in the near future. Pat Lacey, working at a Girls' Remand Home in the London area, was thinking of relinquishing this post to go abroad when last heard of. Betty Foster is living in Copenhagen where she is teaching English. Mickie Grenfell who, as reported in our last issue, married a Dutchman, is living in Rotterdam. Jean Hammond, who married an officer cadet from the Naval College at Quorn, is now a mother. Cynthia Foxworthy was last heard of when with the Pay Corps at Brighton. Mrs. Helen Mulligan (née Brown), visited Brand Hill during January, when she was expecting to sail for the U.S.A. on the *Queen Mary* at the end of January, or beginning of February. Cpl. Jean Hoatson is at the Records Office in Leicester. Pte. Doreen Mallett is on a Clerks' training course at Reading.

At Christmas time, which, by the way, was the quietest in the history of W.O.Y.G., we received cards from several old friends, including "Mac" McGeachy, who has since written from Davidson College, Davidson, N. Carolina, where he is now teaching American, English, European and ancient history. He says that he is finding his stay in England, where he visited such places as Avebury, Bath, St. Albans, Stonehenge, Richborough Castle, and many English Cathedrals, invaluable in connection with his present work. He tells us that Fred Allred is teaching at Meredith College for Girls in the same State, and is living at 2212 Hope Street, Raleigh, N. Carolina. He regrets that he has not heard from Forbes Sibley since they were discharged together at Washington on November 17th. Forbes wrote to us during January from his wife's parents' home at 15, Matthews Street, Pontiac, Michigan. He says that he arrived home to find that General Motors, where he had hoped to work for a while in the truck plant, had been on strike since November 20th, consequently he has been unemployed. His work at the University of Michigan was due to begin on February 20th. In the meantime he had been completing an unfinished course in solid geometry as a prerequisite for entering the University. In addition, he has been punching up his algebra and chemistry. He still spends quite a lot of time on music; considers himself fortunate in having become so intimately acquainted with us and living in our country; plans to come over with his wife Ruth, as soon as he can. This may be in the summer of 1947, but depends on so many things that it is no more than a contemplation at present. He wants to know if The Association intends to issue an Address List as there are numerous members to whom he would like to write occasionally. George Hoare is living at 36, Sellwood Road, Northcourt, Abingdon, Berks., and is working in that district as a radio serviceman. His pal, Jack Gillatt, has returned to his home in Hull where he is working on bomb-damage repairs. He says he misses some of the boys but is glad to be living in his own home again, and finds further consolation in the absence of shift-work.

Norma Domina, ex-Room 61, wrote at the end of December to say that she expected to leave for America soon, and that her future address would be Gnell Glen Chinchilla Farm, Big Bear Lake, California.

Mr. Tomkins, who was a regular contributor to the B.S.M., under the *nom-de-plume* of "Snikmot", also wrote at the end of last year. He is still with Cable and Wireless Ltd., and is living at 11, Etsome Terrace, Somerton, Somerset. He says he is a bit sore at having helped to put the Socialist Government in power now that they have nationalised "the finest firm any man worked for ever"; mentions the fact that there are a lot of names appearing in this column which are unknown to him, but the conscripts, unfortunately, are; has mixed views with a strong negative inclination towards rejoining the Civil Service, but is keeping a weather eye open for alternative employment which does not entail night-work. Often thinks back to BMR days which he really enjoyed on duty and off. Asks whether the canteen queues are like they used to be, and whether it is still running at a loss.

Mrs. G. France writes from 7, Cumberland Terrace, Rhu, Dumbartonshire, where she is staying for the present in order to be near her husband who is stationed in the vicinity.

A letter from Sigmn. Freeman solves a minor mystery. After three months treatment for psycho-neurosis he is due for discharge shortly. He wishes all at BMR a happy New Year.

Margaret Gibbins wrote from c/o 50, Tennyson Avenue, Manor Park, London, E.12. She was posted to C.O.D. Chilwell about six months ago.

A letter from Enid Sharp, written on January 21st, says she has travelled around a bit since leaving BMR. She welcomes "The Woygian" which revives old memories of many happy days spent in the company of friends at Y. Was expecting to be demobbed in March.

Miss M. A. Hall, ex-D Watch, No. 3 Wing, is also glad to receive the Magazine and news of BMR. Her present address is 59, North Road, West Bridgford, Nottingham.

A letter from Jimmy Hunter, now living at 27, Double Street, Spalding, Lincs., says he has not run up against anybody since leaving BMR, and does not expect to in that part of the world. He has rejoined his old firm as assistant factory manager, and now realises that there is much more in controlling staff than he had ever imagined. He sends his best wishes to Eddie Sims, and other old friends.

Barbara Stockwell, ex-canteen staff, is now working as a cook at the Victoria Hotel in Leicester. Margaret Ellingworth, recently discharged from the Wrens, is back at her old job in the Group Office. Ex-Sgt. Peggy Chaffin, now Mrs. Joe Simonite, is working in the Pay Office, and Joe is employed in the C.R.R. whilst awaiting his demob. Norman Wells, our pre-war M.T. driver at Chatham, is back on his old job after returning from service with the Army overseas. There have been several other recent additions to the civilian staff, including George Beeke, now demobbed from the R.N. We extend a hearty welcome to all.

Ex-Sgt. Glenys Phillips, demobbed on January 1st, writes to say that she is working for the Post Office in London, and finding it very hard after the very easy five years in the A.T.S. She is now living at 11, Emlyn Gardens, Shepherds Bush, London, W.12, but before leaving Reading, she had the pleasure of meeting Dicky Ackhurst, who is working for Messrs. Vickers-Armstrong and looks much fitter than he did.

We have had no recent news of Dick and Rita Wildblood, who now have a small son, Christopher Michael. Dicky obtained his release to take up farming. We sympathise with Lois Seal, who, having just got her second stripe, was released on compassionate grounds owing to the sudden death of her mother. Jock Harper sends word that he is still alive and kicking, and likes BMR much better now that it is only a memory. Jimmy Rogers and Nobby Clarke left us during February and have returned to their pre-war jobs with Gaumont British. Lewis Whittaker, and Freddie Bond, both ex-I Corps, have returned to their peace-time occupations. Lewis, after serving at Shenley and F.M., to his old job at Ryland's Library, Manchester, and Freddie, released under Class B, is teaching classics at a school in Bolton. Ex-L/Cpl. Mary Sheldon is still working. Her husband is now demobbed, but their efforts to find a house have been unsuccessful. "Molly" Morgan, ex-D.F.C., is at Kallia Marine Airport, on the Dead Sea. He flew out to Cairo in a Dakota during December, 1944, and after four months point-to-point working there, was posted to Kallia as ground Radio Officer i/c. Last August, the Officer i/c of the airport was posted to Basra, and as there was no replacement available, Molly got the job. He is now extremely busy and happy. His work now is mainly administrative, leave, pay, conditions, etc., for a staff of one English coxswain, one Armenian clerk, two Arab clerks, two first class operators, one Arab, one Jew, one second class junior operator, Arab, one meteorologist observer, Arab, one night watchman, Arab, and fourteen Arab labourers. The Radio Room is equipped with four 250 watt, and two 50 watt transmitters, one S.X.28, one Hallicrafters "Skybuddy", an A.C. Hermes transreceiver, R/T and W/T, and four rectifiers, but Molly doesn't see it for days on end. There are eight services a week touching the airport by Short's flying boats, between Durban and Calcutta. The airport's immediate responsibility is Kallia-Cairo, westward, and Kallia-Habbaniyeh, eastward. Molly has a fully-furnished bungalow with cooker, refrigerator, and radio, has a native cook and servants, and is awaiting the arrival of his wife who would spend her summers in the cool of Jerusalem in preference to the heat of the Jordan Valley. Molly says he got into the B.O.A.C. just in time, as the job is dying and no more recruits are being taken.

Syd Harris, ex-C.R.R., is living at 73, Cambridge Road, Girton, Cambs., and travels to and from Biggleswade daily. Prior to this he was relieving at Surbiton, Esher, and during Christmas at Luton, where his hours were 09.00-21.00 excluding travelling time. He had hoped to get away from Biggleswade but it seems that after the departure of Mr. Watson, who is now at Ipswich, there was a tightening up, so Syd has to stay where he is. Ex-Cpl. Pamela Edmundson, living at Harrow, Middx., and working in her old office after tiring of doing nothing, says that she misses old friends. Her husband came home in September for 28 days, but is now back in Italy and is not expecting demob. until about October. A very informative letter from Alick Berry says that Bill Baker is managing to wrest a living from an ungrateful world under the title of W. Howard Baker & Co., Manufacturers' Agents, Export and Import. I understand that on leaving BMR he spent several idle weeks sun-bathing at Margate, but I suppose even Bill could not go on doing this indefinitely. Jack Colville is an outside salesman for Ever Ready batteries in York. Bill Jones is back in his pre-war job and flat in Birmingham. When I saw the *Daily Express* headline on February 25th, which read: "Mutineers Fire Wrecked Prison. Seized as they run from flames by Ralph Champion", I wondered if he had become a prison warder, but according to Alick, he is pulling down a four figure income covering front page stories for the *Daily* and *Sunday Express*. In spite of this affluence he has no house, and is working shifts 15.00-23.00 etc. He is the father of a new baby, Christopher Dale. Mrs. Vera Adams (ex-runner) wished to convey her best wishes to all her friends at BMR, especially Peggy McCarthy, Alec, Micky, Ina, and D Watch (Barrow). She is living at 11, Ashfield Road, Dunscroft, Nr. Doncaster, and has met several ex-A.T.S. friends in civvy street, including Joan Pusey and ex-Pte. Morris. She hopes Bob and Cecile Downer will be very happy. Some of the numerous promotions have already been mentioned in the foregoing items. Congratulations to all concerned, and also to C.S.M. "Red" Yalden, C.S.M. Joan Myall; Sgts. Pearl Kaitcer, Molly Gould, and Pat Murray; Cpls. Joan Priestnall, Yvonne Bams, Helen Convey, Joan Morley, Evelyn Penter, Pam Denny, Levitt B., Griffiths J., Leedham R., Collier V., and Smith A.; L/Cpls. Muriel Dick, Hine J., and Robson. L/Cpl. Mabel Marple, Ptes. Barbara Lulham and "Tommy" Tucker, have obtained Class "B" releases. The first named to return to the Civil Service, and the others to take up nursing. Departures among the male military include C.Q.M.S. Hedley, posted to F.M. and replaced by Sgt. (now C.Q.M.S.) Rogers E., Dvr. Wilson, G., Dvr. Etherington A., and Sigmn. (Casanova) Jones E. (Class "B"). Cpl. Craig W., Cpl. Page L., Sigmn. Foot, Sigmn. Sandell (Class "A"). Sgt. Joe Kearney, L/Sgt. Phillips E.; Cpls. Marlow, Goldstraw, Jones S., and Ralph; L/Cpls. Roberts, and Smythe; Sigmn. Blair, Muirhead, Shindle, Baston, Johnson A., Lamb, Barrett, Northcott, Morton, and "Topper" Brown. (The two last-named are back with us as civilian I.M's.) Dvrs. Baker, Puttock, and Suett. Incidentally, Jean Baggott is coming back after her demob. leave as a civilian clerk. Congratulations and best wishes for future happiness to L/Cpl. Jean Sargeant, who was married to T/Sgt. Carr, of the U.S. Army Air Corps, on February 3rd, at the Catholic Church, Walthamstow.

A letter from Pte. Blake at War Office Signals, and expecting demob. in March, gives news of ex-Pte. Miller who was posted to Edinburgh, and obtained her release under Class "B", ex-Cpl. Angela Raub (née Wiffen), who is now in America, and has a baby girl, Patricia, and Pte. Mary Paine, who became Mrs. Spiers just before Christmas. Her husband is in the R.E.M.E. Pte. Blake says that most of the T.P. operators there would prefer to be back at W.O.Y.G. Eight of them were posted to F.M. at the end of January, where they should see some old familiar faces since all of our conscripts have been posted there, and are back at the old job. Lew Owen, on a ten weeks' infantry course at Carlisle, is the only exception. All the acting L/Cpls. lost their stripes on being posted, but there are numerous aspirants for commissions. So far only McPhearson has attended W.O.S.B. Harry Bartlett referees quite a few football matches, and is still keeping his hand in (his pocket?) with the pools. The "Weasel" continues to supplement his income by making beds for a nominal fee, although I hear that he has fallen a victim to alcohol. After standing on a table in an Ossett pub at a farewell "do", and rendering "The Lost Chord", he took Pete Gardner, Bernard Norwood, and Harry Bartlett out to celebrate the passing of his B2, and squandered over a pound on beer. DeLab now possesses an Austin 7 of ancient origin with which he nearly murdered several people when at Shenley. "Auxiliaryilary" is living at 24, Longridge Road, Earls Court, S.W.5. She is training for dancing once again, and teaches at Dover on Friday mornings. Sat next to Dudley Truin at a performance of "The Third Visitor" in which Hugh Pryse was playing. Has met Jean Murray several times, and Margaret Bell, who was posted to Edinburgh, her home town. Also met Don Linder and Geo. Lowes, spent a few hours with them, and was amused at the idea of the uniform being on the other sex for a change.

Chas. (Bankroll) Dobson attended a Gilbert and Sullivan Opera at Leicester on March 5th, in the company of "Red" Yalden. Possibly these two have more in common than just being "townies"? I very much regret that numerous items of news have been crowded out of this issue, but don't let this keep you from thumping those tom-toms. Cheerio for now.

"The Chronicles of St. Upid"

MENTION was made in the last number of "The Woygian" of a suggested bound volume of "St. Upid". It was felt that such a book would provide members with an interesting souvenir of their sojourn with W.O.Y.G. Arrangements have now been made for the publication of this volume, which will comprise the complete series of "St. Upid" articles, dating from the original Chicksands "screeds" right through to the chapter which appeared in the first number of "The Woygian". The book, containing forty chapters, with characteristic illustrations by "Wilk", will be handsomely bound with title in imitation gold, and enclosed in an attractive dust-jacket. The price will be **Six Shillings,** post free.

An assured sale of at least two-hundred-and-fifty copies was considered essential before the plan could be adopted, and judging from the number of preliminary orders already received, it seems likely that this number may be exceeded. Naturally, a comparatively small edition such as this cannot be produced anywhere nearly so cheaply as impressions which run into many thousands.

The printing trade, like most others, is far from normal yet, and thus, although the book is now in production, considerable delay is expected in the binding department. As a result it does not appear likely that the volumes will be ready for despatch before late in June. In these circumstances, beyond our control, your patient indulgence is sought.

The author does not feel justified in attempting to personally finance a project of this size and has therefore arranged for orders to be taken on a subscription basis, under the auspices of the Woygian Association. On April 8th the precise number of volumes to be printed has to be decided and, as this will depend on the total orders then received, if you require a copy, please send in your form immediately. You will find one enclosed with this Magazine. Don't leave it until too late, as no guarantee can be made to meet any orders received after **April 8th, 1946.**

The Digby Chronicles

I SAID to Steve: "What do you mean to wear at your Annual Dinner?" Steve, busy with the crossword puzzle, said nothing. So I tried again—"The Reunion ——" I began. Steve leapt at the word. "Reunion!" he cried. "That's it!"

"Yes, dear," I said, pleased at being recognized. "What are you going to wear?" Steve looked at me in utter astonishment. "Wear?" he said incredulously, "whatever do you mean?" Evidently he had not heard me and had taken my remark for the solution of some tiresome clue. "The Reunion Dinner," I began again, **"what are you going to wear?"**

Steve registered no enthusiasm. "Nothing special," he volunteered. "You had a suit made out of my dress clothes, and my Home Guard uniform is full of moths. No choice but a lounge suit. Unless,"—he became sarcastic—"you suggest I wear my gardening jacket and dungarees?"

Before I could answer, the telephone rang. "Now, who can that be?" I wondered. Steve went to the 'phone. A short, heated conversation floated in from the hall, then Steve returned looking annoyed, and sank back into his chair again, picking up the puzzle as he did so. "Wrong number" he muttered grimly, and buried himself into the intricacies of Clue 20 Across.

I tried again. "The Anniversary Dinner——" I began. A reply was in the act of coming to Steve's lips in a none-too-flattering tone, when a cry from upstairs hauled me to my feet. "That's Gilly," I exclaimed, "he wasn't very well when I put him to bed." "Over-eating," muttered Steve, deep in his crossword. I left the room and found the cause of the trouble was just that. (However does Steve know these things without even trying to guess?) I spent about half-an-hour with Gilly, and then Susan and Judy woke up, rather peevish at discovering it was not yet morning. Then I went downstairs again.

"Steve," said I, still trying, **"what are you going to wear?"** No answer. I looked over at his chair to find it vacant——two minutes later Steve came in with the dog. "Barking outside," he remarked.

I still don't know what Steve is going to wear!

K. L. B. P.

ASSOCIATION NEWS

THE last three months having seen a large number of departures from Beaumanor, we are now approaching the time when the Woygian Association should begin to function on its peace-time basis. At a recent joint meeting of the committees at Beaumanor it was decided that it would now be best for the three committees to operate separately, as originally planned, and for the joint meetings at Beaumanor to be discontinued. Of the Central Committee, Miss Joan Rogerson (Hon. Sec.) and Mrs. P. L. Edmundson are at their homes in London, and Capt. Abels (Hon. Treasurer) is expected to arrive in this country soon. Of the Midland Committee, all but Mr. T. Pollard are now home. The Scottish Committee is not yet so settled, as three of its members are still away from home. Nevertheless, it is intended that all three committees will get together during the next few months to plan re-union activities in their respective areas for next Autumn and Winter. We hope to hold the First Annual General Meeting in London next July or August, and mean to make this occasion an informal re-union. More news of this will be given in the next Magazine.

Miss Rogerson, having recently been demobbed, is taking over the secretarial work at her home, but for the time being any Association correspondence should continue to be addressed to the Hon. Sec., c/o Beaumanor Park.

We have been delighted to receive letters from many members during the past few months, and are sorry that in one or two cases we were unable to reply personally, other than to send receipts for subscriptions. So we trust that all who have written to us will accept our best thanks, and be assured that we have been greatly encouraged by your expressions of approval of the Association and its Magazine. We hope that more members will follow your good example. All news of members received by us in this way is, of course, passed to "Ollie" Pearce, for inclusion in his columns, and thus eventually to your Woygian friends.

It is intended to publish a list of members when our members have settled down after demob. or release. In the meantime, if you wish to write to a fellow-Woygian but do not know his or her address, send your letter c/o the Association at Beaumanor Park, and we shall be glad to re-direct it. We shall also be glad to seek and pass on to you news of any ex-colleague of whom you would like to hear.

Membership now totals about six hundred. This is very satisfactory, but even so, represents probably not more than 50% of those who could be members. If you know of an ex-Woyg friend who is not a member, please recommend him or her to join—it is never too late. The Hon. Sec. (c/o Beaumanor Park) will be glad to supply full details to any prospective members.

Each member should now have received from us a Rule Book, an official receipt for the Membership Fee and Subscription, and a copy of each of the three issues of the Magazine published so far—Autumn and Christmas, 1945, and the present issue, except that Joint Members and Ordinary Members whose husbands or wives are Associate Members are sent only one copy for each pair. We hope that all these reached you safely. Supplies of the first issue ran out some time ago, and we regret that we were unable to send copies to new members who joined during the past two or three months.

We extend our best wishes to all those who have been demobbed. or released in 1946; we hope to hear from you some time that you are settling down happily in normal civilian life.

BEAUMANOR MUSIC CLUB

WITH most of the Club's members now gone from Beaumanor, I feel it is time to wind up its affairs, and to dispose of the stock of choral music acquired during its four years' existence. I have, in fact, already started the process of disposing of the music, by giving to several members, some of whom left recently, a selection of our favourite songs. I also sent a number to Mr. Charles Brown, at Bristol, to give him some assistance, of which I feel all ex-members would approve, in his task of reviving the moribund Choral Society at his new P.O. branch. Incidentally, I have no recent news, but I learned just before Christmas that the Choir was to give a carol recital to inmates of the local hospital, so we can assume it is now well on its feet!

There still remains a considerable amount of music, so if any ex-member would like to have copies of some of the songs—"The Blue Danube", "Heraclitus", "Viking Song" and others—I should be pleased to post them to him or her. I shall have to effect this share-out on a "first-come-first-served" basis, so please write to me soon, at Beaumanor, and let me know which songs you would like. I will do my best to satisfy individual requests, though I cannot, of course, offer any guarantee.

About £2 remains as the balance of the Club's funds, and I propose to use this to pay for packing and posting, so there is no need to forward any money when asking for the music.

And so ends a happy and, judged by war-time standards, long association. I think we shall all retain memories of those many pleasant sing-songs and gramophone programmes on Wednesday evenings during the war years, first at Quorn Church Room and later at the "Hurst". The "pioneers" will remember, too, with much pleasure and perhaps a certain feeling of pride, the birth of the Choir—the male-voice chorus who regaled Woygians at the Christmas party in Loughborough Town Hall, in January, 1942, with their lusty renderings of "Down among the Dead Men", "The Mermaid" and other hearty ditties (but not forgetting John Smyth's soulfully pathetic performance in "My Bonny"!). We shall remember the socials at Quorn Church Room which began and ended each season, and the summer rambles, with their regular climax in the splendid teas provided by Mrs. Neale at Blakeshay Farm.

I hope that the Woygian Association will help to keep these memories alive, and that many of us will meet again at its re-unions.

Best wishes to all ex-members of the Music Club.

HARRY DODD.

THE WOYGIAN

Beaumanor Park,
Woodhouse,
Nr. Loughborough, Leics.

WE are very pleased to publish in this issue a contribution by Kay Price, one of the B.S.M's. stalwarts, which unfortunately was crowded out of the Christmas Number at the last moment. This "Digby" episode is noteworthy as being Kay's first attempt at writing following her serious accident last August. We were delighted to see Kay in these parts again recently—of which Ollie has more to say in his notes.

Maurice Reed's highly diverting exposition of life in khaki arrived after we had gone to press last time, but, although its matter has been somewhat out-dated by the march of events, it is, we feel, none the less worthy of inclusion in our pages.

With the appearance of the third number of our magazine the dispersal of members of The Woygian Association is well under way. From now on this journal must play an increasingly vital part in keeping our widely distributed membership *au fait* with the progress, activities and opinions of their fellows. That it has already begun to fill this need is evident from the letters we receive. Mrs. P. L. Edmundson, lately of "A" Watch, 2 Wing, and a member of our Central Committee, now at home in London, says in a recent letter: "I really do look forward to receiving it, for once one leaves, it's strange, one longs to be back with all one's friends, and this magazine is the only way to keep in touch with all that happens". Our American friends, Forbes Sibley and "Mac" McGeachy, also emphasise how gratifying it is, in receiving the Magazine "across the Pond", to read of the doings of their old comrades.

Now that readers are scattering across our islands, the need for a greater variety in our contents is evident in order that this journal may be as representative as possible. If yours is an unusual job, or if you have some uncommon experience to relate; perhaps an engaging hobby; or an entertaining trip; an article, poem, or story which would interest or amuse fellow-Woygians, please send it along. But make it as brief as possible. And don't for goodness sake excuse yourself on the grounds that you "can't write". "The Woygian's" literary standard is not high, and after all, if your attempt is *that* bad it can soon be knocked into shape.

Finally, do keep Ollie well supplied. Remember that often an item of news about yourself or any friends with whom you have maintained contact may seem insignificant enough to you but would nevertheless greatly interest others with whom you and your coterie might have lost touch. Even though you only glimpse Gladys Greenshank or Victor Vulture on a railway platform it will interest *someone*, and very often you may be the only channel for a certain piece of information. Or, if you are entirely devoid of news, at least drop us a line occasionally and tell us what you think of the Magazine, with any suggestions you can offer.

Cheerio for now. Contributions for Summer No. by June 1st, please.

The Editor.

SOLUTION TO OUR CHRISTMAS CROSSWORD.

ACROSS.—1, Beaumanor Park; 7, Ages; 8, Opal; 9, Once; 10, Union; 12, Ensure; 14, Gutter; 15, Exiles; 17, Boche's; 20, Faint; 21, Barb; 22, Mast; 23, Haul; 24, Loudest signal.

DOWN.—1, Barometer; 2, Urge; 3, Assure; 4, Owning; 5, Phonetic; 6, Rear; 7, Acts; 11, Crossbill; 13, Uplifted; 16, Shifts; 17, Bathes; 18, Heal; 19, Halo; 21, Bung.

The Woygian Crossword is held over owing to lack of space.

Printed by John Corah & Son Ltd., and published by E. C. Millhouse for The Woygian Association.

The WOYGIAN

BRIDGEWOODS 1939 CHICKSANDS 1945 BEAUMANOR

Vol. 1   Summer 1946   No. 4

JOURNAL OF THE WOYGIAN ASSOCIATION

President:
Lt. Col. M. J. W. Ellingworth, O.B.E., D.S.M., R. Sigs.

Vice-Presidents:
Major H. F. Jolowicz. Mr. G. M. Spooner.
Jnr. Cdr. I. F. Romer, A.T.S. Mr. C. O. Smith.

Chairman of the Association:
Mr. R. W. Hilder.

Honorary Secretary: *Honorary Treasurer:*
Miss J. Rogerson, Capt. G. E. M. Abels
71, Burnway, (*at present overseas*).
Hornchurch, Essex.

Honorary Editor:
Mr. E. C. Millhouse.

Central Committee:

Mr. E. W. Dobson. Mr. H. Dodd. Mrs. P. L. Edmundson,
  10, Lancaster Av., 27, Wood End Avenue,
  S. Woodford, E.18. S. Harrow, Middlesex.

Midland Zone Committee: *Scottish Zone Committee:*
Mr. J. A. Kearney, Mr. G. G. Cooper,
 53, Baker Street, Manchester, 12. 9, Abbotsford Place, Stirling.
Mrs. A. A. Sockett, Miss J. C. Donlon,
 "Fairfield", Llandevaud, Knockondie, Kirkcolm,
 Nr. Newport, Mon. By Stranraer.
Mr. T. Pollard, Miss S. J. M. Murray,
  13, Church Hill, Edinburgh, 10.
Miss M. Reynolds, Miss A. Robertson,
 11, Lyndhurst Road, Birkdale, Brae Cottage, Old Rattray,
 Southport, Lancs. Blairgowrie, Perthshire.
Mr. L. Whittaker, Cpl. R. Symington, A.T.S.,
 164, Haughton Green Road,
 Haughton Green, Manchester.

Honorary Auditor:
Mr. A. H. Appleton,
12, Temple Gardens, Cuxton Road, Strood, Kent.

ASSOCIATION NEWS

THE Honorary Secretary, Miss Joan Rogerson, is now in London and all correspondence should be addressed to her at 71, Burnway, Hornchurch, Essex. Only matter exclusively for the Chairman or Editor should now be addressed to Beaumanor.

Mr. Harry Dodd, of the Central Committee, has also returned to London. All members would wish to thank him for the yeoman service he has rendered to the Association during the inaugural year and wish him the best of fortune at his new post.

Many letters have been received by the Chairman and the Editor during the past months from members giving information which has been recorded and subsequently passed to Ollie for his "What's He Doing Now?" pages. Now that the majority of members have left Beaumanor it is even more important that everyone should write once in a while to maintain the link with the past and give information of current events. The Association owes a great deal to Ollie Pearce's untiring efforts sifting and condensing the information, but as he says, "it is worth it, because one feels it is appreciated".

The First Annual General Meeting of the Association will be held in the Autumn, notice of which will be given later. Motions to be put at the Annual General Meeting must be received by the Hon. Secretary not later than 31st July, 1946.

A motion has been received from a member, and, subject to amendments, the Annual General Meeting will be asked to confirm: "That in view of the difficulties of the inaugural year when the Committees were unable to function properly owing to the gradual process of demobilisation and release, it is proposed that all Officers and Committees be re-elected *en bloc* for the year 1946-47".

All members are reminded that subscriptions for the year 1946-47 are due and payable on 1st July. It is hoped that all will pay promptly and ensure receiving a copy of the Autumn and subsequent issues of the Magazine.

R. W. Hilder—Chairman.

Midnight Masquerade

By ERIC W. DOBSON.

"DO you believe in ghosts"? I wonder how often that question has been put; how many and how long have been the discussions and arguments whose subject has been the supernatural.

Do *I* believe in ghosts? Well, I'll tell you a tale, and let you judge for yourselves.

A friend of my father owns an old country house, or perhaps I should say a mansion, and years ago we used to go there for week-end parties.

You know the sort of place: long three-storeyed building in grey stone and red brick, with wings (added in the seventeenth century), gables, lattice windows, an ornamental lake; "with statues on the terraces and peacocks strutting by", and lawns like billiards tables, and rose-gardens boxed by impenetrable holly hedges.

The house to which I am referring is one of these, and, to round off what every country seat deems necessary to complete its inventory, it has a ghost.

The brief but lurid legend concerns a murderous ancestor and an erring wife, now doomed to roam the house as a ghost, and said to resort to violence in her efforts to leave one particular room should she enter it. This room is spoken of, in inverted commas and with horrified, bated breath, as the Haunted Bedroom.

Ah! dear reader, I can see you now, racing ahead of my story in shrewd anticipation as to the connection between the haunted bedroom and your narrator. Yes, you're right. I *was* allotted the HBR.

It was during one particularly crowded party, and, as becomes such a small social lion as myself, it was sleep in the HBR or go home!

Of course, I was assured that the vicious lady seldom walked or made herself felt (I trembled at that last word; "heard" would have suited me better), and was told that providing I touched nothing except where necessary, everything would be all right.

Imagine me, then, in fear and trepidation, entering the HBR in order to dress for dinner, on the evening of my arrival.

A gloomy room, somewhat over-furnished, with a thick pile dingy carpet and a huge canopied four-poster bed; with a long dressing table complete with speckled mirror, and deep, dark, dismal cupboards; with a tall-boy and wardrobe fit to hold twenty years of clothing at our present rations, but with a cheerful fire in the spacious grate and four candles burning somewhat unsteadily in the breeze from a partly-opened window. These, with the electric light, made the room a blaze of warm colour, cutting shadows to a minimum.

Of course, the very reputation of the room made me susceptible to its ghostly (I nearly wrote "ghastly") influence, but I dressed, somewhat hurriedly, and suffered no ill results. And that night, with the warning so solemnly reiterated as I stole hesitantly to my bed, I felt rather as if I were spending the night at Madame Tussauds as, with the earnest admonitions ringing in my ears, I crept gingerly between the sheets.

As the canopy settled around me with a rustle I noticed, with curiosity, a thick rope, with tassel attached, swinging at the head of the bed. I didn't dare to touch it, naturally, and, after blowing out the candle on my bedside table, I soon went off into a deep sleep, aided, no doubt, by my tiredness after travelling.

Well, reader, here you go guessing again, I suspect, but this time you're wrong, because I spent a perfect night without a single ghostly interruption, and although I was the subject of curious glances at breakfast the next morning, no comments were passed and no questions asked.

The second night wasn't quite so pleasant, however, because I had summoned sufficient courage to wonder what would happen if I pulled that rope behind the bed, and, in consequence, I had a series of horrible dreams in which I was swung high over the roof on the rope, plunged deep into the lake with the rope, cast over a terrible bottomless chasm by the rope, and, finally I awoke in time to prevent myself being hanged from a beam in the ceiling, at the rope's end.

I was so annoyed by my dreams that I vowed that, come the next bedtime, I would pull that rope before I went to sleep.

I meant to approach my host, nonchalantly, and say: "Look here, Sir, what *would* happen if I hauled on your hefty hawser?" But his repeated warnings of "verboten" still rang in my ears, so I dared not.

Well, I imbued myself with an unusual amount of dutch courage after dinner that evening, and, determined as I was to take the bull by the horns (or the rope by its tassel) I must confess I was distinctly nervous as I went into my room at bedtime.

I undressed slowly, sipping an extra nightcap, and looked around me. Every detail of that room seemed to stand out vividly as if some trick photography was at work lifting each article into the midst of a halo of clarity, focussing upon my retina the very cracks in the walls, and a small cobweb in a far corner.

The carved bedposts looked almost animate and the firelight flickered fitfully, showing me a picture of a man swinging on a gibbet in the coals, then changed, and the winking embers formed themselves first into a donkey pulling a cart, and then into a fire-ridden house from whose windows streamed festoons and garlands of belching flame. Did *you* ever see pictures in the fire when you were very young and alone in a house, and quite a bit nervous?

"Well, this is it," I forced myself to say. Here let me assure you that, despite the influence of good pre-war whisky, I was in a blue funk. Timorously I undressed, and as I turned out the electric light, snuffed three candles and took the fourth to my bedside table, my hands shook violently, the knuckles showing strained and white; my face was clammy and my tongue clove to the roof of my mouth.

I climbed into bed, the evil rope swinging sluggishly, insolently, with the movement of some great tropical creature lazily swaying in a brief jungle zephyr, or like the dock-side hawser of a ship at rest, moving restlessly and rhythmically with the gentle motion of slow lapping water.

It had a single coloured thread woven into its plaits, like a strand of auburn in an old grey head, incongruous, yet compelling. The strand had severed just above the tassel whose tawdry, gold-braided ends were laden with dust.

As the rope swung so did the weight of the tassel retard its reach and bump first against one bedpost and then the other, beating out a solemn, slow tattoo in a vaguely ominous monotone.

"Merciful heavens," I thought, "I can't stand this suspense any longer!"

I drew a deep breath and blew out the candle, and, as the blackness leapt menacingly at me from every corner of the room, and the walls seemed to approach upon me, with wide-staring eyes for I knew not what, and with perspiration running down my chin, I grasped the rope with palsied, shaking hands, and pulled !——

The electric light came on again.

THE WOYGIAN

BEAUMANOR PARK,
WOODHOUSE,
NR. LOUGHBOROUGH, LEICS.

THIS number contains four extra pages, representing a $33\frac{1}{3}\%$ increase over our previous issues. Naturally, this means a considerable inroad into our funds, for printing has not yet become any cheaper, but it does provide Ollie with facilities for unloading the veritable avalanche of "Gen" he continues to amass. So keep him well stocked, folks, and we'll do our best to give you as large a magazine as possible. Also, don't forget that the greater the Association's membership the bigger dividends it can pay in this and other ways; so please do your bit in harrying those of your friends who have neglected to join. If you don't save your magazines, why not post this copy to a non-Woygian ex-Woygite?

I would like to thank all who have written during the past quarter, not forgetting those who took the opportunity to enclose a few lines with their "St. Upid" order forms. I am sorry it is not possible to answer all of these individually, but you may be assured your letters were greatly appreciated and, wherever they contained items of general interest, were passed to Ollie. Many thanks also for the numerous expressions of approval of *The Woygian*.

Response to the announcement of *The Chronicles of St. Upid* has been very gratifying, and about 350 copies have so far been ordered. Bearing in mind that through an unexpected delay in distribution of the Spring Number members were not given much time in which to return their forms, and because a number of people who had expressed a wish to have a copy did not send in orders, I have decided to have a limited number of extra copies printed. These will be distributed on a "first-come-first-served" basis, so if you want a copy please let me have your order with remittance for six shillings without delay. Production is now well under way and I hope to obtain delivery by the end of the month. The book is bound in dark green cloth, titled in gold, and enclosed in a durable neutral-tint jacket printed in green. With "Wilk's" typically humorous drawings, an autographed foreword by the Prophet Osee, and the complete series of "Gospels", I have tried to make this a worth-while and enduring souvenir of your sojourn in the Promised Land.

We have been able to include some fiction in this number. Eric ("Spooky") Dobson contributes a characteristic effort, and there is at last something from a new quarter in our scattered feminine membership—but far be it from me to call *this* fiction!

THE EDITOR.

All Autumn Number contributions by September 1st, please.

"What's He Doing Now?"

By OLLIE PEARCE.

To most of us a common phrase familiar in the doubtful days,
Now as we go our sundry ways, a different meaning it conveys,
Remote from that elusive "he", confined instead to you and me,
Therefore the word must also be interpreted at times as "she".

I WOULD like to thank those members who have supplied me with news for this issue, and apologise for the fact that some of it is somewhat stale owing to lack of space in the Spring Number.

Our deepest sympathies are extended to Mr. Peberdy, of the C.R.R. staff, whose son died on March 9th, whilst serving with the M.E.F.

I am sure readers will share our regret on learning of the accident at her home during April, as a result of which Miss Margaret Ellingworth sustained injuries to the right hand, necessitating an immediate operation which was performed at the Leicester Royal Infirmary. Margaret, who keeps amazingly cheerful, has now been moved to Oxford, and is to undergo a further operation on May 29th. Her address is: Sturges Ward, Wingfield Orthopædic Hospital, Headington, Oxford. She is learning to write with her left hand, and welcomes opportunities to practice.

We are pleased to be able to report that Tommy Hill is up and about again. We have seen him at BMR on a couple of occasions, and notice that he is putting on weight. He will probably be back at work in a few weeks' time.

"Topper" Brown, of the I.M. Shop, had a spot of bad luck recently when he broke his ankle, but he was back at work soon afterwards with his foot in plaster.

Births. To ex-Cpl. Betty Sargeant, née Mendoza, who is living in a flat at Streatham, on March 2nd, a son.

To ex-Pte. Noeline Leadbeatter, at Birmingham, on March 11th, a son. Her husband is still serving with the R.A.F.

To Charles and Mary Brown, at Southampton Borough Hospital, on March 30th, a daughter, Gillian.

To Sigmn. and Mrs. F. A. Lee, at Barnet, on April 8th, a daughter, Frances Diana.

To Mr. and Mrs. Eddie Sims, on April 12th, a son, Paul Trevor.

To Mr. and Mrs. Ron Denny, on April 28th, a daughter, Angela.

To Mrs. Brittle, née Vickers ("Vicky"), at the end of April, a daughter.

To Mr. and Mrs. Malcolm Spooner, a daughter, Heather Evelyn. Sorry I cannot publish the exact date—the Colonel has mislaid the card—but it was some time in April.

To Bob and Cecile Downer, a daughter, Hilary.

To "DAK" and Mrs. Kirkby, at Worthing, on May 18th, a son.

Congratulations to all concerned.

Marriages. Ex-Sgt. Sally Hullett (Commns. Wing), on March 9th, to a member of the Palestine Police Force.

Ex-Pte. D. Claret, at Eaton, Bucks., on March 30th, to W/O James Norman.

Ex-Pte. Frances Garner, at Hinckley, on April 4th, to George Hurman.

Ex-Pte. B. D. Hodgson (2 Wing), at the Loughborough Registrar's Office on April 10th, to F/O K. Treleaven Blewitt.

Ex-Pte. M. Colville, at the Barrow-on-Soar Registrar's Office on April 20th, to Lester Kanefsky, of the American Merchant Navy.

Pte. "Midge" Dawson (3 Wing), at Egglescliffe, Co. Durham, on May 4th, to Capt. R. Tiplady, R.E.M.E., Indian Army.

"Kim" Taylor and Beryl Minter, at Broadstairs, on May 14th. Beryl, formerly of the C.R.R., was demobbed during March.

We offer our congratulations and best wishes for future happiness.

Other News. A letter, dated March 19th, from ex-Sgt. "Micky" Marshall, says that she was expecting to be married on May 4th to Mr. Edward Sockett, and that her future address would be: "Fairfield", Llandevaud, Nr. Newport, Monmouthshire, where she was staying at the time of writing.

Pte. Pat Hughes, of the Plotting Room, and Sigmn. Roy Fullager, ex-Sutton Valence, are to be married on July 6th at Pat's home in Edmonton, London.

A letter from Joan Cook, whose address is 117, Zetland Road, Doncaster, Yorks., points out an error in the last issue. She is not at Knockholt, although she did contemplate the possibility. She is teaching at a school just outside Doncaster, working hard, and says that she gets very tired after a real day's work; is inclined to agree with Glenys about the ease of Army life, but doesn't think she will join up again just yet! Joan is only teaching until such time as she is able to enter college, but it seems that there is a long waiting list. "Dusty" Smith is also waiting to enter college, but Joan has no other news of her excepting that she is out of the Army, and is back at her home in Norfolk.

When in London a little while ago, Joan met Nan Stevenson and "Goldie" Rackham, both demobbed, with their husbands home again. Thanks for the letter, Joan, I have conveyed your salaams, which are reciprocated.

Major Clifton paid us a brief visit during March. He is out of the Army, and is a director of one of the Brush subsidiary firms in London.

Miss Robinson, who was a member of the C.R.R. staff when a Junior Commander in the A.T.S., is now working with the Y.W.C.A. in Italy.

Mrs. Cook, better known to our readers as Kathleen Blake, writes from 74, Lavender Hill, Enfield, Middlx., to say that she is expecting to leave for Australia shortly.

Although this is rather ancient history, some of our readers may not have heard that "Dixie", one of the first contingent of A.T.S. operators to arrive at BMR., became the wife of a R. Signals Officer and now has a son and heir who should be getting quite a big lad by now. "Dixie" was commissioned after leaving us for service overseas.

Ex-L/Cpl. Jean Sargeant, whose wedding announcement appeared at the tail end of the Spring number, is now on her way to Kentucky to join her husband.

Alf. Main, ex-C.R.R., has a house-decorating business in Loughborough, and is being kept very busy.

Lois Seal is now back at her pre-war job with the L.C.C. as a clerk.

Eric Upton, who left us on April 13th, is now fiddling in Yarmouth.

Peggy Cracknell is going to America, and will become a G.I. bride on arrival.

Ex-Cpl. May Haskayne has been on a two months course of teleprinting, slip-reading, and touch-typing in London, with a view to becoming a G.P.O. telegraphist. She is to be married in August. Ex-L/Cpl. Elsie Everett was on the same course. May has gone to Whitchurch, and Elsie is going to Sandridge.

"Appie" Appleton, living at 12, Temple Gardens, Cuxton Road, Rochester, says he is glad to be away from shift work. He found it difficult to get used to his old job after such a long spell, but is now quite comfortably settled. Some of his work necessitates trips into the country, but most of it is done in the office.

Ex-L/Cpl. Tegwen C. Jones writes from 11, Gordon Road, Cardiff, and sends her best wishes to all old friends, both civilian and A.T.S. Says it is good to look back on happy days. She is thoroughly enjoying being back in civvy street, and resumed her pre-A.T.S. job in a Sub Post Office on April 1st.

We had a few lines from "Chick" Henbest, who said he had heard from Glenys Phillips and was looking forward to seeing her in the near future to talk over the hectic days of the "Bull Ring" at Woodhouse. He mentions that he has met most of the BMR lads who were called up. His address, which he thinks will be permanent until his demob., is: 2598369 Cpl. J. Henbest, S.O.M.T.C. R. Signals, Lyndhurst, Shenley.

Ex-Pte. May Knight, née Nichol, sends us her new address, 78, Kingsholm Road, Gloucester, and says she is very pleased to hear about old friends through *The Woygian*. Long may it last.

Bill Hayward wrote from his home after spending seven weeks in hospital at Shenley. He said he was expecting to reach F.M. eventually, and was hoping to attend W.O.S.B. He would very much like to hear from old friends. Letters to 12, Staff Houses, County Police H.Q., Sutton Road, Maidstone, would be forwarded.

Eileen Salter, of 17, Malleson Road, Liverpool, says she hadn't realised how welcome news of old friends contained in *The Woygian* would be, such a short time after her release.

Harry Appleton, Financier, Exchange Buildings, Gt. King Street, Dumfries, writes of the good, bad old days at BMR, but admits getting a nostalgic yearning for it now and again. Says he is always interested to hear how all those he knew here are getting on. Hopes to meet them and have a pow-wow some time, so has become a member of the Association, as also has Freddie (Trombone) Burgess.

Jean Ozon, née Herron, ex-A.R.13, sailed for Canada on April 3rd, per s.s. *Aquitania*. Her new address is: 54, Shore Road, Dartmouth, Nova Scotia. She says that Mrs. Norma Ramsay, née New, is now a reception clerk at "The Chequers", Newbury, Berks. Her husband, who is abroad with the R.A.F., is expected home in June.

"Wilk", who has just had a £200 a year raise, wonders how he managed to live on the pay of an E.W.A. He sends his salaams and mentions that he has seen Dudley Truin, Lew Owen, and Claude Deakin, who is now dishing out demob. suits. Wilk's address is: 50, Streatham Common North, London, S.W.16.

Joan Rogerson says she spent the first month following her demob. visiting people in various parts of the country, after which she tried, unsuccessfully, to find a residence nearer London, where she is working again in the *Sunday Times* West End office. Her address is: 71, Burnway, Hornchurch, Essex, and she sends her regards to all old friends.

Len Moore, back at his old job in the Treasury, says BMR and all it means seems many a mile and many a moon away, for which he has no regrets. He does a certain amount of night work, but does not mind this as it is a sleeping watch. He is expecting an increase in the family in June. He met Eddie Bland recently, who was on the dole at the time, but has since joined the same training school as May Haskayne. Len's address is: 21, Roman Road, Ingatestone, Essex.

Margaret Webb is now working for a National Savings Committee in Kensington.

Sid Crick has settled down very well in Sheffield where he was a bus conductor but is now driving, and trying to pick out a 50-1 winner in his spare time.

We received a very interesting and unexpected letter from Mrs. Rowe, better known to the older members of our community as Hazel Wardle, or "Nutty", of the Canteen at Fort Bridgewoods. She had a copy of *The Woygian* passed on to her by ex-Sgt. Beattie Thorp, and as a result has become a member. "Nutty" was one of the first 35 A.T.S. girls to arrive in Egypt, and was stationed at El Maadi for almost three years. She passed out as a first class cook after a course near Jerusalem which was attended by a very cosmopolitan class representing the Women's Services. She spent a summer leave in Palestine and saw all the places of interest, excepting Galilee. Married in Egypt in 1941, demobbed in December, 1943, and was mentioned in despatches for service overseas. Her present address is: 33, Watkin Road, Folkestone.

"Deadly" Truin, writing from 15, Medway Gardens, Wembley, says that the "Wilkie" touch is discernible in the present McLean's ads. He then deals at length with the progress of "The Author", and from the description we gather that he is an improved character, but Dudley seems undecided whether this is attributable to the Army, or Billie Brown. He hears regularly from Harry Appleton, who met Jock Colville in Glasgow at Christmas time. Dudley also gives us further news of Hugh Pryse, who has appeared in a couple of films, one of which was "Top Secret" with Ralph Richardson. Hugh took the part of an eminent Civil Servant, and his success was probably due to having had plenty of practice. He also appeared in "The Third Visitor", "Treasure Island" (with Jean Forbes-Robertson), and "Mary

Rose" at the Granville Theatre, Walham Green. He then went to the New Lindsey Theatre Club, Notting Hill, where he appeared in Priestley's "The Long Mirror", and is at present playing in "Pick-up Girl". By the way, Dudley is going into hospital soon for some treatment or other.

Peggy McCarthy sailed for Canada on March 3rd. We have since heard that she arrived safely and has had a second honeymoon.

"Casanova" Jones, now living at 31, Springwood Avenue, Huddersfield, is hard at work as a G.P.O. engineer. His fiancée, Pte. A. E. Mudd, ex-A.R.13, was in the Pay Corps at York, but has probably been demobbed by now. He says he saw Freddie Hartland, who was stationed in Huddersfield for a little while before going to Italy. Another old member of A.R.13, Pte. Nutton, married Jack Mansfield, of London, and spent her honeymoon on the South Coast. She was a L/Cpl. in the Pay Corps at Nottingham, but I expect she is out of the Army now.

Maurice Reed wrote to say that he met Molly Wilkinson, ex-T.P. operator, when he was on leave. She was demobbed last October on compassionate grounds, and she wishes to be remembered to all old friends, including Olive, Pat, and Lew Owen.

Chris Pendlebury writes from 48, Alexandra Road, Reading, to say how pleased she was with the baby garments she received from Pte. Vera Sayers, who is leaving the A.T.S. to take up nursing, and also from Pte. René Akeroyd. The baby was christened on April 28th, Pte. Crawford being godmother.

Nan Brown returned to her old job on April 15th after a holiday of seven weeks duration, some of which she spent with Maimie Gray, ex-Alexandria and Kedlestone. They did a lot of travelling and discovered that thumbing lifts in Scotland is a cinch; even civilians do it in places where alternative transport is scarce. They arranged a meeting with Margaret Rees, ex-"D" Watch, in Edinburgh, where she was stationed at the time, and Marion Cameron, ex-"A" Watch, unexpectedly joined the party. She had also been posted to Edinburgh, and had just arrived from the Orkneys. Needless to say, much chin-wagging ensued. Nan's present address is 351, Clepington Road, Dundee, but she is expecting to move into a recently-acquired bungalow just outside the city. Her job, which she says is very interesting, is to compile the "Forthcoming Events" list for the chief editors of a firm of publishers who include in their publications such literary masterpieces as "The Wizard", "Hotspur", "Rover", etc. Nan says she enjoys slipping into bed every night after lounging all day on a soft chair. Nice work, if you can get it!

Gwen McElrea, née Storey, writes to say that she sailed from Southampton on May 18th, in the *Stirling Castle* bound for Sydney via Port Said and Bombay. Her future address is: Card Street, North Rockhampton, Queensland, Australia.

Jacqueline Sarre, writing from "Fortafayre", Havelot, St. Peter Port, Guernsey, says both she and her sister enjoy reading *The Woygian* very much. They have both settled down to civilian life. Lucille is back at her old job as a typist, and "Jackie" is working with the British War Relief Society on the Island. The date for her wedding with Sub. Lieut. Norman Wicks, R.N.V.R. (ex-Quorn Hall), has been fixed for August 8th. She says that the Islands are practically back to normal, but there are still many families needing help.

Vera Ballard, ex-Pte. (Commns. Wing) who was posted to Preston almost a year ago, wrote from 67, London Road, Stockton Heath, Warrington. She informs us that Judy Foster was married in January to a Belgian R.A.F. officer, and is now keeping house in the wilds of Wiltshire. Also that Ptes. Slarke and Tidmarsh have been demobbed, and Pte. Finnegan who went to War Office Signals. Vera became engaged in March to ex-Sgt. F. G. Sanders, R. Signals, of East Dulwich. He was demobbed in February, and they are hoping to be married some time this year if they can find a place to live! Vera says that civvy street isn't too bad, but she often wishes she were back in the A.T.S.

A very long and detailed letter from Constable W. J. Cecil, c/o British South African Police Force Depot, Salisbury, S. Rhodesia, describes, for the benefit of those of us who have forgotten, with the passing years, what it is like to go abroad with the Services. Having come to the conclusion that he could no longer adhere to office routine, he forsook his pre-war occupation, joined the B.S.A.P., and embarked for Durban per R.M.S. *Alcantara* on

March 27th, arriving on April 23rd. Then followed a train journey of approximately 1,500 miles to Salisbury via Johannesburg, and Bulawayo. He is now under training and the course he describes is identical with that of the Army with the addition of "Police and Law", and Native Languages. He says that all sorts of food are plentiful, cigarettes 2/- for 50, and all types of "booze", excepting English beer, are cheap compared with our prices. He mentions that his brother Reg. is now in the R/T section of the R.A.F., having got his release from the "underground movement" after ten months. Wally sends his regards to members of the Music and Dancing Clubs, and also to Roy Hardy, Roy Aldridge, Johnny Hodge, Jimmy Hewson, and Bill Hayward.

Kay Price writes from Pudner's Cottage, Poughill, Bude, Cornwall, to say that she is having difficulty in obtaining a passage to Australia. Latest suggestion by the shipping agents is that she should fly from London to New York, and on to San Francisco, thence by U.S. boat to Sydney. She is still in touch with several old BMR friends, including Yvonne Bams, who is meeting some opposition in her attempt to get a grant for training as a radiologist. Kay sends her salaams to anyone interested, especially to Ted, and Joe Blake.

Mrs. Vera Jackson, née Winzer, is living with her mother-in-law at 22, Cross Street, Kettlebrook, Tamworth, Staffs., and is getting on very well. Her husband was demobbed recently. She doesn't meet many old BMR friends in that part of the world, but is hoping to have a long gossip with some of them at a proposed re-union of Hut 102, Brand Hill, in London, on June 3rd.

Rosemary Price says it is grand to be back at teaching again, but finds it a bit wearing on her feet dealing with hoards of children aged from 2 to 4½ years. Her address is: National Children's Home, Alverstoke, Nr. Gosport, Hants., and she says it is a marvellous place. Five minutes from the sea, and within easy reach of London. She gets every week-end off from Friday night, plus all school holidays. Is waiting for her fiance to be demobbed (Group 40), when she hopes to be married. Says she will miss teaching, but is not sorry to be away from BMR. Sends her regards to anyone still here whom she knows.

Kathleen Snell, née Sutcliffe, writes from 139, Clifton Common, Brighouse, Yorks. She says that reading the last *Woygian* made her long to be back, and describes how she was chased by a man whilst returning home late one night. After rousing the village with shouts of "Help! murder!" she clouted him on the head. (She doesn't mention where she got the ladder from, or whether she was carrying it at the time.) Says she finished up by chasing him, spurred on by the natives shouting encouragement from the windows; but he got away, so Ray got three days compassionate leave to console her. She wishes to be remembered to all old friends, especially Freddie Fox.

Joan Turner, ex-BMR and B.W. teleprinter operator, married, within ten weeks of meeting, Sgt. Bill Shaw, of the R.A.S.C. Depot, at Longwood, Nr. Winchester, to which unit she was transferred after spending a considerable time in hospital getting over the after-effects of air raids at B.W. She worked for a short while at Associated Press, London, on teleprinters, where she found herself siting next to Julie Causer. Joan and her husband are now living at Bishop's Waltham and are frequent visitors to the Denny household.

Jimmy Rogers visited BMR during the Easter period and says that there is a definite boom in all trades connected with the British Film industry. This brings me to the many queries I have received about the item in the Spring Number concerning "Nobby" Clarke. Members are expressing surprise and saying they had no idea that "Nobby" had been a film star, and could I name any of his pictures, etc. First of all, you have got the wrong "Nobby". This one was a member of the A.R.13 staff and returned to Gaumont British, where he was a technician. The "Nobby" you have in mind has also left us to take up a managerial position with the Magnet Stores (North London) Ltd., Enfield, Middlx., but we have had no news of him since his departure.

The B.D.C. accounts were balanced by Stan Brister (Hon. Treas.) and John Dodd (Chairman). What funds remained were spent on the farewell party for the "dear departed" mentioned in the Christmas Number. Space prevents publication of a balance sheet, but the auditors are satisfied that all the funds were spent, all debts paid, and the account square(d).

All past members will probably join us in conveying sincere thanks to "Exauxiliaryilary", whose enthusiasm did so much to make the B.D.C. a success. The Club was formed in the Spring of 1942. Organizing Committee was as follows: Messrs. Carrington, Catchpole, Hamilton, Millhouse, Appleton, H., and Hilary, representing the A.T.S. The O.C. gave valuable assistance in providing the pick-up, amplifier, and loud speaker used throughout. Thanks to all concerned. Twenty gramophone records survived the ordeal, and suggestions as to their disposal are welcome.

I have not heard much lately about the lads who were called up, apart from Maurice Reed's news on another page. Pete James has been in and out of hospital for the removal of cysts from his neck. "Zombie's" attentions, and later letters, to Mrs. Snell's sister, remain unanswered. Norman Hobbs unearthed from somewhere R. Signals reports of morse tests, at about five w.p.m., of such well-known characters as Doreen Lister, Betty Bickett, and Hilary Fry, who was remembered by one or two of the instructors at Shenley.

Hugh Dias left us on May 8th. He received his calling up papers within 48 hours of arriving home. Sorry, John, but the guinea pig appears to have died!

Whilst the recent world's snooker championship was in progress, a well-known elderly bachelor received a telegram addressed to him at Beaumanor, and signed: J. Davis; but it had nothing to do with snooker.

Messrs. Cockram, Dart and Francis have left us, but we have had no further news of them yet.

Mr. Hadler took over the duties of D/F Officer on March 17th, on the departure of Capt. A. G. Billington (demobilised).

Lieut. Harris was demobbed on April 23rd, and Capt. Edwards on May 14th.

Harry Dodd did his last duty at BMR on April 14th. He has gone back to the G.E.C. as an accountant.

Joyce Woollett is resuming her old job on June 3rd and is looking forward to getting settled down again. She is glad to be home and enjoys getting a good rest every night, but misses the girls, and the fine times she had with them, very much.

Madeline Taylor, née Saunders, has returned to her old job with Cadbury's, and hopes to get a house within the next fifty years. She has seen "Bungy" Williamson several times, but not to speak to.

Mr. Cyril Jones (D/F Wing) will be leaving us on May 31st to resume research work at the National Physical Laboratories.

The civilian canteen continues to flourish, and queues are now practically unknown. The staff does its very best to make the place as cosy as possible, even to the extent of adorning the tables with flowers. At the moment it is being debated whether we can afford to subsidise char-a-banc trips out of the profits, but no decision has yet been reached.

The following left us during March: Sgts. Barbara Ramage, Molly Gould, Pat Murray, "Dotty" Walton (9, Sunny Bank, Micklefield, Leeds), Eleanor Lockhart; Cpls. Helen Clegg, Joan Bradshaw, Ann Smith, Joan Morley, K. M. Tew; L/Cpls. Mina McLeod, Joyce Dady, Peggy Hinton, Mabel Oldfield, Ruth Mabbs, Ann Neville, J. Griffiths, C. F. R. McIntosh, G. E. King, A. Watmough; Ptes. N. A. Brook, J. Cox, I. M. Fairley, E. P. Grainger, M. Green, M. Hawdon, D. Hipkiss, J. Irvine, V. M. E. Jones, D. M. Kemp, E. M. Knight, M. E. Motley, M. E. Napier, B. E. Naylor, M. Pollard, B. E. Read, K. M. Scott, E. Stafford, B. Waters, M. F. Wright, E. Young, E. L. W. Charles, F. M. Coutts, M. E. Dakin, M. A. Fabray, C. R. Gray, G. B. E. Green, M. Hancock, I. C. Harper, L. Hoppe, D. A. Howick, P. M. Keats, M. C. Lievesley, M. O. Long, L. McGeever, M. W. Rutherford, J. I. Samples, E. E. Sherwood, M. E. Siddall, R. Simpkin, P. M. Smedley, L. A. Taylor, O. Williams, Mabel Smith, Barbara Sharp, Rene Goldsmith, Doris Chetham, Joan Moderhak, Joyce White, Winnie Teasdale, Hazel Ormrod, Pauline McNichol, Dorothy Jowett, and Heather Garland. From the Plotting Room, Cpl. Connie Scovell and L/Cpl. Joyce Brinn.

The following left us during April: Sgts. Yvonne Bams, Pearl Kaitcer, Celia Allan, Dot Spencer; Cpls. Jean Donlon, Joan Priestnall, Evelyn Penter, Levitt, Leedham, Eastham; L/Cpls. Stone, Muriel Dick, Rodwell, Brown; Ptes. Askew, J. Clarke, Joan Edgell, F. Blake, Chris Ballingall, A. Wigham,

Eileen Allison, Nesta Bailey, Kay White, Betty Smith, N. Chambers, J. Taylor, P. Thiele, M. Carr, E. Norwood, Molly Wallond, Isobel Frame, Elsie Axten, and McIntyre.

The following left us during May: Cpls. Helen Convey, Pam Denny, J. Withers; L/Cpls. Devey, Gladys Humphries; Ptes. A. Stephenson, I. Howat, C. J. Aitken, M. F. Jillions, L. E. Green, F. M. Potter, K. M. King, D. E. M. Webb, M. McKinnon, Olive Spinks, Freda Tootell, B. A. Snow, and M. Pounder. Class "B" Release: Pte. A. D. Tarr.

A.T.S. promotions are still as "screwy" as ever. Before I can tell you that a certain private has been appointed Lance Corporal, she is a Corporal; anyhow, here is the position to date: Sgt. Freda (see what I mean) Smith, M.T. Section, and Alice Young; Cpls. Beatrice Ritchie, Jill Hine, Russell, Jenny Shaw, Henson, M. S. Wyllie, and Ivy Walton; L/Cpls. M. Twigg, M. Dunnett, Ann Gillieson, C. M. Kinnaird, I. Sinclair, W. Smart, K. Walker, J. Watson, B. Cook, M. Wrightson, E. Jones, K. M. Dunnett, Binning, Markwick, E. McIndoe, A. McDougall, Maggie Reilly, Olga Roch, E. I. Stone, Hilda Gee, Sylvia Stephenson, M. Ritchie, Ithan Timms, Auchterlonie, Vince, M. J. Matthews, H. M. Leishman, H. M. O'Hara, and Ann Gray (Clerk). I accept no responsibility for what might happen between now and the date of publication.

A batch of girls has just arrived from F.M. complete with dossiers giving particulars of recent employment, one of which reads: "Special research work for Major Donaldson". I wonder if she included a pack of playing cards in her equipment?

Departures among the male military include C.S.M. Joe Simonite, who will be back after his demob. leave; C.Q.M.S. Frank Winter, posted to Durham. His wife has given up her position in the office and has gone to live in Bromley, Kent; C.Q.M.S. Foy, who was in hospital on his original demob. date; Cpl. Marshall (Charlie) posted to F.M. on March 14th; Cpls. D. E. Goldstraw, S. Jones, J. Ralph, and L/Cpl. W. G. Smythe, demobbed on March 8th.

Sgt. "Ticky" Tyler was posted to us on March 11th.

Tony Eeles (I.M.) and Sigmn. W. H. Butterfield have been appointed L/Cpls.

Whilst plodding through the long list of A.T.S. departures, I was thinking of an amusing story I heard recently concerning a daughter who had returned home after "seeing the world". She was entertaining her boy friend in the drawing-room when her mother opened the door suddenly, paused on the threshold, and exclaimed: "Well, I never did". "Oh, mother," replied the daughter, "you *must* have."

That's all this time, folks. Let's hear from you.

A Flat, a Baby, and I

By CHRIS. PENDLEBURY.

To those members of "C" Watch, Brand Hill, and 99 Squad who know me well, nothing I say in this screed will come as a surprise, nor will it strain their credulity. To those who do not know me well, or at all, let me say that it has happened.

WHEN I left the nursing home, six weeks ago, with my small daughter, life looked quite rosy. I had acquired by under-the-counter activities a four-roomed flat in the same house as my mother; and, after all, a four-roomed flat wouldn't be difficult to run, and the baby would fit into the routine quite easily. What blissful ignorance!

I spent what was left of my first day at home with Mother and returned to my own flat and to bed at ten p.m., leaving her in charge of the baby for the night. At 5.45 the next morning the alarum went off and I leapt from bed with the vigour which I usually display at that hour in the morning (could never understand why I was always late for breakfast on the morning shift!) There was no hot water available, so, to make the baby's feed I had to boil the water from cold. I looked carefully over the electric cooker—I had never used one before—found a knob, and turned it on to heat. But it didn't. It was twenty minutes later, by which time I had practically taken the cooker to pieces, that I discovered that in order to heat the hot plate, one had to first turn on the power. There was then a ten minutes interval whilst the kettle boiled, and I hunted feverishly for the baby food—and in vain. Eventually I decided that I must have left it with Mother, and went down to look.

When I went, still continuing my search, into the room where the baby should have been, the cot was empty. Someone had kidnapped the child!

I rushed into mother's room to tell her the good news, to find her sitting up in bed feeding the baby. She had made the bottle the night before, and only had to warm it up. How long did that take? Oh, less than five minutes.

It was then 6.30, so I went back to bed until 8 a.m., but before settling down I experimented with the bedside lamp. A luxurious contrivance, which I had to get out of bed and switch on and off from the door.

At 8 a.m. the day began in earnest, with breakfast. After spending half an hour taking the toaster to pieces to find out why it didn't work, I put three pieces of bread under the grill and a saucepan of water on the hot plate. It was then I discovered that I had left the kettle on, containing the water originally intended for the first feed. There was now a large hole in the bottom. After dropping the kettle into the rubbish bin, and dropping an egg into the saucepan (No, "C" Watch, I didn't drop off to sleep), I went into the sitting-room to lay the table. Someone had pushed a daily paper under my door, and after laying the table, I sat down and smoked a cigarette and read the paper until someone came in to tell me that the house was on fire. We followed the smell until we reached my kitchen, where I removed three pieces of blackened toast from under the grill.

Breakfast that morning consisted of the hardest boiled egg I have ever eaten, and bread and butter, washed down with a solution of warm water and bicarbonate of soda.

Then it was time to bath the baby. I will add here, in self-defence, that I hadn't even seen the baby bathed before. Owing to an unfortunate illness, I didn't see her from the fourth day until I brought her home at nearly three weeks.

Having collected the infant and begun bathing operations, I had to go and look for the soap. It wasn't until the baby was actually in the bath that I remembered the towel, and it wasn't until the baby was out of the bath that I realised that I had forgotten her clean clothes. Then the door bell rang.

At last bathing, dressing and feeding of screaming, indignant baby were successfully accomplished. I lit a cigarette and surveyed the chaotic state of my living-room.

Eventually I cleared it up, washed up, and tackled a pile of washing, some of which I filed for future reference. Finding that time was short, I could only manage a snack before feeding the baby again—after which a little sleep was indicated, had not plaintive wails kept drifting through my window. After moving the baby to the extreme end of the garden, once more I retired. This time, after a quarter of an hour, my mother came in to announce cheerfully: "Today is the last day you can get your rations, or you won't get them at all". "All right", says I, "I'll get them at the shop round the corner later". Mother then informed me that I couldn't do that because I wasn't registered there. She named a shop some distance away and an early start would be necessary.

My transactions in the shop were drowned by yelling of the baby, so I rocked the pram. A woman who looked as if she was a spinster with middle-age spread came over and told me that one shouldn't rock the pram—the baby would always want to be rocked. So the baby yelled and the shop assistant raised his voice and endeavoured to explain the intricacies of the civilian ration books. Apart from the rations I bought a lot of things that I didn't want, from cocoa to mustard, because the assistant was so anxious to let me have them. And he gave me such a charming smile when he presented me with the bill.

In the process of putting forty-five-shillings-and-sixpence-halfpenny-worth of groceries in the well of the pram, I stood the baby on her head. I hastily flattened her again before the large unmaternal woman came back to tell me that one shouldn't stand babies on their heads as they had a soft spot. Being my child, this baby has more than a soft *spot*!

On the way home I met a friend with her six-months old-baby. She took one look in the direction of the pram and exclaimed: "For goodness sake put the pram hood down or you'll suffocate the child!" I put it down. Nearer home I met my aunt, who implored me to put the hood up before the baby died of exposure. At home I met mother, who greeted me with: "What on earth have you got the hood up for? Give it air".

I spent the evening unpacking. By the time it was feeding time again the flat looked like a bomb-site. However, I spent five minutes pushing things abstractedly into cupboards, drawers and under the bed—I still can't find anything.

The 10 p.m. feed was a nightmare. Nothing that I did would wake the baby up. At 10.30 the radio played non-stop dance music and I dozed with the baby during the sweeter numbers, and dug her furiously in the ribs during the jam-sessions. At last I laid the baby down, got my supper and took it to bed with a book. My enjoyment of both was somewhat marred by violent explosions coming from the baby's cot—she had hiccoughs.

At 12.15 I set the alarm for 6 a.m. and went to sleep. At 2 a.m. the alarm went off; at 4 a.m. the baby registered sounds indicating hunger; at 5.30 a.m. I fed her.

So this was Glorious Motherhood!

Soliloquy

By 2602296 SIGMN. CHRISTOPHER BARNES.

APRIL is here. Tomorrow we shall have been toy soldiers for six months, which seems quite an appropriate moment to survey an eventful half-year.

Haddock will always bring back poignant memories to me. Within twenty minutes of our arrival at the reception centre at Huddersfield we were presented with it, but *not* with eating utensils. That was our first real glimpse of the Army—eating fish with fingers, pencils, penknives or anything we had with us.

The next day we moved on to Ossett. There, in a derelict textile mill, we were plumped into industrial Yorkshire at its best—rows and rows of dour chimneys, blackened houses, dank and cheerless streets. Not all the poetry of Mr. Royle could convert us.

Army life for the "first batch" began in earnest at the G.S.C., Lichfield. Here we had everything from cookhouse-fatigues to route-marches; from assault-courses to gas-chambers; from rifles to bren-guns (brr!); from queue-in-the-mess to queue-in-the-Naafi. Life there was exciting and dangerous, for if one's neck was not broken in the assault course one's kit might disappear in the night. It would be difficult to pretend that we enjoyed the six weeks there, but we made the best of them. There are pleasant memories as well as unpleasant ones, and those of us who took part in the "F" Coy. Concert Party, "A Chord in F", found plenty to do in our limited spare time. Crowning irony in the repertoire of the choir at this concert was Elgar's "Song of Liberty"!

Then there were the week-end visits to Loughborough. Two months ago it had been: "Never go near the place again", but now they went, and came back sheepishly muttering something about "degrees of badness", "change", etc.

Shenley seemed almost a dream camp after the indignities of the G.S.C., but even within fifty miles of their homes some of the lads still trekked to Loughborough! Shenley memories are many, and on the whole, pleasant. They include the hospital (don't they, Mr. Jellings?), the tube-station at Edgware, evening play-readings, and a never-to-be-forgotten corporal—"Chippy" (Yer can't win, mate!). They include, too, daily struggles with the intricacies of "E and M" enlivened by the erudite wit of Messrs. Antrum and Bartlett. Moreover, they include what was for many of us the first Christmas at home for years. We enjoyed Shenley, and the end of our course came all too early.

Now we are back at the old grindstone again, this time at "F.M". instead of "BMR." It all seems much the same as it was before: the disciples of

Karl Marx, Beethoven, Churchill, Patience Strong, Kipling, and Aneurin Bevan cannot be stilled by khaki, and the night air of Yorkshire is rent by their arguments just as once was that of Leicestershire. The same faces are there, and their personalities have not changed much, either. In six months we have seen the world, but if some of our impressions of it have been greyer than we expected we have learned to laugh at that greyness and thus to lighten it.

Anyway, six months have gone, and our release Group number is only 67!

CQ WOYGIANS

de STAN BRISTER.

IT is known that several members of the Woygian Association are interested in Amateur Radio, and it is to them that these notes are addressed.

Now that the ban on amateur transmission has been lifted it is quite possible that some ex-members of W.O.Y.G. are operating their own stations in various parts of the country.

Mr. T. ("Snubby") Pollard, G2AYY, has already reported active, and we should be pleased to hear from **Jimmy Hunter, G6HU**; **Bob Sharpe, G2HMI,** and any other member who may be active or interested. It is hoped to organize regular schedules between these stations, and the 160-metre band is now available and provides an ideal opportunity.

At the Beaumanor end **G6AK** is active on 160 metres and looking around for familiar call-signs. It is expected he will shortly be joined by **Mr. E. Pethers, G6QC.** Possibly **Ken Cook, G2KK**; **Norman Shuttlewood, G6NS,** and others will also help to strengthen the network at this end.

There are also several licensed experimental receiving stations, including **Messrs. A. C. ("Kim") Taylor, BRS8648**; **J. Morton, BRS9209**; **John Ellingworth, BRS10???**; **Simpson, BRS10481**; and **"Bing" Throsby, BRS8336,** all of whom no doubt would be willing to assist.

On July 1st, frequencies will be available in the 40-metre band, and this will further increase our scope and opportunities for organization. At present it is impossible to give more exact or detailed information, but we hope very soon to be able to furnish particulars of crystal-controlled transmitting frequencies of all active stations. It is hoped that a local Radio Society will be formed as soon as the necessary accommodation is acquired. Will interested members please write and inform us as to their activities and forward any suggestions which they consider might be helpful?

In the meantime, we shall be looking out for you on 160 metres and hope to QSO in the near future.

73's **G6AK**.

Plus ça Change

HARROGATE,
YORKS.

DEAR MR. EDITOR,

TO be quite honest, if I merely wrote "It's still the same as ever" and left it at that, you could quite easily imagine for yourself how life is going for those who will, I suppose, be called "The Lucky Seventy Eight", for the rest of Woygian posterity. Transplant us from Hildebrand Barracks, our present comfortable domicile, and put us down again in Garat's Hey or Brand Hill, and you'd hardly know the difference. It's true that opinions differ about our luckiness—to hear the same cries: "What's he doing"? "What's he like"? "That your bloke, Geoff"? (the latter an unlikely contingency nowadays) is not, in the view of the majority, a good thing. I would be asked by the rest, I feel sure, to note in parenthesis that the cries have not the same volume, frequency or urgency of other days. But one hears them at times, and nostalgic memories bloom. So did they bloom some time ago when the Prophet Osee himself walked in. He stretched out his hand and blessed many of his former disciples, and now all we're waiting for is the sudden entry of Harry Dix with a curt request to "put that crossword away and get your hand turning". That, dear Mouse, would complete the picture—so Pete Gardner says, anyway. And then come on the third truck of "B" Watch's convoy up to "work" (still "work" as opposed to "duty" —old names are diehards). Close your eyes, and with a thrill of horror if your name happens to be Jimmy Hunter, you'll recognise the well-beloved chariot of Mr. Barkus—the scuffle of wrestling in the back seat, and loud and at times harmonious renderings of "Green Grow the Rushes-Ho"! And the theme song of Woygians: "The Deacon went Down". As a matter of fact, we've spread "The Deacon" over each spot of the country that has yet been blessed with our presence, and if now and again we introduce the old "Pear Tree" atmosphere to some suffering public-house we feel that our efforts are not being wasted, and that there is still goodness under the sun.

I won't enlarge upon certain incidents; suffice it to say that where cause for celebration has been found good and sound, honours due have been paid in the traditional manner.

Numerically, however, we are not the same. Apart from those of whom you already know, George Lowes, Phil Roberts and Jimmy Purdie, Fred Vickers, "Zombie", Pete Kingsland, and Googie Withers (ex O/S) have gone abroad—all, I think, to Minden. We expect news from them to you, and after they've read this I hope they'll sit down and write a few lines. Noel Royle and Ron Blease are at pre-OCTU at Wrotham, together with Sandy Le Gassick, "MacP" and John Duly (the last three all ex O/S). We've not had much news from them either, and we should be interested to know, Noel. . . .*

For the rest, we're all still here; even Ron Smith, Jimmy Dodd, Pete Dooge and one or two other unfortunates, who have been dragged back from other units to the bosom of the army's W.O.Y.G. equivalent. By the way, we all had a visit the other day from Lew Owen, who is in the "I" Corps— at present at Rotherham. He's happy and still the same, too. He confesses with tears in his eys that he "misses all the lads".

So there you are, Mouse. I've not told you all by any means. But what I have told you can give you a fairly complete idea of life here for us. Since ". . . Plus ça rest le meme", I can do no better than to say "Au revoir", as

MOGGY.

* Hear, hear! Did you pawn your pen for the ring, Noel?—*Ed*.

"Drop your end and have a look at this"
—A Wilk Cartoon

Printed by John Corah & Son Ltd., and published by E. C. Millhouse for The Woygian Association.

The WOYGIAN

BRIDGEWOODS **1939** CHICKSANDS **1945** BEAUMANOR

Vol. 2   Autumn 1946   No. 5

JOURNAL OF
THE WOYGIAN
ASSOCIATION

President:
Lt. Col. M. J. W. Ellingworth, O.B.E., D.S.M., R. Sigs.

Vice-Presidents:

Major H. F. Jolowicz.   Mr. G. M. Spooner.
Jnr. Cdr. I. F. Romer, A.T.S.   Mr. C. O. Smith.

Chairman of the Association:
Mr. R. W. Hilder.

Honorary Secretary: *Honorary Treasurer:*
Miss J. Rogerson,   Mr. G. E. M. Abels
71, Burnway, .   5, St. Cuthberts Road,
Hornchurch, Essex.   London, N.W.2.

Honorary Editor:
Mr. E. C. Millhouse.

Central Committee:

Mr. E. W. Dobson.   Mr. H. Dodd.   Mrs. P. L. Edmundson,
    10, Lancaster Av.,   27, Wood End Avenue,
    S. Woodford, E.18.   S. Harrow, Middlesex.

Midland Zone Committee: *Scottish Zone Committee:*

Mr. J. A. Kearney,   Mr. G. G. Cooper,
53, Baker Street, Manchester, 12.   9, Abbotsford Place, Stirling.
Mrs. A. A. Sockett,   Miss J. C. Donlon,
"Fairfield", Llandevaud,   Knockondie, Kirkcolm,
Nr. Newport, Mon.   By Stranraer.
Mr. T. Pollard,   Miss S. J. M. Murray,
    13, Church Hill, Edinburgh, 10.
Miss M. Reynolds,   Miss A. Robertson,
11, Lyndhurst Road, Birkdale,   Brae Cottage, Old Rattray,
Southport, Lancs.   Blairgowrie, Perthshire.
Mr. L. Whittaker,   Cpl. R. Symington, A.T.S.,
164, Haughton Green Road,
Haughton Green, Manchester.

Honorary Auditor:
Mr. A. H. Appleton,
12, Temple Gardens, Cuxton Road, Strood, Kent.

The First Annual General Meeting of
The Woygian Association
will be held at
THE THREE NUNS HOTEL, ALDGATE HIGH STREET, LONDON, E.C.3.

(Nearest Underground: Aldgate or Aldgate East.   Buses: 15, 23, 25a, 25b, 96, etc.).

On SATURDAY, 26th day of OCTOBER, 1946 at 2-30 p.m.

AGENDA.

1. Chairman's Address.
2. To receive the Report and Accounts for the year ended 31st July 1946.
3. To consider the following Resolution :—
   "That in view of the difficulties of the inaugural year when the Committees were unable to function properly owing to the gradual process of demobilisation and release, it is proposed that all Officers and Committees be re-elected *en bloc* for the year 1946/47".
4. Any other business.

J. ROGERSON,
Hon. Secretary.

Split-Second

By ERIC W. DOBSON.

THE railway bridge stood bleak and gaunt, only a few miles from Paris, high above the meandering Seine, stretched across the cold river. All but one of its occupants were covered in blankets draped across greatcoat-clad shoulders in an endeavour to keep out the bitter, snow-laden east wind. At either end stood a sentry, his back turned upon the central group gathered at one side of the track, where the outstanding figure was the one person clad only in a pair of ragged trousers and an even more disreputable singlet.

He stood erect and proud despite the cold, his hands bound tightly behind him, a hempen noose loosely encircling his neck; for Francois Gascoyne, the leader of a nearby underground resistance group, was being hanged by the Nazi soldiery. For three long and dangerous years he had defied detection, organized many of those acts with which we are all so familiar; and now he was caught and would, in a minute or so, swing between the rail-ties on the end of a German rope.

He gazed without seeing at the Nazi captain upon whose word he would be launched into oblivion; he saw only his wife, Marie, and his children, left only a mile or so away. What would become of them now ? Would the Nazis haul them off to concentration camps, or hang them, too, as they had done to so many innocent women and children ?

"It's funny," he thought, "that they are so near, and yet so very distant. Supposing, when I'm pushed over, that the rope should break. I'd fall into the river, and make a bid for life!"

His reverie was interrupted by a guttural word of command, and brutal hands thrust him forcibly outward. He murmured a brief prayer as he fell and it was miraculously answered. He felt a jerk at his neck but continued falling, turning like a wind-sped leaf, until his body hit the cold Seine with a splash and sank like a stone. The searing, biting cold, and the torturing rope around his throat gave him the strength of a madman. He struggled, it seemed, for hours, when suddenly his hands became free, and, clutching and tearing at the rope about his neck, he kicked out for the surface.

He was nearing his limit when his lungs sucked in air, and the noose floated away in the current; but he retained sufficient of his senses to realise he'd be a target for every rifle and revolver on the bridge. Gulping in the precious air, he submerged and swam with the stream, rising only for hasty breaths. Vaguely, in his ringing ears, he could hear shouts and little popping noises which told him he'd been sighted and was being picked off like some waterlogged buck. All around him bubbles frothed as a stream of bullets came at him like hornets.

Diving deeply, he swam obliquely across the stream and emerged under the shelter of trees far from the shouting Nazis who were still pelting the river with lead. He crawled on to the grassy bank, half-frozen, half-dead, but jubilant at having outwitted the Nazis, and, rising to his feet, staggered, by ways familiar since boyhood, towards his village and his family.

As he reached his cottage and called a glad greeting, his wife, with tear-stained face, came through the door to meet him. Almost falling in his eagerness, he swayed towards her and collapsed in her arms as a white, blinding flash thrust itself like a sharp knife across his eyes.

* * * * * *

Back on the bridge the Nazi captain gave a satisfied smirk as his little squad of murderers marched off, and the lifeless body of Francois Gascoyne, accursed leader of the deceitful underground forces, swung gently in the wind, suspended from a rail-tie by a good, strong, German rope.

"What's He Doing Now?"

By OLLIE PEARCE.

To most of us a common phrase familiar in the doubtful days,
Now as we go our sundry ways, a different meaning it conveys,
Remote from that elusive "he", confined instead to you and me,
Therefore the word must also be interpreted at times as "she".

I FEEL certain that members will not object to my devoting a little space to one who, although never a member of this community, was well known to so many of us in No. 2 W/T Coy, Sarafand. I refer to the late William Charles Logan Harvey, more familiarly known as Erb, who volunteered for active service with the Royal Signals at the outbreak of war, and was taken prisoner in the battle of the Slim River. He was put to work on the construction of a railway, contracted malaria, dysentery, and beri-beri, and died in a Japanese hospital. His wife was not officially notified of his death until two years afterwards, the only information received prior to this was from the padre who conducted the burial service. No personal effects were returned. Erb leaves two sons, one aged 10, and the other 7 years.

Truro Municipal Council, for whom he worked as City Hall caretaker and ceremonial mace-bearer, reduced his wife's rent by 3/- per week.

Members of the staff who were with us at Chicksands will be sorry to hear of the death, on July 18th, of Rear Admiral Miller at the age of 71. He joined the Royal Navy in 1890, and retired in 1926.

I regret to announce that Mr. H. P. Davis (Horace), in in Ward No. 2, Markfield Sanatorium, suffering from T.B. Owing to the considerable expense etc., involved in travelling, his relatives, who live in the South, are only able to visit him at very frequent intervals, and it is hoped that some of Horace's pals will rally round and relieve the monotony of the long, dreary months in hospital. Visiting days are Wednesday, Saturday, and Sunday. Books etc., would be appreciated.

Miss Margaret Ellingworth, still as chirpy as ever in spite of all, came home during August, but will probably have to return to hospital in September.

Members will be sorry to learn that Bill Smart, who left us about two years ago, has been in bed for the past seven weeks suffering from rheumatic fever after falling down the steps of the Empire in Loughborough. I understand that he has been too ill to be moved to hospital.

Our chairman, Mr. Reg. Hilder, has just returned from an illness of several weeks duration bringing with him a pile of correspondence from members.

Births. To ex-Sgt. Hazel Jones, née Webb, on April 30th, a son, David Anthony.

To Mr. and Mrs. Fred Wells, early in June, a daughter, Lynda Ann.

To Sigmn. and Mrs. Denis Brett, during June, a son, Colin.

To Mr. and Mrs. Len Moore, at Bristol on June 23rd, a son.

To Di Brandle, who husband was a P.O.W. in Siam, on August 9th, a daughter, Marilyn Dinah.

To Mr. and Mrs. E. D. Smith, on July 22nd, a son.

To Joan and "Skim" Simpson, on August 8th, a son.

To Sigmn., and Mrs. Greenwood who will be remembered by her old A.T. friends as Pte. Doris Elliott, on August 10th, a son, Richard Martin.

I also hear that Eddie Bland has a son, but no details are known.

Congratulations to all concerned.

Marriages. Pte. McRoberts, at Moston (Lancs.) Parish Church, on June 1st, to Mr. H. J. Price.

Pte. A. R. Hutchings, at Sidmouth (Devon) Parish Church, on June 1st, to Mr. Frederick Morrison.

Sigmn. Desmond Jones and Joyce Harraden, during June.

Pte. C. Bennett, on June 4th, to Mr. Frederick Edwards of London.

Pte. J. West, at Bury, Lancs., on June 5th, to Mr. Jack Vincent Edwards.

Pte. Pat Hughes and Roy Fullager, at St. James' Church, Edmonton, on July, 6th.

Pte. B. Paterson, at Leith, Scotland, to Cpl. Fred Smith.

L./Cpl. A. M. Taylor, at Mosley Street (Manchester) Registry Office, on July 20th, to Mr. Bloomfield. They are now living at 25, Claribel Street, Ardwick, Manchester 11.

Miss Barbara Stockwell (ex-Canteen Staff) at St. Paul's Church, Woodhouse Eaves, on August 31st, to Cpl. George Edward Tebbutt of the R.A.S.C. They may be going to Germany in the near future.

Mr. E. R. Roberts (Bob) and Miss Irene Facer, at the Loughborough Congregational Church, on Sept 7th. Bob gave a "Stag party" at Beaumanor on Sept. 5th which was so successful that it ended as a staggering party for some of the participants. The happy couple are honeymooning at Eastbourne.

We offer congratulations and best wishes for future happiness, also to the undermentioned newlyweds from whom we have received no details;

Ex-Cpl. May Haskayne, ex-Pte. Freda Tootell (August), Sigmn. Pete Gardner and Ann (August 26th?), ex-Cpl. Grace Flowers (August 31st) has a house in Hayes. "Casanova" Jones and Nancy Mudd whose wedding, at Stockton-on-Tees, is believed to have taken place on July 20th. Their future home is in Huddersfield.

Local Gossip. Kathleen Bridgman is to marry her Bill on October 7th.

Joan Holden is to marry a Mr. Chas. Howard of Ealing, where they already have a house, on October 19th.

Sigmn. Bobby Burr is to marry Miss Mary Walsh, who is a clippie on Allen's buses, on October 12th at Rothley.

Barbara Marquiss is being married on October 26th. Her fiancé, who was a P.O.W. in Germany for 4½ years, comes from Woodhouse Eaves, but is at present working in Leeds. They may probably be in this locality at the end of September.

Rumour has it that Ron Blease is to be married shortly, and also that Lynne Symington is trying to make up her mind.

Joyce Bringloe is engaged to a member of the R. Signals who was on a course at BMR about a year ago.

Maud Dunn (Canteen Staff) is wearing a new engagement ring which was presented to her recently by Mr. F. E. Elliott who works at the G.P.O. in Loughborough.

"Micky" Marshall, who became Mrs. Sockett on May 4th, spent her honeymoon in London and then proceeded to the little hamlet in Wales where she now lives. She has not been worried by rationing so far, and says that cooking chickens etc., is mere child's play after all her recent practice. "Micky" intends to visit her home town (Nottingham) shortly. Her husband works in Newport, and they are hoping to get a house of their own.

Some members will no doubt be interested in the information contained in a letter from the Officer i/c R. Signals Records to Mr. H. Dodd concerning the W.T. Reserve, which states: "It is unlikely that you will be required for military service excepting in the case of grave national necessity." It should be noted that Mr. Dodd is 30 years of age.

Major Donaldson has been demobbed and has returned to the G.P.O. A farewell party held at F.M. on August 21st was attended by Major Wort.

Capt. Abels has had his demob leave but is still bewildered by the business of being a civilian.

Capt. Siddall arrived home on August 3rd, and Capt. Johnny Mace is also back in this country.

A small contingent of our A.T.S. girls took part in the London Victory Parade on June 8th. Their names are:—C.S.M. Lorna Galbraith (Admin.), Cpl. Jean Hodgson (H.Q.), L/Cpl. "Winkie" Smart (Operator), and L/Cpl. Margaret McAslan (Runner).

With the increasing possibility of BMR becoming our permanent station, several members of the staff have recently joined the present-day "Quorn Hunt" in which the "hounds" endeavour to run estate agents to earth. Personally I can't think of a better substitute for foxes. This eternal hunt for somewhere to live was the direct cause of the Battle of Brand Hill.

On the evening of August 14th, the local military authorities, having learned of our intention to become squatters, sent a small party of troops to occupy the camp. During the following morning, whilst the said troops were demolishing seven of the huts, the wires between BMR and the "Battle House" were very much alive and decidedly hot, with the result that the troops were withdrawn and the remainng 21 huts were allocated to the most deserving of our families by a Housing Committee of disinterested persons. A further four families have just joined the pioneers, and it is hoped that further accommodation will be available on this site in the not-too-distant future.

Thanks are due to the O.C. and Major Wort for turning defeat into victory, to the Barrow-on-Soar Rural District Council for their splendid co-operation and promptness in effecting alterations and installations, and to the Housing Committee for the manner in which it tackled its unenviable task.

We are now recruiting on a permanent post-war basis, so if you have any acquaintances who are interested in our racket, Y not give them our address?

Messrs. Norris, Burch, Plowman and Wilkes have returned from outstations, and recent intakes include "Tim", the last of the Kenneallys.

Bob Yaxley, who left us in June, hasn't missed a day in the air since joining the B.O.A.C. Being on a short run like Liverpool-Ireland makes it necessary to work seven days per week to put in the required number of flying hours. "Dak" Kirkby left us on 27th July, and has joined up with the same outfit.

Charlie Leedham left at the end of August to beome a school teacher.

George Beeke left on September 2nd, and is working on a cross-channel steamer.

"Big" Harman left us on September 6th, and "Old Tom" Newton (Cleaner) has retired.

On July 5th, the "Merry-go-Round" Quiz programme finished ahead of time, and introduced a member of the Blue Mariners Dance Band (none other than Freddie Burgess) to be shot at. Much amusement was caused when Freddie was gonged for every question. The President and all members of the Woygian Association hang their heads in shame, especially in his mixing up of Josephine, who was a mistress of Napoleon, and Joan of Arc, who was a lady of unquestionable virtue. By the way, Freddie was in this locality at the end of June.

Other ex-members of this community seen here during June were Joyce Lawson, Mrs. Richardson (Jean Dennis), Joan Rogerson and "Rosie" Rostron. Eddie Philpott who left us in June and was called up almost immediately, is in the Tank Corps. He paid us a visit during August, as did Mabel Cage and "Ex-auxiliaryilary". The latter had previously been to Harrogate but had not seen any of our boys because she had forgotten that they were there!

I have been asked if I can supply any news of "Spike" Forster, last seen attired in Scout uniform, sitting beside the driver of a dilapidated shooting-brake, and heading in the direction of Maidstone. Can anyone oblige please?

With the formation of the Beaumanor Amateur Radio Society we are hoping to contact many old friends, either at home or overseas. We might even get in touch with our American friends, from whom we have not heard for some time.

A.T.S. departures during June were as follows: Cpls. Moira Byrne, V. Collier (Collie), "Johnny" Wheeler, and Beatrice Richie; L/Cpls. Hilda Gee, Olga Roch, Ithan Timms, Maggie Reilly, Noreen England and Sylvia Stephenson; Ptes. Sheila Byrne, C. May, L. Newell, Rhoda Pippen, F.L. Wood, G. Clarke, J. Berridge, Bishop, Blacklock, Bradbury, Elliot, Hawkins, Hawley, McMillan, Potter, Partridge, Potts, Spence, Randall, Thickett, Tiplady, (née Dawson), and Morrison, (née Hotchings).

July: Sgts. Pat Hyatt, and Joyce Long (née Strawford); Cpls. Jill Hine and Schofield; L/Cpl. Evelyn Woodhouse; Ptes. V. Gordon, F. Ballantyne, J. Dilley, G. Hadden, D. Sharpe, H. Walker, C. Blair, D. Hall, G. Miller, M. Sharples, M. Walshe, Betty Nimmo, J. Edwards (née West), E. Price (née McRoberts), and C. Edwards (née Bennett).

August: Sgts. "Monty" Gregory, Mary Adamson (Clerk), and Aston; Cpls. Muriel Hancock, Stella Fulford, and C. Inglis; L/Cpls. C. Kinnaird, Norrie MacFarlane, D. O'Hara, A. Bloomfield (Cook) and Margaret McAslam (Runner); Ptes. J. Bangham, S. Hood, F. Lees, O. Mort, F. Watt, C. A. Brown, V. Ellis, H. Seath, B. Smith, M. Fell, M. Gilliland, E. Harvey, W. Irving, M. McElroy, A. Murray, M. Steel, M. Norris, H. Gourlay, P. Silvester, I. Stewart, J. Nicholls, Enid Felgate, Pat Fullager, M. Keeling (S.B.O.), M. Pollock (Runner), E. Nichols (Orderly), and G. Schofield (S.B.O.). Class "B" Releases: Pte. M. Godfrey to University, Pte. H. Wardle, nursing; Pte. W. Taylor, to pre-war job.

September 3rd: Cpls. Ivy Walton, Pam Watkinson, J. Bryant, I. Shand, and M. Wrighton; L/Cpls. D. Markwick, H. Leishman and I. Sinclair; Ptes. E. Anderson, H. Drake, V. Ansell, L. Fitzsimmons, K. Sunderland, S. Hodges, W. Harris, D. Picken, B. Mostyn, M. Findlow, Yvonne Abbott and Betty Meadows.

Nancy Watt ("I" Corps) was demobbed on August 15th, and Maud Wood is hoping to get a Class "B" Release and return to University in October.

Promotions: L/Cpls. McIndoe, Watson and Twigg to Cpl; Ptes. Jean Jenkins and M. Richie to L/Cpl.

Postings: Pte. L. Burns to Manchester (compassionate), Pte. Duff to Aberdeen (compassionate), L/Cpl. Ann Gray, (Clerk) to R.A.S.C., Kensington; Cpl. Belcher (H.Q.) to York as P.T.I.; Ptes. Janet Fourdrinier and Carrie Robb to the London Area; L/Cpl. Gillieson, Ptes. Henry, Brabben, Stocker, McCafferty and McCall to other units. Cpl. Jenny Elliot to the Middle East; Drivers Shackelton and Tricklebank, overseas.

Ptes. Blackshire and Graham, also L/Cpl. K. Dunnett have remustered as P.T.I.'s.

Driver Lynne Sage is to spend six months in Paris with the M.T.C.

Barbara Sharp is training in Loughborough Hospital.

Kathleen Cook sailed for Australia on June 21st. Barbara Winfield is going to South Africa with her family in the near future. Beryl Wardlow, who spent the last ten months in the Pay Corps is now demobbed, as also is Shirley Stilliard who never returned from compassionate leave. Jean Chapman (née Hammond) was in Loughborough recently with her baby. Both are looking very well.

The most tragic occurrence in A.T.S. circles was the posting of Pte. Barrett (Berolli) the hairdresser.

Male military releases: May 25th, L/Cpl. Bob Black and Sigmn. Turner. June: Sigmn. J. Atkinson, now back as civvy I.M., Sigmn. J. Johnson, D. Mitchell, A. Nightingale, S. Yellon, C. Storey, and Dvr. T. Pickles. Class "B" Dvr. B. Stewart. July: L/Cpl. Bill Butterfield, Sigmn. Jock Ellis, and A. Foskett. August: Sigmn. H. Howell, R. Townsend, L. West, and E. McClory.

Promotions: L/Cpl. Tony Eeles to Cpl, Sigmn. Duggie Vessey and Chris Turner to L/Cpl., Dvrs. Dunn and Grimmett to L/Cpl.

Sgt. "Ticky" Tyler was posted to F.M. on June 20th.

It is with deepest regret that we announce the death of recently- promoted Cpl. R. E. Meeks, on September 9th, from pneumonia.

Val Jones is still a lady of leisure, but Beryl Thomas, Joan McEntyre, Aileen Tunnington and Margaret Rees are back at the old office routine. They all get fed up at times and wish they were back, as also does Barbara Marquiss who works in the Leeds Rates Dept.

Jock Hamilton ran into ex-Cpl. Turner (T.P. B.W.) and her husband in the *Mafeking Hero*, Bishops Waltham, during August. They are living in that district at present.

George Howarth (P.O.) and his young lady were also staying in the vicinity at the time.

Jean Donlon, 35, Lilybank Gardens, Glasgow. W.2., who was in London for Pat Fullager's wedding, spent the week-end with Noreen England, and visited the Prince of Wales Theatre with Capt. Billington. On the way she met Jean Sarfaty (W.A.A.F., ex-BMR D.F.X.). Jean is working and attending evening classes until she returns to University in October. She finds civvy street greatly changed and often wishes she were back in her old job at BMR.

Marion Lind ('J' Hut) visited Nottingham recently, and, having nothing in particular to do, decided to take a "Mystery" coach tour. She eventually found herself in Loughborough with an hour to look around. She is eager to go to Nottingham again, in the hope that there may be a trip to BMR!

Several members may be interested to learn that Mr. K. White, ex-Billeting Officer, is suffering from paralysis following a stroke.

Other News. I should like to offer my thanks to the writers of the correspondence from which most of the following items were extracted, and also to those members who have furnished me with news verbally.

The majority of the letters contain greetings from old friends, some collectively and others by name, but space prevents me from mentioning individual greetings, which have been passed on where possible. Another common feature of these letters is the eagerness with which the writers anticipate the Association's first re-union.

Myrtle Waterfall, who was demobbed on January 9th, spent her last two months in the A.T.S. on a clerk's training course at Aldermaston. She then completed a seven weeks course learning to become a G.P.O. S.B.O. During this time she lived at the Y.W.C.A. in Torquay, but now has a flat (facing the sea) at the Spa Hotel, Stitch Hill, Torquay, and is working in the G.P.O. there. She has the use of a "New World" Cooker, and enjoys performing her domestic duties but finds rationing a problem. She would be glad to hear from old friends.

Hilda Yeoman is back at her pre-war job in National Health Insurance, but is hoping to go to an Emergency Training College soon. She says that she misses the old days at BMR. Her present address is: 87, Ashford Road, Eastbourne.

When last heard of, Jean Murray was expecting a compassionate discharge to relieve her invalid mother of housekeeping duties. Doubtless "Jay" Johnson could furnish more recent news if he would talk.

Jean Rowan, living at 8, Benton Lodge Avenue, Newcastle-on-Tyne 7, is taking up nursing at the Victoria Hospital, Blackpool.

Mildred Penn is finding civvy street quite dreary even after six months of comparative freedom, and wishes she were back at BMR. An odd pint with Mr. and Mrs. Mager, or even a glimpse of Freddie Fox would lighten her life a little. She is working as a shorthand typist in a stuffy office where nobody knows anything about Army life, and living at 68, Idmiston Road, West Norwood, S.E.27.

Betty Bicket, 128, Ladybarn Lane, Fallowfield, Manchester 14, is back at her work with the Manchester Education Committee and enjoying it immensely.

Jane Clark, née Birrell, has been extremely busy with domestic affairs during the first year of married life which otherwise has been uneventful. She finds that housekeeping, even with rationing, is not so terrifying as she had anticipated. Her address is: The Lodge, Colinsburgh, Fife.

Margaret Alderton, "Hilmarjim," Godmersham, Canterbury, has "settled again into the normal placidity of a civil servant." There are plenty of other ex-service people in her office so she should feel quite at home. She has not run across any Woygians since leaving BMR excepting Marguerite Randall, Phyl Turner, and Joan H. Rogerson.

As reported in the Summer number, Hugh Pryse is appearing in the social play "Pick-Up Girl" at the Prince of Wales Theatre, Piccadilly, where Tony Mosley is a member of the orchestra. The play, which is based on juvenile sex delinquency, was the subject of a two page article in *Picture Post* of August 10th, and Hugh, who plays the part of father to the chief character, appeared in one of the accompanying photographs.

Winnie Teasdale, living at 22, Henderson Road, Sunderland, has been back at work for three months and misses the old gang very much. During a week's holiday in July she stayed at South Ealing with Joan Morley, met Nan Knight, Olive Spinks, and Ithan Timms, who were on demob leave, also Yvonne Bams, Joyce and Kathleen White. Winnie also spent an evening in West Hartlepool with Marjorie Wright and her guest, Joy Berridge, who was also on demob leave. Ithan Timms, and Beryl Worledge, who is stationed in the vicinity, have both visited Winnie at her home, and she is hoping to arrange a meeting with Muriel Dick and Lexy Burns in Newcastle soon.

Kay White is to be married in September, Muriel Dick is free-lance designing for textiles at her home, and Yvonne Bams is doing two months farm work prior to becoming a student in Radiography at the London Cancer Hospital in October.

Sigmn. Merritt ("The Colonel") with the 8th Army Signals in Klagenfurt, Austria, has a cushy job in the section office learning to make out ration strengths, and typing Daily Orders with one finger. He has been there since June, before which he was at Dalton, Yorkshire, where he met Hugh Dias doing some good work in the plate wash-up.

Mick Francis is back at his old job in Bristol where Bob Collins spent a week's (demob?) leave with him recently.

Pte. Sara Crawford of 82, Delancey Street, Regents Park, N.W.1., who left here on compassionate posting to R.E.M.E. Command Workshops, has recently returned there from a Formation College course.

Joan Kidd, 171, Rugby Road, Dagenham, has resumed her old job at Unilever House, Blackfriars, and doesn't think civvy street is all that it is cracked up to be. Took part in a minor re-union during August, with Mildred Penn, Joan Goodall, and Joan Moderhak. Would be pleased to hear from old pals.

Joan Woollaston now living at 3, Field Street, Willenhall, Staffs., paid a visit to this locality at August week-end and stayed with her old A.T.S. friend Kay Peacock who became Mrs. Tailby, and lives at School Lane, Quorn.

Vera Ballard informs us that Ptes. Joan Pond, Hazel Pearson, Mavis Brown, and Audrey Green are now stationed at H.Q., B.A.O.R., Bad Oeynhausen, where they have settled down quite well and are enjoying life very much in spite of the fact that none of them has been paid since arriving in Germany. However, they are managing very well, thanks to the value of cigarettes in that country, and are taking lessons in horseback riding during their spare time.

Ex-Pte. Blanche Stanton is now living with her husband, who returned from India recently.

Beryl Brock and Brenda Robinson have both become engaged, the latter on her 21st birthday, but no other details are available, excepting that Beryl's fiancé hails from her home town—Bebington, Wirral.

Ex-Pte. Slarke has settled down to her civvy job and seems to be enjoying life. Her boy friend has returned from Italy, and is stationed at Rugby awaiting his demob.

"Ginger" Talbot is living at 7, Brothers Street, Blackburn, and working in the Borough Engineer's Office there. His wife, who will be remembered by old members of 4-cum-7 Wing as "Tich" Warren,, has a job on the administrative staff of Phillips Radio. On "V" Day they were visited unexpectedly by Sigmn. Don Barber and the occasion was celebrated in the usual manner.

"Bobbie" Lord, 28, Burney Avenue, Surbiton, Surrey, has returned to her job in the Licences Dept. of the Surrey County Council. Her fiancé arrived in England recently. She is hoping to be married in the Autumn, and go to Canada with him when he returns. Pauline McNichol spent a week-end of her demob leave with "Bobbie", who has also met "Bambi" Bamford, now in the A.T.S. Records Office at Winchester, and wishing she were back at BMR.

Mrs. Hazel Jones (ex-Sgt. Webb) and her husband are living at 15, Cranes Park Avenue, Surbiton, where they are frequently visited by Mr. and Mrs. Staddon. Fred and Kay, who often mind Hazel's small son when she has an evening out, are hoping to get a house shortly. Hazel says she finds family life much more interesting than the A.T.S., and her sisters also prefer Civvy Street. Betty is working in the Food Office at Southampton where she lives with Gladys, who became Mrs. Earl. Betty's fiancé "Andy," another old Wogyite, is a lieutenant with the Worcestershire Regt., in Burma.

Audrey C. Wright, who left us on being posted to Shenley, found her way to F.M. before being demobbed in January. She recalls happy memories of when the A.T.S. first invaded BMR, but, in common with several other members, gives no up-to-date news of herself other than her address, which is, 72, Button Hill, Eccleshall, Sheffield 2.

Jock Harper and his wife, of 328, Knightswood Road, Glasgow, would be pleased to see any old BMR friends who may chance to visit their city.

Harry and Doreen Dodd, having been unable to secure accommodation in the vicinity of Hendon, are living at his parents' home, 10, Lancaster Avenue, South Woodford, E.18. Harry travels to and from Hendon daily, a journey which takes $1\frac{1}{2}$ hours each way. He has heard from Peter Carrington, who is still with Cable and Wireless on the Embankment, and studying for a technical ticket. His hours are 8 till 4 daily, with half-day Saturday, and he has warm praise for married life. Says he wouldn't revert to "digs" for all the tea in China. Doreen Dodd had a minor re-union in London with Joyce Askew, Susan Weir, and Terry Armour at whose home in Pinner Susan was spending a holiday.

"Chick" Henbest, whose "permanent" address was published in the last issue, now informs us that he is going to Austria but hopes to be demobbed by the end of the year. He applied for the posting to escape from Stalag Goldberg at Shenley. Letters to his home address, 11, City Way, Rochester, Kent, will be forwarded.

Mary Billett, now with the Control Commission in Germany, is endeavouring to see as much of that country as possible in spite of the continual rain which makes everyone feel at home out there. She is also hoping to visit Mrs. den Bakker, née Grenfell, in Rotterdam. Mary's address is, CEO Selection Board, Control Commission for Germany (BE), Lubbecke, B.A.O.R. She has met Hermione Baker, who is at Bunde; and No. 1 Special Wireless Co., Minden, is within easy reach should she ever feel homesick.

That inseparable pair, Margaret Webb and Joyce Dady, are working together at H.M.V. Showrooms, in Oxford Street, London, and although their work affords them plenty of food for the soul, they are getting worried about the serious shortage of eligible males.

Whilst on the subject of inseparables, Peggy Cracknell, has decided against going to America to marry, and after a few weeks' holiday at Gwen Sidwell's home, during which time Peggy helped to solve the problem of staff shortage, she agreed to stay permanently and is now doing her best to satisfy the needs of customers in the private bar, whilst Gwen copes with a similar task in the dining room. Under present conditions neither of them should be overworked, in fact I understand that they spend most of their time sunbathing on the roof. They also see quite a lot of Pam Denny who lives in the vicinity, and is at present housekeeping at home.

For the benefit of ex-Trowbridge members, Gwen informs us that Rita Soal, who is still living at Byfleet, has another daughter.

Molly Gould, 1, Newnham Road, Edgbaston, Birmingham 16, resumed her old job with Birmingham Corporation on 1st June after a most enjoyable seventy-four days demob leave during which she and Mary Billett spent an evening with Alicia Scott, now a civil servant in London. Mollie settled down much better than she expected, and finds that even after four years she can still type. She appreciates being home again, especially when going to bed every night.

Olive Spinks, 83, Trentham Street, Southfields, S.W.18, is working at the Board of Trade in London, Joan Dadswell is making favourable progress, and should be out of hospital by the end of August, and Joan Morley is back at her old job as Cashier (uncaged), at the Woolwich Equitable Building Society, whilst anxiously awaiting the result of her efforts in a recent matriculation exam.

Kay Price, who was met by our editor during his recent holiday in Cornwall, is practically her old self again and getting very bored with having nothing to do. There has been no further development in her proposed trip to Australia. She is keeping in touch with several old BMR friends, and tells us that Mabel Marple is working at the Ministry of Civil Aviation.

Pamela Edmundson has settled down with her husband, who was demobbed in July, at 27, Woodend Avenue, Harrow, Middx. During May and June, Pam, after crossing France and Switzerland, toured Italy with her husband. They visited Milan, Udine, Trieste, Venice, Florence, Rome, and Lake Como. She says she was greatly impressed by the scenery, particularly of the Alps, and the sight of the orange groves. She also expressed surprise at the Italian shops, crammed with all the pre-war luxuries which we in this country have almost forgotten. Pam also had the exciting, but somewhat frightening, experience of broadcasting on the B.B.C. Forces Network.

After making the belated discovery that the duties of an Infantry Officer call for a certain amount of physical exertion, Noel Royle escaped from Sandhurst on production of a pair of flat feet which he had been saving for such an emergency, and is now training for a commission in the Pay Corps. "Billie" has given up her secretarial work with the Evesham Coroner in anticipation of a blessed event, and is now living in a flat at 49, Whitley Road, Eastbourne.

Dot Spencer is doing part-time work as a private secretary with her pre-A.T.S. employers in Northampton.

Walter Bland, who left us in May to rejoin his wife and daughter at their home in Shefford, is, I think, working in Bedford.

Jimmy Hunter has left the job of assistant factory manager in Lincolnshire, but expects to return there in the Autumn. He is now at the London office of the same firm. His address is, 63, Aintree Crescent, Barkingside, Essex. After regaining possession of his house by a Court order, Jimmy had a busy time repairing the damage caused by flying bombs. He was in Loughborough at Whitsun but didn't see any of the old gang.

The "lucky 78" are gradually being distributed over various parts of the earth, and although this policy, which is spoiling so many beautiful friendships, may not be popular, its fairness is commendable. After all, why should F.M. be so favoured, even if it was less fortunate during the war? Bob Talbot, after passing a W.O.S.B. at Oxshott, obtained a Class "B" release. Maurice Reed, Ted Sandy, Duc Downer, and Denis Brett were posted to Basic O.C.T.U. at Mons Barracks, Aldershot, on June 18th. Maurice Reed and Ted Sandy lost their rifles on the way down but seem to be doing well, and according to more recent news, "Moggy" has completed his battle course, having climbed most of the Welsh mountains in full pack.

"Duc" Downer and Denis Brett decided that the concentrated "bull" at Mons Barracks, so familiar to its original occupants, was not worth the prize, which incidentally, prolongs the successful candidates' stay in the Army. They were therefore returned to F.M. at their own request.

Peter Tuke, R.A.S.C., was also at Aldershot on a Basic Course which should have finished during August.

Harry (Big Game) Bartlett was to have gone on a draft for the Middle East (Cairo) on August 1st, together with Norman Rees, Roy Nicholls, Jimmy Dodd, and Reg Weaver, but seems to have got left at the post with five complete strangers. He is expecting to accompany them to Gibraltar. Harry was originally under the impression that his destination would be Cyprus and with that idea in mind he read a large book about the island. I understand that he has disgustedly reverted to "Form".

Norman Rees is reported to have married whilst on draft leave in July. Rumour has it that he had only known the girl a week!

"Ginger" Lowes, "Zombie" Knott, Phil Roberts, Peter Kingsland, and Fred Vickers are in the Kiel Canal area. They left England during the Easter period and were originally at Minden. They are enjoying life immensely, work day shifts only, and do no fatigues, the normal chores being performed by German women and other hired labour. At one transit Camp they even had a band to play to them during meals. "Ginger" is expecting to get home in September for 19 days leave.

Derek Basnett has been hanging his hat up to Maurice Reed's sister, Margaret, who was in the A.T.S. at F.M. Pete James was a rival for Margaret's affections but, owing to the fact that he was involved elsewhere, he was forced to withdraw. He has reaffirmed his vow to remain a bachelor. I hear from another source that Derek is to marry a Miss Ayliss of Maidstone in September!!

Geoff Nicol is living a gentleman's life nowadays. He and Connie (as glamorous as ever) have a place in Harrogate, and Geoff lives out.

Ron (Shaker) Smith is trying to wangle some leave to help with the harvest.

Several of the 78 have suffered the indignities of C.B., one for walking across the R.S.M's. "Holy Carpet", another for wasting edible (?) meat. Johnson (Nuts) made the sad mistake of being caught without a pass on one of his visits to Loughborough. He has also, together with Sigmn. Smith, N.L., and Tomlinson, gained undying popularity amongst his comrades for showing what can be achieved on a kit inspection, to the delight of the powers that be, and the chagrin of the aforesaid comrades, who, having listened to the congratulations etc., had then to emulate this high standard of "bull".

"Snubby" Pollard spends every day off in his native Burnley pursuing his hobby. He recently contacted California on one of these "busman's holidays".

Tubby Fagg, Bill Hayward, Jack Mitchell, and Bert Ashman attended W.O.S.B. during July. Tubby, after smashing up the obstacle course by sheer brutality, was covered with bumps and bruises.

The Weasel, who has taken to singing songs (respectable and otherwise) in a loud and unmelodious voice, has declared that it is a punishable offence for anyone to call him by that name. He recently produced his little red book and loudly announced the dates on which he bought those two memorable cups of tea.

Latest suggestion from F.M. is that a copy of *St. Upid* be chained in the Set Room, and the "Lesson" be read by one of the scribes at the commencement of each watch.

Yes, maybe they are a little more mad (an inevitable development in this racket), but otherwise unchanged and unanimous in their desire to get out of the Army.

Joe Fisher, 13, Scotch Street, Whitehaven, says how glad he is to read of the activites of old friends, to whom he sends his regards. He introduces a new member in the person of Alf Thompson who will be remembered by most Woygians, particularly by the local tennis enthusiasts. Alf's address is, 4, Oakbank Avenue, Whitehaven.

"Bobbie" Percy, Tollgate House, Woodhatch Road, Redhill, was demobbed on August 9th, after a spell with A.T.S. Records at Winchester.

Dorothy Craig, 12, Highbury Avenue, Linthorpe, Middlesbrough, expresses her sincere appreciation of *The Woygian*, and explains, in rhyme, her reason for not producing any contributions, but gives us no news of her activities.

Molly Wallond, Latters Farm, Tudeley Hale, Tonbridge, is going to Germany to take up a post with the Control Commission. During her demob leave she spent a day with Joan Williams, née Nixon, at her flat in Streatham, who, she says, is perfectly happy with her pretty, ten-months-old baby, Patricia Anne. Joan's husband is still in the R.A.F. but is billeted at home.

Anne Neville, 39, Alvis Avenue, Herne Bay, is working in the G.P.O. at Canterbury as a T.P. operator. She says that civvy street has not come up to her eager expectations, and she now appreciates the difficulties in rationing and accommodation which have beset so many for so long.

Maida Hancock, 4, Salmon Street, Sheffield 11, who was demobbed in March, spent an enjoyable eight weeks' leave before starting work with the Sheffield City Police. Her job, which she finds interesting, is still connected with wireless but is all R/T. She has no desire to be back in the A.T.S., but misses the girls to whom she sends her very best wishes.

"Freddie" Crawford, 15, Westville Road, Thames Ditton, who was always very keen to go abroad, has obtained a post as English-speaking shorthand typist to a Norwegian Import Company in Oslo, and hopes this is only the first step in her travels round the world.

Sigmn. Eric Page (14418978) is now with No. 3 Line Section, Att. No. 1 Coy., Palestine Command Signals, M.E.F., where he has been since Jan. 3rd, excepting for a short stay in Maadi, during which he spent a couple of pleasant evenings with Cpl. Bill Hayes. Shortly after arriving at his present Unit, Eric met Sigmn. Sargeant who says that he is to spend a leave in Palestine with Sigmn. Eldridge, now stationed in Cairo.

Vera Jackson has just come out of hospital following an operation for appendicitis which she says has left her a trifle wobbly. The proposed re-union of Hut 102 girls had to be cancelled at the last moment, but will probably take place in the near future. Vera is keeping in touch with Joan Wattis, née Nickson, whose husband is now home, and they are living at Leamington.

Nancy Wigham and Agnes Potter, holidaying in Cornwall during July, were hoping to round off their holiday by holding a re-union in Durham with Joy Berridge and Marjorie Wright. Nancy informs us that Louie Green, ex-"B" Watch, Garats Hay, became Mrs. Chadwick on June 20th. Her husband plays football for Middlesbrough where they live.

The following items come from two anonymous, ex-A.R. 13 members: Joan Turner née Thackrah now has a baby daughter, Susan Joan, born in January. Her husband was recently demobbed and at present they are living at Barrow-in-Furness.

Eileen Thurston, now demobbed, is engaged to Sigmn. Douglas Saxby, stationed at Harrogate. They hope to be married early next year. Meanwhile, Eileen will go back to her old job at Newcastle-on-Tyne.

Margaret Appleby is expecting a "happy event" in September. Her husband was due to be demobbed at the end of June.

Mary Russell, Anne Ransom, and Gladys Edgeson are all demobbed and back at their old jobs, the former in Glasgow, and the others in London.

When last seen, Betty Vance was driving her father's car in Croydon.

Rosemary McNair is married but no details are known.

With the exception of Ina Mitchell, last seen at Harrogate, all former members of A.R.13 are demobbed. Further information would be welcomed.

That's all this time folks. Remember, your letters are always appreciated even if they don't all get answered, but I know you will understand why. Cheerio, and keep writing.

CQ WOYGIANS

I would like to thank all those who answered the "CQ" which appeared in the last issue of *The Woygian*; the response was certainly prompt, and it is hoped that this spirit of enthusiasm and co-operation will be maintained.

A very interesting letter from our old friend Norman Hobbs was most welcome and encouraging. He reported reception of G6AK at Harrogate, and welcomed the formation of an Amateur Radio Section. Jimmy Hunter also promised his full support and hoped to be settled down in London shortly when he would very soon have a station "on the air". Since receiving Jimmy's letter we have been in communication by radio, thus making the first Woygian contact. Jimmy sends us the following "flash" about the event:

RENEGADE WOYGIAN RETURNS TO THE FOLD—BY RADIO (FOR 20 MINUTES)

On July 17th, 1946, history was made. Two hitherto mortals are now immortals. Stan Brister, G6AK, and Jimmy Hunter, G6HU, succeeded in making radio contact at 21.15 BST. Reception was 100% both ways, and, thanks to previous training, both could read each other's morse! At the close of the QSO, during which loving greetings were exchanged, both operators went their separate ways to celebrate—Stan to night duty and Jimmy to bed.

In the last *Woygian* I expressed the hope that it would soon be possible to form a radio club, and I am now able to state that the club is in being. Due to the O.C.'s generous co-operation and assistance the Beaumanor Amateur

Radio Society is now established and its transmitter will soon be in operation on all amateur bands. It is hoped that schedules may be arranged with our American friends at a later date. An experimental and research section under the able guidance of Major Wort promises to be a very interesting feature of the Society's activities. The Engineer-in-Chief, G.P.O. has approved the request for a transmitting licence, and the allotted call-sign is eagerly awaited. The station will be open for schedules at all convenient times, a point which may be of special interest to those ex-Woygites who are expecting to be posted!

Kim Taylor, BRS8648, has successfully completed his examination and now awaits his transmitting licence. Bill Backhouse has also persuaded the P.M.G. to grant him a licence and awaits his call-sign. G6AK is at present QRT owing to change of QRA. The station will be active again shortly from Brand Hill Camp, Woodhouse Eaves, and the transmitter will no longer be portable!

73's de STAN BRISTER,
Hon. Sec. B.A.R.S.

ASSOCIATION NEWS

THE Hon. Treasurer, Mr. G. E. M. Abels, is now in London and in future all Subscriptions should be paid to him. His address is 5, St. Cuthberts Road, London, N.W.2.

Members are reminded that Annual Subscriptions for 1946/47 were due and payable on 1st July, 1946. In accordance with Rule 14 no further issues of the Magazine will be dispatched to those members whose Subscriptions are outstanding.

Some cases have arisen, particularly with the last issue, where members have not received copies of the Magazine. While it is recognised that some errors may have been made by those responsible for dispatching the Magazine, many members have neglected to inform the Hon. Secretary of their change of address. Magazines undelivered are not returned by the Post Office. Please inform the Hon. Secretary immediately of any change of address and every care will be taken to ensure that all paid-up members receive a Magazine.

The Torch is handed on

FOREST MOOR,
YORKS.

DEAR MR. EDITOR,

CONGRATULATIONS to the original Scribe of the "Lucky 78" who has left us to join the small number of our party at OCTU. It is with some trepidation that I take up the pen he has laid down, for the standard he set was a high one.

Greetings to all Woygians from those of us still at Harrogate. No longer are we 78 even if we are still Lucky, for some have wandered, and the Deacon can now be heard going Down in many widely separated quarters of the globe. Here, on the whole, our life goes on much the same; the only major alteration in the last few months has been that we are now a Stag Party, a fact often lamented by the Don Juan element among us. It is still the same; so much the same that we sometimes have to remind ourselves it is no longer necessary to set our alarm clocks before going to bed, nor to pump our bicycle tyres at 5-30 on wet and windy mornings. Old ghosts haunt us on and off duty, and the sinister figure of the C.S.M. merges easily into that of an equally sinister landlady.

Many still make the trek to Loughborough, and someone there was once heard to enquire whether "those fellows do any work or whether they are always on leave?" In answer to that I would point out that our duties do not stop at watch-keeping but embrace all the traditional military rigmarole of "spit-and-polish", beds in a straight line, kit blancoed, brasses polished, uniform toenails, etc. In other words, even when we're off, we're on. But we do not complain for we know that it is this that has made the British Army what it is, and this that has coloured so much of the map red.

The floor of Harrogate's Cairn Hydro is a likely place to find members of the B.D.C., while some of those who were members of the Choir and Music Club attend weekly record recitals. Those preferring more cosmopolitan pleasures than the ones offered by respectable Harrogate are to be seen in less respectable Leeds. Others ramble on the glorious Yorkshire Moors (I had to promise to say something complimentary about Yorkshire this time; these dour Northerners are sensitive about their county).'

In conclusion, may I say how much pleasure we were given by the appearance of *St. Upid* in book form. Somehow or other it seems to conjure up only happy memories of WOYG and it has given us many a nostalgic chuckle.

Cont'd on next page.

THE WOYGIAN

BEAUMANOR PARK,
NR. LOUGHBOROUGH, LEICS.

FOR various reasons, including the Chairman's illness, and the completion of arrangements for the Annual General Meeting, publication of this number has been somewhat delayed, for which, our profound apologies.

Ollie continues to receive splendid support for his feature, nearly ten pages of which ought to have effectively kept him out of other mischief this time. Members still seem chary of sending other contributions for *The Woygian* however, which is very disheartening and, I might say, embarrassing, for I have again had to call on the fluent pen of Eric Dobson to provide a last-minute story. A description of the London Victory Parade, by one of the Beaumanor contingent who participated, was expected but has unfortunately not come to hand.

In order to stimulate interest I have decided to invite contributions on a selected topic for each issue, publishing the one, or more, adjudged of greatest interest to the general membership. The theme for the Christmas Number is: MY PERSONAL ANGLE ON THE WOYGIAN ASSOCIATION. Here is an opportunity for members to make known any pet ideas they may have for the conduct, development and improvement of our Association (always bearing in mind the limited funds at our disposal, of course!). Contributions should not exceed 650 words, and will be considered solely from the "interest" standpoint. I would also welcome "fillers" in the form of jokes, couplets, or brief verses, preferably with a "Woygian" flavour.

The Chronicles of St. Upid. All ordered copies were dispatched during July and early August, so I trust everyone has received theirs safely. A few people have written acknowledging their copies and expressing approval of the production. To quote just one who says: "I can't tell you what pleasure I found in reading them and remembering old times." is sufficient indication that all the work involved was to good purpose. My only regret is that I cannot satisfy those who are still asking for copies, as the last of the extra hundred I had printed was disposed of some weeks ago.

Very many thanks to all who have written during the past quarter. Believe me, all your letters have been greatly appreciated, and if some of them have not been answered it has not been entirely unconnected with the fact that during July the palatial *Woygian* Editorial Offices had to be dismantled and re-erected in another part of Luff, their vital importance not being sufficient to deter the owners from excercising their rights under the Furnished Apartments Hazards.

A full report of The A.G.M. will appear next time.

THE EDITOR.

All Christmas Number contributions by December 1st, please.

THE TORCH IS HANDED ON *(cont'd.)*

Ah, well; dawn is approaching. The first pale rays of the morning sun have penetrated the windows of the set-room. The ancient cry of "Wakey-wakey!" is heard once more in the land, and soon we shall totter forth into the chilly Yorkshire air for our seven-miles ride back to bed. All good things, even night duties, come to an end.

Best Wishes from us all and especially from

2602296 CHRISTOPHER BARNES.

WOYGIAN CROSSWORD

ACROSS.

1. Reason for Ministry of Health's most urgent business. (7, 6)
7. Member of deer family (4)
8. Quality of wireless reception. (4)
9. Close. (4)
10. Fix up transport for a journey? (5)
12. Idols. (6)
14. Make good. (6)
15. Swiss town. (6)
17. Everyone's in this, though it's just the fellow going to "send". (6)
20. You can make me the subject of this. (5)
21. Was once the "home" of Woygians. (4)
22. Reel back . . . (4)
23. . . . . while time hardly marches on to transmit! (4)
24. These often cause interruption of radio reception. (13)

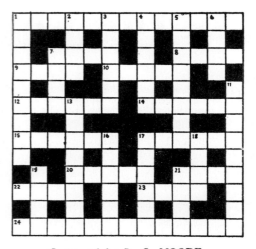

Composed by L. C. MOORE.

DOWN.

1. THEIR GAME (Anag.). (9)
2. Receivers, perhaps. (4)
3. Things change for an unpopular shift. (6)
4. One who diets more quickly? (6)
5. Legendary. (8)
6. One over the eight! (4)
7. One way to catch flies. (4)
11. People who use 2 Down are called—(troops are included). (9)
13. Atomic composite. (8)
16. The road is a rendezvous. (6)
17. There may be a catch in them. (6)
18. Results of ransacking, though there's nothing in the lot. (4)
19. Network. (4)
21. Well-known technical achievement of the War. (4)

Printed by John Corah & Son Ltd., and published by E. C. Millhouse for The Woygian Association.

The WOYGIAN

BRIDGEWOODS 1939 CHICKSANDS 1945 BEAUMANOR

Vol. 2   Winter 1946/7   No. 6

WOYGIAN ASSOCIATION—BALANCE SHEET 30th JUNE 1946.

	£ s. d.		Cash at Bank and in hand.	£ s. d.	£ s. d.
Sundry Creditors	20 5 0		In hand	3 3 5	
Members Subscriptions paid in advance	4 0 0		At Bank	38 19 0	
					42 2 5

Income and Expenditure Account, for the period 26th April, 1945 to 30th June, 1946.

Income:

	£ s. d.	
Membership Fees	28 4 0	
Annual Subscriptions	65 19 0	
Donations	7 7 6	
Post Office Savings Bank Interest	13 8	
Miscellaneous Receipts	8 6	
		102 12 8

Expenditure:

	£ s. d.	
Cost of printing the *Woygian*	63 11 5	
Rule Books	7 10 0	
Stationery and Printing	4 13 10	
Postage and Sundry Expenses	9 0 0	
		84 15 3

Balance, being excess of Income over Expenditure 17 17 5

£42 2 5

Report of the Auditor to the Members of the "Woygian" Association.

I have audited the Balance Sheet of the "Woygian" Association, dated 30th June, 1946, with the books and vouchers and certify the same to be correct. I have verified the Cash at Bank.

(*Sgd.*) A. H. APPLETON, Hon. Auditor.

12, TEMPLE GARDENS, CUXTON ROAD, ROCHESTER, KENT.   24*th September*, 1946.

First Annual General Meeting of
The Woygian Association

THE Chairman, in his opening remarks, welcomed those present, mentioning in particular the President, Lt. Col. M. J. W. Ellingworth, and Major H. F. Jolowicz (Vice-President). He then proceeded to trace the history of the Association from the beginning up to the present time, naming those responsible for its creation and those who had helped during the first difficult year of its life. The Chairman then named various parts of the world where Woygians had made their homes. The difficulties of holding reunions during the past year were explained and he hoped that conditions generally would soon improve so that functions might be arranged free from the many restrictions of the present time. In conclusion the Chairman read two letters he had recently received from members overseas.

The President, Lt. Col. M. J. W. Ellingworth then addressed the Meeting and said how he applauded the idea of the Association and wished it every sucess for the future. He suggested that some form of badge should be worn by members in order that membership of the Association might be recognised.

The Report of the year 1945/46 was made by the Chairman as follows:—
564 Applications for Membership were accepted and 525 Ordinary and Associate (Class 1) Members paid their Annual Subscriptions. 45 Associate (Class 2) Members paid one shilling each. Donations amounting to £7 7s. 6d. were received. 600 Copies of the Magazine had been printed each issue and of the last number 500 had to be posted to members. The cost of the Magazine was rather high and this would have to be carefully considered in the future.

The Accounts for the year 1945/46 were read and explained by Mr. A. H. Appleton (Hon. Auditor), and their adoption was proposed by Mr. J. Reid and seconded by Major H. F. Jolowicz.

The Resolution proposed by Mr. C. W. Dobson and seconded by Mr. R. G. Denny: "**that in view of the difficulties of the inaugural year when the Committees were unable to function properly owing to the gradual process of demobilisation and release, it is proposed that all Officers and Committees be re-elected** *en bloc* **for the year 1946/47**", was put to the meeting and carried unanimously.

It was proposed by Mr. Smith and seconded by Mr. H. Dodd: "**that Mr. A. H. Appleton be re-elected Hon. Auditor for the year 1946/47**".

Mr. A. H. Appleton raised the matter of the three-zone system which he considered too vast to operate satisfactorily, and suggested that town or area representatives, on whom the responsibility of arranging functions would rest, would be better. Mr. Smith supported this idea.

The question of the financial position of the Association in relation to the high cost of the Magazine, was discussed, and to avoid raising the annual subscription, Mr. P. Dart suggested that it should be published that the annual subscription was **a minimum** of 2/6d. and some members might then subscribe more than 2/6d. This was supported by Mr. A. H. Appleton.

Mr. J. R. Pearce raised the question of admitting certain people to the Association, who were excluded by the rules, but had strong claims for membership. It was proposed by Mr. H. Dodd and seconded by Major H. F. Jolowicz: "**that an addition to part 3(b) of the Constitution be made as follows: (III) Any person, sponsored by two Ordinary Members of the Association, whose work during the War period was, in the opinion of the Committee, closely associated with that of the group**". Passed unanimously.

The proceedings then terminated.

AUTUMN CROSSWORD SOLUTION.

ACROSS.—1, Housing famine; 7, Stag; 8, Tone; 9, Mews; 10, Hitch; 12, Totems; 14, Recoup; 15, Geneva; 17, Caller; 20, Theme; 21, Fort; 22, Leer; 23, Emit; 24, Thunderstorms.

DOWN.—1, Hermitage; 2, Sets; 3, Nights; 4, Faster; 5, Mythical; 6, Nine; 7, Swat; 11, Operators; 13, Electron; 16, Avenue; 18, Loot; 19, Mesh; 21, Fido.

Through the Looking Glass

By LEON DE BUNK.

RENAISSANCE.

IT was the occasion of a recent pilgrimage—as is our pious annual custom—to the once palatial, now empty, grass-covered and neglected Editorial offices of the old B.S.M. Suddenly, entering through a mellow, moss-grown doorway, we found the Editor sitting alone; alone at the scene of his former triumph, silent with the dreams of fairer days. A chill wind blew in through the broken window panes; a rat scurried through the dust at our feet, and then, slowly turning towards us, *La Souris* spoke; his voice was low and faltering.

"De Bunk," he said, "We need you; we need all the strength you got. You gotta go in dere wid us; you gotta go in dere and win."

"You know us," he continued, "We're just little guys," and his frail hands trembled as he spoke. "Yeah, just ordinary little guys. We didn't want this fight; we wanna live ordinary decent lives; we want the ordinary decent things—Coca-Cola, ice-cream sodas, the Ball Game, juke boxes, Thanksgivin', Crosby and Sinatra, and"—with a profoundly religious light shining in his eyes—"The American Constitution."

At this, sad old cynics that we are, we were moved; bravely we tried to brush away a tear that trembled in our (left) eye. Suppose they *had* stopped caring? Suppose they never *had* asked about us? Suppose they *never* answered our letters? Even the Editor hadn't shown much enthusiasm when we wrote saying that we had seen three ex-Woygites (not to speak to) in Upper Tooting. And he hadn't even printed our announcement that we had a job with the Min. of Ag. and Fisheries as a Filing Clerk (Grade III), and a one-roomed flat (shared kitchen) in Grimsby, and that we thought bread-rationing was awful.

But this call was something big; something bigger than all of us. Through our tears we smiled and nodded, perhaps a little uncertainly. At that he seemed content; and a slow smile broke over his grizzled old face.

And from now on you rabble can take it that our implacable pen is raised in eternal opposition to the present decadent Romanticist trend in English Letters, never to be sheathed again until the pure light of Truth and Reason shines once more unchallenged over the . . . . . . etc., etc.

SCOOP.

Serious speculation amongst the more imaginative was, in the old days, much concerned with the likely result if Old Cornwallis ever succeeded in relieving that anxious frustration that delineates so clearly his otherwise homely English pan, by finally withdrawing his cutlass from its scabbard and perhaps spiking an odd supervisor or two out of sheer elementary sense of justice. Contemplating the barnacled old Empire-builder one day of late, the question was suddenly answered to us in a moment of Pauline clairvoyance.

First on the scene after the occurrence would, of course, be the ace correspondent of the *Daily Excess*, viz:

Correspondent: "And now could you please say a few words for our readers?"

Cornwallis: "Aw, Gee, I dunno; it ain't nothin' really."

Correspondent: "Sure, sure. That's swell. Now, what's your favourite radio programme?"

Cornwallis: "Aw, Gee, I guess Bix Sweeterblast and his Voodoo Hotsox; dem boys sure do send it solid."

Correspondent: "Yeah, that's fine. Now, how long have you been a regular reader of the *Daily Excess*?"

Cornwallis: "Aw, Gee, I ain't no highbrow; I don't do no readin' but de Funnies—me an' all de boys back dere in Valhalla, we're one hundred per cent fer dis guy Buck Ryan!"

And the resultant headlines in the next edition:

VITALISED STATUE'S AMAZING £50,000 PLEA FOR SWING-STRIP-CARTOON JAMBOREE.

DRAMATIC SCENE AS LONE REPORTER SCOOPS EXCLUSIVE *EXCESS* INTERVIEW.

MOTHER'S CRY—"I ALWAYS KNEW ERNIE COULD DO IT."

With write-up beginning, inevitably:

"Somewhere to-night in the sheltered heart of Hampshire, a grey-haired old lady will be sitting by her wireless-set . . . . "

THOUGHT FOR TODAY.

Everyone finds fault with his memory, but none with his judgement.
—La Rochefoucauld.

"What's He Doing Now?"

By OLLIE PEARCE.

To most of us a common phrase familiar in the doubtful days,
Now as we go our sundry ways, a different meaning it conveys,
Remote from that elusive "he", confined instead to you and me,
Therefore the word must also be interpreted at times as "she".

MANY thanks to members who have supplied me with material for this issue, and my apologies to those whose letters remain unanswered.

Special greetings to old friends who are precluded, by reason of ill health, from enjoying this festive occasion to the utmost. Among these is Miss Margaret Ellingworth who is undergoing a series of skin-grafting operations. Her address is: Montague-Burrows Ward, Wingfield Orthopædic Hospital, Headington, Oxford. Horace Davis, still in Markfield Sanatorium, is making satisfactory progress, and wishes to thank members who have sent him books, etc.

Bill Smart, who came out of hospital in November and has been confined to bed ever since, was taken to his home in Wales by road ambulance on December 4th.

Births. To Joe and Peggy Simonite, on October 14th, 6 lbs 1 oz of daughter, Pauline Margaret.

To "Taffy" and Mrs. Evans, at Somerville Nursing Home, on November 6th, 7¼ lbs of daughter, Megan Elizabeth.

To Margaret Appleby, on October 8th, a son, David John.

To "Cathie" Gibson, ex-'A' Watch, Brand Hill, and now Mrs. Morgan, a daughter, Patricia Mary.

To Joyce Thomas, née Kempin, ex-Canteen staff, at Somerville Nursing Home on October 8th, a daughter, Susan Margaret.

Congratulations to all concerned.

Marriages. Ron Blease and Miss L. R. Howe of Cecil Road, Rochester, at St. Margaret's Church, Rochester. Mr. J. Blease, brother of the bridegroom, was best man. The honeymoon was spent in Devon.

"Bobbie" Percy, on October 5th, to Petty Officer Dick Snare, and now living at Tollgate House, Woodhatch Road, Redhill, Surrey.

Frances Potter, ex-'D' Watch, Brand Hill, early in November.

Kathleen White, ex-'C' Watch, Brand Hill, at Caterham, Surrey, on September 10th, to Mr. David Jones, a farmer.

Freda Tootell, who recently became Mrs. Dolan and is now living at 30, Hazel Grove, Hereford.

Pte. M. Quick, at the Presbyterian Church, Gateshead, on August 31st, to Mr. John Wallace Green.

Pte. D. Gould, at the Parish Church, Stockport, on August 31st, to Mr. Ronald Shields.

Miss Anna Martin, at Ayr on November 27th, to James Sproat, R.A.F. Jean Russell and Jessie Bell were guests at the wedding.

Pte. S. Wilkins (S.B.O.), in Essex on September 21st, to Mr. Herbert Frank Wright. (About time somebody caught up with that guy!)

Betty Garwood, in London on October 27th, to Chris Viljoin, R.A.F.

Bill ("78") Hayward, to Miss Betty Heighway, ex-A.T.S. (but *not* ex-B.M.R., emphasizes the groom), at All Saints' Church, Maidstone, on November 2nd. The wedding was a choral affair, and among those present were Pete James, "Duc" and Cecile Downer, and Roy Aldridge.

Monty Gregory, ex-A.T.S. sergeant, at St. Bartholomew's Church, Blackburn, on November 9th, to Sigmn. Desmond ("Ginger") Wilcox. The honeymoon was spent at Cleveleys.

Pte. D. Mennell, medical orderly, who recently became Mrs. Miller.

We offer our congratulations and best wishes for future happiness.

Forthcoming Marriages, Engagements, etc. Mr. J. Griffiths, E.W.A. and our red headed runner Pte. Mabel Base (not the original Scarlet Runner), are to be married on January 1st, 1947. They have been fortunate in securing accommodation locally.

Driver Dorothea Elam and Sigmn. Marshall, both ex-W.O.Y.G., have become engaged and are to be married next July.

Miss Lynda Reid has become engaged to Morris Wilson of Glasgow. The wedding will take place in Arbroath on March 22nd.

Rita Harrison has become engaged to Bill Simpson, R.A.F.

Maisie Brown was seen recently wearing a brand new engagement ring, but the identity of the "lucky" man is not yet known.

Tegwen Jones, who transformed "Bobbie" Percy's wedding into a re-union, is to be married in the near future but no details are known.

Ex-Pte. Mary Spiers, née Paine, is expecting a happy event in April.

Mrs. Jackson (Vera Winzer), is also expecting to improve the birthrate in March.

Congratulations to all concerned, and to Mr. and Mrs. "Tubby" Blundell who celebrated their Silver Wedding anniversary on November 4th.

Other News. Ex-members of 'C' Watch, Barrow, will probably be interested to hear that Helen Streather is married and has an infant. She is a squatter at an A.A. site in Sutton Park, near Birmingham.

Latest news of Kay Price, received early in December, concerned her trip to Australia, which she is now making by air all the way. She hopes to be back in three or four months to take a course of Shorthand/typing at Pitman's in London.

Mr. and Mrs. "Ginger" Talbot, address in last issue, would like to hear from "Snikmot". They are also hoping that Geoff Nicol might find time to pay them a visit.

"Tich" is still communicating with her old pal Joan Shepherd who became Mrs. Wilson just before being demobbed last year. Incidentally, "Tich" made the acquaintance of Monty Gregory when the latter went to work at Phillips Radio, Blackburn. Monty's husband is still at F.M., but may be sent overseas at any time.

Kay White's wedding was the occasion of a minor re-union. Her chief bridesmaid was Doris Cooper, ex-driver at Garats Hey, and among the guests were Ivy Walton, Joyce White, Nesta Bailey, Ithan Timms, Olive Spinks, and Joan Morley. After taking their leave of the newly-weds, they did a show in the West End, and later in the week attended a performance of "Pick-up Girl", where they saw Hugh Pryse and Tony Mosley.

No recent news has been received of Miss Ida Romer. The last issue of *The Woygian* was returned marked "Gone away". It is believed that she has gone to Canada.

A minor re-union of ex-A.R.13 personnel was held recently in London and attended by Jimmy Rogers, Dora Davies, Flo Mason, Gladys Edson, Ann Ransom, Norma New (now Mrs. Ramsey), Garet Kirkwood (now Mrs. Hemy, and her husband Lieut. Hemy.

Mary Russell and Lynda Reid meet each week in Glasgow and are occasionally joined by Gwen Harvey. Mrs. Burns, formerly Gladys Douglas, has settled down with her husband in Essex. Nora Vaughan, née Boyes-Varley, wishes to convey her regards to other ex-A.R. 13 members. Kit Roberts and Meg Lloyd have taken up children's nursing and are at present in the Princess Louise Home for Children, at Esher, Surrey. Jean Rowan has given up nursing and is now working at the Empire Pools, Blackpool.

Betty Meadows, 2, Hardman Street, Milton, Stoke-on-Trent, is back at her old job in the potteries. She is working hard and attends evening classes twice weekly. Has put on weight since her demob. and in consequence has been having some difficulty in obtaining clothes. She has been getting around with Jean Jenkins who is also living at Stoke.

Vera Ballard had a fortnights holiday in September during which she visited London, Mersea Island (near Colchester), Cambridge and Canterbury with her fiancè. She also went to the Palladium with Betty Slarke to see "High Time". Has been busy during the past few weeks making herself some clothes, her latest accomplishment being a winter coat. She has taken up photography as a hobby but is having difficulty in obtaining printing-out paper. Has heard from Joan Pond who is with the A.T.S. in Germany and hoping to be demobbed very soon.

Belated congratulations to May Haskayne who was married on June 24th to Mr. Chris. Biddle. The honeymoon was spent at Blackpool, and their present domicile is in Cheshire. Sorry it missed the last issue, but some people are so secretive. Reminds me of the proverb about A Wiseman keeping a still tongue, which will probably sound Dutch to members other than those ex-A.R. 13.

During October we received the first news of Annabella Robertson since her departure. She resumed her old occupation as a milliner in February, and was soon placed in charge of the department. She is finding the life vastly different after four years in the A.T.S., and experienced some initial difficulties which made her think it would have been easier to have stayed in uniform. Her address is: Brae Cottage, Old Rattray, Blairgowrie, Perthshire, and she makes frequent business trips to Glasgow and London. She spent an evening in Dundee during March with Margaret Napier who was on demob. leave. About this time there was a small re-union in Glasgow which was attended by Jean Wright, Jeanette Irvine, Olive Russell, Kathleen Mills and Estelle Flett. Bella is hoping to be able to renew old acquaintances when the Association holds a re-union. I understand from Harry Dodd that steps are being taken to arrange this, and it will very likely take place in London early in the New Year. Harry, who spends most of his time to-ing and from-ing, met Jock Forrest in the tube a few weeks ago. Jock is still with de Havilands and is now working at Burnt Oak, Edgeware, which is not far from Harry's place of employment. Jock is living in Bayswater and looks as contented and prosperous as ever.

Mary Billett is seeing quite a few familar faces in Germany. She met Mollie Wallond at a party in Buckeburg, and went to Rotterdam to visit Mickie Grenfell who is now back in Penzance. She also met Dvr. Tricklebank who has managed to get back on troop carriers after suffering the indignity of driving staff cars.

Mary was over here in October, and met Mamie Gray and Nancy Smith in Edinburgh. Great racket this B.A.O.R., excepting for the poor old taxpayer!

Mrs. K. G. Cook wrote from 9, Murdock Street, Brunswick West, N.10., Victoria, Australia, and says that it is very much like England out there. Up in the country it is more like Scotland but a bit greener. The winter is the greenest part of the year as the grass is scorched by the sun in summer. Most of the dwelling places are wooden bungalows and the people are very friendly. The housing situation is almost as acute as it is in England and there is much overcrowding. Kathleen considers herself lucky to have half a bungalow, entirely separated from the other half. Food is very plentiful and nobody seems to go short of anything. Butter and meat are in shortest supply, and tea and sugar are also rationed. The tea ration is the same as ours, but they get twice as much sugar. Knowing how much the English like their tea, K's neighbours have given her quite a bit. Gwen McElrea also wrote from Australia which she says is a fine country. She is rapidly becoming a "fair dinkum Aussie" but still retains nostalgic memories of Blighty and the good old days at B.M.R. Gwen sends her regards to all who remember her.

Forbes Sibley, writing from his latest address, Apartment 7, Veterans' Housing Project, Ann Arbor, Michigan, says he misses B.M.R. very much and considers himself extremely fortunate in having had the opportunity of meeting our community, learning our customs, and enjoying our scenery, photographs of which he has pasted in an album. He is happy to have made so many new friends whose views on things political and social he especially appreciated. He says that American newspapers contain much propaganda adverse to Britain, but after 26 months in this country he is sufficiently acquainted with the truth to be able to spot phoney reporting and ill-informed writing on things British. He is looking forward to coming back as soon as he can, to visit England and Scotland, and meet old friends again. His wife, Ruth, is equally anxious to visit this country. Forbes is now a student at the University of Michigan where he is studying chemical engineering. The University is very crowded owing to the thousands of returning veterans who are taking advantage of the "G.I. Bill of Rights" under which the Government pays the veteran a monthly stipend whilst he attends college, as well as paying for his tuition and cost of books outright. Of the 18,000 students there, 3,000 are engineers, and of these 80% are veterans. Ruth is working for the county welfare society, and between them they are just managing to keep their noses above water during this period of inflation which is seriously affecting the cost of living. They are both proud owners of three-speed Raleigh cycles, made in Nottingham; and British bikes of all makes, which are commonly seen on the campus of the University, are very much in demand as they outshine, by far, American made machines. Forbes says he would have enjoyed being at the first annual meeting of the Association. He is still in communication with friends made at B.M.R. and during his leaves in other parts of the country, but, like ourselves, has not heard from Fred or "Mac" lately.

Jean Ozon says she found the last issue of *The Woygian* more interesting than any previous number and describes it as a breath of air from the old country. She has travelled quite a bit since her arrival last April, and has met many fellow countrymen and women. She is enjoying her new life and is still in touch with a few comrades of Garats Hey-days.

No. 2602356 Sigmn. H. Bartlett is now with Special Wireless Troop, R. Signals, Gibraltar, which was visited recently by our president, who made the return trip by air. Harry arrived at the beginning of September in a land of comparative plenty, where cigarettes are 1/- for 20, grapes 9d. per lb., and beer is in good supply. Wrist watches are also cheap but cannot be sent out of the country. He is keeping his hand in as a football referee and has started a pool club on Zetter's coupons which have to be sent in a week before the matches are played. Some of our members will be interested to learn that Sgt. "Tubby" Turrell, M.M. is in the same section, where incidentally, night watches are unknown.

Charlie Leedham, who has become a member of the Association since leaving B.M.R., wrote from 135, George Street, Hull, where he has settled down. He is still waiting to enter college, but doesn't anticipate this before Christmas. Says school teaching is a good life although he felt strange during the first month when taking a class of 45 boys. At present he is only taking a few lessons each week, the remainder of his time being spent as assistant to other teachers. He is hoping to do some free-lance writing after getting through College. He has heard from Bill Baker who is still flourishing in the car racket.

Other new members include "Nobby" Clarke, ex-Supvr., "J", etc., now living at 29, Putney Road, Enfield, Middx. "Nobby" paid us a visit on November 20th and seems to be doing very well as manager of the Magnet Stores (N. London) Ltd. He said his car had gone on to Leicester, but didn't mention whether it was Allen's or Prestwell's.

2392115 Sigmn. Peter Kingsland, No. 1 Special Wireless Reg., R. Sigs., B.A.O.R., has also become a member. There is little other news of the "78". Flat-footed 2nd Lieut. Royle of the Pay Corps was seen in this vicinity during November; Signalmen Antrum, Barnes, Dooge, Gardner, Hyder, Pearce F., Saunders, Smith, R.E., Snell and Stevens, A.K., were here on a course, from September 17th until November 1st; "Blondie" Hewson went to Basic O.C.T.U. at Aldershot on November 5th, and John Ellingworth followed on December 6th. Bill Hayward wrote from Cairo on December 9th, where he, together with Pete James, Derek Basnett, Ron (Cpl.) Blease, Bern Norwood and "Tubby" Fagg, was hoping to go on to Cyprus but afraid it might be the Holy Land. Also in Cairo with another draft, similarly bound, are Sgt. Tyler, "Doodlebug" Tomlinson and N. L. Smith. Bill sends greetings to all friends at B.M.R. and elsewhere, and adds that he thinks Egypt "Sphinx".

Readers will undoubtedly be interested to learn that I have at long last, and with considerable difficulty, overcome official opposition and obtained permission to publish the meaning of QWW. My case was that, since it has lost its significance to a large percentage of our members who have left the station, there can now be no harm in acquainting them with the meaning of something with which so many of them came into contact during the war years. No longer will it be necessary when relating their war experiences to the uninitiated, to make vague and guarded references to "QWW, sometimes followed by two letters, etc.". Obviously this information may also prove invaluable to some of our members who are still serving at this station. The true meaning of QWW FP is: Quorn Water Works-Fire Point.

There have been numerous arrivals and departures, both Military and Civilian, but I do not propose to publish a complete list as the majority of the names would be unknown to our readers. Charlie Leedham left us on August 31st, Mr. D. O'Neill-Johnson on October 2nd, Miss Margaret Ellingworth relinquished her appointment in the Group Office on October 14th, Mr. Norman Shuttlewood left on October 18th, Mrs. Batchelor on October 26th, Mr. Connolly to take up school teaching, on November 2nd, Tommy Adkins on November 9th, Mick Gilbert, ex-I.M. Staff, on November 19th when he was called up for service with the R.A.F., Mr. J. Atkinson, ex-Army and Civilian workshops, on December 7th. There has been a considerable number of new entrants among whom is Pat Hughes, now Mrs. Fullager, who came back on December 9th as a civilian S.B.O. Messrs. Andy Plowman (August), Blenkinsop, W. (Sept.), "Duggie" Fairbanks (Nov.—since resigned), and Paddy Foley (Dec.), rejoined from outstation duties. Mr. Page (Bill), left here on August 2nd for outstation duty at Newton Morrell.

Congratulations to Mr. Herbert Abraham on his promotion to S.E.W.A. with effect from September 1st, and seniority from 1942.

No Military personnel are expected to remain here after the end of the year, and the O.C. and Major Wort are to don civvies again on January 1st.

Demobilisations during September: Sigmn. J. Bews, Dvrs. T. W. Evans and G. N. Davies. October: Sigmn. J. Parkinson, Dvrs. F. Blackburn and E. Partridge, Signalmen R. C. Greenwood, A. H. Gibbs, and F. A. Lee (Draughtsman).

Miss A. Fowler, Miss H. Macaulay, Miss R. Fowler and Miss "Babs" Nash have all been demobbed during the last few weeks. Other A.T.S. releases are as follows: October: Sgts. Alice Young and Margaret Heaton, Cpls. Marjorie Russell, Joyce Saunders, Jenny Shaw, J. Watson, G. Balls (Runner) and "Butch" Kidger (Cook). Cpl. Wyllie, due for release on October 16th, broke her leg on the 9th, and was detained. L/Cpls. M. Matthews, E. Lloyd-Jones, and M. Bruce (Runner). Ptes. F. Coulthard, Betty Digby, Liddell, J. Baker, D. Ball, P. Barnett, J. Bushnell, E. Gordon, G. Harrison, V. Higgs, E. Lycett, D. Lycett, F. Amster, M. Young, M. Garton, M. Hunter, J. Whiteley, K. Wood, B. Judd, S. Kendrick, H. Wakeman, Jean Jenkins (D.F.P.), A. Scott (S.B.O.) and Wright née Wilkins. November: C.S.M. Lorna Galbraith, Sgt. F. G. Smith (Driver), Ptes. S. Auchterlonie, C. M. Ash, E. Bell, J. Bond, D. Carpenter (Runner), J. Clifford, J. Knifton, J. Lord, Letter, E. Mann, L. E. Nicholls, A. B. Piercy, J. A. Povey, "Winkie" Smart, K. Walker, D. Willis, H. D. Bell, J. H. Bedford, M. Derbyshire, J. Gilheney, J. Graham, C. Morss, C. E. Osborne, D. Scaife, B. C. Stanton, M. A. Todd, U. Vince, M. Wilmer.

December: Cpls. Kay Henson, Betty Smart and M. Robson. Ptes. C. Murray, J. Vulliamy, M. Lind, B. R. Cook, D. Wall, S. Hotchkiss, M. Merry, B. Bethell, K. Boagey, E. Morris, J. MacDonald, J. Allatt, Olive Appleford, D. Davies, F. Doyle, K. Godding, J. Jackson, J. Scurrah, K. M. Smith, D. Wade, E. Whitlock, and H. Wildish.

C.S.M. "Red" Yalden will be leaving us for demob. on December 20th.

The few remaining A.T.S. operators are at present employed from 0700-1300, and 1300-1900 hours only.

Ruby Day spent a week-end here during September, and Major Donaldson paid us a surprise visit on October 6th.

The latest local counter-attraction to the floods is ice hockey at Nottingham, and trips are made on Friday evenings. You get plenty of goals for your money, but very few of them are scored by the home side!

A photograph was taken recently, and a copy appears herewith. The main feature is that it represents 150 years of "Y" service shared by Messrs. Hadler, Sparkes, Kirkman, Hawkes, Blundell, Major Wort, The O.C., and Mr. Abraham. When postcards were being canvassed locally, one member of the staff in declining the offer said he could stand the sight of 'em individually or even in pairs, but this was too much!

Reg. Cecil has escaped from the mines on the grounds of flat feet, and is now in the R.A.F. His present address is 3076838 A. C. Cecil, R.A. S.H.Q. (V.H.F.) Signals, R.A.F., Linton-on-Ouse, Yorks. His experience as a Bevin boy was not as bad as he had anticipated, and he considers himself fortunate in having shared the hard life of such a grand set of men. He also praises the spirit of comradeship shown by the Bevin boys in the hostel at Mansfield where he stayed. He joined the R.A.F. on January 2nd as a wireless operator R/T. At present he is operating a mobile V.H.F. set with a range of 100-124 megacycles, and also taking bearings on aircraft which require a homing bearing. He misses the B.M.R. music club and the dancing classes, for which he is very grateful to Hilary, as they have enabled him to spend many an enjoyable evening. He sends his regards to all old friends including Peter Dooge, Roy Hardy, Roy Aldridge, Johnny Hodge, Bill Hayward, and Jimmy Hewson. Reg., whose demob. number is 64 by virtue of his mining service, intends to join his brother in the Rhodesian Police on his release. He asks us to extend a family Christmas greeting to Wally from all at home.

As reported elsewhere, the first Annual General Meeting of the Association was held in London on October 26th. The following members attended: Lt. Col. Ellingworth, Major Jolowicz, Mr. Reg. Hilder, Miss Joan Rogerson, Mr. and Mrs. Abels, Mr. and Mrs. H. Dodd, Mr. A. H. Appleton, Miss Pam Edmundson, Joan Griffiths, Avril Wiseman, Elsie Knight, Betty Haynes, Myrtle Waterfall, who travelled from Torquay, Mr. and Mrs. R. M. Smith, Mr. Patten, ex-I.M. Shop, now with the G.P.O., and his wife who will be remembered as Cpl. Davenport when in the A.T.S., Peter Dart, ex-I.M. Cpl. Vannerley, John Reid, accompanied by Messrs. Pick and Helder, late of Stn. X, who have now become members, and myself. After the meeting, the O.C., Messrs. Hilder, Appleton, Mr. and Mrs. Dodd and myself went in search of tea (YES, Tea.). We boarded a Victoria-bound bus which was promptly rammed from behind by a private car and rendered *hors-de-combat*. This necessitated a transfer, but the drivers of following buses looked us over and drove straight on. Perhaps the locals are not entirely wrong after all!

The following spot of nonsense was inspired by an actual incident. The principal character was the 16-year-old daughter of the house at which I am billeted. Under similar circumstances, I can visualize any of the Harry Dodd—Chas. Brown fraternity having an apopletic fit. Must tell you of the sweet young thing, whose love of crooners, jazz and swing, occasioned an unkind remark by devotees of Grieg and Bach. That she was "lowbrow", they implied. She (contradictingly) replied:

"In addition to liking both fugue and cantata, My favourite piece is the Moonlight Sinatra."

Thats all for now folks, so I will sign off, wishing you a happy Christmas and a prosperous New Year.

VORPOSTEN MELDUNG

LIFE, for the six thrice-exiled exiles now resident in the comfortable quarters recently vacated by *Deutsch-Krieg-Marines* does not seem to have progressed much beyond the unending monotony of our late residence in Beaumanor's pastoral surrounds. Our somnolent night-duties seem very similar to their Beaumanor counterparts—indeed, except for the rather persistent cries of "You ought to be able to; they can in Blighty", (that from a two-striped equivalent of Harry Dix), one could almost imagine our workplace to be the sepulchural interior of "H".

Back in the old days (notice an affectionate, half-yearning ring about that phrase?), our chief concern was how to get out of civvies and into the Army; now it's the other way round. Whereas in those days the main topics for discussion were Noel's latest *faux pas* in the B.S.M., or the varied antics of one or two other eccentrics—Dick Whitford, the Weasel, Col. Merritt, the Puritanical Purehearts (thanks, Noel), the now extinct Bull-ring clique, and others—nowadays our hearts and minds are turned to matters of high import in the business world. I refer, of course, to Black Market Bartering. There is much checking of facts and comparing of notes concerning the current values of cigarettes and coffee in terms of *Deutsch* cameras and binoculars—the latter always a good line provided you can negotiate the efforts of the quick-witted officials in the Customs shed. My own smuggling activities have already suffered heavy losses in one sharp encounter, but that's another story.

Continuing Moggy's efforts to herald the presence of Beaumanor Fiends in the wilds of Yorkshire in the form of debauched renderings of "The Boys of Beaumanor", and other ethereal compositions, we, in our small way (Zombie's deep bass bellowings, Ginger Lowes' "Sinatra" tones, and the liquid beauty of my own, Pete Kingsland's, and Phil Robert's vocal efforts), have allowed the "Deacon" to go down in many peaceful villages of the Fatherland. Imagine our delight when, after a few particularly brilliant renderings of some of the more obscene B.M. roundelays, a wise-looking *Deutscher* was heard to remark that he supposed we were singing old English folk-songs. Ah well, praise comes very slowly to the talented. I would add, in passing, that my sense of the 'correctness' of things was rudely jolted when, during a tour of bomb-shattered Hamburg we burst into song with: "Oh Mary, this London's a wonderful sight".

The Prophet Osee's appeal to ops. anticipating demob. to continue this job in Civvy Street by writing direct to O.C. Beaumanor Park is causing much amusement and not a little violence. Its prominence on all our notice-boards constitutes a real danger to us ex-civvy ops. Its premier appearance caused such a frenzy of anti-civvy-demonstrations that it became necessary to conduct our social affairs *en bloc* as a means of protection. Time has mellowed their reactions and now, when passing us, the average op. merely expectorates and remarks to his companion in a half-pitying voice: "That's one of those civvy ops.—doesn't look a simpleton, does he?"

Ah yes, times have changed; whereas during our Basic Training at Lichfield a modest reference to our frightfully mysterious civvy job was all that was necessary to turn our fellows agog with admiration, now, among the Army equivalents of our civvy breed, we have to make extensive efforts to conceal our civilian occupation, lest we bring down the scorn of our fellows on our heads. But the mere mention of our astronomical Age-and-Service Group number is enough to make us targets for unending scorn and a host of pitying glances. To the oft-repeated question: "What did you do in Civvy Street?", our reply is: "Oh, I was a Civil Servant", and then we discreetly turn the conversation into other channels.

So, my wartime comrades of Beaumanical insanity, I leave you, with many *Bitteschon's* and *Dankeschon's* and other recently-acquired *Deutsch* phrases, together with the hope that your present fate is not as bad as ours.

Leben Sie wohl,

FRED VICKERS.

Ell-dorado

ELL has been refurbished. It is a sight for sore I.M.s; a Planner's Dream in glorious, gorgeous Technicolor.

Most of you will recall past epics of planning at B.M., but nothing even remotely touching this for sheer splendour, for downright efficiency, and for absolute unadulterated luxury has ever before been attempted, much less achieved, within this power-packed perimeter. Old standards have been ruthlessly cast aside; previous stumbling-blocks spurned; no stone has been left unturned to make this the Ewas' Utopia, the Supervisors' *sanctum sanctorum*.

As this is being written Ell has not yet entered on its new span of life, but your scribe having been privileged for a few moments to cross the sacred threshold; to sully its glistening floor with his infidel boots; and to feast his gentile eyes upon some of its as yet silent mechanism, it does not require a lot of imagination to visualize it in its heyday.

And so, as I relinquish my grasp of the modernistic, chromium-plated door-handle, leaving the ghastly imprint of my pagan thumb (Oi! 'Arry. Wheer's yer dooster?), I see this place as a pulsating, throbbing hub of superbly co-ordinated industry. The elegant, futuristically-designed ash-trays, plugged in to the lustrous benches so that their alignment shall not be disturbed, are symbolic of all that is Ell.

Here is a switch-panel. This switch connects Mr. McGraft's left nostril to a board at the far end of the room where sits an omniscient being who sniffs the odours that assail McGraft's nose. At the deft touch of another switch a purple bulb glows and he is seeing with McGraft's right eye. A green light glimmers, and he listens to the simultaneous beat of McGraft's right pulse and his left heart, superimposing or not, at will, the anxious flutterings of his epiglottis. And this is but a fraction of the marvels of Ell. A microphone before McGraft enables him to speak direct to Whitehall 1212, croon over the N.B.C. Network, or swear modishly at the omniscient one, what time the latter is measuring both of Corkman's feet for Saxone, double-checking Hill-mouse's weight, and extracting a couple of decayed molars from the heavy jaw of an ecstatic Dingfield. By means of further switches Card is engaged in a furious "battleships" duel with Fannington, Wax is ordering his breakfast eggs double-fried, and Patchcoal is electro-dynamically inflating his bicycle tyres by remote control for a quick getaway on super-ultra-long-weekend.

Yes, it is all very lovely—idyllic, in fact. If there is a snag at all it is the solitary black button on the omniscient one's much-bestudded poly-chromatic panel. Very few are aware that deep, deep in the earth beneath Ell reposes a time-bomb . . . . . .

E.C.M.

EDITORIAL NOTE.

IT is with genuine regret that I have to announce that I am resigning the position of Editor of *The Woygian* following publication of this issue.

As my successor (to whom I wish all good fortune) has not yet been appointed, intending contributors to the Spring Number should send their "copy" to the Secretary. Gossip may, of course, still be sent direct to Ollie at Beaumanor.

We are pleased to revive a popular B.S.M. feature, *"Through the Looking Glass"*, in this number. Best Wishes for 1947 to all Woygians everywhere, and thanks, V.B., for the Xmas Card.

Printed by John Corah & Son Ltd., and published by E. C. Millhouse for The Woygian Association.

The WOYGIAN

BRIDGEWOODS 1939 CHICKSANDS 1940 BEAUMANOR

| Vol. 2 | Summer 1947 | No. 7 |

WOYGIAN ASSOCIATION

THE FIRST

Annual Dinner and Dance

will be held on

SATURDAY, NOVEMBER 22nd, 1947

6.0 P.M. TO 11.30 P.M.

at the

"NEW INN"
WESTMINSTER BRIDGE ROAD, LONDON, S.E.1

(adjoining County Hall)

(Nearest Underground Stations—
Waterloo and Westminster)

INFORMAL DRESS   +   +   PRIVATE BAR

TICKETS 15/- EACH

●

Applications for tickets, on the enclosed form, to be sent with remittances to the Hon. Treasurer. Accommodation is limited so APPLY NOW !

Members from any zone may attend.

(It is not expected that latest M.O.F. regulations will necessitate any change in the programme as planned).

THE WOYGIAN

ASSOCIATION

President :
Lt. Col. M. J. W. ELLINGWORTH, O.B.E., D.S.M.

Vice-Presidents :

Major H. F. JOLOWICZ   Mr. G. M. SPOONER
Jnr. Cdr. I. F. ROMER   Mr. C. O. SMITH

Chairman :
Mr. H. DODD,
" Colin-Hurst," 168 Station Road,
Hendon, London, N.W.4

Honorary Secretary :   *Honorary Treasurer :*
Mrs. P. L. EDMUNDSON,   Mr. J. DODD,
27 Wood End Avenue,   82 Newbury Gardens,
S. Harrow, Middlesex   Stoneleigh, Surrey

HERE at last is another issue of " THE WOYGIAN "—the first since the Winter 1946/7 issue. I have no doubt many of you have been wondering whether the Association had "passed away." I am glad to say that this is not so, though we have just emerged from a financial crisis (to use a topical expression) brought about by the fact that by last May half of our members had not paid their subscriptions for 1946/7. Forgetfulness was probably largely to blame, encouraged perhaps by the lack of insistent reminders. Thus, the reason for the non-appearance of the Spring issue, and for the lateness of this Summer issue (which will, in the circumstances, have to be regarded as the Summer-Autumn issue) is simply that funds have until very recently been quite insufficient. Fortunately a circularised appeal met with a fairly good response and the finances are now in better shape—hence the present issue.

The moral is, I hope, plain to you all, so please *do not delay in sending to the new Hon. Treasurer, Mr. J. Dodd, your subscription for* 1947/8. What is to you as an individual, a small matter, easily overlooked, is of vital importance for the continuation of the Association and its Magazine, and obviously we cannot carry on without funds. Please complete the enclosed form and send it with your remittance to the address shown on the form. If you happen to know of any members who have not responded to the appeal for overdue subscriptions (the number is rather disappointingly high), and who will therefore not be receiving copies of this issue, please persuade them to pay up and thus renew their membership. New members will also be welcome, and I hope you will lose no opportunity to gain them for the Association. I might point out here that as the result of a resolution passed at the Annual General Meeting in London last year, persons who had some connection with WOYG during the war years, but who did not actually work in the Group, may be admitted to Associate Membership, subject to sponsorship by two Ordinary Members and the approval of the Committee. All enquiries should be addressed to the new Hon. Secretary, whose address is given above.

Please note that, in order to economise in postage, receipts for subscriptions will usually be sent with the next issue of the Magazine.

RE-UNION. I am very glad to announce that the first Re-union will be held in London on Saturday, November 22nd. Full details appear on page 2, and you can book your ticket by filling up the appropriate parts of the enclosed form and sending 15/- with your subscription. Accommodation is strictly limited, and you are warned that unless you apply immediately, you may be disappointed. For the same reason, the only non-Woygian guests we can allow must be restricted to one friend of each Ordinary Member (Class A) only. I am sure you will have an enjoyable evening, meeting some of your old Woygian friends again in pleasant surroundings, as festive as the "New Inn" manager can make them in these days of austerity. I hope it may be possible for some of our members from the North and Scotland to be with us then.

It is hoped to plan re-unions in the Midland and Scottish zones next winter. With our scattered membership, this will not be an easy matter, but members in the two zones can help by letting us know as soon as possible whether they would be interested in a re-union in Manchester, Glasgow or Edinburgh, or any other convenient centre. Any suggestions, especially regarding a suitable place for a re-union, would be most welcome. If your response to this request is encouraging, the Zone Committees will be asked to make arrangements, of which you will, of course, be notified in good time. So the possibility of a re-union in the Midlands or North of England and in Scotland, is therefore, in the first place, up to you. If you want one, write and tell us so. Please enclose a note with your subscription, or write direct to me.

MAGAZINE. You will be glad to know that Mr. E. C. Millhouse will, as soon as he has found some solution to his accommodation problem in London, resume as our Editor, and both he and I hope that this will be in time for him to deal with the next issue. I have had the benefit of his assistance in the preparation of the present issue.

Don't fail to keep Mr. "Ollie" Pearce at Beaumanor well supplied with items of news of yourself and other Woygians. You are not doing your bit for the Association if you don't pass to him occasionally some news for his columns, no matter how unexciting.

This is perhaps an appropriate point at which to offer our congratulations and best wishes to Flora and Ollie on their recent marriage. I take particular pleasure in doing on your behalf in print what Ollie has himself done so often for many of *us*! Ollie makes a somewhat oblique reference to the happy occasion on a later page.

Contributions to the Magazine in any form will be welcome, particularly more lengthy accounts of any interesting experiences you have had since WOYG days.

It seems that a few members who were entitled to do so, did not receive copies of the last issue. The Secretary will be pleased to forward copies to them on application. Copies of all previous issues, except No. 1 (September, 1945), are still available and will also be sent on application by any member, price 6d. each post free.

The next issue of the Magazine will be the Christmas, 1947 number. All contributions for it must be received not later than 1st December; news items should be sent, as before, to Mr. "Ollie" Pearce, at Beaumanor, and other contributions to me at Hendon.

HONORARY OFFICERS. Mr. R. W. Hilder, Chairman of the Association since its inception, resigned in May, and at a Committee meeting in London soon after, I was appointed to succeed him. Our thanks are due to Mr. Hilder for his pioneer work for the Association as originator and founder of the scheme.

Mr. Graham Abels resigned as Treasurer in June, and my brother, **Mr. John Dodd**, has been appointed by the Committee to succeed him. All subscriptions, etc., should now be sent to Mr. J. Dodd, at the address shown above.

Miss Joan Rogerson, Secretary since September, 1945, is returning to Woodhouse to take up a post at Maplewell Hall, and so is resigning as Secretary. Mrs. P. L. Edmundson, already a member of the Committee, is taking over; enquiries and all matters relating to change of name or address, etc., should now be sent to Mrs. Edmundson. (Any changes noted on the enclosed form and sent to the Treasurer will, of course, be handed on to the Secretary.) Our thanks must also be extended to Miss Rogerson and to Mr. Abels for the work they have done for the Association in the first two difficult years of its life. I am glad to say that Miss Rogerson will be keeping in touch with the Committee.

The Central Committee in London has been strengthened by the addition of Mr. Dudley Truin.

LIST OF MEMBERS. The idea of issuing a complete list of members' names and addresses has not been abandoned, but postponed until a more propitious time. In the meantime, the Secretary will be pleased to re-direct any letters for Woygian members via her address at Harrow, and help members to get into touch with one another in any other way possible.

Finally, I should like to send my good wishes to all members, with special mention for those overseas. I am looking forward to seeing many of you at the Re-union on November 22nd.   *H Dodd*

"What's He Doing Now ?"

By OLLIE PEARCE

To most of us a common phrase familiar in the doubtful days,
Now as we go our sundry ways, a different meaning it conveys,
Remote from that elusive " he," confined instead to you and me,
Therefore the word must also be interpreted at times as " she."

AS most of your are no doubt aware, the Association has, in the past few months been so near to insolvency that another issue of the magazine this year was at one time considered to be out of the question. However, thanks to the unbounded energy of Mr. Harry Dodd and his London colleagues, here we are again.

Personally, I had not anticipated going to press again for some considerable time and had therefore destroyed most of my notes, so please don't be too critical if some of the items are lacking in detail.

Members of BMR staff, particularly those who served at Chatham, were shocked on March 12th to learn of the sudden death of Mrs. Blundell, following a road accident at Rochester, Kent. Mr. Blundell is one of the oldest and most respected members of the staff, and we offer our sincerest sympathy in his tragic loss.

BIRTHS.

To Gilbert and Mrs. Glanville, at Radmoor Nursing Home, on December 18th, a daughter, Stephanie Yvonne.

To Noel and Billy Royle on December 18th, a daughter, Bronwen Ann.

To Wally and Mrs. Ratcliffe, also during December last, a daughter, Barbara.

To "Blanco" and Mrs. White, in London, on January 23rd, a son, Alan David.

To John and Kaye Dodd, at Birmingham, on January 30th, a daughter, Anne Marilyn.

To Mr. and Mrs. Richardson, on February 6th, a daughter, Jennifer Helen. This probably won't mean a thing unless I explain that Mrs. Richardson used to be Jean Dennis.

To Paddy and Doreen Kelly, at The Alexandra Nursing Home, Twickenham on February 17th, a daughter, Patricia Doreen.

To Mr. and Mrs. Jackson (née Vera Winzer) on March 30th, a daughter, Sandra.

To Graham and Daphne Abels, on June 2nd, a daughter, Diana Maureen.

To Arnold and Winnie Manington, at the Mountsorrel Nursing Home, on July 2nd, a son, Christopher Arnold.

To Dick and Mrs. Whitford, on July 25th, 8 lbs. 10 ozs. of daughter, Penelope Jane.

To Ernest and Irene Siddall, at Radmoor Nursing Home, on June 8th, a daughter, Jane. Ernest returned to the G.P.O. on demobilisation and is now an Assistant Regional Inspector in the Brighton area. He and his family are hoping to take up residence in their new house at Patcham by the end of August.

To Dan and Mrs. Hawkins, at Portsmouth, on June 7th, a daughter, Frances Ann.

To "Topper" and Mrs. Brown, a daughter, Susan Patricia.

Congratulations to all concerned.

MARRIAGES.

Peggy Cracknell was married at Leicester on Christmas Eve to a young man whose name I can't remember. He hails from North Cheam, where they are making their home.

Jack Morton of the I.M. Staff and Paddy Picken, ex-A.T.S. BMR, were married at Bristol on January 25th.

Ex-Pte. M. S. Metcalfe, late "D" Watch, Brand Hill, and now living at Ainsworth Vicarage, Bolton, Lancs., was married at Ainsworth Parish Church, on April 19th, to Flt./Lt. G. S. Johnson-Heaps, R.A.F.V.R.

Gwen Sidwell was married at North Cheam, Surrey, on May 17th, to Mr. Ronald Gibbs, ex-Paratroop Sergeant. (Thanks for the cake Gwen.)

Betty Theresa Robinson, ex-Plotting Room Staff, was married at St. Bartholomew's Church, Westgate, Chichester, on May 26th, to Mr. John Henry Seal.

Ex-Driver José Randon, BMR and B.W., was married at Tamworth-in-Arden, on May 21st, to Mr. Michael Gould.

Miss Jean Rowan, ex-A.R.13, of 91, Marple Road, Stockport, was married on June 12th, to Mr. Alan Pridgeon of Offerton, Stockport.

Ex-Sub.-Lt. Paul Martin Shearman, R.N., a former member of BMR staff and now with the Cossor Radio Company, was married at Quorn Parish Church on June 14th, to Miss Janet Squire of Loughborough Road, Quorn. The reception was held in the Church Room, and the honeymoon was spent at Bournemouth.

Norma Double, ex-Plotting Room Staff, was married at St. Mary's Church, East Bergholt, Essex, on June 28th, to Mr. Gordon F. Grimsey. The reception was held at Victory Hut (the name is purely coincidental) and their new home is at Latinford Hill, Stratford St. Mary, nr. Colchester.

Ex-Driver Dorothea Elam and ex-Sigmn. Marshall (Linesman) both former members of W.O.Y.G., were married at St. Paul's Church, Tottenham, on June 29th, and are now living in Scotland. Eileen Fisher was bridesmaid, and among the guests were Mary Morriss, Betty Colvill, Billie Lillywhite, and Tony Eeles. Under the circumstances it was only natural that the reception developed into a minor re-union of the BMR Military section.

Miss Janet Wallace Irvine, of Rushden, a former member of "D" Watch, Quorn, was married at the Parish Church, Quorn, on August 8th, to Mr. Norman John Thornton, of Park View, Quorn. The reception was held at Park View, and the honeymoon was spent in the Isle of Man.

CORRECTION. Readers may remember that I published in the last issue the meaning of the letters QWW FP. One young lady disagreed so strongly with this interpretation that she accompanied me to Leicester on May 3rd to prove her own explanation, which, as far as I could gather after the previous night's Stag Party, had something to do with changing her name to Flora Pearce. Lois Seal travelled up from London for the occasion.

We offer congratulations and best wishes for future happiness also to the undermentioned, details of whose weddings are not available.

Ex-I Corps Cpl. Lilian France, now Mrs. Ball, "Ebor," Cote Lane, Hayfield, nr. Stockport.

Miss N. A. Brook, now Mrs. Harrison, 26 Wakefield Road, Staincross, nr. Barnsley, Yorks.

Miss Frances Blake, now Mrs. F. Southgate, 24 Foyle Road, Tottenham, London N.17.

Ex-L/Cpl. E. B. McGlashan, now Mrs. A. Williams, 16, Blithdale Road, Abbey Wood, London S.E.2.

Miss Olga Roch, now Mrs. E. D. Churchill, 40 Gwyddon Road, Abercarn, Mon.

Miss J. F. Howat, now Mrs. Gross, c/o 238, Hollybrook Street, Glasgow, S.2.

Miss Betty M. Smith, now Mrs. Walker, 14 Lycett Road, Liverpool 4.

Miss Kathleen J. Bridgman, now Mrs. Cox, 80, Ellington Road, Ramsgate.

Miss Gladys Douglas, now Mrs. G. Bunn, 76, Dewey Road, Dagenham, Essex.

Miss Norah Perrin, ex-Commn. Wing, now Mrs. Hughes, 51, Edmund Road, Saltley, Birmingham 8.

Miss Barbara Marquiss, now Mrs. Preston, 55 Kirkstall Avenue, Leeds 5.

Miss Joyce Bringloe, now Mrs. Norris, 2, African Villas, Loose, Maidstone, Kent.

Miss Jean Hoatson, whose married name and present address are unknown.

FORTHCOMING MARRIAGES, ENGAGEMENTS, ETC.

The engagement is announced between Captain Thomas Hildyard Beaumont, Royal Signals, elder son of the late Richard Henry Beaumont, and Mrs. Beaumont, of Kempston, Bedford, and Margaret Mary, younger daughter of Lieutenant-Commander M. J. W. Ellingworth, O.B.E., R.N. (retd.), and Mrs. Ellingworth, of Woodhouse, Leicestershire.

The foregoing is an extract from *The Times*, August 14th, 1947. Captain Beaumont is at present stationed at Garats Hey.

Miss Joan Edgell has become engaged to Mr. C. G. Miller, at present serving in the R.A.F. Joan is looking forward to his return to civvy street in spite of his high group number. Apart from seeing Beryl Groves and Margaret Jillions quite regularly, life at BMR seems very remote, and she has settled down to her old job again. There have been times when she wished she was back, but thoughts of an occasional dig in the ribs from Lilian Lederman during the small hours, have helped her to change her mind.

Miss Mary Rodwell, of 90, Westfield Road, Wellingborough, is to become Mrs. E. E. Tuck on September 6th next.

Miss Audrey Holland is to become Mrs. H. A. Carless on September 13th next. Her new address will be 17 Lancaster Road, Upper Edmonton, London N.18. She wants to know if Rosie from the " Rose and Crown " thinks this sufficient reason for a G.H. Sergeants' celebration.

Congratulations to all concerned.

OTHER NEWS.

We are pleased to welcome back Tommy Hill after yet another operation which we hope will be the last.

We are also pleased to see that "Hobby," convalescing after an operation in Loughborough Hospital, is looking so well.

Congratulations to " Pip " Peerless, whose award of the B.E.M., in recognition of his work at BMR, appeared in the 1947 Birthday Honours List.

On February 24th, poor old "Laddie," who had been showing distinct signs of advancing years, was taken to Loughborough and put to sleep. He had been amongst us so long that he seemed part of the place, and his absence was very noticeable for some time. However, the severe winter was obviously increasing his suffering, and his end was mercifully accelerated.

Writing from 234, Birchgrove Road, Birchgrove, Swansea, Glam., where she and her husband are living with her parents, Nancy Childs, née Rundle, ex-I Corps, says she gets a lot of pleasure from reading about old friends, and though she is very glad to be in civvy street again, W.O.Y.G. holds lots of good memories. After being demobbed in February, 1946, she worked for six months in an engineer's office in London and lived at Earls Court, very near to Exauxiliaryilary, whom she often met whilst shopping. She frequently saw Avril Wiseman, who was training at the London School of Stenotyping, and may now be teaching. Nancy married an ex-R.E.M.E. Sergeant, whom she met in the Nuffield Club. She says she was pleased to hear of Barbara Marquiss's engagement and would welcome news of Val Jones, Joyce Bringloe, and the old crowd from Dorothy Walton's hut.

When last heard of six months ago, Charlie Leedham was living at 135, George Street, Hull, E. Yorks., finding school work very interesting, but having great difficulty in managing on £180 per annum. He mentioned that "Con" Connolly was at a training college in Staffordshire.

Chris Pendlebury, who has moved to 2, The Hollies, Haigh, Wigan, Lancs., is anxious to learn the whereabouts of Barbara J. Smith, and Beryl Worledge.

Margaret Dart is now living in Main Street, Woodhouse Eaves.

Betty Colvill, ex-Driver, is working in London as a private secretary, but finds it very difficult to settle down to a job which keeps her indoors most of the time, and sometimes yearns for a D.R. run to Stn. X. Her address is 7, Raleigh Court, The Avenue, Beckenham, Kent.

Bob Sharp, 137, Coronation Street, Sunderland, writes to say that he had hoped to contact BMR on the air but so far has not heard any of our amp dissipators. I have met several people round here who wish they could say the same thing! However, Bob intends to keep on trying. His call-sign is G2HMi.

The following newspaper extract will probably be of interest to several of our readers: " Mrs. Betty Bavin, youngest daughter of Mrs. and the late Mr. Percy Hills, of 20, West Street, Havant, has been awarded a certificate of merit for good services and devotion to duty in the A.T.S., attached to the Royal Corps of Signals. She was demobilised with the rank of company sergeant major on her marriage to Schoolmaster C. Bavin, R.N., and now lives at Glazebury, Lancs. As Betty Hills, Mrs. Bavin was well known as a golfer. She won several trophies before the war and represented Hampshire at the game. Her father, who died three years ago, was professional at the Gosport and Alverstoke Golf Club for many years."

Exauxiliaryilary, who is still living at Earls Court, says she has met Jimmy Edge on two occasions in the vicinity of St. Albans, and that he was married at Easter time. She also met " Jay " O'Neill-Johnson in Cambridge and had a long chat. Incidentally, " Jay," who is now a B.A., visited BMR earlier in the year, but unfortunately I missed him. Hilary says she would very much like to pay us a visit, but at the time of writing (May) she was saving hard for a summer holiday in Norway.

Bobby Snare, née Percy, whose husband is still in the Navy, writes to say that she is looking forward to the proposed re-union in November, and adds that by that time she will be a proud mother.

Miss Myra Hall, who became Mrs. E. Trappit, left this country with her husband at the beginning of February this year and has now settled down in her new home at Borden, Western Australia.

From Italy comes a spot of news sent in by 2392124, Sigmn. Merritt (" The Colonel ") who appears to have been found out at last. He is now an O.W.L., and says he is amused by the fact that so many of the 78 are still working away at the old job, whilst he is having a nice cushy time. With him are Johnny Hodge and Roy Hardy, presumably two of the objects of his amusement. He mentions that Cpl. de la Bertauche and Les French are in Austria, also that Jack Mitchell has a stripe, and is an enthusiastic " Ham " using the call-sign OE9AD. " Punky Wallah," and others who have served east of Suez, will be interested to learn from the " Colonel " that owing to the intense heat in Italy, the troops there wear nothing but a pair of shorts when on duty. He says that the sweat rolls off him when he thinks of work, but maybe this has nothing to do with the climate? I am publishing his address: No. 2 Wireless Troop, c/o 3 Agra (Field), R. Signals, C.M.F., as he is anxious to hear from Noel Royle. Incidentally, Flora and I saw quite a lot of Noel, Billie, and the baby in Eastbourne during May. Noel was having some trouble with his teeth which he turned to good account in the shape of a couple of extra days' leave.

Kay Price came down for the day on Sunday, May 11th, and we spent a few hours together. Kay, now living at 245, Cromwell Road, S.W.5, was looking very well after her trip to Australia and mentioned that one of her fellow passengers was Mrs. Ley, who flew to this country to attend her husband's murder trial. In spite of the fact that there are no food shortages, and that shopping generally is like a dream come true, Kay, who visited Adelaide, Brisbane and Sydney, says she prefers England.

Captain Johnny Mace, who eventually finished up in China, is now back in civvy street, and is training to be a " vet " at the Royal Veterinary College. He is living in a small bachelor flat near Regents Park, but finds little time for work as it takes all his time getting the beer and rations in His address is, The White House, Regents Park, London, N.W.1.

News of the 78, who are now widely scattered, has reached here in scraps at odd times, and by devious routes. Congratulations are due to Ted Sandy (now with S.E.A.C.), and John Ellingworth (awaiting posting from O.C.T.U.) on being commissioned. I believe " Moggy " Reed also qualifies for similar congratulations, but have been unable to confirm this. I did hear that he was transferred to the R.A.S.C.

Jimmy Hewson, formerly at O.C.T.U. in Catterick, was returned to his unit during March for disciplinary reasons, and is now in Singapore. He is thinking of taking up dancing as a career and before leaving this country was studying for his gold emblem. He wishes to thank Hilary for her early teaching, sends best wishes to all Woygians, and would be glad to swap letters with any of his old cronies, particularly Pete Kingsland.

Hugh Dias, now in " Signal Squadron, British Forces in France, has been enjoying himself in " Gay Paree."

Norman Johnson returned to the fold as a civilian for three months, during which time he was on compassionate leave. He went back into uniform in March.

Sgt. Lew Owen was on leave from Germany just before Christmas, and again in June, when he paid us a visit. He is still the same, excepting that his criticisms of administration are no longer restricted to one small government department, and have now reached international level. I doubt whether we shall still be occupying Germany when he is Prime Minister, so we shan't have the pleasure of seeing how easy it is to transform a combination of rabble and rubble into Utopia overnight.

Sam Murgatroyd and " Duc " Downer have joined Harry Bartlett in Gibraltar. Mrs. Downer, probably better known to most readers as Cecile Groves, flew out to join her husband just after Whitsun. Mrs. Bartlett's boy is expecting to come home on leave during August.

Cpl. Pope paid us a visit a couple of months ago whilst on leave from Austria.

According to information received in May, the following are in Sarafand under the command of Lt.-Col. Du Cros: Ron Blease, who, having lost his " Draft conducting " stripes, is once more a Sigmn. He has had a very fine collection of stripes in his time, totalling eight. He is co-editor with Jimmy Dodd of the unit newspaper, " New Sarafand Star." At Christmas, Jimmy, then L/Cpl., was in charge of the bar which, as usual, did a roaring trade. I heard recently that he is now a sergeant, but I am not sure whether this is correct. " Tubby " Fagg is believed to be employed on the maintenance staff there. There have been several departures from Sarafand, including Bill Hayward and Bernard Norwood to Cyprus, where they met up with " Curly " Hendley, Mike Albon, Johnny Elcombe and L/Cpl. " Googie " Withers. The last named is now attached to the R.A.F. D/F Section, Canal Zone, Egypt, and the other three, who were also D/F employed, left Cyprus for an unknown destination. Bernard Norwood is employed as a storeman, for which he has been given a stripe. Other departures from Sarafand include Pete James, Derek Basnett, Smith N. L., and " Doodlebug " Tomlinson (whose sister is a nurse at Sarafand base hospital) to Habbaniyeh, where they joined Roy Nicholls, Weaver and Norman Rees. Also with this gang is Sgt. " Ticky " Tyler, who was on a train from Cairo to Palestine when it got blown up. He was in the coach next to the one that got the blast, and had to return to Egypt to attend the enquiry. Before sailing from England, " Ticky " was seen at Thirsk with " Mickey " (Tweedledum) Hunt, ex-runner. " Dickey " (Tweedledee) is reported to have left for the U.S.A., so it seems that Pete Kingsland has been written off.

During their stay in Palestine the lads were reminded of the " grips " on the Palestine Police Force, given by Dick Whitford back in '44 when some of them were keen to join. After doing sentry duty on the main gate with a tommy gun, checking traffic in and out by day, and working a searchlight by night as a change from set room duties, they weren't so keen. It is interesting to learn that the Christmas Eve pilgrimage from Sarafand to Bethlehem is still made. Two of last year's pilgrims were Bill Hayward and Derek Basnett. The fact that the annual Donkey Polo and Football matches are still played on Christmas Day is also interesting, but the absence of any records prior to 1939 is not really surprising. I expect our successors obliterated all traces of us long before the arrival of the present occupants.

" Snubby " Pollard came home from Austria for demob at the end of March. Owing to an error by Signals Records, his 4 years and 63 days reserve service with W.O.Y.G. was reckoned towards A and S group, but they are not likely to fall for that one again.

Geoff. Nicol has a nice soft number overseas (255) and is liking it.

It is true that the " Weasel " had a stripe, but whether he still has it, or whether he has got any more, I don't know.

Letter to the Editor

THE following was received by Mr. Millhouse some time ago, as you will see from the date, and is reprinted here with his permission as a fine example of what the British business man can achieve in the face of almost overwhelming difficulties. All who know Mr. Jimmie Hunter will safely assume that he has made even greater strides since the time of writing—but we will not venture to suggest in what direction the strides have been made!

63, Aintree Crescent
Barkingside,
Essex.
/9th October, 1946

dEaR mOuse,

I thOUghT y&o wouLd likE to SeE h%w i Am PRogRes4ing IN tHe bus£ness wor/d. GLad to sAY wE ar4 vEry BUSy inSplte of COntr&ls, stc. and a£e veRy shorT od StaFf. So much sO thAt i Am haVinG to dO mi Own TY½ing but aM ver5Y pleaSed t) s(@y i aM get/ing on Quits weLl althOuHh I oCcasionAlLy MakE misT@ke@.

Howeber aM plEaseD to say i Am Improing GrAdu@l3y. I THink typIcg is TOO easy to lcarn to BoTHer—abOut Cl(@)ss4s sO DeCIded t% teaCh myselF, thereBy Sav3ng MonEY.

ONe of OUr Typists is trYLng to TeacH me—buT we Dont getOn verY Fas/ at Typing) otHerWise We arE Getting on sWeLl and coNsIderIng I have Been At it)TyPing(for Only 14 m)nthS i DonT recken iAm doIng tOo Bad.

All THe bEst foR NOW ! wiLl LeT yoU know / h(@)w igetOn.

YOurs,
jIm£y HUn¼eR,

P.s. IGnor? the Mist@kes, it''s thE MacHine, nOt me

(Coont'd from previous page).

Ray Snell was drafted to Palestine recently, and with the closing down of F.M. in the near future, several more of the 78 will probably be going overseas for the last few months of their service.

Cpls. Don Barber and Dennis Brett are at Garats Hey with 10 Special Operators Training Squadron, familiarly known as SOTS.

There have been numerous arrivals and departures at BMR since the last issue, but only a few of them will be of any interest to our readers. John Dodd left us in January and is getting on well at his new job, salesman for a timber firm, which he says has good prospects, variety, interest, and the privilege of deciding where, when, and for how long he works. The only snag is the present shortage of timber. He and Kaye are sharing a bungalow at Stoneleigh, Surrey, with Kaye's sister and brother-in-law.

In February we said good-bye to Jack Wilkes, ex-Sutton Valence and George Curd. George is now a free-lance carpenter and wood turner. He and Netta are still living in Quorn.

Joe Cleveland and " Ginger " Sprakes left us early in May for four months detached duty. By the time this appears in print they will probably be back, and all those people that are so anxious to know, will be able to see where Joe is.

" Mouse " left us in June to take up an appointment with Customs and Excise in London. We shall be hearing more from him as soon as he gets settled in his new environment.

"Lofty" Burch and Horace Davis left during July. The latter, after several months in Markfield Sanatorium with T.B., from which, we are glad to report, he has now recovered.

Mrs. Molly Cook and Mrs. Lynda Weller (née Courtnage) are back at their old jobs in the T.P. room as civilians, and Bill Page has returned to the fold once more.

In spite of the alleged unpopularity of this place among people who have served here, we still get quite a lot of visitors. Jimmy Rogers paid us another visit at Whitsun, and July visitors included Mr. and Mrs. Greenwood, who are now living at Clonan Cottage, Hebden Bridge, Yorks., Mrs. Batchelor who is keeping the home fires burning at Leigh-on-Sea, whilst Roy is living at 13, Porchester Terrace, Paddington, W.2, in order to be within reasonable distance of his work at Stn. X., Harry Dodd, ex-Cpl. Mabel Cage, and ex-Cpl. Jean Twigg. Ex-Sigmn. Bill Hurrell was here early in August and Ina Hunter, ex-Commns Wing, is frequently in the district, but her interest is centred in Barrow.

Sonya Warren is working in Holborn and sharing a flat in Bayswater with "Bobbie" Packham. Miss Marion Lind, 19, Sandcliffe Road, Wallasey, Cheshire, sends her best wishes to all Woygians. Miss Patricia W. Finnegan is shortly leaving the country. Miss Marjorie F. Wright's new address is "Foscote," 43, All Saints Avenue, Maidenhead, Berks. Mrs. Norma N. Domina has changed her address to 1055, Myrtle Drive, San Bernandino, California, U.S.A. Eric Upton's present address is c/o Winter Gardens Ballroom, Wellington Pier, Great Yarmouth. He has had another addition to the family. Miss Barbara Woodman, ex-I Corps, has moved to Common Down, Lydeard St. Lawrence, near Taunton, Somerset. Joan Pond, ex-Commns Wing, is back in England and demobbed. She became engaged in January to a gentleman from Egham whom she met in Germany. Hazel Pearson, ex-Commns Wing, signed on for a further six months at B.A.O.R., H.Q.

Vera Ballard, whose mother died in January following an unsuccessful operation, is working for Richmonds Gas Stove Co., Ltd., housekeeping for her father, and acting as caretaker in a block of offices. I should think that little lot ought to keep her fully occupied. Hugh Pryse has at last succeeded in obtaining a flat at 2, Sydney House, Woodstock Road, Bedford Park, W.4. He has been very busy lately in the film world and has parts in "The Weird Sisters" (Elstree), "A woman In The Hall" (Pinewood), and "The First Gentleman." Talking of films reminds me, the last news of Paddy Kelly dates back to January, when he was seen dozing in the manager's office of the Odeon at Kettering.

Alec Berry is struggling with an executive job at Nottingham, whilst Henry Lewis and Ralph Champion dine together at the Savoy in spite of the shortage of newsprint, and the drop in tobacco sales.

Mrs. "Maddie" Taylor is now living at 14, Avenue Road, Astwood Bank, Redditch, Worcs. She gave up work last September and went to Folkestone for three months' holiday. Although she hates admitting it, there are times when she is homesick for BMR. She is entirely alone all day, and often doesn't have an opportunity to speak to anyone. (Punishment indeed!) To counteract this loneliness, "Maddie" has adopted a mongrel. She has heard from Mrs. Probert (née Joyce Spotswood, "A" Watch, 2 Wing, overseas) who has got a house in Jersey, where her husband is hotel barman. She has a daughter, Pamela, and says that Marjorie Reynolds, formerly of the same watch, is hoping to leave England later this year with her two children, to join her husband in the Sudan.

Outwardly, BMR has not changed a great deal. Most of the life has moved Westwards and is centred around "H" and "L" Huts, but "I" and "K" are not entirely deserted. The former is used for training purposes and the latter is occupied by the aforementioned SOTS. "J" Hut is closed, and the weeds are coming up between the paving stones here and there. The canteen is gradually being transformed into a new set room. the existing canteen (T.P. Rest Room) is fast becoming inadequate and will soon be left for more suitable accommodation in the house itself. Here also is the future venue of the administration offices, and possibly some accommodation will be made available as a hostel. The lawn between the old offices and the house has been turned into a bowling green, which has proved extremely popular, and is in use daily. There are also facilities for cricket practice, and this also takes place daily. The surrounding countryside is a little more deserted, and the old familiar sight of A.T.S. fratting with Yanks is now no more, but it is quite common to see the local girls with their Jerries.

TAILPIECE. The conversation had embraced various subjects, and eventually turned to bull-fighting. One particularly miserable-looking member of the party, who had hitherto been silent, was asked if he had any knowledge of the subject. " I know all there is to know about it," he replied. " I work for the War Office."

Cheerio folks.

FADE-OUT

By ERIC W. DOBSON

OF course, it was stupid of me in the first place, but I still think it was Dick's fault it all happened.

It all began when I was digging my jungle garden, somewhere between Barrow and Sileby. I came across a course of bricks which, I presumed, was once a pathway, but as I removed first one layer and then another— not without a deal of grunting and cussing. incidentally—it dawned upon me that this was no path, laid and forgotten, but something much more substantial. Well, to cut a long yarn short, as the A.T.S. girl said when she nibbled off the end of her wool, it *was* something more substantial; in fact, I was prising up the roof of a subterranean chamber. My intense excitement and eager expectations, my rapid hopes of treasure, and frantic efforts to dive into the unknown cache were all sadly brought to an end when all I discovered was a pile of rubble and dust and a small wooden chest, broken open, containing a parchment and a bottle. These I carefully removed and examined under my high-pressure three hundred candle-power lamp (*advert.*), but couldn't make much of the writing on the parchment, it being faded and in old-fashioned lettering.

However, when Dick came along that evening we got down to it, to coin a phrase, and managed to roughly decipher the screed as being an explanation of what was in the bottle. This claimed to be no less than an elixir " bye wich a manne may become as a ghoste and floate at will throughout the Worlde, suffering no ill therebye, but preserving all his wittes."

Although obviously not written on the top floor of the Empire State Building, this still sounded like a stall storey—sorry, story— and when Dick said " What about trying it?" I imagined he was joking. (Joe King, of course, is another bloke altogether, and no relation to Nosmo.) However, we took the lid from this beastly, black, bulging bottle and had a quick sniff.

" Har-har," I said, with a sneer (or a jeer, please yourself), " it's only rum." for there was the only too familiar bouquet wreathing across my kitchen—self-contained, with such a lot of clever gadgets (self-advert.). The kitchen, of course, not the rum.

Dick agreed with me as usual, and we thought, " Well, here's the room, choom, and here are we; what are we waiting for?" thus showing our ignorance of grammar by splitting our infinitive just as we intended to split the bottle. Choosing two of my best liquer glasses—well, two cups, if you *must* be correct—we poured a tot into each and drank " good and 'earty."

It was warming and tasty, and I smacked my lips and looked at Dick with a grin. He didn't look too well, funnily enough; somewhat pale and somehow transparent, and as my grin changed to a startled stare he slowly but surely faded to noughts. (No kidding or cooking this time, either!) His cup still hung there in mid-air, like one of those fake photographs, but there was no Dick.

"Wow!" I thought, "wassermatterwidchew?" and gave myself a hasty survey; or at least, attempted to, for I, too, even poor little me, *nearly* the skinniest bloke in Jay, was missing. There I was; I could feel myself, I could see, and presumably I could hear, but where was my bee-yutiful body? "Eh, Dick," I whispered, being as it were much awed, "can you hear me?"

An equally timid voice answered: "Yes, I can hear you all right, but where the dickens *are* we?"

"In the umpteenth dimension, I reckon," I parried, "but how the —well, how are we going to return to normal?"

"Heaven knows," he answered. "Let's read that blinking parchment again.

Being so newly-transposed it was awe-inspiring to see that parchment unroll itself and the two cups float across to keep it from rolling up again as we manipulated the thing. There wasn't a blinking word about an antidote; not one small part of a word which would reprieve us. We spent an hour discussing what we should do, and finally decided to try fresh air. We found great difficulty in negotiating the furniture and all those natty gadgets (ex-self advert.), and bumped into one another several times. Just then my wife came up the front garden.

"Hiya, Pat," I said cheerily. "Wotcher, Mrs. Dee," said Dick in his usual bluff manner, but nary an eyebrow did she stir, never a glance did she give to show she'd heard us.

"Blow me down," said Dick, " she can't hear us, even if we can hear each other!"

Pat had placed her heavy shopping bag on the ground, so, being daring, I walked across, picked it up quite normally, took it in and put it on the kitchen table. Of course, Pat, seeing it sail merrily through the air, gave a yell that rent the echoes. Hastily I grabbed a pencil and a piece of paper and began to write an explanation. When Pat's incredulity and horror had changed to womanly curiosity, she began to follow the swiftly-moving pencil, and gradually the whole ghastly situation dawned on her.

"Can you hear me?" she said, and I wrote: "Yes."

"Well, what are we going to do?" she quavered. "Blowed if I know," I scribbled. And there we were for quite a while, she talking and me writing.

It's three months since that memorable day, and Dick and I are still invisible. The problems we've overcome have been terrific, and poor Pat has nearly been certified several times, explaining to various people where I am.

I'll admit it has its advantages. You can get on a Barkus bus without paying, and visit the Empire for nothing, too, but it's a bit awkward having to wriggle your pencil all the time you're on watch just to prove to Joe that you haven't gone for another break, and it's hard to get Glan to hand over the weekly pay packet to thin air. It's very nice not having to shave or dress before coming to work, but it's a bit hard to find a place in the canteen queue for bacon and beans, especially when Snowy will keep pushing. It's wonderful not having to do the shopping or put the kids to bed, but it's deuced awkward dodging traffic and folk who can't see you.

Taken on the whole it's not too bad, but I can't help feeling sorry for the blokes in Aitch when Dick's on duty!

Anyhow, I expect I'll be haunting you some time. Cheerio!

CQ WOYGIANS

IN the absence of Stan Brister (on leave), I am writing these few notes, which I know, will interest our ex-Woygian "Hams."

We duly received our club licence some six months back, with the call-sign G3BMR, but unfortunately our club-room became temporarily unavailable at about the same time, so we were unable to "get going."

However, we have now got our "H.Q." back again, complete with all the necessary gear, and with our sky-wire hoisted to the top of "Lofty Cook at the far end, we hope to be soon "rattling the cans" of ex-Woyg "Hams" both at home and abroad, so "stick around" chaps, "you may hear summat."

The following Woygians are now active from their own QRAs at Brand Hill Camp (the local QRM factory): Stan Brister, G6AK; Ken Cook, G2KK; Jimmy Collins, G3DCM; Billy Backhouse, G3AON; "Kim" Taylor, G3BBE; and "Skim" Simpson, G3CAA. We also have Mr. Miller, G4MM, who operates from Loughborough.

The "B.A.R.S." entered for the "S.W. Magazine" 1.7 M/c Club transmitting contest last November, under the call of G6AK, and finished eighth out of a total of about 30 clubs. We had a very enjoyable time during the contest, with Major Wort and a few other stalwarts "burning the midnight oil" on the key, and we had some 260 contacts during the week.

We hope to have more to tell you of our activities next time, meanwhile we shall be hoping to QSO ex-Woygian "Hams" so "Wot-sa blokes?"

Vy 73
de TED PETHERS (ex-G6QC),
Hon. Sec. B.A.R.S.

Stop Press News

Miss Marguerite Petrie (ex-Garats Hey) married Mr. Kurt Wiseman (whom she first met whilst in Loughborough) at Southport on Friday, 8th August. They have managed to find a flat in London.

Mrs. Bobby Snare now has a daughter, Susan Jane, born July 5th.

Miss Joan Rogerson, until recently Hon. Secretary of the Association, is about to take up a post as Under-Matron at Maplewell Hall, Woodhouse Eaves, now a hostel for Loughborough College students. The fact that Miss Lorna Galbraith (ex-C.S.M. Admin.) has for some time held a similar position at Quorn Hall, also a Loughborough College hostel, may be taken as more than purely co-incidental! Joan is looking forward to seeing any Woygian members when they are in the district. Joan, by the way, had a pleasant holiday recently at Filey with Ann Kerr.

Another minor re-union was held in the West End of London on Saturday, 15th August, when Dudley Truin, Ralph Champion, Paddy Kelly and Bill Baker met, drank, talked, ate and drank again. Other Woygians who were to have joined them were Alick Berry, detained at work in Nottingham by last-minute developments, "Wilk," who was on holiday, "Mouse," who was visiting his family at Ware, and Bob Yaxley, who wired his regrets from Frome, having landed there instead of Northolt, as expected, from Amsterdam. Ralph Champion is now, by the way, News Editor of the "Sunday Express."

Tony Moseley married Miss Julie Causer (ex-Comm. Wing) recently.

Miss Marguerite Randall, formerly of No. 2 Wing, B Watch, became Mrs. Richard Addiscott, on 19th July. Her address is 34, Coldharbour Lane, Kemsley, Sittingbourne, Kent.

Mr. Jack Colville is now managing a wireless shop in Ealing, London.

One day early in August, Stephanie Saubolle walked into the office in London where Doreen Dodd works. When Doreen looked up and found Stephanie on the client's side of the desk, her astonishment was equalled only by Stephanie's! The inevitable news-swapping followed. Stephanie is hoping to be married in October, but this depends on finding accommodation. As a result of this meeting, Stephanie is now a member of the Association.

Mrs. H. L. Norrie, formerly Miss Heather Brewer, of B Watch, No. 4 Wing, Brand Hill, now lives at No. 2 Site, Skyways Ltd., Dunsfold Aerodrome, near Godalming, Surrey, having moved recently from Bournemouth.

Miss " Bunny " Bunyard, ex-C.S.M. Comm. Wing, who was with WOYG from Chatham days onwards, now works at the British Launderers' Research Association in Hendon, and lives at Hampstead.

A very recent letter from Bill Hayward to Mr. Millhouse gives up-to-date news of several of the "78" which amends some of the points mentioned by Ollie on another page. The Smith brothers, L/Cpl. Antrum, Ray Snell, Fred Pearce, " Tubby " Fagg, Ron Blease and Bernard Norwood (the latter now Cpl. i/c Q Stores) are at Nicosia, Cyprus. Bill Hayward and Chris Barnes are at Famagusta, Cyprus, where Jimmy Dodd is now Sergeant i/c S/R. L/Cpl. Peter Dooge is in Egypt, as is " Curly " Hendley, now L/Cpl. in place of " Googie " Withers, who has left on Liap. Bill says that there are now no BMR lads at Sarafand, and makes wistful (or wishful?) mention of demob. in 6 months' time. He says that it has been *jolly* hot at Famagusta lately.

Miss Nan Brown (No. 2 Wing, A Watch) recently spent a week at Brighouse, Yorks., with Mrs. Kathleen Snell (née Sutcliffe). Kathleen **had** previously visited Nan's home in Dundee, where they had a re-union with Miss Susan Weir and Miss Nan Stewart ("Stewpot" to Hut 3-ites). Susan is expecting to be sent to a Ministry of Labour office in London soon.

A LAST MINUTE REMINDER.—Send your Subscription for 1947/48 and your application for a Re-union ticket NOW. Delay is dangerous!

Printed by The Chandos Press and published by H. Dodd for the Woygian Association.

THE WOYGIAN ASSOCIATION

THE FIRST ANNUAL

DINNER & DANCE

held at

"THE NEW INN"

WESTMINSTER BRIDGE ROAD, LONDON, S.E 1

on

SATURDAY, 22nd NOVEMBER, 1947

Autographs

DANCING

8 – 11.30 p.m.

to

"The Adastrals"

DANCE BAND

+

Light Refreshments
at 9 p.m. approx.

+

PRIVATE BAR – Open to 11.30 p.m.

Menu

Soup

+

Poultry

+

Roast and Creamed Potatoes

Vegetables in Season

+

Sweet

with Ice Cream

+

Coffee

The WOYGIAN

BRIDGEWOODS 1939 CHICKSANDS 1945 BEAUMANOR

Vol. 3   Spring 1948   No. 1

WOYGIAN ASSOCIATION

A GRAND

RE-UNION WEEK-END

WHITSUN 1948 • MAY 15th and 16th

WILL BE HELD AT

BEAUMANOR PARK

(BY KIND PERMISSION OF
Lt.-Col. M. J. W. ELLINGWORTH, O.B.E., D.S.M.)
WITH THE CO-OPERATION OF THE BEAUMANOR STAFF CLUB

SATURDAY, 15th MAY

DINNER & DANCE

6.30 p.m. (for 7) to 12 midnight

INFORMAL DRESS + REFRESHMENTS DURING DANCING + BAR

TICKETS 9/6 EACH

Transport to Quorn, Loughborough and Woodhouse Eaves available at midnight

---

SUNDAY, 16th MAY

BUFFET TEA

4 to 6 p.m.

FOLLOWED BY INFORMAL DANCING

TICKETS 2/6 EACH

Combined Tickets for Both Functions 11/6 each

Applications for Tickets, on the enclosed Form to be sent to the Treasurer, Mr. J. Dodd, at the address shown on the Form, with the appropriate remittance enclosed.

NOTE :— Each Ticket will incorporate an Official Pass for entry into Beaumanor Park; make sure therefore that you bring yours with you and have it ready when applying at the gate to be admitted.

Early application is recommended, as numbers must be limited.

Details of final arrangements are subject to M. of F. approval but it is not anticipated that any major change in the programme will become necessary.

THE WOYGIAN

ASSOCIATION

President :
Lt. Col. M. J. W. ELLINGWORTH, O.B.E., D.S.M.

Vice-Presidents :

Major H. F. JOLOWICZ	Mr. G. M. SPOONER
Jnr. Cmdr. I. F. ROMER	Mr. C. O. SMITH

Chairman :
Mr. H. DODD,
"Col'n-Hurst," 168 Station Road,
Hendon, London, N.W.4.

Honorary Secretary :	*Honorary Treasurer :*
Mrs. P. L. EDMUNDSON,	Mr. J. DODD
27 Wood End Avenue,	82 Newbury Gardens,
S. Harrow, Middlesex.	Stoneleigh, Surrey.

THIS is in many ways a "Re-union" number of the "Woygian"—it includes accounts of the very successful first re-union held in London on 22nd November last, with a reproduction of the photograph taken when we were seated for dinner, and it also contains full details of the Re-union Week-end to be held at Beaumanor next Whitsun. Within these pages you can also renew the acquaintance of old friends of the B.S.M.—Leon de Bunk, and our own chronicler, St. Upid, in a very welcome and appropriate additional chapter to the famous war-time Chronicles. We are also pleased to include an account by Mr. Jimmie Rogers of " what he is doing now," and hope that the example set by him, and by Mrs. Chris. Pendlebury in an earlier issue, will be followed by other members with something interesting to say about their post-war jobs and experiences. This is, you will agree, exactly the type of contribution, apart from news items for Mr. Ollie Pearce's columns, needed to help in keeping the "Woygian" a specially interesting and "live" magazine.

The Whitsun re-union week-end, of which preliminary notice was given in my Christmas letter to members, is now definitely arranged (details are set out opposite), and I am sure that many members will be glad of the opportunity to meet again in the old familiar surroundings. Beaumanor's central position should make it a reasonably convenient rendezvous for members from most parts of the country, though it will, of course, involve travelling. As far as accommodation is concerned, it is felt that many members will have friends in the district with whom they can stay, and for that reason we are not attempting any special arrangements. If, however, you are unable to stay with local friends, we would in the first place suggest that you apply to any of the following as soon as possible : —

Quorn Guest House (formerly the " Old Bull's Head " of A.T.S. days).
Bull's Head Hotel, Quorn.
Manor House Hotel, Quorn.
King's Head Hotel, Loughborough.
Sunnyside Private Hotel, Baxter Gate, Loughborough.
Great Central Hotel, Great Central Road, Loughborough.

There are also, I believe, several Guest Houses in Woodhouse Eaves, and if you have any friends in Woodhouse Eaves, you may be able to obtain their help in booking at one of them. If your applications are unsuccessful, let us know without delay, as it may be possible to make arrangements with the help of certain people at Beaumanor. I would stress the importance of early action in the matter, to save disappointment.

An encouraging feature during the past few months, particularly since the Re-union in November, has been the steady increase in membership—a good augury for the continued success of the Association. I hope that all members will do all they can to bring in their ex-Beaumanor friends who are not already members, in time for the Whitsun Re-union. A note to the Hon. Sec., Mrs. P. L. Edmundson, enclosing 3/6 (1/- Membership Fee, 1st Annual Subscription, 2/6) is all that is necessary to join, and back numbers of the Magazine will be sent to all new members.

My request, in the last issue, to hear from any provincial members interested in a Re-union in Manchester, Glasgow or Edinburgh, met with a response which in itself was not specially encouraging (about a dozen members wrote to express interest in a Manchester function, and about six in a Glasgow or Edinburgh function), but coupled with news received through contacts made since the November Re-union, is sufficient to show that a Manchester and a Scottish Re-union would stand a good chance of success. However, I hope to see many members from the North, and perhaps Scotland, at the Whitsun Re-union, and to have a talk with some of them on this matter, so that we can form some plan for provincial re-unions next winter.

Mr. Millhouse has not yet found it possible to resume as Editor of the "Woygian," but I have again had his help in the preparation of this issue.

The next issue of the Magazine, Summer, 1948, will appear in July or early August. All contributions must be received by June 15th—news items to Mr. Ollie Pearce at Beaumanor, and others to me at Hendon.

The Association's Hon. Auditor, Mr. A. H. Appleton, has recently audited the acounts to 31st December, 1947, and copies of the final accounts will be sent with the Summer, 1948, magazine, to any member on application to the Hon. Secretary or myself.

HARRY DODD,

Chairman.

Through the Looking Glass
By LEON DE BUNK

FRANCHISE

At risk of making ouselves even more unpopular with all those progressive Glaswegian filing-clerks and Streatham typists who so often in the late Era of Romance brought tears and laughter to our dimming eyes, we must again repeat our sad conviction that for all their breathless assimilation of 19th Century Bluebooks, Marxist dialectics, Fabian pamphlets, and P.E.P. Reports, the average British home-girl is not yet up to her cosmic responsibilities; notwithstanding all the earnest lecturing that tousle-headed Blomsbury girls mete out to Middle West cowhands on subsidised tours, the last few weeks show conclusively that Bagehot is still right: a woman loves a Marriage more than a Ministry.

Which makes us wonder a little wryly if there isn't some way, short of actual participation in the suffrage that feminine high spirits could be satisfied. It may be that the girls have too vast an energy: Fashions, Film-Stars,

Cosmetics, Romance and Procreation would be diversion enough for the average male were he capable of the mystico-religious approach that women bring to these subjects. But the girls want the Vote as well. The consequence is an hourly threat of disaster: the existence of a Floating Vote which can be relied upon at any time to go bubbling and gurgling away in response to any old promise of a couple of extra tins of Dried Milk, has produced a state of affairs where no members of the Cabinet dare make a public reference to the British Housewife, without having first instructed the Party Whips to lay on a properly timed outburst of spontaneous cheering from the boys.

The urgent need for the immediate discovery of a new male film-star and/or feminine hair-style will be readily apparent to every responsible thinker present.

JUBILEE

Concurrent with our writing of these soft-sweet numbers falls the B.B.C. 25th Anniversary junketings. In its usual shy, self-effacing fashion, the B.B.C. is only devoting twenty four hours of the day to arch-hystical recollections of that day when Stuxrt Hxbbxrt's braces, strung, in heroic improvisation between the wireless masts at Savoy Hill, alone made it possible for the Basutos of the Upper Zambesi Basin to hear the finish of the 1927 Boat Race; or, alternatively, how the impeccable standards of B.B.C. (circa 1936) in the wording of the Saturday variety programme announcement from " The B.B.C. present Music Hall!" to " Ladies and Gentlemen, Music Hall!"

In our view the honest sociologist may be forgiven if he doesn't quite share the B.B.C.'s extrovert self-satisfaction, but finds himself instead toying with slide-rule and graph-paper in an attempt to assess the average daily incident in heavily populated areas of scurvy and creeping paralysis attributable solely to B.B.C. broadcasts. He will remember sadly the Government White Paper (Cmd. 2496, 1943) giving details of that ugly incident in 1941, when a broadcast of " Workers' Playtime " from a foctory canteen in Heckmondwyke struck down 90 per cent. of the population within twenty miles, twisting infants, adults, and the aged into grotesque attitudes of paralytic agony. Only the bobby-soxers survived unaffected; the slow rhythmic motion of their gum-chewing jaws being the one stable element in a sea of mortal chaos.

TRUAMA

Apropos of schizophrenia, currently, together with Chopin's 24th Prelude and the first ten bars of Rachmaninoff's Second, occupying the undivided attention of film makers on both sides of the Atlantic, we feel that our own experiences in this field might be of interest to the above-mentioned gentry.

Returning by bus one fog-bound night of late from a performance of the films " Spellbound " and " The Seventh Veil," we were much startled when an elderly fellow passenger suddenly turned towards us and asked in quiet tones why the hell, in view of the fact that the ship was on fire, we didn't launch the dinghy. Remembering that to insist upon scholastic logic at such times is ill advised, we said that we'd just given the order, but that trade union regulations wouldn't allow the crew to do it until 10 p.m., and in the meantime, could we please have his name to check the passenger list.

He replied with some fervour that if we, as skipper of the " Beagle," couldn't keep the crew in order—trade union or no trade union—he'd dispatch a full report of the matter to the Admiralty by the first fast sloop available. And that, further, if we who had been dining with him four times a day for the past six months couldn't remember his name was Charles Darwin, we ought to see a psychiatrist at the next port.

At this we began to look round for the conductor—the chap was obviously pretty far gone. We happened to have been Charles Darwin ourselves—for weeks.

THOUGHT FOR TO-DAY

" Wherever there is a creed, there is a heretic round the corner, or in his grave."   A. N. WHITEHEAD.

"What's He Doing Now?"

By OLLIE PEARCE

To most of us a common phrase familiar in the doubtful days, Now as we go our sundry ways, a different meaning it conveys, Remote from that elusive " he," confined instead to you and me, Therefore the word must also be interpreted at times as " she."

ONCE more I must apologise to the writers of those letters which remain unanswered, and convey my thanks to all members who continue to supply me with items of new for this column. I would also like to take this opportunity of thanking the senders of Christmas Cards addressed to the community at B.M.R.

It is with profound regret that we announce the death, on November 7th, 1947, of Adrian Paul, aged three months, infant son of Tom and Chris Pendlebury, to whom we extend our deepest sympathy.

Members will be very sorry to learn that Tommy Hill returned to hospital at the beginning of January. We sincerely hope that he won't have to stay long.

Fred Gardner and Sam Sams have had rather lengthy spells in hospital since our last issue. The former returned to duty just after Christmas but still has several pounds of plaster on his chest, and the latter is convalescing after an operation for the removal of gall-stones. "Topper" Brown went on the sick list with a duodenal ulcer early in the New Year.

We hope it will not be long before they regain normal health.

BIRTHS.

To Mrs. Norman Wicks, née Jacqueline Sarre, in Guernsey, on October 10th, a daughter, Susan Penelope. "Jackie" and her family have since moved to No. 2, Sheldon Road, Edmonton, London, N.18.

To "Di" Brandle, on October 15th, a son, Peter Alan.

To Mrs. Peter Hedgeland, née Margaret Willett, on October 7th, a daughter, Jean Margaret.

To Mr. and Mrs. E. J. Waldron, at Gorseinon Maternity Hospital, on August 12th, a son. "Eddie," of the G.P.O., who served at B.M.R. and B.W., will be remembered for his prowess on the tennis courts.

To Margaret Worrall, née Savage, on December 25th, a daughter, Diana Margaret.

To Mrs. E. B. Williams, née McGlashen, on December 9th, a son, Geoffrey.

To Mrs. McElrea, née Gwen Storey, in Queensland, Australia, during May last, a son, Alan.

To Mrs. Bowman, née "Dottie" Jones, at Chattanooga, Tennessee, on December 28th, 1946, a son, David Noel.

To Mrs. Caruso, née Hilda Brownlow, at Salamanca, New York State, on November 22nd, a daughter, Beverley Jean.

To Mrs. Coppin, née May Wesson, a daughter, Sheila. May also has a small son, Alan, but birth dates are unknown.

To Mrs. Cowell, née I. Jolley, now living at 59, Morley Road, Leyton, London, E.10, on October 8th, a daughter, Isabel Doris.

To Mrs. Jones, née Hazel Webb, early in November, a daughter, Marion Lesley.

Congratulations to all concerned.

MARRIAGES.

Miss Margaret Mary Ellingworth, at St. Mary's-in-the-Elms, Old Woodhouse, on October 11th, to Captain Thomas Hildyard Beaumont, Royal Signals. The honeymoon was spent in London. Margaret is to accompany her husband when he leaves for service overseas in the near future.

Miss Elizabeth Vance, during October, to a Mr. Edwards, one time Naval Cadet stationed in Quorn. Present address: 32, Horsley Road, Chingford, Essex. Betty wishes all old friends a happy and successful New Year.

Mis Joan Elliott, at Crouch End, London, on July 5th, to Mr. Roland Prout. Present address: "Cromwell," May Avenue, Canvey Island.

Miss Mabel Findlow, on June 28th, to Mr. William Bowers.

Miss Bessie Mostyn, on December 20th, to Mr. Ronald Brooks, of Chingford. The honeymoon was spent at Blackpool. Present address: 1, Scholars Road, Chingford, London, E.4.

2392124 Sigmn. V. F. Merritt, at Graz Garrison Church, Austria, on December 20th, to Maria Maurer. Present address: Martenaugasse 47, Graz.

Miss A. J. Kidd is now Mrs. Bennett, and is living at 58, Priory Road, Southpark, Reigate, Surrey.

Miss Joan H. Rogerson (ex "A" Watch) on April 7th last, to Kenneth Anderson, of Sheffield. Phyl Turner also ex "A" Watch, a cousin of the bridegroom, was one of the bridesmaids, and Betty Bicket was among the guests.

Miss Joyce Askew married Mr. Robert Nicholls at St. John's Church, Great Easton, near Dunmow, Essex, on February 7th. The reception was held at the Foakes Memorial Hall, Dunmow, and the honeymoon was spent at Bournemouth. They have since taken up residence in a bungalow at Malden, Essex. The wedding provided on opportunity for "Hut 3, Garats Hey" re-union.

Congratulations and best wishes for future happiness to all concerned.

FORTHCOMING MARRIAGES, ENGAGEMENTS, ETC.

Miss Eileen Hollis, ex "B" Watch, 2 Wing, who is back at her old job in London, is to be married soon.

Mrs. Sockett, née Micky Marshall, is expecting a happy event in May. She has succeeded in obtaining a flat at 39 St. Anns Hill Road, Nottingham, where for the first three months of occupation she and her husband slept on the floor owing to the non-delivery of their new bed. Micky wishes to be remembered to all ex-members of the Sergeants' Mess at Brand Hill.

Miss Phyllis Turner has become engaged to Mr. John Blamire and hopes to be married in July.

Congratulations to all concerned.

OTHER NEWS.

There have been many changes at B.M.R. since the last issue of the "Woygian." All the administrative offices and the Canteen are now situated in the house itself. The old offices and the old canteen (ex-T.P. Rest Room) are affording hostel accommodation for some members of the operating staff, whilst others are domiciled in the upper storeys of the house.

What was once the Officers' Mess is now the Canteen, and the old O.R.'s rest room is set aside for social functions. The offices are situated on the first floor and are approached by way of the "baronial staircase," which, it will be remembered, is overlooked by a large stained glass window.

The official opening of the manor was celebrated with a house-warming party on September 20th last.

During the afternoon, children of the staff took part in races, etc., on the lawn, and after tea in the canteen, were entertained at a nigger minstrel show given by members of the staff in the main hall. The highlight of the afternoon was the visit of the ice-cream man, at which time marshalling of the children became extremely difficult.

In the evening it was the turn of the adults to enjoy themselves, which they did in the accustomed fashion. Judging by the number of unfamiliar faces, there must have been a lot of gate-crashers, but on the whole the party was a great success.

On August 23rd, the coming of age party of Margaret and John Ellingworth was held in the old O.R.'s rest room, and among the many guests were representatives of each department of the group. The room was very tastefully decorated, and the buffet, which must have taken hours of painstaking work to prepare, resembled a series of coloured art plates from Mrs. Beeton's cookery book. Midway through the evening, ice-cream in the shape of a cake was served to the guests, and later, an iced birthday cake with 21 candles was cut by the twins, using the O.C.'s naval sword. An appropriate toast, proposed by Major Wort, was answered by John, who left this country shortly before Christmas, and is now serving in Cyprus.

The next noteworthy event at B.M.R. was the Christmas/New Year Party which was held on December 31st.

On this occasion, the canteen and recreation room were seasonably decorated, whilst the main hall, in which was a huge Christmas tree, was illuminated by coloured lights. The tree was laden with presents for 120 children of the staff, and was lit up by a spotlight from the balcony. About 70 of the children who reside locally, played games during the afternoon, and after tea they were entertained by a professional magician. Then came the distribution of the presents by Father Christmas, a role which was very ably filled by Ted Newmarch at about three hours' notice.

The evening was spent in dancing to the excellent music of a three-piece dance band recently formed by members of the staff, and party games for adults, which caused considerable amusement to participants and onlookers alike. All who were able to attend voted the occasion a great success, even though one of the prizes, a bottle of hair cream, did get mixed up with some of the drinks!

November 22nd, saw the first annual re-union of the Association in the shape of a dinner and dance held at " The New Inn," Westminster Bridge Road. Ninety people attended, and the dining room was filled to capacity. It was a tonic to renew so many old acquaintances, and to see everybody present so obviously enjoying themselves. Great credit is due to the chairman and his committee for putting on such a well-organised and pleasantly memorable function.

The following is a list of those present: Lt.-Cmdr. and Mrs. Ellingworth, Major Wort, Mr. and Mrs. Batchelor, Mr. and Mrs. Harry Dix, Miss Wagon, Mrs. Jessie Reeves, Messrs. Reg. Hilder, Charlie Dobson, Ron Denny, Arthur Barkus, and Mr. and Mrs. "Ollie" Pearce, all of whom travelled down from Woodhouse by Barkus, together with Miss Maud Dunn and Mr. L. P. Jones, who looked in later in the evening.

Major and Mrs. Jolowicz, Mr. and Mrs. Harry Dodd, Mr. and Mrs. John Dodd, Mr. and Mrs. Pam Edmundson, Mr. and Mrs. Dudley Truin, Mr. and Mrs. Paddy Kelly, Mr. and Mrs. Peter Patten, Mr. and Mrs. Miller (née Joan Edgell), Mr. and Mrs. Seal (née Betty Robinson), Mr. and Mrs. Kuhlmeyer (née Avril Wiseman), Mr. Freddie Burgess and Miss K. Starling, Miss Betty Haines and Mr. Smakowski, **Miss Dorothy Swale (from Manchester)** and Mr. Jimmie Rogers, Miss H. M. Kirby and Mr. P. B. Murtagh, Miss Pam Denny and Mr. Guy Charter, Miss Hilda Price and Miss Bond (both from Birmingham), Miss Nan Brown and Miss Nan Stewart (who travelled overnight from Dundee by coach), Miss Susan Weir (also from Dundee), Miss Betty Bicket (from Manchester), Mrs. **Kathleen Snell, Mrs. Mulgrew (née Peggy** Cracknell), Mrs. Gibbs (née Gwen Sidwell), Mrs. Graham (née "Dicky" Jones), Mrs. Earle (née Gladys Webb), Mrs. Wykes (née Joan Bailey), the Misses Beryl Groves, Margaret Jillions, Ruby Day, Lois Seal, Lilian Lederman, Lorna Galbraith, Joan Rogerson, Beattie Thorp, Vera Ballard, Glenys Phillips, Mildred Penn, Olive Spinks, Kay Price, Betty Meadows, Jean Jenkins, Audrey Cruikshank, Hilary Fry, Elsie Knight, Joyce Askew, Betty Colvill, "Billie" Lillywhite, and Eve Dennis, Messrs. Millhouse, **" Wilk,"** Cairncross, Peter

Vannerly, Mick Foy, Peter Dart, "Apple" Appleton, Barber (ex Sgt. A.R.13) John Reid and Brodie Helder (both ex-B.P.) and Major " Jack " Frost.

After dinner speeches were made and appropriate toasts proposed in turn by the Chairman, President, and Secretary.

Telegrams expressing regret at their inability to attend, and best wishes for a successful evening, were received from Pete James, Roy Aldridge, Ron Hyder, Norman Smith, Derek Basnett, Steve Stevens (A.K.), Stan Saunders and Pete Tomlinson at Habbaniyah; Harry Appleton at Dumfries ; Phil Roberts, Pete Kingsland, George Lowes, Norman Obz, Johnny Rastus Hedley, Fred Vickers, Bobby Burr, Cyril Baker, Don Linder, Moggie and Zombie, " in the land of the other end, where, far from the influence of Cornwallis, they listen to the pullets call from the barnyard, the gannets and greenshanks cry from the river, while a lonely vulture hovers above." These were read out by the Secretary, Mrs. Pam Edmundson, who proposed the toast " absent friends." After being photographed, the company spent a most enjoyable evening dancing, drinking, and endeavouring to swap news with as many people as possible in the short time available. Freddie Burgess was in his usual party mood, and did much to keep things going with a swing, especially after he had induced the trombone player to let him " have a go." There was much autographing of menu cards, and "Wilk" was in great demand for his sketches of "A little Bovril," etc.

Towards the end of the proceedings a draw was held and prizes were won as follows : —

Black handbag, Miss Bond; shoulder bag, Mrs. Doreen Kelly; flower ornament, Mrs. Doreen Dodd; box of darts, " Wilk"; box of darts, Miss Joyce Askew; 50 cigarettes, Mrs. Jessie Reeves; 50 cigarettes, unknown; compact, unknown. All the prizes, with the exception of the cigarettes, were kindly presented by Mr. Dudley Truin. The party broke up at about 11.30 p.m., and after some hasty farewells, we went our respective ways, our particular detachment arriving home at about 5 a.m. on Sunday morning, thoroughly worn out, but with the feeling that it had all been worth while.

Twelve months ago, in the daily papers, there appeared an account of the death of one, Margaret Webb, aged 27, who was electrocuted in the bath at her flat in South Kensington. I am happy to be able to announce that this is not the Margaret Webb who was in the A.T.S. at B.M.R. during the war, although a lot of us were under that impression for some months.

Miss Joanna Jones, better known to Woygians as Joan Rees, ex-"A" Watch, Garats Hey, made her stage debut at the Manchester Intimate Theatre last season. She was training as a student actress when, owing to the sudden illness of Miss Jean Forbes Robertson, Joan was called upon to play the important part of Nina in " The Seagull." Although she had never completely rehearsed the part she gave a first-rate performance, to the delight of the audience and the producer, Andre Van Gyseghem. Now a fully-fledged student, Joan is appearing as Rosa in " A Hundred Years Old," by Serafin and Joaquin Quintero. We wish her every success in her future career.

"Mouse" seems quite happy in his new job, but has not yet been successful in finding accommodation for his family, and is therefore back in "digs." He has renewed many B.M.R. contacts in London, including Tony, Julie, and little Simon Moseley, who are living in Streatham, Fred and Kay Staddon, who acted as god-parents to Hazel Webb's (Mrs. Jones) new daughter recently, and Ralph Champion who is now the " Sunday Pictorial's" star reporter at a salary of £2,000 a year. Incidentally, Fred Staddon often sees Freddie Hirstwood, and also saw Lew Owen with his mother, in the vicinity of Waterloo during January.

Kay Price, who was taking a course in shorthand and typewriting, has accepted a part-time clerical job with Pitman's Correspondence College, and has the option of becoming fully employed when her health permits.

George Kenneally left us at the end of August and is now with the B.O.A.C. at Wadi Halfa in the Sudan. Duggie Vessey and John Adam left during September, "Kim" Taylor during November, Paddy Foley in December, and Bert Norris at the beginning of February. The latter now has a clerical job at the Board of Trade in London.

Among recent arrivals are Tom Chapman, "Chick" Last, D. J. Williams and Philip Cooper, all of whom were with us before joining the forces. Incidentally, Tom Chapman got married during January. Some of the "78" are out of uniform, "Tubby" Fagg and Geoff Nicol have been seen in the district recently, and I believe Ted Sandy is also back in civvy street. By the way, Horace Davis, who was forced to resign owing to ill-health, is returning to the fold shortly.

Sgt. De la Bertauche, Cpls. Harry Pope and Jack Mitchell, L/Cpl. Roy Hardy, Sigmn. French, Hodge and Merritt, of 12 Wireless Squadron, R. Signals, British Troops in Austria, are all sweating on demob., and would like to hear from their friends at Hamburg.

Second Lt. le Gassick wrote from India during November, when he was expecting a move to the Middle East. After leaving Harrogate in April, 1946, he went to a pre-OCTU at Wrotham, and got mixed up with a draft for India, where he arrived in July of the same year. He was commissioned in April, 1947, since when he has found life very pleasant indeed.

The only person he has met who is likely to interest any of our readers is a Captain Norman Coslett, an ex-O.C. of the training company at Trowbridge, who is married to an ex-A.T.S. girl. Sandy is anxious to renew his acquaintanceship with Noreen England.

Don Barber and Dennis Brett left Garats Hey recently on demob leave. Hugh Dias is now stationed at Bielefeld in Germany, and after seeing what is left of Essen, Cologne, Dusseldorf and Osnabruck, he says that accounts of the bomb damage there are masterpieces of understatement. He deplores the fact that children have to live under such terrible conditions, half starved, half wild, having barely enough energy to play with a ball when they can find one.

Pete James, writing from Habbaniyah, says there are 18 men in the detachment there, 9 of whom are ex-B.M.R. Their names are published in the account of the re-union excepting for Sgt. "Ticky" Tyler, who is i/c of the section. He should have left for home in October, but seems to have missed the boat.

"Steve" Stevens intends to marry Miss Daphne Osborne of Lenham, near Maidstone as soon as he is demobbed, a couple of photographs of Maurice Reed's sister Margaret, adorn Derek Basnett's bedside locker, and there was some rumour about Norman Smith having become engaged to a young lady with whom he used to be very friendly when at B.M.R., but it seems to have died down lately.

Stan Saunders was made L/Cpl. shortly after his arrival last June. The whole contingent is looking forward to demob in the Spring, in fact, it is their main interest.

Pete James had hoped to attend the re-union, but as "Blighty" leave was stopped, he was unable to make it.

Norman Hendley, who is serving somewhere in the Middle East, has broken his wrist and is, at the moment, unable to write. This should give him a fairly long rest from operating duties.

Miss Phyllis Turner, ex-"A" Watch, Garats Hey, says she couldn't settle down in her old job at Messrs. Boots offices in Nottingham, so took a one year course in Youth Leadership at University College, Nottingham, where she met her fiancé who was a fellow student. She is now Deputy Warden at the Youth Centre in Witney, Oxon, and is looking forward to teaching English in the experimental County College there. Her fiancé is now a youth leader in

Wolverhampton. Phyllis sends her best wishes to all the old "A" Watch gang, particularly those of Hut 2.

Kathleen King, ex-"D" Watch, Garrats Hey, is working at Cable and Wireless in London, and was surprised when Helen Bell arrived there to start work as a typist. Kathleen became engaged last June to a Mr. Ken Taylor, ex-R.A.F. (but not Wymeswold), and like everyone else, she is looking for somewhere to live. She would welcome news of Elizabeth Thomas and Beryl Martin which should be addressed to her at 23 Tantallon Road, Balham, London, S.W.12.

Betty Rose, now Mrs. E. Lambert, has been lucky enough to get a house of her own, but had the great misfortune to lose her baby daughter, Penelope when she was only one day old.

"Maggie" Rees, who spent her holiday in Quorn, says the old place isn't what it used to be, she also says that Nancy Childs (Rundle) now has an infant, but no further details are available.

Hugh Pryse is still busy making films. He recently appeared in "Easy Money," and also one of the Paul Temple series.

Celia Allan is at Washington Hall College, near Chorley, Lancs., and is training to become a teacher. She hopes to specialise in Arts and Crafts, English and History. If successful at the end of the course, Celia intends to apply for a post in the London area. She mentions the fact that Alma Batten is married, but is unable to give any details.

Noel Royle is due for demob in February but intends to stay on until the summer. Just before Christmas he produced Noel Coward's "Hay Fever" in Manchester. The cast were all members of his unit, and the show was a great success. Billie travelled up from Eastbourne for the occasion.

Rene Akeroyd is now a Corporal in a Signals Office at Blacon Camp, Blacon, Chester.

Sara Crawford expects to enter Girton in October to read Economics.

Philip Wade is now in the British Society of Medicine, 1, Wimpole Street, London, and Alan Carr has a job as teacher-cum-curator in Edinburgh. Both were war-time members of the C.R.R. By the way, Philip had a daughter in February of last year.

Betty Luff writes from 22, Brooklands Avenue, Wimbledon Park, S.W.19, where she keeps herself fully occupied with her housework and her "farmyard" comprising one dog, one cat, and eight chickens. She has a daughter, Jane, born on December 26th, 1946.

Betty informs us that Marjorie Wright, ex-"B" Watch, Brand Hill, was married on June 14th, 1946, and is now Mrs. Jones.

May Wilkins, née Stark, and her husband are living at 10a, Ridgmount Gardens, Tottenham Court Road, London.

"Dak" Kirkby has been around quite a bit since leaving Woygland, breakfasting in London, lunching in Malta, dining in Cairo or Lydda, and nipping smartly across the equator, he finds life with Skyways much more lively than at B.M.R. on a Sunday afternoon duty. He has, however, done infinitely more night duty than he ever anticipated. His trips have included Southern Rhodesia, Dar-es-Salaam, Karachi, Baghdad, Basra, Abadan, Damascus, and of course Cairo, which he has got to know fairly well. Since the cholera epidemic Lydda has been substituted for Cairo, but owing to the unrest in Palestine, crews are confined to the airport whilst there. In October he did a two-week tour of Italy taking in all the sights at Milan, Venice, Pisa and Rome, then flying over Vesuvius and Capri. On the return journey he spent a night in Nice and two nights in Brussels. "Dak" has met some interesting personalities in the course of his duties. He was on the plane which brought Elliot Roosevelt from Berlin to London, and was presented with a gold watch by H.R.H. Emir Feisal of Saudi Arabia, in common with all other members of the crew which flew him to Cairo.

Joan Cook has taken the final examination for her teaching certificate, but I do not know how she made out. She recently spent an evening in London with "Dusty" Smith, Jenny Denne, and Ann Law, who is living at "Golden Seal," Tatsfield, Westerham, Kent, and has just become a member of the Association.

Other new members include Miss Alys Crompton, ex-"I" Corps Cpl., living at "Almayar," 18 Sandileigh Avenue, Withington, Manchester 20; Miss Gladys Bunyard ("Bunny"), 2, Lancaster Drive, Hampstead, London, N.W.3, who until recently was the at British Launderers' Research Association, Hendon; and Major Jack Frost, who was at Trowbridge, Sarafand, and India. His present address is "Kingsmead," 8, Clifford Grove, Ashford, Middx., and he sends his kind regards to all who remember him. Incidentally Hilary Fry made his acquaintance in Prestatyn early in the war.

Tony Eeles, ex-I.M. Workshop, is studying for an examination of the Royal Institute of Chartered Surveyors. He is living at "Meltonia," Burton Road, Melton Mowbray, and though quite close to B.M.R., has been too busy to pay us a visit so far.

Miss Susan Weir, ex-"A" Watch, 2 Wing, was transferred from the Ministry of Labour, Dundee, to the Ministry of Works, Victoria, London. She started there on the Monday following the re-union, so her journey from Dundee was one-way. Two colleagues were transferred with her, and she is sharing a bed-sitting room in Ebury Street, Victoria, with one of them. Since moving to London, Susan has contacted Joyce Askew, Doreen Dodd, Pam Edmundson, and Terry Armour, all ex-Hut 3, Garats Hey.

"Exauxiliarilary" achieved fame recently as one of the cast in a 15-minute film on the subject of dancing, which is to be shown first in the News Theatres, then on the Odeon circuit, and subsequently in Australia. She says it was a thrilling experience and she felt quite important, especially as one of the two Max Factor make-up men attending her has the reputation of being the greatest make-up artist in this country.

Mrs. Allen (Peggy Kaye), 12 Plimsoll Road, Finsbury Park, London, N.4, says she is fully occupied these days with household and business duties and has not seen any of the B.M.R. crowd, excepting Joe Cleveland and Tony Moseley, since she left.

Freddie Burgess, writing about the re-union, says: "I never thought during the war years that I should get a thrill in a get-together fight so soon after the war."

He was playing with Dr. Crock and his Crackpots (of "Ignorance is Bliss" fame) before Christmas, has just finished three weeks in panto, and hopes to be touring with Dr. Crock in the near future.

Ex-R.S.M. Hedges ("Tara"), now living at 114, Annington Road, Tamworth, Staffs., sent her best wishes for the success of the re-union, which she regretted being unable to attend.

Miss Jeanne Baker, ex-"B" Watch, Garats Hey, of 18 Sale Street, Hoyland Common, near Barnsley, was bridesmaid at the recent wedding of Miss B. E. Stanton, also ex-"B" Watch. No other details of the wedding are available.

Ginger Talbot has been fortunate enough to get a house, but Tich has been very ill in hospital for a few months. We are pleased to hear that she is now on the road to recovery. Ginger informs us that Snubby Pollard is engaged to be married, but gives no details.

He (Ginger) also met Freddie Bond, ex-"I" Corps, in Bolton, where he is working.

Miss Joan Woollaston is working as a comptometer operator at a steel works in Willenhall, Staffs, and says she is happy at this job which is her second since demobilisation.

Mrs. Muriel McAra is living at 25, Gosford Road, Port Seton, East Lothian, a small fishing village ten miles from Edinburgh where she is hoping to get a house. She now has two children to look after and they take up most of her time, but she is hoping to be able to farm them out at Whitsun in order to attend the proposed re-union at B.M.R.

Chris Wardle, ex-Cpl. Runner, wishes all Woygians the very best of luck in 1948. Her present address is 11, Headlam Street, Newcastle-on-Tyne 6.

Joe Fisher, who is at the Whitehaven Post Office together with Alf Thompson, wrote us a few lines at Christmas time in spite of being up to the eyes in Christmas Cards. He says he has heard from several of the G.P.O. staff who were with us during the war, including Sandy McBurnie, Fred Dickinson, Percy Hooten, Tommy Bancroft, Frank Dadson, Victor McGlen and Joe Bell.

"Mac" McPherson paid us a flying visit this month (February). He is now with the G.P.O. at Bishop Auckland, and Betty Coulthard, ex-"D" Watch, is a clerk in the same office.

Mrs. Walker, née Betty Smith, met Joan Kitson in Liverpool a few weeks ago. After her demob in 1945 Joan joined her husband in Tripoli. She was very interested in what Betty had to tell her about the Association, and has now become a member. Her address is c/o Capt. E. C. Kitson, H.Q., B.M.A., Tripoli, M.E.L.F. (1).

John Reid recently received a small lift up in banking circles, and now has a flat above his business premises in Hare Lane, Claygate, Esher, Surrey. He also has a first-rate garden, and appreciates the advantages of living on the job, especially in the morning when coming downstairs to the office in carpet slippers! He received a food parcel from Forbes Sibley a few weeks ago, but has not heard from either of our other American friends.

Jane Clark writes from Loch Ericht Dam, Rannoch Stn., Perthshire, where she is living a somewhat isolated life with her husband, who works for the Grampian Electric Supply Company. They have a small modern house among the hills, four miles from their nearest neighbour, and 13 miles from Kinloch Rannoch, the nearest village. However, they are quite snug and perfectly contented with the wireless, a good book, and their own fireside. They also have a small car, so civilisation is not completely remote.

"Jay" Johnson was farming for most of last summer, but managed a break of five weeks during which he had a glorious holiday in the wilds of N.W. Scotland, with Jean Murray. He has met several ex-C.R.R. staff lately including Maud Wood, who is a student in Edinburgh, and Ruth Yule, who is a dress designer in London. He also stayed with the Watsons, who have a fairly large house near Ipswich, with four acres of garden. "Jay" tells us that Mary Innes is living at Annat, near Fort William, and is working in a shop.

Mrs. Rowe, "Nutty" of the canteen at Chatham, is working in the upholstery workshop of Messrs. Plummer Roddis Ltd., in Folkestone. She has been there a year now and is in charge of the workroom, with five girls working under her supervision. She is also secretary of the local Savings Club, and although fully occupied is perfectly happy. She wishes all old friends of "Bridgewoods" days a happy and prosperous New Year, and hopes to meet some of them again at Whitsun.

Bob Yaxley is still flying with Skyways Ltd., and enjoying it immensely. He has been to most European cities, made frequent trips to South Africa, and recently returned from a tour of South America. In common with other aerial Radio Officers, he gets plenty of time at home, in fact he only works about 100 hours per month. He wrote me a very long and interesting letter describing his travels, which I regret I cannot deal with more fully in this issue. The most important item of news he had to offer was the arrival of his third son, Bruce, but he didn't say when. Congratulations Bob and Marion, but remember Bath needs more than three for its Rugby team! Another spot of news from Bob was that he met old "Steve" Stephens in Castel Benito. He was homeward bound on a B.O.A.C. plane with a view to taking his wife out to Teheran, where he works on a B.O.A.C. W/T Station.

Miss Margaret Lievesley, ex-"D" Watch, has a most interesting job at the American Consulate in Manchester and really enjoys doing it. She interviews applicants for visas to visit the U.S.A., and attends to the necessary clerical duties. This naturally brings her into contact with all sorts of people including a sprinkling of celebrities. Recently she interviewed Miss Cicely Courtneidge, and the whole cast of the show "Under the Counter," followed a little later by the D'Oyly Carte Opera Company.

Margaret seems to have plenty of time to get around, having visited Mollie Siddell in the Isle of Man, Olga Forshaw at Barrow-in-Furness, and Tomi Thomas at Llandudno.

Mollie is receptionist-cum-secretary to an Air Charter company, Olga devotes her time to household duties and afternoon bridge parties, and Tomi is working in the offices of a dairy machinery factory.

Margaret hears regularly from Aileen Tunnington, who last summer dived fully clothed into the river from a punt which was heading towards a 6ft. waterfall, with her fiancé and two dogs on board. The punt "shot the rapids," but there were no casualties. Aileen had a ten-minute swim before being hauled to safety.

[Continued on page 18

What I am Doing
By JIMMIE ROGERS

THE Re-union Dinner in London a short while ago, brought back several memories, both sweet and sour. (By sour, I mean the separation brought about by war, from our dear ones: SWEET!—the good times we had on the Q.T.—less said the better perhaps! For my part a great deal of pleasure was derived from just seeing and chatting with "old friends" trying once more to drink them under the table. This more or less brings on the topic "What am I doing now."

Well, I am now back in my own Industry, one of helping to bring some amusement into people's lives—FILMS! I am one of J. Arthur Rank's unheard of little men, trying to make an honest copper, honest! My job is that of Technical Adviser in charge of production of 16mm. films, which really means we reduce British films (both features and educational shorts) to home movie size. These films are used by N.A.A.F.I., Road Show Agents, Schools, Ships, and are exported all over the world. They are also sold or hired to all classes of people, but unfortunately, they are still far too expensive for the average working man, let alone the poor Woygian. We are now in the process of producing such excellent films as "LATITUDE AND LONGITUDE," both in Technicolor and Black and White, children's films, purely meant for training, but embodied with a good story in Drama, Morals, Efficiency, Escapism, disguised under Amusement and with perfect educational value. Other subjects are Biology, Physics, Chemistry, Plant Life, Fresh-water Fish and Bacteria, namely AMŒBA, CŒLENTERATA POLYP—far too numerous to mention them all.

Perhaps a little more of where I fit in myself would be of more interest to most folk. I start by searching for material from which to work, i.e., a Master Print, if possible in perfect condition. I then have to decide who or what laboratory could handle that particular job to our best advantage. At the same time everyone concerned in producing the best quality, in sound, picture, quantity, speed are put to work and make their reports, together with physical condition of material at hand which, when compiled, leaves me the task of selecting the best possible method to adopt, to procure the highest quality print.

It is then given to the Laboratory selected by method of quality of past work in the particular field and put into production. Other points to bear in mind are clean competition, speed, prestige, loyalty to one's firm and, of course, one's own advancement, if ambitious.

We have at our disposal some of the finest equipment in the country for producing good sound and facilities to check our work when complete.

We have three small theatres with viewing projectors and on receipt of all finished work, it is viewed and passed, and every copy treated with wax to make its life very much longer.

On receipt of a first copy, the Technical staff involved in the making are gathered together and any faults are corrected, and not until satisfied that the best results are obtained, do we carry on producing the prints required. When this work is complete, the reports are produced, a Technical one which is distributed to all those likely to become connected with the film throughout the building, which enables them to accept or reject when doing their particular job. The other report is of subject and story which is carefully watched in regards to sales and so forth, which goes out of my sphere, being concerned only on the Technical side.

With this work all completed, the finished product is passed over for Library use and from then on the work begins to flow evenly—this, of course, had to be watched all the time for general wear and tear; negatives wear out or get damaged in one way or another, and have to be watched very carefully.

It would be hopeless to try and explain everything in this brief article as there are years of practice and techniques involved.

Well, that is my job now—rather different from life at Beaumanor, but not really a great deal more interesting, as I was one of the lucky ones, having a job with more variety than most of you, and as I said at the very beginning, it had its good points! Or did I?

THE SECOND EPISTLE OF
St. Upid TO THE Woygians

NOW it came to pass that the peoples of Brit knew the rigours of Peace in full measure, even so that they yearned for the carefree days of War. And the mighty hosts of Woyg having dispersed over the face of the land and across the oceans, some even of the Hard Core girded up their loins and adventured into the Outer World.

But notwithstanding their deliverance out of bondage, many among the Woygites, thus departed, desired to Keep in Touch, and to learn the Gen concerning the Inmates and the Outmates. Wherefore they gave alms unto Cornwallis and were henceforth called Woygians.

And the moon rotated exceeding oft, and the seasons came and went; and at uncertain times the parchments of Cornwallis flowed forth throughout the land, bearing unto the scattered hosts the Griff according to St. Oli and exhortations to Cough Up. And oftimes a still, small voice cried in the wilderness: How about a Do?

Now it came to pass a Crisis or so later, in the reign of Kripz, that a new leader arose in the Tribe. For Aridod, even he who exhorted the Nightingales, and was now a merchant in Lon, rose up and beat his breast, crying: How about a Do? And he gathered together certain of the Renegades and they went into a mighty Huddle. And when they had schemed their schemes they gave forth this proclamation unto whomsoever had Coughed Up and were worthy to be called Woygians: Come ye, come ye unto the city of Smowk, and assemble for a mighty Do.

Thus it came to pass, upon a certain day night unto the nuptials of the daughter of the King, that all roads led unto the inn called Noo, which lieth in the shadow of Ben. And the Prophet Osee mounted upon the chariot of Barkus (who forever delivereth the carcase) and, taking with him Missizee and Eswort upon his right hand, and nigh unto a score of Hard Core for whom there was Nil Activity, journeyed down through the wilderness into Spivilization.

And likewise many among those who had cast aside their pencils and their rubbers came also: divers among them from afar off; from the shires of Iawx and Lanx, yea, even from the land of the Scots; and Bang went full many a Saxpence.

Now, the multitude being assembled, and their Whistles being Wetted, the serving-maids appeared and spread a feast before them, even unto five courses, which was the law according to Strachi. And when they had Taken the Edge Off, Aridod rose up and Gripped them; and the Prophet Osee went on a Round Slip. Likewise the maiden Spam exhorted them to consider Absent Bods and spake unto them the words which Peoh and Kablanwylis had borne thither from Ari the fruit man, and from Mogi and Zombi and their tribe in the land of Baor, and from certain others of the Seventy Eight who dwelled night unto Babylon.

Now there appeared before them a certain merchant with his Picture Box. And mounting on high upon a ladder he exhorted the multitude to watch the Dicky Bird. Which was Quite a Change from hearkening for him. And when the merchant had performed, the multitudes retired into a lower chamber for the Odd Noggin. And when they returned, save for sundry who tarried for the Even Noggin, they perceived that the Decks were Cleared and they forthwith Cut a Rug.

Now one among them was Fredi, even he of the Push Pull Amplifier. But because a grievous mischief had been visited upon him he was without his Gadget. For it is written that Fredi and his Push Pull had descended from a certain upper chamber with exceeding great haste; even more quickly than he purposed. Thus, because he had brake his own, did Fredi borrow the Push Pull of Jon, the brother of Aridod. And now he raised it up and gave forth mighty Oompahs.

And there was a certain traveller, Dudli; even he of the Flicks of Luff, who had long cast off the patches from his elbows, and was even blessed with a Homburg. And he came bearing rare gifts, and saith: Let the peoples draw lots for these at one shekel a time or Four for Half a Dollar, that the great Tribe of Woygian may grow rich. And when the peoples saw the gifts they marvelled at them and straightway Fell for It, Hook, Line and Sinker. And the Prophet Osee summoned the maiden Spinx, and, crying unto the multitudes: Get a Load of This, he commanded her to draw forth the Lucky Numbers. And when he called aloud the first Number which she drew, the wife of Dudli cried: Is my face red? For behold, that number is mine. But the Prophet had sinned and committed Faux Pas; for the Number was the Number of another not of the kin of Dudli. Which, peradventure, was Just as Well.

And the moon rose high, and the shadows of Ben grew less; and the night lengthened, and the waters of the publican of Noo grew short; and certain among the multitudes grew exceedingly Unsteady. And accordingly all the peoples joined together their hands and raised up their voices singing: **Olangzyn**.

Thus it came to pass that they called it a Day. And it was indeed a Day. And as they went forth into the night and mounted upon their chariots, they were glad in their hearts. For Aridod had made a prophecy. And the prophecy of Aridod was: Upon the feast of Wit, even in the House of Bo where we suffered our bondage, there shall be another, and better, and greater Do.

A Note from the Hon. Treasurer

WITH few exceptions, every mail delivery since last October has brought me at least one subscription, and with it, most probably, a personal note. As you can guess, I have been unable to reply to every one, but whenever possible I have made an attempt. So those of you who did expect—in vain— a note from me—humble apologies, and please accept my thanks for your good wishes, and also for the news items. The latter I have forwarded to Ollie. And that, by the way, is a suggestion to all who have little time for correspondence. When you post me your subscription, include with it a few lines of news items, either of yourself or fellow-Woygians, with whom you are in contact. I will see that Ollie receives them for inclusion in his column in the next issue of the Magazine.

Amazing as it may seem many of you have sent in a second subscription for this year. This willingness to pay twice is very welcome—but I have played fair! I have carried forward the amounts for the 1948/49 subscription. You can check this on the receipt which should accompany this copy of the Magazine (if you have not already received it with previous correspondence.) Of course, I need hardly say that donations to the funds, over and above subscriptions, are very acceptable and helpful.

I am looking forward to seeing many of you at the Whitsun "Do."

All good wishes,

JOHN DODD.

Die Zweite Vorposten Meldung
By FRED VICKERS

SINCE my last report from here, our brood of Beaumaniacs has increased somewhat. In addition to George Lowes, Zombie, Phil Roberts, Pete Kingsland and myself, the strain has been improved with the addition of Moggy Reed (complete with the usual combination of Briar and Bruno), Norman (67 positions) Johnson, Cyril Baker and Norman Hobbs.

To those of you music lovers who were fortunate enough in the past to attend a recital by Norman Hobbs, I can give assurance that this fine musician's virtuosity has not waned since he played before attentive audiences in "H" Hut during the period of our late exile at B.M.R. His arrangement of " Good King Wenceslas " still has the same tone and flowing movement that he had in those far away days. Moreover, his new setting of " God Save the King " surpasses anything he ever did, and our equivalent of "H" Hut resounds to hearty but well-mannered applause. Of course, his audience is rather different nowadays. Where once a Hobbs recital brought forth the gratifying spectacle of Claud Deakin nearly swallowing his pipe in an apoplectic fit, or a resounding chuckle from Wilk (the latter not quite so gratifying), friend Hobbs now performs before an audience of " Joskins " (translation—soldiers who have seen little service). This, however, does not deter him and he plugs steadfastly on with his complete repertoire of two tunes as mentioned above.

Norman J's "67 Positions" are canvassed around in such the same manner and degree of intensity (which includes the usual "intimate" explanations and diagrams) as they were formerly.

One subject which has received much of our attention is the local language, and we are all linguists of no mean standing, so that, upon being asked by a native the other day, whether we knew what the time was, we were able, after very little hesitation, to answer him with a complete sentence in his native tongue. This sentence, as well as being perfectly pronounced (we had rehearsed it for about two hours just that day), was grammatically, absolutely word perfect. Our answer was "Nein, mein Herr."

Following in the footsteps of the Lew Owen/Ron Smith combine, is one Cyril Maker, ex-O/S Bod. For, like his Masters, Cyril has proved himself to be a master in the art of improvisation. Witness his impressive showing on his latest assignment—the decoration of our large mess hall. Cyril's recipe for this task was as follows: take a few dozen rolls of W.D. toilet paper, drape them attractively around the hall, add a few Christmas trees and, lo and behold, the job is done. The successful completion of this job earned for Cyril a hearty round of applause from the whole unit, including the C.O.

The military authorities do not seem to appreciate the sterling worth of James T. Hewson, or perhaps they have concluded that one "Monty" at a time is enough for any army. However, don't worry unduly, Jimmy, Robert Helpmann seems to be making quite a good living out of your chosen profession and we can certainly do with two Helpmanns.

It occurs to me that Noel Royle is going to encounter some difficulties in the future. How is he going to preach "freedom for the working class" when he himself is a particularly outstanding blossom on the army's class distinction tree? Losing such a fine champion of the cause of us men in the street is a hard blow and I am sure you will all join me in the shedding of a silent tear for the passing of our great leader into the ranks of the privileged classes. (Sounds of weeping off-stage and the slow majesty of the "Internationale" followed by the firing of a hundred-gun salute simultaneously from the Yorkshire Moors and Ipswich)

Well, that is the lot for the present, so cheerio.

"What's He Doing Now?" *continued*

Bobbie Snow spend her time at home coping with domestic duties, and has occasional scheds with Marjorie Dancey and Margaret Rees. Bobbie and Marjorie spent their summer holiday together in Jersey.

Margaret Worrall, née Savage, wrote me quite a long letter containing a detailed account of the disorganisation which has occasioned in her household since the advent of Diana Margaret, and foresees a similar upheaval in the routine of Mabel Bowers, née Findlow, who is expecting a happy event in April, and has been working in an office as well as in the house, and doing the shopping.

The latest innovation in the social life of B.M.R. is "Overseas Night," the first of which took place on February 11th, when ex-Sarafand members of the staff competed with those who had served in other stations abroad, for what has been named the "Beaumonti Shield." The occasion was reminiscent of a feature in the life of 2 W/T Company in bygone days when its members competed regularly with the Palestine Police for a similar shield. The name "Beaumonti" is slightly different from the original, which was phonetically the same and was borrowed from a brand of local beer.

The competition, indoor games and a pint-sinking relay race, was won by the ex-Sarafands, who hold the shield until the next meeting, due some time in March. The evening finished in traditional style with the singing of all the old songs associated with overseas units.

Well, that's about all the news, folks. Cheerio for now, see you at Whitsun.

THE RE-UNION AT THE "NEW INN" LONDON, S.E.1

on 22nd November, 1947

Photograph reproduced here by permission of Horne's Photo Press, 284a Pentonville Road, London, N.1, from whom copies may be obtained, price 5/- (10in. by 4in.) and 7/6 (15in. by 5½in.) post free.

Printed by THE CHANDOS PRESS, *Edgware, and published by* H. DODD *for the Woygian Association.*

The WOYGIAN

BRIDGEWOODS **1939** CHICKSANDS **1945** BEAUMANOR

VOL. 3   AUTUMN 1948   No. 2

An Earlier Summer

The English summer with all its rigours has set in, as somebody once remarked, and, as the rain splashes endlessly on, it is not unnatural that the thoughts of some should wander away to a year ago.

Those ex-Woygites who found themselves in Cyprus will be left with a host of memories, pleasant as well as unpleasant. Each will have his own, and mine, already jumbled into the drawers with neglected photographs, letters and diaries, seem dusty and remote. Yet some come back.

Memories of the long days of sunshine and great heat, of bathing in the royal blue Mediterranean, of the ancient churches of Famagusta, of Bill Hayward arguing with all comers into the small hours of the morning. Of Bellapais Abbey and the ruined castle of St. Hilarion in the summits of the purple Kyrenian Mountains, of "Curly" Hendley after the demob party, Ron Blease's gay shirts, our camp at Famagusta flooded and muddied by winter storms, John Ellingworth as Orderley Officer, the colourful peasants with their mules and donkeys, the old ships from the fishing ports, mountain sheep and armies of goats, cheerful talk and endless chatter. Of the Gothic cathedrals of Famagusta and Nicosia, now used as mosques, the countless little windmills that watered the plain, Winter Sports at Troödos, Barnabas' Salamis and Paul's Paphos, the broken stones that were once the Temple of Venus, Paul Antrum and the camp cat eating the night-duty fish ration; of little cafés, black coffee, wines and the inevitable egg and chips, of oranges and many other fruits, but mostly oranges, the Turkish bazaars and oriental pageantry of parts of Nicosia, fantastic twanging music from the scores of Scheherezade, a solitary cuckoo in the forests of the mountain foothills, the little English church in Famagusta, night duties, fatigues, blancoing and loud-mouthed sergeant-majors.

Finally, of a boat that came to take us away, of the perilous journey on a landing craft, and of Cyprus slipping away into the night. The little island had again become a dim rock on the skyline, and, later, just somewhere on the map.

Better, perhaps, to put them back in the drawer, with their dust and yellowing photographs. But let nobody say the army gave him nothing at all!

CHRISTOPHER BARNES.

The Beaumanor Re-Union

During the Whitsun week-end, we who linger on in the place which to so many Woygians is now but a distant memory, were blessed with a brief foretaste of glorious summer weather. Beaumanor Park presented a most pleasing spectacle with its abundance of rich foliage and its lawns spreading like thick green carpets on either side of the path leading from the house to the fountain which sparkled in the brilliant sunshine.

Such was the setting for the second Woygian re-union which commenced early on Saturday evening with a gathering of the clans in the main hall and, inevitably, at the shrine of Bacchus.

Before going to the canteen (formerly the Officers' Mess) for dinner, a photograph was taken of the group outside the front entrance of the house. At 6.30 p.m. nearly 150 members and friends sat down to an excellent dinner prepared by Mr. L. P. Jones and the canteen staff. The menu was as follows:— Tomato Soup, Cold Chicken and Ham, Green Salad and New Potatoes, Ice Cream, Buttered Rolls and Coffee. After short speeches by the Chairman and President in turn, the company adjourned to the library (which is now used exclusively for social functions) where dancing, drinking and reminiscing ensued until about 12.30 a.m.

As the original list has been mislaid I cannot claim 100% accuracy, but the dinner party looked something like this:—Lieut. Cmdr. Ellingworth and Mrs. Ellingworth, Major and Mrs. Wort, Mr. and Mrs. Harry Dodd, Mr. and Mrs. John Dodd, Miss G. Dodd, Mrs. Pam Edmundson, Mr. and Mrs. Dudley Truin, Mr. Les Hadler, Mr. and Mrs. Bob Roberts, Mr. and Mrs. Alec Keenlyside, Mrs. L. P. Jones and her niece Doreen, Miss Wagon and her friend Miss Tyler, Mr. Cairncross, Miss Betty Bickett, Mr. Pete James, Mr. and Mrs. Ray Snell, Mr. Hugh Dias, Miss Nan Brown, Mr. Harry Appleton, Mr. Tom Chapman, Mr. and Mrs. Bernard Norwood, Mr. Norman Hobbs, Miss Glenys Phillips, Mr. "Chick" Henbest, Mr. and Mrs. "Ginger" Talbot, Mr. and Mrs. Pete Gardner, Miss Knight, Miss Flackfield, Miss Edna Timon, Mr. Peter Hart, Mr. Norman Hendley and two friends, Mr. Phil Cooper, Mr. Ron Hyder, Mr. Horace Davis, Mr. and Mrs. Geoff Nicol, Mr. and Mrs. Ron Blease, Mr. Lew Owen, Mr. Chris Barnes, Mr. Howard Jellings, Mr. and Mrs. George Reeves, Mr. A. Walton, Miss Freda Smith, Miss Joan Rogerson, Miss Lorna Galbraith, Miss "Red" Yalden, Miss Ruby Day, Mr. and Mrs. Ernest Siddells, Mr. Jimmy Rogers, Mr. and Mrs. Glanville, Mr. and Mrs. "Jock" Miller, Miss Elsie Everett, Miss Howard, Miss Willcock, Miss Newell, Miss Heald, Miss Charter, Miss Digby, Miss Marjorie Burton, Mr. A. Bennett, Mr. Reg. Hilder, Miss Mary Innes, Mr. and Mrs. Alf Main. Mr. A. H. ("Appie") Appleton, Mr. and Mrs. Ball, Mr. Blundell, Mr. and Mrs. Hives (well known to several of our younger male members), Miss Celia Hives, their daughter, was unable to attend the dinner but came in time for the dance. Mr., Mrs., and Miss Callaway, Mr. Fred Hearn, Miss Betty Meadows, Miss Audrey Cruickshank, Miss Margaret Bruce, Mr. N. L. Smith, Mr. Dan Hawkins, Miss M. Bennett, Miss Jean Jenkins, Miss Vera Ballard, Mr. Tony Eeles and Miss Fisher, Mr. and Mrs. Jack Morton, Mr. Pete Vannerley, Mr. "Topper" Brown, Miss Thomas, Miss Forshaw, Mr. Bench, Miss Lievesley, Miss McEntyre, Miss Snow, Mr. and Mrs. Preston, Mr. Taylor, Miss King, Miss Muriel Dick, Miss Winnie Teasdale, Miss Olive Spinks, Miss Joan Dadswell and her sister, Miss Joan Priestnall, Mr. and Mrs. "Ollie" Pearce.

Several other people attended the dance among them being Mr. and Mrs. C. O. Smith and their daughter Joy.

Unfortunately, the original programme for the evening which had been arranged by Mr. Harry Dix, had to be abandoned owing to his unavoidable absence. His daughter, Ann, was suffering from scarlet fever at the time and he was in quarantine, but Mr. Lew Owen volunteered to deputise as M.C. at a moment's notice.

Mr. Dudley Truin again very kindly provided the prizes for a draw in which Miss Wagon, Mrs. Pearce and "Chick" Henbest won handbags. I am unable to give details of the other prizes or names of the winners as I was very busy when the draw took place. One telegram, in characteristic style, read as follows:—" Woe is me that I am not come forth but my shekels are weighed and found wanting. Greetings O friends, let there be a heck-uv-ado. St. Upid."

On Whit-Sunday afternoon most of those who were at the dinner returned for a get-together and buffet tea in the grounds, and several people who were unable to attend on the previous evening took advantage of the opportunity to renew old acquaintances. Among them were Mr. and Mrs. Greenwood who came down from Yorkshire, Mr. and Mrs. J. H. Mulgrew, Mr. and Mrs. Gerry Dalton, Mr. and Mrs. "Duc" Downer, Mr. and Mrs. Hicks, Mr. and Mrs. Victor Hartill, Ted Newmarch and numerous others. The main feature of the afternoon session, particularly from the feminine point of view was the presence of members' offspring, and much interest was centred around some of the latest models.

In the evening the bar was re-opened and music for dancing was supplied by gramophone pick-up, but as most of the visitors had rather long journeys ahead of them, the proceedings did not continue much beyond 9 p.m.

Our thanks are due to the organisers for once more affording us the opportunity of meeting old friends, talking over old times, and exchanging current news.

I end this account of the re-union on a sad note. Many members who sojourned in the vicinity of Woodhouse Eaves will remember Fred Walker. To those who frequented the Pear Tree, Fred was an institution, and all who were at the dinner will recall the cheerful figure in a white jacket who attended to our liquid requirements.

I am sure that all who knew him will be most sorry to learn that he passed away on Saturday, July 17th, at the age of 60. He had been far from well for a long time, and his death was due to Cirrhosis of the liver.

OLLIE PEARCE.

"What's He Doing Now ?"

To most of us a common phrase familiar in the doubtful days,
Now as we go our sundry ways, a different meaning it conveys,
Remove from that elusive " he," confined instead to you and me,
Therefore the word must also be interpreted at times as " she."

AFTER three years of excellent work for the Association, Ollie. now weighed down by many additional duties. has decided that the time has arrived for him to take a rest. I'm sure all of you will join in thanking him for his great help in getting the magazine on its feet, and will look forward to hearing more of him in future days. Certain it is that nobody feels his departure more acutely than I, who have now to discover how and where Ollie collected such a wealth of facts and figures about you all. Having read through his vast effort in the last issue I sat despairing before a typewriter, staring at the neat heading. " What's he doing now?" wondering if the machine would answer, and after resisting the temptation to state finally that " he's doing nothing," I set about recording what now follows. Ollie's little verse has been left in it's original position and form, partly so that Ollie will still be remembered and partly so that you may realise that this is intended to be the same column.

BIRTHS (lamentable lack of same).

To Mr. and Mrs. Roy Fullagar, a daughter, Anne Patricia, on Saturday the third of July. Pat was formerly Pat Hughes, and most of you will remember her as a diminutive switchboard operator.

To Mr. and Mrs. Bert Norris, on July 12th, a son, name at present unknown.

To May Knight, ex-C Watch Garats Hey, on June 2nd, a daughter, Gillian Dinah.

To Hilda Gee, formerly of C Watch, Garats Hey, twins, reported to have been born in Stockport. This item of news has a certain vagueness about it, but I trust that if it is true she will accept our congratulations together with those above.

MARRIAGES.

Miss Joan Morley, formerly of C Watch, Brand Hill, on the 10th of July, to Mr. Stewart Thorburn. Unfortunately the place of the ceremony is unknown, but the bride wore a two-piece suit of blue, with flowers and veiling in her hair. After honeymooning in Scotland they will depart for Khartoum in the autumn, where Joan will be able to help her husband in his laboratory.

Miss Maud Dunne, well known to all who used the canteen, was married to Mr. Tommy Creber on May 3rd, at Barrow Register Office. The honeymoon was spent in London. Maud still works in the canteen, and Tommy, who is an operator, can often be seen, lending a husbandly hand.

Best wishes for the future to these lucky people, and I trust Woygians will be considerate enough to arrange more weddings for the next issue.

ENGAGEMENTS.

Jane Harvey, ex-C Watch, Garats Hey, is at present at Station X, and is getting married next Easter. The name of the future husband and any details concerning the event are at present unknown.

Betty Digby, ex-D Watch, Quorn, will fly to India soon to be married, but again no further information is available.

Susan Weir, ex-A Watch. Garats Hey, has become engaged to Mr. R. D. Deayton. Susan is at the Ministry of Works, in London.

Kay Statham is to be married on September 1st. Her future husband is a market gardener in Essex, and Kay is very fortunate in having a home ready for her. Pretty good hunting.

Ron Hyder, once more back at the old place, will be married on December 18th, to Miss Gwen Ward of Aldringham, Suffolk, who has recently been demobbed from the WAAF. Later they will live at Ron's former billet in Woodhouse Eaves.

Curly Hendley, also back again, intends to marry Miss Betty Mehegan, of Merthyr-Tydfil, but at present will not divulge any detailed information. Many ex-Signal bods will remember Betty in the ATS at Shenley.

Yet another venturer is Ted Sandy, who has become engaged to Miss Marjorie Brett, of Ham Street, nr. Ashford. Ted, recently returned from SEAC, where he served as a Lieutenant, has not rejoined the group, but has gone back to his previous job in a Maidstone bank.

Congratulations to all those mentioned above.

GENERAL NEWS.

There have been several more events of interest at Beaumanor, since the last issue, the most notable being the general return of the '78' from the forces. They came singly at first, then later in batches of six or seven, until at the end of May it was possible to see familiar faces on every watch. Nearly forty have returned and the total list of re-instatements is as follows:

  December—Tom Chapman, Dave Williams, Phil Cooper.
  January—Chick Last.
  March—Geoff Nicol.
  April—Bobby Burr, Harry Pope, Bill Hayward, Jimmie Purdie, Duc
      Downer, Bing Bingham, Roy Hardy, Roy Ward, Curly Hendley,
      Norman Johnson, John Duly.
  May—Norman Rees, Roy Aldridge, Roy Fullagar, Bern Norwood, Ron
      Hyder, Stan Saunders, Rastus Hedley, Steve Stevens, Don Linder,
      George Lowes, Moggy Reed, Pete Tomlinson, Norman Smith,
      Johnny Hodge, Paul Antrum.
  June—Zombie Knott, Smiler Smith, Fred Pearce, Bookie Bartlett, Pete
      Gardner.

Apart from these Horace Davis returned after his long illness and now seems to be in good health again. He tells me he made quite a bit of spare cash while in hospital by making and selling rugs and backing the right horses with the profits. Lucrative as it may have been, however, Horace is glad to be out again and is at present enjoying himself in the wilds of Darlington where he is engaged on out-station duties.

Underground OBZ writes to say that he is an in-patient at the University College Hospital, London, and that he will be rejoining the group when he is fit again. Hurry up and get well again, OBZ; we hope to see you soon.

Chick Last and Zombie Knott did not stay long with us this time. Chick is leaving in June to go to D.W.S., and Zombie a fortnight after his arrival to join the Kent County Constabulary. The best of luck to them in their new jobs.

Many of the returned bods are living in the House and many horrors are seen in that ancient place, the most shocking by far being Moggie Reed's bow tie, worn with a red spotted shirt and brown corduroy trousers. Then there is Johnnie Duly's remarkable moustache and Paul Antrum. Paul, by the way, has issued a statement in which he says that severe action will be taken against anyone who dares to address him as the Weasel. Apparently he decided, as a L/Cpl., to free himself from undignified titles and the familiarities of his subordinates. Anyway, beware of the Weasel.

For the rest, many fellows have been married since they left for military service and are now busily trying to settle down in rooms. The housing scheme has not developed further, but many people are looking forward to the happy day when they will move to Woodhouse Eaves.

An event of great importance was the Woygian Reunion which was held at Beaumanor at Whitsun. It was a two day party, starting with a dinner and dance on the Saturday and following with a tea dance on Sunday. The weather was more than kind and tea on the lawn with the fountain playing was very peaceful and pleasant. I'm sure many found it that way after the strenuous excitement of the previous evening. As I believe a full account of the occasion is being prepared for this issue I'll say no more now except to express the hope that many more reunions may be held in the future, and I'm sure that you hope so too.

Pete James, 84 Hersham Road, Walton-on-Thames, Surrey, is one of the "78" who has decided not to return although he often misses the company he has been used to for so long. At present he is employed by The Package Sealing Co., Ltd., of Acton, as a tool salesman. He says its a bit wearing on the feet and doesn't seem to be very profitable. In his letter Pete says " the only drawback is the pay " and explains that his commission for the first week came to 12/- and his expenses to 12/4½ making a loss of 4½d. However, he's quite optimistic and feels sure he'll do better when he has made more contacts. He should think of trying Fallowfield where, I believe, he has a greater incentive to work hard.

Of the others who haven't come back, Ron (Shaker of Shakejack entertainments) Smith is trying to make both ends meet in a butcher's business in Rochester, and Lew (Jackson) Owen is with a firm selling American washing machines. Pete Kingsland is with the Marsham Tyre Co., at Maidstone, and Jimmy Hewson is 50% of the office staff of a Rochester plastics firm. He tells us he is in charge of the firm's advertising.

Phil Roberts, at one time rival of Derek Basnett and Pete James for the hand of Moggy Reed's sister, Margaret, has taken to insurance and is in the same Rochester office as Den Brett. They probably spend much time gripping about the Harrogate days.

A letter from Chris Barnes gives the news that Ron Blease and Reg Cecil (late of Ernie Bevin's Underground Movement) are with him on a course at Bletchley, and that Ginger Catchpole, who left Beaumanor in April, and Dosser Dawes are nearby with D.W.S. Desser and his wife. Madge, are fortunate in having a cottage not too far away from the station. They recently spent a week-end in Loughborough and are hoping to be back for another short break soon.

Vera Ballard, ex-T/P Staff, writes from 1 Walker Street, Warrington. Lancs., to say how much she enjoyed the Reunion, and to express the hope that future ones may also be held at Beaumanor. It is understood that Vera is leaving before the end of the year to stay with relatives in Canada.

In a long and interesting letter, Heather Norris (née Brewer) says she is living in a caravan (not the first ex-Woygian to do so) on the edge of the airport at which her husband is working. She says that electricity is on tap, making life there a simple and comfortable business, and she is lucky enough to have bathing facilities on the spot. The only addition to the family so far is an English Springer Spaniel who keeps Heather busy most of the time taking him for walks. She also says that she hears occasionally from Hazel Ormrod and Beryl Groves both of whom became engaged last year (to whom is at present unknown), and from Lizzie Redpath who has suggested a holiday together in Sussex. In March, Heather met Joan Miller (née Edgell) in London and they hope to spend a week-end together sometime in August. Heather's address is No. 23, No. 2 Site, Skyways Ltd., Dunsfold Aerodrome, Nr. Godalming, Surrey. She sends good wishes to all Woygians.

Pamela Hooton, formerly of B Watch, Brand Hill, has been getting around quite a bit. Last year, with Moira Clarke and another friend, she hitch-hiked across France and spent a couple of days in Switzerland before returning home. She must have enjoyed it because she intends to have a similar holiday this year. Last time she was seen she looked very well and happy, and seemed to be enjoying her duties as secretary to the Air Correspondent of the Daily Mail.

Pat Fullager gave up her job as an S.B.O. in March in preparation for the birth of Anne Patricia whose arrival has been recorded.

Connie Nicol has also given up her T.P. job for much the same reason.

Ann Gardner, wife of Purity Pete, remains with us on T.P. work, but as Geoff and Peter had so much in common in their Army days (both were on extremely soft jobs in Istanbul), it is quite likely that they will keep together now. Peter has put on plenty of weight in the last couple of years and it seems that his Turkish Delight certainly agreed with him.

Since the last issue, Commander Ellingworth has again become a Grandfather with the birth of a son, Timothy, to his eldest daughter, Joyce, who lives at Southbourne.

Margaret, who was married in October of last year, has recently flown to Germany to join her husband.

Seen recently on the beach at Bournemouth were Joan Pusey and her small offspring, and Tony and Julie Mosely with young Simon. Tony is still playing with the Debroy Somers band at the Prince of Wales Theatre

Mr. and Mrs. Siddell with Ann ($2\frac{1}{2}$) and Jane ($1\frac{1}{2}$) are off to Canada. Irene will travel later than her husband, who is believed to have gone in July. Sister Joy is still here as an S.B.O.

Joyce Pope is now a typist in the group office, and Elsie Everett who was a L/Cpl. on D Watch, Brand Hill, is now a civilian T/P operator. She spent some time as an S.B.O. with the N.F.S. in Leicester.

Ex-C.S.M. Red Yalden is now employed in the office of an Aircraft Factory at Farnborough, Hants.

Joe Cleveland left Beaumanor in June to commence duties at Stn. X and Wally Ratcliffe left at the same time for new life. Joe was fortunate in getting a flat in Harrow where he is now living, and when he came back for a brief visit, he seemed well pleased with his new situation.

Johnny (Lord John) Godfrey chose Stn. X in preference to a return to Beaumanor, and is now efficiently answering the phone at that establishment. Fortunate S.B.O.'s sometimes hear his mellow voice at this end.

Gussie Whatmough, who met Commander Ellingworth at Southbourne, has married a Vicar but which one or where I know not.

Ex-runner Margaret Bruce, writes from 25 Kingtree Avenue, Cottingham, Nr. Hull, to say how much she enjoyed the reunion, and wishes to thank all those who helped to make it a success. She says it was good to see the old familiar faces: I imagine she has a close memory of the old familiar face of Pete James.

" Jay " Johnson, ex-CRR, is doing forestry work in the wilds of Scotland.

Exauxiliaryilary recently appeared in a ballet and mime show given by members of the Dancing Academy which she attends, at the 20th Century Theatre, Notting Hill, W. London. It will be a sad day when news of Hilary doesn't appear in the magazine.

Somewhat different news comes from Muriel Dick, ex-C Watch, Brand Hill and Garats Hey, who suffered a great loss on the death of her mother, and who now has to look after the family. I'm sure everyone will wish her the best of luck for the future.

Word from afar brings news of American friends, Forbes Sibley and Mac McGeachey. Forbes is studying for a degree in chemical engineering at Michigan University. He and his wife hope to be able to come to Britain in the not too distant future.

Mac is teaching at Davidson College, North Carolina, and at the time of writing (June) was sweltering in a heat wave with the temperature over 90 degrees. (We might mention, Mac, that we here have had a steady heatwave, too; the last part of July was the hottest for many years.) Mac says he enjoys reading news of Beaumanor and of old friends in the Woygian.

Both Forbes and Mac express their regret that it was not possible for them to be at the reunions but they assure us they attended in spirit.

It is understood that Noel Royle (now a civilian but lately a Lieutenant in the Pay Corps) fell into the sea while boating at Bournemouth and ruined his uniform. Noel is a notoriously bad letter writer, which accounts for the fact that details of his present position are somewhat vague. I can only suggest that he might be tramping the Yorkshire Moors, or sitting in the " Swan " at Delph trying to find out what other people see in Daddy Wordsworth.

Alec Berry, now with the Nottingham Gas Co., was in Loughborough a short time ago.

"Molly" Morgan, of " Shack Teas " fame is still with BOAC, but there is no clue to his present whereabouts. Possibly fitting in with this is the fact that Sam Murgatroyd, who sometimes cheered the good man's lonely hours, has not been heard of since he arrived home from Gibralter in April.

Big Bill Baker, the chap who stood beside Churchill in many a grim battle, is running a taxi business at Westgate-on-Sea, where he lives (6 The Courts).

Wally Cecil has a stores job at Rochester, and Spike Forster is working for the Rochester Gas Co.

Olive Spinks, in a very welcome letter, gave the news of the weddings of Joan Morley and Kay Statham, and tells of regular C Watch meetings at the Coventry Street Corner House on the first Wednesday of each month. Those present at these meetings include Joan Dadswell, Kay Price, Ithan Timms, Sara Crawford, Joyce White, Sylvia Stevenson, Ivy Walton, Yvonne Bams, as well as the two already mentioned. Olive achieved two ambitions last year, one to be in Paris for Easter and the other to spend New Year's Eve at the Chelsea Arts Ball.

She sends salaams to all Woygians and especially to the Sabians.

Since he left Beaumanor, Capt. Burgess has travelled far and seems to have enjoyed his many experiences. Towards the end of the war he was with a mobile recording unit, of which Gordon Crier, the well-known B.B.C. producer, was a member, in Brussels, and made records of troop shows. At the end of hostilities he moved to Hamburg and became a talent scout and audition officer at an Army broadcasting station.

After Demob he accepted a temporary job with the Foreign Office, and spent a very pleasant year in Iceland in charge of visas. The main drawback there, he says, was the cost of living which was four or five times as high as that in England. Eventually he transferred to Amman in Transjordan where he is still in charge of cypher and archives. During the Palestine crisis, Capt. Burgess had more work than he could comfortably cope with and he was often working at midnight.

At another time, however, he found the opportunity of taking a motoring holiday between Amman and Beirut, during which he sampled the pleasures of Eastern cabaret, finding it to his taste but rather expensive.

Norma Domina (née Isaacs) has hit the headlines recently (English Bride . . . American Beauty) in the American periodical, *Ladies Home Journal*. Several pages are devoted to the story of her life from the day she came to Quorn as a wireless operator up to the present, and there are many pictures of her, her husband and their baby, John, at their home in California, where they have a Chinchilla farm. After carving through the usual heavy "blurb," it is possible to deduce that the Dominas are very happy. Certainly Norma has a lovely home and an expensive wardrobe, and seems to enjoy experimenting with the American way of life.

Derek Basnett has started work at the Bank of England. He gets home to Rochester at the week-ends and was recently met by Ron Hyder in Chatham.

Hwfa Price is at present playing in "All My Sons," at the Globe, Haymarket. Jack Colville is still with Frays at Hammersmith.

That is all the news available this time. It would be greatly appreciated if, in some odd moment, you would let us know what you are doing and how you are getting on with life. Even if you think it is not worth mentioning there is usually somebody who would like to hear about you.

Cheerio for this time.

DUC.

Again the Digby's

"YOU know, Joanna," said Steve's sister Gillian, " it's nearly four years since you inflicted on us your unruly brood, and the affable bogy who is my brother and your husband. We're a long-suffering lot, we Beaumanorites (or Woygians, as we now are) but there are things that you *must realize*." The voice was accusing. "I didn't know it was so long," I countered feebly. "And what must I realize, anyway?"

"In April, 1944, we first had to endure those three brats," declared my sister-in-law, "Judy's fourth birthday. Susan was six, and Gilly was two. And where are we now?"

"Well, where?" I asked.

"In exactly the same place," was the retort. "As far as your writings are concerned, Time has stood still. We still hear about their veriest infancy. Presumably they aren't like Peter Pan, and *have* grown older. Well, what about them?"

"Oh," I answered, "Oh yes. Well, I really can't tell you very much about Susan these days. She's at Boarding School now, you understand. I only see her in the holidays, and then she won't talk of anyone but her music master. He's bald, and he lisps, but Mr. "Thmith" is the one man in her life. Incidentally, we're going to have her take up music seriously if she goes on having such a bent for it—and if she wants to, I mean."

"These embryo passions—" murmured Steve's sister, wiping her chin. "Well, what about Judy then? She's nearly eight now, I suppose?"

"Yes," I answered. "But you wouldn't know her, Gillian. She's *changed* so. She used to be such a fat, engaging little bundle, with a lot of coppery curls, and now she's all gawky and leggy, like a half-grown colt. And heaven knows if her hair will ever grow curly again—if it ever grows at all, that is. A wretched child at school cut it all off last week and Judy encouraged her to cut it even shorter. And she's awfully stupid at her lessons —especially maths. Do your remember how she couldn't understand a bead-frame?"

"She takes after her mother in that, then," remarked Steve, suddenly sauntering in. "But of course, she won't find such a marvellous husband as her mother did, will she?"

"Conceited beast," remarked Gillian to her brother. Steve ignored her.

I reached for my mountain of mending. "No dear," I answered tranquilly. "But there—at the moment she doesn't care for your type. She wants either a Pirate or a Piano-tuner, she tells me."

"Oh well," commented Steve, failing to find his pipe in his pocket and sauntering out again in search of it, "three months ago it had to be a chimney-sweep or a nigger-minstrel. At least she's realised that there *are* white men too, on the earth."

As he went out, Mrs. Buckett (our "daily" and still going strong) came hurrying in. She looked more like a rubicund scarecrow than ever, and her crumpled red face creased even further into myriad lines of smile as she beheld Gillian, who had been away for so long.

"Hullo, Mrs. Buckett," greeted Gillian. "Remember me? How are you and how's Gladys?"

"Oh, she's lovely," cried Gladys' mother happily. "Settled in New York, and mother of twins. Ever so happy."

"So she really did marry Gary Cooper, the jeep-driver, did she?" said Gillian.

Mrs. Buckett shook with laughter. "Lor' Miss," she exclaimed. "You must mean Bert Parky! Yes, we did think 'e looked like Gary Cooper just at first, didn't we! Yes—she's married 'im and gone out to America as one of these GI Brides. I can't say I wasn't anxious about 'er at first, you know. But I needn't 'ave worried, and I'm goin' over to visit 'er one of these fine days." She bustled out again, and Gillian turned back to me.

"But you haven't said a word about Gilly," she persisted. I sighed. "Gilly!" I exclaimed. "Oh my dear! He's terrible! Six is such a trying age for little boys! At the moment he has lost one of his front teeth, and as for his clothes—well, he either ruins them or grows out of them. I expect you noticed how ragged Steve looks? Well, that's because I spend so many of his coupons buying things for Gilly. And most horrible of all, he keeps—"

But I need not have continued. The door flew open and a streak of white careered across the carpet and under Gillian's chair. It's red eyes and long tail were visible even as it went. After it came a grimy, tousled urchin who grovelled under the chair where Gillian was now standing, clutching at her skirts.

"Gottim!" declared Gilly in muffled tones of triumph from under the chair. "Mum, please may I—"

It was not until Gilly and his red-eyed pet had departed that Gillian resumed her seat and composed herself once more.

"No," she remarked feelingly at length. "I take back what I said. Don't write about the children as they grow up. They were so much nicer four years ago. Don't you agree?"

"But no," I replied. "And I'm very much obliged to you for telling me how to write about them now. After all, I could never have thought of a little incident like there has been just now, could I? Now it is all simple. I just need to write down the things that really happen. Thank you, Gillian."

And while Gillian cast up her eyes, I went on with my mending.

K. L. B. P.

Matewa Reflections

(Looking forward to looking back)

THE first of a series of reprints from the Beaumanor Staff Magazine, by courtesy of Mr. L. P. Jones and Mr. E. C. Millhouse, formerly of the B.S.M. Editorial Board.

I remember, son in days of yore,
When youthful—I was but a score—
I dwelt in Woygland, land of wonder,
While a common foe split towns asunder.
We cared not then for tyrant's wrath,
With hair askew and lips afroth,
For on our work we'd concentrate,
To bring about the present state
Of peace and friendship o'er the earth
Of joy and happiness and mirth.

Our work was arduous; none could know
Our untold misery and woe;
"They also serve who sit and wait,"
I served—my trousers shone like plate.
We sat through all the hours God made,
We toiled while watching daylight fade,
And even as the dawn came creeping
And birds and beasts alike were sleeping,
Still we sat and laboured on,
Tired and weary every one.

Not all the time was melancholy;
At times, nay frequently, t'was jolly.
We had our football, cricket, dancing,
Beery hops and much romancing;
With women to relieve our sorrow
We worried not about the morrow.
And so, on looking back, my son,
I think that I should like to run
Back to the days I thought were hellish,
But this time every hour I'd cherish.

"NOSWEH"
(B.S.M., April, 1943)

STOP PRESS.—We regret to announce that Mr. Jimmie Griffin (Rigger) passed away in London on Sunday, 1st August. The funeral was to take place on Thursday, 5th August, and Mr. L. P. Jones was attending on behalf of the Staff of Beaumanor.

Printed by THE CHANDOS PRESS, EDGWARE, *and published by H. Dodd for the Woygian Association.*

The WOYGIAN

BRIDGEWOODS **1939** CHICKSANDS **1945** BEAUMANOR

Christmas 1948

THE WOYGIAN
ASSOCIATION

President :
Lt. Col. M. J. W. ELLINGWORTH, O.B.E., D.S.M.

Vice-Presidents :

Major H. F. JOLOWICZ   Mr. G. M. SPOONER
Jnr. Cmdr. I. F. ROMER   Mr. C. O. SMITH

Chairman :
Mr. H. DODD,
161 Hermon Hill,
South Woodford, London, E.18

Honorary Secretary :   *Honorary Treasurer :*
Mrs. P. L. EDMUNDSON,   Mr J. DODD,
27 Wood End Avenue,   29 Arras Avenue,
S. Harrow, Middlesex   Morden, Surrey

Honorary Editor :   *News Items to :*
Mr. E. C. MILLHOUSE,   Mr. R. E. DOWNER,
103 Runnymede,   c/o Beaumanor Park,
Merton Abbey, London, S.W.19   Leicestershire.

Overdue Subscriptions

It is a matter for great concern that at the time of going to press (end of November) no less than 180 members—one half of our present membership—have not yet paid this year's subscription, and have ignored my request in the last issue to pay it promptly and save us the trouble and expense of reminders. A copy of this issue is being sent to all members, even though half of them are not entitled to receive one, and I hope that overdue subscriptions will be sent to the Treasurer without further delay. Otherwise a serious situation will arise and it will be doubtful whether the Association can continue. No further magazines will in any case be sent to those ignoring this final appeal. The enclosed form shows whether *you* still owe this year's subscription.

Re-unions

Details are set out on the back page of two re-unions arranged for next year, as well as a new venture—the Theatre Party on January 29th. Miss Jean Murray has been able to make preliminary arrangements for an Edinburgh Re-union Party on February 12th, and final details will be posted to all Scottish members early in the New Year. (If any other member would like to have these details, please let Jean, or myself, know in good time.) I hope all members will do their best to support us in these functions, as we are committed to minimum numbers in the case of the London Dance and have booked a block of fifty seats at the theatre. Should the latter experiment prove successful, we will follow it up with a similar party later in the year. Suggestions as to the type of show to be chosen will be welcome.

Beaumanor Re-union Photograph

The photographers have now agreed to accept further orders for an indefinite period, so it is not too late to apply for a copy now—send 5s. 6d. to the Treasurer. Overseas members may wish to take advantage of the extension.

Increase in Subscription Rate

As from 1st July next year, the annual subscription will be increased to 4s. 6d. I much regret that we find it necessary to do this, but it has been evident for some time past that with the subscription at 2s. 6d. the Association's income has not been sufficient to guarantee the magazine expenses, and

the general running costs. The two main reasons for this situation are:
(1) Recent considerable increases in printing costs, and
(2) The decrease in membership, from over 600 in 1945 to about 360 at present.

No. (1) cannot be helped, but many of us can do something to remedy No. (2) by obtaining new members and by encouraging ex-members to rejoin by sending the current year's subscription plus 1/- re-application fee. I assure you that we will reduce the subscription rate just as soon as it is possible to do so. I feel you will agree that the Association is well worth keeping going, and that at 4s. 6d. per year it is not an expensive luxury.

The position of members who have paid several years' subscriptions in advance will be made clear to them when those for 1949/50 are requested in the next issue of the magazine.

We have decided to simplify the present somewhat complicated membership classification, and from 1st July onwards there will be only one class of membership, each member paying the 4s. 6d. subscription, except that the "joint membership," where both husband and wife were at Beaumanor, will continue. Husbands, or wives, who were not at Beaumanor will be regarded as Honorary Members, no additional subscription being payable. There will be no alteration in membership reference numbers.

Treasurer's Address

Please note that the Treasurer, Mr. J. Dodd, has changed his address to that shown above. This change should be a permanent one, as he and his family are settling down in their own house at last.

Best wishes to all members for Christmas and the New Year.

HARRY DODD (*Chairman*).

Frailty, Thy Name Is Woyg

By SERVICK

ON the whole, a pen is assumed to be an inanimate object with no mind of its own, and certainly no opinions worthy of a mention in the *Times Literary Supplement*. This pen, however, like its owner, is one of those types who talk merely for the sake of talking and, like its owner, never knows when to stop ; furthermore, it cannot be suppressed. The other day it started arguing with a mysterious part of me which could possibly be classified as my Subconscious Self or perhaps, my Inner Man. It doesn't much matter, as long as the name suggests something more or less detached from myself ; thus I am cleared of any responsibility for anything it might have to say. So, we will call it my " Mysterious Being." One last word before I let them take over. All writs for libel and so forth, will be forwarded to . . . ." Mysterious Being," c/o SERVICK, etc.

As we turn up the volume control, " Pen " is just reciting some mutilated fragments of Omar Khayyam. Just sit back and listen to this recording of their conversation that I made at the time.

Pen : " Here with a *crimson form* and furrowed brow,
A civvy suit, a six-to-two—and thou
Beside me toiling in Lough's wilderness—
And wilderness is paradise enow."

Mysterious Being (*hereinafter known as M.B.*): " Well, what was that about?"

Pen : " Have you noticed that in spite of strongly-worded war-time promises to the contrary, almost all of the ' 78 ' are back at Beaumanor. Frailty, surely thy name is Woyg?"

M.B. : " Whatever frailty their violated promises are proof of, it's nothing compared to that of Servick."

Pen : " Now what has he done?"

M.B. : " Rejoined the army for another three years, remember?"

Pen : " Oh that!"

M.B. : " That short rejoinder sounds suspiciously like an attempt to dismiss the subject."

Pen : "A word in your ear, M.B., old man. Present exiles at Beaumanor

3

are suffering terrible hardships, they are going 'back-to-nature.' I've heard horrible rumours of straw beds and stable floors and what not, but even with the comparative comfort of our wartime exile, would *you* like to go back to those Loughborough Landladies, Paste Sandwiches and rotate week?"

M.B. : " No, but he could've joined Zombie in the police force. Nice bright uniform, plus the self-importance that goes with it, and just you think of the number of cyclists who never stop at ' HALT ' signs."

Pen : " That's no use to him, they want strong men in the police force, not anæmic scribblers. Y'remember old Pete J.?"

M.B. : " The chappie who wanted to join the police force after his demob?"

Pen. : " That's him, he was awfully keen on the P.F. and further, he swore in language most foul, that he'd rather shoot himself than go back to Bmnr., but although we sent him the necessary lethal weapon, ready loaded, he's still alive and merrily working . . . back at the old place. S'pity really, because Pete has such a natural ' Wot's all this 'ere ' manner about him."

M.B. : " Servick could've sold tools with friend OBZ, not to mention that soft typists' job that he nearly settled at the War Office."

Pen. : " Mmm . . . that was rather peculiar wasn't it. First the W.O. chappie promised him a good job in London, then, after he had been in touch with Bmnr., he suddenly discovered that he hadn't any jobs for him at all."

M.B. : " Somebody at Bmnr. probably decided that soft jobs don't suit Hobby, and anyway it was too near his home, so he, also, had to return to the fold."

Pen. : " Of course with the Duc and Moggy it's different, they probably returned in order to improve their literary abilities. Bmnr. is such a useful place for that sort of thing."

M.B. : " No, I think not. Look at your mighty Duc . . . a mere peddler of gossip, and as for Moggy; did you read that bit about his bow tie?"

Pen. : " Well, Frankie-the-crooner and Moggy-the-scribbler/poet physically resemble each other. Both can conceal themselves behind a broomhandle."

M.B. : " Yes, but a bow tie on a red spotted shirt! Not to mention the corduroy bags."

Pen. : " Yeah, these literary types! I wonder if the cords and the bow tie are also red spotted. But that's enough on that subject, we mustn't forget that poets and scandal disseminators are all-powerful. With but a few strokes of their vitriol-laden pens, they can send Servick to Coventry."

M.B. : " It's rather late for worrying about that, for these very words will probably accomplish that beyond all your wildest dreams."

Pen. : " Oh, you do know that our conversations are not exactly private; shall we switch the scrambler on?"

M.B. : " No, I shouldn't bother; besides, if he has this printed it won't do him a bit of good, for nobody will ever speak to him afterwards, but I wouldn't put it past him. These army types are all the same; do anything to get into print."

Pen. : " Next time we manage to contact Servick we must discuss the small matter of a scale of fees for the right to submit our enlightened conversation for publication. As somebody once so aptly remarked . . .
' What frenzy has of late posses'd the brain,
Though few can write, yet fewer can refrain.'

And since Servick is not one of the ' few,' and certainly not one of the ' fewer,' what else can he write about? After all, once you have read the scandal, births, deaths and marriages, what else is there in the magazine?"

M.B. : " What about writing something in the ' My Post-war Job ' series?"

Pen. : " Most emphatically . . . No. The only people who write in that series are those who are proud of their jobs; besides, who could possibly be interested in the Army? No; his occupation must be kept quiet."

M.B. : " I couldn't agree more! However, getting back to the subject of civvy jobs suitable for him, he could've joined Ralph Champion on the staff of the *Sunday Pictorial*. Servick could get just as indignant as Ralph on the subject of Blackmarket Babies."

Pen.: "In thick black type on the front page an' all! But really, when you think of it, after Ralph's superlative effort in his wartime essay on the Prophet Osee and How He Invented Wireless, Blackmarket Babies should have come easy to Ralph."

M.B.: "Another job that Servick could've done would be that of helping Lord John to make tea and answer the 'phone at Stn. X. ' Stn X heah, who is theah? No, this is not the O.C., this is the Office/Tea boy and switchboard operator '."

Pen.: "Ha, ha, very funny, I'm laughing my head off."

(At this point there is a noise similar to that of dried peas rattling in a colander, followed by a crash.)

"Pen" retrieves his head and the conversation continues.

M.B.: "I intercepted some yearning thoughts lingering through his brain, the other day, something about Christmas at Bmnr., and, when you were writing something about the 'H' Hut wolves in full cry in and around 'J' and 'K' Huts in wartime Christmas days, his mouth was absolutely dripping!"

Pen.: "It was an old 'manor' custom, wasn't it? and even so, I don't think he ever took part in them."

Myself (butting in): "Thanks, Pen old man, I'll remember those few kind words."

M.B.: "He was too bashful, scared stiff of the female element, I know for a fact that he lived in daily fear of one coming along with the desire to 'mother' him, indeed, it's entirely due to my constant vigilance that he remains a free man to-day."

At this point in the proceedings, I flung the pen down; it broke into a thousand pieces. M.B. was last heard muttering at great length on the subject of stupid idiots who haven't the courage to sally forth into the brave new world of civilian life and its associate paste sandwiches and 'rotate' weeks.

"WHAT'S HE DOING NOW?"

By DUC DOWNER

To most of us a common phrase familiar in the doubtful days,
Now as we go our sundry ways, a different meaning it conveys,
Remote from that elusive "he," confined instead to you and me,
Therefore the word must also be interpreted at times as "she."

MANY thanks to all those who have written in the past few weeks and who have helped tremendously to make this column worth while with their interesting letters. There was news from all parts of England, from Scotland and the Channel Islands, and I'll see that all letters that have not yet been answered will be dealt with in the very near future.

Very soon after the last issue was published I was quietly but firmly informed that the Globe Theatre, where Hwfa Pryse was appearing in "All My Sons," is in Shaftesbury Avenue, and not Haymarket. With apologies to those who believe it to be a sad neglect of general education, I must admit that I don't know my "London." (I've got him right this time.)

One other apology, and that to Norman (Underground) Hobbs. Owing to a misunderstanding it was not recorded that he was present at the Whitsun Reunion. Harry Dodd writes to say that no booking was made for him, but he was definitely there and it can only be hoped that he didn't slide in without a ticket.

Woygians have done just a little better this time in the matter of producing young members but the time-honoured custom of marriage seems to be out of favour with the tribe, resulting in my being able to record only one wedding in this issue. However we can do nothing about it, being already married ourselves, so must just hope that more things happen for next time.

BIRTHS.

To Micky Sockett (née Marshall), a son, Robert Edward, on April 14th.

To Marguerite (formerly Pte. Randall of B Watch, Garats Hey) and Richard Addiscott, a daughter, Mary Susan, on the 29th of June.

To May Knight (formerly of C Watch, Garats Hey), a daughter, Gillian Dinah, on the 2nd of June.

To Mr. and Mrs. C. McPherson, a son, but no further details are available.

MARRIAGE.

Vera Ballard, ex-T. P. Staff, has become Mrs. Fitzgerald, but I am unfortunately unable to give any further details.

Congratulations to those mentioned above.

GENERAL NEWS.

In September there appeared on the Beaumanor scene two more familiar faces, those of Underground Obz and Pete James, arriving to recommence duties again after their splendid efforts to avoid work of any sort had failed. Obz, returning after an illness from which he appears to have recovered, was reinstated, but Pete had to be classed as a new entrant since he had spent a few months after his demob., trying to be a salesman.

In July, Arnold Manington left the Group to take up again his former occupation with Boots the Chemists. He is at a local branch and he still lives at Quorn.

Pete Gardner withdrew his wife, Ann, from the T.P. Room in August, and is now studying child psychology with Geoff Nicol.

Don Linder obtained a Government Grant, and departed for Hull University in October. He is taking a course in Social Science, and writes to say that so far he is enjoying it very much. He has a very comfortable billet where extremely good food is served; and those of you who knew Don will recognise that this is a most important point.

In August a special benefit night was held at Beaumanor for Mrs. Jimmie Griffin whose husband died so suddenly on August 1st. A feature of the occasion was the arrival of Freddy Burgess with a team of his colleagues from "Dr. Crock and his Crackpots," appearing that week in Leicester, with the result that the Beaumanor Canteen became the objective for buses and cars from many miles around. Many people were turned away.

Ginger Talbot and "Tich" have left Blackburn and are now living at 20 Boston Road, East Ham, London, E.6. I don't know the reason for their move south but, being of a trusting nature I shall presume that they like it better down there.

Hugh Dias is at a teachers' training college in Strawberry Hill, Twickenham. Letters will reach him at 19 Popes Grove, Twickenham, Middlesex. When he has finished his course he hopes to get a post in his native Carlisle.

Jean Murray, formerly of the I-Corps and C.R.R., has done extremely well this year. She gained her M.A. during the summer with Spanish and Psychology as her subjects, and celebrated her success with a six-weeks holiday in Spain. Jean was hoping to get fixed up with a suitable job in, or near, Edinburgh. As her letter was written a few weeks ago it is probable that she is now settled, but in any case we send our congratulations and best wishes for the future.

Joan Thorburn, formerly Joan Morley, whose marriage was recorded in the last issue (I apologise for calling her Jean on that occasion) writes to say that she is already settled in Khartoum where her husband. "Stew," is a lecturer in Chemistry at the Gordon Memorial College and the Kitchener School of Medicine. Joan left England on August 29th by air, and arrived at Wadi Halfa on August 30th, after a night stop at Malta. This was her first experience of air travel, of which she says, " it is quite the most comfortable, cleanest and quickest method of travelling yet devised." Joan's plane was a Viking, and she enjoyed every minute of her journey. Her train journey from Wadi Halfa to Khartoum, however, was not so comfortable, clean or quick and took thirty-six hours to complete. At the time of writing it was a trifle hot and sticky but Joan was expecting conditions to improve with the advent of the cool season.

Joan, who was of " C " Watch, Brand Hill, and later of " B " Watch, Garats Hey, sends greetings to all who may remember her, and especially to Ollie and Flora and to the " Olive Spinks—Joan Dadswell—Muriel Dick—Yvonne Bams Crew " of which she was a member. Letters for her should be addressed c/o Gordon Memorial College, Khartoum, Sudan.

At home again, it must be recorded that Roy (Bachelor) Aldridge is away on holiday at Bournemouth with Eileen, a nurse at the Zachary Merton Convalescent Home. An engagement is predicted.

Matt Mathias, still with the Group, is hoping to be married at the end of March or the beginning of April to Miss Betty Harper of Loughborough.

Betty is a swing pianist and has been a member of the George Hames Accordeon Band and a xylophonist with the Blue Aces Dance Band. Matt seems to be booking himself a continuous performance.

Smiler (brother of Shaker) Smith is energetically "wife-hunting." He has tried several different types in the last couple of months and finally seems to have settled for something in the willowy line from his home town.

Howard Jellings writes to say that he is engaged in a London Hospital and being kept very busy with the new National Health Scheme.

Marguerite Addiscott (the birth of her daughter has been recorded in the appropriate place), writes to say that her baby, Mary, was awarded a silver christening mug, given by the Sittingbourne and Milton Urban District Council to the last baby born before the new Health Scheme came into operation on 5th July. Marguerite has been fortunate in getting a farm cottage, which, she says, is small but very comfortable, and her address is 2 Meresborough Cottages, Rainham, Kent.

Micky Sockett, as well as telling of the birth of her son, which has been recorded, gives a few weights and measures: Bobbie, as the baby is called, was rather small at birth but has made up for it since and at six months weighed eighteen pounds. He has blue eyes and fair hair and is not a bit like his mother. (As I have no idea how much a small son should weigh at the tender age of six months I make no comment of my own, leaving it entirely to female readers and Pete Gardner to judge the merits of the baby, but from the tone of Micky's letter I gather that she is satisfied.)

Micky goes on to say that she was unable to attend the Whitsun reunion because she was at that time in the process of "acquiring" a house and had to move in quickly before anyone realised it was changing hands. Her new address is "Holmer," 20 Duke Street, Arnold, Notts., and she would welcome any news as she now never sees any Woygians. Micky would especially like to hear from (or of) Dot Lavers and Madeline (née Saunders), and she wishes to be remembered to all who were at Brand Hill, especially "D" Watch.

Arthur Skinner recently worked for a while in the wardrobe department of a film studio and was there during the filming of "Bonnie Prince Charlie." After that he decided there was something in the acting business and is now studying at the Guildhall School of Dramatic Art.

Hwfa Pryse, to whom I have already tendered my apologies for transplanting his theatre, has now finished at the Globe, and hopes to be starting work in a new film at Nettlefold Studios, Walton-on-Thames, in the near future. He recently played in the film version of "Calling Paul Temple" and in "Christopher Columbus." The former was shown to the Royal Family at Balmoral.

Alick Berry seems to be in hiding in the Ealing area and is travelling for Ewart's Geysers.

A long and complex letter has arrived from Guernsey. From Lucille Sarre, formerly of "D" Watch at May Cottage, Quorn, it contains much interesting news of meetings with other Woygians and of a holiday in Scotland. In July Marjorie Wass stayed with Lucille in Guernsey for a week and a little later Isabell Harper also spent a week there. At that time, too, Lucille's sister Jaqueline (Jackie) was home on holiday with her husband, Norman, and their baby daughter, Susan, so between them they had a pretty good party. In September Lucille came to England and spent a few days at the home of Eva Cooper in Welling, Kent. Eva sailed for Canada on the 29th September to take up an appointment in Alberta. She expects to be away for two years.

The next stop for Lucille was Paisley where she spent a very pleasant week with Isabell Harper. Together they explored Edinburgh Castle, St. Giles Cathedral and met Isabel (Bill) Stewart. As Lucille had not seen her for three years the few hours spent together were no doubt filled with much gripping. "Bill" herself is doing very well. She is teaching in a mixed school and is in possession of a three-roomed flat. Both "Bill" and Isabell have met Eva Cooper's friend, Bessie Bell, in Glasgow.

At the end of September Lucille returned to London, spent a few days with sister, Jackie, and visited Evelyn Kaye who has a flat in Canonbury and who was expecting an addition to the family on about October 16th. (Doubtless further news of this will arrive in time for the next mag. but at the moment I'm afraid I have no further details.)

At that point I presume that Lucille returned to Guernsey, but not before she had had a very Woygian holiday; and after tracing her movements, I hope correctly, I'm wondering why I don't start a private detective agency. Lucille's address is " Fortafare." Havelet, St. Peter Port, Guernsey, C.I.

Talking of " Bill " Stewart just now reminded me that the other one, late of Newark Street, Greenock, has got himself a job at Church House, Westminster, so London members might bump into him sometime. His address is 155 Brunswick Square, W.C.1.

While in London recently, Pete James and Obz met Ralph Conge Champion and gripped him over a cup of tea. Ralph likes his present job very much as it is full of interest and gives him a chance to get around a bit. He saw Tubby Fagg in London a short while ago and says he seems to be quite happy working at a new job which has something to do with underground cables.

Roy Nicholls hasn't come to light lately, but when last heard of he had just started in the insurance business.

On the other hand, Dudley Truin has unearthed Noel Royle. He is employed by the Dental Estimates Board, a branch of the Ministry of Health, giving the O.K. to the dentists' charges. Wife, Billie, says he is not too keen on it, but at least he now has one of his gods as his boss.

Dudley ran into Mac McKie, the P.O. Liaison Officer, had a coffee with him in Great Yarmouth, and now has supplied me with news of some of the P.O. chaps who were with us during the war.

" Jock " Smith is Telephone Manager at Dundee, and Herbert Taylor is Postmaster at Spinney Moor, Bishop Auckland. C. McPherson is also something that I can't read because of Dudley's writing, at Bishop Auckland, and he now has a son. McKie himself has retired and lives at Great Yarmouth.

Dudley doesn't say how he himself is getting on, but I have no doubt that he is trotting along nicely and trust so anyway.

Another member of the P.O. staff is mentioned by Miss A. D. Blake, who writes from 99 Bonchurch Road, Brighton 7, Sussex. She says that she mentioned one day in the office that during the war she worked to G.M.T., and subsequently discovered that Mr. Chitty did, too—at Beaumanor. He was with the P.O. staff. In her letter, Miss Blake says she never meets any of her old friends and would doubtless like to see any who happen to call in at Brighton at any time.

Kath Cook (Blake) is doing very well in Australia and would always be pleased to hear from old friends. Unfortunately, I haven't got her address at present but will put it in if she would care to send it.

Bobbie Snare (née Percy) is at present living in the wilds of Scotland at 12 Gordon Street, Hopeman, Morayshire. Hopeman is so small that Woodhouse Eaves would look like quite a town beside it. It is on the coast, a trifle breezy at present, but rather pleasant, Bobbie hopes, in the summer. She is there to be with her husband who is in the Navy.

Bobbie would like to have been at the reunion but has just had to say, " well, maybe next time "; she enjoys reading the magazine and would like to be remembered to all her old gang of " D " Watch, Quorn.

Bobbie says that " Teg " Jones, now Mrs. Williams, is getting along very well, and has a flat in Cardiff. Bobbie and her baby, Susan, paid her a visit in July and quite naturally spent much time discussing Woygland days.

Bob Yaxley is doing charter work with B.O.A.C. and is certainly getting around a bit, a recent trip being to Tanganyika.

George Kenneally has resigned from B.O.A.C. to take an airline wireless job in Rhodesia. He was in Vienna just before he resigned where he had a super-furnished flat and where drinks and cigarettes were plentiful and fabulously cheap. However, the fact that foreign governments are installing an increasing number of their own staffs at airports and the ominous political situation in Europe made it advisable to leave, and George now hopes to settle in Rhodesia for all time.

Earlier on I mentioned Ginger Talbot's trek south. I have since discovered that he is at the Mullard Radio Valve Works in Mitcham and that he is searching for a house in that area. Ginger Junior is expected in November.

During his travels, John Dodd bumped into a now very slender and youthful edition of Mabel Marple. As Mrs. Dormer she is living with her husband at 34 Charleville Road, W.14, and, until they find a house of their own, Mabel is continuing her job at a National Health Office in Acton.

In July, Anne Kerr came down from Falkirk to spend a week with Jimmie Rogers. On one particular day they had a very hectic time, starting with a short tour of " the sights of London," followed by a visit to the Denham Film Studios and ending with a pre-arranged all-A.R.13 Party. Those present at the " do " were Mrs. Ramsey, Gladys Edgson and her friend, Eileen Thurston, Mary Reardon, and Eve Dennis. Of these, Eileen is married and will be a mother in November, and Mary is also married and living at Ilford.

Maud Wood, Ex-I Corps and C.R.R., is now teaching small tough children in an Edinburgh school.

Ruth Yule married in July, John Aitken, a B.O.A.C. pilot and is living in Bournemouth.

Lynne Symington has gone back into what they fondly call " Government Communications," and Anne Stewart is working in W. H. Smith's in Glasgow.

These last few items were copied straight from a last minute letter from Jean Murray. Jean, whose address is 13 Church Hill, Edinburgh, enlarges a little upon what I've already said about her, saying that during her holiday she spoke only Spanish, and that she had a glorious time with lots of swimming, dancing and, of course, bull-fights.

Both Moggy Reed and Geoff Nicol have recently written to the Press, ticking about the lateness in starting the orchestral concerts at the De Montfort Hall in Leicester. The occasion that really set them off (there have been many others in the past) was when the Lord Mayor of Leicester himself caused the delay. Both letters were printed, one in each of the Leicester evening papers, but all Moggy's references to the Mayor were cut out. It seems, then, that if one is a Lord Mayor, one can ruin the evening enjoyment of people by causing them to miss the last movement of the Symphony, and not be criticised for so doing. That by way of showing you how indignant the lads were about it.

That seems to be the end of the news list for this time. Many thanks once again for your letters and I hope you'll always let me have what news you may get from time to time because it does really help a lot.

Have just heard that we must offer our congratulations to Roy Aldridge who, as predicted, became engaged while at Bournemouth.

Cheerio for this time and a Merry Christmas.

Duc.

LOOKING BACK
The second of a reminiscent series of " B.S.M." contributions.

Birds of Prey

by Archangel (B.S.M., December, 1944)

TIME. Anywhere between 0600 and 2200.
PLACE. Somewhere in England!

WITH conspiratorial and secretive air about him first op. whispers urgently to second op., then in challenging voice says that the " bloke " he's got is *theirs,* so keep off! Third op. then turns round and does in sneering voice, " Oh? Well, we got 'im on 'ere, see?". First op. sways backwards a bit at concentrated venom contained in third op's. voice, but quickly rallying, exclaims in utter amazement, " Well, blimey! We 'ad 'im when 'e first started." " Well, s'ours—and 'e's on 'ere anyway," repeats third op. with stubborn tenacity, and commences writing.

First op. then begins to rise from chair with determined look on face when second op. suddenly goes mad and thumps him back again; at the same time he juggles with some sheets in front of him and mutters something about letting them have the flaming thing because he's got another. Whispered council of war is then held between first and second ops. which lasts at least three seconds, then first op., as though he were delivering an ultimatum, says, "All right then, we'll 'ave the other ' bloke ' who's in the same place." Tired voice of sixth op. then intervenes, who says in one of those soft, goading ways that we've had it for the last half hour, old man!

Following this announcement, several things happen simultaneously. Second op., maddened almost beyond endurance, flings pencil on to table and says in exasperation, " Tch!" and at the same time valiantly overcomes terrible impulse to hurl things about room. Meanwhile, first op., his lips being drawn back in savage, animal snarl, is noisily sucking air in between tightly clenched teeth. But at last, when able to speak coherently, he renders such fine oration about things in general, and sixth op. in particular, that all those who are able pause to listen and also to memorize any words that still remain unknown to them—which are few. Exhaustion soon sets in, however, and when it does, first op. declines all further interest in matter and sulks for next hour.

Thus, at end of said hour, first op. changes technique. He gets up and takes sneaking looks at what ops. three and four, five and six, seven and eight are doing, disdainful expression on face the whole time. Suddenly, he screams back to chair like a comet, his teeth being bared in fiendish grin and eyes alight with insane gleam, to have another little whisper with second op., who is by now thoroughly frightened and wishing he was out of it all.

Whispered conversation being over, first op. starts to write; precisely thirty seconds later insidious voice of sixth op. states, in no uncertain manner, that the " bloke " *he's* got now is *his*! First op. then gets up with satisfied smirk on face, the very moment he's been living for having arrived, and sneers back, "Ah! See? S'ours; we got 'im ,ere old cock—so you flaming well wrap it!"

And so, at this stage it is fitting that we leave these two gallant gentlemen to carry on; they are working once more in complete harmony. Just take a last look at them—they're like a couple of vultures gloating over their prey, and if they could crow, or cluck, or whatever it is that vultures do—they would.

Through the Looking-Glass
By LEON DE BUNK

CONVERSION

EX-WOYGIAN anthropologists, following their Frazer, will have noticed with bemusement the changes of tribal organisation currently in progress in the species " homo sapiens." The function of high priest and soothsayer, formerly held by medicine man, druid, Atheling, king, Pope, prime minister, press lord (in that order) has been usurped (circa 1947) by the Film Star. Where formerly a cabinet minister, a brace of archbishops and a bevy of duchesses would have sufficed for the inauguration of the Tribal Feast Day, now, no Cup Final, no Appeal for Alcoholic Curates, or Festival of Scug-Rivetters, can be formally opened without the officiation of the latest meteor in the Elstree heavens. Our own conversion is perhaps typical:

Detraining at Manchester in the small hours a few weeks back after a gruelling jaunt from London in a compartment shared with an asthmatical traveller in fish-and-chip ranges, ten drunken Glaswegian stokers, and the UNO delegate for Byelo-Russia, we. arch-conservative that we were, were foolishly provoked to see across the platform a six-foot banner placard proclaiming " Manchester welcomes Miss M*RGAR*T L**KW**D." A few minutes later we were quietly inscribing in a corner of the placard : " But this doesn't include L. de Bunk," when a couple of Elstree bums picked us up.

" Just for dat," they said, " you can present de flowers! An' no squawkin', or you ain't goin' ta get no free tickets!" The even menace in their voices was enough.

And when, next day, they forced us on to the platform with the orchids trembling in our hands, it wasn't a second before our fears were forgotten, and like all the fifty million others we were in love with *her*. " Yes, this time it's real," we thought, and in no time at all she was stroking our grey old head and was telling us, without our even having to ask, all about her latest picture.

EVANGELIST

Conversing the other day with a leading British bigamist (the sport was lately statistically confirmed as, after cricket, the second British national sport) we mentioned a paragraph recently in the Press recalling one of the last recorded instances, in 1801, of the sale at Knaresborough of a wife by her husband. The price, in the days before Ricardo's feathery whimsies banished straight dealing from the market place, showed a quaint but tenacious understanding of real values: the fee demanded was "sixpence and a quid of tobacco."

But the bigamist didn't think it amusing. "Even allowing," he declaimed, with darkening brow and burning eye, "for the lapse of time and the change in moral climate, it is impossible to grasp how our gifted race, the heirs of Drake and the progenitors of Dean Inge, could have sunk to such bestiality; the heart rebels, the conscience grieves, and sanity cries out even at this late hour for justice!" For a moment he paused, and when he spoke again the agony in his voice had been replaced by hope. "But, happily in this hopeful and enlightened age we have cast aside those pagan horrors; we are men revivified, we have new horizons. Through the work of the British Bigamists' Association and its affiliated bodies, the triumph of progress is assured; after years of misunderstanding and persecution we are at the point of triumph. At the first Bigamist Congress, to be held in the Albert Hall next month, we shall appeal to the country with a policy and a programme. A Bigamist Vote, a Housing Drive for Bigger Bigamist Houses, a National Advisory Council on Bigamy, and an increase in invisible ink production for Bigamists' Marriage Certificates!"

As we began to elbow our way through the enthusiastic crowd which had by this time gathered round him, the speaker thrust a slip of paper into our hands. "And as for wife-dealing," he said, "the little calculation on that paper will prove that at present-day world food prices, you couldn't possibly manage more than a five-per-cent. average yearly rake-off!"

THOUGHT FOR TO-DAY

"Snobbery is the pride of those who are not sure of their position."
—Braley.

THE BITTER, BITTER LESSON LEARNED BY
The Unfortunate Josiah Thoussel
By YONC

TO say that Josiah Thoussel jumped would be an exaggeration. To say that he was not startled would be a mere toying with the truth. For the truth is that Josiah Thoussel, known more familiarly within the limits of a fairly narrowly described circle as "Josh," was not the jumping kind. He was a large, heavy, plasticiny sort of man, impervious alike to shocks, alarums, excursions, the political implications of atomic energy, T. S. Eliot, the coming of Spring and the oriental mysticism of Scriabin. He knew nothing of the Pope, the Quantum Theory, the growing of potatoes or the Salvation Army. It has been authoritatively stated that many people have gone through life wasting their sweetness on the desert airs of similar abysmal ignorances. But whereas many of them, had they had the chance, would have displayed an interest that can only be called fanatical in one or several of the fascinating topics mentioned, and would with diligence and application have made of themselves world renowned authorities in their particular chosen sphere, Josiah Thoussel would have done neither of these things. For he was like a not very complicated machine built for one functional set of actions, and to that set he stuck with the unconscious diligence of one of those rubber suction things that you can stick on to other things for no other reason than that you like the noise that it makes when you pull it off, and the imagination of a codfish. The only concessions he made to his own humanity were the necessities of a purely animal existence.

Although he did not know it, and would have been unmoved by the knowledge if he had, Josh's great-great-great-great-great-great grandfather had described "Paradise Lost" as a "vile, despicable, dung-spreading attempt at justification of idolatrous popery; a noisome vehicle of the foul-winded fiend himself, a bastard of words and grammar designed to twist the vitals of all that is pure, and to remain forever in the damnation of eternal fire as a loathesome, pox-ridden monument to filth, lust, fornication and atheistical praters and hypocritical word-vendors." The ancestor had also spent his savings on buying as many copies of "Paradise Lost" as he could lay hands on so that after putting the pages to an unmentionable use he could burn them with due ceremony in the ruins of the nearest monastery. His name had been Abimilech Thou-shalt-rule-them-with-a-rod-of-iron-and-break-them-in-pieces-like-a-potters-vessel. He was a Puritan.

Later and less pious generations had, for the sake of convenience, concertinaed their forefather's rather unwieldy surname and had compromised their consciences and reverenced Abimilech's shade by naming all their offspring after the more militant characters in the Old Testament. The concertina process which they had employed had squeezed the nobility both from their name and from their natures, leaving behind a surname with little merit but a vague suggestion of French ancestry, a family tree of ever-diminishing luxuriance of character of which Josiah was the latest tattered twig, and a complete lack of family interest in "Paradise Lost."

The more perspicacious of my readers will readily apprehend therefore that it could have been no small, trumpery event of everyday life that caused Josh if not exactly to start, at least to feel within himself those actions engendered by a working combination of eye and ear which, when confronted with something out of the usual run of things cause a normally constructed human being involuntarily to constrict the muscles of the body in that natural reaction so familiar to everyone caught with their metaphorical pants down.

The reason for this internal disorder, so unusual in Josiah Thoussel, will now be described.

A man leading a horse had appeared on the drive in front of him.

That description will now be elaborated for the more curious of my readers.

A horse being a horse all the world over (with the possible exception of that zoological curiosity, the Manchurian horse) little can here be added to the many and erudite descriptions of horses that have already been written and which, no doubt, have already been closely perused by those of my readers interested in bloodstock, fetlocks, withers and the like.

The man whom Josh had observed to be leading the horse must, on the imperatively-voiced advice of a well-known poet, be treated with a more studious attention to detail, if only because a sharp rap over the knuckles is threatened for anyone who may presume to reject this excellent advice. Although those of us who know him would have said that he would be the first to qualify, Josh may not be said, even by the strictest of judges, to merit such punishment in this particular instance.

For by the man and by his general appearance Josh was undoubtedly stirred more profoundly than ever before, and the last, final, pitiful remnants of his Puritan forebear's expletive and ejaculatory abilities found utterance in a gem-like word of restrained if powerful beauty.

"Lumme," said Josh.

Beginning at the top of the man we shall follow the excellent advice offered by the King of Hearts to the White Rabbit and "go on to the end and then stop." Or, if the odd reader prefer it, we shall move from head to toe, giving, *en passant* as it were, a brief résumé of those features which seem to the writer to have an outstanding characteristic of some kind, or which may seem to him for one reason or another to have those degrees of out-of-the-ordinary attributes which qualify them for the adjective "unusual." If unusual features be mentioned, a detailed analysis of the attributes making them so out of the ordinary as to be called unusual will not be given because it is assumed by the writer that the reader has a reasonably sound working knowledge of the degrees of oddness and can decide correctly whether a particular feature is unusual or not. It may serve as a send-off and as a general indication of the standard of identification required if the writer begins by saying that the man's head was crowned with a large-brimmed hat of dark-green velvet upon which, fastened with an emerald clasp made of the left foot of a hawk was an ostrich plume, and that these are unusual features. The ostrich plume nodded. This is by way of being a catch feature, because although an ostrich plume on a hat of green-velvet clasped thereto by an emerald clasp made of the left foot of a hawk constitute as fine a set of unusual features as the most exacting reader could wish to have, the fact that the ostrich plume nodded is not unusual. Ostrich plumes always nod.

From a wide-brimmed hat of green velvet (the writer is going back it will be observed, because the last bit was a sort of practice—rather like MacDonald Bailey practising sprint starts except that this will be slower) from beneath a wide-brimmed hat of dark-green velvet upon which, clasped with an emerald brooch made from the left foot of a hawk nodded an ostrich plume, the glossy curls of a carefully made wig protruded. The wig framed a blue-eyed merry face and the smiling mouth was partly concealed by a soft, carefully trimmed moustache and beard. The head was doing that cliché about being set proudly on a slim but wiry torso. Over the shoulders and partly concealed by a green velvet cloak, lined with cloth of gold, which swept outwards and downwards as far as the waist like the one that Guy Fawkes always wears in the fireworks advertisements, was a finely woven collar of white lace, caught together at the throat with a brooch, partner to the one worn in the wide-brimmed hat to keep the nodding ostrich plume in place, the one on the hat being the left claw and the one at the throat being the right claw on account of they both came from the same bird. The tunic or jerkin was sewn with tiny pearls in a complicated pattern and the doublet of cloth of gold was undoubtedly slashed in several places. The apparition wore knee-high boots of soft brown leather with gloves to match rather like a Marshall and Snelgrove pair: very fine handsome gloves with little dangly bits along the seam of the gauntlet like the ones Roy Rogers wears when it's cold. On the little finger of the left hand he wore outside the glove a large-stoned ring. If any reader has not yet guessed that a long rapier swung at his waist (or will swing when he begins to walk in a minute until it hits him on the ankle with a blow that can only be described as shrewd and he puts his hand on the hilt to steady it) then that reader should stop a little while and go back and begin a pretty stiff piece of self-criticism.

Everyone is excused for not knowing the next bit which is that on his right wrist he carried a tiercel-goshawk, hooded, proud and beautiful.

Josiah Thoussel had taken in these sartorial curiosities a good deal more quickly than the writer has been able to distribute them to his readers, mainly because Josiah had not the detail-loving eyes that are undoubtedly the highly commendable possessions of those readers. Josh gazed in a way that may have appeared to anyone not fully acquainted with the circumstances extant at that time as the essence of rudeness with nothing in his eyes but a bulbous lack of belief in what they saw. As he stared the man whistled softly through the moustache that has already been described as being carefully trimmed and partly concealing the smiling mouth, and although Josh did not recognise the melody for characteristic reasons already set down in some detail, people in the know would have recognised it immediately as "Greensleeves," before Vaughan Williams arrange it.

Josh's "Lumme," falling with half-apologetic bump as if it were aware of it's own limitations as a form of self-expression, broke the spell that had bound the two of them to speechlessness.

The man stopped whistling.

"That word," he began abruptly, "is not, I trust, symptomatic in its ugliness and lack of grace of the present condition of human intelligence." Josh did not reply, being a founder-member of that particular set of people who aspire no higher than the occasional use of "irrelevant" for "irrevelant" and who consider as wasted the addition of one word per year to their personal vocabularies.

Apparently unmoved by Josiah's silence, the stranger spoke again.

"I shall explain myself with all simplicity. I may be described albeit somewhat inadequately, but certainly with a degree of accuracy, as a psychic phenomenon."

The less circumspect reader will remark thoughtlessly that Josiah may have been unwilling to make official comment at that stage upon a statement well calculated to have confounded even one more well-versed than he was in the procedure more usually adopted for behaviour warranting the generally approved application of such Continental quelquechoses as "sang-froid" and "blasé."

The more discerning reader, however, will be inclined to dismiss such superficial nonsense, going with that reader's well-known thirst for fundamentals more deeply into the heart of the problem of Josiah's hitherto unexplained silence, pointing a reminding finger in passing at the already carefully delineated evidence that Josh was a man who knew how to express himself, if monosyllabically and a thought bluntly, at least effectively, and putting forward the cogent and laudably succinct opinion that Josh did not make a reply constructed of such words and grammatical machinations as are necessary for the conveyance of intelligent thought because he was unable to. Ten out of Ten for that reader, who may leave earlier.

For of course (readers staying late will excuse that "of course," but they will be the first to admit that they deserved it and may discover consolation in the fact that it is intended in no way as a sneer or as calumnious reference to their own less mature abilities). Of course Josh was unable to reply. Any capable student of phonetics will be pleased to support the writer and to corroborate his proposition that the first necessity for sustained speech on any given subject, apart from a reasonably sound knowledge of that subject, is movement of the lips, which movement, ineffective as it may be in itself for the production of certain sounds, needs to be ably abetted by co-ordinated movements of the jaw and by complementary, equally well co-ordinated changes in the formation of the tongue.

The less discerning will therefore shake their respective heads in self-deprecation when the writer tells them what they should long ago have discovered for themselves: that the understandable surprise experienced by John at the startling nature of the announcement by the apparition had loosened those muscles customarily employed in maintaining the lower jaw in a close proximity to the upper, and he was in that well-known literary, but seldom seen physical state of open-mouthed amazement.

Should any reader experience a passing doubt concerning the inability of the human being to speak when the facial condition described is present, then the writer sharply advises that reader to emulate Josiah's expression and to attempt with all seriousness and diligence to say, "Popocatepetl."

"I have come back," said the apparition abruptly, "because for some three hundred years I have suffered the tortures and agonies consequent upon forgetfulness. You shall set my mind at rest with all possible expedition. You are of course," he continued complacently, "acquainted with my poetry, if not with my appearance. You mind the work of Robert Herrick?"

Josiah Thoussel's acquaintanceship with poetry being of that particularly limited kind that has been nurtured of late years on the nauseating productions of that dark-haired school who have re-discovered at frequent intervals that "you" has an aural relationship with "blue" and who are capable of disgusting the grammatical susceptibilities of all readers with such non-British emotionalisms as "I wish that it was you," and the formal beauties of cement mixers, he could in all honesty and after moments of piercing self-analysis do no more than shake a still wordless head.

It seemed at first that Mr. Herrick considered this dumb negation in the light of a particularly rich form of humour, for he laughed with good-natured heartiness, damned himself if it wasn't the goodliest quip he'd heard since Will Shakespeare himself had asked him if he should compare him to a summer's day, and slapped his thigh so heartily that if Josh had not had well founded fears for his own personal welfare he might with perfect justice have feared for the other's bodily health.

But when it began to dawn upon the laughing embodiment of Mr. Herrick that Josh's impassioned denials were not the mere good-natured carrying too far of a not very good joke, his attitude changed, his laughter dropped into that particular vein favoured by the nineteenth century school of villain actors and he was once observed to be stroking the carefully trimmed moustache that partly concealed the now non-smiling mouth.

"Once more, sweet chuck," he said softly, "what was it that I advised that ye should gather while ye may?" The issue still further confused, and Josiah's mental abilities now at the lowest of a very low ebb, he could still no more than wag his sorry head from side to side.

"By thine own head art thou condemned, thou ignorant fool," thundered Herrick, with eyes that might, without too tenuous an extension of the imagination, be described as flashing. "Thou art condemned as an unæsthetic, laughter-lacking vandal, and a sound application for William's phrase about being fit for treasons, stratagems and spoils. I shall punish thee in the name of all the Muses, and as a salutory example to all who pass their lives as thou, in thoughtless mud and mental slough. Thou shalt not go forward more. Retrogression shall be thy lot; thou shalt live backwards in time."

He hissed the last sentence, leaning forward and thrusting his face close to Josh's in a most appropriate way.

Suddenly he placed his hands on Josh's shoulders and twisted him around once. "Go," he said.

For a moment Josh realised no change. His head continued to wag to and fro. Then it stopped, and his mouth closed.

"Emmul," he said, and began to walk backwards up the drive.

Memorabilia

PROBABLY one of life's greatest compensations is the fact that we tend to retain the happier memories, and that time conduces to obscure the unpleasant ones; or perhaps many of the latter seem less grim with the passage of time.

Who among us who have left Beaumanor behind will deny some almost nostalgic recollections of those war-time days? Who, even among those who have convinced themselves it is an episode best forgotten, can disown any warm memories?

If we allow it, the mind travels easily back into those strange, in some ways almost unreal times: the memory, once jogged, unleashes a surprising flood. The Canteen, with its interminable queues; the hustle and clatter, the various cliques and factions buzzing at their sundry tables. Saturday morning "inspections"; the inception of A.T.S. slacks; Freddy Burgess' frequent outbursts in "H"; a half-completed crossword between the leaves of a pad. These, and a myriad other shapes tumble about the mind's kaleidoscope. Perhaps one recalls a tortuous journey around the perimeter in the dark, small hours; or the bleak depravity of everywhere on emerging from a night of N.H.R. Yet has one forgotten the Town Hall at the height of a "Do"; the Mayor's Parlour; or the Empire coffee-room, hub of Woygite activity in Loughborough? Maybe you wandered afar, to Leicester or Nottingham; through Bradgate's broad acres, or amid the beauty of Charnwood; or perhaps the Victory, Empire and Odeon were the limits of your world. Was there ever a period when the "Boot" did not echo to the Woyg vernacular?

Can you smell those brilliant daffodils beside the drive; taste that two a.m. tea; feel the pressure of those headphones; see Cornwallis grinning vacuously into space? Can't you hear the "juke-box" intoning the preciseness of a certain authority, to be abruptly interrupted by a staccato announcement from a "mighty atom"; or a flood of gibberish from one of those Scottish N.C.O.s?

Then, of course, we all have our personal memories. Is it not therefore intensely worth while keeping alive the Woygian Association and, besides tangible reunions from time to time, this Magazine, which, circulating among us all, revives, enriches and preserves the memories of our war-time fellowship? And how can it best fulfil this purpose? Not, surely, so much by printing the ordinary magazine-type of story (for in any case our space is severely limited) but, in addition to all the Gossip our scribe can garner, those personal, essentially Woygian scripts; items which, if they do not recall those times, reveal the writer as one who once shared the reader's way of life. I am sure there is something *you* can send along, if you will only make the effort, the not very arduous effort. Shall I be hearing from you? All contributions for the next issue should reach me not later than May 16th.

The Woygian sends to Woygians everywhere Heartiest Christmas Greetings and the Best of Good Wishes for the New Year.

THE EDITOR.

A Woygian Party will visit the
"CRAZY GANG" SHOW
"TOGETHER AGAIN"
AT THE
VICTORIA PALACE THEATRE
(nearest Underground Station—Victoria)

On SATURDAY, 29th JANUARY, 1949
at 8.30 p.m.

Meet at "The Windsor Castle" (opposite the Theatre) from 7.15 p.m. onwards   Snacks obtainable

SEATS — 3/6 EACH

Applications for tickets to be sent to the Treasurer, on the enclosed form, with remittance. PLEASE SEND STAMPED & ADDRESSED ENVELOPE for your ticket. Only 50 seats available, so early application is advisable.

A Dance
WILL BE HELD ON

SATURDAY, 26th MARCH, 1949
6.30 (for 7) to 11 p.m.

AT THE
"MECCA" CAFE
11/12 BLOMFIELD STREET, LONDON, E.C.2
(nearest Underground Stations — Liverpool Street and Moorgate)

TICKETS — 9/6 EACH
(Including Buffet Refreshments)

DRESS OPTIONAL   BAR (open from 6.30 p.m.)

Blomfield Street is off the end of Liverpool Street furthest from Bishopsgate. Use the Broad Street exits from Liverpool Street Underground Station. Applications for tickets to be sent to the Treasurer on the enclosed form, with remittance.

Numbers must be limited, so early application is recommended.

All members and their friends welcome.

A RE-UNION PARTY
WILL BE HELD IN
EDINBURGH

On SATURDAY, 12th FEBRUARY, 1949
3.30 to 6 p.m.

Full details will be sent to members in Scotland early in the New Year.

In the meantime . . . . KEEP THIS DATE FREE !

(Organiser: Miss S. J. M. Murray, 13 Church Hill, Edinburgh.)

Printed by The Chandos Press, Edgware, and published by H. Dodd for the Woygian Association.

The WOYGIAN

BRIDGEWOODS 1939 CHICKSANDS 1945 BEAUMANOR

Summer 1949

★ See page eight

THE WOYGIAN
ASSOCIATION

President:
Lt. Col. M. J. W. ELLINGWORTH, O.B.E., D.S.M.

Vice-Presidents:

Major H. F. JOLOWICZ
Jnr. Cmdr. I. F. ROMER

Mr. G. M. SPOONER
Mr. C. O. SMITH

Chairman:
Mr. H. DODD,
161 Hermon Hill,
South Woodford, London, E.18

Honorary Secretary:
Mrs. P. L. EDMUNDSON,
27 Wood End Avenue,
S. Harrow, Middlesex

Honorary Treasurer:
Mr J. DODD,
29 Arras Avenue,
Morden, Surrey

Honorary Editor:
Mr. E. C. MILLHOUSE,
103 Runnymede,
Merton Abbey, London, S.W.19

News Items to:
Mr. R. E. DOWNER,
c/o Beaumanor Park,
Leicestershire.

RECENT EVENTS

THEATRE PARTY

On Saturday, 29th January, twenty-six Woygians were "Together Again" to witness the broad humour of the Crazy Gang show of that name at the Victoria Palace. Bud Flanagan was unfortunately absent from the cast through illness, but this did not deter the rest of the Gang from putting on a show which, though undoubtedly not everybody's cup of tea, produced belly-laughs from quite unexpected quarters. Even the outraging of the Chairman's well-known modesty was belied by several suspiciously Dodd-like guffaws. However, the delicacy or otherwise of the show had not been a primary consideration in its selection; the idea had been to provide an opportunity for a get-together in pleasant and not too expensive circumstances, and on this score the experiment may not be deemed to have failed. The party congregated, from 7.15 onwards, in the *Windsor Castle*, opposite the theatre, for a chat and refreshments before proceeding to the show at 8.30 p.m. The party comprised: Mr. and Mrs. G. E. M. Abels, Mr. A. H. Appleton, Miss W. Burke (a new member enrolled at the theatre), Mr. P. Dart, Mr. and Mrs. H. Dodd, Mr. J. Dodd, Mr. and Mrs. J. Edmundson with Pam's parents, Miss L. Gray, Miss J. M. Jenkins and friend, Miss E. M. Knight, Mr. E. C. Millhouse, Mr. and Mrs. P. Patten, Miss K. Price, Mr. and Mrs. G. K. Talbot, Mr. and Mrs. D. Truin, Mr. W. P. Vannerley and partner.

E. C. M.

SCOTTISH REUNION

Thanks to the enthusiasm and hard work of Jean Murray and Muriel McAra, a Woygian Re-union was held in Edinburgh on 12th February, and was thoroughly enjoyed by the Old Woygians who were able to be present—Doris Hall, Frances Watt, R. McKinnon, J. Baird, Jean Wright, Janette Irvine, Marion Lauder, Anne Kerr, Mary Adamson (ex-Admin. Staff), Anne Stewart, Nan Brown, Maimie Gray, Stella Haig (née Hood), Nancy Watt, Margaret

Bell, Maud Wood, Catherine Turner, Jean Murray, William Smith (an old inhabitant of Thurso Outstation) and Alan Carr. Telegrams were received from Harry Dodd and the London Committee and from Denis Johnson in Argyllshire, and Jean Murray had letters from Jane Clerk, Mary Innes, Lynne Symington, Winifred Melville, K. S. Adam, and Isabel Harper, all of whom were unfortunately unable to come to Edinburgh.

It was a bitterly cold day and, as we huddled round the roaring fires, one thought struck us all—how reminiscent the scene was of the Garat's Hey Naafi—all that was lacking was a stove in the middle of our circle, decorated with a few scattered cups of tea and coffee (still firmly believed by ex-patrons to be the same beverage, the only difference being that " coffee " used to cost ½d. more per cup than " tea ").

A gathering such as this needs, of course, no entertainment, and—aided by Nan Brown's photos of Beaumanorites, a copy of *The Chronicles of St. Upid.* and Jean Murray's Scottish Standard heavily marked Top Sec. and bearing the signatures of many former fellow-slaves)—we provided our own entertainment by talking over the old days until our tongues were almost blistered.

Considering all the energy that had gone into our conversation, it seems incredible at this date to remember that we finished the very happy afternoon by " dancing " an Eightsome Reel!

CATHERINE TURNER.

LONDON RE-UNION

At the *Mecca Cafe*, Blomfield Street, E.C.2, on Saturday, 26th March, forty-five members assembled for a " do " in the well-remembered " Shake-Jack " tradition. Up to the interval the proceedings were on free-and-easy lines, with dancing to Charles Dellar and his Westenders, a licensed bar, and ample opportunity for reminiscing. Following buffet refreshment at 8.30 p.m., and the tardy arrival of Lew Owen (the Jack half of the now Medway-famous Shake-Jack M.C. team), delayed by over-indulgence in high-pressure salesmanship at the *Ideal Home Exhibition* and brandishing free packets of washing-powder as peace offerings, the show was organised in the true Shake-Jack manner, with Paul Jones, elimination, and novelty dances, and various prize-worthy games including one especially enjoyable episode when Roger Deayton, Pete James, Mr. Kuhlmeyer and Betty Haines' gentleman friend, having been given the opportunity to fashion the most amazing samples of millinery on the heads of Doreen Dodd, Hilary Fry, Betty Haines and Mrs. Kuhlmeyer out of crêpe paper, had the tables turned on them when the ladies whipped out a load of cosmetics and proceeded to gild the undeniably lily-like milliners with what can only be described as reckless abandon. In another event Dudley Truin won himself a tin of blacking for having, in the opinion of the judges, the dirtiest shoes on the floor—a tribute, no doubt, to his calling. Lew Owen lost no opportunity in awarding his packets of washing-powder by way of advertisement for his employers. The very enjoyable evening wound up with " Auld Lang Syne." Messages of regret at inability to attend were received from a number of members including the President and Major H. F. Jolowicz. Members present were: Mrs. Peggy Allen, Mr. Alick Berry, Mr. and Mrs. Bunn, Miss Joan Dadswell, Mr. P. Dart, Mr. and Mrs. R. Deayton (née Weir), Mr. Hugh Dias, Mr. Charlie Dobson, Mr. and Mrs. H. Dodd, Mr. J. Dodd, Mrs. Pam Edmundson, Mr. J. Frost, Miss Hilary Fry, Mr. John Godfrey, Miss Betty Haines and friend, Mr. Pete James, Miss Jenkins, Mr. and Mrs. L. P. Jones and relative, Mr. and Mrs. Kuhlmeyer (née Wiseman), Miss Ann Law, Mr. E. C. Millhouse, Mr. Lew Owen, Miss Glenys Phillips and Mr. W. Chick, Miss Kay Price, Mr. Maurice Reed, Mr. John Reid, Mr. Jimmy Rogers, Mr. and Mrs. Seal (née Robinson), Mr. and Mrs. R. (" Shaker ") Smith, Miss Olive Spinks, Mr. Bill Stewart and fiancée, Mr. Dudley Truin, Miss Evelyn Woodhouse. Through illness Mr. Edmundson, Mr. and Mrs. P. Patten, Miss Dorothy Swale and Mrs. Truin were prevented from attending.

An excellent flashlight group photograph was taken during the evening, copies of which at 5s. and 7s. 6d. may be obtained from Cecil Walden, Ltd., 45, Gerrard Street, Shaftesbury Avenue, W.1.

E. C. M.

"WHAT'S HE DOING NOW?"

By DUC DOWNER

To most of us a common phrase familiar in the doubtful days,
Now as we go our sundry ways, a different meaning it conveys,
Remote from that elusive "he," confined instead to you and me,
Therefore the word must also be interpreted at times as "she."

Thanks once again for those who wrote to give me news of bods from near and far, and the usual apologies to those who have not yet had a reply. This goes especially to Lucille Sarre in Guernsey, who wrote a long and useful letter many months ago. Although all her news was included in the last issue, I have not yet got around to answering the letter and will do my best to remedy this at once. I still rely more than ever now, as you spread out, change your addresses, get married, and many things that cause you to slide from view, on your letters, so if you only have yourself to talk about, spare a moment to chalk it down and post it off to me. As I have said before, there is always someone who is glad to hear of your activities, strange as that might seem to you.

Before proceeding with births and marriages, there are, I regret to say, sadder events to record.

Jack Colville collapsed in the street in London on 25th April with hæmorrhage of the lungs, and died in Ealing hospital on 3rd May. He had been suffering for a long time with T.B. but had taken no steps towards a cure. He was buried in Scotland on 5th May. Jack left Beaumanor to work in London at the end of the war, but is well remembered, and the news of his sudden death was a shock to many people here. His friend, Alick Berry, visited him at the hospital.

Mr. Lewis Whittaker, late Staff Sergeant, I-Corps and C.R.R., and one of the original founders of the Woygian Association, died at a Llandudno nursing home on 8th October, 1948, after a month's illness believed caused by heart disease.

A fuller note of this deeply regretted event appears in another part of the Magazine.

At Beaumanor we have seen the departure of old friends for service overseas. Amongst those who sailed a short while ago were Moggy Reed, George Billingsly, Ron (R.P.L.) Smith, Eric Dobson, Jock Cameron, Paddy McGrath and Bob Stevens, with Slap Reedman in charge of the party. There was quite a bit of excitement before they left and one or two became positively boat-happy. Doubtless heavy seas have done something by now to relieve their high spirits, but we do hope they enjoy the trip, and are anxiously awaiting news of how they are settling down. They had a farewell "do" at Beaumanor, and I doubt if even the Bay of Biscay could do more than that party to upset their equilibrium.

A few bods may be interested to know that at a recent meeting it was unanimously decided to resign *en bloc* from the C.S.R.O.A. and to apply for membership of the Civil Service Union.

Springtime seems to have arranged a great number of weddings and births and they will now be recorded with all the details available at the time of writing.

First, special congratulations to one of Woygians vice-Presidents, Major Jolowicz, who was recently appointed Regius Professor of Civil Law at Oxford. His address is now All Soul's College, Oxford.

ENGAGEMENTS

From *The Scotsman*: The engagement is announced between George Girdwood, only son of Mr. and Mrs. H. A. Stewart, and Shelagh Jean Morven, younger daughter of Dr. and Mrs. R. R. Murray, 13, Church Hill, Edinburgh 10. Jean was formerly in the I-Corps at Garats Hey.

MARRIAGES

On 2nd April, at the Emanuel Church, Loughborough, Ron Mathias to Miss Betty Harper, of Loughborough. The bride wore a dress of white French crêpe, a full length veil and a head-dress of orange blossom. The reception was at the "Bull's Head," Shelthorpe, and the honeymoon was spent in

Bournemouth. Matt left Beaumanor on 20th May for compassionate reasons. I understand that he feels it necessary to look after his father. His address will be 32, Quarry Road, West Side, Wandsworth Common, London, S.W.18, and though he hasn't yet got a job in the big city, he shouldn't find life boring at home. His wife is a musician and dancer and a member of two concert parties.

Lexy Burns was married in April at her home village in Northumberland, to Alexei Slansky, and went to Devon for her honeymoon. Lexy and her husband hope to get a house soon.

Susan Weir (late of Hut 3, Garats Hey) became Mrs. Roger Deayton on 1st March. The wedding was at Carnoustie, Scotland, and Frances Watt was one of the bridesmaids. The honeymoon was spent at Dunblane. A reception was held at the Mecca Cafe, Chancery Lane, on 2nd April, for the benefit of the bridegroom's relatives living in the South who could not make the long journey to Carnoustie. This function was attended by Doreen and Harry Dodd. Susan and Roger now live at 29, Pembroke Gardens, Kensington, London, W.8.

Norman (Curley) Hendley was married at Leicester on 26th March to Miss Betty Mehegan of Merthyr. The honeymoon was spent at Lewes.

One from the past: In October, 1947, Eileen Salter was married to Tom Moffatt. It was an all-Signals affair, both the groom and the best man, Bill Baillie, being members of 55 Squad, S.O.T.B., Trowbridge. After living in one room for a few months, they succeeded in getting a two-roomed flat. Eileen says, " It's somewhere to call our ain wee hoose—it's wee all right, but it's home." The address is 19, Dunkeld Road, Perth, Scotland.

It was reported in the last issue that Vera Ballard had become Mrs. Fitzgerald, but no details were then available. Vera has since filled in the gaps. Her husband's name is Jim and the wedding was in August, 1948, fifteen months before they had planned, to fit in with Jim's leave. He is stationed on the Gold Coast. The reception was held at Walton Hall, the home of Lord Daresbury, where some forty wedding photos were taken. Vera says, " For the information of T.P. staff, my marriage was not the result of another flirtation. It started early in 1943 . . . when we haunted the Woodgate Canteen." (Loughborough for Romance!)

On 28th August, 1948, at Hersham, Walton-on-Thames, Joan Pond (" C " Watch, T.P.) to Basil Vowler. No further details are available, but their present address is 17, Beverley Close, Addlestone, Surrey.

BIRTHS

To Geoff and Connie Nicol, on 19th November, 1948, at the Bond Street Maternity Hospital, Leicester, a son, Timothy. Because of housing difficulties Connie went to live with Geoff's parents in Snodland, Kent, but recently they have been more fortunate and have secured accommodation in the district.

To Peter and Ann Gardner, on 15th January, 1949, a son, Andrew. Ann spent quite a time being ill at the beginning of the year, but she seems back to normal again now. Peter, of course, is the perfect father.

To Joyce Nicholls (née Askew, late of Hut 3, " A " Watch, 1/2 Wing, Garats Hey), at the W. J. Courtauld Hospital, Braintree, Essex, on 26th March, 1949, a daughter, Margaret Anne.

To Gwen McElrea (also late of Hut 3, Garats Hey), at Rockhampton, North Queensland, Australia, a daughter, Margaret. The exact date is not known, but Margaret appeared early this year, and is Gwen's second child.

To Jo Bennett (née Kidd and late of " C " Watch, Garats Hey), on 6th March, 1949, a son, William, or " Bill " to his friends. Jo's address is now 58, Priory Road, South Park, Reigate.

To Aline and Douglas Saxby, on 13th November, 1948, a daughter, Julie Kathleen. Aline says that even on present-day rations, Julie weighed 8lb. 11oz. and adds that she just couldn't wait for the appearance of Prince Charles. Her husband, Douglas, may be remembered. He was an operator at Harrogate after the war, when his own section had been disbanded.

To Mr. and Mrs. Robert Bigg (née Betty Slark, '" C " Watch, T.P.), on 8th August, 1948, a daughter, name unknown.

To Ken (Ginger) and Mavis (Tich) Talbot, on 13th November, 1948, a son, John Richard. (The same date, I notice, as Aline Saxby's daughter,

Julie.) The Talbots have recently bought a house at 100, Lakehall Road, Thornton Heath, Surrey.

To Winifred Leadbeater (née Forkin, and formerly of " C " Watch, Garats Hey), on 25th July, 1948, a son, name at present unknown. Winifred sends " good wishes to Woygites " and says that Elsie Goodbrand (née Ford, also of " C " Watch, Garats Hey), has a son born in August, 1948. Again the name is not known.

Eileen Moffat (see Marriages department), gives the news of the following "A " Watch births:

Hilda (Doo-ey) Brown is now Mrs. Terry and the proud mother of Lynne.

Joyce Bacon (née Baillie) has a son, Leonard William, who is about a year old.

Mabel Spires (née Banks), has a two year old daughter, Susan.

Nan Squire has a son, but his name and age, and Nan's married name are unknown.

It is believed that Bungy Williamson, a founder member of the notorious " Bull Ring," who was last heard of in Hull, has a daughter.

It's good to be able to record so many of these events. There are probably many more, and I shall be pleased to hear of any that have not yet come to light.

Congratulations to everyone who has helped to make such a long list of events. Now on to General News.

Mr. and Mrs. Roy Batchelor (Mr. ex I-Corps, and Mrs. ex Group Office) sailed for Canada on 7th May. It is a permanent move and for the next four months their address will be 33, Electric Street, Ottawa, Ontario, Canada, and after that time c/o Communications Branch, National Research Council, Ottawa, Canada. We certainly hope they enjoy their new life over there.

Kath and Ray Snell have recently moved into a flat in a spacious old converted house in Brighouse, Yorkshire, Kath's home town. Kath is still working at the local office of the Prudential, and Ray is engaged on research in gramophone reproduction apparatus with a Brighouse firm.

We were sorry to hear that Nan Brown (ex " A " Watch, 1/2 Wing, Garats Hey) had a nervous breakdown some time ago, but we are glad to say that she has now recovered.

Dudley Truin tells us that Paddy Kelly is now sales manager for a group of twenty-three boot and shoe shops. These shops are widely spread over the country, and Paddy spends much of his time travelling to visit them. He and his family now live in Colchester, Essex.

Still in connection with Dudley Truin, Pete James writes to say that he is now a member of the Truin organisation, as a travelling salesman. We remember that Peter was a travelling salesman once before, at the cost of fourpence a week, and we wish him more success this time. One or two people will notice the significance of the fact that his first trip was to Manchester. After that he will go to Leeds and then to the West country. We still expect to see him back at Beaumanor eventually.

Bettina Woodward writes to say she has just returned to England after she has spent a year in Georgia, U.S.A. Bettina had been on a visit to the relatives of her Paratrooper fiancé, who was killed in the Ardennes gap. She had kept up correspondence with his family and finally managed to obtain a passage. She thoroughly enjoyed her visit and whilst there made many friends and was lucky enough to spend five weeks in Miami. She enjoyed it so much, in fact, that she is now considering emigrating and living there permanently.

Jean Murray (ex I-Corps, Garats Hey) writes to give news of her engagement, which has been recorded in the appropriate place. The paper used was prominently headed " Health and the Soil " (published quarterly, 2s. 6d., annual subscription 10s.), and it appears that Jean now does all the editorial and secretarial work on this magazine. For your information, Jean, Moggy, at the time of writing, is somewhere on the high seas, and Ron Blease is at the Government Communications Headquarters, in London. Jean says she still has the souvenir card of the New Year's celebration for the year when the Pantomime " Spiderella " was produced with Ron Hyder as the heroine. It certainly seems a long time ago now. *(Continued on page eight.)*

IMPORTANT NOTICE

Subscriptions for the year beginning 1st July, 1949, are now due and should be sent without delay to the Treasurer with the enclosed form, duly completed. We regret the necessity to increase the subscription from 2s. 6d. to 4s. 6d.; as explained in the last issue, this is largely due to the severe drop in membership in the last two years.

During the past year, in spite of urgent reminders from us, a further 100 members failed to pay their subscriptions, leaving us with an effective membership of 270. It is obvious that we cannot go on indefinitely losing almost a third of our membership each year, and at a recent meeting the Committee decided that we have now reached the minimum number with which the Association can be run on the lines of the past two years. It was therefore decided that:—

If less than 250 members have paid their 1949-50 subscriptions by 1st November next, the present Chairman and Committee will resign and place all the Association's records and funds in the hands of the President.

Thus, if this course proves unavoidable, any members who have ideas for reviving the Association can communicate with the President at Beaumanor. We undertake to return all 1949-50 subscriptions either in full or possibly minus a small sum to pay for postage, etc., in returning subscriptions.

After paying for the printing and distribution costs of the present Magazine, the current funds will be no more than a few shillings, so that in any case the possibility of a Christmas Number depends entirely on the receipt of 1949-50 subscriptions. With 250 members paying subscriptions of 4s. 6d. each, the Association's income will be just sufficient to enable us to publish the Magazine at six-monthly intervals.

We earnestly hope that all 370 members to whom this magazine is being sent will pay promptly both the new year's subscriptions and, where appropriate, last year's as well. (Once again, we are sending the magazine to the 100 members who have failed us, in this our last attempt to put the Association on a sound footing.) Reports and comments which reach us convince us that many ex-Woygites look forward to receiving the Magazine every few months and to hearing news of old friends, both via the news columns in the Magazine and at re-unions arranged by us, and that a keen regret will be felt should the winding-up of the Association prove unavoidable after four successful years, particularly as the prospects for reviving it would seem extremely remote. Though some members may consider lack of interest as the reason for the drop in membership, we are quite sure that in many, perhaps most, cases the reason is nothing more than the lack of energy necessary to obtain a postal order and post it to the Treasurer—surely a very small part to play compared with the considerable amount of work which Committee members carry out in the running of the Association.

If we reach the requisite minimum of 250 members by 1st November, we shall take this as a vote of confidence in us, and continue to do our utmost to keep the Association and its Magazine running successfully. Comments and suggestions of any sort will, as always, be welcome.

The whole matter is therefore entirely up to you. If you want the Association to continue—send in your subscription now!

Beaumanor Re-union. Some members, particularly those who attended the Dance in London last March, will know that the possibility of another re-union at Beaumanor this Autumn was being discussed. Unfortunately, mainly because of difficulties at Beaumanor which could not be overcome in time, this has not proved possible, but we hope it may be possible to arrange one for next year, perhaps at Whitsun again (but only if the Association survives its present crisis and if we have 250 members by 1st November). We will report on the matter in the Christmas Magazine (again assuming that we are able to publish then).

Edinburgh Re-union. It seems that the first Edinburgh re-union, held on 12th February last, was a great success, and congratulations are due to

Miss Jean Murray and Mrs. Muriel McAra on arranging the first provincial Woygian Association function. A report on it by Miss Catherine Turner appears on another page. We hope that this pleasant affair may be repeated

Mr. Lewis Whittaker. Many members, especially those who were in C.R.R., will be very sorry to learn of the death of Mr. Lewis Whittaker at a nursing home in Llandudno on 8th October, 1948, after a short illness. Lewis, then a Staff Sergeant in the I-Corps, was one of the sponsors of the scheme for the formation of the Association, and gave valuable help in the preparations for launching the Association in 1945.

Major H. F. Jolowicz. All members will wish to join me in offering to Major Jolowicz, one of the Association's Vice-Presidents, our congratulations on his recent appointment as Regius Professor of Civil Law at Oxford University. This is an appropriate moment at which to say that Major Jolowicz has always taken a great interest in the Association and his help and encouragement have been much appreciated by the Chairman and Committee.

HARRY DODD (Chairman).

"WHAT'S HE DOING NOW ?" contd.

From time to time somebody writes to say that they have " bumped " into an old aquaintance in London, and the latest one is Harry Dodd who, while in a Northern Line tube train, caught a glimpse of " Bosun " Sleeper standing on King's Cross Underground station. They just had time for a quick sign of recognition before Harry was whisked away on his journey.

Don Linder is still ploughing through his course at Hull University, and apart from his studies, which he says take most of his time and energy, he has gained a full hockey blue. When he last wrote he was relaxing for a few days in Kent.

Joan Woollaston writes to say that she had a very enjoyable day in London, where she went to see Eileen Hollis (ex " B " Watch, No. 2 Wing). They hadn't met for two and a half years and Joan says it was grand to talk about old times. We've no doubt at all that they found plenty to grip each other about, but apparently they hadn't time in one short day for it all because Joan is hoping that Eileen will be able to visit her at her home at 3, Field Street, Willenhall, Staffordshire.

Joan tells us that Kay Peacock (Tailby) now has her own house at Queniboro, which is about six miles from Leicester.

George Kenneally still seems quite happy in his job in Rhodesia. He hopes to have his family with him very shortly.

Bert Norris met Mouse recently and gave him the very sad news that his wife, Mary (née Watson), went into hospital early this year with pneumonia and pleurisy, and that it has since been discovered that she is suffering from T.B. Bert says that she is likely to be in a sanatorium for about a year. We are very sorry to hear of their misfortune and wish Mary a complete recovery in the shortest possible time.

Mrs. Den. Bakker complains that there is never any news in the column about 524 Coy., A.T.S. What about scribbling a few lines, 524 Coy.? We would certainly like to hear from you.

Miss Robinson, formerly Junior Commander, I-Corps, is now managing her own hotel. The address is unknown, but don't be surprised if you find a familiar face at that place where you plan to stay this year.

Another former Junior Commander, I-Corps, Miss Ida Romer, was met recently by Mrs. Daphne Abels. She is working at Kemp's Biscuit Factory, and living at Park Road, Hendon. At the time of this meeting, Anne Childs was staying with her.

Johnny Mace is now living at Kew and is training to become a Vet. He was married in March, but owing to the lack of further details, the event has not been recorded in the usual place.

Marion Lind sends " good luck " to the Woygian Association. She is now secretary to three specialists in Rodney Street, Liverpool, and in spite of the long hours, enjoys her job very much. One of her charges is an eye specialist, and Marion comments on the crowds of patients he has in these days of free service. " Resembling a rugger scrum, or a Beaumanor Canteen stampede," she says. I suppose it was a bit of a scramble at break times in the old days I know that we used to make split-second calculations in an attempt to get ahead of the khaki contingents. We usually lost.

Jane Clark wrote to say how delighted she was at the prospect of a re-union in Edinburgh. She expected the arrival of her baby in the Spring, but so far there is no further information available.

Olga Churchill and her husband spent six months searching for a house, and were lucky in finding just what they wanted. In January, complete with young daughter, they moved into No. 7, Claremont Crescent, Rumney, Cardiff.

Bessie Mostyn, now Mrs. Brooks, is living at 1, Scholars Road, Chingford, E.4. She hasn't any news, she says, and spends all her time shopping, cooking and cleaning, and hoping for a house.

Hilda Price works at Cadburys, Bourneville, and sends good wishes to all Woygians everywhere. She enjoys the Magazine, but misses the fun of A.T.S. life, and is hoping to replace some of it by joining the T.A. Hilda hasn't been well lately, but we hope she is fully recovered now.

Chris Wardle has now become Mrs. T. Mason, and sends " Best wishes to all Woygians," but no details of her wedding. Her new address is 11, Headlam Street, Newcastle-on-Tyne, 6.

Joan Turner (née Thackrah, of A.R. 13) now has a house of her own and two daughters to keep her busy—Susan, aged 3, and Wendy Elizabeth, who was born on 25th May, 1948. Joan's address is 25, Windsor Street, Barrow-in-Furness, Lancashire, and she sees, occasionally, Olga Forshaw (ex " A " Watch, Garats Hey), who lives quite near to her.

Norma Domina, living in California, hopes to be home in time for the next re-union, and adds, " It would be a thrill to meet old friends again."

A very long and very rambling letter from Bill Hayward explains that he is now a fully fledged Police Constable in the Kent County Constabulary. He hasn't yet done any active duty, having, at the end of a rigorous training course, found it necessary to take a spot of sick leave in Brighton. The same old Bill!

Jimmy Hewson has a new job on the advertising staff of the East Kent Gazette. He intends to marry on 18th June.

Len Owen and Ron Smith are still in the Medway area. I would be pleased to hear from them if they can spare a moment to write.

Dudley Truin has made brief appearances in Loughborogh of late, Ron Blease and his wife stayed for a few days, and Hwfa Pryse, playing a fine part in the Paul Temple film, has been on view in Leicester.

Glenys Phillips left London last June to work for the Ministry of National Insurance, and her address is now 38, Glebelands, Hakin, Milford Haven, Pembs., S. Wales.

To end with, there are several new addresses:—

Mrs. C. J. Blamire (née Turner, " A " Watch, 1/2 Wing, Garats Hey), 121, Probert Road, Wolverhampton.

Mrs. A. Bratt (née Rostron, ex C.S.M., Garats Hey), 38, Roscow Avenue, Bolton, Lancs.

Tom " Snubby " Pollard, 147, Woodgrove Road, Burnley, Lancs.

Lynne Symington (ex I-Corps), c/o Mrs. Humm, 34, Hartland Drive, Ruislip Manor, Middlesex.

Mrs. Connie Ewens (née Scovell, ex W.A.A.F., Switchboard), 41, Penns Road, Petersfield, Hants. ... ...

Mrs. J. A. Norris (née Bringloe), 82, Union Road, Clapham, London, S.W.4.

Mr. J. Morton (ex I.M.), 39, Holt Drive, Loughborough.

Mrs. K. M. Jones (née White), 3, Winders Hill, Godstone, Surrey.

Rachel Clare, Dixon Cottage, Hayton Bent, Nr. Ludlow, Salop.

That's all for this time, except to say " LETTERS PLEASE."

Memorabilia

Confronted with the Editor's recent request for memories of war-time Woyg, I shut out the wind and sleet and spent a nostalgic evening by the fire, immersed in old diaries and a heap of **B.S.M.'s**. Why, I wonder, did we ever complain of dullness or boredom in those days? The hosts of old faces and memories, all fantastic and all a little mad, which came to life around my wintry fireside can surely never have been dull?

My earliest memory is of my first day at Beaumanor, way back in—well, years ago, anyway; of my initiation into the ritual of Barkus, and the songs, new to me in my innocence, that were soon to become so familiar, and which were to be taken up in tents and Nissen huts far away; of the first sight of the entrance to Beaumanor, guarded by two lusty Alsatians. And the house itself, which never failed to thrill me. "Aychut," with its atmosphere of super-boffinism, and the canteen, with its iron-hard rolls, cold, sour, weak tea, and cracked mugs. Back by Barkus again to the digs, to be greeted with, " Oh, 'ullo me doock! Yer moost be starved! I'll mash soom tea."

It went on like that for three long years, the songs in the bus, the dogs at the gate, the set-room clock, the noble game of " Battleships," the canteen, all became a part of a familiar, not to say monotonous routine, and even the wild antics of such people as Messrs. Baker, Burgess, Royle, McNulty, Fox and Antrum became accepted as part of the calendar. Poor Paul Antrum, or whichever of his labels you prefer! It is hard to find a *B.S.M.* without a mention of his name; his value to morale must have been immense.

Very pleasant memories come back of evenings spent at *The Hurst*, where Harry Dodd strove manfully to persuade us we could sing. Did he persuade himself? Anyway, the sound of Thor Smiting with his Hammer and Odin with the Leather on his Knee warmed many long winter evenings. Then there were the summer rambles, mostly across Charnwood Forest. Some of us grew very fond of the Forest, of Old John, Hangingstone Rocks, the ruined home of Lady Jane Grey, deer feeding in the bracken, and egg teas at Blakeshay Farm; and those rambles taught at least one that the country around Loughborough was not all dull and flat. Sometimes we went to the lovely Monastery of St. Bernard, locked away amidst the trees of Charnwood. Here, on one occasion, I had the questionable honour of being introduced to Mr. Hore Belisha, spending a few weeks of political exile in contemplation. Or to the lovelier and far older priory of Ulverscroft, to me one of the most perfect of ancient monuments; poetry in cold, grey stone.

Only the other evening the B.B.C. broadcast a recording of Loughborough's carillon, and my mind went back to frosty evenings in Woodhouse Eaves, when the hymns on the bells could be faintly heard across the fields. That led me on to the little church on the rocks at Woodhouse Eaves; to a service there one Easter Day when all the daffodils in Leicestershire seemed to grow from the ancient stones; and to the celebrated occasion when I was supposed to have raided the church offertory box!

Mention of music reminds me of many happy hours at Leicester's De Montford Hall, especially of a crowded, excited audience on the eve of V-J Day, when Solomon played the Emperor Concerto; and of that other historic occasion when Wally Cecil's bicycle pump competed with Solomon's piano. Of cycle rides back to Woodhouse Eaves on summer evenings, and of a long trudge from Barrow through swirling snow. At the Dancing Class, of which I was not a regular member, I used occasionally, under pressure, to shamble round with the expert guidance of Hilary Fry. It is not her fault if at least one member of her class cannot dance a step now!

Christmases; the dancing in the canteen, surreptitious meetings between " H " and " K " huts, and Freddie Burgess in festive mood. To me, the most memorable was Christmas, '45, my last there; a time of hard frost and thick fog which lasted for days, draping every leaf and blade of grass with tinsel. On Christmas Eve the moon sparkled through the fog, and all Charnwood seemed a forest of dazzling Christmas trees.

Few will think of Beaumanor without some bitter reflections on their " home-life." " There are no such things as good digs," said one profound philosopher, " only bad digs and worse digs." Two memories of my stay in Victoria Road, Woodhouse Eaves, with Ted Sandy, persist—the time when the landlady went out for the day and removed the valve from the radio; and the time when we decided she hadn't left enough marmalade for breakfast, and knocked a jug off the shelf at 5 a.m. " The rain's debating," " Will yer 'ave a swill?" and other classic phrases, are now seldom heard.

So the reminiscences might go on, but, when all is said and done, our share in the history of Beaumanor is puny. The walls which sheltered Richard before Bosworth, and Herrick as he dreamed of Julia, would not crumble with five years of the mad crowd who disported there during the war. They will be there when we are long forgotten.

I, for my sins, am still engaged on the same old job, though not at Beaumanor, and I can tell you that times have changed; things are not what they were. We are growing older and, sadly, saner.

I enjoyed reading the Editor's notes on what he remembers, and noting his suggestion that other people should disclose theirs also, here we go:—

5.20 a.m. Winter morning. Deep snow. Black darkness. Group of operators waiting for Barkus Bus, and one of them saying that just before the alarm went off he was dreaming he was laying under a palm tree, and a beautiful native girl was feeding him with grapes.

Memory of the operator who said he had given up smoking because he considered it a waste of beer money.

The story told by Bill Baker about the man who had bought a bike from him, and came back and said, " I don't know how you do it at the price, Mr. Baker."

An old saying written in a crude country hand over the fireplace of a Woodhouse pub, " Every age has its beauty."

Memory of the Operator who, on being told by the landlady's daughter that she was expecting a baby, asked her whether she was going to marry the man, to which she replied, " No, I don't like him."

A picture in my mind's eye of two A.T.S. girls in tennis shorts against the perfumed beauty of a Woodhouse April morning. Blossom against blossom. As much spring as the lilac.

Of everybody's sadistic joy when a middle-aged G.P.O. operator, confused with snow and black-out, lost his way and fell into Beaumanor's icy stream.

Of a startled breakfast canteen watching white-faced swift Walter MacNulty fighting a man twice his strength.

Of my wonderment at first witnessing an old operator imperturbably covering a full speed Light Blue.

Tubby Tomkin's story of the native girl at Aden (I pay *you*).

Old Fred's throwing-out cry at the *Pear Tree*, " Away to the Woods boys and girls."

A brightly lit room full of young men and girls at a Soar House party.

Odd memories, but they brighten the past.

" RAZ."

Through the Looking-Glass

CULT

A televised view of the annual Cup Final orgy at Wembley served to remind us yet again that Sport, as an alternative to Parliamentary Democracy, is a political ideal that first began to haunt the mind (for want of a better word) of the Island Race several generations before the Reform Bill of 1832. this yearning, still not *quite* satisfied, leads to those regular pronouncements from the Bench of Bishops and House of Lords to the effect that if Stalin, Hitler, Mussolini and the Kaiser had learnt to play cricket, football and/or darts, the Great, the Last or the Next War could never have happened or happen.

Although reluctant to question your deepest spiritual convictions we, outcast that we are, must maintain the opposite thesis, viz.: that if Stalin, Hitler, Mussolini and the Kaiser had learnt to play any popular English game, the above-mentioned conflicts would have been longer, more bitter, and even less conclusive; only one slightly ameliorative change might have resulted: the justifications would have been more ingenious. The mentality that defends coursing on the grounds that the dogs have to run hard to catch the hare (the struggle thus not being one-sided) would (and does) present the atomic bomb as the last word in human beneficence without even pausing to swallow hard.

Our own observations on the cinema-screen have led to the conclusion that ice-hockey matches (for example) produce approximately one free fight per minute among the players, and one of the rules of ladies' indoor cycle race-meetings appears to be to tear off the referee's pants some time towards the end of the proceedings. As for preventing war; it is well known that the visit of the Moscow Dynamos a couple of years ago almost led to the withdrawal of Ambassadors and the mobilisation of the Fleet, and on more than one occasion in the past the appearance of a new pace bowler in a Test Match has nearly caused the secession of Australia from the Commonwealth.

Although unschooled in the ways of politicians, it is as obvious as the scent of a fried fish shop that the first thing an enlightened twentieth-century government should do with its sportsmen is to keep them safely at home; and, as a further precaution, ban the overseas sale of sports equipment as potential war-material.

In all this we find only one spark of comfort: the Russians can't be contemplating war just yet. If they were they'd have sent a team to last year's Olympic Games to provoke a suitable international incident.

MUSIC NOTE

Listening the other day to the first performance of a new orchestral work whose name now eludes us (was it Hohlakov's Concerto in A for Flute, Cymbals and Jew's Harp?) we were for the first time constrained to doubt the omniscience of Dr. Johnson. His well-known dictum, "Sir, music is the least disagreeable of all noises!" is clearly open to question. After five minutes of the above, the noise of a diesel-driven circular-saw cutting through a bag of six-inch nails would have sounded like celestial harmony.

THOUGHT FOR TO-DAY

"A small house agent's clerk with one bold stare,
One of the low on whom assurance sits
As a silk hat on Bradford millionaire."—T. S. Eliot.

In Extremis

The Chairman's remarks on another page give ample food for thought. Are we about to witness the demise of the Woygian Association? If we are, I for one am sure the most fitting epitaph will be the one so many Woygite activities earned—Apathy.

I don't think many people realise the tremendous amount of work put in by Harry Dodd, with the assistance of his small committee, all, mark you, volunteers, since he brought about the renaissance of the Association when it almost met an early death in May, 1947. But all the labour in the world will not avail without *support*. There has been a loyal and enthusiastic core, but a large percentage of the membership has had to be cajoled, threatened, and enticed with free copies of the Magazine before they would belatedly renew their subscription. Not, I am sure, out of sheer indifference, between which and apathy there is a fine distinction—the letters we get and the encouragement we receive from personal contacts at re-unions indicate very much to the contrary—but because of procrastination, dilatoriness, or any other polite word for laziness.

Is it to be wondered at that the committee is now calling for a vote of confidence? It must be very galling to Harry Dodd, after all his gratuitous efforts in reviving a near-corpse, to watch the life-blood ebbing away again, for, make no mistake, subscriptions are the very life-blood of an organisation such as this; and there comes a time when the heart, willing as it may be, has insufficient blood to keep it going. That is the point we have almost reached.

If you are one of the dilatory subscribers the remedy is yours—now. If you are one of the "faithful," and feel sufficiently strongly about the matter, you can still help by rousing some of your more lethargic acquaintances, particularly those who are no longer effective members. When this Association was inaugurated we had *six hundred and fifty members*; to-day we have little more than a third of that number. However you look at it—IT'S UP TO *YOU*, NOW.

Being optimistic enough to hope we shall issue forth from the printers again at Christmas-time, I should like all contributions to reach me not later than 12th November.—THE EDITOR.

Printed by The Chandos Press and Published by H. Dodd for the Woygian Association.

OTHER WOYG INTERCEPT STATIONS

A large number of ATS Wireless Operators Special worked at Kedleston Hall and Forest Moor on intercept duties. The latter were billetted at Queen Ethelburga's College in Harrogate.

The school was named after one of the strongest characters in early Saxon history. Ethelburga married a heathen converted him and persuaded the people of her new kingdom to accept the teachings of St Paulinus and the Roman tradition of Christianity. This in itself was an achievement in an area where Celtic Christianity (that of St Aidan and Cuthbert) was the lingering tradition temporarily eclipsed by the paganism of Edwin and his predecessors. The beautiful York Minster now stands on the site of the first Christian wooden church erected by Edwin and Ethelburga in their capital Eioforwic. When Edwin was killed Ethelburga escaped back to Kent to Cantwara from whence she had travelled as a young bride in 625 AD. She had lived in a palace on the Derwent river in Yorkshire and ended her life in the abbey she founded at Lyminge in Kent. Her niece St Hilda was later responsible for bringing England into the mainstream of Roman Christianity which linked England with Europe in the Middle Ages.

Kedleston Hall, near Derby

Jun Cdr Dorothy Coggan was one of the very first squad posted to Kedleston and they became operational in Nov 1942. She had been called up into the ATS in June 42 and after one month's initial training at Pontefract Barracks (Yorks.) three of them (out of an intake of 360 ATS) were posted to Trowbridge Barracks to train as Special Wireless Operators and she became part of Squad 24 (photo in the Y Compendium, opp. P.158). After three months' training they were posted to Kedleston Hall in Oct 42. They arrived there in the dark and in pouring rain (7 miles from Derby) with nobody expecting them and the accommodation huts not built. They found a skeleton staff (ATS) had arrived only a week previously and nothing had been organised. The Pioneer Corps were building huts. The cookhouse and 2 or 3 wireless huts were ready and a mass of aerials were visible some distance away.

It was very cold in Derby in the winter of 1942 and the small fuel ration was inadequate for the stove in the hut. Luckily they were in the end hut with the woods beside them from which they could gather fallen wood.

They did Morse etc every day including Saturdays and Sundays and took their B3 and/or B2 Operators exam in November, and the E & M and Procedure the following week. With trade tests behind them they started operational shift working on 30 Nov 1942. Unlike Beaumanor there were no permanent civilian operators. They covered the North African campaign—Italian and German Army and Air Forces.

Gradually the station became organised. The male signalmen were very few; four shifts of ATS did the operating with a male Signals Sgt i/c of each hut. Male 'T' "I" Corps officers arrived. About the middle of 1943 a number of the ATS at Kedleston went to Cairo, returning to Kedleston about a year later.

A conversion course for Japanese Morse was held early in 1943 and she thinks she recollects that Japanese traffic was received there with the additional aerials that were installed.

After VE-Day of course the function altered and it became a centre for learning Urdu—language training in preparation for the posting of Signals groups to India. In view of the Hiroshima bomb etc this posting did not take place.

Dorothy Coggan left Kedleston in June 1943 for OCTU and was posted to Forest Moor in March 1944. In 1993 she recalls:

'Queen Ethelburga's School evacuated their buildings just outside Harrogate in the early 1940s when it became an ATS Training Centre where newly called-up ATS did one month initial training. I'm not sure when it was taken over as accommodation for Signals—possibly 1943.

I was posted there in March 1944, the set-up was quite different from Beaumanor in that all the operators were Army Signals. The photograph of the NCOs of "C" Watch shows seven signalmen, who together with two or three male officers per shift made up the male complement as I remember it. The rest of the operators were ATS with a couple of ATS officers to each watch.

All the admin side, messing, Q, sick bay etc was at Queen Ethelburga's and due to the large numbers most of the ATS were accommodated in huts built at the back of the main buildings. There were four main companies (for each watch of course) comprising about 170/200 ATS plus NCOs and Officers, and also the HQ Coy. Transport of each shift was in the larger Army lorries to the Forest Moor Signals station about ten miles away.

Last year I re-visited Harrogate and Q.E.'s College still stands the same, 50 years on, surrounded by moors and not built up at all. The lovely chapel within the grounds, which we used with our own padre, Rev Marshall, still stands in good shape.

No. 24 Squad, ATS

Photo of Staff of Forest Moor at Queen Ethelburga's College.
The 2 i/c was Major Sidney Wort, Royal Signals. He had served pre-war as an NCO at Sarafand and was back in uniform as second in command at Forest Moor.

Back Row
| Sub | Assist/Adj | Sub | Sub | Sub | Sub | | Sub |
| M. Harwood | K. Sharles | P. Neal | Robbins | B. Fulton | B. Granville-Barker | | ? |

Row 3
| Nursing Sister | Lt L. Hobday | Lt ? | Sub ? | Sub ? | Sub ? | | |

Row 2
| Sub B. Bairnsfather | Sub V. Hindmarsh | Capt "Q" | Capt Clarke | Capt Falkener | J/C Lawrence | Lt ? | Capt Lamb |
| Sub D. Coggan | Lt R. Evans | | | | | | |

Front Row
| J/C Ambrunenil | Capt ? | J/C Dyer | Major ? | S/Cdr Abelwhite | Col Davey | Major Wort | Major Silk | J/C M.O. | Capt Macnab. | J/C Crombie |

The duty watch, missing from the photograph, include J/C J Wade, Sub M Abbott, Sub J Care, Lt T Rosney, Lt R Hancock, and Padre Marshall and J.C.D. Rossbottom i/c Catering.

804

"C" COY A.T.S. HARROGATE, 1944

The photograph shows 166 A.T.S. Special Operators and seven R.Signals supervisors at Queen Ethelburga's College. There could be 50 more on duty or on leave.

This is only a small proportion of the thousands of A.T.S. operators who captured from the ether often through atmospherics hundreds of thousands of cipher messages for the cryptographers at B.P.

'Members of No. 3 ATS Y Wing at Kadleston Hall, Feb 1943'

Pat Gardiner   Margo Osborn
Dorothy Dunn   Myrtle   "Chips"
               Willis   Ellis
Valerie Beston

Gathering wood for the hut stove

'War Office Y Group, Forest Moor, Harrogate 1944/45 NCOs of "C" ATS with Royal Signals NCO's'

Back row 3rd from left Cpl O'Sullivan, No.7 Cpl Molly Morgan
Middle row 2nd from left Cpl A. Kay
Front row No.3 Sgt Grant (later CSM), No.4 RSM, No.5 Sgt Burley (later CSM), No.7 Cpl Jamieson

W/T RED FORM.

S.1319.

Ship or Station.	Set	2	Date.	10.6.42	Operator's Remarks.*	
	Opr.	JB	Time Ended§		Q.S.A.	3
	Tot	cd	Frequency & System.			
	From†	PGL				

All before the Text: C 1035 KR 4 TLE ITL 247 BFP RST

TSNOC	AYCNG	REPOF	MTAEC
QERFE	NGISF	RMTNE	RRANG
OLNXF	YSTUP	SLNBR	AYZTL
SDAPB	RUFGE	MNSOU	GTVAW
FXNLG	UTYSM	BNRSL	ANUGL
RTPGQ	LPHRE	FGDRK	SLNOI
SDXNA	KJWYB	LZRFT	BTSNM
FHOTM	GLKZY	ARLFN	ULNPF
OTDEP	FGUBR	TCGAZ	YTHOS
ILNPG	RTFMN	SNPLU	VRLNK
PTRQG	SFNAR	GPTZT	FPEST
GEQSN	TRPOQ	NLSKB	JOLNU
BSTLD	RP		

Do not use Left Margin.

KNOCKHOLT

To cope with the increasing amount of top-level Fish traffic from the Geheimschreibers a purpose-built intercept station, the Foreign Office Research and Development Establishment under Commander Kenworthy, was located at Ivy Farm high on the downs outside Knockholt Pound in Kent. More than 600 skilled operators logged signals sent by Teleprinter to BP.

Patricia Barnett was posted from SOTB at Douglas, Isle of Man to Knockholt, on 1 June 1944 with eighteen other members of the ATS.

"For the last two months we had been introduced to the Murray telegraph code and were now accomplished 'slip readers'. The sets we had used were only for morse interception. None of us had seen an Undulator. We were told at Knockholt we would be under the direction of the Foreign Office. Whether or not this was correct none of us knew what was going on.

The flying bomb attacks were at their worst in June 1944 and it was understood that we were to relieve some of the civilian staff to give them a rest. We were billeted in a house in Grassy Lane, Sevenoaks but not for long as we had to make way for another ATS unit (not Signals) whose billets had been hit by a flying bomb. They moved into our nice clean house whilst we were shifted to Dell House which had to be cleaned before we could settle in!

The staff at Knockholt were civilians, including ex-servicemen who had been invalided from the Forces. Everyone was very kind to us. We were divided between three watches which worked very long hours and it was here that we commenced operating the sets. These consisted of two sets stacked (usually AR 88s), an undulator, a teleprinter and a machine that punched holes in a vellum tape, the latter two machines were only of use if the signal was good. We read and logged the message preambles and Remarks but once the QEP and Number came up the messages were rolled up, marked with the QEP number and despatched to the Slip Reading Room.

In August we were posted to Kedleston Hall where the "Ops Block" consisted of two set rooms, a slip reading hut and a room which housed teleprinters plus vellum tape machines, linked to Bletchley Park. One of the set rooms intercepted Japanese "Kana" morse and the other intercepted Geheimschreiber communications. In the latter room there were between twelve and fourteen AR 88 sets.

We worked in pairs, one of us covering Berlin and the other covering another European town. The various station-pairs were given code-names of different Fish: the ones which I can remember being covered were:—

Gurnard—Berlin/Bucharest
Bream —Berlin/Milan
Barbel —Berlin/Paris(?)

The work procedure was much the same as at Knockholt but we worked fewer spells on duty because there were four watches doing 8-hour shifts, changing every two days.

In the Spring of 1945 we were all posted from Kedleston, some back to Knockholt others to Harrogate because Kedleston Hall was to be used as a training centre for ATS "Y" Signals personnel who had volunteered for service in India. However with the ending of hostilities in the Far East in August, they were not required.

I was stationed at Knockholt when the war finally ended. Latterly the maps on the walls of the set room showed the Geheimschreiber stations closing down or converging on Berlin. They ceased operating immediately the war in Europe was over".

The qualifications for Wireless Operator Special were exacting and the examinations were stiff:—

Army Form B 171—13

ROYAL SIGNALS

QUALIFICATION SHEET FOR OPERATOR (SPECIAL) (GROUP B)

Subject	Group D Class III	Class III	Class II	Class I
1. Knowledge of principles and practice as specified*	A	B	C	D
2. Sending and receiving WT (see Note E):				
(a) Send for 10 minutes at the rates shown—groups per minute—Messages with text in cipher	10	12	15	20
(b) Receive for 15 minutes each of the following, at the rates shown—groups per minute—				
(i) Messages with clear text in a foreign language	15	20	23	25
(ii) Messages with text in cipher	15	18	20	23
3. Log writing for 15 minutes	F	G	G	G
4. British procedure	H	H	H	H
5. Foreign procedure	J	J	J	J
6. Instruments (other than wireless):				
Cells, primary and secondary	K	K	K	K
Telephone, magneto	L	M	N	N
Switchboard, universal call	L	M	N	N
7. Wireless instruments:				
Reception sets	O	P	Q	Q
Direction-finding sets	—	R	R	S
Communication sets	—	T	U	U
8. Map reading	V	V	W	W

* Tests to be by simple written questions and answers, but men who fail may be examined orally.

NOTES.

A.—A general knowledge of the principles of :—

Units of electricity, structure of the atom, conductors, cells, current flow, Ohm's law, series and parallel connections, the effects of electric current, magnetism and electro-magnetism, condensers, the nature of sound, microphones and telephone receivers.

B.—Includes A and, in addition, a general knowledge of the principles of :—

Simple telephony and telegraphy, elementary alternating current, propagation of wireless waves, and reception of wireless waves.

C —A more detailed knowledge of A and B above and, in addition, a general knowledge of the principles of :—

Simple wireless transmitters and receivers, valve theory, ammeters and voltmeters, power supply and accumulators.

D.—Includes C above and, in addition, a general knowledge of the principles of :—

Aerial arrays, tuned circuits, straight and super-heterodyne receivers, amplifiers, frequency-changing, rectification, modulation, wavemeters and signal generators.

E.—(a) Each group to consist of the equivalent of five letters, figures and special signs being counted each as $1\frac{1}{2}$ letters.

(b) Messages for cipher tests to be made up as follows :—

  (i) 80 per cent. to contain, as text, groups of 5 letters only.
  (ii) 10 per cent. to contain, as text, groups of 5 figures only.
  (iii) 10 per cent. to contain, as text, groups of 5 mixed letters and figures.

(c) Rates allow for turning over and inserting carbons.

(d) In the "sending" test all messages will be in cipher and consist of the equivalent of approximately 100 letters. No uncorrected errors are allowed ; not more than the following total number of corrected errors are permissible in the test :—

| Group D | 12 | Class II | 7 |
| Class III | 10 | Class I | 5 |

(e) In the "receiving" test all messages will consist of the equivalent of approximately 200 letters and tests will be conducted as follows :—

Group D, Class III and Class II : An accuracy of 98.5 per cent. required.
Class I : An accuracy of 99 per cent. required.

(*f*) Signal strength and interference to be as follows :—
  (i) Group D and Class III—signal strength R4, interference R3.
  (ii) Class II and Class I—signal strength R3, interference R3.

In each case both signal and interference strengths to be relative to a background noise approximating to that experienced during normal watch-keeping. The interference to be on a different note.

F.—Log writing :—
  (*a*) Using special WT form and special WT log, record all signals and messages from a group of at least two WT stations separated by not more than 20 kc/s, and working to each other.
  (*b*) All transmissions to be recorded in the log with an accuracy of 80 per cent.
  (*c*) The two stations to be working on different notes with variable signal strengths and at speeds of sending not exceeding 15 w.p.m.

G.—Log writing on " live " traffic :—

Includes F and, in addition, carrying out an operational task on a " live group " of stations. The degree of proficiency for Classes III, II and I, will be " satisfactory," " good," and " very good " respectively.

H.—Group D and Class III : Knowledge of formal message procedure as required for sending and receiving short messages by WT.

Class II and Class I : Knowledge of procedure, as laid down in Signal Training Pamphlets, for sending and receiving all types of messages by WT (except duplex working).

J.—Knowledge of procedure signals, methods of working and types of traffic. Group D to include the procedure of one foreign country ; Class III, two ; and Classes II and I, three. The degree of skill for Classes II and I to be " good " and " very good " respectively.

K.—Use and care. Render inert cells active, connect up in series or parallel and test voltage.

L.—Unpack, connect up, adjust, operate and repack in working order, including changing cells, microphone capsules and similar components not requiring the use of tools.

M.—Includes L and, in addition, locate and rectify an external fault, i.e. one that does not necessitate dismantling any part of the instrument.

N.—Includes M and, in addition, locate an internal fault, e.g. a broken lead that is not visible.

O.—Be able to operate a high-grade communication receiver on a fixed frequency and be familiar with the controls. Connect up; locate and rectify an external fault not requiring the use of tools.

P.—Includes O and, in addition, be able to effect rapid changes of frequency and use a frequency meter.

Q.—Includes P and, in addition, be able to change valves and components not requiring the use of tools.

R.—Be able to set up and operate a DF set; locate and rectify minor external faults. Take a bearing on a station of given frequency and call-sign.

S.—Includes R and, in addition, be able to carry out initial and routine calibration, and plot position from bearings obtained by two or more DF stations.

T.—Connect up; adjust, tune to a given frequency, and know the capabilities and range of the set.

U.—Includes T and, in addition, locate and rectify an external fault, change a valve, and be capable of netting a group of three stations.

V.—(a) Point out on a map the conventional signs for objects enumerated.

(b) From a map point out on the ground points and objects selected on map and *vice versa*.

(c) Measure shortest distance from points A to B on a map according to scale.

(d) Measure on a map the distance from one point to another by road.

(e) Set a map without compass :—
 (i) By the ground
 (ii) By the sun.

(f) Set a map by compass.

(g) Describe a point on a gridded map by means of a map reference and *vice versa*.

W.—Includes V. (a) Determine if a point A is visible from a point B by studying contours, but without drawing a section.

(b) Take a bearing with a protractor on a map.

(c) Take a bearing with a compass and measure it on a map with a protractor.

(d) Convert true, grid and magnetic bearings.

(e) Be able to find way across country, or by road, from point to point.

(f) Work out simple time and distance calculations from point A to point B by road on a map.

(80 4718) Wt. 57576—1998 1100 4/44 H & S Ltd. (80 2718) Gp. 393